Abstracts of Death Notices (1833–1852)
and
Miscellaneous News Articles
(1833–1924)
from the *Maine Farmer*

by
David C. Young
and
Benjamin Lewis Keene

HERITAGE BOOKS
2019

HERITAGE BOOKS

AN IMPRINT OF HERITAGE BOOKS, INC.

Books, CDs, and more—Worldwide

For our listing of thousands of titles see our website
at
www.HeritageBooks.com

Published 2019 by
HERITAGE BOOKS, INC.
Publishing Division
5810 Ruatan Street
Berwyn Heights, Md. 20740

Heritage Books by David C. Young and Benjamin Lewis Keene:

*Abstracts of Death Notices (1833–1852) and Miscellaneous
News Articles (1833–1924) from the* Maine Farmer

Heritage Books by David C. Young:

CD: Death Notices from Freewill Baptist Publications 1811–1851

CD: Marriage and Divorce Records from Freewill Baptist Publications 1819–1851

CD: Freewill Baptist Vital Statistics, 1811–1851

Heritage Books by David C. Young (with Elizabeth Keene Young):

Marriage and Divorce Records from Maine Freewill Baptist Publications, 1819–1851

Stackpole's History of Winthrop, Maine, with Genealogical Notes

Heritage Books by Benjamin Lewis Keene (with Elizabeth Keene Young):

Marriage Notices from the Maine Farmer 1833

International Standard Book Number
Paperbound: 978-0-7884-0599-0

CONTENTS

FOREWORD

Newspapers can be a major source of vital records for genealogical research in Maine. David Colby Young, my husband, and Benjamin Lewis Keene, our nephew, have completed a project, originally started over half a century ago by the National Youth Administration. Working under the supervision of Clarence A. Day, Extension Service, University of Maine at Orono, the three students who did the original abstractions were: Oscar R. Martin, class of 1940; Carlton B. Payson, class of 1941; and J. Herbert Roberts, class of 1942. At that time the *Maine Farmer* collection was under the supervision of Mr. Louis T. Ibbetson, librarian of the University of Maine, and Miss Theresa R. Stuart, librarian of the Maine State Library, who deserve recognition for giving permission to copy from the issues in their possession. Special appreciation is due to the NYA authorities and Dean Arthur L. Deering of the College of Agriculture, University of Maine, for their interest and support.

The task was originally financed by the National Youth Administration, under the local direction of Philip J. Brockway. It was abandoned when funds were no longer available. It later continued through the interest of Arthur L. Deering, director of Agricultural Extension Services, University of Maine. Miss Eleanor Lounsbury deserves much credit for her patient and painstaking typing.

The Maine Farmer Company ran a 2x2 inch advertisement on March 23, 1916, "*Maine Farmers* Wanted - Our files lack volumes 10, 11, 19, and 21. We would like to correspond with anyone who has a complete file of *Maine Farmers* for any of the years mentioned 1842, 1843, 1851, 1853. The Maine Farmer Co. Augusta ME."

It is interesting that *The Kennebec Journal* of Augusta, Maine, has a whole year (1842) missing from its microfilm collection. The editors found that the original typescript did not include issues for: 1848, 1851, part of 1852, and July 4, 1840, to December 5, 1840. They were able to incorporate the missing records except for issue Aug. 6, 1842, and one issue in 1843.

Death, birth and other vital records compiled from the *Maine Farmer* cover the entire state of Maine, but most are from the Kennebec Valley. Both professional and amateur genealogists should find them useful, not only for the information contained, but also for the clues they give to finding further information.

Elizabeth Keene Young
P.O. Box 152
Danville, ME
Dec. 1995

PREFACE

In 1833, there were six other agricultural papers in the United States. Only three (*New England Farmer*, 1822; *The Country Gentleman*, 1831 and the *Maine Farmer*, 1833) of the seven papers survived in any form in 1900. The *Maine Farmer*, established in 1833 by Dr. Ezekiel Holmes, was published weekly for nearly a hundred years and devoted to the interest of agriculture and mechanic arts.

The *Maine Farmer* was originally called the *Kennebec Farmer*, and its first issue was dated January 21, 1833. At that time, there was already a different paper being published, called the *Maine Farmer*. That paper went out of print a short time later and the *Kennebec Farmer* changed its name to the *Maine Farmer* on March 18, 1833.

William Noyes (born 15 Mar 1809, died 16 Mar 1882, age 73 at Biddeford, ME) was the first printer of the *Maine Farmer*, and the head of the firm Wm. Noyes and Co. When Mr. Noyes and Company started the *Maine Farmer* the subscription list was 200. The editors of the *Maine Farmer* downplayed William Noyes' role and seemed to put him in the shadow of Dr. Holmes, who, according to them, was the real father of the paper. Dr. Holmes was a benevolent man, but with no head for business. Mr. Noyes was the businessman, and for more than fifty years was connected with the Maine press. Noyes entered the printing office of Joseph Griffin of Brunswick, ME, and served an apprenticeship of seven years which terminated in 1821. After his graduation he worked in Boston, Nashua and Hallowell. William Noyes was the printer of the *Farmer* for the first eleven years, and sold out to Mr. Russell Eaton of Augusta, ME, at no profit. In 1845, in company with the late Louis O. Cowan, Mr. Noyes started the *Union* at Biddeford, ME, later called the *Union and Journal*. They were burned out in 1847; the following year the partnership was dissolved and Mr. Noyes opened a job printing office in Biddeford. He subsequently engaged in several newspaper enterprises, the last of which was the *York County Independent* at Saco, ME. In 1880 he retired and returned to Biddeford.

The *Maine Farmer* moved several times. It was published at Winthrop from 1833 to January 27, 1837; at Hallowell from February, 1837, to October 9, 1838; at Winthrop again from October 16, 1838, to the end of 1843. In 1842, the paper size was made larger. The paper was split into two publications, the *Maine Farmer and Mechanic's Advocate* (new series) and the monthly *Maine Farmer*. Both of these papers were printed in Winthrop and Portland for the years 1842 and 1843, however, the monthly *Maine Farmer* was short lived. While the weekly *Maine Farmer* was being printed in Winthrop and Portland, Francis Ormond, Jonathan Smith and Dr. E. Holmes were the editors.

In January 1844, Mr. William Noyes sold out to Russell Eaton, who moved the paper to Augusta where it was located to until 8 June 1924. Mr. Eaton was a practical printer, in the prime of manhood and had considerable experience in publishing papers. His subscription list ran from the hundreds into the thousands and the paper took the first rank as the organ of the farmers of Maine. In 1858, after publishing the paper for fourteen years, he sold out to Homan and Manley, former owners of the *Gospel Banner*. The *Maine Farmer* was published by them until 1861, when on account of poor health, Mr. Manley sold his half of the business interest to William S. Badger. Mr. Homan continued his interest until 1878, when he sold out to his nephew, Joseph H. Manley. On the death of Dr. Holmes in 1865, Dr. Nathaniel T. True took charge as agricultural editor. On April 6, 1869, the job went to Mr. Boardman, who held the position until 1879, when he left to become the editor of the *Bangor Commercial*. Dr. William B. Lapham then became agricultural editor of the *Maine Farmer*.

At first the paper gave little attention to its news columns. They were generally managed by the agricultural editor and the publishers. Mr. Seavy, during his brief connection with the paper, attended to the news department, which was later administered by Mr. Robbins. After the purchase of the property by Mr. Eaton more attention was paid to news gleaning and Dr. Holmes, Benjamin F. Robbins, Eli Manley, Russell P. Eaton and W. S. Gilman were among the news department personnel. Mr. Homan conducted the news department from 1858-1872; Dr. W. B. Lapham, 1872-1878; J. H. Manley, 1878-1881; and Howard Owen, 1881-1882.

In 1913 William H. Davis was manager and editor of the *Maine Farmer*, with Clare H. Harvey as assistant editor. On November 27, 1913, the Maine Farmer Company was changed to Charles W. Carson and Company, with C. H. Harvey as managing editor until March 11, 1915, when the name, The Maine Farmer Company, was once again used with C. H. Harvey as editor and manager.

In 1921, the Guy Gannett Corp. owned both the *Press Herald* and the *Maine Farmer*. The *Maine Farmer* was printed until June 8, 1924, when it merged with the *Sunday Press Herald*. It was a supplement to *Portland Press Herald* Sunday edition from June 15, 1924, to July 26, 1925. The publication is now called the *Maine Sunday Telegram*.

The publishers of the *Maine Farmer* considered their paper a fine example of family values and high moral standards. As we read the paper today, the statement made on November 10, 1892, seems humorous: "The (Maine) Farmer's advertising columns were watched with care then as now and we find no advertisement of a dangerous or harmful character, no announcements of New England rum for sale, or creatures in the form of men advertising their wives as having left THEIR BED and BOARD...." But in actuality the *Maine Farmer* had many ads for "Dr. Green's Nervura" and other so-called "patent medicines." Before the the Federal Food, Drug, and Cosmetic Act was adopted "patent medicine" formulas were kept secret but were in fact mostly alcohol. With its strong temperance feelings this paper most likely would not have endorsed these narcotic-based medicines in the same way if they had known the formulas. However, the *Maine Farmer* did print many ads in the form of news articles with drawings of people endorsing these "patent medicines." The names of the people endorsing the drugs with their portraits can be found in the special index for 1833-1924.

In the 1800's rope was made from the hemp plant. The *Maine Farmer* advocated the growing of hemp as an agricultural cash-crop in Aroostook County for the purpose of making cloth. The *Maine Farmer* stated on November 10, 1887, "We were glad, Tuesday to greet our old friend, Capt. John H. DREW of Farmingdale, Maine, who is enjoying for a few weeks the delights of home, having recently arrived in Boston, Massachusetts, from Manila, after a year's voyage bringing a cargo of HEMP. In about three weeks he will sail from Philadelphia for Samatra loaded with oil." Again, the paper would not have endorsed the growing of hemp if the publishers had known of the narcotic uses of hemp.

* * *

For the convenience of the reader, the words "in this town" have been replaced, when possible, with the actual name of the town in which the paper was published. Accounts of gifts of wedding cake to the editor and similar references usually have been omitted.

The Maine Farmer obtained some of its information from other newspapers. Most entries, death notices or news articles include the source of the information. We have so noted the source in brackets [ ]. The date in brackets is the date of the issue of the paper in which the item appeared.

The editors would like to thank Mrs. Bonnie Collins of the Maine State Library for furnishing us with a copy of the typescript, and the University of Maine Library for permission to publish this work. We would also like to thank Nicholas Noyes of the Maine Historical Society, and Danny Smith of Gardiner, Maine, who deserves our appreciation as well.

The editors have made a great effort to be correct. We have copied the important information so there is no need to check the newspaper. However, those who require a photocopy can write to Bates College Library, Lewiston, ME. For a small fee a photocopy can be obtained. If you require a photocopy of the issues which were not microfilmed you may be out of luck, as neither the Maine State Library nor the Maine Historical Society have copy services for the public.

David C. Young
P. O. Box 152
Danville, ME

ABBREVIATIONS

adm	administrator(s)/ administratrix(es) of estate	ggch	great grandchild
		h/o	husband of
ae	age	inst	instant (of this month)
AmRev	Revolutionary War veteran	JP	justice of the peace
		m	married
b	born	mer	merchant
bro	brother	m/o	mother of
ch	child, children	nat/o	native of
c/o	child of	pb	probably born
commr	commisioner(s) of estate	pd	probably died
consort	wife or spouse	relict	widow
d	died	schr	schooner
d/o, dau/o	daughter of	sis/o	sister of
estnot	estate notice	ult	ultimo (of the previous month)
exe	executor(s)/ executrix(es) of estate		
		w/o	wife of
f/o	father of	wid/o	widow of
gch	grandchild		

AALL [*sic*] Jane 50 w/o Col John A at Great Falls in Gorham NH [6 Feb 1845]
ABBOTT/ABBOT Abel of Andover MA fired upon on the turnpike [10 Oct 1837]
    Abiel 58 at Waldo Plantation ME [19 Aug 1836]
    Achsah 15 yr d/o Philip A at Dixfield ME on 10th ult [10 July 1841]
    Anna Elizabeth inf d/o of Rev Samuel P A at Farmington ME [5 Sept 1844]
    Benjamin 87 first in the Harvard class of 1786, Preceptor of Philips Academy in Exeter
        for more than 50y [*Salem Gazette*] [22 Nov 1849]
    Betsey 17 yr at Boston d/o Isaac A of Norway ME [29 May 1845]
    Catherine M 26 w/o Ezra A Jr at Jackson ME [19 Aug 1847]
    Charles H [in?] a house destroyed by fire on Thurs at Glenburn ME [18 May 1839]
    Elizabeth 20 at Belfast ME [12 Sept 1850]
    Eunice 44 w/o Abiel A at Sidney ME [21 May 1846]
    George Esq 37 at Thomaston ME [15 Aug 1850]
    George F 8y gs/o William ABBOTT Esq, his parents of New Orleans, at Bangor ME
        with mother on a visit, drowned in Bruce's Mill Pond at Bangor ME [8 Aug 1844]
    Harriet (VAUGHAN) Mrs 41 w/o Rev Jacob A at Farmington ME [30 Sept 1843]
    Henry 92 AmRev at Boothbay ME [2 Jul 1846]
    Isaac Dea 91 AmRev at Andover ME [5 Aug 1836]
    Isaac Esq 57 at Jackson ME [27 Mar 1851]
    Jacob Esq 70 at Farmington ME [4 Feb 1847]
    Jacob Rev of Windham drowned on Sun last and Mr DINSMORE shared his fate [*Exeter*
        NH Letter] [14 Nov 1834]
    James abt 80 of Franklin ME wandered away from home, killed by a falling tree on 25th
        ult (reported by R TINKER Esq) [*Ellsworth Democrat*] [10 Feb 1848]
    John Wilson Capt; Shipwreck of brig *Sarah Lovett* of St. Stephen NB Canada, on 22 Dec
        the wreck was fallen in with by the brig *Ann*, TODD Capt of Shelburne & the two
        survivors taken on board & landed a day after at Barrington NB. The following died:
        Capt John Wilson ABBOT, 2nd s/o Mr George ABBOTT, merchant of this parish ae
        19y 2m 12d. Chief mate Mathew CLINDENIN of St David NB Canada ae 26y. 2nd
        mate, Wm. HELMS, an English lad. Seamen: William ALLEN of St Stephen ae abt
        17; HOLLAND, a young man belonging to St. Andrews & George
    John Esq 84 formerly of Brunswick ME at Andover MA [15 July 1843]
    Joseph 16 s/o Otho ABBOTT of Belfast ME lost overboard from schr *Watchman* on 16th
        ult on the passage from New York to Bermuda [13 Apr 1848]
    Joseph 80 at Livermore ME [21 Jan 1833]
    Joseph R Esq 68 at Augusta ME on 11 Jan [16 Jan 1851]
    Martha Ann 17 at Hallowell ME [7 Oct 1843]
    Mary 82 at Farmington ME [14 June 1849]
    Mary Kimball 4 only c/o Isaac C A at E Thomaston ME [19 Feb 1846]
    Moses 63 at Windsor VT on 12 May [23 May 1850]
    Otho 63 at Belfast ME [11 Mar 1852]
    Philip abt 80 of 1st settlers at Rumford ME [10 Apr 1841]
    Rufus H 32 at Augusta ME [23 Oct 1851]
    Samuel S Rev 34 at Farmington ME on 29th June [12 July 1849]
    Thankful 73 wid/o Constant ABBOTT at Vassalboro ME on 13 May [1 June 1848]
    Wheeler 36 s/o Isaac ABBOTT of Norway ME at Boston MA [7 Sep 1848]
    William Esq 73 of typhus fever of Bangor ME on 25th ult [6 Sept 1849]
    William Jr 23 a native of Castine ME at New Orleans LA [3 Oct 1837]
    William of North Berwick ME while on return from Dover NH on Tues fell from his
        team, not thought to live [30 Jul 1842]

ABBOTT (Cont.) - see FARWELL, HASTINGS

ABERCROMBIE - see TURRILL

Abolitionists - see FISLAR

ABORN Ebenezer 31 at Knox [25 Sept 1851]
> Joan 39 w/o Fred A at Augusta ME on 13 June [28 June 1849]
> Emma Nouse 3y 4m d/o F ABORN at Augusta ME on 8 Oct [14 Oct 1852]

ABRAHAM Mrs 26 w/o Robert A at Eastport ME [20 Mar 1845]
> Mary Mrs 86 at Augusta ME [9 Dec 1852]

ACHORN Calista 17 at Waldoboro ME [9 Jan 1841]
> Mary G 15y 6m hanging herself "nothing unusual in her conduct on the day of her death. She was as cheerful as usual." at Thomaston ME on 2d inst [*Recorder*] [24 Sept 1842]

ADAMS Adeline C 29 w/o Charles A at Levant ME [3 Jan 1850]
> Amos 98 AmRev pensioner at Madison ME [27 Mar 1845]
> Andrew at Wayne Indiana shot his bro, Martin A [16 Oct 1851]
> Benjamin Capt 56 of Pittsfield ME at Hallowell ME [22 Mar 1849]
> Betsy 24 at Belfast ME [9 May 1844]
> Charles 24 at Rumford ME [27 Nov 1845]
> child 21m c/o Mr E H ADAMS, endured a long sickness, a few days since discharged from its bowels three common sized suspender buttons, three smaller ones, one button mould, one pearl button &, most remarkable, a piece of cork the size of a small walnut! The child is now doing well. [*Woonsocket Patriot*] [30 Oct 1841]
> Clarissa 24 w/o Elias A Esq at Greene ME [7 Nov 1837]
> Eliza a girl employed by Mr DALLERY's jewelry factory in Williamsbury NY, accident with filling a lighted lamp Jan HANNA burnt and died also Jane THOMAS seriously burnt [4 Sept 1851]
> Eliza K 38 w/o Augustus ADAMS Esq at Farmington ME [26 June 1851]
> F Esq, OR Emigrants (a letter, to Philadelphia 19 May '45) "I left (Oregon) emigrants above the main crossing of Kansas abt 100 miles from (Independence) on Thurs, 15 May; cannot tell precise number of souls, abt 300 families and an immense quantity of stock &c Five Co of dragoons started from Leavenworth for Ft Lairrul and South Pass day before yesterday" [*Phil Ledger*] [19 June 1845]
> Francis 69 at Brunswick ME [29 Jun 1839]
> George of Cornish ME knocked down by a horse on Sat, (Mr ADAMS's) physician on Sun "symptoms of returning consciousness, but hopes of recovery slight" [*Portland Bulletin*] [*Portland Advertiser*] [27 May 1847] [3 June 1847]
> Hannah 31 w/o Joseph A at Kennebunkport ME [3 Mar 1838]
> Harriet in the family of Mr C B MORTON, a shoe dealer at Augusta ME committed suicide [12 Aug 1843]
> Harriet W 43 w/o W B A Rev at Lewiston Falls ME (Jan 17) [30 Jan 1841]
> Isaac Esq 60 at Portland ME [11 Jul 1834]
> Isaac Esq 72 at Gilead ME [7 Dec 1848]
> J Q "on Camden and Amboy RR (between New York and Philadelphia) on 8th inst abt 4 miles from Hightstown and 14 from Amboy, axle broke, 24 persons in the car (among them J Q ADAMS of MA) all of whom escaped uninjured. Another car thrown against the one above named; forced from the rail, (a Mr STEDMAN of NC) killed and 9 others seriously injured, one of whom has since died." [23 Nov 1833]
> James Esq abt 50 at Norridgewock ME on 30th ult "the Independent Order of Odd Fellows attended his funeral in large numbers. He held the office of P.G. in the lodge at the time of this death." [*Mann's Physician*] [14 Sept 1848]
> John a deserter from the service of Uncle Sam in Boston MA, enlisted during the war, retaken and delivered up to his officer but on his way to New York in the steamer

ADAMS (Cont.) *Bay State*, jumped overboard directly in front of the paddle wheel and
  drowned [5 Aug 1847]
  John abt 45 at Greene ME [25 Dec 1838]
  John Esq s/o John Quincy A at Washington City [7 Nov 1834]
  John late of Greene ME est notice, Jabez PRATT adm [17 Aug 1839]
  John President of USA ae 91 died 4 Jul 1826 [5 Aug 1836]
  John Q 19 a clerk to Darwin CHAFFIN, who keeps the gentlemen's furnishing store,
    hanged himself at his boarding house of George GIBSON, left a mother living in
    Watertown MA [*Boston Post*] [6 June 1844]
  John Quincy 81 d 23 Feb a native of Braintree MA left a wid, dau of the late Col Joshua
    JOHNSON of MD - one son, Charles Francis A of this city - and several grand-ch.
    [*Atlas*] [2 Mar 1848] and among 1000's who came to Washington were colored
    people of Philadelphia who asked permission of the mayor to let them make some
    public demonstration [*Woonsocket Patriot*] [9 Mar 1848]
  John W the missing soldier found and sent from Charlestown on Fri to Brunswick ME
    his native place who enlisted 12 mos ago for the Mexican War, lost an eye and
    wounded in the knee, the jaw and stomach [*Boston Bee*] [4 May 1848] [27 Apr 1848]
  Joseph H 14 formerly of Pittston ME at Wiscasset ME [2 Nov 1848]
  Julia 19 of thin shoes on 17 Apr 1838 (stated on her epitaph in New Jersey) [*Gospel
    Banner*] [26 Oct 1848]
  Lemuel 56 at Farmington ME [17 May 1849]
  Lydia of Carratunk plantation w/o Seth ADAMS suicide on the 3d inst by taking poison,
    left 9 ch, youngest only 4 months [*People's Press*] [19 Jul 1849]
  Martha 79y 6m 12d w/o Moses A, the mother of 14 ch, all whom lived and married, 11
    still live to mourn her loss, grandmother of 106, ggm of 47 at Wilton ME on 3 Feb
    [17 Feb 1848]
  Mary A 27 w/o William F A at Belfast ME [16 Sept 1852]
  Mary 5 d/o Amos A at Portland ME 26 Dec 1844
  Mary Ann w/o Charles F A and d/o Jacob AMES of Chesterville at Seabrook NH [17 Jun
    1847]
  Mary F 18 at Farmington ME [11 Nov 1847]
  Michael 53 at Thomaston ME [5 April 1849]
  Mr of St Louis last week had a finger bit entirely off his left hand by a young colt [5 Oct
    1839]
  Mr the firm ADAMS and STACKPOLE in TX from Portland ME [7 Aug 1851]
  Olive B late of Greene ME est notice, Jabez PRATT exec [20 Apr 1839]
  Paulina Butts 64 w/o Caleb A at Brunswick ME [8 April 1852]
  Rebecca 22 at Limerick ME on 14th ult [21 Aug 1838]
  Samuel late of Wilton ME, est notice, Comfort ADAMS exec [29 June 1839]
  Sarah abt 66 yrs w/o Joshua A at Wales ME [21 Aug 1838]
  Sarah d/o the late Josiah ADAMS a boat on the morning of 2d inst having on board 25
    persons struck upon "Hunt's Rock" ... 19 persons including children drowned ... all of
    whom resided in Portland (ME) or at York Point. [*Portland Advertiser* and *The St
    Johns City Gazette*, 2d Aug] [14 Aug 1838]
  Solomon nearly 70y of the oldest inhabitants of Farmington ME on his way to market in
    (Hallowell) and Gardiner ME thrown from his gig in the descending of a hill in
    Vienna ME [*Hallowell Advocate*] [16 Nov 1833]
  Stephen 35 at Edgecomb ME [21 Aug 1842]
  Susannah 45 formerly of Uxbridge MA at Greene ME [9 Sept 1852]
  Thomas A 23 late of Farmington at Goshen OH [18 Nov 1836]
  Thomas Esq 64 formerly of Castine ME at Roxbury MA [13 Jan 1848]

ADAMS (Cont.) Weston Pela Rev former pastor of the Congregational Church in Danville at Danville ME [30 Oct 1841]

William W Esq 25 youngest s/o Capt Josph C Adams of Bloomfield at Marthasville, Warren Co, MO on 2nd ult [19 Sept 1844]

ADAMS - see JEWETT, LaFAYETTE, MUSSENDEN, THOMPSON

ADDINGTON Charles C drowned at Niagara Falls [5 Jul 1849]

ADDISON Charles C 8 mo s/o Cornelius and Mary E A at Readfield on April 12 [22 April 1847]

ADLE children (two) of Cornelius A of the canker rash now prevalent [8 April 1833]

African youth - see JONES

African - see BRAKELEY

Afro-American Revolutionary soldiers - see BAILEY

AGIN William a drunken demon of Boston MA last week deliberately emptied a kettle of boiling water over the shoulders and bosom of his wife in one of his moments of unreasonable anger. Sent to the House of Correction for 6 months. [7 Sept 1839]

AGRY Elizabeth w/o John A Esq at Hallowell ME of typhus fever [2 Jan 1841]

Elizabeth (Mrs) 44 at Bath ME [22 Jan 1839]

John Esq 80 at Hallowell ME [13 Jul 1848]

Thomas Esq 63 at Bath ME [8 Jan 1852]

AIKEN Daniel 120 married 7 times had 570 gch and ggch - 370 boys and 200 girls at Wexford Canada West [18 May 1848]

William 16 of Bath ME lost overboard from schr *Oliver* on 10th inst on passage from Albany to Providence [25 Nov 1852]

AIKEN - see SIMS

AKELEY Elizabeth 68 consort of Samuel Akeley at Rumford ME on 20th inst [23 April 1842]

ALBEE Ebenezer at Wiscasset ME [21 Sept 1848]

John 42 at Hallowell ME [25 Nov 1843]

Jonathan 100 yrs an AmRev pensioner at Lexington ME [27 Mar 1845]

Obadiah Capt 86 AmRev formerly of Wiscasset ME at Hallowell ME [16 Dec 1852]

Sarah Mrs 58 at Bath ME [3 June 1852]

ALBERTI - see THOMPSON

ALBERTSON Savory 16 of PA belonged to the US ship *Preble* died with the African fever at Porto Grande Island of St Vincent Cape de Verds on 9 Dec [10 Apr 1845]

ALDEN Mr of Canton ME found dead in the boom [an area surrounded by a floating varrier or a log jam] at Brunswick ME missing from Canton since last fall, recognized by the clothing [15 Jul 1847]

Spooner Esq 68y 9m at Newburgh ME [29 June 1848]

ALDEN Miss abt 25y a relative of Augustus ALDEN Esq and residing in his family took her own life [*Hallowell Standard* of the 28th inst] [4 Jan 1844]

Augustus Esq 70 at Hallowell ME [24 Jan 1850]

Austin 56 of protracted illness a native of Gorham at Winthrop ME on 13th inst [21 Feb 1841]

Caroline 25 yrs w/o Darius A at Augusta ME [27 Mar 1838]

Charles Thomas 18 mo s/o Darius A at Augusta ME [23 Jan 1838]

Charlotte 22 yrs formerly of Gorham ME at Winthrop ME on 16th inst [4 Sept 1845]

Harriet N 16 d/o Martin A at Winthrop ME on 16th inst [26 June 1835]

Lewis 52 at Dresden ME [8 Nov 1849]

Peter O abt 70 at Brunswick ME [25 Feb 1843]

Thankful abt 52 wid at Turner ME [3 April 1835]

ALDEN - see LEONARD

ALDIS Asa of St Albans VT formerly Chief Justice of advanced age on Sat the 16th inst [25 Nov 1847]

ALDRICH Elias T 41 native of Livermore ME at Memphis TN on 7 Oct [1 Nov 1849] three brothers since dead at TX from ME [7 Aug 1851]

ALEXANDER Abigail 82 at Hallowell ME [24 Jul 1851]
> boy s/o Washington A of starving [*Woodstock (VA) Tenth Legion*] [13 Sept 1849]
> Hacker 22 of Bowdoin ME mate of brig *Charles* at Wilmington NC [12 Mar 1846]
> Joseph 59 at Hallowell ME [4 April 1850]
> Joseph 60 at the hospital in Augusta ME of Brunswick ME [18 July 1844]
> lad 13 s/o Mr ALEXANDER by lightning while in a boat off Harpswell ME on Thurs the 3d inst [*Forester*] [17 Jul 1845]
> Mr Lord Sterling at Albany [*The Cincinnati Advertiser*] [16 Sept 1847]
> Stanwood Esq 59 at Richmond ME [2 Sept 1852]

ALGER Laura G 37 w/o Lyman A, merchant of Clemsford, and d/o Mr Dean HOWARD of Winthrop ME at Saxonsville MA on 20th ult [21 July 1843]

ALL Levi married Miss Jane WRIGHT "all right" [*Concord Freeman*] [10 Sept 1842]

ALLARD Henry abt 22y an unmarried man accident at Pepperell Mills [*Biddeford ME Advertizer*] [26 June 1851]

ALLBEE Benjamin 74 at Windsor ME on 6th inst [18 Feb 1847]
> Martha Jane 27 w/o O F ALLBEE at North Anson ME on 13 Feb [22 Feb 1849]

ALLEN Albert 27y of Norridgewock ME at Winthrop ME on 1st Sept [13 Sept 1849]
> an infant c/o Dr F ALLEN at Hallowell ME [11 Sept 1845]
> Andrew and Daniel ALLEN and Israel GREGORY Jr all drowned on New Years night, while passing the channel from Seal Harbor to the Muscleridges, near Thomaston ME. The first two left families [16 Jan 1841]
> Benjamin of Rome ME at Belgrade ME, near Chandler's mill drowned in Long Pond [the *Lewiston Journal*] [2 Jan 1851] and [5 Aug 1852]
> Betsey 16 d/o Capt Samuel ALLEN at Dresden ME on the 2nd [17 Dec 1842]
> Betsey w/o Charles ALLEN at Corinna ME [2 Sept 1852]
> Capt 47 left a wife and family of Thomaston ME [15 June 1848]
> Charles 70 at Vassalboro ME [28 Oct 1843]
> child abt 1y of Bangor ME c/o James ALLEN on Wed [28 Nov 1844]
> Daniel 56y at Augusta ME [9 Jan 1838]
> Daniel 93 AmRev pensioner at Winthrop ME [13 Jan 1848]
> Daniel O abt 33 at Winthrop ME on Mon last [10 Apr 1836] [29 Jan 1836]
> Daniel attended 80 successive shearings, since the year 1760, when ae 5 yrs [18 Jul 1840]
> Ebenezer 84 AmRev at Montville ME [19 Aug 1843]
> Ebenezer abt 20 at Stillwater Mills at Cherryfield ME by drowning [20 June 1844]
> Elias B 23 at Windham ME on 7th inst [1 Oct 1842]
> Elizabeth 57 w/o Samuel ALLEN at Thomaston ME [8 Jan 1852]
> Elsie 77 wid/o Woodard ALLEN at Litchfield ME [15 May 1851]
> Ephraim W Esq 66y at Newburyport MA, for 30y editor and publisher of the *Newburyport Herald* [26 Mar 1846]
> Ezra 75 at Augusta ME on 20 Jan [6 Feb 1851]
> George G 23 s/o Freeman ALLEN of Madison ME at Matamoras [24 Sept 1846]
> girl abt 7 of Bangor ME d/o Mr ALLEN drowned [29 Jul 1843]
> Hannah abt 35 at Winthrop ME [20 Mar 1835]
> Hannah B w/o Frederick ALLEN Esq at Gardiner [27 Apr 1848]
> Helen Victoria abt 4y d/o Major Daniel ALLEN at Fairfield ME [26 Aug 1843]

ALLEN (Cont.) James a sick sailor of Camden ME was transported by Capt RICHARDSON of Deer Isle in an open carriage 12 miles from Pembroke to Eastport ME. His last words were "It was cruel to bring me so far when I was so sick!" (from the *Kennebec Journal*) [*Eastport Sentinel* 22nd inst] [6 Aug 1846]

Jennet 43 w/o Isaac ALLEN at Turner ME on 20th ult [26 May 1839]

Joan 42 w/o Jacob ALLEN and sister to Mrs ROLFE at Turner ME on 14 Nov of typhus fever [10 Dec 1842]

Jonathan 21y 3m s/o Parson W ALLEN at Litchfield ME [6 May 1847]

Joseph 79 at Portland ME [19 Sept 1844]

Josephine Mrs 24 of Chelsea MA d/o Benjamin KING at her father's house at Winthrop ME [26 Apr 1849]

Lydia 37 d/o Sylvanus ALLEN Esq of Nantucket at Strong ME of consumption while residing with her friends [26 Sept 1837]

Lydia Mrs 77 by her clothes taking fire at West Waterville ME on 3 Apr at the res of William H HATCH Esq [13 Apr 1848]

Macon B of Portland ME (& formerly of Boston MA) a colored gentleman at first not admitted to the Maine Bar on the grounds not a citizen of Maine, yesterday admitted in the District Court, to practice as an Attorney and Counsellor at Law in the Courts of this State. [*Portland American*] [5 Sept 1844]

Maria Malleville 16 d/o Dr William ALLEN at Brunswick ME [11 Feb 1833]

Mr B of Rome ME and Mr SCRIBNER of Mt Vernon ME drowned while skating on Long Pong (sic), near Chandler's Mills in Belgrade ME. A letter from Mr S dated 9th inst "I take pleasure informing you that I don't believe one word of the above statement so far as it relates to myself nor can I make any one else believe it" Mr ALLEN drowned on Sun. [*Lewiston Journal*] [16 Jan 1851]

Mr the Attorney General of TX from Kennebec Co ME [7 Aug 1851]

N H Dr 28 at Gray ME [21 Feb 1841]

Nancy G T 29 w/o Capt Robert A of the US Army and d/o Hon William P PREBLE of Portland.ME at Portland ME [20 Aug 1846]

Nathaniel Capt 78 at North Sedwick ME [20 Nov 1851]

Norris 24 s/o Elder Datus ALLEN at Industry ME [15 Jan 1852]

Oliver T 21 at Perry ME [19 Nov 1846]

Phebe 18 d/o George ALLEN drowned off Nantucket on the 24th ult [2 Aug 1849]

Ruth Clefford 27 at East Readfield ME of pulmonary consumption [24 Oct 1840]

S Holman a printer 30y 6m formerly of Winthrop ME s/o Eliab ALLEN at Natick MA [14 June 1849]

Sally abt 78 wid/o Benjamin ALLEN at Corinth ME on 17th instant [2 Dec 1847]

Samuel Rev 55 of Deer Isle ME at Levant ME on 8th ult [4 Jan 1834]

Sarah 75 w/o Mr Daniel ALLEN at Winthrop ME on Sun last [31 Jul 1838]

Susan 50 w/o George W ALLEN and d/o the late Capt William ROBINSON at Augusta ME on 12 Nov [18 Nov 1852]

Susanna 62 w/o Deac Jos B ALLEN at Monmouth ME [22 Mar 1849]

Thomas tobacconist, committed suicide on 23rd ult by throwing himself from Charles River Bridge [*Boston Atlas*] [1 Jul 1836]

Velina S 7y 8m d/o George ALLEN at Augusta ME on 5 Oct [16 Oct 1845]

William 78 AmRev at China ME [18 Apr 1834]

William Capt 86y 10m of Industry ME at the res of Dr COOK at New Sharon ME [ap Nov 1842]

William R 26 formerly of Smithfield ME at Bloomfield ME [12 Apr 1849]

Woodward 88 at Litchfield ME [4 Jan 1849]

Zebulon Esq 75 at Farmington ME [9 Jan 1838]

Zylpha 52 at Augusta ME on 27th inst [30 May 1844]

ALLEN - see ABBOTT, BRYANT, MAXAM, SIMS

ALLEY Alfred Capt Capt formerly of Nantucket at Vassalboro ME [17 May 1849]

> Ephraim of St George ME found floating in the dock near Pratt's wharf the appearance of a sailor or stevedore abt 25 and had red hair and whiskers, left a wife and 2 ch, one of the crew of schr *North Carolina* [*Traveller*]

> John of St George ME one of three Maine men who drowned at Norfolk VA of the crew on the schr *May Flower*, HUPPER Capt [11 Nov 1847]

AMEDEY John B Capt 49 at Hallowell ME [12 Dec 1844]

AMES Benjamin 58 at Houlton ME on 28th ult [9 Oct 1835]

> Benjamin F Capt 22y of Osterville [*sic*], Barnstable loss the schr *Saluda*, AMES Capt of Boston MA, all the crew perished excepting the mate, Peter PETERSON of Hyannis [*Boston Journal*, Feb 5] [13 Feb 1845]

> Benjamin Rev abt 82 at St George ME [4 Sept 1845]

> David 87 old paper maker at Springfield is dead. All the paper used bore the stamp of "Ames" [19 Aug 1847]

> Hannah upwards of 90y severely burnt the day before by her clothes taking fire at Yarmouth ME on Mon of last week [24 Apr 1851]

> John J second officer from Belfast ME lost on the brig *Linden*, a sea disaster, Griffith Capt [19 Nov 1842]

> Lucy 78 wid/o Ezra A at Farmington ME [13 Mar 1851]

> Mary Jane 28 d/o Daniel and Mary AMES at Lewiston ME [20 Mar 1851]

> Mellen C 23 at Herman ME [14 Nov 1850]

> N P 44 biographical sketch, manufacturer of swords and fire-arms ... [*Springfield Republican*] [6 May 1847]

> Nancy 63 w/o Phineas AMES at Jefferson ME very suddenly [23 June 1852]

> son /o Jacob AMES 12 killed on the afternoon of the 4th by being thrown out of a wagon, the wheels passing over his breast. Copied from the *Belfast Journal* of (Belfast?) ME [13 Jul 1848]

> W 21at Freeman ME [14 Sept 1839]

AMSBURY Charlotte T 23 w/o Capt Thomas AMSBURY at Camden ME [26 June 1851]

ANDERSON Abigail C abt 10y d/o Ephraim ANDERSON at Augusta ME [28 Dec 1833]

> Almira 19 w/o Joseph ANDERSON Jr at Eastport ME [2 Jul 1846]

> Angeline S 17 at Norridgewock ME [31 Jul 1845]

> Dr of TN invented a hempcutter. [not a death notice] [21 Nov 1834]

> Francis Julia 7 d/o Mr ANDERSON, a teacher, of clothes catching fire while attempting to toast bread at Alleghany, parents moved from Philadelphia PA [28 Oct 1836]

> Henry F 35 of Skowhegan ME at the US Marine Hospital Chelsea MA [16 Dec 1852]

> J Mr a seaman of Maine lost overboard from ship *Henry Clay* on passage from Cronstad to New York [12 Feb 1842]

> James 84 at Lisbon ME [11 Oct 1849]

> Jane B 61 w/o Martin ANDERSON Esq at Waterville ME [8 June 1848]

> Jeremiah 21 of Eden ME lost from brig *Franklin* [17 May 1849]

> John of Wiscasset ME bro of Governor A in his bed yesterday morning, committed suicide, but report is contradicted [*Bath Tribune*, 2d] [30 Sept 1847]

> Robert (Sr) 87y 5m AmRev at Lewiston ME (see page 87 and 375 Elder's History of Lewiston ME) [30 Sept 1843]

> Samuel a seaman of Trenton ME belonging to schr *Mary Ann* of Ellsworth ME lowering a boat in Portsmouth NH harbor last Wed [6 June 1840]

> Sarah Mrs 62 at Baileyville on 10 June [18 Jul 1850]

> William 30 at Limington ME [8 June 1848]

ANDRE - see HALL

ANDREWS Abiezer 77 at Paris ME [6 Jan 1848]

ANDREWS (Cont.) Charles Hon 38y 2m representative in Congress and formerly speaker in Maine house of representatives at Paris ME [6 May 1852]

Eliza Frances d/o Horace and Sarah A ANDREWS at Augusta ME [17 Dec 1846]

Ephraim 90 AmRev at Guilford ME [5 June 1845]

Horace Augustus 10 s/o H A ANDREWS [27 Sept 1849]

James over 70 at Warren ME [29 Jan 1848]

Jane 19 and Juliet MILLER 13y dau's/o Ira ANDREWS and Samuel MILLER at Wallingford CT drowned [5 Jul 1849]

Joanna over 102y at Gloucester MA [11 Feb 1847]

John Esq 52 at Wales ME on 1 Jan [18 Jan 1849]

Joseph Jr 7 of an injury received by being jammed between the railroad cars s/o Joseph ANDREWS at Lewiston ME [4 June 1851]

Josiah Esq of Perry NY a native of Augusta ME s/o Major Mark ANDREWS, in feeble health left his home for Philadelphia PA died 16th inst [2 Dec 1847]

Mark Major 88 AmRev born at Taunton MA, moved from Augusta ME to Perry NY [8 June 1848] and on 16th inst [25 May 1848]

Mary 40 w/o James ANDREWS at Lisbon ME [14 Mar 1837]

Nicholas died at the Hospital at South Boston MA [2 Aug 1849]

Ruth Mrs 84 consort of Major Mark ANDREWS formerly of Augusta ME at Perry NY [6 May 1847]

ANNABLE Frances Ann 3y 11m d/o Harrison W and Ann S ANNABLE [12 Nov 1846]

Robert 57y 5m at Augusta ME on Tues [4 Nov 1847] and laborer from our office, wheelman of our power-press ever since in operation, suffered himself by the allurements of strong drink, but the Washingtonian reform commenced, among the first to embrace it, signed the pledge. Fare thee well, Robert! [4 Nov 1847]

Mr a cabinet maker, lost in a fire his wife and two dau's (from the *North Groton MA Letter*) [26 June 1851]

Mrs and her 2 ch burned to death on Fri, Mr A procured a quantity of gum and turpentine to manufacture into varnish, put the articles in a kettle on the stove to heat and went to the barn for the purpose of milking, returned to the house a flash fire around the room, dressed in woolen clothes not much injured at Groton NH [*Meredith Bridge Democrat*] [3 Jul 1851]

ANNAS Lydia 20 of Bethel ME at Lewiston Falls ME [8 Feb 1844]

ANNIS Samuel 84 at Camden ME [20 Dec 1849]

ANTHON - see COLT

ANTHONY John C formerly of (Augusta ME) funeral attended by the Sabattis Lodge I.O. of Odd Fellows, a member at Portland ME on 10th [15 Jan 1852]

ANTHONY and **GABRIEL** negroes hanged at Lexington KY last week for murder of Joseph LYON [4 Sept 1851]

ANTHONY child an infant of Mr John ANTHONY at Augusta ME on Mon morning [5 Sept 1844]

Jacob of Cohoes and his wife and John LYMAN and his wife and son of Rochester, Mrs ANTHONY cut in two, LYMAN badly injured and his wife and son slightly and the driver not injured and only one of the horses killed on Thurs afternoon the western train crossing Broadway struck the barouche [4 Sept 1845]

John C 2y 4m only s/o Capt J C ANTHONY late of (Augusta ME) at Saco ME at the Thorton House on 8 Jan [17 Jan 1850]

John C Capt formerly of Augusta ME at Portland ME on 10 Jan [15 Jan 1852]

ANWELL - see BALCH

APPLETON Daniel Esq 91 at Buxton ME [25 Mar 1836]

Ivory of Vassalboro ME at San Francisco CA on the day of his arrival [17 Jan 1852]

Moses MD 76 at Waterville ME [17 May 1849]

APTHORP Mrs a letter from Mr SMITH published in the *Missionary Herald*, announces
    death at Panditeripo Ceylon on 3 Sept last [3 Jan 1850]
APPLEBY Levi of Bowdoin ME saved from drowning when the steam packet *New England*
    sank. It left Boston for Bath and Gardiner ME and had an accident with the schr
    Curlew on 31 May [12 June 1838]
APPLETON Ivory of Vassalboro ME at San Francisco CA on the day of his arrival [17 June
    1852]
APPLETON - see PACKARD, WEBSTER
ARCHER Mrs w/o Andrew ARCHER complained of being unwell and in a few minutes a
    corpse at Fairfield ME [*The Skowhegan Clarion*] [3 Jul 1845]
    Abigail Mrs 67 w/o Andrew ARCHER Esq formerly of Salem MA at Fairfield ME on 27
    May very suddenly of disease of the heart [5 June 1845]
    Andrew Esq 69 at Fairfield ME on 18 June, moved to Fairfield ME from Salem MA in
    1806 [1 Jul 1847]
ARCHIBALD Rebecca 63 at Bath ME [10 Feb 1848]
ARDEN Dr of New York in Prussia in an railroad accident [27 Feb 1851]
AREY J Capt of Frankfort ME of schr *Independence* d in wreck on Pumkin Rock off
    Damescove Island, one of the oldest shipmasters on the river. Also drowned was Mr
    ORCUTT of Bucksport, who was one of the crew. Another cew member, Mr HARVY
    of Frankfort remained upon the rock two days, when he made a raft of some of the
    deck plank and succeeded in reaching an island and obtained assistance and has
    returned to Frankfort [21 Jul 1843]
ARMISTEAD W K Brevet Brigadier General, Colonel of the US 3d Regiment of Artillery
    on 13th at Upperville VA [30 Oct 1845]
ARMISTEAD - see TAYLOR
ARMSBY Ira 27 at Farmington ME [4 Oct 1849]
    Nathan Esq at Farmington ME [25 Jul 1840]
    Sarah C Mrs 57 wid/o N ARMSBY of Farmington ME at Bloomfield ME [15 Aug 1844]
ARMSTRONG John Gen 81y of Redhook Duchess Co NY died on Sat last secretary of war
    under Mr MADISON's administration [15 Apr 1843]
    John General, author of the *Newburg Letters* and the historian of the War of 1812, nearly
    the same age as Gov Morgan LEWIS, married a sis/o John LIVINGSTONE [31 Jul
    1841]
    John L (b 2 Nov 1809) s/o the late Wm ARMSTRONG Esq of Readfield ME at
    Pearlington MS (see pp. 707-708 Stackpole's *History of Winthrop ME* 1994) [24 May
    1849]
    Samuel T abt 66 was Lt Gov of MA and for a while acting Gov of MA died at Augusta
    ME [11 Apr 1850]
    William Esq 73 at Readfield ME [10 Aug 1848]
    William passengers lost or missing and also one cabin and two deck passengers on 7th
    inst the steamboat *New York*, bound from Galveston to New Orleans wrecked in a
    hurricane, 17 persons drowned [24 Sept 1846]
ARMSTRONG - see YOUNGBLOOD
ARNO Sally 43 at North Bangor ME [15 Aug 1850]
    Tobias late of Leeds ME, Rufus MARSTON adm [10 June 1852]
ARNOLD Abraham 29 at Augusta ME on 22nd [6 Mar 1845]
    Albion P Capt 36 at New Sharon ME on 22 Feb [25 Feb 1847]
    Benedict named in ledger of J JENNINGS 1777-1800 [St Johns paper NB] [12 Apr 1849]
    Benjamin 72 at Gorham ME [30 Aug 1849]
    Betsey Mrs 43 w/o Edwin ARNOLD at Sidney ME [9 Mar 1839]
    Charles A 2 youngest c/o John ARNOLD at Augusta ME [9 Apr 1846]

ARNOLD (Cont.) child 3y of Shirley ME s/o Wilson ARNOLD accidentally shot by the discharge of a gun in the hands of George FRANCIS, a boy 10y [*Gospel Banner*] [18 Nov 1847]

Hannah Mrs 60 at Augusta ME [21 Nov 1834]

John 93y 6m at Monmouth ME [9 Sept 1847]

Minerva T 54 w/o J H ARNOLD at Augusta ME on 13 May [20 May 1852]

Samuel 20 s/o Wilson ARNOLD at Augusta ME [3 Sept 1846]

ARNOLD - see BRIMIJION, GETCHELL, PETTIS, YORK

ARNOLD's - see RICHARDS

ARNOLD's Expedition to Canada, lumber-men, in woods vicinity of Dead River ME, traces of ARNOLD's passage from Kennebec to Canada visible, paths cut through forests, can be distinctly traced, Chain Lake, fragments of boats now some 70 yrs since ill-fated expedition, among the last acts performed by ARNOLD. The boats built at Augusta ME, and taken to the Lake for the army to cross over [*Danvers Courier*] [17 Jul 1845]

Aroostook Co - see PARSONS

ARRAS Sarah 70 at Danville (now part of Auburn) ME [20 Jan 1848]

ARRAS - see ATWOOD

ARRIS William H abt 30 at Augusta ME on 11th inst formerly of Lisbon ME [16 Dec 1852]

ARSKIN James abt 50 at Hallowell ME on Wed last committed suicide by hanging [4 Apr 1837]

ASHFORD Sarah 51 w/o Robert ASHFORD at Litchfield ME on 13th ult [16 Nov 1839]

ASHLEY Senator from Arkansas died [4 May 1848]

ASHMUN Phineas Esq 86 at Brooks ME [3 June 1852]

ASHOTON - see DUNCAN

ASTOR John Jacob sick is not expected to recover [30 Jul 1842]

ATHEARN Jesse 33 at Starks ME [10 Aug 1848]

ATHERTON Mr (not death notice) of Hartford CT on Wed of last week made 100 horse shoes, in one hour and 47 minutes including a stoppage of six minutes. Done at one fire with 2 helpers, one to blow and the other to strike, [*The Boston Post*] [21 Feb 1837]

ATKINS Joseph S 48 struck by lightning, son with him, knocked down but will recover at Mt Vernon ME [31 Jul 1851]

Mary G 25 w/o Charles W ATKINS at Mt Vernon ME on 3 Mar [6 Mar 1851]

ATKINSON Alexander from Savannah GA 5 negroes of the late Alexander ATKINSON of Camden Co GA hanged on Mon the 6th inst on the plantation of the deceased, where the murder of their late master was committed. Buried under the gallows. [11 July 1840] [25 Jul 1840]

Anna 57 at Buxton ME [5 Feb 1852]

Mary 60 at Montville ME [17 Feb 1848]

Mary J 35 at Montville ME [17 Feb 1848]

Samuel 55 of Montville ME at Winthrop ME on 16 May [29 May 1851]

William of Maine had three fingers taken off at the linseed oil mill at East Boston MA [17 Jul 1851]

ATWOOD B C commission merchant of (Bangor ME), On a visit to his farm in Glenburn ME, thrown down and the wheel of the chaise passed over his head causing immediate death [*Bangor Democrat*] [12 Nov 1842]

Mary S 53 of Thomaston ME at Augusta ME [20 Apr 1848]

Nathan abt 50y of Buckfield ME by hanging himself on Sun last [*Oxford Democrat*] [5 June 1841]

ATWOOD (Cont.) Thomas 69 (b 18 Sept 1811 s/o John and Joanna {ARRAS} ATWOOD) at Lisbon ME [see Davis, *Cemetery Records of Lisbon ME*] [17 Apr 1851]

ATHEARN Hannah 84 at West Bath ME [12 Dec 1850]

ATHENS William 87 AmRev at Lisbon ME [21 June 1849]

ATHERTON Phebe Mrs 85 formerly of MA at Hallowell ME [15 Oct 1846]

ATKINS David A 9y s/o Mr J V ATKINS at Portland ME [26 Aug 1845]
  Deborah Mrs 32 on the 6th inst at Hallowell ME of consumption [3 Apr 1838]
  James S 26 of New Sharon ME at Pekin IL of bilious fever [16 Oct 1838]
  William of Hallowell ME at American Valley CA on 8 Oct [9 Dec 1852]
  Zaccheus 39 of Roxbury MA late of New Sharon ME at Matanzas Cuba [3 Aug 1841]

ATKINSON Anna 57 at Buxton ME [5 Feb 1852]
  Dinah Mrs 73 w/o Richard ATKINSON at Madison ME [26 Aug 1843]
  Eunice B 37 w/o T M ATKINSON at Mercer ME [2 Dec 1847]
  Mary of Winthrop ME, took a quarter of an ounce of arsenic on Sat morning which caused her death [*Lowell Herald*, 4th inst] [13 June 1844]
  Richard 83 at Madison ME [20 May 1847]

ATWOOD Emily Mrs 24 w/o C M ATWOOD at Gardiner ME [28 Nov 1844]
  George 35 at Fairfield ME [18 Oct 1849]
  Hannah 82 w/o Mr Solomon ATWOOD at New Gloucester ME [15 Apr 1836]
  John 66 at Lisbon ME (a native of New Gloucester ME) [7 June 1849]
  Matilda 17 at Fairfield ME [9 Aug 1849]
  Moses 67 at Temple ME [1 Oct 1846]
  Thomas on Tues his farm house and buildings burned at Lisbon ME [*Lewiston Journal*] [16 Aug 1849]

AUBLEY Nelson m Miss Eliza LITTLE in streets of Palmyra by Squire J F MAHAN. Traveling westward, the old folks refused consent, thus travelled on until the families with their wagons parted, the lady escaped from her parents and followed her lover. The opposition of her parents nearly drove her to a state of distraction, so her lover drove her to the state of Illinois [*Missouri Courier*] [28 Oct 1843]

AUSTIN Aaron of Thomaston ME injured by being run against and thrown down by a wagon and has died since [10 Oct 1837]
  Benjamin 20y 8m s/o Edward AUSTIN formerly of York ME at Gardiner ME of consumption [10 Apr 1838]
  Betsey 16 at Vassalboro ME [11 Sept 1845]
  Betsey E 17y d/o Robert and Desiar AUSTIN at Vassalboro ME 29th ult [14 Aug 1845]
  Charles between Fort Independence and Thompson's Island drowned; one of 27 boys of the Farm School [7 May 1842]
  David died at Indian Bar Tuolumne River in CA on 26 Oct [4 Dec 1851]
  Desais 63y 9m w/o Robert AUSTIN at Vassalboro ME on 14 Sept [25 Nov 1852]
  Mary 44 w/o Cyrus ASTINE at Belgrade ME on 19th ult [2 Mar 1848]
  Mary E Mrs 21/24? at Readfield ME on 19 May [27 May 1852]
  Mercy 42 at West Gardiner ME [16 Jan 1851]
  Moses A late of Belgrade ME, est notice, Leonard AUSTIN adm, and Judith AUSTIN, widow [25 Mar 1852]
  Mr in West part of Gardiner ME suicide on Tues last, in good circumstances as to property, but was impressed with the belief should come to want [15 May 1838]
  Stephen Fuller this country to be convulsed in civil war, in consequence of imprisonment of founder of Austin's colony, accused by Mexicans of having excited the colony to insurrection and driving away Mexican troops, undergoing trial in Mexico City and fears are entertained for his life, if executed will be revenged and civil war will be the result (*New Orleans Mer Adv*) (N.B. returned to TX in 1835; d 1863) [16 May 1834]
  William B 34 at Cherryfield ME [15 June 1848]

AUSTIN (Cont.) William B Esq 37 at Cherryfield ME [18 May 1848]

AVERILL Clementine E 31 w/o Hiram AVERILL at East Readfield ME on 27 June [6 Jul 1848]

    Emma Jane 10m only child of Mr Moses AVERILL at Gardiner ME [31 Aug 1833]

    Sarah widow 62 formerly of York ME at Gardiner [23 Sept 1836]

AVERILL - see CUNNINGHAM

AVERY Albert 18 belonging to Bath ME attached to ship *Danvers* lying at Long wharf went on board Fri but has not been seen since [*Boston Atlas*] [25 Nov 1847]

    Dudley 37 at North Anson ME [2 Mar 1848]

    Ezekiel 96 AmRev at Wiscasset ME [21 Mar 1850]

    Franklin 9 youngest s/o widow AVERY at Belfast ME [16 Apr 1842]

    John of Whitefield ME thrown from his wagon on Mon last breaking both of his legs, recovery is doubtful [16 May 1837]

    Sutton 26 at Whitefield ME [6 May 1836]

AVRILL Elijah abt 18y of Upper Stillwater ME s/o Carr AVRILL drowned on Wed last at Pushaw Falls driving logs [1 Jul 1847]

AYER Caroline Isabella 23 w/o Samuel AYER at Waterville ME [1 May 1845]

    Jane 20 w/o John AYER and d/o Benjamin NUTTING of Norridgewock ME at Embden ME [27 Jan 1837]

    Moses 68 at Embden ME [3 Jan 1850]

    Moses Dr 62 of Bangor ME at Augusta ME on 1st inst at the Insane Hospital [1 Jul 1847]

    Tristam 50 at Biddeford ME [2 Jan 1851]

AYLETT Elizabeth Mrs 74y d/o the unrivalled orator Patrick HENRY at Fountainbleu King William Co [VA?] on 24th Sept [12 Nov 1842]

AYERS - PERKINS

AYRES James on the mill pond on the Chautauque River for a sail on the night of 21 Jul the boat upset all five drowned age 17y to 20y (see also PERSEY, CRIPPIN, DALEY) [7 Aug 1851]

    John E and Jonathan PERKINS and William LEACH Jr engaged in the lobster fishery and flat bottom boat capsized all drowned at York ME on 20th ult [11 May 1839]

AZELIUS Adam the Nestor of scientific men in Sweden at Upsal on 30th of last Jan 86 [8 Aug 1837]

- B -

BABB Ann 41 w/o James BABB at Corinna ME [18 June 1842]

BABB Jedidah Mrs 29 at China ME [18 Sept 1835]

BABB Elijah abt 20y on the Presumpscot river at Saccarappa village (Westbrook) ME on Sat afternoon, of four persons - two females. Mr Preston DAY plunged into the river. Nearly lifeless when rescued. [*Eastern Argus*] [20 Apr 1848]

BABE the pirate - see TUCKER

BABBITT boys 14 and 9, girls 12 and 6 c/o Dyer BABBITT at Castleton KY consumed by house fire on the night of 17th ult [10 Oct 1840]

BABCOCK/BADCOCK John a printer 91y and fellow workman of Benjamin FRANKLIN at Baltimore MD [18 Nov 1843]

    Mary 55 d/o the late Jeremiah and Anna (Pettingill) BADCOCK of Augusta ME at Bangor ME on 25th ult (see p. 711 Stackpole's *History of Winthrop ME*, 1994) [10 Jan 1850]

    William 51 at Northfield [9 Sept 1847]

BABCOCK/BADCOCK (Cont.) William R Rev of Westerly RI accepted an invitation to become the rector of Christ's Church at Gardiner ME [8 Aug 1840]

BABCOCK - see MOSES

BABER Ambrose Dr killed by his own prescription, the druggist sent the medicine with a message that whoever took the medicine would be killed. The patient refused so the Dr swallowed it himself to show the sick man it was safe. The Dr died as the quantity of prussic acid was eight times greater than it should have been. (reported in the *New York Tribune*) [26 Mar 1846]

BABSON Richard and Jacob KELLEY, an iron founder killed on top of the cars of the Boston and Maine Railroad near Dover NH [16 Jul 1846]

BACHELDER Alanson 18 s/o Ezekiel BACHELDER at Madison ME [27 Mar 1845]

C G of Hallowell ME saved from drowning when the steam packet *New England* sank. It left Boston for Bath and Gardiner ME and had an accident with the schr *Curlew* on 31 May [12 June 1838]

Charlotte 38 w/o James R BACHELDER at Readfield ME on 10 Feb [14 Mar 1834]

girl 5y formerly of Levant ME d/o widow Elizabeth BACHELDER at Dover ME burnt to death [*Dover Observer*] [19 Oct 1848]

Mary of Jay ME saved from drowning when the steam packet *New England* sank. It left Boston for Bath and Gardiner ME and had an accident with the schr *Curlew* on 31 May [12 June 1838]

Nathan 78 at Hallowell ME [20 June 1850]

Ruth 77 w/o Thomas BACHELDER formerly of London NH at Windsor ME [19 Sept 1837]

Sally 64 w/o Deac Allen BACHELDER at Fayette ME on 7 Feb very suddenly "NH papers please copy" [18 Mar 1852]

BACHELDER - see BATCHELDER, ESTY, WELLS

BACHELLER John Milton abt 21 formerly of Farmington ME at Somerset KY [26 Aug 1852]

BACHELOR George Albert 24 formerly of Hallowell ME at Exeter NH [11 Jul 1834]

BACKUS Elizabeth M 38y 8m w/o Francis BACKUS at Farmington ME [1 Nov 1849]

BACON Alvan Dr 77 at Scarboro ME [31 Aug 1848]

David Dr 74 at Buxton ME [8 June 1848]

Eben Esq 81 at Waterville ME [14 Jan 1847]

Eben F Esq 45 at Waterville ME late Sheriff of Kennebec Co ME [13 Nov 1841]

Eliza Jane 23 at Waterboro ME [11 Jul 1850]

Mary B Mrs 32 w/o Dr Alvan BACON Jr at Skowhegan ME [20 May 1843]

Mr and Mrs WALKER, both married persons, and having families in London, eloped together, and took passage in the *Ocean Monarch* for America, either burned or drowned [12 Oct 1848]

Rebecca Mrs 56 w/o Benjamin BACON at Greenwood ME [20 Jul 1839]

Rufus I 23 youngest s/o Dr David BACON, a grad of West Point, of brain fever [27 Aug 1846]

Timothy 87 AmRev at Gorham ME [29 Nov 1849]

BADGER Abby Jane 2 at Augusta ME on 9th inst at Augusta ME [20 Sept 1849]

Abigail 86 formerly of Palmyra ME wid/o John BADGER at Canaan ME [17 June 1852]

John 72 at Palmyra ME [25 Jul 1844]

P D of Peterborough NH lost his wife and ch in newly painted house hazardous to their life [20 Mar 1845]

BADLAM Otis Gould a teacher in penmanship left Augusta ME on Wed morning 21st ult at 5 o'clock, nothing heard of him. All his effects in his room, in condition which indicated nothing more than an absence for a morning walk. Abt 5' 8", rather dark

BADLAM (Cont.) hair, fair complexion, wore a frock coat and a pair of spectacles. Information directed to the subscriber.... Darius FORBES of Hallowell ME [21 Sept 1839]

BAGLEY George 15 s/o Enoch Bagley Jr killed by the falling of a tree at Troy ME [18 Jul 1840]

Joseph Mrs w/o Joseph BAGLEY at Brunswick ME [25 Nov 1847]

Leonard of North Searsmount ME at San Francisco CA [8 Jan 1852]

Margaret Ann H Mrs 30 w/o John S BAGLEY formerly of Portland ME at New York City on 13th inst [29 Apr 1843]

Philip Esq of Newburyport MA of the oldest citizens and AmRev at the battle of Bunker Hill, in a chair while perusing a newspaper in the store of Mr BROWN on Merrimack St [*Newburyport Herald*, 24th] [2 May 1844]

BAGOT Charles Sir after a brief reign as Governor General of the Canadas died at Kingston on the 9th inst [4 Mar 1843]

BAILEY Abigail 86 wid/o John BAILEY of Portland ME at Vassalboro ME [28 Feb 1837]

Albert S 30 at Freeport ME [24 June 1852]

Ann 17 at Auburn ME [31 Aug 1848]

Betsey Mrs 46 w/o Asa BAILEY at Farmington ME [2 May 1844]

boy abt 17y of Terre Haute Indiana by accidental discharge of gun on 15th ult s/o Major BAILEY [13 Apr 1839]

Capt of his whaling ship the *Gen Williams* with 5 of his crew, all drowned [1 Apr 1843]

Carleton B 18 oldest s/o Capt Samuel G BAILEY at Pittston ME [31 Oct 1844]

Charles G 30 at Dexter ME [10 Dec 1846]

Charles W abt 30 a native of Freeport ME at New Orleans on 21st [7 Oct 1847]

Daniel 78 at Augusta ME on 20 Jan [22 Jan 1846]

Deborah 73 w/o Nathaniel B at Pittston ME [27 Mar 1851]

Edward A 4 s/o Charles M B at Winthrop ME [16 Aug 1849]

Edward formerly of North Yarmouth ME at Galveston TX [12 Sept 1844]

Elijah Capt abt 90y for more than 40y past the postmaster in Groton on the 24th ult. Husband of "Mother BAILEY," the heroine of Stonington, who gave her petticoat to be made into cartridges when the British bombarded. She still survives.[In those days, "cartridges" used in muzzle-loaders were made out of cloth or paper which held the powder and ignited it when lit by a spark.] [*New Haven Register*] [14 Sept 1848]

Ellen Maria 16m d/o Daniel and Emeline BAILEY at Augusta ME [9 Aug 1849]

George 3rd mate of the *Cortez* by a whale; Mr SOULE 2d mate leg broken and Mr BROWN 1st mate arm badly cut. Whaling casualty, the ship *Condor* which arrived at New Bedford MA on Tues from a whaling cruise at Maui, 4 Nov ship *Cortez*, Capt SWIFT of N Bedford [16 Mar 1848]

George W 10m s/o Isaac BAILEY at Augusta ME [12 Feb 1846]

Harriet 65 w/o Hon Jeremiah BAILEY at Wiscasset ME [14 Nov 1850]

Humphrey 85 at Sidney ME [25 Dec 1851]

Isaac 43 at Augusta ME on Sat morning last [4 Feb 1847]

Jane w/o Rev Giles Bailey formerly of Winthrop ME at Brunswick ME on Tues morning last [17 Sept 1842]

John 68 formerly of Wiscasset ME at Alna ME [22 May 1845]

John S 25 at Farmington ME [9 May 1850]

Maria 42 at Washington ME [5 Sept 1850]

Martha 2 d/o Charles M BAILEY at Winthrop ME on 5 Aug [9 Aug 1849]

Mary Bailey 86 w/o Seth BAILEY at Freeport ME [5 Sept 1850]

Mirabel 70 w/o Mr H BAILEY at Sidney ME [18 Jul 1840]

Mr the late Mayor of Houston TX formerly of Augusta ME [7 Aug 1851]

BAILEY (Cont.) Nancy 26y of Merrimac to be married Mr DREW of Concord VT, but died before the wedding [*Nashua Oasis*] [2 Mar 1848]

Ozias C Mrs abt 35 at Farmington ME [12 Aug 1852]

Prince 87 AmRev at Leeds ME bp Africa 1751 alias Prince DUNSWICK, of Hanover MA in 1780, took master's name (BAILEY) to enter military [10 Apr 1838]

Sarah Louisa 11m 23d at Augusta ME on 8 Dec [18 Dec 1845]

Simon Colver 2y 6m youngest s/o Daniel BAILEY at Gardiner ME [12 Mar 1846]

BAILEY - see MEGQUIER, WHITTIER

BAINBRIDGE William Commodore 60 an old and honored officer of the Navy at Philadelphia PA on 27th inst [10 Aug 1833]

BAKER a boy 4y and a girl 7y c/o Cyrus BAKER, playing near a cart body when it suddenly fell upon them killing the girl instantly and seriously injuring the boy, who died on Tues at Ludlow VT, she on Sat of last week [20 Nov 1851]

Abraham of Providence RI at San Francisco CA on 11th Oct [4 Dec 1851]

Agnes Mrs abt 67 at Bingham ME [15 Aug 1844]

Betsey C 30 at Sidney ME on 16 Nov [13 Feb 1851]

Betsey P 59 w/o Col Daniel BAKER at New Sharon ME [27 June 1844]

Brown Major 69y 7m at The Forks (North of Carratunk, Somerset Co) on Kennebec River ME [18 June 1842]

Edward 91 at Waterford ME [25 June 1846]

Frances P 5 or 6 of Orrington ME d/o Peter C BAKER an accident with fire [10 Dec 1842]

Gardiner Bowen 4y 5m of Solon ME s/o Col Howard BAKER on the 4th instant by the wheel of a load cart passing over his body [*People's Press*] [20 May 1847]

George Folsom 2y 9m s/o Edward W BAKER at Portland ME [21 Jul 1843]

Hannah Pond 48 w/o Sewall BAKER at Litchfield ME [26 Dec 1844]

Helen Mrs 37 w/o Henry BAKER at Winthrop ME after a short but distressing illness [30 Apr 1846]

infant abt 15m of Eliot ME c/o Rev John BAKER drowned [*Portsmouth Messenger*] [14 June 1849]

Isaac of Hermon ME on the Levant Rd the barn set on fire on Sat evening 4th inst, a boy the supposed incendiary is under arrest [16 Sept 1847]

John 18 s/o widow BAKER feared drowned [*Kennebunk Gazette*] [24 July 1835]

Joseph Rev 75 at Moscow ME on 1 Jan [8 Jan 1852]

Joshua, boatman when between Fort Independence and Thompson's Island drowned a party of 27 of the boys of the Farm School on Thompson's Island accompanied by a teacher and boat-keeper [7 May 1842]

Maria 25 w/o Major Reuel BAKER and d/o James CROSBY Esq of Albion ME at Whitefield ME [4 Jan 1849]

Maria w/o Reuel BAKER and only d/o James CROSBY Esq of Albion ME at Whitefield ME [14 Dec 1848]

Martha 62 at Calais ME [6 June 1850]

Mary Ann 26 d/o the late Mulford BAKER at Sidney ME [5 Aug 1843]

Mercy Mrs abt 75 relict of the late Capt Shubael BAKER at Sidney ME on 23rd ult [5 Sept 1844]

Mulford 50 formerly of Dartmouth MA at Sidney ME suddenly [29 Jul 1843]

Nabby 75 at Portland ME [13 Nov 1845]

Nancy A Mrs 28 w/o Benjamin F Esq of Norridgewock ME at Athens ME [19 Aug 1852]

Olive C 17 of Palmyra ME clothes took fire while carrying a brand to the school house [1 May 1851]

Phebe Mrs 78 at Augusta ME [7 Sept 1839]

BARCLAY (Cont.) knowledge of any of our friends and forced to put into Tampico and made prisoner and I am to be shot together with 29 others, tomorrow morn at 7. Give my love to my bros and sis; I hope you will not mourn for my death, as I shall die perfectly happy. [29 Jan 1836]

BARDER Mrs w/o Mr B fell into fireplace, 3 little boys (ch of the deceased tried to save her) at St John New Brunswick Canada [7 May 1842]

BARKER Abijah Capt and grandson, Henry C BARKER s/o Isreal A BARKER, of Brooklyn and Martin HOLLY lost from the schr *Ellen*, while at anchor off New Hamburg, run down by the steamboat *South American* on Tues night (from the *NY Commerical*) [14 Aug 1851]

Carr 93 AmRev at Dresden ME [28 Jan 1833]

David Esq of (Exeter ME) engaged in writing its history, doubtless make an interesting book, and one that will command a remunerating local and general sale. Exeter is a flourishing farming town, and one of the oldest Penobscot Co. [*Bangor Democrat*] [28 Aug 1851]

d/o Isaac B of Tiverton RI married on Wed eve on 26th ult, eve a gang of fellows saluted bride at her res, by firing guns, drumming on kettles, &c, greatly to the annoyance of the inmates, Mr B remonstrated with them to no effect, Mr B, seized his gun and fired it into the crowd, shot five or six of the assailants, dispersed the gang, shot Samuel NEGUS, matter is to be legally investigated. [10 Feb 1848]

Eliakim wounded by the discharge of a cannon one arm blown off and received a wound in his side at Saratoga Springs on 4 Jul [25 Jul 1834]

Francis 17 at Bangor ME [11 Feb 1834]

Francis 60 of Calais ME of cholera Sacramento CA on 10 Nov [2 Jan 1851]

Jeremiah MD 84 at Gorham ME [9 Oct 1835]

John 57 formerly of Portland ME formerly landlord of the Cumberland House and then the Mansion House in (Augusta, ME) at San Jose CA on 26 Mar [13 May 1852]

John 77 at East Thomaston ME [30 May 1850]

John Edward 3y second s/o Albert BARKER at Portland ME on Wed [11 Dec 1841]

Lydia widow 80 at Vassalboro ME [4 Nov 1852]

Mary Abby 2y 7m c/o Dr C H BARKER at Wayne ME on 21 Jul [14 Aug 1851]

Mary abt 60 w/o Isaac BARKER at Norridgewock ME [13 May 1852]

Pamelia 35 w/o Col Nathan BARKER at Saccarappa Cumberland Co ME [4 Dec 1841]

Phebe A Mrs 49 w/o Dr John BARKER at Wilton ME [8 Apr 1843]

Tryphosa 25 d/o Caleb BARKER at Pittston ME [30 May 1850]

widow BARKER place burnt at Pittsfield MA on 19th [6 June 1840]

William M 28 at Cornville ME [28 Sept 1848]

BARKER - see HAM

BARNARD Anna 58 at York ME [9 Sept 1847]

Deborah 84 widow of Capt Andrew BARNARD formerly of Nantucket MA at Bloomfield ME on 2 Aug [9 Sept 1852]

Elijah abt 40y drowned in Salem (MA?) signed the Washingtonian pledge on Wed, got a job at Danvers, but some time after having been induced to drink, and was seen intoxicated the night he was drowned [7 May 1842]

George G vs John J GAUL and Mary H, his wife for breach of promise on the part of the lady. Damages laid at $5000. Verdict $1000 at New York Circuit Court on Thurs [24 Jul 1835]

John 35 at the Kennebec Arsenal in Augusta ME [10 Jul 1845]

Leonard 52 at Union ME [14 Aug 1851]

Lucius member of the Senate from the County of Lincoln at Augusta ME [30 Jan 1838]

Nathan F 19 of Augusta ME at Chelsea MA [10 June 1852]

BARNES Abigail 83 w/o Elbridge G BARNES at Bowdoin ME [18 May 1848]

BARNES (Cont.) Elizabeth Ann 32 d/o James BARNES at Sumner ME [28 Nov 1850] family had booked passage from New Orleans LA up the Mississippi on the *Ben Sherrod*; put their baggage on but missed the boat, which subsequently sank. In 1821, this same family, with dau then 3 or 4 took passage in packet *Albion* for Liverpool, however left in the ship *James Crooper*, Capt REED, which sailed a few days after the *Albion*. The *Albion* crew and passengers was a total loss. (Copied from the *New York Express*) [13 June 1837]

James Jr 22y 6m at Sumner ME [3 Feb 1848]

Jane 67 w/o Abel BARNES at Camden ME [30 Apr 1842]

John ill since the last of Jan and in the care of Dr E NICHOLS, but last Sat advised by one "Dr WESTLAKE," professing to be a physican to take cold baths [5 Aug 1843]

Josiah 92 AmRev patriot at Dudley MA [19 Aug 1843]

Lydia 84 wid/o Joseph BARNES at Lubec ME [20 Feb 1851]

Oliver of Portland ME lost at sea from the ship *Susannah Cummings* on 13 Dec [2 Apr 1846]

Sophronia 41 w/o Capt William BARNES at Belfast ME [19 June 1841]

Warren F 21 at Woolwich ME [8 May 1851]

William Capt 40 committed suicide on 24th by cutting his throat [9 May 1844]

BARNET Phillip E in OH thus announces himself as a candidate, has a wife and 13 children - poor - afraid to steal - too lazy to work - and would like to be elected constable." [11 Mar 1847]

BARNEY Francis a French Canadian abt 45 committed suicide in the house on Oak St on Fri morning by cutting his throat. For a long time intemperate (*Temp Gazette*) [25 Jul 1840]

Mrs and George WELLS while crossing the prairie killed by lightning near Prairieville Pike Co MO on Thurs the 14th [5 Jul 1849]

BARRELL Ann J 16 d/o Elijah BARRELL Esq at Greene ME [29 June 1848]

Elizabeth 47 w/o Samuel F BARRELL Esq at Richmond ME [28 Aug 1851]

George G Esq consul of the USA for the port of Malaga, native of Maine at Barcelona on 12 Nov [29 Jan 1839]

BARRELL - see PETTINGILL

BARRETT Daniel 50 of Northport ME at Camden ME [30 May 1844]

Daniel 89 at Camden ME [16 Jan 1851] and 90 at Camden ME [12 Dec 1850]

Fanny 40 w/o James S BARRETT at Sumner ME [21 May 1846]

George proprietor of the New England Farmer at Boston MA on 20th ult [1 Apr 1836]

I 70 at Weld ME [12 Oct 1848]

John Capt 55 at Sumner ME on 22nd ult [14 Mar 1840]

John MD 40 at Portland ME of consumption [30 Apr 1842]

Joseph 43 formerly of ME and s/o the late Oliver BARRETT at Boston MA on 1st Dec [13 Dec 1849]

Joseph 49 formerly of Hallowell ME at Boston MA [13 Dec 1849]

Louisa Miss found on the evening of 2d Nov in the water at the head of Patten's Bay in Surry ME. The coroner's inquest held by Byron W DARLING Esq of Hancock Co, the verdict drowned [9 Dec 1843]

Lucy 37 at Camden ME [27 June 1844]

Mary Ann 22 w/o Wright BARRETT at Sumner ME on 5th inst [30 Nov 1839]

Mr 2nd mate of the bark *Mary* of and from London for St Andrews New Brunswick Canada went ashore near Moose River, Trescott ME night of the 4th inst and went to pieces. Part of the sails and rigging saved. Mr BARRETT was drowned [27 Nov 1845]

Mrs of Wilton ME w/o Oliver BARRETT near dwelling of Sherburne DEARBORN Jr at Bedford on Sat last [copied from *Amherst (NH) Cabinet*] [30 Jan 1851]

BARRETT (Cont.) Oliver 79 at Hallowell ME [23 Dec 1843]

Pamelia abt 40 at Canaan ME [23 May 1844]

Sarah widow 62y 6m at Saco ME [22 June 1848]

Susan w/o Amos BARRETT at Union ME on the 16th ult after a very short illness [7 Mar 1834]

BARROW Alexander Hon of Louisiana at Baltimore MD [7 Jan 1847]

BARROWS Betsey formerly of Augusta ME w/o Capt Elisha BARROWS at Waterville ME on 11 Sept [27 Nov 1845]

Horace A Deac 43 at Harrison ME [24 June 1852]

John Esq 50 formerly of Winthrop ME at Monmouth ME on 5th inst [8 Aug 1834]

John Stuart 54 counselor at law at Fryeburg ME [31 Jul 1845]

Mrs died of cholera w/o Putnam BARROWS at Hampden ME [*Bangor Daily Whig*] [16 Aug 1849]

Peter 86 AmRev at Camden ME [29 May 1841]

BARRY James seaman 23 native of Eastport ME, a recruit of receiving ship *Columbus* at the Naval Hospital in Chelsea MA of pulmonary disease [12 Feb 1842]

William T our minister to Spain and late PM General died in England [23 Oct 1835]

BARSTOW A Capt of Newcastle at CA [18 Nov 1852]

Benjamin 71 at Damariscotta ME [22 Aug 1850]

Clara Fae 23 w/o Capt Benjamin Master of the ship *Osceola* of New Castle on July 15th at San Francisco CA [19 Sept 1850]

Mary w/o Capt B Barstow at Nobleboro ME [2 April 1846]

BARTER Capt saved himself by clinging to the boat and the boy Winthrop SARGENT picked up nearly exhausted. Shipwreck, 4 lives lost on the schr *Cevo*, Capt Pelatiah BARTER (from the *Kennebeck Journal*) [25 May 1839]

BARTHOLOMEW Mrs by lightning while asleep in bed with her husband (Eben G BARTHOLOMEW) and child, Mr B received but a slight shock, the child severely burnt at Harlem Winnebago Co IL [24 Jul 1851]

BARTELS Charles A J 21 of Portland ME 1st officer lost overboard from brig *Cazelle* [14 May 1846]

BARTER Thomas 35 at Wiscasset ME [24 Sept 1842]

BARTLETT Benjamin C 37 at Portland ME [27 Feb 1845]

D A Mr at Amoskeag NH on Fri last taken by mistake a quantity of oil of juniper, died 30 minutes after swallowing the poison [21 Jul 1843]

Easter 44y w/o Capt Thomas BARTLETT at Augusta ME [22 Mar 1849]

Hannah 49 w/o Lemuel BARTLETT at Madison ME [29 June 1848]

Harriet J 16 at Hallowell ME [14 Oct 1852]

James Monroe 16 at Litchfield ME [25 Dec 1845]

Jane Mrs 82 at Augusta E on 21 Sept [26 Sept 1850]

Jason R 37 formerly of Hope ME at New York NY on 30th ult [15 Apr 1833]

Joseph 59 at Bangor ME [11 Jul 1844]

Knott 22 at Thomaston ME [10 Jan 1850]

Lucy Jane 14m only c/o Gilmore C and Margaret J BARTLETT at Augusta ME on 25 Sept [2 Oct 1851]

Margaret Ann 24 w/o Erastus BARTLETT and d/o Silas LEONARD Esq at Augusta ME on Fri last [14 Jan 1847]

Martha 93 at Paris ME [1 June 1848]

Mehitable H Mrs 28 d/o the late Benjamin CARLETON at Camden ME [28 Oct 1852]

Rosannah 35 w/o William Y BARTLETT and d/o Nathaniel and Susannah WENTWORTH at Belgrade ME on 10 Oct [16 Oct 1851]

Rufus 87 formerly of Plymouth MA at Norway ME [3 Aug 1848]

Sarah B 45 w/o Dr Alonzo BARTLETT at Litchfield ME on 26 May [19 June 1851]

BARTLETT (Cont.) Solon Esq native of Maine, resident of Louisiana, nominated for
Congress by the Democrats. Mr B educated in a printing office, some years published
the *NY Constellation* [4 Oct 1849]
son abt 4y s/o Capt Joshua BARTLETT Jr at South Thomaston ME [*Thomaston ME
Recorder*] [11 June 1846]
Susan 40 w/o William BARTLETT at Westbrook ME [12 Jul 1849]
William Esq of Newburyport MA left to the Andover Institution the sum of $50,000; to
his 21 grandchildren $20,000 each .... he died at age 93 [20 Nov 1841]
BARTLETT - see DUNTON
BARTON Alfred Esq 54 at North Anson ME [28 June 1849]
Asa Esq 54 at Norway ME [24 Feb 1848]
Elijah 45 at Windsor ME [6 Apr 1839]
Jabez Aiken Rev "Artium Magister" (Master of Arts) of the Latheria Mission Conference
Society in Monrovia is dead [25 Dec 1841]
John 18 s/o Hannon BARTON drowned at Worromontogus Mills on Fri last [18 Jul
1834]
Philena 17 at North Anson ME [22 May 1851]
Ulmer B 26 of Sebasticook ME at New Orleans LA [21 Sept 1848]
Virgil R abt 18 at Augusta ME on 28th June [1 Jul 1852]
BASCOM Charlotte of Cambridge MA saved from drowning when the steam packet *New
England* sank. It left Boston for Bath and Gardiner ME and had an accident with the
schr *Curlew* on 31 May [12 June 1838]
H H Rev of cholera, but this needs confirmation at Baltimore MD [2 Aug 1849]
BASFORD Emeline Delia 1y c/o Emeline C and William P BASFORD at Pittston ME on
12th Nov [4 Dec 1851]
John 74 at Livermore ME [18 Feb 1847]
Jona 65 Dixmont ME [22 June 1848]
Joseph Sylvester 7y 3m c/o Emeline C and William P BASFORD at Pittston ME on 14
Nov [4 Dec 1851]
Reuben 76 at Monmouth ME on 27 Apr [8 May 1851]
BASMER Charlotte 40 at Brunswick ME [27 Nov 1838]
BASSE Mr lawyer at Brownville TX and a large land holder is from Farmington ME [7 Aug
1851]
BASSETT Martha A 28 a widow at Vassalboro ME [17 Sept 1846]
Samuel lately received a severe wound while engaged in sawing lathes at Barre MA He is
now doing well [7 Aug 1851]
BASSETT - see McCARTNEY
BATCHELDER Benjamin 86 at Belfast ME [25 Dec 1851]
Benoni T abt 25 of Meredith NH born without legs and with only one arm! Came up to
the door of our office last week in a wagon, cracked his whip and went off as smart as
some men would go with four legs. [*Belknap (NH) Gazette*] [1 Jul 1843]
Emerson abt 38 at Bath ME [25 Dec 1851]
Joshua 57 at Levant ME [29 Aug 1844]
Phineas 82y 7m AmRev native of London NH at Garland ME on 12th inst [23 Jul 1842]
BATCHELDER - see also BACHELDER
BATEMAN Simon 79 a planter of TX and Matthew JETT murdered in their sleep, likely by
J SHULTZ [13 Feb 1845]
BATES Abigail L 23 w/o Asa S BATES at Fairfield ME [4 Jan 1849]
Amanda Delora 20m d/o Charles BATES at (Winthrop?) ME on Thurs morning last [5
Mar 1842]
Caleb 64 at Greene ME [22 Aug 1844]

BATES (Cont.) Isaac C funeral at Senate chamber at Washington DC [27 Mar 1845]

Jabez R Capt - see Jobish R Col

James 55 of Norridgewock ME at Fairfield ME on 22nd Jan [8 Feb 1849]

Jobish R Col (Jabez R) AmRev 89 at Leeds ME [NB, in the Navy in AmRev, see Capt Jabez R BATES p. 406 Mower's *History of Greene ME*] [1 Nov 1849]

John 62 at Avon ME [22 June 1839]

John at Leeds ME [7 Nov 1840]

Margaret w/o Charles A BATES at Norridgewock ME on 2nd inst [17 Jul 1845]

Marinda 30 w/o Henry BATES at Green ME [15 Mar 1849]

Mary Ann d/o Charles A and Ellen A BATES at Norridgewock ME on 18th [29 Apr 1847]

Mrs w/o Joseph BATES at Winthrop ME [3 Apr 1835]

Richard an employee of the mill at the power works of Mr JAMESON on Falls Road about seven miles from Baltimore MD blown up on Sat last [22 Sept 1840]

Richard P 68 at Eastport ME [24 Sept 1842]

S Mrs of Norridgewock ME saved from drowning when the steam packet *New England* sank. It left Boston for Bath and Gardiner ME and had an accident with the schr *Curlew* on 31 May [12 June 1838]

Solomon Capt 51 at Athens ME [14 Nov 1844]

William B 22 of Fairfield ME at Westbrook ME on 22nd inst [2 Oct 1835]

BATES - see GOULD

BATTIE Robert Capt 73 at Thomaston ME [3 Dec 1846]

BATTS Sarah 15m d/o Oliver BATTS at Saco ME [1 Jan 1846]

BAUMER Henry Capt 25 at Thomaston ME [20 Apr 1848]

BAUMSEY - see ROBINSON

BAUN Herman 27y married only two weeks on Fri, German worker employed in the Sugar House at Boston MA, fell through the scuttle from the upper story to the cellar, six stories, employed only 2 days. [16 Oct 1851]

BAXTER Daniel Capt 33 at San Francisco CA on 7 Oct [20 Nov 1851]

James Hon of Stanstead Lower Canada (Quebec) committed suicide on last Sat, a native of VT (copied from *NY Com*) [19 Dec 1837]

Stacy of Maine at sea on board US Frigate *Columbia* of small pox [23 Apr 1846]

William 20 s/o Rev J E BAXTER at Wilton ME [8 Feb 1844]

William E 22 eldest s/o Rev John E BAXTER at Wilton ME [23 Jan 1845]

BAYLIES William G 63 left a fortune at over $200,000 at Boston MA *[Boston Traveller* 15th] [23 Nov 1848]

BAYANT Betsey 83 at Nobleboro ME wid/o Nathaniel BAYANT [N.B. Dodge's *Old Bristol Vital Records* on p. 50 has changed the spelling to "BRYANT" by using Census records] [15 Oct 1846]

BEACH Joseph of cholera at Tariffville CT and Benjamin BALL at Thompsonville, where he had gone to give information of Mr BEACH's death *[Hartford Times]* [29 Nov 1849]

BEAL/BEALE Abby F 33y 10m w/o A T BEAL at Augusta ME on 5 Mar [18 Mar 1852]

Daniel 75 at Farmington ME [24 Jul 1851]

Hannah 8 c/o Zina and Charlotte B at North Anson ME [22 Jan 1846]

Lucy H 54 w/o Horatio B at Bangor ME on 26th ult [4 Jan 1834]

Lucy Jane 16 c/o Zina and Charlotte B at North Anson ME [22 Jan 1846]

Martha Ann (Mrs) 40 at Portland ME [11 July 1844]

Martha J of Norway ME lost her right hand at the Paper Mill *[Norway Advertizer]* [22 Feb 1849]

Mary Jane 33 yrs d/o Japeth B at August ME on 6th inst of consumption [30 Jan 1845]

BEAL/BEALE (Cont.) Mary w/o E S BEAL at Lewiston ME [2 May 1850]

   Mehitable 66 w/o Japhet B at Augusta ME on May 18 [23 May 1850]

   Mr was killed at Winchester VA by a biting horse [17 Jul 1851]

   Olive 10 c/o Zina and Charlotte B at North Anson ME [22 Jan 1846]

   Sarah T 36 w/o Oliver S at Bangor ME [14 Feb 1850]

   Zenas Dr 59 at Searsport ME [25 Jan 1849]

BEALS Agnes 84 mother of 11 ch, 76 gch, 46 ggch and 2 gggch at Leeds ME on 13 Feb [26 Feb 1852]

   Alfred 25 formerly of Wiscassett ME at Portland ME on 21 Oct [4 Nov 1852]

   Freeman and 2 sons found drowned in the West Quoddy Bay. Bodies picked up on the flats between the Narrows and West Quoddy Head. They belonged to Jonesport ME. [*Eastport Sentinel*] [6 Nov 1838]

   Mary P 1 yr 9 mo d/o Albert T B at Augusta ME on 27 April [2 May 1850]

   Polly 44 w/o Luther B also left 12 ch at Turner ME [27 Nov 1841]

   Roscoe L 4y 7m s/o George and Almira J BEALS at Leeds ME on 16 Feb [4 Mar 1852]

   Thirsey abt 80 wid at Turner ME [5 Feb 1852]

   William Esq 51 formerly of Wiscasset at Portland ME [19 June 1851]

BEAN Albert S 16 s/o Josiah P B at Winthrop ME on 28 April [9 May 1850]

   Bethiah 22y w/o Nathan BEAN and eldest d/o Dea Samuel SMITH at St Albans ME [12 Sept 1840]

   Charles T a stone cutter death by hydrophobia [*Boston MA Bee*] [11 Jan 1849]

   Cynthia 41 w/o Theodore B Esq at Sullivan ME [29 July 1847]

   Daniel Jr 23 at Brownfield ME member of Montezuma lodge of Odd Fellows [16 Jul 1846]

   David late of Sidney ME [4 Mar 1852]

   Elizabeth C Mrs 46 at Limerick ME [18 June 1846]

   Elizabeth Mrs 86 at Bath ME [16 Sept 1847]

   Florentine M 22 w/o Ira BEAN and d/o Obed WING of East Livermore ME at Livermore Falls ME on 15th ult [28 Dec 1848] and [1 Feb 1849]

   Henry Warren 21 formerly of Oldtown ME at Boothbay ME [19 Oct 1839]

   Ivory Capt abt 50 of New Sharon ME at Strong ME on 25th ult [7 May 1842]

   Jane 3y d/o Peter and Ann BEAN of burns at East Boston MA [11 Sept 1851]

   Joseph 38 at Lincoln ME [7 June 1846]

   Laura Maria 1 yr d/o Geo W B at East Livermore ME [23 Apr 1846]

   Mary 51 w/o Joseph BEAN at Belfast ME [15 June 1848]

   Polly S Mrs 19 at Livermore ME [21 Aug 1841]

   Serena 52 w/o Daniel BEAN Esq at Bancroft, Aroostook Co ME [12 June 1851]

BEAN - see QUIMBY

BEANS Moses at Cuyahoga Falls laboring under mental derangement for several weeks past ... attempted to cut his throat and later attempted to leap 70ft received no injury [*Summit OH Beacon*] [8 Jul 1847]

BEARCE Ezekiel abt 28 drowned in Winthrop Great Pond on 4th inst [11 July 1837]

   Josiah W 19 yrs and 9mos s/o Alvin B of Canton ME drowned in Rumford ME on 17th inst [1 May 1845]

   William H of Winthrop ME maybe the lawful heir of the JENNINGS property being the oldest male heir in that line. His mother was a JENNINGS. Isaac and Samuel JENNINGS came to Plymouth many yrs ago and from them sprang a numerous progeny in the old Colony from which they have spread over the whole Union. Mr Bearce is a hearty old octogenarian. "the JENNINGS est $40,000,000 or 8,000,000 pounds in England" [21 Aug 1851]

BEATH Jonas T 23 of Boothbay ME at Chelsea ME [5 Aug 1843]

BECK Charles H 5 yrs 11mos s/o Capt Charles H B at Augusta ME [25 Feb 1847]

BECK (Cont.) F abt 23 of Augusta ME drowned in the Kennebec River near Gardiner ME
     from schr *Sidney* on the 22nd [2 Oct 1838]
     Frances Lewellar/Francis Llewellyn 10 mos d/o Joseph and Mary B at Augusta ME
          [29/22 Apr 1847]
     Hannah Mrs 67 wid/o Thomas BECK at Augusta ME on 11th inst [21 Aug 1851]
     Martha Helen 6 c/o Joseph S BECK at Augusta ME on 22 Feb [9 Mar 1848]
     Michael W 27 at Portsmouth NH late proprietor of the *Saco (ME) Democrat* [1 April
          1843]
     Thomas 70 at Augusta ME on 9 Aug [14 Aug 1851]
BECKETT John of Lewiston ME and Mr L MERRILL, who went out in the ship *Capital*,
     came back as passagers in the *Crescent City*. They were members of the Lewiston
     Falls Company [27 Dec 1849]
     Mary 68 w/o William B at Belfast ME [16 Sept 1852]
     Thomas 21 of Lewiston ME at Hallowell ME on 3rd inst [30 Nov 1839]
     William 78 at Belfast ME [9 Dec 1852]
BECKETT House - see DAVIS
BECKFORD Mary Mrs 45 of Brookville ME at Augusta ME [18 Nov 1847]
     Sarah 52 w/o Capt John B at Eastport ME [6 Feb 1845]
     Susan 22 yrs w/o Coleman B at Lubec ME [29 May 1845]
     William author of *Yathek*, see sketch repinted from *the Buffalo Commercial Advertizer*
          [12 Sept 1844]
BECKWITH - see MEADS
BEDELL - see WOOD
BEDLOW - see WILEY
BEEBE - see JENKINS
BEECHER George Rev of Scioto OH pastor of the 2d Presbyterian Church accidentally
     killed himself s/o Rev Dr BEECHER now on a visit to Boston MA [*Scioto OH
     Gazette*] [15 Jul 1843]
     Harriet w/o Rev Dr B at Winter Mills near Cincinnati OH on July 7 of consumption [24
          July 1835]
     Rev Mr of Jacksonville college preached an abolition sermon in the Presbyterian church
          at Alton IL on 31st ult which caused so much excitement that military were ordered
          out in front of the church to protect it. [28 Nov 1837]
BEECHER - see SPEAR
BEEDE Nancy 62 w/o Rev Thomas B at Farmington ME [22 Feb 1844]
     Nathan abt 68 at Phillips ME [8 May 1851]
BEEDY Peter 50 at Phillips ME [18 July 1850]
     Thomas Rev 77 at Farmington ME [28 Dec 1848]
BEEMAN Hannah Mrs 70 yrs at Hallowell ME [14 Aug 1845]
     Harriet R 22 d/o Stephen B Esq at North Bridgton ME [14 May 1846]
BEGS c/o Life B abt 4 yrs at Warren ME [29 Jan 1846]
BELCHER Benjamin 24 at Farmington ME [2 Oct 1845]
     Harriet J 22 w/o Capt David P B at Camden ME [25 Dec 1845]
     Lodoiskey (LEAVITT) 21 w/o Alex B (Jr) at Winthrop ME [see p 275 Stackpole's
          History of Winthrop ME] [18 Jan 1849]
BELCHER - see TITCOMB
BELDEN Jonathan H 39 at Hallowell ME [22 Mar 1849]
     Jonathan Rev 70 at Hallowell ME [11 Jan 1844]
     Martha 89 widow of Rev Jonathan BELDEN at Hallowell ME [22 Apr 1852]
BELFORD Louisa Miss 26 yrs at Portland ME [2 Jan 1845]
BELL George Esq 87 at Newcastle ME [18 Jan 1849]

BELL (Cont.) John Hon former Gov of NH at Chester NH [8 Apr 1852]
    John member of Congress from NH and subsequently gov of that state, at Chester NH on 22 Mar 1836 [13 Jan 1837]
    Joseph Esq 72 at Cherryfield ME [8 Apr 1852]
    Margaret 87 at Eastport ME [12 Apr 1849]
    Olive 23 w/o George BELL at Eastport ME [25 May 1848]
    Thomas 13y 6m s/o Henry C DONNELL of (Bath ME) eating some mushrooms [*Bath Times*] [16 Sept 1847]
BELL - see BONTON
BELLOWS Ithemar Dr 65 at Freedom ME [9 May 1850]
    Mr of Framingham on Fri by the Worcester Railroad train [20 Dec 1849]
BELLETTI - see LIND
BELSFORD Nathan of Hopkinsville KY fell down a well, a faithful old negro, TOTA went after the body but was also killed [31 Aug 1839]
BELTON Thomas 36 at Gorham ME [25 Sept 1851]
BEMENT Walter P Maj abt 60 at Dexter ME [3 Sept 1846]
BEMER Waterman 3y 7m s/o Willaim BEMER at Waldoboro ME [15 Jan 1848]
BEMIS Almedia Mrs 24 w/o Jacob BEMIS and d/o Benjamin CORSON of Athens ME at Hebron WI [13 Apr 1848]
BENDALL G A of Boston MA saved from drowning when the steam packet *New England* sank. It left Boston for Bath and Gardiner ME and had an accident with the schr *Curlew* on 31 May [12 June 1838]
BENJAMIN Billy Col 64 at Livermore ME [10 May 1849]
    Caroline Emmons 6y 10m d/o David BENJAMIN at Livermore ME on 7 Feb [15 Apr 1833]
    Charles 38 at Winthrop ME on 10th inst [16 May 1834]
    Charles Henry 10y and 5m s/o Samuel and Olivia BENJAMIN on 9 Jul [18 Jul 1850]
    Tabitha widow of the late Lt Samuel BENJAMIN an officer of AmRev at Livermore ME on the 20th ult [18 Jul 1837]
BENNER Leander his father, Charles BENNER of Waldoboro ME on 17 Nov 1851, relinquishing all claims to Leander's service during his son's minority and will no longer pay any more of the son's debts [27 Nov 1851]
    Mary Ann 26 at Damariscotta ME [11 Nov 1852]
    Phebe Mrs 75 at Thomaston ME [12 Aug 1847]
BENNETT, Andrew - see RENNET, Andrew [14 Dec 1839]
BENNETT/BENNET Abigail 70 w/o Jahn BENNET of Winslow ME at Augusta ME [19 Mar 1846]
    Almond 22 at Thomaston ME [8 Jul 1847]
    Areal M 24 formerly of Troy ME at Belfast ME [28 Feb 1837]
    Cynthia A 26 w/o Samuel BENNETT at Augusta ME on 15th inst [27 Apr 1848]
    Elisha 49 formerly of New Bedford MA and more recently of Chesterville ME at Savannah MO on 11 Jan [14 Mar 1844]
    Elizabeth 15 at Ellsworth ME [14 Nov 1844]
    Elizabeth W widow 97 formerly of MA at Jackson ME [25 Sept 1841]
    Jonathan 70 at New Gloucester ME [16 Jul 1846]
    Leonard 26 at Eastport ME of NS (Nova Scotia?) [11 Feb 1847]
    Mary E 43 w/o Col William BENNETT at Ellsworth ME [11 May 1848]
    Mary Mrs 78 at Norway ME [9 Aug 1849]
    Mr Rev of Woburn settled upwards of 25 yrs graduated at Harvard College in 1818 committed suicide [25 Nov 1847]
    Nathaniel 86 at Guilford ME [28 Oct 1852]

BENNETT/BENNET (Cont.) Stephen a colored man arrested in Columbia PA on claim of being a fugitive slave from Baltimore MD the prop of Capt Edward B GALLUP. Judge KANE rendered up the fugitive to his master. BENNETT was afterwards purchased for about $700 and set at liberty. [6 Feb 1851]

   Tamson W 37 w/o George BENNET at North Yarmouth ME [15 Aug 1840]

   William seaman of MA lost on the brig *Linden*, a sea disaster, Griffith Capt [19 Nov 1842]

BENNETT - see BUCK, EDGECOMB, WILSON

BENNOCH Archibald P 22 at Stillwater, Orono ME [5 Oct 1839]

BENOIT Mrs at Lower Canada left 6 ch all under 11 yrs, also Mrs McDONALD of LC killed in a mill accident both left ch [16 Oct 1841]

BENSON Abigail 83 wid/o Ichabod BENSON of Livermore ME formerly of Middleboro MA, schooled mid the trials and adversities of the days of the AmRev, subsequent to the peace came to Maine with her husband... at (Winthrop ME) on 26th inst [29 Sept 1840]

   Elizabeth Mrs 36 at Winthrop ME [24 Feb 1848]

   Ichabod 77 AmRev, arose apparently well, went out to attend to his affairs as usual, and was soon after found dead upon the ground [5 Aug 1833]

   Mary Jane 27 at Greene ME [21 Mar 1850]

   Mrs 81y (b 9 Aug 1768) of Minot ME w/o Elnathan BENSON formerly of Hebron ME on her birthday spun 13 skeins of good yarn from common wool rolls, and would have done 14, had it not been for the failure of the wheel-band. Walked during the past season, from res in Minot to Hebron ME a distance of 7 or 8 miles. [*Portland Argus*] [1 Nov 1849]

   Peleg Dr 82 a native of Middlebury MA the 1st physician who ever settled in Winthrop ME [12 Oct 1848]

   Robert seaman of Maine, fell from the foreyard, on board US frigate *Potomac* [2 Jul 1846]

   Stephen Deac 75 at West Waterville ME [2 Sept 1852]

   Thomas colored and Edward F DOUGLASS convicted of murder of the mate of the bark *Glen*, executed in the rear of the Tombs NY [31 Jul 1851]

BENSON - see WOODCOCK, PAGE

BENT Silas 21 at Belfast ME [24 Aug 1848]

BEOTTGER Mr his wife and 2 ch of poison, emigated to America from Prussia [*Baton Rouge Gazette*] [22 Feb 1849]

BERKIMER Lucy A 46 at Bath ME [1 Oct 1846]

BERRY Abigail 53 w/o Joseph BERRY Esq at Thomaston ME [17 Jul 1845]

   Anna 78 at Saco ME [9 Mar 1848]

   Arthur C of Gardiner ME saved from drowning when the steam packet *New England* sank. It left Boston for Bath and Gardiner ME and had an accident with the schr *Curlew* on 31 May [12 June 1838]

   Arthur W abt 30 formerly publisher of the *Gospel Banner* at Dixfield ME [1 Jul 1847]

   Daniel late of Home, Almyra Witham of Woburn MA [18 Jul 1852]

   Edward Alonzo s/o Robert P BERRY to be a young giant, weighs 134 lbs and is only 8yrs growth [15 Aug 1844]

   George 91 at Greene ME [19 Mar 1846]

   girl ae 22 [*sic*] d/o widow Elizabeth BERRY at Brunswick ME [18 Jul 1844]

   Hannah 78 at Kennebunk ME [10 Feb 1848]

   Harriet 47 at Gardiner ME very suddenly [2 Jul 1846]

   Harriet 50 sis/o Capt Arthur BERRY of Gardiner ME, an apoplectic fit or a disease of heart [2 Jul 1846]

BERRY (Cont.) Isabel 38 at Bangor ME [5 Feb 1842]
    Jacob N of Brunswick ME at CA on 22 Nov [13 Feb 1851]
    John A Dr of Saco ME accidentally shot by a fowling piece in the left arm near the shoulder will likely recover [20 Nov 1838]
    John 101 AmRev at Trenton, Monmouth, Brandywine, Germantown, Brooklyn Heights and Valley Forge in 1777 and at the surrender of Lord CORNWALLIS at Yorktown in 1781, died at Patterson Creek Hardy Co VA [28 Aug 1845]
    John 77 at Fayette ME [14 Aug 1845]
    Jonathan 43 at Fayette ME [1 Apr 1847]
    Joseph 49 at Bangor ME [11 Jan 1840]
    Louisa 18m d/o Joseph S BERRY at Augusta ME [19 June 1845]
    Lydia 18 at New Sharon ME [1 Feb 1844]
    Nathaniel life guard of (George) WASHINGTON, of Pittston (ME), born 22 Dec 1755, enlisted on 7 Jan 1777 and drafted into W's body guard in Mar 1778, served 22 mos, enlistment expired returned to ME, at the taking of BURGUOYNE, age of 87, he fully retains his body and mental power [the *Gardiner Ledger*] [3 Dec 1842] and died 94y 8m AmRev at Pittston ME on Aug 20th [29 Aug 1850]
    Nicholas at Brownville ME on 5th inst [17 Dec 1846]
    Richard (about 65) and respectable member of the Baptist Church at Shiloh, Camden Co NC? died during the divine service at that place on Sun last (from the *Elizabeth City, NC Advocate* of Tues) [22 Oct 1842]
    Rosella abt 23 at Winthrop ME on Sat last [5 Sept 1841]
    Samuel 73 at Auburn ME [6 Dec 1849]
    Sebastain M 5m s/o A W BERRY at Augusta ME [1 Oct 1846]
    Sophia 55 wid/o Rufus BERRY at Bath ME [29 Jul 1847]
    Stephen Capt of Bath ME late master of ship *Harriet* at New Orleans on 25 May [6 June 1852] and [10 June 1852]
BESSE Ellen E 16m at Augusta ME [10 Sept 1846]
BESSY Ephraim S his father, Jonathan BESSE, hereby relinquished his son .... witnessed by O W BLAISDELL at Leeds ME on 1 Oct 1843 [21 Oct 1843]
BEST Mr drinking and driven home in the bottom of the sleigh. Placed in a stall and wrapped in buffalo skins. In the morning his neck swollen as to tighten his cravat to strangulation and his face suffused with blood. He died soon after at Ogdensburg [1 Feb 1849]
BETSON James S 26 at Gardiner ME [4 Apr 1850]
BETTES Jeremiah 80y AmRev and a pensioner under the act of June 1832 at Biddeford ME [21 Dec 1833]
BETTS Thaddeus Senator from CT at Washington DC on Tues morning the 7th [18 Apr 1840]
BIBBER James 89 AmRev at Freeport ME [29 Jan 1846]
BICKFORD Celia Frances 18 at Hartland ME [25 Sept 1851]
    Elizabeth widow 92 at Limerick ME [26 June 1851]
    James 25 at Gardiner ME [9 Sept 1843]
    Joseph 47 at Litchfield ME formerly of Portland ME [24 May 1849]
    Lydia A 21 of Newburgh ME [21 Feb 1850]
    Moses 67 at Smithfield ME [1 Jul 1852]
    Mr the mixing mill at the Gorham powder works blew up the week before last killing him, in the employment of Mr WHIPPLE for over 30y [*Argus*] [9 Oct 1851]
BICKMORE Solomon 70 at Appleton ME [19 Mar 1846]
BICKNELL Alfred of Augusta ME left for CA (gold mines) [*Gospel Banner*] [15 Feb 1849]
    Edward G 26 at Augusta ME on 29 May [1 June 1848]

BICKNELL (Cont.) Elizabeth L 29 d/o Nathaniel BICKNELL of Hartford ME at Belfast
    ME [22 Aug 1844]
    Louisa 36 w/o Nehemiah B BICKNELL at Turner ME [3 Sept 1846]
    Mary 77 wid/o Simeon BICKNELL of Hiram ME at Harrison ME [8 Jul 1843]
    Samuel 70 of Bloomfield ME in his barn on Sun evening of last week an afliction of the
        heart [24 Jan 1850]
    Sullivan 43 at Hebron ME [26 Sept 1850]
    William at Hartford ME [5 June 1841]
BICKNELL - see CHASE, HAYFORD
BIDDLE James of the United States Navy at Philadelphia PA on Sun [12 Oct 1848]
BIGBY John abt 70 in crossing the Androscoggin River on the ice on the evening of 15 Dec
    at Turner ME [15 Jan 1842]
BIGLOW - see HOLMAN
BIGELOW Abba 26 at Bloomfield ME w/o Jonathan S BIGELOW [24 Oct 1850]
    Betsey 18 at St Albans ME [9 Mar 1848]
    Elmira 38 w/o Israel S BIGLOW Esq of Mayfield ME at Brighton [11 Nov 1847]
    John 72 formerly of Worcester MA at Livermore ME [28 Oct 1847]
    Polly 74 w/o George BIGLOW at Bloomfield ME [15 Nov 1849]
BILCH Mr fireman and 6 persons on the steamboat *George Collier* on 6th inst on her
    passage from New Orleans to St Lewis MO [25 May 1839]
BILLINGS Dexter 33 and his son 10m at Northport ME [25 Jul 1840]
    Dexter 33 at Milton Plt Oxford Co ME [4 June 1846]
    Eliza R 43 w/o Charles BILLINGS at Waterford ME [10 June 1847]
    Hannah J 22 at York ME [9 Sept 1847]
    Joe 42 at Hope ME [10 Feb 1848]
    Phineas Capt 78 at Northport ME on 27 Dec [16 Jan 1851]
BILLINGS - see news on Hemp
BILLINGTON Amanda 25 w/o Nathaniel BILLINGTON at Winthrop ME [18 Mar 1852]
    Josiah abt 20 s/o Seth BILLINGTON of Winthrop ME at Dexter ME on Tues of last
    week [11 Apr 1840]
BINGAM Abel and Lucy WRIGHT a maid entering St Stephen's Church last Sun Abel B, a
    widower stepped up to Lucy and said "will you marry me to-day?" She blushing said
    "Yes Abel!" Published and married at noon by Rev Thomas J SALTER [*The
    Middletown CT Sentinel*] [3 Sept 1842]
BINGHAM Ozias Capt 95 AmRev at PA [3 Apr 1845]
BINNEY Amos late Navy at Boston MA [21 Jan 1833]
BIRD Aaron 20 of Minot ME at Augusta ME [15 June 1839]
    Sally Mrs 81 at Belfast ME [19 Feb 1852]
BIRNEY James G recently executed at Louisville a deed of manumission to 20 slaves which
    descended to him from his father, recently deceased [5 Oct 1839]
    Mr a number of citizens in Cincinnati OH on the 12th ult entered the printing office of a
    Mr BIRNEY, publisher and proprietor of an abolition paper and destroyed his press
    [5 Aug 1836]
BISBEE Betsey Mrs 17 at Buckfield ME [25 Jul 1844]
    Betsey W 17y 2m w/o D S BISBEE at Buckfield ME [4 Jul 1844]
    Hannah 79 w/o Rouse BISBEE at Woodstook ME [6 June 1850]
    Moses 87 at Waterford ME [19 Feb 1852]
    Olive 56 w/o Mark BISBEE at Oxford ME [26 Dec 1844]
    Thomas abt 14 at Waterville ME [30 May 1844]
    William W 20 s/o Moses BISBEE of Bridgton ME at Pueblo Mexico [7 June 1849]
BISHOP Ann 51 w/o William BISHOP at Belfast ME [30 Sept 1847]

BISHOP (Cont.) George of Bangor ME drowned at McQueen's Mills [13 May 1852]

Hannah 35 w/o Jos S BISHOP at Wayne ME [1 Nov 1849]

James death by cholera at Venice [5 Sept 1834]

Martha Mrs 36 w/o Nathan BISHOP Esq and d/o Dr Moses and Martha WING at Wayne ME on the 14th inst [22 Jul 1833]

Martha O 22 at Biddeford ME [3 June 1852]

Mr attempt to revive the *Alton Observer*, an abolition paper. Mr LOVEJOY also killed. 7 others wounded. The mob succeeded in destroying the *Observer* press at Alton IL [28 Nov 1837]

Nathaniel of Winthrop ME to be the oldest Methodist now living in Maine, listened to Rev Jesse LEE and join the class formed in Monmouth on Nov 1794 [11 Jul 1850]

Susan 44 w/o Cyrus BISHOP at Winthrop ME after a long illness [7 Mar 1844]

Thomas S 90 AmRev of Avon ME on or abt 25 July [*Hartford Times*] [14 Aug 1851]

BISHOP - see MILES

BISSEY Jonas Rev a Methodist minister at New London PA struck by lightning, just finished his sermon in the act of reaching for his hymn book when struck down, several of the audience were stunned. The building sustained no damage. Left a wife and 2 ch [28 Aug 1851]

BITTUES Arno, for more than 20 yrs a citizen of Augusta, late a res of Hallowell ME on Thurs drowned in a small stream outlet of Belgrade pond near the bridge, buried on Fri with masonic honors, native of France, believed [23 Jul 1846]

BIXBY Amos formerly of Columbus OH shot himself on 3d Nov near Marshall Clark Co IL leaving a paper, had meditated the act for 15 years. Left personal property to the amount of $3000 and 480 acres of land valued at nearly the same amount. His friends reside in ME. [*Sat Courier*] [14 Dec 1839]

Catherine 20 w/o C BIXBY at Skowhegan ME [21 Feb 1850]

Mrs w/o late Deac BIXBY at Norridgewock ME [31 Jul 1851]

BLABEN Lydia 44 w/o Nathaniel BLABEN at Wells ME on 28th ult [5 Dec 1834]

BLACK Clarissa 50 of Newry ME at Augusta ME [28 Sept 1848]

Cloud - see KATH-LA-MO-HEE

David 2nd abt 18 at Sedgwick ME [4 Mar 1847]

Eleanor 42 w/o Joshua BLACK at Searsport ME [27 June 1850]

James Capt 87 at Augusta ME on 24 Dec [30 Dec 1847]

James Jr 54 at Augusta ME on 14th inst [6 Mar 1845]

Peter and John executed in the harbor of San Francisco CA on the 23d Oct by order of court martial [20 Dec 1849]

Rhoda 54 wid/o James BLACK Jr at Augusta ME on 13th inst [25 Jan 1849]

servant - see CARY

William P formerly of (Augusta ME) at Charleston SC on 16 Feb [6 Mar 1851]

BLACK - see DURHAM, STARKEY

BLACK - see BOYER, BROWN, CARTER, CATO, colored, FREEBODY, GRIFFIN, HANCOCK, HAWKINS, HETH, JACKSON, JOHNSON, LONSTRETH, LUNDY, MERRIGOE, MILLER, OVERTON, RICHARDSON, SMITH, THOMPSON, WASHINGTON, WILLIAMS, WILSON

BLACKINGTON Benjamin 75 at East Thomaston ME [25 Apr 1850]

Eleanor 72 at Thomaston ME [16 Apr 1846]

Elizabeth 68 at Thomaston ME [19 Oct 1848]

James 67 at East Thomaston ME [16 May 1850]

Levi W 63 of Attleboro MA at Winthrop ME (RI papers please copy) [17 Jul 1851]

BLACKMAN Col shot through the head while on horseback on his way to the North Fork [21 Aug 1851]

BLACKMAN (Cont.) Nathan 59 at Sidney ME on 30 May [20 June 1850]

BLACKMER Celina P 73 wid/o Mr Joseph BLACKMER at Bath ME [23 Feb 1839]
Joseph last 2 or 3 yrs, imagined should come to want although possessed of a handsome property. So depressed with his idea, last 14 days of his life refused all sustenance at Woolwich ME on 15th inst [25 May 1848]

BLACKSNAKE Gov a grand sachem of the Indian nation, Alleghany Reservation a nephew of Jospeh BRANT and uncle of Red JACKET, born near Cayuga Lake 1749, being 96y, at battles of Fort Stanwix Wyoming &c, friend of Gen WASHINGTON and in his camp 40 days at close of the Revolution - appointed chief by him, and now wears suspended from his neck a beautiful silver medal presented to him by Gen WASHINGTON bearing the date 1796 [20 Mar 1845]

BLACKWELL - PATTEN

BLACKWELL Asa 52 at Fairfield ME [2 Nov 1848] and [26 Oct 1848]
Asa Esq abt 50 at Litchfield ME [6 Aug 1846]
Chloe 16 d/o William BLACKWELL at Skowhegan ME [4 Feb 1847]
Elizabeth 67 w/o Joshua BLACKWELL at Madison ME [17 Sept 1846]
Elizabeth a female doctor graduated at the Geneva Medical College on 23rd ult, with high honors and received the degree of MD, her thesis: ship fever. Miss B studied medicine with Dr ELDER of Philadelphia PA [23 Feb 1849] and [26 Apr 1849] and opened an office in New York, 2 yrs back in Europe, studying and practicing in hospitals. [23 Sept 1851]
Fanny 39 w/o Asa BLACKWELL at Madison ME [6 June 1834]
girl abt 6y d/o Franklin B suddenly killed in Winslow ME by a cart body falling upon her at Winslow ME [*Eastern Argus*] [5 Aug 1843]
Sylvanus 27 at Wayne ME [18 May 1848]
Sylvanus 70 at Wayne ME suddenly [13 Apr 1848]
Thomas E 35 at Waterville ME [22 June 1848]

BLAGDEN John 90 at Etna ME on the 16th ult of apoplexy [2 May 1834]

BLAIR General on the evening of the 1st Apr, representative in congress from South Carolina, shot himself through the head with a pistol at Washington DC "His disease was *mania a pota* or insanity occasioned by intemperate drinking" [11 Apr 1834]
Mr of Dresden ME drowned at Eastern river bridge on Tues of last week, victim of rum [25 July 1840]
Robert 99th year of age at Readfield ME [12 Sept 1840]
Robert the only 2 living "Life Guards" of WASHINGTON in the procession on the 4th of July in Newburg ME, R B and Benjamin FATON on entering the church bore an American flag, followed by 6 other AmRev - united ages being 551 years. [3 Aug 1839]

BLAISDELL Delilah 46 at Lewiston ME [9 Aug 1849]
Elijah 83 at Sidney ME [25 Jan 1849]
H C 18y 8m s/o Eleazer and Harriet BLAISDELL at Waterville ME on 3d Feb [3 Apr 1851]
Mary 56 w/o Sanborn BLAISDELL at Rockland ME [17 Apr 1851]
Mrs d/o John LADD at Winthrop ME of consumption [4 Mar 1843]
R S 85 formerly of Hampden ME at East Thomaston ME [19 Nov 1846]
Samuel 77 a native of York ME, moved to Sidney ME and died at Bristol ME [12 Aug 1847]

BLAISDELL - see BLASDELL, DAY

BLAKE Abagail E 23 at Monmouth ME on 28 Dec of consumption [15 May 1845]
Abigail 43 w/o Joshua BLAKE at Mt Vernon ME [28 Mar 1850]
Ann Mrs 34 w/o Augustine BLAKE Esq at Monmouth ME on 3rd inst [23 Oct 1838]
Augustine 40 from the effects of heat at Monmouth ME [26 Jul 1849]

BLAKE (Cont.) Caroline F infant d/o of Increase and Sarah BLAKE at Farmington ME [19 Feb 1846]

Col a citizen of East Brewer ME 86 walked from res to Bangor distance of 7 miles on the 15th inst in the space of two hrs [30 Jan 1851]

Daniel abt 45 at Turner ME on 28 Oct after a short and very distressing sickness [6 Nov 1841]

Dudley L of Augusta ME on board schr *Semers* on 14th ult at Savannah from New Orleans of consumption [4 Feb 1847]

Eben 68 formerly of Winthrop ME [29 Apr 1852]

Edward Esq 66 at Hartford ME [29 Jul 1843]

Elias 60 at Gray ME [30 Apr 1846]

Emeline A abt 24 at West Waterville ME [5 Apr 1849]

Ezekiel 22 of Bath ME at Chelsea Hospital [9 Oct 1835]

Frederick 14 at Calais ME [8 Feb 1844]

George 72 at Boston MA [23 Oct 1841]

Hannah 45 w/o Eliab BLAKE at Augusta ME [19 June 1845]

Hannah 54 w/o Robert BLAKE at Salem ME [3 May 1849]

Hannah 77 wid/o Joseph BLAKE at Gorham ME on 27th inst [5 Feb 1842]

Hannah 90 widow of Nathaniel BLAKE at Gorham ME [15 Mar 1849]

J of Lynn MA saved from drowning when the steam packet *New England* sank. It left Boston for Bath and Gardiner ME and had an accident with the schr *Curlew* on 31 May [12 June 1838]

Jenett 71 at Brunswick ME [6 June 1837]

John 15 s/o widow Catherine BLAKE formerly of Hallowell ME at Boston MA [26 Sept 1840]

John AmRev 90 at Gardiner ME on 20th inst [3 Feb 1848]

John Capt 38 at Harpswell ME [24 Apr 1845]

Johnson of Augusta ME at Pensacola FL [11 Jul 1834]

Joseph Jr 32 at Gorham ME [31 Jul 1835]

Lavina 46 w/o John BLAKE Esq at Mt Vernon ME [6 May 1843]

Lydia 18 of Turner ME d/o Daniel BLAKE at Minot ME on 29th ult [11 Jan 1840]

Martin R 32 formerly of Monmouth ME at New York City on 27 June [14 Aug 1851]

Mary 69 at Portland ME consort of Nathaniel BLAKE [21 Jul 1843]

Mr killed in Midland Railway in England [28 Aug 1851]

Mrs 112y died in 1824 at Portland ME [19 Feb 1846]

Mrs 77 w/o Capt Whiting BLAKE at Warren ME [21 Aug 1842]

Nathaniel 90 at Gorham ME on 28th [11 Mar 1843]

Oliver abt 60y fell in a fit and striking his forehead upon a curb stone, died instantly at Portland ME on Sat morning while crossing Middle Street at the junction of Exchange Street [22 June 1848]

Sally 69 a widow at Gorham ME [3 Dec 1846]

Sylvanus L 44 at Calais ME [8 Feb 1844]

Thankful 89 at Harpswell ME the mother of Capt BLAKE [24 Apr 1845]

Thatcher 65 at Foxcroft ME [9 Nov 1839]

Thomas Dawes Dr 81 at Farmington ME [29 Nov 1849]

Thomas F drowned between Fort Independence and Thompson's Island with a party of 27 boys of the Farm School on Thompson's Island accompanied by a teacher and boat-keeper [7 May 1842]

W Mr first officer on the brig *Granite* drowned at sea [15 June 1839]

Walker Capt 64 at Union ME [10 Sept 1846]

William an American merchant of the firm of Heart and Co New York found drowned with marks of violence in the Thames River (London England) [2 Oct 1838]

BLAKE (Cont.) William deck passenger of Boston MA accident happened on board the steamboat *George Collier* on the 6th inst on her passage from New Orleans to St Louis MO [25 May 1839]

Willing Capt 82 AmRev [18 Jul 1844]

BLAKE - see LIBBY, Love (the law of Love)

BLAKELY Hannah C 17 at Appleton ME [27 Nov 1851]

BLANCHARD Abigail B 17 d/o Jesse BLANCHARD Esq at Madison ME [19 Aug 1847]

Aradra 80 w/o Solomon BLANCHARD at Dresden ME [21 Feb 1850]

Asa 79 at Gardiner ME [21 Dec 1848]

Eunice w/o Merrill BLANCHARD and only d/o Deac Benjamin WESTON formerly of Madison ME at Woodstock New Brunswick Canada [11 Dec 1841]

Frances C abt 25 w/o Capt Paul G BLANCHARD at North Yarmouth ME [8 May 1845]

Hallowell B 20y 6m eldest s/o Bradford and Ann BLANCHARD at East Pittsfield ME on 3d inst (Maine, Boston, New York, and California papers please copy) [20 May 1852]

Hannah abt 60 w/o Captian John BLANCHARD at Pittston ME [22 Jan 1852]

Jane Prince 99 w/o Joshua BLANCHARD at Cumberland ME [14 Feb 1850]

Leonard at Pittston ME [8 May 1851]

Lydia 77 wid/o of Asa BLANCHARD at Gardiner ME [26 Sept 1850]

Maria 11 d/o Jesse BLANCHARD Esq at Madison ME [19 Aug 1847]

Samuel Deac 74y 3m formerly of Bowdoinham ME on 3rd inst at Plymouth (ME?) [18 June 1846]

Seth Capt 26 of North Yarmouth ME lost overboard from brig *Forest* on her passage from Belfast ME for Havana Cuba [4 Jul 1837]

Shepard 62 of Searsport ME found dead, verdict by apoplexy [21 Dec 1848]

Solomon Capt 55 at Richmond ME 10 inst; faithful pilot of the Kennebec [23 Dec 1847]

Sophia L 22 d/o Capt Beza BLANCHARD at Cumberland ME [10 Oct 1837]

BLANCHARD - see deaf and dumb (deaf mute), WINTHROP

BLANDING Obadiah 22 of New Sharon ME at Augusta ME, a member of Olive Branch Division Sons of Temperance [2 Aug 1849]

Obadiah 89 at Mercer ME on 25 Dec [22 Feb 1849]

BLASDELL Ruth 61 at Sidney ME [19 Oct 1839]

BLETHEN Isaac of Dover ME at his hall, the Penobscot Tribe of Indians will perform Indian Dances, among will be the Great Mohawk Dance as performed by the Mohawk Tribe of Indians at their festivals. The Indians have been encamped in Dover during the winter. [*Piscataquis Observer*] [8 Mar 1849]

BLIN Martha J d/o the Captain, passenger lost on the *Maine* of Bath ME, James BLIN of Dresden ME, master [16 Oct 1841]

BLIN - see HAMMOND

BLINN Lewis 29 at Bangor ME [8 Jan 1836]

BLISH Bloomy D 36 w/o Arthur BLISH at Augusta ME on 20 May [22 May 1851]

James Capt 59 at Hallowell ME [29 Apr 1847]

Mary Ann 24 w/o Arthur BLISH at Vassalboro ME on 5 Jan of consumption [27 Mar 1845]

Susan B 35 w/o Wells E BLISS at Pittston ME [29 Aug 1850]

William T Capt of Vassalboro ME at New Orleans on 28 Jan [7 Mar 1840]

BLISS Addison B 18 only s/o Moses B BLISS Esq of Pittston ME at Gardiner ME on 17 June [3 Jul 1851]

Hannah Cordelia 25 w/o Zeba F BLISS at Lewiston ME [31 Jul 1851]

John of Wilbraham left at our office last week some shingles taken from the roof of his barn on the 9th inst; remained 104y, put there by his grandfather, Ensign Abel BLISS in May 1740 [*Springfield Gazette*] [15 Aug 1844]

BLODGETT Joseph 91 at East Pittston ME [6 Jul 1848]

BLOOD Elizabeth 77 w/o George BLOOD at Gardiner ME [10 Aug 1848]

M Rev of the Congregational Church 51 at Bucksport ME [22 Apr 1852]

Nathaniel F 28 a miner formerly of Lincolnville ME at Cannon Creek near Georgetown CA [9 Sept 1852]

BLOOM William at Bath ME [14 May 1846]

BLOOMFIELD - see BALCH

BLOSSOM Libbeus Deac 67 on 6 Nov at Scarboro ME [4 Dec 1845]

Lydia 65 w/o General Alden BLOSSOM at Turner ME [24 Jan 1850]

Rebecca 62 w/o Libbeus BLOSSOM on 3 Nov [4 Dec 1845]

Thomas J 28 of Turner ME on board steamer *Golden Gate* between Panama and San Francisco CA [15 Apr 1852]

BLOSSOM - see SAVAGE

BLUE Hannah 73 widow at Monmouth ME on 8 Sept [10 Oct 1840]

Jacob P Capt 31 at Monmouth ME [28 Mar 1840]

BLUNT Arthur C 22 at Union ME [9 May 1850]

Caroline Fletcher 14 c/o Oliver C and Sarah F BLUNT at Bingham ME on 3rd Nov [6 Feb 1845]

Henry M 39 at Augusta ME on 4 Jul [15 Jul 1852]

Isaac 23 s/o Eben BLUNT at Union ME on 1 Apr [12 Apr 1849]

Nathan w/o Nathan BLUNT and d/o Elijah GROVER of Solon ME at New York [26 Feb 1846]

Oliver C 23 at Norridgewock ME [4 Jan 1834]

Oliver C 12 c/o Oliver C and Sarah F BLUNT at Bingham ME [6 Feb 1845]

BLY Charles a printer formerly of Saco ME at Boston MA [5 Mar 1846]

BOARDMAN George W 22 at Isleboro ME of yellow fever [16 Sept 1852]

Holmes A Esq at New Sharon ME [5 Nov 1846]

Margaret Ann 27 w/o Thomas BOARDMAN at Frankfort ME [27 Sept 1849]

Mary 90 widow at Ilesboro ME [12 Aug 1847]

Naomi H 26 w/o Andrew BOARDMAN and eldest d/o late Jesse SAVAGE at Lexington ME on 3 Aug [23 Aug 1849]

BOARDMAN - see WASHINGTON

BODFISH Lucinda w/o Calvin P BODFISH at Fairfield ME [1 Jul 1852]

William of Gardiner ME 42 of cholera Sacramento CA [2 Jan 1851]

BODMAN - see VINCENT

BOGGAR a Frenchman in Tazewell County IL discharged two pistols at his wife, shot himself in the head and died instantly, wife recovered although one of the balls lodged in the skull. [16 Nov 1839]

BOGGS Oliver abt 28 at Warren ME [18 June 1846]

BOHANAN Mercy 70 w/o Daniel BOHANAN at Calais ME [21 June 1849]

BOIES Eliza B of Solon ME vs J H McALISTER of St Stevens New Brunswick Canada at the term of Supreme Court at Norridgewock for breach of promise of marriage. Verdict of $1200 for the plaintiff [*Norridgewock Journal*] [24 Oct 1834]

Eliza M w/o Ithamer E BOIES at Skowhegan ME [12 Feb 1852]

Jane 28 at Milltown (village in Calais ME) [17 Oct 1850]

BOLKOM Ebenezer Major formerly of Waterville ME at Marietta Hotel Cobb County GA [28 Mar 1844]

BOLO John W 33 at Farmington ME [16 Apr 1846]

BOLSTER boy 9y of Rumford ME s/o Otis C BOLSTER Esq a cask of powder set on fire [18 Nov 1836]

BOLTON Capt of the US sloop of war *Jamestown* [5 Apr 1849]

    Caroline Mrs 88 at Augusta ME on 23rd ult [9 Dec 1852]

    Frances A E 19 w/o Samuel BOLTON and d/o William and Margaret WINCHELL of Bradford ME at Allagash ME on 13 Dec [9 Jan 1851]

    Francis Davis 3 s/o George BOLTON at Augusta ME on 20 Mar (New Hampshire papers please copy) [3 Apr 1851]

    Harriet Mrs 41 at Augusta ME on 21st ult [18 Dec 1845]

    James abt 60 at Augusta ME on 1st Oct [16 Oct 1851]

    James late of Augusta ME, his est notice Joseph W PATTERSON exec [14 Oct 1852]

    Sarah 28 w/o James BOLTON at Augusta ME on 19th inst [28 June 1849]

BOMSBOTTOM - see KNIGHT

BONAPARTE Joseph the younger, a Roman prince by the title of Prince of Musigrand eldest gs/o Joseph BONAPARTE (not an obit, see article) [22 May 1845]

BONAPARTE - see NAPOLEON

BOND Benjamin Franklin printer abt 46 formerly of Hallowell ME at Boston MA on 9 Mar [20 Mar 1851]

    Francis Eugene Esq 38 only s/o the late Hon Thomas BOND of Hallowell ME at Bangor ME [24 Sept 1846]

    John H by accident in a mill at Portland ME [8 July 1852]

    Lois H 19y 7m w/o Henry BOND and d/o Gideon POWERS of Augusta ME at Boston MA on 10th inst [23 Dec 1847]

    Susannah 77 widow at Saco ME [27 Mar 1845]

BONNEY Abby 25 w/o J E BONNEY at Winthrop ME very suddenly [4 Oct 1849]

    Alden 41 at Turner ME [19 Aug 1847]

    Anna Mrs 85 at Turner ME [2 Jan 1851]

    Isaac, his child 14m at Winthrop ME [18 Sept 1835]

    Nancy 69 w/o Beriah BONNEY at China ME on 22 Aug [5 Sept 1850]

BONTON Mary Ann P Mrs 34 w/o Rev N BONTON at Concord NH and d/o the late Hon John BELL of Chester [9 Mar 1839]

BONTON - see story

BOOBIER Andrew 78 at Lewiston ME (spelling of the name has been changed to BUBIER, d 12 May 1847 buried in Crowley Cemetery at South Lewiston) [10 June 1847]

BOOBAR girl 9y of Linneus Aroostook CO ME d/o David W BOOBAR [*Temperance Gazette*] [26 June 1841]

BOODY Lydia M 14 youngest d/o Edmund BOODY at Winham ME [23 Jul 1846]

BOOKER Algernon S 22 at Bowdoinham ME [16 Sept 1847]

    Charles A formerly of Augusta ME at San Francisco CA [14 Oct 1852]

    child of Richard BOOKER at Hallowell ME [18 Jul 1844]

    Frederick 22 at Bowdoinham ME on 13th inst [11 May 1839]

    Jacob 46 at Gardiner ME [25 Dec 1841]

BOONE Daniel and his wife reburied at Frankfort KY, Sat 13th inst, 15,000 to 20,000 persons present, the remains were born on a hearse drawn by four white horses and attended by Col E M JOHNSON and other distinguished men as pall bearers. The Methodist Conference attended and after appropriate religious exercises an eloquent and thrilling address was delivered by Hon J J CRITTENDEN [2 Oct 1845]

BOOTH Kirk Esq a distinguished manufacturer from England, died of apoplexy as he was about to get into his chaise at Lowell MA [25 Apr 1837]

    William 67 at Cornville ME [29 Jul 1852]

BOOTHBAY Lemuel 44 at Saco ME [12 Dec 1837]

BOOTHBY Adhah 13y 10m s/o Mrs Sally and Mr Samuel BOOTHBY of typhus fever at Turner ME on 4 Aug and buried on 5 Aug at 6pm [28 Aug 1842]

BOOTHBY (Cont.) Charity 54 w/o Capt Cyrus BOOTHBAY at Embden ME [3 June 1847]
Charlotte 52 w/o Ichabod BOOTHBY at Livermore ME [23 Nov 1848]
Elizabeth 87 w/o William BOOTHBY at Limerick ME [3 Feb 1848]
Isaac abt 61 at Leeds ME on 20 May (extended notice) [3 Jul 1835]
Jane 42 w/o Isaac BOOTHBY 42 at Leeds ME [4 Jan 1849]
John Jr 23 youngest s/o Elder John BOOTHBY at Saco ME [10 Jan 1850]
Lydia J 16 d/o I BOOTHBAY Esq at Leeds ME [7 June 1849]
Sally 13y 10m d/o Sally and Samuel BOOTHBY at Turner ME of typhus fever on 3 Aug
in the evening [28 Aug 1842]
Samuel Esq at Buxton ME on 8th inst by suicide, considered the wealthiest man in
Buxton ME [23 Dec 1843]
BORDEEN Lewis of Maine landed sick at (Gloucester MA), from schr *Alice R*, of Eden ME
at Gloucester MA [27 Jan 1848]
BORDEN Mrs w/o Laderich BORDEN, an estimable inhabitant of Fall River, drowned her
2 youngest ch, ae 3y 6m and ae 1y, in a cistern, and then took her own life. Mrs B has
within a few days shown undeniable evidence of an unsound mind (N.B. Lizzie
BORDEN born 1860 was from Fall River MA also) (see also page one of *Lewiston
Sun Journal* 15 Jul 1995) [11 May 1848]
BORNHEIMER Almira 26y 5m w/o Joseph BORNHEIMER 2nd at North Waldoboro ME
[24 June 1852]
Henry 42 at North Waldoboro ME on 27 June [12 Jul 1849]
Mary 63 at North Waldoboro ME on 22 Feb [4 Mar 1852]
BORNHEIMER - see ORFF
BOSS John Capt and Mr STAPLES drowned off the schr *H M Johnson*, new, of Castine ME
dragged her anchors and went ashore on Little Deer Isle, night of 4th inst and stove
stern and received considerable damage. Next morning, in carrying off an anchor, the
boat was upset and the two men were drowned [27 Nov 1845]
BOSTON boy 12y run over by one of the Bangor ME engines at the alarm of a fire on Sat
last, his thigh was broken, the sum of $40 was immediately collected among the
members of the company and sent to the widowed mother of the boy [16 May 1840]
Francis 96y after a widowhood of eight weeks married Mrs Nancy JONES 33y at
Baltimore MD on the 11th inst, each wearing the bloom of the black rose of
Hindostan [3 June 1843]
Franklin abt 45 at Augusta ME on 3rd inst [13 May 1847]
Lucretia B 47 at Bangor ME [3 Aug 1848]
Thomas 86 AmRev at Kennebunkport ME [8 Feb 1844]
BOSWORTH Bradley of Vernon CT struck on his head receiving injuries, fell backward
out of a wagon up a steep hill. [21 Aug 1851]
Charles A 19m s/o Richard T and Sarah A BOSWORTH at Augusta ME [4 Feb 1847]
Dorcas 46 w/o James BOSWORTH at Solon ME [25 Sept 1845]
Robert 52 at Bath ME [29 Jul 1852]
Sarah Mrs 70 at Bath ME [28 Aug 1851]
BOULTER Wordsworth Capt formerly of Moscow ME 48 at Bangor ME [28 Sept 1848]
BOUNEY Emily w/o Mr I N BOUNEY at Winthrop village ME on Wed last [18 Dec 1838]
BOURK Cyrus 55 at Litchfield ME [13 Apr 1848]
Joseph M 28 of Hallowell ME at New Orleans [11 Feb 1847]
BOURNE William Col 43 at Wells ME [7 Sep 1848]
William of Bangor ME on shipboard [21 Oct 1852]
BOUTWELL Levi Franklin of Leverett s/o Levi BOUTWELL on the 8th ult suicide with a
gun [*Greenfield (MA) Gazette*] [*Portland Am*] [25 Jan 1844]
BOUTELLE Artemas 21 of Waterville ME at Pinckneyville (IL) [13 Nov 1835]

BOVEY Elizabeth 12 d/o John BOVEY at Wiscasset ME [18 Apr 1844]

Susan 45 w/o Samuel C BOVEY at Bath ME [4 June 1846]

BOWDEN George with his wife and child and Emma KEELER crossing the river at Castine on Mon last to Brooksville side, the boat upset and the women and child drowned. Mr B saved in a very exhausted state [*Boston Courier*] [28 Oct 1843]

Theodore 72 at Norridgewock ME [18 Oct 1849]

BOWDITCH Charles Albert 14 s/o Horace BOWDITCH at Augusta ME on 8th inst [11 Oct 1849]

Nathaniel at Boston MA [27 Mar 1838]

Nathaniel author of one of the best works on navigation ever published died at Boston MA [27 Mar 1838]

BOWEN Henry R of Castine ME lost of overboard from the jibboom on the ship *Maryland* from Rio Janeiro to Baltimore MD on the 29 Sept [22 Nov 1849]

John Howard 6m s/o John C BOWEN Esq at Bucksport ME [11 Apr 1837]

Phebe w/o William BOWEN at Eastport ME [6 Nov 1846]

BOWERS William of Warwich RI drowned on fishing trip at Providence RI on 18th [6 Jul 1839]

BOWES Hannah E 16 at Washington ME [12 Mar 1846]

BOWKER Hannah Almira 37 w/o Joseph BOWKER at Phipsburg ME [21 Nov 1837]

James Esq 58 at Paris ME [3 June 1847]

James Major 73 at Phippsburg ME [28 Oct 1852]

Levi 88 AmRev pensioner at Machias ME [12 Sept 1850]

BOWLER Clara Augusta 33 w/o Edward BOWLER Esq at Lee [26 Sept 1850]

girl 2y 5m d/o Isaac BOWLER Esq at Winthrop ME [16 Oct 1841]

Hannah abt 72 wid/o Deac J BOWLER at Palermo ME on 27 May [24 June 1852]

Joseph Dea 69 smallpox at Palermo ME [16 Jan 1851]

BOWLES Abigail Mrs 85 formerly of Martha's Vineyard MA at Winthrop ME [15 Feb 1849]

Ann 2y 6m d/o Joshua BOWLES Esq at Wayne ME on Tues evening last [7 Feb 1834]

Francis J at Wayne ME [15 Jan 1839]

Gardiner 15y s/o Isaac BOWLES Esq of consumption at Winthrop ME [8 Jan 1846]

Joseph Deac 69 at Palermo ME on 9 Dec [9 Jan 1851]

Lucius Q C Hon 54 of Machias ME at Roxbury MA on 27th ult at the res of his bro after a short but severe illness of the prevailing influenza epidemic [8 Jul 1843]

Thomas Esq 66 at Bath ME [7 Aug 1851]

BOWMAN Abial S 10 s/o Abial and Syrena E BOWMAN at Kennebec ME [10 Apr 1851]

Cynthia 22 w/o Joshua BOWMAN on 4th inst at Augusta ME [11 Oct 1849]

James a merchant of Gardiner ME late a res of St Louis MO fell into the cellar of a new house, fractured his skull, the gentleman who owned the land made a check out for $500 for the relief of the widow of the deceased and said he would send more if necessary. [16 May 1840]

Marcellus 2y 4m s/o Joseph BOWEN Esq at Vassalboro ME [28 May 1846]

Sarah 72y w/o Thomas BOWMAN at Augusta ME on 18th ult [1 Nov 1849]

Sarah 82 w/o Elihu BOWMAN at Fairfield ME [29 Apr 1852]

Thomas Esq 63 of Augusta ME at Dresden ME [13 June 1837]

BOWYER- see GEORGE

BOX BROWN - see BROWN

BOYCE Francis and William F BOYCE, 2 bros from Amoskeag Village attempting to gather driftwood in the Merrimack River, both drowned, shoemakers 21 and 18, on Fri last [*Manchester Mirror*] [4 June 1851]

BOYD Gen also Prof S QUIMBY, John NIX Esq and a young man an aid of the Marshal of the day, all citizens of Ithica NY and others wounded in the explosion of a cannon on the 4th of July [17 Jul 1845]

Thomas Capt 57 of Wiscasset ME at Boston MA [20 Nov 1835]

William N 62 at Wiscasset ME [22 Aug 1844]

William M 77 at Wiscasset ME [4 June 1846]

BOYER colored man from Elkton MD on Wed last in Philadelphia from poisioning effects of shot left in a bottle of cider. The shot used in cleansing the bottle, remained in it by accident. [7 Mar 1840]

BOYGA Manuel dying declaration of the Pirates signed by companions Angel GARRIA, Manuel BOYGA, Juan MONTENEGRO, Manuel CASTILTE [10 Jul 1835]

BOYINGTON/BOYNTON/BOYTON Abby Louisa 14m only d/o D J and F D BOYNTON at Augusta ME on 21 Jan [30 Jan 1851]

Daniel J of Monmouth ME [2 Nov 1852]

Edward H 19 at Bangor ME on 6th Oct [16 Oct 1846]

Flora A 15 d/o Daniel and Francis BOYNTON at New Portland ME [2 May 1850]

Franklin 20 at Augusta ME on 11th inst [23 Mar 1848]

James 29 drowned in Alna ME [12 Feb 1852]

Mary 57 w/o H M BOYNTON Esq at Brooks ME [27 Dec 1849]

Mary E Mrs 26 at Jefferson ME [6 May 1852]

Samuel 82 AmRev, soon after joined army in 1775, captured by the British and carried to Halifax and remained six months in close confinement, died at Cornish ME [7 Mar 1837]

Sarah 3 only c/o T H BOYTON of Dover ME at Norridgewock ME [11 Feb 1847]

Sarah 32 w/o Thurston BOYNTON at Dover ME [8 Apr 1852]

William D 15y at Orrington ME [29 Jul 1836]

BOYINGTON/BOYNTON - see FROST, TOWLE

BOYLES Edward Mrs 40 at Thomaston ME [8 Jan 1852]

Mrs 40 w/o Edward BOYLES at Thomaston ME [8 Jan 1852]

Rebecca 45 w/o Capt J BOYLES at Belfast ME [21 May 1846]

Sarah E 19y 5m d/o Capt Ichabod BOYLES at Belfast ME [6 Feb 1845]

BRACE Charles L abt 25 an American citizen lately incarcerated in a dungeon in Austria on charge of being a political spy, a native of Hartford CT family moved to New Milford CT, was later released [14 Aug 1851]

BRACKETT Benjamin F of Waterville ME at sea en route to Central America [12 Feb 1852]

Daniel 59 formerly of Tuftonborough NH at Newmarket NH, extensively known for his extraordinary size, weighing previous to his sickness between 500 and 600 pounds [2 May 1837]

Emily 25 at Belfast ME [20 Jul 1848]

James 81 AmRev at Phillips ME [24 Apr 1845]

Joshua 87 AmRev pensioner at Limington ME [28 June 1849]

Samuel shot on Peck Island on Mon [*Eastern Argus*] [14 Jan 1847]

Willard abt 30 at Winnegance (village in Phippsburg) ME [9 Dec 1852]

BRADBURY A Capt 35 at Thomaston ME [27 Nov 1845]

Andrew of ME 25 of cholera Sacramento CA on Nov 5 [2 Jan 1851]

Benjamin B 28 at Biddeford ME [16 Dec 1852]

Daniel 74 at Portland ME [17 Jul 1845]

Daniel 86 at Athens ME [12 Dec 1850]

Enos 52 at Minot ME [1 Feb 1849]

Jabez 43 a member of the executive council of ME at Hollis ME on 13th inst [27 May 1836]

BRADBURY (Cont.) James Dr 73 formerly of Parsonsfield ME at Windham ME [22 Feb 1844]

Jeremiah Esq 69 at Calais ME [28 Dec 1848]

John Capt of Newburyport MA at San Francisco CA on 3 Oct [20 Nov 1851]

Lucius Esq 36 at Eastport ME [25 Jul 1850]

Marion B 16 at Brownfield ME [22 Jan 1846]

Mrs abt 33 w/o John BRADBURY at Fairfield ME [17 Jul 1851]

Nathan C 16 only s/o Dr N A BRADBURY at Sweden ME [25 Oct 1849]

Rhoda 70 w/o Daniel BRADBURY at Portland ME [28 Nov 1844]

William 81 at Chesterville ME [10 Dec 1846]

BRADEEN Jane 77 at Cornish ME [8 Apr 1847]

Sarah w/o Oliver BRADEEN at Waterboro ME [9 Jul 1846]

BRADFORD A 63 at Turner ME [25 Nov 1843]

A abt 53 at Turner ME on 22 Sept [4 Nov 1843]

Alvira 33 w/o William BRADFORD at Turner ME on 28 Sept of consumption [6 Nov 1841]

Benjamin F 25 at Livermore ME [25 Jul 1844]

boy of St George ME s/o Capt BRADFORD drowned [26 Apr 1849]

Chandler 87 at Turner ME [22 Mar 1849]

Isaiah 73 at Cushing ME [20 Nov 1851]

Joseph Capt 78 at St George ME [16 Apr 1846]

Judith widow 72 at Turner ME [10 Dec 1842]

Mary T Capt 59 w/o Capt George BRADFORD at Portland ME on Sun morning [16 Oct 1838]

Mrs w/o Doctor BRADFORD late of Boston MA at Augusta ME on the 11th very suddenly [12 Dec 1844]

Thomas Esq successor to Benjamin FRANKLIN, one of the oldest printers in the Union, in the 94 yr of his age at Philadelphia PA [29 May 1838]

William 36 of consumption at Turner ME on 12 Oct [6 Nov 1841]

BRADISH Gen alias Count ELIOVITCH, the notorious impostor who figured largely in Philadelphia, Portland and some other cities, in Servia calling himself Consul General of the USA. The American Minister at Constantinople properly denounced him as an impostor [*Boston Bee*] [27 July 1844]

BRADLEY Dan Hon 72y a judge [23 Oct 1838]

George of Andover his wife, and a ch 3 or 4, Mrs B seriously injured, the carriage fell upon her on the Boston and Maine Railroad on 12th Fri [*Boston Traveller*] [18 Sept 1845]

George V on Mon last arrested by Constable THURSTON and brought before Mr Justice LUMMUS on the charge of polygamy, 3 wives living, ordered to recognize in $600, to appear at the next term of the Court of Common Pleas and in default committed to jail in Salem [*Lynn Forum*] [10 Aug 1848]

James 23 at Gardiner ME [9 Sept 1843]

Samuel Esq 89 AmRev at New Sharon ME [17 Jul 1851] and [7 Aug 1851]

Samuel Esq 47 formerly of Hollis ME at Saco ME on 26 June [12 Jul 1849]

BRADSHAW Jos at Philadelphia PA on 27th at Barnum's Museum broke his neck [6 Sept 1849]

Robert E abt 22 and William A SIMPSON of Charlestown MA 2 miners murdered for their money by a party of Mexicans at Chilian Gulch. Both MA men. [11 Sept 1851]

BRADSTREET John 35 formerly of Palermo ME, in the attempt to cross Presque Isle stream on the ice near Bradstreet's mill, in Aroostook Co on 25th ult [14 Dec 1848]

Lovina 36 w/o R T BRADSTREET at Palermo ME [3 Jan 1850]

Moses Jr abt 26 at Palermo ME on 25 Jan [7 Jan 1850]

BRADSTREET (Cont.) Samuel G 16 s/o William BRADSTREET at Gardiner ME [23 Dec 1843]

Simon 76 at Gardiner ME [24 Oct 1844]

Thomas Esq 37 of Jefferson ME at Albion ME [30 Jul 1846]

William building consumed with its contents, fire Departments of (Gardiner) and Pittston ME, saved the surrounding buildings. The building occupied for Mechanics' Shop and the oldest in the village, built by Gen DEARBORN in 1785 and occupied for many yrs as his res. During the time that he occupied it, he received a visit from Louis Philippe and TALLEYRAND at Gardiner ME *[Gardiner Fountain]* [18 May 1848]

BRADY Anna 100y 6m at Montville ME [22 Jul 1847]

BRAGDON Celinda w/o Seth P BRAGDON and d/o Nathan WHITNEY of Augusta ME at Cornwall NY on 3 Apr of consumption [4 May 1848]

Charles R alias BRADLEY in jail in Boston MA awaiting trial on charges of bigamy, is suspected of being the murderer of Col HENLY at Portland ME nearly three yrs ago, Lucy Ann Jones BRAGDON's second wife, has made to officer WHIPPLE some important disclosures. She says that BRAGDON came to this city with her in 1843 - she being on her way to see her friends at Newcastle ME ... [2 Jul 1846]

Marion 13 s/o Seth P BRAGDON at Augusta ME [8 Jul 1852]

BRAGG Allen 6 s/o Mr H BRAGG fell from the bridge near Stone Grist Mill into the flume and was drowned *[Gardiner Ledger]* [27 May 1843]

Daniel 57 at Vassalboro ME [4 Jan 1849]

Emeline 19th year at Canaan ME on 15th inst [7 May 1842]

George W 31 s/o Nehemiah BRAGG at Foxcroft ME [5 Aug 1852]

Ingalls Esq 64 at Andover ME [26 Dec 1840]

Matthew 71 at Vassalboro ME on 14 Mar [3 Apr 1851]

BRAINARD Abigail H 25 w/o Rufus A BRAINARD at Hallowell ME [27 Mar 1845]

C small pox introduced into New Sharon by a person who caught it in Boston MA. One case occurred in Augusta ME [21 Dec 1839]

Charles 5 s/o Isaac at Winthrop ME [12 Apr 1849]

Dr late of King's Mills, Whitefield ME, suicide by means of opium [5 Aug 1843]

BRAKELEY Dinah wid/o Pero BRAKELEY, a native of Africa, supposed near 100 yrs old [18 Sept 1835]

BRALEY Russell 60 at Gardiner ME [3 Apr 1845]

Sumner 36 formerly of Gardiner ME at Lewiston ME [22 Aug 1850]

BRAN Thomas 47 at Gardiner ME [19 Apr 1849]

BRANDTNOR girl d/o Dr George H BRANDTNOR killed by a cat *[Pottsville PA Emporium]* [13 June 1844]

BRANT James Lt executed at Havana Cuba, the body shipped to New Orleans on the 16th ult [4 Sept 1851]

BRANT - see BLACKSNAKE

BRANCH Betsey 57 w/o Palmer BRANCH at Augusta ME on 8 June [19 June 1851]

Eliza H 15 youngest d/o Palmer BRANCH at Augusta ME on 5 June [10 June 1852]

Elizabeth 22 d/o Palmer and Betsey BRANCH at Augusta ME [26 Dec 1850]

Sarah 83 w/o the late Samuel BRANCH at Augusta ME [12 Mar 1846]

Susan A 8 d/o Palmer BRANCH at Augusta ME [27 Feb 1841]

Tibbetts Franklin 9m at Augusta ME [2 Sept 1852]

BRANERD Fanny Mrs 73 wid/o Reuben BRANERD at Winthrop ME on Sabbath morning last [5 Aug 1856]

BRATLY Mr died going over Niagara Falls *[NY Cou and Enq]* [12 June 1835]

BRAWN Eliphalet 75 at Vienna ME [26 June 1851]

BRAWN (Cont.) James 61 at Skowhegan ME [2 Dec 1852]
Reuben 41 at Bloomfield ME [15 Nov 1849]
Sarah 19 at Norridgewock ME [3 May 1849]
BRAY Miss abt 40y fell into a fire and burnt to death at South Dover ME [21 May 1842]
Nathaniel at his kiln in Poland ME, burnt last week 35 casts of lime of superior quality,
which proves beyond a doubt that there is abundance of lime rock in that region at
Poland ME [1 Aug 1837]
William at Bloomfield ME [23 Jan 1845]
BRAZER John Rev Dr 57 of Salem MA, the North Church a Unitarian clergyman died of
chest and organic disease of the heart on 26 Feb last [19 Mar 1846]
BRAZIER Nancy Ellen abt 29 w/o Nathan BRAZIER at Abbot ME [19 Dec 1844]
BRECKENRIDGE Robert Gen at Lexington KY [12 Oct 1833]
BREAKIRON Warwick abt 15 s/o Jacob BREAKIRON accidentally killed [*Morgantown VA
Journal*] [1 Apr 1843]
BREATHITT John Hon Gov of Kentucky [*Washington Globe*] [28 Mar 1834]
BRECK Fdw'd [*sic*, most likely Edward?] Esq at China ME [12 Oct 1848]
BRECK Mrs Edward at China ME [30 Jan 1851]
BREESON - see BURNS
BRENT - see OLD PHIL
BRESILLON Sabine of Etampes (France) attempting to assassinate MONTAUBAND, who
insulted her at a ball; at the dance the gentleman was to kiss the opposite lady, but
when it came to MONTAUBAND's turn instead of embracing his partner, he kissed
his own hand. The insult committed in the midst of the young girl's companions
produced a very forcible impression on her mind ... she was sentenced three years
hard labor [*Gazette des Tribunaux*, Paris] [28 Nov 1834]
BRETT Mr in a stage accident [*Portland Advertiser*, 1st inst] [5 Oct 1833]
Pliny F 24 at Oldtown ME [9 Mar 1848]
R F formerly of Phillips ME at Marysville CA [23 June 1852]
BRETTURN William A Esq of Livermore ME at Augusta ME on Sun last [19 Sept 1837]
BREWER Hannah 75 wid/o Gen John BREWER at Robbinston ME [30 Oct 1851]
Mary T 32 w/o Cyrus A BREWER at Brewer ME [12 June 1845]
Silas 37 of Boothbay ME on board ship *Paul Jones* [*sic*] on 18th ult [16 Sept 1847]
BREWER - see MUSSENDEN
BREWSTER Benjamin 72 at West Camden ME [8 Feb 1849]
Dr an American dentist in Paris France, sent for to operate on the teeth of the Imperial
family in Russia, received costly presents and the title of Baron as a mark of regard
for his ability. He resides in Paris France [30 Sept 1843]
James 32 of York ME on Tues the 19th inst in the shipyard of Capt George MOULTON
by the falling of a section of vessel's frame (or in ship carpenter's phrase, a rib) upon
him, whilst assisting in moving it on the ice [28 Jan 1847]
Lydia hung herself at Lowell MA, a factory girl [27 Jul 1839]
William Capt 62 at Camden ME [18 Mar 1852]
William Jr 26 at Parkman ME on 22 Aug [16 Sept 1843]
William abt 23 of Thomaston ME lost overboard from schr *Hero* of Thomaston ME on
19th ult off Eaton's Neck [14 Nov 1844]
BRIANT Joel 78 at Hollis ME [8 Aug 1850]
BRICK Albert 11m c/o the late Augustus BRICK at Augusta ME [3 Dec 1846]
Augustus abt 34 at Augusta ME, buried with the honors of Odd Fellowship [20 Aug
1846]
Caroline 2 d/o S S BRICK at Augusta ME [24 Apr 1845]
BRICKETT Rizpal E 26 w/o Dr G BRICKETT at Mechanic Falls ME [24 Jan 1850]

BRIDGE James Hon 68 at Augusta ME on Sat morning last [31 Jan 1834]

Mary w/o William S BRIDGE of Milford ME at Tyngsborough MA [26 Mar 1846]

William S Esq 69 at Milford ME [14 June 1849]

BRIDGES Isaac 32 at Bluehill ME [23 Sept 1847]

Edmund 89 AmRev at Castine ME [2 Oct 1851]

BRIDGES - see Love (The Law of Love)

BRIDGMAN Grant abt 22y s/o Clark BRIDGMAN of Westhampton on Thurs, found abt half a mile from home lying on the ground with one of the runners of the sled resting on his back, dead [*Greenfield Gazette*] [1 Feb 1844]

BRIDGHAM Orrah 9 d/o Dr T W BRIDGHAM at Leeds ME on Sun last [26 Mar 1842]

T W Dr 54 at Leeds ME on 23rd inst member of the House of Representatives [5 Aug 1847]

BRIER Eunice S 33 w/o Moses W BRIER at Belfast ME [25 Feb 1847]

BRIGGS Anna Fiske 6y 9m d/o Dr Cyrus BRIGGS at Augusta ME on 2 May [8 May 1851]

boy 15y of Roxbury MA administered by his father, Rev Mr BRIGGS, a quantity of opium pills which he supposed to be a common cathartic [22 Feb 1840]

Catharine 70 at Newport ME [14 Sept 1835]

child of Ezra BRIGGS Jr 1y at Winthrop ME on Fri last [27 Nov 1836]

Daniel 74 at Minot ME [23 Feb 1839]

Ezra 73 at Winthrop ME [7 Mar 1844]

George W abt 19 s/o Luther BRIGGS at Locke's Mills, Greenwood ME while engaged in sawing laths [*Norway Advertiser*] [8 June 1848]

Hannah 36 w/o Philip A BRIGGS at Auburn ME [6 Feb 1851]

Hart 22 at Livermore ME of the typhus fever [10 Feb 1842]

Jennet 23 at Turner ME [6 Nov 1838]

John 68 at Turner ME [19 Aug 1847]

Joshua Esq 61 of Robbinston ME at Eastport ME [4 June 1846]

Lucy Ann 8y 9m d/o George BRIGGS at The Forks Somerset Co ME [7 Oct 1847]

Martha E 16 d/o Alden BRIGGS Esq of Pembroke MA at Augusta ME on 15 Mar [20 Mar 1851]

Mary 71 w/o William BRIGGS at Augusta ME [30 Dec 1847]

Mary 80 at Winthrop ME [6 Apr 1848]

Matilda 77 consort of Abiather BRIGGS at Parkman ME [12 Aug 1843]

Mr of ME listed in deaths in CA [23 Sept 1851]

Nathaniel 87 at Jay ME [20 Mar 1851]

Rowland 57 at Winthrop ME on 22 Dec [26 Dec 1840]

BRIGGS - see RAY

BRIGHAM Miranda 43 w/o Cyrus BRIGHAM Esq at West Minot ME [5 Mar 1846]

Stephen Capt 96y born 13 May 1754 in Worcester Co MA, AmRev at Bunker Hill, in 1790 he moved to (now Oneida Co) died at Vernon Oneida Co NY on the 11th inst [1 Nov 1849]

Thomas S Dr abt 75 at Wayne ME on 16th ult [6 June 1844]

BRIGHT Harvey S 14y 7m of Bath ME at Woolwich ME [30 May 1844]

BRIMHALL Sarah Mrs 100y 21d at Sanbornton NH [24 Jul 1845]

BRIMIJION Phebe Mrs 78 w/o Thomas BRIMIJION at Bowdoin ME on the 15th of Jan [1 Feb 1844]

Thomas 89 AmRev, Boston tea party in 1773, battle of Lexington 1775, Bunker Hill, at taking of BURGOYNE and served under ARNOLD, until he turned traitor [1 Feb 1844]

BRINSMADE Elizabeth 35 w/o P A BRINSMADE at Kolua, Sandwich Island (Hawaiian Islands) [30 Jan 1841]

BRINSMADE (Cont.) Horatio Clark 2y s/o P A and E S BRINSMADE at Hallowell ME on
    the 6th inst after a distressing attack of croup which lasted 5 days [14 Nov 1837]
BRISCOE Judge four score and ten married Miss DRAKE, a sweet sixteener! La! what's
    the gal thinkin' on? [*The Lexington (MO) Telegraph*] [7 May 1846]
BRISCOE - see CHAMBERLAIN
BRISTOL William US District Judge since 1826 at New Haven CT on 7 Mar 1836 [13 Jan
    1837]
BRITTON Jonathan 84 at Otisfield ME AmRev [26 Dec 1844]
BRITTON - see STEPHENSON
BROAD Wilmot 24 s/o Thaddeus BROAD at Albion ME on 19th Oct [1 Nov 1849]
BROAD - see HATCH
BROCKAWAY Joseph 59 at Sangerville ME [25 Dec 1851]
BROCKWAY William s 22 s/o Abel BROCKWAY [12 June 1845]
BROOKINGS Pauline Irene 21 w/o Capt Samuel H BROOKINGS at Hallowell ME [15 Jan
    1846]
BROOKS Abel 70 at Robbinston ME [17 June 1847]
    Charles C 24 at Farmington ME [17 Aug 1848]
    Charles deck passenger a serious accident happened on board the steamboat *George
        Collier* on the 6th inst on her passage from New Orleans to St Louis MO [25 May
        1839]
    Elvira H 40 of Strong ME at Farmington ME [25 Jul 1844]
    Fidelia C 45 w/o Rev John S BROOKS of Mendi Mission and d/o the late Eleazer
        COBURN Esq of Bloomfield ME at near Sierra Leone Africa [30 May 1850]
    Gardiner 41 at Belfast ME [29 Apr 1847]
    Georgiana E 17y 6m d/o Henry A BROOKS at Augusta ME [2 Sept 1852]
    Jonas 89 at Wiscasset ME [10 Oct 1850]
    Lt of the 8th infantry by being thrown by his horse at Fredericksburg TX a few weeks
        since [9 Aug 1849]
    Lovina B 17y 4m of Augusta ME at Uxbridge MA [21 Oct 1847]
    Martha 41y w/o J C BROOKS at Portland ME [23 Jan 1845]
    Mr of South Berwick ME at the quarries in Rockport [*Boston Mail*] [31 May 1849]
    Peter C 83 one of the oldest citizens of Boston MA and the richest man in New England
        on 2d inst [11 Jan 1849]
    Susan 62 w/o John BROOKS at Farmington ME [17 Jul 1841]
    William C 73 at Norway ME [28 Feb 1850]
BROCQUE Seldon J deck passenger of Poland died a serious accident happened on board
    the steamboat *George Collier* on the 6th inst on her passage from New Orleans to St
    Louis MO [25 May 1839]
BROWN Aaron of Wilton ME skull badly fractured at Moose Head Lake ME recently by the
    fall of a tree. [1 Feb 1840]
    Abel Rev and an African, once a slave, who accompanied him while giving a lecture last
        week at Northampton; a disgraceful riot occurred, Rev B and the negro escaped
        [*Hampden Post*] [25 Mar 1843]
    Abigail 47 w/o Samuel BROWN at Winslow ME on 8th inst [21 Feb 1841]
    Affia 36 (died ae 35 on 27 Apr 1846, married 12 Aug 1832) w/o James BROWN at
        Buxton ME (see Maine Old Cemetery Association records and York County Marriage
        Records at Maine State Archives) [8 Oct 1846]
    Alden 25 of Bath ME at Boston MA [19 Apr 1849]
    Benjamin Esq 68 formerly of Vassalboro ME at Bangor ME [19 June 1845]
    Betsey S 23 d/o Philbrick of (Augusta) ME at Lowell MA on 13th of May [3 Aug 1848]

BROWN (Cont.) boy abt 15 s/o Henry BROWN Esq while shooting in Northport, with
    another lad about 13y s/o Capt George W BROWN accidentally shot into the thigh of
    the other, the lad is not expected to recover [*Belfast Journal*] [4 Nov 1843]
    boy abt 8y s/o Daniel BROWN, through Wiscasset ME on Mon evening of last week, the
    boy got on behind and as the stage slewed around a corner precipitated against a stone
    post and his brains immeditately dashed out [*Bath ME Times*] [31 Jan 1850]
Caroline M 19 d/o Capt Andrew BROWN at Hallowell ME [12 Mar 1842]
Catharine 54 at St Stephen New Brunswick Canada [17 Apr 1835]
Charles C at Sebasticook ME [9 Mar 1848]
Charlotte widow abt 63 at Albion ME [16 May 1850]
Clarissa Ann 20 at Freeman ME [30 Aug 1849]
Daniel 90 at St Stephens New Brunswick Canada [17 Apr 1835]
Daniel by a wheel passing over his body [22 Oct 1846]
Ebenezer of Jay ME committed suicide [*Hallowell Free Press*] [17 Oct 1834]
Eliza w/o Amos BROWN, principal of the Gorham Academy and Teachers Seminary at
    Gorham ME on 3 Feb [15 Feb 1840]
Elizabeth 37 at Bath ME [4 Jul 1837]
Elizabeth Frost 14 d/o Capt Andrew BROWN at Hallowell ME [3 Oct 1844]
Elizabeth widow 85 formerly of Charlestown MA at Sidney ME on 20th Nov [7 Dec
    1833]
Elzina B 27 w/o Bradish B BROWN Esq at Monson ME [24 Dec 1846]
Emeline 16 d/o Capt Andrew BROWN at Hallowell ME [30 Jul 1846]
Ephraim 40 at Corrina ME [7 Dec 1839]
Esther 39 w/o Daniel BROWN at Kennebec ME [29 Jul 1836]
Eunice wid/o Capt Thomas BROWN formerly of Portsmouth NH at Kittery ME [22 Apr
    1843]
Ezra of Stowe found in the road leading from Stowe to Concord on Fri 31st Mar, Col W
    E FAULKNER, the coroner was called and Patrick COLE was arrested and charged
    with the murder. [*Atlas*] [20 Apr 1848]
George black man 19y sought the felicity of calling his, the charming, yellow-skinned
    Mary CRANE, who it seems preferred another. Last Sat evening he visited her, when
    in a fit of desperation, he fired at her a pistol lodging a ball in the back of her head,
    and instantly discharged another pistol into his own mouth the ball cutting his under
    lip and breaking the jaw bone. Mary CRANE is only 17y. [*Bangor Democrat*] [2 Dec
    1847]
George C abt 42 at Bath ME [16 Sept 1852]
Helen Uphema 8y 1m d/o Daniel BROWN at Hallowell ME [5 Aug 1847]
Henrietta 17 of Augusta ME at Ripley ME while on a visit to her friends [5 Feb 1839]
Isaac a fugitive slave from MD before the courts in PA, arrested on a warrant from the
    Gov of MD charging him with a felony, a second requisition was sent from MD, the
    Gov of PA revoked his warrant to Judge PARSONS and issued another; but by
    oversight no warrant was obtained from Judge PARSONS, under this second warrant
    from the Gov; and the 1st being revoked, there was no authority to hold the slave. [3
    June 1847]
Isaac C 30 partially insane and died by his own hand at Belfast ME [16 May 1837]
James 2d 94 AmRev pensioner at Porter ME [12 Feb 1852]
James 55 at Nobleboro ME [7 Mar 1840]
James at Orland ME [4 Feb 1833]
Jane 19 w/o Geo of Oldtown, he left her, when she found him he didn't recognize her
    dressed as a man, he claimed married to his paramour, her funds gone enlisted as
    ship cook out of Boston, DOW Capt. Not suspected a female in male attire, until at

BROWN (Cont.) Mt Desert ME, discovered the cook wore stays, was conveyed ashore and ladies in the neighborhood gave her fare to Oldtown [*Hancock Co Democrat*] [11 Nov 1847]

Jesse 73 at Vienna on 25 Mar (NH papers please copy) (13 May 1852]

Jesse of Poland ME arrested, having been accused of poisoning his wife and a girl named (Rachel) BAILEY with whom he had held "criminal intercource" He was later acquitted of the death of Rachel BAILEY at Poland ME [21 Feb 1837] [2 May 1837]

Joel of Violet Fairfield Co OH struck by lightning in the open air on the 4th inst and killed instantly. It is remarkable some silver which was in his pantaloons' pocket at the time of the accident could not be found afterwards [4 Jul 1834]

John 140y a native of Ireland but for the last 50 years a citizen of New Jersey died at Mansfield NJ [19 Aug 1836]

John 40 recently of Bangor ME at Exeter ME [10 Aug 1839]

John 60 formerly of Frankfort ME at Bradley ME [31 May 1849]

John 96 AmRev at Bangor ME [29 Apr 1852] and [3 June 1852]

John Col 65 at Belfast ME [5 Sept 1844]

John M 64 at Atkinson ME [21 Nov 1850]

John T abt 26 found in the barn of Mr Cotton BROWN suspended by his neck and dead at Sangerville ME suicide [*Piscataquis Farmer*] [18 Jan 1844]

John W 31 at Bath ME [17 Aug 1848]

Joseph abt 60 at Vassalboro ME [9 Sept 1852]

Josiah 63 at Jackson ME [13 June 1844]

Levi Esq 51 at Waterford ME [30 Dec 1847]

Levi Towle 27 at Belfast ME [26 Dec 1834]

Margaret abt 6y d/o Elijah and Margaret BROWN, drowned in a tan vat [19 Sept 1837]

Maria K 33 w/o Dr T H BROWN at Paris ME [10 Dec 1846]

Martha Jane 31y 8m w/o William BROWN at Brownville ME on Sun morning Apr 8 [8 May 1838]

Mary (Polly DAILEY) (see p. 304 Stackpole's *History of Winthrop ME*) 62 w/o Jeremiah BROWN at Winthrop ME on 19th ult [6 Mar 1835]

Mary late of Vienna ME, est notice, Samuel BROWN exec [30 Sept 1852]

Mary N 15 d/o John and Thankful BROWN at Windham ME [30 Sept 1847]

Molly 81 at Monmouth ME [27 May 1847]

Moody 87 AmRev at Cornish ME on 9 Jul [4 Sept 1851] and [6 Nov 1851]

Mr married abt three months ago, committed suicide [9 Dec 1836]

Mrs w/o B F BROWN of Biddeford ME drowned near her res Mon forenoon last [16 Sept 1843]

Nancy 54 w/o Capt M BROWN at Waterford ME [23 Nov 1848]

Phebe T 12y and 6m d/o Samuel and Mary W BROWN at Chester ME on 27 June of consumption [8 Jul 1852]

Philena D 24 w/o James B BROWN at Norridgewock ME [7 Nov 1850]

Rachel 85 wid/o Andrew BROWN AmRev at Gray ME [20 Mar 1845]

Samuel D 27 at Winthrop ME on Fri last [18 Apr 1837]

Samuel H of Ipswich by trade a carpenter on the Fresh Pond Rail road [13 May 1843]

Sarah 82 wid/o Nathan BROWN at Mt Vernon ME [7 Oct 1843]

Seth after an illness of 36 hours at So China ME [15 Oct 1846]

Stephen P Esq of Dover ME lost his hand in the cards in his factory, the amputation performed by Dr S LAUGHTON of Foxcroft ME [*Dover Observer*] [25 Jan 1849]

Susannah 80 w/o Titus O BROWN at Norway ME [13 Nov 1851]

Susannah Mrs 93y 7m at Farmington ME [1 Oct 1846]

Timothy 76 at Solon ME [19 June 1851] and [4 June 1851]

BROWN (Cont.) two sisters one of them not expected to survive at Woonsocket by the bursting of a lamp [*Prov Sentinel*] [3 Sept 1846]

W W and George and J C DUDLEY of Hampden ME at the Adams House of Boston MA and were robbed of $3000 of gold dust on Wed. They had returned from CA being passengers on the *Crescent City* (from the *Eastern Argus* of Portland ME) [31 Jul 1851]

widow 95 at Skowhegan ME [5 Aug 1847]

BROWN - see BAGLEY, BAILEY, CARTER, DRAPER, DURGAN, HOVEY, SIMON, THOMAS, YOOSTLING

BROWNELL David at Fall River MA stabbed in a quarrel by Wescott SPRINGER. The wounded man is not expected to recover [*New Bedford Mercury*] [2 Mar 1848]

BROWNING Cyntha [Cynthia?] the famed Kentucky giantess seven feet high and proportionate in size died on 30th ult at Flemingsburg KY [21 Aug 1845]

Miss 17y and 7ft of Fleming Co KY and Porter the Giant is said to be 7' 3" in his stocking feet [*Maysville Monitor*] [19 Dec 1837]

BRUCE Liscolm who kept in Tremont St Boston MA was instantly killed by the explosion of a soda reservoir [*Boston Cultivator*] [13 Jul 1839]

Mrs of Alna ME w/o Charles BRUCE of Alna ME depressed by the long sickness of her husband and others of her family put a period to her life on Fri last [21 Dec 1839]

Phebe 66 at Bath ME [1 Apr 1847]

Robert of Augusta ME a seaman on board brig *Lucy* on 10 Sept of African fever on passage from Africa to New York [30 Sept 1852]

BRULON Mrs Knight of the Legion of Honor, crested by Pres of French Rep, b 1771 and officer res Hotel des Invalides last 52y, dau, sister, and wife of military, who d in active service in Italy. Her husband d at Ajaccio in 1791, after 7y service. In 1792 she entered husband's Regt, (42d Inf) ... was permitted to continue notwithstanding her sex, wounded at the siege of Calvi. In Oct 1822, promoted to Ensign.... [9 Oct 1851]

BRYAN Edward and Eliza of Utica NY drowned on 2d inst at Trenton Falls [16 Aug 1849]

BRYANT Allen 18 c/o James and Lydia (MASON) BRYANT at Industry ME (see p 523 *A History of Industry ME* by Wm Collins Hatch 1893) [21 Nov 1850]

Alvin 10 or 12 s/o Leander BRYANT at Saco? village ME *drowned* [*Saco Union*] [2 Jan 1851]

Charles M 42y of Saco ME fell through the floor of a saw-mill on the 24th ult at Biddeford ME on Mon last after suffering two weeks, left a wife and ch [*Saco Repository*] [7 Nov 1844]

David Capt 70 at Dover ME [26 Apr 1849]

Diana 32 at Dover ME of consumption [10 Aug 1839]

Edward L the 1st officer 22 s/o Cushing BRYANT Esq of Damariscotta ME at San Francisco CA died on board the brig *Col Fremont* on 22 May [17 Jul 1851]

Gridley of Boston MA saved from drowning when the steam packet *New England* sank. It left Boston for Bath and Gardiner ME and had an accident with the schr *Curlew* on 31 May [12 June 1838]

Hezekiah 61 at Turner ME on 4 Dec of the typhus fever, father to Mrs ROLFE who died on 4 Nov and Mrs Joan ALLEN died 14 Nov [24 Dec 1842]

James 36 of Long Island NY belonged to the US ship *Preble* and died with the Africa fever at Porto Grande Island of St Vincent Cape de Verds on 8 Jan [10 Apr 1845]

James Alvan 25 c/o James and Lydia (MASON) BRYANT at Industry ME [21 Nov 1850]

Joseph 89 AmRev at Baldwin ME [8 Apr 1847]

Luther 31 at Union ME [9 Jan 1841]

Lydia Ellen 7y c/o James and Lydia (MASON) BRYANT at Industry ME [21 Nov 1850]

Lydia (MASON) 50 w/o James BRYANT at Industry ME [21 Nov 1850]

BRYANT (Cont.) Mary H 89 w/o Daniel BRYANT at Gardiner ME [18 Jul 1850]

Nathaniel 74 at Gardiner ME [24 Oct 1850]

Nathaniel at Saco ME [20 June 1844]

Spencer at Portland ME [6 Apr 1839]

William abt 15y while tending a grist mill at Turner ME on Mon the 28th ult [2 Nov 1833]

BRYANT - see BAYANT

BUBIER Esther 35 at Hallowell ME [12 Aug 1847]

BUBIER - see BOOBIER

BUCHANAAN Boon 113y "a colored man" at Washington Co PA at the poor house, was a waiter in the army at Braddock's defeat 1775 [1 Oct 1846]

BUCHANAN John Hon in the 71y Chief Justice of the State of MD at Woodland on Wed last [*Hagerstown Torchlight*] [21 Nov 1844]

BUCHMAN Thomas died [25 Dec 1841]

BUCK Hosea B 30 at Guilford ME on 16th inst [2 Jan 1841]

James M 28 at Paris ME [18 Nov 1836]

Jane 30 at Fryeburg ME [3 Oct 1850]

Jonathan Capt 67 at Buckfield ME [7 Mar 1850]

Lewis A 20y s/o Stephen and Ruth BUCK at Bethel ME [8 Jul 1852]

Maria 18 of Bucksport ME at Bradford ME [4 June 1842]

Moses 21 s/o Esther and David BUCK Esq at Canton ME on 14 May [17 Jul 1851]

Sarah abt 23 of Bath ME at Winthrop or Portland ME on 7 Sept and inserted erroneously before, should have stated 78 [17 Sept 1842] [1 Oct 1842]

Silva left a girl with a BENNETT family at the head of Cayuga Lake; after some time there was no trace of Mrs BUCK. The well educated girl 17 is at Ovid Seneca Co and advertises for her parents and relatives [15 May 1835]

BUCK - see DURHAM

BUCKER Alexander a Senator in Congress from the state of Missouri, about a fortnight since of the cholera at Cape Girardeau. His lady of the same disease about the same time. [8 Jul 1833]

BUCKINGHAM Edwin junior editor of the *Boston Courier* at sea on his return from Smyrna [3 June 1833]

BUCKLAND Josiah abt 13y found on the 6th inst in a field a mile and one half east of the village, shot through the body, by accident by Moses C ELLIOT, found by an elder bro [*Hampden Whig*] [18 Apr 1834]

BUCKLEY Laura J abt 39 w/o Charles S BUCKLEY at Augusta ME on 13th inst [16 Dec 1852]

Timothy abt 25 killed by accident at Lewiston ME a native of Cork Co Ireland [29 Apr 1852]

Ralph E 8m s/o Charles S BUCKLEY at Augusta ME on 5 inst [11 Sept 1851]

BUCKLIN Nathaniel Capt abt 60 at Camden ME while on a visit to his friends [6 June 1840]

BUCKMINISTER David Capt 63 at Saco ME [14 June 1849]

Friend of the Ploughman a warm friend to husbandry recently connubialized now off on a honey-moon excursion. Last heard from at Niagara Falls [6 Jul 1848]

BUCKNAM Amos 30 at Eastport ME [22 Apr 1836]

Olive 69 at Solon ME [3 Jul 1838]

BUCKNER Mrs A Mr C married Miss BUCKNER last week, on that evening Mrs B, the mother of the bride, had a large quantity of custards made and sent them to the house of her married ch. On Sun Mrs FOSTER, her dau taken ill and died. [*Philadelphia Commercial Herald*, Louisville KY 12 June] [4 Jul 1834]

BUDSON Charles C 1m s/o Joseph BUDSON at Bangor ME [12 June 1845]

BUELL Parker of Mendon NY recovered at a recent Circuit Court a verdict of $1600
against Falcon P POWERS for the seduction of his daughter. Such enemies to virtue
ought to be kept upon oat-meal gruel and to give them a smart appetite, receive a
cowhiding three times a day, immediately before eating. [*The Rochester (NY)
Democrat*] [10 Oct 1844]

BUFFUM William by the bursting of a grindstone at the scythe factory at Nasonville RI on
28th inst [3 Feb 1848]

BUGBEE Professor while looking abt a whale ship at Bridgeport CT accidentally fell and
instantly broke his neck. [1 June 1839]

BUKER Carver 23 at Castine ME [5 Mar 1846]

Lovina P 22 at Bowdoin ME [17 Sept 1846]

BULFINCH Benjamin S an aged journeyman printer, a native of Philadelphia, known from
Maine to GA was drowned near Newwark OH a few days ago [2 May 1840]

Jeremiah 86 of Waldoboro ME at Augusta ME at the insane hospital [3 Dec 1846]

BULLARD O A his biography with line drawing from the *American Biographical Sketch
Book* and other authentic sources, born 25 Feb 1816 at Howard, Steuben Co NY [13
Nov 1851]

Judge late Rep from New Orleans LA died on 18th ult was a native of MA [1 May 1851]

BULLEN Franklin 22 at New Sharon ME [1 Jul 1847]

Priscilla 24 wid/o Joseph BULLEN at Swanville ME [25 Apr 1850]

Thankful 85 wid/o Joshua BULLEN at New Sharon ME [20 June 1850]

BULLEN - see MOORE

BULLOCH Douglass killed at Madawaska, Aroostook Co ME by Mr WELCH [11 Nov
1847]

BULLOCK Jeremiah Elder 62 at Limington ME [10 Jan 1850]

Mary Elizabeth 17 of Bristol RI d/o Ebenezer BULLOCK, death in the card room of the
Poksnoket Steam Mill [*Bristol (RI) Phenix*] [12 Dec 1844]

BULLOCK - see WAYNE

BUMP George W 27 at Farmington ME [19 Dec 1850]

Z 86 at East Livermore ME [15 Apr 1852]

Zepheniah 2nd 25 at the Forks of the Kennebec River, Somerset Co ME [8 Mar 1849]

BUMPUS Z 86 at East Livermore ME [15 Apr 1852]

BUNHAM Joseph Capt 46 of New Castle ME at Boston MA [9 Dec 1852]

BUNINGTON Charles abt 28 at Augusta ME on 23 Oct [4 Nov 1852]

BUNKER Betsey 77 a widow at North Anson ME [2 Oct 1851]

Capt of Bristol RI a letter from Abraham OSBORN dated of Edgartown MA on 28 Dec
the *O H Perry* of Sullivan ME was lost [9 Jan 1851]

David 72 at Portland ME on 29th ult [9 Jan 1845]

Mary Ann abt 20 w/o David Y BUNKER of Exeter NH at Mechanicsburg OH [26 Dec
1850]

Nathaniel 73 at Bath ME [26 June 1851]

Rufus abt 35 at Hallowell ME [6 Oct 1843]

Rufus H P 24 at Bath ME [27 Jul 1848]

Susan D 38 at Bath ME [20 Mar 1845]

BURBANK Daniel E pastor of the 1st Baptist Church and society of Winthrop ME 27 at
(Winthrop ME) on Mon last [31 Oct 1840]

BURDICK - see VARSE

BURGESS Benjamin is now 100y at Wayne ME [1 May 1851] and 101y 3m at Wayne ME
on 13 June [5 Aug 1852]

Hiram 21 at China ME on the 6th inst [1 May 1838]

BURGESS (Cont.) Jabez and son drowned, his son abt 9y at Pocasset [*Providence Courier*]
[14 Aug 1838]
Jonathan in Vassalboro ME by falling a tree [29 Jan 1846]
S W D P 14 at Phipsburg ME [27 Aug 1846]
Seth 56 at Phipsburg ME [6 Aug 1846]
Zima H 27 at Phipsburg ME [19 Nov 1846]
BURGIN John Hon 80 at Eastport ME [5 Mar 1846]
BURGOINE - see MOORE
BURGOYNE - see BERRY, BUTLER, BRIMIJOIN, COOLIDGE, CHURCHELL,
DENNIS, FORD, SCHUYLER, WHIDDEN, WHITCOMB
BURGUOYNE- PHELEPS
BURHAM Henry when between Fort Independence and Thompson's Island drowned a party
of 27 of the boys of the Farm School on Thompson's Island accompanied by a teacher
and boat-keeper [7 May 1842]
BURKE Edmund Keene of Mobile a most unfilial young reprobate, recently ridden on a rail
by the citizens of that place, for breaking two of his father's ribs, and running away
with a third; that is to say he ran away with his old father's young wife his own step-
mother, and married her! (from the *Louisville Journal*) [16 Oct 1838]
Edmund, 4 editors in Congress at present viz Luther SEVERANCE of Augusta ME;
Edmund BURKE of Haverhill NH; John WENTWORTH of Chicago IL; and Volney
E HOWARD of MS [18 Jan 1844]
Michael at Gardiner ME [19 Aug 1852]
BURKER Nathan of Gouldsboro ME lost overboard from schr *Ann Denman* night of 19th
inst in L I Sound [7 Jan 1847]
BURLEIGH Hannah C 51 w/o Josiah BURLIEGH Esq at Ripley ME [27 Nov 1845]
BURLEM Frederick a native of Germany at Bangor ME by the breaking of a grindstone [25
Nov 1852]
BURLEY Nancy 64 w/o Col Moses BURLEY formerly of Palermo ME at Linneus ME [31
Jan 1850]
Robert from Sanbornton NH shot himself at the Fulton House last week, bar-keeper for
some time [21 Dec 1833]
BURNETT Rebecca 64 at Gorham ME [1 Feb 1849]
BURNHAM Asa Elder 60 formerly of Sebec ME dropped down dead after returning from
mowing his field at Garland ME [19 Aug 1852]
J E Rev 33 at Dover ME [7 Mar 1850]
Owen 40 at Bridgton ME [17 June 1836]
Rebecca 66 consort of Hon John Burnham ME member of Executive Council of Maine at
Orland ME on 21st ult [4 Mar 1836]
Thomas S 46 of Lubec ME on board brig *Quoddy Belle* on 16 Apr [4 Jul 1850]
BURNS Jane 38 w/o John BURNS at Thomaston ME [11 Feb 1847]
John a bricklayer killed, 5 Irishman arrested: Patrick RAGAN; Sylvester PHILLIPS;
John BREESON; James KAY and Archibald MULHOLLAND [Philadelphia paper]
[1 May 1845]
Sarah 88 at Hallowell ME [13 Aug 1846]
William Esq editor of the *Sunday Dispatch* at New York s/o Mrs Deborah BURNS of
Gardiner ME [27 June 1850]
BURR Aaron 81y formerly Vice Pres of the USA on Staten Island on Tues in Sept 1836
[*Boston Atlas*] [23 Sept 1836] [13 Jan 1837]
Edward 17 s/o Martin BURR at Mercer ME [26 Nov 1846]
Edwin H 17 at Mercer ME [28 Oct 1846]
Hannah 35y 6m w/o C C BURR at Embden ME [28 Nov 1850]

BURR (Cont.) Jane 17 wid/o Luther BURR [26 Nov 1846]

    Perez 57 at Eastport ME [20 Feb 1851]

    Samuel his house struck by lightning at Woolwich ME on Fri last and a little girl abt 7y was killed [*Eastern Argus*] [21 Aug 1845]

BURR - see DORROGH, KEEN/KEENE

BURRELL/BURRILL Calvin of Northampton on the 25th inst of injuries sustained on the Camden and Ambody Railroad by the late unfortunate and careless accident [12 Oct 1839]

    Crooker 39 at Dover NH [5 Feb 1852]

    Franklin 10m s/o Columbus BURRILL at Augusta ME on 13th inst [22 Feb 1849]

    I Crooker 39 at Dover ME [5 Feb 1852]

    John 90 AmRev at East Sanderville ME [15 Oct 1842]

    Mary wid/o Deac Humphry 82 at Skowhegan ME [16 Jan 1845]

    Mr 23, had one of his thumbs blown off and his right arm lacerated by the premature discharge of a cannon on the 4th. It is feared that he may also lose his eyesight. at Newmarket [17 Jul 1851]

    Rhoda 18 at Clinton ME [24 June 1847]

    Samuel 37 at Clinton ME [25 Mar 1847]

    Sarah F at China ME on 29th ult [6 Feb 1841]

    Sarah Mrs 24 formerly of Camden ME at Boston MA [10 June 1843]

    Susan w/o Jerome BURRILL at Fairfield ME [1 Apr 1843]

    Unity (WHITE) 39 w/o Hiram BURRELL at Winthrop ME very suddenly (see p. 659 Stackpole's *History of Winthrop ME*) [25 Sept 1841]

BURROWS James a native of Maine very suddenly on Mon morning on board the *Galveston* at New York [24 Feb 1848]

    Stephen at Three Rivers Lower Canada [22 Feb 1840]

BURSLEY Abigail L H 39 w/o John S BURSLEY at Chesterville [13 Mar 1845]

BURT James P 16 s/o Peirce BURT of Pittston ME on Shell Island FL of yellow fever [30 Dec 1843]

    Mary widow 76 at Skowhegan ME [15 June 1839]

BURTON Edward S 27 s/o the late J BURTON Jr printer of Bangor ME at Linton China Empire [4 Mar 1847]

    Elizabeth 34 w/o Joseph BURTON and d/o Jesse ROBINSON of Waterville ME at Hallowell ME [8 Aug 1834]

    Ellen Gardner 19 d/o Joseph BURTON Esq at Augusta ME [17 Dec 1846]

    George a negro, on Sat evening fell from the maintop mast head of the bark *Louisa*, lying at the wharf between Lombard and South Street and was instantly killed. The fatal result of a drunken wager, BURTON betting that he could climb to the top of the flag staff, when he reached the cross trees, he grew dizzy [*Philadelphia Ledger*] [27 May 1843]

    Hutchins G Gov in Lincoln Co, NC on 21 Apr 1836 [13 Jan 1837]

    James Esq 73 of the oldest residents of Augusta ME, Postmaster of Augusta ME 40 year ago [13 Nov 1838]

    James Jr abt 45 at Bangor ME [20 June 1837]

    Mary 80 wid/o James BURTON at Augusta ME on 26 May [1 June 1848]

    Mary Elizabeth 19 at Bangor ME on 25th ult [9 Oct 1845]

BUSBY Mr a butcher shot by a rifle ball in a riot in St John New Brunswick Canada at the recent Municipal Election. The military had to be called out before order could be restored. The *Calais Advertiser* adds that now all the elections there are scenes of riot and bloodshed. [29 Mar 1849]

BUSH Alfred W of New London CT at San Francisco CA [8 Jan 1852]

BUSSELL Abby C 3 d/o William and Catherine BUSSELL at Vassalboro ME on 4 Mar [18
    Mar 1852]
   Abigail abt 23 at Vassalboro ME on 18th ult of consumption [4 Sept 1845]
BUSWELL Abigail 76 w/o Ebenezer BUSWELL at Hallowell ME [10 Apr 1851]
   Caleb 22 at Solon ME very suddenly [27 Jan 1837]
   girl 6y of Louden Hill in (Hallowell) ME d/o Elanor BUSWELL accidentally killed. Mrs
      B lost her husband abt one yr ago by drowning [*Hallowell Gazette*] [11 Dec 1851]
   James at Winthrop ME [4 Apr 1834]
   William I 20 at Hallowell ME [20 Sept 1849]
BUTLER Augustus 33at Farmington ME on 10th [22 Aug 1850]
   Benjamin 73 at Cornville ME [16 Oct 1851]
   Calvin L 25 formerly of Bangor ME at New York suddenly [4 Nov 1847]
   Charles Henry 3 s/o Capt E L BUTLER at Chesterville ME on Oct last [2 Nov 1849]
   Cornelius 31 at Norridgewock ME [5 Mar 1846]
   Edward Esq 70 at Farmington ME [10 May 1849]
   Elijah Jr 42 at Hallowell ME [10 Sept 1846]
   Emeline Mrs at New Portland ME [31 Aug 1839] Eugene A 14m c/o Alonzo BUTLER at
      Augusta ME [9 May 1850]
   Feruel Mellen 2y 2m s/o Thomas and Amanda BUTLER at Dead River on 19th Dec [4
      Jan 1849]
   Gorham 50 at Union ME [30 Sept 1836]
   Hiram P 10 s/o Capt E L BUTLER at Chesterville ME in Oct last [22 Nov 1849]
   Jane P 16 d/o Rev John BUTLER late of North Yarmouth ME at Hallowell ME on 8th
      inst [21 Jan 1843]
   Jeremiah Rev 71 at Farmington ME [31 Jul 1851]
   Joanna B 44 w/o Walter BUTLER at Rockland ME [17 Jul 1851]
   Judith 51 w/o William BUTLER at Thomaston ME [6 Mar 1838]
   Lovey (Lovie Sherman PEASE) 83 at Farmington ME (see p. 401 *Butler's History of
      Farmington ME*) [1 Apr 1843]
   Maria Antoinette 6y 8m d/o Ralph BUTLER at Augusta ME [25 Nov 1847]
   Mary Ella 23m d/o Ralph BUTLER at Augusta ME [1 Apr 1847]
   Mina R 28 d/o Phineas BUTLER at Rockland ME [8 Aug 1850]
   Nathan N Capt 50 at Hallowell ME on 13 Feb [20 Feb 1851]
   Phineas 92 of Thomaston ME, oldest of the 5 gg gparents of a ch in Searsmont ME b 7
      Sept 1849, AmRev at BURGOYNE's surrender at Saratoga 17 Oct 1778, surviving
      gg gparents: Mrs Phineas BUTLER; Mr and Mrs Thomas ROBINSON of Liberty
      ME; and Mrs Elizabeth ULMER of Thomaston ME. The age 92, 85, 88, 88, 85
      respectively, also living three g gparents and 4 gparents. [22 Nov 1849]
   Phineas 94 AmRev at Thomaston ME [28 Oct 1852]
   Samuel Elder 64 formerly of New Hampshire at Monmouth ME [18 May 1848]
   William 51 formerly of Farmington ME at Bear Creek Upper Canada [29 Nov 1849]
BUTLER - see JUNKINS, McVEAN
BUTMAN Benjamin Esq 89 at Dixmont ME on 8th inst AmRev at Bunker Hill battle [24
   June 1843]
   Susannah 88 at Dixmont ME [8 Jan 1846]
BUTMAN - see SIMS
BUTTER - see BUTLER
BUTTERFIELD Charles engineer of Thetford VT on 30th ult, a culvert washed out,
      engineer, fireman, conductor, and breakman, 2 latter on the tenth car from the
      engine, saw light disappear, rushed towards last car (20th car) and saved their lives,
      16 cars followed engine into the chasm and literally smashed to atoms, on Passumpsic

BUTTERFIELD (Cont.) Railroad (reported in the *Haverhill Republican* and then reprinted in the *Manchester Mirror*) [6 Nov 1851]

Franklin 48 formerly of Sidney ME at Molunkus ME [31 Aug 1848]

James Col of Tyngsborough, a mill-wright run over by the cars in that place on Mon last and instantly killed, has left a wife and children [*Lowell Journal*] [7 Dec 1848]

John 60 at Paris ME [25 Nov 1836]

Joseph Esq 86 at Milford ME on 15th ult, of 1st settlers and among the earliest emigrants into the county of Penobscot [11 June 1842]

Mary 43 at Sidney ME [16 Oct 1841]

Moses murdered his wife and 2 youngest ch, while 2 others of the family only saved themselves by flight for murdering his family "to sure them from eternal ruin, at the approaching end of the world!" committed to gaol in Paris ME [*Eastern Argus*] [1 May 1841]

Nancy T 29 w/o Robert BUTTERFIELD at Bowdoinham ME [5 Apr 1849]

BUTTERS Abiel of Wilmington MA saved from drowning when the steam packet *New England* sank. It left Boston for Bath and Gardiner ME and had an accident with the schr *Curlew* on 31 May [12 June 1838]

BUTTS Abraham 19 at Waterville ME [11 Jul 1844]

George Henry 4w s/o Pierce and Mary Ann BUTTS at Pittston ME [27 June 1837]

Sarah Ann Mrs 21 at New Portland ME [11 Jul 1844]

BUXTON George 15y 5m s/o Capt J BUXTON at North Yarmouth ME on 8th [19 Mar 1842]

James 92 at Falmouth ME [10 June 1833]

Jeremiah Esq 68 at North Yarmouth ME on 19th inst [31 Jul 1835]

BUZZELL Jacob barn burned down at Newfield ME on Wed last week, Sargent DREW was arrested on Thurs upon suspicion of having set the fire [20 Feb 1851]

Mary Mrs 56 formerly of Parsonsfield ME at Biddeford ME [5 Feb 1852]

Sarah Mary 4 only d/o Stephen P and Sarah BUZZELL at Vassalboro ME [3 Aug 1841]

Stephen 65 formerly of East Kingstown NH at Vassalboro ME [30 May 1844]

Susannah 86 wid/o Jonathan BUZZELL at Winthrop ME [1 Feb 1844]

William abt 80 at Winthrop ME on 1st inst [9 Jul 1842]

William B 54 at Fayette ME [12 Dec 1844]

BUZZLE Gorham 29 formerly of Mt Vernon ME at New Bedford MA on 16th ult [8 Jul 1843]

BYARD John 38 of Sedgwick ME master of the brig *Lucy H Chase* in Eastport Harbor [14 Oct 1852]

BYER Hannah 100y at Calais ME [27 May 1836]

BYRAM Benjamin 26 at Bath ME [26 Aug 1847]

Henry Dr 58 at Eastport ME [2 Mar 1848]

Mary 28 w/o Erastus D BYRAM at Guildford ME [2 Jan 1845]

Miriam 16 d/o Major S B BYRAM of Dover ME at North Yarmouth ME [28 Nov 1850]

Sarah H 38 w/o Major S B BYRAM and d/o Henry CARLTON Esq of Augusta ME at Dover ME [8 June 1848]

- **C** -

CABBETT boy 6y s/o Lewis CABBETT of West Dedham MA [*Norfolk Democrat*] [19 June 1845]

CACY Hannah 32 wid/o Zenas CACY at Fayette ME [18 Feb 1833]

Caddo Indian - see KATH-LA-MO-HEE

CAHILL James abt 30 eastern bank gave way burying him, born in Parish of Killard, County of Clare Ireland, left a wife & one ch [*Gardiner Advertiser*, Extra 5 Feb] [14 Feb 1850]

CAIN boys two s/o Capt David CAIN of Clinton ME drowned near Noble's Ferry at Fairfield ME [3 Feb 1848]

N Rev 83 at Clinton ME [22 Feb 1849]

CALAR Joseph of Waldoboro ME lost overboard from ship *New England*, Capt LOWELL of Bath ME on her passage from James River [11 Nov 1843]

CALDEN Velina H 48 w/o Benjamin CALDEN at Kennebec (now Manchester) ME [16 Dec 1852]

CALDERWOOD Louisa Mrs 43 w/o J CALDERWOOD at Camden ME [20 May 1847]

CALDWELL Capt the mail rider between Monterey and Santa Barbara killed, left St Yeub [*sic*] on the 22d June, his body found a day or two afterwards with several bullets in it [21 Aug 1851]

John A abt 38 formerly of (Kennebec Co, Maine) died at Vandalia IL [21 Aug 1845]

Maria B Mrs 35 w/o John CALDWELL 2d at Oxford ME [9 May 1844]

Marritt Professor abt 30 formerly principal of Wesleyan Seminary at Readfield ME at Carlisle PA [23 May 1837]

Merritt Prof of Dickinson College at Portland ME [22 June 1848]

Susan Stanwood 11m 2w d/o John S & Mary E CALDWELL at Belfast ME on Fri on 12th inst [25 Sept 1845]

CALEF/CALIFF Mary 24y d/o Josiah CALEF Esq of Saco ME at Mobile AL of consumption [6 Mar 1845]

Mary Mrs 71 w/o Capt John CALEF at Portland ME [15 Feb 1844]

Samuel 75 from Camden to Islesboro ME on 23d ult, frozen to death [29 Jan 1852]

CALER Mary 60 w/o Christian CALER at Waldoboro ME [10 Apr 1835]

CALL boy 17y in a cart accident s/o Mr CALL a wood-wharfinger of Charlestown MA [16 May 1840]

CALLENDER Mr of York suddenly on his way home from Harrisburg PA (from the *Philadelphia Bulletin*) [10 Apr 1851]

CALLEY William of Belfast ME fell into the hold of a vessel & broke his neck [1 Aug 1850]

CALVERT Richard 75 formerly a resident of Pittston ME at St John New Brunswick Canada on 4 June [10 Jul 1845]

CAME Sarah M abt 25 w/o Mark CAME at Standish ME [18 Sept 1845]

CAMERON Simon Gen, cashier of the Branch Bank at Middletown PA injuried on the Philadelphia & Wilmington Railroad [23 Sept 1841]

CAMMET Joseph 18 at Albion ME [25 Feb 1843]

CAMPBELL Abigail Mrs 75 w/o Daniel CAMPBELL at Bowdoin ME of a cancer in her mouth [9 Dec 1847]

Anna M 4 only d/o Simeon & Emily CAMPBELL at Sidney ME on 21 Oct [4 Jan 1849]

Annis Capt 74 at Belfast ME [27 Dec 1849]

Daniel Rev formerly a lawyer in Winthrop ME at Orford NH settled as minister 70y [25 Oct 1849]

Dr of Watermoreland [*sic*] VT riding home from Chesterfield on Fri his horse stumbled and threw him with such great force it broke his skull [3 Aug 1841]

Edwin of Cherryfield ME by the accidental discharge of a gun while hunting [1 Aug 1840] & [8 Aug 1840]

Elizabeth 74 at Bath ME [13 Aug 1846]

George W 80 twice a US senator from TN & appointed secretary of the treasury by President MADISON in 1814 at Nashville TN [9 Mar 1848]

CAMPBELL (Cont.) John of Westerly RI at San Francisco CA [8 Jan 1852]
   Martha Mrs 35 at West Bath ME [9 Mar 1848]
   Melinda B 23 w/o William CAMPBELL & d/o Ezra FISK Esq of Fayette at Lowell MA
      on 19 Dec 1839 [4 Jul 1840]
CAMPBELL - see RINGOLD
CAMPLIN person of a party of young men & women, seven in number started from
      Campobello for Casco Bay Island on a pleasure excursion & drowned, see also
      WILSON & PARKER. The name of those who were saved are George NEWMAN,
      Benjamin PARKER and Maria WILSON [*Eastern Democrat*] [24 Jul 1835]
   Sarah Mrs 70 w/o James CAMPLIN at Eastport ME [10 Apr 1845]
CANE James 3y 6m s/o John CANE at Augusta ME on 3 Sept [13 Sept 1850]
CANNELL Philip 79 at Standish ME [17 May 1849]
CANNON John M Esq mayor of the Northern Liberties PA on Thurs morning of
      consumption [3 Oct 1844]
   Mr murdered by a Spanish woman, later hung at Downieville, Sacramento Valley CA on
      7th inst [21 Aug 1851]
CAPEN A Mrs w/o Gen A CAPEN at Gardiner ME [29 May 1845]
CAPIN boy 19 s/o Gen CAPIN drowned at Moosehead Lake ME on Thurs last [2 Jan 1851]
CAPPERS Belinda 42 at Garland ME very suddenly [5 June 1845]
   infant child of Mrs Belinda CAPPERS at Garland ME [5 June 1845]
CARD Elizabeth B 63 w/o Francis CARD at Brunswick ME [22 Jul 1852]
   Mary 88 at Norridgewock ME [29 Apr 1836]
   Nancy Mrs 32 w/o Mr George W CARD [28 Jan 1843]
   Sally 83 at Gardiner ME [4 Mar 1847]
   Thomas 22 at York ME [28 Mar 1844]
   Thomas 62 at Woolwich ME [5 Nov 1846]
CARD - see CRAWFORD
CAREY Caleb 60 at East Machias ME [1 Feb 1849]
   Ezra Deac 60 at Turner ME [8 June 1839]
CAREY - see MOUNTS
CARGILL Henry 70 at Newcastle ME [5 Dec 1837]
CARL Solo 18 of Maine at San Francisco CA on 6 Oct [20 Nov 1851]
CARLETON Caroline T 31 w/o S D CARLETON at Camden ME [16 Oct 1845]
   Conrad 48 at Thomaston ME on 24th ult at the hospital of smallpox [3 Feb 1848]
   Daniel W 14m at Woolwich ME [29 May 1845]
   Ellen L 7y d/o Osgood CARLETON at Augusta ME [3 Dec 1846]
   Hannah 63y & entirely blind, a native of Charleston MA killed in NY by her own son,
      (from the *Argus*) [5 June 1841]
   James H Lt of Bangor ME & Lt George EVANS s/o Senator EVANS of Gardiner ME.
      Both of the Dragoons under Col MAY, Lt C being in command of the first Co, his
      Capt absent on account of sickness. Lt C's 2 horses shot, & himself stunned by a rock
      thrown up by a ball, striking his head... "The two officers in the army under Gen
      TAYLOR at the great battle of Buena Vista were from Maine" [*Bangor Whig*] [20
      May 1847]
   Joseph 69 at Hallowell ME [23 May 1840]
CARLETON - see BARTLETT
CARLTON child of Osgood 1y at Augusta ME [19 Aug 1847]
   Clarissa P 40 a wid/o Guy CARLTON Esq & d/o Nehemiah PIERCE Esq of Monmouth
      ME at Sangerville ME on 16th inst [9 Apr 1842]
   Cynthia 74 w/o Ebenezer CARLTON at Winthrop ME [10 Apr 1851]
   John K 26 at Whitefield ME [11 Jul 1850]

CARLTON (Cont.) M A lady saved from drowning when the steam packet *New England* sank. It left Boston for Bath & Gardiner ME and had an accident with the schr *Curlew* on 31 May [12 June 1838]

    Mary 98 mother of Mr Ebenezer CARLTON at Winthrop ME on Fri last [6 Nov 1841]

    Rosellen 7m d/o Robert CARLTON Esq at Dresden ME on 9 Nov [4 Dec 1851]

    Samuel Capt 86 at Whitefield ME on the 25th ult [7 Dec 1839]

    Samuel Edward 4 s/o Henry CARLTON at Belfast ME [10 May 1849]

    William 25 at Wiscasset ME [21 Sept 1848]

CARLTON - see BYRAM

CARMAN Thomas H 61 at Rockland ME [21 Oct 1852]

CARMER Thomas 57 at Waldoboro ME [14 Nov 1850]

CARNELL - see WOOD

CARNEY James 17 at Thomaston ME accidentally shot one of his associates while gunning [27 May 1847]

    Lucinda P 44 w/o Capt James CARNEY at Richmond ME [23 Jan 1851]

    Mark 37 at Dresden ME [22 Jan 1846]

    Richard Esq of Norfolk VA recently deceased bequeathed $13,000 to various religious societies & emancipated all his slaves giving each of them $150, with a request that they would emigrate to Liberia [15 Oct 1842]

CARON Thomas abt 30 an Irish laborer on the Portland & Kennebec Railroad run over by the gravel train one day last week about two miles from that city (Bath) [*Tribune*] [19 Jul 1849]

CARPENTER child of Rev Mark C of Keene NH a bean in the glottis, though Dr TWITCHELL was in attendance fifteen minutes after the accident (from the *Boston Times*) [30 Oct 1841]

    John a sail boat left Baker's Folly on Mon for Newport capsized, see HAWKINS [*Providence Journal*] [5 Aug 1843]

    Sarah S 8 d/o George S CARPENTER at Augusta ME on 5th inst [20 Sept 1849]

    Seth G 25 at Windham ME [25 Apr 1844]

    Susan 51 w/o Simon CARPENTER at Waterboro ME [4 Jul 1850]

    Thomas J 22 native of Maine death at New Orleans of yellow fever at Charity Hospital died on 13 Sept [2 Nov 1848]

CARR Anna 86 at Shaker Village New Gloucester ME, one of the founders of the society of Shakers for abt 70 yrs [11 Nov 1852]

    Benjamin late of Readfield ME [27 Jul 1839]

    Daniel 39 at Mt Vernon ME on 1st June of consumption [8 Jul 1852]

    Daniel "Forgery, libel & slander, circulated in (Winthrop ME), the past week, a letter, purporting to be written by Mr. CARR, & directed to Mrs Ruth (May) (Metcalf) MARR, to be genuine by a certain individual. Said letter is a forgery. Therefore the sum of 50 dollars will be paid to anyone who will direct the infamous writer, so that he may be brought to justice (signed) Daniel CARR (dated) Winthrop 25 Jul 1843" [29 Jul 1843]

    George W 25 a member of United Brothers Division Sons of Temperance at Winthrop ME on 4 May [10 May 1849]

    J W formerly of Maine at St Louis MO on 7th inst [27 June 1844]

    John 76 at Portland ME [6 Feb 1845]

    Joseph Esq 85 at Bowdoin ME [25 Apr 1850]

    Justus S killed by John PATTEN & son at Ellsworth ME [1 Aug 1840]

    Lydia C 37 w/o William W CARR at Hallowell ME [28 Mar 1850]

    Mary 44 at Augusta ME on 14th inst [22 Feb 1849]

    Mary Mrs 81 at Hallowell ME [27 Apr 1848]

    Mehitable 76 at West Waterville ME [1 Feb 1849]

CARR (Cont.) Michael went on board the steamboat *Madison*, got into difficulties with the hands on board, who put him ashore, injured & died [9 Apr 1842]

Mr by upsetting his load of wood into a snow drift at Dexter ME [30 Jan 1851]

Polly Mrs 70 w/o Daniel CARR at Rumford ME [28 Jan 1847]

Robert Dr 69 at West Minot ME [29 Jul 1852]

Roxana M 38 w/o Benjamin CARR at Thomaston ME [31 Aug 1848]

Samuel 64 formerly of Winslow ME at Wilkes GA on Oct last of bilious fever [8 Apr 1843]

Samuel 70 at Hallowell ME [14 Sept 1833]

Stephen late of Mt Vernon ME est notice, Betsey CARR adm [4 Mar 1852]

CARR - see KNOWLEN

CARRIER Abraham abt 19 or 20 s/o John C killed by the discharge of a gun in the hands of Nathan HANNAH [*Rockingham (VA) Register*] [9 Oct 1846]

CARROL - PEABODY

CARROLL Charles 35 at Augusta ME on Fri last [22 Jul 1847]

James 83 at Augusta ME on 23 Apr [2 May 1850]

James & John PEABODY both of Maine at New Orleans of cholera [1 Feb 1849]

Julia 17m d/o Martin CARROLL at Augusta ME on 17th inst [27 May 1847]

CARSLEY Isaac at Wilton ME [6 Mar 1851]

CARSON Augustine 19 at Skowhegan ME [10 Jul 1851]

John of the steamboat *Governor* [*Bangor Whig*] [7 June 1849]

Seth T seaman of Belfast ME lost overboard from schr *Melrose* on passage from Turks Island to Belfast ME [5 Dec 1850]

CARSWELL Samuel G "*The Exeter News Letter* received from Mr Samuel G C of Deerfield, 4 squash - product of one seed, planted by the side of his mill, produced 383 ft of vines, and yielded 116 squash." of Deerfield NH? [16 Nov 1848]

CARTER Abigail B 23 w/o H L CARTER at Augusta ME [8 Jan 1839]

Caroline 29 at Augusta ME [30 May 1834]

Charlotte M 37 w/o J S CARTER at Waterville ME [20 Feb 1851]

Emily 16y formerly of Knox ME at Saco ME [7 Aug 1845]

Fred Stearns s/o John S CARTER at Waterville ME [20 Sept 1849]

Isaac Capt 65 at Augusta ME [26 Oct 1839]

James rescued by a boat near by, being able to swim, see also LOUD & CARTER on Mon the 5th inst abt 11 AM, while three men in a boat fishing between Bar Island & Cox's Cove [*Lincoln Patriot*] [17 Aug 1839]

Jane 15 at Skowhegan ME [1 Feb 1849]

Joel abt 22 drowned between Bar Island and Cox's Cove [17 Aug 1839]

John Capt 66 at Belfast ME [8 Apr 1852]

John T 42 at Augusta ME on Thurs last "a colored man" [25 July 1844]

Lydia A 54 w/o Dr Timothy CARTER at Bethel ME [26 Dec 1844]

Martha Mrs 74 at Etna ME [4 June 1842]

Mary P 71 w/o the late John T CARTER [19 July 1849]

Mr of Ipswich MA drowned in the Kennebec River at Pittston ME [*Blade*] [1 Oct 1846]

Prince E 31 at Searsport ME [12 Aug 1847]

Sarah abt 70 yrs w/o Ezra CARTER at Scarborough ME [31 July 1845]

slave escaped from Mobile to New York, & disclosed the plot among the slaves which resulted in fatal conflagration at Mobile, a letter to a Mobile paper from Abel BROWN, secretary of the NY Abolition Society, gives the plan concocted by the negroes, the whole city of Mobile burnt to ashes if not for the interposition of some Christian slaves. [12 Aug 1843]

T J Hon a member of Congress from Oxford Dist ME [27 Mar 1838]

CARTER - see SMITH, WALES

CARTON Samuel 70 at Phillips ME [8 May 1851]

CARVER Alice d/o Eleazer CARVER Jr at Leeds ME on the 10th inst [31 July 1845]
    Emily Jane 8 yrs and 10 mos at Milo ME on Jan 8 [21 Feb 1850]
    Hannah 89 wid/o Thadeus CARVER at South Vinalhaven ME [3 Aug 1848]
    Jane w/o Wm CARVER formerly of Leeds ME at Milo ME [6 May 1836]
    Wells 50 at Etna ME [23 Jan 1841]

CARVILLE William II 28 of Lewiston ME at San Francisco CA [14 Nov 1850]

CARY black servant 114y another AmRev character Gen WASHINGTON's colored servant,
    buried on Sun the 4th inst at Greenleaf's Point, an ostler [person who takes care of
    horses; also spelled "hostler"] to Gen W & served at the passage of the Delaware &
    battles of Brandywine & Trenton [10 June 1843]
    Caleb 61 at E Machias ME [18 Jan 1849]
    Harriet 46 w/o Dr R H CARY formerly of Vassalboro ME at Chelsea MA [28 Oct 1852]
    Margaret Pyne 8 d/o Robert H and Harriet C at Vassalboro [1 Jul 1852]
    Maria S 45 w/o Dr Nelson H CARY of Yarmouth ME at Gardiner ME [18 Sept 1851]
    Mr Rev of Topsfield MA the Salem MA police court upon a charge of having married
    two minors without consent of their parents trial in Oct [28 Aug 1851]
    widow 85 at Brunswick ME [5 Sept 1841]

CASE Abigail Page 19 eld d/o Dr Isaac CASE at Levant ME [14 August 1841]
    Harriet 38 w/o Arvin CASE & d/o John PINKHAM at Sidney ME on 10 Sept [18 Sept
    1851]
    Isaac Rev 91 at Readfield ME [2 Dec 1852]
    James of Hallowell at sea by drowning [15 June 1839]
    John 75 at Norway ME [19 Oct 1848]

CASEY Mr head literally rammed to pieces by a "bucket cutter" in a saw mill at Milltown
    last week. He survived only a few monments. (from the *Calais ME Journal*) [23 Sept
    1851]

CASH Martha 28y w/o James CASH on 15th inst drowned at Windham ME left 2 ch, one
    but 6m old [22 Nov 1849]

CASLOW Thomas by an embankment caving in near where he was working on the
    Androscoggin & Kennebec Railroad [*Lewiston Journal*] [23 Dec 1847]

CASON John 9 (an adopted s/o Benjamin GODFREY) of Etna ME by the falling of a tree
    on him on Wed last [11 Mar 1843]

CASS - see VALE

CASSAN - see ROLERSON

CASSIDY - see COAN

CASTILTE Manuel dying declaration of the pirates signed by companions Angel GARRIA,
    Manuel BOYGA, Juan MONTENEGRO, Manuel CASTILTE [10 Jul 1835]

CASTLEMAN Capt saved his wife & 2 ch - one of his ch & his father lost only 50 lives
    saved, 150 lives lost on the steamer *Ben Sherrod* [30 May 1837]
    James Col & his son, Stephen of Clarke Co VA held to bail in the sum of $5000 each to a
    charge of whipping a negro to death 23 Sept 1851]

CASTNER Huldah M 24 w/o Col John T C and d/o Gen Danny McCOBB at Waldoboro
    ME [4 Sept 1838]
    J T Gen 40 at Waldoboro ME [5 Dec 1850]
    Martha M 22 w/o Capt A W C at Waldoboro ME [18 Oct 1849]

CASWELL Alice 77 widow at Leeds ME [19 Aug 1847]
    Amos 23 at West Camden ME [3 June 1852]
    Asa 83 AmRev at Burnham ME [10 Dec 1846]
    Catherine W 18 d/o Zabina C at Harrison ME on 7 ult [10 June 1843]
    Elmina Mrs 29 at Farmington Falls ME [11 July 1844]

CASWELL (Cont.) Joseph 91 AmRev at Strafford [5 Mar 1846]
    Lendall S Col 38 at Farmington ME [4 Dec 1845]
    Rhoda (Mrs) 42 at Auburn ME [7 Oct 1852]
    Simeon 81 yrs 6 mos AmRev patriot at Harrison ME [7 Nov 1844]
CATEN c/o Thomas C 18 mos at Pittston ME [22 Aug 1844]
CATES Esther 72 at Thorndike ME [17 June 1836]
    Henry at Machias Port ME [10 Feb 1848]
CATHCART - see JENKINS
CATLIN Dolly Mrs 27 at Waldoboro ME [17 Sept 1846]
    Emily 29 w/o Edwin CATLIN at Waldoboro ME [4 Nov 1847]
    Prof of Hamilton College last week of dysentery [25 Oct 1849]
CATO Jonathan Rev "colored preacher" formerly a slave at Newmarket NH [22 Feb 1840]
CATON - see DORROGH
CAUDLE Mrs living within 15 miles of Mobile AL weighs 460 pounds, being 40 pounds
    heavier than the Hon Dixon LEWIS, member of Congress from that state. She is the
    mother of several ch of unusual size, enjoys fine health & is good tempered. It is
    impossible to imagine a Mrs CAUDLE answering physically to such a description. [4
    Dec 1845]
CENTER Emily 41 w/o William CENTER at Brunswick ME [31 May 1849]
CHACE - see LINCOLN
CHADBORNE/CHADBOURNE/CHADBORN Albert 6m s/o Owen CHADBORNE at
    Saco ME [4 Sept 1845]
    Ann 15 at Vassalboro ME [15 Jul 1847]
    Bela L abt 13 of Eastport ME s/o I R CHADBOURNE Esq on Fri afternoon by the
    accedental discharge of a gun [*Eastport Sentinel*] [20 Apr 1848]
    Frances T 60 w/o Benjamin CHADBOURNE Esq at Standish ME [14 May 1846]
    Israel sheriff of York Co of Alfred ME fell from his wagon, in Shaker Village on Thurs
    last was seriously injured. "Twas thought his thigh was broken" (from the *Saco*
    Herald) [12 Nov 1842]
    Jacob H 83 at Greene ME [28 May 1846]
    John B 24 at Vassalboro ME on 26 Mar of consumption (Ohio papers please copy) [10
    Apr 1851] & John B 24 at Vassalboro ME on 27 Mar [3 Apr 1851]
    Simeon Deac 96y 6m AmRev at Lyman York Co ME [3 Dec 1846]
CHADBOURNE - see ROBERTS
CHADWICK Adevesta M 8y d/o Zelofus & Hannah CHADWICK at China on 1st Mar [22
    Mar 1849]
    Sylvenus 67 at China on 5 Mar [22 Mar 1849]
CHAFFEY Capt & his bro killed & the cook's leg broken the British brig *Chaffey* of Deer
    Isle Passamaquoddy left Lubec 21 Dec for the West Indies took the gale on the night
    of 22d between Cape Sable & George's Bank [*Boston Advertiser*] [10 June 1850]
CHAFFIN John formerly of Buckfield ME at Boston ME [20 Jul 1848]
CHAFFIN - see ADAMS
CHAMBERLAIN Ann 23 d/o Nathaniel CHAMBERLAIN at Foxcroft ME [2 Oct 1841]
    Benjamin 79 at Clinton ME very suddenly [1 Mar 1849]
    J W while engaged in blasting on the rail roadeast of (Portland) on Wed last, severely
    injured in the face by the premature discharged of a blast [*Portland Argus*] [17 Feb
    1848]
    Jeremiah Rev & Pres of Oakland College MS by George BRISCOE, a student, who then
    committed suicide [18 Sept 1851]
    John 78 at Hallowell ME [19 Feb 1852]

CHAMBERLAIN (Cont.) Lavina Mrs 31 w/o Calvin CHAMBERLAIN Esq & d/o the late Nathaniel PHILBRICK of Mt Vernon ME at Foxcroft ME [30 Sept 1843]
   Rebecca abt 70 widow at Turner ME very suddenly on 22 Sept [16 Oct 1841]
   Samuel abt 56 of Foxcroft (Dover-Foxcroft) ME in his chaise on Fri last his horse took fright, overturned & threw Mr C to the ground as to break his back, survived only till the next morning, a highly respectable citizen of Foxcroft & formerly a resident of Charlestown MA (copied from the *Bangor Whig*) [19 June 1838] & Samuel Esq 54 of Foxcroft ME at Guilford ME [19 June 1838]
   William 61 at Damariscotta ME [24 Jan 1850]
CHAMBERS D the conductor, injured in the back, not expected to live, accident on the Fresh Pond Railroad [13 May 1843]
CHANCE Mrs Dr PARSONS of Macon GA informs the *Telegraph* "that about a week since, a Mrs CHANCE of Burke Co GA was safely delivered of three children at a birth, all of common size & perfectly formed. Two were united from the axilla or armpit to the upper part of the hip bone. The union Dr P states is perfect. One child is living; the two which are united survived their birth a short time only, & are in preservation." [31 Jul 1845]
CHANCELLER William of Charleston MA lost overboard from propeller *Spaulding* at Grand River on the night of the 22d [30 Oct 1851]
CHANDERTON Phoebe 8y d/o of a weaver at Falsworth, drowned herself in a pit abt 200 yards from her father's dwelling [*London Times*] [6 Nov 1835]
CHANDLER Aaron 30 at Norway ME [22 Nov 1849]
   Abigail w/o Abel CHANDLER at Turner ME of consumption [25 Sept 1835]
   Charles Henry 26 eldest s/o John A CHANDLER Esq at Augusta ME of consumption [27 Nov 1841]
   Delia W 20 w/o John A CHANDLER at Augusta ME [27 Jan 1837]
   Eliza 42 w/o Benjamin CHANDLER at Starks ME [27 Mar 1845]
   Elizabeth Ann 45y w/o Hon Anson G CHANDLER [8 Dec 1847]
   Enos T abt 21 at Winthrop ME on 6 May [8 May 1851]
   Eunice P Esq 27 w/o John A CHANDLER at Augusta ME [5 Feb 1842]
   Fanny 58 at Paris ME [1 Apr 1852] & [1 Mar 1852]
   Fayette an upright honest man at Winthrop ME [28 Feb 1837]
   Florinda w/o Jonathan CHANDLER at Turner ME [22 Jan 1852]
   Frederick B a printer 23 s/o Enos CHANDLER of Winthrop ME at Augusta ME at the res of Rev B F ROBBINS on 21 Jul [31 Jul 1851]
   George 30 oldest s/o late John A CHANDLER of (Augusta) ME near Augusta Jackson Co Arkansas [4 Sept 1851]
   Jacob 65 at Norway ME [25 June 1846]
   James M when between Fort Independence & Thompson's Island drowned a party of 27 of the boys of the Farm School on Thompson's Island accompanied by a teacher & boat-keeper [7 May 1842]
   Jemma 70 a widow lady seized with apoplexy at the res of her son-in-law, Samuel WHITEHEAD. Her daughter Mrs W was so shocked by the spectacle, she complained of a headache & also fell dead on the instant at Elizabethtown on Fri evening [*Newark Advertiser*] [15 Aug 1844]
   John 104y at Jacksonville AL [25 Apr 1850]
   John 35 at Belgrade ME [21 Sept 1848]
   John A Esq 51y formerly clerk of the courts of this county at Norridgewock ME on Sun night last [15 Oct 1842]
   John abt 85 at Winthrop ME on Sat last [14 Nov 1837]
   John Esq 65 at Belgrade ME [24 June 1847]

CHANDLER (Cont.) John Gen formerly senator in Congress from ME at Augusta ME on Sun morning last [2 Oct 1841]

John H 25 at Winthrop ME of consumption [12 Oct 1833]

John S P 28 a native of ME at New Orleans on 1st inst from accidental drowning [2 Mar 1842]

Joshua 95 AmRev pensioner a native of Duxbury MA & formerly lived in North Yarmouth ME at Rochester MA [9 Dec 1852]

Maria 24 w/o Calvin CHANDLER at Winthrop ME on Wed morn last of consumption [23 May 1834]

Mary Mrs 40 w/o Benjamin CHANDLER at Starks ME [28 Jan 1847]

Mary Mrs 82 wid/o Gen John CHANDLER of Augusta ME [24 Sept 1846]

Mary Mrs w/o Addison CHANDLER at Avon ME [22 June 1839]

Milton 44 at Winthrop ME on 10th inst of consumption [19 Oct 1833]

Nathan N 24 at Monmouth ME of consumption [28 Aug 1845]

Noah Esq 67 formerly of Wayne ME at Lewiston ME [20 Nov 1851]

Peleg Esq 73 at Bangor ME [28 Jan 1847]

Reuben Jr abt 25 at West Sumner ME [9 Nov 1848]

Sarah 88 wid/o Col Moses CHANDLER at Farmington ME [6 Feb 1851]

Seth Dr 73 at Minot ME of fever on the 9th ult [2 Mar 1839]

Winchester 7 s/o Joel CHANDLER at Winthrop ME [13 Feb 1835]

CHANDLER - see KEUCHETT, LOVEJOY

CHANEY Betsey 39 w/o Isaac CHANEY at Hallowell ME [17 Feb 1848]

Luther 76 at Wilton ME [25 Sept 1851]

Luther P 11 at Solon ME [14 Jan 1847]

Seth Freeman Rev 25 formerly of Farmington ME at Unadilla Forks NY [11 Nov 1843]

CHANEY - see LINSCOTT

CHANNING Dr Unitarian divine in Benington VT last Sun of typhus fever, his remains are to be carried to Boston MA for interment [15 Oct 1842]

CHAPIN H B Rev at Lewiston Falls ME pastor of Congregational Church in that town [14 Nov 1840]

John 100y 6m 13d at Ogdensburg NY, the hero of 3 wars [21 Dec 1839]

Mr & Miss, died of cholera with the HAMILTON family, Mr FRISHIE, Mr PAGE & Mr COLE. Mr CHAPIN & Mr COLE were from CT & engaged in the sale of clocks. They, with 2 other boarders, fled to Warsaw to escape the disease, but all 4 sickened and died immediately there. A letter from Carthage IL gave a list of 12 persons of the house of Mr HAMILTON, a hotel-keeper; all of whom all died within a few days. [14 Aug 1851]

Jeremiah Rev 1st President of Waterville College at Hamilton NY [29 May 1841]

CHAPMAN Alanson B 3y 2m c/o Elijah CHAPMAN at Moscow ME [25 Sept 1845]

Asa B 1y c/o Elijah CHAPMAN at Moscow ME [25 Sept 1845]

Julia F Mrs 20 w/o John CHAPMAN at Pittston ME [6 May 1847]

Margaret Mrs 62 at Starks ME [19 Sept 1834]

Margaret Mrs 76 at Gardiner ME [5 Sept 1844]

Mary Ann 19 at Newcastle ME [27 Jul 1848]

Mary T 29 w/o Samuel H CHAPMAN at Bethel ME [20 Jul 1848]

Michael at Nobleborough ME [16 May 1837]

Miss abt 12y [*Keene Sentinel*] [26 June 1838]

Mr res in the family of Mr Henry COWLES at Sandisfield taken home to his fields in Tolland, Mr C & his mother shortly afterwards died. Mr Solomon SACKETT's family, six persons, all of fever & Mrs SACKETT & her brother died. Mr WHITNEY's family with sickness at the southern part of Sandisfield MA & the

CHAPMAN (Cont.) adjoining portions of Norfolk CT a malignant fever has prevailed
   [*Hartford Columbia*] [12 Sept 1844]
   Wilford perished on the schr *Thomas*, SPROULE Capt of Belfast ME [25 Mar 1843]
   William H abt 20 at St Albans ME [6 June 1840]
CHARLES - see HAMLIN
CHASE Ann Elizabeth 23 w/o Dr R M CHASE at Canaan ME [13 Feb 1851]
   Aulger 47 at Hartland ME on Tues last [29 Sept 1840]
   Benjamin 25 at Camden ME [2 Dec 1843]
   Catharine 74 w/o Benjamin CHASE at Augusta ME [19 Dec 1837]
   Charles an old res of Bennington VT while engaged in chopping abt 200 rods from his
      house caught under a falling tree & instantly killed [27 Nov 1851]
   Davis 47 at Bingham ME returned from CA [2 Sept 1852]
   Eleazer 60 of Buxton ME at Gray ME [2 Apr 1846]
   Elizabeth 76 w/o Thomas CHASE at Fryeburg ME on 28 Mar [6 Apr 1848]
   Elizabeth 87 relict of Robert CHASE at Skowhegan ME [17 Feb 1848]
   Elizabeth (SAUNDERS) born 27 Oct 1738/9 at Boston MA, married 3 times died on
      10th inst [*Boston MA Transcript*] [29 May 1845]
   Eunice 10 w/o Col L CHASE at Turner ME [15 Oct 1842]
   G W when between Fort Independence & Thompson's Island drowned a party of 27 of
      the boys of the Farm School on Thompson's Island accompanied by a teacher & boat-
      keeper [7 May 1842]
   Hannah 106y w/o Hon Stephen CHASE, her ggch numbered 160, & 130 of her
      descendants walked in her funeral train at Unity ME [24 Jul 1845]
   Hannah 40 w/o Col N Col N CHASE & d/o Noah BICKNELL of this town (Augusta)
      ME at Sidney ME on 12 Feb [21 Feb 1850]
   Hannah M 53 w/o Dr Hall CHASE at Waterville ME after a short but severe sickness [1
      Apr 1843]
   Hezekiah 60 at Unity ME [20 Apr 1848]
   Hooper house destroyed by fire on the 22d ult at Limington ME [9 Jan 1851]
   Jerusha Wadsworth 46 w/o Simeon CHASE formerly of East Winthrop ME at Fayette
      ME on 26 June [1 Jul 1852]
   John Babson 23 at Brooks ME [16 Oct 1851]
   Joseph M 6y s/o John W CHASE at Portland ME [26 June 1845]
   Josiah 67 at Limington ME [3 Jul 1851]
   Julia Frances 18 d/o Capt Arthur L CHASE of Augusta ME [9 Apr 1846]
   Lucy Mrs wid/o William CHASE at Augusta ME on Sat last [12 Dec 1844]
   Mary Mrs 40 at East Winthrop ME [12 Aug 1847]
   Mr foreman formerly of Elliot ME, 3 persons wounded during the explosions but not
      fatally: Mr PIERCE, engineer, and THOMPSON & KELLEY at Deer Island Hospital
      the steam boiler exploded on Wed (see story of details) [*E Argus* of Portland ME] [1
      Jan 1852]
   Mr just returned from Mexico murdered at Kesar Falls, Parsonsfield ME [*Banner*] [22
      Feb 1849]
   Nathaniel of the AmRev 87y made the prayer & address, Jonathan RECORDS 99y
      AmRev struck the 1st spade, Josiah PARRIS Esq 80y wheeled off the 1st load at the
      ceremony connected with breaking ground on the Buckfield Branch Railroad says the
      Oxford Dem on the 31st ult [14 Dec 1848]
   Oliver 65 at Hallowell ME [18 Jul 1850]
   Richard seaman lost overboard from ship *Splendid* of Eastport ME [14 May 1846]
   Sarah H 48 at Bluehill ME [25 Dec 1851]
   Sarah Mrs 43 w/o Rev Mark L CHASE at Monroe [11 Nov 1847]
   Stephen Esq 62 Consellor at Law at Fryeburg [5 Dec 1844]

CHASE (Cont.) Thomas 88 AmRev pensioner, served in the Navy under John Paul JONES
in the celebrated action between the *Bon Homme Richard* & the *Serapis* [2 May 1844]

Thomas abt 85 at Clinton ME [18 Feb 1847]

Thomas J s/o Col D CHASE drowned at Atkinson ME in the Piscataquis River [*Bangor
Democrat*] [30 Aug 1849]

William abt 45y of North Berwick ME on Fri 9th ult [5 Feb 1852]

William at Augusta ME [7 Oct 1843]

William J 17 s/o William CHASE at Hallowell ME on 13th inst [20 Apr 1848]

CHATRES the family of, only 10 miles from Tallahassee FL. The Indians burned the house
& murdered his wife and ch, Mr Chatres escaped by a back door. The Indians were
pursued but were not caught at the last dates [3 Aug 1839]

CHEESEBRO Gilbert of Stonington CT by a singular accident [14 Aug 1851]

CHEEVER Nathaniel Dr 29 of Hallowell ME on brig *Espelata* on 23d ult, passage from St
Jago Cuba to Philadelphia PA, returning to the US after an unsuccessful attempt to
regain his health [21 Nov 1844]

CHENEY George 6m s/o George H CHENEY of Portland ME at Winthrop ME on Sat last
[1 Jul 1836]

Marion Prentice 14m only c/o George H CHENEY [11 Sept 1835]

CHENEY - see DAVIS

CHESLEY Henry R 9m s/o Daniel & Abigail CHESLEY at Jay ME [31 Aug 1848]

CHESSMAN Daniel Rev 54 formerly pastor of the Baptist church in Hallowell ME died at
Barnstable [8 June 1839]

CHICK Abner 40 at Waterville ME [18 Mar 1852]

Harriet M Mrs w/o Thomas C CHICK at Hallowell ME [4 Dec 1835]

Isaac 88 AmRev at York ME [15 Feb 1849]

James H Capt a native of Bangor ME at Mobile AL [14 Nov 1850]

Naomi 11 d/o Henry CHICK of Litchfield ME at Charleston MA [4 Apr 1840]

Newell B formerly of Bangor ME at New Orleans of yellow fever [22 Feb 1844]

William 25 at Dixmont ME [9 Nov 1848]

CHILD Alice Wainwright an infant d/o James L CHILD Esq at Augusta ME on Sat last [18
Jan 1844]

Capt by an accident on board the steamer *Narragansett* on her way from Providence to
Boston MA several persons badly scalded [24 Aug 1839]

Daniel C Capt 27 eldest s/o James I CHILD Esq in Oregon in Mar last [29 May 1851]

Edward S abt 10y only s/o the late Elisha CHILD had a fatal accident [7 Nov 1844]

Greenville H Esq formerly of Augusta ME now a res at San Francisco Upper CA & an
inspector of customs appointed by Gov DANA a commissioner for upper CA to take
depositions acknowlegement of deed, powers of attorney, proof of claims &c to be
used and recorded in the state of ME (news, not an obit) [10 June 1850]

Greenville s/o James L CHILD Esq of Augusta ME left some time ago for the gold
mountains in CA [*Banner*] [15 Feb 1849]

Horace 4y 5m youngest c/o James L CHILD Esq at Augusta ME on the 5th inst of croup
[9 Jan 1845]

James Esq 78 of the oldest res at Augusta ME [4 Apr 1840]

John P 20 late of (Hallowell ME) at New Orleans [13 Feb 1838]

CHILD - see JUDKINS, PRESTON

CHILDS Amos 85 AmRev at Vassalboro ME [18 Mar 1847]

Ansel T 34 at Norridgewock ME [27 Mar 1845]

Elizabeth 70 wid/o Willard CHILDS at Eastport ME [12 Feb 1852]

John H 27 at Norridgewock ME [25 Dec 1850]

Mary 89 a widow at Chesterville ME [15 Jan 1839]

CHIPMAN Louisa 24 d/o Joshua & Hannah CHIPMAN at New Portland ME [20 Mar 1845]

William 89 AmRev at Oxford ME [19 Apr 1849]

CHISAM Charles Philip 16m s/o William H CHISAM at Augusta ME [29 Aug 1844]

CHISHOLM John died of dropsy at East River [*Pictou Nova Scotia Chronicle*] [17 Jul 1851]

CHISOLE Edward 50 at Bangor ME on 20th ult [13 Feb 1845]

CHITTENDEN Martin formerly a member of Congress and Governor at Williston VT [26 Sept 1840] & [5 Dec 1840]

CHOAT/CHOATE Abraham Deac 78 [23 May 1837]

Francis 37y 8m s/o Moses CHOAT at Whitefield ME on 15th last of consumption [24 Apr 1838]

Moses abt 46 at Whitefield ME on 28 May [4 June 1851]

Sarah Ann 27 w/o Isaac C CHOATE at Whitefield ME [24 June 1843]

CHREEVES John a painter shot through the head, during the Irishmen Riots [16 May 1844]

CHRISTIE George single abt 32y on commerical wharf, a steward of the schr *Accumulator* of Gloucester MA [*Portland Advertiser*] [26 Mar 1846]

CHRYSTLER Jacob 80 one of WASHINGTON's life guards at Philadelphia PA [28 Aug 1838]

CHURCH a child 15m of Mr CHURCH at Hallowell ME [5 Sept 1840]

David 61 at Farmington ME [17 Aug 1848]

Henry of hydrophobia, skinned a fox found in a barnyard in a feeble state a few weeks before s/o Daniel CHURCH of Farmington ME [16 May 1837]

John 85 at Farmington ME on 12th ult [10 Apr 1838]

Mercy A 20 at Augusta ME on 31 May [15 June 1848]

Nancy 59 w/o Isaac CHURCH at Augusta ME [12 Aug 1852]

Samuel 84 at Augusta ME [18 Jul 1840]

Susannah 89 w/o the John CHURCH of 1st settlers of Farmington ME at Mercer ME [16 May 1844]

CHURCH - see DOYLE

CHURCHELL Daniel 73 at Solon ME [17 Jan 1850]

Jabez 85 AmRev & pensioner, battle of Saratoga when BURGOYNE surrendered [2 Sept 1843]

CHURCHILL Angelia L 15 d/o Alfred D CHURCHILL at Augusta ME [4 Jan 1849]

Catherine 23 formerly of Wiscasset ME at Gardiner ME [8 Jul 1836]

Jabez 86 formerly of Middleboro MA AmRev with WASHINGTON at Trenton & Princeton died at Hartford on 21 Jan [13 Feb 1841]

Mary Frances abt 3 child of Joseph P CHURCHILL at New Portland ME [3 Apr 1845]

Polly abt 20 at Paris ME [23 Oct 1838]

Susan 18 at Wiscasset ME very suddenly [7 May 1842]

CHURCHILL - see PIERCE [16 Jan 1851]

CHUTE Mr of Otisfield ME recently committed suicide [*Norway Advertiser*] [14 May 1846]

CILLEY Benjamin 85 AmRev at Brooks ME [16 Oct 1845]

Deborah P Mrs 35y wid/o Hon Jonathan CILLEY & d/o the late Hon Hezekiah PRINCE at Thomaston ME [24 Oct 1844]

Jonathan Hon Rep in Congress from the Lincoln Co ME Dist on 24 Feb in a duel with Mr GRAVES of KY at Washington DC [6 Mar 1838]

CIST Charles Esq who is engaged in taking the census at Cincinnati says "I found a lady who, at the age of 29, had 14 children, the oldest being born on her 14th birthday. And other - a case more remarkable - in which her son stood by her side within a few

CIST (Cont.) months as old as she was when married and the mother not yet 26 yrs. Consequently the mother was about 13 when married! [11 Jul 1840]

CLANCY David of Bath ME saved from drowning when the steam packet *New England* sank. It left Boston for Bath & Gardiner ME and had an accident with the schr *Curlew* on 31 May [12 June 1838]

William bit by a mad dog at Quebec Canada [11 Jan 1840]

CLAPP Asa 86y of Portland ME [*Eastern Argus*] [27 Apr 1848]

farm the mansion house on the "CLAPP Farm" (so called) in Scarboro ME destroyed by fire on Sat last. [27 Apr 1839]

Mrs of Newcastle ME w/o Maj Nathaniel CLAPP committed suicide on Wed 8 Nov, she had been at the insane hospital in Augusta ME. left a husband & 6 children [30 Nov 1848]

CLARCK Samuel of Parkman ME poisoned on the 21st ult by the use of Blue Flag Root in Syrup, life despaired of by himself. (says the *Dover ME paper*) [19 Aug 1843]

CLARE Albert Capt formerly of Nantucket at Vassalboro ME [17 May 1849]

CLARK/CLARKE Aaron of Pembroke a seaman of schr *Ashland* drowned on Wed at Brimmer's Wharf at Brewer ME [19 Oct 1848]

Alexander 95 at Brooks ME [23 Feb 1839]

Benjamin 48 at Augusta ME on 15th inst [22 Feb 1849]

Capt of the schr *Bay State* (of & from St George ME) tells of the wreck of schr *Frederick* of Boothbay ME, took from her 4 persons Joshua REED, Master; Capt PINKHAM; Gustavus REED & Joseph READ both seamen [*Eastport Sentinel*] [4 Apr 1850]

Charlotte 48 w/o W L CLARK at Augusta ME on 20 Oct [30 Oct 1851]

child of William CLARK 4 at Augusta ME [3 Dec 1846]

Clement 18 at Wells ME very suddenly [1 Jul 1847]

Dr an American physician sickness at Havannah (Havana Cuba) more than 20 deaths by yellow fever have occured [28 Feb 1834]

Ebenezer 81 at Limington ME [5 Oct 1833]

Elizabeth B 44 w/o William CLARK Esq at Hallowell ME [1 Apr 1856]

Ellen 2y c/o Henry & Emeline CLARK at Augusta ME on 11th inst [20 Dec 1849]

Ellen L 18 at Augusta ME [10 Feb 1848]

Ezekiel of the schr *Banister*, body found drowned [5 Jul 1849]

George by trade a rigger on the brig *Eagle* at Central wharf fell from the main to masthead & died in a few hours, he left a sick wife & two children (*Portland Advertiser*) [30 Oct 1841]

George H 22y s/o Capt Isaac CLARK of Belfast ME at East Boston MA of smallpox [7 Oct 1847]

Hannah 97 widow had 12ch 40gch 85ggch 6gggch at Vassalboro ME on Apr 25 [4 May 1848]

Harriet 5y d/o Henry & Emily CLARK at Augusta ME on 9 Jan [17 Jan 1850]

Harrison G O 30 of Winthrop ME on passage from Panama to San Francisco CA [17 Oct 1850]

Henry P s/o Elisha CLARKE Esq, editor of the *Bath Telegraph* at Bath ME [27 Aug 1846]

Horace Marston 16y formerly of Dover NH at Lewiston ME [10 Jan 1850]

Ichabod Esq 88 one of the brave men who fought at Monmouth at his res at Westfield Nova Scotia Canada on Tues last [5 Feb 1846]

James a printer by trade & now the editor of the *Iowa Reporter*, the newly appointed Gov of Iowa [not an obit] [4 Dec 1845]

James C 19 at Washington ME at the res of his father of consumption, a printer, lately workman in the *Bath Telegraph* office [25 Nov 1843]

CLARK/CLARKE (Cont.) James Gov late of Kentucky on the morning of Tues 27th *ult* [*Frankfort Argus*] [14 Sept 1839]

James married Miss Mary E PHILLIPS formerly of the Missouri House, Little Rock at Fort Smith on Sun night last. We are informed that the happy man has some four or five wives besides the new one, & the lady we know to have some two or three living husbands besides CLARK [*Arkansas Int*] [1 Jan 1846]

James Rev by being thrown from his wagon while on his way to the church, serving at St Catherine's Upper Canada on the 19th ult [15 Aug 1840]

Jane 52 w/o William G CLARK at Augusta ME [30 May 1850]

Jane T 24 d/o Reuben CLARK at Unity ME [9 May 1834]

Joel 37 at Hallowell ME [19 June 1845]

John 83 AmRev at Sandbornton NH [1 Feb 1844]

John D of Augusta ME boatsteerer, by a whale on board whaling bark *Hope* 18 Mar 1846 [25 Mar 1847]

John L in Providence was an exchange broker committed suicide on Mon [*Providence Journal*] [5 Aug 1836]

John M 23 formerly of Solon ME at Livermore ME [3 Oct 1844]

John W 34 of Hallowell ME at Bingham ME [11 Oct 1849]

Josiah 75 at Brunswick ME [1 Jul 1836]

Julia A 35 w/o Samuel CLARK at Sidney ME on 15th inst [27 Jan 1848]

Lewis 67 at Searsmont ME [1 Feb 1844]

Lucretia 24 at Windsor ME on 29th inst [30 Mar 1848]

Lucy Ann 21 of Readfield ME at Augusta ME [11 June 1845]

Martha L 51 w/o Thomas CLARK at Newport ME on 7 Apr [6 May 1852]

Mary 25 at Palermo ME on 8th inst [21 Feb 1841]

Mary 53 w/o Rev Atherton CLARK at Sangerville ME [10 Aug 1848]

Mary Ann w/o J W CLARK at Norway ME formerly of Sutton VT [14 Feb 1850]

Mary Mrs formerly of Blanchard ME at Maumee OH [9 Jul 1846]

Mary W P 42 w/o Benjamin CLARK late of Harrison ME at Lewiston ME [12 Feb 1852]

Moses a representative to the state legislature, fell into the MILLER delusion, & committed suicide. [*The New Hampshire Patriot*] [7 Nov 1844]

Mr s/o Jona CLARK of Moultonboro NH at Sandwich of typhus fever, the 7th person in his family who has died of the same disease within a few months [8 Feb 1844]

Nancy 76 widow of William CLARK late of Damariscotta ME at Pittston ME [25 Dec 1851]

Nathan Capt 83 at Wiscasset ME [4 May 1848]

Nathaniel 64 at Limington ME [23 May 1850]

Olevia formerly Olevia CROSS, wid/o William CROSS late of Hallowell ME, application for dower in the real est of said deceased [27 June 1844]

Oliver late of Belgrade ME est notice, Sarah CLARK adm [29 Jul 1852]

Orlissa Esq 52 w/o Thomas CLARK Esq [7 Oct 1847]

Otis 39 s/o Owen & Jemima CLARK at Vassalboro ME on 1 Feb [15 Feb 1844]

Peter H abt 27 while walking on the railroad tracks in Oxford ME [6 Aug 1852]

Rebecca 69 w/o Eph CLARK at China ME on 17 Mar [3 Apr 1851]

Samuel 71 at Pittston ME [12 June 1851]

Samuel C 75 at Belgrade ME on 16th ult [13 May 1847]

Samuel L MD of Bangor ME formerly of Winthrop ME at the Northampton Water Cure Establishment [4 Sept 1851]

Samuel W 64 at Portland ME [17 Aug 1848]

Sarah 50 at Bangor ME [13 Mar 1835]

Sarah L w/o Joseph CLARKE and dau/o Widow McCAUSLAND of Augusta ME at Windsor ME on 29 Mar [27 Apr 1848]

CLARK/CLARKE (Cont.) Sarah Mrs 75 at Wiscasset ME [10 Apr 1835]

Sarah of Bath ME saved from drowning when the steam packet *New England* sank. It left Boston for Bath & Gardiner ME and had an accident with the schr *Curlew* on 31 May [12 June 1838]

Sarah P 44 w/o William P CLARK at Glenburn ME [11 May 1848]

Sarah Pepperell 89y 8m at Hollis ME [19 Mar 1846]

Silas Capt 44 of Camden ME at Key West FL on 4 Nov [16 May 1850]

Sophila F 3y 6m d/o Samuel & Betsey CLARK at Augusta ME on 23 Sept [30 Sept 1852]

Thomas 21 s/o Alfred CLARK of Augusta ME lost overboard from brig *William Crawford* on 6 Jan from Bath ME to Wilmington NC [26 Feb 1852]

Thomas A of Lebanon ME met his death Tues 16 Aug in a very unexpected manner. While in the act of throwing a stick of wood upon a pile of his feet slipped & he fell backwards, his neck striking upon a small stick ...instant death [*Morning Star* (Freewill Baptist newspaper)] [2 Sept 1847]

two boys 9y & 16y near Rondout NY slept on board of the father's boat on the 25th, their father & others being on shore, the boat was burnt & the boys burnt to death [16 Oct 1851]

Uriah 62 at Hollis ME [19 Aug 1852]

William 70 at Damariscotta ME [10 Oct 1850]

William Gov, the associate of Merriweather LEWIS in a tour across the Rocky mountains to the Pacific in 1803, died at St Louis MO [2 Oct 1838]

William S drowned between Thompson's Island & Fort Independence one of 27 boys of the Farm School [7 May 1842]

CLARK - see IRVIN, MEGQUIER, RUSSELL, STODDARD

CLARY Margaret 48 at Gardiner ME [21 Feb 1850]

Mary Jane 24 of Jackson ME at Troy ME [15 Aug 1844]

Nancy w/o Robert CLARY at Jefferson ME [15 Jul 1836]

Robert 91 at Jefferson ME [1 June 1848]

Sarah Rosetta 18 d/o Robert & Ruth CLARY at Belfast ME [27 June 1850]

CLAXTON Alexander commander of the American Squadron in the Pacific died at Talcahuano on 7 Mar his remains were conveyed to Valparaiso where interred on 12th. He has left a wife & child [5 June 1841]

CLAY Abigail 46 w/o Jona CLAY at Augusta ME on 29 Mar [3 Apr 1851]

Henry his negro servant, Levi, who accompanied him on his visit to the north, was induced to run away from his master at Newport & that he voluntarily returned to him at Boston & was very kindly received. [13 Sept 1849]

Jonatha 86 at Vassalboro ME [4 Feb 1847]

Porter Rev 71 last surviving full bro/o of Hon Henry CLAY at Camden Arkansas on 16th ult [21 Mar 1850]

Richard Esq 69 at Gardiner ME [12 Oct 1848]

Samuel 57 at Gardiner ME [8 June 1848]

CLAYTON Jonathan abt 25 at Strong ME [20 Mar 1851]

CLEAVELAND Cymbia Ann 24 at Bloomfield ME [28 Nov 1837]

Ebenezer 66 at Camden ME [10 Jul 1851]

John of Embden ME left home on Mon of last week for Waterville ME, his horse & wagon found the next morning in a field in Fairfield ME, but he still missing [6 Jan 1837]

John found in the mill stream abt a mile from the spot where seen last fall at Fairfield ME [*Somerset Journal*] [23 May 1837]

Josiah Capt of Oswego Tioga Co NY traveled a distance of 450 miles to be in the Bunker Hill celebration on the 17th died on Sat last at res of Samuel C HUNT in Charlestown. In the 90th yr a native of CT. The 1st man killed in that action,

CLEAVELAND (Cont.) received his wound from a cannon ball, fired from the *Glasgow*, while reclining on the green sward at the side of Clark. [*Mercury Journal*] [8 Jul 1843]

Lydia abt 50 w/o Capt Benjamin at Embden ME [22 Jul 1836]

Moses P MD 33 eldest s/o Professor C of Bowdoin College at Natick MA of typhus fever [27 Oct 1840]

William H 31 at Embden ME [22 Jan 1846]

CLEAVES a child of Paul CLEAVES at Brunswick ME [27 Nov 1838]

Hannah 82 widow of the late Capt Jonathan CLEAVES at Saco ME [12 June 1845]

Hannah widow 70 at Biddeford ME [16 Aug 1849]

Jesse S 24 s/o Samuel CLEAVES at Kennebunkport ME on 28 Nov [25 Dec 1835]

John 81 at Kennebunkport ME [14 Mar 1844]

Leonard 27 oldest s/o Samuel CLEAVES of Kennebunkport ME [25 Dec 1835]

Mary 72 w/o Joseph CLEAVES at Lyman ME [16 Apr 1850]

Robert ordinary seaman 27 of New Orleans belonged to the US ship *Preble* & died with the Africa fever at Porto Grande Island of St Vincent Cape de Verds on 8th Dec [10 Apr 1845]

CLEFLIN A 44 at Richmond ME [17 Jan 1850]

CLEMENS Hiram A 16 s/o J CLEMENS at Berwick ME [5 Dec 1850]

Mary w/o CLEMENS at Berwick ME [5 Dec 1850]

Samuel 23 s/o J CLEMENS at Berwick ME [5 Dec 1850]

CLEMENT George W 20 s/o Job CLEMENT of Waldo Plt ME died at Augusta ME [22 Nov 1849]

Susan Mrs 76 Fryeburg ME [10 Oct 1850]

CLEMENTS Elijah Capt 89 of Frankfort ME formerly of Somersworth NH at Monroe ME on 3 Aug [22 Aug 1850]

Elizabeth 83 wid/o Capt Elijah CLEMENTS at Monroe ME [20 Feb 1851]

Enoch 50 at Knox ME [16 Mar 1848]

Sylvia 62 formerly of Waterville ME at Dexter ME [6 Mar 1851]

family killed by Indians near the Livingston's Ferry on the Suwanna at Jacksonville FL [9 May 1837]

CLEVELAND Rachel Caroline 20 w/o Samuel T CLEVELAND at Camden ME [27 Nov 1851]

Susan P 25 d/o Zimri CLEVELAND drowned off Nantucket [2 Aug 1849]

CLEVELAND - see KNOWLEN, McKENNEY

CLIFFORD Climena 27 w/o John N CLIFFORD at Augusta ME [23 Aug 1849]

Clymena C 3 d/o John N CLIFFORD at Augusta ME [21 Oct 1852]

Frances 89 at Bath ME [9 Sept 1852]

Hannah 77 at Montville ME [17 Jan 1850]

John 82, the 1st white male child born in Prospect ME & his widow 78 the 1st white child born in Belfast ME [2 Jul 1846]

Joseph 39 at Montville ME [27 Nov 1838]

Mary 77 at West Bath ME [9 Mar 1848]

Mary Elizabeth 54 w/o G C CLIFFORD at Dover ME [25 Dec 1845]

Mary Jane w/o John H CLIFFORD at Augusta ME [10 Sept 1846]

Mary Mrs 57 at Augusta ME [14 Mar 1850]

Rhoda 84 at Montville ME [17 Aug 1848] & [3 Aug 1848]

Samuel N 27 formerly of Augusta ME at Midville GA on 3 May [27 May 1847]

Sarah 72 w/o John COOK at Oxford ME [30 Oct 1851]

Sarah Thomas 20 w/o Richard CLIFFORD at Waterville ME [3 June 1833]

William H of Bath ME seaman on board schr *Challenge* from Wilmington to Providence, the vessel put into Newport to bury him [30 Apr 1846]

CLIFFORD - see FORBES

CLINDENIN - see ABBOTT

CLIPFELL Mr 89y killed with an iron bar by his son 51 who then blew his brains out with a gun. They long lived together & the deeds were in consequence of the gentleman remonstrating with the son upon his intemperate habits at Colon MI [18 Nov 1847]

CLOCK Abigail 50 wid/o Lewis CLOCK at Winthrop ME [8 Feb 1840]

CLOUD - see WRIGHT

CLOUDMAN Mr portraits recently taken in this village by Mr C, we believe of Portland ME, striking & true likenesses of the individuals, good artist [3 June 1843]

Warren 28 of Portland ME at South Berwick ME [23 Sept 1852]

CLOUGH Asa A 25, John E CLOUGH 18, Elias P CLOUGH 16 all sons of Capt Asa CLOUGH, John E RANLETT 19 s/o Capt Samuel RANLETT, and Charles Clark 22 s/o Samuel CLARK of Newport ME were all drowned. The only one saved was Simon RANLETT at Momouth Centre ME five men drowned on Wed last week (9th inst) [17 Jul 1851]

Benjamin Esq 75 AmRev at Monmouth ME [25 Jul 1840]

Capt in command of a whaler out of New Bedford into San Francisco CA & writes home to say has gold enough & is coming home. The Capt is the s/o Asa CLOUGH of Monmouth ME & distinguished himself some 3 yrs ago by recapturing his ship from the natives [*Kennebec Journal*] [25 Jan 1849]

Caroline 31 w/o Gorham CLOUGH Esq at Freedom ME [30 Jan 1845]

David abt 19 at Monmouth ME on Sun night last [13 Feb 1841]

Elizabeth D 37 w/o Allen G CLOUGH at Madison ME [12 Nov 1846]

Greenlief H 21 s/o Isaiah CLOUGH at Litchfield ME [24 Oct 1850]

Henrietta 17m d/o Asa CLOUGH at Monmouth ME [31 Oct 1840]

Isaac 77 at Brunswick ME [6 Nov 1851]

John 87 at Phillips ME AmRev [20 May 1847]

Mehitable widow 77 at Lewiston ME [29 June 1848]

Molly 74 widow of Benjamin CLOUGH Esq at Monmouth ME [22 Mar 1849]

Sarah 22 at Hallowell ME [6 May 1843]

Thomas M 14 s/o James S CLOUGH at Readfield ME [26 Mar 1846]

Tobias 27 s/o Isaiah CLOUGH at Litchfield ME [23 Oct 1845]

CLOUSE Mary 82 at Waldoboro ME on 1st ult [13 May 1843]

COAKLEY Lydia S 25 w/o Joan COAKLEY at Bath ME [28 Oct 1847]

COAN Samuel Capt 55 drowned at sea on the 25th inst & also Daniel PENDERGRAST 16; Nathaniel PAINE 15; John RIDLEY 13; Andrew CASSIDY 17; William ORTRA 15 formerly of Charlestown. The bodies of all except the last named have been recovered. Thomas SANDERSON, Barnabus GROZIER & Capt COAN's two sons were the four persons saved at sea from the schr *Brenda* of Provincetown. Reported by Capt. COOK of schr *Mary Elizabeth*. [*Bee*] [6 May 1847]

COBB Amasa H 19 s/o Mrs Elizabeth COBB of Dover ME at Memphis TN [6 Jan 1850]

Charles E 18 member of Waterville college (Colby College) at Solon ME [13 Aug 1846]

Charles Esq 48 at Portland ME [2 Mar 1848]

Cordelia 21 w/o A E COBB at Danville (New Auburn, Auburn ME) [27 Mar 1851]

Cynthia Ann 34 w/o Anson B COBB at Biddeford ME [7 Aug 1845]

Ebenezer 67 formerly of Gorham ME at Alna ME [4 Jan 1844]

Elias of Solon ME at Boston MA [3 Aug 1848]

Ellen Augusta 8y d/o Thomas COBB at Portland ME [8 May 1845]

Henry 60y of Mt Desert ME formerly of Goldsboro ME suicide on Mon by drowning no family [29 June 1848]

COBB (Cont.) J married Miss Mary KORNN by Rev FAY, will admit that a COBB is never valuable as when joined in close union to KORNN [*Richmond Star*] [26 June 1841]

Jerushua 86 at Union ME [14 Oct 1843]

John 73 at Turner ME [29 Oct 1846]

Lois Mrs 63 at Portland ME [5 Dec 1844]

Martha 24 w/o Lorain COBB at Winthrop ME [13 Feb 1845]

Nancy W 24 w/o A B COBB at Dover ME? [24 Aug 1848]

Smith 76 at Portland ME [16 Jul 1846]

Theresa only d/o Lewis COBB at Winthrop ME [15 Apr 1847]

widow 55 at Brunswick ME [9 Oct 1841]

COBB - see WALTON

COBBET Jacob 59 at Belfast ME [8 Jul 1836]

COBURN Abi 73 at Farmington ME [25 Jul 1840]

Charles 21y principal of Bloomfield Academy at Bloomfield ME [14 Nov 1844]

Charles 48 at Lewiston ME on 9 Oct of consumption [30 Oct 1838]

Eleazer 33 at Bloomfield ME on 10th inst [21 Mar 1850]

Eleazer Esq 57 at Bloomfield ME [23 Jan 1845]

Jesse Deac 83 at Greene ME [24 Feb 1848]

lad abt 23 of near Pushaw Lake out in a boat with his bro 13y, driving across the lake to Dollar Island, the elder bro drowned, 1st person known to have drowned in the Lake for 20 yrs past [*Bangor Whig*] [2 Sept 1847]

Mercy 66 widow at Lewiston ME [11 Jul 1850]

COBURN - see BROOKS

COCHRAN Benjamin of Dover Piscataquis Co ME killed by a bull on 28th ult [*Bangor Whig*] [8 Jul 1847]

Deborah Ann 60 w/o John COCHRAN at Atkinson ME [12 June 1838]

John one of the famous "Boston Tea Party," born in Boston MA and removed to Belfast ME a number of years since. [*Belfast Republican Journal*] [23 Nov 1839]

Lewis B 27 at Mt Vernon ME [5 June 1858]

Mary 86y 10m at Belfast ME [31 Jan 1850]

Mary Elizabeth 16y at Winthrop ME [1 Oct 1842]

COCHRAN - see DORROGH

CODMAN Richard Capt 72 at Portland ME on 9th inst [14 Sept 1833]

COFFEE John Gen member of the present Congress at Georgia [13 Jan 1837]

COFFIN Daniel 26y s/o James COFFIN of Leeds ME drowned in Androscoggin River on the 19th ult [4 Sept 1835]

George 25 of Brunswick ME at sea [2 Oct 1846]

Helen Olcot 13 d/o Nathaniel COFFIN Esq at Wiscasset ME [14 Dec 1833]

Isaac 5th of the Navy list at Cheltenham England on the 23d of Jul [31 Aug 1839]

James D who kept a fancy goods store at 78 Washington St & George DANA Jr s/o George DANA Esq of Long Wharf at Boston MA on Mon the two men were drowned [5 Aug 1843]

Katharine D 25 w/o A K COFFIN [22 Jul 1847]

Mary 57 w/o Capt Daniel G COFFIN at Vassalboro ME [26 Aug 1852]

Mary L 31 w/o Daniel P COFFIN at Eastport ME [5 Dec 1850]

Mrs w/o William COFFIN at Temple ME [7 Oct 1852]

Prince Capt of Nantucket MA crew of whale ship *Awashonks* of Falmouth ME at Fejee Island [6 May 1836]

Rear Admiral 73y on Sun the 17th ult at Dover [14 May 1842]

S P a merchant charged with having seduced & ranaway with the wife of Mr HUNT of North Carolina, $500 reward is offered [*US Gazette*] [12 Nov 1846]

Tristram 23 lost overboard from Norfolk pilot boat *Henry Clay* [22 Feb 1844]

COFRAN Mrs killed at Pembroke NH on Sat 23d inst [8 Jul 1833]

COGDON George 82 AmRev at Wickford RI [31 Dec 1842]

COGSWELL Charles N formerly Senator of ME & chosen a delegate to the Baltimore (Democratic) Convention to be held in May next, died at South Berwick ME [28 Oct 1843]

COLATON Patrick 38 at Augusta ME [28 Feb 1834]

COLBATH - see HOPSKINS

COLBURN Ann Maria 30 w/o Silas B COLBURN at Richmond ME on 13 June [15 Jul 1852]

 Charles D 3y 8m s/o Capt Eben COLBURN at Belfast ME [6 Feb 1845]

 Ebenezer 85 of Belfast ME at Frankfort ME [12 Feb 1846]

 Joseph late of Windsor ME est notice, Horace COLBURN exec [20 May 1852]

 Thomas 90 AmRev at Wilton ME [19 Oct 1848]

 Zerah "the Mathematician" & a talented preacher, b 1 Apr 1804 at Cabot VT, in his 6th yr taken to Danville, Montpelier and Burlington, had opportunity to witness the readiness & correctness, gave answers to questions that required long & careful attention of well instructed mathematician. He was a Methodist minister. He died 2 Mar 1839 at Norwich [*Vermont Watchmen & Journal*] [27 Apr 1839]

COLBY Abigail 40 at Denmark ME [25 Oct 1849]

 Benjamin Capt 68 at Embden ME [16 Jan 1841]

 Charles in a railroad accident at Dover NH [20 Mar 1851]

 David Jr 22 at Madison ME [30 Dec 1847]

 Ebenezer Esq 67 at Webster ME [20 Aug 1846]

 Hannah widow 93 at Bath ME [20 Apr 1848]

 Harriet E 3y 10m d/o Thomas & Charlotte COLBY at Augusta ME on 19th inst [22 Nov 1849]

 John of Bath ME at New Orleans of consumption [9 Jan 1845]

 Martha 30 at Madison ME [4 June 1846]

 Melvina Augusta 2y 7m d/o Thomas & Charlotte COLBY at Augusta ME [12 Nov 1846]

 Philip Rev 71 formerly a merchant of Vassalboro ME at North Middleborough MA on 27 Feb [10 Apr 1851]

 Robert 2 young men abt 19 - R C s/o Joshua COLBY & Thomas LUNT s/o William LUNT left (Newburyport) on Wed the 2d inst in the afternoon on a gunning excursion. Probably both drowned the same night they left home. [*Newburyport Herald*] [26 Nov 1842]

 Sally 46 w/o John COLBY at Madison ME [17 Apr 1838]

 Samuel 90 AmRev pensioner at Westport ME [11 Feb 1847]

COLCORD Caroline 41 at Waterville ME [15 Jan 1852]

 John 50 at Berwick ME [29 Mar 1849]

 Thomas H 43 at Fairfield ME [19 Aug 1852]

COLE a child of John COLE at Windsor ME [19 Sept 1837]

 Albert Rev 36 at Saco ME [3 Apr 1845]

 Angeline 22 at Athens ME [26 Dec 1834]

 Betsey P 23y 9m w/o Harrison COLE at Sebasticook ME [29 Apr 1847]

 Calvin 50 at Hallowell ME [26 Aug 1847]

 Calvin at Paris ME on 15th inst [17 Jul 1841]

 Catherine an inmate of the Lawrence poor house starved herself to death [26 Apr 1849]

 child 2y burnt such a manner as to cause its death on 5th inst c/o Solomon COLE Jr of Parkman ME [30 Oct 1838] [4 Dec 1838]

 Daniel Maj 82 at Saco ME [5 Jul 1849]

 Dr an attempt on Wed last week to destroy the family of Dr COLE of Williston VT, arsenic in the well [9 Oct 1835]

COLE (Cont.) Edward Capt of Frankfort ME on 7th of Sept left in a small lap streak boat which had a cuddy forward, left Martinicus on the 28th ult ... since then nothing has been heard of him...*[Argus]* [19 Oct 1848] [Editors' note: Lap streak, also known as lap strake, means built with overlapping planks or strakes on a boat's frame. A cuddy is a small covered area over the forward part of an otherwise open boat. See the book, *Maine Lingo* by John Gould, publ. in Camden, ME, by *Down East Magazine*, 1978.]

Esther 54 w/o Capt Cephas COLE at Waldoboro ME [17 Sept 1846]

Hannah 56 w/o Samuel COLE at Hollis ME [14 Mar 1850]

Henry C 19m s/o Joseph R COLE at Vassalboro ME on 5 Feb [26 Feb 1852]

Isaac D a master carpenter formerly of South Boston MA fell from a barn in Bath ME on Mon afternoon, doubtful whether he would recover [27 Nov 1845]

Isaac of Greene ME found in the pond near his res on Tues supposed suicide (from *Lewiston Journal*) [29 June 1848]

Isaiah 80 AmRev one of Gen WASHINGTON's life guards, battles of Monmouth & Lexington, died at Waldoboro ME [28 Oct 1836]

Joseph G Hon Judge of the District Court 52 at Paris ME on 12 Nov [20 Nov 1851]

Joseph H 29 s/o Edward COLE at Cornish ME [20 June 1850]

Joseph Palmer 2y 8m s/o J R & Sophia COLE at Vassalboro ME [31 Jan 1850]

Mr died in the drifts of snow at Sebago ME a week ago last Sat *[Argus]* [12 Feb 1846]

Mr died of cholera with the with the HAMILTON family, Mr & Miss CHAPIN, Mr FRISHIE, Mr PAGE & Mr COLE. Mr CHAPIN & Mr COLE were from CT & engaged in the sale of clocks. They, with 2 other boarders, fled to Warsaw to escape the disease, but all 4 sickened and died immediately there. A letter from Carthage IL gave a list of 12 persons of the house of Mr HAMILTON, a hotel-keeper; all of whom all died within a few days. [14 Aug 1851]

Nathan, s/o Sumner COLE of Vienna ME, for ten dollars bought of his father his time until he is of age... [16 Apr 1846]

Nathaniel 2d was living in the dwelling belonging to P M PIERCE Esq, COLE had owned the house but the love of Rum put it into the hands of the rumseller. While COLE was intoxicated & his wife was not home he died in the house fire. [4 Apr 1834]

Rebecca L 54 w/o William COLE at Waldoboro ME on 5 Oct [25 Oct 1849]

Rev Mr his lady & child of Hallowell ME saved from drowning when the steam packet *New England* sank. It left Boston for Bath & Gardiner ME and had an accident with the schr *Curlew* on 31 May [12 June 1838]

Samuel W Esq late editor of *New England Farmer* died at Chelsea MA [11 Dec 1851]

Sarah 17 at China ME [18 Sept 1835]

Simon formerly of (Skowhegan) ME drowned in Long Pond last week *[Skowhegan Press]* [30 Nov 1848]

Thomas on Sat at his res at Catskill NY [2 Mar 1848]

William 61 at Thomaston ME [3 May 1849]

William Esq 54 at Buckfield ME on the 6th inst [17 Jul 1841]

COLE - see YORK

COLEMAN Henry Rev at Islington near London the day before sailed *[Boston Daily Advertiser]* [6 Sept 1849]

James 70 at Anson ME [7 Mar 1850]

negro killed his wife in Broadway NY last summer by cutting her throat has been sentenced to be hung on 12 Jan 1839 [4 Dec 1838]

COLGAN James 30 at Gardiner ME [24 Jan 1850]

COLLAMORE boy abt 19y s/o Capt COLLAMORE & Dexter THOMAS 21 of French's Beach were drowned at Lincolnville ME on Sat last, nine persons were in the boat

COLLAMORE (Cont.) which had swept the cable to the anchor of a new barque, which was parted in the gale of Fri night (from the *Belfast ME Journal*) [4 Dec 1851]

COLLIER Albert or Albert COLLINS seaman fell from the foretop gallant yard on 15th inst & was killed on board ship *Canton* of Wiscasset ME on the passage from Palermo to NY [6 Feb 1845]

 Charles B 34y 6m at Turner ME on 7 June [29 Jul 1852]

COLLING Daniel 89y AmRev at Industry ME [14 Aug 1845]

COLLINS Benjamin F 21 of Vassalboro ME lost overboard from brig *Orbit* off Cohasset Rocks Cape Cod [29 May 1841]

 Charles Hon at Newport RI on Sun morning last [26 June 1845]

 Daniel 94 AmRev pensioner at Harmony ME on 2 Feb [13 Feb 1851]

 Hannah E 17 d/o Joseph W COLLINS at Portland ME [20 Feb 1845]

 James Esq 70 at North Anson ME [15 Apr 1847]

 John 80 a member of the Society of Friends at Durham ME [24 Jul 1845]

 Joseph 89 AmRev at Gardiner ME [21 Dec 1848]

 Lucy 25 w/o Otis COLLINS at Embden ME [15 Feb 1849]

 Lydia Ellen 4 d/o George COLLINS at Gardiner ME [17 Aug 1848]

 Mary H 22 at Farmingdale ME [11 Nov 1852]

 Richard Esq abt 70 at Millbridge ME [28 Oct 1852]

 Sewall B 21 at Gardiner ME [15 June 1848]

 Timothy of Penobscot ME on the bark *J W Coffin* on 16 Apr passage from Panama to San Francisco CA [4 Jul 1850]

COLLINS - see DIXON

COLMAN Henry C Esq US Consul at Tobasco, had arranged passage for home but died before the vessel sailed [30 May 1840]

 Joseph J 27 at Hallowell ME [5 Aug 1852]

 Mary 70 consort of Deac Jos COLMAN at Vassalboro ME [24 June 1843]

 Mr known for his improvements on the pianoforte died at Saratoga on Sat last [17 Apr 1845]

 Sophia Mrs 45 at Hallowell ME [9 May 1844]

colored girl - see PEARCE

colored - see ABBOTT, ALLEN, BUCKANAAN, DAVIS, JACKSON, JOHNSON, McFARLAN, MORRIS, OVERTON, RANDOLPH, REMOND, SMITH, TUCKER, WILLIAMS, WILSON, YOUNG

COLSON Ebenezer 64 at Bath ME [5 Nov 1846]

 person of Bath ME drowned at sea [15 June 1839]

COLT J C sensible people in New York have doubted the death, Dr HOSACK has testified that he knew COLT & the man is dead! [17 Dec 1842]

 John C fourteen years a voluntary exile from the parental roof. [30 Oct 1841] He was the grandson of the late John CALDWELL of Hartford & s/o Christopher COLT of Hartford & his sister suicided in 1837 [30 Oct 1841]

 John C married Miss Caroline HENSHAW by Rev ANTHON witnessed by Sheriff HART, David GRAHAM Jr, Samuel COLT (his brother), Justice MERRIT, Robert EMMET and John Howard PAYNE. To be hung at 4PM killed himself by stabbing. On Thurs, COLT wrote a long letter, and sealed it up, with directions that it should be opened by his child when it becomes old enough to read. [26 Aug 1841]

COLTON George H the proprietor & editor of the *American (Whig) Review* died at his res in New York on Wed evening, He had been ill for more than a month of typhus fever. He was in the 29th yr of age [9 Dec 1847]

 Walter Rev at Philadelphia PA [6 Feb 1851]

COLVIN child c/o William D COLVIN at Huron from the *Sundusky OH Clarion* [5 Sept 1834]

COMBS David 57 of West Waterville ME at Newport FL on 5 Feb [4 Mar 1852]
　　Jonathan Esq 56 at West Waterville ME [29 Nov 1849]
COMINGS Charles 45 at Eddington ME [25 Jul 1840]
　　Chloe T 23 d/o Samuel & Mary COMINGS formerly of Sidney ME at Boston MA on 23
　　　　Sept [15 Nov 1849]
　　Coolidge 78 at East Eddington ME [7 Sep 1848]
　　Harriet Elen & Sarah d/o Deac Lemuel COMINGS at Greene ME [24 Oct 1840]
　　Sarah 83 a widow at Eddington ME [18 June 1846]
COMSTOCK Grover S Rev missionary of the American Baptist Board at Ramree Arracan
　　died of the Asiatic cholera at Akyab on the 25th of Apr [*Watchman*] [5 Sept 1844]
　　Mary A 19 of Lubec ME at Augusta ME on the the 8th inst [16 Aug 1849]
CONANT Abraham 70 at Frankfort ME [15 Mar 1849]
　　Andrew 70 formerly of Alfred ME at Dexter ME [20 Jul 1848]
　　Clementine w/o Winslow CONANT at Lewiston ME [21 Oct 1847]
　　William Horace R 23 from Charlestown MA at Sacramento City CA on 21 Dec of
　　　　typhiod fever [14 Feb 1850]
CONARD Jacob 14 a native of Santa Cruz & shipped at Machias ME on board barque *Lucy*
　　Ellen, Capt CATES was accidentally drowned yesterday in Ashley River [Charleston
　　News, 29th] [10 Aug 1848]
CONDON Albert seaman lost overboard from schr *Only Daughter* from Lubec for New
　　York on 7th inst [26 Aug 1843]
　　girl abt 6y burned to death accidentally d/o Thomas I & Sarah CONDON at Dixmont ME
　　　　(from *Bangor ME Jefferson*) [15 Nov 1849]
　　Julia Ann run over by a horse team of Mr BURNS, to see her father, Joseph C, & on
　　　　returning not waiting until the team had passed, attempted to run across & struck by
　　　　the pole of the cart, knocked down & the wheels passed directly over her neck
　　　　(*Thomaston Rep*) [31 Aug 1839]
CONE A P 35 w/o Rev C C CONE at Saco ME [28 Aug 1851]
CONFORTH Mary w/o Robert CONFORTH & d/o John HASKELL at Waterville ME on
　　15th inst [4 Dec 1841]
　　Robert 77 formerly of Readfield ME at Johnson RI on 31 Oct [19 Nov 1842]
CONLEY Patrick a laborer upon the St Lawrence Railroad frozen to death on Sun last at
　　Danville (now part of Auburn) ME, left a wife [4 Mar 1847]
CONNELEY Mr 80 at Brunswick ME [17 Jul 1835]
CONNELL Francis P 82d yr of age native of Mecklenburg Co VA entered the service at age
　　16, served under Gen LaFAYETTE, who in 1781, had been entrusted with the
　　principal command in VA at Hanging Rock Lancaster District SC on 25th ult [2 Dec
　　1843]
CONNER Jesse at North Wayne ME [1 Jan 1852]
　　John abt 36 of Maine at New Orleans [22 Feb 1849]
　　Joseph found nearly dead in the lane near the house of Arthur COUNCE, by blows upon
　　　　the head [14 Mar 1844]
　　Mary 24 d/o John CONNER at Hartland ME [22 Oct 1846]
　　Wilson Rev a Baptist minister died in his pulpit [10 Oct 1844]
CONNER - see KNIGHT
CONNERS - see ROLERSON
CONNOR Catharine 42 w/o Thomas CONNOR at Augusta ME on Tues morning last [10
　　Sept 1846]
　　George 18m s/o Thomas CONNOR at Augusta ME [30 Sept 1852]
　　James 47 at Augusta ME on Sun last [25 Feb 1847]
　　Louisa 45 w/o Thomas CONNOR at Fairfield ME [24 June 1847]

CONNOR - see JEFFRIES

CONROY Bridget on Tues last near the village of Hyde Park NY by a piece of rock, thrown from a blast, falling through the roof of their house. The rock weighed 1000 pounds. [6 Mar 1851]

CONSTOCK - see SIMON

CONVERS Marian Mrs 67 at Bath ME [12 Aug 1836]

CONVEY James 55 a native of Ireland at Pittsfield ME [1 Apr 1852]

CONY child of John CONY at Augusta ME [8 Apr 1833]

    Daniel 90 officer AmRev at Augusta ME on 20th inst [29 Jan 1842]

    Elizabeth 51y w/o Daniel J CONY at Farmington ME [16 Mar 1848]

    Martha 82 w/o Hartson CONY at Farmington ME [14 Nov 1850]

    Mercy H 31 consort of Samuel CONY Esq & youngest d/o Joseph SEWALL Esq of Farmington ME at Old Town on 9th inst [15 Apr 1847]

    Sabra 36y w/o Samuel CONY at Augusta ME [3 Apr 1845]

    Samuel Gen formerly Adjutant General of Maine at Augusta ME on 8th inst after a protracted illness [27 Nov 1835]

    Susan B abt 70 wid/o Gen CONY & eldest d/o the late Hon Daniel CONY at Augusta ME on 12 May [22 May 1851]

    Susannah 81 consort of Hon Daniel CONY at Augusta ME [9 Nov 1833]

CONY - see PEARCE

COOK Isaac abt 17 youngest s/o Thomas COOK at Norridgewock ME [17 Sept 1846]

    Abigail Cressey 57 w/o Benjamin COOK Esq of Gardiner ME [6 Dec 1849]

    Charlotte A 2y 4m d/o Fuller G COOK of Boston MA at Waterville ME [28 Aug 1841]

    Christian a lad whilst swimming in Parker's pond near Fairmount Philadelphia PA on Sun afternoon was accidentally drowned. He was with a party who went out to steal cherries. "The wages of Sin" [3 Jul 1845]

    D G Esq of Number 11 (Ashland) Aroostook Co ME his tavern house consumed by fire on the 29th ult [23 Aug 1849]

    Eli 77 AmRev at New Sharon ME [16 Sept 1836]

    Elijah & Charles PALMER both of Friendship ME lost overboard from brig *Proxy* on passage from Thomaston to Norfolk [14 Jan 1843]

    Jacob Decon 60 at Exeter ME [9 May 1840]

    Joanna wid/o Samuel of Norridgewock ME [24 Apr 1845]

    John 69 member of the Society of Friends at Vassalborough ME on 15th inst [30 May 1834]

    John killed in the Irish & Native American (not American Indians more likely English-born in American) Riots in Philadelphia PA *[Dollar Newspaper]* [18 July 1844]

    Julia abt 20 accident in a cotton factory in Chester *[Northampton Courier]* [14 Aug 1835]

    Mr killed in a building during the thunder shower on 12th at the grist mill in Washington VT by lightning 23 Sept 1851]

    P M 26 s/o Dr COOK at Auburn ME [30 Oct 1851]

    Polly 74 w/o Capt James COOK at Orland ME [22 Apr 1847]

    Samuel 73 at Starks ME [6 Mar 1841]

    Sarah 69 w/o Samuel COOK at Houlton ME [30 Jan 1851]

    Sarah E 25 at Hallowell ME [28 May 1846]

    Stephen 27 at Casco ME [20 June 1844]

    Valentine left a large family of ch of Dearborn (now part of Oakland, Rome, and or Belgrade ME) on returning from Augusta ME called at Mr Philbrick's tavern & ordered his supper, death by choking on a large piece of meat at supper at Sidney ME on 18th ult *[Augusta Gospel Banner]* [12 Dec 1837]

    William of Albany while eating at the dinner table on 4 Jul [25 Jul 1834]

COOK - see ALLEN, PALMER

COOKE Anna Frances 2y 2m d/o George F & Margaret COOKE at Augusta ME [19 Sept 1850]

COOL Abigail 77 w/o late John COOL at Waterville ME on 30 Mar [13 Apr 1848]
   John 89y 6m 10d at Waterville ME on 8th Oct [29 Oct 1846]
   Loring 42 at Waterville ME 42 [5 Dec 1850]

COOL - see CURTIS

COOLAN - see COOPER

COOLBERTH Joel 24 & William COOLBERTH 19 lost overboard from schr *Francis* from Machiasport ME to Boston MA [21 Sept 1839] & Capt ROBINSON told us in *Eastern Argus*, buried at sea, the schr *Francis Robinson*, master of Thomaston ME from Machias Port for Boston MA put into Boothbay last week. When off Damariscotta River reefing the mainsail, they lost two men overboard [21 Sept 1839]

COOLBROOTH Samuel & his son drowned near the mouth of Scarboro River ME the boat probably sunk, when the ballast was discharged & she rose and drifted ashore on Fletcher's Neck in Biddeford ME [16 Oct 1841]

COOLIDGE Charles 18m youngest s/o Merritt COOLIDGE at Hallowell ME [5 Sept 1844]
   Henry of Framingham MA on Sat last of poison communicated to his blood by a razor with which he shaved himself soon after the face of his deceased father. The father AmRev, pensioner advanced beyond 80 [*MA Ploughman*] [30 Oct 1841]
   Jerusha 74 w/o Daniel COOLIDGE at Livermore ME [7 Sep 1848]
   Lucy 97 wid/o Thomas COOLIDGE at Livermore ME [7 Nov 1850]
   Mary H 40 w/o C H COOLIDGE at Buckfield ME [17 Jul 1851]
   Silas 79 AmRev & pensioner, at Bunker Hill & surrender of BURGOYNE & exception of some short intervals, out during the whole war, died at Trenton on 13th ult [27 June 1834]

COOMBS Albion 47 at Augusta ME [28 Jan 1847]
   Ardon W 25 at Brunswick ME [5 Nov 1846]
   Betsey A 18y at Parkman ME [26 June 1845]
   Ephraim 65 at Bangor ME [3 Aug 1848]
   girl 6y of Vinalhaven ME d/o Paul M COOMBS burnt to death by clothes catching fire [14 Aug 1851]
   J C Capt at Bowdoinham ME [16 Jan 1851]
   Robert 84 at Islesboro ME [20 Jul 1848]

COOMBS - see GALLAGHER

COOPER Betsey Mrs 49 wid/o Alexander COOPER at Pittston ME on 7 Nov of consumption [11 Dec 1851]
   Clara M 20 dau & last surviving c/o Alex COOPER at Pittston ME on 5th Dec at the res of her Uncle William COOPER of consumption [11 Dec 1851]
   Ezekiel Rev 84 of Philadelphia PA supposed the oldest minister of the Methodist Episcopal Church in the US having been in the ministry 62 yrs [4 Mar 1847]
   James Fennimore 62y wanting one day to be the great American novelist, of English parentage born in Burlington NJ, grad of Yale College in 1805, married a sister of Bishop DeLANCEY of Western NY in 1811, after he left the the Navy ... died at his res at Cooperstown NY on 14th inst [23 Sept 1851]
   John a baker, James COOPER, his brother, Andrew COOLAN & John SMITH, a party of New Yorkers were drowned near Blackwell's Island. The three last were seamen & shipmates. Three others were picked up by two men in another boat. [23 May 1834]
   John Jr 24 at Norway ME [9 Nov 1848]
   Joshua 25y an Indian conveyed to the hospital from Fulton St & recovery is doubtful at South Boston MA [2 Aug 1849]
   Martinboro 23 at Pittston ME [16 Jan 1851]
   Sally L 69 w/o Jas N COOPER Esq at Pittston ME [18 May 1848]

COOPER (Cont.) Samuel Professor at Shepperton [11 Jan 1849]

COOPER - see TAYLOR, WEBSTER

COPELAND Boice of Cushing ME crushed between two mill logs at the Creighton Sawmill at Warren ME he left a wife & one child (Copied from *Thomaston Recorder*) [24 Apr 1838]

Franklin of Roxbury MA? saved from drowning when the steam packet *New England* sank. It left Boston for Bath & Gardiner ME and had an accident with the schr *Curlew* on 31 May [12 June 1838]

COPP Hannah Mrs 86 at Eastport ME [20 Feb 1851]

CORBETT Hannah L 71y 8m w/o Isaac M CORBETT at Brunswick ME [11 Feb 1847]

John Esq 69 at Farmington ME [19 Feb 1846]

Rufus 77 at Farmington ME [26 Dec 1850]

CORDON George of Cushing ME found dead on 24th ult (see story) [6 Feb 1851]

CORDWELL Sanford B 24 at Paris ME [29 Jan 1846]

CORLISS Emma Jane 31 w/o Joseph CORLISS at Bath ME [28 Jan 1843]

Joseph 42 at Bath ME [12 Dec 1850]

Lucy Mrs 80 at Lewiston ME (NB the *VR of Lewiston ME* p. 206 "d 29 Dec 1849 ae 78 a widow mother of Samuel CORLISS, recorded by E P Tobie, Town Clerk ") [10 Jan 1850]

CORNELIUS Lewis "death of a Giant" 50y, 6ft 3in high & weight 685 pounds at Milford(?) PA [16 Oct 1841]

CORNEY Loran of Surry ME on passage from Panama to San Francisco CA [26 Feb 1852]

CORNWALLIS - see BERRY, PERKINS

CORRIGAN - see MORACY

CORSON Thankful (WHITNEY) 74 (d/o Benjamin & Nancy [HINKLEY] WHITNEY & 1st wife of Zebulon COURSON of Lisbon ME) at Lewiston ME [20 Mar 1851]

CORSON - see BEMIS

COSTELLOW Mr a laborer on the Androscoggin & Kennebec railroad, had his thigh fractured a few days since by a stone thrown in blasting. (not a death notice) [23 Mar 1848]

COSTLOW Orin B 3y 4m only child of Elwell COSTLOW at Dresden ME on 21st Nov [4 Dec 1851]

COTHRAN Augustine W 25 at Edgecomb ME [18 Nov 1852]

COTIE - see KIMBALL

COTTER Joseph 40 at Damariscotta ME [3 Aug 1848]

COTTLE Dolly 22 at Windsor ME [25 Jul 1844]

Edwin 2 s/o Charles & Elias COTTLE at Readfield ME [6 Sept 1849]

Isaac late of Sidney ME est notice [10 June 1852]

Matilda 16 at Bucksport ME on 8 Dec [12 Feb 1836]

Rhoda (MANCHESTER) 95 (wid/o Isaac COTTLE & d/o Thomas & Eunice [NORTON] MANCHESTER) [see also *Stackpole's History of Winthrop ME*, p. 728] at Kennebec (formerly Winthrop/Readfield, now Manchester) ME on 19 Sept [2 Oct 1851]

Sally 40 w/o Samuel COTTLE at New Portland ME [23 Jan 1845]

COTTON Edward 63 at Saco ME [4 Apr 1837]

COUCH Elizabeth 55 w/o George COUCH at Hallowell ME [6 Feb 1851]

Hannah 91 at Hallowell ME [4 June 1851]

John 70 at Hallowell ME [12 June 1851]

William 16 at Hallowell ME [15 Aug 1844]

COUILARD Samuel 81 at Frankfort ME on 18 Mar [10 Apr 1851]

COUILLARD Charles 78 formerly of Bath ME at Kennebunk ME [7 Jan 1847]

COULIER Ben 29 an intemperate man at Brunswick ME of apoplexy [13 June 1834]

COULTHARD John 82 married Miss M MARSHALL, a "blooming rose" of sweet 22y,
    they immediately set for America [*The Mark Lane (England) Express*] [6 June 1844]

COUNCE Mary 84 at Thomaston ME [15 Nov 1849]

COUNCE - see CONNER

COURSER Elias abt 65 at Dover ME [10 Dec 1846]

COURSON - see CORSON

COURTLAND W D 28 of ME at New Orleans [30 Sept 1847]

COUSIN Martha 31 w/o Capt Nelson COUSINS at Lubec ME [15 Mar 1849]

COUSINS John Francis c/o John COUSINS at Belfast ME [12 Dec 1837]
    Mary 49 w/o Capt Joseph formerly of Kennebunk ME very sudden & unexpected at Eden
        (Bar Harbor) ME on 1st inst [25 Jan 1840]
    Mary Frances c/o John COUSINS at Belfast ME [12 Dec 1837]

COVEL Dorcas 76y 10m w/o Nathan COVEL at Bath ME [20 Nov 1845]

COVELL Rebecca 46 d/o Nathan COVELL at Bath ME [1 Jan 1846]

COVER Abigail Mrs 39 at Bethel ME [1 Feb 1849]

COVILL Mary Mrs while passing from one room to another fell dead at Fairfield ME [*The
        Skowhegan Clarion*] [3 Jul 1845]

COWAN Alice W 13m d/o L O COWAN at Augusta ME on Sun morning last [5 Sept 1844]
    Samuel of Moose River an Irishman hunting moose with Jacob NEWTON, accidentally
        killed by a shot from the rifle of Ephraim WITHAM of the Forks [19 Jul 1849]

COWART Mrs w/o Lewis COWART of cholera as did the youngest child & the nephew by
        the name of WRIGHT. Also James G POWELL is dead, of emigrants from Monroe
        Co. GA, 34 whites & 43 negroes left for TX, they were in all six families POWELL;
        COWART; WALKER; JONES; HILL; & HILL [letter post-marked Cottle Louisiana
        on 9 Feb] [*Macon GA Messenger*, 4 Apr] [19 Apr 1849]

COWEN Amelia A 36 d/o Isaac COWAN Esq of Sidney ME at Autuaga Co AL on 5 Jul [5
        Aug 1852]
    Betsey 72 at Gardiner ME [7 Dec 1848]
    Hannah 80 w/o Ephraim COWEN at Glenburn ME [29 Feb 1844]
    Judith G 58 at Farmington ME [4 Oct 1849]

COWEN - see SANFORD

COWING Calvin 83 AmRev at Lisbon ME [25 Apr 1844]

COWING - TIBBETTS

COWLES - see CHAPMAN

COX Aurelius A 22 at Thomaston ME [1 June 1848]
    Edwin S 28 s/o William COX of Norway ME at Fayette IL [16 Apr 1846]
    Ellen M 18 youngest d/o George COX Esq at Vassalboro ME [5 June 1845]
    Hugh 76 AmRev at Gardiner ME [25 Dec 1835]
    Israel Capt 94 at Bristol ME [25 Apr 1850]
    James 80 at Hallowell ME [22 Feb 1844]
    John mate of Thomaston ME lost overboard, from schr *F Copeland & Co* on passage
        from Thomaston to Norfolk [27 Nov 1851]
    little child of clothes taking fire at Bath ME [*Bath Mirror*] [17 Jan 1850]
    Mr died during a fire [*The Cleveland Plaindealer*] [4 Oct 1849]
    Simon Rev 51 at Rockland ME [6 Feb 1851]
    William 73 at Norway ME [22 Apr 1847]

COX - see KNIGHT

COY Cyrus 48 s/o the late John COY of Minot ME at Swanton OH [29 May 1845]
    Daniel 82 at Readfield ME on 5 Oct [18 Oct 1849]
    Martha N 9 d/o Elbridge at Augusta ME [20 Dec 1849]

COY (Cont.) Nathan of Oxford ME drowned [5 Jul 1849]
    Sylvia 3m 2w at Augusta ME on 27 Sept [7 Oct 1852]
    Tryphena 31 w/o Elbridge G at Augusta ME on 31 Jul [5 Aug 1852]
    Typhene 11m at Augusta ME on 26th inst [5 Aug 1847]
COZZENS Augustus D 21 mate of bark *Ovando* of Belfast ME at sea on Feb 21 on passage
    from Boston to Havana [31 Oct 1850]
CRAGIN Molly of Embden 78 at New Portland ME [4 Apr 1850]
CRAIG Charles H 22 s/o Col Daniel CRAIG at Readfield ME on 25 Oct, returned from CA
    just two weeks before his death [31 Oct 1850]
    David 75 at Augusta ME [9 Jan 1845]
    Edwin 12 s/o Hiram CRAIG at Augusta ME on 8 Mar [22 Mar 1849]
    Elias Esq formerly of Augusta ME at Fayette ME [23 May 1837]
    Ezekiel 56 at Saccarappa ME [26 Feb 1852]
    Jesse 87 at Augusta ME on 9th inst [18 Nov 1852]
    John S 23 at Belfast ME [14 June 1849]
    Matilda 75 w/o David CRAIG at Augusta ME [14 Oct 1843]
    Nancy 52 at Readfield ME on 21st Sept [5 Oct 1839]
    Olive 78 wid/o Elias CRAIG at Fayette ME [12 Oct 1848]
    Sarah w/o Jesse CRAIG at Augusta ME [15 Aug 1834]
    Sophia A 22 at Farmington ME [12 Apr 1849]
CRAM Emily J w/o Sewall CRAM Esq attorney at law at New Sharon ME on 13th inst [3
    Oct 1840]
    George of Whiting & another man burnt to death at Trescot on 17th inst, a short way
    from Mr WILCOX's at Trescot who discovered the camp on fire, Mr CRAM a young
    unmarried man & the other man left a wife & children [1 Feb 1840]
    George W of Bradford the crew of the *Traveller* supposed lost [16 Oct 1851]
    Hannah L 41 w/o Stephen CRAM 2d at Mt Vernon ME on 10 Oct [21 Oct 1852]
    Harrison W 18y 6m s/o Gen Varnum CRAM at New Sharon ME [5 Feb 1839]
    Huldah P 25 w/o R CRAM Esq at Bridgton ME on 16th ult [10 Jul 1845]
    Olive 82 widow of John CRAM at Kennebec ME [27 Mar 1851]
    W C a native of Bath ME, 3rd officer of whaleship *Formosa* at the US Hospital Honolulu
    Hawaii Islands on 22d Nov [17 May 1849]
CRAMMER Charles 27 at Waldoboro ME [12 Dec 1850]
CRAN David abt 50y of Centre Harbor NH suicide on Wed last by hanging himself left wife
    & 5 children [30 Jul 1842]
CRANE Abigail 12 formerly of Mt Desert ME at Roxbury MA [23 Sept 1847]
    Abner 40 at Winthrop ME of consumption on Sun night last at Winthrop ME [25 Dec
    1841]
    John abt 55 at Fayette ME [4 Jan 1844]
    Mary Miss at Temple on 1st inst of consumption [6 June 1840]
CRANE - see BROWN, STEPHENS
CRARY Lucy 86 wid/o Joseph CRARY at Jackson ME [15 Aug 1844]
CRAVEN Virginia Ann Nesbit Mrs 26 w/o Lt Thomas Tingley CRAVEN & eldest d/o Hon
    J F WINGATE at Hallowell ME on Sun last after a long illness [9 May 1837]
CRAVES John 66 formerly of Topsham ME at Moscow ME [3 Sept 1846]
CRAWFORD Abel Esq 86 "death of the White Mountain Patriarch" The paper stated "His
    name has long been identifed with the White Mts" [24 Jul 1851]
    Criscinda S 32 w/o John W CRAWFORD at Winthrop ME [28 Oct 1852]
    Henry 60 member of the Sidney Div of Sons of Temperance at Sidney ME on 16 Dec [9
    Jan 1851]
    James 73 at Brunswick ME [26 Mar 1846]

CROSBY (Cont.) John Gen LXXXVI (86) at Hampden ME on 25th ult [10 June 1843]
Jonathan abt 25 at Embden ME [7 Oct 1852]
Lucy abt 60 at Norridgewock ME [17 Apr 1839]
Mr a Kennebecker in Newfoundland, a brick-layer & learned his trade in Albion ME
where he was born. At the age twenty years he gave his father a hundred dollars for
"his time" and with a pack on his back started for Bangor ME. Here his industry
earned him a good living and in a year or two he was sent to St John New Brunswick
Canada as foreman of a gang of Yankee mechanics ....(see article not an obit) [11
Nov 847]
Rebecca 24 w/o Hanford CROSBY at Albion ME [4 Jan 1849]
Rebecca w/o Major T H CROSBY at Augusta ME [7 Jan 1847]
Ruth 75 wid/o Eben CROSBY Esq at Hampden ME [7 Mar 1850]
Sarah H 36 at Belfast ME [14 Mar 1840]
William 82 the oldest lawyer & judge probably in ME at Belfast ME on 31 Mar [15 Apr
1852]
William of No 4, South of Springfield ME shot accidentally by Major Luther TURNER
of Lincoln village ME [*Bangor Whig*] [26 Feb 1846]
CROSBY - see BAKER, ROLERSON
CROSS Abigail 46 w/o William CROSS at Vassalboro ME on 10th Mar [27 Mar 1851]
Augusta 5y c/o Francis & Mary CROSS [3 Dec 1846]
Bethiah 67 w/o Samuel CROSS at Vassalboro ME on 24th inst [4 Apr 1845]
Caleb 96 AmRev pensioner at Vassalboro ME on 27th ult [11 Feb 1843]
Col his murdered body found four miles from Rio Grande TX [14 May 1846]
Edward Bean 3y 6m s/o Gershom & Mary CROSS at Vassalboro ME [11 Mar 1847]
family lost in a flood by the breaking up of ice in the Des Moines River [Keokuk (Iowa)
papers] [12 Apr 1849]
Joseph 19 & Rhoda 10 both c/o Samuel CROSS at Foxcroft ME of the canker rash [29
Feb 1840]
Judith Mrs 68 consort of William CROSS [9 Sept 1843]
Lois 72 w/o Jona CROSS at Vassalboro ME [9 Dec 1843]
Margaret 5y 3m only d/o Simon & Mary J CROSS at Windsor ME on 26 Jan [6 Feb
1851]
Mary S 45 w/o Francis W CROSS at Augusta ME on 19 Sept [28 Sept 1848]
Mercy 68 w/o Caleb CROSS at Vassalboro ME on 30 Mar 1839]
Mrs of New Gloucester ME w/o Col Joseph CROSS on Tues morning 4th inst committed
suicide [*Lewiston Journal*] [13 Jul 1848]
Rev Mr at Hallowell ME [1 Aug 1840]
Rev suicide by drowning he was a Baptist minister (from the *Temperance Gazette*) [1
Aug 1840]
Rhoda 10 c/o Samuel CROSS at Foxcroft (now Dover-Foxcroft) ME of the canker rash
[29 Feb 1840]
Samuel 71 at Vassalboro ME on 28 Mar [10 Apr 1851]
Sarah "the sweetheart of an old soldier" a bill to grant a pension passed by the House of
Representatives of PA last week 45 to 36 [11 Mar 1833]
Theodore 8 c/o Francis & Mary CROSS [5 Dec 1846]
Wheeler of Sebec ME at Grey Eagle City CA on 31 Jul [9 Oct 1851]
CROSS - see CLARK
CROSWELL Henrietta 26 w/o Dr Thomas CROSWELL at Newport ME [16 May 1850]
Mr drowned at Oldtown ME [22 Jul 1852]
William Dr, the rector of the Church of the Advent at Boston MA of an attack of
apoplexy [13 Nov 1851]
CROUCH Alden 36 of Rockland ME at sea on board schr *Lucretia* [22 May 1851]

CROUCH (Cont.) infant of Italy Hill the child's parents left home with the infant to visit some relatives in Jerusalem - It being a very cold day they bundled up very warm. On arriving at their friends, the young mother commenced telling how "very quiet the baby was during the whole ride." On uncovering it she beheld her infant a corpse [*Penn Yan Democrat*] [8 Jan 1846]

CROUSE Hannah of OH now 11y & weighs 300 pounds at Washington DC 5' 2" height & measuring 5' 1" around the shoulders & 21 inches round the arm [1 Jan 1846]

CROWELL Baxter abt 60y of Canaan ME found dead in his barn at the end of a rope, left a wife & a large family ch, most if not all of whom have arrived to the age of manhood [29 Jul 1843]

    Daniel Capt 62 at China ME on 11 Nov [6 Dec 1849]

    Emily M 39 at Waterville ME on 10 Aug [22 Aug 1850]

    James of Levant ME lost his right hand in a mill accident [16 Dec 1843]

    Keziah 84 at Whitefield ME a widow [3 Oct 1850]

    Manoah AmRev pensioner at Waterville ME [25 Mar 1847]

    Moses 40 formerly of Boston MA at New Sharon ME on 24 Mar [1 Apr 1847]

    Nancy R 39 w/o Rev William C at Waterville ME [15 Nov 1849]

    Nathan 65 formerly of (Augusta) ME at Sidney ME [12 Apr 1849]

    Patience 29 w/o Nathan CROWELL at Augusta ME on Sun last [6 Mar 1838]

    Rhoda S 24 at Dexter ME [19 Mar 1846]

    Thomas 90 a native of Ireland & AmRev at Brunswick ME [5 Dec 1844]

CROWLEY Mr the second mate of the *Lexington*, after drifting about 50 miles on a bale of cotton, got ashore on Long Island, not far from River Head. The *Sag Harbor Corrector* gives the following particulars: It appears from CROWLEY's account, that the boat was first discovered to be on fire off Huntington at abt 7 - that he soon took to a plank, but shortly left it for a bale of cotton, on which he drifted until Wed evening, when he landed at New Gully & made his way to the house of Mathias HUTCHINSON - having drifted ... abt 50 mi & absolutely sleeping at times. He wore two flannel shirts but had on no shoes or hat. Every care was taken of him at Hutchinson's. It was thought he will lose some of his toes & one finger on which he had a ring which impeded the circulation [1 Feb 1840]

CROZIER William killed in the Irish & Native American (not American Indians more likely English born in American) Riots in Philadelphia PA [*Dollar Newspaper*] [18 July 1844]

CRUCE Mary Ann Mrs 53 at Bath ME [19 Sept 1850]

CRUCH Elsy Ann 7 d/o & Ephraim 12 s/o Capt Ephraim CRUCH at Thomaston ME [19 Dec 1834]

CRUMWELL Elizabeth 36 at Bath ME [15 Jul 1836]

CRUSER Mr of Rossville, Staten Island lost with his wife in his house fire [8 Mar 1849]

CULLEN James 43 at Gardiner ME [26 Jul 1849]

CUMMINGS child 1y of Alexander CUMMINGS at Winthrop ME [7 May 1842]

    Daniel 66 at Paris ME [18 Feb 1847]

    Deborah 56 w/o William CUMMINGS at Greenville ME [28 Dec 1848]

    Eliza M 31 at Levant ME [20 Jan 1848]

    Joseph P 27 s/o Daniel CUMMINGS of Portland ME at Natchez MS [30 May 1844]

    Lemuel Deac at Greene ME [1 Apr 1852]

    Lemuel Decon 82 at Greene ME [1 Apr 1852]

    Lewis L an Engineer on Lewiston & Waterville Railroad at Winthrop ME [8 Apr 1847]

    Lydia L 18 d/o John & Nancy CUMMINGS at Standish ME [27 Nov 1851]

    Mary S ae 32 w/o Leonard CUMMINGS at Albany [29 Oct 1846]

    Richard 90 AmRev at Waldoboro ME on Sun last [21 Sept 1839]

CUMMINGS (Cont.) Seth G 48 of Belgrade ME at San Francisco CA on 3 May [24 June 1852]

CUMNER Hannah 57 w/o Rev John CUMNER at Wayne ME on 5th inst [16 Dec 1852]

CUNNINGHAM Allen perished in the flames of the fire, house of Anson MEIGS & occupied by Eben AVERILL on Tues morning on 29th of July at Vassalboro ME [7 Aug 1851]

Louisa 43 of Belfast ME at Calais ME [21 May 1845]

Louisa abt 37 at Augusta ME on 5 Apr of consumption [17 Apr 1851]

Martha M d/o Eben CUNNINGHAM at Swanville ME [8 June 1839]

Mr blown up in some blasting operations at St Louis and his entrails torn out, yet he survived at the last accounts. [23 Nov 1839]

Robert seaman of Newcastle ME fell from aloft & was drowned overboard from ship *Canton* 3rd in going into Boston harbor [12 Feb 1842]

CURATE Jacob Rev of Wilton MA horsewhipped by two persons in the public square of Wilton MA, for courting a young lady & then refusing to marry her. The floggers, the father & brother of the slighted damsel. Being a reverend the gentleman's offense was considered the more aggravating, as he had 2 yrs boarding & lodging out of the gentlemen, while paying his addresses to the lady [5 Apr 1849]

CURLE - see FISLAR

CURRIER Alfred a seaman of the schr *Ceylon*, CROOKER Capt of Hallowell ME, succeeded in lashing himself to the wreck & was taken off by the *Comet* & carried safely to New Orleans [4 Apr 1844]

Betsey w/o David CURRIER Esq at New Sharon ME [16 Nov 1848]

child of Jeremiah CURRIER at Windsor ME [19 Sept 1837]

Eben M 23 formerly of Hallowell ME at Bloomfield ME on 7 May [16 May 1850]

Edward J of Newburyport MA (son of the Capt Edward CURRIER) the crew of the *Traveller* supposed lost [16 Oct 1851]

Elizabeth C 28 w/o George CURRIER at Montville ME on 20 May [27 May 1852]

Harriet 21 at Norridgewock ME [1 Apr 1847]

Israel 18 drowned while bathing [3 Jul 1841]

John abt 60 at Winthrop ME on Wed evening last [8 Apr 1833]

Joseph 39 at Auburn ME [19 Dec 1844]

Mary 73 w/o Ephraim CURRIER at Cornville ME [30 Jan 1845]

Mary Jane 5y 5m d/o E G & Mary CURRIER at Winthrop ME [29 Aug 1850]

CURRIER Nathaniel 72 at Mt Vernon ME on 13th inst [27 Sept 1849]

Sarah 32 at Winthrop ME on 9th inst [25 Sept 1838]

Thomas 76 at Skowhegan ME [13 Mar 1851]

CURRY - see NASON

CURTAIN - see DORROGH

CURTIS Aaron 30 at Prospect ME [20 Apr 1839]

Abigail 55 w/o David C at Harpswell [11 Nov 1843]

Benjamin Capt 28 at Bowdoinham ME [6 Apr 1839]

Christiana 47 w/o Dr Henry C sister of Pres of USA at Hanover Co VA on 13th inst [29 Jan 1842]

Edmund 45 at Mercer ME [15 Nov 1849]

Elijah a stage driver from Bangor disappeared about a fortnight since. After he had been absent eleven days, his body was found floating on a pond in the town of Dexter (ME) having a stone tied to it which was not of sufficient weight to prevent it floating when in a state of putrefaction. The coroner's verdict was suicide by drowning. [1 Aug 1837]

Elizabeth 70 w/o Willard CHILDS at Eastport ME [12 Feb 1852]

Elizabeth abt 4 yrs d/o David C at Bath [15 May 1845]

CURTIS (Cont.) Freeman C 24 at Bath ME [18 Oct 1849]

girl of Biddeford ME d/o Noah CURTIS found murdered in the woods a few miles from her father's house [29 May 1841]

Harriet Lee 41 w/o David C at Bath ME [20 Aug 1846]

Henry s/o Ebenezer & (Sarah DINGLEY) CURTIS of Newburgh ME killed on Sat, engaged in clearing a winter road near his father's res, with a bro, (perhaps Levi Dingley CURTIS b 24 Mar 1819, d 29 Mar 1901, his oldest bro) and endeavoring to escape the falling stump of a tree, received its whole weight on his head [*Bangor Mercury*] [14 Jan 1847]

Jacob W 26 at Hampden ME [6 Feb 1851]

James Esq 69 at Winthrop ME on the 16th [26 Dec 1837]

James Jr 28 eldest son of James CURTIS Esq of Winthrop ME at Para on the Amazon, had been between two or three years established in that place as a blacksmith [28 Jan 1833]

Jeremiah his house burnt at Calais ME [22 May 1841]

Jeremiah 51 at Biddeford ME [29 Mar 1849]

John C 43 at Brunswick ME [4 May 1848]

Joshua of Perry ME fell from aloft on board the schr *Lucy* of Pembroke lying in the stream died [*Traveller*, 26th] [2 Sept 1847]

Julia abt 20 d/o Rev Thomas C of the Baptist Church in Bangor ME, went to Portland ME in a consumption abt 6 weeks since & fell a victim to that insatiable disease [22 Jul 1836]

Levi 69 at Bowdinham ME [19 Jul 1849]

Lucy C Mrs d/o the late John COOL 55 at Jackson ME on 12 Mar [13 Apr 1848]

Nancy H 36 w/o George A CURTIS late of Boston MA at West Newton MA on 25 Jan [14 Feb 1850]

Reuben B Rev a Methodist minister, near loss of life at Solon village ME on New Year's Day (from *People's Press*) [22 Jan 1846]

Richard H a native of ME chief mate on board ship *Prentice* drowned an hour after leaving Boston MA from New Orleans [25 Apr 1844]

Samuel 48 at Alton ME [20 June 1850]

Sarah widow 38 at Freeport ME on 28th ult [11 Mar 1843]

Turner I give to my son, Robert CURTIS, his lawful right to trade for himself from this time until he is 21 & that I shall pay none of his debts ... He must pay me $30 at Monmouth ME [30 May 1837]

Turner of Monmouth ME lost his barn by fire on Tues the 4th inst [13 Feb 1845]

William by overeating at Spitalfields England [28 Oct 1842]

CURTIS - see GOUGH, HAMILTON, THOMAS, WHEELER

CUSAC Patrick 25 at Gardiner ME [16 Oct 1851]

CUSACK Luke 3y 9m (*sic* see Mary) s/o John CUSACK at Gardiner ME on Sun of scarlet fever [9 May 1844]

Mark 6y 10m s/o John CUSACK of Gardiner ME of scarlet fever on Fri last [9 May 1844]

Mary 4y 11m d/o John CUSACK of Gardiner ME of scarlet fever on Fri last [9 May 1844]

Mathew 3y & 6m (*sic* see Luke) c/o John CUSACK of Gardiner ME of scarlet fever on Fri last [9 May 1844]

Michael 1y 8m c/o John CUSACK of Gardiner ME of scarlet fever on Fri last [9 May 1844]

CUSHING Caleb Esq 61 at Brunswick ME on Fri last [24 Apr 1838]

Elizabeth 75 at Topsham ME on 27th ult [10 June 1843]

Esther 17 at Freeport ME [5 Sept 1850]

CUSHING (Cont.) Francis D 28 of the firm of C CUSHING & Co at Brunswick ME on 16th
inst [26 June 1835]

Hannah 68y 4m w/o Martin CUSHING & d/o the late Dummer SEWALL Esq of Bath
ME at Winthrop ME on 27 Aug [3 Sept 1842]

Harriet Irven 22y 6m w/o Hiram CUSHING at Augusta ME on 22 Apr [4 May 1848]

Horatio 31 at Bloomfield ME [14 Nov 1844]

James M 22 at Bangor ME [27 Mar 1845]

John N Capt 70 the father of Hon Caleb CUSHING at Newburyport MA [18 Jan 1849]

Loring Capt 53 at Augusta ME on Sat last [27 Jan 1848]

Louis T 35 a worthy & much lamented citizen at Brunswick ME on 18th ult suddenly of
influenza [13 Mar 1838]

Mary F 22 w/o Hiram CUSHING of Augusta ME at Vassalboro ME [11 Sept 1845]

R T of Thomaston ME on board ship *Massachusetts* on her passage from Thomaston ME
to New Orleans on 16th ult of consumption [8 Feb 1840]

Sarah A 35 w/o Rev James CUSHING at South Berwick ME [7 Aug 1845]

Thomas 61 at Phipsburg ME [20 Feb 1851]

Tileston 79 at Bath ME [25 Mar 1847]

CUSHMAN Ada Mrs 38 at Hallowell ME [19 Oct 1848]

Ann 33 d/o Deac Andrew CUSHMAN of Monson ME at Foxcroft (now Dover-Foxcroft
ME) [17 June 1852]

Caleb 84 at Paris ME AmRev [1 Apr 1833]

Col 66 at Bridgton ME [25 Oct 1849]

Dorcas H 42 w/o Isaac CUSHMAN at Leeds on 11 May [23 May 1850]

Elihu 78 at Augusta ME on 7 Jan [18 Jan 1849]

Eliza M 21 at Montville ME [27 Jul 1848]

Gideon 95 at Hebron ME left ten children & about 80 grandchildren, 100 great-grand [22
May 1845]

Harriet 43 w/o Dr CUSHMAN at Brunswick ME [15 Aug 1844]

Joshua of Winslow ME a member of the house of representatives on Mon [31 Jan 1834]

Lucy w/o the late Joshua CUSHMAN at Winslow at the res of her son [4 Feb 1847]

Mary 22 w/o Alexander CUSHMAN & d/o James MORRILL of Buckfield ME at
Buckfield ME [27 Jul 1839]

Samuel 59 59 at New Gloucester ME [14 Jan 1847]

Solomon P Dr 43 at Brunswick ME [7 Nov 1844]

Widow 83 at Turner ME on 30 Jan [19 Feb 1842]

CUSHMAN - see JOY, THOMAS

CUTLER Abby D 26 w/o J L CUTLER Esq at Farmington ME [13 May 1847]

E G Rev 34 pastor of the 1st Congregational Church of Belfast ME at Reading PA [14
May 1846]

Hannah (MOORE) w/o w/o Hon Nathan CUTLER at Farmington ME (see p. 451
Butler's *History of Farmington ME*) [8 May 1835]

Mary Jane 24 w/o Reuben CUTLER at Strong ME [8 Apr 1847]

Nancy S 31 w/o Josiah CUTLER at Strong ME [27 Jan 1848]

Samuel A of North Yarmouth ME lost overboard from ship *Macedonia* on 23 Apr on her
passage from Mobile to Boston MA [15 May 1835]

Zilpha 29 w/o John L CUTLER & d/o Hon Reuel WILLIAMS of (Augusta) ME at
Farmington ME on 25 Jul [31 Jul 1851]

CUTTER Charles E 22 s/o Deac J CUTTER at Sebec ME [19 Oct 1848]

John 77 at North Yarmouth ME [6 June 1844]

Simon Col 54 at Saccarappa ME from an injury a fortnight since from a circular saw in
his works which resulted in his death [1 Oct 1842]

Wilmot 30 at Wiscasset ME [25 Mar 1836]

CUTTER - see ABBOTT

CUTTING Jonah Capt 80 AmRev & one of the 1st settlers of Guilford VT [31 Dec 1842]
    Samuel Col 51 at Guilford VT [31 Dec 1842]

CUTTS Charles 77 a US senator at the res of his son in Fairfax Co VA on 25th inst
    [*National Intelligencer*] [5 Feb 1846]
    Hannah 63 at Saco ME [26 Aug 1847]
    Joanna 56 w/o Richard CUTTS at Kittery ME [21 Dec 1848]
    Joseph abt 70 at Kittery ME drowned [18 Nov 1852]

CYPHERS John 76 at Sidney ME [4 Dec 1851]
    Mr 90 at Eastport ME [9 Oct 1845]

- D -

DADMUN/DADMAN George Lyman 20m s/o Jeduthan & Lucy DADMUN at Winthrop
    ME on 4th inst "papers in MA please copy" [16 Apr 1842] [N.B. There is a Jeduthan
    Dadman listed in the 1850 Census of Holliston MA)

DAGGETT Abigail 80 at Farmington ME [5 Nov 1846]
    Angeline 15 at Houlton ME on 27 Sept [24 Oct 1850]
    Bradford B s/o Col Samuel DAGGETT of New Vineyard ME drowned on Thurs last
        while bathing in the Sandy River at Farmington ME [24 Jul 1841]
    Ephraim G from Hope ME at Roxbury MA [*Boston MA Bee*] [19 June 1851]
    Isabel 18m c/o Aaron & Bethiah DAGGETT at Appleton ME [19 Apr 1849]
    Louisa W 23 w/o Samuel DAGGETT at Industry ME [27 Jan 1848]
    Mehitable 50 w/o Benjamin DAGGETT Esq at Palmyra ME [9 Oct 1851]
    Morrell 5 c/o Aaron & Bethiah DAGGETT [19 Apr 1849]
    Oriville 8 c/o Aaron & Bethiah DAGGETT at Appleton ME [19 Apr 1849]
    Warren 39 of Winthrop ME on passage from Panama to San Francisco CA on 10th Jul
        [17 Oct 1850]

DAILEY Abiel MD 70 at Monmouth ME [23 Oct 1845]

DAILY Mr killed & another Mr MITCHELL s/o Capt MITCHELL of the steamboat
    Osceola was wounded in an accident at the Washington Navy Yard [*Magnetic
    Telegraph*] [*Baltimore Pat*, Thurs] [19 Feb 1846]

DAIN William 91 at Bath ME [24 May 1849]

DALE Dr bro/o Major who fell in FL died very suddenly on 16th ult at King George Co VA
    returning from the funeral of a friend with his little son, observed to check his horse
    so violently as to throw him down. The Doctor then fell forward to the ground &
    never spoke again [16 Dec 1843]
    George 20 of ME of cholera Sacramento CA on Nov 5 [2 Jan 1851]
    John 69 at Alna ME [23 Apr 1842]
    Lieutenant connected with the Dead Sea exploring party is dead [21 Sept 1848]

DALEY Daniel on the mill pond on the Chautauque River for a sail on the night of 21 Jul
    the boat was upset all five were drowned age 17y to 20y (see also AYRES, PERSEY,
    CRIPPIN) [7 Aug 1851]

DALLAS Com s/o Alex J DALLAS & bro/o Mr D, the Democratic VP candidate on board
    the flag ship of the squadron from the effects of a third attack of paralysis [5 Sept
    1844]

DALTON Anna of Cambridgport MA saved from drowning when the steam packet *New
    England* sank. It left Boston for Bath & Gardiner ME and had an accident with the
    schr *Curlew* on 31 May [12 June 1838]
    James M 39 of Baltimore MD s/o William A DALTON at Augusta ME at Washington
    DC on 2 Nov by accidentally falling from the platform of a railroad car [19 Dec 1850]

DALTON (Cont.) Mary Ellen 20 at Gardiner ME [26 Apr 1849]

> Mr "sentenced a few days since to a fine of one dollar and thirty days imprisonment for beating his wife" at Northampton Co PA [29 Feb 1840]

> Paulina A 41 w/o P A DALTON at Norridgewock ME [27 Mar 1851]

DALTON - see WEST

DALY Catharine P 21 w/o Captain Zebedee S DALY at Augusta ME [30 Jul 1846]

> Sophia abt 36 w/o Isaac S DALY Esq at Livermore ME [23 Oct 1845]

DAM Robert 17 s/o Samuel DAM at Passadumkeag ME [30 Nov 1839]

DAMON Dolly widow 77 at Gardiner ME [2 Jan 1851]

DANA Judah 72 at Fryeburg ME [15 Jan 1846]

DANA - see CHILD, COFFIN

DANAHA - see DOYLE

DANFORTH David killed on the Lowell Railroad on Tues afternoon last [10 Jul 1835]

> Emily S d/o Asa DANFORTH of Norton MA at Winthrop ME on 31st of Jan [21 Feb 1837]

> Joseph 57 at Salem in the street on his way to meeting on Sun 26th ult [8 Feb 1840]

> Newland S 29 at Lagrange ME [4 Feb 1846]

> Philip seaman of Freedom ME on board schr *Albert* from Bangor ME on 27th ult was knocked overboard by the fore boom & drowned [9 Jul 1842]

DANGLE - see CRAWFORD

DANIELS Columbia B 22y & 10m at Paris ME [31 Oct 1844]

> Harding abt 50y left widow & ch of Holliston killed crossing the Milford Branch railroad [27 Dec 1849]

> James of Cooks Manor, Upper Canada. His family was awakened by a severe shock like that of an earthquake on the night of the 17th ult. In the morning it was discovered that a meteor, judged to be about three times the size of an ordinary farm house had struck the earth some 80 rods distant from Mr. D's dwelling with a force which buried its entire bulk about 8 inches below the surface. (Believe it or not) Reported in the *Boston Transcript* of Wed and *Portland Advertiser* [23 May 1840][11 Apr 1840]

> John 78 at Paris ME [11 Oct 1849]

> Rebecca w/o James DANIEL formerly of Paris ME at Bethel ME [2 Apr 1846]

> Susan 78 at Paris ME [4 Feb 1843]

DANOVER Hannah widow 90 at Lewiston ME [17 Apr 1851]

DARLING Benjamin 47 at Phipsburg ME (NB head of a large mulatto family, see Rev Charles N SINNETT's typescript *Benjamin Darling of Casco Bay, Maine* at ME State Library [30 Sep 1847]

DARLING - see BARRETT

DARLINGTON Lt of the US Navy found dead in his bed at Portsmouth NH [20 Mar 1845]

DARROW Abigail 87 formerly of York at Belfast ME [24 Feb 1848]

DASCOM Elbridge 42 at Jay ME [16 Sept 1852]

DAVEE Thomas former Congressman at Blanchard ME on 11th inst [25 Dec 1841]

DAVENPORT Abraham 73 a native of Hallowell ME at Mobile AL [20 Nov 1838]

> David at Augusta ME [11 Jan 1843]

> Elijah Capt at Jay ME on inst [3 Feb 1848]

> Emeline abt 30 w/o John DAVENPORT at Hallowell ME [17 Apr 1845]

> Frederick 24 or 25 married Mrs Amelia SPRUILL 58 or 60, the bridegroom is a perfect cripple & has been so from a child. The bride is worth something like 30 or 35,000 dollars, & Mr D is a poor man. At Tyrrell NC a short time since [16 Sept 1843]

> Joanna 69 w/o Jonathan DAVENPORT at Hallowell ME at Hallowell ME on Tues last. "Portsmouth paper please copy" [8 May 1838]

DAVENPORT (Cont.) Ruth 40 consort of Cyrus DAVENPORT formerly of Bridgton ME & d/o William DOANE formerly of Greene ME at Cincinnati OH [10 Jul 1845]

Thomas J of MA, with six other persons had been murdered by Indians, the mail from the steamer *Columbia* from Oregon arrived at San Francisco CA to report. [20 Nov 1851]

DAVIDSON Sarah G 19 at Lexington ME on 13 Aug [26 Aug 1852]

DAVIDSON - see HASEITH

DAVIES E G of Augusta ME left for CA (gold mines) [*Gospel Banner*] [15 Feb 1849]

DAVIS Abel 19 formerly of Norridgewock ME at Lowell MA [11 Nov 1847]

Abel 45 at Danville (now part of Auburn) ME [10 Dec 1846]

Abigail 70 w/o Rufus DAVIS at Hallowell ME [8 Feb 1849]

Abner 38 at Waldoboro ME [23 Apr 1846]

Alexander abt 14 drowned on the evening of the 5th while skating on the ice of the pond near (Winthrop ME) [9 Dec 1836]

Amey 73 wid/o Asa DAVIS late of New Sharon ME at Winslow ME [5 Apr 1849]

Ann 30 d/o Amos CARVER formerly of Freeport ME at Winthrop ME [14 Oct 1847]

Ann G 38 formerly of (Winthrop ME) at Toronto Canada on 3 Aug at the res of her bro-in-law, George H CHENEY, formerly of Portland ME [28 Aug 1842]

Anner E Mrs 65 at Bath ME [5 Feb 1846]

Avesta A 15 d/o Jona DAVIS at Chesterville ME [27 Jan 1848]

Benjamin C 23 at Augusta ME on Sun last [17 Sept 1842]

Betsey 61 at Augusta ME [21 Feb 1850]

Betsey abt 50 at Warren ME [5 Aug 1843]

Catherine 71 formerly of Gorham ME at Farmington ME [1 Aug 1837]

Charles 42 at Wilton ME on 3rd inst [18 Nov 1852]

Charles F 28 of Charleston MA at San Pablo CA of cholera on 5 Sept [13 Feb 1851]

Charles "colored" s/o Levi DAVIS of Augusta ME [11 Apr 1844]

Charlotte 21 d/o Capt Benjamin DAVIS at Belfast ME [5 Aug 1852]

Daniel 23 at Norway ME [4 Apr 1850]

Daniel Esq 73 formerly solicitor general of the Commonwealth of MA at Cambridge MA [13 Nov 1835]

David 75y 6m at Lewiston ME [16 Jan 1851]

David Capt 68 at Industry ME on the 26th of Aug [3 Oct 1837]

David L 34 at Gardiner ME [1 Mat 1845]

Delia 48 w/o Major Nathaniel DAVIS [17 June 1847]

E 52 at Newcastle ME [27 Jul 1848]

Elizabeth 30 w/o E I Vassal DAVIS late of Washington City at Wayne ME [19 Dec 1840]

Elizabeth 65 w/o S Davis Esq at Mount Vernon ME [8 Oct 1846]

Elizabeth 84 at Bloomfield ME [31 Oct 1834]

Ephraim 77 his father, Capt Isaac DAVIS of Acton MA shot by the British troops at Concord Bridge on the memorable 19 of April in 1775, he died at South Solon ME [22 Jan 1846]

Eunice 72 w/o John DAVIS at Fairfield ME [23 May 1840]

Eunice 79 w/o late Benjamin DAVIS & formerly w/o Joseph LAMBERT at Readfield ME on 8th inst [18 Nov 1847]

Frances M A 76 wid/o Samuel DAVIS Esq at Augusta ME on 21 Mar [1 Apr 1852]

Francisco 31/34 at Dover ME [29 Apr 1852]

George 25 & unmarried reported death by suicide of Rev DAVIS by letter dated South Berwick ME 16 Jan 1844 [1 Feb 1844]

George 38 of Parsonsfield ME came to his death on Thurs of last week, left a wife & 3 ch [*Limerick Repository* (Freewill Baptist)] [30 Dec 1847]

DAVIS (Cont.) George Capt of Somerset Co MD born with but one visual organ or at least there was nothing like a ball in the socket of the other, continued this way until 10 or 12 yrs of age, when a small, but perfect eye began to form in the hitherto sightless socket; it increased in size until now (1840) can see with it clearly & distinctly. [*The Baltimore Sun*] [18 Jul 1840]

Hamden (b 4 June 1814, d 21 Sept 1849 s/o Richard & Abagail {PARKER} DAVIS) at Litchfield ME, see p. 97 Clason's *History of Litchfield ME*, Heritage Books 1992 [11 Oct 1849]

Hannah widow 87 at Buxton ME [3 June 1843]

Henry 115, colored, at Dearborn Co, the papers stated was a servant to Gen George WASHINGTON, "It appears to us that every descendant of Ham who deceases now-a-days at the advanced age, has been a servant of Gen WASHINGTON. Three of his servants have died within the past year. Are there any more of the same sort left!" [22 Feb 1849]

I S 34 at Poland ME [29 June 1848]

Ichabod 22 at Saco ME [24 Sept 1846]

Isaac Capt 88 AmRev at Lisbon ME [7 Jan 1847]

Isaac S 34 at Poland ME [13 Jul 1848]

James Jr 49 at Augusta ME [29 Jul 2843]

James of Fairfield ME drowned at Moosehead Lake, abt three weeks since [24 Jul 1845]

Jane Ann 21 d/o Simeon & Jane DAVIS at Standish ME on 27 Oct [15 Jan 1852]

Joanna 32 at Kennebunkport ME on 15th inst [24 Jul 1835]

John A 15 youngest s/o Dr Joshua DAVIS at Belgrade ME on 24th Apr [3 May 1849]

John 25 of Augusta ME lost overboard from schr *Henry Freeling* on 4th inst [30 Mar 1848]

John W Esq Clerk of the District Court of the USA at Boston MA [28 Nov 1834]

Jonathan Esq his large wooden dwelling house in the village near the depot & out building were consumed by fire on Tues afternoon known as the BECKETT House (from the *Lewiston Journal*) [31 Jul 1851]

Joseph late of Rome Kennebec Co ME at Swan's Island Plt in Hancock Co ME on 26th ult, friends can receive any info by addressing to Benj STINSON at Swan's Island [21 Oct 1836]

Joseph W Capt 49 formerly of Maine for the last 12 yrs a res in New Orleans master of a steamboat on 27 Nov [5 Mar 1842]

Joshua 19 of Sidney ME at sea on the *Tristan* whaling ground in the Pacific Ocean [6 June 1837]

Lolby blowing rocks in a well of Joseph CRESEY of Gorham ME on Thurs last an accidental explosion took place by which one of the workmen Mr Zachariah LIBBY almost instantly killed & Lolby DAVIS so horribly mangled that his life is despaired of [*Eastern Argus*] [2 Nov 1839]

Louisa M 28 w/o John W DAVIS at Palmyra ME [26 Apr 1849]

Lucinda 37 w/o Daniel DAVIS & d/o the late Capt James TOWARD at Freedom ME on 3rd [9 May 1850]

Lucy 78 w/o Francis DAVIS at Readfield ME on 13 May [16 May 1850]

Lyman E 26 formerly of Winthrop ME at Holliston MA [25 Jul 1850] Margaret 42 at Bath ME [26 Sept 1837]

Martha D abt 32 formerly of Fayette ME at Lowell MA on 30 Sept [14 Oct 1843]

Mary 87 w/o John DAVIS of Shapleigh ME at Wellington ME [11 Jan 1849]

Mary Jane 32 w/o Capt Francis DAVIS at Thomaston ME [30 May 1837]

Mary M 14m d/o Franklin DAVIS at Augusta ME [7 Sept 1848]

Moses Esq 63 at Edgecomb ME on 19th ult [16 Nov 1839]

DAVIS (Cont.) Mr killed by accident at the William REID mill of Carmel ME [*Bangor ME Whig*] [30 Nov 1848]

Mr s/o Moses DAVIS of Augusta ME by drowning en route from Bucksport ME by sailboat to Augusta ME [17 June 1852]

Nathaniel Esq 46 on Mon of last week at Industry ME skull fractured by machinery in the clover mill [*Farmington Register*] [28 Oct 1843]

negro the second cook on board of the steamer *Buckeye State*, the fugitive slave of Mr MOORE of Louisville KY [21 Aug 1851]

Prof of the University of VA [5 Dec 1840]

Rachel 78 wid/o Increase DAVIS formerly of Brookline MA at Lubec ME [2 May 1844]

Rhoda S 23 at Belfast ME [27 June 1850]

Sally widow 30 at Solon ME [24 Jan 1834]

Sally 68 w/o James DAVIS at Rome ME [11 Jul 1844]

Samuel l/o Mt Vernon ME, Henry DAVIS & James DAVIS execs of the est [4 Mar 1852]

Sarah C Mrs at Belgrade ME [13 June 1843]

Sarah Elizabeth 18y 5m d/o Simeon & Jane DAVIS at Standish ME on 13 Sept [30 Sept 1852]

Sarah Jane 37 at Fairfield ME on 1 Dec [16 Dec 1847]

Sarah W 23 w/o Elias DAVIS Jr at Gardiner ME [8 Feb 1844]

Shubael 72 at Milo ME [17 Aug 1848]

Thomas A at Brookline [*Boston Bee*] [27 Nov 1845]

Thomas 84 at Farmington NH [20 June 1834]

Thomas 85 at Hallowell ME [28 Nov 1844]

Triphena 22 w/o Arba P DAVIS at Waterville ME [16 Jan 1851]

Wendall 84 AmRev at Farmington ME [11 June 1846]

Westly s/o William DAVIS Jr of Eddington ME thrown off, the wheel passed over his head, the fatal accident occured on Tues last [13 Jul 1839]

William 81 AmRev at Eddington [1 Oct 1846]

William 97 AmRev at Palermo ME [22 Jul 1847]

William B 35 formerly of Winthrop ME at Mexico ME? [12 Dec 1850]

DAVIS - see FOSTER, JENKINS, LEYDEN, RIDLON, SLATER, SIMMONS, slave, WOODMAN

DAWES Abner 47 at Anson ME [30 Dec 1847]

Charles 51 at New Gloucester ME [11 Oct 1849]

Gideon Esq 77 at New Gloucester ME [24 Dec 1846]

DAY Benjamin Capt 76 at Fryeburg ME [5 Sept 1850]

Clara Adelma 7y 7m d/o Randall & Phebe DAY at Greene ME on 1 Apr [22 Apr 1847]

Daniel Deac 73 at Damariscotta ME [7 June 1849]

George 18 at Hallowell ME [18 June 1842]

Isaac Newton 7 s/o Henry DAY at Winthrop ME [25 Sept 1851]

Lurana 17 at Augusta ME on 8th inst [15 Mar 1849]

Mary 84 at Phipsburg ME [6 May 1852]

Mary F 28 w/o Edwin E DAY of Boston MA & d/o Jeremiah BLAISDELL of Sidney ME at Augusta ME on 30 June [8 Jul 1852]

Mary Mrs 84 at Phipsburg ME [6 May 1852]

Ophelia abt 26 at Lisbon ME [22 June 1839]

Patience w/o Asa DAY at Belfast ME [24 June 1852]

Rebecca 53 (a native of Livermore ME) w/o Andrew N DAY (formerly of Strong ME, see *Descendants of Robert & Mary DAY, who came to Ipswich MA from England in the 1630's* by David C Young & Barbara {DAY} Harasko unpublished 1977) at Dexter ME [4 Dec 1851]

Robert H 18m s/o Henry DAY at Augusta ME [10 Sept 1846]

DAY (Cont.) Sarah widow 95 at East Winthrop ME [23 Oct 1845]

Thomas 29 s/o Elijah DAY of Hallowell ME at Honolulu Sandwich Islands (Hawaii) [11 Sept 1845]

Thomas J 28 at Stow ME [12 Aug 1852]

DAY - see BABB, DORROGH

DAYERS Gerard Dr suicide at the Norfork House, abt a yr since the doctor thrown from a gig his arm & skull fractured [*Transcript*] [29 May 1835]

DAYTON Elias B of Elizabethtown NJ AmRev at New York on Sun [5 Feb 1846]

De OCA Montes recently executed at Havana Cuba for attemping to bribe a pilot to assist LOPEZ in his invasion of that island, died like a hero [29 May 1851]

DEAF MUTE - see HILL, LOVEJOY, MEYER, MORSE, THOMPSON, TRUE

DEAF & DUMB, leg broken on Fall River RR near Middleboro, A card of N B BORDEN Esq, Boston Journal says, map of the New England on back in pencil "This man is bound to Cape Cod, to go fishing" perhaps came from the Madawaska Settlement, in eastern part of ME to Boston, on arm in India ink the letters E.B. In his wallet the name Bela M BLANCHARD, Coxsackie also Jacob MARCHESSON [10 June 1852]

DEALY Charles Carroll 9 s/o James DEALY at Augusta ME [13 Mar 1845]

Mrs of Jackson Co MO the mother of 28 ch, by one husband, ought to have a township of land given her. If the children follow suit they will soon fill it [10 Aug 1848]

DEAN a boy 6y s/o Joseph DEAN of Madison ME one day last week by falling of a cart body [9 Nov 1839]

Benjamin 28 at Lincolnville ME [3 Feb 1848]

Emma A 6m d/o Thomas DEAN at Augusta ME [30 Mar 1848]

James 70y at Burlington VT on the 20th inst Professor of mathematics [*NY Tribune*]

Jonas Capt 89 at Thomaston ME [9 Apr 1846]

Jonathan Capt 75 at Thomaston ME [26 Mar 1846]

Laura 20 d/o Col Andrew DEAN at Belfast ME [24 Jan 1850]

Lucinda abt 14 at Paris ME [13 Jan 1837]

Mary 27 w/o Charles P DEAN at Danville (New Auburn, Auburn ME) [8 May 1851]

Miss at New York burnt to death in attempting to replenish a lighted spirit lamp [14 Sept 1839]

William H 24 s/o Asa DEAN at Paris ME [7 Oct 1852]

DEAN - see SIMON

DEANE Anna & Harrison youngest c/o Samuel DEANE at Madison ME on 29 Apr [6 June 1840]

Catharine B 29 w/o Samuel DEANE at Hallowell ME on 29 Apr [5 Oct 1839]

John G formerly the land agent for ME at Narraquagus of bilious colic [23 Nov 1839]

Mary F 14 d/o Samuel & Catherine B DEANE at Hallowell ME on 8th inst of consumption [28 Dec 1839]

Rebecca P 13 d/o John G DEAN at Ellsworth ME [31 Aug 1833]

Sarah Shepard 14m only d/o M C & H A DEAN at Winthrop ME on 27 Dec [8 Jan 1852]

Thankful 44 d/o Cyrus DEANE at Temple ME [23 Oct 1851]

DEARBORN Benjamin 48 a lawyer from ME at New York Hospital [8 May 1835]

Benjamin 70 at Winthrop ME on Thurs last [1 May 1838]

Edwin Burbank 6m s/o George H DEARBORN of Winthrop ME at Waterville on Sun last [16 Oct 1841]

George of Corrinna ME drowned at Upper Stillwater (Oldtown) ME [*Bangor ME Whig*] [23 Jul 1846]

Greenleaf 19 at Hallowell ME [23 Dec 1843]

Greenleaf Lt Col US Army at Brattleboro VT [1 Oct 1846]

DEARBORN (Cont.) Hannah 17 at Hallowell ME [23 Dec 1843]
  Henry Alexander Scammell Gen born 3 Mar 1783 in NH & removed to Kennebec Co ME
    in 1784. His father twice elected to Congress from Kennebec Dist; prior to 1801,
    educated at William & Mary in VA, in 1807 m Miss LEE of Salem, mayor of
    Roxbury MA when died, res of son-in-law, A W H CLAPP Esq on 29 Jul at Portland
    ME, left a widow, two sons & a dau [*Portland Advertiser*] [31 Jul 1851]
  Henry S Esq 26 studied the profession of the law in (Winthrop) admitted to practice at
    the bar in Waldo Co, formerly a physician in Monmouth ME at Hope ME [25 Jan
    1840]
  Jeremiah 83 at Parsonsfield ME [20 Feb 1851]
  John 71y 10m at Windsor ME on 4th ult [3 June 1852]
  Joseph Jr 38 at Buxton ME [5 Sept 1834]
  Louisa 58 at Limerick ME [16 Sept 1847]
  Martha Jane 24 w/o John O DEARBORN & d/o John MOOERS Esq at Vienna ME on
    20 Jul [10 Aug 1848]
  Nancy 30 of Winthrop ME at Augusta ME of scarlet fever on 7th inst [19 Sept 1837]
  Sally 47 w/o John DEARBORN at Parsonsfield ME [11 Jul 1850]
  Susan 40 d/o Frederic DEARBORN at Augusta ME on 21 Aug [29 Aug 1850]
  Warren P s/o Henry DEARBORN Esq of East Pittston ME at Rio de Janeiro on 20 June
    [15 Aug 1850]
DEARBORN - see BRADSTREET, FOLLET
DEARING Samuel Deac 71 at Webster ME [2 May 1850]
DEARTH - see KNOWLTON
DeBUIRETTE Isaac married 3 times, d 1708, head of mercantile house, DeB's from an old,
    noble, reformed family of the county Hennegan on the Raine, who, till the Duke Alba
    of Spain tyrannized over the Netherlands, had possession of a large property, was
    obliged to leave. Had 7 ch: Daniel b 1665; John William b 1668 who married Miss
    COMPENING; John North (a half brother of the former) b 1682 (from the
    Merchant's Magazine) [3 Jul 1841]
DECKER Joseph R 29 at Gardiner ME [13 June 1850]
  Kendall 34 at Smithfield ME [8 Feb 1849]
  Nathaniel at Gardiner ME [26 Oct 1848]
DECKER - see GARRET
DeCOSTER Esther K 25 of Hartford ME at Northampton MA [18 Dec 1845]
DeCOSTUR 4 sons of Henry DECOSTUR the eldest of whom 9y, truly this is an afflicted
    family, the youngest child, a dau 19m also is dangerously sick at Buckfield ME [20
    Nov 1838]
DEERING Abigail 45 w/o John DEERING of Portland ME at Augusta ME at the Insane
    Hospital [9 Jul 1846]
  George 36 merchant at Portland ME [29 July 1833]
  James 84 at Westbrook ME [3 Oct 1850]
  Jane (Mrs) 70 at Pittston ME [1 Apr 1847]
  Samuel 68 on Feb 6 at Gorham ME [16 Feb 1839]
DEETS Daniel abt 43 drowned when drunk [15 Nov 1849]
DeFOREST girl drowned at Niagara Falls [5 Jul 1849]
DeGROOT - see GARRET
DEITER - see DYSON
DeLANCEY - see COOPER
DELANO Amaziah 92 AmRev at Gray ME [28 Nov 1850]
  David P of Bath of the corps of sappers and miners at Camargo [14 Jan 1847]
  Helen M 3y 4m d/o A DELANO at Skowhegan ME [1 June 1848]

DELANO (Cont.) Jabez 87 AmRev at Livermore ME [5 Oct 1848]

Joanna Mrs 78 at Portland ME [3 Apr 1845]

Lewis Capt of Woolwich first officer of *Columbus* of Bath ME of cholera at New Orleans [24 May 1849]

Seth 87 AmRev formerly of Winthrop ME at Berlin ME on 27th ult [9 Oct 1838]

DELANO - see LEAVITT

DELANY Mr M R a full blooded negro admitted to medical school of Harvard University, the third of his color abmitted this season. [16 Jan 1851]

DELAVAN E C The brewers of Albany (NY?) commenced a suit against DELAVAN for articles published in the *Temperance Recorder*, the ingredients used so offensive not a fit drink for any decent being. The case turned on the truth of an article published by the defendant in Feb 1835, charging the plaintiff for several years of filthy & impure water in malting. And the jury returned a verdict for the defendant with cost. [16 May 1840]

DeLYON - see SIMS

DEMDSEY Dennis abt 3y at New York [30 Sept 1843]

DEMERICK Louisa of Dresden ME saved from drowning when the steam packet *New England* sank. It left Boston for Bath & Gardiner ME and had an accident with the schr *Curlew* on 31 May [12 June 1838]

DEMING Mr of Rock Hill on the Hartford & Willimantic railroad [13 Dec 1849]

DeMOSS - see YOOSTLING

DEMSEY William of Boston MA lost & drowned. The barque *William Fales*, Capt William THOMES of this port (Portland ME) was lost in Well Bay ME on Wed evening at 9 o'clock, 13 persons on board, eight were lost including every officer. Through the attention of our friend, George M FREEMAN of Cape Needick (Old York, where the barque drove) [26 Feb 1842]

DEMUTH Julia F 21 at Thomaston ME of consumption [13 May 1836]

DENHOLM Mr a merchant of Quebec Canada who started for Boston MA to take the last steamer for Europe, found on the 20th inst, near Great Falls NH [31 Jan 1850]

DENISTON Sarah 77 w/o Robert DENNISTON at Augusta ME [14 Dec 1839]

DENNARD Alexander 10y of Barthone Co AL suicide hung himself [11 Sept 1841]

DENNET/DENNETT Augustus D 18 yrs 6 mos at Etna ME on 10th inst [7 Oct 1843]

Francis 22 of Milo ME at Calcutta Asia of sunstroke [1 April 1843]

H of Bridgton ME arose at 12 o'clock at night, went down into the bar-room with a candle in his hand and just as he was opening a door, uttered a loud scream and fell dead. At Franklin House at Portland ME on Wed last [*Argus*] [15 June 1848]

James 71 at Dover ME [11 Mar 1852]

John 87 at Buxton ME [18 Feb 1847]

Judith 39 at Dover [12 Aug 1852]

Moses Esq 76 at Bowdoin ME [17 Dec 1846]

Mr of Hollis ME store house destroyed by fire on Sun morning last abt five o'clock. Mr D lost all his farming tools, 75 bushels of corn &c. The fire, set by a bro of Mr D, termed "foolish" [*Eastern Argus*] [30 Oct 1845]

Rebecca widow at Lewiston ME [8 August 1850]

Samuel 33 at Belfast ME [24 Jun 1852]

Sylvester 28 at Kittery ME [9 Sept 1847]

DENNIS Adonijah 86 of Hardwick Worcester Co AmRev & present at the surrender of BURGOYNE, under Gen LINCOLN & during the Revolution served at Saratoga, Stillwater & Fort Independence in our harbor on the 30th ult [*Boston Bee*] [10 Oct 1844]

DENNIS (Cont.) Charles attached to brig *Frances Ellen* fell to his death [*Portland Advertiser*] [4 May 1848]

Cornelius one of Parker & Whitney's waiters, met with a most painful, and it is feared, dangerous accident, last evening. With abt a quart of alcohol in a tin he undertook to burn a cluster of flies on the ceiling of the eating saloon, but the pan getting too hot for his fingers, he thoughtlessly let it tip over and the entire contents of burning alcohol fell upon his head, face, neck, and arms, scalding them in the most shocking manner. (*Post*) [2 Oct 1838]

Elizabeth 14 d/o Capt Nathaniel DENNIS at Litchfield ME [27 Jul 1848]

Ezekiel of Gardiner ME lost overboard from brig *Levant* [28 Jan 1847]

James 65 at Portland [24 Oct 1844]

Littleton P at Washington City on 15th inst house of representatives from Maryland [25 Apr 1834]

Louisa E 7 yrs d/o Mrs Mary Dennis at Augusta ME on 31 Mar [1 May 1845]

Mary B/R at Augusta ME on 18th inst [1 May 1845]

DENNISON a lad 12y s/o Isaac W DENNISON of NJ [31 Jan 1834]

Charlotte Woodman 18 d/o Maj Andrew and Mrs Lydia D at Brunswick ME of consumption on 9th inst [19 June 1835]

Harriet Newell 19 at Farmington ME [17 Sept 1846]

Henry of New York the ship *Jacob Perkins*, Capt SHOOF, from Crostadt reported on 22 inst fell in with the wreck of brig *Washington*, RIDER Capt [*Transcript*] [2 Oct 1835]

Joseph Jr 22 at Augusta ME on 4th [20 Jul 1848]

Solomon 75 at Brunswick ME [20 Jul 1848]

DENNISON - see HINKSON

DENNY George 18 of Carmel Putnam Co executed for the murder of an old man on Fri last [*NY American*] [22 Aug 1844]

DENSMORE Hannah J 26 w/o B L DENSMORE at Bowdoinham ME [27 Jan 1848]

DENVILLE John 8y at the Asylum for the Blind at South Boston MA [16 Sept 1843]

DEPEW Henry 97 a native of New England AmRev, fought in the battle & surrender at Yorktown [*NY Jour Com*] [30 Apr 1846]

DEPONTE Lorenzo L of the NY University at New York [22 Feb 1840]

DEPUTY Jacob 117y 9m 15d of Sussex Co near Milford in Delaware on 5 June [3 Aug 1848]

DERBY Jonathan of Lowell MA drowned from on board the steamboat *Choctaw* on her passage up the Yazoo River nearly opposite the Little Sunflower River (from Vicksburg Missouri paper) [5 Dec 1834]

Sarah 87 formerly of York ME at Belfast ME [28 Nov 1837]

DeROY - see BALCH

DESHA Joseph Hon Ex-Gov of KY at Georgetown KY [19 Nov 1842]

DESHON Fidelia W 28y 7m at Camden ME [29 Jan 1846]

Moses 82 AmRev at Waterboro ME [11 Dec 1845]

Sarah B 45 at Calais ME [22 Feb 1849]

DeSOTO Benardo convicted of piracy in Boston MA in 1834 & pardoned by Pres JACKSON is the master of a steamboat at Havana [2 Oct 1838]

DEVEREUX Charles B of Prospect ME lost overboard from schr *Illuminator* from Prospect for Beverly [14 Nov 1844]

DEXTER Abigail 45 w/o Freeman DEXTER at Winthrop ME on 17 Feb last [3 Apr 1845]

Freeman abt 65 at Winthrop ME on Mon last [5 Dec 1840]

Loton N 22 at at Dover [17 Jan 1850]

Nancy B abt 22 d/o Isaac DEXTER at Winthrop ME on the 2d inst [13 May 1843]

Nancy C 32 w/o Rev H V DEXTER at Calais ME [12 Apr 1849]

DEXTER (Cont.) Olive 35 w/o Stephen DEXTER at Sangerville ME [24 Aug 1839]
   Samuel of Maine seaman lost overboard from schr *Mary Eleanor* of Baltimore on
      passage from Pornambuco [*sic*] to Baltimore MD [8 Mar 1849]
DEXTER - see PETTINGILL
DICKENSON Mr of Wiscasset ME a ship-carpenter employed in Messrs DRUMMOND &
   TRUFANT shipyard died accidentally [*Bath Tribune*] [16 Aug 1849]
DICKER Aunt 100 at Winthrop ME [20 June 1850]
DICKEY Hannah R 35 w/o H G DICKEY at Vassalboro ME suddenly [15 Apr 1847]
DICKINSON D W member of Congress from TN died 27th ult near Franklin TN [1 May
   1845]
DICKSON David member of the present Congress from Mississippi at Little Rock,
   Arkansas on 9 Jul [13 Jan 1837]
   Mr at Macon GA his negro house burnt to the ground recently and a negro man, his wife
      and child perished in the flames. [21 Dec 1839]
DIGBY Levi Capt 89 AmRev at Harpswell ME [27 Feb 1845]
DIGGLES Peter at New Sharon ME [23 Nov 1848]
DILINGHAM Mr abt 21 of Camden ME committed suicide at Belfast ME [*Belfast Journal*]
   [25 May 1848]
DILL Dorcas M 9 at Phillips ME [18 June 1846]
   Enoch 48 at Gardiner ME member of Warren Division Sons of Temperance [22 Oct
      1846]
   Sally widow 88 at Lewiston ME [9 May 1850]
DILLER Isaac fell down in convulsions while at the plough, John JOHNSON carried him
   home & both died within an half an hour at Susquehanna township Dauphin Co PA
   on Thurs of last week [4 Jul 1834]
DILLINGHAM a son of Barnard 2 at Warren ME [19 Sept 1834]
   Dexter 33 at Auburn ME [1 Feb 1849]
   Edward H 27 s/o Joshua DILLINGHAM Esq at Camden [20 Nov 1845]
   Joshua of Batesville, Arkansas bitten by a tarantula, while asleep & died in consequence
      [14 Sept 1848]
   Lemuel 59 formerly of Camden ME at Belfast ME [6 Nov 1845]
DILLON Susan abt 17 poisoned herself by taking a large quantity of solid corrosive
   sublimate, which she placed on an apple, and ate as it were like food [Philadelphia
   Paper [*sic*]] [20 Nov 1835]
DIMMOCK Henry native of Limington York Co ME, editor of the *North State Whig* was in
   a duel with Dr TOMPKINS at nine miles of Weldon near the VA line on Thurs,
   exchanged one shot at eight paces. The quarrel grew out of an article which appeared
   in the *North State Whig* of which Mr D is the editor [*Norfolk Beacon* 20 Jul] [23 Jul
   1846]
DINGLEY Charles 86 at Waterville ME [25 Oct 1849]
   George 3y s/o Capt Jabez DINGLEY at Hallowell ME [12 Sept 1837]
   Hannah a poor woman, in 1717, not far from New Haven (CT?) house buried in snow for
      6 or 8 days, but at last discovered by her neighbors by the smoke of her fire coming
      through the snow, dieted a la Graham, on potatoes & dried corn & warmed up with
      chairs & tables. [5 Feb 1846]
   Harvey E 30 of Providence RI at Stockton CA on 30 Jul [9 Sept 1852]
   Lydia Ann 7 d/o William DINGLEY at Lewiston ME [30 Sept 1847]
   Nathaniel 57 at Winslow ME [18 Dec 1845]
DINGLEY - see CURTIS
DINSDELL Sarah 78 at Portland ME a widow [9 Jan 1835]
DINSLOW Cynthia 38 w/o Joseph DINSLOW at Richmond ME [23 May 1837]

DINSMORE David 77 at Anson ME [25 Nov 1852]

    Elizabeth w/o John DINSMORE at Augusta ME on 8th inst [14 Sept 1848]

    Isaac 61 at Thomaston ME [9 Aug 1849]

    Lucretia T 3y only child of Simon & Sarah J DINSMORE at Norridgewock ME [5 Dec 1844]

    Rachel 27 at Richmond ME [26 Apr 1849]

    Reuben 61 at Norridgewock ME [15 Apr 1847]

    Robert Esq abt 50 at Anson ME [29 Aug 1837]

    William W Deac of South Norridgewock ME engaged in holding a horse rake dropped down dead [3 Aug 1848]

DINSMORE - see ABBOT

DIX Eunice 14y 3m d/o William DIX at Lincoln ME [15 May 1845]

DIXON Lavina Mrs death by using laudanum & creosote for a toothache [25 Apr 1840]

    Samuel & Woodbury D (brothers) & John COLLINS on a fishing excursion, the 20th inst off Cape Neddick harbor York ME, Woodbury D 20 & John COLLINS abt 20y drowned. Samuel D only survivor [1 Jul 1843]

    slave Riot & Rescue in New York [23 Apr 1837] [2 May 1837]

DIXON - see RIPLEY

DOANE Elisha 80 at Hampden ME [19 Mar 1846]

    Rachel 73y 11m w/o Elisha DOANE at Hampden ME [19 June 1841]

DOANE - see DAVENPORT

DOAR John Capt 50 at Belfast ME [14 Oct 1847]

DOCKENDORFF Walter 70y 8m at Windsor ME [27 Apr 1848]

DODD Elizabeth Mrs 111y born on board a British ship-of-the-line in the Bay of Biscay, her father killed fighting the battle of "George I." At the close of the American war, came with the loyalists to NB in 1784 at St Stephens New Brunswick Canada [*St Andrews NB Standard*] [16 Aug 1849]

    Stephen 75 AmRev at Augusta ME [28 Oct 1836]

DODGE Daniel Andrews 7 & Helen 8y 3m c/o Samuel E & Ann H DODGE at Vassalboro ME on 23 Apr (New Hampshire papers please copy) [6 May 1852]

    Eunice G 31 w/o Samuel DODGE at Weld ME [8 Aug 1850]

    James seaman of Bangor ME 16y lost overboard on 16th ult [18 Apr 1840]

    Jonathan 79 at Sedgwick ME [30 Jan 1851]

    Josiah W 46 at Thomaston ME [8 Mar 1849]

    Morris 81 at Edgecomb ME [22 Jan 1846]

DOE Abram Cotton 20 at Bingham ME on 8th inst of consumption [5 June 1845]

    Calvin W 17 at Parsonsfield ME [1 Oct 1846]

    Charles Richmond only s/o Jedediah DOE at China ME [13 May 1843]

    D Watson Rev 38 at China ME [25 June 1843]

    Ellen Jane 17 d/o E G DOE at Augusta ME on 27 Oct [6 Nov 1851]

    Isaac 33 s/o Deac of South China ME at Mobile AL on 1st Feb [15 Jul 1852]

    Mary 88 wid/o Simon DOE at Fairfield ME [28 June 1849]

    Mary Ann 35 w/o Amos W DOE at Paris ME [24 Jul 1845]

    Mary Ann abt 20 at Hallowell ME [4 Apr 1844]

    Nathaniel 70 at Vassalboro ME [17 May 1849]

    Serena 34 at Augusta ME [16 May 1837]

    William 7y 6m only s/o Wm M DOE of Augusta ME at Boston MA [6 May 1847]

DOGARD Abraham 118y 4d at Maury Co TN, never drank spirits or was sick nor took medicine, was once bled out of curiousity ... retained all the faculties and memory until his death [29 Jul 1833]

DOGGETT Mr 1st mate & Christopher GOODALL, seaman entangled in the hawser of
  ship *Beatrice* of Boston MA while being towed over the bar at New Orleans 17 Dec
  each had a thigh broken & GOODALL died in ten minutes [24 Jan 1850]

DOLAN Thomas between Fort Independence & Thompson's Island drowned one of 27 boys
  of the Farm School [7 May 1842]

DOLAND John of Boston ME was saved the barque *William Fales*, Capt William THOMES
  of this port (Portland ME) was lost in Well Bay ME on Wed evening at 9 o'clock, 13
  persons on board, eight were lost including every officer. Through the attention of our
  friend, George M FREEMAN of Cape Needick (Old York, where the barque drove)
  [26 Feb 1842]

DOLBIER Charles Esq 54 at Boston MA on Mar [13 Apr 1848]

DOLE Abby Elizabeth 2 c/o Albert G DOLE Esq at Augusta ME [26 Mar 1846]
  Abner 83 at Limerick ME [24 May 1849]
  Andrew Capt 78 at Newfield ME [9 Mar 1848]
  D N 67 at Hallowell ME [20 Mar 1841]
  Ebenezer Deac 71 at Hallowell ME [17 June 1847]
  Ebenezer Jr 30 at Hallowell ME [18 June 1846]
  Elizabeth 33 w/o Isaiah DOLE at Bloomfield ME [20 Mar 1851]
  Elizabeth 74 widow of Hon John DOLE at Alna ME [15 Jan 1852]
  Emily Ballard 36 w/o Rev Daniel DOLE, principal of Mission Boarding School at
    Panahou Honolulu [5 Dec 1844]
  infant child of Carleton DOLE at Augusta ME [1 Apr 1833]
  John 69 at Alna ME [16 Apr 1842]
  Margaret L 40 w/o E G DOLE at Hallowell ME [19 Apr 1849]
  Mr was drowned at Newport on 16th [29 Sept 1840]
  Nancy 57 wid/o D N DOLE at Hallowell ME on 6th inst [17 Oct 1844]
  Samuel Muson 2y s/o Eben G DOLE at Hallowell ME [29 Aug 1837]
  Sarah 26 w/o Nathaniel B DOLE & d/o Rev B HEDGE of Readfield ME at Alna ME [20
    Mar 1838]

DOLLAND Rt Rev Dr 63 Roman Catholic Bishop of New Brunswick Canada on 29th ult at
  Fredericton NB Cand a native of of Ireland [18 Sept 1851]

DOLLEY Roxanna E 12 at West Livermore ME on 11 Sept [15 Oct 1846]

DOLLOFF David 81 at Mt Vernon ME on 8 Mar [18 Mar 1852]
  Richard 91y 10m AmRev at Rumford ME [27 Nov 1845]

DOLLY - see SMALL

DOLPH Harvey F of Thomaston ME at New Orleans on 23 Sept [4 Dec 1835]

DONAHUE John trial for an assault with an attempt to kiss one Mary GORMAN, whom he
  alleges is his second cousin ... The court found John guilty & fined him $1 & cost...
  [*Providence Journal*] [12 Oct 1848]

DONALD James M of crew died shipwreck & four lives lost on the schr *Cevo*, Capt Pelatiah
  BARTER [25 May 1839]

DONAVAN Daniel 54 an Irishman employed in blasting rocks, left a wife & 4 children,
  Young FALES met a similar fate on 8th inst [*Thomaston Recorder*] [21 Aug 1845]

DONNELL Benjamin B 29 at Bath ME [30 Sept 1836]
  Charles H 17 at Bath ME [24 June 1847]
  James Capt 71 at Wells ME [18 Mar 1836]
  Jane 74 at Bremen ME [10 Feb 1848]
  John 68 at Bath ME [1 Jan 1846]
  Jona S Esq 72 at West Bath ME [21 Dec 1848]
  Mary M 19 w/o William M DONNELL at Bath ME [16 Jul 1846]
  Nathaniel 93 at Bath ME [28 Sept 1839]

DONNELL (Cont.) Silas 30 at Windsor ME on 24 Aug [5 Oct 1839]
Thomas 72 at Bath ME [27 Dec 1849]

DOOLITTLE Edith 82 at Waterville ME [30 Apr 1846]
Julia Ann 39 wid/o Oren DOOLITTLE at Waterville ME [12 Sept 1850]
Ophelia 14 eldest d/o Oren DOOLITTLE at Waterville ME [2 Sept 1847]
Orrea [sic] 42 at Waterville ME [27 Jan 1848]

DORAN Mrs gas for a toothache, well the operation worked but the person died (from the *New Orleans Delta*) [17 Apr 1851]

DORE Phebe 45 w/o Charles DORE at Dover [22 Jan 1836]

DORMAN Daniel mutilated on the 30th ult at Cherryfield while charging a rock in the bed of the river also a Mr BEAN's eye were badly injured. Daniel's left hand & arm were amputated & four days later he was walking about town. (*Ellsworth Advertiser*) [22 Aug 1834]
Israel 62 at Mercer ME [21 Feb 1850]
Israel 86 AmRev at Kennebunkport ME on 27th ult [14 Feb 1837]
Jesse saw-mill & shingle machine & a barn burnt in Winslow ME near Southwick's tannery [*Watervillonian*] [19 Feb 1842]
Sarah Miss 83 at Kennebunkport ME on Thurs morning 18th ult [*Saco Democrat*] [11 Mar 1847]
Thomas 76 at Kennebunkport ME [17 Aug 1848]

DORMER Enoch of ME of cholera Sacramento CA on Nov 5 [2 Jan 1851]

DORR Cynthia A 25 at Anson ME [21 Mar 1850]
Jane 89 relict of William DORR of Hallowell ME at Augusta ME on 10 Aug [23 Aug 1849]
S H of Boston MA saved from drowning when the steam packet *New England* sank. It left Boston for Bath & Gardiner ME and had an accident with the schr *Curlew* on 31 May [12 June 1838]
Stephen S 28 formerly of Bingham ME at Augusta ME on 25 Feb [28 Feb 1850]
William 84 AmRev & native of Roxbury MA at Augusta ME [22 Sept 1840]

DORROGH Mary & Sarah SMITH, Matty SMITH & child, Peggy COCHRAN, Mary CATON, Charles CURTAIN, Mary CURTAIN & child, Mary HOGAN, Nicholas PHREMBA, Thomas MEHONY, Dennis O'BRIEN, Mary HICKLY, Fanny O'BRIEN, old lady, boy, John & Eliza HOGAN. Crew lost John DAY, seaman, Charles FORD, seaman, Mary BURR, stewardess were all lost on the *Royal Tar* by fire crossing Penobscot Bay about two miles from the Fox Islands [4 Nov 1836]

DORSEY Michael abt 20 at Bath ME drowned [8 Jul 1852]

DORSON Thomas 25 a mariner at Eastport ME [14 May 1846]

DOTEN Alvin 35 at Sumner ME [11 Apr 1850]
Mary Ann 23 at North Yarmouth ME [6 Jan 1848]

DOTY Alfred Edwin 16m only c/o Charles & Priscilla DOTY at Augusta ME formerly of Montville ME [6 Sept 1849]

DOUGHERTY James killed in the Irish & Native American (not American Indians more likely English born in American) Riots in Philadelphia PA [*Dollar Newspaper*] [18 July 1844]
Mr contractor on this Tide Water Canal injuried on the Philadelphia & Wilmington Railroad and little hope of his surviving (from the *Baltimore Patriot*) [23 Sept 1841]
Mary C 26 w/o Capt Truxton DOUGHTERY at Bangor ME [2 Dec 1847]

DOUGHTY Amos 82 at Hallowell ME [14 June 1849]
Ichabod 90 AmRev at Brunswick ME [27 Feb 1845]

DOUGLAS Solomon 22 a shoemaker at Brunswick ME committed suicide [*Eastern Argus*] [1 Oct 1846]

DOUGLASS Wm S Elder, FWB before Abiel CUSHMAN Esq, JP at Springfield 3d inst, complaint of Elizabeth B D, an attempt to ravish Priscilla N D, 10th Feb, complaint of Mary B D for a rape alleged 29th of June, ordered the former charge, $2000 & on latter, $5000 with sureties, failing committed to jail (Bangor ME) 4th inst, girls named above daus of accused, & their father, res years ago in Eddington ME [*Bangor Whig*] [23 Jul 1846]

Abigail 57 w/o Capt James DOUGLASS at East Thomaston ME [10 Dec 1846]

Albert 14, Alden M 17 on 18 May, & Alpheus 12 on 25 Apr c/o Levi & Jane DOUGLASS at Monroe ME [27 June 1850]

David 24 at Litchfield ME [23 May 1840]

Ebenezer B the son of Israel DOUGLASS, left his father's house without permission, the father forbids all persons from harboring or trusting him on his account of Hallowell ME [12 Sept 1837]

Joseph 45 at Gardiner ME [16 May 1850]

Mary E 22 w/o John W DOUGLASS at Gardiner ME [26 Aug 1852]

DOUGLASS - see BENSON, MILES

DOUTY Oaksman 44 at Sangerville ME of consumption [12 Sept 1844]

DOVE Rev purchased 20,000 acres of land in Cattaraugus Co NY with a view to settle an Irish colony [15 Nov 1849]

DOW Charlotte 18 d/o Lyford DOW at Dover [10 Dec 1846]

Climene 20 c/o John DOW [1 Apr 1847]

Daniel Rev 77y 5m of Thompson CT on 19th ult (see obit) [16 Aug 1849]

Franklin 43 at East Vassalboro ME [1 June 1848]

Hannah C w/o E W DOW at Milo ME [18 Sept 1851]

Jabez 56 formerly of Salisbury MA at East Livermore ME [1 June 1848]

Jane widow housekeeper of the dwelling house of Major Samuel GEORGE perished in the flames at Seabrook MA the house destroyed by fire on Mon of last week [16 Sept 1847]

Jonathan 87 at China ME on 24 June a member of the Society of Friends [5 Jul 1849]

Jonathan Col 61 at Prospect ME [4 Apr 1834]

Levi Esq 77 at Waterville ME [5 Apr 1849]

Lorenzo an itinerant preacher for the Methodist, native of Coventry CT & had travelled in England Ireland & USA more than 30y, died at Georgetown on 22nd inst [21 Feb 1834]

Lucinda 21 at Palermo ME [3 Jan 1850]

Mary 11 c/o John DOW at Sidney ME [1 Apr 1847]

Mary F 20 w/o William C DOW at Waterville ME [2 Nov 1848]

Noah 40 at Milo ME on 15 Nov [22 Nov 1849]

Roxanna 26 w/o Amos DOW Jr at Hampden ME [18 Jul 1844]

Sally 36 w/o Noah DOW at Milo ME [18 Jul 1840]

Samuel 25 at Wilton ME [19 Oct 1848]

Sophia 18 c/o John DOW at Sidney ME [1 Apr 1847]

DOW - see SWETT

DOWES Joseph H 42y of Linneus ME while felling trees on 30 June left a wife & 7 ch, formerly of New Hamphire [23 Jul 1842]

DOWNE Nathaniel H Capt 74 AmRev pensioner at Bangor ME [6 Feb 1838]

DOWNER Mary Ann 16y only d/o Joseph DOWNER at Newport ME [25 Apr 1844]

DOWNES Joseph 67 at Waterboro ME [3 Feb 1848]

Sidney of Worcester MA drowned left 2 ch [*Bath Tribune*] [19 Jul 1849]

DOWNES - see MESERVEY

DOWNEY Patrick 88 at Nobleboro ME [22 Jan 1852]

DOWNING a son of Rev Isaac DOWNING 13 drowned in Phillip ME while bathing [5 Jul 1849]

Charles S abt one year s/o Sumner DOWNING at (Winthrop ME) [12 Sept 1840]

Charles S abt 1y at Winthrop ME [12 Sept 1840]

John 40 at Bangor ME [11 Jul 1844]

Laura L 31 w/o Amos DOWNING at Winthrop ME on 16th ult [7 Mar 1837]

Mrs w/o Mr Amos DOWNING at Winthrop ME on Thurs morning the 16th inst [28 Feb 1837]

Nathan 21 of Auburn ME drowned at West Cambridge on Sun, employed of Mr J H HUTCHINSON [19 June 1845]

Rachel S 40 w/o Rev Isaac DOWNING at Phillips ME [20 May 1847]

DOWNING - see VERRILL

DOWNS Lucy T 29 w/o Charles M DOWNS formerly of Mercer ME at Manchester MA on 18 Jan [22 Feb 1849]

DOXTATER Peter 92 at Adams Jefferson Co NY, during the French & Indian War taken from his parents at the age of 6y by the savages and held a captive in Canada for three years [7 Jan 1843]

DOYEN Lydia 36 w/o John D & stepmother of Dorcas D, murdered in New York by young ROBINSON. She went by the name of Ellen JEWETT at Augusta alms house [13 Jan 1837]

DOYLE John Capt 35 of Belfast ME at Eastport ME [9 Sept 1843]

Michael 86 AmRev pensioner at Bowdoin ME [4 June 1846]

Perley H formerly of Belfast ME after an accident at the Navy Yard in Charlestown MA [*Belfast Signal*] [13 Jul 1848]

Thomas "the man with five wives" arrested on a charge of bigamy. In Feb last married to a girl named Eliza KEGAN by Rev Dr VARELLA. In Apr married Miss Mary CHURCH by the Rev Dr DANAHA. [N.B. the paper does not name his other three wives] [14 Aug 1838]

DRAKE - see BRISCOE

DRAPER Ebenezer during the thunder storm on Thurs the electric fluid struck an old fashioned clock in his house, and stripped it of its externals, leaving the works beating as regularly as ever. The same shock struck Mr DRAPER, stripped the skin from his leg, tore the sole off his boot, and stretched him on the floor senseless. While Mr DRAPER's mother & a neighor named BROWN were attempting to revive him they were stunned by a second shock. Mrs D being considerably injured. Another lady in the room fainted either from fright or from the influence of the electricity. At Attleborough MA [17 Jul 1851]

DRESS Mrs of Wayne township Schuylkill Co PA w/o Michael DRESS is the mother of 24 children & is only 38y old [28 Sept 1848]

DRESSER Richard 88 AmRev at Buxton ME [30 Apr 1846]

DREW Alvan of Liberty ME a carding and clothing mill destroyed by fire last week with all its contents. The mill belonged to DREW & Joseph FRENCH [*Bangor Whig*] [12 Oct 1839]

Eliza 38 w/o Samuel W DREW at Augusta ME on 15th inst [29 May 1838]

Gustavus in the county jail on Thurs night, a hatter by trade, had a wife & 4 small ch [8 Jul 1843]

Joseph 77 at South Thomaston ME [24 May 1849]

Julia Parris 11y d/o Rev William A DREW at Augusta ME on 20th ult [4 Mar 1843]

Lemuel 81 formerly of Liverpool Nova Scotia Canada at Hallowell ME (see p. 735 *Stackpole's History of Winthrop ME* by David C Young, 1994) [1 Mar 1849]

Lucinda 45 at Hallowell ME on 27 Aug [6 Sept 1849]

DREW (Cont.) Mary 30 at Limerick ME [10 Jan 1850]
    Susan 5m at Winthrop ME on Sun 23 Feb [27 Feb 1845] & [6 Mar 1845]
    William 87 at Dover NH on 15 May [29 May 1851]
    William abt 16 of Chelsea ME at sea the nephew of William A DREW, editor of the
       Gospel Banner [16 Dec 1852]
DREW - see BAILEY, BUZZELL, KENISON/KENISTON
DRINKWATER Amy 68 w/o Capt Micajah DRINKWATER at Northport ME on 11 Feb
    [22 May 1851]
    Ann Maria 37 w/o William DRINKWATER at Portland ME [27 Feb 1845]
    Captain of North Yarmouth ME, master of schr *Don Nicholas* on board at New York the
       11th inst [26 Aug 1847]
    Edward 64 at Webster (now Sabattus) ME [17 Aug 1848]
    Micajah Capt 68 at Northport ME on 29 Apr [22 May 1851]
    Olive 66 w/o Capt DRINKWATER at North Yarmouth ME [2 Sept 1847]
    Phillip Capt 40 at Camden ME [8 June 1848]
    Samuel 74 at Northport ME [7 Jan 1847]
DRISCOLL - see TAYLOR
DRIVER Mr administered to himself a powerful dose of lobelia, seized directly after with
    spasms & in 15 minutes a corpse at Wilmington NC [21 Aug 1841]
DROMGOOLE Gen elected representative to congress in VA died [6 May 1847]
DROWNING J R of Buffalo NY on the 15th ult married to Mary A STRAW this time that
    would hold him up. "The Drowning catching a Straw" [29 June 1848]
DRUMMOND Damaris 77 w/o John DRUMMOND at Winslow ME [18 Sept 1851]
    James abt 63 at Bristol ME [20 Jan 1837]
    Martha 76 at New Portland ME [22 Mar 1849]
    Mary 36 w/o Capt DRUMMOND at New York city on 18th inst on ship *Rappahannock*,
       from Liverpool of consumption, her remains were taken to Bath for interment [30
       Sept 1847]
DRURY George of Prescott, & Mr DUELL of West Brookfield, passed a grizzly bear, 1500
    lbs, which bit nearly through the body of DRURY, carried him 15 feet, bit his head
    tearing the scalp, then made for DUELL. DUELL stopped the bear with bullets at 10
    yards. DRURY was carried abt 3 miles on a litter & was on his feet again in 4 weeks
    at the date of the letter able to work, from CA written near the north fork of the
    American River, Nov last [*Amherst Express*] [20 Mar 1851]
DUBOIS Joseph of Schenectady in crossing with his team, a branch of the Mohawk, became
    entangled in the harness & drowned, a year ago lost his wife & two children [5 Aug
    1836]
DUCET child of Charles DUCET, from the effects of a scalding by falling into a hot water,
    one day last week at Bath ME [14 Jan 1847]
DUCKET John "the Tender Husband" held to bail in Philadelphia on Wed for fifteenth
    time, for assault & battery on his wife [31 Dec 1842]
DUDLEY Andrew J 22 eldest s/o John DUDKEY Esq at Waite Plantation ME (in
    Washington Co) [3 June 1852]
    Catharine R 37 w/o Edmund DUDLEY [7 Feb 1850]
    Chandler A 22 of ME at New Orleans [30 Sept 1847]
    Dr of Gardiner ME found on Fri last in the woods in Windsor, with a stab in his side. His
       body brought to (Gardiner ME) this morning [*Gardiner Transcript*] [2 Oct 1851]
    George & J C DUDLEY & W W BROWN of Hampden ME at the Adams House of
       Boston MA, robbed of $3000 of gold dust on Wed, returned from CA being
       passengers on the *Crescent City* [*Eastern Argus*] [31 Jul 1851]
    Gilman 32 at Mt Vernon ME [1 May 1835]

DUDLEY (Cont.) Gilman Capt 63y & 9m at Kingfield ME [4 Dec 1851]

Lovina 22 at Mt Vernon ME [19 June 1841]

Lydia French 31 w/o Dr Albion S DUDLEY & d/o Amasa MANLEY Esq of Augusta ME at Dedham MA on 19th inst [29 Nov 1849]

Paul Esq of Milford ME & a native of Roxbury MA at Orono ME, AmRev at the battle of Lexington [11 Mar 1847]

Rosina 27 w/o Charles DUDLEY at Farmington ME [21 June 1849]

Samuel D Rev his descendants may lay claim to a Dudley estate in England. The person not named died intestate (without a will) leaving $150,000,000. Rev S. D. DUDLEY was the first Dudley to America, to New England in 1630, m Mary, d/o Gov WINTHROP & d in 1643. He m twice & by his wives had 15 ch. He claims consanguinity w/ Robert D, Earl of Leicester, the profligate & God-abandoned favorite of Queen Elizabeth (the 1st) & from the fam of the later, person to whom we have alluded as leaving such an immense fortune, said to have descended [*Bee*] [30 Sept 1847]

Sarah 22 w/o William K DUDLEY at Readfield ME [21 Feb 1850]

Sarah E 19 at Mt Vernon ME [18 Nov 1843]

DUELL - see DRURY

DUFFY William an explosion at the Pyrotechine Works in Jersey City [17 Jul 1851]

DUGAN Amelia P 79 formerly of Walpole MA at Gardiner ME [22 Feb 1849]

DULEY Sampson S 11 s/o James Duley at Starks ME [19 Sept 1834]

DUMMER Joseph 70 at Augusta ME on 18th inst [28 Mar 1844]

Judith Greenleaf w/o Joseph Dummer & d/o the late Richard DUMMER of Hallowell ME at Weld ME [3 Aug 1839]

Richard Gorham 27 formerly of Hallowell ME at Weld [7 May 1846]

Shubael Capt 34 s/o Joseph DUMMER Esq of Augusta ME at Jackson County FL [7 Oct 1843]

DUMONT J T P 50 at Hallowell ME on 5 Oct [14 Oct 1852]

Louisa Perley 24 eldest d/o Hon J T P at Hallowell ME [22 Jul 1852]

DUNBAR Asa 80 at Warren ME [20 Nov 1851]

David Capt 78 at Penobscot ME [27 Mar 1841]

Joshua 75 at Belfast ME [11 Nov 1852]

Luther 18 of Castine ME seaman on board ship *St Louis* on 4th inst, the passage from New Orleans to Boston MA [16 Jul 1842]

Nancy abt 35 w/o Thomas DUNBAR at Fairfield ME [12 Sept 1834]

DUNBAR - see SMITH, SPEAR

DUNCAN Charles by lightning on the *Saxonville*, Capt RICHARDSON on his passage to Calcutta. The man was alias Thomas ASHOTON, a native of Edinburgh [*Boston Atlas*] [1 Nov 1849]

Col Inspector General of Army died at Mobile on 6th inst [19 Jul 1849]

Deborah 78 wid/o Samuel DUNCAN at Kittery ME [3 May 1849]

Elizabeth 30 at Bath ME [16 Oct 1846]

George W Capt 50 at Rockland ME [18 Dec 1851]

lad 12 of Auburn NY s/o Mr DUNCAN was accidentally shot [12 June 1851]

Mary Ann 34 w/o John DUNCAN at Lincolnville ME [6 June 1850]

Mr Franklin FLYE, Putnam SIMONTON, & John TYLER. On Sun last six young men, abt the age of 23 took a boat at Camden harbor to go to French's beach, Lincolnville, where a vessel lay to which some of them belonged. Four drowned & two were saved. The two saved were George HODGMAN & a brother of the Mr DUNCAN drowned. [*Belfast Journal*] [20 Apr 1848]

Sarah M Mrs 60 at Bath ME [24 Apr 1851]

DUNCAN - see WORTH

DUNDAN Patrick in railroad accident also Batt REAGAN; James O'MALLY, & James
   McGRATH [*Burlington Free Press*] [29 Jul 1847]

DUNHAM Benjamin S Rev 47 pastor of the Baptist Church of Parkman ME [9 Apr 1846]
   Hannah 52 w/o Benjamin DUNHAM at South Leeds ME (extended notice) [27 Feb 1835]
   Harris B of MA in CA at dry diggings Abaco on the 22 Sept [20 Nov 1851]
   Jane 30 at Paris ME [26 Sept 1850]
   John 60 at Northport ME [1 Feb 1849]
   Mary 29 w/o Daniel DUNHAM at Bath ME [19 Sept 1850]

DUNKERSOLY George a young Scotchman on Mon afternoon of last week on the Norwich
   & Worcester railroad near Webster [2 Oct 1851]

DUNLAP Andrew Esq late US District Attorney in MA at Salem MA [7 Aug 1835]
   Archa 69 at Embden ME [14 May 1846]
   Caroline 6y 5m d/o Richard T DUNLAP Esq at Brunswick ME [16 Jan 1845]
   Harriet 43 w/o Gen R T DUNLAP at Brunswick ME [24 Apr 1851]
   Hugh 100y 6m at Brunswick ME [2 Jan 1851]
   John 27 s/o R T DUNLAP Esq at Brunswick ME [6 Apr 1848]
   John Capt 66 merchant at Portland ME on Thurs evening [30 Jul 1842]
   Samuel Deac 94 at Brunswick ME [5 Aug 1836]
   Samuel F of ME at San Francisco CA [29 Jul 1852]

DUNLAP - see slaves

DUNN Anna 88 w/o J DUNN at West Poland ME [23 May 1844]
   Benjamin Col 67 at Saco ME [11 Oct 1849]
   Christopher at Belgrade ME [4 Apr 1850]
   Christopher of Belgrade ME killed by lightning, bayonet hanging horizontally against
      the wall, & at the moment when his shoulder was near the bayonet, the electric fluid
      passed from the point of the bayonet to his body, killing him [*Journal*] [31 Aug 1848]
   Edward murdered in the street at Newark NJ on Mon night by a girl named Margaret
      GARRETY. She had been seduced by E DUNN under promise of marriage. [14 Aug
      1851]
   Emily 16y 11m d/o Nathaniel & Betsey DUNN at Belgrade ME on 21 Aug [3 Sept 1846]
   John Jr 36 at Hallowell ME [4 Apr 1844]
   Jonah abt 70 at Belgrade ME [23 Sept 1847]
   Joshua 88 AmRev at Poland ME [6 Jul 1848]
   Josiah abt 59 formerly sheriff of Cumberland Co at Poland ME on 3 inst [11 Feb 1843]
   Louisa w/o Moses Esq at Hollis ME on the 5th inst [15 Jan 1842]
   Martha 29 w/o Aaron DUNN at Paris ME [24 Dec 1846]
   Mary Jane 18y 11m at Belgrade ME on 4 Jul d/o Nathaniel & Betsey DUNN [3 Sept
      1846]
   Nancy 59 w/o Hon William DUNN at Poland ME [19 Mar 1846]
   Rosina 17 d/o Hon Josiah DUNN at Poland ME [16 Dec 1836]
   Thomas fell overboard from a vessel in Bangor ME harbor on Sat the 15th Nov & was
      drowned [27 Nov 1851]
   Tryphena 23y & 9m d/o Nathaniel & Betsey DUNN at Belgrade ME on 8 Jul [3 Sept
      1846]

DUNN - see MORSE

DUNNELS Ira of Hamilton MA feared fatal accident on Thurs last [*Boston Journal*] [1 Nov
   1849]

DUNNING Anna 58 widow at Harpswell ME on 1st inst [4 Mar 1833]
   Hannah w/o Col John A DUNNING & d/o Philip OWEN Esq of Brunswick ME at Minot
      ME [23 Oct 1841]

DUNNING (Cont.) John the sawmill owned by John DUNNING in Charleston ME consumed by fire on Tues night the 11th inst [27 Apr 1839]

Leman 60 at Augusta ME [7 Sept 1833]

Leman abt 55 of New Haven CT at Augusta ME of cholera Morbus after an illness of 6 days [24 Aug 1833]

Margaret 106 at Brunswick ME [6 June 1837]

Minot near own dwelling on Fri last, left his partner united but little more than two yrs of Brunswick ME *[Eastern Baptist]* [21 Feb 1837]

Mrs 48 w/o Robert DUNNING at Thomaston ME [16 Jul 1842]

DUNSWICK - see BAILEY

DUNTON Dellora 30 w/o John B DUNTON & d/o Hon Thomas BARTLETT at Hope ME [7 Dec 1848]

J Mr of Franklin MA kicked by a horse on 2 Jul died on 3 Jul [19 Jul 1849]

Mary Ann 36 w/o Hartley at Concord [15 Nov 1849]

DURBIN H J Rev, bro/o Rev Dr DURBIN of NY city by a falling of a limb of a tree while passing from Greensburg Indiana to the Railroad on the 11th ult. Remains taken to Madison Indiana [4 Sept 1851]

DURBOROW W mate perished in shipwreck of the schr *William Polk*, Mr HAMILTON Capt, the Capt alone escaped *[Philidelphia Exchange Book]* [23 Jul 1846]

DURELL Obed 46 at Oldtown ME [7 Aug 1851]

DUREN Sarah 74 wid/o Reuben DUREN at Augusta ME on 23 Oct [2 Nov 1848]

DURESS Catherine Mrs & 5 of her ch drowned on board the brig *Tilton* of Boston MA, Capt GREENLAW laden with lumber from Calais ME for Providence RI. Capt G states while lying to in a gale on Fri the schr struck on Marsfield Beach (where she now lays). Crew was all saved. The vessel was a total loss, principal of the cargo saved. [14 Sept 1839]

DURGAN Alexander 45 a native of Ireland yesterday afternoon at the marble works of Robert J BROWN *[N Y Gazette]* [30 Oct 1845]

DURGIN Horace 19 at Belfast ME [22 Apr 1852]

DURHAM George of Belfast ME lost the house & barn by fire, s/o Jona DURHAM, who lost two barns though the same means *[Republican Journal of Belfast]* [12 Nov 1842]

Jane 90y 10m; Elizabeth DURHAM 89; Mary BLACK 87; Ann BLACK 82y 9m; Rebecca BUCK 80y 9m; and Jenet STEVENSON 78y 8m there are now living in (Belfast ME) & vicinity, the six sisters listed above *[Belfast Signal]* [1 Feb 1849]

Mary 25 of Belfast ME at Monroe ME [1 Apr 1844]

Mary 51 formerly of Belfast ME [25 Jul 1844]

Narcissa 19 d/o William DURHAM at Frankfort ME [7 Sept 1833]

Sarah widow 85 at Greenfield ME [9 Jan 1851]

DURNELL Henry of ME at New Orleans [7 Oct 1847]

DURRELL Benjamin 86 at Kennebunkport ME [29 Apr 1836]

Orrell abt 26y of Maine drowned herself in the Hamilton Canal on Fri evening, had received the attentions of a young man, who deserted her a few weeks since. [25 Jan 1849]

DUTCH John 91 at Salem, the oldest person of that place [30 Sept 1836]

DUTTON Almira 5y 8m d/o James W DUTTON at Avon ME [2 Nov 1839]

Benjamin 46 at Hallowell ME [16 Jul 1846]

Ephraim 63 at Augusta ME morning [15 Aug 1844]

Helen S 10 w/o Nathaniel C & Betsey DUTTON at Augusta ME on 12 Mar [18 Mar 1852] & [25 Mar 1852]

John 72 after an illness of four days at Vassalboro ME [13 Nov 1845]

Kesiah H 30 w/o Charles DUTTON at Waterville ME on 14 Sept [30 Sept 1852]

DUTTON (Cont.) Lucy widow 61 at Sidney ME on 1st inst of consumption [17 Aug 1839]

Lydia Harriet 19 at New Sharon ME [18 June 1846]

Mary 64 relict of Deac John DUTTON at Augusta ME [7 June 1849]

Mr drowned at Sidney ME on Mon evening last [11 Jul 1834]

Nancy S 33 at Sidney ME on 30 May of consumption [8 June 1839]

Robert 29y 9m at Bangor ME [2 Dec 1843]

Samuel P 31 of Bangor ME at New York NY on 19 inst [30 Dec 1836]

Thomas Jefferson of Starks Somerset Co ME left home in Apr 1842 to vicinity of Brunswick ME & left in the fall for the logging swamp, has left a wife & 3 ch. Direct a letter to William E FOLSOM Esq of Starks. Mr D is abt 37y 5' 6", rather fleshy, of light complexion, black eyes & light hair. Newspapers in & out of the state & also in Upper & Lower Canada requested to give the above an insertion [2 Dec 1843]

DUTTON - see HOIT, WAIT

DWELLEY - see LAPHAM

DWIGHT Theodore 82 formerly member of Congress from CT, editor of *Albany Daily Advertiser* & *NY Daily Advertiser* [18 June 1846]

DWINAL A Capt 82 at Leeds ME [22 Aug 1844]

DWINELL Jacob Capt 58 at Minot ME [30 Oct 1851]

DYAR Joseph of Middlebury MA killed on 22d ult by being run over by a pair of horses [7 Mar 1850]

Rev of the Episcopal Church late of Whitehall drowned at the Chasm of Ausable (High Bridge) near Keeseville NY. His body had not been recovered on the 2nd inst [15 Aug 1844]

DYER Amelia 47 w/o Isaac DYER at Baldwin ME [23 Sept 1847]

Asa 77 at Skowhegan ME [13 Feb 1851]

Asa abt 25 at Vinalhaven ME on 26th ult in a gun accident [10 Dec 1842]

Augusta M 20 d/o James & Betsey DYER at New Sharon ME on 28 Sept [18 Oct 1849]

Elder 74 at Phillips ME [8 Apr 1847]

Emily 20 d/o Jones DYER at Augusta ME [31 Aug 1839]

Hannah 100 at Calais ME [3 June 1836]

Henry 21 at Jackson ME [17 Jul 1851]

Israel Esq 64 at Cape Elizabeth ME [3 Oct 1850]

John Capt 68 at Brooksville ME [19 Feb 1852]

Jonathan 77 at Sidney ME [19 Feb 1852]

Lemuel Capt 61 of this city last Thurs from the effect of a wound received in the woods at Hiram ME about a week previous [*Zion's Advocate* (of Portland? ME)] [28 Jan 1847]

Lovina L 28 wid/o William DYER at Farmington ME [10 Aug 1848]

Mary 38 w/o Henry DYER at Montville ME [3 Jul 1851]

Mary 60 formerly of Durham ME at Lisbon ME [8 May 1851]

Mr pilot of the cutter *Veto* while engaged in firing a salute on the wharf in the hour of Washington's birthday, was mutilated by the bursting of the cannon, having both of his legs blown off. There is no hope of his recovery. At Castine ME on 22d inst [7 Mar 1840]

Priscilla S 9 d/o Christopher DYER at New Sharon ME on 15 Oct 1843 [14 Nov 1844]

Rebecca 49 at Lewiston ME [23 Nov 1848]

Roscoe B 7y only s/o Benjamin & Mary DYER he dug & ate (supposing it to be artichoke) the root of "wild parsnip - Pastinaca Sylvestra" a poison of almost electric energy at Cape Elizabeth ME on 12th (from the *Portland E Argus*) [24 Apr 1851]

Sarah 23 Sarah A Mrs at Belfast ME [25 Feb 1843]

Susan 53 w/o Christopher DYER at New Sharon ME on 19 Oct [14 Nov 1844]

Susan M 19 d/o Christopher DYER at New Sharon ME on 31 Aug [14 Nov 1844]

William 26 at Farmington ME [4 Mar 1847]

DYER (Cont.) William 39 at Skowhegan ME [4 Nov 1847]

DYER - see PEARCE, WATERHOUSE

DYSON Dunbar S of New Orleans made a draft (check or note) on a house in (New York NY), it was endorsed by George B DEITER. When the draft was presented for payment in Wall St on Fri it was found that both the drawer & endorser had become victims of the epidemic which is now raging so fearfully in New Orleans [11 Jan 1849]

- E -

EAMES Alfred 69 at Madison ME [18 Dec 1851]

> Benjamin 20th year s/o Rev Benjamin EAMES of St George ME at New Orleans [13 Nov 1835]
>
> Daniel 37 at Camden ME [12 Aug 1852]
>
> Jacob 98 AmRev at Swanville ME [11 Dec 1851]
>
> John 30 at Dover ME [26 Dec 1840]
>
> Lucy 82 w/o late Jacob EAMES formerly of Wilmington MA at Woolwich ME on 6 Feb (Western papers please copy) [12 Mar 1842]
>
> Mark 79 at Appleton ME [28 Mar1850]
>
> Sarah J 20 at Farmington ME [11 June 1846]

EAMES - see WOODWARD

EARLE Mr a young man had one arm frightfully injured and his body was so severly burnt the *Union* newspaper (Saco) well says, that it is likely to cost more lives to celebrate our independence than it did to obtain it at South Berwick ME on the Fourth (of July) [17 Jul 1851]

EASTMAN Ann C 85y 6m at Strong ME on 28 Mar [8 Apr 1852]

> Ann E 21 d/o Richard EASTMAN at Hallowell ME [22 Apr 1852]
>
> Anne E 24 d/o Richard EASTMAN at Hallowell ME [22 Apr 1852]
>
> Comfort widow 77 at Rumford ME [16 Oct 1845]
>
> David 50y Esq formerly of this county at Auburn Sengamon Co IL [20 Mar 1845]
>
> Enoch Capt 34 at Thomaston ME [27 Nov 1845]
>
> Frances A 21 d/o Hon Samuel at Strong ME on 31 Oct [18 Nov 1847]
>
> Jacob Deacon 86/87 AmRev at Hampden ME [1 Feb 1849]
>
> Jacob Capt 87 at Exeter ME [13 June 1850]
>
> Job Esq town clerk of Norway ME house fire at midnight, Wed 4th inst & Mr E (90? yr), wife, gdau, & Mr Shephard RICHARDSON's wife & mother barely escaped, fire caught from hot ashes in a wooden vessel, Norway lost Town Records, the law library & valuable books & papers, which were kept in the town clerk's house. [N.B. Often when genealogists are told the old town records were lost in a fire, the Norway records were lost in 1842] [11 Jan 1842]
>
> John 45 of Charleston ME at Augusta ME on 23d [28 Jan 1847]
>
> John Major 52 at Jackson ME [10 Jan 1850]
>
> Lydia 19 at Pownal ME [15 Jul 1847]
>
> Mary 19 d/o John EASTMAN at Bradford ME on 26 Nov of consumption [4 Dec 1838]
>
> Moses S 15 at East Parsonsfield ME [11 Mar 1847]
>
> Sarah 85 at Gardiner ME [19 Dec 1850]
>
> Thomas abt 80 formerly of Winthrop ME & more recently of Palermo ME at Auburn IL [14 Nov 1840]
>
> Willis C 22 at Exeter ME [2 Apr 1846]

EASTWOOD Palmer R late of Waterville ME minor hiers: Clara A, Caroline A & Lydia F EASTWOOD [22 Jul 1852]

EATON Affa 52y 2m formerly of Wells ME at Belmont ME [27 Feb 1845]

Barnabas 68 at East Pond Plantation [18 Jan 1840]

Benjamin one of the only two living "Life Guards" of WASHINGTON in the procession on the 4th of July in Newburg. Benjamin EATON & Robert BLAIR, on entering the church, bore an American flag, followed by six other AmRev, their united ages being 551 years [3 Aug 1839] & Benjamin EATON 85 at Cadceback [perhaps should be Goddenbackville?] Orange Co NY, the only survivor of WASHINGTON's life Guards [19 Nov 1842]

Betsey 84 at Brunswick ME [5 Aug 1836]

Ebenezer a seaman on board schr *Nancy Maria*, Mr LOW Capt of Bucksport ME, Mr EATON fell a distance of abt 40 feet from one of the yards of that vessel. The vessel was lying at Harpswell on Tues last and he was injured so seriously - breaking a leg and dislocating one of his wrists - that his life is despaired of (from the *Argus*) [3 Aug 1839]

Ebenezer Esq 70 AmRev at Wilton ME [13 Nov 1838]

Eliab 80 AmRev at Srong ME on 2d ult [10 June 1843]

James D 29 a printer at Bangor ME [18 Dec 1851]

James Moorfield 8y 7m last surviving child of George & Ann T EATON at Boston MA on 3 June [11 June 1846]

John abt 18 of Falmouth ME the coroner Thomas NORTON held inquest Sat afternoon last on John EATON's body, he had shipped as cook on board the schr *Sarah*, and had been missing from said vessel. He was subject to fits and supposed drowned (Portland *Argus*) [4 June 1851]

John Hancock 1y s/o Russel & Mary Ann EATON at Augusta ME [7 Sept 1833]

Joseph Capt 73 at Camden ME [19 Mar 1846]

lad 6y s/o Mrs EATON attempted to climb upon a cart body, crushed him instantly to death at Sedgwick ME on Thurs 22d inst [*Hancock Democrat*] [5 Aug 1847]

Lucy A 81 w/o Capt Nathaniel EATON at Camden ME [27 Mar 1845]

Lucy Perkins 18m d/o Russel & Mary Ann EATON of Boston MA [22 Oct 1842]

Mary 57 d/o William EATON Esq of Worcester MA at Boston MA [9 Sept 1847]

Mary 90 wid/o Samuel EATON at Thomaston ME [22 Oct 1846]

Mary S 59 w/o Parker EATON at Plymouth ME [3 Aug 1848]

Moses 60 dropped dead in the road at Sedgwick ME [16 Jul 1846]

Moses 78 formerly of Brunswick ME at Rome ME [28 Mar 1844]

Mr 77y engaged to walk 1000 miles in 1000 hrs [13 Aug 1846]

Mrs abt 45 w/o Aaron EATON at Belfast ME [13 Feb 1845]

Mrs of Exeter ME found almost burnt to a cinder, married but 24 hours. The funeral sermon pronounced by Rev E G CARPENTER [*Bangor Whig*, 5th] [15 Jan 1846]

Olive V 31 d/o Isaac EATON of Chesterville ME at Eaton MA on 12 Mar [27 Mar 1851]

Rowland L abt 22 a member of the sophomore class of Bowdoin College [1 Jul 1833]

Thomas G 10 s/o Thomas EATON Esq at Bath ME on 1st inst [14 Sept 1839]

Warren of Farmington ME 28 at Nashua NH [13 Jul 1848]

EAYRS Joseph Esq 35 at Swanville ME [17 Sept 1846]

ECHORD girl 11 of Black Rock on the plains gathering strawberries in a field attacked by villains, on Mon last [*Black Rock Advocate*] [29 Jul 1836]

EDDY Amanda M 15 at Skowhegan ME [11 May 1848]

Celia 80 wid/o Ibrook EDDY at Eddington ME on 23rds ult [18 June 1842]

Miss one of three ladies thrown from a chaise by the fright of the horse. Miss Eddy had a broken leg, Mrs SMITH w/o Noah SMITH Jr of Calais ME hurt, Mrs Fuller of Milltown ME escaped with slight injury at Baileyville ME on Sat last [8 Aug 1840]

Mrs abt 60y saw the flood coming & returned to her bed, wrapped herself up in her bed clothes. The house was borne down the stream & she extricated herself in safety at the

EDDY (Cont.) factory village of James F SIMMONS on Pochasset Brook River. Samuel
RANDALL called the warning but the dam gave way before he reached the village
[*Providence Journal*] [18 Apr 1840]
William by falling from from a beam in his barn at Corinth ME [5 Feb 1852]
EDES Almira 37 w/o Joseph EDES Jr at Temple ME [24 Oct 1850]
Edward H Rev pastor of the Unitarian Society in Kennebunk ME and previously for
several years in Augusta ME at Boston ME [19 June 1845]
Elizabeth Augusta 18y 4m d/o George V EDES publisher of *Piscataquis Farmer* at
Foxcroft [5 Dec 1844]
Peter Esq 83 at Bangor ME on 29th ult probably the oldest printer in the USA, resided in
Augusta many years, & published a paper [11 Apr 1840]
Thomas Col 58 at Otisfield ME [3 June 1847]
EDGECOMB Jno A of Mystic CT listed in deaths in CA [23 Sept 1851]
Joel 36 at Bath ME [23 Sept 1836]
Julia 22 at Parsonsfield ME [3 Jul 1845]
Margaret 80 at Bath ME [8 Feb 1849]
Robert 75 at Gardiner ME on 25th ult [6 Jan 1848]
Sarah 81 at Bath ME [29 Apr 1847]
William 16 & Ebenezer BENNETT 14 both belonging to Alfred Gore found frozen to
death in Alfred [*Saco Union*] [12 Mar 1846]
EDGERLEY Anthony W 38 of Tuftonboro NH at Meredith NH on 7 Oct [21 Oct 1852]
EDGEWORTH Maria Miss a novelist died on 21st May at Edgeworthtown Ireland [14 June
1849]
EDLIN Walter of Prince George's Co MD was accidentally shot & died [10 Apr 1851]
EDMUNDS Elanson 48 of Corinth ME at San Francisco CA [7 Mar 1850]
EDSON Alexander Dr bro/o Calvin E, spending a few days in this village exhibiting his
shrunken proportions. The Dr ae 18 weighed 125 lbs since decreased at ae 42
skeleton weighing only 50 lbs. The oldest dau weighs upwards of 200 lbs & the oldest
son (the celebrated Calvin or "Bony EDSON") weighed before his death less than 45
pounds [*VT Patriot*] [14 May 1846]
Calvin "living skeleton" at the time of his death his body weighed less than 50 lbs, after
burial it was stolen by some medical students at Randolph VT [26 Oct 1833]
EDWARDS B W Major one of the administration candidates for governor died at his
plantation in Holmes Co MS on the 19th Aug [26 Sept 1837]
Charles B 18 of Greene on board bark *Detroit* on the passage from Havana to Boston MA
on 9th inst [29 Feb 1844]
George L 26 at Lyman ME [3 June 1852]
Johnson 24 of West Gardiner ME formerly of (Augusta) ME at Sacramento City CA on
10 Feb [8 May 1851]
Joshua 82 AmRev at West Gardiner ME [17 Aug 1833]
Lothrop 47 at Otisfield ME [15 Apr 1847]
Nathaniel 49 at Gardiner ME [19 Sept 1844]
William & Mr HILL the two colored men with their families who had their house
damaged by lightning on Congress St near the foot of Mt Joy in Portland ME [19 Aug
1843]
EGAN Catherine 84 at Hallowell ME [7 Mar 1844]
EGERTON Sally formerly of Nobleboro ME at Winthrop ME [26 Nov 1846]
EGERY Newell W 5 s/o Thomas EGERY at Bangor ME [14 Aug 1841]
EGHERT - see SCOTT

EHLERES Gerhard killed in the Irish & Native American (not American Indians more
likely English born in American) Riots in Philadelphia PA [*Dollar Newspaper*] [18
July 1844]

ELA Mary 19 at Canaan ME [8 Aug 1844]

ELBRIDGE Otis Esq of Boston MA his name must be added to the sufferers on the
Lexington (from the *New Haven Herald*) [7 Mar 1840]

ELDEN Alcestes 25 at Hollis ME [20 June 1844]
Caroline R Mrs 24 w/o Jones R ELDEN & d/o Daniel FAIRFIELD at Waterville ME on
Thurs last [24 Feb 1848]

ELDER Francis 71 formerly of Portland ME at Clinton ME [14 Jan 1847]
Isaac 71 at New Portland ME [25 Jan 1849]
Josiah L 38 of Westbrook ME cut his throat with a razor in James CAMPBELL's cellar
on Fenwick St, he has a wife & four children in Westrook. He had been unwell for a
week or ten days & is supposed to have been somewhat deranged. It was reported
attempt to commit suicide [*Lowell Courier*, 8th] [17 Feb 1848]

ELDER - see BLACKWELL

ELDERT Hannah 23 plaintiff in a breach of promise of marriage, George WEEKS, a
widower over sixty was the defendant. The verdict in her favor damages $2000 & six
cent cost [*NY Standard*] [29 Apr 1833]

ELDRACHER Alois a German carpenter 25y of Providence died [2 Dec 1836]

ELDRED Hannah 45 d/o late Thomas ELDRED Esq at Belgrade ME [17 May 1849]

ELDREDGE Ruth H vs Samuel PHILLIPS in the breach of promise case in the Supreme
Court of Rhode Island damages for the plaintiff in the sum of $5,000 [10 Apr 1841]
Dorcas 46 w/o Winthrop ELDRIDGE at Bingham ME [13 May 1852]
Frederick his house consumed by fire & his father, David ELDRIDGE abt 65 died in the
fire at Hyannis MA (from the *E Argus* of Portland ME) [23 Sept 1841]
Peter H 45 at Portland ME [1 May 1845]
Sally 29 at Eastport ME [27 June 1844]

ELDRIDGE - see BALCH

ELIOVITCH - see BRADISH

ELKINS Smith 19 of Milburn drowned in Kennebec River while engaged in rafting logs to
the mills [1 Aug 1834]
William 72 at Windham ME [14 Jan 1847]

ELLENWOOD Joseph 66 at Thorndike ME [22 Nov 1849]

ELLET William of Townsend ME killed by the late explosion in New York [14 Feb 1850]

ELLIOT Abba Josephine 13m d/o Washington ELLOIT at Bath ME [9 Oct 1845]
child of James ELLIOTT at Brunswick ME [27 Nov 1838]
Daniel 77 at Mercer ME on 26 Nov [10 Jan 1850]
James S 55 at Brunswick ME [9 Nov 1848]
Jesse D of the US Navy 62y disease of the heart at Philadelphia PA [18 Dec 1845]
John H 21 at Thomaston ME [8 Nov 1849]
John W 79 & 5m at New Vineyard ME [3 Oct 1844]
Nancy 19y d/o Isaiah & Elizabeth ELLIOT of Hartland ME at Old Town ME on 19th ult
[6 May 1843]
Oliver 102y 6m a soldier of the French War of 1756 & AmRev at Mason NH on 5 Mar
[18 Apr 1837]
Rosanna 34 w/o Gustavus ELLIOT & d/o Rev James JAQUES of Dixmont ME at
Worcester MA [29 Aug 1850]
Simeon seaman of Maine lost overboard from brig *Ponce* [7 May 1846]
Simon abt 30 seaman on board bark *Carmeltitia* [7 Jan 1847]
Stephen 36 at Brunswick ME [8 May 1845]

ELLIS Benjamin B abt 40 at Madison ME [7 Nov 1850]
    Betsey 66 at Waterville ME [22 Aug 1840] & [22 Sept 1840]
    Charles H 45 formerly of Waterville ME at Sacramento City CA [19 Sept 1850]
    Eben 52 at Canton Point ME [26 Dec 1840]
    Edmund 30 of Waterville ME Sacramento CA on 5 Nov [2 Jan 1851]
    Elijah P 6y s/o Deac Wm E of Old Town fell from a saw mill into the river and was
        drowned on Mon last [18 Nov 1843]
    Elizabeth Clark 1 only child of Amasa T ELLIS at Augusta ME [26 Oct 1839]
    Evelyn H 28 w/o William B ELLIS of Sidney ME at Dexter ME on 7 June [8 Jul 1847]
    Georgianna 9m d/o Russell F ELLIS at Augusta ME [9 Oct 1851]
    Joseph 44 at Madison ME [21 Mar 1850]
    Manoah 74 at Prospect ME [21 Nov 1834]
    Mary Ann 24 w/o Almander ELLIS at Augusta ME [24 Jan 1850]
    Olive widow 89 at Augusta ME on 21 Feb [29 Apr 1852]
    Philip Esq 60 at Canton ME on 25 June [12 Jul 1849]
    Robert 80y 8m AmRev at Sidney ME [17 Dec 1846]
    Russell of Waterville ME saved from drowning when the steam packet *New England*
        sank. It left Boston for Bath & Gardiner ME and had an accident with the schr
        Curlew on 31 May [12 June 1838]
    Sally 35 of Smithfield ME at Augusta ME on 7 Mar [22 Apr 1852]
    Sophia Stewart 26 w/o Dr Edwin ELLIS at Farmington ME [19 Apr 1849]
    Thomas H Capt 29 s/o late Dr J R ELLIS at Augusta ME on Mon night last [21 Dec
        1848]
ELLIS - see HEWINS, RYAN
ELLISON Robert S an imposter married (by the consent of her parents), left his wife in a
    strange place without friends or money, which the villian appears to have had a
    plenty of, between $5,000 to $6,000 in gold, the rascal under the assumed name of
    Robert MORRIS is now on passage to Liverpool on ship *Ajax* in the steerage on the
    13th inst [19 Sept 1834]
ELLSLER Louis death of the celebrated clown on 18 Mar at the theatre of Porto Cabello [6
    May 1847]
ELLSWORTH Elizabeth W 15 d/o Jeremiah Ellsworth Esq [14 Aug 1845]
    Hitty 47 w/o Hartson Ellsworth at Strong ME [4 Mar 1852]
    Jacob Deacon 74 of Bridgton ME at Bath ME [15 Oct 1842]
ELMES Mary D 21 w/o Carlton D ELMES at Hallowell ME on 25th [5 June 1845]
ELMES Sarah w/o Charles D ELMES at Washington Tazewell Co IL of cholera & four of
    their ch, Mrs ELMES was formerly of Augusta ME (Taunton papers please copy) [16
    Sept 1852]
    two young men belonging in Thomaston by the names of LOVEJOY & ELMES drowned
    of schr *Granville*, SNOW Capt near George's Islands at the mouth of George's River
    [16 May 1837]
ELNATHAN Mr nearly 50y an intemperate man lived alone, in a house fire [*Springfield
    Gazette*] [29 Apr 1847]
ELWELL Henrietta 14 d/o Benjamin ELWELL at Gardiner ME [21 Jan 1843]
    John Esq formerly of Bath ME at Bangor ME [5 Aug 1847]
    Miranda 17m d/o Charles ELWELL at Portland ME [2 Oct 1835]
    Payn Deacon 73 at Waldoboro ME [5 Sept 1840]
ELY D Henry Dr on Wed last the New Haven Palladium announced his marriage which
    took place on the evening previous. Today we are called upon to announce his death!
    Married on Tues night & died on the following Sun noon (yesterday!) [8 May 1841]
EMERSON Ann 32 at Portland ME [8 Feb 1844]

EMERSON (Cont.) Benjamin D 33 at Hallowell ME [11 Oct 1849]
   Charles W 39 at Bristol ME [29 Jul 1852]
   child 6y of Saco ME c/o William EMERSON nightclothes caught fire [3 Dec 1842]
   Edwin of West Bradford ME s/o the late Rev Joseph EMERSON on board ship *Lenore* at
       Matanzas on 9 May [3 Jul 1841]
   Eliza 4 d/o William EMERSON at Belfast ME by her clothes taking fire [8 Jan 1836]
   Elizabeth 27 w/o Orrin EMERSON at Hallowell ME on Sun evening last [30 May 1837]
   Elizabeth F 17 eldest d/o Rev Charles EMERSON at Bangor ME [4 Jul 1844]
   Emily 24 w/o J P EMERSON of Salmon Falls NH at Mercer ME [5 Aug 1852]
   George of Danville (now Danville Corner Rd, Auburn, ME) working on the North
       Turner Bridge over the Androscoggin River fell from the top of the bridge, lain
       seventeen days in paralysis of the spine & no hopes for recovery (N.B. he died 1 Dec
       1840 or 1839 the s/o Jonathan & Hepzibah EMERSON according to Starbird's
       Records of Danville ME) [23 Nov 1839]
   Hannibal Ingalls 15m s/o John P EMERSON at Mercer ME [11 Mar 1847]
   Henry 77 formerly of Georgetown ME at Norridgewock ME [22 Feb 1844]
   Jeremiah 80 at Durham ME [8 Jan 1852]
   Jonathan 72 at Poland ME [16 Dec 1836]
   Jotham abt 40 formerly of Norridgewock ME at Dover [8 Jul 1852]
   Mrs of Reading MA w/o David EMERSON from a fall in barn [16 Aug 1849]
   Nancy S 24 at Wayne ME on 21 Apr [10 May 1849]
   Samuel MD 87 AmRev at Kennebunk ME [21 Aug 1851]
   Stephen L abt 21 at Hermon ME on 25th ult [10 June 1843]
   William 85 AmRev at Machias Port ME [15 June 1848]
EMERY Ann 23 residing at the lower part of the town with her mother & four sisters died
       in the Globe Mill on Mon at noon [*Newburyport Herald*] [12 Oct 1848]
   Ann T 67 w/o Hon Nicholas EMERY at Portland ME [10 Feb 1848]
   Asenathan M 7 d/o Thomas EMERY clothes taking fire at Kennebunk ME [7 Dec 1833]
   Betsey 22 hung herself with a skein of yarn [*Belfast Signal*] [5 Mar 1846]
   Briggs H 72y 7m at Fairfield ME on 10th inst [4 Jul 1840]
   Charles 22 of Fairfield ME at Bath ME [21 Nov 1834]
   Darius Deacon 49 formerly of Bloomfield ME at St Albans ME [12 Oct 1839]
   Diadamia 37 w/o Joseph EMERY at Fairfield ME [12 Dec 1850]
   Edwin Wilson 7m s/o Hon Daniel EMERY at Hampden ME on 12th inst [2 Jul 1842]
   Elbridge 28 at Belfast ME [9 Sept 1847]
   Eliphalet 40 at Poland ME [22 Jan 1846]
   Elizabeth 53 at Biddeford ME [13 Nov 1845]
   Elmira Crosby 2y 9m d/o Hon Daniel EMERY at Hampden ME on 23d inst [2 Jul 1842]
   Elvira & her mother on 12 inst went to Newfield ME in a wagon, to do some shopping &
       on their return, called at Mr SWEAT's, a son-in-law of Mrs EMERY, discovered that
       they had left the goods purchased at the store & immediately returned for them. On
       his return trip the wagon upset & Mr EMERY died as did Miss EMERY 9 or 10 days
       after. [*Great Falls (NH) Transcript*] [1 Aug 1844]
   Hannah 90 at Buxton ME [8 Feb 1844]
   Hester Ann 35 d/o Joshua EMERY at Portland ME [19 Mar 1846]
   James 20 of Portland ME at Augusta ME [5 Mar 1846]
   Jeremiah Esq 93 at Acton ME [7 Sep 1848]
   John 96 at Bloomfield ME [9 Mar 1848]
   Joseph 51 at Fairfield ME [4 Nov 1852]
   Joseph D Esq 56 at Augusta ME on 15th inst [18 Nov 1847]
   Mary Jane 30 eldest d/o the Hon Nicholas EMERY [21 Feb 1841]
   Ruth 48 w/o Maj Joseph EMERY at Bloomfield ME on the 12th inst [25 Apr 1844]

EMERY (Cont.) Sally 43 w/o Daniel EMERY at Limington ME on 5th inst [28 Jan 1843]

Sally 78 w/o Briggs H EMERY at Fairfield ME [20 May 1852]

William B 17 s/o Benjamin EMERY, feared found a watery grave [*Kennebunk Gazette*] [24 July 1835]

EMLEN Samuel Esq of Burlington NJ has left a legacy of $15,000 for the education of "colored" youths [3 Apr 1838]

EMMET - see COLT

EMMONS a child 16m c/o Joshua EMMONS at Bath ME on Sun last [23 Oct 1838]

Caroline R 53 w/o Benjamin EMMONS at Hallowell ME [8 Aug 1850]

Ellen E W 18 d/o William EMMONS at Augusta ME [14 Mar 1834]

Lydia 18 at Bath ME [20 May 1836]

ENA Gen whose funeral [at Cuba?]attended by all classes of citizens and by representatives of all foreign countries including that of the United States of America [18 Sept 1851]

ENO Hannah a little girl caught lately in the machinery of a cotton factory at Hartford CT and so dreadfully mangled died within 30 min [14 Sept 1839]

ERSKINE Mary Jane 42 w/o James ERSKINE at New Castle ME [26 Aug 1847]

Rosanna 53 at Jefferson ME retired to bed in as good health as usual & died at 9 o'clock the next morning [8 Jan 1836]

Samuel at Bristol ME [14 Mar 1837]

Sarah 19 w/o John ERSKINE at Pittston ME [10 Sept 1846]

ERSKINS Christopher 84 one of the first settlers of Palermo ME [25 Feb 1847]

ESTABROOK Mrs 66 w/o Col T S ESTABROOK at Brunswick ME [5 Sept 1841]

Rev Dr of the Methodist Episcopal Church at Fort Smith in Arkansas on 21 Jul his wife died on 24th [21 Aug 1851]

Thomas 18 occasioned by a accidental blow while at work in a lath machine at Belfast ME [30 May 1837]

ESTES Elizabeth L 34 at China ME [12 Feb 1846]

Eunice 25 w/o Jonathan ESTES at East Monmouth ME on 13th inst [22 Jul 1852]

Huldah A 19 at Bethel ME [25 Jul 1850]

Isabella M 35 w/o Jonathan ESTES formerly of Buxton ME at Corinna ME [8 Feb 1844]

Louisa 21 w/o Valentine M ESTES at China ME on 11 Jul [22 Jul 1847]

Louise 22 d/o Stephen ESTES at Bethel ME [14 Oct 1852]

Mary widow 90 at Durham ME [23 May 1850]

ESTY Danford youngest s/o Aaron ESTY of Belgrade ME formerly of Winthrop at East Winthrop ME on 31 Oct [4 Nov 1843]

Edward 68 at Waterville ME on 30 Nov [1 Jan 1839]

Mary 35 w/o Francis ESTY & d/o Nathan BACHELDER Esq of Hallowell ME at New York City [1 Mar 1849]

Mrs w/o Aaron ESTY at Winthrop ME on the 20th ult [5 Sept 1840]

Solomon 63 at Augusta ME on 27 Oct of a cancer on the face [16 Nov 1848]

EUSTIS Abraham 57 commander of the 6th Military Department of the US Army [8 Jul 1843]

George formerly of Hallowell ME at Cincinnati OH on 9th ult [11 Apr 1844]

EVANS Benjamin 100 AmRev formerly of Somersworth at Kennebunk ME [13 June 1844]

Daniel Esq 75y 6m father of Hon George EVANS at Hallowell ME on 14th inst after a painful illness of 6m [26 Nov 1842]

Frederic of Gardiner ME saved from drowning when the steam *packet New England* sank. It left Boston for Bath & Gardiner ME and had an accident with the schr *Curlew* on 31 May [12 June 1838]

H B 35 late of Boston MA at San Francisco CA on 18th inst [14 Feb 1850]

EVANS (Cont.) James a seaman perished in shipwreck of the schr *William Polk*, Mr HAMILTON Capt, the Capt alone escaped [*Philidelphia Exchange Book*] [23 Jul 1846]

Mary E 3 d/o James P EVANS at Augusta ME on 21 ult [5 Oct 1848] [12 Oct 1848]

Mr a young man employed in McQuesten's Mill near Lover's Leap in this city, this morning caught his arm in the chain used for hauling up logs, & was carried to the wheel, the chain passing over his body and crushing him in a shocking manner. His life is despaired *of [Bangor Mercury]* [21 Jan 1847]

Oliver in 1786, now nearly 50 yrs ago was granted an exclusive right to run steam wagons in that state (PA) for a limited number of yrs. [18 Mar 1833]

Sarah 10 d/o Henry EVANS at Foxcroft ME [19 Dec 1844]

Sarah 30 of Harmony ME at Hallowell ME [11 Apr 1850]

Susan 46 at Winthrop ME on Fri 1st inst [16 Mar 1839]

EVANS - see CARLETON, CILLEY, MULVIN

EVELETH Alpheus W 22 at South West Bend Village (Durham ME) [29 Oct 1846]

Isaac 83 at New Gloucester ME [21 Oct 1843]

J H & lady of Augusta ME saved from drowning when the steam *packet New England* sank. It left Boston for Bath & Gardiner ME and had an accident with the schr *Curlew* on 31 May [12 June 1838]

John Dea 76 at Augusta ME on 19th instant [30 Mar 1848]

John Henry 37 formerly of Augusta ME at Newton MA of smallpox [8 Aug 1850]

Joseph 75 at Danville ME (now part of Auburn) on 2d inst [21 Oct 1843]

Sally Hale 78 wid/o Deacon John EVELETH at Augusta ME on 24th ult [1 Nov 1849]

EVERETT Ebenezer Esq 54 at Montville ME [22 Jan 1836]

Josiah 88 AmRev pensioner at New Portland ME [18 May 1848]

Moses Esq 18 s/o Ebenezer EVERETT at Brunswick ME [4 Jul 1840]

Stevens Rev formerly pastor of the Unitarian Church & society in Hallowell ME at Dorchester MA [11 Mar 1833]

EVERETTE Charles Dr of Albemarle Co VA d Oct last, left his 33 slaves to be settled in Liberia [22 Mar 1849]

EVERTON John abt 86 at Guilford ME [12 June 1851]

EWERS Mary 23 at Richmond ME of consumption [3 Jul 1838]

EWING William Capt 26 of Lisbon ME of yellow fever on board brig *Empire* on her passage from Pt Petre to New Orleans [23 May 1844]

- F -

FAIRBANKS Amos of Somerville by the express train on the Fitchburg Railroad [*Atlas*] [20 Sept 1849]

Calvin Rev pardoned out of the Kentucky penitentiary after 4 yrs confinement for abducting slaves in connection with Delia A WEBSTER. His father, Chester FAIRBANKS of Genessee NY died at Frankfort KY of cholera brought on by exertions for the release of the son. [30 Aug 1849]

Charles Everett 17m 20d only c/o Daniel A & Elizabeth W FAIRBANKS at Augusta ME on 10th inst [25 Jan 1849]

c/o Columbus FAIRBANKS abt 2y at Winthrop ME [31 Aug 1833]

David 75 at Winthrop ME [23 Sept 1852]

Dennis 16 at Phillips ME [4 May 1848]

Elias formerly of Gardiner ME at Skowhegan ME [17 Apr 1838]

Elijah 67 at Winthrop ME on 8 May [16 May 1850]

Elijah 80th yr one of 1st settlers of Winthrop ME on 1st inst [13 May 1836]

FAIRBANKS (Cont.) Elizabeth abt 76 wid/o Elijah FAIRBANKS of Winthrop ME at Monmouth ME on the 27th ult [7 Aug 1838]

Frances Allen 15 d/o Calvin FAIRBANKS at Brunswick ME [16 Sept 1847]

Levi abt 34 of Monmouth ME left his home on the 3d & arrived in Boston MA on the 4 Nov last, any information about him may be addressed to his mother, Joanna FAIRBANKS, Monmouth ME or his brother, Henry FAIRBANKS, Portland ME. A reward was offered. [*Times*] [20 Jan 1848]

Marcia A 20 youngest d/o Elijah FAIRBANKS at Winthrop ME on 20th inst [30 Dec 1847]

Martha 72 wid/o Hon Jos FAIRBANKS at Farmington ME [8 Oct 1842]

Mary 25 d/o Joseph FAIRBANKS at Monmouth ME [13 Aug 1846]

Mary E abt 30 w/o Dr J L FAIRBANKS at Monmouth ME [7 Feb 1850]

Miss abt d/o Elijah FAIRBANKS at Winthrop ME [13 May 1833]

Nathaniel Col abt 85 AmRev at Wayne ME [3 Apr 1838]

Rachel E Jr 34 w/o Joseph FAIRBANKS Jr at Farmington ME [3 Oct 1844]

FAIRBROTHER Elizabeth C 18 at Waterville ME [5 Dec 1850]

James 80 at Skowhegan ME [1 Apr 1847]

FAIRFIELD Ann 100 sis/o the late Rev John FAIRFIELD, formerly minister of the 1st Parish of Saco ME at Wells ME on 31st ult [20 June 1834]

Catharine Ellen 3y 3m youngest child of H A FAIRFIELD at Augusta ME on May 31st [6 June 1850]

Daniel 60 at Waterville ME on Thurs last [24 Feb 1848]

Ephraim C Esq 28 at Patten Aroostook Co (*sic:* Patten is in Penobscot Co) ME on 21 June [18 Jul 1844]

George J US consul and only bro/o the late Hon John FAIRFIELD of ME at Buenos Aires, Argentina on 8 May [20 Jul 1848]

Martha 34 sis/o the Hon John FAIRFIELD at Saco ME [4 Sept 1838]

Mary 18 at Waterville ME [11 Mar 1833]

Mary 51 w/o John FAIRFIELD at Troy ME [21 June 1849]

Mr killed in the Irish & Native American (not American Indians more likely English born in American) Riots in Philadelphia PA [*Dollar Newspaper*] [18 July 1844]

Senator died [*Portland Argus*] [20 Jan 1848]

Sumner Lincoln the poet lately found drunk in the streets of Philadelphia & sent to prison for want of bail [29 May 1841]

Susan C 25 eldest d/o Daniel FAIRFIELD at Waterville ME [15 Oct 1846]

Walter abt 14y s/o Gov FAIRFIELD drowned in Saco River, near Gray's Point, his friend the s/o Edward RUMERY is thought to have drowned also [7 May 1842]

William Dr formerly of Saco ME at Exeter ME? [19 Feb 1846]

FAIRFIELD - see ELDEN, WHITMAN

FALEN boy of Solon ME s/o Mr FALEN, fell into a well 20 feet deep, a few days since. He descended head foremost & remained in that position until his mother descended upon the stones & rescued him from his perilous situation. [*Skowhegan Clarion*] [5 Apr 1849]

FALES Benjamin D 25 of Thomaston ME at New Orleans LA on 21 May [15 June 1848]

David Esq 81 at Thomaston ME [25 Sept 1845]

David S Esq 69y 10m at Thomaston ME [2 Apr 1846]

Edward of Thomaston ME seaman on brig *Hollander* at Rotterdam [22 May 1835]

Elisha 51 w/o Elisha FALES at Thomaston ME [20 Nov 1845]

Hannah 30 w/o Burton FALES at Thomaston ME [22 June 1848]

Holmes 27 at Thomaston ME [1 June 1848]

Jesse 70 at West Mt Vernon ME "New Hampshire papers please copy" [22 Apr 1852]

Samuel H 40 at Thomaston ME [20 Feb 1851]

FALES (Cont.) Stephen K 41 formerly of Thomaston ME at Bangor ME [30 Jan 1841]
    Susan 51 at Thomaston ME [13 June 1844]
FALES - see DONAVAN
FALL Hannah 35 w/o George W FALL at Gardiner ME [21 Nov 1850]
    Martha 28 w/o David FALL at Albion ME on 2 Aug [21 Aug 1851]
FAREWELL Polly Mrs 40 at Bethel ME on 13 Mar [20 May 1852]
FARGO Elisha 85 at Whitefield ME [18 Apr 1850]
FARLEY boy 8 of Coleman Upper Canada s/o Ebenezer FARLEY supposed attacked by
    wolves about 4• miles from home in the neighborhood of Steep Mtn [18 Apr 1840]
    Caleb Capt 102y 5m at Hollis NH [6 May 1833]
    William J Esq 37 at Thomaston ME [29 June 1839]
FARMER Abram 52 at Temple ME [24 Apr 1851]
    Jacob 40 at Temple ME [3 June 1847]
    John Esq 49 a distinguished antiquary at Concord NH [28 Aug 1838]
FARNHAM Alvin A 5y & Ann Augusta 3y c/o Mr FARNHAM at St Louis MO by the
    explosion of a can of spirit gas [*N O Times*] [11 June 1846]
    Enoch C 27 at Albion ME on 26 Oct [2 Nov 1848]
    Enoch Hon at Albion ME [18 Sept 1838]
    Helen 52 w/o Thomas FARNHAM at Bath ME [28 Oct 1852]
    Henry Martin 2y s/o Samuel S FARNHAM at Augusta ME [8 May 1845]
    Horace 20 at Sidney ME on 1 Nov [7 Dec 1848]
    John W 31 at Danville ME (now part of Auburn) [14 Nov 1850]
    Jonathan 81 AmRev at York ME [4 Apr 1837]
    Jotham 47 at Sangerville ME [19 June 1851]
    Lucinda 20 at New Portland ME [25 Jul 1840]
    Nathaniel 89 AmRev at Mercer ME [6 June 1844]
    William 30 at Palmyra ME [15 May 1851]
    Zebedee Capt 74 at Woolwich ME [31 Aug 1839]
FARNSWORTH Meroe 43 w/o Hon D FARNSWORTH at Norridgewock ME [2 Jan 1845]
    Parker abt 20 of Pembroke s/o Joseph FARNSWORTH Esq fell through the ice on Sat
    evening 2d instant [*Eastern Argus*] [16 Dec 1843]
    Peter G Esq 39 at Pembroke ME/MA? [N.B. There is a Peter Farnsworth in Bedington,
    Washington Co, ME in 1840.][27 Dec 1849]
    Rosaline 25 w/o A J FARNSWORTH at Bath ME [23 Sept 1852]
FARNUM Alfred 30 of the firm of Farnum & Barker of Boston MA at Rumford ME [23
    Mar 1848]
    Clement M 20 of Boston MA and of the senior class in Bowdoin College at Brunswick
    ME on 17th inst [30 Dec 1843]
    Mary Hall 35 at Alfred ME on 2nd inst [21 Aug 1838]
FARR Clarissa G 21 w/o Dr G W FARR at Lisbon ME [21 Oct 1847]
FARR Hannah 37 w/o DR G W FARR at Lewiston ME [19 Feb 1852]
FARRAR Calvin Capt 76 at Windsor ME [10 Aug 1848]
    Ephraim 60 at Ripley ME [15 Nov 1849]
    Janet 17 and 8 mos d/o Mason C and Catharine M FARRAR at Augusta ME on 7 Mar
    [18 Mar 1852]
    Janet 17y 8m d/o Mason C & Catherine M FARRAR at Augusta ME on 7 Mar [18 Mar
    1852]
    Jonas 43 of Augusta at Middle Fork of the American River CA [18 Nov 1852]
    Jonathan Esq 67 at Dexter ME [27 Mar 1839]
    Joseph second officer of brig *Cleveland* of Harmony ME at sea by a fall [22 May 1851]

FARRAR (Cont.) W Wallace 11y 6m adopted s/o Jonas & Dolly FARRAR at Augusta ME on 3 Mar [18 Mar 1852]

FARRAR - see HALEY

FARRELL Sarah 30 at Almshouse on Sun after being assaulted by her son, Owen FARRELL [*Traveller*] [3 Feb 1848]

Thomas of ME at the New York Hospital on 26 August [4 Dec 1838]

FARREN David Esq 80 yrs at Brunswick ME [18 Feb 1847]

FARRIN Mary Jane 25 w/o C D FARRIN at Norridgewock ME [7 Dec 1848]

Richard 86 AmRev soldier at Bowdoin ME [18 Sept 1845]

FARRINGTON Charles a merchant stabbed severely & lies in a critical state from a riot at Manchester NH between the American (English) & Irish, a man named John McMAHAN arrested [29 May 1851]

Edwin G W 17 mos s/o Betsey and Leonard FARRINGTON at Augusta ME on 6th inst [27 June 1844]

John 84 AmRev pensioner at Bath ME [19 Dec 1840]

Leonard abt 50 at Augusta ME on 18th Apr [1 May 1851]

Leonard late of Augusta ME Adinoram J REYNOLDS adm of est [29 July 1852]

Lucetta R 41 w/o Pliny FARRINGTON at Brewer ME [27 Jul 1848]

FARRIS Harriet N 32 w/o Elbridge P FARRIS at Gardiner ME [22 June 1848]

Hartwell 27 at Gardiner ME [30 Aug 1849]

FARROW John 90 AmRev at Washington ME [15 Apr 1847]

Martha Jane 17 d/o John FARROW at Bath ME [23 Oct 1835]

FARWELL Abby 28 w/o Joseph FARWELL Esq at Rockland ME [23 Dec 1852]

Ann 28 at East Thomaston ME [4 Dec 1838]

Capt of Vassalboro ME arrested in New York on charge of having kidnapped four Africans on the coast of Africa with intent to make them slaves, discharged, it having been proved that they entered his service voluntarily [30 Oct 1838] & [25 Sept 1838]

Capt "*Baltimore Sun* account not correct. 20 Apr schr *Mary Carver* of Plymouth MA (not ME) at Beribay, on the west coast of Africa, the officers were induced ashore to see camwood, seized & delivered over to women & ch, stripped, tied to a tree, & pelted with stones, while men of tribe boarded & murdered the crew" *Kennebec Journal* says "Capt F's res in Vassalborough, in Kennebec Co, wife d/o Joseph R ABBOTT Esq [3 Sept 1842] (see story "More of the African ...") [*Kennebec Journal*] [18 Jan 1849]

Edward Augustus 35 formerly of Dixfield ME at Sutterville Upper California in Dec last [8 Nov 1849]

Frances Jane 18 d/o Hannibal FARWELL at Greene ME (see p. 564 Walter Mower's *History of Greene ME*) [18 Oct 1849]

Henry Gen 65 at Dixfield ME [18 Mar 1847]

Josiah 60 at Pittsfield ME [1 Apr 1852]

Thaddeus H 23 principal editor of *Hallowell Free Press* at Dixfield ME [28 Jan 1833]

FARWELL William Capt 73 at Vassalboro ME [7 Jan 1847]

Z Jr 25 or 30y killed by the unexpected explosion of a pistol & was an only son, absent at the West on business for two years. He had a sister at Waltham MA (from the *Christian Freeman*) [25 Jul 1840]

FASTES Betsey Mrs at Portland ME [20 May 1836]

FATE S A Dr of Huntington IN brought a suit against a Mrs LAVALLY, a widow lady who was house-keeper of the late Chief RICHARDVILLE of the Miami Indians & laid his damages at $2000. A verdict in favor of the broken-hearted doctor of $150 [30 Oct 1841]

FATOR Stephen 82 at Limerick ME [12 Sept 1850]

FAUGHT Rebecca 67 at Sidney ME on the 9th inst [20 Aug 1846]

 Samuel S Jr 25 at Sidney ME on 11 Sept [18 Sept 1851]

FAULKNER Patrick a native of Ireland, had 2 bros in Ireland, died in Boston MA [*Boston Transcript*] [12 Sept 1844]

FAULKNER - see BROWN

FAVOR George C 28 of Dexter ME at Newport ME [28 June 1849]

 John 50 at Dexter ME [26 Oct 1848]

FAXON Mydia/Lydia? wid/o Luther FAXON formerly of Bridgewater at Belfast ME [18 Oct 1849]

FAY - see WHITNEY

FEATHERSTONHAUGH - see PEARCE

FELKER Augustus 21 at Solon ME [11 Nov 1852]

 John Capt 37 at Biddeford ME [20 May 1843]

FELL G H 25y a native of Newburyport MA on the *Falcon* on the 29th ult [news late from CA] [16 Aug 1849]

 Jesse 56 at Rostraver PA, of unusual size weighing when living 500 pounds [14 Sept 1833]

FELLOWS Albert Dearborn 7w infant c/o of Dearborn & Hannah F FELLOWS at Fayette ME on 27th ult [7 Oct 1847]

 Dearborn 40 at Fayette ME [12 Apr 1849]

 Eliza 76 w/o Aaron FELLOWS at Chesterville ME on 7 Jul [26 Jul 1849]

 Emeline D 23 d/o Isaac FELLOWS at Fayette ME [29 May 1851]

 Moses 60 at Vienna ME [27 Nov 1838]

 William E 25 of Oswego NY arrested in Canada & transported to Van Diemanland for political offenses has just returned home with $12,000 in gold dust. After liberated from Her Majesty's penal colony, he went to Oregon & thence to CA where he met with a better vein of fortune's favor. [28 Mar 1850]

 Zina C 1y 8m s/o Cyrus & Mary C FELLOWS at Augusta ME on 16 Feb [26 Feb 1852]

female sailor - see BROWN

FENDERSON Mary Ann 46 w/o Nathaniel FENDERSON Esq at Scarboro ME [6 Dec 1849]

 Peletiah 80 AmRev at Scarboro ME [9 May 1837]

FENNER James 77 for many years Gov of RI died at Providence RI [23 Apr 1846]

FENNIN John seaman 39 from ME at New York hospital [8 May 1835]

FERGUSON Emma J 27 at Gardiner ME [16 Jan 1851]

 Mr an unmarried Irishman and railroad worker, killed on Wed near the Western depot by a the bank of dirt falling upon him [*E Argus* of Portland ME] [7 Aug 1851]

FERGUSON - see GULLIVER

FERNALD Oscar W 3y of Eliot ME s/o Owen & Eliza T FERNALD burnt to death by his clothes taking fire in the absence of his mother on the 18th ult [*Argus*] [2 Oct 1851]

 Sarah 85 wid/o Capt George FERNALD at Portland ME [2 Nov 1848]

FERRAN Mrs 73 w/o William FERRAN at New Vineyard ME [30 Dec 1843]

FERRIAUD Lareut at Greene River 25 ch by one wife, no abortions [a letter from Fort Kent reported great doings in Madawaska, the French part of the territory] [17 Oct 1844]

FERRIN Rebecca 55 at Topsham ME [1 Apr 1852]

FESSENDEN Thomas G Esq the able editor of the *New England Farmer* at Boston MA on Sat evening the 11th inst of apoplexy [21 Nov 1837]

FESSENDEN - see SWETT

FEYLER George 50 at North Waldoboro ME [31 May 1849]

 Mary Ann 38 w/o Zenas FEYLER at Waldoboro ME [9 Jan 1841]

FIELD Avis A 15 d/o Benjamin G FIELD at Augusta ME on 10 Mar [1 Apr 1852]

FIELD (Cont.) Bohan P Esq 68 of the oldest members of the Waldo bar at Belfast ME on 13th inst [25 Mar 1843]

Charles Dr 34 a native of North Yarmouth ME at Plymouth MA [18 Sept 1838]

Francis of Portland ME killed in a railroad accident [1 Jul 1852]

Josiah of Bloomfield ME on Dead River a jam of logs [*Clarion*] [3 June 1847]

Obadiah 57 at Sidney ME on 9 Sept [21 Sept 1848]

Rachel 94y 3m 21d widow at Greenwood ME [12 Feb 1846]

Reuel 23 a native of Mercer ME for the last two years a merchant in Mercer d at Mobile of consumption [21 Dec 1839]

Thomas G 31 at Augusta ME on 14 Feb [1 Apr 1852]

Zachary 80 at Freeport ME [11 Apr 1850]

FIELD - see SMITH, WILSON, WOODBURY

FIELDS Ezekiel & Jack FIELDS, with their 2 sons caught in a prairie fire, the two men & one of the boys were lost in the fire. The other youth saved his life by rushing through the flames to their windward. [*Cherokee Advocate*] [12 Dec 1844]

FIFIELD Eunice 38 w/o Elbridge FIFIELD at Bethel ME [8 Nov 1849]

Hannah E 23y 6m at Pittsfield ME [3 June 1847]

Mary 83 widow at Readfield ME [16 Feb 1839]

FILES Esther Mrs widow 81 at Gorham ME [21 Mar 1844]

FILLEBROWN James Esq 64 at Readfield ME [18 Jul 1850]

Joshua 24 a merchant drowned in Readfield ME on Sun 2nd inst while skating on the pond in that town [11 Dec 1838]

Thomas 80 AmRev at Winthrop ME on 14th inst (see p. 366 Stackpole's *History of Winthrop ME*) [20 June 1844]

FILMORE Joseph one of 27 boys of the Farm School drowned between Fort Independence & Thompson's Island [7 May 1842]

FINN D Mrs of Gardiner ME saved from drowning when the steam packet *New England* sank. It left Boston for Bath & Gardiner ME and had an accident with the schr *Curlew* on 31 May [12 June 1838]

Edward 110 at Whitefield ME [22 Apr 1847]

FINSON Thomas Deacon 65 at Bangor ME [27 Mar 1845]

FISH Eliza Mrs at Bath ME [25 Mar 1847]

John O 21 at Bath ME [20 Nov 1851]

Prudence Chapman 17 d/o George FISH at Augusta ME [28 Mar 1837]

Rebecca 82 at Lincoln ME [10 Jan 1850]

Ruth 65 formerly of Bloomfield ME at Bangor ME [16 Apr 1846]

FISHER Abiathar 61 at Bath ME [20 Sept 1849]

Almira Frances 4 youngest c/o John FISHER at Augusta ME [4 May 1839]

Asa Deacon 57 at Webster ME (now Sabattus) [10 Dec 1846]

Elijah abt 90 AmRev found dead in bed at Livermore ME on 28 Jan [19 Feb 1842]

Frances D 44 w/o Capt John FISHER at Arrowsic ME [26 Feb 1846]

Jane widow of Henry FISHER at Bowdoinham ME [14 May 1846]

Jonathan Rev 79 at Bluehill ME [7 Oct 1847]

Mary 50 d/o Elijah FISHER at Livermore ME on 21 June [10 Jul 1841]

FISHER - see GOLDSMITH, joke, MOSES

FISK Abner at Wells ME [20 Apr 1839]

David 16y 2m at Readfield ME [28 Sept 1839]

Mary 38 w/o Thomas FISK at Fairfield ME on 10 Sept [14 Oct 1847]

Shubael M 25 at Parkman [19 Dec 1837]

Wilbur Rev, President of the Wesleyan University at Middletown CT [9 Mar 1839]

FISK - see CAMPBELL

FISKE Cynthia abt 66 at Whitefield ME [26 Dec 1850]

FISLAR Wm of Lincoln Co MO & free negro man, Richmond, living here a long time
caught by Capt McDONOUGH, off in a skiff, with a slave belonging to Mr CURLE,
abt to convey to IL. [*St Louis Republican*] [13 Nov 1845]

FITCH Mary w/o James FITCH formerly of Wiscasset ME at Washington ME [28 Nov
1834]

FITCH - see GOULD

FITE - see LEVIN

FITS Roswell Capt 65 at East Brewer ME [3 Aug 1848]

FITTS Sarah 93 at Bath ME [6 May 1847]

FITZ Warren C & Antonio SILVIER were in an affray that occurred on board the schr *H W
Williams*, Russell ELLIOTT master on 22 Sept last, while lying in the harbor of
Three Rivers at Prince Edward's Island. Mr SILVIER was killed. FITZ is abt 17y
whose paretnts reside at Cabotville, Springfield, P.E.I. [*Boston Journal*] [14 Oct
1847]

FITZGERALD George Esq 75 at Fairfield ME [3 Jul 1851]
John 44 at Portland ME [28 Nov 1844]
Michael 62 at Foxcroft ME [26 Apr 1849]

FITZGERALD - see WOOD

FLAGG Caroline 22 at Winslow ME [4 Jul 1850]
Elizabeth M 28 w/o James FLAGG 2nd at Augusta ME [11 Jul 1837]
Fanny Widow 67 at Benton ME on 24 Apr [1 May 1851]
Lydia P 42 at Dover ME [3 Jul 1845]
Mary Frances 8m only d/o Benjamin R & Mary A FLAGG at Augusta ME on 25 Apr [2
May 1850]
Mr of NH jumped from a window on the third story of the tavern of Mr HASEY in
Bangor ME on Fri afternoon & broke his thigh in two places. Was still alive at press
time. (from the *Bangor Whig* of Saturday) [16 May 1840]
Timothy Esq of the firm of Flagg & Gould, printers at Andover MA [24 June 1833]
Vester G (WILLIAMS) 45 w/o Nehemiah FLAGG at Augusta ME on Tues last (see p.
298, *Vital Records of Augusta, ME, to 1892,* Auburn: Merrill & Webber Co., 1933-
34, by Ethel Colby Conant.) [30 Aug 1849]

FLAGG - see BARBER

FLAGNER Henry 30 at Belfast ME [22 Apr 1852]

FLANAGAN John seaman 34y of New York belonged to the US ship *Preble* & died with
the Africa fever at Porto Grande Island of St Vincent Cape de Verds on 12 Dec [10
Apr 1845]

FLANDERS Daniel W 21 of Sangerville ME at Charlestown MA [22 May 1851]
Jeremiah 64 at Garland ME [4 May 1848]
Mary A d/o Rev Thomas FLANDERS at Sangerville ME [27 Aug 1846]
Moses 55 at Cornville ME [30 Jan 1845]
Thomas Jr 24 at Cornville ME on Sun 23rd ult [12 Sept 1840]

FLANNEGAN John abt 60 at Bangor ME by lightning [15 May 1852]

FLEMING John killed in a railroad accident [31 Aug 1839]

FLETCHER Anna 53 at Augusta ME [20 Feb 1835]
Betsey Ellen 3y 3m d/o Merriam A & Ahusha B FLETCHER at Palermo ME on 13 Apr
[22 Apr 1852]
Charlotte & her bro, deck passengers of England on board the steamboat *George Collier*
on the 6th inst on her passage from New Orleans to St Louis MO [25 May 1839]
Ephraim abt 70 one of the electors for president in 1832 at Lincolnville ME [11 Dec
1835]

FLETCHER (Cont.) Hannah 67 at Lincolnville ME [28 May 1842]

    Hannibal 22 from bleeding at the lungs at Bingham [23 Sept 1836]

    Jeremiah 83 at Wilton ME on the 14th Oct [7 Dec 1839]

    Levi Esq formerly of Bingham ME at Charleston MO [8 Oct 1846]

    Lois 46y 10m w/o Joseph FLETCHER at Searsmont ME on 25 June [9 Jul 1846]

    Lydia 26 w/o Joseph FLETCHER at Augusta ME [30 Aug 1849]

    Lydia abt 28 at Augusta ME [9 May 1844]

    Mr of Quincy MA & Mr GROVER both killed last evening (20th inst) digging a well [*Bay State Dem*] [7 Oct 1843]

    Parker 65 at Augusta ME [23 Mar 1848]

    Rebecca abt 60 at Augusta ME on 20 Jan [24 Jan 1850]

    Rhoda 41 at Bloomfield ME [5 Dec 1837]

    Robert 92 the oldest man at Augusta ME [14 Sept 1848]

    Susan 48 w/o Capt F FLETCHER at Augusta ME [26 Sept 1837]

    widow 98 at Bloomfield ME [18 Jan 1849]

    William 46 at Bloomfield ME [5 Dec 1837]

    William Esq 48 at Linconville ME [17 Oct 1850]

FLING - see ROLERSON

FLINT Betsey widow 86 at Strong ME [3 Dec 1846]

    Levi 88 AmRev pensioner formerly of Norridgewock ME at Sebasticook ME [27 Mar 1845]

    Nehemiah abt 55 at Norridgewock ME on 29 Mar [11 Apr 1850]

    Sarah 66 w/o Dr Thomas FLINT at Farmington ME [24 Aug 1833]

    Sarah J 23 w/o Francis FLINT at Waterville ME [24 Oct 1850]

FLINT - see LARKIN

FLITNER Francis Esq 76 at Pittston ME [18 Apr 1850]

FLOOD John of Eastport ME body found drowned at the end of Mr Marks' wharf in St Stephen [19 Aug 1847]

FLOWERS John F 4 s/o Capt John FLOWERS at Belfast ME [30 Sept 1847]

FLOYD Betsey 36 w/o Nathaniel FLOYD at Hallowell ME [29 Aug 1834]

    Eliza Ann 26 at Winthrop ME on Fri of last week (see p. 368 Stackpole's *History of Winthrop ME*) [21 May 1842]

    Mary 63 wid/o Samuel FLOYD at Saco ME [31 Oct 1850]

    Mr a bricklayer 57y of Romsey "the heaviest man in England exceeded 32 stones or 348 pounds" died on 17th inst [28 Oct 1842]

FLY Elijah 52 at Unity ME [19 Feb 1852]

    John A 40 of Cornish ME while engaged in walking on the bridge across the Ossipee River near Col John WARREN's accidentally struck on the head by a stick of timber & immediately precipitated into the river & drowned, left a wife & children on Mon the 22d inst [*Eastern Argus*] [9 Jul 1846]

FLYE Ephraim S 45 at Camden ME [25 Jul 1850]

    Franklin, also: Putnam SIMONTON, John TYLER & Mr DUNCAN, on Sun last 6 men, abt the age of 23 took a boat at Camden harbor to go to French's beach, Lincolnville, where a vessel lay. Four drowned & two were saved. 2 saved: George HODGMAN & a bro of the Mr DUNCAN drowned. [*Belfast Journal*] [20 Apr 1848]

FOGG Abigail C w/o Samuel L FOGG at Auburn ME [11 June 1846]

    boy 7 of Wales ME s/o Moses FOGG formerly of (Augusta) ME killed by a cart accident [11 Nov 1843]

    Dudley Jr 22 s/o Dudley FOGG at Readfield ME [22 June 1839]

    Elias 27 at Saco ME [20 Jan 1848]

    Ephraim 69 at Augusta ME on 21st inst of consumption [4 Jul 1844]

FOGG (Cont.) Harriet 52 w/o Phineas FOGG at Appleton ME on 17th May [27 May 1852]

Isaac 63 at Limerick ME [11 Feb 1847]

Jane 27 at Augusta ME on 9th inst [18 Nov 1852]

Jesse L 47 at Monmouth ME [7 June 1849]

Jonathan Esq of Montville ME his joiner's shop struck by lightning, no insurance [3 Aug 1841]

Joseph 45 at Readfield ME on 17th inst [28 Aug 1842]

Mary 19 d/o Levi FOGG at Brunswick ME on Sat last of consumption [12 June 1836]

Mary 28 w/o Timothy FOGG & d/o John MILLER Esq at Thomaston ME [20 Nov 1835]

Mary 63 relict of Ephraim FOGG at Augusta ME [30 Sept 1847]

Mary Ann 28 w/o Samuel C FOGG at Readfield ME on 2 Dec [19 Dec 1850]

Mary of Eliot ME on her way home from Portsmouth NH to Eliot ME with Dr WILLIS in a wagon accident, she broke her lower jaw in two places, injured her eye & it is feared she was harmed internally. Dr W fortunately escaped unhurt [*Portsmouth Messenger*] [14 June 1849]

Nancy 23 at Gardiner ME [29 Mar 1849]

Newell 60/66y on 16 May (see p. 58 Harry H Cochrane's *History of Monmouth & Wales ME*) [24 May & 7 June 1849]

Olive F 83 wid/o Rev Caleb FOGG at Monmouth ME [14 Aug 1845]

Ruth 83 w/o Samuel FOGG at Cornville ME [18 Feb 1846]

S D Capt of East Winthrop ME "The person who took a pair of ladies shoes from Masonic Hall at the late Cattle Show & Fair is requested to leave them with the owner" [14 Nov 1840]

Samuel 76 at Freeport ME [16 May 1837]

Samuel D 30 at Winthrop ME [29 June 1848]

Sarah Elizabeth 16 d/o Dr James FOGG at Limerick ME [25 Sept 1851]

Solomon H 22 at Bath ME [21 Oct 1836]

Tabitha 57 wid/o Isaac FOGG at Limerick ME [30 Aug 1849]

Washington M 5 s/o Capt Robinson FOGG at Bath ME [8 Aug 1844]

FOLEY Thomas of Bath ME a native of Ireland, left a wife & a large family of ch [*Bath Tribune*, 9th] [15 Feb 1849]

FOLGER Harriot 9y 8m d/o Uriah A FOLGER at Sidney ME on 8 Jan [21 Jan 1843]

Mary Ellen 10m d/o Francis M & Eliza J FOLGER at Augusta ME on 1 Oct [7 Oct 1852]

Mary Frances 5y d/o Uriah A FOLGER at Sidney ME on 18th inst [28 Jan 1847]

FOLKS John seaman of New York lost in a sea disaster on the brig *Linden*, GRIFFITH Capt [19 Nov 1842]

FOLLANSBEE Abiel P 76 at Waterville ME [4 Mar 1852]

Mayo 30 w/o Charles FOLLANSBEE at New Sharon ME [18 Mar 1847]

FOLLETT/FOLLET Jesse Jr abt 17 a runaway apprentice from George H DEARBORN of East Winthrop ME [14 Aug 1835]

Lewis 60 at Paris ME [22 Oct 1846]

Michael late of Winthrop ME his minors, heirs were: Mary FOLLET; Abigail SUTHERLAND; June FOLLET; Sophrona FOLLET & Rhenance FOLLET [28 Aug 1835]

Miss 3 children of Mrs FOLLETT passengers lost or missing on 7th inst when the steamboat *New York*, bound from Galveston to New Orleans was wrecked in a hurricane, 17 persons drowned [24 Sept 1846]

Sophronia 18 at (Winthrop ME) on Mon last after a short illness [3 Oct 1840]

FOLSOM Abigail widow 85 at Strong ME [23 Jul 1846]

Ann G L 32 w/o William FOLSOM Esq at Madison ME [10 Jul 1851]

Ann Quincy 37 d/o Nathan B FOLSOM of Bangor ME at Etna ME [17 June 1847]

Augusta A 22 d/o James FOLSOM at Augusta ME [4 Apr 1850]

FOLSOM (Cont.) Benjamin 43 editor & publisher of the *Eastport Sentinel* at Eastport ME on 9 Jul [22 Jul 1833]

Dennis H two months s/o Robert H & Vashti A FOLSOM at Winthrop ME on 29 Sept [7 Oct 1847]

Eliphalet abt 50 at Monmouth ME on Mon last [3 Jul 1841]

Hiram Esq 48 at Monson ME [12 Aug 1852]

Jackson Jr abt 21 at Mercer ME [10 June 1847]

John L 43y 6m s/o Peter S FOLSOM Esq of Mt Vernon ME at Lowell MA on 5 Apr [22 Apr 1852]

John L 43y 6m s/o Peter S FOLSOM Esq of Mt Vernon ME at Lowell MA [22 Apr 1852]

Margaret Quimby 22 d/o Israel FOLSOM at Strong ME on 16 Sept [23 Dec 1847]

Mr a workman at the Upper Stream Mill at Bath ME drowned on Wed last [6 Nov 1838]

Nancy Albina 14y 29d at Augusta ME of consumption [15 Apr 1847]

Sally 54 w/o Nathan B FOLSOM at Bangor ME [16 May 1844]

Samuel 88 at Cornville ME [7 Mar 1850]

Samuel L 38y 6m s/o Peter S FOLSOM Esq of Mt Vernon ME at Lowell MA on 26 Jul [22 Apr 1852]

Stephen 30 at Eastport ME [13 Aug 1846]

FOOTE Mary A 59 w/o Capt William P FOOTE at Waterville ME [17 June 1847]

Merchant Ranger 3y 10m s/o William & Rosanna FOOTE at Wilton ME on 7 Mar [18 Mar 1847]

Susan 56 w/o William FOOTE at Bath ME [2 Dec 1847]

William 63 at Bath ME [19 Feb 1852]

FOOTMAN Charles 5 s/o Orin & Sarah FOOTMAN at St Albans ME drowned [30 Aug 1849]

FORBES Daniel 75 at Paris ME [29 June 1848]

Hannah 92 at Paris ME on 10 Jan [16 Mar 1839]

Lovina 20 at Brooks ME [5 Sept 1850]

William late of Benton ME, est notice, John B CLIFFORD adm [25 Mar 1852]

FORBES - see BADLAM

FORD Abby E 15y & 6m at Gardiner ME [24 June 1847]

Abigail M of Boston MA, died at Augusta ME on 26th ult on her way to visit her friends at Mt Vernon ME & her remains were taken to that place (Mt. Vernon). [11 Dec 1845]

Abner 93 at Mayfield ME on 22 May [4 Jul 1850]

Agnes C 24 w/o R H FORD at Wayne ME [14 Nov 1840]

Betsey 46 w/o James FORD at East Livermore ME [23 Aug 1849]

Charles 88 AmRev died at Sumner ME. Moved from Pembroke MA in 1783 to Sumner, then a wilderness [18 June 1846]

Charles E 24 s/o Dr E J FORD of Gardiner ME at Boston MA [4 Nov 1847]

Elisha J Jr 25 at Gardiner ME [6 Nov 1845]

Eliza Ann C 33 w/o C A FORD at Waterford ME [25 Mar 1847]

George 36 at Limerick ME [7 Dec 1848]

Henry (the boy) perished on the schr *Thomas*, SPROULE Capt of Belfast ME [25 Mar 1843]

John 93 AmRev at Sturbridge MA, under Gen GATES in 1777, at Ticonderoga & a veteran who compelled Gen BURGOYNE to surrender his army [28 Aug 1845]

John formerly of Hallowell ME a laborer on the water works in Boston MA on the 16th inst by the falling of a stone blown from the ledge in which he was at work [*Boston Traveller*] [24 Aug 1848]

Lydia (SIMONS) 82y wid/o Nathaniel FORD formerly of Duxbury MA at Readfield ME (see p. 746 Stackpole's *History of Winthrop ME* 1994) [13 Nov 1838]

FORD (Cont.) Mary Ann 19y 10m d/o Benjamin FORD at Sangerville ME [22 Aug 1850]
    Ruth 70 at Readfield ME [25 Feb 1847]
    Sophia 47 w/o Robert FORD at Readfield ME on 19 May [13 June 1850]
    William Jr 62 (s/o William & Elizabeth [TARR] FORD) at Lewiston ME [5 Feb 1852]
    William R 20 s/o Marshall & Susan FORD at Lewiston ME [8 Jan 1852]
FORD - see DORROGH
FORESTER Thomas Dr 83 at Limington ME [1 Mar 1849]
FORSYTH John Hon, secretary of state under Van Buren's administration died at
    Washington last night as he has been sick for some time with bilious fever [30 Oct
    1841]
FORWARD John fireman crew lost & missing on 7th inst when the steamboat *New York*,
    bound from Galveston to New Orleans was wrecked in a hurricane, 17 persons
    drowned [24 Sept 1846]
FOSBENNER - see MOORE
FOSS a child 3y c/o Thomas D FOSS at Saco ME [12 Dec 1837]
    Charles L 19 at Buxton ME of consumption [11 Jul 1840]
    Christopher C Esq 34 at Milo ME the postmaster of that place [16 Dec 1843]
    Clarrisa 21 w/o John FOSS at Monmouth ME on 15 Aug [22 Aug 1850]
    David 24/21 at Waldo ME [27 May 1852]
    Eleanor 44 w/o Joseph FOSS at Saco ME [28 Feb 1850]
    Elizabeth 19 at Hollis ME [6 Feb 1845]
    Elizabeth d/o Thomas FOSS at St Albans ME [3 Apr 1851]
    Joseph 76 at Saco ME [12 Apr 1849]
    Joseph Col at Wales ME [26 Dec 1850]
    Louisa B 10 d/o Jabez FOSS at St Albans ME [16 Jul 1846]
    Margaret Laura 12y 9m d/o Rev Walter FOSS at Leeds ME on 25 Feb of erysipelas [11
    Mar 1852]
    Mary 79 widow at Saco ME [6 June 1850]
    Mehitable w/o Uriah FOSS at Winthrop ME [14 Feb 1850]
    Mrs 41 w/o Asa FOSS Esq left a husband & 4 ch at Wayne ME on Jan last [27 Mar
    1835]
    Oren 20 s/o Jeremiah FOSS of Wayne ME at Quincy MA [30 Oct 1841]
    Phinehas Harmon whereas my son, Phinehas H FOSS, has left without my consent ....
    Phinehas FOSS of Livermore ME on 1 Apr 1835 [3 Apr 1835]
    William 15 or 16 of Portland ME nephew of Capt THOMAS saved when the barque
    William Fales, Capt William THOMES of this port (Portland ME) was lost in Well
    Bay ME on Wed evening at 9 o'clock, 13 persons on board, eight were lost including
    every officer. Through the attention of our friend, George M FREEMAN of Cape
    Needick (Old York, where the barque drove) [26 Feb 1842]
FOSTER Abigail 32 w/o Franklin FOSTER at Boston ME on the 25th ult [6 Nov 1838]
    Abigail 35 at Belfast ME [24 Apr 1846]
    Abigail 40 d/o Otis FOSTER at Winthrop ME [3 Oct 1844]
    Anna 58 w/o Capt Benjamin FOSTER at Bowdoin ME [6 Feb 1845]
    Anna 84 w/o Asa FOSTER at Newry ME [18 Sept 1851]
    Charles abt 36 native of Winthrop ME & formerly of Boston MA at Hallowell ME on Fri
    evening the 25th of May [17 Jul 1838]
    Daniel 70 Naval officer at Newburyport MA, a subordinate officer of the troops under the
    command of Gen LAFAYETTE [7 Sept 1833]
    Daniel M 29 at Pittsfield ME [13 Jul 1848]
    Edward 28 of VT at San Francisco CA on 7 Oct [20 Nov 1851]
    Ezekiel Gen 47 at Pembroke of consumption [28 Oct 1843]
    Frances S 23 d/o Thos FOSTER at Bristol ME [6 Jan 1848]

FOSTER (Cont.) Hannah 94 at Chesterville ME [28 May 1846]

James Deacon 80y 6m at Augusta ME on 10th Aug [17 Aug 1848]

John A 25 at Leeds ME on 29 June [7 Aug 1845]

John of Bristol ME seaman lost overboard from schr *Ashland* [7 May 1846]

Joseph S Esq 62 at Poland ME [11 Mar 1852]

lad s/o Maximillen FOSTER drowned on Sun of last week at Canaan ME [15 Jul 1847]

Margaret S 27 w/o Charles FOSTER at Brunswick ME [15 May 1845]

Mary 46 w/o Ichabod FOSTER Esq at Presque Isle Plantation Aroostook Co ME [24 Jul 1845]

Mary 58 at Thomaston ME [26 Sept 1850]

Mary 82 formerly of Kingston MA wid/o Capt Samuel FOSTER at Vassalboro ME on 29 Feb (Massachusetts papers please copy) [18 Mar 1852]

Mr the murderer of his wife acquitted and set free, but only for a minute or two, tried for the murder of his wife last year, whom he killed with a negro whip. He was a planter worth $90,000 & gave Eli HUSTON, one of our first lawyers $3,000 to get him clear of the gallows ... a mob whipped, tarred & feathered him ... at Natchez [13 Feb 1835]

N B Esq Esq at Belfast ME [24 Apr 1845]

Nancy Mrs 62 at Belfast ME [19 Feb 1852]

Parker 85 AmRev at Elliot ME [21 May 1846]

Rachel F 83 formerly of Nantucket wid/o Steward FOSTER of Winthrop ME Litchfield ME [11 May 1848]

Richard 57 at Bremen ME [24 June 1847]

Sarah 29 w/o Herman FOSTER & d/o Zadoc DAVIS at Bangor ME on 27th ult [14 Aug 1841]

Stephen 76 1st white child ever born in Winthrop ME at Winthrop ME [16 Apr 1842]

Stephen C 28 of the state convention lately held in CA, born at East Machias ME removed to MO thence to Pueblo de los Angelos CA & in CA three years. [29 Nov 1849]

Steuart 83 at Winthrop ME on 21st inst [24 Aug 1839]

widow 94 at Chesterville ME [11 June 1846]

William H being engaged in clearing a jam of logs, slipped & fell into the river & drowned, at Kezar Falls, Ossipee River in Parsonsfield ME [7 May 1846]

FOSTER - see BUCKNER

FOWLE Charlotte 48 at Hallowell ME [12 June 1833]

FOWLER Alexander H organ-builder of this city (New York) was reported "another survivor from the *Lexington*!" then reports come from Mobile printed in the *NY Journal of Commerce* that the letter had been a hoax, written for the poor motive of adding to the trouble of his widow. [4 Jul 1840]

Bartholomew D 27 at Skowhegan ME [13 May 1852]

George W, E S FOWLER, Charles S PARSONS, & Hiram HARDISON of Sangerville ME tried to cross the Aroostook River on a raft, Geo FOWLER drowned. C S PARSONS, E FOWLER & H HARDISON got ashore to safety at St Croix River. [13 Jul 1839]

Isaac C of brig *Belfast* from Searsport ME at San Francisco CA on 6 Jan [21 Mar 1850]

Jedediah 69 at Pittsfield ME [15 Jul 1852]

Matthew/Mathew 80/79y AmRev pensioner at Unity ME on 27 Apr [14/28 May 1842]

Mr was found dead from poison, had purchased and swallowed 2 ounces of laudanum. They tried to save him the usual ways without effect. It was recommended to use electricity. The wire was applied to the chest, and a shock given him, when he rose up, but sank slowly back again. Another shock was given, when he rose up and exlaimed "oh!" and again fell back. On the 3rd shock he rose up and remained in a

FOWLER (Cont.) sitting posture. He soon asked for drink, and was supplied with tea and coffee. In the course of an hour he had almost entirely recovered. [13 Jul 1839]

Rebecca 55 at Hallowell ME [1 Feb 1844]

Susannah (STACY) 51 formerly of Winthrop ME (wife of Joseph FOWLER, see p. 385 *Stackpole's History of Winthrop ME*) at Sangerville ME on Sun last [31 Aug 1833]

William P formerly of Augusta ME at Brunswick ME [29 Apr 1847]

FOWLER - see JONES, PEARCE, SAWYER

FOWLER - see PARSONS

FOWLEY John 19 at Gardiner ME [19 June 1851]

FOX Charles J Esq 30 author of the sketches of the West Indies & history of Dunstable died at Nashua on Tues of consumption [26 Feb 1846]

Daniel of Sebasticook ME accident in the woods on Tues last died on Fri [*People's Press*] [4 Mar 1847]

Elijah 86 at Monmouth ME [24 June 1847]

Henry & Jonathan NIXON & John RICKET the 3 men drowned by a deluge of water while working nearly three hundred feet underground at the bottom of a coal mine near Pottsville PA called the Spohn's tract. The 1st account named "Three Englishmen NINON, FOX & (name missing)" drowned [15 Aug 1844] [22 Aug 1844]

Mr the British Minister about to marry a sister of the Russian Minister's lady, the Miss WILLIAMS. The bridegroom in this match, should it occur, will be age abt 50, the bride abt 16 [1 May 1841]

FOX - see HARE

FOY Dolly S 59 w/o John L FOY at Gardiner ME [15 Aug 1850]

Mary J 34 at Gardiner ME [3 Jul 1851]

FOYE lad Fri in Fore St in a fatal affray between some lawless youngsters & several fisherman whom they attacked in the street. The latter retired to their vessels but being pursued one of them procured a gun loaded with shot which he discharged among the assailants. It hit a lad named FOYE who died (as told by the *Zion's Advocate*) [2 Nov 1839]

Lucy 77 relict of John FOYE of Augusta ME at Hallowell ME on 12 Oct [13 Nov 1838]

sons two s/o J G FOYE in Brunswick ME poisoned on Thurs by eating the roots of American Hemlock (*Cicuta Maculata*) which they found in a brook near their dwelling ... they are expected to recover [*Brunswick Journal*] [23 Apr 1846]

William 30 at Wiscasset ME [29 Jul 1847]

FRANCIS Catharine Rebecca 31 w/o Charles S FRANCIS & d/o Jesse JEWETT Esq of Windsor ME at New York City on 14th inst [25 Sept 1841]

Mary R 55 wid/o Major FRANCIS at Bangor ME [20 Feb 1845]

Robert 92y at Hallowell ME, born 27 Jul 1742 at Astrid England [28 Nov 1834]

William Major 65 formerly of Portland ME [25 Jan 1844]

FRANCIS - see ARNOLD, HAZELINE

FRANCISCO Manuel a boy of Maderia belonged to the US ship *Preble* & died with the Africa fever at Porto Grande Island of St Vincent Cape Verde 11 Dec [10 Apr 1845]

FRANKLIN Benjamin sketch by George BANCROFT [30 Jan 1841]

Cornelius E 16 of Attleborough MA of the crew of the schr *Woodcock*, CLEMENTS, master, arrived the day before from the straits of Belle Isle at Mt Desert on Mon the 3rd two boys were crossing to Cranberry Isle ME in an open boat, this sailboat capsized, one drowned & one saved J H HUTCHINGS of Kennebunk ME 13 was the saved lad (from the *Portland Advertiser*) [22 Oct 1842]

Eleanor Ann (PORDEN) born 1795 w/o Sir Jan FRANKLIN [4 Mar 1852]

John Sr in search of by Moses H GRINNELL [21 Feb 1850]

FRANKLIN (Cont.) Walter S, clerk of the US House of Representatives at Lancaster PA [9 Oct 1838]

FRANKLIN - see BABCOCK, VAUGHAN

FRAZIER William 31 formerly of Boston MA at Gardiner ME [18 Jul 1837]

FREDERICK Diantha M 7y 9m d/o William & Rhoda FREDERICK at Starks ME on 23 Dec [24 Jan 1850]

    family lost in a flood by the breaking up of ice in the Des Moines River [*Keokuk (Iowa) papers*] [12 Apr 1849]

    Jerusha 100 wid/o Joseph FREDERICK at Starks ME on 22 Oct [26 Dec 1850]

FREEBODY Catherine a colored woman at Hartford CT on 6th left $100 to four religious societies, $200 to another & $100 to the African Society of Hartford for the support of the ministry [24 Apr 1845]

FREED Mr in the Irish & Native American (not American Indians more likely English born in American) Riots in Philadelphia PA [*Dollar Newspaper*] [18 July 1844]

FREEMAN Abby W 19 at Norridgewock ME [25 Jul 1844]

    Alexander 21 s/o Col Ebenezer FREEMAN at Monmouth ME on 11th inst [21 Mar 1837]

    Barnabas 82 at Fairfield ME [30 Oct 1851]

    Charles a American giant died in London hospital [27 Nov 1845]

    Cyrus 33 l/o Gorham ME at Farmington ME [28 Nov 1840] & [5 Dec 1840] & on 8th inst of typhus fever [21 Nov 1840]

    Delphinia 15 at Poland ME [25 Jul 1844]

    Ebenezer 36 at Hallowell ME [21 Oct 1847]

    Edmund 73 at Brunswick ME [4 Jul 1837]

    Enoch 20 of Providence lost life on the brig *Washington*, RIDER Capt, [2 Oct 1835]

    Hannah w/o Capt S FREEMAN at Falmouth ME [16 Nov 1848]

    Harriet E C 39 w/o Rev Edward FREEMAN, chaplain of the Maine state prison at Camden ME [22 Jul 1852]

    Henriette abt 18 her body discovered in the Penobscot River at Hampden ME, her parents reside in Bucksport ME [26 Aug 1852]

    Hiram D abt 30 at NH state prision on 17th ult, native of Monmouth ME was committed for passing counterfeit bank bills, Hillsborough Co, 17 Oct 1843 [1 May 1845]

    James 78 at Orrington ME [20 May 1847]

    James Rev 76 at Newton MA in his 54th yr of ministry [27 Nov 1835]

    John 87 AmRev pensioner at Monmouth ME [4 Nov 1847]

    Jonathan B 23 at Fairfield ME [3 May 1849]

    Lydia 67 widow of Capt Nathaniel FREEMAN of Saccarappa ME at Brunswick ME [9 Oct 1841]

    Mr employed as a blacksmith on the railroad in the town of Gilead ME near NH line shot his wife on Wed last, after she retired to bed with her child & servant girl. The bed clothes were raised up & he aimed at her heart but the charge took effect in her arm, lacerating it in a shocking manner. He then ran into a field about a mile from the house & cut his throat (from the *Portland Eastern Argus*) [19 June 1851]

    Nancy 59 w/o Abraham N FREEMAN Esq at Norridgewock ME [24 Apr 1845]

    Nathaniel Deacon 92 at York ME [20 June 1834]

    Nathaniel Russell 27 formerly of Norridgewock ME at Sandwick MA, of the firm Hinckley & Freeman [3 Sept 1846]

    Reuben Capt 80 at Mt Desert ME [19 Sept 1850]

    Rhoda 76 wid/o Joshua FREEMAN at Fairfield ME [19 Feb 1852]

    Russell Hon of Sandwich ME formerly of Clinton Kennebec Co ME at Boston MA [12 Feb 1842]

    Samuel abt 80 at Hallowell ME [28 Aug 1845]

FREEMAN (Cont.) Sarah 45 at Fairfield ME [7 Oct 1847]
Thomas 73 a deacon at Portland ME [28 Oct 1847]
Thomas formerly of Hallowell ME at Montgomery AL [20 Mar 1841]
FREEMAN - see HANDY, RANSOM
FREME Mrs of Brattleboro VT perished in the flames with her home she was a widow [31 May 1849]
French Canadian - see BARNEY
FRENCH Benjamin 65 at Palmyra ME [5 Oct 1839]
Betsey 48 w/o C FRENCH at Salem [8 Mar 1849]
Charlotte 70 at Belfast ME [7 Jan 1847]
Charlotte S 60 at Belfast ME [21 Jan 1847]
David 73 at Turner ME on 27 Jan [19 Feb 1842]
E W merchant formerly of Turner ME at Waterville ME [10 Aug 1839]
Estes W 28 at Waterville ME [31 Aug 1839]
Gibson 86 AmRev at Quincy MA [11 Dec 1841]
Greenlief at Winthrop ME [11 Dec 1841]
Isaac 59 formerly of Winthrop ME at Kingfield ME on 26th ult [13 Mar 1841]
J K Dr 73 at Thomaston ME [9 Aug 1849]
Jacob 72 at Porter ME [3 Jul 1851]
Joseph H 18 of Athens ME at San Francisco CA on 11 Jul of cholera, arrived in CA but the day previous to his death [9 Sept 1852]
Joseph of Liberty ME a carding and clothing mill was destroyed by fire last week with all its contents it was his mill & Mr Alvan DREW's [*Bangor Whig*] [12 Oct 1839]
Lewis 41 at Dresden ME [17 Aug 1848]
Lydia M 30 w/o Emery FRENCH at South Chesterville ME on 8 Aug [16 Aug 1849]
Mary 33 w/o Charles S FRENCH at Chesterville ME [13 Jul 1848]
Mary 33 w/o Nathaniel FRENCH at Belfast ME [23 Nov 1833]
Mary 72 w/o Jacob FRENCH at Porter ME [3 Jul 1851]
Mary R 28 w/o George FRENCH at Andover ME/MA? [2 Oct 1835]
Mehitable 44 w/o Moses FRENCH formerly of Ossipee NH at Bingham ME [4 Sept 1845]
Moses 54 at Montville ME on 12 Feb [21 Feb 1851]
Mrs of Saco ME w/o Loring FRENCH committed suicide on the 2d inst by taking laudanum, left husband & 5 children [8 Feb 1844]
Nicholas D Esq 33 formerly of Montville ME at Bellville OH [29 June 1839]
Polly 26 w/o Capt David FRENCH at Mount Vernon ME [6 May 1843]
Ruth A 23 d/o the late Moses FRENCH of Montville ME at Gardiner ME on 1 Jan [21 Feb 1851]
Samuel 76 at Prospect ME [16 Sept 1852]
Samuel T 38 at Concord NH, probably the largest man in the state, if not New England, his weight 430 lbs, death by obesity [*The Courier*] [22 Feb 1840]
Sarah Arabella 21 w/o A S FRENCH at Dexter ME [30 Apr 1846]
Sarah Mrs 66 at Prospect ME on May 1st [18 May 1848]
Sarah Mrs 94 at Canton ME [6 Feb 1851]
Seba 69 at Dexter ME [11 June 1842]
Seth at Chesterville ME [7 Feb 1850]
Thomas abt 25 of Sidney ME a carpenter fell off the Kennebec Dam at Augusta ME & died [*Argus*] [9 Sept 1836]
William abt 15 of Bucksport ME lost overboard from schr *Henry Crosby* [15 Aug 1850]
French - see PERRO, Slavery
Frenchman - see BITTUES

FRENGER George 68 married Miss Frances McFarland MERCHANT 14 [a Georgia paper] [23 Mar 1848]

FRICK Henry 50 of PA died, another member of Congress [14 Mar 1844]

FRIE Robie 60 at Montville ME [15 Jul 1852]

FRIEL a child abt 4y belonging to widow O FRIEL of Portland ME playing on the wharf fell & death by drowning [13 Jul 1839]

FRIEND Phineas 80 at Etna ME one of the 1st two settlers of that town [13 Dec 1849]

FRINK J N Dr 36 at Portland ME [24 Oct 1844]

FRISBEE Harriet 18 d/o James FRISBEE at Kittery ME [27 Mar 1845]

FRISHIE Mr, died of cholera with the HAMILTON family, Mr PAGE & Mr COLE. Mr CHAPIN & Mr COLE were from CT & engaged in the sale of clocks. They, with 2 other boarders, fled to Warsaw to escape the disease, but all 4 sickened and died immediately there. A letter from Carthage IL gave a list of 12 persons of the house of Mr HAMILTON, a hotel-keeper; all of whom all died within a few days. [14 Aug 1851]

FRITH Joseph B, printer of Wiscasset ME at Kennebunk ME [20 May 1847]

FRIZZELL Tamas 53 w/o John FRIZZELL at Starks ME on 18th ult [14 Dec 1839]

FROHOCK Ann Maria 26 w/o D K FROHOCK at Smithfield ME on 15 Sept of consumption [14 Oct 1847]

FROST Abel recently of Bangor ME & formerly of Monmouth ME informed by a letter printed in the *Eastern Republican* to the postmaster of Bangor ME from J F ROBINSON PM of Campte LA giving the account of Mr A F's death [16 May 1837]

Abigail 71 w/o Moses FROST at Monmouth ME on 27 Sept after a short illness of the Society of Friends (Quakers) [14 Oct 1843]

Ann Emery 66 consort of Major William FROST at Topsham ME [13 June 1840]

Benjamin 23 of ME Sacramento CA on 8 Nov [2 Jan 1851]

Benjamin 80 at Belgrade ME on March 31 [26 April 1849]

Betsey 72 widow at Litchfield ME [13 Sept 1849]

Charles Rev 50 at Bethel ME [28 Feb 1850]

Eliza T 48 w/o William FROST at Norway ME [11 Sept 1851]

Esther w/o John FROST at Winthrop ME [10 June 1852]

George Frederic 17 at Gorham ME on 30th ult of consumption [12 Sept 1840]

John 76 at Norway ME [15 Jan 1846]

Josiah 40 left a wife and three children at Caghnawaga Pond near Monmouth Centre ME [12 June 1838]

Mary 25 w/o Joseph at Leeds ME [18 Nov 1843]

Mary abt 50 w/o Wm FROST at Norway ME [18 April 1850]

Mary Mrs 68 at Norway ME [15 July 1852]

Miss of MA got $365 of Mr SNOW for breach of marriage promise, he courted her a year & had to pay at the rate a dollar a day for it. "He got frost bitten" (copied from *Worcester Telegraph*) [28 Oct 1847]

Moses 64 at Gorham ME [10 Oct 1850]

Nathaniel abt 40 at Camden ME [25 July 1850]

Nathaniel supposed murdered by fellow workman of the *Mobile Advertiser*, Charles BOYNTON. Both natives of New England. BOYNTON served his time in New Haven & is abt 23y, 5' 9", thick set, black hair & eyebrows. The *New Haven Herald* in re-publishing the acount of FROST at Mobile says, "The perpetrator of the dreadful deed, whose proper name is Charles R S BOYINGTON, is a native of Litchfield in this state (CT)." [6 June 1834]

Obadiah E Esq 42 at Topsham ME [8 Aug 1849]

FROST (Cont.) Phebe Elizabeth 19 eldest c/o Isaac and Sarah W FROST at Weld ME on 17
June [30 Sept 1852]

Rebecca 80 widow of Jacob FROST at Norway ME [11 Feb 1847]

Rebecca Ann 2 yrs 2mos d/o Nathaniel B and Julia A FROST at Wayne ME on 16th ult
[17 Dec 1846]

Simon 37 at Lubec [15 Mar 1849]

Sophia 55 w/o Elder Henry FROST at Cornville ME [16 Mar 1848]

Stoddard J of New York city killed in a cart accident at Redding CT on Fri last [7 Nov
1840]

William D 17 of Orrington at Chelsea Hospital [9 Oct 1835]

Zepheniah 65 at Norway ME [3 Aug 1848]

FROTHINGHAM William an apprentice to Joseph ALLEY of (Lynn MA) abt 18y his
throat cut in his bed while asleep [*Lynn Record*] [15 Aug 1834]

William Rev 75 at Belfast on June 24th [8 July 1852]

FROVER Hadassah Mrs 52 at Machias ME [2 Mar 1848]

FRYE Abiel 27 at Fryeburg ME [6 May 1836]

boy 4y s/o Ensign FRYE drowned at Haskell's Corner by accidentally falling into an old
cellar [*Skowhegan Press*] [20 May 1847]

John Jr 17 of Wiscassett ME lost overboard from bark *Smyrna* on passage from Savannah
to Boston [25 Feb 1847]

Mary 32 yr w/o Jonathan L FRYE at Belfast ME [5 Dec 1844]

Mary M 23 d/o late Mr Dean FRYE at Lewiston ME [27 Nov 1835]

Phebe 29 yr 6mos w/o Benjamin FRYE at China [16 April 1846]

Rowland 80 formerly of East Vassalboro ME at Nashville[*sic*], Hillsboro Co., NH, on 25
Oct [6 Nov 1851]

Samuel Dr 61 at St Andrews [14 Oct 1847]

fugitive slave - see HAWKINS, GORSUCH

FULLER Benjamin 84 at Norway ME [28 Mar 1850]

Charles of Lewiston ME in the woods in Masardis ME a week ago last Fri, wounded by
stub of a bush which entered his abdomen, died the next Mon [*Lincoln Observer*] [6
May 1847]

c/o F A FULLER Esq at Augusta ME [8 Oct 1846]

David Capt 73 at Lewiston ME [13 June 1850]

Edward 47 at Jay ME on 10 Aug [31 Aug 1848]

Edward Esq 20y of Readfield ME only s/o William C FULLER of Bradford NH at
Hopkinton NH on 9 Oct 1840 [31 Oct 1840]

Eliza W 17 d/o Eben FULLER at Augusta on Sept 25 [4 Oct 1849]

Emily 35 w/o Hiram FULLER at Boston MA on 10th inst [23 Dec 1852]

Enoch 87 AmRev soldier at Winslow ME [5 Mar 1842]

Francis 94 formerly of Readfield ME at Vassalboro ME [1 July 1843]

Franklin of Rockland ME at sea washed from schr *Senate* [24 Apr 1851]

Frederick A Esq 42 at Augusta ME on 29th ult [1 Feb 1849]

George G a native of ME at Natchitoches [24 Oct 1844]

Given 46 at Warren ME [20 May 1847]

Hannah Harriman 1 yr at Bath ME d/o Dr A J FULLER of Searsmont ME [25 Sept 1845]

Henry A 20 s/o Dr A P FULLER at Albion ME [16 Jan 1851]

Henry W Hon judge of probate of the county of Kennebec at Boston on Fri eve of last
week [6 Feb 1841]

Isaac 82 at Jay ME [24 Apr 1851]

John Maj 83 AmRev officer at Pittsfield VT [9 Mar 1839]

John W 19 at Livermore ME [25 Jan 1840]

Luda M w/o Rev Caleb FULLER of Hallowell ME at Wayne ME [31 July 1845]

FULLER (Cont.) Margaret 54 w/o Joseph FULLER at Brunswick ME [4 Dec 1851]

Mary Emily 18 mos d/o J and Harriet FULLER at Corinth on 4th inst [17 Sept 1842]

Mrs abt 76 w/o Francis FULLER at the town farm at Winthrop ME [18 July 1840]

Mrs one of three ladies thrown from a chaise by the fright of the horse Miss Eddy had a broken leg, Mrs SMITH w/o Noah SMITH Jr of Calais ME was hurt. Mrs Fuller of Milltown ME escaped with slight injury at Baileyville ME on Sat last [8 Aug 1840]

Nancy 71 yrs 6 mos w/o Lawrence FULLER at East Livermore ME[21 Aug 1845]

Nathaniel 97 yrs formerly of Plymouth MA at Oxford ME [19 Dec 1844]

Robert W 32 of Winslow ME at Pittsfield ME [13 Mar 1851]

Rosina 10m d/o Edward & Harriet T FULLER at Jay ME on 3 Aug [31 Aug 1848]

Samuel abt 54 yrs at New Portland [15 Feb 1840]

Samuel Capt at Thomaston [26 Nov 1846]

William W Esq 56 at Oregon City IL on Aug 17 formerly a lawyer at Hallowell and editor of the old *Hallowell Gazette* [13 Sept 1849]

Wm Henry 27 s/o Leonard FULLER of Farmington ME at sea on Feb 19th on board bark *Lady Knight* of Portland ME [13 June 1850]

FULTON Mrs w/o John FULTON seized with a fit fell across a water pail & her neck resting upon the edge of the pail, thus strangled to death at Tariffville CT on Fri [26 Oct 1848]

FURBER Eliza Ann 26 at Clinton ME [28 Mar 1834]

FURBER William 28 a native of Belfast ME first officer of ship *India* at sea on Aug 5th off Java Head [2 Apr 1842]

FURBISH Albert 2 yrs c/o Samuel FURBISH at Bangor ME on 13th [20 May 1843]

Betsey Mrs 86 yrs 6 mos formerly of Berwick ME at Webster ME [14 Jan 1847]

Dennis 28 yrs at Green ME on 24th Feb last [23 Mar 1839]

Greenlief W 5 yrs s/o Webber FURBISH at Hallowell ME on 4th inst [16 Jan 1839]

James 6 yrs c/o Samuel FURBISH at Bangor ME on 11th [20 May 1843]

FURBUSH Hannah 32 at Elliot [6 Feb 1845]

Mr the head ostler (person who cares for horses) terribly burnt in attempting to make his way past the front of the stable, his recovery will be slow and doubtful & Mr SULLIVAN of Charlestown also severely burned ... Stables belong to Doolittle's city tavern [*Boston Bee* 16 Aug] [21 Aug 1845]

FURGERSON S 80 at Gardiner ME [24 Jan 1850]

FURGUSON Eunice 41 w/o Stephen FURGUSON at Gardiner ME [11 Nov 1843]

FURLONG Patrick 30 at Augusta ME[19 Dec 1850]

FURNISS Richard 110 died in 1810 at Cushing ME [19 Feb 1846]

- **G** -

GAFFNEY John of the brig *Juno* wrecked [16 Apr 1846]

GAGE Eliza Ann abt 19 d/o Isaac GAGE at Waterville ME [24 Jul 1841]

Isaac his barn burned in Waterville ME on Sun 16th inst, all at church except Mrs GAGE, who discovered the fire [3 June 1847]

J T E Dr 42 late of Edgartown MA & formerly of Augusta ME at San Francisco CA on 4 Apr [27 June 1850]

John Capt of Monroe ME at Clarksville TN [19 Dec 1837]

Lucretia B w/o Franklin GAGE MD & d/o the late Hon Thomas BOND of Hallowell ME [29 Jan 1846]

Sarah Jane 30 w/o Frederick GAGE at Chesterville ME [6 Mar 1851]

Thomas E Capt 82 at Augusta ME, owned & commanded a vessel confiscated by the French prior to 1800 [10 Dec 1846]

GAINES Elizabeth 55 at Saco ME [2 Dec 1836]
    Gen the oldest officer in the army, commander of the Southwestern Military Division,
    died of cholera [14 June 1849]

GALE Charles H 13 s/o late Smith L GALE at Augusta ME on Mon last [12 Aug 1847]
    Stephen E 17 s/o the late Smith L GALE at (Augusta ME) on 10 Oct [19 Oct 1848]

GALIGHAN Mary 1y d/o Patrick & Jane Ann GALIGHAN verdict: death from accidental
    suffocation in a tub containing some water rendered at New York [30 Sept 1843]

GALISON [*sic*, the spelling of the name should be GALLISON] John of Foxcroft ME This
    is the 1st death by drowning of any person employed of the firm Fiske & Norcross on
    Merrimack River [*Concord (NH) Statesman*] [25 May 1848]

GALLAGHER Ann - alias Ann GALLAGER, on Sat last died at the house of Mrs
    MERRIAM, in Fruit St Court. Verdict of jury: death by violence on Sat 25th of Mar
    inst between 6 & 7 PM in consequence of an abortion produced by an operation,
    which operation was performed upon her with an instrument in the hands of Dr John
    Stevens at his house in Howard Street, on Wed evening 15 Mar 1848, for the purpose
    of producing an abortion. Dr Stevens was accordingly arrested on Coroner's warrant,
    brought before the police court and held to bail in sum of $5,000 to answer at the next
    term of the Municipal Court. Miss COOMBS, the principal witness for government,
    having acknowledged that she received $20 at Dr STEVENS's house to leave the city,
    was ordered to find surety in $1000 for her appearance as a witness.... copied from
    the *Boston Traveller* [13 Apr 1848]

GALLAN Michael on the Pennsylvania Railroad over the Alleghany Mtn [4 Jul 1834]

GALLATIN Albert 89 at the res of his son-in-law on Long Island on Sat 12 Aug. A native
    of Geneva, Switzerland & came to this country in 1780. For many years a member of
    Congress [23 Aug 1849]

GALLAUDET T H Rev known as the friend of the Deafmute died on Wed at Hartford [18
    Sept 1851]

GALLOPP Benjamin A 50 at Thomaston ME [30 Apr 1846]

GALLUP Joseph A Dr 80 at Woodstock VT on 12 Oct, the founder of the Medical
    Institution of that place [25 Oct 1849]

GALLUP - see BENNETT

GALVIN George I Esq an invalid in search of health, recently died. Capt GOULD, the
    master of the vessel in which Mr Galvin sailed, and Mr HODGDON, a passenger in
    the same vessel, victims to the yellow fever - Mr William BAKER, who left here abt 1
    ago, from the same. [7 Dec 1839]

GAMMON Hannah 36 w/o Ezekiel D GAMMON at Portland ME [19 Dec 1844]
    Joshua 82 of Cape Elizabeth ME AmRev at Portland ME [13 Mar 1845]
    Samuel 86 at Hartford ME of lung fever, had from his youth enjoyed a remarkable degree
    of health having worked every year for 80yrs [30 Mar 1839]

GAMMONS Rebecca 46 w/o Capt James GAMMONS at Belfast ME [30 Jan 1845]

GANNET Benjamin a pensioner in right of his wife, Deborah SHURTLEFF, enlisted in Apr
    1781, served 2y in a MA regiment honorably discharged after seriously wounded at
    Tarrytown, 1783. She married, received a pension & her husband now claimed her
    pension as in the case of widow of AmRev. The bill passed without any opposition.
    [*Transcript*] (She had a Maine connection) [26 June 1838]

GANNETT Joseph Tinkham 1 s/o Joseph F & Mary E GANNETT at Augusta ME on 11th
    inst [20 Sept 1849]

GANTER Mrs of sickness near Augusta GA [16 Nov 1839]

GARCELON Cressulia J 23 d/o late Mark GARCELON at Lewiston ME [16 Jan 1851]
    Hannah N 18y d/o Capt Mark GARCELON at Webster ME [27 Oct 1840]
    James Rev 59 at Lewiston ME [24 Oct 1850]

GARCELON (Cont.) Jane 48 w/o Capt Mark GARCELON at Durham ME [18 Mar 1847]
  Lucy 43 d/o late Peter & Catherine GARCELON at Lewiston ME on 14 inst of
    consumption [23 Jan 1841]
  Maria 88 w/o William GARCELON at Lewiston ME [11 Jul 1850]
  Mark Capt 57 at Lewiston ME [9 Jan 1851]
  Washington 40 at Harpswell ME [21 June 1849]
  William 87 (ae 89y 7m s/o James & Deliverance (ANNIS) G, The additions from notes
    by his grandson, Col William Garcelon, early historian of Lewiston and father of Gov
    Garcelon, died on 20 Jan 1851) at Lewiston ME [30 Jan 1851]
GARCELON - see LEMONT
  Emily Newell 8m 20d at Winthrop ME on 4th ult [7 Feb 1834]
  Emma 37 d/o R H GARDINER Esq at Gardiner ME [16 Jan 1845]
  Hepsebath 88 wid/o Capt Peleg GARDINER formerly of Nantucket at Vassalboro ME [1
    June 1848]
  John S Dr of Gardiner ME on board US *Alleghany* on passage from New Orleans to
    Norfolk [15 Mar 1849]
  Lucy 23 d/o R H GARDINER Esq at Gardiner ME [2 Dec 1847]
  Nancy T Mrs 48y 8m at Hope ME [26 Feb 1852]
  R H Esq his elegant mansion destroyed by fire on Tues last [28 Nov 1834]
  Robert abt 50 & James, his son abt 20 left their homes in Harpswell ME on the 21st to go
    to Ragged Island in a small boat, the boat was picked up the following Sat on North
    Yarmouth Island, the men are supposed drowned [12 Feb 1836]
GARDINER - see JONES, UPSHUR
GARDNER Alexander mate of Nantucket MA crew of whale ship *Awashonks* of Falmouth
    ME at Fejee Island [6 May 1836]
  Benjamin 42 at Northport ME [12 Feb 1836]
  c/o Walter GARDNER ae 10 at Palermo ME on 5 Apr [12 Apr 1849]
  Lydia B 14 only d/o Robert GARDNER 14 at Hallowell ME on 10th inst [17 Apr 1845]
  Mary 43 w/o Alexander GARDNER at Augusta ME [5 Apr 1849]
  Prince 20 s/o Alexander GARDNER at Augusta ME [14 June 1849]
  Robert 81 at Hallowell ME [19 Feb 1846]
  Sarah 81y relict of Jona GARDNER at Carthage ME [16 Mar 1848]
  Warren Deac at Pembroke ME [14 Mar 1850]
  William 75 formerly of Boston MA at Portland ME [7 Oct 1843]
GARDNER - see WILLIAMS, WINTHROP
GAREY Sarah Jane at Dover [14 Nov 1844]
GARFIELD Mary E 21 d/o Mr A GARFIELD [31 Jul 1845]
GARLAND Benjamin Esq 69 at Levant ME [22 Jan 1852]
  James 22y run over by the cars in Portland ME on Mon of the last week & has since died
    [23 Sept 1851]
  Mary Ann 24 w/o John U GARLAND at Winslow ME [5 Apr 1849]
  Olive 53 w/o Jona GARLAND at Winslow ME [9 May 1850]
  Theodotia 18 at Oxford ME [28 Aug 1851]
GARLAND - see SAWYER
GARNAGE Jonathan AmRev 90y of Fryeburg ME at the battle of Bunker Hill & present at
    the Bunker Hill celebration & lost his reason from the excitement produced by the
    occasion in which state he died, without any other apparent disease (from the Hill's
    New Hampshire Patriot) [2 Sept 1843]
GARNER - see LORAINE

GARRET Hiram 19y convicted at NY week before last of having two wives, married Mary Jane DeGROOT, when but 16 & last April married Eliza DECKER his 1st wife being still alive [1 June 1848]

GARRETY - see DUNN

GARRIA Angel dying declaration of the pirates signed by companions Manuel BOYGA, Juan MONTENEGRO, Manuel CASTILTE [10 Jul 1835]

GARY Harriet F 25 w/o Luther GARY at Bradford ME [26 June 1838]

GASELIN Jacob 45 at Hallowell ME on 4th [20 Jul 1848]

GASLAND Mary 68 at Vassalboro ME in a small puddle of water [2 May 1837]

GASLIN Aaron H 22 at Vassalboro ME [25 Jan 1844]

    Flora A 1y 7m d/o B F & Sophia GASLIN at Augusta ME on 4 Sept [18 Sept 1851]

    Martha R 34y 9m at Vassalboro ME [6 Sept 1849]

GATES Alfred 81 at Carroll ME formerly of Paris ME [26 Feb 1846]

    Hezekiah Dr of cholera at St Louis on 22 June a native of Norwich CT & had been the senoir editor of the *Valley Farmer* [13 Sept 1849]

    Mr Brevet Major of the 8th infantry of cholera at Fredericksburg TX on 28th June [9 Aug 1849]

    Simon 93 at Worcester MA on 2 Feb [15 Feb 1849]

GATES - see FORD, SCHUYLER, WORTH

GAUBERT Harriet 60 w/o John GAUBERT at Richmond ME on 3rd inst [8 Feb 1849]

    Mary Estelle 4m 2w only ch of Alonzo & Sarah E GAUBERT at Augusta ME on 10 Sept [16 Sept 1852]

GAUL - see BARNARD

    Dr lately in Boston MA in conversation with a friend attributed his disease to poison contracted from handling the remains at the Medical College believed to be those of Dr PARKMAN [31 Jan 1850]

    Elizabeth 81 w/o Seth GAY at Gardiner ME [19 Jul 1849]

    Jabez Esq 81 at Farmington ME [29 Apr 1852]

    Jesse Deac 90 at Denham MA the oldest person in that town, his wife died in June 1836, married 66y 6m [31 Oct 1837]

    Leonard 15 s/o Eliphas GAY of Farmington ME drowned at Lewiston ME [*Lewiston Journal*] [5 Jul 1849]

    Martha W 32 at Hallowell ME [6 May 1852]

    Mary 68 w/o Rufus GAY Esq at Gardiner ME [26 Oct 1839]

    Mary Mrs 101 at North Bridgton ME [11 Apr 1850]

    Rufus Esq 83y 6m at Gardiner ME on 6 Nov [11 Nov 1852]

    Seth Jr Capt 50y 7m at Gardiner ME [19 Sept 1844]

    Thomas Esq 65 at Gardiner ME [29 Jul 1852]

GAYLORD Jesse 44 a pallbearer at the funeral of Mrs JOHNSON of Bristol CT [6 Feb 1851]

GAYLORD - see RIGAN

GAZLIN Sarah 62 at Vassalboro ME on 5th inst [8 Jan 1846]

GENNES - see JENNESS

GENNINGS Sophia 50 w/o Rufus GENNINGS at Industry ME [14 Nov 1850]

GENTHER Charles unmarried of Waldoboro ME at Bremen ME on Tues on 1st inst 4 persons drowned while sailing from Long Island in Bremen ME towards Friendship ME [17 Apr 1851]

GENTHNER child 17m of Waldoboro ME c/o Isaac GENTHNER scalded by drinking hot coffee from nose (spout) of a coffee pot on Mon morning of last week, death in few hours [*Patriot*] [21 Dec 1839]

GEORGE Mrs w/o Francis GEORGE at Leeds ME [15 May 1835]

GEORGE (Cont.) Hannah an old lady upwards of a 100 called upon the President of the United States last week in New York. Seen every President of the USA, shaken hands with WASHINGTON and was quite delighted to see the present incumbent (VAN BUREN). She walked without assistance from her res & escorted back by Robert W BOWYER. [20 Jul 1839]

George IV - see VINCENT

GEORGE - see DOW

GERALD - see LARKIN

German - see BEOTTGER, GROE, JEFFRIES, SACH, WENDENBURG

GERRISH Andrew of Goldsboro ME missing for some time found at sea with a rope tied to his neck [1 Aug 1834]

George B 39 at Freeport ME [3 Oct 1850]

Sally wid/o Joseph M GERRISH at South DOVER ME [11 Nov 1847]

Sarah 22 d/o William GERRISH Esq at Durham ME [10 Jan 1850]

Sarah Ann 14y 4m d/o Nathaniel GERRISH at Milford ME on 20 Aug [29 Aug 1840]

Sophia 35 w/o William GERRISH at Durham ME [10 Jul 1835]

GERRY Ann Mrs 86 relict of Elbridge GERRY, one of the signers of the Declaration of Independence at New Haven on 17th ult [29 Mar 1849]

Deborah 71 w/o Abel GERRY at York ME [14 Feb 1837]

Morgan L encourages people to settle in Aroostook Co. and tells those who would like to move or "have a desire to emigrate to the far west, I would advise (before going) to take a look into the Aroostook, I ground barley in my mill the 5th Aug, raised this season by Thomas CASY of Benadicta Plt, who says that he could have had it at the mill the last week in July. I have abt ten acres of corn, ... Golden Ridge Plt No 3 (now Sherman Aroostook Co ME) 28 Aug" [*Bangor Democrat*] [16 Sept 1847]

GETCHELL Abby L 19y 11m at Augusta ME on 15th inst [27 Sept 1849]

Abigail 80 at Augusta ME [18 Feb 1847]

Abigail K 58 w/o Abel GETCHELL at Waterville ME [5 Oct 1848]

Bradford 26 at Litchfield ME [1 Apr 1852]

Catherine 25 d/o Dennis GETCHELL at Augusta ME on 15th inst [21 Mar 1844]

Clara Augusta 1y d/o Nahum GETCHELL at Saco ME [9 Oct 1845]

Elisha 36 at Brunswick ME [27 Nov 1838]

Hannah 45 at Wells ME [21 Dec 1848]

Hannah 80 w/o Isaiah GETCHELL at Wells ME [21 Dec 1848]

Horace 14 s/o Arthur L GETCHELL at Augusta ME [26 Nov 1846]

Joshua of Wells ME his buildings burnt on Wed & his son lost in the fire [learned from the *Child & Co Express*] [*Traveller*] [24 Dec 1846]

Julia W 18m d/o Arthur L GETCHELL at Augusta ME [29 May 1845]

Louisa 18m d/o Ansel L at Augusta ME [22 May 1845]

Mary 31 at Hallowell ME [4 Apr 1837]

Mary 37 w/o Andrew GETCHELL at Litchfield ME [16 Dec 1847]

Mary Frances 4y & a boy abt 6 of Brunswick ME c/o Abizer GETCHELL went a short distance from their home to procure fuel. The girl attempting to re-kindle the flame, set her clothes afire, she died in 14 hours [*Brunswicker*] [16 Dec 1843]

Philena 39 w/o Arthur L GETCHELL at Augusta ME on 6 Oct [12 Oct 1848]

Ruth Mrs 69 formerly of Sidney ME at Palermo ME on 4 Apr [12 Apr 1849]

Sarah W ae 36 w/o G H GETCHELL Esq at Vassalboro ME on 4 Sept [12 Sept 1850]

Seth 90y 8m AmRev under Gen ARNOLD at Pittsfield ME [8 Aug 1844]

Sumner W 37 at Augusta ME on Sat last [21 Jan 1847]

Thomas Capt of Northport ME drowned, the master of the sloop *Alert* of Lincolnville ME, left a son Thomas H GETCHELL Jr & 6 other ch & a widow [*Thomaston ME Gazette*] [29 Apr 1847]

GETCHELL (Cont.) William 13y death caused by a tree falling on him at Windsor ME s/o
  Hiram GETCHELL [30 May 1834]
GETCHELL - see MOULTON
GEYERS - see SAVAGE
GHERKIN C H Prof of music at Norfolk VA [28 Aug 1851]
GIBBS Achsah 69 wid/o Deac Peltiah GIBBS at Augusta ME on 9th inst [25 Jan 1849]
  Elisha 82 AmRev at Foxcroft ME [3 June 1836]
  Franklin of Bridgton on Wed night 23rd inst [*Portland Advertiser*] [31 Aug 1848]
  Mr one of the emigrants from Lynn to CA returned by the last steamer bringing with him
    ten pounds of gold dust. As an offset he states that the passage out cost him $150 &
    he paid a doctor's bill of $700 just before leaving CA [10 Jan 1850]
  Silence 85y 5m at Foxcroft ME on 28th ult [12 June 1838]
GIBERT Capt dying declaration of the pirates signed by companions Angel GARRIA,
  Manuel BOYGA, Juan MONTENEGRO, Manuel CASTILTE [10 Jul 1835]
GIBSON - see ADAMS
GIBSON Abel Esq 92 at Brownfield ME [26 Aug 1852]
  children Mrs GIBSON of the same county as the HUDSONS (Marshall Co, Mississippi?)
    presented her husband with five children in two births the *Natches Free Trader*
    reported [12 June 1838]
  Eliza A 6y 3m d/o Zeakariah GIBSON at Brownfield ME on 28th ult [10 Jul 1835]
  John W 21 at Bangor ME [28 Oct 1836]
  Lydia 39 w/o Capt John D GIBSON at Perry ME on 5th of consumption [26 Nov 1842]
  Phebe 70 w/o Samuel GIBSON at Sebasticook ME [16 Nov 1848]
  Rebecca 64 w/o John GIBSON "colored" at Portland ME [27 Mar 1845]
GIDDINGS Andrew R Esq 73y 9m at Danville ME (now part of Auburn, but still called
  Danville Jct) (see Androscoggin Historical Society for his papers & diaries) [15 Jul
  1847]
  Stephen 73 at Bangor ME [25 Jul 1850]
GIFFORD boy 7 s/o R S & Abby W GIFFORD perished in the flames the *New Bedford
  Mercury* says that the dwelling house of David WING in Westport near the Hicks'
  Bridge was discovered to be on fire on Tues morning [11 Jan 1849]
  Jacob abt 25 at Sidney ME on Mon night fell from the yard of a river boat while furling
    the sail & drowned [30 Oct 1845]
  Maria M 20 at Fairfield ME [6 Aug 1846]
GILBERT Caleb 69 at Turner ME [25 Oct 1849]
  Levi J s/o Henry GILBERT of Leeds ME given his time until age 21y etc [26 Mar 1836]
  Martha 56 w/o Charles G GILBERT at Leeds ME [21 May 1846]
  Mr killed by accident on board US steamer *Michigan* by the premature explosion of a gun
    firing a salute in honor of the President at Erie PA [6 Sept 1849]
  Sewall 42 at East Thomaston ME [19 Oct 1848]
GILBRETH Benjamin F 32 formerly of Augusta ME at Charleston SC on 1st Oct [16 Oct
  1851]
  J Esq at Farmington ME [21 Dec 1848]
  Martha 88 wid/o Patrick GILBRETH at Belfast ME on 19th ult [13 Feb 1845]
GILCHRIST Joseph of Thomaston ME the 1st officer of the *John Hancock* fell from the top
  of the mast & drowned on 28th ult [7 June 1849]
GILE infant c/o Asa GILE Esq at Readfield ME [5 Mar 1846]
  Stephen 81 of the oldest citizens of Alfred ME [2 Sept 1847]
  Thomas 79 of the oldest native citizens of Alfred ME [2 Sept 1847]
GILES Mary W 25 at Portland ME [22 May 1835]
GILKEY Caroline 35 w/o Freeman GILKEY at Houlton ME [31 Jul 1851]

GILKEY (Cont.) Thomas 78 at Isleboro ME [23 Dec 1847]

GILL Deborah A 28 w/o Capt Charles GILL at Farmington ME [13 Mar 1845]

Thomas in CA buried in Tukey's Plains, said to be from Maine or Cape Cod [29 Nov 1849]

Victoria Jane 2y 3m d/o Charles & Sarah GILL at Augusta ME on Thurs [25 Sept 1845]

GILLCHREST Peggy abt 52 at St George ME of smallpox [20 Nov 1841]

GILLCHRIST - see THOMAS

GILLET Austin H G 16 a member of Amherst College & s/o Rev Dr GILLET of Hallowell ME at Amherst MA [25 Dec 1838]

GILLETT Eliphalet Rev 80 at Hallowell ME [26 Oct 1848]

Grace Hanfield 24 d/o the late Rev Dr GILLETT of Hallowell at Rochester NY [31 Jan 1850]

GILLEY Dorcas 90-100 at Augusta ME wid/o John GILLEY who died in Augusta 25yrs since at age 124 [28 Mar 1840]

John born in Kilkenny, West of Cork Co Ireland, married at age 80y, 2nd wife (Dorcas), who was upwards of 25y when she married him, he died at Augusta ME on 9 Jul 1813; see also *American Advocate* issue 17 Jul 1813, and *Transcript* issues dates not known [*The Piscataquis Farmer*] [5 Nov 1841] [19 Feb 1846]

GILLIAME Col killed after the battle between the Indians & the Oregon Regiment by the accidental discharge of a rifle. There were 50 Indians killed & many wounded. The Americans (The Oregon Soldiers) had ten wounded, none killed. [10 Aug 1848]

GILLPATRICK - see GILPATRICK

GILMAN Allen Esq 80 at Bangor ME [23 Apr 1846]

Anna 71 wid/o Joseph GILMAN at Mt Vernon ME on 15th [27 Sept 1849]

Anna 88 at Albion ME [21 Sept 1848]

Bela 57 at Mt Vernon ME on 3 Apr [15 Apr 1852]

Betsey 83 wid/o Nathaniel GILMAN 83 at East Mt Vernon ME on 20 Oct [11 Dec 1851]

Caleb abt 75 at Smithfield ME [27 Mar 1851]

Charlotte W 27 d/o N GILMAN Esq at Waterville ME [21 Oct 1847]

Dennis at Mt Vernon ME [8 Jul 1852]

Emily R 24 at Hallowell ME [25 Jul 1844]

George 37 at South Berwick ME [9 Sept 1847]

Gideon 75 born in Exeter NH & res Hallowell ME 60y [16 Jan 1845]

girl d/o Josiah GILMAN of scalding [*Dover Farmer*] [3 Sept 1846]

John L abt 80 at Smithfield ME [20 May 1852]

Jonathan 84 AmRev at Searsmont ME [22 Jan 1836]

Jonathan Sherman 11m s/o Jona C & Zeruiah D GILMAN at Dover NH [12 Oct 1839]

Lucy Dummer 9y 11m d/o S K GILMAN Esq at Hallowell ME on Tues last of scarlet fever [17 Jul 1838]

Lydia W 37 w/o John GILMAN at Milo ME on 17 Jan [8 Feb 1849]

Martha 101 at Norridgewock ME [11 Apr 1850]

Martha Mrs 72 at Monmouth ME [4 June 1851]

Mary Jane 34 d/o Josiah & Mary Jane GILMAN at Sebec ME on 24 Jan [22 Feb 1849]

Mary M 16 d/o Nicholas GILMAN at Wells ME [24 Apr 1835]

Mrs 89 wid/o Eliphalet GILMAN at Hallowell ME [26 Feb 1846]

Nathaniel 40 drowned at Shad Rips Oldtown ME [27 June 1850]

Nathaniel 88 of Exeter NH held several public offices, bro/o Gov GILMAN [11 Feb 1847]

Peter 82 AmRev pensioner at Norridgewock ME [17 Oct 1834]

Polly 65y 3m w/o Stephen GILMAN Esq at East Mt Vernon ME on 12 Sept [23 Oct 1851]

Samuel Deac 86 at Exeter NH [25 Sept 1838]

GILMANTON Levi one of the justices of the Supreme Court lately married an Indian
    princess, brought up in the family of Theodore DAVIS Esq of Gibson's Creek,
    Missouri. She d/o late Fox chief named KEOKHERSHA, The Black Bear. Mr Davis
    received her into his family in 1823 when she was but 7 years of age (*St Louis Obser*)
    [22 Aug 1837]

GILMER - see slaves, UPSHUR

GILMORE Addison 48, president of Western Railroad died Fri at Watertown MA of
    disease of the heart, left a wife & two sons & two dau he was a native of VT (copied
    from *Boston Post*) [23 Jan 1851]

    child abt 1y c/o John K GILMORE of Brewer ME died of clothes taking fire on Sat last
    [*Bangor Whig*] [16 Sept 1847]

    Hepsabeth S abt 30 w/o Dr Langdon GILMORE at Gardiner ME [13 Feb 1851]

    Huldah 46 w/o John GILMORE at Leeds ME of consumption on the 16th of July [15 Aug
    1840]

    Joseph 74 at Wells ME [21 Jan 1847]

    Martin of Belfast ME on board steamer *S S Lewis* [28 Oct 1852]

    Samuel 79 AmRev at Brewer ME [20 Mar 1845]

    Sarah E abt 17 d/o Martin GILMORE [8 May 1845]

GILPATRICK Amelia 42 at Hallowell ME [6 Jul 1848]

    Caroline A 18 at Hallowell ME [4 Sept 1851]

    Emeline 21 at Hollis ME [30 May 1844]

    John the first officer of Trenton ME, lost overboard from schr *Tangier* on the passage
    from Boston MA to Charlestown [15 Jan 1846]

    Martin 1st officer of Portland ME lost & drowned the barque *William Fales*, Capt
    William THOMES of this port (Portland ME) was lost in Well Bay ME on Wed
    evening at 9 o'clock, 13 persons on board, eight were lost including every officer.
    Through the attention of our friend, George M FREEMAN of Cape Needick (Old
    York, where the barque drove) [26 Feb 1842]

    Rosanna 24 at Farmingdale ME on 23 Nov [9 Dec 1852]

    Samuel (born 5 Jul 1796 s/o James & Elizabeth G) at Lisbon ME (they lived in Webster,
    later called Sabattus) [20 Feb 1851]

    Thomas 42 at Bath ME [28 Jan 1847]

GILSON Mrs of Schenectady her remains discovered a few days since, two miles below
    Athens, one of the passenger of the lost steamboat *Swallow* [the *Albany Evening
    Journal*] [6 Nov 1845]

    Nathan 62 formerly of Brooklin NH at Winthrop ME on the 8th inst [14 Mar 1834]

GINNES - see JENNESS

gipsy - see LEATHERS

GIVEN David 78 at Brunswick ME [17 Jul 1835]

    George Tyler 12y 5m at Gardiner ME [1 Jan 1846]

    John A 38 at Brunswick ME [25 Nov 1852]

    John S of Boston MA saved from drowning when the steam packet *New England* sank. It
    left Boston for Bath & Gardiner ME and had an accident with the schr *Curlew* on 31
    May [12 June 1838]

    Mahala w/o Capt Robert GIVEN at Brunswick ME [23 Dec 1852]

    Mary 82 at Wales ME [13 May 1847]

    Robert Capt formerly of Brunswick ME at Philadelphia PA on 14 Feb [7 Mar 1837]

GIVEN - PENNELL

GLASS Adeline 22 w/o Samuel M GLASS at Oldtown ME [10 Feb 1848]

    Consider (b 15 Nov 1759 at Duxbury MA, & formerly a res of Pejepscot, later called
    Danville, now part of Auburn ME) 83y 3m at Guilford ME [8 Apr 1843]

    George K 29 at Gardiner ME [4 May 1848]

GLASS (Cont.) Rufus P 33 s/o Henry GLASS late of Gardiner ME at Bowdoinham ME [25 June 1846]

Samuel M 27 late of Oldtown ME at Gardiner ME [23 Aug 1849]

GLAZIER boy 8y of Castine ME s/o Joseph GLAZIER on 24th inst by an upsetting of an ox cart [31 May 1849]

Joseph Jr 22 drowned in Castine ME on 29th ult, found in the bottom of his boat with his face in the water [15 Jul 1847]

GLEASON Jonas 56 at Eastport ME [11 Oct 1849]

GLIDDEN Albert abt 23y suicide by hanging himself near the edge of the woods & near his father's house in Palermo ME on the 12th inst [*Belfast ME Journal*] [6 Jul 1848]

Ann Webber c/o Samuel GLIDDEN at Gardiner ME [14 Mar 1840]

Arixena S 31/34 w/o Peter L GLIDDEN at Lewiston ME [18 Mar 1852] & [25 Mar 1852]

Deborah 86 wid/o Jeremiah GLIDDEN at Winthrop ME [12 Mar 1846]

Elisha H 23 at Nobleboro ME [6 Jan 1848] & Elisha W 23 c/o John C GLIDDEN Esq of Freedom ME at Damariscotta ME [16 Mar 1848]

Gideon 59 at Hallowell ME [4 Mar 1852]

Gideon 76 AmRev at Bowman's Point at Hallowell ME on the 5th inst [21 Dec 1833]

Lydia 24 of Sebec ME at Ellsworth ME [14 Nov 1844]

Mary F 15 c/o John C GLIDDEN Esq of Freedom ME at Damariscotta ME [16 Mar 1848]

Susan 72 of New Castle ME at Alna ME [19 Dec 1850]

GLIDDEN - see HUNTOON, NORRIS

GLIMES Isaac S 18 s/o David GLIMES of Gray ME at Boston MA of smallpox [12 Feb 1846]

GLOVER George S abt 53 at Thomaston ME [17 Jul 1845]

James 78 at Sumner ME [14 Jan 1847]

Lucy Jane 36 w/o Capt Thomas GLOVER at Camden ME [20 Nov 1851]

GLOYD David Col 83 at East Thomaston ME [27 Dec 1849]

GNESS J A Mr of Barnwell Dist SC on 18th ult by a slave he was attempting to chastise [10 Apr 1851]

GODDARD George A Esq 38y left a wife [*Boston Atlas*] [22 May 1845]

Israel 62 at Vassalboro ME [9 Sept 1843] & [23 Sept 1843]

John Col on Mon afternoon of last week a violent tornado passed over part of Orono ME destorying his timber barn [31 Jul 1845]

William G Prof 52 of Belles Lettres Brown University [26 Feb 1846]

GODDING Jonas 83 formerly of Watertown MA at Jay ME on 23rd June [30 Aug 1849]

Josephine 23 w/o Ensign GODDING at Livermore ME [27 Sept 1849]

GODFREY John 62 at Topsham ME [4 June 1846]

Sophia 50 at Bangor ME [1 Jul 1836]

Sylvia abt 20 w/o Capt Adams G at Augusta ME [10 Apr 1845] & d/o Thomas PECK at Augusta ME on 4th inst [17 Apr 1845]

GODFREY - CRAWFORD, CASON

GODNEY Rachel 107 d at 91 Seventh Ave. A grand dau/o the lady states "born at Manaroneck, Westchester Co 1741, parents Indians, her father belonged to the Tappan tribe & her mother a Mohegan, married a Malay, & had two ch, one of whom is is 77y and is the mother of this witness. At 99y old Rachel went from Haverstaw [*sic*] to New Haven. The mother of deceased also lived to 107y." [*New York Journal of Com*] [7 Dec 1848]

GODWIN Colman Gen 70 at Rumford ME [16 Sept 1852]

GOGGINS Mr 84 at Saco ME [20 May 1847]

GOING John married Mrs A HEAD "Going ahead" [*Concord Freeman*] [10 Sept 1842]

GOLDER Caroline 40 w/o William GOLDER at Waterville ME [20 June 1850]

GOLDSBOROUGH Robert H a US senator at Elkton MD on 10 Oct [13 Jan 1837]

GOLDSMITH Mr the cook perished in the flames at Brownstown PA, Abraham FISHER, the contractor & Henry FISHER, his son had just returned with funds to pay his hands [7 Aug 1851]

GOLDSTEIN - see JEFFRIES

GOLDTHWAITE Charles 20 at Augusta ME [14 Oct 1836]

Mary 83 w/o Timothy GOLDTHWAITE at Augusta ME [9 Nov 1848]

GOOCH Jedediah 65 at Kennebunk ME [11 Nov 1852]

Joel & Mr HENDERSON of Alexander ME by entering a foul well [19 Aug 1852]

Richard Esq 31 editor of *Southern Planter* at Airfield VA on 13th ult [19 June 1851]

Samuel Esq 52 register of probate for Aroostook Co at Houlton ME [2 May 1844]

GOODALE Hannah C 56 w/o Enoch GOODALE at Saco ME [14 Mar 1850]

Helen Nason 13m d/o D H GOODALE of Winthrop ME at Harpswell ME [27 June 1840]

John 82 at Clinton ME [19 Aug 1852]

Prudence H 76 w/o Ephraim GOODALE at Orrington ME [21 Feb 1850]

GOODALE - see THURSTON

GOODALL Christopher seaman & Mr DOGGETT, 1st mate entangled in the hawser of ship *Beatrice* of Boston MA while being towed over the bar at New Orleans 17 Dec each had a thigh broken & GOODALL died in ten minutes [24 Jan 1850]

GOODELL Bartholomew 102y 16d at Belmont ME [13 Mar 1851]

GOODENOW John Lt 92y 8m AmRev at Hiram ME [12 Sept 1844]

GOODEY John 24 at Lisbon ME (s/o John G GOODY) [5 Apr 1849]

GOODHUE Nancy Jane 4y 8m d/o David & Hannah GOODHUE at Sidney ME on 21st inst of canker rash & scarlet fever [1 Oct 1846]

GOODNO Maria B 31 w/o Dr D H GOODNO at Hallowell ME on 11th [20 Jul 1848]

GOODNOW Harriet E P Esq abt 14 only c/o William E GOODNOW Esq at Norway ME [24 Apr 1845]

GOODRICH Charles F 8m s/o Charles F & Lucinda W GOODRICH at Vassalboro ME on 29 Sept [23 Oct 1851]

Daniel 64 one of the 1st settlers of the town, had for abt 2 yrs a cancer, & trusted his life in the hands of a person who undertook to cure it "By the job." The disease immediately grew worse and he finally died of starvation not having been able to swallow anything for the last 14 days of his life, at Canaan ME on 25 Aug [19 Sept 1840]

Jeremiah 73 at Canaan ME on Sat 27 Apr [23 May 1844]

Jonathan 75 also on the same night his wife 74 at Canaan ME on 25 Mar [11 Apr 1850]

Mrs 74 w/o Jonathan GOODRICH at Canaan ME on 25 Mar [11 Apr 1850]

Polly 77 widow of Levi GOODRICH at Bingham ME [4 Mar 1852]

Samuel has given his son, David GOODRICH his time & declared him to be free to trade for himself etc from the 12th Mar 1839 and thereafter [13 Apr 1839]

Miss & Miss LINDSEY attempting to cross the river near St John New Brunswick Canada found upon the ice frozen to death [28 Feb 1850]

GOODRIDGE Caroline 21 of Belgrade ME at Providence RI on 15 Aug [11 Nov 1847]

Eleanor 20 d/o Nathan GOODRIDGE at Clinton ME [10 June 1852]

Isaac 56 at Belgrade ME [11 Nov 1847]

Lovina abt 37 w/o Christopher GOODRIDGE at Rome ME on 27 Apr [29 May 1851]

Mary 60 a widow at Canaan ME [11 Jan 1849]

GOODWIN a son of Mr G by lightning while sitting at the door of his father's house at St Albans ME [1 Aug 1834]

GOODWIN (Cont.) Allen M 5m c/o Joshua & Sophia GOODWIN at Palermo on 10 June
[20 June 1850]

Amos C Esq of Saco attorney at law at Augusta ME on the 22nd [1 Feb 1840]

Ann 40 w/o Capt George W GOODWIN at Foxcroft ME [11 Nov 1847]

Benjamin 2y 7m s/o Reuel GOODWIN at Hallowell ME [18 Mar 1833]

C Mrs 42 w/o John GOODWIN at Baldwin ME on 11th inst [15 Aug 1840]

Charles H 19 an apprentice to Franklin of Pittston ME, a blacksmith, drowned [*Gardiner
Fountain*] [19 Jul 1849]

Daniel A 16 at Biddeford ME [18 Jul 1844]

Daniel F abt 13 a runaway apprentice from Reuben BASFORD of Monmouth ME [28 Jan
1833]

Downing 71 of Lewiston ME a native of Wells ME at Baldwin ME [20 Mar 1841]

Eliza A 41 at Augusta ME on 10th inst [17 Apr 1845]

Eunice of Gardiner ME saved from drowning when the steam packet *New England* sank.
It left Boston for Bath & Gardiner ME and had an accident with the schr *Curlew* on
31 May [12 June 1838]

Hannah 69 a widow at Hollis ME [21 Jan 1847]

Jacob 93y 6m formerly of Great Falls NH at Dover [5 Nov 1846]

James M Esq 39 at Biddeford ME [15 Oct 1846]

Jane 60 w/o Caleb GOODWIN at Clinton ME [5 June 1835]

Jeremiah 46 at Augusta ME on 10th inst [22 Jul 1847]

Joseph Perkins 4y s/o S B & Eliza GOODWIN at Augusta ME [17 Sept 1842]

Lydia 72 wid/o Daniel GOODWIN at Hollis ME [30 Apr 1842]

Martha 69 of Hallowell ME at Dorchester MA [9 Apr 1846]

Mary 30 w/o George GOODWIN at Weld ME [21 Dec 1839]

Moses at Hartford ME AmRev [9 Feb 1839]

Mrs C 42 w/o John GOODWIN Esq at Baldwin ME on 11th inst [15 Aug 1840]

Nathan 59 at Buxton ME [28 Oct 1852]

Priscilla 48 w/o Moses GOODWIN at Pittston ME [8 Feb 1849]

Sally 50 w/o Benjamin GOODWIN on 1st inst [17 Dec 1842]

Sarah D 9 d/o Jermiah & Melinda GOODWIN at Augusta ME on 7th inst [22 Jul 1847]

Thomas 36 w/o Hon Thomas GOODWIN 2nd at South Berwick ME [28 Mar 1844]

GOODWIN - see RAY

GOODYEAR Miles M 30 formerly of Hampden CT at Yuba CA on 12 Nov [14 Feb 1850]

GOOKIN Abigail 69 at Scarboro ME [29 Jan 1836]

Daniel injured on Boston & Maine Railroad at Malden MA? body conveyed to Biddeford
ME [17 Jul 1851]

GOOLD Thomas abt 70 resided in the western part of Philadelphia PA working near
Columbus tavern [*Philadelphia Chronicle*] [30 Apr 1846]

GORDAN Elijah Col of Aroostook Co ME in a letter dated 7 May says; "There is now full
three feet of snow in woods, and the knolls are just beginning to get bare in the fields.
The mail from Houlton to Fort Fairfield, is to-day carried in a sleigh." [20 May 1847]

GORDEN Jonathan 80 at Readfield ME while being shaved [26 Mar 1846]

Samuel A 34 at Hallowell ME [6 Mar 1845]

widow 80 at Saco ME [20 May 1847]

GORDON Benjamin 71 at Biddeford ME [8 Oct 1846]

Caleb abt 80 AmRev at Augusta ME [15 Jul 1833]

Chester Herbert 13m c/o Josiah & Belinda GORDON at Farmington ME [13 Feb 1851]

Isabel 16 of Readfield ME at Pittston ME [18 Dec 1845]

GORDON Jonathan Esq 42 at Abbot ME [14 Oct 1852]

Josiah 90 AmRev at Searsport ME [31 May 1849]

Miram 85 widow of Caleb GORDON at Augusta ME [7 Oct 1843]

GORDON (Cont.) Rosannah 20 w/o Sylvester GORDON at Hallowell ME [4 Oct 1849]
    William 45 at St Albans ME suddenly [17 Jan 1850]
GORHAM Calvin 60 at Lewiston ME [7 Mar 1850]
    Hannah 80 wid/o David GORHAM at Norway ME [20 Apr 1848]
    Josiah 83 AmRev at Richmond ME [3 May 1849]
    Julia Ann 21 d/o Dr C GORHAM at Lewiston ME [27 Nov 1835]
    Turana wid/o Dr C GORHAM of Lewiston ME at Turner ME [14 Oct 1852]
GORMAN - see DONAHUE, PETTINGILL
GORSUCH Edward the owner of two fugitives from Baltimore Co accompanied by his two
    sons, the deputy US Marshall from Baltimore, two US officers from Philadelphia for
    the purpose of arresting the fugitives ... we learn the colored population in the vicinity
    having been informed of the nature of the visit ... resolved to stand their ground.
    Edward GORSUCH, the owner of the slaves was shot Dead in the encounter.
    Dickerson GORSUCH, who was likewise shot & died there from. Joshua GORSUCH,
    mortally wounded, Dr Thomas PRINCE shot & badly beaten - feared he will die.
    Messrs Nicholas HUTCHINSON & Joshua NELSON managed to escape to
    Philadelphia PA. Two or three of the negroes were also shot in this fearful Fugitive
    Slave Riot at Christiana Lancaster Co PA on Thurs last [18 Sept 1851]
GOSLING Mrs w/o Henry GOSLING, restaurantor of Nassau Street last Sat morning
    became the mother of her twenty-fourth child at New York [5 Aug 1847]
GOSS Almira J 22 of Kents Hill (Readfield) ME at St Albans ME [8 Jul 1847]
    Dorcas 51 at Danville (now part of Auburn) ME [27 Dec 1849]
    Herbert L 3 s/o Leonard GOSS at Augusta ME [8 Aug 1850]
    Jonathan 46 at Levant ME [4 Jan 1850]
    Thomas Esq 75 at Pittston ME [1 Apr 1843]
    William H 22 at Lewiston ME [3 Jan 1850]
GOSSUM Abiel at Paris ME [21 Jan 1833]
GOTT Benjamin of Mt Desert ME drowned himself from the "Porcupine Island"
    Frenchman's Bay some time in May. He was insane [18 June 1846]
    Rhoda 75 w/o William GOTT at Leeds ME [2 Jan 1851]
GOUD John C 20 at Topsham ME [26 Oct 1848]
GOUDY Amos 61 at Bristol [31 Mar 1844]
GOUGH Hannah Mrs 109y 11m 15d on Sun conversed with every President of the United
    States. When George Washington Parks CURTIS was here whe was sent for to go &
    see him, but was too feeble to accept the invitation [*NY Express*] [30 Oct 1845]
    John B the temperance lecturer not Dead nor likely to die at present though the papers
    have had him as Dead as a smoked herring. Is now at Roxbury [24 Sept 1846]
GOULD Abel 27, 2nd mate of Lisbon ME, the names of the officers & crew as per the
    Custom House list, the ship *Jacob Perkins*, Capt SHOOF, which arrived his morning
    from Crostadt reported that on 22 inst Cape Cod WSW 55 miles fell in with the
    wreck of brig *Washington*, RIDER Capt [*Transcript*] [2 Oct 1835]
    Anna Leonora 8m d/o William & Martha A GOULD at Bristol NH on 19 Aug [2 Sept
    1852]
    Bethiah 42 w/o Charles GOULD at Lisbon ME on 7 Aug [23 Aug 1849]
    Betsey of Lewiston Falls ME 24 of dysentery Sacramento CA [2 Jan 1851]
    boy of New Sharon ME s/o Oliver GOULD swallowed a cent, after four days Dr P DYER
    was called upon & removed the cent [28 Sept 1848]
    Cardelia at North Leeds ME on 8 Oct with brain fever [19 Oct 1839]
    child of Mr GOULD drowned in Seven Mile Brook at New Portland ME on Tues last.
    The child was abt 3y (from *Skowhegan Sentinel*) [23 Mar 1839]
    Cynthia 50 at Dixfield ME [6 Nov 1845]

GOULD (Cont.) Daniel 72 at New Sharon ME on 10 Sept [8 Oct 1845]
    Dennis 86 at Pittston ME [12 Feb 1852]
    Dorothy 73 w/o Nathaniel GOULD Esq at New Sharon ME [6 May 1843]
    Edward 34 at Rockland ME [12 Sept 1850]
    Eli 56 of Baltimore MD a native of Leeds ME at California on 5th Oct [29 May 1851]
    Elizabeth 72 w/o Dennis GOULD at Pittston ME on 26th ult, the third d/o Peletiah
        WARREN, early known as among the first settlers of Gardiner ME [29 Mar 1849]
    G F saved from drowning between Thompson's Island & Fort Independence one of three
        of 27 boys of the Farm School taken off by a boat from the schr *H B FOSTER* of
        Machias ME, then coming up the harbor from Trinidad [7 May 1842]
    George A of Gardiner ME on Sat last; Capt Andrew FITCH d same day; George O
        BATES of Springfield MA & Thomas PENDERGRAST, of Ireland d same day. 1st
        officer Mr ROLLINS, a nephew of Capt James ROLLINS of Hallowell ME & two
        foreigners taken off wreck on Sat 28th ult by the schr *Minnesota*, Capt Gilbert M
        LEIGHTON, who brought them to (Boston) last evening, the brig *Natahnis* (of
        Pittston ME), was shipwrecked [8 Feb 1849]
    Horace 4y 9m s/o Horace GOULD at Winthrop ME of measles [19 Feb 1846]
    Isaac 88 at Leeds ME on 5 Feb [19 Feb 1852]
    Jesse 82nd AmRev at Hamilton Butler Co OH on 12 Jan [6 Mar 1838]
    John 38 of Portland ME at Alms House (*E Argus*) [20 Jan 1848]
    John 69 at Wilton ME [4 Oct 1849]
    Joseph 69 at Leeds ME [16 May 1837]
    Joseph Esq 63 of Lincolnville ME at Belfast ME on 30th ult [14 Dec 1833]
    Julia 26 w/o Elias GOULD at Porter ME [1 Apr 1847]
    Lucy 22 w/o William GOULD at Pittston ME on 26 Oct [13 Nov 1838]
    Lucy J 32 w/o Andrew GOULD at New Portland ME [1 Jan 1846]
    Lucy widow 85 at Norridgewock ME [15 Jan 1846]
    Mary 53 w/o Nicholas GOULD at Hollis ME [20 Apr 1848]
    Melinda 14 d/o Asa GOULD at Hallowell ME [12 Aug 1852]
    Moses formerly of Nashua NH near Sacramento City CA [20 Nov 1851]
    Nancy 30 w/o Harrison GOULD at Leeds ME [1 Apr 1847]
    Peltiah 69 8m at Leeds ME on 7 Apr [29 Apr 1852]
    Richmond H 36 of Belgrade ME at Augusta ME at the Insane Hospital on 18 Nov [28
        Nov 1850]
    Samuel 70 at Corinth ME [1 Feb 1849]
    Samuel 80 at Dixmont ME [26 Oct 1848]
    Samuel Esq 77 at New Portland ME [4 Jul 1844]
    Sarah 55 at Portland ME [8 Feb 1844]
    Simeon 62 at Leeds ME on 30th ult [8 Aug 1834]
    Susan D 13 of Dixfield ME at Bath ME [14 Feb 1850]
    Thankful 73 w/o Silas GOULD at Wilton ME [11 Apr 1834]
    William 83 at Hope ME [2 Sept 1852]
GOULD - see BARBER, NASON, STARBIRD
GOULDING Nancy P 29 at Perry ME [15 Feb 1849]
    Peter Esq 66 at Perry ME [29 Nov 1839]
GOUTS Susan has made Isaac B ROWLAND pay her $1000 (the Washington MD Court
    has so ordered) for promising to marry her & then refusing. Susan sold Isaac for a
    pretty good sum these "hard times" [21 Dec 1839]
GOVE Dorothy Jane 25 d/o Elias GOVE at Readfield ME on the 18th ult [6 Feb 1838]
    Elias 76 at Readfield ME [17 June 1852]
    George W S 23 at Readfield ME on 14 June [10 Jul 1845]

GOVE (Cont.) Jonathan Capt 37y 7m at Readfield ME of consumption after a severe
   sickness of 8 months [24 Dec 1842]
   Mary A 31 w/o Capt A I GOVE at Augusta ME on 21 Sept [2 Oct 1851]
   S D of Manchester NH at San Francisco CA [8 Jan 1852]
   Simon 25 at Limington ME [16 Sept 1852]
   William 80 at Augusta ME on 7 June [13 June 1850]
GOW Eliphalet abt 30 s/o Deac James of Hallowell ME at Waterville ME [8 Aug 1837]
   James 78 at Hallowell ME [18 June 1842]
   John L the Whigs of Washington Co PA have nominated him for Congress, a native of
      Hallowell ME & the eldest s/o the late Deac GOW [*Kennebec Journal*] [23 Jul 1846]
GOWAN John a well known citizen of Baltimore lately committed suicide [23 May 1834]
GOWELL James 58 at Danville (now part of Auburn) ME [2 Aug 1849]
GOWEN James 57 at Westbrook ME [29 Apr 1852]
   John F a letter to the *Courier* from him stated he was raising the wreck of the United
      States steamship *Missouri*, sunk in the Bay of Gibraltar [*Boston Journal*] [4 Mar
      1852]
   two ch of John GOWEN, both died in one day & interred in one coffin, his only ch at
      Montville ME [21 Aug 1841]
GOWER Edwin 11m only d/o Davis N & Susan GOWER at Vassalboro ME on 17 Mar [18
   Mar 1852]
   Florinda W 20 at Minot Corner ME [27 Jul 1839]
   Haskell 37 of Gray ME at Havana Cuba on 29 Oct [6 Dec 1849]
   Richard Elder 51 at Hartland ME on 18 Jul [1 Aug 1850]
   Susanna Mrs 70 at Industry ME [29 Feb 1844]
GRACE Thomas 21 at Bath ME [18 Dec 1851]
GRADY - see ROLERSON
GRAFFAM Stephen W 45 formerly of Lewiston ME at San Francisco CA [21 Mar 1850]
GRAFTON Lucy 78 of Cushing ME at Thomaston ME [6 Jul 1848]
GRAHAM George 56 at Milton [17 Jul 1851]
   George A a machinist of So Boston MA shot at Havana Cuba [18 Sept 1851]
   Seth a machinist of Maine found near Abbott's wharf with a junk bottle lying by his side
      containing New England rum, an inquest was held before Coroner Mace SMITH at
      South Boston MA the verdict - exposure, caused by intemperance [29 Feb 1840]
   Sylvester Dr of "bran-bread notoriety" died abt 50y at Northampton on Wed [18 Sept
      1851]
GRANDIN Jane Maria Mrs 33 at New York City on 25th ult & youngest d/o the late
   Stephen LEE formerly of Portland ME [15 Jan 1842]
GRANGER Charles Francis 3 s/o Charles GRANGER at Augusta ME [19 Sept 1850]
   child 18m infant child of Charles GRANGER at Augusta ME [26 Sept 1850]
   Edward L Esq of the firm of Lewis P MEED & Co of Augusta ME at Pittsford VT on 1st
      Dec [10 Dec 1846]
   Frederick abt 12 or 13 s/o Joseph GRANGER Esq, playing abt the frame of a new
      building on Germain St on Wed fell from the ridge-pole to the ground 18 or 20 feet,
      Dr PORTER who is attending him said the lad was in a very critical condition it is a
      wonder he was not killed on the spot [*Calais Advertiser*] [30 Mar 1848]
GRANT Azor H 24 at Bath ME [29 Jan 1836]
   Betsey L 20 w/o William S GRANT of Gardiner ME at Augusta ME on 18 Mar & d/o
      Alvah JOSSELYN Esq of this town [22 Mar 1849]
   child 18m c/o Jotham GRANT burnt to death in (Portland?) on 28th ult. This was the
      2nd child in Portland on that day [13 Apr 1839]

GRANT (Cont.) Daniel 43 drowned at Bar Mills in Hollis ME on 24th inst, the body has not been found, whoever may find the same will confer a great favor to the mother by sending word to Samuel McKENNEY of Saco ME & will be suitably rewarded. [*Saco Democrat*] [2 Dec 1847]

Desiah M 24 of Freeport ME at Scituate MA [26 Nov 1842]

Edward abt 40 at Augusta ME [28 June 1849]

Elisha 90 at Bridgton [11 Jan 1849]

Elizabeth V 66 w/o John GRANT at Prospect ME [18 Jul 1850]

Enoch 15 at Ellsworth ME by drowning [24 June 1852]

Franklin 18 youngest s/o Samuel C GRANT Esq at Hallowell ME [19 Aug 1852]

Hannah Mrs 58 at Sebasticook ME [21 Oct 1847]

James 68 at Westbrook ME [2 Jan 1851]

John J M 20 s/o Rev Mr GRANT at Litchfield ME on the 4th inst [13 Aug 1842]

Joshua 80 at York ME [16 Nov 1848]

Josiah 48 at Frankfort ME [15 Jul 1843]

Mrs a letter from Persia, announcing the painful news of her death, w/o Dr G at Oromiah [*New York Commercial*] [8 June 1839]

Mrs of Stoverton Muskingum Co OH found lately lying upon the fire in her room quite Dead [*Zaneville Journal*] [1 Jan 1846]

Patience 80 wid/o James GRANT at York ME [19 Aug 1852]

Peter 66 at Gardiner ME [8 Jul 1836]

Sally Ann 22 w/o Josiah GRANT at York ME [12 Nov 1845]

Samuel 73 at Freeman ME [6 May 1852]

Thomas J of Black Brook in (Piscataquis Co ME) formerly of Old Town Penobscot Co ME killed near his res on 19th ult by falling a tree (from the *Piscataquis Observer*) [11 Dec 1851]

Valentine A at Exeter ME [30 Nov 1848]

William 35 formerly of Rome ME drowned at Frankfort ME [15 Jan 1852]

GRANT - see WILSON

GRAVES Albert 21y formerly of Richmond ME at Bangor ME on 17th ult [11 Nov 1836]

c/o David & Hannah GRAVES of Litchfield ME badly scalded by tipping over a pot of beans, funeral by Elder P RIDLEY [4 Nov 1847]

Eliza F Esq 20 d/o Charles GRAVES at Wayne ME [14 Oct 1847]

Jacob Esq 68 of Vienna ME at Augusta ME on 24th inst while attending as juror at Supreme Judicial Court of lung fever [5 Feb 1842]

John 88y 8m at Kingfield ME on 1st Apr [9 May 1850]

Mary Ann 31 wid/o Joel H GRAVES at Bowdoinham ME [29 Jul 1852]

Mr of Kentucky died [5 Oct 1848]

Mrs w/o George A GRAVES of Guilford CT death by clothes taking fire [19 Feb 1846]

Nathaniel on 28th of May left the res of his father in South Thomaston ME and is now missing, he was 23y old (the *Rockland Gazette* in Maine) [17 Jul 1851]

Sarah 64 w/o Jacob GRAVES Esq at Vienna ME [27 Feb 1838]

Zelpha w/o William GRAVES at Topsham ME [18 Feb 1847]

GRAY Andrew 80 at Waterboro ME [14 Mar 1850]

Betsey 79 consort of Andrew GRAY at Waterboro ME [8 Nov 1849]

David of Castine ME seaman of the brig Mary of Southport ME drowned [*Newport News*] [24 Dec 1846]

E F Mr of Portland ME a constable fell Dead while washing himself on Mon [26 Feb 1846]

Elizabeth Miss of Solon ME (whose previous absence had already been announced) found on the banks of Charles River at Newton Corner. It is supposed that in a fit of insanity she left Boston MA & threw herself into the river [6 Nov 1851]

GRAY (Cont.) George Esq of Boston found Dead in a railroad car...supposedly of apoplexy at Andover MA on Thurs afternoon 18 Nov 1843

George W 6 s/o John GRAY at Vassalboro ME on Tues last of canker rash [25 Feb 1833]

Henry killed 22y belonged to Lubec ME runover by a locomotive at Taunton on Tues morning 25th ult [17 Apr 1851]

Isabella 27 at Gorham ME [15 Aug 1844]

James 25 at Readfield ME on the 7th ult [15 Apr 1833]

Jesse 55 at Brooksville ME [12 Feb 1846]

John 62 at Belfast ME [9 Nov 1848]

John Col 50 at Dixmont ME [20 Dec 1849]

John H one of the Tehuantepec surveying party devoured by a shark while bathing in the Pacific Ocean, he was formerly of Atkins, Stedman & Co of Boston MA [4 June 1851]

Leonard of Bristol ME at New Orleans on Jul last [2 Sept 1836]

Lucy A 32 w/o William GRAY at Gardiner ME [16 Jan 1851]

Luria Ann 34 w/o William GRAY at Gardiner ME [23 Jan 1851]

Martha M Mrs 35 d/o Isaac & Alice COWEN of Sidney ME at Mulberry AL on 1 Aug [8 Aug 1850]

Melinda 48 w/o Wesley GRAY Esq at Concord [23 May 1850]

Nancy 23 w/o Therel GRAY at Waldoboro ME on 19 May [8 June 1848]

Peter T Dr at Jefferson ME on 7th inst was the rep in the legislature at the last session and was indisposed thro' the winter [29 May 1838]

Reuben Mrs 75 at Anson ME on 27 Sept [17 Oct 1844]

Sally 21 at Plymouth ME on 20 June [13 Jul 1848]

Samuel A age 23 at Gardiner ME on Sat on 30 Mar of consumption [16 Apr 1844]

Turner 24 s/o Guy & Miner GRAY of Dead River Franklin Co ME at Concord NH on 26 June [15 Jul 1852]

William H 15 s/o Capt H GRAY of Hallowell ME on Board schr *Orlinda* on the passage from Boston to Norfolk [11 May 1848]

GRAY - see KNIGHT, PERKINS

GREASON Margaret 63 at Hallowell ME [11 Oct 1849]

Wilson 54 at New Portland ME [14 Mar 1850]

GREATON Leonard Major 60 at Starks ME [22 Nov 1849]

GREELEY/GREELY Arthur Young 6 years only s/o Horace GREELEY of cholera [26 Jul 1849]

Aurilla A 20 d/o Burnham C GREELEY at Augusta ME on 18 Aug [26 Aug 1852]

Bathsheba F 33 w/o Burnham C GREELEY of Augusta ME at Palermo ME on 15th inst [23 Aug 1849]

Daniel Esq 69 at Foxcroft ME [23 Jan 1845]

Fanny 40 w/o Enos GREELY Esq at Palermo ME [20 June 1850]

George 28 at Belfast ME [6 Jan 1848]

Jonathan Esq 84 at Palermo ME [26 Aug 1852]

Joseph Esq his sawmill & grist mill at Mercer ME totally consumed by fire on Fri afternoon (from the *Somerset Journal*) [11 Apr 1834]

lad s/o Philip GREELEY Esq saved from drowning by Ezra HARTFORD [27 Jul 1839]

Nancy w/o Rev Allen GREELEY at Turner ME on 30 June [15 Jul 1833]

Samuel 33 at Gardiner ME [29 June 1839]

Samuel 73 at Hallowell ME [6 Jan 1848]

Sarah Jane Mrs at Palermo ME on 2 Dec after an illness of four years d/o Dr E P HUNTOON [31 Dec 1842]

William 65 at Belfast ME [28 Mar 1850]

GREELEY/GREELY - see HACKER, TAYLOR

GREEN Abigail w/o Joseph GREEN at Pittston ME of an advanced age [6 Aug 1846]

> David 53 at Norridgewock ME [14 May 1846]

> Eunice 54 at Byron ME [5 Apr 1849]

> Ezra Dr born in Malden MA 17 June 1746, graduated in 1765, NH regiment AmRev a surgeon in June 1775 to last of Dec 1776, joined the army on the retreat before the enemy, as they advanced from Quebec by way of North River to Montreal. In Oct 1777, he enlisted as surgeon on board the *Ranger*, of 18 guns, Capt (John) Paul JONES ... He now resides at Dover NH 99y on 28 June last [*Dover Gazette*] (not an obit) [30 Oct 1845]

> Fidelia 13 d/o Norrel GREEN at Dead River ME [13 June 1850]

> Gardiner Esq of Topsham ME board ship *United States* on her passage Bath ME to New Orleans of consumption on 10th Jan off the Balize, remains carried to New Orleans [8 Feb 1840]

> George & Joseph 10m, twin children of Capt George GREEN at Pittston ME [14 Jan 1847]

> Hannah Mrs w/o Jonas GREEN of Wilton ME killed by lightning a week or two since. She was on a visit at the house of Philbrick MARSTON in Harrington [*Portland Advertiser*] [2 Oct 1845]

> Harriet 16 d/o Stephen GREEN at Fairfield ME [28 Aug 1851]

> Isaiah B 22 formerly of Turner ME of typhus fever at Sagna La Crande in Cuba [29 May 1845]

> J C Dr 45 at Turner ME on 9 Jan [8 Feb 1844]

> Josiah 82 at Wilton ME [14 Mar 1850]

> Leonard H of Portland ME at San Francisco CA on 3rd May [11 Jul 1850]

> Lydia 81 wid/o Joseph GREEN at Winton ME [21 Feb 1851]

> Martha 82 at Deer Isle ME [1 Feb 1849]

> Mary 27y 9m consort of Joseph GREEN at Bowdoinham ME on 14th inst [23 May 1844]

> Mr of Newbury the engineer killed in the steam when boiler exploded [28 Oct 1843]

> Nathaniel 66 at Topsham ME on 2d inst [13 Apr 1848]

> Robert & Anthony HAMILTON of New York had a duel with rifles "Either because the rifles were not loaded or the marksmen were no blood was spilt" at Bladensburgh [18 Dec 1841]

> Sarah a widow 74y 10m at Starks ME [2 Jan 1845]

> Susan 25 at Saco ME [15 Jul 1847]

> Thomas AmRev of Stoneham at Stoneham on Tues of last week [*Concord Freeman*] [22 Oct 1842]

GREEN - see CRAWFORD, HALL, THOMPSON

GREENE Albert H 2 s/o William S GREENE at Augusta ME [13 June 1850]

> Benjamin 75 formerly of South Berwick ME at Athens ME at the res of his son [24 Oct 1837]

> Charles judge of the probate court for Somerset Co abt 46 at Athens ME on 24 Aug [2 Sept 1852]

> Henry 52 printer formerly of Augusta ME at Portland ME on 28 Mar [5 Apr 1849]

> Jonathan S 74 AmRev at Jackson ME [27 June 1834]

> Roscoe G surveyor of the port of Portland ME at Portland ME [26 Dec 1840]

> William A lost on the *Lexington*, $15,000 found on his body and in the hands of the coroner [1 Feb 1840]

GREENE - see WILLIAMS

GREENLAW Ebenezer 44y of Bristol in this county committed suicide on 22d of this month cutting his throat with a razor [13 June 1834]

GREENLEAF Asa at Hallowell ME [18 Jul 1847]

> Caroline 15 of Mercer ME at Augusta ME on 1 June [15 June 1848]

GREENLEAF (Cont.) Ebenezer Esq 70 at Williamsburg ME [8 Jan 1852]

Hannah Dennison 57 w/o Eben GREENLEAF Esq [13 Apr 1839]

Henry 63 at Boothbay ME [7 Nov 1850]

John 23 native of Bangor ME at Marine Hospital at Chelsea MA [14 Jan 1847]

John 90y 7m AmRev of the 1st on Sandy River & form/o Wiscasset ME present at surrender of both Gen CORNWALLIS & BURGOYNE died at Starks ME on 4th inst [18 June 1846]

Louisa 33 w/o John GREENLEAF at Wiscasset ME [30 Dec 1847]

Lydia G 83 at Williamsburgh ME of erysipelas [4 Apr 1834]

M P Dr a physician of West Newton on Sun [*Traveller*] [3 Feb 1848]

Moses abt 55 at Williamsburgh ME of erysipelas [4 Apr 1834]

Perry abt 22 at Mercer ME by a fall from a barn he was repairing at Mercer ME [22 June 1839]

Thomas C Esq age about 45 at Bristol ME? [18 Dec 1845]

GREENMAN Mr who keeps a public house near Fonda NY having refused of a Sunday liquor to another named Mr THOMAS, words ensued & as GREENMAN was shutting the door upon him, he received a stab in the abdomen which proved fatal [21 Dec 1839]

GREENOUGH Hannah B 32 at Kennebunk ME [3 Jul 1835]

Henry 21 at Saco ME [23 Jan 1851]

Thomas 90 the last of tribe of Nobscuretts, in (Yarmouth MA) ... alive the ashes of their nationality, since the 1st withering influence of the whites felt upon their shores [21 Mar 1837]

GREENWOOD F W P Rev of King's Chapel Boston MA at Dorchester MA on 2nd inst [12 Aug 1843]

George Albion O 23 formerly of Farmington ME at Albany [9 Dec 1843]

Gilman 42 late of Boston MA at Boothbay ME [20 Nov 1851]

James H 22 of Calais ME at Sacramento CA [18 Mar 1852]

Malinda 20 at Industry ME [17 May 1849]

Mary Ann 15 at Industry ME [26 Aug 1847]

Nathaniel 85 at Farmington ME [19 Nov 1846]

Sarah 31 at Brunswick ME [17 Jul 1835]

Sarah Jane 26 formerly of Farmington ME at Industry ME [8 Mar 1849]

GREGORY Isreal Jr three men drowned on New Years's night, passing channel Seal Harbor to Muscleridges near Thomaston ME, the others were Andrew & Daniel ALLEN who left families [16 Jan 1841]

GREMILLION Mr on Wed 14th ult [*The Point Coupee Tribune*] [19 Feb 1846]

GREY Julia S 33 at Denmark ME [21 Jan 1847]

GRIEVE John Mr & Mrs "the bodies of two unknown persons found shot & frozen in the woods near Quincy MA a few weeks since .... have been identifed as above of Zanesville OH who mysteriously disappeared from that place last Oct and were supposed to have been drowned. They were both noted for their romantic freaks. [6 Mar 1851]

GRIFFETH Nancy 45 w/o John GRIFFETH Jr at Livermore ME on 28th ult [7 Mar 1843]

GRIFFIN Celia 35 at Bangor ME [14 Nov 1844]

Ebenzer 68 at Vienna ME [29 Jan 1839]

Eliza G 25 at Gardiner ME (died 11 Apr 1852 d/o Reuben & Fanny [Hill] GRIFFIN) [N.B. see also *Morning Star* issue 5 May 1852 & Dean Stakeman's *Maine Black Population* at Bowdoin College of Brunswick ME] [29 Apr 1852]

John an Irishman died at New York of chloroform [1 Feb 1849]

Joseph 21 fell overboard from schr *Mars Hill* at Bangor ME on Thurs last, his body had not been found [23 Jul 1842]

GRIFFIN (Cont.) Mr 74 at Vassalboro ME [2 Mar 1848]

Peter T 25 at Belfast ME [22 Feb 1844]

GRIFFIN - see KNIGHT

GRIFFITH Boyden 2 at Dixfield ME [6 Nov 1845]

Mary 81 at Livermore ME [9 Apr 1846]

GRIFFITHS - see CRAWFORD

GRIMES Nancy 5 s/o Capt GRIMES at Hallowell ME [31 Oct 1844]

GRIMMELL Caroline w/o Daniel H GRIMMELL at Norridgewock ME [17 Apr 1838]

GRINDLE William Capt 80 at Belfast ME on 4th inst [17 Dec 1842]

GRINNEL Cornelius 33 at Union ME [1 Apr 1833]

Patience w/o Bailey GRINNEL at Union ME [11 JUl 1834]

GRINNELL Experince 87 at Belfast ME [3 Apr 1851]

GRINNELL - see FRANKLIN

GRISWOLD Mr a Baptist clergyman killed in consequence of offense taken at some of his remarks [the *Cincinnati Chronicle*] [8 May 1841]

Oliver 56 of Fryeburg ME at Limerick ME [7 Dec 1833]

GROE Dederick deck passenger of Germany on board the steamboat *George Collier* on the 6th inst on her passage from New Orleans to St Louis MO [25 May 1839]

GRONING Adolph, importer, of Pearl Street killed by the falling walls caused by the explosion at New York NY [24 Jul 1845]

GROSLAY Dr an eminent physican of Opelousas a victim of cholera [10 Aug 1833]

GROSS David missing since Jul last then insane, wore a long beard & his father, John GROSS, is anxious to hear from him of Jay ME [2 Jan 1851]

Otis C 49 at New Gloucester ME [2 Aug 1849]

Samuel 20 late of Brunswick ME at Bangor ME [8 Apr 1843]

GROSSE Mary B 79 w/o Joshua GROSSE at Orland ME [14 Nov 1850]

GROUS Rufus at East Monmouth ME buried alive last Sat [9 Sept 1847]

GROUSE Joseph 34 of North Yarmouth ME lost overboard on 7th ult from ship *Perdonnet* in the Mississippi on passage New Orleans to Boston MA [11 Jul 1844]

GROVER Andrew of Bowdoinham ME a seaman at sea 8th inst on board brig *William Purington* from Guadaloupe for Wilmington [5 Mar 1846]

Eli 33 at Norway ME [3 Oct 1850]

Eliza 14 d/o Joseph GROVER at Phillips ME of smallpox [11 Sept 1851]

Joseph Jr 24 at Phillips ME of smallpox [11 Sept 1851]

Mrs 60 w/o Jos GROVER at Phillips ME of smallpox [4 Sept 1851]

GROVER - see BLUNT, FLETCHER

GROVES John 85 at Wiscasset ME [11 June 1846]

Widow her dwelling house situated abt one mile westward from Wiscasset Village totally destroyed by fire & melancholy to relate, the lady owner & her brother - Mr Reuben YOUNG were both consumed in the flames! They were aged people - upwards of 75y [*Bath Times*] [18 Nov 1847]

GROWER Martha Jane 22 at Industry ME [18 Jul 1837]

GROWS John Jr 18 at Brunswick ME [1 Jul 1836]

GROZIER - see COAN

GRYMES Fitzhugh & four negro men left Aquia Stafford Co VA for his home in a sailboat & were all drowned by the upsetting of the boat, *The Alexandria Gazette* so stated on 13th ult [7 Feb 1850]

GUBTILL Benjamin 28 of Hermon ME drowned in Hampden ME on 27th ult [30 Dec 1847]

GUILD boy s/o Davis GUILD at Augusta ME [18 Jul 1837]

Emma Jane 3 d/o Cyrus GUILD Jr at Augusta ME on 9th inst [28 Dec 1848]

GUILD (Cont.) Virgil Esq 37 postmaster of Pineville SC on 26 May s/o Cyrus GUILD Esq
    of Augusta ME [11 Jul 1837]
GUILD - see WHITTIER
GUILFORD William 61 at Saco ME [21 Mar 1850]
GUILLIVER David 29 at Fairfield ME [18 Mar 1852]
GULLIFER Hannah 34 at Fairfield ME [9 Apr 1842]
GULLIFORD Hugh (Irish) 30 at Augusta ME on Mon last very suddenly [3 Feb 1848]
GULLIVER David 29 at Fairfield ME [18 Mar 1852]
    Sampson also Stephen WHITE, Isaac HALL & Mr FERGUSON drowned at Gordon
        Falls on Penobscot River [*Bangor ME Whig*] [14 Aug 1845]
GUMWELL James at Palmer MA his house struck by lightning on the 8th inst & his wife
    killed. One of the ch stunned by the stock but has since recovered. [27 Jul 1839]
GUPTILL Alice Mrs 57 at Porter ME [29 Jul 1847]
    Polly 51 at Belgrade ME on 9 Apr [1 May 1851]
    Thomas H 4y 6m only s/o Dr W N GUPTILL of Clinton ME at Albion ME [27 Jul 1848]
GURGESS Merinda G 21 at Vassalboro ME [24 Apr 1851]
GURLEY John A 43 of New York City at Hallowell ME [3 Sept 1846]
GURNEY child of South Abington MA c/o David B GURNEY accidentally run over by a
    hayrack on Fri 25th ult, the cart weighed abt eight cwt & 6 or 8 persons on it yet
    wonderful to relate the child was not seriously injured although the wheel passed over
    her stomach & head [7 Aug 1851]
    Sarah 52 at Fayette ME, "she was Deaf & dumb" (Deaf mute) [19 Sept 1844]
GUYER Sergeant in the Irish & Native American (not American Indians more likely
    English born in American) Riots in Philadelphia PA [*Dollar Newspaper*] [18 July
    1844]

- H -

HACKER Anna 92 wid/o Jeremiah HACKER of Salem MA at Brunswick ME, for more
    than 50y a member & highly esteemed elder of Durham monthly meeting of Friends
    [21 Aug 1835]
    Joseph late of China ME est notice Josiah H GREELEY adm [17 June 1852]
HACKETT Minerva 42 w/o Jacob HACKETT at Danville (now part of Auburn) ME [21
    Mar 1850]
    Nelson abt 19 died by gun accident at Manchester CT [28 Aug 1835]
HADLEY Aaron C 76 at Unity ME [19 July 1849]
    James V 47 at Augusta ME on 2 Sept [5 Sept 1850]
HAGER Ezekiel 77 at Union ME of the early settlers & during his life caught & killed 49
    bears [*W Yankee*] [1 Apr 1833]
HAINES Isaac of Passadumkeag ME his tavern house & two barns also other buildings
    burned last Thurs [*Bangor Mercury*] [16 Sept 1847]
    John A 25 at Hallowell ME [14 Nov 1840] & [21 Nov 1840]
    Lewis abt 35 at Readfield ME on Tues last of consumption [10 Oct 1834]
    Miss the young lady who married in London one of the Chippewa Indians, under the care
        of Mr CATLIN, arrived in New York on their way to the Indian territories [12 Sept
        1844]
    Nathaniel Esq late editor of the *Eastern Republican* at Bangor ME [16 Dec 1836]
    Walter 37 at Winthrop ME on the 15th inst [23 May 1840]
    Walter 68 at Dexter ME [28 June 1849]
    William P Esq 3m 13d at Saco ME [20 Mar 1845]

HAINS child 3y c/o widow Content W HAINS at Winthrop ME of scarlet fever [16 Apr 1842]
> Daniel 58 at Hallowell ME on the 1st inst of consumption [17 Jul 1838]
> John Capt 52 at Readfield ME [27 June 1844]
> Nancy Mrs 56 at Readfield ME [20 June 1850]

HALAM Col killed in Mexican War [22 Jan 1836]

HALE David Esq 74 of Turner ME at Waterford ME on 6th inst suddenly [19 Feb 1846]
> Enoch Dr 53 formerly of Gardiner ME at Boston MA on the 12th inst [30 Nov 1848]
> Harriette 25 at Winslow ME on 3 Aug [19 Aug 1852]
> Jonas 50 at Madison ME [5 Jul 1849]
> Maria Miss (sister to Mrs Robert TRINIMAN & Mrs MANITON) on the morning of 2d inst was on board with 25 persons when the boat struck upon "Hunt's Rock" 19 persons including ch drowned all of whom resided in Portland (ME) or at York Point [*Portland Adv*] [*The St Johns City Gazette* of 2 Aug] [21 Aug 1838]
> Olive 90 AmRev at Waterford ME [20 Mar 1851]
> Oliver 90 at Waterford ME [16 Oct 1851]
> Philena 36 w/o Eusebius HALE at West Waterville ME [26 Feb 1846]
> Philena D 17 d/o Rev Eusebius HALE at Bradford ME [5 Feb 1852]
> Robert of Yorkshire England has risen to the height of eight feet & weighs 462 lbs His father was 6'6" & his mother 6' & still the son can look down upon them. [11 May 1848]
> Sarah J an article in *Godey's Lady's Book* for August, takes strong ground in favor of the practice of medicine by females. She was a female doctor. [14 Aug 1851]
> Sarah w/o S HALE at West Waterville ME [20 May 1847]
> Thomas Esq 60 at Anson ME [5 Jul 1849]
> William 65 at Limerick ME [7 June 1849]

HALE - see WRIGHT

HALEY Elizabeth 92y 11m 10d wid/o Capt Pelatiah HALEY at Topsham ME [1 Apr 1836]
> Hiram 23 at Saco ME [5 Feb 1852]
> Joel 32 at Portland ME [31 Oct 1844]
> John T 62 formerly of Lubec ME at Biddeford ME [28 Oct 1852]
> Joshua Deac at Webster ME (b 1776, d 1849 left a wife, the former Mary FARRAR, & ch, see *History of Webster* by David C YOUNG) [25 Jan 1849]
> Oliver Esq of Frankfort ME drowned, a representative in the last legislature from Frankfort, left a wife & several ch [*Republican Journal*] [14 Aug 1845]

HALL Abigail 80 widow at Turner ME on 25 Apr [14 May 1842]
> Arad 29 at New Castle ME [22 Aug 1850]
> Benjamin a poor man, turned out homeless with his family when at Frankfort ME on Tues the house took fire [*Belfast Signal*] [16 Jan 1851]
> boy abt 13 s/o late W N HALL drowned at Brunswick ME [15 Jul 1847]
> Caroline 18 at Pittston ME on the 27th ult [13 Mar 1845]
> Caroline Amanda 7 d/o Ezekiel HALL at Thomaston ME [19 Feb 1846]
> Desire widow 85 at Bath ME [21 Dec 1848]
> Eartha C at Portland ME [9 Dec 1847]
> Elbridge removing stones & the pry left under one swung around causing almost instantaneous death [6 Nov 1845]
> Elijah 64 at Thomaston ME [13 Aug 1846]
> Elijah Maj 69 of a cancer in the mouth at Norway ME [13 Jan 1837]
> Elinor widow 62 at Camden ME [20 Jan 1848]
> Emily J 28 at Norway ME [21 Nov 1844]
> Ezra 37 at Belfast ME [26 Dec 1850]
> Frye 62 at Belfast ME [16 Aug 1849]

HALL (Cont.) George 23 of South Thomaston ME at Panama New Grenada [31 May 1849]

George at Nobleboro ME on 30 Sept [11 Nov 1836]

Hannah 86 relict of Dr John HALL at China ME [8 June 1848]

Helen M 18 d/o Gen Daniel HALL at Gorham ME [16 Dec 1852]

Henry E 10m s/o Capt James B HALL at Augusta ME [17 Oct 1850]

Isaac H C 28 of Abbott ME 4 men burnt to death in a camp in Plt No 4 on Great Works Stream HALL left a wife & 2 ch [13 Feb 1835]

J Page 25 at East Hallowell ME [8 Feb 1844]

James Capt 32 at Thomaston ME [21 Jan 1847]

Jarvin while sharpening a mill saw at Lower Falls at Brunswick ME injured on Sun [*Portland ME Adv*] [12 Sept 1837]

Jerushua R 17 d/o Seth & Lydia HALL at Nobleboro ME [22 Jul 1852]

John 21 of Belfast ME at the house of Mrs GREEN on Mon [15 Jul 1843]

John 70 at Woolwich ME [5 Apr 1849]

John Dr 82 formerly of Warner NH AmRev pensioner at China ME [13 May 1836]

John L 23 of Augusta ME on board ship *Norman* on passage from San Francisco CA to Panama on 30 Sept [24 Oct 1850]

John one of 27 boys of the Farm School drowned when between Fort Independence & Thompson's Island [7 May 1842]

Joseph A of Boston MA in CA [21 Aug 1851]

Julia 18 d/o Zaccheus HALL at Corinna ME [7 Mar 1840]

Levi Col 64 at Gorham ME [21 Feb 1851]

Lewis 82 at Thomaston ME [20 Nov 1845]

Lucy 38 formerly of Belmont ME at Camden ME [23 Jul 1846]

Lydia 68 at Damariscotta ME [22 Jan 1852]

Lydia w/o Gilman H at Athens ME [16 Aug 1849]

Mary 20 w/o Sparrow HALL at Bowdoinham ME [6 Apr 1848]

Mary 61 at Portland ME [12 Sept 1844]

Mary Ann 24 w/o Captain Samuel B HALL at Damariscotta ME [20 Mar 1851]

Mary Jane 25 d/o Deac Peter HALL at Rockland ME [26 Aug 1852]

Moses Esq 64 at Westbrook ME [16 Nov 1848]

Mr married Miss LITTLE "an interesting matter is before the NY legislature as present. So far as the lady was concerned it was a joke, but the youth held her to her bargain & her friends have the matter before the legislature [16 Apr 1846]

Mrs thrown through the railing of the bridge during an accident, but fortunately rescued at Portland ME [6 Feb 1851]

Polly 67 w/o Randall HALL at Anson ME [7 Mar 1850]

Rebecca 19 d/o Neal HALL at Brunswick ME [7 Aug 1845]

Robert F Esq at Augusta ME on Thurs morning [5 Sept 1841]

Samuel abt 40 formerly of Northport ME found dead in Boston MA, in a fit caused by intemperance. [25 May 1839]

Sarah 98 at Litchfield ME [4 Jan 1849]

Sarah an insane woman of Lexington ME who made away with herself on Sat 16th inst by jumping into Seven Mile Steam at North Anson ME [*People's Press*] [28 Oct 1847]

Sherburn 19 s/o Deac Daniel HALL of Rumford ME at Newton MA on the 21st of Mar last (extended notice) [12 June 1841]

Stephen N 24 at Brunswick ME [25 Nov 1847]

Susan A 20 d/o Paul P HALL at Augusta ME on 3rd inst [16 Sept 1847]

Thomas 16 s/o Thomas HALL formerly of Bath ME at Nobleboro ME on 23rd ult [15 Apr 1843]

Timothy 60 at Litchfield ME [6 May 1847]

HALL (Cont.) Timothy Dr 87 AmRev surgeon & an eye witness to the execution of Major ANDRE, died from being thrown from a wagon at East Hartford CT on the 6th inst [22 Aug 1844]

William 16 s/o Col Joseph HALL member of Congress from ME at Salem MA on 12th inst [28 Feb 1837]

William N 55 formerly of Brunswick ME at Bangor ME [28 Jan 1847]

Ziba 78 formerly of Belfast ME at Athens ME [24 Sept 1846]

HALL - see GULLIVER, SMITH, WRIGHT

HALLETT Elisha Esq 53 at Augusta ME on 14th inst [20 Jan 1848]

Elisha Esq 90 AmRev prisoner confined in the Jersey prison ship in the harbor of New York, after the war he settled on west side of Snow Pond in ME died in Waterville ME [14 Oct 1847]

J Lorenzo 23 s/o late Elisha HALLETT Esq of Augusta ME at Mobile AL on 10 Mar [25 Mar 1852]

Marcia A 17y 9m d/o late Elisha HALLETT Esq of Augusta ME at Suffield CT [13 May 1852]

Olive 18 of Waterville ME at Hallowell ME [15 Jan 1846]

Thankful S 39 w/o Watson F HALLET at Augusta ME [18 Jul 1834]

HAM Abner 21 at Hallowell ME on Mon the 27th ult [7 Mar 1837]

Betsey widow of James HAM formerly of Bath ME at Hodgdon ME [9 May 1850]

Elizabeth 80 sis/o John HERRICK at Lewiston ME [11 Apr 1834]

Harvey s/o James HAM at Hodgdon on the 29th [9 May 1850]

Jacob 62 at Portland ME [11 Dec 1835]

James 58 formerly of Bath ME at Hodgdon ME on 18th of March [8 May 1845]

Joseph 71 at Hallowell ME [17 Aug 1848]

Joseph late of Hallowell ME est notice, Joseph M HAM adm [3 June 1852]

Judith 51 w/o Col Ebenezer HAM & (d/o Jacob & Martha [ROSS] BARKER) at Lewiston ME [8 May 1851]

Julia A 26 w/o J Edward HAM at Farmington ME [10 Aug 1848]

Sarah Mrs 81 at Gardiner ME [30 Jan 1851]

Tamosa B 41 w/o Francis HAM at Exeter NH [29 Aug 1850]

HAMBLEN Amos 56 at Farmington ME [6 May 1843]

Lydia 18 w/o Levi HAMBLEN at Sumner ME [26 June 1851]

HAMBLET Charles killed at Lowell on Mon by being caught in the wheel of one of the Merrimac Mills [6 June 1840]

HAMBLETON Richard drowned at Bangor ME [12 Dec 1840]

Simeon 19 at Parkman ME [29 Feb 1844]

HAMBLIN Hannibal 24 formerly of Livermore ME at Pearlington Hancock Co MS at the res of Gen P R R PRAY [29 Aug 1837]

Mary 47 at Buxton ME [18 Mar 1836]

Mary S 20 d/o Amos HAMBLIN at Farmington ME [30 Nov 1848]

HAMILTON Anthony & Robert GREEN of New York a duel with rifles "Either because the rifles were not loaded or the marksmen were no blood was spilt" at Bladensburgh on Sat last [18 Dec 1841]

Frances A 19y at Vassalboro ME [1 Nov 1849]

Hannah 73 w/o John HAMILTON at Windham ME on 10th inst after a short illness [18 Nov 1847]

John Capt 51y by drinking half a pint of bedbug poison *[Portland Advertiser]* [24 June 1847]

John Decator 26 at Vassalboro ME [1 Nov 1849]

Mrs & two dau's, son and a female relative (name cut off), died of cholera with Mr FRISHIE, Mr PAGE & Mr COLE. Mr CHAPIN & Mr COLE were from CT &

HAMILTON (Cont.) engaged in the sale of clocks. They, with 2 other boarders, fled to Warsaw to escape the disease, but all 4 sickened and died immediately there. A letter from Carthage IL gave a list of 12 persons of the house of Mr HAMILTON, a hotel-keeper; all of whom all died within a few days. [14 Aug 1851]

Richard 75 AmRev & a member of the Christian Church at Searsmont ME on 7th inst [27 June 1834]

Sarah Jane 27 w/o James HAMILTON at Lewiston ME [14 Nov 1850]

wid/o Alexander HAMILTON a visit to Arlington House. Mr CURTIS having been the play-fellow of her eldest son. Mrs H is the d/o the late Major Gen SCHUYLER AmRev of Albany & in her 88y, visit to the seat of Government is made with a view to the disposal to Congress of the Hamilton Papers, which contain more than 100 letters from Gen WASHINGTON that have never been published ... [*Alexandria Gazette*] [20 Feb 1845]

William Deac 86y 8m AmRev at North Yarmouth ME [12 Apr 1849]

HAMILTON - see MACOMB, NEWELL

HAMLEN Amanda Malvina 26 formerly of Augusta ME at Magnolia FL [20 Mar 1841]

Asa William 15 s/o Charles HAMLEN at Augusta ME [31 May 1849]

Augustus 8 formerly of (Augusta ME) s/o Charles S HAMLEN at Boston MA [12 Oct 1848]

Hobart 4 s/o Henry HAMLEN at Augusta ME [1 Oct 1846]

Jane C 63 of (Augusta) ME at St Stephens New Brunswick Canada [13 Jul 1848]

John 58 a native of (Augusta ME) at Magnolia FL [23 Aug 1849]

Matilda R 5 d/o John HAMLEN at Augusta ME [6 Aug 1846]

Nathaniel R 6 s/o Nathaniel HAMLEN Esq at Augusta ME [6 Aug 1846]

Salley Craig 62 w/o Lot HAMLEN at Augusta ME on 15th inst [27 May 1847]

Sarah 74 w/o Perez HAMLEN at Augusta ME [9 May 1844]

Sarah 87 wid/of Perez HAMLEN at Hampden ME [7 Mar 1850]

HAMLET Justus dwelling house burnt on 7th inst at Solon ME [21 May 1842]

Phebe 60 w/o Hon John HAMLET at Solon ME [19 Dec 1840]

HAMLIN Ebenezer 67 of Orono ME at Augusta ME [18 Nov 1847]

girl little d/o Levi HAMLIN at Tremont burned to death [8 Jan 1852]

Lizzie 6 d/o Charles H & Caroline HAMLIN formerly of (Augusta) ME at Boston ME on 20 June [29 June 1848]

Mr on Wed night last a fire broke out in Lovell ME, the house is owned by Mr Charles WHIPPLE [23 Jul 1842]

Sarah 9m c/o Gorham HAMLIN at Gardiner ME [31 Aug 1833]

Susan 68 wid/o Hannibal HAMLIN Esq at Waterford ME on 19th inst [16 May 1840]

Theophilus Esq 75 at Augusta ME [23 Apr 1842]

HAMLIN - see Maine Information

HAMMATT William Major 68 at Bangor ME [8 Oct 1846]

HAMMON John 36 at East Thomaston ME [5 Nov 1846]

HAMMOND Abby 20 at Foxcroft ME [27 Jan 1848]

Elbridge H 18 of Guilford ME escaped from the flames & ran two miles to the house of Mr PRATT, when he arived he was in almost a perfect state of nudity. HALL, RANDALL, LIBBEY & HAMMOND were the four men burnt to death in a camp in Plt No 4 on Great Works Stream [13 Feb 1835]

Eliza P 25 w/o Isaac A HAMMOND at Sidney ME on 21 Nov [6 Dec 1849]

Helen Maria 31 w/o Charles H HAMMOND at Bangor ME [25 Jan 1844]

Jefferson "Schr *Maine* of Bath (ME), master James BLIN of Dresden (ME), bound from Kennebec for Boston MA, loaded with wood, potatoes and hay, with a crew of four besides the captain, and three men and four women passengers, on Monday last about 9 a.m. parted cables and drove out of Portsmouth harbor - threw over deck load of hay

HAMMOND (Cont.) - slit fore sail and drifted into the hay - at 9 p.m. struck Cohasset rocks
& bilged afterwards came ashore on Scituate beach, about three miles North of the
Light. Vessel total loss. Part of the cargo saved. The following were lost: Jefferson
HAMMOND of Jefferson ME; John POTTLE and Mahala MOOD of Pittston;
Lucinda and Octavia LRASH (sisters found drowned in the cabin) of Whitefield ME;
Martha J BLIN d/o the captain, Passengers. Lewis PUSHARD of Wiscassset,
Seaman" (N.B. the name LRASH, most likely should be LASH?/TRASH?/TRASK?)
[16 Oct 1841]

Jonathan Esq 61 at Elliot ME for several yrs a member of the legislature [6 Nov 1838]

Joseph of brig *India* of Eastport ME at Bathurst Africa on 7 Sept [21 Nov 1850]

Joseph 2nd mate of the brig *India* 25y died on 2 Sept native of Saco ME From the coast
of Africa the brig *India*, Capt HANSCOMB arrived at this port this morning
(*Philadelphia Bulletin*, 31st) She left Bissau West Coast of Africa 23 Jan & arrived at
Port Praya Cape de Verds on 12 Feb [10 Apr 1851]

Joseph 80 at Buckfield ME [15 Apr 1852]

Lydia 25y 6m at Albion ME [11 May 1848]

M A Miss 31 at Mechanic Falls (then part of Poland or Minot) ME [24 Jan 1850]

Rebecca Mrs 81 at Paris ME [22 Feb 1844]

Sarah abt 22 at Phillips ME on 28th ult [18 Nov 1836]

Thomas S of ME second officer on board the *Panama* passage New Orleans to Boston
MA [2 Oct 1835]

Zeno L 5m only child of Isaac HAMMOND at Sidney ME [30 Jul 1846]

HAMOR Mary Angelia 16 eldest d/o William HAMOR at Eden [26 Dec 1834]

HANCOCK John a colored man beat a colored woman in Philadelphia PA, Mary
WASHINGTON, John was arrested & held to bail [30 Nov 1848]

William AmRev at Buxton ME [23 Dec 1836]

HANDEN Mr we learn by the stage driver, HANDEN killed in Farmington on Sat last, H &
Mr PARKER were engaged in cutting wood [*Skowhegan Clarion*] [28 Dec 1848]

HANDY Ebenezer Dr of Steuben ME his house burned [27 May 1843]

Elizabeth 37 w/o Captain William HANDY of Sandwick MA? & Abraham W
FREEMAN of Norridgewock ME at Wilbraham MA [23 Sept 1847]

Elizabeth wid/o Nathan HANDY at Wayne ME [11 Dec 1841]

Hannah w/o Deac E HANDY at Steuben ME [27 Jan 1848]

HANES Ephraim 102 at Eden ME on 25 Dec 1836? [23 Jan 1837]

James Monroe 22 at Burnham ME [8 June 1848]

Martha Ann 25 w/o Benjamin F at Gardiner ME [18 Dec 1852]

HANGLEY Jerry an Irishman by a falling embankment at Bangor ME [23 Dec 1852]

HANKS Edson Corporal of Company E, 1st US Inf 26y s/o Jacob HANKS of (Augusta) ME
at the city of Mexico on 14 Mar [13 Jul 1848]

HANLY Benjamin Esq 24 at Appleton ME [8 Jan 1852]

John Col at Bristol [19 Dec 1840]

Michael 92 at Appleton ME [18 Dec 1851]

HANNA Mrs her family consisting of 9 persons attacked with the disease known as "Milk
Sickness" & eight Dead. Four negroes had also died from the same cause. [*Richmond
(KY) News Letter*] [6 Dec 1849]

HANNA - see ADAMS

HANNAFORD Anna C 20m only d/o William & Jemima HANNAFORD at Augusta ME on
21 Mar [1 Apr 1852]

Mary Jane abt one yr at Winthrop ME on 3rd inst [13 Aug 1843]

William 21 at Monmouth ME on Mon last [1 Aug 1840]

HANNIFORD David 77 at Alna ME [20 Feb 1845]

HANSCOIN John B dwelling house at Dead River Upper Mills consumed by fire the 2d inst together with all the house contained excepting two feather beds [4 Mar 1836]

HANSCOM A F 22 at Elloit ME [15 Aug 1850]

James 38 at Albion ME on 28th ult [11 Sept 1841]

Martha 28 at Elliot ME [2 Jan 1845]

Mary 27 w/o Deac Michael HANSON at Unity ME [2 Sept 1843]

Mary 53 w/o Deac Alpheus HANSCOM at Elliot ME [23 Jan 1851]

HANSON Andrew 67 at Fairfield ME on the 12th inst [20 Jul 1848]

Andrew late of China ME est notice Nancy HANSON exec [27 May 1852] & Stephen JONES adm [2 Dec 1852]

Barthena 33 w/o Robert HANSON at Bath ME [21 Mar 1834]

Benjamin steward of Frankfort ME fatal shipwreck of the schr *Argus* on Plum Island Capt CROCKETT of Frankfort ME was the captain [2 Jan 1851]

E 80 at Windham ME [24 Feb 1848]

Eliza abt 19 d/o Stephen HANSON [14 Aug 1845]

Elizabeth 45 w/o Moses HANSON at Winthrop ME [22 Mar 1849]

Elizabeth abt 4y c/o Moses HANSON at (Winthrop ME) of scarlet fever [16 Apr 1842]

Isaac Jr 18 of Hallowell ME committed suicide [2 Jul 1849]

J W now engaged in writing a history of the Kennebec Purchase & the towns of Gardiner & Pittston ME. [N.B. Rev HANSON's *History of Gardiner ME* was published in Gardiner ME by William PALMER in 1852) [10 Apr 1851]

John E 43 of Buxton ME fell from the mow in his barn on Mon the 7th inst [19 Aug 1843]

Julia 68 at Waterboro ME [21 June 1849]

Leonard P his father, Nathan HANSON, stated "as my son absolutely refuses to hear to any advice from me or follow any of my directions, I shall pay no debts of his, signed Nathan HANSON of Winthrop ME" [2 Apr 1842]

Lydia L 33 w/o John Hanson at Jay ME on 6th Apr [25 Apr 1850]

Mr of Durham ME 37y ago left wife & family, married & blessed with 2 ch. Meanwhile, his disconsolate wife married again, then her second husband died, left two ch. Mr H made his appearance in (Lewiston?) where his former wife & ch have resided for several years past. Some time previous to his return, Mr H had lost his second wife. [*Lewiston Journal*] [17 June 1847]

Oliver Esq 54 at China ME on 19 Oct [18 Nov 1852]

Paul 67 at Readfield ME on 1 Apr [10 Apr 1851] & Paul late of Readfield ME est notice Margaret HANSON adm [11 Mar 1852]

Phebe a maiden lady of between 60 & 70 discovered lying in the front entryway of the house Dead, from a gunshot wound in the neck, she had resided with an old bachelor brother in the part of Rochester called Mederborough [30 Sept 1843]

Thomas B 34 at Bath ME [5 Dec 1844]

William of the Forks Somerset Co ME at Lowell MA on his way home from CA [22 Jul 1852]

HANSON - see HOWARD

HAPGOOD Sprout 57 at Augusta ME on 23 Sept [4 Oct 1849]

HARASKO - see DAY

HARBACK Thomas abt 65 at Camden ME [25 Jul 1850]

HARDEN Freeman 65 at Thomaston ME [7 Dec 1848]

Sarah Mrs 80 at Gardiner ME [11 Dec 1851]

HARDING Charles Esq clerk of the common council for several years & a member of the Cumberland bar abt 25y [*Portland Argus*] [19 Jul 1849]

David S 25 s/o Capt Neh HARDING of Bath ME at New Orleans [31 Oct 1837]

Elisha Dr 54 at East Thomaston ME [16 May 1850]

HARDING (Cont.) Eliza B 21 at Standish ME [4 June 1846]

Emeline Libby 18y 7m d/o James & Martha HARDING at Standish ME on 25 Aug of typhoid fever [30 Sept 1852]

Frederick A 16 at Auburn ME on 3 Dec [22 Mar 1849]

Mary W 60 w/o Capt Nehemiah HARDING at Bath ME [25 May 1848]

Nathaniel 25 at Bath ME [30 Jan 1845]

Rachael R 47 w/o Capt Nehemiah HARDING at Bath ME [31 Jan 1834]

Robert Capt 74 at Brunswick ME [21 Aug 1851]

Spencer 42 at Gardiner ME [22 Aug 1844]

William 19 at Bath ME [5 Nov 1846]

HARDISON - see PARSON

HARDY Clara Frances 2 d/o Albert HARDY at Augusta ME [23 Sept 1852]

Esther 25 at Gardiner ME [6 Nov 1845]

Manly 71 formerly of Bucksport ME at Bangor ME [5 Apr 1849]

Mrs 100 having travelled on Feb 11th in the evening about two miles over a hill on foot on the snow crust, lost her shoes & wore out her stockings, came to a house which was fastened and no person within, left her staff at the door and went into a barn yard, near the house, half a mile distance from any other house, where she wrapped her cloak around her feet and lain herself down - and was there found next morning frozen to death (from the *Haverhill Repub*) at Springfield NH [7 Mar 1840]

Sullivan at Bremen ME [16 Mar 1848]

HARE Michael in the United States just 100 soldiers of the AmRev on the pension list over one hundred years of age. The oldest man on the list is Michael HARE of Union Co PA 115y [15 Oct 1842]

Michael 116 AmRev at Union Township NY [1 Apr 1843]

Mr eloped not long since from New York with a Miss FOX & Mrs HARE has got divorced from him on that account. "The HARE & the FOX" [9 Mar 1848]

HARFORD - see GREELY

HARLOW Benson 21 at Hebron ME [23 Jan 1851]

Ephraim working upon the Quequeshan Mill, lost his balance & precipited some sixty or seventy feet into the wheel pit, survived the shock (retaining his reason) about four hours on Wed morning last [*Fall River Monitor*] [5 Dec 1844]

Hannah 79 wid/o Reuben HARLOW at Easton [21 Nov 1850]

James of Auburn, Cumberland Co ME, brought into the Portland market a few days since, a pig only eleven months old weighing three hundred & forty pounds [1 Apr 1843]

Lydia 101y 8m 22d, left 10 ch, 87 gch, 220 of 4th gen, & supposed abt 20 of the 5th, as late as last fall a sister in MA 100y & another 97y [24 Sept 1846]

Philemon Esq 79 at Auburn ME [25 Nov 1852]

Polly 37 w/o Chandler HARLOW at Parkman ME [9 Jan 1851]

HARMAN Betsey 33 w/o Eben HARMAN at Buxton ME [26 Dec 1834]

Harvey J attorney at law died at Lower Sundusky OH? [5 Sept 1834]

HARMON Betsey 84 a widow at Brownfield ME [12 June 1851]

Daniel 65 at Eaton NH on Jan last [15 Apr 1843]

Frances J 18 at Saco ME [26 Aug 1847]

Joseph 50y of Gorham ME on Wed last riding in a wagon & accidentally shot by his gun [*Eastern Argus*] [26 Oct 1848]

Josiah 82 AmRev at Corinna ME [26 June 1845]

Luther, died after a squabble about the water pail in a grog shop in Union ME with a Mr ROBBINS & a 3rd person. The 3rd person took down H, R then kicked H 3 times in the temple. The man holding down H said to R "I am not going to hold H down for you to kill him" H got up, said he was much hurt & started for home, a short

HARMON (Cont.) distance...could not speak, but pointed to his temple [*Belfast Republican*] [26 Feb 1836]

Sally 68 w/o Francis HARMON at Durham ME [11 Dec 1845]

William 88 AmRev at Gorham ME [18 Jan 1849]

HARNDEN Capt as the steamer *Belle* was leaving the camp-meeting ground on Tues evening last, while assisting in pushing the boat off, accidentally caught in the machinery & died [28 Sept 1848]

HARPER Chancellor one of the strongest minds in South Carolina died [4 Nov 1847]

Phillipa 80 death by clothes taking fire at Pembroke [11 Dec 1835]

HARRADEN Lucy Ann 24 w/o Daniel HARRADEN at Belfast ME on 30th [15 Aug 1840]

HARRDISON [*sic*] - see FOWLER

HARRIDEN Sarah A 22 at Alna ME [6 Nov 1851]

Thomas 59 at Alna ME [6 Nov 1851]

HARRIMAN Apphia Coombs 17 d/o Josiah HARRIMAN at Gardiner ME [15 Oct 1846]

Benjamin F his house at Bucksport ME lost by fire [18 Jan 1849]

Elmira B 42 w/o Capt Jonathan HARRIMAN at Bucksport ME [17 Jan 1850]

Joab 75 AmRev at Windsor ME [27 June 1834]

John drowned in the Kennebec River opposite the US Arsenal in Augusta ME on Sun morning last. His parents are said to reside in Litchfield ME [25 Jul 1844]

Mary 50 w/o Jonathan HARRIMAN at Bucksport ME [10 Dec 1846]

Peter 90 at Bucksport ME [1 May 1851]

HARRIMAN - see HUTCHINS

HARRINGTON Ann Maria 14 d/o Andrew HARRINGTON at Eastport ME [13 Feb 1845]

Charles 18 at Eastport ME [11 Feb 1847]

Charles Esq 56 at Thomaston ME [23 Dec 1847]

child abt 8 c/o Mr HARRINGTON drowned [*Bath (ME) Tribune*] [29 June 1848]

Elizabeth 41 w/o Robert HARRINGTON at Eastport ME [19 June 1851]

John seaman of Bath ME lost overboard from schr *John Bell* on 4th ult in the Bay of Chaleur by a heavy sea which broke over her while riding at anchor [3 Aug 1848]

Lucy 36 w/o William HARRINGTON at Eastport ME [6 Nov 1845]

Lucy formerly a resident of Amesbury & d/o Moses HARRINGTON died recently at Cornish NH. She was sick three years and a half and confined to her bed two yrs & five months. She had an illness which made her bones soft ....she lay in bed only two feet and four inches .... ribs broke, collar bones broke, her under jaw, hands, feet ... upon a post mortem examination, not a sound bone was found. All were so softened as to be easily cut with a knife ... (from the *Amesbury Transcript*) [29 Feb 1840]

son a boy abt 11 years of age drowned at Dresden ME on Wed last at Parker's Head ME drowned a few days since [29 June 1848]

HARRINTON Walter 23 drowned near Dog Island, left a young wife & a large circle of relatives to mourn his untimely death. His body has not been recovered [*Eastport Sentinel*] [2 Jul 1846]

HARRIS a little boy was killed by a cart passing over his head s/o Edward HARRIS (from the *Philadelphia (PA) Gazette*) on the 18th inst [4 Apr 1834]

Ansel D 30 formerly of Lewiston ME at Waupan WI [8 Aug 1850]

Charles Edward 7y 8m c/o Samuel L & Abba C HARRIS formerly of Augusta ME at Washington DC on 22nd Jan [7 Feb 1850]

Charles M of ME at San Francisco CA [5 Feb 1852]

child of Mr Pliny HARRIS at Winthrop ME on Fri last [22 May 1845]

E J Rev, pastor of the Baptist Church at Waldoboro ME [16 Oct 1851]

Ella Louise 9 youngest child of Samuel L HARRIS at Augusta ME [22 Aug 1844]

Frank W 5 oldest s/o Samuel L HARRIS Esq at Augusta ME on 3rd inst [12 June 1845]

HARRIS (Cont.) James 29 at Brunswick ME [16 May 1850]

Jane 50 w/o Nathaniel HARRIS Esq at Greene ME [26 Dec 1850]

John 14 only s/o Elbridge HARRIS Esq of Bangor ME by drowning [22 Jul 1852]

Josiah Esq 75 at East Machias ME on 17th inst [3 Jul 1845] & 75 at East Machias ME on 2nd ult [10 Jul 1845]

Judge killed by lightning near Montezuma Indiana [1 May 1851]

Lemira [*sic*] M Mrs abt 22y of Coeymans w/o Sylvester HARRIS & d/o Martin SLOCUM of Manchester VT took passage from Coeymans on board the *American Eagle* with the intention of passing the night with relatives in Troy & then the following morning in the stage to Bennington...no trace of her has been discovered...has been missing on the 13th inst (now two weeks since) [*Albany Argus*][4 Sept 1845]

Lewis W 28 at Poland ME [23 Sept 1847]

Mary 67 w/o John HARRIS at Pittston ME [7 Mar 1850]

Mercy 15 d/o N HARRIS at Jay ME [27 Nov 1845]

Morris 50 at Monroe ME [18 Jul 1850]

Moses at Greene ME [26 Sept 1840]

Mr a missionary to New Zealand killed & eaten by the savages, shared the fate of LYMAN & MUNSON see also - WILLIAMS [2 May 1840]

Orelia B 25 w/o Rev Jerome HARRIS at Prospect ME [26 Feb 1852]

Rebeckah w/o Martin HARRIS at Turner ME on 23rd ult [9 May 1844]

Samuel A only s/o Pliny HARRIS of Gardiner ME at Augusta ME on 19 Jan of inflammation of brain [25 Jan 1849]

Sarah 97 wid/o Stephen HARRIS at Gorham ME [11 Mar 1852]

Stephen 62 broke his neck by a fall while attempting to mount his horse from a fence at Rowley MA [9 Oct 1838]

William 28 at Turner ME [30 May 1850]

William 64 at Portland ME [20 June 1844]

William E late of Waterville ME at Danville VT [29 May 1851]

William of Swanville ME lost overboard from schr *Lenity* [*sic*] on the passage from Sag Harbor [1 Aug 1844]

Willie Fitzgerald 13m child of Samuel L & Abba C HARRIS formerly of Augusta ME at Washington DC on 22rd Jan [7 Feb 1850]

HARRIS - see LEONARD, NEWMAN, WILLIAMS

HARRISON Benjamin Dr 34th year of life s/o Gen HARRISON at North Bend died very suddenly on Tues evening 12th inst at father's res [4 Jul 1840]

Gen born on the 9th Feb 1773, now nearly 68yrs old [2 Jan 1841] & died at the President's House in Washington DC on 4 Apr 1841 at 30 mins before one o'clock in the morning (N.B. President William Henry HARRISON's term of office was 12 & one half hours short of 31 days) [10 Apr 1841]

Henry K Capt 81 at St George ME [27 Dec 1849]

John B of 3rd Ave NY on Thurs afternoon by a kick from his father's horse while unharnessing [7 Nov 1840]

Samuel 73 at Kennebunk ME [15 Jul 1843]

HARRISON - see news on Hemp, PIKE, TYLER, THORNTON

HART Richard P met with a singular death in New York recently, in a vapor bath when the curtain which enclosed it took fire. A servant threw upon it what he considered a glass of water, but it was alcohol, which so increased the violence of the flames, as to burn Mr HART to a degree that caused his death [18 Jan 1844]

HART - see COLT

HARTFORD Jane 36 w/o Gen Benjamin HARTFORD at Lovell ME [16 Mar 1848]

Lucy M 51 at Augusta ME on 20 Apr [29 Apr 1852]

Mary widow 75 aft a 13y illness at Augusta ME on 18 Dec [2 Jan 1851]

HARTSHORN Edwin B 22 of Walpole MA at Augusta ME on 24 June [6 Jul 1848]
   Lucy 92 a widow at Brownville ME [30 May 1850]
HARTT John seaman a native of Edinburgh Scotland drowned in the harbor while
   attempting to swim from the shore to a vessel on the 3d [*Eastport ME Sentinel*] [15
   Jul 1847]
HARTWELL Edward 96y 6m 26d AmRev at St Albans ME on 29 Mar [25 Apr 1844]
   Horace Herbert 5m only s/o William B & Eliza J HARTWELL at Augusta ME [26 Jul
   1849]
   Lydia 93 at St Albans ME [16 May 1837]
   Lysander W 36 formerly of St Albans ME at Sebec ME [31 Jul 1851]
   Philena S 38 w/o John S HARTWELL at Gardiner ME [28 Feb 1837]
   Stephen 57 formerly of Bloomfield ME in Wisconsin [15 Oct 1846]
   William B Esq 35 of Augusta ME purser of the US frigate *Falmouth* at sea on 12 Jul
   three days out of Rio de Janiero of apoplexy [22 Nov 1849]
HARVELL William 57 at Madison ME [4 June 1851]
HARVEST John H 82 AmRev at Waldo Plantation [7 Aug 1835]
HARVEY David Esq 57 at Atkinson ME [21 Oct 1843]
   John 71 formerly of Winthrop ME at Freedom ME [5 Aug 1843]
   John Esq 65 at Monmouth ME [1 Jan 1846]
   John of Jefferson ME frozen to death in the road on his way home from a neighboring
   grocery store, intoxicated [*Augusta Age*] [25 Jan 1849]
   Judith 77 a widow at Freedom ME [4 Jul 1850]
   Lady w/o Sir George HARVEY, governor of Nova Scotia & d/o Lord LAKE, a peer of
   England at Halifax NS Canada on 10th inst [24 Apr 1851]
   Mr one of 13 old AmRevs present & took a part in the celebration of the 4th inst (4 July)
   at Utica. Twelve of them rode in the procession. The youngest of the twelve is 72 &
   the oldest 92 & the aggregate ages is 976 abt the same as that of old Mr
   MATHUSELAH. The 13th was a Mr HARVEY of Frankfort. He looked of the others
   as "boys" for he himself had a son aged 82 [23 Jul 1842]
   Robert perished on the schr *Thomas*, SPROULE Capt of Belfast ME [25 Mar 1843]
   Samuel late of Winthrop ME est notice Oakes HOWARD adm [16 Dec 1852]
   Sarah A 41 at Brunswick ME [21 Sept 1848]
   William Jr 23 formerly of Hallowell ME at Peru IL on 28th ult of bilious fever [9 Nov
   1839]
HARVEY - see news, VARNUM
HARVILL John 90 at Calais CA [14 Aug 1851]
HARWELL Derrick of Langdon on Wed [*Keene (NH) Sentinel* of the 17th inst] [5 Feb
   1846]
HARWOOD James 61 at Wilton ME on 12 Jan (MA & NH papers please copy) [23 Jan
   1851]
HASEITH James the cook, David WATKINS the 2d steward of the fore cabin; Alexander
   TURNBULL, bar keeper & John SUMNER, watchman on Cunard wharf (from the
   Boston Bee). Four lives lost on Tues night the 25 Nov, they left Cunard wharf East
   Boston MA for steamship *Asia*, 5 men all but Henry DAVIDSON met a watery grave
   [11 Dec 1851]
HASELTINE Harriet J 18 at Gardiner ME on Sun last [12 June 1838]
HASEY John 88 at Bristol [18 Feb 1847]
   Martha 32 w/o Edward W HASEY at Oldtown ME [26 June 1845]
HASKELL c/o Mrs Jane HASKELL 7days old at China ME [18 Apr 1834]
   Arseneth 51 w/o Orrin HASKELL at Livermore ME [9 Nov 1848]

HASKELL (Cont.) Calvin of Worcester MA died of suffocation - "a piece of a doughnut into his windpipe" [17 Jul 1851]

Daniel 22 hunting & gunning accident at Deer Isle ME on 20th ult [11 Mar 1847]

Drusilla abt 35 w/o J HASKELL at Norridgewock ME [3 May 1849]

Eunice 78 at Augusta ME on 23 Aug [29 Aug 1850]

Harriet 29 w/o Niles HASKELL & d/o John WOODS of Bloomfield ME at Newburyport MA [13 Mar 1845]

Jacob at Wayne ME [4 Apr 1850]

Joseph 84y AmRev at Thomaston ME [23 May 1844]

Joseph Capt 62 formerly of Gloucester MA at West Gardiner ME on 5 Dec [13 Dec 1849]

Louisa 18y 5m d/o Mrs Paulina HASKELL at Greene ME on 9th Nov [21 Nov 1850]

Mary 24 w/o John HASKELL at East Thomaston ME [6 Apr 1839]

Mary Ann 14 at Auburn ME [14 Aug 1851]

Mary J 36 formerly of Hallowell ME at East Livermore ME [5 Oct 1848]

Mary Jane 29y w/o John HASKELL & her child 7d at China ME [18 Apr 1834]

Mercey 46 w/o Jabez HASKELL at Warren ME [7 Aug 1851]

Moses 67 at North Yarmouth ME [16 Nov 1833]

Mrs 86 formerly of Gorham ME wid/o Jon HASKELL at Knox ME on 19th ult [11 Mar 1843]

Nathan S 34 at Know ME [16 Mar 1848]

Rufus 66 at Augusta ME [7 Nov 1840]

Sarah 83 a widow at West Gardiner ME [5 June 1835]

Sarah Jane 20 d/o Benjamin & Abigail HASKELL at China ME on 22 June [28 June 1849]

Sarah Louisa youngest c/o William S HASKELL at Augusta ME on Sun last [27 Mar 1838]

Verteline 20 d/o Oren HASKELL at Livermore ME [27 Sept 1849]

William 47 at Greene ME [13 June 1844]

William 77 formerly of Bath ME at Gray ME on 27th inst [9 Apr 1842]

William E 17 s/o Benjamin HASKELL drowned on Thanksgiving day while skating at China ME [11 Dec 1838]

William Jr abt 30 at Canton ME on 7th inst [25 Jan 1840]

HASKELL - see CONFORTH, WATSON

HASLAM Mr, When the storm was at its height, he was about to enter a stable on horseback, had not passed the door an instant, before the gable end fell in with a heavy crash. Had he been a second or two later, he must have perished. The paper titles the story "Serious Tornado" *[The Baltimore Chronicle* of Wed] [5 June 1838]

HASSLER Edward shot himself through his head at the American Hotel in New York *[Daily Bee]* [20 June 1844]

HASTINGS Flora the same lady which has been in the circle of gossip in the courts of London died [3 Aug 1839]

girl, d/o William HASTINGS of Jamaica, Mr H & family visiting Mr Lucius ABBOTT of Londonderry and the d/o Mr H & her cousin, Mr ABBOTT's son, a little older than herself were amusing themselves together...playing with a loaded gun which accidentally went off killing the girl at Londonderry last week (reported in the *Brattleboro Eagle* on 25th May) [4 June 1851]

Hannah 65 at Hope ME [21 Oct 1847]

James 77 one of the first settlers of (Brewer) ME [4 Feb 1847]

Moses 90 a native of Natick MA at Sidney ME [1 Jan 1839]

Mr of MA died at Virginia Springs [9 Jul 1842]

HASTY Andrew 43 at Waterboro ME [29 Jul 1847]

HASTY (Cont.) James Major 84 at Standish ME [24 Jul 1835]

HATCH Abigail 79 w/o John HATCH at Lewiston ME on 21 Aug [9 Sept 1852]

Abigail S 23 w/o Asa D HATCH at Thomaston ME [17 Jul 1845]

Adaline 2y 4m d/o Lemuel & Eunice HATCH at Augusta ME on 18th inst *"Zion's Advocate* please copy" [24 Feb 1848]

Alexander 17 s/o Dr A HATCH at China ME [27 Mar 1841]

Alvah 44 at Waterboro ME [9 May 1850]

Benjamin Col formerly of Bath ME at East Pittston ME [2 Dec 1852]

Daniel E 27 at Belmont ME [25 Dec 1851]

Dennis his blacksmith shop & shoe manufactory of Mr ROBB & store of A P HUBBARD Esq were burnt at Springvale ME [14 Aug 1851]

Hawse 50 at Medybemps [2 Jul 1846]

Horace M 1y 6m youngest c/o Dr A HATCH at China ME [20 May 1847]

Howland 78 at Bristol [29 Jan 1846]

James M 33y 10m at Bowdoinham ME [4 Dec 1845]

Julia A 17 d/o Dr Alex HATCH at China ME [28 Sept 1848]

Laura Jane 22 at Knox ME [12 Sept 1850]

Mary 11m d/o Roland HATCH at Thomaston ME [9 Jul 1842]

Mary Jane 25 d/o Thadeus BROAD at Albion ME on 12th inst [23 Mar 1848] & [16 Mar 1848]

Nathaniel employed as teamster at the new Almshouse in Cambridge while mentally deranged with typhiod fever threw himself from a 4th story window. He was of Lisbon ME (copied from the *Boston Bee*) [22 May 1851]

Sally 52 w/o Col Benjamin HATCH at Bath ME [17 Feb 1848]

Sarah 73 w/o Zenos HATCH Esq at Bowdoinham ME [17 Sept 1846]

Sarah H 22 at North Berwick ME [30 Sept 1847]

Sarah Jane 5y 4m d/o Thomas W & Sarah R HATCH at Liberty ME on 21 Sept [14 Oct 1852]

Sophronia 15 d/o John HATCH at Lisbon mE [27 Nov 1851]

Susan 46 w/o Ira HATCH at Vassalboro ME on 30 Aug [9 Sept 1847]

Sylvanus Deac 90 at Unity ME [9 Jan 1851]

Thomas 41 at Bangor ME [3 Aug 1839]

Thomas of Saco ME injured while blasting for the railroad last week, may have lost his sight [23 Sept 1841]

Walter Capt AmRev at Belfast ME [30 Jan 1841]

William A 32 at Bangor ME [24 June 1836]

Zacheus Lt 83 at Jefferson ME on 22nd inst AmRev [6 May 1833]

HATCH - see ALLEN

HATHAWAY Avis B 34 w/o Lorenzo HATHWAY at Norway ME [17 Oct 1850]

Hiram H 2y 6m s/o late Samuel HATHAWAY at Worcester MA [28 Jan 1833]

J Mr of Machias ME 65y with his wife 62 & 8 ch & son of his children's children belong to the "California Packet" Colony, formerly a millman in ME. He & his family appear to be in excellent health, & are busily engaged on board the ship with the rest of the young company. [21 Feb 1850]

Lydia F w/o Lorenzo HATHAWAY at Norway ME [15 Jan 1846]

Mary S W 41 w/o Rev G W HATHAWAY at Bloomfield ME [29 Mar 1849]

Thankful B w/o Ezra HATHAWAY of (Wilton) ME at Wilton on 24th inst [10 Aug 1839]

HATHAWAY - see GABRIEL, PARKER,

HATHORN Andrew M 26 a member of Nequasset Tent International Order of Redmen at Woolwich ME [11 Mar 1847]

James 85 at Palermo ME [15 Aug 1844]

HATHORN (Cont.) John 81 of the first settlers of Dresden ME at Richmond ME [16 Nov 1848]

Mary Mustard 11 d/o Charles HATHORN at Palermo ME [22 Jan 1842]

Sarah Ann F 19 d/o Charles HATHORN at Palermo ME of consumption [4 Mar 1847]

HATHORN - see WOODWARD

HATHORNE Emma L 19 at Eastport ME [13 Nov 1835]

Silas 62 on the 20th [5 Feb 1842]

Solomon of Milford ME at CA [18 Nov 1852]

HAVEN Benjamin S of Portsmouth NC 17 , the names of the officers & crew as per the Custom House list, the ship *Jacob Perkins*, Capt SHOOF, which arrived his morning from Crostadt reported that on 22 inst Cape Cod WSW 55 miles fell in with the wreck of brig *Washington*, RIDER Capt [*Transcript*] [2 Oct 1835]

Horace 21y of Portsmouth NH last week left $3,000 to Harvard College [2 Dec 1843]

HAVENER Nancy S 47 w/o Jacob L HAVENER at Belfast ME [3 Jul 1851]

HAVILAND Eliza 36 w/o F F HAVILAND at Waterville ME [3 June 1847]

HAWES Abijah abt 50 at China ME [26 Sept 1850]

Charles N 17 of Hallowell ME lost overboard from schr *Henry Freeling* on 4th inst [30 Mar 1848]

Clymena P 28 at Augusta ME on 16 Feb [19 Feb 1852]

Clymeria S late of Vassalboro ME est notice Oliver P WEBBER adm [4 Mar 1852]

Eliza 46 w/o David HAWES at Vassalboro ME of consumption after an illness of more than twenty years [10 Dec 1846]

girl abt 4y of Hampden ME d/o Rev Hervey HAWES burnt when her clothes caught afire [11 Dec 1835]

Gustavus W formerly of Boston MA s/o William HAWES of North Yarmouth ME at Alton IL on 6 Jan [1 Feb 1840]

Isaac 75 at Vassalboro ME on 16 Aug [29 Aug 1840]

Isaiah 75 at Vassalboro ME on 31 May (MA papers please copy) [10 June 1852]

Joseph 56y 9m at Troy ME of consumption [10 Feb 1848]

Margaret 77 w/o Abijah HAWES at Union ME [6 May 1833]

Mary Ann Moore Mrs about 19 w/o Joel HAWES at Bucksport ME [4 Feb 1847]

Sarah 78 at Vassalboro ME [19 Nov 1846]

Tasmin Mrs 72y to a day at Vassalboro ME [31 Oct 1844]

Thomas 72 at Vassalboro ME on 9 Feb [21 Feb 1834]

HAWES - see WEBBER

HAWK Black remains stolen & Gov LUCAS issued a requisition for them, found in the hands of an anatomist at Quincy, the desire & expectation is that they should be deposited in the Burlington burial ground. The Indian mode of burial is to build a pen of round poles about 10' by 3'; the pen built as high as the shoulders of a man when sitting on the ground. In the west end the mighty B H was placed in sitting posture with his face to the rising sun his gun, tomahawk & blanket placed by his side, the pen covered over, leaving the head & neck exposed to the weather; his face painted red & striped off with black [*Burlington (Iowa) Hawkeye*] [30 Sept 1843] & assassination of Keokuck by young B H, an entire fabrication [*The Chicago American* of the 6th inst] [27 Jul 1839]

HAWKES Abigail Mrs 76 at Kennebec (now Manchester) ME on 15 Nov [15 Jan 1852]

Elizabeth 27 w/o Nathaniel HAWKES & d/o Josiah & Mary MAGOON at St Albans ME on 6 Feb [6 Mar 1851]

John 38 at Hallowell ME on 3d inst [17 Sept 1842]

Mary W 24 w/o Isaiah J HAWKES & d/o Josiah & Mary MAGOON at St Albans ME on 8 Nov [6 Mar 1851]

wife & child family of Nathaniel HAWKES at St Albans ME [3 Apr 1851]

HAWKINS Daniel, colored, claimed as the slave of William M RISTEEN of Baltimore MD was surrendered to his owner by US Commissioner INGRAHAM of Philadelphia PA The fugitive was arrested at Lancaster Jail where he had just served out a sentence for larceny [7 Aug 1851]

Henry a sailboat which left Baker's Folly on Mon for Newport capsized & he drowned, see CARPENTER [*Providence Journal*] [5 Aug 1843]

Minerva 21 d/o Henry HAWKINS of Oxford ME at New Orleans on 2 Nov [25 Nov 1852]

HAWKS James 22 of Thomaston ME at sea from schr *Frances Ellen* [12 Mar 1846]

Mary 41 w/o Major Eben HAWKS at Bloomfield ME [6 Feb 1845]

HAWLET Benjamin B 31 at Bucksport ME [6 Jul 1839]

HAWLEY S Elder, End of the World Postponed!!!, Elder H, of the Millerites & preached at the dedication of that so called Tabernacle in Boston MA, has published in the *Signs of the Times* the world is not to come to an end until the year 1847. The leader of this humbug (we declare we cannot think of any other name), has always insisted that the end will happen in 1843 ...[*Boston Transcript*] [4 Jan 1844]

Walter his son & grandson all instantly killed in bed when their house was struck by lightning three miles west of Ridgefield Church in CT [8 Aug 1837]

HAWSON - see ROCKFELLE

HAYCOCK Mrs of Milltown (Calais?) ME nearly had her leg broken on Tues last while getting out of her carriage, by a drunken fellow driving his wagon against her & her leg otherwise badly injured. Mrs H is a poor widow & has a large family to look after, which renders her misfortune truly deplorable [11 May 1848]

HAYDEN Charles 79 at Winslow ME [25 June 1842]

Charles H 41 of Eastport ME at Calais ME [30 Oct 1851]

Henry 24 formerly of Castine ME at Exeter ME [13 Feb 1851]

John of Newfield ME his wife & infant & his wife's sister in the sleigh, the mother & child instantly cut into pieces by the Maine Railroad (upper road so called) on Sat while the train was passing through Newmarket NH [11 Dec 1845]

Luther 85 at South Thomaston ME [28 Oct 1852]

Marie 10 eldest d/o John HAYDEN at Bath ME on Sun the 24th ult [4 Jan 1844]

Mr in his case the jury discharged, 9 for conviction & 3 for acquittal in helping a runaway slave [26 June 1851]

HAYDEN - see SCOTT

HAYES Benjamin F 5 c/o Elihu HAYES at Augusta ME [2 Nov 1848]

Caroline 3 c/o Elihu HAYES at Augusta ME [2 Nov 1848]

Charles Esq at Bangor ME [3 Aug 1839]

Daniel 37 one of the owners of the steam mill, killed by the balance wheel, left a wife & one child [*Dover NH Gazette*] [1 Apr 1836]

Edmund 24 recently from Bowdoin College, res of Portland ME, drowned off the steamer *Ohio* [*Cleveland Herald*] *The Umpire* stated last evening he drowned at 7 a.m. Wed at Cleveland OH, belonging to Industry ME. His bro is a Congregational clergyman at Frankfort ME [*Portland Argus*] [10 Aug 1848] [24 Aug 1848]

Elijah Esq 42 at Gorham ME [6 Jan 1848]

Jane 81 wid/o Deac John HAYES formerly of North Yarmouth ME at Turner ME [17 APr 1851]

Lydia S 24 at North Yarmouth ME [22 Jul 1836]

Mrs w/o John H, a carpenter, found in a Brooklyn street, chains on legs & taken to the Police Office, the mother of 12 children (6 living with her) her husband had been in the habit of ill-treating her which led her to drink to excess; that in consequence of this intemperate indulgence he had for three weeks past, chained her to the floor of her bedroom. Her children had aided her escape [New York paper] [19 Feb 1846]

HAYES (Cont.) Rachel Mrs 29 at Garland ME [1 Feb 1849]

Reuben 60 at Berwick ME on 3d inst [21 Aug 1838]

Susan R 26 w/o George P HAYES at Saco ME [8 Feb 1844]

William R Esq at native of VT died at Barbados [2 Sept 1852]

HAYES - see ROLERSON

HAYFORD Elizabeth Mrs 29 d/o Nathaniel BICKNELL at Belfast ME [8 Aug 1844]

Gustavus Esq 76 at Canton Mills ME on 19th ult [17 Aug 1848]

HAYNES Elijah Esq of Gorham ME struck with paralysis on Thurs last at Moderation Mills [*Eastern Argus*] [30 Dec 1847]

Lucretia 22 w/o Albert Q HAYNES at Bethel ME [22 Jul 1852]

Mary abt 62 wid/o Mr Jacob HAYNES at North Yarmouth ME [20 May 1843]

Pritchard W 26 killed at the wheel on board bark *Diligence* on 15th Jan [11 Apr 1850]

HAYWARD Elizabeth 54 w/o Daniel HAYWARD at Winthrop ME [23 Apr 1846]

Elizabeth abt 21 at Winthrop ME [4 Sept 1838]

George station agent on the Fitchbury Railroad shot at Lincoln MA? [*Boston Advertiser*] [2 Jan 1851]

John 22 of Gardiner ME d near Brighton Station [25 Nov 1852]

Libeus 53 at Augusta ME on 13 Jul of typhoid fever [2 Aug 1849]

Mary 65 at Hebron ME [1 Feb 1849]

Pelez 19 of Winthrop ME s/o Daniel HAYWARD on the Sweet Water River on his way to CA [11 Nov 1852]

HAYWOOD Lucy Ann 27 at Weld ME on 20 Feb [21 Feb 1851]

Rebecca 84 widow at Winthrop ME on Fri last [14 Aug 1841]

Timothy 66 at Waterville ME [26 Aug 1847]

Z B Mrs w/o Mr Z B HAYWOOD at Calais ME [10 Apr 1845]

HAZELETON Gilman 20y a brakeman on the Lowell Railroad killed accidentally last week, a native of Springfield NH [29 Mar 1849]

HAZELETON - see LEONARD

HAZELINE Isabel Eustus 26 w/o William B HAZELINE & d/o David FRANCIS Esq of Boston MA at Gardiner ME [24 Aug 1848]

John 70 at Gardiner ME [14 Sept 1848]

HAZELTINE Arad 47 late of Nobleboro ME at Searsmont ME [19 June 1841]

HAZEN Samuel S 31/34 formerly of Bridgton ME at Readfield ME on 15th ult of consumption [13 Jan 1848]

HEAD James abt 16 at Waldoboro ME [12 Sept 1834]

Jonathan 74 formerly of Waldoboro ME at Warren ME [28 Aug 1841]

Rebecca 86 w/o Moses HEAD AmRev at Barnard ME [18 May 1848]

HEAGAN Maria 40 w/o Samuel HEAGAN formerly of Phipsburg ME at Prospect ME [22 Jul 1833]

HEAL Josiah 33 at Calais ME of consumption [27 Jul 1839]

Josiah 6m s/o Josiah HEAL at Calais ME [6 Jul 1839]

HEALD Caroline 19 d/o Capt Jonas HEALD of Madison ME at Winthrop ME [16 Oct 1845]

Daniel 44 at Bingham ME [15 May 1851]

Lucy 86 w/o Lt Thomas HEALD at Norridgewock ME [4 Feb 1847]

Lydia Ann 19 of Georgetown ME at Bath ME [4 Sept 1845]

Mary 87 wid/o Capt Oliver HEALD at South Solon ME [13 Apr 1848]

Oliver 80 AmRev at Madison ME on the 31st ult [21 Aug 1838]

Paulina eldest d/o Eben HEALD Esq at Anson ME [28 Aug 1838]

Thomas 82 at Norridgewock ME [14 Jan 1847]

Thomas 86 AmRev pensioner at Norridgewock on 5 Feb [28 Feb 1850]

HEALD (Cont.) Thurston 6 s/o widow HEALD at Norridgewock ME [27 Nov 1845]

  Thurston Maj 45 at Norridgewock ME on 14th inst [4 May 1839]

  Wellington of (Norridgewock) ME s/o Deac Ezeliel HEALD had his clothes caught in
  the gear of Mr J W SAWTELLE's grist mill ... it is thought he will recover
  [*Norridgewock Journal*] [6 Feb 1835]

HEALEY Mr 75 went to a spring a few rods from his house for water & not returning was
  found with his head in the water, drowned, at Raymond ME [10 Nov 1846]

HEALY Eliphalet 79 AmRev at Thomaston ME [26 Oct 1833]

  girl burned by breaking a fluid lamp of (Wiscasset? ME) on Mon [*Lincoln Miscellany*] [6
  Feb 1851]

HEARD Barshaba 92 at Anson ME [13 Apr 1848]

  Daniel 77 at Hallowell ME [5 Sept 1844]

  Philemon his house fire near Main Stream in Harmony ME newly built [1 Apr 1843]

  Sarah 85 wid/o Joseph HEARD at Berwick ME [19 Aug 1836]

HEARSAY George T Col abt 40 formerly of Augusta ME at Springfield LA on 16 Nov [14
  Dec 1833]

  Lucy 80 wid/o Capt Nathaniel HEARSAY at Farmington ME [6 May 1843]

HEATH Andrew Mrs 63 at Bath ME [2 May 1850]

  Clarinda 29 at Sidney ME on 29 Sept [17 Oct 1840]

  Eunice 63 wid/o Samuel HEATH at Litchfield ME [25 Nov 1847]

  Hannah E 28 wid/o Charles HEATH Esq 28 at Phillips ME on 10 Sept [21 Sept 1848]

  John Capt 38 at Salem ME [30 Dec 1843]

  Mary Mrs 74 at Augusta ME on 26 Dec [3 Jan 1850]

  Mrs 45 w/o Josiah HEATH at Augusta ME [3 June 1833]

  Randolph 36 at Augusta ME on 15th inst [28 June 1849]

  Samuel 28 a native of ME at Washington TX after a lingering sickness [28 Oct 1836]

  Samuel Dr 73 at Jefferson ME [14 Aug 1835]

  Sarah abt 24 d/o Andrew at Bath ME on 20th ult [3 Apr 1835]

  Sarah Jane B 24 at Whitefield ME [6 Jan 1848]

  Selmna [*sic*] A 12 at Augusta ME on 12 Aug [4 Sept 1851]

  Simeon abt 50 at Hallowell ME [13 June 1834]

  William Esq 70 at Litchfield ME [28 Aug 1841]

HEATH - see Negro

HEBER Richard Esq died in England on the 4th ult [23 Nov 1833]

HEDGE Barnabas 93 formerly of Yarmouth MA at Vassalboro ME [7 Sept 1839]

  Horace B 24 at Augusta ME [25 Apr 1837]

  Sarah 26 w/o Rev B HEDGE of Readfield ME at Alna ME [13 Mar 1838]

HEDGE - see DOLE

HELMERSHAUSEN Matilda Williams formerly of Calais ME at Damariscotta ME on
  30th ult [14 June 1849]

HELMS Andrew the pilot of the steamer *Wilmington* (the New Orleans papers state) was
  blown overboard and the 1st & 2nd engineer & four other hands were killed. [21 Dec
  1839]

HELMS - see ABBOTT

HEMANS Mrs on 16th ult at Dublin [10 Jul 1835]

HEMENWAY Thomas 84 at Union ME [4 Mar 1847]

HEMINGWAY Phineas 79 s/o the late Rev Dr HEMINGWAY of Wells ME at Acton ME
  on 3rd ult [28 May 1842]

HEMLEN Mrs over 60y wid/o Lewis HEMLEN, her 6 brothers last week seen in (Augusta)
  ME, the oldest over 60y. They had not been all together before since the AmRev. Four
  of them were out in the American service in that war. Four of them live in this county

HEMLEN (Cont.) & are well known here; the others in MA. Their names are CRAIG, - Moses, Elias, Elijah, Jesse, Enoch & David. *[Kennebec Journal]* [7 Sept 1833]

HEMMENWAY Louisa Mrs at Belgrade ME [29 Aug 1834]

Hemp - see news

HENDER Jerusha 76 at Wilton ME formerly of Camden ME [18 Dec 1845]

HENDERSON Alice 48 w/o John HENDERSON Esq at Rockland ME [19 Sept 1850]
  Almira A 24 at Farmington ME [14 Nov 1850]
  Andrew F Esq, the president of the steamboat line scalded severely & wounded in the head on the *Medora*, Capt SUTTON. He appeared to be doing well last night [23 Apr 1842]
  Clara Bell 8m d/o Dr J HENDERSON at Saco ME on 21st inst [5 Aug 1847]
  Josiah Dr 80 at Farmington ME [16 Oct 1845]
  Mary 71 w/o John HENDERSON at New Portland ME [22 Mar 1849]
  Mary Jane 30 w/o Capt James HENDERSON at Thomaston ME [25 Apr 1850]
  Mr drowned of East Thomaston ME. The schr *Potomac* mentioned as having been lost, belonged to East Thomaston ME and was capsized on Sun afternoon on the 2nd inst in Long Island Sound, opposite Smithtown and all on board perished. [1 Jan 1839]
  Mr of Alexander ME with Mr J S PHILLIPS & Mr Joel GOOCHAND killed last by entering a foul well [19 Aug 1852]
  Samuel H 30 of New Portland ME drowned in Penobscot River [30 Jul 1842]
  Stephen in his will he directed that his slaves should be sent to Liberia by the American Colonization Society ... [14 Aug 1845]

HENLY Col attacked & robbed at Portland a few days since died on the 17th inst [28 Oct 1843]

HENNESY - see ROLERSON

HENRICH Mr killed in 1819 a man had just died in the valley of Munster, who confessed committed the murder of HENRICH in 1819, for which his wife & son were convicted, and executed at Colmar. The son said to the clergyman who attended him. "It is impossible that God should allow this execution to take place, for I always loved my father & am perfectly innocent." *The Journal du Bas Rhin* (in Germany) [29 Feb 1840]

HENRY Abigail 49 w/o George HENRY at Bowdoinham ME [20 Jul 1839]
  Dr died at Pendlebury near Manchester [28 Oct 1836]
  John A Rev 32 at Ludlow VT [30 Dec 1847]
  Sir Admiral 76y at Brighton on 9 Feb [28 Feb 1840]
  William A passed midshipman US Navy attached to US ship *Preble* as acting master, who died at this place 15 Dec 1844 of disease contracted on the coast of Africa [10 Apr 1845]

HENSHAW - see COLT

HERBERT James 90 father of Thomas HERBERT of Richmond ME & James HERBERT of Waldoboro ME died in England [20 June 1844]
  William O 21 late of Rowley MA at Sacramento City CA on 26 Dec [14 Feb 1850]

HERD - see WOOD

HERRERA - see PANA

HERRICK Benjamin Capt of Surry Hancock Co ME on passage from Panama to San Francisco CA [26 Feb 1852]
  David Capt 38 at Gardiner ME [6 Nov 1845]
  Ebenezer member of Congress at Lewiston ME [18 May 1839]
  Elizabeth Mrs 67 formerly of Gloucester MA at West Gardiner ME [28 Aug 1851]
  Emily a widow 31 at Farmingdale [6 May 1852]
  Hannah 47 w/o Hon Eben HERRICK of Lewiston ME at New York [31 Oct 1837]

HERRICK (Cont.) Huldah 70 at Sedgwick ME [16 Jul 1846]
 Israel of Poland ME from a cannon burst on the 4th of July had his right limb so horribly
  mangled he lost his leg to the hip joint *[Lewiston Journal]* [13 Jul 1848]
 J Gen abt 70 at Hampden ME [1 Nov 1849]
 John Esq 82 & his sister Mrs Elizabeth HAM 80 (The Herrick Tavern still stands on
  Main St in Lewiston built 1800, see Elder's *History of Lewiston ME*) [11 Apr 1834]
 Letitie Ann abt 19 w/o Isaac C HERRICK at Glenburn ME [21 Aug 1845]
 Lucy 37 at Greene ME [13 Feb 1851]
 Mr J L s/o Hon Ebenezer HERRICK at New York of smallpox [9 Mar 1839]
 Nancy Mrs 62 at Sedgwick Bay ME [30 Nov 1848]
 Oliver Esq 70 at Lewiston ME [15 Jul 1852]
HERRICK - see WOODMAN
HERRIN Andrew 68 at Skowhegan ME [15 Jul 1847]
 Appleton 33 s/o Samuel HERRIN of Exeter ME at Brownville ME [10 Jan 1850]
 Asa 44 formerly of Skowhegan ME at Garland ME [10 June 1847]
 Daniel 100y 8m AmRev at Charleston ME [28 Sept 1839]
 Samuel abt 40 at Augusta ME [19 Dec 1844]
HERRING Augusta L 35 w/o S S HERRING of Bangor ME at Paris ME [17 June 1847]
 Clara 47 w/o Daniel HERRING at Norway ME [12 Aug 1852]
 Crissian deck passenger of Germany died when a serious accident happened on board the
  steamboat *George Collier* on the 6th inst on her passage from New Orleans to St
  Louis MO [25 May 1839]
 John his family consisting of himself, wife. father, mother, 6 ch & a hired man came near
  losing their lives. The eldest son had died. Upon inspection of the flour in the barrel,
  a quantity of white lead was found intermixed at LeRoy NY [1 Jul 1836]
HERSAY Nathan 43 at Corinth ME [5 Dec 1850]
HERSEY Benjamin 33 at Minot ME [14 Oct 1852]
 Hiram 12 at Topsham ME drowned [24 Dec 1846]
 James 67 at Farmington ME [31 Aug 1848]
 James Gen 3rd 32 at Sumner ME [8 Jul 1847]
 John A Dr 60 formerly of Farmington ME at New Orleans on 27 Mar [3 May 1849]
 Zadok 98 AmRev pensioner at Pembroke [7 Feb 1850]
HERSEY - see NORCROSS, PERKINS
HERSHAM a child 7m c/o John HERSHAM at Augusta ME [1 Apr 1847]
HERSUM Ann M 8 d/o widow Lydia HERSUM at Belgrade ME on 27 Feb [13 Mar 1851]
 James late of Belgrade ME, Tamson HERSUM widow [5 Feb 1852]
HESELTON Sarah 21 w/o Reuben HESELTON Jr at Gardiner ME [13 Nov 1851]
HESKETH John K 33 s/o John HESKETH at Hallowell ME on 24th ult [8 Aug 1837]
HETH Joise [*sic*] 162y at New York on 14th ult "no mistake," ailing for abt a week with a
 cold & went off in a quiet tranquil manner ... [4 Mar 1836]
 Loise [*sic*] Miss, the nurse of George WASHINGTON & who is 161 yrs of age will be in
  Boston MA in a few days. Her age is proved by the most authentic documents -
  among which are certificates from very aged & respectable persons now living & the
  original bill of sale from WAHINGTON's father [*Post*] [4 Sept 1835]
HETING Esther 78y w/o Benjamin at Norway ME [25 Apr 1844]
HEWES Henry M printer in firm Watson & Hewes at Boston MA on 27 ult [11 May 1848]
 Isabel 5 youngest c/o V H HEWES formerly of Augusta ME at Boston MA [2 Sept 1847]
 John drowned in Madison Pond left wife & 6ch at Madison ME on Fri morning last [19
  Aug 1847]
 Nathaniel H 18 s/o Virgil H HEWES of Boston MA at sea on 5 Dec on passage from
  Batavia to Boston MA [23 Mar 1848]

HEWES (Cont.) Paoli Capt 80 at Belfast ME [29 June 1848]
> Sarah 61 w/o Solon HEWES at Augusta ME [12 Oct 1833]
> Solomon 67 of Augusta ME at Boston ME [4 Jul 1834]
> Thankful 30 w/o Virgil H HEWES at Augusta ME [30 Sept 1836]

HEWETT Charles 25 at Fayette ME had just returned from St Louis MO [14 Aug 1845]
> P Mr his dwelling house destroyed by fire one morning last week, several small children suffered considerably from the cold, having to leave their beds without their clothes at Livermore ME [26 Mar 1836]
> Patience K 78 w/o Deac WATERMAN HEWETT at West Camden [10 Jan 1850]
> W Deac 84 at West Camden ME [18 Sept 1851]

HEWEY Bethiah Mrs 90 at Webster (now Sabattus) ME [7 Sep 1848]
> Lucy w/o William HEWEY at Phillips ME [15 Apr 1847]

HEWINS Amasa at Augusta ME on Feb 16th [24 Feb 1848]
> Daniel Webster 7y 3m s/o Daniel & Zeruiah HEWINS at Augusta ME on 16 May [6 June 1850]
> Harriet A E 22 w/o Franklin A HEWINS & d/o late Dr Joel R ELLIS at Augusta of consumption on 3rd inst [13 Nov 1845]
> Martha M 43 w/o James HEWINS at Augusta ME [6 Aug 1846]

HEWINS - see WOOD

HEWS Owen 20 of Portland at Augusta ME at the insane hospital [20 Nov 1841]

HEYWOOD Almira L 21 d/o Nathan HEYWOOD Esq of Troy OH at Freedom ME [1 Apr 1852]
> Dudley 46 formerly of Skowhegan ME at Milwaukee WI on 25 May [15 Jul 1852]
> Lydia 83 wid/o Rev Joshua HEYWOOD at Camden ME [11 Sept 1851]
> Mary w/o Dudley HEYWOOD of WI & d/o Asa WYMAN Esq of Skowhegan ME at Skowhegan ME [23 Oct 1845]

HIBBARD Calesta Elizabeth 26 d/o Isaac HIBBARD at Farmington Falls ME [30 Mar 1839]
> Martha 20y of North Hadley MA while singing with a choir in Congregational Church [3 Jul 1851]
> Mr 8 persons killed by the bursting of the boiler, thought to be the only one of the crew to be saved in the loss of the steamboat *Pulaski* about 40 miles to the southward of Wilmington NC [3 July 1838]

HICKLY - see DORROGH

HICKS Franklin 35 at Belfast ME [26 Dec 1834]
> Samuel Capt 64 at Thomaston ME [3 May 1849]
> Sarah 14 a passenger in one of New York canal boats knocked overboard while passing through a dam. An elder brother, 18 tried to save her & both were drowned [17 June 1836]

HIGENS Andrew killed by a shot through the head, one of the laborers on a line of the Baltimore & Ohio Railroad which recently attacked a shanty [10 Apr 1851]

HIGGINS A 60 at Farmington ME [18 Jan 1849]
> Archibald now 123y settler of Athens TN and the oldest man of TN (N.B. likely was not the oldest) fought in the AmRev, recieved a wound in his leg at the battle of Georgetown, "lived to see the 5th generation of his own blood," wife died abt 40 yrs ago, father among the 1st that came from Ireland & was killed by Indians together with his mother & oldest sister [*New York Spirit of the Times*] [9 Sept 1847]
> Azbach 47 w/o Jedediah HIGGINS at Lincoln ME [19 June 1851]
> Hannah 57 w/o Jesse HIGGINS at Eden ME 1st death which has taken place in that town for more than a year [6 May 1836]

HIGGINS (Cont.) Hartwell 15 left his father's home & has not since been heard of, light complexion, light hair, light blue eyes, has a scar upon his forehead near the hair ... reward for information ... Abner HIGGINS of West Waterville ME [14 May 1846]

Jordan L 1st officer of Lisbon ME died on board bark *Franklin* from injuries recieved by being knocked overboard from schr *Manchester* [11 Apr 1850]

Levi 50 at St Albans ME [23 Jan 1851]

Levi of Richmond ME seaman on schr *Texas*, Capt BROWN which vessel put into that port (Nassau) from St Mary's to Havana Cuba on 10th ult [12 Dec 1840]

Lydia abt 40 w/o Aaron HIGGINS of Farmington at Norridgewock ME [10 Oct 1844]

Nancy 18 d/o Major Edmund HIGGINS at South Berwick ME [7 May 1846]

Sarah T 7 c/o Stephen HIGGINS at Augusta ME [21 Jan 1847]

Silas formerly a member of the FL house of representatives, AmRev [*Burlington Free Press*] [19 Oct 1848]

Susannah 88 at Bath ME [23 Dec 1847]

William Henry s/o Solomon HIGGINS at Bath ME [19 Dec 1834]

HIGGINS - see KNIGHT

HIGH Abigail Mrs 74 at South Berwick ME [26 June 1851]

HIGHT Ann Maria 21 at Athens ME [18 Jan 1849]

Dennis 24 s/o Hanson HIGHT of Norridgewock ME at CA on 23 Oct [1 Jan 1852]

George N 24 formerly of Wayne ME at Boston ME [2 Sept 1847]

Lydia Ann 18 d/o Dr Samuel C HIGH at Hollis ME on 11th inst [25 June 1842]

Sarah 17 at Athens ME [30 Oct 1838]

HIGHT - see YALLALEE

HILBORN girl youngest d/o Seth B HILBORN at Portland ME [14 Aug 1845]

HILDRETH Mr of Gardiner ME on Tues week of lockjaw the result of a dreadful wound in the thigh inflicted by a circular saw on which he fell while it was in motion [30 Sept 1847]

Susan J 19 d/o Daniel & Elmira HILDRETH at Gardiner ME [14 Aug 1851]

Thaddeus 28 at Gardiner ME [23 Sept 1847]

William 28 formerly of Gardiner ME at Boston MA [20 Mar 1851]

HILDRETH - see LIBBY [14 Aug 1851]

HILL Alfred arrested on the complaint against him for the violation & murder of a child not 9 yrs old, whom he had taken from the poor house in Newmarket ... Although there was no direct evidence against HILL, the circumstances were so strong against him, that he was committed to jail to await the action of the Grand Jury in Feb next on Tues last 17th ult [*Exeter (NH) News Letter*] [4 Nov 1843]

Betsey 69 w/o Joseph H HILL Esq at Norridgewock ME on 17 June [28 June 1849]

Caroline Mrs 20 w/o John HILL at Lyman ME [30 Sept 1847]

Elizabeth 57 w/o Hon Thomas A HILL at Bangor ME on 28th ult [11 Jan 1840]

George 56 at Buxton ME [30 Sept 1847]

George a native of Newburgh ME at sea 1 June on board bark *Undine* on passage from San Francisco to New York [2 Sept 1852]

girl 18m from the effects of several percussion caps, which she swallowed d/o Robert HILL of Baltimore MD [1 Aug 1840]

H of Bangor ME saved from drowning when the steam packet *New England* sank. It left Boston for Bath & Gardiner ME and had an accident with the schr *Curlew* on 31 May [12 June 1838]

Hannah w/o John HILL at Augusta ME [12 Dec 1837]

Isaac 78 father of ex-gov HILL at Ashburnham MA [11 Jan 1844]

Jacob Esq 68 at Sabattisville ME [3 June 1852]

James shot accidental [*Woodville (MS) Republican*] [30 Apr 1846]

Jane 63y 10m at Gardiner ME formerly of Portland ME [2 Dec 1837]

HILL (Cont.) John 85 a Deacon at Elliot ME [28 Oct 1852]
John abt 16 accidentally shot with a pistol s/o William HILL at Etna ME on Fri [24 Jul 1851]
John H 32 at Winthrop ME [26 Mar 1842]
John L Capt 50 at Phipsburg ME [9 Sept 1847]
Joseph A 38 at Waterboro ME [29 Nov 1849]
Josiah Dr surgeon dentist formerly of Calais ME at Norway ME [14 Mar 1850]
Livonia H 29 at Saco ME [19 June 1851]
Louisa A Mrs 28 w/o Lawson HILL at Paris ME [9 Dec 1847]
Lydia 79 at Saco ME a widow [3 June 1843]
Mark 48 at Auburn ME [4 May 1848]
Martha Ann 32y 7m d/o Joseph & Mary HILL at Belgrade ME on 31 Mar [29 Apr 1852]
Mary A Mrs 46 at Brunswick ME [27 Jul 1848]
Mary Jane 18 d/o Jonas HILL at Fayette ME [26 June 1851]
Milo of (Mt) Vernon (ME?) at San Francisco CA [8 Jan 1852]
Nancy B 23y 5m w/o Mark L HILL Esq at Bangor ME [18 Apr 1834]
Nathaniel 78 at Greene ME [13 Jan 1848]
Nathaniel S 40 at East Readfield ME on Dec 7th of consumption [13 Jan 1848]
Rebecca Mrs 89 wid/o Thomas HILL a native of Weston MA at Gouldsboro ME [6 May 1843]
Thomas M of US Army & s/o Hon Mark L HILL at Phipsburg ME on Sat [24 Jul 1838]
Timothy 55 a convict at Thomaston ME state prison, of Kennebec Co, Deaf & dumb (Deaf mute), death by a blow upon his head from a cord wood stick ... [5 Feb 1836]
widow 88 at Kennebunk ME [16 Dec 1836]
Wilson 18 s/o James HILL at Norway ME [12 Nov 1846]
HILL - see COWART, EDWARDS, GRIFFIN, WILLIAMS
HILLMAN Charles of Boston MA in CA [21 Aug 1851]
HILLS Julia A 27 w/o Ilock HILLS at Biddeford ME [2 Dec 1852]
Mrs abt 45 w/o Samuel at Union ME [28 Oct 1836]
HILTON Alfred 22 at Washington ME [20 Nov 1845]
Almeda 26 at North Anson ME [30 Aug 1849]
Benjamin Esq abt 73 at Anson ME [31 Jul 1845]
Daniel T 61 at Cornville ME [15 Apr 1847]
Ebenezer Col 61 at Wiscasset ME [19 Sept 1844]
Isaac 46 at Kennebunk ME [19 June 1851]
Isaac W 37 d/o Mason C & Catherine M FARRAR at Augusta ME on 23 Feb of consumption [18 Mar 1852]
Joicy Ann d/o Rufus HILTON at Boothbay ME [1 Jan 1846]
Lydia Mrs 91 at Wiscasset ME [20 Apr 1848]
Mary 68 at Hallowell ME [14 Dec 1833]
Mary Mrs w/o James HILTON at Starks ME [13 May 1847]
Mary Olivia 2 yrs 3 mos youngest d/o Edward W and Diantha T HILTON at Augusta ME on May 4 [10 May 1849]
Morrill 85 AmRev soldier at Wiscasset ME [21 Mar 1840]
Moses 59 at Wiscasset ME [3 July 1835]
Nath'l 42 at St Albans ME [13 Sept 1849]
Nehemiah 81 at Farmingdale ME [7 Oct 1852]
Priscilla L w/o C E HILTON of Belfast ME at Hallowell ME [10 Apr 1851]
Rufus Henry 16 formerly of Wiscasset ME s/o Rufus HILTON at Boothbay ME on 12th inst drowned [*Bath Tribune*] [3 June 1847]
Sarah H abt 17 of Norridgewock ME at Lowell MA [16 Oct 1845]

HILTON (Cont.) William 87 AmRev at Solon ME first settler of that town and ever since resided there [6 Aug 1846]

HILTON - see PAGE

HINCKLEY Almira 29 w/o John H HINCKLEY Esq & d/o the late Rev Paul RUGGLES of Carmel ME at Hermon ME on 7 Aug [29 Sept 1840]

Anna abt 72 at Readfield ME on 21 May [6 June 1850]

Zelopha N 40 w/o Capt Benjamin L HINCKLEY at Hallowell ME [2 May 1844]

HINCKLEY - see HINKLEY

HINDS Barton 18 s/o Capt Nimrod & Lydia HINDS at Dover ME [27 May 1852]

Benjamin Capt 82 AmRev at Madison ME [15 Apr 1836]

Betsey B 45 w/o Peter HINDS formerly of Bloomfield ME at Howland ME [25 May 1848]

Josiah D Capt 44 formerly of Belfast ME at Penn Hospital PA [30 May 1850]

Rebecca 26 w/o Arthur HINDS formerly of Dover ME? at New Hudson NY on 3 Sept [25 Sept 1851]

HINES Mary E 11m d/o Mr Jesse HINES at Bangor ME [12 June 1845]

HINGLEY/HINCKLEY(?) Mary 42 w/o William HINGLEY at Lewiston ME [23 Dec 1852]

HINKLEY Abigail 84 wid/o Shubael HINKLEY formerly of Hallowell ME at Richmond ME [23 Jan 1845]

Almira 29 w/o John H HINKLEY & d/o the late Rev Paul RUGGLES of Carmel ME at Hermon ME on 7 Aug [29 Aug 1840]

Austin 20 at Hallowell ME [13 June 1837]

Benjamin 15 s/o Enoch H HINKLEY of Bath ME fell through the ice on the flats on Wed at Bath ME & was drowned [30 Dec 1847] & [6 Jan 1848]

child of John HINKLEY at Brunswick ME [5 Sept 1841]

Cyrena 45 w/o Nicholas HINKLEY at Monmouth ME [6 Feb 1851]

Ebenezer Capt 71 at Hallowell ME [19 Aug 1852]

Elizabeth 68 at Hallowell ME [14 Dec 1848]

Elizabeth C Mrs 79 at Lisbon ME [22 Oct 1846]

James Deac abt 70 at Hallowell ME on 8th inst [18 Apr 1840]

L B Capt 40 at Augusta ME on 13 Aug died suddenly [17 Aug 1848]

Leonard 26 explosion of steamer *Sagamore* Sacramento CA at State Marine Hospital on Nov 6th [2 Jan 1851]

Mary 44 w/o David HINKLEY at Gardiner ME [28 Nov 1850]

Mary J 24 at Gardiner ME [16 Dec 1847]

Matthew 68 at Bath ME [30 Jan 1845]

Samuel B 6y 3m s/o Reuel HINKLEY at Vassalboro ME on 31 Jan [18 Feb 1847]

Seth abt 24 at Mercer ME [17 Apr 1838]

Smith Rev 54 at Monmouth ME on 1 May [20 May 1852]

HINKS Winslow at Bucksport ME [8 Apr 1847]

HINKSON Julia C Mrs 22 d/o Col Andrew DENNISON of Brunswick ME at Bath ME [6 Apr 1848]

HINMAN Hiram about 15y hung himself with a bridle at Southbury [1 May 1841]

HISCOCK Albert 9m s/o Richard & Sarah HISCOCK at Farmington ME [3 Oct 1844]

Jane widow 47 d/o the late Mary & John WHEELER of Chesterville ME at Wilton ME [2 May 1844]

Mary Jane 26 w/o Capt A HISCOCK of Newcastle ME at sea on passage from France to the United States [13 Jul 1848]

William 89 of the first settlers of Strong ME [5 Aug 1852]

HITCHCOCK Alanson of Green River, Great Barrington MA found Dead & headless supposed lain down with his head upon the rail while intoxicated [24 Jul 1851]

Benjamin Thaxter 19 s/o the late Dr Gad HITCHCOCK of North Yarmouth ME at Portland ME [6 Mar 1845]

Edward of Charlestown drowned on the 25 Dec in CA [14 Feb 1850]

Jonah of Westminster VT hung himself on the evening of Fast in that state. Religious melancholy is ascribed as the cause. [27 Apr 1839]

HITCHCOCK - see WINSLOW

HIXON John B shot a short distance from Benton MS by his father-in-law, Lewis LOTT. HIXON had maltreated his wife, who had sought refuge in her father's house, when HIXON had been forbidden, in consequence of which he threatened violence upon the persons of his wife, Mr LOTT, & other members of his family. [1 May 1845]

HOBAN James Esq the attorney of the United States for the District of Columbia died [*Intelligencer*] [29 Jan 1846]

HOBBEY Joseph C Dr 25 at Winslow ME of consumption at the res of his father on the 2nd of the 9th month [1 Oct 1846]

Lucy N 22 at Winslow ME on 15 Oct [12 Nov 1846]

HOBBS Eunice 22 d/o Thomas & Lydia HOBBS at Wells ME [12 Feb 1852]

George of Camden ME of the schr *Lucy Blake*, when off Catham on the 28th inst was killed by the accidental discharge of a gun. His remains were carried to Edgartown MA for interment [10 Oct 1837]

Harrison of Kendall's Mills at Pishons Ferry in an accident at Fairfield ME [14 May 1842]

Joseph 48 at Biddeford ME [15 Apr 1852]

Josiah Col 87 AmRev at Falmouth ME [15 Nov 1849]

Nancy Mrs 59 w/o Jeremiah HOBBS at Norway ME [24 June 1847]

Nathaniel 55 at Waterboro ME [29 Nov 1849]

HOBIN Patrick 49 at Eastport ME [11 Feb 1847]

HOBSON Frances A 20 w/o Joseph L HOBSON at Hollis ME [1 Apr 1852]

HOBSON - see LORD

HOCK - see PROCK

HODGDON Abba M 17 at Bath ME [25 Nov 1847]

Abram 65 at East Livermore ME [28 Oct 1847]

child 8m c/o S HODGON at Gardiner ME [9 Oct 1845]

Daniel M seaman of Boothbay ME lost overboard from schr *John Bell* on 4th ult in the Bay of Chaleur by a heavy sea which broke over her while riding at anchor [3 Aug 1848]

David Wilson 17m s/o Samuel HODGDON Jr at Gardiner ME [3 Oct 1840]

Israel 80 at Parsonsfield ME [12 Mar 1846]

Joanna Mrs 34 w/o Samuel HODGDON at Gardiner ME [29 Oct 1846]

Lydia Mrs 55 at Shapleigh ME [31 Jul 1851]

Sullivan 43 at Gardiner ME [21 Feb 1851]

HODGDON - see BAKER

HODGE L W 25 at Dexter ME [13 June 1850]

HODGES Brooks a fishhook accidentally entered his heart & killed him instantly when his horse was starting suddenly near Purysbury AL. He left one step child and his widow, whose previous husband was killed two yrs ago by a fall from a horse [1 May 1851]

child 4m c/o Daniel HODGES at Hallowell ME [5 Sept 1840]

Eleanor 75 at Ellsworth ME [12 Nov 1842]

Elizabeth Mrs 48 w/o Ezra HODGES & d/o Capt Joseph KERSEY formerly of Alna ME at Hallowell ME on 14th inst [23 Sept 1847]

HODGES (Cont.) Ezra 90y 9m of Hallowell ME at Vassalboro ME on 28th Sept at the res of his dau [9 Oct 1851]

Isaac 25y 9m s/o Barnum & Phebe HODGES of Winslow ME at Breman ME on 13 Nov [11 Dec 1851]

Mehitable 71 w/o Ezra HODGE the mother of 22 ch almost all whom are living at Hallowell ME [17 Oct 1834]

S 70y of Foxboro MA killed in a railroad accident [1 Nov 1849]

HODGES - see NELSON

HODGKINS Charles of Portland ME saved the barque *William Fales*, Capt William THOMES of this port (Portland ME) was lost in Well Bay ME on Wed evening at 9 o'clock, 13 persons on board, eight were lost including every officer. Through the attention of our friend, George M FREEMAN of Cape Needick (Old York, where the barque drove) [26 Feb 1842]

Ellen 7 d/o T M HODGKINS at Bangor ME on 10th inst [16 Mar 1848]

Ellen C 2m d/o Samuel V HODGKINS at Augusta ME [16 Jan 1846]

John Capt 78 at Bath ME [20 Mar 1835]

Judith M 40 w/o Sumner HODGKINS at Albion ME on 9th Aug [22 Aug 1850]

Lucy A 30 w/o Capt J R HODGKINS at Gardiner ME [30 Apr 1846]

Lucy R 62 formerly of Bath ME at Salem MA [23 May 1844]

Mrs w/o William HODGKINS at Brunswick ME [13 Jan 1837]

Rollins B 25 at Augusta ME on 14 Jul [18 Jul 1850]

HODGMAN Clarissa 23 d/o Amos HODGMAN of Jefferson ME at Boston MA of smallpox [12 Feb 1846]

Job Capt 45 at Camden ME [15 Jul 1843]

HODSDON Abby Elizabeth 13 at New Portland ME [9 Mar 1848]

Daniel 46 at Hollis ME [29 Jul 1847]

Mercy S 24y 9m at Milo ME on 13 Jan [7 Feb 1850]

Moses 79y 6m at Levant ME [27 Nov 1845]

HOE Lt a duel with Lt ROSS of the US Navy at Pensacola FL It terminated "honorably" - one wounded in the heel of his boot & the other shot through the hat [26 Oct 1839]

HOEZER - see Van HOEZER

HOFFSES Mr 90 at Waldoboro ME [15 Oct 1846]

HOGA Stephen three of Mrs children drowned on board the brig *Tilton* of Boston MA, Capt GREENLAW laden with lumber from Calais ME for Providence RI. Capt G states while lying to in a gale on Fri the schr struck on Marsfield Beach (where she now lays). Crew was all saved. The vessel was a total loss, principal of the cargo saved. [14 Sept 1839]

HOGAN Julia A 31 w/o Capt William H HOGAN at Bath ME [13 Jan 1848]

Rev of the Methodist persuasion murdered on Pinelog Creek, Cass Co GA on the night of the 9th ult at his own house by his miller, named Western JENKS [8 June 1839]

HOGAN - see DORROGH

HOIT Abigail 17 d/o Holland & Lucy HOIT of North Anson ME at Augusta ME on 17 Sept at the res of John L DUTTON [2 Oct 1851]

HOLAND Ansel of Sandwich MA crushed to death by a stone weighing about a ton falling on him [30 Mar 1848]

HOLBROOK David 86 at Prospect ME [30 Jan 1851]

Emma J 3y 3m d/o Asa C & Sarah J HOLBROOK at Fairfield ME on 26 Aug [14 Dec 1848]

George B of MA at San Francisco CA on 7 Oct [20 Nov 1851]

Harriet Ellen wife of S C HOLBROOK Esq at Mercer ME on 15 Mar [27 Apr 1848]

Mary Jane 22 w/o Israel HOLBROOK at Gardiner ME [12 Jul 1849]

HOLBROOK (Cont.) Mrs drowned at Langley's Factory Pond [*Times*] [20 Sept 1849]
  Samuel abt 45 at St Albans ME [3 Apr 1851]
  Simon abt 48 at Brunswick ME [7 Jan 1847]

HOLDEN Charles W in CA on 13 June, of the *Holden's Dollar Magazine* [27 Sept 1849]
  Daniel Esq 86 AmRev pensioner at Sweden ME [16 Aug 1849]
  Elizabeth G 45 w/o Charles HOLDEN at Portland ME [16 Jan 1851]
  Ezra one of the editors of the *Philadelphia Saturday Courier*, a native of Oxford Co
    [*Portland Transcript*] [2 Apr 1846]
  Hiram, a child. A brute in human form, named James QUITLY passing down Roosevelt
    St quite intoxicated encountered the lad HOLDEN on the sidewalk, playing. The
    villain seized the child, dashed his head against the pavement. The child not expected
    to survive. [*NY Sun*] [9 Oct 1838]
  James W 24 at Moose River Somerset Co ME [9 Aug 1849]
  Samuel 70 at Waterville ME [11 Mar 1833]

HOLDRIDGE Mrs (not an obit) a lady sailor, the w/o Capt N HOLDRIDGE of the packet
    ship *US* arrived on Tues her 13th voyage across the Atlantic. "We think she is fairly
    entitled to a command having in every instance sailed as the mate of Capt H" [*NY
    Courier & Enquirer*] [23 May 1837]

HOLLAND Elbridge G 42 at Camden ME [10 Jan 1850]
  Hannah 72 w/o Joseph HOLLAND at Vienna ME very suddenly [18 Mar 1847]
  James M 29 at Canton ME [28 Oct 1847]
  John 76 at Lewiston ME [8 Aug 1850]
  Joseph AmRev pensioner at Vienna ME [18 Mar 1847]
  Mary A 24 at Waterville ME [14 Aug 1851]
  Mary Louisa 7 d/o Capt Joseph HOLLAND at Canton ME [4 Apr 1850]
  Mary w/o Gen Richard HOLLAND of Brunswick ME at Lewiston ME [13 Mar 1845]
  Mr also Mr McCLORY in an accident at Pittsburg ME on Fri [3 Dec 1846]

HOLLAND - see ABBOTT

HOLLEY Hepsibah abt 24 d/o Capt John HOLLEY at Farmington ME [16 May 1844]
  Park 94 at Bangor ME [6 June 1844]

HOLLIS David 56 at Bingham ME [5 Feb 1852]
  Isaiah W 27 at Kingfield ME [26 Nov 1846]
  Thomas J of New Sharon ME a seaman lost overboard on 17 Apr in the Kennebec River
    from brig *Harriet Newell* [3 May 1849]

HOLLOM Emanuel 86 a native of Stockholm Sweden at Sebec ME [27 May 1847]

HOLLY - see BARKER

HOLMAN George 12y s/o the late Dr HOLMAN of Gardiner ME on Wed between the
    hours of 3 and 4 in the afternoon, he left his home in Bolton MA in pursuit of
    squirrels. About 6PM cries were heard at the village for help and the boy was
    discovered about 100 rods from the street sitting upon a wall and calling to people to
    come and get him. Upon reaching him it was found he had broken his leg just below
    the hip. He had tied one of his suspenders around his leg and crawled probably forty
    rods over very rough ground and climbed to the top of a stone wall on the edge of the
    woods. Drs BIGELOW & HOLMAN were called & the boy is doing well [22 May
    1851]
  Mr of ME on the bark *Undine* from Panama to San Francisco CA [5 Feb 1852]
  Nathaniel abt 25 of Canaan ME a member of Medical School at Brunswick ME [4 Apr
    1834]
  Polly 76 wid/o Capt Jona HOLMAN at Dixfield ME [26 Oct 1848]
  Samuel C 29 of PEI Canada formerly of St John New Brunswick Canada & late of
    Boston MA at Augusta ME on 6 Oct [14 Oct 1852]
  Silas Dr 61 at Gardiner ME [26 Sept 1850]

HOLMES Asaph 41 at Kingston MA after a long period of suffering borne with exemplary
    Christian fortitude [27 Mar 1845]
    Asenath 2y d/o Allyn HOLMES at Gardiner ME [19 Sept 1840]
    Caroline F w/o Hon John HOLMES at Thomaston ME [30 Oct 1851]
    child of Allyn HOLMES at Gardiner ME [8 Aug 1844]
    Ebenezer 61 at West Waterville ME on 6 Oct of quick consumption [28 Oct 1842]
    Elizabeth 65 w/o Davis Esq at Bath ME [26 Mar 1846]
    Ezekiel Dr 64 of Winthrop ME on 9th inst (see obit) [16 Feb 1865]
    Gershom 87 AmRev at Auburn ME [22 Jan 1852]
    Hazael 23 at Belfast ME on 8th inst [24 Jan 1834]
    Henry Smith 21 at Kingston MS [3 Sept 1842]
    Horace F 22 at Frankfort ME [27 Aug 1846]
    Horace P 38 at Dover [5 Sept 1850]
    Issachar Snell 27 s/o Isaac SNELL of Winthrop ME at Augusta ME on Sat night last [2
        Sept 1841]
    J Mr of Kingston lost his pocket-book. Found by Michael SHEEHAN, a poor Irishman.
        Mr H told of the recovery, who upon examination of same, found all as he lost it, &
        learned Sheehan compelled to sell his boat, with which he got a living to pay the
        funeral expense of his wife; Mr H very generously gave him the $13 in the pocket-
        book & then added a $5 bill as a reward for his honesty. [*Atlas*] [4 Oct 1849]
    Jerusha 78 widow of the late James HOLMES at Oxford ME [27 Jul 1848]
    John 35 at Eastport ME [6 Jan 1848]
    Joseph formerly of North Yarmouth ME accidentally killed at Hampden ME while
        employed in the paper mill. He has left a large family. [*Boston Bee*] [9 Jan 1845]
    Lewis of Weymouth in accident, left wife & two or three children [*Boston Post*] [14 Aug
        1845]
    Lucinda 24 w/o Dr George HOLMES at Belmont ME [24 Apr 1851]
    Mrs w/o William HOLMES burned to death in their house at the Forks ME [9 Dec 1852]
    Nathaniel 75, father of the editor of the *Maine Farmer* at Kingston MA [16 Nov 1848]
    Orpheus 23 s/o Capt Samuel HOLMES of Peru ME thrown from a train of cars &
        instantly killed at Boston MA [29 Jul 1852]
    Sally 62 w/o Hon John HOLMES at Alfred ME on 6 Dec [18 Dec 1835]
    Sophia 64 at Bath ME [21 Aug 1851]
    Thomas 70 at Berwick ME [20 Dec 1849]
    Thomas 96 AmRev at Mercer ME on 25th Feb [8 Mar 1849]
    William B s/o the late Hon John HOLMES at Alfred ME [19 Dec 1850]
HOLMES - see JENKINS, PURRINGTON, news on Hemp
HOLT Abel 45 at Weld ME [21 Feb 1851]
    Chloe 81 w/o Darius HOLT at Norway ME [8 Nov 1849]
    Eliza 56 w/o Jonah HOLT Esq at Bluehill ME [9 Dec 1847]
    Ephraim of Bethel ME of drowning in Songo Pond on Thurs [25 May 1848]
    Hannah 57 w/o Capt Isaac HOLT at Clinton ME [1 Jan 1852] & [18 Dec 1851]
    James not been found yet, fatal shipwreck of the schr *Argus* on Plum Island [2 Jan 1851]
    Jeremiah 94 one of the first settlers of that town at Bluehill ME [26 Aug 1847]
    John a machine maker "entered a grocery in (Paterson) on evening last week, and called
        for something to drink, believing him already intoxicated, refused him, the proprietor
        attempted to lead him away, but before they had, expired immediately. He was a very
        intemperate man." [*The Paterson Intelligencer*] [29 Apr 1836]
    Moses 74 at Paris ME [22 Feb 1844]
    Nehemiah 44 at Portland ME [11 Jul 1844]
    Osborn 15y at West Bethel ME killed by a train of cars passing over him completely
        severing his body 23 Sept 1851]

HOLT (Cont.) Phebe 78 at Weld ME on 28 Dec [21 Feb 1851]
   Uriah Esq 74 at Norway ME [5 Jul 1849]
HOLTON - see joke
HOLWAY Elizabeth 77 w/o Barnabas HOLWAY at Fairfield ME [20 Apr 1848]
   Gideon of Fairfield ME died at the dwelling house of H A MOORE in Skowhegan ME on
      Thurs last at his dinner, choking of apoplexy [9 Oct 1841]
HOMAN Charles Sewall 11m 1w only child of senior publisher of the *Gospel Banner* at
      Augusta ME on 7th inst [10 Sept 1846]
   Charles Sewall 4y 6m only s/o Joseph A HOMAN at Augusta ME on Fri evening last [11
      Sept 1845]
HOMAN Samuel abt 28 formerly of Boston MA at Hallowell ME on 14th inst [17 Sept
      1846]
HOMANS Mary 41 w/o Capt Samuel HOMANS at Vassalboro ME [30 Oct 1841]
   Samuel Capt 58 at Augusta ME on 15th inst [22 Feb 1849]
   Stephen 82 at Vassalboro ME [29 Oct 1846]
HOMANS - PRAY
HOMES Henry Esq 69 senior partner of the late firm of Homes, Homer [*sic*] & Co at
      Middleborough MA [30 Oct 1845]
   Lewis of East Weymouth thrown from the driver's seat & killed [7 Aug 1845]
HOOD Patty 73 at Lynn MA [7 Sept 1833]
HOOK Charles S 24 a member of Division No 33 Sons of Temperance at Searsmont ME
      [28 Jan 1847]
   Joseph Capt of Skowhegan ME millwright died suddenly [27 Aug 1846]
   Sarah 68 wid/o Capt Joseph HOOK at Skowhegan ME [8 May 1851]
HOOKE Josiah S Dr 40 s/o Josiah HOOKE Esq of Castine ME at Adrian MI [30 May
      1844]
HOOKEY John 66 at Brownfield ME [17 Jul 1851]
HOOPER George Bates 1y 7d s/o Capt John & Christina HOOPER at Greene ME [22 Apr
      1847]
   Jacob abt 55 formerly of Augusta ME at Manchester MA [19 Mar 1846]
   James 65 at Paris ME [14 June 1849]
   James Elder at Paris ME pastor of the Baptist Church [7 Jan 1843]
   James of North Castine ME discovered his store to be on fire & the Post Office was also
      lost [*Bangor Courier*] [28 Mar 1844]
   Mrs 55 w/o Henry HOOPER at North Anson ME [10 Jul 1851]
   Rachel 19 at Freeport ME on 25th ult [13 Aug 1842]
   Samuel 72 at Saco ME [19 June 1851]
HOOTON Bridget 12 died on Thurs at South Boston MA [2 Aug 1849]
HOPKINS Allen 49 at Hampden ME [21 Jan 1833]
   child of Joel HOPKINS Jr of cholera at Hampden ME [*Bangor Daily Whig*] [16 Aug
      1849]
   Erastus Rev of Northampton lost a fine little boy abt three yrs old [*Worcester Journal*]
      [20 Apr 1848]
   Hannah Jane 23 w/o Theophilus HOPKINS at Orneville ME [17 Jan 1850]
   James a seaman lost overboard from brig *Catharine Nichols* on passage from Matanzas
      to Hopkins [3 June 1847]
   James D Esq with the exception of Chief Justice MELLEN, the oldest practitioner at the
      Cumberland bar also departed this life at Portland ME [27 June 1840]
   John 65 at Orland ME [23 Nov 1848]
   Joseph F abt 24y formerly of Bucksport ME on 4 Oct in or was of Portland ME [11 Dec
      1851]

HOPKINS (Cont.) Judith widow 38 at Brunswick ME [24 June 1843]
  Lewis at Jefferson ME on 2d inst [19 June 1838]
  Lewis P 28 at Kennebec ME [26 Aug 1852]
  Myrick & son of Gardiner ME saved from drowning when the steam packet *New England* sank. It left Boston for Bath & Gardiner ME and had an accident with the schr *Curlew* on 31 May [12 June 1838]
  Robert 26 formerly of Jefferson ME at Calais ME [10 June 1836]
  Solomon 56 at Biddeford ME [23 Dec 1852]
  William T has recently "taken to himself a rib" (a wife) in Lumbergor alias Bangor ME by the name of Eunice COLBATH [24 Sept 1846]
HORN Charles 46 at Augusta ME [20 Nov 1845]
  Nancy 63 formerly of Castine ME at Somerville MA on 18th ult [9 Dec 1852]
  Paul 61 formerly of Rochester NH at Hallowell ME on 10th inst of consumption [4 Feb 1833]
  Wentworth 61 at Berwick ME [26 June 1851]
  William B s/o James HORN of Vassalboro ME at Louisville KY [31 Oct 1840]
HORNBECK Maria J Mrs appointed Postmistress of the Allentown PA office in place of E R NEWEARD resigned. Mrs H is the wid/o Hon John W HORNBECK & has a large family dependent upon her for support. [22 Mar 1849]
HORNE Anna 50 at Saco ME d/o John HORNE [26 Nov 1846]
  John 78 at Saco ME [26 Nov 1846]
HORR Alexander 2 s/o Phillip & Mary HORR at Waterford ME [8 Aug 1850]
  Anna 74 w/o Deac John HORR at Portland ME [22 Nov 1849]
  Isaac 83 at Waterford ME [27 May 1847]
HORTON David W of Boston MA saved from drowning when the steam packet *New England* sank. It left Boston for Bath & Gardiner ME and had an accident with the schr *Curlew* on 31 May [12 June 1838]
HOSACK - see COLT
HOSKINS James W Rev of the Universalist Society at Bangor ME [17 June 1833]
  Joseph "took from the keel one of the crew a Scotchman, with an American protection, purporting to be the only survivor" stated the ship *Jacob Perkins*, Capt SHOOF, which arrived his morning from Crostadt reported that on 22 inst Cape Cod WSW 55 miles fell in with the wreck of brig *Washington*, Rider Capt [2 Oct 1835]
HOSMER Ann Mrs 33 at Weld ME [20 Feb 1851]
  David of Acton taken up alive died in the afternoon, on his way to work on the Fitchburg road as an "axe man" accident on the Fresh Pond Railroad [13 May 1843]
  Edward 2y 6m at Camden ME [23 Apr 1842]
HOSUN James abt 25 an unmarried man formerly of Lebanon ME one of the hostlers belonging to the stable connected with the Patterson House. Two years ago his brother was accidentally killed. Coroner PRATT held an inquest on the body & the verdict of "accidental death" was rendered [*Boston Bee* 18th] [23 Nov 1848]
HOUDLETT John D 3 s/o Capt Washington HOUDLETT at Whitefield ME [29 Jan 1846]
  Lewis 75 at Dresden ME on 8th inst [21 May 1846]
HOUDLETTE Frances 16 d/o Capt Edward E HOUDLETTE at Dresden ME [5 Jul 1849]
  Mary E 6y 8m d/o Cavalier HOUDLETTE Esq at Dresden ME on 18 Jul [9 Aug 1849]
HOUGH James recovered $200 of John REED, for saying the sausages in which he Dealt, were made of Dead hogs, &c - We should think that sausages made of live hogs whould produce an awful squealing in the frying pan. (from a Southern paper) [21 Dec 1839]
  John compelled by the S P Court, sitting in Cincinnati, to pay $1700 for seducing Ann Maria ROBERTS. A few days after another verdict was rendered against him for

HOUGH (Cont.) promising to marry Sarah WATSON. His account stands thus: For seducing Miss ROBERTS $1700, for promising Miss WATSON $2,700 total $4,450. According to this account breach of promise is considered in Ohio, worse than seduction [12 Feb 1846]

    Mary 51 formerly of Lebanon NH at Bowdoinham ME [8 Apr 1836]

    William of Manchester NH accidentally shot on Fri of week before last at a shooting match [12 Oct 1848]

HOUGHTON Adaline Mrs 20 at Weld ME [20 May 1852]

    Amanda 18 youngest d/o the late Rev Josiah HOUGHTON at Winthrop ME on the 1st inst [7 Dec 1839]

    Cynthia 24 w/o Euclid HOUGHTON formerly of Gardiner ME at Troy ME [24 Dec 1846]

    Douglass Dr state geologist of Michigan drowned near Eagle River, Lake Superior on the 13th ult [6 Nov 1845]

    Edwin R 21 s/o Euclid HOUGHTON of Gardiner ME at Baltimore MD at the hospital [11 Jan 1849]

    Hannah 36 of Weld ME at Augusta ME [2 Mar 1848]

    Hannah 84 at Weld ME [20 Feb 1851]

    Josiah 3y s/o Rev Josiah Houghton at Fayette ME [18 Feb 1833]

    Josiah Rev 48 of the Baptist Church in Turner village at Turner ME on Tues last on 22d inst [29 May 1838]

    Nancy 23 at Gardiner ME [10 Sept 1846]

    Richard Esq the editor of the *Boston Atlas*, when seized with a fit of apoplexy [*Argus*] [24 Apr 1841]

HOULY Sarah 44 d/o William HOULY at Bristol [18 Feb 1847]

HOUSE boy abt 12d s/o Ezekiel HOUSE at Turner ME on 13 Feb [5 Mar 1842]

    child 2y c/o David HOUSE at Winthrop ME [31 Aug 1833]

    Isabel E 28 w/o Melzer HOUSE of Brunswick ME at Augusta ME [N.B. a Melzer HOUSE m 11 Jan 1798 Mehitable MALLET at Brunswick ME, see VR pp. 125, 379, 13 & a Melzer HOUSE married Eliza CONDON, who was born 17 May 1790, d 21 Mar 1867 or 57 had ch: Daniel b 1836; Joan & Alfred; James; Mary E; & Alfred b 15 Jul 1848 (VR *329 Brunswick ME*)] [25 Apr 1834]

    Joseph 68 at Turner ME [24 Sept 1842]

House of Hanover - see Saxe-Coburg-Gotha

HOUSTON Emily A 25 w/o A G HOUSTON at Monson ME [30 Jul 1846]

    Hannah M ae 5y d/o Joseph HOUSTON at Belfast ME [29 Apr 1836]

    John 80 of Exeter NH at Portland ME [11 Jul 1844]

    Samuel Gen "Reported by way of Jackson TN from Texas, Gen Samuel H shot, in personal recontre, by the speaker of Texas house of representatives - no hope entertained of his recovery. H a member from St Augustine Co." (N.B. if so he did recover as Sam HOUSTON was later elected president of Texas in 1841-1844 & was after that a senator to the US Congress & did not die until 1863) [1 Feb 1840]

HOUSTON - see FOSTER

HOVEY Amos 81y Gen AmRev Patriot at Salem MA on Thurs [30 Oct 1838]

    Anna 75 w/o John HOVEY Esq of Augusta ME at Mount Vernon ME on the 11th inst [18 Jul 1834]

    Clarissa 42 w/o Edwin S HOVEY Esq of Wiscasset ME at Orono ME [10 Oct 1850]

    David T 25 of ME Sacramento CA in Nov [2 Jan 1851]

    Ebenezer late of Augusta ME, est notice &/or probate notice Susan BROWN & Ruth WILLIAMS, daughters of the deceased [5 Feb 1852]

    George H 16m at Farmington ME [18 Sept 1845]

    Harriet 24 at New Sharon ME [1 Feb 1844]

HOVEY (Cont.) Henry B at Boston MA on 24th June [4 Jul 1850]
Isabella S 31 w/o Henry B HOVEY at Augusta ME on 10th inst [28 Mar 1844]
John Esq 89 for many years register of deeds for Kennebec County at Mt Vernon ME [8 May 1851]
Samuel 72 at Augusta ME on Fri last [25 Jul 1844]
HOW baby about six months of Washington HOW exercising in a baby jumper last Mon, when the hook, attached to the ceiling, gave way and falling upon the child's head penetrated the brain and caused its death in a short time at Templeton MA? [*Boston Transcript*] [12 Oct 1848]
HOWARD a child of Daniel HOWARD at Winthrop ME on Sun night last [6 Jan 1837]
Anderson S 32 at Readfield ME on 28th Aug [12 Sept 1850]
Andrew executed last Wed at Dover NH for the murder of Phebe HANSON in Sep 1843 [16 Jul 1846]
George 60 of smallpox at Castine ME [30 Jan 1841]
Hannah A 42 w/o Oaks HOWARD Esq at Winthrop ME of consumption [13 Dec 1849]
Joseph 63 at Hiram ME [20 Jan 1848]
Joseph 93 AmRev at Brownfield ME [27 Nov 1851]
Libbeus at Augusta ME on 13th inst [19 Jul 1849]
Mr from Maine an early member of Congress from TX of Kennebec Co? & Mr PILLSBURY moved to TX from Penobscot Co? ME [7 Aug 1851]
Polly 58 w/o Dean HOWARD of Winthrop ME at Mt Vernon ME on 30th ult [6 May 1836]
Rowland B abt 44 at Leeds ME on Thurs last funeral Sun at 11 o'clock [2 May 1840]
Sarah Jane 41 w/o Alex H HOWARD [7 May 1859]
Theodore abt 19y at Thomaston ME [26 June 1845]
Volney E of MS, one of four editors in Congress at present, viz: Luther SEVERANCE of Augusta ME; Edmund BURKE of Haverhill NH; John WENTWORTH of Chicago IL; & Volney E HOWARD of MS. HOWARD native of ME, we believe. He resided in Norridgewock, Somerset Co, some ten or twelve years since, & was a "smart boy" though the people of that section did not appreciate his merits. HOWARD has a younger brother off south. [18 Jan 1844]
W James distinguished vocalist died at Philadelphia PA on Sat [18 Apr 1844]
Warren Deac of North Leeds ME family rhyming, has a family of eight lively children ...the roll call makes quite a song per se (of themselves) Just listen while we call it: Luther Summers, Melvin Clark, Lucy Mitchell, Merillo Marks, Elmina Augusta, Mary Jane, Dexter Waterman, Hannah Lane .... [11 June 1846]
Zipion late of Winthrop ME est notice, Daniel HOWARD exec [1 Jan 1852]
HOWARD - see PERKINS
HOWE Abigail 37 w/o Ephraim HOWE at Frankfort ME [20 Nov 1851]
Abigail abt 38 w/o Curtis O HOWE Esq at Mexico ME [30 Nov 1839]
boy 11y s/o Gilbert D HOWE was shot on Fri last at East Machias ME by the carelessness of another boy, he survived till Sun [*Eastport Sentinel*] [30 Mar 1848]
Charlotte B 67 at Augusta ME on 26 June after an illness of twelve weeks [4 Jul 1850]
Christopher Capt 69y formerly of South Berwick ME at the Henry S THATCHER barn fire in Saco ME [17 Apr 1841]
Daniel G 29 at Damariscotta ME [31 Oct 1850]
Eleanor 77 at Leeds ME [21 Feb 1851]
Eliza 31 d/o Dr Timothy HOWE at Turner ME [10 June 1836]
Franklin 28 at Lincoln ME [3 Jul 1851]
Isaac abt 40 at Solon ME [25 Nov 1852]
John his house & barn burned in the absence of himself & his wife at Abbott ME they were formerly of Portland ME [20 Aug 1846]

HOWE (Cont.) Lucinda 33 w/o Henry HOWE at Paris ME [15 Jan 1846]
  Rhoda 53 w/o Leonard M HOWE at Dover [10 Jan 1850]
HOWE - see SMITH
HOWELL Silas A 100y 10m at Portland ME [21 May 1846]
HOWES Charles Albert 8m s/o Henry S HOWES at Bangor ME on 7th inst [20 May 1843]
  Edward abt 65 at Bingham ME on 12th May of consumption [5 June 1845]
  Eleanor 56 at Bingham ME on 11th inst [3 Jul 1838]
  Eliza 27 w/o Capt Levi HOWES at Richmond ME [23 Dec 1847]
  Eliza B 48 w/o James HOWES at New Sharon ME [22 May 1851]
  J S 32 of Bingham ME on board steamer *Constitution* on 7 May [8 Jul 1852]
  James 56y 9m at Troy ME [2 Mar 1848]
  Samuel H abt 50 late master of the steamer *State of Maine*, died this morning of brain
    fever at Cambridgeport [*Traveller*] [29 Mar 1849]
  Thomas Capt a steamboat commander between Bangor & Boston MA at Chatham MA
    [26 Aug 1843]
HOWLAND C J 32 senior editor of the *Daily Bee* at Boston MA [23 Jul 1846]
  girl d/o Capt Benjamin F HOWLAND burned to death by a lighted fire-cracker [*New
    Bedford Mercury*] [12 June 1849]
  Joseph 70 at Vassalboro ME on 7th inst [18 Jan 1840]
  Joseph 70 member of the Society of Friends (Quakers) a res of Vassalboro ME 54y, but a
    native of Pembroke MA at Vassalboro ME on 7th inst [18 Jan 1840]
  Mr one of the editors of the *Boston MA Bee* died [23 Jul 1846]
HOXIE Abel 77 of the Society of Friends (Quakers) at Fairfield ME [24 Apr 1845]
  Ann Mrs 19 w/o Abel HOXIE at Fairfield ME [6 Mar 1841]
  child abt 4 c/o Major E HOXIE at Bloomfield ME [27 Mar 1838]
  John H 31 at Augusta ME [30 Sept 1852]
  Rhoda 50 w/o Arnold HOXIE at Fairfield ME [16 Sept 1852]
  Stephen Esq at Milton VT on 21st Dec last [22 Jan 1842]
HOYT Anna 84 at East Vassalboro ME [24 Jul 1838]
  boy 12y drowned of Portland ME s/o Reuben HOYT [26 Apr 1849]
  Ebenezer Capt 33 of Vassalboro ME at sea on board schr *Delta* on her passage from
    Magnolia to New York four days out from Key West [21 Jan 1833]
  Eunice C 39 w/o Thomas C HOYT & d/o Pelatiah VARNEY at Vassalboro ME on 21
    Mar of apoplexy [28 Mar 1850]
  Lewis 24 wounded on his foot while sharpening rails on 27 Apr at New Portland ME on
    5th inst [23 May 1837]
  Mr tavern keeper & wife & child died at Huron [*Sundusky OH Clarion*] [5 Sept 1834]
  Sally 65 w/o Eliphalet HOYT Esq at Readfield ME (on 17 Mar 1850 see p. 756
    Stackpole's History of Winthrop ME by Young & Young, 1994) [28 Mar 1850]
  Stephen Capt 63 formerly of Augusta ME, at Vassalboro ME on Sun morning 15th inst a
    long illness, also next evening, Mrs Anna HOYT, his mother 84, buried in one grave
    [24 Jul 1838]
HOYT - see TAYLOR
HUBBARD a child 5 of Mr È HUBBARD at Hallowell ME on 2d inst [13 Feb 1838]
  Ebenezer B 25 s/o Richard HUBBARD at Fayette ME on 3 Mar [13 Mar 1851]
  Eugene Weston 13 youngest child of Ezekiel HUBBARD at Hallowell ME [30 Oct 1838]
  Henry Clarke in 73 yr of age, a Baptist minister for nearly 40y, died in the pulpit at South
    Kingston RI on 9th inst [29 May 1841]
  Jonathan H Hon 81y rep to Congress 1809-1811 & 1843-1845 was judge of the Supreme
    Court at Windsor VT [11 Oct 1849]
  Mary 80 relict of the late Gen Levi HUBBARD at Paris ME [20 Mar 1845]

HUBBARD (Cont.) Mehitable 43 w/o John HUBBARD of North Berwick ME at South
    Berwick ME [3 Apr 1838]
  Melvin 25 at Fayette ME [28 Oct 1847]
  Olive 86 wid/o Dr John HUBBARD at Hallowell ME [28 Oct 1847]
  Philena 54 w/o Richard HUBBARD at Fayette ME on 19 Feb [13 Mar 1851]
  Richard 76 AmRev at Acton ME [22 Apr 1836]
  Sophronia 23 at Fayette ME on 20 Oct [16 Dec 1847]
  two c/o John HUBBARD lost when his house burned at Bucksport ME [23 Sept 1852]
HUBBARD - see HATCH
HUCKINS Elizabeth Ann 19 w/o Henry HUCKINS at Lubec ME [6 May 1847]
  Emerson 4 s/o Eli HUCKINS at Lubec ME [6 May 1847]
  Isabel 33 w/o Hiram HUCKINS at Lubec ME [6 May 1847]
HUDSON lad while firing a small cannon in the street in Brooklyn NY on the 4th of July
    had one of his eyes destroyed by a piece of metal in consequence of this explosion
    [*New York Farmer & Mechanic*] [17 Jul 1845]
  Mrs w/o Mr J C HUDSON delivered 3 promising ch at a birth. The citizens with
    becoming liberality donated them a section of land of Mississippi in Marshall Co
    [*Natches Free Trader*] [12 June 1838]
  Ripley of ME fell overboard from the *Prometheus* & drowned [15 Apr 1852]
  Samuel surveyor general of lumber for Penobscot Co ME at Bangor ME [11 Nov 1836]
HUDSPETH Caroline married William PEEVY in MS by Rev Jos BELL [*Natchez Free
    Trader* on 11th inst] [11 Jan 1849]
HUFF Joseph 77 at Saco ME [23 May 1850]
  Josiah 64 at Kennebunkport ME [21 Dec 1848]
  Thomas 108 at Hartland ME [13 June 1844]
  William Mrs at Norridgewock ME [10 Apr 1851]
HUGH D T 104 of the Boston Tea Party thought to be dead at Albany NY [*Albany Argus*] [1
    Oct 1842]
HUGHES Joseph of Saco ME a discharged soldier at sea on passage from New Orleans to
    New York [24 Aug 1848]
HULL Jesse R charged with starving his own mother to death, supposed to be merely to
    release himself of the burden of keeping her, shut her up in a cold room, without food
    until she literally starved to death, having first gnawed the paper from the walls at
    Mendon IL [17 Feb 1848]
HULL - see JENKINS
HUME Baron 82 nephew of David HUME & author of an elaborate work on the criminal
    jurisprudence of Scotland at England [2 Oct 1838]
  George 32 at Waterville ME [22 Aug 1834]
  James Esq 92 at Earlstown Scotland [20 Jul 1839]
  Nancy widow of John HUME formerly of Waterville ME at Calais ME [6 May 1847]
HUMES Charkes Franklin c/o Charles & Ann HUMES at Augusta ME on 24 Jan [30 Jan
    1851]
  Henry Allen c/o Charles & Ann HUMES at Augusta ME on 22 Jan [30 Jan 1851]
HUMPHREY Melintha Augusta 14m youngest d/o James & Elizabeth HUMPHREY at
    Augusta ME on 19 Sept [23 Oct 1851]
HUMPHREYS Frederick Whitmore 13 s/o Gen John HUMPHREYS at Brunswick ME last
    Sat afternoon [23 Nov 1848]
  Gen J C 8m at Brunswick ME [8 May 1845]
  Lovicea 16 d/o Gen John HUMPHREYS at Brunswick ME [20 Nov 1845]
HUNNEFORD William Prescott 2y 5m c/o William HUNNEFORD at Augusta ME [11 Mar
    1847]

HUNNEWELL George tried last week at East Cambridge MA for setting fire to his mother's house in Aug 1846, the house consumed with his brother Leonard in it! They jury rendered a verdict of "guilty" & he was remanded back to jail to await sentence of death [23 Dec 1847]

Julia 18 d/o Richard Hunnewell at Solon ME [25 Jul 1850]

Rebecca 91 at Solon ME [2 Oct 1851] & Rebecca Mrs 94 at Solon ME [13 Nov 1851]

William 64 at China ME on 6th inst [16 Apr 1846]

HUNT Bernard 17y while diving struck his head against something in the bed of the river, injuring him so that he died the next day at Philadelphia? [5 Aug 1843]

Bradbury W Esq 11y of Manchester NH was drowned in the Merrimack on Wed last [3 Aug 1841]

Edwin N 2 s/o Levi HUNT [30 Jul 1846]

George R abt 3 s/o Elias & Selina B HUNT at Lincoln ME on 22 Sept [30 Sept 1852]

Jeremiah 70 at Brunswick ME [2 Aug 1849]

John 90 AmRev at Cape Elizabeth ME [27 Nov 1845]

Lovina A 22y d/o Jonathan J HUNT at Bangor ME of consumption [13 Mar 1835]

Luara Mrs of Broadalbin Montgomery Co NY through *the Amsterdam Intelligencer*, husband, Josiah HUNT, has left her bed & board & strayed away to parts unknown. She warns all girls, old maids & widows, not to meddle with or marry him, on penalty of the law, and all newspapers "throughout the world" to lay the foregoing information before their readers, who will please perceive that we have complied with her request. [8 May 1835]

Martha F 30 w/o W H HUNT at Montville ME [27 Jan 1848]

Mary 101y 7m at Pittston ME [18 Mar 1847]

Mary w/o William HUNT at Kingsbury ME [21 Oct 1847]

Philena w/o Capt George C HUNT late of St John New Brunswick Canada at Bath ME [27 May 1852]

Samuel 99 at Kennebunkport ME [22 Apr 1836]

Sarah Mrs 76 at Alna ME [12 Sept 1840]

Sherburne 29 at Thorndike ME [17 June 1836]

two children 3y & 2y suffocated at home by a fire which took in a clothes press of Little Falls they were the c/o Rev Isaac HUNT of the Methodist Episcopal church [13 Nov 1845]

William Mrs w/o William HUNT at Township Number 3 on east branch of Penobscot River [21 Jan 1843]

HUNT - see CLEAVELAND, COFFIN, TUCKER, WATSON

HUNTER Alfred Esq 31 at Clinton ME in consequence of an injury received in running a raft over Sebasticook Falls [13 Jul 1839]

Antionette Elizabeth 28 w/o J H HUNTER of Topsham ME at Chesterville ME [12 Dec 1850]

Betsey 26 at Farmington ME [19 Nov 1846]

Henry 76 a Deacon at Bristol [9 Apr 1846]

J P of Gardiner ME saved from drowning when the steam packet *New England* sank. It left Boston for Bath & Gardiner ME and had an accident with the schr *Curlew* on 31 May [12 June 1838]

James 48 at Strong ME [6 Mar 1851]

Martha Ann 32 d/o Adam HUNTER at Topsham ME [16 Sept 1843]

Sarah 95 wid/o Arthur HUNTER at Topsham ME [28 May 1846]

Sarah w/o Daniel HUNTER at Topsham ME [26 Mar 1846]

Thomas 75 at Topsham ME [7 May 1846]

HUNTING Caroline 20 at Corinth ME [28 Feb 1850]

Mary 27 w/o Rev J P HUNTING at Parsonsfield ME [22 Jan 1852]

HUNTING (Cont.) Sally Ann 32 w/o Samuel W HUNTING [11 Oct 1849]

Sarah E 11y 8m d/o Rev Enoch HUNTING at Guilford ME [25 June 1846]

HUNTINGTON Edward 77 knocked from his cart into the street and then beaten to death by a gang of Irishmen at New York. Eight Irishmen were reported arrested. [8 Feb 1840]

Isaac 75 of Woodbridge CT during the snow storm of Fri week lost his way & falling into a ditch perished [11 Jan 1849]

Jabez W late congressman of CT died on Tues at Norwich [11 Nov 1847]

Sarah E 25 w/o Cyrus HUNTINGTON at Hallowell ME [11 May 1848]

HUNTLEY Mr father of Mrs SIGOURNEY died at Hartford a few days since [31 Aug 1839]

HUNTON Betsey 64 at Readfield ME (d/o Christopher & Catherine TURNER & wid/o Peter HUNTON Jr, see pp. 761 & 821 *Stackpole's History of Winthrop, ME* by Young & Young, 1994) [1 Mar 1849]

Betsey wid/o Peter HUNTON late of Readfield ME, having made application for an allowance out of the personal est of the said deceased [14 Oct 1836]

Henry W 6y 5m s/o Wellington & Sarah HUNTON at Wayne ME on 2d Aug [9 Aug 1849]

Peter (Jr) abt 60 at Readfield ME (born June 1769, d 6 May 1836, see p. 761 *Stackpole's History of Winthrop ME* by Young & Young, 1994) [13 May 1836]

Sarah W 1y 2m only d/o Wellington & Sarah HUNTON at Wayne ME on 13 Aug [22 Aug 1850]

HUNTON/HUNTOON - see STEVENS, WOODBURY

HUNTOON Caroline 27 w/o E D HUNTOON at Hallowell ME [14 Nov 1850]

Jonathan G formerly governor of ME (born 14 Mar 1781 at Unity plt NH s/o Josiah & Hannah (Glidden) HUNTON) The spelling of Hunton was changed to "Huntoon" about 1840. See *Stackpole's History of Winthrop ME* p. 765 at Fairfield ME [23 Oct 1851]

Rachel abt 44 at Readfield ME on 19th ult [2 Sept 1843]

HUNTRESS boy abt 5y s/o of the widow HUNTRESS who lives in Brackett St in Portland ME [*Portland Argus*] [16 May 1844]

Mr 27 fatal accident at Biddeford ME [*Saco Democrat*] [26 Oct 1848]

HURD Lucy 68 w/o John HURD at Swanville ME [21 Oct 1852]

Maria Ellen married Henry W SEINE the bride was but 15y, married by Rev Mr PIERCE at Peoria IL on 12th ult (This is fulfilling the juvenile adjunct that children should be seen & not heard) [19 June 1851]

Moses of South Thomaston ME, tells us a "Pumpkin story," which is worthy of record; He raised from one seed last season, a vine 513 ft long, which produced 19 pumpkins, weighing four hundred and twenty pounds. (copied from the *Thomaston Gazette*) [16 Nov 1848]

Paul 88 at Dover [23 Dec 1852]

William 33 at Hallowell ME on Fri last [26 Sept 1838]

HURLBERT Thomas 60 at Eastport ME [3 Jan 1850]

HURLEY Daniel 41 at Bangor ME [21 Jan 1847]

HURLY John 50 an Irishman killed on Thurs by the falling of an embankment [*Lewiston Journal*] [19 June 1851]

HURST Mr of Avon OH his res destroyed by fire on 12th inst consuming Mrs HURST, who was very sick at the time. Mr H was also much burnt in an attempt to rescue his wife [31 Jan 1850]

HUSBAND "A Woman with Ten HUSBANDs, "There is now living in one of the chief towns of NH, a woman who has had ten husbands, all of whom are now living upon

HUSBAND (Cont.) the best terms with her and each other. The woman is highly respected among her neighbors, who see nothing to censure, but much to approve....the lady referred to was a Mrs HUSBAND, who lived very lawfully with Mr HUSBAND & 9 little HUSBANDs. [*Washingtonian*]" [2 Sept 1847] [N.B. The 1840 Census of Dover NH p. 536 & p. 543, lists three families of HUSBANDS: Ann, Charles, and Edward HUSBAND.]

HUSE Jesse Mrs formerly of Farmington ME at Lowell MA w/o Jesse HUSE Esq [18 Dec 1845]

Joseph Dr 25 at East Thomaston ME [6 Nov 1838]

Joseph Dr 74 of the early settlers at Camden ME on 30 June [15 Jul 1847]

Sally 78 widow Enoch HUSE at Temple ME on 27 Jan [13 Feb 1851] & [21 Feb 1851]

HUSSEY Augustus fell Dead on the 8th Oct at the battle of Molino de Rey, struck with a musket ball was the s/o M B HUSSEY, *The Bangor Whig* contains a letter from the city of Mexico, written by W R TITTLE of Canaan ME to M B HUSSEY of Houlton ME giving the account [23 Dec 1847]

Elizabeth 65 at Dover [23 Dec 1852]

Huldah 40 at Vassalboro ME [11 Sept 1845]

Jane S 39 w/o Batchelor HUSSEY & d/o Ezekiel SMALL of Vassalboro ME formerly of Limington ME at Houlton ME [19 Dec 1844]

Rebecca R 57 w/o Capt Benjamin F HUSSEY at Fairfield ME [16 May 1850]

Susan 66 w/o Timothy HUSSEY at Athens ME [17 Apr 1851]

Susan S 30 w/o John HUSSEY at Augusta ME [20 Nov 1845]

HUSTED J B Rev of Bangor ME saved from drowning when the steam packet *New England* sank left Boston for Bath & Gardiner ME and had an accident with the schr *Curlew* on 31 May [12 June 1838]

HUSTON David 68 at West Waterville ME [26 Sept 1850]

James G yeoman of the Preble formerly an orderly sergeant in the US Marine Corps & citizen of Brooklyn NY belonged to the US ship *Preble* & died with the Africa fever at Porto Grande Island of St Vincent Cape de Verds on 21 Dec [10 Apr 1845]

HUTCHINGS a lad 14 was killed by lighting s/o Jonathan HUTCHINGS on the 9th inst [11 July 1844]

Abigail 20 d/o Whicher HUTCHINGS at Lovell ME [20 Nov 1851]

Ellen 13 at Penobscot ME [23 Oct 1838]

Ezra Esq 76 of Bangor ME held a plough all day of the 14th inst in ploughing the field with a span of horses [*The Bangor Whig*] [28 Jan 1843]

Hannah 51 wid/o Charles HUTCHINGS at Kittery ME on 22d Jan, home from a visit, unwell & called a neighbor, took some herb tea & retired, next morning was found a corpse [12 Feb 1842]

J H 13 of Kennebunk ME picked up by a small boat after being in the water over half an hour nearly exhausted at Mt Desert on Mon the 3rd two boys were crossing to Cranberry Isle ME in an open boat, this sailboat capsized, one drowned & one saved. The boy who drowned was Cornelius E FRANKLIN (from the *Portland Advertiser*) [22 Oct 1842]

HUTCHINS Andrew Capt 65 at Gardiner ME [20 Feb 1851]

Charles 6 s/o Hanson HUTCHINS at Brewer ME by drowning [22 Jul 1852]

Eliza 28 w/o Leonard HUTCHINS & d/o Silas HARRIMAN of Sebec ME at Hampstead NH on 4th inst of typhus fever [24 Sept 1842]

Ezra 79 at Bangor ME [31 May 1849]

John 22 s/o James & Cynthia HUTCHINS of China ME at Vassalboro ME [31 May 1849]

Jotham abt 19 at Atkinson ME on 1 May [12 June 1838]

Martha Ann 15 d/o William & Hannah HUTCHINS at Turner ME [17 Dec 1846]

HUTCHINS (Cont.) Samuel R Esq 55 at Atkinson ME [27 Aug 1846]

Sarah abt 25 w/o John HUTCHINS of Unity Gore at Freedom ME [7 Nov 1850]

Simeon 81 AmRev at Kennebunk ME [26 Aug 1846]

William of Boston ME saved from drowning when the steam packet *New England* sank. It left Boston for Bath & Gardiner ME and had an accident with the schr *Curlew* on 31 May [12 June 1838]

HUTCHINS - see JENKINS, MUSSENDEN

HUTCHINSON a boy 12 s/o Capt Isaac HUTCHINSON fell from building in Portland ME on Tues [29 May 1851]

Abby J of the HUTCHINSON Family singers married Ludlow PATTON s/o Rev Dr PATTON of New York on Wed evening [8 Mar 1849]

Asa 89 AmRev at Fayette ME on 26 June [10 Aug 1848]

Benjamin 13 & George STEVENS 14y s/o Jacob STEVENS drowned at VassalboroME [18 Jul 1834]

Israel 85 AmRev at Hallowell ME on 12 June [27 June 1850]

Rebecca Mrs 32 at Bath ME [29 Jul 1852]

Samuel 26 on 9th ult at Buckfield ME on the 9th ult drowned [6 May 1833]

Samuel at Readfield ME (see p. 766 *Stackpole's History of Winthrop ME* by Young & Young, 1994) [14 Nov 1844]

Stephen 63 at Buckfield ME [12 Sept 1850]

Stephen pilot of the steamboat *Bangor* in the Eastern Steamboat Co, left a wife & several ch in Portland ME [13 June 1837]

William 24 at Winthrop ME on Fri last [26 Aug 1836]

HUTCHINSON - see DOWNING, GORSUCH, McNEAL

HUTTON William abt 50 on Fri afternoon last lost overboard from schr *Enterprise* near Northern Harbor on passage from St Stephen for Deer Island, New Brunswick. His sons James & Henry were all his crew. [*Eastport Sentinel*] [3 Feb 1848]

HYDE Jonathan 80 at Bath ME [31 Oct 1850]

Jude 71 at Brunswick ME [16 Mar 1848]

Priscilla 68 w/o Dr John A HYDE at Freeport ME [16 May 1844]

Samuel A Esq of Bangor ME at Augusta ME [16 Oct 1845]

- I -

IDEDA John deck passenger of France on board the steamboat *George Collier* on the 6th inst on her passage from New Orleans to St Louis MO [25 May 1839]

ILSLEY Ferdinand 39 formerly of Portland ME at Eastport ME [23 Oct 1835]

IMANUEL - see CRAWFORD

Indian War - see WAYNE

Indian - see BLACKSNAKE, COOPER, HAWK, KATH-LA-MO-HEE, ORONO, PETERSON, ROSS, VALENTINE, VINCENT, WAWCONCHOCAUNIFCAW, WHITE, WILBUR,

Indians - see DOXTATER, FATE, GODNEY, HAINES, NEPTUNE, PAULSOOSUP, RICHARDSON, ROSS, SCOTT, WARR

INGALLS Charles 68 at Waterville ME [15 Aug 1850]

Ebenezer of Sullivan ME fell overboard from ship *Bolivar* of Portsmouth NH for Cadiz one day out at sea [4 Jan 1840]

Laura 3y 7m d/o Amos INGALLS at Mercer ME [17 Apr 1838]

Robert A 31 at Waterville ME [18 Mar 1852]

Samuel 50 at Hebron ME [23 Jul 1846]

Susan 25 w/o Henry INGALLS Esq at Wiscasset ME [1 Apr 1852]

INGERHAM Abigail 82 wid/o Moses INGRAHAM at Augusta ME on 28 Jan [12 Feb 1852]

INGERSOL John T 23 of Eastport ME lost overboard from bark *Massasoit* on her voyage from Surinam to Gloucester MA [15 Feb 1849]

Nathaniel 81 of New Gloucester ME at Bangor ME [2 May 1834]

INGERSOLL J R Hon "Medals for the Soldiers" proposes to form medals of the brass balls captured from the Mexicans & award them to officers & soldiers who served in Mexico [6 Jul 1848]

INGHAM Nancy 51 w/o Daniel INGHAM at Bath ME [3 Oct 1850]

Rebecca 80 wid/o David INGHAM at Farmington ME [30 Nov 1848]

INGLEE Ebenezer Deac 87 at Machias ME [4 Dec 1851]

INGRAHAM Abigail 39 w/o Capt Samuel INGRAHAM at Augusta ME [21 Mar 1834]

Abigail 82 wid/o Moses INGRAHAM at Augusta ME [12 Feb 1852]

Beniah 42 at Augusta ME on 22 Aug [31 Aug 1848]

Hannah abt 80 w/o Capt Josiah INGRAHAM at Thomaston ME [16 Jul 1842]

Joseph Esq 90 at East Thompson ME [16 Nov 1848]

Josiah Capt 88 at Thomaston ME [15 Feb 1849]

Lewis s/o Joseph INGRAHAM at Union ME [8 Aug 1834]

Lucy abt 82 at Thomaston ME [27 Aug 1846]

Luther abt 40 supposed drowned in the Kennebec River on Sat night [24 Aug 1833]

Lydia A 16y of Camden ME at Gorham Seminary [4 Sept 1845]

William Stone 46 s/o Joseph INGRAHAM Esq of Portland ME at Scarboro ME in a state of mental derangement 26 yrs [28 Mar 1834]

INGRAHAM - see HAWKINS

INIS John 78 at Bath ME [1 Apr 1836]

INMAN Henry the distinguished painter at New York City [5 Feb 1846]

INNIS Abby O 78 at Bath ME [10 June 1843]

Abigail 57 w/o James INNIS at Bath ME [20 Jan 1837]

IRELAND Celar 33 at Cornville ME [1 June 1848]

Eleanor 79 at Skowhegan ME [20 Mar 1851]

Francis W 27 s/o Joel IRELAND of Byron at Cambridgeport MA on 12 Sept [1 Nov 1849]

John B Esq at North Newport [30 May 1850]

Randall 22 s/o Benjamin IRELAND of St Albans ME in CA at the Northern Mines on 22d Oct [2 Dec 1852]

Sarah 19 d/o David IRELAND at Bloomfield ME [30 May 1837]

IRISH Cornelius Rev 70 at Union ME [11 Nov 1852]

James H 23 s/o Gen James IRISH at Gorham ME [25 June 1846]

Irish - see BANIN, CARON, DOVE, FAULKNER, GOULD, GRIFFEN, HOLMES, McCARTY, O'BRIAN, O'DOUGHERTY, MAHON, O'FLAHERTY, POWERS, SHEA, WALKER

Irishman - see BROWN, BURNS, CAHILL,CROWELL, DONAVAN, DURGAN, HANGLEY, HIGGINS, KELLEY, McLANEY, MURRAY, NEWELL, WHEELER

IRVIN - see MITCHELL

IRWIN John C buried in the graveyard near West Lebanon, discourse by Elder W CLARK, had the remains of his 1st wife moved to the same graveyard ... the body found petrified, the story [Mr WOODFORD of Warren Co OH printed in the *Eaton Register*] [31 Jul 1845]

ISELAND Vesta Jane 3y 3m at Byron ME [8 Apr 1847]

- J -

JACK Almira 33y 6m w/o James M JACK Esq at Topsham ME on 24 May [4 June 1851]
   Elbridge 28 at Topsham ME [18 Nov 1852]
JACKET - see BLACKSNAKE
JACKMAN Anna 97 at Eastport ME [13 May 1847]
   Persis 27 w/o David JACKMAN at Turner ME [10 June 1836]
JACKSON Absalom died up river in a logging accident, belongs over in St Stephen New
      Brunswick Canada, left a wife & family [*Calais Advertiser*] [8 June 1848]
   Andrew Gen on 8 June 78y at Hermitage [19 June 1845] & [26 June 1845] & President
      died (NB the 9 Nov 1839 issue of the *Maine Farmer* states that "Nashville papers to
      18 Oct make no mention of the death or sickness of Gen JACKSON. The late report
      of his decease was doubtless without foundation") [2 Nov 1839]
   Barsena E 23 at Hallowell ME on Thurs last [8 Aug 1837] & consort of A JACKSON &
      d/o Deac Daniel WEEKS of Jefferson ME (see obit) [15 Aug 1837]
   Bartholomew 89 AmRev at Wales ME [24 Oct 1837]
   Caleb 78 formerly of N Bridgewater MA at East Winthrop ME [16 Sept 1847]
   Charles W formerly of Maine at Lowell MA on 21th ult [9 Oct 1851]
   child abt 1y of Charles JACKSON at Winthrop ME [14 May 1842]
   child of Oliver JACKSON at Winthrop ME [26 Feb 1846]
   David Jr 24 s/o David & Sarah JACKSON at Newburgh ME [27 Aug 1846]
   Elener [*sic*] Mary 18 at Belfast ME [25 Feb 1843]
   Elizabeth 90 widow of Jos L JACKSON at the Forks ME [15 Mar 1849]
   Emily W 17 d/o David & Sarah JACKSON at Newburgh ME [27 Aug 1846]
   Hannah 66 wid/o John JACKSON formerly of Middleboro MA at Winthrop ME
      (Plymouth Co papers please copy) [4 Sept 1851]
   John S 27 formerly of Winthrop ME at Philadelphia PA on 15th inst of consumption [30
      Jan 1841]
   Jonathan K 30 at Winthrop ME on 2d inst [13 Aug 1842]
   Joseph 83 AmRev at Newry ME [25 Sept 1835]
   Martha J 20 at Bath ME [18 May 1848]
   Mrs Caleb 62 at East Winthrop ME [27 June 1844]
   Nancy w/o Robert L JACKSON formerly of Winthrop ME at Rockland ME [24 Oct
      1850]
   Nicholas 100y "colored" at Howard District MD, a servant of Gen WASHINGTON
      during the AmRev war [6 Mar 1845]
   Ralph T 50 at Castine ME [26 Dec 1840]
   Samuel 66 at Belfast ME [2 Jan 1845]
   Samuel Esq 63 at Jefferson ME [22 Oct 1846]
   Samuel Jr 41 formerly of Belfast ME at Portsmouth NH [6 Nov 1838]
   Sarah 54 w/o Thomas JACKSON at Winthrop ME on 17th ult [17 Apr 1845]
   Sarah 68 w/o Patten JACKSON at North Yarmouth ME [10 Feb 1848]
   Sarah Ann 21 w/o Harrison JACKSON at Troy ME [23 Dec 1847]
   Sarah E 21 at North Yarmouth ME [21 Nov 1840]
   Sarah E 21 at North Yarmouth ME [21 Nov 1840]
   Susan Mrs abt 90 wid/o Bartholomew JACKSON at Wales ME [23 Jan 1838]
   Thomas 67 at Bath ME [6 Apr 1848]
   Thomas 82 at Pittston ME [17 Aug 1833]
   Thomas T 22y 9m at Richmond ME [13 May 1847]
   William 64 at Montville ME [31 Oct 1850]
   William H abt 22 at Livermore ME at Apr 28 [14 May 1842]

JACKSON - see WARR

JACOBS Benjamin F 50 at (Augusta) ME on 6th inst at the Alms House [13 Jan 1848]

Charles 17 killed by a falling tree at Mexico ME on 14th ult [Oxford Democrat] [4 Apr 1840]

child 9m of Reuel JACOBS at Augusta ME [18 Feb 1847]

child of Elijah JACOBS at Winthrop ME [5 Aug 1836]

Mary Frances 2y 7m only c/o Reuel JACOBS at Augusta ME [11 Mar 1847]

Mrs of Norway ME w/o Jacob PARSONS on Fri of last week [Norway Advertiser] [5 Aug 1847]

Thomas 77 at Winthrop ME [8 Jan 1846]

JAMES John 21 at Bingham ME [2 Oct 1845]

John 21 of Pittston ME knocked overboard & drowned [Gardiner Blade 25th ult] [4 Nov 1843]

Judge of Kentucky senate killed by Hopson BINFORD, being the 4th victim of a feud that existed between the JAMES & BINFORD families at Columbus on the Mississippi River [10 Aug 1839]

Mrs w/o Samuel JAMES at Smithfield ME [19 Feb 1846]

JAMESON Isaac 23 s/o Capt W JAMESON at Windsor ME [19 Sept 1837]

Margaret 27 w/o John JAMESON at Bath ME [31 Jan 1850]

Peter 70 at Cushing ME [7 May 1846]

JAQUES - see ELLIOT

JAQUISH Mrs 58 at Brunswick ME [27 Nov 1838]

JARVIS John H 65 of Castine ME at Boston MA [24 Jan 1850]

Mrs w/o the Rev Dr JARVIS, trouble with her husband or he with her, with her daughter went to the Roman Catholic Church at Brooklyn NY [30 Oct 1841]

JARVIS - RUSSELL

JASPER Olive 29 at Minot ME [16 Mar 1848]

JAY Peter A oldest s/o John JAY at New York [4 Mar 1843]

JEFFERDS Charles C 24 of Kennebunkport ME at Rochester NY [27 June 1844]

JEFFERSON Thomas President ae 84 of USA on 4 Jul 1826 [5 Aug 1836]

JEFFERSON - see PERKINS, SMITH

JEFFORDS Susan Olive 23 d/o Nicholas JEFFORDS at Brooks ME [8 Jul 1847]

JEFFRES Samuel M AmRev at Wells ME [18 Mar 1847]

JEFFRIES Mr the driver of the stage thrown, Prof SHERMAN a skull fractured; Mr Pleasant SMITH of Nashville TN doubtful will survive; a German named W GOLDSTEIN, a merchant of Philadelphia, recovery doubtful [Nashville TN Banner, 27 June] [19 Jul 1849]

Sally a colored girl and d/o a white woman, Ann CONNER. Mrs. Conner tried to sell her own daughter in to slavery. The mother claimed her daughter was her slave; however, the Baltimore, MD, courts ruled in favor of Sally Jeffries releasing the girl. [9 Apr 1842]

JELLESON Elizabeth 93y 6m 2d wid/o George J at Waterboro ME [25 Dec 1845]

Betsey H 30 w/o Abel J at Biddeford ME [11 Nov 1852]

JELLISON Theodore Esq 54 at Calais ME [16 May 1844]

Webster abt 17 at Ellsworth ME by drowning [24 June 1852]

JEMISON - see CRAWFORD

JENISON Silas H Hon Gov of VT died at Shoreham on Sun 30th ult [11 Oct 1849]

JENKINS Capt 68 formerly of Quincy MA at Pittston ME [28 Aug 1835]

Hiram Esq 28 at Wales ME on 6th inst [21 Aug 1838]

John 51 at Skowhegan ME [27 June 1850]

JENKINS (Cont.) John editor of the *Vicksburgh Sentinel* killed in the streets during a
    political quarrel [5 Oct 1848]
    Jos 62 at Madison ME [5 Jul 1849]
    Nathan 37 native of Kittery ME employed at the Charlestown Navy Yard where he
    accidentally died [12 Nov 1846]
    Paul, Thomas HULL, William HUTCHINS, Jonathan CATHCART, William HOLMES,
    Sophia BEEBE, Phebe JONES, Mirah DAVIS at Quaise, Nantucket the poor house
    burned on the 20th inst [*New Bedford Bulletin*] [29 Feb 1844]
    Sarah 54 at Skowhegan ME [17 Aug 1848]
JENKS Nancy 37 at North Yarmouth ME [14 Jan 1847]
JENKS - see HOGAN, KIMBALL
JENNESS/JENNIS/GENNES/GINNESS Benjamin 76 at Readfield ME [26 Aug 1843]
    Hannah (TURNER) 61 w/o Benjamin JENNESS at Winthrop ME (see p. 771 *Stackpole's
    History of Winthrop ME* by Young & Young, 1994) [20 Jul 1839]
    James 38 of Winthrop ME on passage from Panama to San Francisco CA on 7 Jul [17
    Oct 1850]
    Jeremiah 48 of Fryeburg ME at Dover NH? [25 Nov 1852]
JENNINGS an English fortune, amounting to the small sum of abt $40,000,000 is likely to
    fall to a gentleman named JENNINGS, now resident at Newcastle ME. It has been in
    chancery nearly fifty years - the interest accumulating. We do not vouch for the truth
    of the rumor, although we have our information from a relative of the gentleman
    named [*Journal*] [5 Feb 1846]
    Asa Esq 43 at New Sharon ME of consumption [20 June 1840]
    Eliphalet Mrs 80 at Farmington ME [30 Jan 1851]
    Hannah 52 w/o John JENNINGS at Livermore ME [10 Oct 1844]
    son 6y of Tappan JENNINGS at Farmington ME [16 May 1844]
JENNINGS - see ARNOLD, BEARCE
JENNISON Ebenezer Esq 76 the postmaster of North Dixmont ME died [5 Nov 1842]
JETT - see BATEMAN
JEWELL child 2 of True JEWELL at Gardiner ME [9 Oct 1845]
    Elijah 33 of Canaan ME at Bloomfield ME [16 Apr 1846]
    Enos Jr 23 formerly of Canaan ME at Cincinnati OH [24 Dec 1846]
    Ersula 32 wid/o Benjamin L J formerly Lewiston ME at Wells ME [15 Jul 1852]
    Harvey B 21 at Litchfield ME [25 Jul 1834]
    lad 6 or 8y of Lewiston ME from a fall [*Lewiston Journal*] [6 Sept 1849]
    Louisa M 25 wid/o Robert W JEWELL of Bath ME at Topsham ME [19 Nov 1846]
    Lydia 75 formerly of Litchfield ME at Vicksburg MS [20 May 1847]
    Nicholas a blacksmith is missing 5' 9" 53y, dark complex, hazel eyes, partly grey hair of
    Newburgh ME (copied from *Portland ME Argus*) [6 Mar 1851]
    Rebecca 7y d/o Jacob JEWELL at Windsor ME [19 Sept 1837]
    Robert W 23 formerly of Bath ME at Gardiner ME [13 Aug 1846]
    Stephen Denny 3m 12d s/o Stephen P JEWELL [24 Oct 1844]
JEWETT Abby K 23 d/o John JEWETT Esq of Farmington ME at Readfield ME [4 May
    1848]
    Abigail 18 w/o John H JEWETT at Machias Port ME [10 Feb 1848]
    Betsey 63 w/o Samuel JEWETT at Hartland ME [31 May 1849]
    Caroline F of Waterford ME at Georgetown MA [4 Feb 1843]
    child 9 c/o John JEWETT at Augusta ME [18 Mar 1847]
    David 63 at Monmouth ME on 2d inst at Monmouth ME eldest s/o Rev David JEWETT
    1st minister of Winthrop ME died Feb 1783, abt one year after being installed pastor
    [9 Jan 1841]

JEWETT (Cont.) Ellen The *Portland Argus* published a letter from Judge WESTON to a professional gentleman in New York, in answer to enquiries made by the latter concerning the early life of Ellen JEWETT. She was received into the Judge's family at ae 14y, as a servant and continued there in that capacity until she was 18y. "...Some little time before she left us, rumors to her disadvantage had reached the ears of Mrs. Weston, which she was led from the protestations of the girl, to believe untrue. ...By whom seduced I do not know. She was visited by no young men at our house, to the knowledge either of Mrs. Weston or myself. She left us in the fall of 1830, passing where she went, as we were given to understand, by the name of Maria STANLEY." [6 May 1836]

Enoch Capt 69 at Pittston ME [12 Mar 1846]

Georgeiana 10m at Augusta ME [22 Mar 1849]

Henry J formerly of Portland ME & one year attorney for Cumberland Co elected senator in TX legislature from Robertstown Co TX and G W ADAMS Esq formerly of Bangor ME a member of the House from the same Co in TX [5 Feb 1846]

Jesse Esq 72 at Windsor ME [3 Sept 1842]

John abt 95 at Readfield ME on 29 Nov one of the 1st settlers of Readfield ME [19 Dec 1837]

John Loring 8y 5m eldest child of John & Sarah JEWETT at Augusta ME [16 Sept 1847]

Jonas 75 at Solon ME [20 May 1847]

Jonas a venerable gentleman abt 80 thrown from his sleigh one day last week & had a thigh broken. It is feared that he will not recover [*Skowhegan Press*] [4 Feb 1847]

Lydia 76 at Alna ME [8 Apr 1847]

Mary Frances 11 d/o Samuel JEWETT Esq at Pittston ME [10 Oct 1840]

Miles 24 of Westport ME drowned near Lower Hurlsgate [19 Apr 1849]

Mrs w/o William JEWETT of Madison ME committed suicide by hanging [*Clarion*] [15 Apr 1847]

Sarah 34 d/o Joshua JEWETT of Norridgewock ME at Bangor ME [29 Jan 1852]

Washington 66 at Kennebec ME on 10 Nov [21 Nov 1850]

William H 19 at Sidney ME on 31 May [20 June 1850]

JEWETT - see DOYEN, FRANCIS

JOHNSON Abel of Vienna ME "appeared to be a sort of Wandering Jew" died at Swanville ME at res of Reuben NICKERSON Jr [15 Feb 1849]

Abigail C 23 w/o A G JOHNSON at Eastport ME [15 May 1845]

Alfred 57 at Winthrop ME on 1st ult [2 May 1834]

Alfred 62 at Belfast ME on 22 Mar [1 Apr 1852]

Alfred Hon 62 at Belfast ME on 22 Mar [1 Apr 1852]

Andrew 4 s/o Joseph JOHNSON at Gardiner ME [3 Oct 1840]

Andrew 75 at Gardiner ME [9 Sept 1843]

Andrew "Worth Noting" the wife (Eliza McCARDLE) of Andrew JOHNSON, now a member of Congress from TN, taught him to read since he has been married! He is a tailor by trade, & is said to be at present a pretty intelligent man. [N.B. the 17th President of the USA] [5 Feb 1846]

boy of Machias ME s/o Charles JOHNSON, while under the influence of chloroform had a thigh amputated . The operation was performed in a little less than one minute by Dr J W MURRAY assisted by Dr PEABODY both of Machias ME [*Eastport Sentinel*] [30 Aug 1849]

boy of Skowhegan ME s/o Hiram JOHNSON drowned [23 Aug 1849]

boy shot by his brother on Sat last, the 2 boys, abt 14y & 8y s/o Peter JOHNSON of Orono ME on Essex St were on a gunning excursion. The oldest boy attempted to fire at some object in a tree, when the rifle missed fire & on bringing it down to examine

JOHNSON (Cont.) the lock it went off & the whole charge of shot entered the neck of the little boy, killing him instantly (see also *Bangor Whig*) [17 Sept 1842]

Charles E 33 formerly of Farmington ME at Fort Atkinson WI [18 Nov 1847]

Charles H 24 at Brownville ME [14 May 1846]

Charles W at Fort Fairfield ME the postmaster of that place [7 Nov 1850]

child of Rev Mr JOHNSON drowned in Seven Mile Brook at New Portland ME on Tues last. The child was abt 3y (from *Skowhegan Sentinel*) [23 Mar 1839]

Daniel 28 at Readfield ME [27 Nov 1851]

David Capt drowned 57 at Harpswell ME on 19th inst [4 Jul 1840]

Elisha 74 formerly of Vienna ME at Dexter ME [15 Feb 1849]

Eliza S w/o Simon JOHNSON at Hallowell ME [24 Jul 1851]

Elizabeth w/o Joshua JOHNSON at Vienna ME [23 Jan 1838]

Heman S 37 at Gardiner ME on 27 Mar [1 Apr 1852]

Henrietta Ilsley 11m d/o Joseph S & Ann W JOHNSON at Farmington ME [3 Oct 1844]

Isaac D 62 of Maine at Cold Spring El Derando CA on 17 Apr [29 Jul 1852]

J Francis Capt 24/21 at Bremen ME [8 Apr 1852]

Jacob 52 at Unity ME [2 Nov 1833]

Jacob Jr purser on board the *Gen Waven* s/o Col Jacob JOHNSON of Brunswick ME on the coast of Oregon on 31 Jan [22 Apr 1852]

James a fugitive slave of Mr THOMAS of Mississippi at Princeton NJ [12 Aug 1843]

James at Starks ME [11 Mar 1833]

John a native of ME at New Orleans [22 Feb 1849]

John & Isaac DILLER fell down in convulsions while at the plough, John JOHNSON carried him home & both died within an half an hour. At Susquehanna township Dauphin Co PA on Thurs of last week [4 Jul 1834]

Joseph P 9 c/o William T JOHNSON at Augusta ME on 3d inst [12 June 1845]

lad drowned between Fort Independence & Thompson's Island one of a party of 27 boys of the Farm School on Thompson's Island [7 May 1842]

Lydia 86 late of Billerica MA at Sangerville ME [11 Dec 1851]

Marcy wid/o Capt Levi JOHNSON formerly of Readfield ME at Brownville ME on 18 Mar [28 Mar 1850]

Mary 25 at Portland ME [19 Aug 1836]

Mary 56 wid/o William JOHNSON of Farmington ME at Augusta ME on 20 June [27 June 1850]

Mary 75 wid/o David JOHNSON at Hallowell ME [22 Mar 1849]

Mary 76 at North Yarmouth ME [18 Nov 1847]

Mary 78 at Jefferson ME [20 Jan 1848]

Mary Ann 24 w/o Samuel JOHNSON of Jackson ME at Dixmont ME [19 Nov 1846]

Mary of New York petitioned Congress for pay for the loss of her husband killed in the Mexican War on the strength of PACHECO's heirs having recovered $1000 for a slave killed in the Florida war. Mary asks for $2000, estimating her husband to be worth as much as two negroes. [22 Feb 1849]

Mary Sophia of Eastport ME at sea [21 Oct 1852]

Mary W 22 widow of Rev Charles JOHNSON late pastor of the Baptist Church in Topsham ME at Templeton MA [9 Sept 1836]

Miranda B 59 w/o Henry JOHNSON at Farmington ME [14 Nov 1850]

Mr abt 17 living in Boston MA stabbed the night of 5th Mar in Federal St [6 Apr 1848]

Mrs a man by the name of Jesse GAYLORD of Bristol CT, a pall-bearer at her funeral died at her funeral [6 Feb 1851]

Mrs from the bite of a cat, hydrophobic symptoms *[The Brockport Sentinel]* *[Boston Courier]* [14 Oct 1843]

JOHNSON (Cont.) Nathan on Wed morning 31st ult a sentry of Fort Fairfield attempted to
fire off his gun as usual, the piece hung fire & when being taken down by the soldier
it discharged & the ball lodged in the side of Mr Nathan JOHNSON, harvesting in a
field a short distance from the fort killing JOHNSON, relieved from his post
[*Woodstock Telegraph*] [*Bangor Courier*] [17 Sept 1842]
Nathaniel 73 at Saco ME [11 Mar 1852]
Nathaniel 80y 5m formerly from MA at China ME on 5th Feb [15 Mar 1849] &
Nathaniel Capt 80 at China ME [8 Mar 1849]
Orinda A d/o Joseph JOHNSON at Gardiner ME [30 Oct 1845]
Peter fell into the river & drowned, attributed to the use of alcohol on Tues last [*Bath
Inquirer*] [5 Aug 1836]
Philomela 47 widow at Winthrop ME on Sat last [15 June 1839]
Phinehas 97y AmRev, reputed the oldest man present at Bunker Hill [1 July 1843]
Porteus Esq 50 at Frankfort ME formerly of Belfast ME [12 Feb 1846]
R D married Matilda MAFFITT a d/o we believe of Rev J N MAFFITT, Methodist
clergyman at Galveston TX on 6th inst [12 Dec 1844]
Rebecca 32 w/o David JOHNSON at Pownal ME [7 Nov 1844]
Rebecca 37 w/o Calvin JOHNSON at New Vineyard ME [2 Sept 1847]
Rhoda 74 of Sebago ME at Saco ME [2 Apr 1846]
Richard M Col in a letter to some of his fellow citizens, who had invited him to a dinner
declining the compliment mentions the death of ten of his family by cholera. [17 Aug
1833]
Samuel 45 at Hallowell ME on the 15th inst general agent for the Maine Missionary
Society formerly of Winthrop ME [25 Nov 1836]
Samuel 75 at Jefferson ME [25 Feb 1847]
Samuel Capt 64 at Wiscasset ME [20 June 1844]
Samuel S 32y a graduate of Waterville College (Colby College) at Ludlow VT on 14 Mar
a victim to consumption [16 Apr 1842]
Sarah M 17y 7m at Augusta ME on 17 Oct [24 Oct 1850]
Simon 67 at Hallowell ME formerly of Lisbon ME [25 Sept 1841]
Susan L 37 w/o Dr Benjamin JOHNSON at Dover [15 Jul 1852]
Susannah 89 wid/o Deac JOHNSON at Winthrop ME on Wed last [30 Nov 1839]
Sylvester of Frankfort ME first officer of schr *Hope* at Norfolk [15 Jan 1846]
Thomas 60 at Topsfield [22 Feb 1849]
Thomas 68 formerly of Farmington ME at New Vineyard ME [16 May 1844]
Thomas 72 at Dresden ME [24 Jan 1850]
Thomas "a colored man" cook; death by drinking a quart of rum belonging to one of
crew at sea on June 1st on board brig *June* [17 Jul 1835]
Timothy Rev 76 at North Berwick ME [20 Dec 1849]
W B of Newburyport MA the crew of the *Traveller* supposed lost [16 Oct 1851]
William 29 s/o Daniel JOHNSON of Gardiner ME at Boston MA [8 Aug 1850]
William arrested in Pittsburg, for getting money under false pretenses. He represented
himself to have once been a slave & had purchased his freedom & was now trying to
raise money to purchase the freedom of his wife & several children [*Boston Bee*] [17
Oct 1844]
William Treby 4y 7m c/o William T JOHNSON at Augusta ME on 6th [12 June 1845]
Zachariah abt 80 for many years a barber in (Augusta) ME on 18 Mar [22 Mar 1849]
JOHNSON - see ADAMS, BOONE, RIGAN, SMITH, TAYLOR, SAWYER, WILSON
JOHNSTON James Lt 84 at Hollis ME [2 Sept 1847]
John 106 at Steubenville ME AmRev [17 Apr 1838]
Mrs formerly of Frankfort ME [27 May 1847]
Thomas Capt 85 at Bremen ME [29 Jul 1852]

JOHNSTONE James 43 standing on a large mass of limestone & endeavoring to break it to
pieces at Barmoor limekiln near Lowick, Northumberland. & Dr TAYLOR of Lowick
stated that death was inevitable. [13 June 1844]

JOICE Lucy Ann Southworth 81 wid/o Asa J of Plymouth at East Boston MA [5 Aug 1852]

JONES Abby Eliza 9m c/o George W JONES at Augusta ME [13 Feb 1845]

Abigail 90 w/o John JONES at Fairfield ME [6 May 1847]

Albert 20 of Seasport ME lost overboard from schr *Fame* on 18th inst on passage from
Norfolk to Boston MA [5 Jul 1849]

Alden ae abt 25y helping in the barn raising in North Turner ME fell off the roof to the
ground and struck his head. He had injured the spinal marrow near the neck, & all
below is without feeling or power of motion although he has his senses. [27 Jul 1839]
He died 22 Aug [7 Sept 1839]

Amos abt 80 AmRev at Unity ME on 20 Apr [14 May 1842]

Apollos 80y a member of Society of Friends (Quakers) at Fairfield ME [15 May 1845]

Bethis widow 82 at Brooksville ME [12 Feb 1846]

boy 12y s/o Benjamin JONES employed at the tannery in Searsmont ME, fell through a
hopper where the tan was turned down & when taken out he had taken so much of the
dust into his lungs as to cause his death in a few hours. [1 Nov 1849]

boy abt 16y of Norridgewock ME s/o Samuel JONES kicked by a horse on Tues the 14th
ult in the abdomen. The boy died in about 12 hours [*Skowhegan Press*] [7 June 1849]

Catharine S 3m d/o the late Charles W JONES at Augusta ME [30 Apr 1846]

Charles 30y 10m at Augusta ME on Sat last [5 Feb 1846]

Charlotte 4y 6m d/o George W JONES at Augusta ME [28 Jan 1847]

daughter 4y of Fairfield ME c/o Elbridge JONES of burns [30 Nov 1848]

Delia Tudor Mrs 23 w/o George JONES Jr of Savannah GA & d/o Robert H GARDINER
Esq at the res of her father in Gardiner ME [15 Jan 1836]

Erasmus A 31 at Frankfort ME [17 June 1852]

Eunice widow 70 at Augusta ME on the 26th ult a dau/o the late Rev Mr FOWLER of
New Ipswich NH [6 June 1838]

Hannah 62 at East Hallowell ME on 11th inst [29 Nov 1849]

Hart 23 s/o the late Mr Hira JONES at Turner ME [26 Mar 1842]

Henry 56 formerly of Turner ME at Bangor ME [16 Oct 1835]

Henry Oscar 6y 9m s/o Eben JONES at Augusta ME [15 Apr 1847]

Hira 54 at Turner ME on 30 Nov [13 Dec 1841]

Irene 35 w/o Benjamin JONES at Readfield ME on 12th inst of consumption [28 Dec
1839]

Ivory 34 at Mercer ME on 12 Jan [8 Feb 1849]

James R 24 at Belfast ME [18 Sept 1851]

Jane 30y 7m w/o Lee D JONES at Madison ME [18 Apr 1850] & Jane 31 w/o Deac D
JONES at Madison ME [28 Mar 1850]

Joanna 40 w/o James JONES at South Solon ME [18 Dec 1852]

John 51y 27d at Searsmont ME [25 Apr 1844]

John 59 at Nobleboro ME very suddenly [15 May 1836]

John 76 of Monmouth ME at Searsport ME [4 Apr 1850]

John 87y of 1st settlers of Fairfield ME [23 Mar 1839]

John honest epitaph in a county graveyard in New Jersey, "here lies buried the body of
John JONES, who never held an office. An honest man" [*Gospel Banner*] [26 Oct
1848]

John L 40 at Clinton ME [15 Jul 1847]

John of Hallowell ME a crazy man burnt to death on the town farm [9 Oct 1841]

John Paul AmRev Navy, article contains vindication of his character [*Charleston
Mercury*] [7 May 1846] See Paul JONES.

JONES (Cont.) John W of Louisville KY sentenced to the penitentiary for living with two wives. JONES said one wife would fight him; but when he got 2 they fought each other & left him in a state of quietude. According to this the temptation to polygamy is strong. [9 Dec 1843]

Lorraine Mrs 35 at Gardiner ME [20 May 1843]

Lydia R Mrs 24 at Weld ME [20 Feb 1851]

Martha 19 of Elliot ME at South Berwick ME [18 June 1846]

Martha abt 18y eldest d/o M Africa JONES at Turner ME [28 Aug 1842]

Mary Mrs 80 at Union ME [18 June 1846]

Mr 3d mate of Falmouth ME 18y the only surviving officer of the crew of whaleship *Awashonks* of Falmouth ME at Fejee Island [6 May 1836]

Mr & Mr WILLIAMS drowned at the Forks of the Kennebec River, J returning from a hunting expedition, when he met with W who invited him to go home with him. In a birch canoe capsized & both perished [9 Apr 1846]

Mrs 42 w/o Galon JONES at Turner ME [13 June 1840]

Nathaniel Esq 60 at Mercer ME on 28 Dec [16 Jan 1851]

Paul An act of justice about to be rendered to the heirs of this naval hero of our Revolution. On the 10th inst the committee on claims in the House, unanimously reported a bill for the payment of salary and rations due for nearly his entire service during the Seven Years' War, as passed & audited by Robert MORRIS, then Minister of Marine & Finance [19 Feb 1846]

Paulina Cony 35 w/o Charles JONES Esq & d/o Hon Reuel WILLIAMS of Augusta ME at Portland ME the 19th ult [10 Jul 1845]

Phineas age abt 30 at Norridgewock ME [15 June 1848]

Rebecca 40 w/o Silas JONES Jr & d/o Peleg TOWNSEND formerly of Freeport ME at Jay ME on 20th ult after illness of nearly 5 yrs [4 Mar 1843]

Reuben 73 at Farmington ME [14 June 1849]

Samuel 51 at Wilton ME [22 Jan 1852]

Sarah E 18 d/o Daniel JONES at Newcastle ME [25 Dec 1851]

Sylvester 60 at Fayette ME [29 Apr 1847]

Sylvia W 16 d/o Nathaniel JONES Esq at Mercer ME on 2d Jul [15 Aug 1850]

Thomas 90 at Hope ME [22 May 1835]

Thomas P Dr 75y editor of the *Franklin Journal* & formerly superintendent of the patent office died at Washington on the 11th inst [6 Apr 1848]

two c/o William JONES at Palermo ME [9 Jan 1851]

Walter Gen lawyer of the city of Washington, & one of the officers of the Colonization Society, has offered his plantation, about two miles from Arlington in the District of Columbia, for the purpose of educating African youth [7 Dec 1833]

William 42 at Palermo ME [9 Jan 1851]

JONES - see BOSTON, CHASE, COWART, GREEN, JENKINS, KINGSLEY, MERRILL, PETERSON, ROLERSON, SMITH

JORDAN Andrew 22y drowned in Lincolnville Pond ME on Wed [5 Mar 1842]

Andrew M of Columbus MS had a giant negro who died at the Exchange Hotel (Louisville). The boy four years old in April last & four feet one inch in height. He was born in MS of parents in no way remarkable for any deviation from the ordinary size *[Louisville Daily Advertiser]* [26 Aug 1843]

Charity 44 w/o Abijah JORDAN at Topsham ME [16 Mar 1848]

Charles F 21 of Thomaston ME first officer of the ship *Leonidas* at Havre on 7th ult [15 Aug 1844]

Dominicus 51 at Harpswell ME [6 Jul 1848]

Elizabeth C 26 w/o Eben S JORDAN at Limerick ME [18 Apr 1850]

Ephraim 32y 8m at Webster (now called Sabattus) ME [14 Jan 1847]

JORDAN (Cont.) Esther 75 w/o Timothy JORDAN at Norway ME [28 Oct 1847]
Hannah 76 at Norway ME [30 Jan 1851]
Hannah 90y 5m at Monroe ME [28 Sept 1848]
Harriet abt 20 w/o Lyman JORDAN at Gardiner ME [22 Jul 1847]
Isabel 29 w/o Jeremiah JORDAN at Mariaville [27 Jul 1848]
James B Capt of the brig *Belfast* from Searsport ME at San Francisco CA on 16 Jan [21 Mar 1850]
James P late of Mt Vernon ME, est notice, Lydia JORDAN widow [20 May 1852]
John of Cape Elizabeth ME gun accident with duck gun, lost one arm [14 Oct 1843]
Joshua at Thomaston ME [25 Jul 1834]
Kezia C 26 s/o Robert C JORDAN at Augusta ME [12 June 1851]
Keziah w/o Capt Rishworth JORDAN 3d at Biddeford ME [17 June 1847]
Mary 61 w/o Deac Robert JORDAN at Brunswick ME [26 Oct 1848]
Mary Jane 20 at New Portland ME [30 Aug 1849]
Mary R 31 w/o Lawrence JORDAN at Saco ME [14 Aug 1851]
Matilda H 29 w/o Anson JORDAN Esq at Raymond ME [27 Apr 1848]
Sarah Mrs 82 at Buxton ME [2 Dec 1836]
JOSE Martin 79 at Buxton ME [20 Jan 1848]
Moses 43 at Dexter ME, by injuries recieved from a threshing machine [23 Jan 1845] & [6 Feb 1845]
JOSS William 76 at Readfield ME [12 Aug 1847]
JOSSELY Alvah 51 at Augusta ME on 22 Nov, for many years proprietor of the Kennebec House [28 Nov 1850]
Ann Foxcroft 6m 2w d/o Alvah JOSSELYN at Augusta ME 19 Jan [24 Jan 1850]
Charles H 28 at Fayette ME [12 Dec 1844]
Eliza Parker 2y 11m youngest d/o Alvah & Eliza JOSSELYN at Augusta ME on the 22 inst [25 Mar 1847]
Marcellus Chandler 2y 6m only s/o Alvah JOSSELYN Esq at Augusta ME on 19th inst [5 Dec 1844]
JOY Ann 26y 9m w/o Samuel JOY & d/o William & Catharine CUSHMAN at Readfield ME on 17 Oct [7 Nov 1850]
Cyrus Esq formerly of Plainfield MA appointed consul from Texas to reside in Philadelphia. He was a partner in law with Hon L C BATES in Northampton and afterwards went to Plainfield to superintend a tan yard, remarking at the time that having practiced "skinning" some years, he now proposed to do the "tanning" [30 Nov 1839]
Huldah 75 at Winthrop ME on 5th inst [14 May 1842]
Jeremiah 67y 4m at Canaan ME on 26 Feb (*Morning Star* please copy) [11 Mar 1847]
Peter 42 at Lubec ME [30 Sept 1836]
Phebe 44 w/o Love JOY at Ellsworth ME [23 Dec 1847]
Polly abt 40 w/o Benjamin C JOY at Winthrop ME on Sun last [6 June 1840]
Reuben 75 at Limington ME [3 Jul 1845]
Samuel 85 at Ellsworth ME [6 May 1836]
JOYCE Lawrence Esq at Richmond ME [25 Nov 1843]
JUDKINS Benjamin J 19 at Fayette ME of consumption [29 Apr 1833]
Ebenezer H 78 at Athen ME [18 Dec 1852]
Elizabeth 29 w/o Moses JUDKINS & D/o Benjamin BUTLER Esq of Cornville ME at Cincinnati OH [13 Dec 1849]
George of Augusta ME lost overboard from the steamer *Sea Gull* in the Columbia River on her trip down from Oregon to CA. It was from this same steamer on her upward trip Mr Daniel C CHILD (whose death was reported the week before) was also lost (from the *Journal*) [4 June 1851]

JUDKINS (Cont.) Henry s/o Major B S JUNKINS of Palmyra ME at Milwaukie WI on 31 Sept [31 Oct 1850]

Hiram A 16y 5m at Augusta ME [1 Jan 1846]

John late of Monmouth ME est notice Washington WILCOX exec [10 Jul 1852]

Jonathan 87 AmRev pensioner at Hallowell ME [22 June 1839]

Mary Josephine 1y 9m d/o Jonathan & Julian JUDKINS at Monmouth ME on 26 Feb [22 Apr 1847]

Mehitable 91 wid/o Benjamin JUDKINS late of Fayette ME. Her descendants now (1848) living are 190 at Ripley ME [19 Oct 1848]

Moses 78 at Greenwood ME [13 Nov 1851]

Peter 36 at Bloomfield ME [19 June 1841]

Philip 103 AmRev pensioner at Parkman ME [29 Jan 1852]

JUDSON Sarah B w/o Dr J at St Helen on 1 Sept on way from Port Louis Mauritius to Boston MA, Dr J has arrived at Boston MA with three children, has been a missionary in Burmah [30 Oct 1845]

JUMPER Sally 63 wid/o James JUMPER Esq at Dexter ME [22 April 1847]

JUNKINS Paul 79 at Saco ME [16 Sept 1836]

JUSTICE Liz d/o Jacob JUSTICE of Swedsboro [sic], 2 lads out gunning & one of the guns was discharged; dau/o Mr JUSTICE abt 15y was sitting on the floor sewing, when her brother, 2 or 3 years older, seized hold of and leveled the supposed unloaded gun at her, saying "Liz, I'll shoot you," she did not fear his gun, as she had heard him discharge it. He pulled the fatal tigger & she died in a few hrs. [reported by the *Woodbury Herald*] [4 Dec 1835]

- K -

KAHERL Orange 60 w/o Thomas R KAHERL at Belgrade ME "during the absence of her husband she committed suicide..." [3 Dec 1846]

KALER Catharine 41 at Waldoboro ME [28 May 1846]

Joseph 68 formerly of Waldoboro ME at Belfast ME [30 Jan 1851]

KALLOCH Clementine Ward 11m c/o A KALLOCH at Augusta ME on 7th inst [18 Nov 1847]

Mortimer L 10 s/o Silas KALLOCH at South Thomaston ME [13 Sept 1849]

KATH-LA-MO-HEE Miss a Choctaw belle, the d/o "Black CLOUD," Caddo chief married Mr Loring F____. She is a full blooded Caddo above six feet in stature [*Arkansas Intelligencer*] [13 June 1844]

KAUFMAN Mr Rep in Congress of TX [6 Feb 1851]

KAVANAGH Edward Gov born Apr 1795 at his late father's est in Newcastle ME, in 1830, he was elected to Congress, he was Catholic (see obit) [15 Feb 1844] [25 Jan 1844]

Michael 36 & John FIELD helping in the moving of a barn belonging to Mr CLARK. During the operation of moving the barn, KAVANAGH & FIELDS partook of the liquor provided for the occasion - soon after they had some words in relation to a goadstick. FIELD struck KAVANAGH & killed him. FIELD has a wife & four children. [*Gardiner Fountain*] [29 June 1848]

Morris of Hallowell ME, visited Readfield ME a few days since & became intoxicated; from which we fear the late vote of that town is not thoroughly executed as it should be. He requested a lawyer to grant a warrant, that he might be committed to jail for the purpose of becoming sober. Instead of a warrant, he was induced to take an emetic, under the operation of which he died. [*Temperance Gazette*] [13 June 1840]

KAY - see BURNS

KEAN John Capt 64 at Hallowell ME [7 Sep 1848]

KEAN (Cont.) family consisting of a mother & her five ch poisoned in Greenville NY by
   drinking tea made of yellow saffron, gathered by the children, supposing it to be
   spikenard. Mrs KEAN died in a few hours afterwards and the recovery of two of the
   children was considered doubtful. [3 Aug 1839]
   William abt 25 of (Limerick?) ME on 5th inst in a pond in Newfield ME while on a
      fishing excurston [*Limerick* (Maine Freewill Baptist) *Repository*] [15 Jul 1847]
KEARMAN Nancy 3 women killed on Tues last near the village of Hyde Park NY by a
   piece of rock, thrown from a blast, falling through the roof of their house. The rock
   weighed 1000 pounds. They were all married. [6 Mar 1851]
KEARNEY Stephen W General of the United States Army died at St Louis [9 Nov 1848]
KEATING R 27 of ME of cholera Sacramento CA on 30 Oct [2 Jan 1851]
KEATON Sarah widow 84 at Belgrade ME on 27 Dec [5 Feb 1852]
   Willaim 49 at Augusta ME on 5th inst [18 Nov 1852]
KEELER - see BOWDEN
KEELY Eliza 14 d/o Prof KEELY at Waterville ME [14 June 1849]
KEEN Anna late of Greene ME, est notice, Stephen W MITCHELL adm [5 Feb 1852]
   Asher 35 at Sumner ME [18 Feb 1847]
   Betsey S 14y 1m d/o James & Judith KEENE at Augusta ME on 29 Nov [22 Apr 1847]
   Chandler 17 s/o Andrew KEEN at Sumner ME [5 Feb 1846]
   Frances 3y 6m d/o James & Sarah at Augusta ME [22 Apr 1847]
   Hart B 21 at Canton ME [5 Mar 1846]
   James Jr of Thomaston ME died [13 Apr 1848]
   Jerusha 64 w/o John KEEN at North Turner ME [3 Jul 1851]
   John 87 at Turner ME on 3 Aug AmRev pensioner [3 Sept 1842]
   Julia A L 30 at Freedom ME on 17 Mar [8 Apr 1852]
   Mary 87 wid/o Benjamin P KEENE Esq at Appleton ME [15 Feb 1849]
   Mary 97 at Bremen ME [25 Mar 1847]
   Mr abt 20 by the falling of a tree at Oxford ME [8 Jul 1852]
   Prince 76 at Windsor ME [23 Apr 1846]
   Reuben Rev 74 at Camden ME [8 Apr 1852]
   Richard Raynal Col of New Orleans a conspicuous character in the disputes which grew
      out of the BURR conspiracy d at St Louis MO [19 Oct 1839]
   Rosanna the mulatto girl to hang on Fri last for poisoning SEELEY reprieved by Gov
      PENNINGTON of NJ [11 Nov 1843]
   Sophia 42 w/o Charles KEENE Esq at Augusta ME on 24 Dec [30 Dec 1847]
KEENE Abner 58 at Windsor ME on 29 Nov of consumption [11 Jan 1840]
   Celena 84 w/o William KEENE at Wales ME [22 June 1848]
   Elizabeth Y 10m d/o Charles KEENE at Augusta ME on 22 Aug [4 Sept 1851]
KEEP Lydia a widow left the house & board of Jacob TOWNSEND of Dixfield ME he
   forbids all persons ... [23 Jan 1841]
KEGAN - see DOYLE KEIF David arrested in Boston MA for the murder of a boy three yrs
   old, the son of his wife by her 1st husband [23 Oct 1838]
KEITH Hampden Esq at Vassalboro ME [5 Nov 1842]
   Heber 7y 10m s/o Alvan KEITH at Augusta ME [26 Nov 1846]
   Sarah 18 at Thomaston ME [10 Aug 1833]
   Thomas Capt 66 of Thomson CT carrying the mail in a chaise from Thomson to Pomfret
      ...family set after him & on overtaking him found him dead in the chaise still holding
      upon the reins of his horse. [18 Sept 1835]
KEITH - see MEDBERY
KELLAM James not found yet, fatal shipwreck of the schr *Argus* on Plum Island [2 Jan
   1851]

KELLAR Andrew F abt 30 of Warren ME at New Orleans [13 June 1850]

Benjamin 53 at Warren ME on Tues of last week (see obit) [16 Jan 1838]

Charles late master of schr *Charles L Vose* at East Machias ME [6 Jul 1848]

David 81 AmRev at Thomaston ME [15 Jan 1846]

George W of Thomaston ME on board bark *Scott Dyer* on passage from Wilmington to Boston MA [25 Sept 1851]

Hannah Mrs 56 at Thomaston ME [11 Dec 1845]

KELLERAN - see slaves

KELLEY Amos abt 35 of Harwich MA & his brother Shubael B KELLEY ... fell to the deck (abt 40') The elder, Amos KELLEY, struck upon his head & shoulder, which fractured his skull & broke his collar bone, died in minutes. The other brother was not injured at all. The deceased has left a wife & three children [*Gardiner Ledger*] [20 May 1843]

an infant 1y c/o David KELLEY at Augusta ME on 11th inst [18 Aug 1850]

Content 80 formerly of Sidney ME at Raisin MI on 3 Feb [21 Feb 1850]

George A 5 c/o David KELLEY at Augusta ME [15 Aug 1850]

James 24 at Augusta ME on 13 Aug [2 Sept 1852]

John in New York from drinking poisoned brandy [10 Apr 1851]

John W 71 formerly of Sidney ME at Raisin MI [18 Sept 1841]

Joseph A 23 at Phillips ME on 24th ult [14 Sept 1848]

Michael of Augusta ME at Bath ME [22 Jul 1852]

Phineas 33 s/o John KELLEY at Augusta ME on 27 Sept [14 Oct 1847]

Roxana abt 33 of Plymouth ME in consequence of ill treatment from her husband, she had 6 children the oldest was 12y, her parents live in Freedom ME & his in Montville ME [6 June 1834]

William 40 an Irishman at West Prospect ME death caused by suffocation in the cabin of a vessel [15 Aug 1844]

Wing abt 46 formerly of Sidney ME at Raisin MI on 19 Feb [21 Feb 1851]

KELLEY - see BABSON

KELLOCH Ball of Warren ME at King William's Co VA [4 Mar 1847]

Harriet abt 28 w/o Rev Amariah KELLOCH at Thomaston ME on 14th inst [29 Jan 1842]

KELLOCK Rachel 18 d/o James at Belfast ME on 13th ult [3 Apr 1835]

KELLOGG Anethusa wid/o Rev Ezra KELLOGG of Maine Conference at Littleton NH [8 June 1839]

Charles 19 s/o David KELLOGG formerly of Thomaston ME died at the Rough & Ready diggings on 27th Sept in CA [5 Dec 1850]

KELLY Abial Jr, the coroner, summoned a jury for the death of Joseph TINUM of Kennebunkport ME, after the jury brought in the verdict of suicide; Mr KELLY died of heart disease [15 May 1851]

James 32 at Lubec ME [23 May 1850]

KELSEY Harriet 22 d/o Moses KELSEY of Knox ME at the Massachusetts General Hospital on 19th inst [28 Dec 1848]

Isaac S Esq 30 of Calais ME at the mines on Stanislaus River CA [1 Aug 1850]

Mary Jane 26 d/o Moses KELSEY of Knox ME at the Massachusetts General Hospital on 17th inst [28 Dec 1848]

Sarah Abby 21 w/o Joel W KELSEY & d/o Joseph MOULTON of Foxcroft ME at Port Huron MI on 16th ult [17 Jul 1845]

Sophia 55 w/o Moses KELSEY at KNOX [31 Jan 1850]

KEMP Alexander 1y c/o Peter KEMP at the corner of 26th St & 3d Ave NY upset a teapot filled with hot tea and scalded himself in such a manner that he died from the effects of the same early next morning. [17 Aug 1839]

KEMP (Cont.) Elijah 69 at Gorham [3 Dec 1846]
KEMPTON John at Farmington ME [19 Dec 1844]
    Lucy Ann 15y 11m at Augusta ME on 29 Sept [4 Oct 1849]
KENARD John 83 at Cornish ME [10 Aug 1848]
KENDALL Amos Hon "A Man of Sorrow" lost a week or two ago his wife's mother, one of
    her sons burnt to death in Missouri by a prairie fire & his son murdered in the streets
    of Washington not long since [1 Jan 1846]
    Anna 70 at Bangor ME [9 Jan 1838]
    Edmund 44 at South Gardiner MA on 18 June [29 June 1848]
    Elias A 21 at Bath ME [26 Sept 1837]
    Eunice 71 wid/o Deac Samuel KENDALL formerly of New Salem MA at Houlton
    Aroostook Co ME on 11 Aug [3 Oct 1837]
    James F shot by one of his fellow laborers reported by *The Placer* of 10 Nov [3 Jan 1850]
    Zebedee Jr 45 at Waldo ME [15 Feb 1849]
KENDALL - see KYLE
KENDRICK Cyrus 11 s/o Seth KENDRICK at Saco ME [27 Mar 1845]
    Ruth D 88 wid/o Capt Samuel KENDRICK at Saco ME [3 Aug 1848]
KENERSON Mary 64 w/o Jonathan B KENERSON at Fayette ME on 8th inst [14 Mar
    1850]
KENISON/KENISTON Sarah/Sally (DREW) 43 w/o Stephen KENISON at Readfield ME
    (see *Eastern Argus* issue 28 Dec 1827) [22 Aug 1844] [8 Aug 1844]
KENNEDY Augusta D 21 at Whitefield ME [14 Jan 1847]
    David 85 at Newcastle ME [31 Jul 1851]
    Eunice 19 d/o John A & Ruth KENNEDY at New Sharon ME [11 Nov 1847]
    Nancy 36 w/o George W KENNEDY at Waldoboro ME [25 Dec 1851]
    Nichols Esq 72 at Whitefield ME [16 Oct 1851]
    Pat 13y died accidentally at North Adams MA? [1 May 1851]
    Sarah 92 at Newcastle ME [29 Jan 1846]
    Thomas F 37 formerly of Whitefield ME at Warren ME on 1 Feb [10 Jul 1845]
    William 19y at Norridgewock ME [31 Jul 1845]
    William Mrs 67 at Jefferson ME [19 Sept 1850]
KENNELL Zebedee father of the postmaster general recently at his res in Dunstable MA
    81y [31 Aug 1839]
KENNEY Barnabas 68 at Dixfield ME on 28 Apr one of the first settlers of that town [11
    June 1842]
    J L Capt 44 at Newcastle ME [6 Jan 1848]
    John Maj 65 at East Dixfield ME [22 Apr 1847]
KENNISTON Elizabeth 80 at Boothbay ME [21 Mar 1844]
KENNON - see UPSHUR
KENNY Elizabeth W 27 w/o William SKENNY at Hallowell ME [16 Oct 1851]
    Mary a servant girl in the family of George CLARK dreadfully burned on Fri by her
    clothes a taking fire ... but she died on Sat morning ... Ferdinand CLARK had his
    hands severly burnt ... at Boston MA [12 Nov 1842]
KENT Frances Maria 4 d/o Hon Edward KENT [28 Sept 1839]
    James 85 in 1798, recorder of (New York) & appointed a justice of the Supreme Court of
    NY & later the chancellor of NY [*NY Jour Com*] [23 Dec 1847]
    Lucy 55y d/o Justin KENT of Portland ME at Augusta ME on 27th ult at the insane
    hospital [11 Oct 1849]
    Mr abt 30 of Sebec ME crossing the mill dam [29 May 1835]
KENT - see MORRISON, slaves

KEOKUCK person, the story of assassination of K by young Black HAWK, an entire fabrication. [*The Chicago American* of the 6th inst] [27 Jul 1839]

KEPPEL Mr at Germantown killed by a pitchfork [10 Aug 1848]

KERR David C Dr at New Orleans LA, Gen JACKSON's physician during the war [21 Nov 1840]

Victor Capt executed at Havana Cuba, the body shipped to New Orleans on the 16th ult [4 Sept 1851]

KERSEY William "A Drunkard Burned To Death" near Greensboro [*Patriot*] [7 Mar 1840]

KERSEY - see HODGES

KESLER Jacob his house in Rochester struck by lightning & killed Mrs KESLER [30 Jul 1842]

KETCHUM John seaman lost overboard from bark *Dutchess* [*sic*] for Mediterranean [28 May 1846]

KEUCHETT George W fell from the jib-boom & the vessel ran over him, the Capt CHANDLER of the barque *Empire*, thinks KEUCHETT belonged to Calais ME [*Portland Argus*] [1 Nov 1849]

KEYES Simon 83 at Weld ME [20 Feb 1851]

KEYES - see KYES

KEYSER Mr death from hydrophobia, bitten in Baltimore, in Jul last by his own dog [21 Sept 1848]

KEZAR George 36 at Parsonsfield ME [6 Jan 1848]

KEZER Amos 2y 7m c/o John KEZER Jr at Winthrop ME on Sat last [24 Sept 1842]

Apphia 22 d/o John KEZER of Winthrop ME at Lowell MA [4 Mar 1847]

John Capt 80 AmRev fought at Bunker Hill at Winthrop ME on 20 Jul [29 Jul 1843]

KEZIER Catherine 94 at Waldoboro ME [7 May 1846]

KIBBEL John found frozen to death in a house in New York City on Mon night [11 Jan 1849]

KIDDER Cyrus S 23 at Skowhegan ME [25 Oct 1849]

Josiah Esq 77 at Hampden ME [16 Nov 1848]

Lucy 64 w/o Hon David KIDDER at Skowhegan ME [11 Sept 1851] & [4 Sept 1851]

Mary A 23 w/o Joseph W KIDDER at Skowhegan ME [8 May 1851]

Mr of Townsend & William C REED of Pepperell sufferers from an accident at the military review from five muskets burst at Lowell MA [9 Oct 1841]

William 26 at Albion ME he died in one week from the day of his marriage [6 May 1836]

KIFER Mr 110y 6m AmRev of 1775 died on 11 Feb at the res of his son at Woodbury Township Bedford Co PA [11 Apr 1844]

KIFF Mrs perhaps killed by her husband at Bucksport ME [8 Aug 1837]

KILBORN Calvin 91 of Princeton married Mrs Susan SANDERSON 71 (heading reads "Vitality in MA") [8 Mar 1849]

Sarah A 27 w/o Augustus KILBOURN of Boston MA at Saco ME [12 Nov 1846]

KILBURN John his barn burnt [*Calais ME Democrat*] [6 June 1840]

John J 39 late of (Augusta) at Fall River MA [17 Dec 1846]

KILGORE Mrs 38 w/o Col John KILGORE at Norridgewock ME [19 Feb 1846]

KILLSA William Esq formerly of Thomaston ME 62 at Canton IL [18 May 1848]

KILPATRICK George 19 a native of ME at sea on board brig *Charlotte* [31 Jul 1835]

lad had his thumb blown off on Fri by the accidental discharge of a pistol & a Mr TIMES engaged in firing a Native [*sic*] salute was injured by the premature discharge of a gun at Philadelphia PA [*The New York Farmer & Mechanic*] [17 Jul 1845]

KILSA Lydia 81 at Thomaston ME on 19th ult [10 Jul 1841]

KIMBAL W H 16y drowning at a skating party on ice made the night before [*Portland Courier*] [21 Dec 1833]

KIMBALL Abba W d/o Abraham KIMBALL at Kennebunkport ME [3 May 1849]

Abraham 77 at Bath ME [27 Jan 1848]

Almira Todd 25 w/o George KIMBALL at Hallowell ME [7 Jan 1847]

Asa Mrs at Livermore Falls ME [20 June 1844]

Betsey 58 w/o Benjamin KIMBALL formerly of Vienna ME at Dixmont ME 17th Jul [22 Jul 1852]

Betsey abt 35 at Winthrop ME on Sat last [23 May 1834]

David 68 at Belfast ME [10 Jul 1845]

Eliza J 22 w/o Albion G KIMBALL at Augusta ME on 8 Mar [15 Apr 1852]

Eunice Mrs 54 at Kennebunk ME [22 Jan 1836]

George 21 at New Sharon ME on 3 Dec [15 Jan 1852]

George Esq 44 formerly of Alna ME at Dixmont on 2d inst [27 Jan 1840]

George T 6 s/o Thomas KIMBALL at Hallowell ME [2 Apr 1846]

Hannah 76 at Bath ME [14 Nov 1850]

Harriet W 39 at Augusta ME on 28 Apr after illness of nearly 6y [4 May 1848]

Harrison 30 at Waterville ME [1 Apr 1847]

James 77 formerly of Passadumkeag at Buxton ME [9 Apr 1846]

Jeremiah killed, John COTIE mortally wounded & a man named JENKS severely wounded by the premature discharge of a cannon at Hanover NH on 4th inst [10 Jul 1851]

John C 19 eldest s/o Thomas KIMBALL at Hallowell ME 4th inst [14 Aug 1845]

Joseph abt 35 at Cornish ME [24 Dec 1846]

Margaret R 26 w/o Otis KIMBALL & d/o William M ROGERS Esq at Bath ME [12 June 1838]

Mariah 28 at Winthrop ME on the 21st ult at the res of Samuel WEBB Esq [2 Oct 1838]

Martha D 48 at Gardiner ME [6 Feb 1851]

Mary 14 at Gardiner ME [6 June 1844]

Mary 36 w/o Hon I K KIMBALL at Rockland ME [3 Jul 1851]

Mary 71 wid/o James KIMBALL formerly of Newburyport MA at Augusta ME on 30 · Apr at the res of Gen Alfred REDINGTON [15 May 1851]

Mila Mrs 75 at Waterford ME [7 Sep 1848]

Nancy 25 d/o Porter KIMBALL Esq at Rumford ME [12 Sept 1844]

Nancy D 50 w/o Capt Thomas KIMBALL at Monmouth ME [7 Sept 1839]

Nancy M 24 w/o William H KIMBALL formerly of Augusta ME at New Sharon ME on 7 Apr [15 Apr 1852]

Nathaniel 86 at Winthrop ME suddenly [28 Oct 1843]

Peter 58 at Rumford ME [10 Jul 1851]

Rebecca 65 w/o Ancil KIMBALL Esq at Dover ME? formerly of Athens ME? [10 Dec 1846]

Roxanna 19 at Gardiner ME [23 Dec 1847]

Sarah F 21st yr a native of Bangor ME w/o W Gustavus KIMBALL at Milledgeville GA on 19th ult [1 Aug 1840]

Seth W 42 at Atkinson ME [6 Jul 1839]

Stephen J merchant at Bangor ME [27 Aug 1846]

Thomas 61 a native of Ipswich MA at Bath ME [31 Jan 1834]

Thomas Henry 16m 21d youngest child of Charles KIMBALL at Hallowell ME on Tues last [18 Sept 1838]

Thomas & Daniel GUILFORD employed in removing a slab pile from the foot of the double saw mill, KIMBALL was killed & GUILFORD came near a similar fate.

KIMBALL (Cont.) KIMBALL left a widow & 4 ch at the Bar Mills Village in Hollis ME on Fri 5th inst [*Eastern Argus*] [25 May 1848]

    William 67 at Vienna ME on 13th Jan [31 Jan 1850]

KIMBALL - see WHITNEY

KINCAID Alexander 7y 5m s/o Alexander KINCAID at Augusta ME on 7 Mar [14 Mar 1850]

    Charles 3 s/o Hiram KINCAID at Augusta ME on 10th inst [18 Jan 1849]

    David 42 at Augusta ME [13 May 1847]

    Henrietta C w/o Horatio N KINCAID at Cornville ME on 23 Aug [4 Sept 1851]

    Susannah 87 wid/o John KINCALD at Chelsea ME on 23 Mar [3 Apr 1851]

KINCAID - see NORCROSS

KINES George T 78 at Hartland ME [1 Jan 1852]

King Louis XVIII - see NILES

King of Denmark on 8 Dec & was born 1762, ascended the throne in 1808, reigned 32y. Christian Frederick, half-brother of the deceased was his successor [25 Jan 1840]

King of Denmark proclaimed that all persons who are born in his dominions shall be free and that all slaves in his dominions on 28th of Jul last, shall be free on the 28th of Jul 1859. West India Islands belonging to Denmark are St John, St Thomas & St Croix. They contain now abt 35,000 slaves. [16 Sept 1847]

King of Prussia. The report of his death is stated by the *London Times* of June 4, to have been premature. [18 Jul 1840] & The King of Prussia is positively dead [25 Jul 1840]

KING Albion K P 25 late of Skowhegan ME at Oxford ME [29 Jul 1852]

    Angelina 20 d/o Capt G W KING at Bloomfield ME [2 Jan 1851]

    Augustus a black man of Mount Joy Hill in Portland, ME, was keeping a house of prostitution. The men of Portland, ME, Mr SWEAT and Capt SNOW of Cape Anne or Cohasset were wounded in a militaia action trying to run the KING out of town. Mr KING and Mr THOMAS were arrested. Officers packed off 5 girls. (*Portland Advertizer*) (*Portland Argus*) [9 Aug 1849] [13 Sept 1849] [20 Sept 1849] [27 Sept 1849]

    boy 6y of Bath ME s/o Francis KING was found drowned [*Bath Times*] [11 May 1848]

    Clarissa 55 w/o Jason KING at Monmouth ME [24 Aug 1848]

    Cyrus 56 at Saco ME [11 Feb 1847]

    E N lady of South Boston MA saved from drowning when the steam packet *New England* sank. It left Boston for Bath & Gardiner ME and had an accident with the schr *Curlew* on 31 May [12 June 1838]

    Edward Gen many yrs member of the legislature of OH & speaker at Cincinnati OH on 6 Feb 1836 [13 Jan 1837]

    Eunice 43y 6m w/o Zenas KING at Hallowell ME [28 Nov 1844]

    Henry C a hatter by trade having a wife & children living at Danbury CT was frozen to death a few nights since on his way home from a tavern where he had been drinking to excess [23 Dec 1847]

    Jonathan Esq 65 at Saco ME [22 Feb 1849]

    Lewis D abt 28 at Monmouth ME [24 Aug 1848]

    Lewis D at Monmouth ME [4 Apr 1850]

    Lorinda 6y d/o Zenas KING at Hallowell ME [23 Dec 1843]

    Lucy 32 w/o James H KING at Bloomfield ME [9 Aug 1849]

    Mary Elizabeth 32 d/o Ex-Gov KING at Bath ME [16 Aug 1849]

    Miss an aged woman native of England brought to the shore alive but immediately expired from fatigue [*Portland Advertiser*] [*The St Johns City Gazette*] [14 Aug 1838]

    Nancy 78 at Bath ME [25 Mar 1847]

    Oliva 53 w/o Benjamin KING at Winthrop ME [2 Mar 1848]

KING (Cont.) Pamelia 45 w/o Jason KING at Monmouth ME on Thurs on 20th ult [5 Sept 1840]

Samuel his blacksmith shop in Monmouth ME burnt to the ground [15 Jan 1839]

Thomas F Rev 42 pastor of the Universalist Society at Charleston MA [28 Sept 1839]

William Hon 84 at Bath ME formerly Gov of ME on 17 June [24 June 1852]

William ordinary seaman of Albany NY belonged to the US ship *Preble* & died with the Africa fever at Porto Grande Island of St Vincent Cape de Verds on 11 Dec [10 Apr 1845]

KING - see ALLEN, WOODBURY

KINGSBERY Judge died when visiting at Gardiner ME [8 Mar 1849]

Charles D 29 at Bath ME [19 Dec 1850]

J H 30 of MA at CA on 28 Dec [13 Feb 1851]

Sarah S 28 at Bath ME [12 Jul 1849]

KINGSLEY Rufus 84 born 1 Feb 1763 in CT, AmRev the death of the "Bunker Hill Drummer," his wife d 29 May at Hartford Susquehanna Co PA on the 26 of May [*Ithaca Chronicle*] [2 Jul 1846]

Rufus of Hartford, Susquehanna Co PA sole survivor of American drummers at battle of Bunker Hill. Error, Daniel JONES 91 who lives with to his son, in Morris Co, just below Stanhope, New Jersey was a drummer in the American army at that battle & was wounded in the calf of the right leg during the conflict, blind for 18y & his wife is 70y. His son is a merchant of Patterson. [*True Sun*] [*Boston Bee*] [22 Aug 1844]

KINHEAD - see TRIMBLE

KINNAMAN - see MYERS

KINNARD George L from Indiana death caused by injuries received from the bursting of a boiler of a steamboat at Cincinnati OH on 1 Dec [13 Jan 1837]

KINNIE Pamelia 39 w/o George KINNIE at Est Vassalboro ME [22 Oct 1846]

KINSLEY Daniel 93 AmRev at Auburn ME [23 Oct 1851]

Leonard of Washington Co ME at Sacramento City CA [1 Aug 1850]

KINSMAN Charles 66 at Pittston ME [29 Apr 1847]

Eleanor 75 of Pittston ME at Windsor ME [19 Feb 1852] & [4 Mar 1852]

Enoch J 22 s/o Gen Joseph KINSMAN at Cornville ME [23 Jan 1845]

John D 44 at Belfast ME [6 June 1850]

Polly 41 w/o Capt T F KINSMAN at Solon ME [28 Feb 1837]

KINSMAN - see KINSMORE

KINSMORE Jacob 18 native of Cornville Somerset Co ME left a father, mother, four bros, & 3 or 4 sisters (the *Clarion* thinks the deceased's name was KINSMAN instead of Kinsmore) [*Calais ME Journal*] [5 Aug 1847]

KIRBY Mr a baker reported killed in a Brooklyn fire [14 Sept 1848]

Nancy w/o Abner KIRBY at Norridgewock ME [16 May 1837]

Rebecca 28 w/o Capt Abner KIRBY formerly of Skowhegan ME at Milwaukee WI [27 Sept 1849]

KIRENS - see PEARCE

KIRK James of Bucks County PA 90 nearly eight yrs AmRev at the battles of Princeton, Trenton, Brandywine & Red Bank & at the surrender of Cornwallis at Yorktown at Philadelphia on the 16th ult [17 Jul 1841]

kissing - see DONAHUE

KITTREDGE Eleanor 68 at Bath ME [3 Sept 1846]

James Rush Esq 69 at Weld ME [22 Jul 1852]

KLANDLES Morgan 21, of gigantic size 6' 2" & stout recently arrived from Ireland taken to the hospital in Duane Street on 17th inst died on 22d attack of cholera [*NY Daily Adv*] [5 Sept 1834]

KNAPP John L 34 at New Portland ME on 15th Mar [4 May 1839]

    Mr sentenced in New York a day or two ago, for stealing a horse & wagon while the owner was taking a "snooze" in a grog-shop [17 Aug 1839]

    Nathaniel 32 at Portland ME [7 Nov 1837]

    William Francis 5y eldest s/o Dr Cyrus KNAPP at Winthrop ME on 27th ult (see obit) [2 Dec 1836]

KNEE Richard suddenly while attending church at Melksham [14 May 1842]

KNEELAND Abner a petition for the pardon of (him), lately convicted of the crime of blasphemy, is in circulation. *The Salem Gazette* says the petition has been revised by Dr CHANNING, who is to head it and that it will be signed by clergymen & others, of all denominations. [19 June 1838]

    Edward 75 at Prospect ME [4 Oct 1849]

    James Capt of schr *Prudence*, perhaps recently drowned at New York by the upsetting of a boat [22 Sept 1840]

    James of Frankfort ME fatal shipwreck of the schr *Argus* on Plum Island Capt CROCKETT of Frankfort ME was the captain [2 Jan 1851]

KNIGHT Abner 2d 48 at Lincolnville ME [11 Mar 1852]

    Amos 48y unmarried of North Wayne ME thrown from his horse on Sun last [4 June 1851]

    Amos 82y 6m at Wayne ME [30 Jul 1846]

    Amos late of Wayne ME est notice William KNIGHT adm [20 May 1852]

    Asenath 48 w/o William KNIGHT at Pittston ME [7 Feb 1850]

    Augusta Ann 2y 9m 20d d/o E M & B R KNIGHT at North Wayne ME on 27 Mar of canker rash & scarlet fever [22 Apr 1847]

    boy 5y drowned of Portland ME s/o Robert H KNIGHT [*Argus*] [8 Apr 1847]

    C L Capt second cabin; Richard CONNER, steward; L Creamer, second cabin; M D COX, first cabin; E A HIGGINS, second cabin; C B GRIFFIN, second cabin. A letter from Capt GRAY of the *Architect* states that six of his passengers had died of cholera [15 Feb 1849]

    Deborah Mrs If she had lived till the 19th of July, would have completed her 105th yr died at Sumner ME on 22d inst [6 Jul 1839]

    Edward 45 at Portland ME [30 Dec 1847]

    Eveline A 19 at Peru ME [21 Mar 1844]

    F 27 at Falmouth ME [2 Nov 1848]

    Francis 54 at North Wayne ME [22 Feb 1849]

    George W 33 at South Berwick ME [29 Jul 1847]

    girl 2y of Portland ME d/o Nathaniel KNIGHT, a teamster, the girl drank from the spout of a tea-pot sitting on the tea table on Sat & died on Mon [5 Apr 1849]

    Hannah Mrs 88 at Fryeburg ME [22 Nov 1849]

    Havery M 29 s/o James J KNIGHT at Casco ME on 9th inst [25 Nov 1852]

    Henry his house burnt [*Calais (ME) Democrat*] [6 June 1840]

    Horace 14 c/o Isaiah KNIGHT at Paris ME [23 Sept 1847]

    Isaac 58 at Portland ME [21 May 1846]

    James T abt 39 at Thomaston ME [20 Nov 1845]

    Jonathan 78 AmRev at Windham ME [2 Jan 1838]

    lad & lad BOMSBOTTOM both abt 7y into a fight last week & K thrown striking his head on a stone & died. He was an only child [*Providence Transcript*] [29 Mar 1849]

    Margaret A 20 at Lincolnville ME [18 June 1846]

    Mr abt 70 of Falmouth ME drowned on Sat near Martin's Point Bridge [13 June 1844]

    Rebecca 87 a widow at Westbrook ME [19 Mar 1846]

    Samuel 24 at Garland ME [21 Jan 1847]

    Susan P 57 w/o Nathaniel KNIGHT at Northport ME [10 Jul 1838]

KNIGHT (Cont.) Thomas R 26 at Portland ME [20 June 1844]

KNIGHT - see NASON, TABER

KNIGHTS John s/o Capt George KNIGHT of (Portland) drowned yesterday afternoon in the
river at Scarborough ME. Out gunning at the time of the accident [*Portland Umpire*]
[14 Sept 1848]

    Miriam 58 w/o Daniel KNIGHTS at Waterboro ME [18 Feb 1847]

    Rebecca 38 w/o Sumner KNIGHTS at Gardiner ME [4 June 1846]

    Stephen Rev formerly of ME at Western NY [29 May 1841]

KNOWLEN Thomas buried on the Penobscot at Passadumkeag, one of the first settlers, the
fall of 1825, left home on an excursion with Jonathan CLEAVELAND, Justus
MICHAELS & Mr CARR. During the next summer CARR returned to the Penobscot
bringing with him KNOWLEN's dog to the banks of the La Pompique, the dog lead
the way, where they found the remains of his master, tied up in his blanket (see
Scenes in the Wilderness #4) [13 Nov 1845]

KNOWLES Eben P 26 at Hallowell ME [27 June 1850]

    Edward O abt 12 of Surry ME [*Transcript*] [12 Nov 1846]

    Henry H 4y 10m suddenly from the effects of a bean lodged in the windpipe at Readfield
ME on 24 Oct [19 Nov 1846]

    James of Georgetown married but a short time sitting with his wife on the wall far as they
supposed from danger, about a 4th of a mile, but one of the rockets struck him on his
left breast directly over the heart, at Washington DC [*US Journal*] [17 Jul 1845]

    Jonathan on Fri evening last abt dusk returning home from the Belfast village, while
crossing a bridge, the wheel went over on one side & threw Mr K, he crawled into the
house of Mr Webster BANKS, taken care of & thence conveyed home, maybe
crippled for life [*Belfast Republican*] [9 Dec 1843]

    Moses B 22 at Belgrade ME on Belgrade ME [9 May 1850]

    Stephen S 34 at Sidney ME [16 Dec 1852]

KNOWLTON Abigail 84 widow at Litchfield ME [12 Dec 1850]

    Andrew 95 AmRev at Nobleboro ME [19 Nov 1846]

    Benjamin 9y 7m eldest s/o Hiram & Lorana KNOWLTON at Liberty ME on 23 Jul [16
Sept 1847]

    Cyrus 19 s/o Isaiah KNOWLTON at Sangerville ME [12 Oct 1848]

    Dean 42 at Farmington ME [1 Nov 1849]

    Deborah 37 w/o J B KNOWLTON at Chesterville ME [25 Apr 1850]

    Ebenezer 60th at Montville ME [4 Dec 1841]

    Isaiah 75 formerly of Sherburne MA at East Sangerville ME on 24 Nov [31 Dec 1842]

    Jere Capt 64 at Northport ME [6 Mar 1851]

    Joseph I abt 30 of Liberty ME went into the woods with a sled & yoke of oxen to procure
a load of bark - Upon his return to the tannery, slipped & the sled passed over him; he
left a wife [3 June 1843]

    Leonard of Montville ME assisted by Henry DEARTH & a younger brother abt 16y went
into their shingle mill, in Sangerville, one morning, two weeks since, & before dark
the same day, prepared the timber, sawed, sorted, & bunched, ready for market,
fourteen thousand pine shingles. They call upon their brother sawyers to beat this if
they can. [*Dover Observer*] [10 Aug 1848]

    Mary T 19 d/o James KNOWLTON at Elliot ME [27 Jul 1848]

    Mehitable 38 w/o Dean KNOWLTON at Farmington ME [26 Oct 1848]

KNOX Achsah H Mrs w/o Rev George KNOX pastor of the Baptist church in Cornish ME
at Cornish ME [*Portland Eastern Argus*] [3 Sept 1846]

    Amos P 42 at Portland ME [15 May 1838]

    Elizabeth 44 w/o Theodore KNOX at East Winthrop ME [17 Apr 1845]

    James 46 at Peru on 29 Jan of consumption [2 Mar 1839]

KNOX (Cont.) Jonathan 82, AmRev, in 31 battles and skirmishes including the battles of Bunker Hill & Saratoga. While serving under Gen SULLIVAN, imprisoned by the Indians at Canada, died at Berwick ME [29 Feb 1840]

Julia Ann 18 of Peru ME at Lowell MA [15 Aug 1844]

Lewis 34 at Augusta ME on 25 Jan [6 Feb 1851]

Mr AmRev at Thomaston ME [16 Sept 1847]

Thomas abt 21, at work in the woods alone, killed by the fall of a tree at Topsfield ME [16 Mar 1848]

William 102y 4m 2w at Berwick ME [12 June 1851]

William 29 at Dover ME? [20 Jan 1848]

KOCH George 99 AmRev at Waldoboro ME [7 May 1846]

KORNN - see COBB

KROSS Dederick deck passenger of Boston MA a serious accident happened on board the steamboat *George Collier* on the 6th inst on her passage from New Orleans to St Louis MO [25 May 1839]

KROUGH Charlotte 22 at East Thomaston ME [30 Apr 1846]

KUHN Sally 74 w/o Charles KUHN at North Waldoboro ME on 12 Jul [22 Jul 1852]

KYAN John H 75 an Englishman of scientific attainments, the originator of Kyanized wood, died in New York City lately of apoplexy leaving a wife & children in London England, he had just prepared a plan for purifying & filtrating the Croton water [24 Jan 1850]

KYES Ebenezer 77 AmRev at Gray ME (sic) on 31st ult [19 June 1838]

Ebenezer 77y 7m 7d at Jay ME AmRev after a painful sickness of about three weeks (see p. 435 Fisher's *S S & Patriots of ME*) [3 Jul 1838]

KYLE Mrs the mother-in-law of Hon Amos KENDALL, accompanied by her son, endeavored to save the fence surrounding the farm, both the son & the old lady were lost in the flames on the prairie about nine miles north of Monticello, Clark Co MO on 22d ult [*MO Reporter*] [25 Dec 1845]

- L -

LaBALLISTER Thomas P 42 at Whitefield ME [8 Aug 1844]

LaBALLISTER - see LeBALLISTER

LABREE Peter 96 at Brentwood NH [17 Apr 1851]

Submit 41 w/o Daniel M LABREE at Wales ME on 15 Oct (Bangor ME papers please copy) [26 Oct 1848]

LACELY Miss abt 17 of Churchtown, Cumberland Co PA by a stroke of lightning on Sun afternoon last [17 June 1836]

LaCROIX Nancy 45 w/o Frederick LaCROIX at Winthrop ME [5 Aug 1836]

LADD Arthur 1y youngest c/o J E LADD formerly of Augusta ME at Portland ME on 13 Aug [28 Aug 1851]

Confort M 27 recently a merchant in Hallowell ME of consumption at Winthrop ME on 19th at the residence of his father [21 Jan 1843]

Elizabeth a pauper of Winthrop ME supported by Simeon LADD of Readfield ME [28 Feb 1834]

Elizabeth formerly of New Hamphire 83 at Winthrop ME [18 Apr 1840]

F B one of the best portrait painters in the country is in town. He is a native of Augusta ME. Those who wish to be painted, & in a life-like style, had better give Mr LADD a call [24 Aug 1848]

Hannah 13 d/o the late Joseph LADD at Augusta ME [6 Nov 1838]

LADD (Cont.) James M 27 of Augusta ME passed Midshipman USN at Naval Hospital Norfolk VA [9 Dec 1847] &his funeral took place at the house of his brother, J E LADD on Sun at Norfolk VA [*Gospel Banner*] [23 Dec 1847][30 Dec 1847]

John 58 at Winthrop ME on Wed last of consumption at Winthrop ME [25 Mar 1843]

Joses abt 80 at Mt Vernon ME one of the 1st settlers [23 Sept 1843]

Julia F 15m c/o John LADD at Augusta ME on 2d inst [13 Jan 1848]

Laura Ann 27 w/o Harvey LADD at Readfield ME [29 Jan 1846]

Lucy 48 at Hallowell ME [25 May 1848]

Rachel 84 wid/o Joses LADD at Mt Vernon ME on 9 Oct [17 Oct 1850]

Thomas 68 at Saco ME [28 Nov 1837]

LADD - see BLAISDELL

LaFAYETTE General 77y on 20 May & born 1 Sept 1757 [*Boston Patriot*, London Papers, Paris correspondent of *NY Journal of Commerce*][27 June 1834]

Mrs 1784, Mr John ADAMS, afterwards Pres of USA in France for a season. His wife called one day on the lady of Gen LaFAYETTE. Mrs LaFAYETTE was modestly dressed, while the American ladies were mostly in very gay attire. One lady whispered to Mrs A, "Good heavens! how awfully she is dressed." Mrs A returned the whisper "the lady's rank placed her above the little formalities of dress." [*Exeter News Letter*] [14 Oct 1847]

LaFAYETTE - see CONNELL, FOSTER

LAIN Abigail 27 formerly of Buxton ME at Saco ME [28 Nov 1837]

LAINE George F abt 21 formerly of Hallowell ME at Boston MA [30 Dec 1847]

Mary P Mrs 45 at Hallowell ME [9 May 1844]

LAIRD - see WRIGHT

LAKEMAN child 6w of Daniel LAKEMAN at Hallowell ME [5 Sept 1840]

Eliza 37 w/o Daniel D LAKEMAN at Hallowell ME [8 Aug 1840]

Sarah 72 formerly of Newburyport MA at Hallowell ME [13 Nov 1841]

LAMB Benjamin 71 at Lincolnville ME [19 Sept 1850]

Cyrus Allen youngest s/o Luther R LAMB Esq at Winslow ME [19 Apr 1849]

George Eld 48 at Brunswick ME on 14th inst [23 Dec 1836]

James 82 at Clinton ME [30 Jan 1851]

Joshua Capt 84 at Lincolnville ME [16 Oct 1851]

Louisa Arabella 10y 10m only d/o Maj Merrick LAMB at Greene ME on 27th ult after a severe sickness of two weeks [17 Dec 1842]

Rufus 22 at Argyle ME [12 Apr 1849]

LAMBARD Francis Todd c/o Thomas LAMBARD at Augusta ME [23 Jul 1846]

Julia Ann 80 w/o Luke LAMBARD Esq at Bath ME [24 Sept 1846]

Nathaniel 80 at Skowhegan ME [29 Aug 1837]

Thomas 86 at Bath ME [27 Dec 1849]

William died of consumption at Augusta ME [2 Mar 1839]

LAMBART Isaac Jr 37 at Durham ME [24 Oct 1850]

Elisha 82y 4m at Norridgewock ME [26 Dec 1844]

Eliza 27 at Monroe ME [21 Mar 1850]

Pamelia 78 w/o late Shebiah LAMBERT at Skowhegan ME [6 Feb 1845]

Prudence 50 w/o Dennis LAMBERT Esq at Dover [21 June 1849]

LAMBERT - see DAVIS

LAMPSON Chapin Capt 86 at West Gardiner ME on 30 Dec [9 Jan 1851]

LAMSON Elmira 20 at Augusta ME on 19th instant [30 Mar 1848]

George 11m youngest child of J S LAMSON at Augusta ME [8 Oct 1846]

LANCASTER Ada Maria 5y 11m d/o Sewall LANCHESTER Esq at Augusta ME [25 Feb 1847]

LANCASTER (Cont.) Ann Maria 18 d/o E M & C D LANCASTER at New Sharon ME on 3 Nov [21 Dec 1848]

     Bartlett Capt 59 at Augusta ME on 28th ult his funeral attended by the Masons & Sons of Temperance of which societies he was a member [10 May 1849]

     Eben 60 at Newport ME? [25 Jul 1850]

     James 100 at China at Alms House on 22d inst one of the very first selectmen of the town (China), when known by the name of Harlem ME [27 Jan 1848]

     Joseph 89y 6m formerly of Durham ME AmRev pens at Richmond ME [10 Sept 1846]

     Josiah Dr 43 at Hartford ME? of consumption [2 Sept 1836]

     Lucy Mrs 65 at Northport ME [3 Jan 1850]

     Mary 59 w/o Thomas LANCASTER at Winthrop ME [13 Apr 1839]

     Mary Jane 33 w/o Charles LANCASTER Esq & d/o late Jos NORTH of Augusta ME at Philadelphia PA [9 Dec 1843]

     Miss 22 of Woolwich ME committed suicide by drowning herself in the Kennebec River on Wed evening last [*Bath Mirror*][10 Apr 1851]

     Thomas G 49 s/o Thomas LANCASTER of Winthrop ME in MO on 1 May [16 Sept 1852]

LANCESTER - PAINE

LANCEY Deborah E 34 formerly of Topsham ME at Webster ME [4 May 1848]

     George Esq 54 at Palmyra [5 Dec 1850]

     Martha 16 eldest d/o Capt Thomas LANCEY at Palmyra ME on Nov 14 [7 Dec 1839]

LANCY Samuel Esq 77 at Palmyra ME [21 Nov 1837]

LAND Lydia abt 55 at Augusta ME on 4 Jul [24 Jul 1845]

LANDER Alden 45 at Waterville ME [25 Mar 1847]

     Margaret 26 w/o Alden LANDER at Waterville ME on 19th inst [28 Aug 1841]

     Peleg 48 at Houlton Aroostook Co ME on 2 Sept, by falling from the framework of a building [9 Oct 1845]

     Prudence 80 w/o Robinson LANDER at Bloomfield ME [2 Oct 1851]

LANDERS Susannah M 9y 6m d/o David LANDERS of Gardiner ME at Bowdoinham ME on 13th inst [28 Aug 1838]

LANDON - see McLEAN

LANE Abigail 26 Kingfield ME [18 Dec 1845]

     Abraham 61 of Anson ME at Embden ME [4 Feb 1847]

     Albert 18 s/o Zenas LANE of Poland ME at Augusta ME [26 Feb 1846]

     Belinda S 13m d/o James LANE at Augusta ME on 24 Apr [4 May 1848]

     Charles B 40 recently from Boston MA originating from Gray ME at Franklin House [*Portland Advertiser*] [19 Mar 1846] & died in Portland ME on Fri last, at Longley's Tavern & taken ill in the stable [*Eastern Argus* of Portland ME] [12 Mar 1846]

     Charles second mate from schr *Majestic* lost overboard of Addision ME [23 Apr 1846]

     child 4y 6m after illness of about 6w at Wayne ME c/o Alpheus LANE [21 Sept 1833]

     Daniel 15 s/o Samuel LANE at Greene ME on 12th [14 Nov 1834]

     Eliphalet 72 at Weld ME on 28 Mar [8 Apr 1852]

     Elizabeth 61 w/o Thomas K LANE at Brooks ME [20 Dec 1849]

     George W 29 s/o John LANE of Readfield ME at Boston ME on 19th ult [10 June 1833]

     Jabez at Hollis ME of smallpox [1 Jul 1836]

     Jeremiah 73 at Fayette ME [7 June 1849]

     Job abt 70 at Danville (now part of Auburn) ME (b 25 June 1766, d 19 Jan 1844 *VR Danville ME*) [8 Feb 1844]

     John 85 at Readfield ME [24 Dec 1846]

     John 95 at Eastport ME [26 Aug 1843]

     John B Esq at Minot ME on 18th inst [26 Nov 1842]

LANE (Cont.) John Esq his dwelling house at Ripley ME destroyed by fire last week with all
     the bedding and clothes of the family [13 Apr 1839]
 Louisa J 16m d/o Barbour & Louisa LANE at Augusta ME [27 Jul 1848]
 Lucy S 22m grand child of Isaac & Mary STEDMAN at Sidney ME on 10 Jul [20 Sept
     1849]
 Ruth 75 w/o John LANE at Readfield ME on 16th inst [5 Feb 1839]
 Samuel 55 at Hollis ME very suddenly [21 Mar 1834]
 Samuel (ae 48 on 9 Aug 1834) at Greene ME [see *American Advocate* 5 Nov 1834][14
     Nov 1834]
 Sarah Louisa Annetta 3y 10m gch of Isaac & Mary STEDMAN [20 Sept 1849]
 Sarah w/o Samuel LANE at Greene ME on 20th [14 Nov 1834]
 Simeon 54 at Oxford ME [21 June 1849]
 Webster 80 at Dexter ME [12 Mar 1846]
LANG Ellen 23 w/o Thomas S LANG & d/o Jacob SOUTHWICK Esq of Vassalboro ME at
     Augusta ME on 13 June [27 June 1850]
LANGDON Joseph 90 at Wiscasset ME [27 May 1847]
LAPHAM Abel 92 at Cornville ME [13 Nov 1851]
 Benjamin 40 of South Boston MA fell asleep in the bottom of the boat & drowned, left
     wife & 4 ch, one of his children, a boy 10y, was with him in the boat & was saved by
     Mr DWELLEY, the boatman [15 Jul 1843]
 Bethiah abt 22 d/o Thomas LAPHAM of Bethel ME [*Norway Advertiser*] [2 Sept 1847]
 Huldah 82 at Auburn ME [19 Oct 1848]
LARA James AmRev pens at Turner ME on 31 Jan [19 Feb 1842]
LARABEE Phebe 19 at Parkman on the 16th ult [14 Dec 1833]
LARADEN Lucy Ann 24 w/o Daniel LARADEN at Belfast ME on 30th [15 Aug 1840]
LAREY - see LARA
LARKIN Abby J 22 w/o J B LARKIN at Danville (now Auburn) ME [20 Jan 1848]
 Henry of Concord was recently poisoned by tincture of aconite, which he supposed to be
     brandy. It had just been brought into the house by his daughter, Mrs GERALD. He
     lived but a few minutes after drinking it. [29 Mar 1849]
 Oliver B of Tyningham MA a passenger in a canal boat near Black Rock, was murdered
     by Jonathan F FLINT, the master of the boat. The dispute respected the pay for the
     passage. [9 Oct 1838]
 Patrick 24 at Farmington ME [15 Apr 1847]
LARKIN - see ROLERSON, WOOD
LARRABEE Ammi 58 at Auburn ME [13 Mar 1851]
 Francis E 22 at South China ME [4 Feb 1847]
 John 55 at Unity ME [23 Nov 1848]
 John Jr 18 of Bath ME s/o Deac LARRABEE accidently shot by another boy in the
     neighborhood of Sewall's Mills on a shooting excursion. Dr T G STOCKBRIDGE
     was called & removed the wad & a portion of that shot & thinks the patient may
     recover. [*Bath Times*] [20 Apr 1848]
 Mary 19m d/o John LARRABEE at Augusta ME on 12 Sept [20 Sept 1849]
 Phebe 43 w/o William P LARRABEE at Dover ME [3 Jul 1851]
 Sarah E 12 d/o Capt John LARRABEE at Bath ME [14 May 1846]
 Sylvia E w/o Capt Samuel LARRABEE & d/o Rev Robert LOW at Winthrop ME at the
     residence of Moses WHITE Esq [25 Sept 1838]
 William 80 at Brunswick ME [25 Nov 1847]
 William A 24 printer of Augusta ME at Bradford ME of consumption on Wed [27 May
     1843]
LARRY Elizabeth 87 at Phipsburg ME [26 Apr 1849]

LASCOMB Gideon Capt 74 at Eden ME [29 Jul 1843]

LASH Augustus T formerly preceptor of Lincoln Academy at Newcastle ME [16 Sept 1847]

LASHER Miss of Ohio recovered a verdict of $130 from Mr SMITH (rather an odd name) for a breach of the marriage promise. S stated the lady wore false teeth. No excuse at all. He should himself have discovered the defect by asking the lady to bite his little finger and if there was a rattling among the ivory he would have known his cue. Such are not legal excuses at all [23 May 1840]

LASSELL Sarah 53 w/o Mathew LASSELL at Norway ME [22 June 1848]

LATHROP Rodney on Wed at Sandusky OH & his 2 dau, Mrs WALTER & Emeline LATHROP ae 15 both of cholera & next door c/o George MAYLE died of cholera [*Cincinnati Gazette*, 25th] [13 Sept 1849]

LATIMER slave the case heard before Chief Justice in Boston MA [12 Nov 1842] & is free [3 Dec 1842]

LAUGHLIN - see LAW

LAUGHTON Cyrene 22 at Augusta ME on 16th inst [27 Apr 1848]

Delia Ann Mrs 26 at Gardiner ME [25 Nov 1836]

James 92 at Bristol a soldier in the old French war & a sergeant AmRev [22 Jul 1833]

LAUGHTON - see BROWN

LAUNDER Thomas of Zanesville OH aroused from his sleep in the middle of the night by a call of a man in the street; fire in the store. Papers on fire, on the same shelf sat a keg of gunpowder which Mr L deliberately seized and carried into the street, & got water & put the fire out, burning his hands badly in the operation...perhaps the only thing that could have saved the lives of his family...[4 Dec 1851]

LAVALLY - see FATE

LAW Mary Ann recovered $600 by a suit in Juniata Co PA against Thomas LAUGHLIN for a breach of promise, previously been awarded $625 by arbitrators [11 Jan 1849]

LAWRENCE Asa 80y died; moved to Wayne (then called New Sandwich) ME on 10 Aug 1786, in May 1838, buried his wife, ch living in Wayne & Sumner ME at Wayne ME on 9 Apr [1 May 1851]

David of Pittston ME master of ship *Meteor* at sea on passage from Apalachicola to Liverpool [1 Aug 1850]

Ebenezer 63 at Fairfield ME [1 June 1848]

Elizabeth 43 w/o Samuel LAWRENCE at Lubec ME [27 May 1836]

Harriet 19 d/o Isaac LAWRENCE at Gardiner ME [25 Sept 1845]

Isaac W 13 s/o John LAWRENCE Jr at Arrowsic ME drowned [3 June 1852]

John seaman of Bucksport ME on board schr *Ellen Perkins* at New York from Sisal on the outward passage [26 Feb 1846]

Julia Ann 31 w/o Franklin LAWRENCE at Fairfield ME [26 Sept 1850]

Moses of Warren ME a passenger on the schr *May Flower*, HUPPER Capt, Moses was one of three Maine men who drowned at Norfolk VA [11 Nov 1847]

Phebe H 45 w/o Isaac LAWRENCE at Gardiner ME [28 Nov 1850]

S A ticket master at North Yarmouth Depot ME met with an accident today which will, it is thought, prove fatal. He was standing on a wooden horse, when a water pipe on which he & others were working struck him on the head & knocked him from the horse. At the last accounts he was senseless & not expected to live through the night (*Portland Advertiser*) [28 Dec 1848]

Sarah J 20y 7m at Sidney ME on 30th ult [14 Aug 1838]

Simeon S Capt of Madison ME on his passage to CA [16 Sept 1852]

Susan 22 d/o Francis & Susan LAWRENCE at Jay ME on 27 Sept [17 Oct 1850]

LAWRENCE (Cont.) William 97 born in Scotland at Bucksport ME sergeant in the Royal Artillery and came to his country with the British Army before the rupture with Great Britian [20 Feb 1845]

LAWRENCE - see ABBOTT, QUIMBY

LAWSON Helen Milleson 11 d/o Albert G & Lydia L LAWSON at Augusta ME on 2d inst [11 May 1848]

Mrs w/o Asa LAWSON at Augusta ME [13 Aug 1842]

LAWTON Barnabas 33 at Augusta ME [28 Feb 1834]

E W Mrs 57 w/o Rev C J LAWTON of Passadumkeag ME at Sangerville ME [4 Sept 1845]

Sarina 35 at Augusta ME on 17 Apr [25 May 1848]

LEACH Henry abt 27 s/o Elder Henry LEACH at Smithfield ME [15 May 1851]

Margaret widow 77 at Jay ME [19 Jul 1849]

Mr of Manchester MA sickness at Havannah (Havana Cuba); more than twenty deaths by yellow fever have occurred [28 Feb 1834]

Thomas 38 at Elliot ME [21 Mar 1837]

William Jr drowned at York ME on 20th ult with John E AYRES & Jonathan PERKINS, engaged in the lobster fishery & their flat bottom boat capsized, each left a family [11 May 1839]

LEACH - PERKINS, WATERMAN

LEADARD Melinda P abt 60 at Dexter ME [6 Mar 1851]

LEADBETTER Emily Fletcher 18 at Bingham ME [24 June 1847]

Lucinda 41 w/o B F LEADBETTER at Concord ME [16 Jul 1846]

LEAR Betsey 27 at Northport ME on 16th inst (see obit) [31 Jul 1838]

LEARNED Mary Hamlin Mrs w/o Charles D LEARNED Esq formerly of Livermore ME at Jackson MS on 17 Nov 1841 [26 Feb 1842]

LEASAGE Isaac of St Leon, in the District of Three Rivers Canada killed in the earthquake [*Montreal Gazette*] [14 Sept 1833]

LEATHERS Nathaniel Merrill wants to change name to Nathaniel Merrill WARREN, abt to leave the state to get married. She would not take his name, he belongs to the proscribed & isolated, but numerous family, its home at Barrington NH. Other members, who have worn the name, & have charged it for the same reason ... We have no recorded information of the family, but heard that it is of gipsy origin. [*Boston Courier*] [5 Apr 1849]

LEAVITT Albert P 22 at Saco ME [23 Dec 1847]

Ann d/o Joseph LEAVITT at Bangor ME on Fri morning [*Bangor Mercury*] [9 Jan 1851]

Benjamin 72 formerly of Buxton ME at Foxcroft ME [19 Feb 1846]

Caleb 67 at Brunswick ME [18 Oct 1849]

child 10m c/o Alvan LEAVITT at Turner ME [25 Mar 1836]

Elizabeth B 44 w/o R H LEAVITT at Pittston ME [22 Apr 1852]

Frederick 19 eldest s/o Caleb LEAVITT at Athens ME [6 May 1847]

Harriet Matilda 22m d/o Colos & Eliza A LEAVITT at Rockland ME [13 Mar 1851]

Isaac 65y at Turner ME on 7 Jan of the congestion of the heart [15 Jan 1842]

Isaiah 76 at Turner ME [27 Mar 1845]

John W 37 at Hallowell ME [5 Feb 1846]

Josiah E 31 at Naples ME [29 Jul 1847]

Mary E late of Sidney ME est notice Amy DELANO exec [23 Sept 1852]

Mary (ELKINS) 91 wid/o Lt Nathaniel LEAVITT, AmRev pens at Limerick ME (d 27 July 1852) [12 Aug 1852]

Prescott 15 s/o Alvan & Susanna LEAVITT at Turner ME [3 Oct 1844]

LEAVITT - see BELCHER

LEAZARDER Mr of Monmouth ME & saw the meteor and informed us of it during that day (13th). He said that the light was full equal to that of the sun. Other people also saw it; It was at 3 in morning [*Portland Advertiser*][23 May 1840] [N.B. A Monmouth Center Cemetery gravestone bears the name Benjamin LEUZARDER, d 1873 ae 83y.]

LeBALLISTER Betsey 25 at Windsor ME on 2 May [22 May 1838]
Thomas 72 at Whitefield ME [25 Dec 1845]

LeBALLISTER - see LaBALLISTER

LEBROKE Henry 4 c/o Jacob LEBROKE at Foxcroft (now Dover-Foxcroft) ME of the canker rash [29 Feb 1840]
James 10 c/o Jacob LEBROKE at Foxcroft (now Dover-Foxcroft) ME of the canker rash [29 Feb 1840]

LECOMPTE Joseph both legs broken, blown high into the air when the steamboat *Medora*, Capt SUTTON, exploded & fell on board the steamboat *Constitution* lying close by [23 Apr 1842]

LeCROG B had 19 children in 18 yrs & of these 5 pair twins [a letter from Fort Kent reported great doings in Madawaska, the French part of the territory] [17 Oct 1844]

LEE Charles AmRev lies at the foot of Gen MERCER's tomb at Christ Church in Philadelphia PA [16 Sept 1847]
Charles of Barre MA lost on board the ill-fated *Lexington*, the draft of his will in his hand was lately found beneath the false bottom of a travelling trunk that had been thrown aside. In the disposition of his property the sum of $2000 was to the town for a library, $6000 to the Unitarian Society, besides $1000 to its pastor [14 Aug 1841]
Eleanor 76 at Phipsburg ME [13 Nov 1845]
H Mr descended the well of Mr SLIFTER near Charlestown VA on Fri last to ascertain the cause of the impurity of the water but without using any precautionary measure to test the character of the air ....before reaching the top he fell to the bottom & was killed ... [2 Oct 1845]
Henry AmRev in VA [16 Sept 1847]
Henry Maj of VA the author of the *Life of Napoleon* at Paris France on 20 Jan Mon [21 Feb 1837]
John T 23 s/o Stephen LEE at Lee ME [22 Oct 1846]
Mr of Maysville KY advertises seven runaway slaves & among them is a female whom he thus describes. "Fanny, the mother of the four children, is about 25y of age, white as white women, straight light hair" [20 May 1843]
Mrs 38 w/o Seward G LEE at Winthrop ME [24 Feb 1848]
Temple wid/o Judge LEE at Wiscasset ME [30 Oct 1845]
Thomas J Esq of Calais & formerly of Winthrop ME at Belfast ME [18 Mar 1836]

LEE - see BISHOP, DEARBORN, Negro

LEECH Jeremiah 68 a native of Minot ME at Sangerville ME [15 Jul 1847]
William H 40 a member of Franklin Division S of T at Augusta ME on 23 Mar [29 Mar 1849]

LEEMAN Ariel 17 s/o Nathaniel LEEMAN at Hallowell ME on 2d inst of scarlet fever [12 Dec 1837]
Charlotte 53 w/o Nathaniel LEEMAN at Hallowell ME [29 May 1851]
David 87 at Windsor ME [15 Mar 1849]
Edwin 24 at Wiscaset ME [9 Mar 1848]
Edwin A 96 at Wiscasset ME [30 Mar 1848]
Eli 45 at Augusta ME [27 Aug 1846]
Martha widow 97 at South Dresden ME on 13 Apr [22 Apr 1852]
Samuel AmRev pens at Bristol ME [20 May 1833]

LeFEVRE Susan Mrs abt 50 at Hallowell ME [18 Jan 1849]
LeGARE Hugh S the Attorney General of the US & acting secretary of state, of indigestion
    or stoppage in the bowels [*Boston Times*] [1 June 1843]
LeGROW Hannah 72 at Windham ME [7 May 1846]
    Benjamin Watkins a politician at Richmond VA last week [15 Feb 1849]
    Martha 18 at South Berwick ME [24 June 1836]
    Thomas Capt 80 at Hallowell ME [28 Mar 1840]
LEIGHTON Charles 68 at Waterville ME [29 Aug 1850]
    Charlotte 18 d/o Andrew LEIGHTON at Elliot ME [18 Feb 1847]
    Elizabeth 34 w/o Abijah LEIGHTON at Eastport ME [23 Jul 1842]
    Ephraim 86 at Augusta ME on 15 Mar [27 Mar 1851]
    Harrison 6 s/o Nathan LEIGHTON at Augusta ME [29 Apr 1847]
    Horace Franklin 9 s/o Nathan LEIGHTON at Augusta ME on the 22d inst [3 Oct 1844]
    Isaac 15 s/o Benjamin at Belgrade ME on 5 Oct [17 Oct 1850]
    Jas R Capt 37 formerly of Mt Vernon ME at Dover [10 Dec 1846]
    Jesse B 30 late master of brig *Osage* of Boston MA & formerly of Cherryfield ME at
        Savannah GA [8 Oct 1842]
    Joel 62 at Bloomfield ME [6 Nov 1851]
    John 69 at Perry ME [7 Feb 1850]
    Mary 30 w/o George LEIGHTON at Eastport ME [27 Dec 1849]
    Nancy 40 w/o Nathaniel LEIGHTON at Gardiner ME [31 Aug 1833]
    Olive T 7y 8m d/o George & Betsey LEIGHTON at Augusta ME on 16 Oct [26 Oct
        1848]
    R F Mrs 46 at Biddeford ME [1 May 1851]
    Sullivan A 10 s/o Ephraim LEIGHTON at Augusta ME on 25 May [8 June 1848]
    Thomas H 50 of Lubec ME drowned between Eastport & Lubec ME left a wife & 13
        children [6 May 1847]
LEIGHTON - see GOULD
LELAND Aurelia M 23 w/o L M LELAND formerly of Templeton MA at Augusta ME [4
    Apr 1840]
    Betsey 37 at Sangerville ME on 1st inst of lung fever [18 Feb 1833]
    Eliza A 21 w/o L M LELAND at Augusta ME [20 Feb 1845]
    George Henry 7m 11d only s/o L M LELAND at Augusta ME on 3 June [5 June 1845]
    Henry 22 formerly of Templeton MA at Augusta ME on Tues last of typhus fever [30 Jul
        1846]
    Joseph 46 at Saco ME [15 June 1839]
    Joseph 82 at Saco ME [8 June 1839]
    Sarah P 72 on 26th at Sangerville ME [26 June 1838]
    Solomon Esq 79 at Dixfield ME [24 Apr 1851]
LEMAN baby 6m s/o Joel S LEMAN formerly of Turner ME at China ME [11 Mar 1836]
    Phebe Ann 56 at Vassalboro ME [6 Dec 1849]
LEMONT Adam 78 at Bath ME [17 Oct 1850]
    Adam 84 at Bath ME [8 Aug 1844]
    Benjamin of Danville (now part of Auburn) ME accident on Mon last during
        construction upon the 17th section of the Atlantic & St Lawrence Railroad: his right
        leg was caught between a very heavy stone & a skid crushing it so badly as to render
        amputation necessary.The operation performed by Dr (Alonzo) GARCELON & Dr
        STEVENS [*Lewiston Journal*] [13 Apr 1848]
    Betsey 57 at Bath ME [16 Oct 1851]
    Betsey T 68 w/o late Capt James W LEMONT of Bath ME at Newport RI [18 June 1846]
    Charles D Capt 33 of Hallowell ME at Chicago IL on 14th of Jan [26 Feb 1846]
    Charles S 15 only s/o Charles B LEMONT at Bath ME [27 Nov 1845]

LEMONT (Cont.) James W Capt 61 at Bath ME [19 Feb 1836]

John H abt 20 at Greene ME [6 Nov 1838]

Mehitible 74 at Bath ME [13 Aug 1846]

Robert 68 at Bath ME [16 May 1850]

Roxanna abt 25 eldest d/o Robert LEMONT at Bath ME [19 Aug 1836]

Sarah Ann S d/o late Samuel S LEMONT of Bath at Portland ME [12 Sept 1844]

LENFEST Abraham 69 (s/o Peter & Lydia (Harris) Lenfest of Lewiston ME) at Palmyra ME [3 Apr 1851]

John 72 at Swanville ME [13 Sept 1849]

LENNAN David 84 at Richmond ME [26 Apr 1849]

James Col at Phipsburg ME [26 Apr 1849]

LENNEL Enoch 43 at Portland ME formerly of Minot ME [12 Aug 1843]

LENOX Robert left to his heirs a well invested fortune of $3,000,000. Left about two million to his only son - the residue to his wife & seven daughters. He accumulated this large fortune himself, beginning with little or nothing (from the *NY Sun*) [8 Feb 1840]

LEONARD Betsey 34 w/o Elkanah LEONARD at Canton ME on the 18th ult [18 Sept 1838]

Caroline abt 23 d/o Silas LEONARD Esq at Augusta ME on 17th inst of consumption [21 Oct 1847]

Elizabeth C 18 d/o Silas LEONARD at Augusta ME on 16th Jul [18 Jul 1850]

Emily Maria 25 w/o Evander W LEONARD Esq at Lexington ME? on 10 May [20 June 1850]

F S of MA he & a companion, Charles HAZELETON waylaid on their way to the Yuba Mines by eleven Mexicans. HAZELETON being well mounted, escaped by fight, but LEONARD thought to have been massacred on the 11th of Oct [*The Alta California* newspaper, San Francisco, of 15 Nov] [3 Jan 1850]

Jane C 37 w/o Edwin LEONARD at Bath ME [18 May 1848]

Lucy F 23 w/o Henry O LEONARD at Worcester MA & d/o Pliny HARRIS of Gardiner ME [9 Sept 1847]

Moses 44 at Sidney ME [4 Apr 1844]

Mrs nearly 101y a lineal descendant of John ALDEN who landed from the *Mayflower* on the Rock of Plymouth & only the fifth in descent at Raynham MA [20 Feb 1845]

Mrs of cholera w/o Sylvanus LEONARD at Hampden ME [*Bangor Daily Whig*] [16 Aug 1849]

Nathaniel 82 AmRev formerly of Middleborough MA at Buckfield ME on 4 Jul 1833]

Watson of Augusta ME left for CA (gold mines) [*Banner*] [15 Feb 1849]

William 80 formerly of Plymouth MA at Monmouth ME on 19 Jan [8 Feb 1849]

LEONARD - see BARTLETT, RATHBORNE

LePLAIN Mr set fire to his barn. He seemed very anxious for the safety of the "hens and swallows." in the back part of Gardiner ME [8 Aug 1840] & [1 Aug 1840]

LERMON Campbell 35 at Bangor ME [27 Nov 1845]

LERMOND John Esq 68 at Union ME [20 June 1840]

Martha 31 w/o Benjamin at Warren ME [23 Aug 1849]

LeROY Herman 82 an eminent merchant & father of Daniel WEBSTER's wife at New York [10 Apr 1841]

LeVENSALLER/LeVENSELLER Adam 74 at Thomaston ME [12 Jul 1849]

Amos at Waldoboro ME [13 June 1844]

Caroline 65 at Waldoboro ME [21 Oct 1847]

LEVERITT Amanda Jane 4m only child of Silas & Eliza A LEVERITT at Rockland ME [1 Jan 1852]

LEVIN Mrs wife of the member of Congress fined in the Baltimore County Court, $30 & cost for horsewhipping a Mr FITE, who had showed love to her daughter by a former husband. Her servant, who held FITE's horse, was fined $10. [6 Dec 1849]

LEWIS Abigail S 56 at Vassalboro ME on 26 Dec [16 Jan 1851]

Andrew 79y 6m at Palermo ME on Oct last of smallpox [9 Jan 1851]

Andrew 80 at Palermo ME [6 Mar 1851]

Capt of the schr *Wave* of Hallowell ME, from St Marks via Key West for New York, with cotton, tobacco & cigars was found ashore at Metemphia Beach, Accomack Co VA on 22d ult The mate died about ten days before; & the Capt being dangerously ill, his crew exhausted, his sails blown away & no one to navigate the vessel, had run her ashore. Capt LEWIS was taken to the house of Mr Thomas CROPPER, commissioner of wrecks and died on 25th. [16 Oct 1838]

Daniel Col 61 at Alfred ME [1 Apr 1833]

Desire 74 w/o Samuel LEWIS at Skowhegan ME on 5 Jan [9 Apr 1842]

Dixon H the New York papers of Wed state his death, United States senator from AL at New York City [2 Nov 1848]

Edwin E on Sun last week by his horse & wagon backing off a steep bank at Waterbury CT [6 Feb 1851]

Francis W of Portland ME on board bark *Jane* the 1st officer [2 Jul 1846]

G 70 at Brunswick ME [3 Feb 1848]

George W 22 of Liberty ME at Appleton ME [14 Nov 1850]

girl 2m d/o Capt William LEWIS at Vassalboro ME [24 June 1847]

Harriet C 2 c/o Prince B & Harriet C LEWIS at Vassalboro ME on 7 Dec [25 Dec 1851]

Harriet E 21 at Hallowell ME [4 Apr 1837]

Humphrey of Waterville ME lost overboard from fishing schr *North Star* of Camden ME on the Banks in the gale of 4th ult [13 Nov 1841]

Jane widow 39 at Hallowell ME [8 Apr 1847]

Jeremiah 52 at Brunswick ME [9 Oct 1841]

Juliett 13m d/o William & Elizabeth LEWIS at North Wayne ME on 22 Aug [6 Sept 1849]

Laura J 21 w/o Warren K LEWIS at Pittston ME [10 Apr 1851]

Lucy 77 w/o Frederick LEWIS at Whitefield ME [11 Apr 1850]

Mary 62 wid/o Capt John L LEWIS at Portland ME [16 May 1844]

Morgan Governor 87 no less distinguised by his civil acquirements than by his services during our two wars, he married a sister of John R LIVINGTONE [31 Jul 1841]

Mrs w/o Alden LEWIS at Whitefield ME [5 Sept 1840]

Osborne L 22 s/o Stephen LEWIS at Whitefield ME [15 Feb 1849]

Samuel 25 at Strong ME [24 Oct 1850]

Samuel 76 husband of Mrs Desire LEWIS at Skowhegan ME on 20 Feb [9 Apr 1842]

Stacy B 5 c/o Prince B & Harriet C LEWIS at Vassalboro ME on 2 Dec [25 Dec 1851]

Stephen 75 at Portland ME [11 Jul 1844]

Susan P w/o Capt William LEWIS at West Waterville ME [19 June 1845]

Temperance 90 a native of Barnstable MA at Waterville ME a widow [28 Jan 1847]

Thomas a seaman perished in shipwreck of the schr *William Polk*, Mr HAMILTON Capt, the Capt alone escaped [*Philidelphia Exchange Book*] [23 Jul 1846]

William 43 at Hallowell ME [2 May 1844]

LEWIS & Brother merchants of TX are from Hallowell ME [7 Aug 1851]

LEWIS - see CAUDLE, CLARK

LEYDEN Patrick an Irish laborer employed by Daniel DAVIS as a brick maker, he died at Horse Tavern by drinking nearly a quart of ice water. But a few days in this country, came from Galway Ireland. [7 Aug 1851]

LIBBEE Francis 86 AmRev at Brewer ME [11 Feb 1847]

LIBBEY Abby G 24y 3m w/o Orin LIBBY & d/o Zebulon BLAKE at Detroit ME on 22 Nov [4 Dec 1851]

Betsey 68 w/o Major Josiah LIBBY of Scarboro ME *[Portland ME Bulletin]* [30 Sept 1843]

Drusilla 81 w/o John LIBBY at Greene ME [12 Oct 1848]

Emily Mrs 39 at Saco ME [17 Jul 1851]

Frances 58 w/o Solomon LIBBY at Brunswick ME [22 Feb 1844]

Franklin abt 27y of Portland ME s/o Deac LIBBY at Kennebunk depot on the 14th inst by being crushed between a tender & a car, connected with Longley & Co's Express. *[Biddeford Herald]* [24 Aug 1848]

Hannah T 21 at Limerick ME [11 Jul 1844]

John 24 of Portland ME drowned at Little Chebeag *[Advertiser]* [27 Aug 1846]

John 85 at Greene ME [1 Mar 1849]

John at North Berwick ME [21 Mar 1837]

Lavina 52y 6m w/o Capt Enoch LIBBEY at Richmond ME on 3d Jan [9 Jan 1851]

Luther of Lebanon ME by a falling of a derrick, struck him on the head at Rockport ME [25 May 1848]

Mary 56 wid/o Joshua LIBBY at Scarboro ME [6 Dec 1849]

Mary Elizabeth 26 w/o Asa LIBBY & d/o Daniel & Elmira HILDRETH at Gardiner ME [14 Aug 1851]

Melissa M abt 2y youngest d/o Reuben LIBBY at North Turner ME on 8 May of canker rash [5 June 1841]

Mercy 23 at Lubec ME [17 June 1836]

Mrs w/o Rev LIBBY at Farmington ME [26 Nov 1846]

Olive 14 at Limerick ME [19 Aug 1847]

Phineas T 31 at Lewiston ME [2 Dec 1852]

Pyper Mrs 27 w/o Rev LIBBY at Farmington ME [26 Nov 1846]

Richard H 74 at Gardiner ME [18 Jul 1837]

Sarah W 20 d/o Caleb LIBBY at Portland ME [21 Aug 1838]

Solomon 66 at Elliot ME [8 Feb 1844]

Stephen Jr Esq, his building containing a grist mill, cabinet shop, lathing machine, together with all the tools &c was destroyed by fire on Wed 30th Oct (from *Saco Democrat*) [23 Nov 1839]

Timothy 21 of Pownal ME 4 men burnt to death in a camp in Plt No 4 on Great Works Stream [13 Feb 1835]

Tying S abt 45 at Vassalborough ME "killed while engaged in rolling logs on the bank of the Kennebec River" [13 June 1837]

William 49 at Danville (now part of Auburn) ME [25 Apr 1850]

William formerly of Gorham ME employed by Mr B WALKER endeavored to turn with a large stick of timber on a pair of wheels, the tongue hit him on the head, killed him. A worthy man abt 26, to be married in a few days, honors of Odd Fellowship at Brighton ME *[Portland Advertiser]*[11 May 1848]

Zachariah blowing rocks in a well of Joseph CRESEY of Gorham ME on Thurs & Lolby DAVIS so horribly mangled that his life is despaired of. *[Argus]*[2 Nov 1839]

LIBBY - see MERRILL

LIDDY John of Thomaston ME while blasting lime rock [3 Jul 1851]

LIGHTFOOT Peter 96 at Waldoboro ME on 3rd [13 May 1843]

LILLY Charles W 10m s/o Thomas LILLY at Augusta ME on 21 Sept [4 Oct 1849]

Mary 57 at Gardiner ME [19 Oct 1839]

LINCH John 26 at Bath ME [22 May 1845]

LINCOLN Benjamin 32 formerly of Boston MA & late professor of anatomy & surgery at
 Burlington College at Dennysville on 26th ult at the residence of his father [13 Mar
 1835]

Betsey w/o Ebed LINCOLN at Bath ME [11 June 1846]

Cotton Esq 80 at Cornishville ME [30 Apr 1846]

Dr of Dennysville ME & Mr D K CHACE of Eastport ME; their health compelled them
 to remain till yesterday, so they missed their passage on the brig *Hayden*, which was a
 total loss. [20 June 1834]

Eben 77 formerly of Hingham MA at Bath ME [9 Sept 1852]

Ezekiel 57 at Madison ME [20 Apr 1848]

Frances J 19 at Bath ME [18 Dec 1845]

George 15 s/o Daniel & Olive LINCOLN at Augusta ME on 28 Feb [13 Mar 1851]

George Capt funeral, interred in Worcester MA [5 Aug 1847]

Isaac 53 at Thomaston ME [5 Sept 1837]

Isaiah Jr 26 s/o Isiah LINCOLN Esq of Corinna ME at Manistee MI on 11 Jan [20 June
 1850]

Jeremiah at Eastport ME [29 Feb 1844]

Jerusha 90 wid/o Royal LINCOLN at Cornish ME [20 Apr 1848]

John K 25 at Thomaston ME [13 Aug 1846]

Joseph Capt commander of brig *Island* of Eastport ME lost overboard off Cape Hatteras
 in the gale of the 1st [26 Mar 1846]

Joseph seaman of Belfast ME at Charleston on board brig *Lucy* [12 Nov 1846]

Loved 95 AmRev pens at Lewiston ME [18 Apr 1850]

Lovey M 71 w/o Jacob LINCOLN at Freeport ME [14 Sept 1848]

Marcia 32 w/o Dr Isaac LINCOLN at Brunswick ME [11 Feb 1833]

Miss abt 20y at Brunswick ME in a railroad accident [12 Feb 1852]

Mitchell Capt 86 AmRev formerly of Hingham MA at Boston MA [19 Sept 1844]

Moses 89 at Perry ME [10 Oct 1850]

Moses B 9y s/o Capt Obed LINCOLN drowned in Bath ME in the dock in front of his
 father's store [27 Aug 1846]

Nathaniel 22 at Litchfield ME [11 Jan 1849]

Nathaniel Capt 61 at Durham ME [20 Mar 1845]

Otis 85 at Perry ME [29 Oct 1846]

Royal 83 AmRev at Cornish ME [25 Apr 1837]

Theodore 70 w/o Hon Theodore LINCOLN at Dennysville ME [6 Mar 1845]

Thomas S 11y at China ME [16 Oct 1841]

William Esq of Worcester an able lawyer died [*Boston Courier*] [14 Oct 1843]

LINCOLN - see DENNIS, WOODBURY

LIND Jenny married Signor BELLETTI in Canada on Fri last (N.B. she was a Swedish
 soprano, one of the famous singers of the 1800's born 1820, d 1887) [7 Aug 1851]

LINDEN Sidney Mrs of VT in CA [21 Aug 1851]

LINDSAY Andrew 45 at St Stephens New Brunswick Canada [17 June 1847]

Henry 41 at Carroll [28 Nov 1850]

LINDSEY H G O Capt 30 at Norridgewock ME [7 May 1846]

Mary 25 w/o Capt H G O LINDSEY of Norridgewock ME at the Insane Hospital
 (Augusta) ME on 11th inst [21 Aug 1845]

Matthew Esq 69 at Wells ME on 13th inst kept a Public House in that place 43y & was
 Postmaster 38y previous to Jan last when he resigned on account of his health [25
 Mar 1843]

Miss & Miss GOODRICH while attempting to cross the river near St John New
 Brunswick Canada were found upon the ice frozen to death [28 Feb 1850]

Nathaniel 82 at Rockland ME [19 Sept 1850]

LINDSEY (Cont.) Susan 48 w/o Col A LINDSEY at Auburn ME [5 Feb 1852]

LINES Ruhamah 25th yr of Dresden ME at Bath ME on 25th ult [4 Jan 1834]

LINN Abigail 55 w/o Nathaniel LINN at Windsor ME on 28 Dec [30 Jan 1851]

Alonzo 18 s/o Joseph LINN of Windsor ME at New Orleans on 19 Jan [31 Jul 1845]

John 29y 9m s/o David LINN of Augusta ME at Bradley ME on 13th June [1 Jul 1852]

Lewis R Dr (U. S. senator) at St Genevieve MO [28 Oct 1843]

Mary Ann 33 w/o David LINN at Augusta ME [22 June 1848]

LINNELL Samuel drowned at Corporation Mills in North Bangor ME [5 Feb 1852]

Samuel L 20 s/o Samuel LINNELL of Palermo ME at Boston ME on 8th inst of smallpox [30 May 1840]

Stephen W 23 at Otisfield ME [9 Dec 1852]

LINSCOTT (Abraham?) attempted to murder his wife (Elizabeth? LITTLEFIELD?) on Mon by cutting her throat, but it did not cause immediate death. She will probably die. Then attempted to cut his own throat with a broad axe, completely, dividing the wind pipe. Intended to murder his family, consisting of wife, mother-in-law, & 5 ch. L was laboring under the effects of delirium tremens at Cornish ME [24 Jul 1851]

Edgar A 6y 7m s/o Hon Joseph A LINSCOTT at Phillips ME [4 Mar 1847]

Joel died by being thrown from a wagon at Alfred ME [1 Nov 1852]

Joshua a bachelor abt 45y of New Castle ME committed suicide on the night before Christmas by cutting his throat with a penknife [18 Jan 1840]

Mary Blake 5y 3m 16d d/o Hon J A LINSCOTT at Phillips ME on 15 Nov [23 Nov 1848]

Sarah 39 w/o Ebenezer LINSCOTT at Damariscotta ME [1 Jan 1852]

Susan H 27 w/o Samuel LINSCOTT & d/o William CHANEY of Whitefield ME at Paris ME on 24th Nov [13 Dec 1849]

William at Jefferson ME [13 Jan 1848]

LINTEN Mr killed on Tues last on the railroad left a wife with 6 ch at Calais ME [*Calais Advertizer*][30 Jan 1851]

LITCHFIELD Capt body picked up 30 miles from Cape Cod on 26th inst, of the schr *Maine* of Cohasset (from the *Boston MA Bee*) [3 Sept 1846]

Clement 3y s/o William & Mrs Wenefree LITCHFIELD at Brunswick ME [19 Sept 1844]

Harriet S 25 at Foxcroft ME [14 Nov 1850]

LITTLE child 14m c/o Deac Josiah LITTLE at Winthrop ME of scarlet fever [7 May 1842]

Doty Esq 87 formerly of Marshfield MA at Castine ME [29 Jul 1852]

Edward & Thomas B and Ira PURRINGTON on the evening of the 3d inst the carpet factory owned by these three men was destroyed by fire at Lewiston Falls ME. Nothing was saved. The fire orginated in the room for drying wood. There was no insurance and the loss is estimated at not less than $7000 (from the *Kennebec Journal*) [8 Feb 1840]

Eliza 41 at Bath ME [14 Nov 1844]

Eliza married Nelson AUBLEY [28 Oct 1843]

Eunice 46 w/o Thomas B LITTLE Esq at Auburn ME [16 May 1844]

Fanny widow 88 formerly of Newcastle ME at Bristol ME [15 Oct 1846]

Henry W seaman s/o Col Henry LITTLE of Bangor ME lost overboard from ship *Oregon* on his passage from Liverpool to New Orleans [4 June 1842]

Luther Esq at Marshfield on Tues last. AmRev pens & first lieut of the *Protector* which ship, it will be remembered engaged with & captured the *Admiral Duff*, a ship of superior force. (from the *Post*) [9 Apr 1842]

Mary D w/o Mr Thomas LITTLE at Nobleborough ME [6 June 1847]

Micajah 88 at East Thomaston ME [6 June 1850]

Otis Major 77 at Castine ME [5 Mar 1846]

LITTLE (Cont.) Rhumah 92y 7m wid/o Capt Joshua LITTLE at Whitefield ME [18 Feb 1847]

Samuel 79 at Pittston ME [11 Jan 1849]

Thomas Esq 44 at Nobleborough ME [20 June 1837]

Timothy Dr 73 at Portland ME [6 Dec 1849]

Valentine Rev formerly pastor of the Congregational Church at Lovell ME at Salisbury NH on 2 June [9 Sept 1852]

William Pitt Fessenden 21 s/o Moses LITTLE Esq at Windham ME [1 Jan 1846]

Willis formerly a periodical dealer in Boston MA executed in Havana Cuba [18 Sept 1851]

LITTLE - see HALL, MOODY

LITTLEFIELD A Z Esq 48 formerly of Skowhegan ME at Sheboyan Falls WI of smallpox [11 Feb 1847]

Aaron 76 at Kennebunkport ME [10 Sept 1846]

Abner 25 at Portland ME [6 Feb 1845]

Abner late of Greene ME (d 24 May 1827 gravestone, Lane Cem, Greene ME & a probate record about minor children dated 1836) [14 Oct 1836]

Charles 50 at Belgrade ME [31 Jan 1850]

Elijah 73 AmRev pens of Durham ME at Little River Village (Lisbon) on 9 Jan, walked half a mile home to village & in conversation fell dead in the street [12 Feb 1836]

Eliza w/o Enoch LITTLEFIELD Esq of Auburn ME committed suicide on Wed last (from *E Argus* of Portland ME) [26 June 1851]

Ephraim 2nd officer of Portland ME lost & drowned the barque *William Fales*, Capt William THOMES, of this port (Portland ME) was lost in Wells Bay ME on Wed evening at 9 o'clock, 13 persons on board, eight were lost including every officer. Through the attention of our friend, George M FREEMAN of Cape Needick (Old York, where the barque drove) [26 Feb 1842]

Eunice 67 w/o William B LITTLEFIELD at Chelsea ME [2 Sept 1852]

Harriet 22 at Sangerville ME [9 Jul 1846]

Horace 5 s/o Ivory LITTLEFIELD at Chesterville ME [26 Feb 1846]

Huldah A Mrs 41 at Alfred ME [27 Sept 1849]

Isaac 72 formerly of Lyman ME at Norridgewock ME [9 Jul 1846]

Jane L 18y 10m d/o William B LITTLEFIELD at Augusta ME [16 Jul 1846]

John H 19 drowned near Frankfort ME [6 June 1850]

Moses 27 one of the crew of the schr *Margaret Ann* arrived at Newburyport on Sun from Castine after eating his breakfast on board ...died on deck was of Penobscot ME where he left a wife & one child [*Traveller*] [14 Oct 1847]

Mrs 82 widow of AmRev at York ME [28 May 1846]

Mrs w/o Walter LITTLEFIELD at Brunswick ME [18 Jul 1844]

Nathaniel 43 at England on the 27th Aug. Merchant of New York, a native of Hallowell ME [12 Oct 1839]

Sarah w/o John LITTLEFIELD formerly of Belgrade ME at Skowhegan ME [25 Sept 1845]

Uriah Jr 22 of Auburn ME s/o Uriah LITTLEFIELD was killed on Tues, accidental [*Lewiston Journal*] [30 Aug 1849]

Zebediah 94 formerly of Fairfield ME at Sheboygan Falls WI on 20 Nov [20 Jan 1848]

LITTLEFIELD - see LINSCOTT

LIVERMORE Sarah 81 relict of the late Maj William LIVERMORE at Hallowell ME on 3d inst [25 Sept 1838]

LIVINGSTON Edward on 23 May 1836 at Redhook NY. A jurist & statesman, member of Congress [13 Jan 1837]

LIVINGSTON (Cont.) Edward Esq at Albany on Tues morning last. Served as clerk of the assembly, district attorney, city representative & speaker of the Assembly [27 June 1840]

George eloped with the w/o Austin McGUIRE, the colored inhabitants of Franklin St New Haven thrown into tribulation. Two departed made manifest their appeal to the tribunal of Justice. It was adjudged that "even exchange was no robbery" & the said McGUIRE & Mrs LIVINGSTON, also agreed to take each other "for better or for worse" & returned on their way rejoicing. *[New Haven Courier]* [12 Sept 1844] [An early account of wife swapping]

LIVINGSTONE John R only one or two years younger than Gov Morgan LEWIS. One of his sisters married Gov Morgan LEWIS & one married John ARMSTRONG. There are in Duchess Co on the Hudson River & within a few miles of each other three veterans of the Revolution united ages are about 260 yrs [31 Jul 1841]

LOANE Adam 45 at Fairfield ME [17 Feb 1848]

LOCK Samuel Esq 49 at Belfast ME [6 Mar 1851]

Samuel Jr 21 at Mt Vernon ME [11 Dec 1845]

LOCKE Anna 68 wid/o Tristram LOCKE at Gardiner ME [12 Mar 1846]

Caleb Esq 33 counselor at law of Gardiner ME at Biddeford ME [10 Apr 1835]

Daniel Mrs at Augusta ME [6 Nov 1835]

Elizabeth H 67 w/o Samuel LOCKE at Hallowell ME on 15 Apr [25 Apr 1850]

Frank S 2y 9m s/o H B & E W LOCKE at Augusta ME [1 Jul 1852]

Hannah 50 w/o James R LOCKE at Mt Vernon ME on 29 May [4 June 1851]

Mary 62 w/o Gen Joseph LOCKE at Bloomfield ME [5 Dec 1844]

LOCKHART John P 35 formerly of Bath ME at Salem MA [28 Aug 1845]

LOCKWELL Andrew 20 of Boston MA drowned in the pond by the upsetting of a boat at East Vassalboro ME [24 June 1847]

LOCKWOOD Mils of Stanwich CT met with a very sudden and lamentable death on the 24th ult. He went into a lot not far from his house, for the purpose of doctoring a horse, and it appears that after he had caught the horse and commenced operating, the animal started off, with Mr M holding on by the mane, but he was soon thrown down and his head coming in contact with a rock, it is supposed he never stirred after [26 Oct 1839]

Noah 91 of the smallpox at Greenwich CT on 8th June; one of the 1st to enter the army at the outbreak of the Revolution [17 Jul 1845]

LOGAN William on the ledge near Sewall's Mills on Mon 15th quite severely injured one of his eyes by the premature explosion of a charge upon the railroad [25 May 1848]

LOMBARD Charles 8 s/o Ephraim H LOMBARD Esq at Readfield ME in consequence of a fall from a horse [16 Jan 1838]

Daniel H the teacher at Chelsea, who lost his life by falling through the ice near Boston MA last week was formerly a resident of Readfield ME [25 Mar 1843]

James 89 at Belgrade ME on 18 May [23 May 1850]

Joseph 27 at Saco ME [29 Mar 1849]

Lucy 35 at West Bath ME [17 Sept 1846]

Mary A 7y d/o D H LOMBARD Esq at Readfield ME [16 Nov 1833]

Mary Ann 19 at West Bath ME [21 Dec 1848]

Solomon H master 28 lost of the schr *Commerce's* crew lost at Truro on Sat last. Also James LOMBARD 26; Solomon RICH 30; Charles RICH 13; Thomas MAYO 23; Sewall WORCESTER 25; John L RICH 14; Elisha RICH 14; Elisha RICH 17; Ezra TURNER 21; Reuben PIERCE 30 all of Truro MA; five of whom married. Up to Tues, none of the bodies had washed on shore [3 Oct 1844]

LONG Capt & Mr STEWART of ME 23, a boat steerer, were washed overboard, loss of the whaleship *Mabile* of New Bedford [*Boston Adv*] [19 Oct 1848]

Edward 45 at Eastport ME [11 Feb 1847]

Henry from southern bondage at New York NY [16 Jan 1851] & sold at Richmond VA for $750 ae 25y an experienced tavern servant [30 Jan 1851] & for sale at Atlanta GA [20 Feb 1851] & arrested for picking a man's pocket & making abolition speeches to his brother slaves. [14 Aug 1851]

Lucy of western part of OH breach of promise against Hiram SMITHSON. Hiram said in his defense that he was willing enough to marry Lucy, but that he was not quite ready; that she was altogether in too big a hurry ... [16 Jul 1842]

Nicholas seaman fell overboard in a gale & lost from *Ellen Perkins* on route from New York to Sisal [26 Feb 1846]

William R the ticket master at the Lowell depot by his head coming in contact with a bridge between Andover & Lowell. His wife & son were with him. [4 Jul 1840]

LONGFELLOW David abt 60 at Winthrop ME on 28 Dec [3 Jan 1850]

Ellen 16 d/o Hon Stephen LONGFELLOW at Portland ME [29 Aug 1834]

George 18m s/o Nathan LONGFELLOW at Augusta ME [15 Mar 1849]

Jacob 81 at Whitefield ME [5 Sept 1850]

John A abt 25 at Winthrop ME suddenly on Mon last [12 Dec 1840]

John Adams abt 2y s/o George A LONGFELLOW at Winthrop ME [14 Mar 1844]

Mary 39 at South Whitefield ME [18 Mar 1836]

Mary P 23y w/o Prof Henry W LONGFELLOW recently of Brunswick ME & d/o Hon Barrett POTTER of Portland ME at Rotterdam on 26 Nov 1835 [29 Jan 1836]

Orlando S 26 at Augusta ME on 16th ult [12 Dec 1844]

Sabe 52 w/o Sewall LONGFELLOW at Augusta ME [13 Aug 1842]

Sally 60 w/o Green LONGFELLOW at Palermo ME [15 June 1848]

Stephen Hon 73 at Portland ME [*Argus*] [9 Aug 1849]

Velina 46 w/o Green A LONGFELLOW at Winthrop ME on 8th Jul [15 Jul 1852]

LONGLEY Albert M 25 at Norridgewock ME on 14th Jul [1 Aug 1850]

Aphia W ae 29 w/o William P LONGLEY at Norridgewock ME [24 Oct 1850]

Benjamin 76 at Norridgewock ME on 16 Apr [29 Apr 1852]

Cnnthia P (*sic:* more likely Cynthia) P 40 w/o Obadiah LONGLEY at Waterville ME [13 Feb 1851]

Columbia Mrs 41 at Paris ME [23 Jan 1851]

Hannah H 25 at Norridgewock ME [16 Jan 1851]

Judith 76 w/o John S LONGLEY at Norridgewock ME [23 Aug 1849]

Meriam 89 relict of Nehemiah LONGLEY at Sidney ME [25 Apr 1837]

Sheldon 23y 11m of Sydney ME at Vicksburg MS [1 Jan 1842]

LONSTRETH Peter notice in the *Germantown PA Telegraph* a few weeks since living as they (see MERRIGOE) did neighbors together & their deaths occurring nearly at the same time, united ages 206yrs at Bensalem Bucks Co [26 Oct 1848]

LOOMIS Erastus 70 at Kennebec ME [20 May 1852]

Hannah 63y 6m widow at Monmouth ME on 2d inst [13 May 1847]

Samuel 60 at Skowhegan ME [5 Aug 1847]

Sarah A 10 d/o Luther LOOMIS at Haydenville burning at school-house [*Springfield Republican*] [2 Jan 1851]

Sarah Anne 40 w/o Prof J R LOOMIS at Waterville ME [11 Mar 1852]

LOPES Emanuel (apprentice) of Malaga, lost in the wreck of brig *Washington*, RIDER Capt [*Transcript*] [2 Oct 1835]

LOPEZ Ricardo executed at San Jose on Fri for the murder of United States dragoon [21 Aug 1851]

LOPEZ - see De OCA

LORA - see LARA

LORAINE C Mr & Mr GARNER & Mr THOMAS all of Washington Co OH on the
evening of 9th says the *Cincinnati Gazette* were seized on the Ohio shore by a body of
men from VA & put in jail at Parkersburg, upon the charge that they had aided the
escaped slaves. In VA, the people of Parkersburg are armed & prepared to repel any
attempt to release the prisoners ... In Washington Co ... to tear down the jail ... [31
Jul 1845]

LORD Abraham 75 at Webster (now called Sabattus) ME [13 Dec 1849]

Abram 40 at Belfast ME [29 Apr 1852]

Abram of Gardiner ME saved from drowning when the steam packet *New England* sank.
It left Boston for Bath & Gardiner ME and had an accident with the schr *Curlew* on
31 May [12 June 1838]

Almira B 25 w/o Capt Edwin LORD at Ellsworth ME [6 Feb 1845]

boy 10 c/o William LORD was killed by accident at his father's mill in Vassalboro ME &
his sister 8 was hurt. [3 Jul 1841]

Edward P 19 drowned at Ellsworth at the head of the Falls on the 5th *inst [Ellsworth
Democrat]* [22 June 1848]

Edwin 21 at Gardiner ME [14 Nov 1844]

Emma Jane 19 at Gardiner ME [18 May 1848]

George 49 formerly of Norway ME at Alexander ME [2 Jul 1846]

Hannah 76 a native of Newburyport MA w/o James LORD at West Gardiner ME on 9th
inst [25 Jan 1840]

Hannah 76 w/o James LORD at West Gardiner ME on 9th inst a native of Newburyport
MA [25 Jan 1840]

Heard Deac 70 at Trenton [21 May 1846]

Isaac 73 at Farmingdale ME [6 May 1852]

Isaac M; On the 28th of Dec in the county of York, two young men, brothers, started
from their father's house in Limington to go to Parsonsfield ME. On passing a piece
of woodland in which men were engaged in felling trees, a large tree fell across the
road, the limbs of which struck both the young men, killing the eldest brother. [1 Jan
1839]

Ivory 30 at Gardiner ME [2 Jan 1841]

James 63 at Limerick ME [20 Feb 1851]

John 47 of Hallowell ME at Brazos Santiago on 1 Mar of cholera [17 May 1849]

Joshua Capt 72 at Gardiner ME [13 Nov 1838]

Julia Ann 29 w/o Augustine LORD at Hallowell ME [10 Apr 1845]

Margaeret 65 w/o Gershon LORD at Harmony ME [11 June 1846]

Martha A 35 w/o Stephen LORD at Hallowell ME on Thurs last of consumption [26 Dec
1837]

Martha E 39 w/o John LORD of Hallowell ME at Winthrop ME on 31st ult very
suddenly [13 Jan 1848]

Mary E abt 22 w/o Alva LORD at Harmony ME [15 May 1845]

Oliver B late of Farmington ME his est notice names minor children: Reuben H LORD,
Olive B LORD & James B LORD [16 Mar 1839]

Peter 68 at his residence in Vassalboro ME on 31st Apr (see obit) [13 June 1837]

Rebecca D 79 at Hallowell ME [3 Aug 1848]

Rev died of cholera at Cincinnati OH on 13 Jul [19 Jul 1849]

Sally 28 at Webster (now Sabattus) ME [27 Dec 1849]

Samuel 48y 10m at Augusta ME on 26th ult [1 Nov 1849]

Sarah H 30 w/o Jos D LORD at Hallowell ME [14 Sept 1848]

Tobias with Jabez HOBSON & Stephen W WOOD as principal owners suffered the loss
fire at Steep Falls on the Limington side ME, the double saw mill, grist mill, together

LORD (Cont.) with a box machine and a number of shingle, lath & clapboard machines were wholly consumed by fire on Sun last [*Union*] [11 Feb 1847]

Wentworth Elder 89 AmRev at Parsonsfield ME [2 Apr 1846]

LORD - see Ellsworth ME

LORETTE Antonio F at Portland ME [20 June 1844]

LORING Hannah 47 w/o Ammi M LORING at North Yarmouth [25 Nov 1836]

Hannah F 64 w/o John LORING at Norridgewock ME [2 Oct 1841]

infant 1y c/o John H LORING Esq at Guilford ME [30 Mar 1839]

James a printer 80 at Boston ME [25 Jul 1850]

John abt 70 a Deac at Norridgewock ME [26 Dec 1850]

Mrs 61 wid/o Lot LORING late of North Yarmouth ME by a fall in her house at Yarmouth ME [17 June 1852]

Richmond Esq 40 at Shirley ME [7 Sep 1848]

LORING - see WATSON

LOTHROP a child of Leander LOTHROP at Hallowell ME [14 Dec 1833]

Achsah 20y at Leeds ME on 9th inst of consumption [22 Apr 1833]

Cornelius W of Taunton MA tending a shingle machine in Raynham when the saw broke & a piece hit Mr L cutting off the main artery of his neck, & producing almost instant death [23 Dec 1847]

David W 42 at Belfast ME [7 June 1849]

George Esq 74 at Leeds ME on 4 Mar [16 Mar 1839]

Leavitt Hon 55 at Leeds ME on 17 Apr [10 May 1849]

LOUD Lydia 20 at Pittston ME [17 Aug 1833]

Silas Capt 35 of Pittston ME at Mobile AL on 1 Jul on board brig *James Marshall* [8 Aug 1850]

Solomon 21 "dround" (*sic*) on Mon the 5th inst about 11am, while three men were in a boat fishing between between Bar Island & Cox's Cove [17 Aug 1839]

LOUGEE J Cowan w/o Alvah T LOUGEE at Stetson ME [14 June 1849]

Louis Philippe - see BRADSTREET [18 May 1848]

LOVE George of Seabrook NH the crew of the *Traveller* supposed lost [16 Oct 1851]

Love (the law of Love) In 1617, the General Court of Massachusetts enacted, that if any young man attempt to address any young woman without the consent of her parents, or, in case of their absence of a neighboring magistrate of the County Court, he should be fined 5 pounds for the first offense, 10 pounds for the second & imprisonment for the third. In 1660, Capt Daniel BLAKE was fined the first named sum, but let off for one pound, conditionally, "for making love to Edmand BRIDGE's daughter without her parent's consent." [20 June 1840]

LOVEJOY Amos Lawrence Esq has been chosen speaker to the House of Representatives in Oregon. Mr. Lovejoy is from Wayne ME & stdied law with Seth MAY Esq of Winthrop ME. [26 Aug 1847 & A letter from Oregon dated 23rd May last, the election for Gov to come off on the 1st Mon of June. Geo ABERNETHY (Whig) & A L LOVEJOY (Dem) the principal candidates ... only issue, Liquor or No Liquor ... Mr L above is the Wayne ME boy of whom we spake two weeks since, no doubt now the Gov. It takes the Yankees to do things. [N.B. Oregon was not a territory until 1848 & a state until 1859] [9 Sept 1847]

Ardeane 4y 8m c/o Charles & Maria LOVEJOY at Augusta ME on 28 Oct [4 Nov 1847]

Benjamin abt 2y s/o Joseph LOVEJOY at Augusta ME [3 Oct 1844]

Betsey 30 w/o Henry LOVEJOY at Sidney ME [3 Apr 1841]

Daniel Rev of Albion ME on Sat last committed suicide by hanging himself [*Hallowell Advertiser*, Aug 14] [17 Aug 1833]

E P at Alton IL late editor of the *Observer* killed a short time since in consequence of an attempt to revive the *Alton Observer*, an abolition paper which has been the cause of

LOVEJOY (Cont.) one or two riots before. Mr Bishop was also killed. Seven other were wounded. The mob succeeded in destroying the *Observer* press. [28 Nov 1837]

Eliza Arris 20 d/o widow Eliza LOVEJOY at Thomaston ME [28 Oct 1847]

Eliza F 45 w/o H B LOVEJOY Esq at Fayette ME on 23 May [10 June 1852]

Enoch 65 at East Thomaston ME [7 Dec 1848]

George H 18m s/o Charles & Maria LOVEJOY at Augusta ME [26 Nov 1846]

Hannah 42 w/o Jesse LOVEJOY at Fayette ME [18 Jul 1840]

Hartwell 28 "a deaf & dumb" (deaf mute) & Henry SAFFORD 17 drowned in Winthrop Upper Pond on Fri last week, Daniel CHANDLER was with them but swam ashore [8 Jul 1833]

Joseph formerly of Sidney ME at Raisen MI on 14 Sept [23 Oct 1845]

Losana 2y d/o Augustus LOVEJOY at Augusta ME on 27 Jan [7 Feb 1850]

Martha 93 widow of Lt John LOVEJOY at Fayette ME [18 Nov 1847]

Mary E 67 w/o Eben C LOVEJOY at Fayette ME [3 June 1847]

Mr drowned from the schr *Granville*, Mr SNOW Capt, near George's Island at the mouth of George's River was one of two men of Thomaston ME the other was ELMES [16 May 1837]

Mr killed in the riot at Alton native of ME, grad of (Colby College). His widow remained senseless, with but little hopes of her surviving the shock. In a late issue dated 19 Dec 1837 "Intimation has been given from several different quarters of persons who are willing to go to Alton IL & take charge of the *Observer*. The *Zion's Herald* states a chergyman of Boston MA is ready for this service." [5 Dec 1837]

Mrs renders her thanks to the people of Winthrop ME village for their kind & successful efforts to find the body of her son who was drowned on Fri last & for their continued attention till the body was buried. [8 Jul 1833]

Nathan Ellis is permitted to trade or act for himself same as if he was 21y signed Nathan LOVEJOY of Wayne ME on 26 Jan 1841 [30 Jan 1841]

Nathaniel 90 at Vassalboro ME [31 May 1849]

Rachael H 11y 11m c/o Charles & Maria LOVEJOY at Augusta ME on 23 Oct [4 Nov 1847]

Tabitha Ann 15m on 11 Jan & Willaim Augustus 6y on 6 Jan the only c/o Jonathan & Mrs Ruth LOVEJOY at Livermore ME [17 June 1833]

Thomas 58 at Kilmarnock ME [25 May 1848]

V R of Gardiner ME saved from drowning when the steam packet *New England* sank. It left Boston for Bath & Gardiner ME and had an accident with the schr *Curlew* on 31 May [12 June 1838]

William 62 of Sidney ME at Eliza City CA on 19 May [29 Aug 1850]

LOVEJOY - see ELMES

LOVELL Caroline w/o Capt Joseph LOVELL at Wilton ME on 9th inst [21 Feb 1837]

David abt 16 s/o Luther LOVELL at Livermore ME [2 Sept 1843]

George abt 17 s/o Amasa LOVELL at Livermore caused by the kick of a colt the 1st part of the summer last [6 Nov 1841]

Hannah B 39 w/o Sewall LOVELL at Abbot ME [2 Jul 1846]

Harriet abt 7y d/o Luther LOVELL at Livermore ME [24 Sept 1842]

LOVERING Cornelia S 23 w/o A W LOVERING at Exeter NH on 19 May [27 May 1852]

Nathaniel 79 a native of Exeter NH AmRev at Winthrop ME on 29 Dec [14 Jan 1843]

Taylor 52 at Lisbon ME (on 25 Apr 1851, VR p 321) [8 May 1851]

LOVETT - see SAVAGE

LOW Betsey 57 w/o Arthur at China ME on 22 Dec [26 Dec 1850]

Daniel 90 at Frankfort ME [28 Feb 1850]

David 91 AmRev at Buckfield ME [11 Oct 1849]

John 33 at Pittston ME [23 Mar 1848]

LOW (Cont.) John 49 at Saco ME [17 May 1849]
    Mary Mrs 82 at Bath ME [6 June 1850]
    Orin 44 at Waterville ME [9 Aug 1849]
    Robert AmRev pens 88 at Livermore Falls ME [20 Jan 1848]
    Samuel Stilman 26 of Bath ME at Quincy [3 Aug 1841]
    Solomon 45 at Norridgewock ME [9 Feb 1839]
    Stephen 82 at Alfred ME [24 Jul 1851]
LOW - see LARRABEE
LOWDER Samuel Capt 83 at Bangor ME [29 Jul 1847]
LOWELL Abner Mrs abt 60 at Hallowell ME [6 Mar 1851]
    Anna 22 w/o W W LOWELL at Calais ME [8 Oct 1846]
    Charles 24 at Chesterville ME on 8 Aug [26 Aug 1847]
    Chloe 45 w/o Joishua B LOWELL at Farmington ME [19 Dec 1850]
    Eliphalet 70 at Bath ME [6 Nov 1845]
    Harriet 26 at Farmington ME [6 Nov 1838]
    Henry of Hallowell ME a seaman lost overboard from brig *Mary Averill* [13 Feb 1835]
    James Capt 49 at Bath ME [16 Apr 1842]
    James Jr 33 s/o Hon James LOWELL at Lewiston ME [15 Aug 1850]
    John 70 at Roxbury MA died of apoplexy [28 Mar 1840]
    John 83 at Bath ME [6 Nov 1845]
    John 89 AmRev at Gardiner ME [26 Nov 1846]
    Julia A H 20 at East Thomaston ME [22 Jan 1839]
    Leonard M formerly of Farmington ME at Abbot ME [12 Oct 1839]
    Martha d/o William Winthrop ME at Augusta ME on Tues last [22 June 1839]
    Mary 56 w/o Oliver LOWELL Esq at Abbott [30 Jan 1851]
    Mrs w/o William LOWELL At Winthrop ME on 29th inst [6 Feb 1841]
    Pamelia 41 w/o David LOWELL at Alna [18 Mar 1836]
    Reuben 68 at Abbot ME formerly of Farmington ME [2 Oct 1841]
    Rosamus K 49 formerly of Thomaston ME at Farmington ME [11 Jul 1837]
    Roscoe 4y s/o James & Eliza LOWELL At Gardiner ME drowned on 11th inst [22 Aug 1837]
    Thomas M 24 at Machias ME [10 Dec Dec 1846]
LOWNEY Hannah 14 d/o N M LOWNEY Esq at Belfast ME [14 Oct 1847]
    William R Esq 64 at Sebec ME [12 Sept 1850]
LOWRANCE Joseph deck passenger of Park County IA a serious accident happened on board the steamboat *George Collier* on the 6th inst on her passage from New Orleans to St Louis MO [25 May 1839]
LOWRY Nancy L 47 of Charlestown MA at Augusta ME on 10th inst [23 Aug 1849]
    Stephen Jr 19 at Charleston MA on 14 Dec [26 Dec 1850]
LRASH Lucinda & Octavia (sisters found drowned in the cabin) of Whitefield ME lost on the *Maine* of Bath ME, James BLIN of Dresden ME, master [16 Oct 1841] [N.B. LRASH we think shouls read TRASH/TRASK]
LRASH - see HAMMOND
LUCAS child youngest of Richard LUCAS at Bath ME [1 Jan 1846]
    Henry drowned one of 27 boys of the Farm School when between Fort Independence & Thompson's Island [7 May 1842]
    Mr 48y was killed while blasting a ledge on Sat last on the railroad near the Richmond line he was a widower & has children living in Boston MA [11 Sept 1851]
LUCE Alsbury 39 at Farmington ME [30 Jul 1846]
    child of Gorham A LUCE at Winthrop ME [11 Sept 1835]
    Freeman 73 at South Newburg ME [3 Oct 1850]

LUCE (Cont.) Leonard 53 at Industry ME [30 Sept 1852]
Seth 83 at Union ME [1 Apr 1833]
Solomon Mrs of New Vineyard ME committed suicide last week by taking laudanum, having become deranged by embracing the doctrines of Millerism. She was the d/o David PRATT Esq & has left 5 or 6 small children [*Norridgewock Workingman*] [7 Mar 1844]
William Esq 39 at Appleton ME [18 Jul 1850]
LUDLOW Prudence 75 at Eastport ME [2 Jul 1846]
LUFKIN Dana 23 s/o Aaron LUFKIN at Mexico ME [4 Mar 1852]
Eleanor 57 w/o Jacob LUFKIN at Rumford ME [22 May 1851]
Jacob B Deac 70 at North Yarmouth ME [2 Nov 1848]
Joseph R Capt 51 at Deer Isle ME [24 Apr 1851]
Moses 90 at Gloucester MA AmRev & two years during the war a drummer in WASHINGTON's Life Guard, at the battles of Lexington, Bunker Hill, Trenton & Saratoga [25 June 1846]
Thomas Capt 23 at the loss of the schr *Orbit* at sea near Isle au Haut on 27 Dec [9 Jan 1851]
LUKE Jonathan 84 at Jay ME [2 May 1850]
LUKIN Dana 23 s/o Aaron LUFKIN at Mexico ME on 31 Jan [4 Mar 1852]
LULL Hester Ann 22 d/o Rev Joseph LULL at Readfield ME [1 Jul 1847]
LUMBERT Mary 16 at Bangor ME [11 Jul 1844]
LUMMUS - see BRADLEY
LUNAR Mr in an explosion at the wagon & plow factory of H A WHITBECK at Chicago IL [28 Feb 1850]
LUNDY Benjamin recently in Hennepin IL. He was a native of New Jersey, was one of the most indefatigable men that ever trod the earth & he did tread it steadily from Maine to Mexico on behalf of the blacks, publishing a paper *in transitu*, amiable in his disposition, courteous in his manners, & of a Christian faith (judging from his practice) he offended few by his zeal & won many by his mildness. (*U.S. Gaz*) [p. 294 #37 Vol VII, 28 Sept 1839]
LUNT Cyrus K 32 at Long Island Hancock Co ME [25 May 1848]
Edwin R s/o Capt Daniel LUNT of Lincolnville ME supposed to have fallen at the battle of Buena Vista as reported among the missing [12 Aug 1847]
Hannah born in 1750 & wanted only a few days of 86y w/o Amos LUNT at Brunswick ME [9 Dec 1836]
Horace 20 a grade of Bowdoin College at York ME on 18th inst [3 Oct 1837]
Lydia 46 w/o John LUNT at Kennebunkport ME [29 Oct 1846]
Priscilla Mrs 92y 9m at Bath ME [8 Feb 1849]
Samuel 35 at Clinton ME [9 Mar 1839]
Sarah 53 wid/o Capt James LUNT at Westbrook ME [6 Dec 1849]
LUNT - see COLBY
LURTON Levi 63 of Skowhegan ME at Provincetown MA [18 Nov 1847]
LUZENBURY Dr restored the sight of a Seminole squaw by an operation at New Orleans [8 May 1838]
LYELL Rev DR 74 rector of Christ Church of New York NY [16 Mar 1848]
LYFORD Abby Maria 2y 2m only child of Francis LYFORD at Hallowell ME [12 Mar 1842]
Betsey 52 w/o Oliver S LYFORD at East Livermore ME [12 Mar 1846]
Betsey abt 19 d/o Oliver LYFORD at Livermore ME [12 Feb 1846]
child infant of F LYFORD at Hallowell ME [11 Sept 1845]
Francis 90y 7m at Livermore ME [18 Mar 1847]

LYFORD (Cont.) Hannah 37 w/o Levi LYFORD at East Livermore ME [9 Nov 1848]
   Mrs 82 w/o Nathaniel LYFORD at East Livermore ME [27 Nov 1845]
   Nathaniel 89 at East Livermore ME AmRev [24 Oct 1850]
LYMAN Caroline B 30 w/o S R LYMAN Esq at Portland ME [21 Mar 1840]
LYMAN - see ANTHONY, SMITH
LYNCH Eben 20 at Bath ME [11 Mar 1852]
   George W 19 at Belfast ME [13 June 1844]
   Jeremiah one of 27 boys of the Farm School drowned off Fort Independence &
      Thompson's Island, PS "Mr MORRISON, the Superintendent of the Farm School, put
      off in a boat, after the disaster, and picked up the bodies of two of the boys, one of
      which, Jeremaih LYNCH, was still alive and was resuscitated. The other was beyond
      recovery" (from the *Boston Courier* of Sat last) [7 May 1842]
   Lydia at Branch Pond [19 Aug 1852]
   Samuel a member of the Hibernia Greens, engaged in cleaning his musket, when he set
      the trigger, pulled it & the entire contents entered the head of his sister Elizabeth
      LYNCH abt 14y [*Boston Bee*] [27 July 1844]
LYNKS George in New York on Sun by falling into the gutter of the street in which the
   scalding water from a distillery was running [9 May 1840]
LYNN Charles H 21y 11m s/o James & Betsey LYNN formerly of Windsor ME at Lee
   Centre IL on 18 Oct [2 Dec 1852]
   Elizabeth 23 w/o Anderson J LYNN at Hallowell ME [19 Feb 1852]
   Joseph 62 at Windsor ME [15 Oct 1846]
   Lydia Ann 17y 5m w/o James R LYNN at Augusta ME [23 May 1850]
LYON Abigail C 65 w/o Tabor LYON at Readfield ME [5 Oct 1848]
   Charles Henry 22 at Augusta ME on 22d ult of smallpox [15 Jul 1847]
   Eliab 86 at Readfield ME [23 Aug 1849]
   Lucy 74 at Augusta ME [8 May 1835]
   Lucy L Dora 4y 3m at Augusta ME on 27 June [8 Jul 1852]
   Mary Abby 2y 4m d/o William H LYON at Readfield ME [27 May 1847]
   Pliny abt 50 at Augusta ME on 26 Jul [9 Aug 1849]
   Rachel 92 of Readfield ME at Farmington ME [18 Jan 1849] & 92 w/o Eliab LYON of
      Readfield ME at Farmington ME [1 Mar 1849]
   Samuel abt 55 at Augusta ME on 8th inst [14 Oct 1847]
LYON - see ANTHONY
LYTELL Robert of Troy ME one of the lumbering gang of the woods left his camp & went
   to Matawamkeag ME to drink. The next day he was found frozen to death by the side
   of the road. Left a wife & five or six children [*Portland Advertiser*] [26 Feb 1846]

- M -

MABEE Benjamin Capt 46 of Eastport ME at New York [12 Feb 1846]
MABERRY H seaman perished in shipwreck of the schr *William Polk*, Mr HAMILTON
   Capt, the Capt alone escaped [*Philidelphia Exchange Book*] [23 Jul 1846]
MACE Mr his barn at Buxton ME burned (copied from the *Repository*) [20 Feb 1851]
   Reuben of Greene Kennebec Co ME, Lucinda MACE, exec [10 Aug 1839]
   Vilera A 30 w/o Richard MACE at Gardiner ME [12 Aug 1852]
MacKENZIE W L late a leading patriot in Canada issued in Philadelphia the prospectus of
   a weekly journal to be established in New York to be called *MacKenzic's British,
   Irish & Canadian Gazette* [3 Apr 1838]
MACKEY Mr of Pike Co killed by one of his negro slaves [29 May 1841]

MACKIE Joseph S 19yr 7mo, s/o the late Capt Andrew MACKIE at sea on passage from Point Petre to Wilmington, fell from main topsail yard on deck, survived only six hours. [21 Mar 1837]

MACOMB Alexander Major General, the General-in-Chief of United States Army died, entered service as cornet of dragoons in 1799 & was in the military family of Gen Alexander HAMILTON ... from the *Madisonian* [10 Jul 1841]

MACOMBER Ard 73 at Monmouth ME (NB b 21 Feb 1780, d 28 Dec 1850, see p. 107 Cochrane's *History of Monmouth & Wales*) [6 Feb 1851]

Ardelia abt 20 at Monmouth ME [24 Aug 1848]

L Augusta 24 at Augusta ME 14 Oct [8 Nov 1849]

Laban L of Natchez, MS, formerly of Gardiner ME at Woodburn, IL 16th ult [16 Nov 1839]

Olive Caroline 3y 20d only c/o O T & Deborah A MACOMBER formerly of Gardiner ME at Burnt Prairie IL on 27 Nov of croup [13 Jan 1848]

Sarah L 31 w/o A A MACOMBER at Dover [29 Feb 1840]

Sarah P 39 w/o George W MACOMBER at Augusta ME [12 Oct 1848]

William at Readfield ME [4 Apr 1850]

MACON Nathaniel 83th year a member of one or the other branches of Congress without intermission almost from the formation of the present government down to the yr 1829 of Carolina near Warrenton on 29th ult [18 Jul 1837]

Madawaska Settlement - see deaf & dumb (deaf mute)

MADDOCKS Abigail G abt 30 w/o Willard L M & d/o John & Mary K MADDOCKS at Belfast ME [27 May 1852]

Austin 28 at Ellsworth ME [9 Sept 1847]

Caleb 82 at Ellsworth ME [22 Apr 1836]

John 80 at Belfast ME [29 June 1848]

Mary 74 w/o late Samuel MADDOCKS at Ellsworth ME on 13th inst [27 May 1836]

Nathan E 21 at Ellsworth ME [29 Jul 1847]

William ab 72 at Ellsworth ME [27 May 1836]

MADDOX Dorcas Mrs 89 at Bangor ME [12 Jun 1845]

Oren 18 of Union ME on the ice of Sennebec Pond at Appleton on the 28th ult, supposed to have fallen & died there on the 21st, the same day he had procured spirits of one MORANG, so that the rum is probably at the bottom of the affair [*Belfast Journal*]

Richard 72 at Chesterville ME on 19th inst of 1st settlers of Chesterville [5 Feb 1839]

MADIGAN Walter 84 at Newcastle ME [1 Feb 1849]

MADISON James the 4th president of the USA (1809-1817) at Montpelier VA on 28 June 1836 [13 Jan 1837] & President of USA died 28 June 1836 86 [5 Aug 1836] & James 84 at Virginia extended obituary [15 July 1836]

Mrs was born in 1776, had married a Philadephia lawyer named TODD, when she was 20y. He died three years after & when 24 she married James MADISON while he was a member of Congress. A son by her 1st marriage still lives in VA [26 Jul 1849]

William 82y a General & AmRev of Madison Co VA the youngest brother of the late Pres MADISON [26 Aug 1843]

MADISON - see CAMPBELL, SMITH, TODD

MAGEE Sutton had his wrist dreadfully wounded & his children were scorched by fireworks at Washington DC [*US Journal*] [17 Jul 1845]

MAGOON Eliza D abt 17 d/o Mr N S MAGOON called upon a dentist to destroy the nerve of the tooth, and for that purpose applied Kreosote, some of which ran down her throat ... she died later (from the *Boston Post*) [21 Dec 1839]

MAGOON - see HAWKES

MAGOYNE Madame 101 at Easton PA 507 descendants [16 Nov 1833]

MAGRATH Mary E 20 at Belfast ME [19 Aug 1847]

MAGUIRE Dr of Winthrop ME & his lady left New York on 1 Mar for San Francisco CA in the steamship *Northerner for Chagres* [29 Mar 1849]

MAHAMMED - see SOOJAH

MAHAN J B Rev & others convicted at Georgetown OH an indictment charging them with the forcible rescue of a negro from Kentucky, sentenced fine of $300 & thirty days imprisonment. [2 Nov 1839]

MAHAN - see AUBLEY

MAHER Michael 24 at Gardiner ME on 30 Sept [5 Oct 1848]

Thomas ordinary seaman 17 of New Haven CT to the US ship *Preble*, with the Africa fever at Porto Grande Island of St Vincent Cape de Verds on 11 Dec [10 Apr 1845]

MAHON John Irish laborer in a destructive fire, 34 horses burnt [*New York Commercial* of Wed] [26 Mar 1836]

MAHON - see WILLIAMS

MAHONEY infant 6 wks c/o Daniel MAHONEY at Augusta ME [14 Mar 1850]

MAHONY Thomas of Augusta ME saved from drowning when the steam packet *New England* sank. It left Boston for Bath & Gardiner ME and had an accident with the schr *Curlew* on 31 May [12 June 1838]

MAINS Martha at Woolwich ME [6 Nov 1845]

MAJOR Isaac drowned, one of 27 boys of the Farm School between Fort Independence & Thompson's Island [7 May 1842]

MALANNA Mary A 17 d/o widow Mary MALANNA at Gardiner ME on 23 Dec [1 Jan 1852]

MALBAN James 70 at Skowhegan ME [5 Aug 1847]

Nathaniel 70 at Skowhegan ME [17 June 1847]

MALBON Betsey abt 50 w/o James MALBON at Skowhegan ME on 22d ult [11 June 1842]

Polly 68 widow of Nathaniel MALBON at Skowhegan ME [7 Aug 1851]

MALCOM Capt of the schr *Edward* of Wiscasset ME bound from Boston MA to Charleston SC was crushed to death on Wed last between the boom & quarter rail...Capt M was of Dresden ME & left a wife & two children. [6 June 1840]

MALOON Isaac 78 of Greene ME on Tues last dropped down dead while attempting to rise from his chair [from *Lewiston (ME) Journal*] [15 June 1848]

MALOY Mr an Irishman murdered near Houlton ME a few days since. His wife, sister & two or three Irishmen have been arrested on suspicion of being the murderers. [5 Feb 1839]

MANCHESTER Capt two of men on the coroner's jury signed a paper exonerating this Capt of the *Lexington*, who was the pilot, from any blame after the fire broke out. [15 Feb 1840]

MANCHESTER - see COTTLE

MANLEY Eli French of typhoid fever on 14th inst member of the Odd Fellows & the Sons of Temperance [19 Jul 1849]

Jason abt 50y of Seaville committed suicide with a gun [*Ellsworth Democrat*] [6 Jul 1848]

MANLEY - see DUDLEY

MANN Beriah Capt formerly of Wrentham MA 73 at Hallowell ME [7 Dec 1848]

Francis 33 formerly of Wiscasset ME at Boston MA of consumption [8 Feb 1840]

MANNING Richard J of South Carolina once gov at Philadelphia PA on 1 May 1836 [13 Jan 1837]

William 82y 3m (formerly the publisher of the *Worcester Spy*) [2 Aug 1849]

MANSEL Joseph on Fri 47y left a wid & 9 ch at Hermon ME [4 June 1842]

MANSFIELD Lydia of Camden ME 24 at Foxcroft (now Dover-Foxcroft) ME [5 Dec 1840]

MANSON James M drowned attempting to cross the river above the dam, in a canoe at Farmington Falls ME on 22d inst [8 May 1841]

MARBLE John of Grafton saved from drowning when the steam packet *New England* sank. It left Boston for Bath & Gardiner ME and had an accident with the schr *Curlew* on 31 May [12 June 1838]

> Samuel F Capt 29 of Buckfield ME at Norway ME [27 Jan 1848]

MARBLE - see WOODMAN

MARBURY - see McVEAN

MARCH George of Keene NH fatally injured last week being jammed between two cars [27 Feb 1851]

MARCHESSON - see deaf & dumb (deaf mute)

MARDEN Alonzo 18 s/o Deac Elijah MARDEN drowned at Atkinson ME in the Piscataquis River [*Bangor Democrat*] [30 Aug 1849]

> Eunice 70 w/o Deac John MARDEN at Palermo ME on 28 Feb (NH papers please copy) [13 Mar 1851]

MARDIN Mr recently employed as ostler at Camden by the Belfast & Thomaston stage proprietors committed suicide at Belfast ME [10 June 1847]

MARINER child 9m of (Winthrop) fell into the fire & burned to death, Mrs James MARINER, the mother was absent at the time [13 Nov 1841]

MARKHAN - see WOOD

MARR Dorothy 84 wid/o Mark MARR at Limington ME [20 Feb 1851]

> Ichabod 83y 9m at Patricktown Plt (Jefferson/Somerville Lincoln Co) ME on 17 May [27 May 1852]

> Mr G a young man from Boston MA on a visit to his friends in North Monmouth ME was accidentally shot while returning a boat from a fishing excursion on Wilson's Pond. One of the party in removing a gun took it by the muzzle & drew it towards him when it went off & the whole charge passed over his shoulder & lodged in the head of Mr MARR, who sat behind him, killing him instantly. [21 Aug 1851]

> Mrs w/o John MARR of Phipsburg gave birth to six children on 27 June, 4 of them dead, two living [*Bath Inquirer*] [16 Jul 1846]

MARR - see CARR

MARRELL James B 23 eldest s/o Jos MARRELL at St Albans ME [17 Apr 1851]

MARROW Susan 5y d/o Zelotes A MARROW at Monmouth ME [21 Nov 1840]

MARSH J died at Lower Sundusky OH? [5 Sept 1834]

MARSHALL Basheba of Sansom St Philadelphia PA death by fire on Sat accident [1 Jan 1836]

> Jane 28 w/o Handen MARSHALL at Paris ME [17 Feb 1848]

> John Chief Justice called to the bench of Supreme Court in 1800 now dead at Philadelphia PA [*New Yorker*] [17 Jul 1835]

MARSHMAN Joshua Rev 69 on 5 Dec 1837 (from *Christian Watchman*) [8 May 1838]

MARSTON Abraham Col 55 at Parsonsfield ME [28 Dec 1848]

> David 93 AmRev at Monmouth ME [6 Feb 1851]

> Elizabeth 90y 10m wid/o I MARSTON at Waterville ME [1 June 1848]

> Hiram abt 16 of Whitneyville s/o Jotham S MARSTON Esq at Whitneyville ME on 30 May [*Age of Augusta ME*] [14 June 1849]

> James R youngest s/o Col Rufus MARSTON at Monmouth ME [3 Feb 1848]

> Nathaniel Capt at West Gardiner ME [3 Feb 1848]

> Simon 69 at Monmouth ME on 26 Sept [10 Oct 1840]

> Theodore Capt 76y 8m at E Livermore ME on 21th ult [28 Dec 1848]

MARTIN Addison Esq his house was struck by lightning on Tues in the Guilford Village ME & his wife, killed while in the act of closing a window [16 Jul 1842]

MARTIN (Cont.) Addison Mrs 43 d/o Oliver OTIS Esq of Hallowell ME rose to close a
window & killed by lightning, funeral delivered by Rev Mr PIERCE of Dover ME &
she was one of the earliest inhabitants of the Guilford Village ME on Tues 5th inst
[23 Jul 1842]

    John cook of sch *Henry* of (Augusta) ME drinking too freely of cold water at
Newburyport MA [3 Aug 1848]

    Mr a ostler at Camden by the Belfast & Thomaston stage committed suicide [*Signal*] [10
June 1847]

    Nathaniel 60 at Belfast ME [3 June 1852]

    Ruth 32 w/o Simon MARTIN at Searsmont ME [1 Jan 1852]

    Stephen of Warren RI saved from drowning when the steam packet *New England* sank. It
left Boston for Bath & Gardiner ME and had an accident with the schr *Curlew* on 31
May [12 June 1838]

MASON Alexander 2y 6m s/o Silas MASON at Fairfield ME on 7th ult [12 Sept 1840]

    Asa 50 to 60y killed accidentally at work [*Worcester Transcript*] [27 Nov 1845]

    Asa Jr 55 at Sidney ME on 21 Feb [2 Mar 1848]

    Benjamin Master Capt 32 & his lady, Mrs Alice J MASON 31, sis/o Hon Henry
TALLMAN, among the number drowned. Capt M's father is a much esteemed citizen
of Lisbon ME, having his res at Little River Village. [*Bath Times*] [30 Nov 1848]

    George W of Davies Co KY arrested a "colored man" by the name of MITCHUM, who
with his wife & children resided about four miles from Vernon. Mr George W
MASON introduced proof to the satisfaction of Mr BASSETT, a justice of the peace
... [13 Mar 1851]

    Hannah Mrs 80 at Augusta ME on 6 Feb [2 Mar 1848]

    Jeremiah Hon formerly US Senator from NH [*Boston Advertiser*] [26 Oct 1848]

    Mary T wid/o Rev Easton MASON formerly of Sweden ME at Biddeford ME [3 Aug
1848]

    Mrs w/o W P MASON at Huron from the *Sundusky OH Clarion* [5 Sept 1834]

masonic honors - see BITTUES

MASTERMAN Benjamin 64 at Weld ME [20 Feb 1851]

MASTERS Caroline 11 d/o Col Andrew MASTERS at Hallowell ME [26 Sept 1840]

MATHEWS Elizabeth 20 w/o William MATHEWS Esq, editor of the *Yankee Blade* at
Winslow ME [3 Feb 1848]

    Mary Mrs 108 at Warren ME [3 Jul 1851]

    Ruth 67 at Augusta ME [6 Jan 1848]

    Samuel B 22 of ME at Sacramento CA on 2 Nov [2 Jan 1851]

MATTHEWS Susan 67 w/o Capt Jona MATTHEWS at Monson ME [6 May 1852]

MATTOCKS John sick with cholera at Herman ME [*Bangor Daily Whig*] [16 Aug 1849]

MATTOX Mr in Union ME of a quarrel for a bottle of rum [*Thomaston (ME) Record*] [19
Dec 1837]

MAXAM Adonijah 97 supposed the last of the band of Ethan ALLEN in the bold
experiment against Montreal in Nov 1765 at Sharon VT on 22d ult [30 Jan 1851]

MAXEY Milton 21 at Union ME [4 Dec 1851]

    Virgil some papers state a native of MD, born in MA, in the vicinity of Providence RI, a
graduate of Brown University, at the same time as his bro, Homer M & the late Gov
PICKENS of SC, s/o Rev Dr Jonathan M (see UPSHUR) [*NY Commercial*] [14 Mar
1844]

MAXFIELD Elvira 41 w/o James MAXFIELD at Mt Vernon ME [23 Mar 1848]

MAXIM Asenath A 23 w/o Jacob MAXIM Jr at East Livermore ME [17 June 1852]

    Sally 35 w/o Converse F MAXIN at Augusta ME on 24th inst [31 Aug 1848]

MAXWELL Martha 68 w/o Joseph MAXWELL at Waterville ME [8 Jan 1852]

MAXWELL (Cont.) Mr of Litchfield ME one of the deck hands on board the steamer *Kennebec River* drowned, the body was recovered in about twenty minutes after, but life was extinct [*Hallowell Gazette*] [8 Jul 1847]

Mr who commenced the battle of Brandywine by opposing Knyphausen's troops in their attempts to cross Chadd's Ford died at Flemington NJ [16 Sept 1847]

MAY - see CARLETON

Mayflower - see LEONARD

MAYHEW Ephraim Mrs 52 at New Sharon ME [25 Sept 1851]

MAYLE - see LATHROP

MAYNARD Charles S 23 at Fairfield ME of consumption [4 Jan 1840]

Miss E K 27 at Fairfield ME [12 Feb 1852]

MAYO boy abt 10y of Eden ME s/o Moses H MAYO accidentally killed [1 Nov 1849]

Mary w/o Nathaniel MAYO at Livermore Falls ME [25 Jan 1840]

MAYO - see LOMBARD

McALLISTER child 2y c/o Zachariah McALLISTER, burned to death in a house fire which broke out 15 minutes after leaving their children in bed. A girl abt 13y saved herself by jumping from the widow. The mother seeing the flames, rushed into the house, but barely time to save another child, about five yrs old at Usher ME [23 Jul 1842]

Guy 48 at Freedom ME [2 Nov 1848]

McBRIGHT James, his mother came over from Ireland, to see him at Lewiston ME, is very anxious to find him. [4 Oct 1849]

McCARDEL Major the *Picayune* annouces Maj, editor of the *Vicksburg Whig* no more - "a bachelor" married a few days ago [20 June 1840]

McCARDLE - see JOHNSON

McCARTNEY & BASSETT, two men most horribly mutilated by the premature discharge of an old cannon. McC dead & B in a critical state. His right arm amputated & also two or three fingers of his left arm [*New York Farmer & Mechanic*] [*Providence Transcript*] [17 Jul 1845]

McCARTY John an Irish laborer injured on Tues by the falling of a bank of earth, doing well yesterday [*Lewiston Journal*] [8 Feb 1849]

Mr a tailor of Oldtown ME run over by the horse carriage of Engine # 17 & had his arm broken [15 Aug 1834]

McCAUSLAND Alexander 31 at Augusta ME on 4 Apr [8 May 1851]

boy 17 of Gardiner s/o Mr McCAUSLAND injured on the Fourth (July) by the accidental discharge of a pistol [18 Jul 1840]

John 20y 6m at Augusta ME on 23 June [17 Jul 1851]

Mary Mrs 88 at West Gardiner ME [21 Dec 1848]

Sarah 16 at Gardiner ME [13 Jan 1848]

Violette 4y 4m d/o Hiram & Betsey McCAUSLAND at Augusta ME on 1st Feb [12 Feb 1852]

McCAUSLAND - see CLARKE

McCHESNEY - see REED

McCLAIN John body found, left a wife & 7 children of Bremen ME at Bremen ME on Tues on 1st inst 4 persons drowned while sailing from Long Island in Bremen ME towards Friendship ME [17 Apr 1851]

McCLEARY William Capt 54 at Strong ME [28 Sept 1848]

McCLENCH John H 76 at Fayette ME [2 Aug 1849]

McCLINTOCK John of Boothbay ME saved from drowning when the steam packet *New England* sank. It left Boston for Bath & Gardiner ME and had an accident with the schr *Curlew* on 31 May [12 June 1838]

McCLORY - see HOLLAND

McCOBB Denny Gen 79 at Bath ME [12 July 1849]

Harriet N 31 w/o Arthur M'COBB at Boothbay ME [8 June 1848]

McCOBB - see CASTNER, MUSSENDEN

McCONKEY - see MILES

McCONNELL Mary 13 at Norridgewock ME [1 June 1848]

McCORMICK A H one of the passengers lost or missing on 7th inst when the steamboat *New York*, bound from Galveston to New Orleans was wrecked in a hurricane, 17 persons drowned [24 Sept 1846]

child abt 8y of Brown's Corner Vassalboro ME severely burned on Sat & died after three days [2 Mar 1848]

Jack a slave belonging to Mr A H McCORMICK of New Orleans shot abt two weeks since when his master being absent, his mistress ordered him to ride a horse that needed exercise. He did so and when at the toll gate of the Shell road, he rode past. One of the keepers called upon him to stop. Jack was injured for life and the affair is to undergo a legal investigation. [26 Aug 1843]

McCOUSON Betsey Mrs 74 at Belfast ME [19 June 1851]

McCOY - see McLNDOE

McCRILLIS Mr "the toll-house at the new bridge near the village of (Belfast) ME was destroyed by fire last Sun morning. The bridge sustains no injury & Mr McCRILLIS's papers & books were saved (from the *Belfast Advertiser*) [24 Jan 1834]

McCULLOCH's company of mounted Rangers overtook on the 10th ult a gang of runaway negroes, near the river Neuces, on their way to Mexico. The negroes challenged by the Rangers to surrender, but refused and in return opened a fire upon the Rangers, killing two & wounding a third very badly. All the negroes were killed. [*The Galveston Civilian* of the 18th] [8 May 1851]

McCURDY John Esq married Miss Sally Ann WORTHING, reported in our last week's paper turns out to be a miserable hoax [*Belfast Journal*] [1 Apr 1847]

McDANIELS Mrs in Hagerstown MD from lock-jaw caused by a slight wound on the finger which she had received a few days previous [18 Sept 1845]

Nehemiah 85 at Cornville ME [17 Apr 1851] & [10 Apr 1851]

McDOANNOUGH girls two d/o James McDOANNOUGH & another girl d/o Samuel CLARK were all drowned at Bosworth's wharf at Boston MA [23 Aug 1849]

McDONAL boy of Earltown (not far from Pictou) nearly killed by a bear, may die (from the *Pictou Mechanic & Farmer*) [5 Nov 1841]

McDONALD Betsey killed on Tues last near the village of Hyde Park NY by a piece of rock, thrown from a blast, falling through the roof of their house. The rock weighted 1000 lbs [6 Mar 1851]

Elizabeth B 26 at Madison ME [10 Apr 1851]

Mrs at Lower Canada left ch & the oldest is not yet fifteen & Mrs BENOIT in a mill accident both left children [16 Oct 1841]

McDONOUGH Daniel slightly injured upon the railroad on the ledge near Sewall's Mills on Mon 15th by the premature explosion of a charge [25 May 1848]

McDONOUGH - see FISLAR

McDORMAND James abt 27 second mate of the barque *Vahalle*, lying at Commerical wharf accidentally fell overboard from the starboard head rail & drowned, native of Eastport ME [*Charleston Courier*, 23d ult] [13 June 1844]

McDOUGAL Mr AmRev buried in New York [16 Sept 1847]

McDOWELL Gov rep to Congress for 8y of VA last Sat near Lexington [4 Sept 1851]

McDUFFIE Abigail Mrs 38 at Woolwich ME [17 Apr 1851]

Betsey (SINCLAIR) Whereas his wife, during his absence last evening, took her infant child & left without his knowlege or consent ... signed Daniel McDUFFIE, Winthrop

McDUFFIE (Cont.) ME 21 Nov 1842 (N.B. on 1 Jan 1844, a Daniel McDUFFIE of Winthrop ME took a mortgage in 1834 & Noah CURRIER gave notice of foreclosure on 1 Jan 1844) (see p. 491 *Stackpole's History of Winthrop Maine*) [10 Dec 1842] [18 Jan 1844]

   David of Winthrop ME arrived at Rochester NH on Sat 1st inst, being unwell, called on Dr J M BERRY, thought the smallpox. Dr B confirmed in his previous opinion, sent for Dr RUSSELL of Great Falls NH, no doubt of the nature of the disease. Mr McD now sick abt two miles from the village [*Dover (NH?) Gazette*] see MEQQUIER [15 Feb 1840]

McELROY Mr of Pittsbury while out riding on the bank of Turtle creek on Sat [11 Sept 1851]

McFADDEN Mr injured on board the *Ruth S Hodgdon* of Boothbay ME during Thurs's storm & later died at the Marine Hospital under the care of Dr WESTERN (from the *Portland Argus*) [21 Mar 1850]

   Amos & Solomon STAITES (the latter a colored man) recently convicted of kidnapping a colored boy 15y of Downingtown PA & taking him to Baltimore with the intention of selling him into slavery. [23 Aug 1849]

McFALLEN lad, "*The Somerset Journal* says: 'We learn also that the Anson bridge, across the Seven Mile Brook, so called, was crried away by the ice, and a boy named McFALLEN, who was standing upon the bridge at the time it fell, was buried beneath the falling timbers and drowned.'" [5 Feb 1839]

McFARLAND Julia 20 w/o Isaac McFARLAND at Waterville ME [26 June 1851]

   Nathaniel 67 at East Trenton ME? [23 Jan 1851]

McGAFFEY George Capt 66 at Mt Vernon ME on 25 Apr [20 May 1852]

McGAHEY Alexander the owner of a plantation at Yazoo MS & Lewis G ROSS, his overseer, have been held to bail, the latter in $2,000 as principle and the former in $10,000 as accessory to the murder of one of McGAHEY's slaves, who was whipped to death by ROSS [3 Aug 1839]

McGAN Mr shot dead by the guard in attempting to escape from Thomaston Prision. He was a swimming when shot. (from the *Jerome's Bulletin* on 6th June) [19 June 1838]

McGAR Hugh of Bangor ME while logging by a tree falling on him at Aurora on the 29th ult [11 Jan 1849]

McGEE child 5y of Westminister 5y on Fri fell head foremost into the well abt 20 ft deep. (Mrs Mc) hearing cries, although poor in health & having a child only 5 weeks old, descended & rescued the child (the *Bellows Falls Gazette*) [14 Aug 1841]

McGEORGE Mrs 95 at St Stephen New Brunswick Canada wrapt in the flames of a house fire (*Calais ME Advertiser*) [14 Feb 1850]

McGLATHRY John 22y native of Searsport ME knocked overboard from the schr *Ottoman* going up the Chesspeake Bay & drowned [*Baltimore American*, Tues] [28 Sept 1848]

McGRATH a boy fell into the water on the Canada side & carried over Niagara Falls on Mon [29 May 1851]

   Michael 52 at Limerick ME [22 Jan 1852]

McGRATH - see DUNDAN

McGUINE poor fellow found dead in a yard in front of our office this morning. He had died some time in the night, and was the prey of rats. We never saw a more horrible, mangled body. The nose, lips, cheeks and eyebrows were all eaten away... (copied from the *Picayune*) [26 Sept 1837]

McGUIRE Joseph of Glenburn ME burnt to death, left a wife & 4 children [*Bangor Whig*] [26 June 1845]

McGUIRE - see LIVINGTON

McHALE Elizabeth 4y at the House of Industry on Fri night at South Boston MA [2 Aug 1849]

McINDOE Thomas an apprentice & Robert McCOY, a mason at work taking down the First Presbyterian Church in Wall St opposite the Express Office of Adams & Co, the first named died & little hope for the other [*NY Cor Bee*] [22 Aug 1844]

McINTIRE Hezekiah 83 at Norway ME [19 Feb 1852] & [4 Mar 1852]

McINTYRE - see OUTERBRIDGE

McKAY Samuel D shot in the Cherokee Nation, a short distance above Fort Smith on the 9th inst [20 June 1840]

McKEAG James Adams at Waldoboro ME [23 Sept 1836]

McKEAN Samuel Gen, late a senator of the United States from PA at Burlington, Bradford Co PA on Tues the 14th inst [1 Jan 1842]

McKECHNIE - see NORTH

McKEEN Alice 76 relict of the Rev Joseph M, 1st president of Bowdoin College, survived her partner 26y at Brunswick ME on 21st inst [4 Apr 1834]

Dustin 3y 4m s/o Hiram McKEEN burned [*Norway Advertiser*] [22 Feb 1849]

Eph 82 at Belfast ME [6 Jul 1848]

Silas Mrs of Bradford VT instantly killed a few days since by leaping from the carriage as the horses took fright from the breaking of the harness and rushed down a steep hill, Mr McKEEN was injured but not seriously [11 Jan 1849]

McKEENAN Daniel of Old Town ME at San Francisco CA [8 Jan 1852]

McKELLAR Catharine E 33 w/o Major A M Jr at South Thomaston ME [3 Oct 1850]

McKENNAN James Hon 42y one of the associate judges of Indiana at his residence of consumption [19 June 1845]

McKENNEY Edward living in the dwelling house owned by W H HENEY of Eastport ME lost the entire home by fire at Deer Island New Brunswick Canada [*sic*] on the night of 20th inst (from the *Eastport Sentinal*) [11 Sept 1851]

Elizabeth 96 at Greene ME [2 May 1850]

Esther 85 a widow at Bath ME [16 Oct 1851]

Isaac 77 at Carmel ME [11 Jan 1849]

James 57y of Embden ME killed on the 2d inst, assisting in raising a frame for his son-in-law, Ashur CLEVELAND, in attemping to put on the plates, one of the broadsides, which was held up by a couple of rafters placed in the braces gave way & fell upon Mr McK & Mr CLEVELAND, killing Mr McKENNEY almost instantly. Mr CLEVELAND although severely injured it is thought will recover. (from *Skowhegan Clarion*) [28 Dec 1848]

John 81 formerly of Saco ME at Biddeford ME [5 Feb 1852]

Mathew 75y at Bath ME [20 Mar 1851]

William Capt of Deer Island New Brunswick Canada [*sic*] his wife given birth to two ch, the first of whom weighed 24 & the last 22 pounds on the day of birth! [*Eastport Sentinel*] [1 Feb 1849]

McKENNEY - see WOOD

McKIM Isaac rep from Maryland at Washington DC on Sun last [17 Apr 1838]

McKINNEY Edward 10 s/o Reuben McKENNEY at Augusta ME [24 Aug 1848]

Frances 74 formerly of Georgetown ME at Bath ME [3 June 1847]

McKUSICK Charity 54 w/o Capt Noah McKUSICK at Cornish ME [6 Apr 1848]

McLAIN Otis 30 at Rockland ME [2 Dec 1852]

McLAINE Sylvia Ann 18 d/o Jesse & Ann M at Farmington ME [10 Oct 1844]

McLANATHAN Thomas 69 at Searsport ME [28 Feb 1850]

McLANE Henry one of Island a party of 27 of the boys of the Farm School on Thompson's Island accompanied by a teacher & boat-keeper drowned when between Fort Independence & Thompson's Island [7 May 1842]

Mr 70 member of Congress from Ohio at Washington DC [4 Apr 1837]

McLANEY John an Irishman drowned in the Kennebec River [7 Aug 1851]

McLAUGHLIN Hugh killed accidentally at Messrs C & E TRULL's distillery in Boston MA [*Boston Bee*] [6 Aug 1846]

James 82 at Madison ME on the 15th ult [4 Jan 1844]

Mr seaman on a schr lying at one of our wharves, was seriously injured on last Fri, thought he will not recover [*Free American*] [19 Aug 1847]

Sarah Frances 2 d/o Albert McLAUGHLIN at Augusta ME on 4 Aug [21 Aug 1851]

McLEAN James a teamster of Milltown, Calais ME was kicked in the stomach on Thurs last, by one of his horses & killed instantaneously. He not even gasped after he received the kick [3 Jan 1850]

John 67 at Alna ME [31 May 1849]

Julia 19 at Hope ME [5 June 1835]

Leatitia E Mrs accomplished and beautiful writer and poetess at Cape Coast Castle Africa (formerly Miss L E LANDON) [29 Jan 1839]

Sarah 22 at Wiscasset [11 Jun 1846]

McLELLAN Anna M 61 w/o Elkanah M at Gardiner ME [3 Oct 1850]

Arthur Capt 83 at Portland [20 Mar 1835]

Bryce 42 of Gardiner ME on board frigate *United States* [22 Mar 1849]

Bryce 74 at Bloomfield ME late judge of probate [14 Oct 1836]

Elizabeth A 5y d/o J H M'LELLAN Esq at Bath [19 Dec 1844]

Jas A of Bath ME saved from drowning when the steam packet *New England* sank. It left Boston for Bath & Gardiner ME and had an accident with the schr *Curlew* on 31 May [12 June 1838]

Nancy A 30 w/o Capt Thomas M at Thomaston ME [16 Jul 1842]

Peter Osgood 27 s/o Gen James M of Bath ME at New Orleans [21 Sept 1839]

Thomas of Portland ME at CA [18 Nov 1852]

Thomas of Portland ME lost & drowned the barque *William Fales*, Capt William THOMES of this port (Portland ME) was lost in Wells Bay ME on Wed evening at 9 o'clock, 13 persons on board, eight were lost including every officer. Through the attention of our friend, George M FREEMAN of Cape Needick (Old York, where the barque drove) [26 Feb 1842]

William of Gorham ME his dwelling house was destroyed by fire on Mon night, he was AmRev, the fire insurance had expired only a day or two before [13 Jan 1837]

Wm 37 at Gorham [19 Sep 1850]

McLEOD David a native of Nova Scotia & workman in the paper mill of Paul ELLIS at South Dedham MA, was killed Mon of last week by being caught in the gearing [27 Nov 1851]

McLUCAS Flora Mrs 46 at Biddeford ME [13 Sep 1849]

McLURE Samuel 45 at Cornville ME [5 Jul 1845]

McMAHAN - see FARRINGTON

McMAHON Daniel 85 AmRev at Georgetown [1 Jan 1836]

McMANNUS Asa Capt 26 master of the brig *Mary Pennell* of Brunswick ME, s/o Robert MCMANNUS died 16 Jul of yellow fever at Vera Cruz [11 Nov 1843]

Precilla ab 28 w/o Robert McMANNUS Capt at Brunswick ME [15 Aug 1844]

McNAUGHT A Mrs 50 w/o A McNAUGHT at Eastport ME [4 Jun 1846]

McNEAL Abigail Mrs 52 12 Jun at res of Jas H HUTCHINSON at Fayette ME [24 Jun 1843]

McNEAL (Cont.) Chastina 34 w/o Daniel McNEAL at Fryeburg ME [5 Apr 1849]

McNEAR James Capt 68 at Bristol ME [7 Dec 1848]
>   Robert 15 at Wiscasset ME [24 Jun 1836]
>   Robert formerly of Bristol at Boston MA [12 Dec 1837]

McNULTY C J late clerk to the house of Congress died on his way to Mexico, he was a hard drinking man is said died from over spreeing [20 Aug 1846]

McQUILKIN - see NASON

McREA William C fireman crew lost & missing on 7th inst the steamboat *New York*, bound from Galveston to New Orleans was wrecked in a hurricane, 17 persons drowned [24 Sept 1846]

McROBERTS Samuel senator in Congress from IL died in Cincinnati on Mon 40y after a short illness, resulting from a cold taken in crossing the mountains on his way home from the session which has recently closed [15 Apr 1843]

McVEAN Charles Esq U. S. district attorney recently appointed in place of Mr Benjamin F BUTLER died at his residence in Albingdon Place, Thurs afternoon. The U. S. district court, on motion of Mr MARBURY, adjourned out of respect to his memory (from the *Tribune*) [28 Dec 1848]

MEAD Willie 3 yr 6mo on 10 Apr at Augusta ME [26 Apr 1849]

MEADE Richard Kidder Esq 50 at Lucky-hit Farm, Frederick CO, VA on Tues 26th ult [25 Mar 1833]

MEADER Joan E 38 w/o John MEADER at Gardiner ME [19 June 1851]

MEADS boy we are told by a gentleman belonging to Lynn MA, that a school mistress in Lynn named BECKWITH tied up the lad by the heels on Sat & whipped him striking him several times on his head, the lad was 8y, he went home & the next morning died [21 May 1842]

MEAGHER William of Whitefield ME saved from drowning when the steam packet *New England* sank. It left Boston for Bath & Gardiner ME and had an accident with the schr *Curlew* on 31 May [12 June 1838]

MEANS Charlie Southwick 10m c/o William P M & Sarah H MEANS at Augusta ME on Sun morning Sept 21st [25 Sept 1851]
>   Eleanor Mrs 79 at Freeport ME [14 Mar 1837]
>   Hannah 82 at Saco ME [17 Feb 1848]
>   Thomas 94 AmRev fought at Bunker Hill w/ WASHINGTON at Etna ME [26 Oct 1848]

MEDBERY Mary C 26 w/o Nicholas MEDBERY Rev d/o Hamden KEITH Esq of Winslow ME at Watertown MA [15 Apr 1836]

MEGQUIER child abt 1yr c/o Dr T L MEGQUIER at Winthrop ME [11 May 1839]
>   Dr & Drs CLARK & BAILEY "Arrangements made with these doctors for vaccinating at the expense of the town those who never vaccinated with effect provided they call upon said physicians .... Moses B SEARS & Francis FULLER, selectmen of Winthrop dated 26 Feb 1840 see also McDUFFIE [29 Feb 1840]
>   John L Hon register of probate for Cumberland Co ME at Portland ME [11 Jan 1840]

MEGRATH 10 mo c/o John MEGRATH at Hallowell ME [29 Aug 1844]

MEHONY - see DORROGH

MEIGS Anna 65 w/o Anson MEIGS on 13 Apr at Vassalboro ME [30 May 1850]

MELCHER Aaron 72 at Falmouth ME [13 Feb 1845]
>   Abner Capt 32 at Brunswick ME [27 Mar 1845]
>   Harriet H Miss 28 at Bath ME [28 Jan 1847]
>   Nathaniel upwards of 70 yrs of Brunswick ME by his son Levi MELCHER 38 in a paroxysm of mental alienation and madness on Mon of last week [1 Aug 1840]
>   Noah 73 at Brunswick ME [5 Aug 1836]
>   Sarah 67 widow at Bath ME [16 May 1850]

MELLEN Alanson Esq 71 at Paris ME [18 Dec 1851]

Frederic s/o Judge MELLEN of Portland ME at Boston ME [22 Aug 1834]

Grenville Esq 41 s/o late Chief Justice MELLEN of this state at New York [18 Sept 1841]

MELLEN - see HOPKINS, NIVINS

MELLUS Susan 40 w/o Daniel MELLUS at Damariscove Island [15 Aug 1850]

MELVIM Mary (WHITTIER) (born 24 Nov 1768) d 83y 6m w/o Samuel MELVIN (see also *Kennebec Journal* 17 June 1852) at Readfield ME [17 June 1852]

Benjamin 79 of the early settlers formerly of Chester NH at Readfield ME on 18 Jan (NH papers please copy) [29 Jan 1852]

Emma Jane B 1y 2mo d/o Samuel and Mary MELVIN at Hallowell ME [3 Oct 1844]

Martha S 31 d/o Benjamin and Eliza MELVIN 21 Feb at Readfield ME [26 Feb 1852]

Mary 14 d/o Josiah MELVIN at Anson ME [20 Mar 1835]

Mary 83 w/o Samuel MELVIN at Readfield ME [17 Jun 1852]

Mary Mrs 44 widow of Samuel MELVIN Esq of consumption 10th inst at Hallowell ME [19 June 1845]

Samuel Esq 50 at Hallowell ME [30 Jan 1845]

MENDALL John 89 at Fairfield ME [6 May 1847]

Thankful 84 widow of John MENDALL at Fairfield ME [6 May 1847]

MENEFEE Richard H Hon formerly a Rep in Congress 11th district in Kentucky died at Lexington KY on last Sat [13 Mar 1841]

MENKIN Solomon 45y in damages to the tune of $6000, for refusing to marry Frances WYATT, after he voluntarily pledged his word to do the same. Miss WYATT is a pretty maiden of abt 16y, sister-in-law to the defendant, & a resident in the same family. [22 Jul 1836]

MERCER Gen AmRev said killed at the battle of Princeton but really died of an epileptic fit in the neighborhood a week after that affair, buried in Christ Church Philadelphia PA [16 Sept 1847]

Milton Capt 34 at Phipsburg ME [6 Nov 1851]

MERCHANT Edward late of Belgrade ME, William WARD adm [29 Apr 1852]

Sarah 43 w/o Joseph MERCHANT 26 Apr at Belgrade ME [10 May 1849]

MERCHANT - see FRENGER

MERIAM John 81 AmRev pens formerly of East Sudbury at Fitchburg MA [19 Aug 1843]

Silas ab 80 at Norway ME [15 Aug 1844]

MERINER Stephen F of Maine lost overboard from ship *Orpheus* while lying to off Coquimbo [25 Feb 1847]

MERITHEW Mary 16 at Gouldsboro ME [14 Jan 1847]

MERO Lydia 86 w/o John MERO at Gardiner ME [25 May 1848]

Rachel 29 at Thomaston ME [30 Nov 1848]

MERRIAM Sarah 20 youngest d/o Deac Joel MERRIAM on 4th inst at Westminster MA [15 Oct 1846]

Sophia 32 at Camden ME [29 Oct 1846]

MERRICK John Esq of Hallowell ME erected at his own expense a meeting house in Dover Penobscot Co ME, which he presented to the Methodist Episcopal Church in that place. The house was dedicated by the society on the 25th *ult [Bangor Mechanic & Farmer]* [4 Mar 1836]

John S 21 a book-keeper of the Sagadohock House formerly of Springfield MA drowned [19 Jul 1849]

John W 24 of Chesterville ME at Milford MA [14 Mar 1850]

lad 16 fell through the ice while skating upon a pond in St Albans (ME) on Thurs last & was drowned [7 Dec 1839]

MERRICK (Cont.) Lt officer of the Texas Army a graduate of West Point, killed on board
    the steamer *Augusta* on the 27th by falling from a yard arm, parents reside in OH [27
    Nov 1845]
    Rebecca V 85 w/o John MERRICK Esq at Hallowell ME [24 Jul 1851]
MERRIGOE Sarah 104 "a colored woman" in Bensalem Bucks Co on 10th inst (*The
    Germanton PA Telegraph*) [26 Oct 1848]
MERRILL Aaron Esq 79 AmRev at Hampton Falls [7 Sept 1833]
    Abel Dr 41 at Phipsburg ME [12 Mar 1846]
    Abigail 34 w/o Dexter MERRILL at Lee [28 Nov 1850]
    Achsah 35 w/o James A MERRILL d/o Walter LIBBY of Durham ME at Falmouth ME
        [13 Jan 1837]
    Alfred 32 printer of the *Christain Mirror* at Portland ME [30 Sept 1843]
    Anna 21 w/o William C MERRILL at Elliot ME [21 May 1846]
    Betsey of Hebron ME w/o Ezekiel MERRILL committed suicide on Fri last week [17
        May 1849]
    boy 3y of Palmyra ME s/o Nelson MERRILL, the youngster weighs 85 lbs, in height 3 ft
        3 inches [*Piscataquis Observer* in Dover ME] [6 Apr 1848]
    Capt 74 at Gardiner ME [24 May 1849]
    Christopher Capt 75 at Brooklyn [8 Apr 1852]
    Daniel 71 at West Gardiner ME [25 Sept 1851]
    Deborah 40 w/o Silas MERRILL at New Sharon ME on 28 Dec 1847 "Lowell (MA)
        papers please copy" [17 Feb 1848]
    Eliza J 28 w/o Daniel MERRILL at Biddeford ME [15 Jul 1843]
    Emma J 24 d/o Daniel MERRILL at Gardiner ME [9 Jan 1851]
    Freelove 28 w/o Albert N MERRILL at Brighton [4 Nov 1852]
    Harriet 28th ult at Pittston ME [9 Dec 1852]
    James Franklin 10mo s/o Amos MERRILL at Augusta ME [19 July 1849]
    Jeremiah 68 at Springfield [27 Apr 1848]
    Job ab 42 at Turner ME [8 Feb 1844]
    John 82 at Buxton ME [21 Jun 1849]
    Jonathan Gen 47 at Frankfort ME [21 Dec 1848]
    Joseph 53 of the firm MERRILL and WINGATE at Hallowell ME [16 Oct 1840] & [10
        Oct 1840]
    Joshua 16 from the accidental discharge of a gun some six weeks since at Oxford ME [21
        Nov 1844]
    Joshua 45 formerly of Cumberland ME on 4th inst at Windsor ME [23 Apr 1842]
    Leonard 42 at Gardiner ME [13 Sept 1849]
    Levi J 47 at St Albans ME [30 Sep 1847]
    Luna 26 w/o Luther MERRILL Jr d/o Hira JONES on 22 Dec at Turner ME [15 Jan
        1842]
    Lydia 37 w/o Leonard MERRILL at Gardiner ME [24 Oct 1844]
    Mary 58 w/o late Moses MERRILL Esq of New Gloucester ME on 2nd inst at Baltimore
        MD [25 Apr 1844]
    Mary 72 wid/o Giles MERRILL of Hebron ME at Saco ME [20 Mar 1851]
    Mary Ann 42 w/o Joseph MERRILL at Gardiner ME [15 Jan 1846]
    Melinda J 31 w/o C MERRILL at New Gloucester ME [1 June 1848]
    Miriam 30 w/o Dr Joseph MERRILL of Durham ME on 1st inst at Hallowell ME [5 Feb
        1839]
    Moses E Capt who fell at the battle of Chapultepec took place on Mon last in Brunswick,
        the deceased's native place. [4 May 1848]
    Mrs 67 w/o Jabez MERRILL at Turner ME [16 Jan 1851]
    Nancy 64 w/o Sam'l MERRILL Esq at Frankfort ME [15 Feb 1849]

MERRILL (Cont.) Otis 15 s/o Joseph MERRILL Dr at Gardiner ME [25 July 1850]
Peter Esq for many years deputy collector of customs at Portland ME [12 Nov 1846]
Polly Mrs 51 at Gray ME [18 Jan 1849]
Roger Esq 72 at Brunswick ME [25 Feb 1847]
Ruth 45 w/o Samuel MERRILL at Livermore ME [6 Mar 1845]
Sarah 45 w/o Stephen MERRILL at Madison ME [8 Mar 1849]
Sarah Louisa 14mo d/o Dr John MERRILL at Thomaston ME [11 Jan 1844]
Silas 24 at Paris ME [24 Aug 1848]
Sinnet ab 18 d/o Calvin MERRILL of consumption on 12 Aug at Turner ME [28 Aug 1842]
Thomas C Rev of Newbury MA former pastor of the Baptist Church in Baring ME on 27 Oct at Sacramento City [7 Mar 1850]
William abt 40 at Norway ME [11 Mar 1852]
MERRILL - see BECKET
MERRIMAN George 18 inflamation of the brain at Richmond ME [1 Aug 1834]
Sylvester Capt of Harpswell ME master of ship *Columbus* of Bath ME of cholera at New Orleans [24 May 1849]
MERRIT - see COLT
MERRITHEW William 94y 6mo at Searsport ME [27 June 1850]
MERRITT Maria ab 21 d/o William MERRITT at Brunswick ME [24 Jun 1847]
MERROW Charles 8 drowned on Mon 24 May [*Gardiner Fountain*] [3 June 1847]
Eleanor w/o James MERROW of Gray ME on 29th ult at Boston MA [23 Dec 1852]
George 47 at Gardiner ME [12 Sept 1850]
Hannah w/o Joshua MERROW at Gardiner ME [17 Oct 1850]
Montgomery 22 at Augusta ME [25 Sep 1845]
Susan M 26 w/o James R MERROW of Augusta ME on 15 Aug at Sidney ME [22 Aug 1850]
William another destructive fire in Monmouth ME on the 19th, he lost his house, barn, sheds &c. Part of the furniture was saved. No insurance. Mr Marrow is a young man just starting in life and the loss of his property is a serious calamity to him [24 Apr 1841]
MERRY Benjamin 19 of Parkham ME at Stillwater ME [2 Nov 1839]
Jonathan 84 at Edgecomb ME [29 Jul 1852]
MERRYFIELD Mary Jane 18 of Porter ME at Saco ME [4 Sept 1845]
MERRYMAN ab 16 a d/o John MERRYMAN at Brunswick ME [18 July 1844]
Ellis Capt of Brunswick ME at San Francisco CA [8 Jan 1852]
Sylvester Capt of Harpswell ME died at New Orleans of cholera [*Bath Tribune*] [17 May 1849]
Timothy Capt 72 at Brunswick ME [24 Sep 1846]
MESERVE Samuel Dea 80 at North Parsonfield ME [8 Jan 1852]
MESERVE - see RANDALL
MESERVEY Emily Jane 18mo d/o Clement MESERVEY at Hallowell ME [8 Oct 1842]
Mr & Mr STRATTON, & Mr DOWNES embarked at Squaw Brook with the intentions of sailing down Moose Head lake in a boat. DOWNES made it to shore but the other two were drowned. The informant stated the two men were the first drowned in Moose Head Lake. [22 Nov 1849]
Sarah D 40 w/o Clement M at Hallowell ME [3 Apr 1845]
METCALF Benj 72 on 10 Jan at Turner ME [8 Feb 1844]
Catherine 17y 6m at New Portland ME [1 Jan 1852]
Eliza D 41 w/o Moses H METCALF 14th inst at Winthrop ME [2 Oct 1838]
Elizabeth 46 w/o Addison METCALF at Lisbon ME [2 Dec 1847]

METCALF (Cont.) Ellen J 17y 10m d/o Moses H & Elias D METCALF at Winthrop ME
on 17 Feb [13 Mar 1851]

J A Dea 49 at Winthrop ME [10 Jul 1845]

John 36 a member of Sabattis Lodge I.O.O.F. at Winthrop ME [12 Oct 1848]

Joseph Dea 85 an early settler at Winthrop ME [15 Feb 1849]

Joseph Esq ab 50 member of fraternity of Odd Fellows at Hallowell ME [28 Jan 1847]

Henry Martin abt 8 oldest s/o Moses H of (Winthrop), his father at work on Sat last at a
saw mill, slipped & killed him (see p. 507 *Stackpole's History of Winthrop, ME*) [20
Mar 1835]

Marcus & Mason, nine persons went out in a sailboat on the Caghnawaga Pond
(pronounced CAWNAWAWGA) near Monmouth Centre, The brothers M were saved
by clinging to the boat. Those drowned were Josiah FROST 40 & three children;
Arthur WELCH 23, Ann WHITMORE 14 d/o Otis WHITMORE of New Sharon ME
& John HUTCHINSON 21 (copied from the *Zion's Advocate*) on Thurs 31 May [12
June 1838]

Olive 26 d/o Moses H METCALF Esq at Winthrop ME [8 Apr 1852]

Sally Mrs 77 of Damariscotta ME at Warren ME [24 May 1849]

Solomon Esq 71y 6m at Monmouth ME on 6 June [12 June 1851]

Solomon late of Monmouth ME, Mason J METCALF adm [26 Feb 1852]

Susan Mrs 48 at Northampton MA [1 Apr 1836]

Willard 23 at Lisbon ME [2 Dec 1847]

meteror - see DANIELS

MEYER Albert J of Buffalo NY, a thesis written & published by for him by the faculty of
the Medical College, in which the propriety of substituting for the present mode of
conversing by signs, used by "deaf mutes", an alphabet of dots and dashes, or lines
similar to those used by telegraph ....(N.B. the term "Deaf Mutes" is used here for the
first time and not deaf & dumb) [31 Jul 1851]

MICHAELS - see KNOWLEN

MICHENER James 60 at Eastport ME [13 Aug 1846]

MIFFIN Mr AmRev the idol of PA at Lancaster PA & buried there [16 Sept 1847]

MIKELL Edward of Edisto Island Two of Mr M's sisters, a niece and several other relatives
were lost in the ill-fated *Pulaski*, June last drowned at Edisto Island C by the
upsetting of a boat [20 Jul 1839]

MILES Benjamin H 25 s/o late Jesse MILES at Newport ME [23 Dec 1847]

Thomas s/o Capt MILES of the New York & Mr WOODBURY/WOODFORD from
French CREEK taken off, Thomas McCONKEY deputy collector & Mrs THOMAS
w/o 2nd mate of the *William Penn* lost, also Amos H BISHOP, Butternuts, Otsego Co
NY; Luther DOUGLASS, Michigan Territory; Mr PALMER, took passage on board
the stage at North East, on 13th inst. 7 out of 9 passagers on the sailboat were lost.
[from the *Erie (PA) Gazette*] [30 May 1834]

MILLAY Joseph D abt 22 at New Portland ME [17 Apr 1838]

Nathaniel of Whitefield ME saved from drowning when the steam packet *New England*
sank. It left Boston for Bath & Gardiner ME and had an accident with the schr
Curlew on 31 May [12 June 1838]

MILLER Abijah 22 s/o Abijah T MILLER at Whitefield ME [15 Apr 1847]

Anna 86 w/o Joshua MILLER at Durham ME [12 Feb 1852]

boy 4y his mother, Elizabeth MILLER stopped out for a pail of water leaving her son in
the care of Mrs Eliza PATTERSON of the same room & while the mother was absent,
the child's clothes caught fire & burnt his back, abdomen & legs before Mrs P could
extinguish them. The boy died the next day. [25 Dec 1841]

Charles Jr ab 50 at Waldoboro ME [21 Nov 1837]

MILLER (Cont.) David 84 at Northport ME [2 Sept 1843] & one of 1st settlers in
(Northport ME) & a descendant of the 1st family settled in Belfast ME [9 Sept 1843]
     Edward abt 30 boat-builder of (Augusta) formerly of Portland ME instantly killed a few
moments since, by giving way of the flooring overhead, letting a large lot of lumber
down & crushing him to death. He leaves a wife & child & has two brothers residing
in Belfast ME. [the first telegraphic despatch from Thomaston to Belfast ME
published in the *Republican Journal*, is dated at East Thomaston the 30th ult] [7 Dec
1848]
     Elias 66 at Kennebec ME on 2 June (RI, MA & Wisconsin papers please copy) [12 June
1851] & late of Kennebec ME (est notice) [5 Feb 1852]
     Elijah 40 at Waldoboro ME [17 Oct 1850]
     Fanny 60 w/o Charles MILLER Esq at Waldoboro ME [26 Nov 1846]
     George 84 at Waldoboro ME [17 Oct 1850]
     J P Col 50y known for his service in the Greek Revolution died 17th ult at Montpelier VT
"Much of his time and money during the last yrs of his life has been spent in behalf of
the three millions of American slaves" [*Woonsocket Patriot*] [11 Mar 1847]
     Jacob 44 at Waldoboro ME [15 Oct 1846]
     James 76 born at Peterboro NH, Gov of Territory of Arkansas at Temple NH on Mon
(from the *Boston Times*) [17 Jul 1851]
     James of Eastport ME onboard whaleship *Neptune* of New London on passage to Pacific
[22 Jan 1846]
     Joel Hon 65 at Thomaston ME [20 Sep 1849]
     John L 22 s/o Abijah T MILLER at Whitefield ME [15 Apr 1847]
     John L 23 member of Franklin Division S of T on 18th inst at Whitefield [25 Mar 1847]
     Lucy 50 w/o John MILLER at Thomaston ME [9 Dec 1847]
     Margaret 69 at Belfast ME [16 Jan 1851]
     Mr of Hempstead, LI on 22d ult in a house fire 4 lives lost, a mother & 3 ch [*Brooklyn
Daily Advertiser*] [1 Mar 1849]
     Mr the agent of Mr STEENBERGEN, whose mysterious disappearance excited so much
notice at the time, went to Quebec, and embarked thence in a vessel bound to
Glasgow, Scotland [3 Aug 1839]
     Nancy 21 at Industry ME [7 Aug 1851]
     Peggy Mrs of Culpepper Co VA, manumitted about 60 colored men, women & children
who passed through Washington on Wed on their way to Baltimore MD to embark for
Liberia Africa. They were to be sent out to Liberia by the Colonization Society. [13
Nov 1851]
     Phineas Esq was a native of CT & a graduate of Yale College & died 7 Dec 1803 p 373
& 381 under heading Mechanic, Memoir of the life of Eli WHITNEY [7 Dec 1833 &
14 Dec 1833]
     Roswell 92 AmRev of Windsor ME died on 28 Jul [*Hartford Times*] [14 Aug 1851]
     Samuel 63 at Belfast ME [27 Jul 1848]
     Samuel and wife, of the measles 3rd inst at Brunswick ME [12 Feb 1836]
     w/o Deac George MILLER at Waldoboro ME [24 Apr 1835]
MILLER - see CLARK, FOGG, THOMAS
MILLETT Elizabeth 76 w/o Solomon MILLETT at Norway ME [9 Aug 1849]
     Joshua Rev 45 at Wayne ME [20 Apr 1848]
     Matilda Mrs abt 65 14th inst at Leeds ME [23 May 1834]
     Wm Col 40 at Leeds ME [11 Jun 1846]
     Wm R 16 at Leeds ME [4 Oct 1849]
MILLIKEN Anna 41 w/o Alexander MILLIKEN at Portland ME [23 Sep 1836]
     Collins R 32 at Saco ME [21 May 1846]
     Eunice 27 w/o Capt Simon MILLIKEN at Scarborough ME [16 May 1837]

MILLIKEN (Cont.) Eunice 33 d/o Abraham MILLIKEN Capt at Buxton ME [3 Jul 1845]
> Ezra C 23 at Biddeford ME [14 Oct 1852]
> George 37 at Boston MA [3 July 1845]
> James 70 at Ellsworth ME [8 Mar 1849]

MILLINTON - see SMITH

MILLS Alex 81 at Greenwood ME [16 Aug 1849]
> Benjamin F 25 formerly of Palmyra ME at Fort Wayne IN [16 Jan 1845]
> John 2d officer of *India* on 28 Dec. From the Coast of Africa the brig *India*, Capt
> HANSCOMB, arrived at this port this morning (*Philadelphia Bulletin*, 31st) She left
> Bissau West Coast of Africa 23 Jan & arrived at Port Praya Cape de Verds on 12 Feb
> [10 Apr 1851]
> Joseph 88 at Palmyra ME [26 Aug 1852]
> Mr made a successful balloon ascension from York PA on the 25th ult but was found
> dead on Sun [28 Aug 1835]
> William 13 s/o James MILLS drowned while bathing 17th ult at Norridgewock ME [3 Jul
> 1841]

MINER Joannah G 31 w/o Dwight MINER 24th inst at Hallowell ME [5 July 1849]

MINK Solomon A 28 of firm of ORFF and MINK 27 Sep at North Waldoboro ME [11 Oct
1849]

MINOT George H 31 formerly of Belgrade ME of yellow fever 28th ult at New Orleans [22
Nov 1849]
> Laura Eliza 1y 3m d/o John S & Olive P MINOT at Belgrade ME on 11 Apr [1 May
> 1851]
> Rhoda Samantha 10mo only c/o James and Rhoda MINOT 3 Apr at Belgrade ME [11
> Apr 1850]

MITCHELL Ann J 21 of Lewiston at Limerick ME [25 Nov 1852]
> Charles the house, barn & out buildings of his at Newfield were destroyed by fire on 6th
> inst & all his farming tools, hay, a hay wagon, sleigh were lost…the furniture was
> saved…no insurance [23 Oct 1838]
> Charlotte Miss of GA appeared on her wedding day dressed entirely in silk of her own
> manufacture - cap, gloves, stockings & dress - equal to the best pongee. [17 Jul 1841]
> c/o Joseph MITCHELL Jr 8 mo at Freeport ME [30 Dec 1836]
> c/o Nathaniel B MITCHELL 15 mo 2 Aug at Augusta ME [16 Aug 1849]
> Elijah S 32 at Jackson ME [16 Oct 1851]
> Frederic of Freeport s/o Josiah W MITCHELL Esq drowned at Rio de Janerio 1 Sept
> 1845 [29 Jan 1846]
> Frederick E 23 s/o Joshua & Mary MITCHELL of Litchfield ME at Richmond ME on 31
> May drowned [15 June 1848]
> Frederick Emerson a ship carpenter abt 22 of Litchfield ME s/o Joshua MITCHELL
> drowned [8 June 1848]
> Hannah L Mrs 26 at Bath ME [13 Nov 1845]
> Harriet N 24 of North Bridgewater MA at Lisbon ME [17 Oct 1844]
> Hazen Esq died [*Bangor Mercury*] [1 May 1845]
> Isaac 35 formerly of Dover ME at Lowell MA [22 Feb 1844]
> J W 20 of ME 13 Jun at San Francisco [29 Jul 1852]
> James 28 s/o Asa by accidental discharge of gun 10th ult at Temple [4 Feb 1833]
> Jameson Mrs 78 wid/o Joshua M on 21st ult at Bath ME [4 Jan 1844]
> Jane C Mrs 26 w/o William E MITCHELL at Bath ME [1 Jan 1846]
> Jesse 60 at Bath ME [21 Mar 1840]
> lad 24y of Pittston ME eldest s/o Enos Mitchell killed in steam sawmill "crushing his
> head to atoms" (from the *Gardiner Transcript*) [6 Nov 1851]
> Levi ab 68 at North Yarmouth ME [5 Mar 1842]

MITCHELL (Cont.) Levi B 24 formerly of Wales ME at Winthrop ME [8 Apr 1833]

Lucy Miss ab 22 at Thomaston ME [21 Aug 1845]

Lydia on Thurs from the bank of Little Androscoggin, near covered bridge in Danville (now Auburn) sled shot into a hole, her sister Helen, 2yrs younger, caught the extended fingers. She requested Helen to let go, not to be drawn in with her. This should serve as a warning to those who are in the habit of sliding and skating upon our rivers at this season of the year. (*Lewiston Journal*) [6 Mar 1851]

Mary 27 w/o Asa MITCHELL at Raymond ME [28 Feb 1850]

Mary G 20 d/o Deac Amaziah & Sally MITCHELL at Wales ME on 18 Jan [30 Jan 1851]

Mary Mrs 59 at Union ME [30 Sept 1836]

Mary Mrs 70 w/o late Zebulon MITCHELL at Mexico ME [4 Sept 1845]

Mr on Wed the 29th ult at sawmill at Kennebec Dam [*Temperance Gazette*] [9 Oct 1841]

Mrs w/o James MITCHELL at Kennebunk ME [2 Dec 1836]

Nancy Mrs 75 at Bath ME [23 Dec 1852]

P R 32 at Dexter ME [1 Nov 1849]

Penaiah D 25 due to accidental discharge of pistol with which playing 24th ult at Mobile [22 Jan 1842]

Phebe Ann M 16y d/o Nathaniel B and Nancy C MITCHELL of Augusta ME on 11th inst at Saco ME [20 May 1847]

Rebecca M 24 d/o late Nicholas L MITCHELL Esq 6th inst at Wiscasset ME [18 Apr 1844]

Sally H 52 w/o Hon David MITCHELL at Temple ME [30 Oct 1851]

Samuel 80 at China ME on 10 Apr [15 May 1851]

Samuel fire in his store at New Gloucester ME [*Lewiston ME Journal*] [8 Feb 1849]

Sarah J P 17 d/o Rev D M MITCHELL at Waldoboro ME on 27th ult [10 Oct 1840]

Seth B 30 editor and proprietor of the *Eastport Sentinel* at Eastport ME [30 Sep 1843]

Susannah 84 wid/o Andrew MITCHEL 19th ult at Temple ME [19 Dec 1834]

William 64 at West Bath ME [10 Oct 1850]

MITCHELL - see DAILY, THOMPSON, KEEN/KEENE

MITCHUM blackman/slave a runaway, Mr MASON of Davies Co KY arrested a "colored man" by the name of MITCHUM, who with his wife & children resided about four miles from Vernon. Mr George W MASON introduced proof to the satisfaction of Mr BASSETT, a justice of the peace... [13 Mar 1851]

MOALE John C Esq, the agent of the steamboat line was on the *Medora*, with his two sons, he had his right foot dislocated & was injured in the side & back. Soon after he was taken home, he expired. Mr Moale's eldest son William, abt 14y was killed & his second son was dangerously injured. [23 Apr 1842]

MOFFATT - see ROALDSON

MONAC Major the officer at the battle of Wahoo Swamp & not Major MORICE as reported Army in FL [23 Dec 1836]

MONECK/MONOCK - see WILSON

MONKS Elias 89 at Hebron ME [4 Feb 1843]

MONROE Nathaniel drowned in Bristol Harbor RI? [5 Aug 1843]

Sally w/o late Abijah MONROE formerly of Livermore ME at Winthrop ME [20 Jun 1837]

MONROE - see SMITH

MONTAUBAND - see BRESILLON

MONTCALM - REPHENBARK

MONTENEGRO Juan dying declaration of the pirates signed by companions Angel GARRIA, Manuel BOYGA, Manuel CASTILTE [10 Jul 1835]

MONTGOMERY Benjamin Capt ab 32 at Thomaston ME [16 Jul 1842]

Miss rescued from the wreck of the *Oraloo*, since died, abt 18y, her sister was on board of the *Oraloo* at the time of the disaster, lies very low at Damariscotta ME [24 Jul 1845]

Mr AmRev buried in New York [16 Sept 1847]

MOOD Mahala of Pittston ME lost on the schr *Maine* of Bath ME, James BLIN of Dresden, master from the Kennebec for Boston MA loaded with wood, potatoes & hay...[16 Oct 1841]

MOOD - see HAMMOND

MOODY Alfred S 22 at Monmouth ME [14 Nov 1837]

Catharine 22 d/o Ezra MOODY at Windsor ME [4 Jan 1849]

Edlon D 32 a native of Monmouth ME & arrived from California only twelve days before his death at Boston MA [6 Nov 1851]

Elias 80 at Webster ME on 20 Sept [2 Oct 1851]

Elizabeth 62 w/o Joshua MOODY at Andover [29 Jan 1839]

Elizabeth C 28 w/o Joseph G MOODY Esq at Augusta ME [22 July 1833]

Elizabeth widow 77 3rs inst at Limington ME [28 Jan 1843]

Emeline B 21 at Norway ME [27 Jan 1848]

Henry 33 on the same evening Mrs N MOODY his wife in a fit of despondency left the house and was found drowned the next morning in Damariscotta Pond near their home at Nobleboro ME [19 Dec 1834]

John 88 AmRev pens at Nobleboro ME [7 Mar 1840]

Joshua 49 at Falmouth ME [28 Nov 1850]

Lemuel Capt 79 for nearly forty years superintendent of the Portland Observatory, in the construction of which he was instrumental at Portland ME [20 Aug 1846]

Lucy w/o George MOODY at Thomaston ME [11 Jul 1834]

Lydia 18 w/o Robert S MOODY on 28 Apr at Windsor ME [6 May 1852]

Lyman H 10m youngest child of E C & Margaret MOODY at Augusta ME on 18 Feb [4 Mar 1852]

Mary J 23 d/o Sam'l MOODY Capt at Saco ME [10 Jun 1843]

Mehitable 43 of Saco ME at Augusta ME [9 Dec 1852]

Mrs 111 died in 1824 [19 Feb 1846]

Mrs w/o Brother MOODY of the Bountry Division, S of T, safely delivered of three children at a birth - one son & two daughters - all of them doing well. Named Love, Purity & Fidelity [*Calais Advertiser*] [22 Mar 1849]

Mrs & three children, a boy 10, a girl abt 7 & an infant abt ten mos perished in the flames in New York NY. A fifth person name not known had arrived from St John's New Brunswick Canada abt ten days since, was a school master by trade & known by the name of John _____. The husband of Mrs MOODEY was one of the 1st who escaped by jumping from a window in the rear... [*Boston Courier*] [22 May 1835]

Nathan Esq 77 at Hallowell ME [9 Apr 1846]

Octavia Mrs 48 at Limington ME [15 Aug 1840]

Patience Mrs 78 of Lincolnville ME at Union ME [7 May 1846]

Rebecca committed suicide by cutting throat with a razor on Tues w/o Enoch MOODY & d/o Stephen LITTLE Esq of Portland ME [22 June 1839] & [6 Jul 1839]

Richard 77 10th inst at Windsor ME [19 Oct 1839]

Sarah 35 w/o James MOODY 25 Jan at Bath ME [6 Feb 1835]

Sarah H 49 d/o late Edmund MOODY Capt at Saco ME [25 Jun 1846]

Wealthy 68 w/o Joshua MOODY at Bath ME [3 Apr 1845]

MOOERS David 89 AmRev at Pittston ME [11 Feb 1847]

Ellen A 13 d/o Timothy MOOERS at Hallowell ME [25 Dec 1845]

William of Vassalboro ME accidental discharge of a gun on Sat the 25th ult [6 Apr 1848]

MOOERS - see DEARBORN, WELLS

MOONEY Mary Adaline d/o John MOONEY Lt USN at Newcastle ME [15 Oct 1846]
Miss 10y at Jersey city accident from gunpowder at house at Bergen St occupied by a number of Irish families (copied from *NY Sun*) [3 Apr 1838]

MOONEY - see SANBORN

MOOR Hector a member of the St Louis bar, convicted at Memphis TN of the abduction of a negro & sentenced to the penitentiary for five years. [13 Dec 1849]
John 68 at Lewiston ME (NB spelling of his name was "MOOAR" b 14 Aug 1780, d 20 Dec 1848) [11 Jan 1849]
Nancy Mrs 31 at Anson ME [29 Apr 1833]

MOORE 9 mo c/o Alden MOORE of Woburn MA at Hallowell ME [29 Aug 1844]
Aaron 79 from being thrown from a wagon 5th inst at Rumford ME [27 Apr 1839]
Abel Capt struck upon the head with a hand spike while at work upon logs near Holeb Falls on Dead River & killed. He was thrown into the river & at last accounts his body had not been found [*Mann's Physician*] [8 June 1848]
Albert of Thomaston ME while at work in the quarries so seriously injured by a fragment of rock, which struck him on the head that he lived but a few hours [*The Thomaston Gazette*] [14 May 1846]
Angeline S 18 formerly of New Sharon ME at Worcester MA [4 Nov 1852]
Benjamin 89 yr 11 d at Sebec ME [18 Jan 1844]
Betsey 69 w/o Capt Leonard MOORE at Sidney ME [18 Nov 1843]
Ebenezer Esq formerly of Gardiner ME elected mayor of Quincy IL [16 May 1840]
Edwin W commodore in the Texan Navy arrested by U. S. authorities of New York & held to bail $1000 for enlisting men in that city for the Texan Army & Navy [11 Jan 1840]
Elsy widow 85 at Gardiner ME [25 Feb 1847]
Eveline 14 d/o Capt John MOORE at Waterville ME [22 Jan 1842]
Frances C 3m d/o I H MOORE at Augusta ME [14 Sept 1848]
Geo Henry 3y s/o George MOORE at Gardiner ME [4 Feb 1847]
Goff 89 AmRev at Madison ME [10 Oct 1850]
Hannah 88th yr on the 7th at her res in Windor Terrace Clifton [2 Nov 1833]
Heman A Gen, member of Congress from OH at Columbus OH on 3d inst [18 Apr 1844]
Henry 20 at Waterville ME [29 Apr 1847]
Ira 35 at Bath ME [20 May 1836]
James a mason of Endicott St, Boston MA stepping on board the East Boston MA ferry boat & slipped & fell between & drowned (from the *Boston Bee*) [9 Oct 1845)
James Jr 23 at Parsonsfield ME on 26 Jan [21 Feb 1851]
James M late of Gardiner ME, Leonard MOORE Jr exec [20 May 1852]
Jeremiah married in 1822, Polly PROUGH, tried to divorce his wife in 1825, on the grounds that he had kissed an unmarried woman, but the Ohio Supreme Judicial Court said no. [18 Mar 1833]
John 74 "beloved & universally repected for his goodness" at Anson ME [15 Feb 1840]
John H 41 formerly of Bath ME at Gardiner ME [8 Apr 1847]
Joseph 61 at Hartland ME [24 Jun 1852]
Joseph 82 at North Anson ME [7 Oct 1852]
Joshua 81 AmRev one of the brave patriots selected by General WAYNE for the taking of Stony Point. He was in seven pitched battles including the capture of BURGOYNE, battle of Monmouth. He was one of the first settlers of Vienna and for eleven years a selectman, 8 Oct at Vienna ME [8 Feb 1840]
Julia Anna 7m d/o Lewis D MOORE Esq at Augusta ME on 27 Dec [8 Jan 1852]
lad abt 11y from Waterville ME drowned [14 Aug 1845]
Lydia Ann 13mo at Bath ME [26 Dec 1844]

MORRILL (Cont.) Samuel late of Winthrop ME, Joanna MORRILL adm [20 May 1852]
    Sophronia 37 w/o John S MORRILL at St Albans ME [13 Aug 1846]
MORRILL - see CUSHMAN
MORRIS Henry Esq High Sheriff of Philadelphia PA died s/o Robert MORRIS the financier
    of the American Revolution [10 Dec 1842]
    James Capt of Portland ME lost overboard from brig *Houston* on passage from Boston
        MA to Wilmington NC [21 Jan 1847]
    Rhoda Caroline 20 of Portland ME at Windham ME [26 Jun 1845]
    Robert a black member of the Massachusetts bar, to be taken up next [26 June 1851]
    Robert Jr a young colored man, made his debut in the court of common pleas in Boston
        MA & acquitted himself with much credit. It is said that there are many lawyers with
        whiter skins & blacker characters than his. [3 Feb 1848]
MORRIS - see ELLISON, JONES, WILLIAMS
MORRISON Hiram 45 at Madison ME [4 June 1851]
    John abt 40 on 14 Sept at Augusta ME [19 Sep 1850]
    John late of Wayne ME, Elisha KENT executor [29 Jul 1852]
    Lydia Mrs 82 at Robbinston ME [11 Sept 1851]
    Mark L 17 s/o Capt Pearson MORRISON of Phipsburg ME on board ship *Kossuth* [19
        Sep 1850]
    Mary M 53 w/o Capt P MORRISON at Phipsburg ME [17 Feb 1848]
    Montgomery 63 at Fayette ME on 10th ult [9 Apr 1846]
    Sarah 56 w/o John MORRISON Esq at Farmington ME on 13 Jan [12 Feb 1852]
MORSE Affa Mrs 37 d/o Col B DUNN at Saco ME [26 Mar 1846]
    Andrew Esq 82 at Bloomfield ME [10 Apr 1851]
    Anna Mrs 68 at Norway ME [16 Jul 1846]
    Asa Mrs 100 at Belchertown MA [2 Dec 1843]
    Catharine J Miss 25 at Portland ME [14 Aug 1845]
    Charles 2nd abt 28 eldest s/o Eliphalet MORSE at Norridgewock ME [27 Mar 1838]
    Charles Col 69y 7mo 30 May at Wilton ME [5 June 1845]
    Charlotte Jane 17 d/o Samuel MORSE at Fayette ME [4 Jul 1840]
    David ab 45 at Livermore ME [5 Jun 1841]
    David L 28 of St Albans on board schr *William M Mier* on passage from the West Indies
        [20 Feb 1851] & [6 Mar 1851]
    Eliza 68 w/o Deac MORSE at Bath ME [24 June 1852] & Eliza 69 w/o Deac William
        MORSE at Bath ME [17 June 1852]
    Eliza S 25 d/o Thomas STEVENS formerly of Augusta ME at Worcester MA [22 Feb
        1849]
    Emma Ann Miss a native of Fayette ME & "pupil at the Asylum for the deaf & dumb"
        (deaf-mute) at Hartford CT [10 Oct 1840]
    George S 7 s/o William H MORSE 24th inst at Augusta ME [5 Jun 1845]
    Henry B 4 s/o William MORSE Jr at Hallowell ME [2 Jan 1835]
    J Capt 77 at Livermore ME [16 Nov 1848]
    Jabez 64 at Mt Vernon ME [5 Oct 1848]
    Jacob abt 83y AmRev formerly of NH on 20 Nov at Augusta ME [2 Dec 1847]
    Jonathan 80 at Phipsburg ME [24 Jun 1836]
    Joseph H of Livermore ME left his father's house in Oct 1847, between 18 & 19y, dark
        complexion, dark eyes & hair & of slim form, s/o Joseph M of Livermore ME want
        information & his return [25 Jan 1849]
    Joshua 22 at Gray ME [27 Dec 1849]
    Lydia A 18 at Lisbon ME [2 Aug 1849]
    Lyman 4mo s/o William H MORSE at Augusta ME [4 Sep 1845]
    Mary Ann 37 w/o Samuel A MORSE Esq on 29th ult at Machias ME [9 Jul 1842]

MORSE (Cont.) Mary G 40 formerly of Hallowell ME at New Castle ME [20 Nov 1851]

Melinda D 18 w/o Samuel & Sarah MORSE of Sidney ME at Hallowell ME [7 Dec 1848]

Miss abt 17 d/o James MORSE at Thomaston ME [9 Apr 1846]

Mrs 70 w/o Ephraim MORSE at Brunswick ME [7 Sep 1848]

Philip 91yr 9mo AmRev & of first settlers of Fayette ME on 17th inst at Fayette [25 Feb 1847]

Rufus W 24 of Livermore ME at Lewiston ME [10 May 1849]

Salley 60 w/o Joel MORSE at Auburn ME [22 Aug 1850]

Sarah Mrs 48 at Hallowell ME [1 Aug 1837]

Vesta L Miss 33 at Paris ME [26 Jul 1849]

William 84 one of first settlers of Hallowell ME at Hallowell ME [2 May 1844]

William Dea 71 at Bath ME [22 July 1852]

William Dea 76 at Dixfield ME [11 Feb 1847]

William H abt 45 of Brunswick ME the senator-elect from Cumberland Co died very suddenly at his residence last Thurs [13 Apr 1848]

William of Bath ME saved from drowning when the steam packet *New England* sank. It left Boston for Bath & Gardiner ME and had an accident with the schr *Curlew* on 31 May [12 June 1838]

Wyman Capt 44 at Bath ME [15 Aug 1844]

MORTON Abigail 101 w/o late Jas MORTON at Bristol ME [7 Jun 1849]

Andrew Capt 37 late master of packet schr *Splendid* at Eastport ME [23 Dec 1836]

Betsey 51 w/o John MORTON at Monson ME [22 Sept 1840]

C B of Augusta on board barque *Blonde* en route from Panama to San Francisco CA [17 Jun 1852]

C Gilbert 18mo only c/o Wm H and Annie C MORTON formerly of Augusta ME on 23 Aug at Hingham MA [9 Sep 1852]

Christina Bennet 77 relict of late Nath'l MORTON, native of Middlebury MA at Winthrop ME [25 Nov 1847]

Christopher s/o Ruben MORTON and a member of the junior class of Bowdoin College at Portland ME [28 Dec 1833]

Clarinda 19 at Norridgewock [1 Mar 1849]

Elsie 60 w/o Reuben MORTON at Norridgewock [14 Feb 1850]

Francis S 9 s/o C B MORTON fishing near the upper dam in this village when the slab on which he was standing gave way fell into water and drowned at Winthrop [20 Jun 1840]

Freeman C 30 at Paris ME [26 Sep 1850]

Geo W 14 mo s/o Wm H MORTON on 13 Oct at Augusta ME [17 Oct 1850]

George A 24 s/o George W MORTON of Augusta ME on 9 Nov at Key West FL [16 Dec 1847]

George W of Augusta ME saved from drowning when the steam packet *New England* sank. It left Boston for Bath & Gardiner ME and had an accident with the schr *Curlew* on 31 May [12 June 1838]

Harriet Maria 3 d/o A B MORTON at Hallowell ME [9 Oct 1841]

Jacob the major general of the state artillery, probably the oldest military officer in the country [*New Yorker*] at New York on 3 Dec 1836 [13 Jan 1837]

James of Bristol ME on board brig *Argo* at Boston ME [25 Sept 1851]

Joseph P 69 at New Vineyard ME [18 Nov 1843]

Livy 78 formerly of Winthrop ME on 19th ult at Middleboro MA [14 Aug 1838]

Lucinda F 31 w/o J P MORTON Esq at Exeter Mills (ME?) [23 Jan 1851]

Mark 19 at Bangor ME [21 Jan 1847]

Mary P 35 w/o Thos MORTON Jr at (Augusta ME) [11 Oct 1849]

MORTON (Cont.) Mordecai 62 a worthy and respectable citizen 9th inst at Winthrop ME [18 Sep 1835]

Priscilla 80 formerly of Middleboro MA w/o late Mordecai MORTON of Winthrop ME at Bloomfield ME [4 Nov 1852]

Richard L 31 one of MA Volunteers 31 at Gardiner ME [5 Oct 1848]

Sophia C Mrs 54 of East Boston MA at Winthrop ME [19 Sep 1850]

Thomas Esq 70 at Jackson ME [13 Jun 1850]

Thomas Jr 50 at Augusta ME on 16 Apr [1 May 1851] & late of Augusta ME [15 Apr 1852]

William 70 at New Vineyard ME [21 May 1846]

MORTON - see ADAMS

MOSES Frederick & Leman two sons of Capt T MOSES of Rouen Island in the Passamaquoddy Bay were drowned but a third brother was saved [*Eastport Sentinel*] [25 Jan 1849]

Henry a journeyman mechanic many years in the employment of Mr BABCOCK,carriage manufacturer, hung himself about 6 o'clock. He was an aged man, unmarried & has no relation in this quarter on Sat at Portland ME (from the *Portland Advertiser*) [22 Oct 1842]

Henry a slave tried before the Hastings Court VA for the murder of Delila FISHER, free mulatto woman & found guilty. He is to be hanged on the 27th of Mar next [5 Feb 1846]

Julia P 5 d/o Oliver MOSES Esq at Bath ME [24 Apr 1845]

MOSES - see RAMSAY

MOSHER Amanda A 7yr 6mo only d/o James H and Sarah T MOSHER 18 Jun of measles at Belgrade ME [12 Jul 1849]

child of Dartmouth NH c/o Dep Sheriff Lemuel MOSHER Esq accidentally poisoned (from *New Bedford Mercury*) [8 May 1851]

Drusilla of Rome ME & her child abt 3y are runaway poor of Joseph WARREN of Rome [1 May 1845]

Elisha 80 2nd inst at Belgrade ME [21 Jan 1847]

Helen Melvina 1yr 9mo d/o Wm Jr and Betsey MOSHER 2 Jan at China ME [4 Feb 1847]

Hugh, John & Daniel a search making for the heirs in this country (USA) to whom an est of 32 million recently descended in England [*The Albany Advertiser*] [1 Apr 1836]

Lodia Ann 9yr 4mo d/o Capt Wm and Freelove MOSHER on 23 Jan at China ME [4 Feb 1847]

Sarah T 36 8m w/o James H MOSHER at Belgrade ME on 29 Feb (Western papers please copy) [11 Mar 1852]

MOSSMAN Aaron 83 AmRev on 27th ult at Thomaston ME [12 Dec 1840]

Myrick Esq 45 at Thomaston ME [28 Oct 1847]

MOTT Thomas 72 of consumption 29 Nov at New Lebanon NY [21 Mar 1840]

MOULTON Benning abt 50 on 17 Sept at Augusta ME [26 Sep 1850]

Daniel 85 at Scarborough ME [15 Mar 1849]

Edwin S on 15 Nov drowned in Saco River [6 Dec 1849] & [22 Nov 1849]

Elizabeth 31 w/o George MOULTON of Bucksport ME at Jackson ME [24 Jun 1847]

Emeline 36 w/o T M MOULTON at Freedom ME [20 Jul 1848]

Emery ab 35 formerly of New Hampshire on 1 Apr at Augusta ME [11 Apr 1850]

Ephraim Capt of Bangor ME on 8 May at San Francisco CA [11 Jul 1850]

James s/o Levi MOULTON Esq & (cound not read) GETCHELL s/o S GETCHELL all of Springfield in this state were crossing one of the Schoodiac Lakes in which they were upset on Sun 10th inst [*Bangor Whig*] [4 June 1846]

Oliver 47 at Embden ME [14 Aug 1851]

MOULTON (Cont.) William 83 at Leeds ME [5 Feb 1852]
 William S 29 at Corinna ME [18 Jun 1842]
MOULTON - see KELSEY
MOUNTFORT Lorenzo of Falmouth ME on Sat morning seriously injured by a falling of the mast [*Lewiston Journal*] [2 Mar 1848]
MOUNTS John who left Halifax about five years ago for USA with the intention of visiting Canada in search of his sister. He has not been heard of since. He is about 30y. His widow sister, Margaret WRIGHT, may be addressed by letter to the care of Thomas CAREY, *Mercury* office Quebec Canada [26 June 1851]
MOWER John 92 (d 1854), William MOWER 84 (d 1854) and Ebenezer MOWER 82 (d 1847) (s/o Jonathan & Elizabeth (Bemis) MOWER of Charlton MA) see W L MOWER's *History of Greene ME* all three are in good health longevity three brothers now living in Green (Greene) ME (reported in the *Lewiston Journal*) [24 Apr 1851]
 Jonathan late of Greene, Kennebec Co (now part of Androscoggin Co) ME, Lora B Stevens adm [20 May 1852]
 Martha G 25 w/o W W MOWER at Jay ME [10 Feb 1848]
 Octavia J 20 d/o Peter S & Nancy MOWER 25th ult at Jay ME [9 Sep 1847]
 Olivette 26 d/o late Aaron MOWER Esq at Greene ME [18 Mar 1852]
 Seward P printer of Bangor 17 Apr on board brig *Allston* at Hampton Roads [16 May 1850]
 Temperance 82 w/o William MOWER at Greene ME [26 June 1851]
MUDGET Catharine w/o Jacob MUDGET at Hallowell ME [24 Aug 1848]
MUGFORD Phebe w/o Rev C MUGFORD at Readfield ME [12 June 1851]
MUHLENBERG H A, candidate for gov of PA apoplexy on Sat at Reading (PS the conductor of Reading train cars informed funeral of Mr M did not take place, about ten o'clock, previous to the closing the coffin, he assumed his natural color & exhibited signs of returning life! Immediate restoratives were applied, such as rubbing &c but all proved useless. It was, he says, a melancholy scene.) [*Cor NY Tribune*] [22 Aug 1844]
MUHLENBERY Major at Grand Ecore [*Natchitoches Chronicle* of the 24th ult] [19 Sept 1844]
mulatto - see DARLING, KEEN, MOSES, SIMS
MULHOLLAND - see BURNS
MULLEN William abt 23y of Embden ME found in the woods in Lexington ME, on his way to see his bro, who lives in Lexington [*People's Press*] [3 Jul 1845]
MULLIKEN Allison 78 at West Gardiner ME [9 Dec 1852]
MULVIN Thomas arrested at an early hour this morning on charge of violating Melinda EVANS of China ME at the Vermont Central Railroad House (*Boston Journal*) [4 Sept 1851]
MUNCEY Rebecca 75 w/o Robert MUNCEY Col at Newcastle ME [7 Jan 1847]
MUNRO Thayus 44 w/o B G MUNRO at Lincoln ME [31 Jan 1850]
MUNROE James President of USA died 4 Jul 1831 73 [5 Aug 1836]
 Moody ab 26 formerly of China ME at Ellsworth ME [14 Nov 1834]
MUNSEY Joseph 72 at Wiscasset ME [28 Nov 1844]
MURAT Achille 46 the eldest son of Napolean's marshal, on 15th inst at his res in Jefferson Co FL [*Floridian* of 17th inst] [*Philadelphia Bulletin*] [6 May 1847]
MURCH Aaron ae 28 at Monmouth ME [9 Aug 1849]
 P Luncas 2nd engineer crew lost & missing on 7th inst the steamboat *New York*, bound from Galveston to New Orleans was wrecked in a hurricane, 17 persons drowned [24 Sept 1846]

MURCHBURK Mr R of PA, a passenger perished in shipwreck of the schr *William Polk*,
Mr HAMILTON Capt, the Capt alone escaped [*Philidelphia Exchange Book*] [23 Jul
1846]

MURDOCK James 98 AmRev pens at Springfield ME [25 Dec 1851]

MURPHY Charles L of Bath ME at California [2 Dec 1852]

Henry of New York fatal shipwreck of the schr *Argus* on Plum Island Capt CROCKETT
of Frankfort ME was the captain [2 Jan 1851]

Michael 22 seaman, a naturalized American citizen killed at Havana [9 May 1844]

Mr on Wed of last week the s/o Judge Murphy of Westerlo [4 Oct 1849]

Mrs her body & that of her son buried on Tues on Long Island NY, says Mr J J
SPROULL, agent of the Underwriters [*NY Herald*] [21 Feb 1850]

Patrick who went to bed with a pistol under his pillow shot himself through the arm
during the night. Patrick should be careful in his selection of bedfellows at Norfolk
VA [19 June 1851]

Thomas 47 of Portland ME at Woodstock ME [28 Feb 1850]

Thomas an Irishman employed in slating the brick stores in water street erected by D
WILLIAMS Esq on Wed last fell from the roof on the back side of the building to the
ground a distance of 50 or 60 feet. He belonged to Boston MA, left a wife & four
children (from the *Age*) [26 Oct 1839]

Thomas probably from Boston MA from falling off roof of building at Augusta ME [2
Nov 1839]

W S Gen at Galveston TX late Charge de Affairs to Texas on the 13th ult of yellow fever
[*Charleston Patriot*] [22 Aug 1844]

MURRAY Lewis a seaman on board schr *Dart* of Deer Isle ME fell from the loft a distance
of about 25 ft & his fall had his head badly cut & his shoulder wounded at Boston
MA [18 Jan 1849]

Lucy B 24y 10m d/o Thomas and Elizabeth MURRAY on 29 Nov at Danville ME [1 Jan
1842]

Patrick an Irishman engaged upon the gravel train on the Androscoggin & Kennebec
Railroad, a gravel car passed over both legs & crushed them so frightfully as to leave
no hope of recovery, save by amputation of both legs above the knee. To this he would
not submit though by so doing he might have a fair chase of recovery. He was alive at
the time of going to press [*Lewiston Journal*] [11 Jan 1849]

Rebecca 75 w/o Col Robert MURRAY at Newcastle ME [21 Jan 1847]

Thomas 65 of bilious colic 12 Mar at Danville ME [29 Apr 1843]

William abt 22 suicide by drowning off the steamer *Kennebec* from New York [17 Jul
1851]

MURRAY - see JOHNSON

MUSSENDEN Abraham Capt of Boothbay ME; George McCOBB; William Ferdinand
McCOBB; Thomas HUTCHINS; and Rufus BREWER supposed loss of five lives of
the schr *Pearl*, Capt MUSSENDEN & James ADAMS 3rd & Ferdinand BREWER
were saved [Boston paper] [12 Apr 1849]

MUSSEY Dolly 92 w/o late Theodore MUSSEY at North Bridgton ME [8 Mar 1849]

MUSTARD James Esq 52 recently of Portland at Brunswick ME [13 Jun 1840]

Joseph Esq 61 innholder at Bowdoinham ME [24 Aug 1833]

Margaret Mrs 66 at Topsham ME [6 Jun 1837]

MUZZEY Edmund Esq abt 60 at Unity ME [23 June 1852]

Meribah T 21 d/o Jacob MUZZEY at East Eddington ME [27 Nov 1851]

MUZZY Amos 51 formerly of Spencer MA 18 Feb at Gardiner ME [11 Mar 1843]

Cephas 18 s/o late Amos MUZZY of Gardiner at Bangor [15 Aug 1844]

Edmund Esq ab 60 at Unity ME [24 Jun 1852]

MYERS Betsey of Warren OH recovered $170 from a whimsical swain named Jacob
    KINNAMAN, for breach of marriage promise. Betsey has made a better bargain, we
    guess than though she had taken the body [24 Apr 1838]
    Elden 19 married Mrs Mary NASH, the mother of 25 children! Oh, scissors! what a
    brave general he'd make [the *Lexington (MO) Telegraph*] [7 May 1846]
MYRICK Daniel H MD 30 at Gardiner ME [4 Apr 1837]
    Peninah Mrs 68 on 8th inst at Kennebec (now called Manchester) ME [16 Dec 1852

- N -

NASH Belinda w/o Deac William N NASH at Steuben ME [27 Jan 1848]
    boy 16 or 17 of Robinston ME s/o Mr A NASH so badly injured by a blow from a
    handspike at work lived but 27 hrs [*Calais Advertiser*] [8 June 1848]
    David 60 fell off load of hay at Montville ME [15 Aug 1844]
    Ellen 2yr 2mo youngest c/o James and Susan NASH at Gardiner ME [16 Jan 1845]
    Susan G 32 w/o James NASH at Gardiner ME [24 Jun 1847]
NASH - see MYERS
NASON Albert G Capt, of Kennebunk ME, the total loss of the barque *Cactus* of Kennebunk
    officers & crew: Francis NASON of do, 1st mate; Benniah NASON of Wells ME 2nd
    mate; Wm H NEWTON of do, cook & steward; Francis W CRODKER, Charles
    NYE, James McQUILKIN, Isaac KNIGHT, Edward GOULD, James CURRY, all
    seaman. Neither the Capt or mate were married [*Traveller*] [1 Apr 1847]
    Edward 91 AmRev at Kennebunkport ME [8 Apr 1847]
    Eliza 22 c/o Nathaniel & Laura NASON at Augusta ME on 26 May [15 June 1848]
    Elizabeth Mrs w/o Bartholomew NASON Esq on the 17th after a long illness at
    Hallowell ME [25 Sep 1841]
    Hannah Eliza 1 d/o Nathaniel & Laura Ann NASON at Augusta ME [2 Nov 1848]
    Harrison 3 s/o Wm NASON on 12th inst at Augusta ME [20 Sep 1849]
    John B 20 at Charleston [8 Feb 1844]
    Lot 65 at Gorham ME on 7th inst [22 Sept 1840]
    Margaret 19 d/o Bartholomew NASON Esq on 7th inst at Hallowell ME [14 Mar 1840]
    Mary J 29 w/o Wm B NASON on 15th inst at Portland ME [26 Oct 1839]
    Mary T 39 w/o J F NASON at Hallowell ME [20 May 1852]
NAY Eben 32 at Skowhegan ME [22 May 1851]
    Mrs Joseph 60 of numb palsey at Skowhegan ME [15 Oct 1846]
NEAGLE John abt 60 a native of Ireland of Ellsworth ME by falling upon the deck of the
    schr *Superior*, Capt LORD. John died the same day, left a wife & several children
    (from the *Ellsworth Democrat*) [6 APr 1848]
NEAL child 14 mo c/o John NEAL Esq at Portland ME [9 Oct 1845]
    David Dr at Gardiner ME [3 Aug 1839]
    Elisha B 26 form/o New Sharon at Danville IL [9 Nov 1839]
    Isaac 62 soldier of the last war at Belmont ME [21 Aug 1841]
    Joseph 66 at West Gardiner ME [18 Dec 1835]
    Joseph C Esq 48 editor of *Saturday Gazette* in Philadelphia PA on 17th inst a native of
    Greenville NH [29 Jul 1847]
    Lydia 45 w/o Goldsmith NEAL at Chelsea ME?/MA? [13 Feb 1851]
    Mary W 38 w/o John NEAL at New Sharon ME [10 Oct 1844]
    Mrs 24 w/o Jere O NEAL at Eastport ME [15 May 1845]
    Richard 83 at Newcastle ME [6 Apr 1848]
    Sarah Jane 20 d/o Isaiah C NEAL at Belmomt ME [20 Nov 1851]
    Thomas L 25 at Bangor ME [28 Oct 1836]

NEAL (Cont.) John B the Democratic candidate for Elector in Waldo County at Monroe ME
    [17 Oct 1840]
Negro Ailsy 120y woman, d/o the celebrated Joyce HEATH, her son, now a man of 92 yrs
    employed in the garden at Green View in Fauquier Co VA at the residence of J A
    LEE Esq [Southern paper] [7 June 1849]
negro, free - see WELLS & THOMPSON
negro - see ANTHONY, ATKINSTON, BELSFORD, BENSON, BRAKELEY, BURTON,
    CASTLEMAN, DAVIS, EDWARDS, FARWELL, GABRIEL, GORSUCH, GNESS,
    GRIFFIN, JEFFERIES, JORDAN, KING, MACKEY, McCORMICK, OLD PHIL,
    SADDLER, SCOTT, SIMS, STRONG, WHITEHEAD, WILLIAMS
negroes - see FISLAR, CARTER, CATO CLAY, FREEBODY, HETH, LATIMER,
    RANDALL, GRYMES
NEIL - see TALBOT
NEIL Horace 13mo s/o John L NEIL at Skowhegan ME [8 Jun 1839]
NEILSON Robert Esq PMWP of the National Division of the Sons of Temperance at
    Baltimore MD [7 Aug 1845]
NELSON Alexander D of Calais ME lost overboard from schr *Declaration* [14 Jan 1847]
    Caroline F 44 w/o LP NELSON at New Gloucester ME [24 Oct 1850]
    child of Bath ME c/o Richard NELSON on Sat from swallowing a bean, lodged in the
        windpipe [*Bath Tribune*] [25 May 1848]
    Florence Ella 2y 5m d/o J R & Abby H NELSON at Winthrop ME on 12 Aug [11 Sept
        1851]
    Isaac 53 of Winthrop ME on 12th inst at Byfield MA gone to visit friends [22 Aug 1840]
    Isabella 59 w/o late Isaac NELSON of Winthrop ME at Saco ME [2 Aug 1849]
    Joanna Mrs 87 formerly of Middleborough MA 1 Apr at Jay ME [18 Apr 1834]
    John Maj 40 of Sebec ME at Sacramento City CA [9 Jan 1851]
    Jonathan 65 at China ME [18 Sept 1851]
    Judge formerly of Castine ME at Orland ME [25 Jul 1850]
    Nancy Mrs 60 at Berwick ME [17 May 1849]
    Persis 81 w/o late David NELSON at Buckfield ME [8 Jul 1847]
    Soloman Deac 69 20 Feb at Georgetown MA [12 Mar 1842]
    Susan R 24 w/o CE NELSON d/o B HODGES on 17 Oct at Winslow ME [4 Nov 1847]
    Thomas of Liberty ME a prisoner for beating his wife will probably be tried for murder
        the abused woman is dead [30 Jul 1842]
    3 bros, county surveyors in TX from Hallowell ME [7 Aug 1851]
NELSON - see CRAWFORD, GORSUCH, WEBB
NEPTUNE John Gov of the Penobscot tribe of Indians 87y married in (Bangor ME) a short
    time since to Miss Mary PAULSOOSUP 73y. The Gov been very successful the past
    few months in hunting, having secured some $500 worth of game & he became so
    elated with his success that he could not refrain from hunting among the women.
    [*Bangor ME Whig*] [4 Dec 1851]
NESMITH Carver P Deputy Grand Worthy Patriarch of the Sons of Temperance of that
    district and Chaplain? of the Grand Division of Maine at Brooks ME. His funeral was
    attended by the members of Pinckney Division to which he belonged.[7 May 1846]
    Isaac 66 formerly of Londonderry NH at Brooks ME [5 Feb 1846]
    Mary 69 w/o late Isaac NESMITH at Brooks ME [14 Oct 1847]
NESS Van Gen 76 at Washington City [19 Mar 1846]
NEUTH Mark 82 at Bloomfield ME [28 Jan 1847]
NEVERS Samuel 21 at Sweden ME [1 Feb 1849]
NEWALL E F of Boston MA died [28 Oct 1842]
NEWBEGIN George 93 AmRev at Parsonfield ME [24 Jun 1852]

NEWBURT Peter 52 at North Waldoboro ME [26 June 1851]

NEWCOMB Alvin 30 at Denmark ME [15 Mar 1849]

    Hannah 60 w/o William NEWCOMB at Milo ME on 11 Mar [20 Mar 1851]

    Sarah C 23 d/o William and Hannah NEWCOMB on 28 Dec at Milo ME [8 Jan 1852]

NEWEARD - see HORNBECK

NEWELL Charles & his wife died at East Burke VT on the 25th ult [16 Apr 1846]

    Ebenezer 67 at Montville ME [21 Oct 1852]

    Emily G 22 at Montville ME [8 Jul 1847]

    Lucinda 33 w/o Albert NEWELL at Litchfield ME [28 Oct 1852]

    Mary of Granby the other day braided fifteen variegated Palm Leaf Hats, of superior quality, and of good size. Her sister, the same day braided thirteen of the same quality and size. They commenced at half past seven in the morning, and finished at half past eight in the evening. [*Northampton Courier*] [3 Aug 1841]

    Nathaniel 50 at Gardiner ME [2 Jan 1851]

    Robert of Herman of Penobscot Co ME found on the 6th inst senseless by the side of the road about four miles from Bangor ME, carried to a house where he died a few days after. An Irishman, Mr HAMILTON, was arrested & jailed [1 Jan 1839]

NEWHALL John B 22y 6mo on 1 Mar at Milltown ME [8 Mar 1849]

NEWLAND Eliza abt 35 at Skowhegan ME [19 June 1851]

NEWMAN A in Pittsburg after a short illness, a member of Congress [13 Sept 1849]

    Eliza 45 at Augusta ME on 29 Sept [5 Oct 1848]

    George B 17 at Bath ME [22 May 1845]

    George H 27 at Hallowell ME [9 Sept 1843]

    Henry S of Boston MA formerly of Winthrop ME 30 at Hallowell ME on 14th [20 Jul 1848]

    Joseph & Jacob S HARRIS rescued by the schr *Seaflower* going from Portsmouth NH to Wellfleet, arrived at Gloucester at Thurs morning with the two young men who were picked up in a wherry off Newburyport bar [16 Oct 1841]

    Sally 91 at Weld ME [2 Oct 1851]

    Samuel P 45 of class of 1816 at Harvard and a professor at Bowdoin for several years on 10th inst at Andover [19 Feb 1842]

    Sarah 23 w/o Thomas W NEWMAN at Hallowell ME [25 Apr 1840]

NEWMAN - see CAMPLIN

NEWTON Amos 11 fell overboard from a small boat while engaged in paddling with a piece of board copied from Eastern Mail at Kendall's Mills (Fairfield) ME on Sat [13 Jul 1848]

    Calvin W 23 at residence of his father at Argle ME [now Argyle Plantation, Penobscot Co.][9 Dec 1843]

    Robert Rev the last forty years, travelled, on the average 9000 miles a year & preached twelve times a week. Total, the distance 360,000 miles - sermons 13,118 [4 Jul 1840]

    Thomas a veteran Congressman for 30 consecutive yrs died 79y [19 Aug 1847]

NEWTON - see COWAN, NASON

NICHOLAS Mr house fire at Eden ME (from the *Portland Advertiser*) [8 Mar 1849]

NICHOLS Amos Esq 55 formerly of (Augusta ME) at Portland ME [23 Mar 1848]

    David Capt 52 of Searsport ME at Boston MA [25 Sept 1851]

    Edwin 24 in Sheepscot Falls ME drowned [12 Oct 1848]

    F W the *Temperance Herald*, published at Portland & the *Washington Herald*, published in Wiscasset have been united. The *Herald* will be published at Portland by F W NICHOLS & his brother. Mr ADAMS still continues as the editor, & will, as usual devote his time & talents to the good cause with unceasing industry. [12 Nov 1842]

NICHOLS (Cont.) Francis ae 23 of Burnham ME on 22nd drowned in the Kennebec River near Gardiner ME from the schr *Sidney* [2 Oct 1838]

Isaac P of Boston MA native of Augusta ME and brothers of Asaph R NICHOLS Esq late secretary of state at Portland harbor ME a few days since [4 Jul 1840]

John Henry 1 s/o Asaph R NICHOLS Esq at Augusta ME on 18 Sept [21 Sept 1848]

Melville Capt 31 native of Bath late master of ship *France* at New Orleans [29 Jul 1852]

Mrs w/o J H NICHOLS Esq drowned at Bath ME on 18th inst on King's Wharf [*Lincoln Telegraph*] [26 June 1845]

Philena w/o Capt Charles NICHOLS at New Castle ME [3 Jul 1851]

Stephen 55 at East Livermore [9 Dec 1852]

William B of Portland drowned with brother, Isaac P NICHOLS of Boston MA at Portland Harbor [4 Jul 1840]

NICHOLS - see BAKEWELL

NICHOLSON John of the United States Navy last night under an attack of the apoplexy, a printer by profession, in Richmond in 1804, but his genius led him into a different destination [*Washington Union*, 10th] [19 Nov 1846]

Susannah 56 w/o Wm NICHOLSON at Thomaston ME [8 Nov 1849]

NICKELS Samuel Capt 56 of Pittston ME at Staten Island [27 Jun 1844]

NICKERSON Abigail E Mrs 26 at Swanville ME [20 Jun 1844]

Albert T 34 at Belfast ME [6 Jul 1848]

Dorcas 35 w/o Eleazer NICKERSON at Swanville ME [24 Aug 1848]

Jabez of Charleston MA on 1st inst at Gardiner ME [15 Apr 1843]

Mary 16 d/o Capt George NICKERSON at East Sangerville ME [11 Jan 1843]

Matilda d/o S H NICKERSON at Swanville ME [16 Apr 1842]

Robert 24 at Gardiner ME [6 Nov 1851]

NICKERSON - see JOHNSON, STEPHENSON, WHEELER

NICKLES Edwin abt 30 of Alna ME drowned in Sheepscot River on the 29th ult [5 Oct 1848]

NICKLESS Mrs ab 23 w/o Joseph NICKLESS on 4th inst at Augusta ME [11 Oct 1849]

NILES Hezekiah long distinguished as editor of *Niles Register* at Wilmington DE [13 Apr 1839]

Mah Rev 41 at Belfast ME [26 Aug 1847]

Mrs w/o the American Charge d' Affaires at Turin; the Paris papers say she died. This lady was born in France & married for the 1st husband Dr SUE, formerly physican to King Louis XVIII & father of the celebrated Eugene SUE. [8 Feb 1849]

Nathan 60 at East Livermore ME [6 Nov 1851]

Thomas of Gloucester MA one of his children by eating poisoned clams [*Traveller*] [29 June 1848]

NIMROD "Alcohol, killed more men than all the armies from the days of Nimrod to our time." (see *Genesis* 10 8-10) [31 Aug 1839]

NINON - see FOX

NIVINS Merrion Miss 62 at the house of Chief Justice MELLEN at Portland ME [27 May 1833]

NIX - see BOYD

NIXON - see FOX

NOBLE Bloomy C 50 w/o John NOBLE at Fairfield ME [30 Jan 1851]

Gov of South Carolina died suddenly at Abbeville SC [2 May 1840]

Harris 28 of Fairfield drowned by upsetting of boat while driving logs in the Kennebec River on 19 May [24 Jun 1833]

Jeremiah 63 at Paris ME [25 Jul 1850]

NOBLE (Cont.) John 30 drowned attempting to cross Kennebec River in canoe at Noble's ferry at Fairfield ME [28 May 1846]

John 81 at Calais ME [19 Aug 1843]

John formerly of Portland ME at Brunswick ME [11 Jan 1840]

Joseph of place not stated. "Alabama, *Dread & Caution* of Mystic bound to this port, drove ashore & were lost in the same gale. The only survivor yet ascertained is Joseph NOBLE." [16 Oct 1838]

Mary Mrs 36 on 16 Dec at Norway ME [22 Jan 1846]

NOLAND John of Boston MA lost & drowned the barque *William Fales*, Capt William THOMES of this port (Portland ME) was lost in Wells Bay ME on Wed evening at 9 o'clock, 13 persons on board, eight were lost including every officer. Through the attention of our friend, George M FREEMAN of Cape Needick (Old York, where the barque drove) [26 Feb 1842]

NOLEN Matthew W of Boston MA died in CA on 6 Oct [20 Nov 1851]

NOLLENS Joseph 50 formerly of Sidney ME at Bancroft Plantation Aroostook Co ME [10 Apr 1845]

NOLMAN John of Albany & Mr WELCH of Troy both blacksmiths had a trial of their skill lately at Albany. Mr NOLMAN turned out in 40 hrs 219 horse shoes, WELCH in the same time 209 [30 Dec 1847]

NORCROSS Eunice widow a town pauper of Fayette ME runaway from Samuel HERSEY of Fayette ME [2 Dec 1836]

Josiah 20 at Farmington ME [2 Sep 1847]

Marcia C 22 w/o William H NORCROSS d/o Alexandra and Susan KINCAID 22nd inst at Augusta ME [1 Jul 1847]

Mary 63 w/o Thomas NORCROSS 14 Jul at Augusta ME [19 Jul 1849]

Mary Jane 32 w/o Adna L NORCROSS at Augusta ME [24 Oct 1844]

Mary Matilda 23 d/o Leonard NORCROSS at Dixfield ME [23 Apr 1846]

Nancy 84 widow formerly of Hallowell ME at Charleston [15 Jan 1852]

Robert C 45 after short illness 26 Aug at Hallowell ME [14 Sep 1839]

Sarah Branch 15mo d/o George A and Helen Z NORCROSS at Augusta ME [13 Sep 1849]

Wm A 3 s/o William H NORCROSS on 25 Aug at Augusta ME [29 Aug 1850]

NORDSTRUM Mary E 18y 6mo at Perry ME [24 Jul 1845]

NORRIS Almira Mrs wid/o Capt NORRIS late of ship *Sharon* at Holmes Hole on 29th ult lighting killed her also Mr Francis NYE, who was at the time in his paint shop [7 Aug 1851]

boys; two young men, s/o Joshua NORRIS of Wayne ME by lightning during the shower on Mon. All efforts to resuscitate the young men proved unavailing. In Winthrop the lightning struck the front yard fence near the house of Mr Jeremiah GLIDDEN, but no further damage was done. [24 Jul 1841]

Emma Louisa 1y 11mo only d/o Woodlin and Maria L NORRIS on 25 Jul at Augusta ME [2 Aug 1849]

J Capt 87 at Whitefield ME [19 Oct 1848]

James F 70 on 6th inst at Monmouth ME [21 Feb 1841]

James M 21 clerk from Maine at New York hospital [8 May 1835]

John 81 at Groton NH [9 Oct 1846]

Josiah Capt 55 at Anson ME [2 Nov 1839]

Otis Esq abt 57 formerly of Monmouth ME at Lansinburg NY on 17 Mar [8 May 1851]

Polly abt 45 w/o Otis NORRIS Esq at Monmouth ME [24 Oct 1840]

Woodin abt 29 member of Sabattis lodge IOOF Sun last at Augusta ME [14 Feb 1850]

Wyatt D 24 s/o Otis NORRIS of Monmouth ME on 9th ult at Schaghlicoke NY [8 Aug 1844]

NORTH Gershom 81 formerly of Augusta ME at New Sharon ME [15 Mar 1849]

Lydia 63 w/o late Joseph NORTH of Augusta d/o late Dr Alexander McKECHNIE of Waterville ME at Philadelphia PA [5 Feb 1842]

Mehitable Mrs 78 18 Apr at Augusta ME [25 Apr 1850]

William A S Col only s/o Late Gen William NORTH on 7th ult at Dunnesburgh NY [11 Dec 1845]

NORTH - see LANCASTER

NORTHEND Harriet w/o Samuel NORTHEND d/o Francis PERLEY Esq of Winthrop 3rd inst at Newbury MA [14 Mar 1840]

NORTON Ann w/o Constant NORTON in the 81st year of her age, after a lingering illness of 48y at Readfield ME on 12th inst [3 Oct 1840]

Betsey 22 w/o Winthrop NORTON at Norridgewock ME [27 May 1852]

Betsey 51 w/o John NORTON at Monson ME[22 Aug 1840]

Betsey 72 w/o Winthrop NORTON at Norridgewock ME [27 May 1852]

Cornelius 70 at Industry ME [28 Jun 1849]

De Have 64 at Madison ME [15 Aug 1844]

Deborah 59 w/o Peter NORTON at Farmington ME [26 Aug 1847]

Deborah Mrs 91 at Farmington ME [1 Apr 1843]

Eliza C late of China ME, Sarah NORTON adm [17 Jun 1852]

Emily Mrs 24 of Norwalk CT afflcted for some years with a disease of the jaw and cheek ... "death from the use of chloroform" the New Haven papers announced [22 Apr 1852]

Ezra C 41 at China ME on 29 May of consumption [10 June 1852]

FC master lost overboard from schr *Royal George* of Thomaston ME [4 Nov 1847]

George E 4 only c/o Edward NORTON at Gardiner ME [30 Oct 1845]

Henry C 12y 4m eldest s/o Ezra & Sarah NORTON at China ME on 29 Apr of scarlet fever (Western papers please copy) [13 May 1852]

Henry S a native of Wales at Macon AL [14 Mar 1844]

Isaac 66 at Starks ME [15 Oct 1846]

Jabez Capt at East Machias ME [14 Oct 1847]

Jacob 2nd 22 at China ME [30 Oct 1835]

Jacob late of China ME, Sophronia Norton adm [2 Dec 1852]

James 27 formerly of Buxton ME at Cornishville ME [12 Mar 1846]

James 67 at Farmington ME [25 Apr 1850]

Keziah 2 d/o Jeremiah NORTON of Strong ME at Farmington ME [23 Sep 1847]

Keziah V 28 w/o Jeremiah NORTON at Strong ME [9 Oct 1845]

M P Judge from Kennebec Co Maine now in TX [7 Aug 1851]

Mary widow 86 at Cushing ME [18 Nov 1852]

Mayhew 66 at Farmington ME [18 Sep 1845]

Michael in bed at the New England house, absent in CA 3 yrs & last fall returned to Mobile AL, arrived in (Boston) MA on Thurs evening on his way to visit his relations at Gardiner ME of sickness contracted while in CA [29 May 1851]

Moses Capt of Addison Point drowned at sea abt 20 Oct [11 Nov 1847]

Mr of Livermore ME injured in Winthrop ME "thrown drown & the wheels of the wagon went over his head" Dr STANLEY was called [17 Jul 1851]

Nathaniel AmRev pensioner at Wiscasset ME [13 Jan 1848]

Polly Miss 65 at Farmington ME [26 Aug 1847]

Sarah late of China ME, Ebenezer LIBBY adm [29 Oct 1852]

Susan Mrs 25 at York ME [24 Jul 1835]

Thomas 75 first male child born in China ME at China ME on 28 Apr [21 Jun 1849]

Winthrop B 38 at Bath ME [20 Mar 1851]

NORTON - see COTTLE

NORWOOD Charles 15 s/o Benj NORWOOD on 21st ult at Eastport ME [13 Feb 1845]
Charles of York ME while unloading a load of screwed hay at the wharf on the 30th ult was injured & died the next day. [13 Sept 1849]
Emeline 20 w/o Winslow NORWOOD at Camden ME [2 May 1840]
Mary Ann 19 w/o Joshua NORWOOD at Bangor ME [10 Jun 1833]
Nathan 24 at Appleton ME [16 May 1850]
NOTT Handel Rev pastor of the Baptist church married Miss Sarah Louise SMITH d/o William P SMITH Esq at Bath ME on 5th ult *[Bath (ME) Inquirer]* [9 Apr 1846]
NOURSE John C 22 eldest s/o Dr Amos NOURSE at Hallowell ME [7 Nov 1844]
Peter Rev 65 late of Ellsworth ME on 25th ult at Phippsburg ME [11 Apr 1840]
NOWELL Esther 67 w/o Samuel NOWELL at Fairfield ME [1 Apr 1847]
Mark 74 at North Berwick ME [22 Apr 1836]
Zachariah 87 at Portland ME [16 Dec 1836]
NOYES Ann Elizabeth Miss 19 at Gardiner ME [20 Jun 1840]
Betsey 45 w/o Rev Robert H NOYES at New Gloucester ME [18 Nov 1836]
Charles by occupation a cooper was a passenger the brig *G W KNIGHT*, Mr MUNROE Capt, which sailed from Portland on Thurs last for Cardenas. NOYES was in the cabin at the time of the disaster and was drowned. The cook died four hours afterwards. (N.B. the ship cooks were often black, and were rarely listed by name.) The Capt & crew were taken from the wreck by the schr *Pilot*, Mr COLBY Capt, of Gloucester MA (*Boston BEE* reported 8th) [11 Jan 1849]
Ebenezer 55 at Portland ME [16 Nov 1848]
George formerly of Belfast ME on 11th ult at Vera Cruz [19 Aug 1847]
Harriet Miss 30 at Norway ME [30 May 1850]
Henry Laurens 28 of Waterford ME at his fathers res at Norway ME [23 Jan 1841]
Hezekiah 38 at Jefferson ME [25 Jun 1846]
James 52 at Brunswick ME [8 Apr 1847]
John W 17y 9mo s/o Enoch NOYES of Jay ME drowned in Androscoggin River near Jay ME bridge on 1st inst [1 Jul 1847]
Mansfield 2m s/o Isaac NOYES at Augusta ME on 8 Nov [23 Nov 1848]
Mary 39 w/o Ward NOYES at Portland ME [23 Jan 1845]
Mary Maria 3y 4mo only d/o Wm NOYES senior publisher of *Saco Union* at Saco ME [27 Aug 1846]
Nathan Capt at Falmouth ME suddenly [14 Sept 1848]
Nathaniel 28 at Westbrook ME [10 Aug 1833]
Nathaniel 52 at Carthage ME [14 Mar 1840]
Reuben of Boston MA drowned in a small stream near Dead River was the agent for the Houston township [*Clarion* 23d Apr] [14 May 1846]
Samuel a grocer of Portland ME hung himself [8 Apr 1833]
Simeon 24 at Carthage ME [8 June 1848]
William (the former owner of the *Maine Farmer*) "the subscriber offers for sale the house he now lives in. There is attached to the house a wood shed, barn & something short of two acres of excellent land, with a small orchard, principally grafted. Said property will be sold at a great bargain." [2 Dec 1843]
NOYES - see SYLVESTER
NUDD Abby F 21 w/o Mr J C NUDD at Winslow ME [26 Feb 1852]
NUTTER James 35 a butcher killed in an railroad accident in East Cambridge, left wife & two children [*Boston Bee*] [14 Feb 1850]
Lucy C 45 w/o Richard NUTTER Esq at Bath ME [25 Nov 1847]
Sarah 67 w/o Abel NUTTING at Madison ME [15 Jul 1852]
Thomas 75y 9mo AmRev first settler of Wilton ME having moved from MA more than fifty years ago died on 13th ult at Wilton ME [4 Mar 1843]

NUTTING - see AYER

NYE Ansel Capt 77 at Hallowell ME [15 Jul 1847]
    Ellis 63 at Clinton ME [31 Aug 1848]
    Emily B 22 w/o Stillman NYE at Union ME [25 Jul 1850]
    Lorenzo D 20 s/o Stephen NYE (N.B. paper printed "Ste;hen NYE") at Fairfield ME [23 Oct 1851]
    Samuel 30 of Saco ME at New Orleans [27 Jun 1844]
NYE - see NASON, NORRIS

- O -

OAKES George J 27 of Boston MA at San Francisco CA on 27th [4 Dec 1851]
    Lucinda 18 of Old Town ME at Lewiston ME [11 Jan 1849]
    Martha 11 d/o Ebenezer OAKES Esq at Lubec ME [17 Apr 1835]
    William Elder 77 at Sangerville ME [15 Jan 1852]
OAKMAN infant 15m c/o Major Ora OAKMAN of Corinth ME in cart accident [*Bangor Whig*] [20 May 1844]
    Joseph Capt of Hallowell 25 Aug of yellow fever at Mobile AL [7 Oct 1847]
OAKS Samuel in the 73 yr of age of West Hamburg NY hung himself on the 19th could not marry a young woman, fallen in love with [19 June 1841]
OBER Lendall W 36 at Sedgewick [16 Jul 1846]
ODIORN Jotham 38 at Lewiston ME [31 Oct 1850]
ODIORNE Samuel Capt 78 AmRev at Litchfield ME [25 Dec 1835]
    Thomas Dr 68 at Augusta ME [29 Aug 1834]
OGDEN David B Esq a lawyer of cholera at New York on Mon [26 Jul 1849]
OGIER Abraham Esq 65 at Camden ME [12 Jul 1849]
    Lewis 88 a AmRev at Camden ME [1 Mar 1849]
OLCOTT Jonathan 93y AmRev of Hartford ME on 17 Jul [*Hartford Times*] [14 Aug 1851]
OLCOTT - see SAWYER
OLD PHIL 115y a negro servant belonging to Mr James BRENT of Charles Co MD on 5th inst [3 Aug 1848]
OLIN Dr Rev president of Wesleyan U at Middletown CT [28 Aug 1851]
OLIVER Andrew W thigh crushed at a stone quarry in Medford MA, took chloroform & had a limb amputated & died in about an hour [*Charlestown (MA) Aurora*] [16 Mar 1848]
    Ichabod 39 at Bath ME [4 May 1848]
    Jane 75 w/o James B OLIVER at Starks ME [7 May 1846]
    John 82 of Bowdoin ME at Gardiner ME [12 Oct 1848]
    Mark 10 of Orland ME s/o Campbell OLIVER by a wound from an axe [*Portland Jeffersonian*] [6 Feb 1835]
    Mary Jane 29 w/o Capt Washington OLIVER at Georgetown ME [28 Nov 1840]
    Richard R 26 of Phipsburg ME drowned in Kennebec River near Coxes Head. He and another man were ascending the river in a loaded Condola [*sic*, should be gondola], a rapid current carried the boat into an eddy. Mr O lived in the village at Parker's Head & left a wife & two ch. [*Maine Inquirer*] [13 June 1844]
    Theodore 20 in the employ of Mr William LAWRENCE, accidentally cut in the main artery of his right leg, died shortly at Boston MA [18 May 1839]
    William 90 AmRev pensioner at Georgetown ME [29 Apr 1847]
    William B 22 druggist of Lowell MA at Augusta ME [7 Dec 1839]
    Wm E 24 at Belfast ME [14 Jan 1847]

OLNEY G W Rev 45 former rector of the Episcopal Church at Gardiner ME on 18th inst at Portland ME [27 Feb 1838]

ORCUTT Josiah Esq at Monmouth ME [22 Feb 1849]

ORFF Susan 36 w/o Benjamin ORFF & d/o Christian & Mary BORNHEIMER at North Waldoboro ME on 21st Feb [4 Mar 1852]

ORFF - see MINK

ORICK Mary ab 30 w/o Wm ORICK on 6th inst at Augusta ME [18 Jan 1849]

ORMSBY Phebe Z 33y 8mo d/o Daniel and Zeruiah P ORMSBY on 17th inst after a long and painful illness [25 Oct 1849]

ORNE Columbus left a widow, Mrs Harriet ORNE, at Gray ME (on 8 Sept 1845) fell dead in his field on Mon [*E Argus* & Maine Historical Society *Gray ME Families* by Nelson] [18 Sept 1845]

David 77 at Gray ME [9 Jan 1845]

ORONO Mrs 115 an Indian died in 1818 wife of Chief ORONO, & Chief ORONO died a few years previous abt 112 at Old Town ME [19 Feb 1846]

ORR James F 19 at Harpswell ME [7 Sep 1848]

Richard 58 at Harpswell ME [3 Aug 1848]

Richard 79 at Harpswell ME [21 Aug 1851]

ORROK William W 40 on 8 Nov at Augusta ME [11 Nov 1852]

ORTTRA - see COAN

OSBORN Isabella T 47 w/o Alonzo OSBORN at Belfast ME [19 Jul 1849]

Milton 24 at Fairfield ME [12 June 1851]

Mrs of Fitchburg MA w/o Abram OSBORN & her daughter, w/o Mr Jacob TOLMAN of West Sterling passed railroad when the horse became frightened & backed the sleigh on to the track by which both the ladies were thrown out in front of the engine, run over & almost instantly killed. The train had been nearly stopped when they were run over. [*Argus*] [9 Mar 1848]

OSBORNE John 47 of Lubec ME, Captain of Forecastle on 27 Oct on board US sloop of war *Boston* buried at Anjier the same day [25 Mar 1843]

widow & son a boat on the morning of 2d inst having on board 25 persons struck upon "Hunt's Rock" ... 19 persons including children drowned ... all of whom resided in Portland (ME) or at York Point. (*Portland Advertiser*) (The *St Johns City Gazette* of the 2d Aug)[14 Aug 1838]

OSBOURNE Judith Mrs 81 at Augusta ME [15 Oct 1842]

Wm 61 at Eastport ME [5 Dec 1850]

OSGOOD 2y 9mo s/o Enoch and Jane OSGOOD on the 9th at Bluehill ME [2 Apr 1842]

Abigail Mrs 85 at Fryeburg ME [5 Mar 1846]

Samuel 67 at Auburn ME [30 Jan 1851]

Abijah 56 at Newburgh ME [10 Sep 1846]

Abijah N 38 of Newburg ME on 1 Mar at New Orleans [30 Apr 1846]

Atwater 16 at Bluehill ME [9 May 1840]

Aurena d/o Dean OSGOOD at Augusta ME [28 Jan 1833]

Brainard 21 at Durham ME [24 Oct 1850]

Caroline G 30 w/o Charles OSGOOD at Gardiner ME [23 Dec 1847]

Charlotte H 12 d/o late Abijah OSGOOD at Newburgh ME [10 Sep 1846]

Ellen Frances 15 last d/o of the late Frances S OSGOOD, Ellen & May (OSGOOD) survived their mother only 15 months [*New York Mirror*] [11 Sept 1851]

Enoch C 24 of London NH at Hallowell ME [7 Nov 1844]

Henry B Esq 30 counsellor at law formerly of Portland ME at Fryeburg ME [2 Dec 1843]

Jacob 65 10th inst at Bluehill ME [2 Apr 1842]

James Jr 27 of Fryeburg ME at Portland ME [22 Jul 1852]

OSGOOD (Cont.) Jonathan of crew, shipwreck & four lives lost on the schr *Cevo*, Capt
  Pelatiah BARTER [25 May 1839]
  Joseph 39 at Portland ME [2 Jan 1845]
  Joshua S of Bluehill ME drowned at Ellsworth ME [6 May 1852]
  Maria Mrs relict of Elbridge OSGOOD late of Machias ME at Durham ME [28 Nov
    1840]
  Nancy 24 w/o Wm OSGOOD 13th ult at Bucksport ME [1 Jan 1836]
  Oliver S 8 s/o Samuel OSGOOD drowned at Bath ME [27 May 1836]
  Sarah w/o Samuel OSGOOD at Bucksport ME [1 Jan 1836]
  William P a young mechanic a few days since rescued a boy 7 or 8 yrs from a watery
    grave at Bangor ME [8 June 1839]
OSMORE Oscar formerly of Readfield ME at Calais ME [30 Nov 1833]
OTIS Amos Dr ab 30 s/o Oliver Otis of Hallowell ME at Monroe ME [15 Aug 1844]
  Clarinda Miss 22 after short illness 23rd inst at Monmouth ME [30 Nov 1833]
  David Capt 82 at Alna ME [15 Feb 1849]
  Eliza w/o Hon E OTIS at St George ME [22 Jan 1846]
  Frances V 36 w/o Hon John OTIS at Hallowell ME [6 Aug 1846]
  Harrison Gray 83 held state & member of Congress offices [*Boston Traveller*, Sat] [2
    Nov 1848]
  James 23 of Brunswick at Bath ME [28 Nov 1840]
  John 2 s/o John OTIS Esq at Hallowell ME [30 Oct 1838]
  Laura D Mrs 26 at Minot ME [14 Nov 1844]
  Mary W 85 widow of Capt Samuel OTIS at Harpswell ME [28 Aug 1851]
  Oliver 76 at Hallowell ME [10 Oct 1844]
  Sarah Mrs 16th ult at Monmouth ME [1 Aug 1834]
OUACKER family all but Mr & Mrs & an infant child lost in the house fire 16, 14, 12, 11,
  & 2 at Brighton OH [4 Sept 1851]
OUTERBRIDGE Capt on the *Minstool* of 156 persons on board, eight only escaped! on
  Tues 18th of May, the ship was bound from Limerick to Quebec was lost on Red Reef,
  the eight persons saved, succeeded in pulling to White Island ... taken off by the ship
  Wellington of Belfast, Capt McINTYRE and carried to Grosse Isle. The Capt, mate,
  & nine of the crew are among the lost. Of the passengers, 47 were male adults & 41
  females. There were 10 infants on board who were lost & 39 male & female persons
  between childhood and the age 14. The *Eastern Argus* of Portland ME called this one
  of the most horrid shipwrecks we have ever been called upon to record [5 June 1841]
OVERBURY Thomas Sr "If we have nothing to boast of ourselves, - if the world has
  neither been made wiser, happier or better through our efforts & instrumentalities all
  that our predecessors effected, can legitimately, reflect no lustre upon us." Sir O, on
  hearing a man boast of his ancestry, remarked that he was like "a potato - the best
  thing belonging to him was under ground." [8 June 1848]
OVERTON Samuel 103 a free man of color at Pasquotank County NC [4 Mar 1833]
OWEN Charles 54 at Danville ME [30 Aug 1849]
  David 72 at Bath ME [28 Jan 1847]
  Edward 11mo at Hallowell ME [5 Sep 1840]
  Hannah widow 80 on 12 Nov at Albion ME [21 Nov 1850]
  Isaac L 35 of Topsham ME at sea [21 Jan 1843]
  Margaret 63 at Bath ME [22 Nov 1849]
  Michael the cook of Bucksport ME drowned in shipwreck & loss of life on schr *Charles
    Henry* of Bucksport ME, Mr COOMBS Capt off Nantucket [*Traveller*] [5 Nov 1846]
  Philip 67 at Bath ME [18 Jul 1844]
  Philip Esq 93 AmRev pensioner at Brunswick ME [7 Jun 1849]
  Robert P Esq merchant of Wiscasset at Wiscasset ME [4 Sep 1838]

OWEN (Cont.) Shem Elder 80 (of Durham, ME) at Danville (New Auburn, part of Auburn) ME [22 Jan 1852]

OWEN - see DUNNING

OWENS Smith seaman ae 27 of ME belonged to the US ship *Preble* & with the Africa fever at Porto Grande Island of St Vincent Cape de Verds on 10 Dec [10 Apr 1845]

OXNARD Thomas Capt for many yrs resident of Marseilles died on 17th inst. During the late war, he was captain of the privateer, *True Blooded Yankee*, and afterward in the merchant service. Those acquainted with him will not be astonished at his last request, which was to be wrapt in the American flag and so interred. His funeral was largely attended and all the Americans in port half-masted their flags, reported from Marseilles on 20 June 1840 [12 Sept 1840]

O'BRIAN Morty of Springfield MA a letter from Ireland informing him that his brother Theodore O'BRIAN somewhere in ME & desirous of ascertaining his whereabouts. Any information of his abode communicate to the *Kennebec Journal* office or to the *Springfield Republican MA* will be gratefully recieved by his friends [*Kennebec Journal*] [17 June 1847]

O'BRIEN Charles living in Orange Street had hand completely shot off with a pistol in Broadway on the 4th of Jul [*New York Farmer & Mechanic*] [17 Jul 1845]

John Hon formerly warden of the state prison at Newcastle ME [10 Oct 1850]

John & wife, deck passengers of New Orleans a serious accident happened on board the steamboat *George Collier* on the 6th inst on her passage from New Orleans to St Louis MO [25 May 1839]

William member of senior class of Bowdoin College 22nd ult at Brunswick [12 Feb 1836]

O'BRIEN - see DORROGH

O'CONNELL - see STEELE

O'CONNOR John 49 at Freedom ME on 18 Apr [3 Aug 1848]

O'DOUGHERTY Patrick Irish laborer lost life in a destructive fire, 34 horses burnt [*New York Commercial* of Wed] [26 Mar 1836]

O'FLAHERTY T J Rev rector of St Mary's (Roman Catholic Church) at Salem died [*Boston Courier*] [9 Apr 1846]

O'MALLY - see DUNDAN

O'MEARA Michael a foreigner found in a shed adjoining the place of his abode in Wiscasset ME [*Lincoln Patriot*] [22 Jan 1836]

O'NEAL Timothy 27 at Gardiner ME [6 Jun 1850]

O'NEIL James killed while unloading a large bell from a cart at New York [16 Jan 1851]

O'REILLY Margaret 3 d/o Gilbert H O'REILLY at Augusta ME [14 Jan 1843]

- P -

PACHECO - see JOHNSON

PACKARD Anna 87 wid/o Deac Eliphalet PACKARD on 29 Aug at Winthrop ME [5 Sep 1850]

Caleb 75 at Readfield ME [24 Jan 1834]

Calvin 19 at Sidney ME on 26 Dec (Boston MA papers please copy) [2 Jan 1851]

Charles a carpenter of Hamburg St drowned left a wife & two ch. Mr P was formerly of Readfield ME [*Boston Traveller*] [8 Jul 1847]

Frances E w/o Prof PACKARD of Bowdoin College d/o late President APPLETON at Brunswick [15 Jun 1839]

H H Capt 34 at Woodstock ME [26 Oct 1848]

Harriet 59 w/o Joshua PACKARD at Readfield (Kent's Hill) ME [30 May 1850]

PACKARD (Cont.) Harriet G Mrs 48 at Hallowell ME [7 Jan 1847]

James 89 AmRev at Noway ME on 19th inst [2 Mar 1848]

James a passenger of Thomaston ME on board brig *Danube* on 11th inst on passage from New Orleans to Boston MA [7 Mar 1840]

Job Deac 86 AmRev & pensioner at Buckfield ME [20 Apr 1848]

Joseph ab 75 at Winthrop ME [11 Apr 1840]

Joshua 33 at Hampden ME [11 Feb 1847]

Keziah widow 92 at Auburn ME [28 Nov 1850]

Nancy Mrs 39 at New Castle ME [27 Nov 1851]

PADDINGTON Sarah 103y born 4 Jul 1746, d 4 Jul 1849 at Princess Anne Co MD [26 Jul 1849]

PADDOCK Capt P his two story dwelling house at Sidney ME on Mon 25th ult burned, late of Nantucket & his son-in-law, Charles WING's buildings adjoining were also lost [*Journal*] [7 Dec 1839]

PAGE Abigail Miss 20 d/o Sewall PAGE of Winthrop ME at Lowell MA [6 Mar 1841]

Benjamin 77 formerly of Gilmantown NH on 13th at Norridgewock ME [4 Mar 1852]

Benjamin Dr 74 at Hallowell ME [1 Feb 1844]

Benjamin M 37 at Brownville ME [14 Oct 1852]

Catharine 27 w/o Elijah PAGE d/o Richard HILTON of Winthrop ME at Livermore ME [15 Jan 1836]

Charles Henry 16 only s/o Levi PAGE on 26 Jun at Augusta ME [15 Jul 1852]

Charles S Esq of Frankfort ME at Providence [9 Oct 1851]

Clarissa 49 w/o James PAGE on 16 Jan at Augusta ME [24 Jan 1850]

Daniel 51 on 5th inst at Augusta ME [10 Jul 1845]

Dorothy Mrs 83 at Belgrade ME [18 Jul 1840]

E C of Orono ME at San Francisco CA [8 Jan 1852]

Elice Mrs 99y 9mo at Cornville ME [27 May 1847]

Elizabeth S 74 w/o I W PAGE on 10th inst at Hallowell ME [23 Dec 1852]

Fanny 45 w/o John C PAGE on 1 Sept at Norridgewock ME [9 Sep 1852]

Franklin 4 s/o James PAGE at Augusta ME [22 Apr 1847]

Hannah 36 w/o John O PAGE at Poland ME [19 Apr 1849]

Hannah 83 at Fryeburg ME [13 May 1847]

Hannah 89 w/o late Maj Edward H PAGE on 23rd ult at Bath ME [4 Jan 1844]

Hannibal N 23 on 9th inst at Winthrop ME [17 Apr 1845]

Harriet Eliza 26 w/o Geo B PAGE at Houlton ME [4 Feb 1847]

Henry 34 at Augusta ME [19 Aug 1843]

Horatio N 23 a member of the United Brothers' Division, S & T at Winthrop ME [12 Oct 1848]

infant c/o Greanleaf PAGE at Augusta ME [15 Oct 1842]

James 43 "fell from the bridge" at Buxton ME on 5 Jul [11 Jul 1840]

Jonathan Dr 66 on 18th inst at Brunswick ME [3 Dec 1842]

Joseph S 41 formerly a travelling agent for (*Maine Farmer*) on 15 Oct at Augusta ME [21 Oct 1852]

Kesiah 82 relict of late Capt Caleb PAGE at Belgrade ME [1 Apr 1843]

Levi 87 18 Apr at Augusta ME [25 Apr 1850]

Louisa Miss 24 at Augusta ME [25 Apr 1837]

Martha H abt 43 w/o Rufus K PAGE Esq at Hallowell ME [9 Oct 1845]

Mary M 16 d/o James and Clarissa PAGE she belonged to Myrtle Union D of T on 24th inst at Augusta ME [1 Mar 1849]

Mr (name cut off), with the HAMILTON family, Mr & Miss CHAPIN, Mr FRISHIE, Mr PAGE & Mr COLE. a letter from Carthage IL gave a list of twelve persons of the

PAGE (Cont.) house of Mr HAMILTON, a hotel-keeper who had died within a few days of cholera [14 Aug 1851]

Mr W H fatal accident [*Belfast Signal*] [27 Feb 1851]

Nathan late of Fayette ME, John Fellows adm [26 Feb 1852]

Newell S of Dexter ME at San Francisco CA [8 Jan 1852]

Rufus of South China ME at Dixmont ME on Tues by the upsetting of the Stage (Shaw's line from Waterville ME). Mr CROCKER, the driver acquitted of all blame. [*Waterville Mail*] [27 Nov 1851]

Samuel 39 formerly of Hallowell ME on 4 Jul of cholera at Chicago IL [26 Jul 1849]

Sarah B 31 at Waterville ME [15 Jul 1852]

Simon 76 formerly of Readfield ME at Lexington [18 Jun 1846]

Simon Col 91 on 21st inst at Dr BENSON's at Winthrop [27 Mar 1835]

Sophia B w/o Peter PAGE at Fairfield ME [1 Feb 1844]

Swasey killed at Thomaston ME on the 22d ult by the falling upon him of one of the stringers of the lower toll bridge [*Thomaston Recorder*] [2 Dec 1847]

William S of Bowdoinham ME first officer of brig *Baltic* at Wilmington NC [9 Jan 1845]

PAIGE Capt part of face carried away by a cannon shot in the battle of Palo Alto died on the 12th inst [23 Jul 1846]

PAINE Abiel W 64 w/o Frederick PAINE Esq at Winslow ME [29 Jan 1852]

Daniel M 19 s/o late John K PAINE at Portland ME [7 Nov 1844]

Edward 62 at Phipsburg ME [16 Mar 1848]

Edward Gen 96 of the earliest settlers of northern Ohio and AmRev d at Painesville [16 Oct 1841]

Eleanor 60 w/o Nath'l PAINE at Augusta ME [14 Oct 1843]

Eunice Mrs 89 relict of Simon PAINE on 3 Jul at Augusta ME [20 Jul 1839]

Hannah 68 at Knox ME [29 June 1848]

Hannah widow 93 at Greenwood ME [4 Jun 1846]

Harriet Amelie 3 youngest c/o Simon PAINE burnt to death in accident on 4th inst at Bowdoinham ME [9 Nov 1839]

Harriet Newell 15 d/o Frederick PAINE Esq at Winslow ME [27 Jun 1837]

Jos 80 at Starks ME [22 May 1851]

Josiah 35 at Calais ME [28 Oct 1847]

Love Mrs 42 consort of John PAINE Esq at Anson ME [13 Nov 1838]

Mary 34y 9mo w/o Robert PAINE at Skowhegan ME [16 May 1844]

Mary Mrs 31 only d/o Thomas LANCASTER of Winthrop ME on 2nd inst at Skowhegan ME [9 May 1844]

Thomas 93 AmRev at Pownal ME [12 Aug 1847]

two children crushed by the fall of a cart body of Brownfield ME c/o Richard S PAINE (from the report of the *Augusta Gospel Banner*) [20 Nov 1838]

William Elder 86 AmRev at Anson ME [5 Nov 1846]

Zebulon of Conway NH been pardoned by the Gov of NH, sentenced in 1846, for 8yrs for having set fire to a barn, convicted on the testimony of a boy who was admitted as state's evidence. It now appears, by a confession of the boy that he was the guilty one & that Mr PAINE was wholly innocent. [10 Feb 1848]

PAINE - see COAN, schr *Mary Ann*

PALAFOX Duke of Saragosso at a very advanced age famous for his desperate defense of that city (Madrid) against the French in 1868 in which 54,000 Saragossians perished. He then sent back the famous answer to the demand for capitulation, "War to the Knife" at Madrid [18 Jul 1847]

PALFREY Warwick Jr Hon 60 for 33 years editor of *Essex Register*, & member of common council of Salem and state senate of MA, at Salem MA [4 Sep 1838]

PALL Joseph injured in an accident blasting rocks in the quarries [*Thomaston Gazette*] [13 Apr 1848]

PALLOCK lad 14 at Philadelphia PA on Mon last engaged in some active play with other boys, in getting over a fence in a hurry he accidentally fell upon a sharp upright cornstalk, which entered his groin and caused his death in 24 hrs. [30 Nov 1839]

PALMER 3y c/o John PALMER at Hallowell ME [5 Sep 1840]

5wk s/o Horatio N PALMER at Belfast ME [29 Aug 1840]

Alonzo F 42 of Hallowell ME lost at sea on board brig *Wanderer* on passage from St Thomas to Wilmington NC on 1st inst [16 Dec 1852]

Anna 5 d/o Andrew and Catherine PALMER at Hollis ME [25 Dec 1845]

Barnabas H Esq 61 at South Berwick ME [15 Aug 1850]

Benjamin B 3 s/o Daniel B and Hannah PALMER on 3 Jan at Wayne ME [17 Jan 1850]

Charles lost overboard brig *Proxy* on passage from Thomaston ME to Norfolk also lost Elijah COOK, both men from Friendship ME [14 Jan 1843]

Emeline A 28 w/o Valencourt B PALMER at Gardiner ME [11 Nov 1843]

Enoch 24 of Whitefield at Sidney ME [9 Aug 1849]

Eulalia 29 w/o Daniel PALMER at Augusta ME on 10 Jan [29 Jan 1852]

Francis 60 at Calias ME [27 Jul 1848]

Gustavus ab 20 s/o Col David PALMER at Athens ME [29 Jul 1852]

Hannah 25 d/o Elisha PALMER at Hallowell ME [22 Apr 1852]

Hannah Mrs 60 at Readfield ME [4 Sept 1851]

Hannah Mrs 70 at Hallowell ME [20 May 1847]

Horace 2 s/o Wm H and Almira PALMER at Albion ME [12 Apr 1850]

J Mr the tavern house kept by PALMER entirely consumed by fire on Thurs, the mother, having two children in her arms, in attempting to escape, was considerably, though not dangerously burnt - one of the children, while in its mother's arms, had its face much burnt [*Bangor Whig*] [11 Jan 1844]

Jacob with five young men all of Machiasport going down the river & drowned. The others rescued by Mr SMART. Mr P was a ship-carpenter & left a large family [14 June 1849]

Julius 22 killed by falling of large stub while chopping in woods at Gardiner ME [18 Mar 1833]

Lucien 24 native of Maine death at New Orleans of yellow fever on 30 Sept at Charity Hospital [2 Nov 1848]

Martha 76 w/o Marlbury PALMER at Litchfield ME [6 Jan 1846]

Mary 60 at Gardiner ME [30 Nov 1848]

Moses Capt 62 on 5th inst at Hallowell ME [21 Aug 1835]

Mr of ME of cholera Sacramento CA on 3 Nov [2 Jan 1851]

Susan 65 w/o Amos PALMER on 31st ult member of Baptist church at Fayette ME [11 Feb 1833]

PALMER - see MILES, WRIGHT

PARCHER Ann 26 w/o Samuel M PARCHER at Winthrop ME [21 Dec 1848]

PARISH Daniel Rev of the Methodist Church, death caused by a tight boot at Newark NJ [4 May 1848]

Joseph Dr, an Quaker no less than 5000 persons & 80 carriages attended the funeral at Philadelphia PA [18 Apr 1840]

PARK Joseph Pope 1y3mo only c/o Rev Calvin E and Harriet T PARK on 14th inst at Waterville ME [23 Apr 1842]

Mrs 59y relict of Mr Mungo PARK died on 31 Jan at London England [28 Feb 1840]

PARKER Abigail M 20 w/o Bartholomew T PARKER d/o Isaac HATHAWAY on 31st ult at Vassalboro ME [8 Apr 1847]

Adeline 44 w/o Capt Samuel PARKER at Bloomfield ME [17 June 1852]

PARKER (Cont.) Alonzo 6 s/o John PARKER at Hallowell ME [5 Sep 1840]

    Alvah 40 at Parsonsfield ME [3 Jul 1851]

    Anslem 40 at Greene ME [21 Mar 1850]

    Betsey 85 wid/o William PARKER Esq at Farmington ME [23 Nov 1848]

    Catharine B 17 d/o John and Eunice PARKER on 30 Apr at New Portland ME [1 Aug 1850]

    Catharine R 34 w/o Levi PARKER at Norridgewock ME [13 Dec 1849]

    Charles ab 24 of Augusta ME eldest s/o Edmund PARKER of Norridgewock ME on 12th ult of yellow fever at Galveston TX [14 Dec 1839]

    Dr formerly member of Congress from Kennebec district at Gardiner ME [14 Nov 1837]

    Edmund AmRev pensioner at Norridgewock ME [9 Dec 1836]

    Edwin 16mo s/o John PARKER at Hallowell ME [5 Sep 1840]

    Elizabeth 62 w/o Matthias S PARKER at Waldo Plantation ME [19 Dec 1844]

    Hannah Mrs 76 at Greene ME [29 Jan 1852]

    Hannah was of a party of young men & women, seven in number started from Campobello for Casco Bay Island on a pleasure excursion & drowned, see WILSON & CAMPDIN [24 Jul 1835]

    James M 53 at Gardiner ME [2 Mar 1848]

    James M Capt 40 of Lubec ME at Holmes (Oxford Co? ME) [5 Sep 1850]

    John 82 at Jefferson ME [22 Jan 1852]

    John one of the oldest merchants in Boston MA died on Thurs, probably left the largest estate, two or three millions, in New England [20 June 1840]

    Lavinia C 22 w/o George H PARKER d/o John GETCHELL on 8 Feb at Vassalboro ME [21 Dec 1850]

    little girl abt 2y of St Albans ME d/o Mr Phineas PARKER during the absence of her mother fell into the fire and was so shockingly burnt that she survived but about three hours (from the *Skowhegan Sentinel*) [7 Sept 1839]

    Margaret widow 88 at Norridgewock ME [14 Mar 1844]

    Mary 20 at Norridgewock ME [23 Nov 1848]

    Mary E 10 at Mercer ME [19 Mar 1846]

    Mary Mrs 99 at Scarboro ME [20 Mar 1851]

    Mr of Southbury CT attacked by a bull, death is likely [12 Aug 1843]

    Olive 62 w/o Thos PARKER at Hallowell ME [17 May 1849]

    Phinehas 64 formerly of Bloomfield ME at St Albans ME [11 Apr 1837]

    Rachel H w/o Lorenzo PARKER at Bath ME [2 Jan 1851]

    Rebecca 84 at Wiscasset ME [6 Jan 1848]

    Richard 12 s/o James PARKER at Industry ME [17 Jul 1841]

    Stacy B abt 50 at Augusta ME [26 Aug 1852]

    Stephen 34 at Patten ME [4 Apr 1850]

    Sybil W widow 89 at Skowhegan ME [18 Mar 1852] & [25 Mar 1852]

    Thomas J 49 at Phillips ME [15 Apr 1847]

    Thomas Jr 43 at Farmington ME [23 Oct 1851]

    Wm Esq ab 87 at Farmington ME [17 Jul 1841]

PARKER - see DAVIS

PARKHURST Augusta 5 d/o Hale and Elvira PARKHURST on 5 Apr at Unity ME [19 Apr 1849]

    John L 61 at Gorham ME [13 Jun 1850]

    Julia A 22 on 18 Mar at Unity ME [12 Apr 1849]

    Lucy 84 w/o late Isaac PARKHURST of Jay ME of towns first settlers on 3 Jul at Livermore ME [24 Jul 1841]

    Nathan 36 at Unity ME [19 Feb 1852]

PARKMAN David 71 formerly of Abbington MA at Solon ME [17 Sep 1846]

PARKMAN (Cont.) George 29y 10m s/o Samuel & Sarah PARKHAM on 23 Nov 1849
  [*Cambridge Chronicle*] [13 Dec 1849]
  Lydia C 8 at Skowhegan ME [21 Nov 1844]
  Lyman P 10mo s/o Alva PARKMAN at Bloomfield ME [19 Feb 1846]
  Mary E 35 w/o Benjamin F PARKER at Palmyra ME [3 June 1852]
  Mr arrested on suspicion of poisoning his wife of Parkman ME [copied from *Somerset
    Journal*] [31 Oct 1837]
  Orrison 35 at Garland ME [2 Jan 1845]
  Shepherd 32 s/o Daniel PARKMAN of Skowhegan ME died of consumption at Garland
    ME [10 Aug 1843]
PARKMAN - see GAY
PARKS James 60 at Richmond ME [5 Mar 1846]
  John D 72 at Bath ME [13 Nov 1845]
  Mary 76 w/o William PARKS at Skowhegan ME [4 Nov 1852]
  Mary Ann 16 of Palermo on 25th ult at Augusta ME [9 Dec 1852]
PARLIN Benjamin L 12 s/o Capt Jonas PARLIN at Norridgewock ME [2 Sep 1852]
  George W 6m s/o Silas W & Sarah PARLIN at East Winthrop ME on 3rd inst [9 Sept
    1843]
  Horace Bradford 3y 8mo s/o Horace PARLIN drowned at East Winthrop ME on 22nd ult
    [7 Oct 1843]
  Ira Esq 34 at Weld ME [20 May 1852]
  Mrs w/o Horace PARLIN Esq at East Winthrop ME [6 May 1843]
  Silas Capt at Winthrop ME [26 Aug 1836]
PARRIS Martin Rev 73 at Kingston MA [7 Dec 1839]
PARRIS - see CHASE
PARRITT Salome B 30 w/o Capt Obed H PARRITT at Eastport ME [16 Sep 1836]
  William Capt 27 of Eastport ME lost at sea on board schr *Rolla* of Boston [14 Aug 1835]
PARROT John F US senator from 1819-1825 at Greenland NH on 9 Jul 1836 [13 Jan 1837]
PARSHLEY Ezekiel 49 at Bath ME [10 Aug 1833]
  Joanna G 72 w/o Joshua PARSHLEY formerly of Gilmantown NH at Brunswick ME [1
    Jan 1846]
  Joseph ae 64 formerly of Bath ME on 27th ult at Sangerville ME [26 Jun 1841]
  Manthano 40 at Bath ME [19 Dec 1850]
PARSONS 6 d/o David PARSON burned to death at North Yarmouth ME [18 Nov 1852]
  Abigail Miss 62 at Norway ME [13 Nov 1851]
  Abigail Mrs 83 at Norway ME [1 Aug 1844]
  Ann 45 at Danville (now part of Auburn) ME [20 Jan 1848]
  C S Messrs E S FOWLER, Charles S PARSONS, George W FOWLER, & Hiram
    HARDISON of Sangerville ME visited the Aroostook Co ME for the purpose of
    purchasing land on which to settle. They arrived at St Croix on the 3d of June almost
    noon and found it impossible to procure keeping for their horses, without taking them
    across the Aroostook River which purpose they constructed a raft & started but the
    current being very strong carried them against a tree which had recently fallen into
    the river & stove their raft & two of them G W FOWLER & C S PARSONS were
    drowned. E S FOWLER was saved with extreme difficulty. The horses swam ashore.
    (from the *Piscataquis Herald*) [13 Jul 1839]
  Capt of Portsmouth NH sickness at Havannah (Havana Cuba) more than twenty deaths by
    yellow fever have occurred [28 Feb 1834]
  Charles S drowned at the mouth of St Croix river while crossing the Aroostook on a raft.
    Also drowned George W FOWLER & E S FOWLER and Hiram HARDISON who
    were with them got ashore [13 Jul 1839]
  Charles T 49 s/o Thomas PARSONS Esq at Boston MA [6 Nov 1835]

PARSONS (Cont.) Clara Sophia 17 d/o Gen Wm PARSONS at Norway ME [12 Aug 1852]
  Clarissa Ann 43 w/o Dr C G PARSONS at Windham ME [19 Dec 1850]
  Davis 86 at Hartford ME [6 Nov 1851]
  Horace 23 of York ME drowned at Boston MA [22 Feb 1844]
  Horace H 22 master of the schr *Favorite*, owned at York ME by the father of the late
    Capt PARSONS, he was drowned [*Atlas*] [22 Feb 1844]
  Jeremiah 65 at Farmington ME [4 Jan 1849]
  John 82 at Norway ME [6 Jan 1848]
  John 85 at Norway ME [16 Dec 1847]
  Joseph Esq 76 at Cornville ME [3 Jan 1850]
  Mr AmRev at Marieta OH [16 Sept 1847]
  Phidilio of Bangor ME at sea en route to California [18 Mar 1852]
  Sally 40 at Cornville ME [5 Jul 1849]
  Sarah 77 wid/o Joseph PARSONS Esq at Cornville ME [9 Oct 1851]
  Westbrook Capt 25 at Edgecomb ME [14 Aug 1835]
  William Capt 90 at Cushing ME [27 Nov 1851]
  William T 20 s/o Oliver PARSONS Esq at Smithfield ME on 27 Apr [13 May 1852]
PARSONS - see CHANCE, FOWLER
PARTRIDGE Anna 23 youngest d/o Amos PARTRIDGE Esq at Augusta ME [28 Jan 1833]
  Moses 73 at Augusta ME [28 Jun 1849]
  Nathaniel 37 at Augusta ME [20 Mar 1841]
  Oceanna A 18 at Gardiner ME [25 Jan 1849]
  Reuben 49 6 Sept at Augusta ME [12 Sep 1850]
  Reuben Henry 1y 4mo s/o Reuben and Charlotte F PARTRIDGE on 30 Apr at Augusta
    ME [2 May 1850]
  Samuel of East Thomaston ME by board falling from a building hitting him on his head
    [5 Sept 1841]
  T J of Barre MA & one child of his own & another child belonging to his sister, believed
    to have been on board the *Lexington* when the vessel was destroyed. Mr P went about
    a year since to Ohio with the intention of remaining, but having abandoned his
    purpose, was on his return to his home. (learned from the *Barre Gazette*) [29 Feb
    1840]
  William 16y 5mo at Hallowell ME [30 Oct 1845]
  William Esq 54 at Gardiner ME [22 Jul 1836]
PATCH Harriet G 21 at Otisfield MA [28 May 1846]
  Sarah J 29 at Otisfield [16 Aug 1849]
PATERSON Jane A abt 20y of Industry ME at Cleveland OH on 10 Nov [4 Dec 1851]
  Mary 92 relict of late Wm PATERSON at Belfast ME, first couple to be married in
    Belfast [6 Nov 1838]
PATTEE Joseph Jr 40 at Smithfield ME [8 Feb 1849]
  Levi L 18y eldest s/o Asa PATTEE of Mercer ME while engaged in rafting logs at
    Greeley's Mills in Smithfield, fell into the stream & was drowned. Every possible
    effort was made to rescue him but all in vain [30 Dec 1847]
  Samuel 63 at Bath ME [8 Nov 1849]
PATTEN Alfred Capt master of barque *Dudley* of Bowdoinham drowned at New Orleans
    [18 Feb 1847]
  Bethia C/Bethiah C 37 w/o Seth PATTEN at Lisbon ME [18 May 1848] & [4 May 1848]
  Caroline 20 w/o Capt Thomas R PATTEN at Pittston ME [5 Dec 1844]
  Daniel 22 at East Brewer ME [11 May 1848]
  E S 22 at Waldoboro ME [15 June 1848]
  Elizabeth 9y 3m d/o A S PATTEN Esq at Dover ME? NH? [22 Sept 1840] & [22 Aug
    1840]

PATTEN (Cont.) John 46 at Portland ME [28 Feb 1834]
    John Jr 26 at Bath ME [18 Mar 1833]
    John of Donnellsville OH by the accidental use of strychnia instead of morphine. He had
        a phial of each, both labelled properly, took a small quantity of strychnia upon the
        point of a pen-knife & did not discover his mistake until he felt the effects of the
        poison [2 Dec 1847]
    Mary Elizabeth 25 w/o John S PATTEN d/o John TREAT of consumption on 24th ult at
        Enfield ME [9 Oct 1849]
    Nathaniel 86 AmRev at Penobscot ME [9 Jul 1846]
    Paulina 20 w/o Stephen PATTEN d/o Thomas BLACKWELL on 10th inst at Fairfield
        ME [23 Mar 1839]
    Thomas R Capt 26 at Bath ME [1 Apr 1847]
    Urbane 31 w/o Joseph PATTEN Jr at Pittsfield ME [6 May 1852]
PATTERSON Samuel 34 at Portland ME [31 Oct 1844]
    David 40 at Biddeford ME [8 Oct 1846]
    Edward 28 of Bangor ME, lost at sea 19th ult aboard schr *Bellino* from Havana [10 Aug
        1833]
    Elizabeth Mrs 88 at Belfast ME [19 Mar 1846]
    Francis W 32 at Belfast ME [11 Jan 1849]
    James G Capt 22 master of brig *Julia* and Helen of Belfast ME on 24th ult at New
        Orleans [21 Oct 1847]
    James H Esq 75 at Dresden ME [22 Jun 1839]
    James of Otisco CT accidentally killed by his own gun [22 Aug 1844]
    Jane 80 w/o late Robert PATTERSON at Belfast ME [4 Jul 1850]
    Mary Jane Mrs 25 at Alna ME [21 Feb 1850]
    Mrs died of cholera w/o Rev Samuel PATTERSON at Hampden ME [*Bangor Daily
        Whig*] [16 Aug 1849]
    Otis Esq 27 at Calais ME [3 Jun 1836]
    Robert 76 at Salem [8 Apr 1847]
    Robert his house comsumed by fire at Waldo Plt ME on the 14 inst, new & two story,
        none was living in it at the time (*Belfast Journal* reported) [31 Aug 1839] & Robert
        of Waldo ME the house belonging to him lost by fire [12 Oct 1839]
    Samuel 49 at Belfast ME [8 Jul 1836]
    Samuel Capt 82 on 4th inst at Augusta ME [18 Jan 1849]
    Sophia 28 w/o Samuel PATTERSON Jr of consumption 1st inst at Augusta [11 Apr
        1840]
    William Jr 40 at Portland ME [28 Aug 1845]
PATTERSON - see BOLTON
PATTON - see HUTCHINSON
PAUL Benjamin 22 at Hallowell ME [14 Oct 1836]
    David 89 AmRev at Lewiston ME [26 Sep 1850]
    Eliza Miss 40 at Thomaston ME [8 Jul 1847]
    Loring M 20 at Saco ME [1 Apr 1852]
    Lucy Mrs 83 at Lewiston ME [6 Apr 1848]
    Margaret 24 w/o Capt W PAUL at Bath ME [21 Aug 1851]
    Mary E 25 formerly of Buxton ME at Biddeford ME [21 Jan 1847]
    Nathaniel 46 a colored preacher and pastor of the Union St Baptist Church in Albany NY
        at Albany NY [21 Sep 1839]
    William 66 formerly of Hallowell ME at Newburyport MA [15 May 1851]
PAULL Sabra 43 w/o James PAULL at Belfast ME [27 Nov 1851]
PAULSOOSUP - see NEPTUNE

PAUSLAND Edmund of Salem MA drowned from on board brig *Lexington*, he left a wife & four children, he was a sober & worthy man (from the *Bangor ME Whig* on 28th) [12 Aug 1847]

PAYNE John 75 at Belfast ME [14 Aug 1851]
John Howard US consul and author of *Home Sweet Home* at Tunis Africa [3 Jun 1852]
PAYNE - see COLT, CRAWFORD

PAYSON George M mate of schr *Louisa*, native of Hope ME and wife Margaret 19 lost at sea on passage from Demerara [14 Oct 1852]

PEABODY Capt master of ship *Rochester* of Bath lost at sea on passage from Liverpool to Charleston [28 Jan 1847]
    Charlotte C 22 w/o Wm S PEABODY at Bangor ME [5 Dec 1844]
    Esther Mrs 87 at Belfast ME [7 Oct 1852]
    John and James CARROL both of Maine of cholera at New Orleans [1 Feb 1849]
    Lucinda 13 d/o Oliver and Catharine PEABODY at Freeman ME [28 Aug 1845]
    Mercy Mrs 85 formerly of Warren ME at Union ME [11 Jul 1850]
    Mr Rev 81 on 14th inst at New Portland ME [25 Nov 1847]
    Samuel a native of Maine jumped overboard from ship *Rousseau*, of New Bedford on 11 Oct 1839 [11 Jul 1840]
    Stephen Hon 77 at Bucksport ME [1 May 1851]
    s/o Col J L PEABODY 5 at Brunswick ME [5 Sep 1841]
    Thomas, the schoolmaster drowned when between Fort Independence & Thompson's Island with a party of 27 of the boys of the Farm School on Thompson's Island accompanied by a teacher & boat-keeper [7 May 1842]
    William H Dr 42 on 2nd inst at Gorham ME [11 Mar 1843]
PEABODY - see JOHNSON

PEACOCK Love 30 w/o James PEACOCK Jr at Gardiner ME [12 Mar 1846]
    Sarah 61 w/o James PEACOCK at Gardiner ME [17 Dec 1846]
    widow 110 at Richmond ME [22 Feb 1849]

PEAKS Thankful 68 w/o Israel PEAKS of Dedham at Bucksport ME [21 May 1846]

PEARCE Thomas master & John SWETT, mate; E STARBOARD & J S CONY, all of (Eastport) & all left w & ch; also a s/o Capt P abt 9; Stephen C TALBOT s/o J C T Esq of East Machias ME; Wm FEATHERSTONHAUGH of Lubec ME; Mr SMITH from the West Indies; Wm FOWLER of Lubec ME; Samuel WIGGINS of St John; Robert DYER, sailor & Collins WARWICK, cook. T, S & the cook interred upon the Island; Mr F to Lubec for burial [*Eastport Dem*] [17 Oct 1834]
PEARCE - see LINCOLN

PEARE widow 100y 11m 15d at Wells ME [31 Oct 1840]

PEARL John 59 at Augusta ME on 7 Nov [20 Nov 1851]

PEARSON David 63 at Fairfield ME [11 Mar 1852]
    Paul Esq 55 at Alna ME [27 Mar 1851]
    Tabitha Miss 74 at Paris ME [18 Feb 1847]
    Thomas J 45 of Dover ME hauling supplies for the lumbermen from the foot of Moosehead Lake to the camps in the woods was so severly injured by the upsetting of his sled as to cause his death on the 7th inst. [20 Apr 1848]
    William Capt 60 formerly of Waterville ME at Clinton ME [11 Jul 1844]

PEASE Abner 27 of New Bedford at Chelsea ME [24 Jul 1851]
    Bradley heirs wanted, letter received at Windor VT from Louisiana, died some months since in the parish of Ouachits, was from VT has a sister living near Lake Champlain, left some $3000 or $4000. [27 Nov 1845]
    Bridget of Brooklyn NY shot by her brother [10 Feb 1848]

PEASE (Cont.) Hannah 68 w/o Timothy PEASE formerly of Farmington ME at Martha's
Vineyard MA [25 Sept 1845]
Henry 6 s/o Daniel PEASE on 3 Jan at Augusta ME [11 Jan 1849]
Mary M 16 d/o Henry W PEASE at Hallowell ME on Mar 11 [20 Apr 1848]
Mary W 57 w/o Simeon PEASE Esq at Cornish ME [10 Oct 1837]
Samuel 77 of Vinalhaven at North Bucksport ME [19 Dec 1850]
widow 100y 11mo 15d at Wells ME [31 Oct 1840]
PEASLEE Sarah 51 w/o Orchard PEASLEE at Chelsea ME [6 Mar 1851]
PEASLEY A 20 at Whitefield ME [24 Jan 1850]
Ezekiel 66 at Whitefield ME on 13 Oct [21 Dec 1848]
PEAVEY Ann 21 of Lubec ME at Gorham Seminary [4 Mar 1847]
John J Esq of Eastport ME the US consul at Pictou Nova Scotia Canada [12 Mar 1846]
Joseph abt 20 discovered by William W ROLLINS of Somersworth NH in his pasture,
likely died abt 27 Dec last, while intoxicated, left a mother res in Manchester NH
[*Dover Inquirer*] [5 Apr 1849]
PEAVY John J Esq of Eastport ME, US consul at Pictou NS at Washington City [19 Mar
1846]
PECK Calvin Dr 57 formerly of MA at Ellsworth ME [8 Mar 1849]
PECKHAM girl of Middletown d/o Joshua PECKHAM on Sun last [*Newport Herald of the
Times*] [30 Oct 1835]
PEEBLES Mary 73 w/o Wm W PEEBLES 23rd inst at Danville ME [1 Jan 1842]
PEET Josiah Rev 71y 6mo for 38 years pastor of Congregational Church in Norridgewock
ME on 18 Feb at N [4 Mar 1852]
PEEVY William married Caroline HUDSPETH in MS on 11th inst in the courthouse by
Rev Jos BELL [*Natchez Free Trader*] [11 Jan 1849]
PEGG Benjamin 100y 10m AmRev died last week near Covington Miami Co OH [23 Apr
1846]
PELKY Lewy 5 s/o Charles PELKY at Augusta ME [19 Jul 1849]
PELLEGREA Gilman 43 at Ripley ME [3 Dec 1846]
PENDERGRASS Edmund 86 AmRev at Durham ME [3 Dec 1846]
PENDERGRAST - see COAN, GOULD
PENDEXTER Nancy R 55 w/o Oliver PENDEXTER at Cornish ME [8 Aug 1850]
PENDLETON Benjamin 41 at Searsmont ME [21 Aug 1851]
Charles Amos 1y 14d only c/o Rev A B PENDLETON of Livermore Falls ME at
Topsham ME [2 Oct 1845]
Lucinda Mrs 87 at Islesboro ME [19 Feb 1852]
Peleg 14 mo c/o widow Sybil PENDLETON at Isleboro ME [26 Oct 1839]
Rebecca C Mrs 55 at Northport ME [11 Jul 1844]
PENFIELD Nathan C 75 at Gorham ME [31 Oct 1850]
PENLEY John abt 35 of Oxford ME a peddler put up on Sat night at Dunn's Tavern on the
Stephens' Plains Westbrook ME after dinner on Sun he walked out & fell dead from
apoplexy [18 Nov 1847]
PENN William Esq 70 great-grandson of Wm PENN founder of Province of Pennsylvania
on 17th ult at London [16 Oct 1845]
PENNELL Harriet N Mrs 27 d/o late John GIVEN at Brunswick ME [30 Oct 1841]
Levi 31 at Buxton ME [18 Apr 1850]
Thomas 28 at New Portland ME [23 Jan 1845]
PENNIMAN John A printer his son 9y saved the life of one of his playmates near Perkins's
Wharf [*Bee*] [15 Aug 1844]

PENNIMAN (Cont.) two brothers drowned of East Thomaston ME the schr *Potomac* mentioned lost, belonged to East Thomaston ME capsized on Sun afternoon on the 2nd inst in Long Island Sound, opposite Smithtown, all on board perished. [1 Jan 1839]

PENNINGTON - see KEEN

PENNOCK Abby 17 a chambermaid, found dead in her bed, a native of Keene NH [*Boston Traveller*] [15 Mar 1849]

PENNY Benjamin 88 AmRev at Wells ME [11 Dec 1845]

boy abt 15 kicked by a horse [*Bangor Whig*] [9 Jan 1851]

Elliot Fletcher 1y only c/o Stephen PENNY at Bath ME [31 Oct 1844]

Selathial 91 AmRev at Sidney ME [21 Oct 1847]

PENNYBACKER Isaac senator from VA on Mon [21 Jan 1847]

PEPPER boy abt 10y a Canadian killed on Smith's Wharf in (Augusta ME) s/o Widow SMITH [14 Aug 1851]

Thomas abt 60 formerly of St Francis, Lower Canada at Augusta ME on 24 Oct [2 Nov 1848]

PERCIVAL Lydia G 32 w/o Sumner PERCIVAL at Waterville ME [2 Sep 1847]

PERCIVAL - RANDALL

PERCY John 77 at West Bath ME [9 Nov 1848]

PERHAM B F 36 of congestive fever 15 Jul at Madison County, Middle Florida [5 Nov 1842]

Elizabeth E H Mrs of Wilton ME at Boston MA [22 Aug 1834]

Eunice S 36 w/o John PERHAM at Farmington ME [19 Apr 1849]

Josiah Deac 70 at Wilton ME [19 Jul 1849]

Josiah & Josiah PERHAM Jr of Wilton ME the principal losers when the Readfield Woolen Factory burned on Fri morning last, loss nearly $35,000 [*Washingtonian*] [21 Aug 1841]

Silas Capt 74 at Farmington ME [18 Jul 1844]

PERKETT - see PERRO

PERKINS Abigail 66 w/o Jona PERKINS on 13 Dec at Augusta ME [19 Dec 1850]

Benjamin 83 from effects of a fall September last 11th inst at East Winthrop ME [25 Jan 1849]

David of Hampton mate of the crew of the *Traveller* supposed lost [16 Oct 1851]

Edward B 23 of Kennebunkport ME at Hollis ME [8 Jan 1852]

Eliphalet Jr ae 60 at Orono ME [26 Dec 1850]

Eliza Ann 24 w/o Job PERKINS on 11 Mar at Augusta ME [14 Mar 1850]

Elizabeth Mrs 42 at Arrowsic ME [30 Jan 1845]

Emeline 35 w/o Richard F PERKINS Esq at Hallowell ME on 6 June [17 June 1852]

Frances Mrs 63 at Augusta ME [19 Aug 1847]

Francis of Boston MA s/o Thomas H PERKINS Jr Esq at Swan Island on the Kennebec River ME was accidentally shot [12 Aug 1843]

Frederick Waldo 4 youngest c/o Richard F & Emeline P A PERKINS on 14 Jul at Hallowell ME [1 Aug 1850]

George W elected to the House from Hallowell ME & R F PERKINS elected to the State House from Augusta ME, they were twins (reported in the *Boston Bee*) [N.B. The *Maine Farmer* says, "a slight mistake Mr *Bee*, George is Richard's senior by some four or five yrs."] [3 Oct 1844]

Jacob 84y formerly of Newburyport MA on the 30 Jul [6 Sept 1849]

Jane 48 w/o Peter PERKINS 28th ult at Frankfort ME [13 Feb 1845]

Jerusha Maria 8y 7mo d/o Luther PERKINS on 26 Aug at Winthrop ME [25 Sep 1835]

John G Hon 56 at Kennebunkport ME [9 Dec 1847]

PERKINS (Cont.) John & Osborne WARDELL, mate; Charles GRAY, cook; Charles
CORNWALLIS, steward; Otis HOWARD & James SNOWMAN, seamen, all
unmarried, the schr *Samuel Noyes* of Castine ME from Frankfort via Castine for
Mariel Cuba fallen in with ship *Erromanga* at Greenock from NY on 22d Feb lat 40
20N lon 67 15W only the master Mr H on board, the 6 member crew perished [20
Apr 1848]

Jonathan, John E AYRES and William LEACH Jr, drowned at York 20th ult. They were
engaged in the lobster fishery, and their flat-bottom boat capsized. Each has left a
family [11 May 1839]

Julia A recovered $3000 of Mr Francis HERSEY for breach of promise by the supreme
court of RI [8 May 1851]

Julia M Miss 24 at Kennebunkport ME [29 Jul 1836]

Lot 45 at Gardiner ME [4 June 1851]

Louisa ab 20 w/o Capt Luther PERKINS at Winthrop ME on Sat last [17 Jun 1843]

Louisa H Miss 19 at York ME [28 Feb 1837]

Luke Deac his blacksmith shop in West Winthrop burnt to the ground (see p. 542
Stackpole's History of Winthrop Maine) [15 Jan 1839]

Luke Deac 78 early settler of town of Winthrop ME, at East Winthrop ME [21 Jun 1849]

Maj a fire occurred in Topsham ME on Thurs moring last which destroyed a stable
opposite the Lincoln Hotel and tannery buildings belonging to Maj PERKINS
together with several small buildings. [*Argus* of Portland ME] [13 Jul 1839]

Marcy Mrs 79 relict of late Capt John PERKINS at Bangor ME [22 May 1845]

Mary Miss ab 20 at East Pond Plantation (Incorp as Smithfield ME in 1840) [8 Jan 1839]

Moses P Capt 40 found drowned in the Cocheco near the landing Sat last at Dover NH [5
Dec 1834]

Mr of Kennebunk ME injured when the mail stage upset near Ipswich MA [20 Apr 1839]

Mr of Lamprey River NH on returning from Portsmouth NH last Fri in a sleigh
undertook to cross the branch of the Piscataqua at a place called Great Bay, New
England ... drowned [*Mer Journal*] [15 Apr 1836]

Mr of Warren ME arose on Thanksgiving morning found mince pie & three cakes on the
widow sill, enveloped in a newspaper, on which were written the names of Mrs
PERKINS' sister & nephew. The cakes were nicely marked each with the name of
one of Mr PERKINS children ... they ate them for breakfast became ill & the Dr was
requested, the timely remedies rescued them ... [3 Dec 1842]

Nancy 45 w/o Deac Jabez PERKINS on 15 Apr at Topsham ME [27 Apr 1839]

Nancy Miss 26 at Hanson [2 Oct 1845]

Nathaniel 85 at Winthrop ME [2 Jan 1835]

Nioma 16 at Winthrop ME on Mon last [24 Oct 1834]

Olive 36 a widow at Gardiner ME [6 Nov 1851]

Rev brief telegraphic despatch from Cincinnati OH on Tues announnced his death, s/o
Samuel G PERKINS of Brookline, left a widow & several ch [*Boston Bee*] [10 June
1850]

Rev Dr of West Hartford CT who is now in his 86y settled in that place 62y, graduated at
Princeton in 1769 & was a classmate of Thomas JEFFERSON [25 July 1834]

Robert 55 at Rome ME [9 Dec 1852]

Ruth Mrs 45 at Phillips ME [6 Feb 1851]

Sarah 45 w/o Bradbury PERKINS at Cornville ME [13 Dec 1849]

Sarah Mrs 58 of Dresden ME at Waterville ME [6 Mar 1851]

William 47 at Wells ME [20 Apr 1839]

PERKINS - see WOOD

PERLEY Austin U 4y 6mo 12d only s/o Ulmer PERLEY on 20 Aug at Livermore ME [23
Sep 1843]

PERLEY (Cont.) Betsey Wood ab 13 d/o Capt Francis PERLEY at Winthrop ME [27 Jun 1840]

Caroline A 38 at Hallowell ME [7 Mar 1850]

Fanny Miss 62 d/o late Amos PERLEY at Winthrop ME [16 Oct 1851]

girl of Lebanon NH d/o William G PERLEY Esq playing with a pen holder having one end in her mouth, fell forward upon the floor driving the pen holder far into her throat, on Sun (from the Lebanon NH *Whig*) [6 Nov 1851]

Hannah widow 98 at Georgetown MA [1 Oct 1842]

Israel 67 formerly of Winthrop ME at Vassalboro ME [14 Dec 1848]

Lucinda 65 w/o Nath'l PERLEY on 16th inst at Livermore ME [26 Mar 1842]

Mary 55 w/o Capt Francis PERLEY & d/o Caleb TITCOMB late of Byfield MA at Winthrop ME on 9th inst [20 Jan 1848]

Mary 68 w/o late Nath'l PERLEY Esq on 7th inst at Hallowell ME [16 Jan 1838]

Mrs w/o Capt Francis PERLEY at WInthrop ME [13 Jan 1848]

Nathaniel 41 at Gray ME [18 Nov 1852]

Nath'l Dummer 24 s/o Maria D and late Jeremiah PERLEY Esq formerly of Hallowell ME at Bangor ME [10 Apr 1841]

Olive 57 at Winthrop ME [26 Sep 1850]

Sarah 85 wid/o Amos P of Winthrop ME at home of her son Israel PERLEY at Vassalboro ME [5 Nov 1842]

PERLEY - see NORTHEND

PERRO Thomas 6y & Mary PERKETT 4y are two French ch accidentally shot by Gilman CREASY 10y or 12y [*Bath ME Tribune*] [25 Nov 1847]

PERRY Albion a young man abt 19y drowned s/o Daniel PERRY Esq of Limerick ME (from the *Eastern Argus*) [31 Jul 1841]

Allen 52 at Biddeford ME [3 Jun 1852]

Ann Mary Mrs 23 at Bath ME [18 Apr 1850]

Betsey 86 at Paris ME [5 Apr 1849]

Capt died [*Kennebec Journal*] [28 Aug 1846]

Capt pilot of Warren RI lost & drowned the barque *William Fales*, Capt William THOMES of this port (Portland ME) was lost in Wells Bay ME on Wed evening at 9 o'clock, 13 persons on board, eight were lost including every officer. Through the attention of our friend, George M FREEMAN of Cape Needick (Old York, where the barque drove) [26 Feb 1842]

Christopher s/o Com PERRY, of the evening of the 17th of the arrival of the ship *Suvia* from the Balize on 5th inst for New York encountered a severe storm in the Gulf on the 8th inst while the storm was raging Lt Christopher R PERRY of the 4th Infantry & 6 of the men died on board & one man was washed overboard [*New Orleans Mercury*] [2 Nov 1848]

Clarinda 19 at Litchfield ME [21 Sept 1848]

David B 34 of Auburn ME at Kennebec Hotel at Augusta ME [28 Jan 1847]

Dearborn 32 at Chesterville ME [13 Apr 1848]

Eli 83 at Phipsburg ME [3 Feb 1848]

Emily H 22 of East Thomaston ME on 15 May at Belfast ME [24 May 1849]

Jessey one of oldest inhabitants of Limerick ME [15 Jul 1843]

Julian Miss 18 d/o Capt Joseph PERRY 8th inst at Orland ME [24 Jan 1834]

Kimball 22 s/o Isaac PERRY Esq of Orland ME at Galveston TX? [13 Apr 1848]

Laura B 29 w/o John W PERRY at Brunswick ME [20 Sep 1849]

Lucy Jane 20 at Norway ME [24 Jun 1847] & 21 d/o John PERRY at Norway [8 Jul 1847]

Mary Jane 22 at Hollis ME [18 Nov 1847]

Sarah B 21 of consumption 25th ult at Paris ME [13 Feb 1845]

PERRY (Cont.) Sarah J Miss ab 21 at Paris ME [6 Feb 1845]

Wilder 69 at Northport ME [21 Mar 1850]

William B of Newport RI reported from CA drowned from sloop *Felecina* on 30 Sept [20 Nov 1851]

Wm 49 of Waterville ME in US Marine hospital at Chelsea [2 May 1837]

PERSEY Garret Jr & Sophronia on the mill pond on the Chautauque River for a sail on the night of 21 Jul the boat was upset all five were drowned age 17y to 20y (see also AYRES, CRIPPEN, DALEY) [7 Aug 1851]

PERSONS Henry C 2y 6mo s/o Richard PERSONS Wed last at Winthrop ME [4 Sep 1835]

PETERMAN Elizabeth of Rochester Fullerton Co Indiana thus notices her absconding husband - "Left my bed & board, last Aug, thereby rendering my expenses lighter, my dear & beloved companion, David PETERMAN, without any just cause or provocation. All the old maids and young girls are hereby forewarned against harboring or trusting him on my account, as I am determined not to be accountable for his debts..." [23 Apr 1846]

PETERS George a lad in Hallam PA s/o D F PETERS Esq attacked the other day by his father's bull [*York Dem*] [31 Aug 1839]

John 27 of Bluehill ME s/o Lemuel PETERS drowned while sailing [*Belfast Journal*] [3 Aug 1848]

John Angell 3y 6mo s/o John A PETERS at Augusta ME [25 Feb 1847]

Simeon P 22 at Bluehill ME [9 Dec 1847]

William Capt 54 native of Portland and shipmaster of port of New York for many years 14 Mar at Barbados [11 Nov 1852]

PETERSON Charles J following a deer at Waquoit Bay, broke through the ice. He & Mr JONES upset in a canoe. John SWIFT went to their assistance, were all finally drawn out by the exertions of SWIFT's wife & an Indian. All were taken from the water. P had perished with the cold, & Mr JONES was insensible and was revived. Their dog & the deer were also frozen to death (learned from the *Sandwich Observer*) [17 Jan 1850]

Chloe 48 w/o Benj PETERSON at Paris ME [22 Nov 1849]

girl 8 of near Whitehall NY d/o John PETERSON frightened to death by her brother ae 14 dressed in a dried bear skin [30 Sept 1836]

Stephen L 35 at Brunswick ME [25 Nov 1847]

PETERSON - see AMES

PETTEGROW Martha 27 w/o Lyman PETTEGROW at Gardiner ME [10 Sep 1846]

PETTINGILL Alfred S of Winthrop ME at St Louis on way home from California [18 Jul 1852]

D Deac 82 at Lewiston ME [12 Oct 1848]

Elona ab 55 wid/o Harvey PETTINGILL 30 Sep at Winthrop ME [4 Oct 1849]

Foxwell F 37 at Augusta ME [18 Nov 1847]

Gilbert W ab 20 supposed of Hampden ME on board ship *India* on her passage home last spring [3 Jul 1845]

Harvey ab 45 on 26th ult at (Winthrop) ME [5 Feb 1842]

Jas M master of the missing brig *Olive Thompson* which left Portland ME for Porto Rico on 4 Nov 1850. Crew Charles H PHILLIPS of Cape Elizabeth ME; Samuel BARRELL of Portland ME; William Monroe DEXTER of Bangor ME; Archible SMITH of Portland ME; John GORMAN of Albany NY (copied from *Portland Advertiser*) [30 Jan 1851]

Luther C Capt 34 16th inst at Augusta ME [27 May 1843]

Mary widow 81 at Augusta ME on 27 June [6 Jul 1848]

Mehitable 60 w/o Elisha PETTINGILL at Livermore Falls ME [19 Aug 1852]

Rosannah 24 w/o E H PETTINGILL at East Livermore ME [16 Nov 1848]

PETTINGILL (Cont.) William 40 on 3 Dec at Augusta ME [11 Dec 1845]
  William Capt 57 at Bath ME [21 Mar 1840]
PETTIS David 83 one of the brave men who accompanied General ARNOLD on his
  expedition up the Kennebec to Quebec in 1775, died at Herkimer NY [25 Dec 1838]
PETTY son abt 11 gun accident s/o Philip PETTY at Westport ME? on Mon last [23 Apr
  1837]
PETTYCREW - see CRAWFORD
PHARRIS Elizabeth A 20 d/o Meltire PHARRIS at Sebec ME [31 Jul 1851]
PHELPS A A Rev 43 at res of Rev E D MOORE at Roxbury MA from Castine ME a week
  since [*Traveller*] [5 Aug 1847]
  Charlotte w/o Rev A A PHELPS at Boston MA [25 Sep 1838]
  Samuel 80 born in Pembroke NH, AmRev for nearly five years, in the battle of Trenton
    and battle of 7th October 1777, at the surrender of Gen BURGOYNE & was
    wounded, died 30 Nov at Byron [18 Dec 1838]
PHILBRICK Alpheus ab 35 in a snowstorm on 13 Jan at Buckfield ME [8 Feb 1844]
  Andrew 21 s/o Walter W PHILBRICK at Augusta ME [25 Dec 1845]
  Asa Russell 17 s/o Thomas PHILBRICK at St Albans ME [19 Sep 1844]
  Benj 22 at Waterville ME [22 Oct 1846]
  Betsey 19 at Farmington ME [10 May 1849]
  George W 23 s/o Walter W PHILBRICK at Augusta ME [13 Mar 1851]
  Hannah W 53 w/o John R PHILBRICK at Waterville ME [19 Apr 1849]
  John G 17 s/o John S PHILBRICK on 1st inst at Augusta ME [16 Sep 1847]
  Marshall formerly of Buckfield ME drowned near Sandwich MA? on Sun by the
    upsetting of a boat [16 Jul 1846]
  Meriam ab 48 wid John PHILBRICK on 15th inst at Standish ME [4 Dec 1841]
  Samuel R 20 graduate of Waterville College, class of 1843 on 16th inst at Waterville ME
    [5 Sep 1844]
  Sylvina E 18 eldest d/o Walter W PHILBRICK at Augusta ME [2 Sep 1843]
  Wealthy 41 w/o Walter W PHILBRICK at Augusta ME [15 May 1845]
PHILBRICK - see CHAMBERLAIN
PHILBROOK Charles on Sun last at Winthrop ME [7 Mar 1834]
  Deborah 27 w/o Jonathan PHILBROOK on 3 Feb at Milford, Penobscot County ME [21
    Feb 1834]
  Elizabeth 84 relict of Daniel PHILBROOK at Bath ME [18 May 1848]
  James 12 s/o Jonathan PHILBROOK drowned while ice skating on the mill pond at
    Standish ME on Wed last week [*Argus*] [30 Nov 1848]
  Milton Esq formerly of Fairfield ME at Texas [5 Oct 1839]
  Robert 80 at Augusta ME on 3 Nov [9 Nov 1848]
  Thomas 34 formerly of Winthrop ME of bilious fever 27th ult at Staten Island Hospital
    NY [14 Nov 1837]
PHILBROOK - see slaves
PHILLIPS Abigail N 37 w/o Calvin S PHILLIPS on 13 Apr at Augusta ME [26 Apr 1849]
  Betsey 44 w/o Jonathan PHILLIPS on 27 May at Turner ME [10 Jun 1836]
  Betsey Mrs 59 at Belfast ME [27 Mar 1851]
  Cushing 66 at Turner ME [19 Aug 1847]
  Edward 64 on 12 Dec at Gardiner ME [1 Jan 1852]
  Elihu B 3 s/o Gardiner PHILLIPS on 10 Oct at Augusta ME [21 Oct 1852]
  Henry Jr 34 at York ME [28 Mar 1844]
  J A 28 w/o John PHILLIPS formerly of New Ipswich NH on 5 Sept at Kennebec ME [9
    Sept 1852]

PHILLIPS (Cont.) J S, Joel GOOCH, & Mr HENDERSON of Alexander ME killed last
    week by descending into a foul well [19 Aug 1852]
    James M found dead in a back road, but seldom traveled in Sanford ME. He came from
        Lawrence MA on Sat last, where he had worked since Dec last as an Iron Machinist
        [*Saco Union*] [15 Mar 1849]
    James of Columbia ME drowned in Narraguagus River in attempting to clear a boom.
        His body is not yet found [14 Aug 1845]
    Jenett 16 eldest d/o Hart PHILLIPS of typhus fever on 4 Sep at Turner ME [24 Sep 1842]
    Leonard ab 25 at North Turner ME [5 Jun 1841]
    Louisa 39 w/o Philip PHILLIPS Esq at Turner ME [7 Jan 1847]
    Thomas 41 on Sun last at the Cross Roads at Hallowell ME [1 Aug 1834]
    William M 28 at Waterville ME [14 Dec 1848]
    Zeruviah Miss 64 native of Hull MA at Belfast ME [7 Oct 1847]
PHILLIPS - see ABBOTT, BURNS, ELDREDGE, PETTINGILL, WHITE
PHINNEY Ann W 35 w/o John G PHINNEY at Augusta ME [11 Feb 1847]
    John 61 at Prospect ME [19 Dec 1850]
    Leonard 33 left a feeble wife and 3 small ch on 10 Feb at Turner ME [5 Mar 1842]
    Samuel 29 at Canton ME [26 Jul 1849]
    William Capt ab 34 late master of schr *Oregon* on 19th inst at Machias ME [4 Jun 1842]
PHIPPS John a hand on board the steamboat *Kennebec* injured by being crushed against the
    wharf & death a few days later [*Boston Times*] [13 Jul 1848]
    Maria 8y accidentally shot by Albert POMROY of Pembroke ME [*Eastern Argus*] [1 Oct
    1846]
PHREMBA - see DORROGH
PICKARD Joshua 65 at Belfast ME [13 Mar 1851]
PICKENS Leonard 26 of Wilton ME on board bark *Clara C Bell*, on passage from Rio de
    Janeiro to New Orleans on 10 Apr of yellow fever [12 June 1851]
PICKENS - see MAXCY
PICKETT - see BALCH
PICKFORD John 79 at Farmington ME [4 Dec 1851]
PIERCE Aaron AE 35 of Peru Berkshire Co MA splitting wood when his axe cut the main
    arteries of his leg & bled to death [27 Nov 1851]
    Alvah M abt 24 died on 24 Mar at Montville ME (s/o Hiram & Nancy PIERCE, buried in
    North Windsor Cem) [4 Apr 1850]
    Ann Augusta 20 at New Gloucester ME [9 May 1850]
    Benjamin Gen 82 & formerly Gov of NH at Hillsboro NH his son is the present US
    senator [27 Apr 1839]
    Capt of brig *Columbia* of Belfast ME, when off Newcastle DE, going down before the
    wind abt 24th inst was knocked overboard by the gaff & drowned. His wife & two
    children were on board [30 Sept 1847]
    Caroline W 27 w/o Dr David Y PIERCE at Pownal ME [31 Aug 1848]
    Charles 73 of Bingham ME while engaged in trimming some willow trees in front of his
    house, fell sixteen and a half feet from one of the branches and struck head first upon
    the hard ground. He was so little injured he returned to his work abt two hrs after the
    accident. He was still very much alive at press time. [*Clarion*] [7 June 1849]
    Charles C s/o Elbridge PIERCE of Farmingdale ME at sea [16 Dec 1852]
    Clarissa P 69y 11mo w/o Nehemiah PIERCE Esq after an 8 year illness 27th ult at
    Monmouth [26 Feb 1842]
    Cyrus 23 at Moscow ME [1 Mar 1849]
    Cyrus 57 at Chesterville ME [8 May 1851]
    Elizabeth Harding Mrs 83 on 6 Feb at Norridgewock ME [21 Feb 1850]

PIERCE (Cont.) George A 8mo s/o Jona PIERCE at Augusta ME [3 Sep 1846]

George W Esq 30 reporter of decisions in the supreme judicial court of typhus fever at Portland ME [27 Nov 1835]

girl 2y & 6m of Lowell MA killed by the upsetting of a stage in New Hampshire last week. There were eleven persons in the stage, but none seriously injured except the child. It had the efforts of Doctors DANE & AYER of New Hampden, who were on the spot in a few minutes after the accident occurred but failed to restore it to life [3 Aug 1841]

Hiram 60 (ae 62) formerly of Ossipee NH at Windsor ME (North Windsor Cem, MOCA record) [7 Oct 1852]

James A "The way they do things in Nova Scotia," the last Nova Scotian papers from Fredericton report, "James A PIERCE, a native of this town & Proprietor of the *Miramichi Gleanor* had been arrested on Speaker's warrant, dragged off to Fredericton thrown into the York Co Gaol for some free remarks on the conduct of Mr WILMOT, one of the members of New Brunswick Assembly" [21 Feb 1837]

Jesse 42 s/o Nehemiah PIERCE Esq of Monmouth ME at Lowell MA [30 Apr 1842]

Job Capt of Hallowell ME at sea [16 Dec 1852]

Jonathan Capt 76 at Townsend [24 Jun 1847]

Lewis 22 only s/o Thos PIERCE Esq at New Orleans [7 Aug 1838]

Malancey F 21 d/o Hiram PIERCE 13th inst at Windsor ME [25 Mar 1847]

Nehemiah Esq 79 6 May at Monmouth ME [23 May 1850]

Peletiah 7 s/o George W PIERCE of hydrocephalus at Vassalboro ME [30 May 1844]

Rev Dr of Brookline died [6 Sept 1849]

Samuel M an Englishman in the employ of Mr CHURCHILL of the Franklin House died on Thurs [16 Jan 1851]

Samuel Watson 20 of Orrington ME, first officer of schr *Vanda* of yellow fever contracted at St Petre Guad died at St Thomas [26 Aug 1843]

Sarah 46 w/o Alvin B PIERCE at Bingham ME [2 Oct 1845]

Thomas Esq 83 formerly of Durham ME at Lisbon ME [11 Jul 1850]

Zilpha of Boston MA saved from drowning when the steam packet *New England* sank. It left Boston for Bath & Gardiner ME and had an accident with the schr *Curlew* on 31 May [12 June 1838]

PIERCE - see CARLTON, COLE, LOMBARD, POWERS

PIERMONT Charles H 43 native of Livermore ME on 7 Oct at Memphis TN [1 Nov 1849]

PIERSON John of cholera 50 Sacramento CA on 8 Nov [2 Jan 1851]

Samuel Esq 93 AmRev at Biddeford ME [3 June 1852]

PIDGIN Diantha J A (RAWSON) 39 widow of Dr J N PIDGIN at Litchfield ME (see p. 257 Clason's *History of Litchfield ME*) [7 Sep 1848]

PIKE Caroline at Norway ME [3 Feb 1848]

Charles 4mo s/o Samuel PIKE 7th inst at Augusta ME [19 Jun 1845]

Charlotee 37 w/o Js S PIKE Esq at Calais ME [11 Nov 1847]

Ella Maria 21m d/o D T PIKE at Augusta ME on 1 Sept 1848 [14 Sept 1848]

Hannah widow 92 at Wilton ME on 13 Feb [13 Mar 1851]

Harrison N(ewell) 25 printer s/o late Dr (Jesse) PIKE of Litchfield ME died of typhus fever on 21st inst at Augusta ME [30 Dec 1836]

Jacob 52 at Strong ME [8 Apr 1847]

Justus 78 at Eastport ME [20 Jun 1844]

Mark T 40 at Saco ME [14 Aug 1851]

Martha L Miss 24 d/o Alfred W PIKE Esq on 15th inst at Brunswick ME [26 Feb 1842]

Mr third officer of the steamer *Acadia* on passage from Liverpool to Halifax [29 Sept 1840]

PIKE (Cont.) Mrs widow of Mr PIKE & d/o Gen HARRISON, lost her res by fire. It was just completed on the Ohio River 3 miles above Cincinnati on the Kentucky shore [20 Mar 1845]

PILLSBURY Albert Larrabee 18mo c/o Wm PILLSBURY at Augusta ME [17 Dec 1846]

Elizabeth Mrs 64 at Parsonfield ME [2 Apr 1846]

Emeline D 37 w/o Geo W PILLSBURY at Rockland ME [17 Oct 1850]

J 22 by suicide at Palmyra ME [10 Aug 1839]

Phebe 69 at Thomaston ME [16 Mar 1848] & [30 Mar 1848]

Timothy one of the representatives in Congress from Texas originally came from Maine. He represented Eastport ME in the legislature a long time ago. He now legislates for the other extreme of the Union [18 June 1846

Weston 18 printer at Cape Elizabeth ME [22 Oct 1846]

William Orlando of Augusta ME left for CA (gold mines) [*Banner*] [15 Feb 1849]

PILLSBURY - see HOWARD

PILSBURY Capt s/o Hon Timothy PILSBURY formerly of this state caught the yellow fever at Vera Cruz & died. He was commander of the steamer *McKIM* [29 Jul 1847]

George L 18mo s/o Capt Joseph PILSBURY, fell into some boiling syrup and the embers lived about 24 hours 11th inst at Jackson [24 Oct 1834]

Martha 33 w/o Capt Dennis PILSBURY at South Thomaston ME [18 Nov 1852]

PINDAR Benjamin 23 of Bangor ME on 7 Jul at Sonora CA [9 Sept 1852]

PINE Stephen 68 at Eastport ME [3 Oct 1850]

PINGREE Ruth Mrs 87 at Norway ME [18 Nov 1836]

Stephen 78 AmRev pensioner at Albany ME [23 May 1840]

PINKHAM Ann Maria 20 at Hallowell ME [14 Jun 1849]

Drusilla Mrs 30 at Augusta ME [30 Aug 1849]

Elijah 25 s/o Noah and Abigail P PINKHAM of Kennebec (now Manchester) ME at North Wayne ME [21 Oct 1852]

Elizabeth w/o Charles PINKHAM on Mon last at Winthrop ME [23 Sep 1836]

Erastus E 22 s/o Richard M PINKHAM at Kennebec ME [17 Oct 1850]

Eri 30 at Dover [3 Jul 1845]

Gracia 45 w/o Abraham PINKHAM at Sidney ME [29 May 1845]

Joseph 49 on 21 Apr at Sidney ME [26 Apr 1849]

Joseph H 45 at Dover [3 Jul 1845]

Joseph late of Sidney ME, Asa Smiley adm [4 Mar 1852]

Louisa Miss 15 d/o Richard M PINKHAM on 23rd ult of consumption at Hallowell ME [30 Jan 1845]

Nicholas of Auburn ME whose head is frosted by the winters of three score years sentenced by the supreme judicial court to the state prison for life for committing a rape on a little girl about 13y! His grey hairs will go down with sorrow to the grave. [14 May 1846]

PINKHAM - see CASE, CLARK

PINKNEY Ann Maria Mrs relict of Hon William ROGERS & the lady sister to the late veteran Commodore RODGERS (from Baltimore papers) [28 June 1849]

PIPER Lucy 52 w/o Jonathan PIPER at Madison ME [12 Nov 1846]

Mrs 81 at Waterville ME [24 Jun 1847]

PIPER Nathan 58 at Rumford ME [9 May 1850]

PIPLEY Betsey 41 at Augusta ME on 24 Sept [5 Oct 1848]

pirate - See TUCKER

PISHON Betsey 49 w/o Frederick PISHON at Augusta ME on 25 Feb [9 Mar 1848]

Edward K 7mo s/o Hiram PISHON at Sidney ME [31 Aug 1839]

PITMAN Mark Esq 74 one of first settlers of Sebec at Sebec ME [25 Jul 1840]

PITTS Caroline F 3 d/o James C PITTS at Augusta ME [8 May 1845]
    infant c/o John A PITTS at Winthrop ME [27 Nov 1835]
    Judith Miss 104y 6mo at Harrison ME [6 May 1843]
    Sarah 62 w/o Shubael PITTS at Augusta ME [9 Jan 1838]
    Seth 90y 6mo AmRev on 22nd inst at Augusta ME [30 Jul 1846]
    William 29 on 16 Sept at Sidney ME [7 Oct 1847]
PLAISTED Charles Everett 3y 7mo s/o William and Maryette PLAISTED on 20th inst of
    dysentery at Augusta ME [27 Sep 1849]
    George 27 at Biddeford ME [25 Dec 1845]
    Ichabod 72 at Gardiner ME [25 Mar 1836]
    James Esq 37 native of Gardiner ME on 9 Aug at Franklin LA [26 Sep 1837]
    Mary Muzzy 10mo c/o John PLAISTED of Searsmont ME at Readfield ME [29 Jul 1847]
    Octavia C 20 d/o Samuel PLAISTED at Gardiner ME [27 Mar 1845]
    Roger 94 AmRev pensioner at Buxton ME [2 Nov 1848]
    Thomas M 22 formerly of Jefferson NH at Gardiner ME [2 Sept 1843]
    Winslow 21 s/o John & Nany PLAISTED at Gardiner ME [21 Feb 1851]
PLEASANTS James former governor of VA and U. S. on 9th ult after painful illness at
    Goochland VA [9 Dec 1836]
PLOWMAN Nancy of Scarborough ME w/o George PLOWMAN on Sat last murdered
    [*Portland Argus*] [12 Apr 1849]
PLUCK Colonel at the Philadelphia alms house last week [12 Oct 1839]
PLUMER John Capt abt 60 formerly of Albion ME at Dover ME [29 Apr 1852]
PLUMMER 4mo c/o James PLUMMER at Augusta ME [1 Oct 1846]
    Abigail H 71 w/o David PLUMMER Esq at Wales ME [13 Aug 1846]
    Alvin Trask only c/o David and Elizabeth PLUMMER at Bradford [1 May 1838]
    Charles S 25 on 10th inst at Augusta ME [21 Mar 1844]
    Christopher 84 at Gorham ME [11 Feb 1847]
    Daniel 57 formerly of Pownal ME at Durham ME [2 May 1844]
    David 72 at Wales ME [9 Dec 1847]
    Emily C ab 6 d/o Adna PLUMMER at Augusta ME [26 Sep 1850]
    Henry of Durham ME lost his saw mill, grist mill &c at Little River Village (Lisbon
      ME); totally destroyed by fire on Mon night 13th; loss probably between two & three
      thousand dollars, no insurance. (from the *Lewiston Falls Journal*) [30 Oct 1851]
    John R his body drifted ashore; the barque *William Fales*, Capt William THOMES of this
      port (Portland ME) was lost in Wells Bay ME on Wed evening at 9 o'clock, 13
      persons on board, eight were lost including every officer. Through the attention of our
      friend, George M FREEMAN of Cape Needick (Old York, where the barque drove)
      [26 Feb 1842]
    Jonathan 52 on 17th inst at China ME [30 Oct 1838]
    Leander G ab 32 at Waterford ME [18 Apr 1850]
    Martha 21 (Martin PLUMMER's name is also listed) at Bloomfield ME [30 Jan 1851]
    Moses 76 at Portland ME [23 Dec 1847
POINSETT Joel R Hon 73y of Statesbury, South Carolina at his res on Fri last [25 Dec
    1851]
POLLARD Alfred T formerly of Vassalboro ME 30 at Phillistle OH [31 Aug 1848]
    George 59 at Hallowell ME [18 Jan 1849]
    John M of Cornville ME thrown from a wagon & so seriously injured as to cause his
      death in about an hour [6 Jul 1848]
    Jonathan 43 2nd inst at Brunswick ME [12 Feb 1836]
    Kendall at Sangerville ME [10 Jul 1845]
    Mary 75 wid/o Barton POLLARD of Albion ME at Bangor ME [4 Sep 1845]
    Moses 81 at Bloomfield ME [20 Feb 1851]

POLLARD (Cont.) Thomas 73 wid/o Thomas POLLARD at Augusta ME [10 Sep 1846]
POLLEYS William Capt 62 of Portland ME at Augusta ME on 7 Apr [29 Apr 1852]
POMROY - see PHIPPS
POND Herbert Mason 17 mos only son of John M and Mary H POND at Augusta ME on 31
    Mar [8 Apr 1852]
    Polly 70 w/o George POND at Monticello ME [12 Sep 1850]
    Samuel M Hon 71 at Bucksport ME [15 Feb 1849]
    Stephen Decature s/o Hon Samuel POND of consumption, resident of New Orleans for
        several years died at Bucksport ME [30 Oct 1841]
POND - see WILEY
POOL Abiah Mrs 74 formerly of Martha's Vineyard MA at Mt Vernon ME on 3 Feb [10
    Feb 1848]
    Eunice J 38 w/o Joshua POOL at Newcastle ME [15 Jul 1852]
    Hannah late of Readfield ME, Nelson POOL exec [25 Mar 1852]
    Jane Mrs 60 Tues last after two day illness at Hallowell ME [25 May 1839]
    Joshua 82 AmRev at Greenwood ME [5 Sep 1844]
    Laura Norwood 15 d/o late Winthrop POOL Esq of Rockport MA Sat last at Hallowell
        ME [30 Jul 1842]
    Lucy N 23 at Hallowell ME [1 Jul 1852]
    Samuel 45 on 13th inst at Readfield ME [30 May 1844]
    Samuel Deac ab 80 at Minot ME [14 Mar 1850]
    William G 42 formerly of Hallowell ME at Rockport MA [30 Sep 1847]
POOLE child 4m s/o Mr W POOLE of Yarmouth MA killed by a cat [13 Feb 1845]
POOLER John Capt ab 62 at Skowhegan ME [25 Apr 1840]
POOLER Pamela A 32 w/o William POOLER at Skowhegan ME [24 May 1849]
POOR Amos Esq 56 at Denmark ME [25 Oct 1849]
    Elizabeth Orr w/o John A POOR Esq at Bangor ME [13 Jun 1844]
    Hannah 51 widow of Samuel POOR at Readfield ME [11 Mar 1852]
    Jonathan D 42 late of Portland ME on 10 Sep at Winslow ME [25 Sep 1845]
    Mr his house in Berlin VT? struck & burnt to the ground 23 Sept 1851]
    Sylvanus 80 at Andover ME [16 Nov 1848]
POPE Edward on Tues last at Bath ME [2 Oct 1835]
    Elizabeth Mrs 77 at Hallowell ME [30 Oct 1838]
    Thomas 86 AmRev formerly of Fairhaven at Halifax [29 Jul 1843]
POPES William Henry abt 14y of South Salem MA s/o Samuel ROPES fatal railroad
    accident, run over & killed (from the *Boston Transcript*) [17 Sept 1842]
PORCH - see THOMPSON
PORDEN Eleanor Ann born 1795 later married Sir John FRANKLIN [4 Mar 1852]
PORTER Aaron Dr 85 at Portland ME [11 Jul 1837]
    Benj J Hon 84 AmRev officer at Camden ME [9 Sep 1847]
    Charles V 23 formerly of Hiram ME on 29th ult Tue at Winthrop ME [8 Apr 1836]
    Commodore the U. S. Minister at Constantinople on 3 Mar [29 Apr 1843]
    Ebenezer Rev 62 president of the Theological Seminary at Andover MA [25 Apr 1834]
    H F Lt of the US schr *Flint* of yellow fever, the s/o the late Com PORTER [*Charleston
        Courier*] [22 Aug 1844]
    Isaac Capt 66 at Augusta ME on 20 Aug [4 Sept 1851]
    Isaac late of Augusta ME, Mary PORTER exec [5 Feb 1852]
    Jefferson C 10 drowned at Great Falls, Gorham ME at the canal lock [4 Jun 1846]
    John B Esq 61 at Lyman ME [18 May 1848]
    Joseph 80 at Kennebunk ME [21 Jan 1847]
    Juliet M 19 w/o Capt I A PORTER at Rockland ME [5 Dec 1850]

PORTER (Cont.) Miss 14y of West Prospect ME clothes burnt on the 13th inst later died [*Bangor Advertiser*] [8 Jan 1836]

    Nehemiah 87 at North Yarmouth ME [5 Mar 1846]

    Peter B 71 at Niagara Falls on the 20th inst [*Buffalo Advertiser*] [4 Apr 1844]

    Samuel Capt 65 at Portland ME [25 Nov 1847]

    Steward Capt ab 60 of Portland ME at Augusta ME [10 Apr 1838]

    William 3 only s/o Rufus A PORTER 21st ult at North Yarmouth ME [18 Dec 1838]

PORTER - see GRANGER

PORTERFIELD Catharine widow 90 late of Westbrook ME at Saco ME [25 Jun 1846]

POST Ann Mrs 53 at Thomaston ME [9 Feb 1839]

    Hannah Mrs 90y 8mo at Thomaston (Owl's Head) ME [22 Jan 1846]

    Mr part of the crew the schr *Potomac* lost, belonged to East Thomaston ME, capsized on Sun afternoon on the 2nd inst in Long Island Sound, opposite Smithtown and all on board perished. [1 Jan 1839]

POTTER boy abt 10 s/o Dr POTTER of Pembroke NH, on Sat last as some Irishmen in the employ of the Suncook Co at Pembroke, were at work digging in the side of a hill, the bank caved in, burying two of the workmen & a little boy (POTTER). They were all three dug out dead! We did not learn the names of the workmen [*Manchester American*] [20 Nov 1845]

    David 61 at Arrowsic ME [22 Jul 1847]

    Elish R Hon member of legislature of Rhode Island and for many years a member of Congress at South Kingston RI [16 Oct 1835]

    Elizabeth 25 w/o Amos B POTTER at Gardiner ME [10 Aug 1848]

    Isaac 76 at Bloomfield ME [21 Aug 1851]

    Isabella A Mrs w/o Robert POTTER of North Carolina lately obtained a divorce from her husband by the legislature of that state. She has since petitioned the county court of Granville to alter her own name & that of her children .... [27 Mar 1835]

    John of Pittston ME lost on the schr *Maine* of Bath ME, James BLIN of Dresden, master from the Kennebec for Boston MA loaded with wood, potatoes & hay ... [16 Oct 1841]

    Mary 57 w/o James B POTTER at Wellington ME [27 Jan 1848]

    Mary Mrs 71 wid/o Hugh POTTER at Gardiner ME [18 Jun 1842]

    Nath'l at Gardiner ME [3 Jan 1850]

    Ray Rev "has held illicit intercourse with a church-sister" at Pawtucket RI [21 Feb 1837]

    Robert Col killed by a ROSE [*Caddo Gazette*] [9 Apr 1842]

    Sally 28 at Gardiner ME [6 Jun 1850]

POTTER - see SIMS

POTTLE Mary 44 w/o Daniel POTTLE at Norway ME [26 Dec 1850]

POTTLE - see HAMMOND

POULSON Zachariah 83 of Philadelphia PA, for many yrs editor & propietor of the *American Daily Advertiser* [8 Aug 1844]

POWELL Capt of Newbury MA listed in deaths in CA [23 Sept 1851]

POWELL - see COWART

POWERS Abigail 82 relict of Rev Jonathan POWERS, former minister of Penobscot, at Penobscot ME [28 Dec 1839]

    Arnold 82 at Bethel ME [9 May 1850]

    Calvin Esq 65 at Sweden ME [27 May 1847]

    Hannah H 26y 7m d/o Gideon & Appha POWERS at Augusta ME on 17th inst [20 May 1852]

    Henrietta H 2y 8mo only d/o Jacob S and Charlotte POWERS on 27 Sep at Sweden ME [4 Oct 1849]

POWERS (Cont.) James indicted for rape on Hannah WELSH the supreme court at Salem, to be tried on Thurs for his life, court deprived of the material witness, he married the girl! James P is a gay bridegroom at large enjoying his honeymoon, instead of a prisoner in the dock on his trail. The parties are both Irish & the young man decent in other repects, & the girl a faithful domestic [*Boston Post*] [20 Nov 1845]

Jonathan 60 at St Albans ME [19 Sep 18]

Jonathan & Sarah R POWERS have by their own free will, come to the conclusion to disolve the bands of matrimony existing between them. Mr POWERS very generously states that if his wife choses "to marry again with any other man," he "shall never interfere or consider it" his "business whom or when she marries." William WHITNEY, Nicholas YOUNGMAN & Simon PIERCE have signed their names as witnesses to his agreement. This is certainly a very curious kind of a divorce. [4 Jan 1840]

Mrs ab 76 at St Albans ME [19 Sep 1850]

POWERS - see BOND, BUELL

PRATT Albion N 17 at Foxcroft (Dover-Foxcroft) ME [1 May 1851]

Almeda 26 at Bloomfield ME [12 Feb 1846]

Anna 65y 8m at New Vineyard ME on 10 Nov 1848 [9 Nov 1848]

Benj T Capt 23 late master of brig *Ceylon* at Bath ME [17 Sep 1846]

Bradford Capt 36 on 11 Oct of consumption at Bowdoinham ME [25 Oct 1849]

Charles 28 of Weld ME at Mexico on the 15th ult [4 Apr 1840]

Charles of Weld ME received an injury on the 15th ult while spending an evening in Mexico ME, which caused his death in abt 32 hrs. He was trying a somerset by drawing himself up on a hook in the ceiling overhead and was abt to turn his hands when the hook drew out & let him to the floor, starting [*sic*, means jerking] the spine. He was abt 28 yrs ... [4 Apr 1840]

Clara 14 d/o Amasa PRATT at Bloomfield ME [26 Dec 1850]

Dan 90 AmRev at Turner ME [31 Jul 1851]

Elam 84 at Bloomfield ME [29 Apr 1836]

Elizabeth 47 w/o Stephen M PRATT at New Vineyard ME on 4 Apr [1 May 1851]

G W 23 at Bloomfield ME [8 Mar 1849]

Henrietta w/o Rev Cyprian PRATT at Brighton ME [7 Aug 1851]

Hiram C 27 at Foxcroft (Dover-Foxcroft) ME [22 May 1851]

Jesse 36 formerly of New Vineyard at Farmington ME [5 Aug 1852]

Jesse 71 formerly of Rochester MA (Boston MA & New Bedford papers please copy) at New Vineyard ME on 25 OCt [9 Nov 1848]

Joseph 90 at Palmyra ME [9 Nov 1848]

Joseph abt 67 of Paris ME found in the river a short distance below below SNO's Falls last Thurs afternoon, under such circumstances as to the belief that he had committed suicide by downing himself. He has children in MA [*Paris Democrat*] [14 Sept 1848]

Joseph Deac 56 at Starks ME [24 Oct 1850]

Levi H at North Yarmouth ME [27 Dec 1849]

Louisa 27 w/o Amasa PRATT at Bloomfield ME [10 Oct 1850]

Lydia 41 w/o William PRATT at Foxcroft ME [11 Jun 1842]

Mary ab 42 at Hallowell ME [19 Feb 1842]

Mrs 100y 3mo w/o late Paul PRATT at New Vineyard ME [30 Dec 1843]

Mrs 51 w/o late Whitcomb PRATT at Bloomfield ME [9 Oct 1845]

Mrs 60 of Foxcroft ME manufactured butter & cheese enough the past season besides doing the work of her family to render her a clear profit of $180 [20 Apr 1839]

Nancy B Mrs 53 at Gardiner ME [25 Mar 1847]

Oscar 3 s/o Diah P on 1st inst at Hallowell ME [7 Mar 1837]

PRATT (Cont.) Phinelias of Saco ME saved from drowning when the steam packet *New England* sank. It left Boston for Bath & Gardiner ME and had an accident with the schr *Curlew* on 31 May [12 June 1838]

    Rebecca 72 w/o Elisha PRATT at Turner ME [19 Aug 1847]

    Sally 41 w/o Thomas PRATT at Fairfield ME [30 Oct 1838]

    Sanford 8 s/o Rev Cyprian PRATT at Brighton ME [7 Aug 1851]

    Sarah B 18 d/o Simeon PRATT on 15 Jan at Freeport ME [14 Feb 1850]

    Sarah w/o Capt Joel PRATT on 17th ult at Foxcroft ME [12 Jun 1838]

    Silas T 24 at Norridgewock ME [15 Jul 1847]

    Simon of consumption at Augusta ME [29 Jan 1846]

    Thaddeus 88 AmRev pensioner at Buckfield ME [2 Sep 1843]

    Timothy Capt, wife & fam on board, died a short time before the arrival of the bark *Abby Baker* of Yarmouth ME at San Francisco CA. Augustus P, his son, died at Sacramento CA on the 30th of last month a victim of the cholera one hr after his bro, Enos on the same inst. Bro William on 3d and a Dutch boy belonging to the ship also died. On 5th Mrs Jane P died and left boy 9y who has been kindly taken charge (see *Sacramento Trans*)] [16 Jan 1851]

    Truman Capt ab 40 formerly of New Vineyard at Lee Co, IL [7 Nov 1844]

    William of ME of cholera Sacramento CA on 1 Nov [2 Jan 1851]

    Wm Deac 70 at Foxcroft ME [20 Dec 1849]

PRATT - see ADAMS, LUCE

PRAY Abraham 74 at Paris ME [10 Jul 1851]

    Abraham 95 at Hallowell ME [1 Feb 1844]

    Cushing ae 30 at Camden ME [22 Oct 1846]

    Edmund formerly of Hallowell ME at Woodstock NH [13 Feb 1838]

    Elizabeth R w/o Dean P, d/o Capt Sam'l SMITH of Hallowell ME at Gardiner ME [10 Apr 1841]

    Joshua Capt 77 at Dresden ME [19 Feb 1852]

    Lucy L 28 w/o E C PRAY d/o Stephen HOMANS at Vassalboro ME [8 Aug 1837]

    Mrs ab 70 w/o Abraham PRAY at Paris ME [1 Jan 1846]

    P Rutilius R Judge 45y of Mississippi at Pearlington Hancock Co MS on 11th ult was a native of Livermore ME [22 Feb 1840]

    Rebecca 58 w/o Edmund PRAY at Augusta ME [11 Apr 1844]

    Sarah M 22 at Brunswick ME [31 Jul 1851]

PRAY - see HAMBLIN

PREBLE Abigail B 28 w/o Samuel PREBLE at Bradford ME [12 Mar 1842]

    Abigail Mrs 55 at Bath ME [28 Aug 1835]

    Eben 42 eldest s/o late Enoch PREBLE of Portland ME at Gorham ME [30 Jan 1845]

    Ebenezer 75 at Gardiner ME [18 Dec 1851]

    Henry 22 of Maine, at New Orleans [30 Sep 1847]

    James ab 67 at Hallowell ME [23 Dec 1843]

    John 24 of Richmond at the mouth of Kennebec River on the brig *Virginia* [13 Nov 1851]

    John 89 at Camden ME [15 Jul 1843]

    Margaret 82 at Woolwich ME [18 Nov 1852]

    Mary Miss ab 100 at Winslow ME [4 Jan 1844]

    Mrs 24 w/o Leander PREBLE at Bradley [28 Oct 1847]

    Oliver 21 at Hallowell ME [18 Mar 1847]

    Sewel of Bowdoinham ME saved from drowning when the steam packet *New England* sank. It left Boston for Bath & Gardiner ME and had an accident with the schr *Curlew* on 31 May [12 June 1838]

PREBLE - see ALLEN

PRENELLE Louis a native of Geneva, Switzerland, at Calais ME [16 May 1844]

PRENTICE Lucretia 30 at China ME [7 Nov 1850]
PRENTISS Caleb Deac 67 at Paris ME [23 Oct 1838]
  Caleb Esq 40 of Foxcroft ME at Paris ME [2 Apr 1846]
  Ruth Mrs 89 at Bloomfield ME [26 Dec 1840]
PRESCOTT Aaron 52 formerly of Vienna ME on 1st inst at Ripley ME [9 Dec 1852]
  Abby 42 w/o Jedediah PRESCOTT at Memphis TN on 10 Feb (Maine & Boston papers
    please copy) [18 Mar 1852]
  Amos a native of Boston MA shot by order of Don Manuel RICO, a revolutionary chief
    now in rebellion against the government of Buenos Ayres [*sic*] (Argentina).
    PRESCOTT was accused of infiltrating the rebel camp as a spy on behalf of the
    government. Mr PRESCOTT was a resident of Buenos Ayres, & had a wife & three
    children (from the *Maine Temperance Gazette*) [4 Apr 1840]
  Benj E 30 at Winthrop ME [27 Nov 1845]
  Caroline 26 w/o Simon B PRESCOTT on 23rd inst at Winthrop ME [26 Sep 1834]
  Charles 30 at Winthrop ME [23 Mar 1848]
  Chas G 24 at New Sharon ME [6 Sep 1849]
  Clara E 34 at Lewiston ME [7 Nov 1850]
  Eben'r 72 of consumption on 16th inst at Monmouth ME [30 May 1844]
  Edward H 3y youngest child of Isaac N PRESCOTT at Monmouth ME on 9 Aug [11 Sept
    1851]
  Elijah 82 one of the early settlers of Winthrop ME at Vassalboro ME on 28 Oct [2 Nov
    1848]
  Elizabeth 58 w/o Samuel PRESCOTT Esq at New Sharon ME [2 May 1844]
  Harrison E 24 at Norridgewock ME [9 Jan 1845]
  Henry abt 50 found yesterday near the mouth of Kenduskeag stream. [*Bangor Whig*] [30
    Sept 1847]
  Henry M Dr 39 formerly of Brunswick ME at Montgomery Co GA [5 Nov 1846]
  Jesse 83 at New Sharon ME [28 Jan 1847]
  Levi 67 on 25 Dec at Readfield ME [3 Jan 1850]
  Lucy 50y 6m w/o Isaac N PRESCOTT at Monmouth ME on 23 Aug [11 Sept 1851]
  Mary 78 w/o Jesse PRESCOTT at New Sharon ME [5 Sep 1841]
  Mary Ann committed suicide by cutting her throat from ear to ear, supposed in a state of
    mental aberration at Norridgewock ME on Mon [31 Oct 1840]
  Mary C 58 w/o Levi PRESCOTT on 15 May at Readfield ME [27 May 1847]
  Olive B Mrs 18 at Augusta ME on 12 Nov [1 Apr 1852]
  Philander C 21 on 25 Mar at Winthrop ME [9 May 1850]
  Sarah C 37 w/o Alfred PRESCOTT at Liberty ME on 9 May [27 May 1852]
  Sarah Mrs 83y 6mo at Arrowsic ME [28 Oct 1852]
  Sewall Jr 39 of St Albans, Somerset Co ME, late county commissioner, member of last
    legislature, died at father's house at Monmouth ME on 14th inst [25 Apr 1837]
  Simon 86 at Corinth ME [13 Mar 1851] & [6 Mar 1851]
  Susan Mrs 54 of Augusta ME at Hallowell ME [8 Oct 1842]
PRESSLEY James 47, fell from a hay loft and broke his neck at Eastport ME [1 Apr 1836]
PRESTON Mary R 54 w/o Hon Warren PRESTON, sister of Mrs L Maria CHILD, 21st ult
    at Bangor ME [7 Oct 1847]
  Sarah Mrs 83y 6mo at Arrowsic ME [28 Oct 1852]
  William Capt late master of American coasting schr *Regulus*, died of coast fever on 14
    May at Monrovia, Africa [1 Oct 1842]
PREW Joseph 34 at Hallowell ME [30 Apr 1846]
PRIBBLE David I hereby give my son, James P, his time, witness, William WOART in
    China ME on 27 Feb 1844 [7 Mar 1844]

PRICE William 96y of age, of the Boston rebels in 1773 aided in throwing the tea at Boston harbor. The fact alluded to by the Rev J MARSH, to his speech at the table. The old veteran was called upon his feet and received with great cheering. He was helped into his carriage, a revolutionary lad in his 85th year. This all occurred at the temperance dinner in Fanueil Hall in Boston MA on the 4th of July. [3 Aug 1839]

PRICE - see THOMPSON

PRIDE Nathaniel Rev 54 at Naples ME [31 Aug 1848]
 Thomas 80 AmRev at Cumberland ME [19 Jun 1845]

PRIEST Jonathan 44 at Biddeford ME [12 Jul 1849]
 Lydia Mrs 70 at Vassalboro ME [14 Nov 1844]

PRIM Lucy Helen 21mo d/o John PRIM at Bangor ME [30 Jan 1845]

PRIME Elizabeth Mrs 66 at Sanford ME [8 Apr 1847]
 Nathaniel Esq 74 of New York [5 Dec 1840]

PRINCE Edward C 29 at Portland ME [6 Dec 1849]
 Hezekiah Hon 73 at Thomaston ME [9 Jan 1841]
 Isaac 85 at Portland ME [21 Jul 1843]
 Isabella Mrs 40 w/o Hezekiah PRINCE on 2nd inst at Thomaston ME [12 Dec 1840]
 L S 28 on 21st inst at Winthrop ME [27 Sep 1849]
 Lucius Capt 30 at Westbrook ME [25 Oct 1849]
 Thomas Deac 91y at Belfast ME [29 Sept 1840]

PRINCE - see CILLEY, GORSUCH

PRINGLE James R for 20y collector of Charleston SC at Charleston SC [8 Aug 1840]

PRITCHARD Margaret 80 wid/o Capt John PRITCHARD at Portland ME [5 Feb 1846]

PROCK boys of Waldoboro ME two s/o Israel PROCK were helping themselves to apples in the orchard of Mr HOCK, when a son of Mr H abt 17y took his gun, loaded with buck shot & fired, both boys were wounded & one died after two days [*Bangor Courier*] [21 Sept 1848]

PROCTOR Abigail F 58 w/o Deac Uriah PROCTOR on 1 Sep at Hartford [13 Sep 1849]
 Jason 37 formerly of New Sharon ME at Augusta ME on 14th [27 Jul 1848]
 Josiah abt 87 AmRev at Waterford ME [27 Jul 1848]
 Mrs 71 w/o Joseph PROCTOR at Waterville ME [12 Aug 1847]

PROPHY John after eating a dinner of fish taken suddenly ill & died next morning, supposed poisoned by the lead, in the glazing of the pot, at Waltham MA on Fri last [8 Aug 1840]

PROUGH - see MOORE

PROUT Loring Mr 87 at Freeport ME [30 Dec 1836]

PROUTY Aaron 74 at Bangor ME [18 Jul 1850]

PRUDEN Geo W 53 formerly of Vassalboro ME at Boston MA [12 Apr 1849]
 Stephen H 24 of Thorndike ME drowned at Fall River MA on 15th inst [30 Dec 1847]

PRUGILLO Ojo Caliente Jose Antonio the census marshal of New Mexico reports this man has 25 children living (13 sons & 12 daughters) by one wife also living in health. He 91 & she 86 [1 May 1851]

PUGSLEY Andrew 78 on 1st inst at Cornish ME [16 Jul 1842]

PULLEN Abigail Miss 37 at Augusta ME [8 Apr 1836]
 Betsey 67 w/o William PULLEN at Portland ME [4 Dec 1835]
 child ab 5y c/o Sumner B PULLEN [25 Jun 1842]
 infant c/o Thomas Stanley PULLEN at Winthrop ME [10 Oct 1834]
 Lavinda C 28 w/o Thomas S PULLEN of fever 21st inst at Winthrop ME [26 Sep 1834]
 Lucinda C 20y 4mo d/o James PULLEN formerly of Hallowell ME died of typhus fever at Franklin MA where she had gone to spend winter with friends [27 Nov 1838]

PULLEN (Cont.) Lucy M 2 d/o Gilbert & S G C PULLEN on 31st ult of dysentery at Augusta ME [13 Sep 1849]

Mary Elizabeth 6 d/o Gilbert and S G C PULLEN on 7th inst at Augusta ME [13 Sep 1849]

PULSIFER Joseph 80 at Bath ME [17 Jan 1850]

PURKITT Henry Col 91 AmRev at Boston MA saw the destruction of the tea in Boston MA [12 Mar 1846]

PURNELL - see WILLIAMS

PURRINGTON/PURINGTON/PURINTON Anna 64 w/o late Jacob PURRINGTON at Foxcroft ME [13 Jun 1850]

(David) of Lewiston ME confined in jail at Wiscasset for debt, committed suicide by cutting his throat with a razor on the night of the 26th ult [*Bath Tribune*] [8 June 1848]

Catherine 43 at Gardiner ME [30 Mar 1848] & Catherine 43 w/o Z S PURINTON at Gardiner ME [6 Apr 1848]

girl 12 of Coleraine d/o Luther PURRINGTON on Sun the 19th ult [*Greenfield Gazette*] [13 June 1844]

Hezekiah 41 at West Bath ME [27 Aug 1846]

Humphrey Esq 68 at Topsham ME [16 Jan 1841]

Isaac Capt of Calais ME on Wed his boat found off Hardwood Island in St Andrews Bay with his dead body in it [*Calais Advertiser*] [26 Apr 1849]

James 26 at Gardiner ME [26 Dec 1841]

James Capt master of brig *Baltic* of Bowdoinham ME, on passage from St Thomas to Wilmington NC [27 May 1843]

Jerome of RI on a visit to his father in Carver & accidentally shot by Augustus HOLMES at Plymouth [*Boston Courier*] [14 Aug 1845]

Simeon H at Portland ME [26 Jun 1845]

Sophia 75 at Bath ME [20 Jan 1848]

PURVIS - see ROALDSON

PUSHARD Lewis seaman of Wiscasset ME lost on the *Maine* of Bath ME, James BLIN of Dresden ME, master [16 Oct 1841]

PUSHARD - see HAMMOND

PUTNAM child 5mo c/o Mrs Harriet PUTNAM at Hallowell ME [29 Aug 1844]

Elizabeth J 33 w/o John V PUTNAM Esq, of consumption at Houlton ME [3 Dec 1846]

Marcia H Mrs 43 w/o Daniel PUTNAM at Belfast ME [29 Jul 1843]

Mr AmRev disabled from active service in very middle of the strife, 1779 by paralytic stroke but survived till 1790, being 72y of age at his death buried at Brooklyn CT [16 Sept 1847]

Phebe H 28 w/o Simeon PUTNAM Jr formerly of Athens ME at East Thomaston ME [27 Sep 1849]

PUTNAM - see SEWALL, SMITH

- Q -

Quaker - see JONES, HOXIE

Queen Elizabeth - see DUDLEY

QUEENY Lake an Irishman, by cave-in while working in canal connected with dam at Augusta ME. He was a worthy and industrious man. [10 Apr 1838]

QUICK James a storekeeper committed suicide by cutting his throat with a razor; he owed at the time of his death $100,000 by the unsuccessful speculations in grains at Belvidere Warren Co NJ [16 May 1840]

QUIMBY Benjamin at Greene ME [4 Jul 1840]
     Daniel of Lisbon ME elopement with Mrs LAWRENCE (see story) [24 May 1849]
     Edwin F Rev 26 Aug at Norway ME [9 Sep 1852]
     infant c/o Robert QUIMBY at Belfast ME [25 Dec 1845]
     J T 43, 4th inst at Belfast ME [17 Dec 1842]
     Martha Ann 23 w/o AM QUIMBY on 28 Aug at Farmington ME [9 Sep 1836]
     Samuel Dr 82 at Mt Vernon ME on 5 June [12 June 1851] & Samuel late of Mt Vernon,
         John BEAN exec [17 Jun 1852]
QUIN William 20 of Camden drowned on coast of Labrador [28 Nov 1850]
QUINBY Stephen 50 at Phillips ME [15 Apr 1847]
QUINBY - see BOYD
QUINCY Mehitable 60 w/o late Marcus QUINCY 9th inst at Portland ME [16 May 1840]
QUINNAM Jacob B 36 of Wiscasset ME at Lafayette City LA [24 June 1852]
QUINT Jacob 40 at Starks ME [20 Feb 1851]
QUITLY - see HOLDEN

- R -

RABB Jesse of Chester ME? at San Francisco CA [8 Jan 1852]
RABEY 3 births at one delivery to Mrs William RABEY, the trio, 2 daus & a son of
     LaFayette Co [12 June 1838]
RACKLEFF Benjamin house joiner near Munjoy Hill Portland ME & James W
     SKILLINGS both killed by the same bolt of lightning Dr SWEAT sent for but arrived
     too late [*Portland Argus*] [31 Jul 1851]
     Charles 37 at Portland ME [5 Dec 1844]
RACKLEY Benj 69 at Greene ME [7 Nov 1850]
RACKLIFF Betsey 52 w/o Col Benjamin RACKLIFF & formerly of Unity ME at Letter P,
     Presque Isle Plt, Aroostook Co ME [20 Jul 1848]
RADDIN James of Edgecomb lost overboard in a gale on 11 Jan from brig *Ajax* on passage
     from Wiscasset ME to Trinidad. Also lost James SAUNDERS of Dresden ME [19 Feb
     1836]
RAEBURN Thomas D Dr 38 on Sun morn the 20th inst at Bath ME [25 Jul 1834]
RAFANEL Augustus 97 a native of France at Mt Desert ME [6 Nov 1845]
RAGAN - see BURNS
RALDERBORN Andrew 4 ch died on the 16th [7 June 1849]
RAMASS girls of New Orleans two d's/o Alderman RAMASS [29 May 1851]
RAMSAY boy drowned in the dock back of Messrs W V & O MOSES Foundry (from *Bath
     ME Mirror*) [7 Aug 1851]
RAMSDELL Achsa wid/o Luther RAMSDELL, late of Leeds ME [17 Jun 1852]
     Ann L Mrs 30 formerly of Hallowell ME on 29 Oct at Lynn MA [8 Nov 1849]
     Luther 18y of Bowdoinham lost overboard from schr *Olive Branch* of Richmond on the
     passage from Portland ME for Boston MA [28 Nov 1840]
     Luther 63 at Leeds ME [5 Feb 1852]
     Mahala B 27 w/o Cyrus C RAMSDELL at Farmington ME [2 May 1850]
RAMSEY James 30 at Waterville ME [21 Oct 1836]
     Martha 63 w/o John M RAMSEY at Portland ME [9 Oct 1845]
RAND James B 65 at Limerick ME [2 May 1850]
RANDALL Albert of Vassalboro ME at sea [16 Dec 1852]
     Elizabeth 72 w/o Rev Joshua RANDALL at Wilton ME [9 Jul 1846]
     Huldah 28 w/o Elbridge RANDALL of Topsham ME at Harpswell ME [18 Oct 1849]
     James 45 at Limerick ME [24 Aug 1848]

RANDALL (Cont.) James 65y of Cambridge run over at So Reading MA by one of the late trains on the Boston MA & Maine Railroad on Fri evening & instantly killed [2 Oct 1851]

John a negro imprisoned in the jail at (Lancaster NH) for robbing the store of Joseph MESERVE. RANDALL was born in Flatbush NY & came here fronm Portland ME. He said he is 32y, 5' 11", very black, high forehead, one of his front teeth is some decayed & the first double tooth on the left side of the upper jaw is gone ... [14 Aug 1845]

John Dr 68 at Boston MA [4 Jan 1844]

Joshua Jr 50 at Dixfield ME [21 Dec 1848]

Merrill Capt 31 of Prospect lost overboard from brig *Sarah* of Bangor ME [11 Apr 1850]

Nathan 53 at Leeds ME [13 Nov 1838]

Phinney abt 80 on 13th at Augusta ME [18 Nov 1847]

Reuben ab 75 on 19 Feb at Augusta ME [1 Mar 1849]

Sally widow 72 formerly of Kingfield at Augusta ME on 2d Oct [16 Oct 1851]

Samuel 25 at Augusta ME [5 Feb 1842]

Samuel 82 AmRev at Vassalboro ME [4 May 1839]

Seth L late of Augusta ME [29 Jan 1852]

Shadrach 78 at Hollis ME [3 Sep 1846]

Solomon 21 of Foxcroft ME four men burnt to death in a camp in Plt No 4 on Great Works Stream [13 Feb 1835]

Sophronia 32 w/o Isaac H RANDALL d/o William PERCIVAL Esq of Vassalboro ME on 10th inst at Augusta ME [14 Mar 1844]

Susan R 34 w/o Capt Otis RANDALL at Bowdoin ME [15 Nov 1849]

Susannah 56 w/o Isaac RANDALL at Litchfield ME [18 Sept 1851]

William 33 at Vassalboro ME [1 Feb 1849]

William 40 on 25 Mar at Monmouth ME [10 May 1849]

RANDALL - see EDDY

RANDLET Joseph Edmund 5y 3mo eldest s/o Joseph S RANDLET at Palmyra ME [3 Apr 1841]

RANDLETT Elizabeth Mrs of St George ME on board ship *Arvum* on passage from New Orleans to Boston MA on 4th inst [27 Jun 1844]

Jane 24 w/o Warren RANDLETT Esq at Alna ME [5 Aug 1843]

Rufus 35 at Mt Vernon ME [2 May 1840]

RANDOLPH John a colored servant born on the plantation of the famous RANDOLPH of Roanoke & long in his service among the four hundred left free in his will proposes to publish *The private Life of John RANDOLPH* [2 Mar 1848]

Mrs w/o of a naval officer married abt six weeks & d/o Mr SMITH at Brooklyn NY on Wed [8 Feb 1840]

RANKEY Nicholas N journeyman tailor res in a 3rd or 4th story room in Greenwich St NY NY arrested, by officer DENNISTON, libeling Margaret E WELLS 13 res at 490 Greenwich st, in an old daub of a transparent window shade, whereon a female figure was said to represent the above Miss W. This the ungallant tailor had placed up at his window to keep the sun out. [New York paper] [7 May 1846]

RANKIN Elizabeth 74 w/o late Sam'l RANKIN at Thomaston ME [14 Feb 1850]

Miss the author of *Texas in 1850* hails from Hallowell, Kennecc Co, ME [7 Aug 1851]

Nathaniel 58 3rd inst at Wells ME [25 Sep 1845]

Sarah 58 w/o Nathaniel RANKIN at Wells ME [25 Sep 1845]

William H 25 at Brownville ME [16 Apr 1846]

RANKO boy of Waterville ME s/o Abram RANKO drowned near the Iron Foundry [*Eastern Mail*] [19 Jul 1849]

RANKS Joseph 24 at Gardiner ME [29 Nov 1849]

RANLETT John E 19 & John E CLOUGH 18, Elias P CLOUGH 16 both sons of Capt Asa
   CLOUGH and Charles Clark 22 at Monmouth Centre ME five men drowned on Wed
   last week (9th inst) [17 Jul 1851]

RANSOM Alexander of Boston MA married Miss Margaretta FREEMAN d/o Rev
   Frederick FREEMAN of Sandwich MA (formerly of this town) [*Plymouth Memorial*]
   see story about elopement [5 Mar 1846]

   T B Col killed at Norwich VT on the 22nd, left a wife & 4 ch, three boys & one girl only
   14m, his oldest son, Dunbar RANSOM is a member of military academy at West
   Point [*Atlas*] [16 Mar 1848]

   Truman B Col the late commander of the 9th or New England regiment together with
   those remains of Capt Martin SCOTT & THOMPSON arrived at Boston on Fri. They
   were received with military honors. [17 Feb 1848]

RASLES Sebastian a missionary of the Jesuit Society at Norridgewock ME on 23 Aug 1724
   killed by the English [24 Jul 1845]

RATHBORNE Frances Amelia 25 w/o William P RATHBORNE & d/o Silas LEONARD
   Esq of Augusta ME at Providence RI on 22 Apr [6 May 1852]

RAWLE William a lawyer & commentator on the Constitution at Philadelphia PA on 24
   Apr 1836 [13 Jan 1837]

RAWSON Azubah B 19 w/o Samuel F RAWSON at Paris ME [2 Nov 1833]

   Ebenezer Col 77 on 26th ult at Paris ME [13 Jul 1839]

   Levi 64 at Paris ME [18 Jan 1849]

   Mary L 53 a widow at Waldoboro ME [4 June 1851] & wid/o Horace RAWSON Esq [12
   June 1851]

   Salisbury F 82 s/o Capt Samuel F RAWSON at Paris ME [12 Sep 1844]

RAWSON - see PIDGIN

RAY Daniel abt 27 & Samuel GOODWIN 32y who left a wife & two ch & Mr BRIGGS abt
   18y tried to save Daniel RAY at Hineburgh VT all drowned [*Liberty Gaz* on the 13th]
   [27 Aug 1846]

   Henry of Knox lost overboard from brig *Adams* on passage from Havana to Boston [17
   Jun 1847]

RAYMOND David H Dr 40 at Milburn [29 Jul 1833]

   Frederick Dr 42 at Bloomfield ME [19 Dec 1840]

RAYNARD Susan 26 at Norridgewock ME [10 Jun 1847]

RAYNES Albert 24 of Lewiston Falls ME died at Sacramento CA [2 Jan 1851]

   boy abt 12 of Lewiston ME s/o Nathaniel RAYNES drowned in the Androscoggin River,
   while bathing on the 8th [*Lewiston Journal*] [N.B. The name Raynes is common to
   the towns of Danville & New Gloucester of then Cumberland Co ME & not common
   to Lewiston] [15 Jul 1847]

   Mary 41 w/o Jona RAYNES at Danville ME [21 Jun 1849

READ Albert H 31 at Strong ME [4 Jul 1850]

   Arthur G of Dresden ME on 7 Sep on board barque *Columbia* on passage from New
   Orleans to New York [22 Oct 1842]

   John Hon 57 22nd ult at Strong ME [6 Jun 1837]

   John P Capt 57 at Lewiston ME [6 Dec 1849]

   Lydia Mrs 70 at Augusta ME [2 Jan 1838]

READ Mary Jane 18 at Buckfield ME [28 Oct 1847]

   Nathan Hon 89 at Belfast ME [1 Feb 1849]

   Noah 87 at Windham ME [25 Apr 1844]

   Oliver 72 at Lewiston ME [11 Jul 1850]

   Susannah 77 w/o Dan READ Esq at Lewiston ME [10 Jun 1847]

REAGAN - see DUNDAN

REASON Charles L an artist of New York elected professor in Central College at
McGranville NY. He is the first gentleman of color who has been elected to a college
professorship in this country [15 Nov 1849]

RECORD Jonathan 101y AmRev the *Oxford Democrat* published a list of Old People in
Buckfield ME, 77 person were said to be over 70 with 30 between 80 to 90 & three
between 90 to 100 at Buckfield ME [17 Jul 1851]

Pamelia 22 at Auburn ME [20 Mar 1851]

Sally 25 at Minot ME [20 Jul 1839]

Sarah 46 w/o Barak R at Strong ME [25 Oct 1849]

Thomas 26 of Buckfield ME at East Stoughton MA [3 Jul 1845]

RECORDS - see CHASE

REDDINGTON George 39 at Waterville ME [10 Oct 1840]

Thomas 82 at Waterville ME [22 Aug 1840]

REDINGTON Asa Esq 83 AmRev at Waterville ME [17 Apr 1845]

Elizabeth 24 w/o Col Alfred REDINGTON at Augusta ME [17 Oct 1837]

Elizabeth G w/o Hon Isaac REDINGTON formerly of Waterville ME at Forestburg NY
[8 Nov 1849]

George 39 at Waterville ME [10 Oct 1840]

Hannah 67 w/o Samuel REDINGTON Esq at Vassalboro ME [30 Jan 1838]

Hannah 78 consort of Asa REDINGTON Esq at Waterville ME [23 May 1837]

Thomas 82 at Waterville ME [22 Sept 1840]

REDINGTON - see KIMBALL

REDLON Daniel 95 at Limerick ME [25 Feb 1847]

REDLON Elizabeth 27 w/o Nathan REDLON Esq at Thomaston ME [18 Feb 1847]

REDMAN Mrs 24 at Bloomfield ME [14 May 1846]

Sophronia 20 at Ellsworth ME [13 Jan 1848]

REED Adraan T 21 d/o Capt Jeremiah REED at Bath ME [23 Dec 1847]

Amelia Mrs 32y 7mo at Union ME [25 Feb 1847]

Amos 94 at Dresden ME [29 Apr 1847]

Andrew Deac 83 at Phipsburg ME [13 Jan 1848]

Archibald 35 Fri night on 16th inst at Pittston ME [27 Feb 1838]

Benjamin a young man from Boothbay ME went out in the *Elvira* from Boston MA &
who had been to Yaba river & returned to San Francisco sick after staying a few days
on board the Elvira, jumped overboard & was drowned. [3 Jan 1850]

Betsey 37 w/o Luther REED at Augusta ME [10 Jun 1836]

Calvin N of Bath ME at San Francisco CA [8 Jan 1852]

Charlotte 22 d/o Hon Nathan REED at Belfast ME [21 Feb 1834]

Daniel 82 at Madison ME [9 Mar 1839]

Deborah Mrs 83 at Dover [15 Jun 1839]

Edward 36 at Belfast ME [21 Aug 1845]

Elisha B 32 at Hartford [14 Oct 1852]

Eliza Jane Carleton 23 w/o Dr A REED at Castine ME [6 Apr 1848]

Eunice widow 98y 8mo at Dresden ME [11 Oct 1849]

Frances 22 of Bath ME on board schr *Peru* at Gloucester Harbor MA [14 Oct 1847]

George 71 one of the city constables and long distinguished for his activity and success as
a police officer at Boston MA [8 Aug 1840]

George AmRev pensioner 87 at Augusta ME [24 Feb 1848]

George W 21 at Woolwich ME [22 Oct 1846]

Henry 33 at Nobleboro ME [16 May 1837]

Isaac G Hon 63 at Waldoboro ME [11 Mar 1847]

J C Capt of the United States army shot himself at Wheeling [4 Dec 1845]

Joanna Mrs 93 at Pittston ME [1 Aug 1840]

REED (Cont.) John a blacksmith made an attack upon his wife & eldest dau with a bar of iron, they escaped, caught two of the younger children whom he killed. Capt James McCHESNEY of Brownsbury was passing by & REED killed him also the Capt McCHESNEY left a large family of ch at Brownsbury Rickbridge Co VA [10 Sept 1842]

Joseph Major 75 at Windsor ME on 18 Apr [22 Apr 1852]

Margaret 54 w/o Ammi R formerly of Kingfield ME at Lewiston ME [13 Jun 1850]

Martha 28 w/o Thomas REED at Gardiner ME [8 May 1851]

Mary E 3 d/o Hiram REED at Augusta ME on 14th inst [21 Dec 1848]

Mrs w/o Elbridge REED at Madison ME [21 Oct 1847]

Polly 55 w/o John REED Esq on 21st inst of consumption at Augusta ME [29 Jul 1847]

Ruth 48 w/o Eliphalet REED at Dixmont ME [23 Jul 1846]

Samuel 50 formerly of Dexter ME at Dover ME [7 Dec 1848]

Samuel 60 at Gardiner ME [6 Jan 1848]

Sarah 66 wid/o David REED at Dresden ME [10 Apr 1851]

Thomas 33 of Boothbay ME at the Marine hospital at Chelsea ME [25 Jul 1850]

W G of NY lost steamboat *Burt* passage from Manchester to New Orleans [23 Apr 1837]

William Maxwell Capt 83y 5mo at Boothbay ME [29 Aug 1850]

William W Col 88y 4m 22d of Dixmont ME was in AmRev and served as orderly sergeant in battles of Trenton, Princeton, Monmouth, Brandywine, White Plains and Yorktown, died at Hallowell ME [22 Feb 1844]

Wm Gordan 37 of Boston MA at Paris ME [29 Mar 1849]

REED - see CLARK, WENTWORTH

REEVES Mary 13 burned in the park, her clothes taking fire from a cracker *[New York Farmer & Mechanic]* [17 Jul 1845]

Mary A 25 at Pittston ME on 29 Mar [17 Apr 1851]

REGAN Mary Ann Mrs at Eastport ME [29 Feb 1844]

REID John A seaman of Bristol ME lost overboard from brig *Margaret* of Boston from New Orleans coming down the Mississippi [25 Mar 1843]

Sarah 58 w/o Wm REID of dropsy 13th inst at Canaan ME [2 Jul 1842]

REID - see DAVIS

REILAY John Capt 104 AmRev on 17th ult at Troy NY [22 May 1838]

REILLY Capt by an address to the Mexican people in the Diario del Gobernio, it appears that only eighteen were hung, including Capt REILLY, whose head was placed on a pike .... [21 Oct 1847]

REMBY Nathaniel of crew shipwreck & four lives lost on the schr *Cevo*, Capt Pelatiah BARTER [25 May 1839]

REMICK Anna A 60 w/o Nathaniel REMICK at Augusta ME [23 Jul 1842] & Anna B 60 w/o Nathaniel REMICK at Augusta [30 Jul 1842]

James Edwin 5mo s/o Jas W and Caroline L REMICK at Augusta ME [28 Jan 1847]

John abt 50 (b Dec 1799, d 17 Dec 1851, left widow & 4 ch s/o William REMICK of Leeds ME) (see *Stackpole's History* p. 564) at Winthrop ME [26 June 1851] (*sic*)

Mercy W 30 d/o Nathaniel REMICK Thurs last at Augusta ME [11 Apr 1840]

Nathaniel 67 at Augusta ME on 8th [27 Jul 1848]

REMOND Mr a colored man, an agent of the Maine Anti-Slavery Society, while lecturing at Orrington ME last week had his chaise and harness very much injured by being cut to pieces with knives. The top of the chaise has five long slits upon the sides and traves, reins, & breeching, were cut in several places. Our Orrington friends should ferret out the perpetrators of this disgraceful outrage. (from the *Bangor Whig*) [2 Nov 1839]

RENNET Andrew abt 86 AmRev pensioner at Troy ME (*sic*) [NB editors think name should have been BENNET not "RENNET"] [14 Dec 1839]

REPHENBARK Tunis 103 one of surviving few who fought before the walls of Quebec at the fall of WOLF and MONTCALM at Sidney NY [12 Oct 1833]

REYNOLDS Arthur C murdered at San Francisco CA in one of the saloons by R C WITHERS who fled to the Sandwich Islands [14 Feb 1850]

Caroline 43 w/o Calvin REYNOLDS at Sidney ME [31 Jan 1850]

Cynthia Carey Miss 19 d/o Timothy REYNOLDS at Sidney ME [7 Nov 1844]

Edward 22 s/o Thomas & Susan REYNOLDS at Sidney ME on 8 Jul (MA papers please copy) [24 Jul 1851]

Edwin H 1y 3mo s/o Marcus V REYNOLDS at Augusta ME [10 Apr 1845]

Francis P 24 of ME of cholera Sacramento CA [2 Jan 1851]

Franklin S 10 s/o Thomas REYNOLDS 24 Sept at Sidney ME [4 Oct 1849]

Hannah Porter 16 d/o Newton REYNOLDS at (Augusta ME) on 11th inst [19 Oct 1848]

John 63 at Eastport ME [9 Jul 1846]

Lydia B 42 w/o Newton REYNOLDS at Sidney ME [2 Oct 1851]

Thomas of Missouri the governor shot himself at Jefferson [7 Mar 1844]

Wm Jr 44 at Minot ME [28 Feb 1837]

REYNOLDS - see FARRINGTON, SAWYER, WOODWARD

RHOADES Aaron 70 s/o Mrs MORSE at Belchertown MA [2 Dec 1843]

Elizabeth 58 w/o Levi RHOADES at Gardiner ME on 30 Mar [8 Apr 1852]

Matilda 21 at Gardiner ME [26 Oct 1848]

RHOADS Aaron of Waterboro ME by the premature discharge of powder, while engaged in blasting rocks on the railroad track, about half a mile from Saco ME. William GOODWIN of Biddeford ME & a Mr PRESCOTT were at the same time considerably injured [29 Jan 1842]

RHOADS - see YOOSTLING

RHODES Chester of Gardiner ME engaged in hauling stone for the paper mill about to be erected in that town, the stone fell upon his leg [*Fountain & Journal*] [9 Mar 1848]

RIANT Joseph 92 at Farmington ME [27 Sep 1849]

RICE Abigail 85 w/o late Richard RICE at Farmington ME [26 Dec 1850]

Alonzo J 7y 9m s/o George G & Rosanna G RICE at Guilford ME on 31 May of consumption [15 June 1848]

Ann R 22 w/o Richard D RICE d/o Stevens SMITH Esq of Hallowell ME on Sun last at Augusta ME [26 Jun 1838]

Benjamin 51 of Monmouth ME on board steamer *Falcon* on passage from Chagres to New York on 24 Jan [6 Feb 1851]

daughter 5mo d/o Benj RICE at Monmouth ME [21 Aug 1841]

Horace W of Oakham MA by a horse running away with a gig at the corner of Wilde's Tavern on Elm St Boston MA [2 Oct 1838]

John W 23 at Hallowell ME [26 Nov 1846]

Margaret B 20y 8mo w/o John H RICE at Hallowell ME [6 May 1847]

Mary 35 w/o Benjamin RICE of consumption at Monmouth ME [12 Feb 1842]

Mr abt 30 was a Thompsonian physician, belonging to Providence RI killed by accident on the Norwich Railroad last Wed, left a wife [*Spy*] [20 Feb 1845]

Noah Capt 56 at Union ME [31 Aug 1839]

Richard 73 at Farmington ME [15 Jan 1839]

Richard Capt abt 60 at Hallowell ME [19 Feb 1842]

Rufus 49 at Hallowell ME [22 June 1848]

Samuel 57 at Eastport ME very suddenly at his store [30 Oct 1851]

Samuel accidenty shot himself but it is supposed the foot may be saved at East Monmouth ME on Mon [*Journal* (Lewiston?)] [23 Sept 1851]

Warren 69 at Wiscasset ME [1 Jan 1852]

William 46 of Monmouth ME drowned [21 Aug 1841] & [30 Oct 1841]

RICE (Cont.) William Esq 67 at Bangor ME [31 Dec 1842]

RICH Amos 88 at Albion ME [15 Apr 1847]

    Calvin of Topsham ME at Rowley on Thurs in the street in a fit [7 Aug 1851]

    Capt - see Schooner *Forest*

    David of Wales ME lost overboard 16th inst from schr *Hylas* on passage from Bath ME to Portland ME [26 Mar 1842]

    George 34 of Hudson NY at Gardiner ME [8 Aug 1844]

    Isaiah 73 formerly of Truro MA at Bucksport ME [21 Jan 1847]

    Joel 27 of Frankfort ME late chief mate of the barque *Rothchild* of consumption at New York [29 Apr 1843]

    Lemuel 79 at Standish ME [17 May 1849]

    Mary Lyman 6mo only d/o Artemas R at North Yarmouth ME [5 Sep 1837]

    Nehemiah Capt 74 at Frankfort ME [12 Jul 1849]

    widow 91 at Jackson ME [31 Jul 1851]

    William 33 of Skowhegan ME formerly of Portland ME at Westbrook ME on 14th inst [26 Sept 1840]

RICH - see LOMBARD, SMITH, LOMBARD

RICHARDS Amos 37 at Bristol [27 Nov 1838]

    Charles 30 at Scarboro ME [2 Jan 1851]

    Charles A of Winthrop ME at Mason Hall, Orange County NC [18 Jul 1840]

    child 6y c/o Thomas R RICHARDS at Portland ME [27 Feb 1845]

    Erastus 39 on 11 Mar at Augusta ME [18 Mar 1847]

    Jacob 63 at Hallowell ME [9 Dec 1847]

    James 27 at Strong ME [24 Oct 1850]

    Joanna 80 wid/o William RICHARDS Esq on 25th inst at East Winthrop ME [3 Jun 1843]

    John 48 at Eastport ME [5 Dec 1850]

    John Esq 55 register of deeds for the county of Kennebec at Augusta ME [12 Dec 1844]

    Loring C 20y 6mo of East Livermore ME on 17 Oct of typhoid fever at Lowell MA [4 Nov 1847]

    Louisa Mrs 20 formerly of Dexter ME of consumption 4th inst at Garland ME [20 Mar 1841]

    Lydia 46 w/o Isaac RICHARDS at East Monmouth ME [26 Oct 1848]

    Martin abt 30 at Belfast ME [21 Aug 1851]

    Mary Matilda 25 d/o late John RICHARDS Esq on 11 Nov at Augusta ME [14 Nov 1850]

    Olive 78 at Roxbury [7 Nov 1850]

    Robert 84 formerly of Norridgewock ME at Levant ME [24 Jul 1851]

    Sally Mrs 81 at Belfast ME [19 Feb 1852]

    Tristram 84 AmRev & at West Point when ARNOLD's treason was discovered, died at Oxford ME [26 Jun 1845]

    William H 18 s/o the late Capt Jos(eph) RICHARDS of Hallowell ME at Mobile AL [10 Oct 1840]

RICHARDSON Abigail 52 w/o Augustine RICHARDSON at Augusta ME [17 Jun 1852]

    Artemas 64 of Hiram ME at Portland ME [20 Jun 1844]

    Asa Capt abt 50; William RICHARSON; Michael H PRESSEY of Deer Isle it is supposed the brig *Ransom* of Deer Isle, from an Eastern port has been totally lost [*Boston Adv*] [5 Apr 1849]

    Astemas of Keene NH sporting with a dirk knife in the bar-room at Lord's tavern, Swansey Factory Village, when he accidentally stuck it into his thigh, cutting the main artery & died [*Keene NH Rep*] [20 Nov 1845]

RICHARDSON (Cont.) child 3y of Canaan ME c/o Mr & Mrs David RICHARDSON was killed in a chaise accident [1 Jul 1843]

Edward 86 AmRev at Jay ME [11 Jul 1834]

Eliza Ann 1y d/o Wm and Olive RICHARDSON on 25 Sep at Clinton ME [7 Oct 1847]

Estabell 6mo d/o Charles RICHARDSON at Gardiner ME [8 Feb 1844]

Eunice 29 w/o Philip RICHARDSON on 14th ult at New Sharon ME [25 Jul 1834]

Ezekiel Col 50 of consumption on 10 Jul at Jay ME [7 Aug 1838]

Hannah widow 87 on 3rd ult at Monmouth ME [6 Feb 1835]

Harriet M 29 w/o Dr M C RICHARSON at Hallowell ME [8 June 1848]

Harriet Miss 20 of Litchfield ME on 10th ult at Ipswich [16 Nov 1839]

Howard 22 found in the upper canal above Tremont Mills, on way to see the Indians, now encamped on "Musquash Island," likely fell & drowned never making it to the camp site. The coroner's jury killed by violence inflicted by some person or persons unknown [*Lowell Mercury*] [12 Sept 1834]

John B master of schr *Arcturus* a native of Deer Isle ME 26 at the Quarantine Hospital, Staten Island NY on 12th inst of smallpox [28 Dec 1848]

Lucy 38 w/o Henry RICHARDSON of Old Town ME at Kennebunkport ME [11 Feb 1847]

Mary Ann abt 35 w/o Albert RICHARDSON at Jefferson ME [8 Jan 1852]

Moses 68 at Portland ME [16 Dec 1836]

Mrs 54 w/o Henry RICHARDSON at Monmouth ME [22 Feb 1849]

Mrs of Augusta ME indicted & convicted, for beating her husband - fined & compelled to give security for future good behavior. See paper for the song "Henpeck'd". [28 Jan 1833]

Richard accidentally at Woburn MA [*Lowell Advertiser*] [23 Nov 1848]

Ruth P w/o Benj RICHARDSON formerly of Monmouth ME at Byron [13 Mar 1838]

Sarah 7 d/o Joel and Mary L RICHARDSON on 8 Feb at Belgrade ME [26 Feb 1852]

Sophronia 29 w/o Joshua B RICHARDSON at Norway ME [1 Oct 1846]

Thias Frances 3y d/o Otis RICHARDSON at Hallowell ME [17 Aug 1833]

W E of Pawtucket 40 , the names of the officers & crew as per the custom house list, the ship *Jacob Perkins*, Capt SHOOF, which arrived his morning from Crostadt reported that on 22 inst Cape Cod WSW 55 miles fell in with the wreck of brig *Washington*, RIDER Capt [*Transcript*] [2 Oct 1835]

William 48, a black man, at the alms house at Portland ME [29 May 1845]

William 59 formerly of Standish ME after short illness on 16th inst at Monmouth ME [28 Mar 1844]

RICHARDSON - see EASTMAN

RICHARDVILLE - see FATE

RICHMOND Cyrus C 30 formerly of Winthrop ME at San Francisco CA [22 Jul 1852]

David Dr at Perkins Erie Co OH formerly of Norwalk CT was attacked by a bull in the field on 19th ult and died the next day [21 Nov 1840]

RICHOU Pierre six in three yrs, three pair twins, all now living at Shattavuoi, 6 miles below the fort [a letter from Fort Kent reported great doings in Madawaska, the French part of the territory] [17 Oct 1844]

RICKER 18mo c/o Moses and Eliza RICKER at Bradford ME [1 May 1838]

Albert 27y of Greene ME s/o Henry RICKER accidental [*Lewiston Journal*] [8 Feb 1849]

Charles seaman of Frankfort ME lost overboard from schr *Edward* on passage from St George to New Bedford [3 Jul 1851]

Ebenezer S 27 at Wales ME [15 June 1848] & [18 May 1848]

Eliza Miss 28 d/o Nathaniel RICKER at New Portland ME [23 Jan 1845]

James 23 s/o Capt Smith RICKER at Wales ME [10 Jul 1851]

RICKER (Cont.) John of Monroe ME one of the passengers on the *Lexington*, employed in
Mr SWEENEY's eating house in Fulton sSreet, on his way to visit his friends, the
number now ascertained to be lost on the *Lexington* is at least 140 [8 Feb 1840]
Mary 68 w/o Benj RICKER at Eastport ME [16 Jan 1841]
Samuel 21 at Frankfort ME [7 Jan 1847]
Samuel H of Monmouth ME death by exposure to the rain, two of his sons were in
company with him & came near sharing the same fate [*Age*] [18 Dec 1845]
Sophronia abt 35 at Auburn ME [20 Feb 1851]
Stephen 80 AmRev formerly of Wells ME at Parsonfield ME [14 Feb 1837]
Timothy 40 of smallpox at Canaan ME [15 Jan 1846]
Tobias abt 89 AmRev pensioner at Buckfield ME [20 Apr 1848]
Tobias Esq 57 at Parsonfield ME [15 Feb 1844]
William C 38 at Bath ME [11 Mar 1852]
RICKET - see FOX
RICKETS - see ROBINSON
RICO - see PRESCOTT
RIDEOUT Alvin 27 at Oldtown ME [16 Nov 1848]
Johnson Elder 36 at Township No 5 ME [10 Aug 1848]
Jos 59 at Bath ME [19 Apr 1849]
Martha J Miss 16 at Bath ME [15 Jul 1836]
Mary Ann 10 d/o Capt Jacob RIDEOUT at Brunswick ME [22 Feb 1844]
Stephen 84 AmRev pensioner on 15th ult at Bowdoin ME [11 Nov 1843]
RIDER Isaac 27 at Brownfield ME [6 Apr 1848]
J M G mate of Bedford NH 28 , the names of the officers & crew as per the customs
house list, the ship *Jacob Perkins*, Capt SHOOF, which arrived his morning from
Crostadt reported that on 22 inst Cape Cod WSW 55 miles fell in with the wreck of
brig *Washington*, RIDER Capt [*Transcript*] [2 Oct 1835]
John B Capt 57 at Thomaston ME [6 Feb 1845]
Louisa abt 13 on 7th inst at North Yarmouth ME [11 Apr 1834]
Magnis 80 at Durham ME [12 Feb 1852]
Obadiah of Bowdoin ME at Mary Meeting Bay by the upsetting of his boat [8 Jun 1839]
William master , the names of the officers & crew as per the customs house list, the ship
Jacob Perkins, Capt SHOOF, which arrived his morning from Crostadt reported that
on 22 inst Cape Cod WSS 55 miles fell in with the wreck of brig *Washington*, RIDER
Capt [*Transcript*] [2 Oct 1835]
RIDER - see SMITH
RIDGELY Capt at Monterey on the 27th Oct [3 Dec 1846]
Commodore death by an attack of gout in the stomach [10 Feb 1848]
RIDLEY Daniel Jr 48 at Wayne ME [14 Mar 1850]
Magnis 80 at Durham ME [12 Feb 1852]
Obadiah of Bowdoin ME picked up in the Kennebec River at the North End of this
village, on Tues last. The Coroner's Jury verdict, came to his death by the upsetting
of a boat, while crossing the Merry Meeting Bay, three weeks since [*Bath Tel*] [8 June
1839]
RIDLEY - see COAN
RIDLON Elizabeth Mrs 72 at Bath ME [2 Jan 1841]
Jemima (DAVIS) 100 wid/o Daniel RIDLON at Limerick ME [25 Dec 1851]
RIGAN Mr & a woman named GAYLORD perished in the flames of the stable of Mr
JOHNSON in New York on the 29 Sept [4 Oct 1849]
RIGBY Hannah 39 w/o George RIGBY at Auburn ME [11 Mar 1852]

RIGDON Sidney the Mormons dissolved their body collected at Kirland [*sic*] OH under Joe SMITH & Sidney RIGDON. These leaders recently decamped with their families in the night. [*The Sciota Gazette*] [6 Mar 1838]

RIGGS Benjamin Esq 87 at Georgetown ME [15 Jan 1846]

Julia 18 at Bath ME [19 Nov 1846]

Marcia 22mo d/o Benj F RIGGS at Augusta ME [22 Aug 1837]

RILEY James Capt 63 author of *Riley's Narrative* d at sea on board brig *Wm Tell* for St Thomas [18 Apr 1840]

RILEY - see story

RINES Llewellyn B 4mo s/o Thomas RINES on 18 Sep at Augusta ME [30 Sep 1852]

Stephen 25 at Augusta ME [30 Apr 1846]

Thomas 70 on 30 Apr at Augusta ME [2 May 1850]

RING Henrietta L 42 w/o Andrew RING Esq at Lubec ME [21 Dec 1848]

Jacob Esq 67 at Searsmont ME [16 Nov 1848]

Roxanna 21 w/o Burnham RING at Gardiner ME [23 May 1850]

RINGOLD Samuel of Maryland promised to Mary Sarah CAMPBELL, but broke his promise, Sarah prosecuted the faithless Samuel, & the court fined him $1500. Guess he thinks by this time - "The Campbells are coming." [12 Oct 1848]

RIPLEY 4 s/o Capt J W RIPLEY at Augusta ME [15 May 1838]

5mo c/o Cyrus H RIPLEY at Paris ME [31 Oct 1844]

Christopher 65 on 23 Dec at Augusta ME [30 Dec 1847]

Eliza 15mo d/o John RIPLEY on 9 Jul at Augusta ME [26 Jul 1849]

Franklin B 16m c/o John S RIPLEY at Augusta ME on 11th Sept [25 Sept 1851]

Henry R 17mo s/o Daniel S RIPLEY on 26th inst at Augusta ME [2 Sep 1847]

Henry R 23 at Augusta ME [13 Aug 1842]

Mr in a railroad accident caused by the carelessness of Robert DIXON [1 May 1851]

Nathaniel Capt 74 formerly of Bridgewater MA at Bath ME [29 May 1845]

Polly 60 w/o Capt A RIPLEY at Washington [26 Sep 1850]

Ruth 63 w/o Christopher RIPLEY at Augusta ME [11 Mar 1847]

Susan 52 wid/o late Ransom RIPLEY at Norway ME [14 Jun 1849]

Thomas H a student of Newton Theological School s/o Rev Thomas B RIPLEY in Kentucky, former pastor of Federal Street Baptist Church in Portland ME [17 Jun 1852]

RISTEEN - see HAWKINS

RIVALS Thomas abt 50 8th inst at Eastport ME [21 Aug 1842]

ROACH Jno [*sic*] Mr 48 at Bath ME [21 Mar 1840]

ROAKS Robert terrible thunder storm, the store of Mr FASSETT struck by lightning at Union ME [12 Sept 1840]

ROALDSON William & his wife, their 4 ch Ellen, Archibald, Jane & Robert & their servant Grace PURVIS all from Leith & Thomas MOFFATT, a child, were so badly scalded as to survive but a few hrs on board the steamer *Lady of the Lake*, Capt NICHOLAS [26 Sept 1834]

ROBB Mary S 23 w/o Thomas P ROBB d/o Jonathan and Jane MORSE of Lisbon ME at Chicago IL [3 Jun 1847]

ROBB - see HATCH

ROBBINS Abiathar 51 at Dresden ME on 19th Nov [4 Dec 1851]

Aldana Miss 20 on 12th at Union ME [10 Jul 1841]

Anna 92 wid/o Luther ROBBINS at Greene ME [13 Sep 1849]

Asa 81 AmRev, 1781 moved from Walpole MA to Winthrop ME until his death [5 Dec 1840]

Asa Esq 48 on 8th inst at Phillips ME [18 Apr 1840]

ROBBINS (Cont.) B F Rev 34 death a former part owner of the *Maine Farmer* at Augusta ME on 5 Aug [12 Aug 1852]

B Mrs 53 at Union ME [10 Aug 1839]

Caleb 73 at Augusta ME [3 Sep 1846]

Chandler Hon 72 formerly of Hallowell ME at Boston MA [6 Jun 1834]

Charles Esq formerly of (Winthrop) ME a worthy man at Greene ME [30 Jul 1842]

Charles G 3y s/o Benjamin ROBBINS 22nd inst at Winthrop ME [28 Aug 1835]

Clark 66 one of the Friend's Society (Quaker) at Sidney ME on 28 Jan [5 Feb 1852]

Eliphalet 80 at Norridgewock ME [11 Apr 1837]

Eliza Ann 32 w/o Daniel ROBBINS at Bath ME [10 Oct 1837]

Ellery F 19mo s/o Rev B F ROBBINS on 10 Oct at Winthrop ME [18 Oct 1849]

Eunice 82 wid/o Daniel ROBBINS on 9th inst at Winthrop ME [18 Nov 1847]

Joel Jr 42 at Hope ME [1 Feb 1849]

Luther Esq 83 at Greene ME [31 Oct 1840]

Margaret 83 at Thomaston ME [21 Sept 1848]

Mr died by accident on board U. S. steamer *Michigan* firing a salute in honor of the President at Erie PA by the premature explosion of a gun. 1st lost both arms & has since died. [6 Sept 1849]

Nath'l 77 formerly of Union at Brunswick ME [18 Jul 1850]

Oliver 55 formerly of Winthrop ME at Phillips ME on 13 Sept [21 Sept 1848]

Oliver Esq 55 at Thomaston ME [14 Aug 1851]

Otis Maj 82 hero of AmRev at Thomaston ME [16 May 1840]

Susan 50 w/o John ROBBINS at Norridgewock ME [16 Aug 1849]

Thomas 86 at Vassalboro ME [8 Apr 1852]

William A 41 at Vassalboro ME of typhoid fever [20 Jul 1848]

Wm H Harrison 7 s/o Simeon ROBBINS Esq at Norridgewock ME [11 Nov 1847]

ROBBINS - see CHANDLER, HARMON

ROBERTS 3 ch lost in the fire c/o Mrs Nancy ROBERTS at Rochester NY on 18th [1 Jan 1846]

Alanson in the act of logging "of intemperate habits, left a wife & family" [19 June 1841]

Ellen 18 of Webster ME at Bath ME [1 Jan 1846]

George 28 at Dover ME [21 Aug 1851]

Huldah Mrs 53 w/o Dr Jacob ROBERTS at Brooks ME [24 Apr 1845]

James 76 formerly a slave at Brunswick ME [23 Jul 1846]

James S 22 at Portland ME [13 Feb 1845]

Joanna 24 w/o Lemuel ROBERTS of Waterboro ME at Alfred ME [17 Apr 1835]

John Esq 65 formerly of Vassalboro ME at Hallowell ME [15 Jul 1847]

Joseph 69 at Gardiner ME [30 Apr 1846]

Lucy P 30 d/o John ROBERTS grand-d/o Capt Jeremiah ROBERTS and Deac Simeon CHADBOURNE, both were in the battle of Bunker Hill. They and the Deac's wife followed Lucy to the grave, each being about 90 on 19th ult at Lyman ME [10 Sep 1842]

Mary Miss 16 d/o John ROBERTS Esq at Vassalboro ME [4 Apr 1837]

Mr at Bowdoinham ME had both his hands & one of his arms blown off by a premature explosion of a cannon on the 4th of Jul, little hopes of his recovery [15 Jul 1843]

Norman E 36 deputy collector of the district of Belfast at Belfast ME [19 Dec 1844]

Phebe S 26 w/o Wellington J ROBERTS at Brooks ME [9 Jan 1845]

Prudence 22 at Buckfield ME (*sic*) [31 Aug 1848]

Prudence 32 at Buckfield ME (*sic*) [24 Aug 1848]

Rebecca 21 w/o Ammi ROBERTS at Durham ME [14 Nov 1850]

Rufus 28 at Waterboro ME [18 Jun 1846]

Sarah 67 w/o Samuel ROBERTS at Lyman [6 Dec 1849]

ROBERTS (Cont.) Susan 28 d/o Elder Joseph ROBERTS at Hartland ME [5 Nov 1846]

ROBERTS - see HOUGH, CRAWFORD

ROBINSON 15y s/o Elwell ROBINSON 5 Jul at Bath ME [18 Jul 1852]

9 d/o Hon Edward ROBINSON at Thomaston ME [2 Nov 1839]

Alfred 36 at Eastport ME [16 Apr 1846]

Alla Anna 4 d/o Sewall G ROBINSON at Vassalboro ME [10 Jun 1847]

Alonzo of Ohio struck on the head by a flash of lightning to all appearance dead. His father immediately rubbed him with milk and water when he became blistered all over, showed signs of life and under the care of a doctor recovered. [7 Sept 1839]

Asa 76 at Paris ME [22 Jan 1846]

Betsey 74 w/o Eld John ROBINSON at Cornville ME [4 Sept 1851]

C of Thomaston ME at sea on the 16th [7 June 1849]

Charles Henry 25 of Vassalboro ME at Augusta ME [15 Mar 1849]

child at Gardiner ME on Fri by her brother accidentally with a gun [16 May 1837]

child less than 3y of Newburyport MA fell backwards into a pail containing two quarts of boiling water, sufferer lived but twenty-four hours. [8 Mar 1849]

Clementine B 33 w/o William ROBINSON at North Vassalboro ME on 13 Jan [23 Jan 1851]

David 35 a member of the Passagassawakeag Lodge of Odd Fellows at Belfast ME [29 Oct 1846]

Edward W of Baltimore MD on Mon buried 3 of his ch, the oldest only nine yrs of age all of whom died within eight hrs of each other of the scarlet fever [14 Feb 1850]

Eliphalet 55 at Brentwood NH [17 Apr 1851]

Elizabeth 57 at Phipsburg ME [10 Oct 1850]

Emeline Miss 41 at Cushing ME [5 Sep 1850]

Eunice 71 w/o Ezekiel ROBINSON at West Gardiner ME [21 Dec 1848]

Frances 5 c/o Thomas and Mary ROBINSON at Augusta ME [26 Nov 1846]

G Chandler 36 s/o Gen Jesse ROBINSON at Waterville ME on 15 Jul [20 Jul 1848]

George 14 s/o William ROBINSON at Buckfield ME [28 Sept 1848]

George A 11y s/o Charles and Rebecca ROBINSON on 6th inst at Newport [25 Feb 1847]

George Esq 27 formerly editor of the *Age* at Augusta ME on Tues morning last [29 Feb 1840]

Gideon 61 16 Sep at Sidney ME [7 Nov 1850]

Hannah 48 w/o Josiah ROBINSON at Cornville ME [20 June 1850]

Harriet D 43 w/o K G ROBINSON Esq formerly of Hallowell ME at St George New Brunswick Canada on 24th ult [13 Feb 1841]

Increase 75 at Sumner ME [11 Apr 1850]

Isaac 66 at Hampden ME on 19th ult [6 Jan 1837]

James 63 at Bath ME [22 Jan 1839]

Jane 67 wid/o Capt John ROBINSON at Thomaston ME [13 Jul 1848]

Jedediah 83 AmRev at Gardiner ME [23 Nov 1848]

Jeremiah 56 at Augusta ME on 10th inst [24 Apr 1845]

John 51 at Vassalborough ME [21 Mar 1834]

John R Capt 75 early settler of Mt Vernon ME formerly of Brentwood NH on 10th inst [28 Aug 1842]

John & Cato RICKETS seaman sentenced to state prision in VA for secreting on board a schooner two runaway slaves. "Who stole the slaves in the first place?" [19 Aug 1847]

Jonathan late of Mt Vernon ME, Gustavus A ROBINSON, adm [20 May 1852]

Joseph 76 at Vassalboro ME [4 Mar 1852]

Joseph F abt 25 of Augusta ME at Mobile AL on 9th ult [2 May 1850]

ROBINSON (Cont.) Lieut of VA of the U. S. brig of war *Somer* of yellow fever [14 Mar 1844]

Louisa P 17 d/o Elijah ROBINSON Esq at Vassalboro ME [14 Aug 1845]

Lucina abt 50 at Trenton Wisconsin on 6 May [7 June 1849]

Lucinda Adeaide 2y 9m d/o Benjamin C ROBINSON at Augusta ME [11 Mar 1847]

Lucy J 30 of Cushing ME at Augusta ME on 15 Mar [29 Mar 1849]

Mary 15 c/o Thomas & Mary ROBINSON at Augusta ME [26 Nov 1846]

Mary 70 at Bath ME [18 Apr 1850]

Mary M C 29 w/o William C ROBINSON at Bangor ME on 21st inst [4 Dec 1841]

Molly 88 wid/o Thomas ROBINSON at Skowhegan ME [21 Sept 1848]

Mrs abt 88 on 7th inst at St George [22 Apr 1843]

Mrs of Port Gibson advertised by her husband "Object of my pity & contempt I defy thee! Ere thou canst attach blameable disgrace to Eliza, her heart will cease to beat. The safety of my empty purse alarms thee more than the vacancy of my honor" [2 Nov 1848]

Nancy 35 consort of Hon Edward ROBINSON at Thomaston ME [8 May 1845]

Pamelia 44 w/o William S ROBINSON at Hallowell ME [6 Mar 1845]

Rhoda 74 w/o Jos ROBINSON at Vassalboro ME on 9 June [14 June 1849]

Robert 93 at New Castle ME [20 Mar 1845]

Robert a carpenter of the *Berlin* & Thomas BAUMSEY, a seaman of the *Berlin* died on board [*N O Crescent*, 23d] [8 Nov 1849]

Sally w/o Nathaniel ROBINSON Jr at Hallowell ME [13 June 1837]

Samuel B 25y 2m of Boston MA at Wilton ME [26 Feb 1846]

Samuel Capt 75 at Oxford ME [20 Jan 1837]

Sarah 10y c/o Thomas & Mary ROBINSON at Augusta ME [26 Nov 1846]

Sarah 55 w/o Rev Ezekiel ROBINSON at Hallowell ME [4 Oct 1849]

Shepard 28 of St George ME at sea on passage from New Orleans to Philadelphia PA [20 Jul 1848]

Sylvanus W Esq of Boston MA at Litchfield ME [4 Oct 1849]

Whiting Dr 75 at Sebasticook ME [4 Mar 1852]

William 70 buried with Masonic honors at Corinna ME [24 Sept 1846]

William Capt 42 at Thomaston ME [9 Dec 1847]

William Mrs at Warren ME [29 Jan 1846]

William of Gardiner ME his house in the village burnt [16 Nov 1839]

William of Lewiston ME at Kingston Upper Canada [27 Mar 1851]

ROBINSON - see ABBOTT, ALLEN, BUTLER, BURTON, DOYEN, Ellsworth ME, FROST

ROBY two boys 13 & 15 of East Monmouth ME s/o Henry ROBY while skating on Winthrop Great Pond, with their elder brother all fell through the ice; however only the eldest was able to save himself [18 Dec 1841]

ROCKFELLE [sic] George his wife & daughter; Mr SAULPAGH, son & daughter; Andrer [sic] HAWON [sic] & two other persons who all reside at Germantown Columbia Co drowned [3 Apr 1845]

ROCKWOOD Emeline 27 at Augusta ME [19 June 1838]

Hiram Esq 32 at Belgrade ME on 13th inst [28 Dec 1833]

Josephus at Augusta ME on 25th [28 Jan 1847]

Salmon abt 40 at Augusta ME on 27th Aug [30 Aug 1849]

RODBIRD Jane Amanda 47 w/o Capt William RODBIRD at Bath ME [27 Dec 1849]

RODGERS - see PINKNEY

RODICK Charles K 17y 2m s/o the late David RODICK at Brunswick ME [3 June 1843]

ROGER Mary reported murdered "a victim to hellish lust & then murder" but by the end of the article Justice MERRITT stated no confession ever had been made & the *New*

ROGER (Cont.) *York Sun* says "Within the past week a report has been quite current that
the girl is alive & in the keeping of her former employer .... [26 Aug 1841]

ROGERS Adam entered 101y (on 22 Feb) of Marshfield MA of 6 brothers five lived to 95 to
100. They were all born in Marshfield & descended from the first settlers of Plymouth
MA. [11 Mar 1833]

Albion s/o Hugh ROGERS 11m at Bath ME [4 Mar 1847]

Alexander Major 92 at Topsham ME [26 Mar 1846]

Andrew Capt Jr of brig *India* of Eastport ME at Bathurst Africa on 26 Aug [21 Nov
1850]

Andrew Esq 68 at Augusta ME [19 Aug 1836]

Andrew master of brig India on 26 Aug From the Coast of Africa the brig *India*, Capt
HANSCOMB arrived at thsi port this morning (*Philadelphia Bulletin*, 31st). She left
Bissau West Coast of Africa 23 Jan & arrived at Port Praya Cape de Verds on 12 Feb
[10 Apr 1851]

Aurelia C 41 w/o Seth ROGERS at Freeport ME [3 Oct 1850]

Beatrice Mrs 63 at Phipsburg ME [9 Apr 1846]

Betsey 84 wid/o Rev Robert ROGERS at Anson ME [4 Jan 1840]

Catharine 29 at Alfred ME [10 Oct 1837]

Catharine C 24 d/o William H & Lydia ROGERS at Norridgewock ME on 16 May [10
June 1852]

Drummond 26 at Bath ME [15 June 1839]

Elizabeth 26 at Belgrade ME on 10 May [16 May 1850]

family the last four of the family named ROGERS who went from New York to CA in
Dec last died, one of fever at Panama, the father & one son died in Oct on the Yuba
River, and on the 30th Oct the remaining son died at Sacramento CA [3 Jan 1850]

George on Sun last [31 Jan 1834]

Harison a carpenter & native of the state of Maine so badly injured by a fall from a
building in New Orleans on the 4th inst that he died in a few hours [1 Jan 1842] &
[15 Jan 1842]

Hugh of Calais ME shockingly mutilated on Tues last while blasting rocks in the field
belonging to George DOWNS Esq at Calais ME [*Calais Advertiser*] [21 Oct 1847]

J P formerly Attorney Gen of ME a distinguished member of the Suffolk bar died at
Norfolk House Roxbury MA [*Bee*] [3 Dec 1846]

James M Esq 66 at Bowdoinham ME [10 Jul 1851]

John 92y 7m AmRev at Mt Vernon ME on 27th Jan [22 Feb 1849]

John L Esq of Gloucester MA of a disease resembling cholera [20 Sept 1849]

John P Capt 50 at Elliot ME [15 Jul 1843]

John S 22 at Litchfield ME [16 Oct 1851]

Jonathan 63 at St Stephen New Brunswick Canada [14 Feb 1850]

Josiah shot in the head & killed by lad SINCLAIR 18 by accident at Litchfield Corner
ME [*Gardiner Fountain*] [22 Nov 1849]

lad 12 s/o Charles ROGERS accidentaly hung himself at Lyons NY [19 June 1841

Levi Esq 48 well known for manys as the keeper of the Mansion House & since then the
proprietor of Augusta Hotel at Augusta ME on Mon last [4 Apr 1837]

Lucretia Page 39 wid/o Col J P ROGERS of Boston MA at Hallowell ME [4 Apr 1850]

Martha 78 at Exeter NH on 15th inst [28 Mar 1840]

Martin 64 at Belfast ME [9 Nov 1848]

Mary 90 widow at Orneville ME [25 Apr 1850]

Miriam P 36 at Freeport ME [5 Sept 1850]

Mrs killed 3 of her ch by cutting heads off with an axe. The dreadful deed done while fit
of mental derangement. The mother of 11 ch, including the 3 killed & says while
under the influence of a distorted imagination, thought doing a charitable action in

ROGERS (Cont.) ridding her husband of the burden of supporting herself & their five youngest ch, at Louisville on the 18th ult [21 Aug 1841]

Nathan at Litchfield ME [1 Jan 1852]

Nathan B Rev, pastor of the Congregational Church at Hallowell ME on 29 Oct [8 Nov 1849]

Noah 48 at Bath ME [17 Apr 1851]

Peter Rev 99y 4m 10d died at Waterloo IL on 4th ult, of Washington's life-guards AmRev [27 Dec 1849]

Polly 35 w/o Robert ROGERS Jr at Dover ME [6 Apr 1848]

Rufus his sawmill was on fire at Topsham ME [2 Jan 1851]

Samuel H 73 at Phipsburg ME [14 June 1849]

Thomas, his wife died [15 Jan 1846]

three children of Daniel R burned to death ae 5y, 3y, & 9m also father at Boston [2 Sept 1852]

W E P 46 formerly publisher of the *Bangor (ME) Courier* at Haverhill MA [7 Dec 1848]

ROGERS - see KIMBALL, RUSSELL

ROLERSON Joseph Capt of Belfast ME & wife & son Charles R & Thomas SHAW & wife, Miss Julia LARKIN, neice of Mr S; Margaret HENNESY; Horace CROSBY of Albion ME; Mr TUCKER native of Philadelphia, & Edward FLING; Thomas GRADY; Peter CONNERS; James CASSAN; George HAYES; Thomas WARREN; John SUMMERS; Isaac JONES a boy, brig *Falconer* of Belfast ME lost on the Southern spit of our bar last Sat 18th inst [*Boston Traveller*] [30 Dec 1847]

ROLFE Charles B of Concord NH in CA on the Stanislaus River on 2 Oct [20 Nov 1851]

David S 45 at Portland ME on Mon on 21st inst of consumption [2 Apr 1842]

Dorothy 71 widow of Henry R at Rumford ME [2 May 1837]

Susannah 25 w/o Mr E R at Turner ME on 4 Nov [10 Dec 1842]

ROLFE - see BRYANT

ROLLINS Ann M 29 w/o Theodore ROLLINS formerly of Hampden ME at East Boston MA [15 Aug 1844]

Capt master of brig *Natahnis* of Pittston ME at Sagua La Grande Cuba on 27th ult [3 Sept 1846]

David deceased in Union ME [29 Apr 1852]

Eben Capt of Pittston ME, master of brig *Sea Flower* at New York in the Marine Hospital on the 2nd inst of yellow fever [22 Aug 1844]

Ebenezer 14y drowned in Richmond (ME) on Sat 16th inst [4 Nov 1847]

Eunice 53 w/o Valentine ROLLINS at Sangerville ME on 21 Apr [15 May 1851]

James 28 at Vassalboro ME [25 Nov 1847]

James O late of Vassalboro ME, Hiram A ROLLINS exec [15 Apr 1852]

Julia A 36 w/o Levi ROLLINS at Albion ME on 26 Aug [12 Sept 1850]

Lydia 91 at Saco ME [4 Apr 1850]

Mary Ann 31 of Pittston ME at Waterville ME on 29 Sept [30 Nov 1848]

Moses H 61 formerly of London NH 30th ult at Hallowell [14 Aug 1838]

Nathaniel 84 AmRev at Hallowell ME [1 Jan 1846]

Sophrina AD 34 w/o Abel ROLLINS at Bath ME [28 Oct 1843]

Spencer M 25 s/o John C ROLLINS at Union ME [8 Aug 1834]

Sumner H 18m twin s/o Jesse & Lucy ROLLINS at Milo ME [20 Mar 1851]

True abt 46 at Pittston ME [20 Feb 1845]

William 61 at Hallowell ME [12 Sept 1840]

William Francis 2 s/o W M & J K ROLLINS at Orono ME on 31 Jul [21 Aug 1851]

William T of Gardiner ME in CA left widow & several ch in Gardiner ME [19 June 1851]

ROLLINS - see GOULD

RONALDSON James a Scotsman and of the first type founders in Philadelphia at Phil [10 Apr 1841]

ROPER Peter of New Bedford MA? at San Francisco CA [8 Jan 1852]

ROSE Allen G 4 c/o George ROSE at Fairfield ME [18 Dec 1841]

Benjamin 92 AmRev at Bangor ME [26 Sep 1850]

Betsey 42 w/o Nelson ROSE at Leeds ME [19 Jul 1849]

Daniel Hon 62 on 25th ult at Thomaston ME [16 Nov 1833]

David J deck passenger of New Orleans a serious accident happened on board the steamboat *George Collier* on the 6th inst on her passage from New Orleans to St Louis MO [25 May 1839]

Joseph Palmer 19 s/o Zebedee ROSE Jr of Livermore ME washed overboard from ship *Genesee* on passage to Ireland [25 Mar 1847]

Mrs 56 wid/o Hon Daniel ROSE at Thomaston ME [3 Oct 1844]

William 36 recently of Rome ME at Augusta ME [4 Jan 1844]

ROSS Benjamin 26 formerly of Bloomfield ME at Bath ME at the Marine Hospital [28 Sept 1848]

Benjamin 73, tailor, buried with Masonic honors at Augusta ME [17 Jul 1845]

boy of St David s/o Charles ROSS & the other the s/o Merrill WITCHER of St Patrick their ages were 17 to 18 & were burnt to death [*Calais Journal*] [15 Feb 1849]

children born 16 Dec 1847 of Texas Co MO c/o Benjamin ROSS mow of St Louis are connected from the breast bone & abdomen, measures twenty inches in height & weighs 20 lbs [15 Mar 1849]

c/o Benjamin ROSS at Augusta ME [8 Apr 1833]

Hannah A 15 d/o late Jas B ROSS at Saco ME [6 Sep 1849]

James B 64 at Saco ME [27 Jul 1848]

Jeremiah C of North Yarmouth ME, seaman lost overboard from brig *Baltic* from Cardenas to Boston ME [30 Apr 1846]

John abt 55 married Miss Mary B STAPLES 18y of Wilmington DL, she of the Society of Friends or did, was given away by her brother & attended by her sister & a niece of John ROSS as bridesmaids, after ceremony a family party of 20 of the ROSSES (all half breed Indians) sat down to a banquet. R is considered to be worth half a million of dollars, soon to his wild home in the south-western prairies. [*Bee*] [12 Sept 1844]

John Cherokee Chief has a Quaker wife who is a native of Philadelphia. We don't know what her color is, but they are now ruralizing at Brandywine Springs Delaware [27 July 1848]

John the celebrated Cherokee chief, has been spending part of the summer at Schooley's mountain with his family ... the 2nd wife of John ROSS himself, was a pretty Quaker lass, we believe from Wilmington DE [*Neal's Gazette*] [7 Sept 1848]

Lewis G & Mr McGAHEY the owner of a plantation at Yazoo MS & Lewis G ROSS, his overseer, have been held to bail, the latter in $2,000 as principle and the former in $10,000 as accessory to the murder of one of McGAHEY's slaves, who was whipped to death by ROSS [3 Aug 1839]

Lt a duel with Lt HOE of the U. S. Navy at Pensacola FL It terminated "honorably" - one wounded in the heel of his boot & the other shot through the hat [26 Oct 1839]

Mary widow abt 40 at Brunswick ME [3 Feb 1848]

Susannah 21 d/o Joseph Ross Jr at Jefferson ME [9 Oct 1845]

Walter 74 at Chesterville ME [5 Mar 1846]

William of Boston ME saved the barque *William Fales*, Capt William THOMES of this port (Portland ME) was lost in Wells Bay ME on Wed evening at 9 o'clock, 13 persons on board, eight were lost including every officer. Through the attention of our friend, George M FREEMAN of Cape Needick (Old York, where the barque drove) [26 Feb 1842]

ROSS - see HAM

ROTHSCHILD Mager Amschel born 1743 at Frankfort-on-the-Main. He had ten children Amschel/Ansel born 12 June 1773, d 1840; Solomon b 9 Sept 1774 res Berlin & Vienna; Nathan b 16 Sept 1777 res London England; Charles b 24 Apr 1788 res Naples; Jacob 15 May 1792 married a dau of the second brother (Solomon) & live in Paris Mager A ROTHSCHILD left his parents in his 11 year, without any fortune, he was, as is still customary in Germany with poor Jews, destined for the business of a teacher (for more see pp. 205-206 *Maine Farmer*) [3 Jul 1841]

    Nathan Mayer 59 a London banker, on Thurs 28th at Frankfort-on-the-Maine He was on a visit to Frankfort to see son's marriage [16 Sept 1836]

ROUNDEY Myron D 18 or 20 killed by accident at Sebasticook on Tues [*Waterville Mail*] [16 Aug 1849]

ROUNDS Lovina H Mrs 28 26th ult at Norway ME [16 Oct 1845]

ROWE Abial 29 at Madison ME [26 Sep 1850]

    Benjamin 64 formerly of Sandy Bay MA at Moscow ME [22 Mar 1849]

    Elizabeth 82 w/o Benj ROWE at Norway ME [4 Nov 1852]

    Elizabeth P Mrs 25 at Greenwood ME [6 Jun 1844]

    Ephraim abt 40 at Smithfield ME [8 Feb 1849]

    Experience 73 w/o John ROWE at New Sharon ME on 13 Jul [31 Jul 1851]

    Hannah Miss 18 d/o Peter ROWE Esq at Belfast ME [17 Jun 1833]

    Harrison the brother of Cyrus ROWE, late editor of the *Belfast Journal* now on his way to CA was killed by Indians at Loup Fork of the Platt River on 23d May [9 Aug 1849]

    Mrs of Roxbury CT burnt in the most shocking manner died a few days since [11 Jan 1849]

    Nathan abt 55 formerly of Oxford ME at Newry ME [28 Feb 1850]

    Peter Esq 70 at Belfast ME [2 Sep 1847]

    Samuel A 29 at Oxford ME [8 Aug 1850]

    Sarah Mrs 61 of Augusta ME at Portland ME [7 Oct 1852]

    Sarah S 35 w/o Cyrus ROWE at Belfast ME [9 Jan 1845]

    Stephen Deac abt 65 at Danville ME [3 Jan 1850]

    Theodore 24 of Maine of yellow fever 19th or 20th ult at New Orleans [7 Oct 1847]

    Webber 86 AmRev at Baldwin ME [21 Feb 1851]

    Winthrop fell down in a fit and expired at East Pond Plantation ME (inc as part of Smithfield in 1840) [8 Jan 1839]

ROWELL Hezekiah 71 formerly of Castine ME at Hampden ME [5 Aug 1852]

    Hiram 36 at Skowhegan ME]4 Apr 1850]

    Joseph 86 at Monmouth ME [7 Oct 1852]

    Mary w/o Col John ROWELL on 20 Nov at Jay ME [12 Dec 1850]

ROWLAND boy of Philadelphia PA s/o Peter S ROWLAND was killed through the carelessness of a physician & the ignorance of an apothecary. The physician wrote for some oil "Resini" but neglected to dot the "i" & made the "e" look like an o, the apothecary put up oil of Rosemary which caused the death [19 June 1851]

ROWLAND - see GOUTS

ROYAL Henry Harrison 10 s/o Bailey ROYAL at Winthrop ME [17 June 1852]

    Mary 71 at Brunswick ME [21 Sept 1848]

RUBY Reuben (formerly of Portland ME) has returned from CA after mining four months. He collected about $3000 worth of gold. [*Portland Argus*] [6 Dec 1849]

RUGG Martha K of Lancaster MA death at Niagara Falls on the Canadian side [*Albany Daily Advertiser*] [5 Sept 1844]

RUGGLES David "a colored man," the most active of the New York "Committee of Vigilance" has been held to bail for improperly interfering in a case of a slave that had robbed his master. [25 Sept 1838]

Thos G 32 at Calais ME [22 Feb 1849]

RUGGLES - see HINCKLEY [29 Sept 1840]

RUIZ Mr of the schr *Prize*. Mr RUIZ, the owner of the slaves on board the schr taken to New London resided in Boston MA several months last year & is well known to many gentlemen there & his connections in Principe are highly repectable. [14 Sept 1839]

RULE girls 12 & 14 d/o Capt George RULE dreadfully wounded by a large dog at Poplis, Nantucket on the 3d inst [15 Aug 1844]

Sarah 30 w/o Capt Geo RULE formerly of Winthrop ME at Nantucket MA [5 Oct 1833]

RUMERY James S 52 at Saco ME [15 Jul 1843]

Pamelia Mrs 76 at Lubec ME [6 May 1847]

RUNDLET Charles 74 at Alna ME [12 Apr 1849]

RUNDLETT Paulina Mrs 49 at Mt Vernon ME on 1 Mar [3 Apr 1851]

Rufus 16 29 Nov at Mt Vernon ME [11 Jan 1849]

Susan 26 w/o Smith RUNDLETT at Waterville ME [12 Dec 1844]

RUNDLETT - see WITHERN

RUNNELLS Harriet C 20y 9mo d/o Thomas and Elizabeth RUNNELLS at Freeport ME [23 Jan 1845]

RUNNELS Gov formerly gov of Mississippi [14 Nov 1844]

Jackson 14 in employ of the mills at New Durham NH caught by a shaft & later died (*Traveller*) [12 Oct 1848]

Rebecca Mrs 77 on 14 inst at Marion [25 Apr 1844]

RUSH Dr he found only one person above the age of eighty who had lived unmarried. [13 June 1840]

Julia 90th yr died last week wid/o Dr RUSH & the mother of Hon Richard RUSH minister to France [27 July 1848]

widow the wife of the late Mr RUSh ae 90, probably the only surviving partner of any of those who signed the Declaration of Independence [4 Nov 1847]

RUSS John Major 75 at Belfast ME [15 Nov 1849]

Mary Mrs 79 wid/o Jonathan RUSS Esq 3 Oct at New Sharon ME [17 Oct 1844]

Rosomund H d/o late Major RUSS of Farmington ME at Carmel ME [16 May 1850]

Ruth H 31 w/o Horatio G RUSS Esq at Paris ME [21 Sept 1848]

William Esq 36 at Paris ME [26 Jul 1849]

RUSSEL Betsey Mrs 69 formerly of Mass at Sidney ME [4 Apr 1840]

Levi 83 AmRev at Waldoboro ME [12 Sep 1834]

RUSSELL Benjamin Hon 83d y of Boston MA many years editor of *the Columbian Centinel*, AmRev [*Boston Advertiser*] [16 Jan 1845]

Calvin 90 AmRev pensioner at Moscow ME [10 Jun 1852]

Charles H of Pittston ME at the Hospital in Honolulu (Sandwich Islands) on 7 Oct [25 Dec 1851]

David 72 formerly of Norridgewock ME at Garland ME [15 Mar 1849]

Eliza 75 w/o late John RUSSELL Esq of Boston MA for many years editor and publisher of the *Boston Gazette* died at Bath ME [22 Jan 1846]

Elizabeth Ann 24 w/o Perkins RUSSELL at East Winthrop ME [18 Mar 1852] & [25 Mar 1852]

Ephraim H 48 of Pittston ME formerly of Bath ME at Staten Island NY [4 June 1851]

George of Troy ME youngest s/o Martin RUSSELL fell from a window in the court house on the 6th inst & did not survive but a few hours. [31 Aug 1839]

Hannah 81 w/o Calvin RUSSELL at Bingham ME [28 May 1846]

RUSSELL (Cont.) Helen Mar abt 10 of Bath ME d/o Charles RUSSELL, & Adelaide
ROGERS d/o Robert B ROGERS of Chelsea MA abt 12y left the residence of Mr
RUSSELL yesterday morning to a walk in the woods ... they were found drowned in
Sewall Stream. [*Bath Tribune*, Sept 9] [21 Sept 1848]

Jane ab 40 w/o Nathaniel RUSSELL formerly of Penobscot ME at Exeter ME [20 Jun
1834]

Jesse 69 at Bath ME [7 Mar 1844]

John killed & one other person slightly injured on the firing a cannon in the honor of the
election of James K POLK [OH Statesman] at Zanesville on the 13th [5 Dec 1844]

John late of Sidney ME, Asa SMILEY adm [4 Mar 1852]

John at Weld ME [21 Feb 1851]

lad & lad CLARK, the two boys both of Dracut MA fell through the ice on Beaver Brook,
Jeremiah THOMAS not yet 9y old s/o John THOMAS with judgement befitting older
heads saved them both. [*Lowell Journal*] [2 Mar 1849]

Lucy 25y 10 m twin d/o Capt William & Sylvia RUSSELL at Farmington ME on 7 Jan
[13 Feb 1851]

Nathaniel Deac 68 at Waterville ME [23 Jan 1851]

Nathaniel P Esq at Nahant drowned himself [*Boston Advertiser*] [13 Jul 1848]

Olive 43 d/o Jonathan RUSSELL of Madison ME at Industry ME [14 Aug 1845]

Olivia P 43 at Damariscatta ME [1 Jan 1852]

Olivia P Mrs 43 at Damariscotta ME [1 Jan 1852]

Sarah w/o Joseph RUSSELL of Boston d/o Hon Leonard JARVIS at Ellsworth ME [26
Mar 1837]

Sylvia 25y 10 m twin d/o Capt William & Sylvia RUSSELL at Farmington ME on 29th
[13 Feb 1851]

William perished on the schr *Thomas*, SPROULE Capt of Belfast ME [25 Mar 1843]

Zilphia S 19 d/o Theodore RUSSELL at Leeds ME [4 Jan 1834]

RUST Eugene G 11m s/o Benjamin RUST at Augusta ME on 21th inst [27 Mar 1851]

Eunice J ab 18 of Washington ME at Hallowell ME [9 May 1850]

Joseph 96 at Wiscasset ME [14 Nov 1844]

Sarah 13 eldest d/o Capt Henry and Mary RUST 6th inst of erysipelas and rheumatic
fever at Norway Village ME [15 Apr 1843]

Sarah 83 wid/o Henry RUST Esq at Norway ME [20 Aug 1846]

RUTTY Edward 48 at Phipsburg ME [25 Mar 1847]

RYAN Michael drowned at Gardiner ME [27 May 1852]

Samuel J C perished in the flames in the house fire of Jos ELLIS at Brooks ME [*Belfast
Advocate*] [6 Nov 1835]

William of the crew of ship *Columbus* sentenced to 2 yrs at Blackwell's Island for mutiny
on Thurs made an attempt to escape by swimming across the East River & drowned
[13 Nov 1851]

RYDER Rebecca 36 w/o Capt Benj RYDER at Belfast ME [2 Dec 1852]

RYERSON Eben'r fell dead while mixing mortar at Portland ME [17 May 1849]

George G 89 AmRev at New York NY on Tues 24 Mar [11 Apr 1840]

RYLAND William Rev 78 chaplain in the Navy [*Washington Union* of Mon] [29 Jan 1846]
at Washington City on Mon [5 Feb 1846]

RYONSON Maria Elizabeth 6y 9mo d/o Edward and Elizabeth RYONSON at Brunswick
ME [6 Mar 1845]

SAWYER (Cont.) Mr his barn & stable burned, Mr GARLAND burned in endeavoring to rescue the horses. Suspicion having fallen upon a Mr Asa CROCKER of having the fire set was arrested and bound over to next supreme court. at Hermon ME on Sat evening 5th inst (from the *Bangor Courier*) [19 Nov 1842]

Rhoda Ann 16y 4m w/o Thadeus SAWYER at Greene ME on 4th ult [25 Jan 1840]

wid/o Joshua SAWYER & d/o James OLCOTT took a bridle in her hand about 11 o'clock to catch a horse in the pasture, found her skull kicked & broken at Swanzey NH on Mon of last week [1 Aug 1840] & [8 Aug 1840]

William 87y 8m AmRev pensioner at Greene ME [13 Mar 1851]

SAWYER - see SEAVER

Saxe-Coburg-Gotha Adelaide Victoria Louisa Princess birth to Queen Victoria House of Hanover & Prince Albert Saxe-Coburg-Gotha in England on 21st ult [2 Jan 1841]

SAYWARD Charles Edward 9 s/o J S SAYWARD at Bangor ME [28 Sept 1848]

SCALES Nathan 6 riding with his father in a wagon & in turning round to look at some object behind fell out and the wheels passed over his head. At Hallowell ME [9 Sept 1843]

SCAMMON Charles W 33 at Saco ME [9 Oct 1851]

SCHELLINGER John 32y from Portland ME where his family resides buried alive, digging a well on Big Rock Creek Kendall Co [*Chicago Democrat*] [8 Jul 1847]

SCHERMERHORN an infant of Lambertville NJ d/o Mr J A SCHERMERHORN lying in her cradle heard to cry violently & upon searching for the cause, it was ascertained that a large rat had entered the apartment & attacked the child. The rat had bitten one hand entirely through in two places, which was much swollen and inflamed. (No death was reported at this time.) [*Newark (NJ) Advertiser*] [9 Mar 1848]

SCHLEGEL Mary Jane of Washington PA on a visit to her friends in Pittsburgh died in accident rolling down Boyd's Hill [12 June 1835]

SCHRACK Michael of Upper Providence accidentally by a colt [*Norristown (PA) Herald*] [2 May 1844]

SCHUYLER Harriet of Albany killed in the streets on Thurs, a niece of Gen Van RENSSALAER [1 Jan 1846]

Mr AmRev who deserves all the credit of the capture of Burgoyne of which he was deprived by Gen GATES assuming the command just as all the arrangements for the battle had been made at Saratoga died at New York in 1804 [16 Sept 1847]

Philip Gen the existence of a box or camp chest left in (Albany) contained information relative to the events with the Am Rev & the history of that period. Mrs Alexander HAMILTON, the surviving daughter of Gen SCHUYLER instituted the search for this long missing box. It was found but it did not list its contents. [19 June 1845]

SCHWARTZ - see SMITH

SCHWENK Charles for seduction of his daughter in Norristown Montgomery Co the verdict was in favor of the plaintiff for $2,500. [10 Apr 1851]

SCOLES - see WARNER

SCOTT James colored indicted in Boston MA for aiding in the escape of Shadrach SIMS, an alleged fugitive from slavery committed to the jury on Thurs after 5 hours ... unable to agree then were again sent out & remained out all night & being still unable to agree they were discharged. The District Attorney then moved for trial in case of Lewis HAYDEN, colored [12 June 1851]

James mate of Halifax Nova Scotia Canada, fatal shipwreck of the schr *Argus* on Plum Island Capt CROCKETT of Frankfort ME was the captain [2 Jan 1851]

Mr AmRev died in KY [16 Sept 1847]

William Walter late of Van Dieman's Land, whither he was sent for his participation in the patriot war & Miss Nancy EGHERT of (Bangor ME?) married by Justice

SCOTT (Cont.) WENTWORTH at the Police Office on Fri. Being acquainted about fifteen
minutes before the ceremony [*Rochester Democrat*] [22 Aug 1844]

Winfield Gen, the party of Iowa Indians, while passing through Elizabethtown NJ visited
the residence of Gen W SCOTT accompanied by Mr T B CATLIN & were
entertained by Mrs SCOTT & her daughters. The party have with them the war chief
of the Iowa nation - and when the Indian chief found that the great chief of his white
brethren lived there, he expressed a wish to see his squaw (his duaghter) & wigwam!
[23 Dec 1847]

Winfield Gen (of the Mexican War) reported 75y old on last Sun, born 15 June 1786
(N.B. also served in the Civil War 1861, the (so called) Aroostook War of Maine in
1839 & the War of 1812) [19 June 1851]

SCOTT - see CRAWFORD, news, RANSOM

SCOVEN Samuel his house burned & his son 4y & a black boy in the flames [*Savannah
Republican*] [25 Jan 1840]

SCRANTON John 68 of Madison ME on 20th inst [*New Haven Herald*] [2 Apr 1846]

SCRIBNER Ellen Nora infant d/o Viril SCRIBNER at Kennebec (now Manchester) ME on
17 Sept [2 Oct 1851]

Mr stating Mr B ALLEN of Rome ME, Mr S of Mt Vernon drowned on Long Pong (*sic*),
near Chandler's Mills in Belgrade ME, received a letter from Mr S dated 9th inst "I
take pleasure informing you that I don't believe one word of the above statement so
far as it relates to myself nor can I make any one else believe it ... Mr ALLEN was
drowned on Sun." [*Lewiston Journal*] [16 Jan 1851]

Mrs at the head of Lambert's Lake poisoned herself to death by taking a dose of wolf
poison [*Calais Advertiser*] [2 Sept 1847]

Sabrina M 19y 10m d/o Isaac J & Rachel THOMPSON of Unity ME (Portland ME
papers please copy) at Freedom ME on 25 Jan [5 Feb 1852]

SCUDDER Harriet w/o Rev John SCUDDER MD & for more than 30 yrs a missionary of
the American Board died & the sister of Rev Dr WATERBERY of Boston MA at
Madres on 19 Nov [31 Jan 1850]

SEAMAN Mr of New York (who came in charge of the two race boats entered for the
regatta), on Tues afternoon as a train from Providence was near Dedham MA, was
thrown from an open freight car by the breaking of the chain & fell upon the track.
The cars passed over him [26 Aug 1843]

SEARS Eleanor Warren died on 28 Mar 1842 almost completed 22nd year. (Will *Christian
Mirror* & *Zion's Herald* please copy?) (see obit) [21 May 1842]

Olive 2y d/o Moses B SEARS at (Winthrop ME) on Wed of last week [22 Feb 1840]

SEAVER a boy abt 10y s/o William J SEAVER bitten on Fri last by a dog belonging to his
uncle; the boy has had medical assistance, the dog was killed & the boy might recover
[*Traveller*] [10 June 1847]

George W a young man from Gardiner ME under the influence of delirium tremens
killed himself in Boston MA [18 June 1846]

Simeon C of Hopkinton went squirrel hunting. Mr SAWYER shot a squirrel in the top of
a tree - but as it did not fall to the ground, Mr SEAVER attempted to support
SAWYER's climb with the breech of his gun, which was loaded. The cock caught in
the bark of the tree & the gun fired passing into the thigh of Mr SEAVER, killing
him on Tues last [*Mercantile Journal*] [16 Nov 1839]

SEAVEY Joseph 18y to sail with a party on Sat last; as the boat was coming up to the wharf,
under full sail, he received so severe a blow on the head from the fall of a timber ...
his life was dispaired of. His head was bruised in a most shocking manner, but he was
living 17 June [*Portland Adv*] [22 June 1839]

Sally 40y of Scarborough ME by suicide at Provincetown MA left husband & several
children [15 Nov 1849]

SEAVY Edwin of Cushing ME, chief mate lost overboard from brig *Kedron* on passage
    from Providence to Thomaston [30 Mar 1848]

SEDGLEY Hannah 71 w/o James SEDGLEY at Readfield ME on 23 Mar [1 May 1851]
    Jotham of Whitneyville on Sat the 19th inst a crew of river drivers, was breaking a
    heavey jam of logs on the Great Falls, the jam started & Mr SEGLEY fell in & went
    over the falls with the logs. He came out a quarter of a mile below alive, but much
    bruised & dangerously injured [*Argus*] [31 Aug 1848]

SEDGWICK Theodore of Stockbridge MA while addressing a public meeting at Pittsfield
    (MA)? was seized with a sudden rush of blood to the head, and shortly afterwards
    expired [30 Nov 1839]

SEELEY - see KEEN

SEIDEARS John 57y of Waldoboro ME suicide [3 Sept 1846]

SEINE Henry W married Miss Maria Ellen HURD the bride but 15y, married by Rev Mr
    PIERCE at Peoria IL on 12th ult (This is fulfilling the juvenile adjunct that children
    should be SEEN & not HEARD) [19 June 1851]

SEKINS Elijah & Enoch 17y & 8y c/o Josiah SEKINS and Miss STICKNEY 18 who
    resided in the sme family but belonged to Hallowell ME drowned at Wescott Pond in
    Swanville ME on 12th inst by the upsetting of a boat [*Belfast ME Journal*] [23 Jul
    1846]

SEMINOLE Squaw born blind, eyes recently restored to sight at New Orleans by an
    operation by Dr LUZENBURY [8 May 1838]

SENTER Robert abt 41y of Bowdoinham ME while out on a gunning excursion on
    Merrymeeting Bay on Thurs night last capsized his float & drowned [19 Apr 1849]

SENTMANAT Francisco de Gen see translation of his letter written to wife a few moments
    before was shot at Tobasco [15 Aug 1844]

SERVATIUS Amelia Mrs a German lady 22y from inhaling chloroform at her residence
    Spruce St NY as a remedy for a toothache [7 Aug 1851]

SEVERANCE Elijah 33 at Milo ME [19 Oct 1848]
    Henry s/o Luther S, editor of *Kennebec Journal* of Augusta ME left some time ago for
    the gold mountains in CA [*Gospel Banner*] [15 Feb 1849]
    Joseph a member of the Society of Shakers, found suspended by the neck in the mill at
    Shaker Village, Enfield NH on 19th inst [6 Apr 1848]
    Luther four editors in Congress at present viz Luther SEVERANCE of Augusta ME;
    Edmund BURKE of Haverhill NH; John WENTWORTH of Chicago IL; & Volney E
    HOWARD of MS [18 Jan 1844]

SEVIER Mr one of the prominent politicians of the country is dead, just been appointed to
    run the boundary line of TX [18 Jan 1849]

SEWALL Eliza 49 w/o Gen Joseph SEWALL at Bath ME [9 Mar 1848]
    Henry Maj Gen XCIII AmRev, personally acquainted with WASHINGTON, to whose
    staff he was for a time attached ... Immediately after the peace, in Sept 1783, he came
    to Fort Western, then Hallowell ME, now Augusta ME & opened a store near that
    place in company with Mr William BURLEY of Beverley MA ... He was town clerk
    of the original town of Hallowell ME in 1788 ... [*Gospel Banner*] [11 Sept 1845]
    Joseph Esq 81 at Farmington ME [13 Nov 1851]
    Joseph Gen 56 at Bath ME [10 Apr 1851]
    Lydia 83 at York ME [20 Mar 1851]
    Thomas Dr one of the oldest resident physicians & well known in Europe as well as
    throughout the USA died of pneumonia [17 Apr 1845]
    William D Jr assisting a little boy down from the ship now building in the yard of Clark
    & Sewall by a misstep both were precipitated to the ground. Mr S struck upon the left
    side of his head just above the temple. Dr STOCKBRIDGE & PUTNAM were called,

SEWALL (Cont.) but he died 25y leaving a wife married but 6mos. (from the *Bath ME Times*) [18 Sept 1851]

SEWALL - see CONY, CUSHING, SIMS

SEWELL Joseph Neal the Lincolnshire giant born 1805 at Horncastle of Taunton. Died on the 4th inst at Swansea & buried in the church yard of Taunton St Mary Magdalen. The deceased was 7'4" & weight was 518 pounds (or 37 stones). (*The Taunton Currier* of England) [18 Apr 1834]

SEXTON Dennis abt 34, a fireman on Fri on the Oldtown ME Railroad left wife & two children (*Bangor ME Whig*) [18 Jan 1849]

SHANE Patrick drowned when between Fort Independence & Thompson's Island, one of a party of 27 of the boys of the Farm School on Thompson's Island accompanied by a teacher & boat-keeper [7 May 1842]

SHANNON James 35 formerly of Saco ME at Louisville KY [27 Nov 1851]

SHAPLEIGH Rebecca P d/o Levi J SHAPLEIGH Esq at Eliot ME on 25th ult [21 Nov 1840]

SHARP Daniel of Colchester VT killed by his horse taking fright when near the railroad crossing at Rouse's Point on Sat [14 Aug 1851]

SHARTTERLEE Benedict Dr a missionary to the Pawnee Indians in the Missouri Terr supposed to have been murdered abt 75 miles from Cantoment Leavenworth by two Indians. His wife, Mrs S, died before she reached the missionary ground (Copied from the *Boston Pat*) [18 Jul 1837]

SHAUR girl d/o Mr Lucius SHAUR while attending her loom at one of the village mills, got entangled by the hair of her head with in the machinery ... There is very little hope of her recovery at Valatia Columbia Co [20 Nov 1845]

SHAW Benjamin Esq 40 at Old Town ME [1 May 1851]

Bethwell P of Durham ME 23 at Marysville CA on the morning on 31st Oct [2 Jan 1851]

child 2y d/o Albert SHAW last Sat from eating cobalt [*Bath Tribune*] [16 Aug 1849]

Cyrus formerly of Middeborough MA but more recently of Plymouth. He was seen in New York City about 4 yrs ago & said he was bound to East Dixfield ME, where he has accumulated a little property. He has resided in Hallowell ME within ten years; & is abt 44y ... information wanted on him so letters addressed to the *Rock* Office of Plymouth MA will be attended to [*Plymouth Rock* MA 10th Dec] [24 Dec 1846]

James H seaman 40 of MA belonged to the US ship *Preble*, by the Africa fever at Porto Grande Island of St Vincent Cape de Verds on 8th Dec [10 Apr 1845]

Jos at Sebec ME [22 Sept 1840]

Luke 59 at Bath ME [17 Feb 1848]

Mr the proprietor of the Tremont House at Galveston TX is a live Yankee from Bath ME & his clerk & book-keeper are of that ilk [7 Aug 1851]

Oren 45 at Paris ME [3 Oct 1840]

Sarah 23 wid/o Nicholas SHAW at Augusta ME on 26 Jan (MA please copy) [6 Feb 1851]

William S 64 formerly of Wiscasset ME at Winthrop ME on 5 Apr [10 Apr 1851]

SHAW - see ROLERSON

SHEA Mr an Irishman on Mon last attempting to get upon the gravel cars when in motion, so drunk [*Lewiston Journal*] [31 May 1849]

SHEAPARD Dr Rev was for 50+ yrs pastor of Congregation Society in Lenox on Mon last 74, said to be the oldest settled pastor in the country [22 Jan 1846]

SHED Mrs in Lunenburg, Worcester Co the deceased as well as her husband, habitually intemperate. In one of her fits of intoxication some years ago, she fell into the fire & burned her foot badly. [12 Oct 1833]

SHEEHAN - see HOLMES

SHELBURN Lord a young English Peer, committed suicide to the disappointment in love. [23 May 1834]

SHELTON Mrs died in spasms [29 Apr 1843]

W H President of the late Brandon Bank drowned himself in Pearl River (from the *New Orleans Republican*) [8 Apr 1843]

SHEPARD Lammus of Amherst NH killed on Wed of last week by the fall of a tree he was cutting [29 Mar 1849]

John 118y 9m 18d at the battles Brandywine & Germantown Flats & wounded at the former. He never received a pension! An ungrateful congress denied him that boon, because he had misfortune to lose his papers in a fire which consumed his dwelling but his children provided for him comfortably in his old age. He died at Akron OH on 3d inst [18 Feb 1847]

SHEPHERD Mary Elizabeth 12y 6m d/o Lemuel & Delia SHEPHERD at Fairfield ME on 20 Aug of brain fever [4 Sept 1851]

Richard 66 a member of the Society of Friends at Vassalboro ME on 22 Apr [11 May 1848]

SHEPLEY Nancy 61 w/o Jona SHEPLEY at Dexter ME [4 May 1848]

SHERIDAN Daniel 19y of Portland ME was in the act of oiling the running gear of the main shaft, when he was struck by the shaft & completely cut in two, killing him instantly. His body was left at Portland ME. Last year his brother, while at work upon the same boat, made a mis-step fell overboard & was so much injured that he died in two weeks. [31 Jul 1851]

SHERMAN Hepsabeth 75 w/o Capt Nathaniel SHERMAN formerly of Nantucket MA at Sidney ME on 14 Feb [13 Mar 1851]

Mrs wid/o Hon Roger M SHERMAN of CT, on the 3d Aug & a liberal contributor to the Colonization Society [22 Mar 1849]

S 51y of Nantucket at San Francisco CA on 29 Sept [20 Nov 1851]

William a little child abt 5y accidentally killed at Camden ME on Mon [*Belfast Journal*] [19 Apr 1849]

SHERMAN - see JEFFRIES, WEAVER

SHERWOOD Mrs 77y an author [6 Nov 1851]

SHILLING Alfred a German lately at Cincinnati OH attempting to carry for a wager eight hundred pounds of pork four hundred yards. He broke down before he had accomplished half the distance, literally realizing the saying of "Too much pork for a Shilling" [11 Feb 1847]

SHIRLEY Jonathan 75 at Fryeburg ME [15 Apr 1852]

SHOREY Charlotte 31 w/o Francis SHOREY at Albion ME [15 Apr 1852]

Samuel of Winslow ME drowned by falling from the steamer *Oregon* on Fri last abt two miles above Augusta Dam [19 Jul 1849]

Susan G 23 w/o George SHOREY at Gardiner ME [2 Jan 1851]

SHORT James married Emeline SWEET "Short & Sweet" [*Concord Freeman*] [10 Sept 1842]

Rebecca 76 d/o Molly PITCHER tells of the story of AmRev "Molly PITCHER" [*Portsmouth Journal*] [29 May 1841]

SHORT - see SIMS, STORY

SHULTZ - see BATEMAN

SHUNK Gov died on 20th inst at PA [27 Jul 1848]

SHURTLEFF - see GANNET

SIAS Jason abt 21 leg badly fractured on his way to Eagle Lake (ME) on 14th ult. Dr McRUER of Bangor ME & Dr DAVISON of Monson ME came to his aid at Ford's Tavern on the Roach River. On the 22d, leg amputated above the knee by Dr

SIAS (Cont.) JORDON of Foxcroft ME assisted by Dr HUCKINS of Monson ME, but died
two days later, funeral at the home of his father, Jeremiah S, at Charleston ME
(copied from the *Piscataquis Obs*) [9 Jan 1851]

Judith 20 at Livermore ME [25 Jan 1840]

SIGOURNEY - see HUNTLEY

SILVIER - see FITZ

SIMINTON - see WOOD

SIMIS Edward D Rev on 15th ult of the University of Alabama [1 May 1845]

SIMMONS Alonzo 43 at Phillips ME [11 May 1848]

boy 6y s/o Gen SIMONS of Waterville ME drowned at Ticonic Falls on Sat [*Waterville Mail*] [19 Oct 1848]

Daniel Rev a Baptist clergyman arrested in Mobile AL last week as a fugitive from
justice charged with having committed homicide, killing H DAVIS in 1822 or 1823
in Tatnal Co, GA [*Mobile Tribune*] [12 Feb 1846]

Frederick W saved from drowning between Thompson's Island & Fort Independence.
The lad said that the boat sunk soon after it capsized. The boat man, Mr OAKES
threw a chair & topmast of the boat to help save one of three of 27 boys of the Farm
School off Fort Independence & Thompson's Island, they were taken off by a boat
from the schr *H B FOSTER* of Machias ME, then coming up the harbor from
Trinidad [7 May 1842]

SIMMONS - see EDDY

SIMON Mrs of Burnah Mrs CONSTOCK of Arrakan & Mrs DEAN of China A letter just
recevied from my brother, N BROWN dated "Sibsabgar, 14 Jul 1843," contains the
names of the deaths of three missionary sisters. W. G. BROWN [*Voice of Freedom*]
[18 Jan 1844]

SIMONS Fred 5 s/o Solon S SIMONS at Waterville ME drowned [19 Oct 1848]

little boy 6 s/o Gen SIMONS of (Augusta ME) in the Kennebec River ME drowned on
Sat last [*Waterville (ME) Mail*] [19 Oct 1848]

SIMONS - see FORD

SIMONTON Abraham 63 at Rockland ME [13 Nov 1851]

Putnam Franklin FLYE, John TYLER & Mr DUNCAN. On Sun last 6 men, abt the age
of 23 took a boat at Camden harbor to go to French's beach, Lincolnville, where a
vessel lay. Four drowned & two were saved. The two saved were George HODGMAN
& a brother of the Mr DUNCAN drowned. [*Belfast Journal*] [20 Apr 1848]

Walter H 55 of Maine at the Sailor's Song Harbor, Staten Island on 23 June [10 Jul
1851]

SIMPSON Jane 54 w/o John SIMPSON of Ellsworth ME at Belfast ME [10 Jul 1851]

William A abt 24 of Charlestown MA & Robert E BRADSHAW abt 22 two miners were
murdered for their money by a party of Mexicans at Chilian Gulch. They were both
MA men. [11 Sept 1851]

SIMS fugitive slave is returned to GA [1 May 1851]

Thomas, De LYON, a slave catcher, w/ Mr BACON received $350. The Capt, mate &
seaman of brig M & J C GILMORE called to prove the prisoner boarded the vessel to
Boston MA. S E SEWALL, for the defense put the following affidavit sworn to by S
"I was born at St Augustine FL, my free papers were left with Morris PORTER of
Savannah GA; that these free papers were obtained in St Augustine by his father a
spaniard. SIMS owes service to James POTTER of Chatham Co GA. He escaped on
22 Feb, a mulatto 5'6" without whiskers. Deposition of Adam STORT stated he
"knew T S as slave of J P, apprenticed 4y by said P, escaped on the regular
northbound steamer from Charleston stopping at boarding house of James AIKEN

SIMS (Cont.) #153, 155 Ann St." SIMS having a wife & ch in Savannah, free & were abt to come to Boston (from *Traveller*) [10 Apr 1851]

SIMS - see SCOTT

SINCLAIR - see CRAWFORD, McDUFFIE

SKEHAN w/o Pierce SKEHAN & only d/o Mr DUNBAR of London. Making 11 in all lost on the wreck of the *Frankin*, the Wellfleet correspondent of the *Courier* gives the above names of persons lost [15 Mar 1849]

SKEHAN - see SMITH

SKILLINGS James W near Munjoy Hill Portland ME & Benjamin RACKLEFF both killed by the same bolt of lightning Dr SWEAT sent for but arrived too late [*Portland Argus*] [31 Jul 1851]

SKINNER Albert in Garland ME by lightning. [*Bangor Whig*] [6 June 1840]
Capt of the *Barbara* lost at sea [*Traveller*] [13 Apr 1848]

SKOLFIELD Samuel of Hapswell ME while loading timber killed by accident, by trade a ship carpenter [12 Sept 1837]

SLADE Hannah B 66 wife of Benjamin SLADE at Hallowell [27 Apr 1848]
Rollin H of CT listed in deaths in CA [23 Sept 1851]

SLATER boy while bathing in the mill brook nearly drowned & saved by Maj Francis DAVIS. The boy was the s/o Nichols SLATER (from the *Temperance Gazette*) [26 June 1841]

Slave, Betsey "A vessel arrived at Boston MA a yellow girl, a slave, belonging in Wilmington NC secreted on board by the mate. The authorities smoked the vessel several times, after loudly announcing that they would smother her if she did not show herself. It was all unsuccessful. She remained secure in her hiding place. During the voyage the girl was fed in the watches without the knowledge of the master" [17 Jan 1850]

Betsey, the yellow girl lately brought to Boston MA in the *Thales* from Wilmington is of a delicate constitution. She left a babe behind her. Her feet were frozen & she suffered much on the passage. [24 Jan 1850]

fugitive - see MASON, MITCHUM

James belonging to Mr DAVIS charged at New Orleans with shooting a white man was tried by a jury of six free-holders, found guilty & sentenced to receive one hundred lashes - 25 lashes every 22 days - to remain in custody in the mean time & wear an iron collar with three prongs for five years [3 Sept 1846]

whipped to death - see McGAHEY

slave - see BROWN, CARTER, CATO, HAYDEN, HETH, LEE, LONG, MOSES, ROBERTS, SIMS, STONE, WARFIELD, WILLIAMS

Slavery "A letter from Springfield IL states that the Supreme Court of IL have decided that all the children born of French slaves in the state since the Ordinance of 1798 are free. This will destroy & wipe away everything like slavery in IL. The opinion was delivered by Justice YOUNG & the bench was divided three being in favor of the opinion & two against it" [13 Mar 1845]

Slavery - see King of Denmark, news slavery

slaves - see BIRNEY, CARNEY, FAIRBANK, FARWELL, LORAINE, MILLER, RUIZ, SOULE, BENNETT, THOMPSON

SLEEPER Mary A 17 at Farmington ME [11 Sept 1851]
Samuel B Capt 39 at Rockland ME [24 Apr 1851]

SLIFTER - see LEE

SLOAN John died of sickness near Augusta GA [16 Nov 1839]

SLOCUM - see HARRIS

SLOCUMB daughters ages 10 & 12 of Mr C N SLOCUMB. The sisters took a kettle of live coals to their bedroom & in the morning one was found dead at Homer NY [8 Feb 1840]

SMALL Amanda L 21 at Bath ME [11 Sept 1851]

Anson 11 s/o Jeremiah SMALL drowned on the 7th ult between Lubec Neck & Eastport Bridge [2 Dec 1852]

brothers; Three boys of Mr Williams SMALL, cabinet maker, strolled up to the Canal at the westerly part of the city (Portland ME) - two of them Howard Malcom 11 & Melvin Wade 8 undressed to bathe. Neither could swim. Howard took Melvin upon his back to carry him across the canal (which was narrow at the point where they were) and when partly across, they fell & before assistance could reach them, drowned. The brother on the margin was younger ran a quarter of a mile to the lock for help. However when help arrived his brothers were dead. [from the *Eastern Argus*] [17 Jul 1841]

Elizabeth G 73 wid/o Joshua SMALL formerly of Truro MA at New Sharon ME suddenly of an apoplectic fit [18 Dec 1851]

George A his large two story house destroyed by fire on the morning of the 21st inst at Raymond ME [6 June 1840]

infant scalded by tea of Union Mills ME c/o Alexander SMALL [16 Jul 1846]

Pamelia P 36 w/o Dr Joseph P SMALL & d/o Increase DOLLY at Rumford ME on 31 Mar [24 Apr 1851]

Samuel 94 AmRev at Phipsburg ME [18 Dec 1851]

Simon C 20 at Addison Point ME [3 Aug 1848]

SMALL - see HUSSEY, BEAN

SMALLEY Jane 74 a widow at St George ME [10 Jul 1851]

SMART Charles S 12y of Camden ME knocked overboard & Mr Thomas SMITH jumped overboard to save the boy, both drowned [*New Orleans Picayune*] [31 Aug 1848]

Isaac a native of Salem NJ supposed to be living in ME, engaged in the lumber business. Thomas Jones YORK of Salem NJ needs to find him. [*Age*] [8 Mar 1849]

James 45 at Vassalboro ME [25 May 1848]

SMART - see PALMER

SMICK William 93y 9m 6d AmRev at Salem Co NJ on 8th ult raised a family of 11 children, 10 of whom he lived to see married & 178 descendants living [23 Apr 1846]

SMILEY Alex 87 at Sidney ME [13 Jul 1848]

Asa 56 a member of the Society of Friends (Quakers) at Sidney ME on 9 Mar [18 Mar 1852]

Benjamin A 21 at Sidney ME on 23 Apr of typhoid fever, eldest s/o Hugh SMILEY, a Son of Temperance, his funeral attended by the members of Sidney Division [29 Apr 1852]

SMILEY - see RUSSELL

SMITH Abraham R 33y of Lyman killed on Wed last by a fall from his wagon. Left a wife & 2 ch. [*Saco Democrat*] [3 Feb 1848]

Andrew G of ME on board steamer *Constitution* on the 16 Oct [11 Dec 1851]

Benjamin Capt formerly of Duxbury MA jumped overboard at New Orleans not long since in a fit of insanity & was drowned [17 Aug 1848]

Bill of the villains who took possession of the schr *Alexander* & murdered a part of the crew near Cat Island ... Bill S who appears to have been the leader in the affair is a native of Maine [13 Feb 1841]

Charles Capt of Charlestown left w & 2 ch; mate Richard MILLINTON of Charleston SC left w & likely ch; seaman John PUTNAM of Newburyport left a large fam; Daniel FIELD of MA; Frederick JOHNSON of Finland; James HALL of Sweden; John RIDER of Sweden; George ___ of N Shields England. Passengers Thomas TOOMEY

SMITH (Cont.) of Ireland; Miss SKEHAN of Ireland both abt 20y; Mrs SKEHAN w/o
    Pierce S & only d/o Mr DUNBAR, London [15 Mar 1849]

Constance 91y 8m at West Mt Vernon ME [29 Jan 1852]

Daniel 32 at Skowhegan ME [28 Dec 1848]

Daniel 93 at Hollis ME [4 June 1851]

Daniel Capt of (Gardiner?) ME died of cholera at Coronstradt Russia left a wife &
    children [*Gardiner Fountain*] [23 Nov 1848]

Daniel D Rev of Gloucester MA tried at Ipswich last week for an assault on Miss Sophia
    JONES, with an intent to commit a rape & acquitted. The *Salem Advertiser* says
    "Thirty witnesses were brought upon the stand, who testified to the good charactor of
    Mr SMITH & the bad character of Miss JONES & a paper was also ruled in the court,
    signed by ninety-six ladies, against her character" [3 Jul 1841]

Delia W 38 w/o George S SMITH Jr Esq at Machias ME [18 May 1848]

Ebenezer 35 at Skowhegan ME [28 Sept 1848]

Elijah 19y s/o Peter SMITH of Biddeford ME drowned near the meeting house eddy last
    Sat, attempted to swim across the river [15 Jul 1843]

Elizabeth of Hodgdon ME w/o Joseph O SMITH at Addison ME [19 June 1851]

Emily J 21 w/o Daniel SMITH at Berwick ME [20 Jul 1848]

Enos of Bucksport ME in a deranged state of mind left home on the 11th instant and has
    not been heard from. He is 26y, 5' 7" high, light complexion - a black jacket and hat,
    blue vest & pantaloons. Please address Seth E SMITH of Bucksport ME (copied from
    Bangor Whig) [21 Sept 1839]

Ephraim 77 at New Sharon ME [25 Sept 1851]

Esther E 24 w/o Capt Isaac SMITH at Camden ME [3 Jul 1851]

George abt 5 s/o Gen F SMITH at Anson ME distressing occurrence, so badly scalded on
    Sat last [*Skowhegan Sentinel*] [21 Feb 1837]

girl abt 4y d/o widow Mehitable SMITH burnt to death on Tues last, in the absence of her
    mother. Her clothes were of cotton. The little sufferer survived abt two hrs at Boston
    MA [11 Dec 1835]

Hannah 27 wid/o Capt SMITH at Hallowell ME [24 Feb 1848]

Harriet 7 d/o Isaac & Pamelia SMITH at Sidney ME on 26 Feb [1 May 1851]

Hendrick G of Worcester MA left home on the 9th of May on a visit to his friends at
    Waterford ME the place of his nativity & return to Portland then to Boston by train,
    however he is missing [*Worcester Spy*] [12 Jul 1849]

Henry 81 formerly of Hallowell ME at Brunswick ME [19 Feb 1852]

Hollis W 24 s/o widow Sally SMITH of Wayne ME at Winthrop ME on 21 Nov at the
    home of Capt B C GARDINER [6 Feb 1851]

Hosea H a teacher of a school in Brewer ME assaulted during school hours by several of
    his scholars armed with unlawful weapons. They were tried before the municipal
    court of Bangor ME & punished by fines & amounting to $25. [27 Feb 1838]

Isaac 35 buried with the honors of Odd Fellowship at Hallowell ME [20 Jan 1848]

Jacob 31 on the brig *Ruth*, lying in Shackford's Cove [*Eastport Sentinel*] [21 Jan 1847]

James a shoemaker left St Stephens NB Canada on Fri last, company of 2 other men, on
    a one-horse shed all in a state of intoxication. Not satisfied with what they had in
    them, it appears they stopped on their way to drink more ... SMITH it appears got off
    his sled, but from being too drunk to get on again, & his companions being drunk did
    not notice left him ...he froze to death [*Calais Advertiser*] [5 Mar 1846]

James the Methodist minister of Fayette ME lost his barn on Fri night the 16th (copied
    from the *Eastern Baptist*) [3 Apr 1838]

Jane 25 w/o William SMITH at Pembroke MA/ME? [11 Dec 1851]

SMITH (Cont.) Jared abt 60 a colored barber died at Wilmington DE on the 9th inst, he had
    purchased his wife's freedom, by industry, punctuality, & care, he lived snugly &
    comfortably, & has left two houses, besides money & personal estate [4 Jan 1844]
Jasial 85 AmRev pensioner at Buckfield ME [8 June 1848]
Jesse Capt 88 of Salem MA death of the last of WASHINGTON's Life Guards on the 4th
    inst [*Salem Register*] [13 June 1844]
Jessy M s/o Lieut J SMITH lost on the Hornet belonging to the *Preble* who died at this
    place 3 Dec 1844 of disease contracted on the coast of Africa [10 Apr 1845]
Joe the Mormons dissolved their body at Kirland OH under Joe SMITH & Sidney
    RIGDON. These leaders recently decamped with their families in the night. [The
    Sciota Gazette] [6 Mar 1838]
John a conductor on the Stonybrook Railraod killed Wed [2 Oct 1851]
John Cotton 81 of Sharon, Litchfield Co, CT President of the American Bible Society [18
    Dec 1845]
John D shipwright found dead in the road on Thurs last at Machias ME. Excessive
    Intoxication is charged with his murder [30 Apr 1846]
John M US Deputy Surveyor of Dubuque IA & Oscar LYMAN both killed by a tree on
    the 24th ult [14 Aug 1851]
John seaman belonging to the U. S. ship *Saratoga* on board the frigate *Macedonian* at
    this place 10 Oct 1844 of disease contracted on the coast of Africa [10 Apr 1845]
Joseph 10y s/o widow SMITH of Portland ME & Abigail CARTER of Andover MA 10y.
    Both houses adjourned at eleven o'clock to give an opportunty to Dr Samuel G
    HOWE to exhibit two of his pupils from the Boston MA asylum for the blind. He
    stated the Legislatures of MA, CT, VT & NH have made appropriations & he wanted
    to show the Maine Legislature what could be done for the blind (from the *Kennebeck
    Journal*) [21 Feb 1834]
Joseph of Colerain MA saved from drowning when the steam packet *New England* sank.
    it left Boston for Bath & Gardiner ME and had an accident with the schr *Curlew* on
    31 May [12 June 1838]
Joseph the Mormon prophet shot dead! [11 July 1844]
Josiah 85 AmRev pensioner at Buckfield ME on 15th inst "Portland papers please copy"
    [1 June 1848]
Judge a year previous divorced from his wife for intemperate habits, and brutal neglect &
    abuse of his family, made a speech at the close of a mass temperance meeting at
    Medina Ohio to say that he was re-united to his wife - the minister exclaiming. "What
    God has rejoined, let neither man nor alcohol sever!" Who will say temperance is not
    of God? [28 Oct 1842]
Judge impeached before the Senate of Illinois, among the charges is one for imprisoning
    a Quaker for refusing to take off his hat in court [18 Feb 1833]
Lois P of Saratoga by hanging herself while insane on account of the death of her kitten
    which was found in her room with this letter "Oh dear! bury my poor little kitten with
    me, as it is to me as an angel from above. O, grant me my wishes. Bury me in my
    back yard until the time expires that I have paid for the houses. Lay my little angel by
    my right side on my right arm. Don't deny my wishes." [2 Nov 1848]
Mathew 28 of Farmington ME at East Thomaston ME [25 May 1848]
Margaret L 26 at Hallowell ME [6 Feb 1851]
Martha Ann 31 w/o Joseph S SMITH at Hallowell ME [18 May 1848]
Mary Ann 42 w/o Charles SMITH at Livermore ME [6 Jul 1848]
Mathias of Norway ME in the snow a short distance from his house [24 Feb 1848]
Mr a fire broke out on Tues morning last in the WATSON & HOOPER store & the
    dwelling house near injured, owned by Mr SMITH of 11 at Houlton ME [5 Nov 1841]

SMITH (Cont.) Mr left home in deranged state of mind found in Frankfort ME somewhat improved in health [*Bangor Whig*] [31 Aug 1839]

Mr saved his wife & one child, only 50 lives saved, one hundred fifty lives lost, one of the most horrible catastrophes this paper has ever been to record on the *steamer Ben Sherrod* [30 May 1837]

Mrs 70 of Northfield MA w/o Mr Adolphus SMITH burnt to death [28 Aug 1851]

Mrs one of three ladies thrown from a chaise by the fright of the horse Miss Eddy had a broken leg, Mrs SMITH w/o Noah SMITH Jr of Calais ME was hurt. Mrs Fuller of Milltown ME escaped with slight injury at Baileyville ME on Sat last [8 Aug 1840]

Mrs wid/o Abijah SMITH Esq on Mon at accidentally shot [*Waterville Mail*] [17 Jul 1851]

N C 23 at Freedom ME [10 Feb 1848]

Nancy 54 at Augusta ME at the alms house [17 Feb 1848]

Nathan 37 of Hampden ME lost overboard from the schr *Francis* of Orrington ME [*Portland Advertiser*] [17 Dec 1846]

Nathaniel 52 at Sand-bar, Moose Head Lake ME [17 June 1852]

Noah & his wife both abt 70 murdered at Petersburg NY [13 Jul 1848]

Otis Dr "beware of a person in Stonington" abt a year, "Dr Otis S, Thomsonian physician," who married the dau/o a respectable citizen, got a horse upon credit, and started for parts unknown, by the discovery of his previous marriages, and had another wife in ME, NH, MA & NY, was an active exhorter at religious meeting in Stonington & vicinity [*New London News*] [9 Apr 1846]

Peter, the names of the officers & crew as per the customs house list, the ship *Jacob Perkins*, Capt SHOOF, which arrived his morning from Crostadt reported that on 22 inst Cape Cod WSW 55 miles fell in with the wreck of brig *Washington*, RIDER Capt [*Transcript*] [2 Oct 1835]

Peter deck passenger of New Orleans a serious accident happened on board the steamboat *George Collier* on the 6th inst on her passage from New Orleans to St Louis MO [25 May 1839]

Peter J of West Randolph MA, the city marshal's office says his wife, Catherine SMITH on Mon absconded from her home, husband & three ch (youngest being but 9mos old) for parts unknown, but probably for this city. She is described as being abt 32y 5' 9" dark brown hair cut short, light gray eyes & walks lame [*Boston Courier*] [16 Oct 1851]

Peter J of West Randolph ME reports at the city marshal's office that his wife, Catherine SMITH on Mon donned a genteel masculine garb, consisting of black frock coat, pants, vest & cap, which she obtained for the purpose & absconded from her home, husband & three children (youngest being but 9mos old) for parts unknown, but probably for this city. She is described as being abt 32y 5' 9" dark brown hair cut short, [Boston Courier] [16 Oct 1851]

Richard abt 60 at Mercer ME [10 Apr 1851]

Sally 64 at West Mt Vernon ME on 16 Dec [29 Jan 1852]

Samuel 75 of Norridgewock ME at Edgartown MA on 25 Sept [5 Oct 1848]

Samuel Bradley Capt 35 of Hallowell ME at San Francisco CA [9 Jan 1851]

Samuel Harrison Esq of Washington DC, The Washington papers annouce the decease, on the morning of the 1st of this venerable citizen in the 74th year of his age, Mr SMITH was the founder & during many years the sole editor of the *National Intelligencer* & a friend of JEFFERSON, MADISON, MONROE & their associates [13 Nov 1845]

Samuel of Westport CT while drawing water fell into the well [24 May 1849]

Sydney C of ME 26 Sacramento CA on 7 Nov [2 Jan 1851]

widow 72 at Bloomfield ME [13 Nov 1851]

SMITH (Cont.) William 26 formerly of Kennebunkport ME at Biddeford ME [3 June 1852]

William Capt 73 born in Maryland died at Northampton [*Northampton Courier*] [5 Feb 1846]

William S abt 18 an apprentice to Mr SCHWARTZ in Bangor ME while engaged in polishing a large circular saw accidentally cut almost two-thirds though his arm. Dr RICH has expressed the hope of saving the arm. [*Bangor Whig*] [3 Feb 1848]

William seaman of Sweden lost on the brig Linden, a sea disaster, GRIFFITH Capt [19 Nov 1842]

SMITH - see BEAN, COOPER, CRAWFORD, DORROGH, DOWNING, GRAHAM, JEFFRIES, NOTT, PEARCE, PETTINGILL, PRAY, RANDOLPH, RICE, WOOD

SMITHSON - see LONG

SMYTHE Alexander fell 50ft from the roof of the brick mill at Taunton on Mon last [24 Jul 1851]

SNELL Eleazer 63 at Starks ME [22 May 1851]

George C 4m s/o E C SNELL at Winthrop ME [23 Mar 1848]

Issachar Dr of (Augusta) in passing a team in his carriage overthrown to the ground head-foremost, dislocating his neck. Dr S was one of the oldest & most successful physicians in Kennebec. He formerly resided in Winthrop ME & was a member of the Rev Dr TAPPAN's Society. [14 Oct 1847]

Samuel Col 27 of Dover NH on the Isthmus on his way to CA [27 May 1852]

SNELLING Jonathan long a master in public schools in Boston MA on Sat 78y [11 Feb 1847]

SNOW Capt of Thomaston ME murdered in his tent at Dragoon Gulch near Sonora CA by two Mexicans on 10 June, weighing some gold dust [7 Aug 1851]

Catherine 25 w/o W R SNOW, publisher of the *Frontier Journal* at Calais ME on 10 Apr [24 Apr 1851]

Henry 32y of Hampden ME at Boston MA by disease contracted in CA [7 Aug 1851]

Joseph Capt of Brunswick ME at London England on 6 Jul [28 Aug 1851]

Joseph of Nova Scotia Canada the crew of the *Traveller* supposed lost [16 Oct 1851]

Mary H 25 at Frankfort ME [20 Jul 1848]

Nathaniel 45 at Gardiner ME [17 Apr 1851]

Robert Capt 60 at Thomaston ME [7 Sep 1848]

SNOW - see ELMES, FROST, KING, LOVEJOY

SNOWMAN Betsey Miss 96 at Weld ME [20 Feb 1851]

SNOWMAN - see PERKINS

SNYDER Andrew 113y AmRev at Intercourse in Lancaster PA on the 1st inst perhaps the oldest man in PA [27 Nov 1845]

SOCKABASIN son of an Indian of Bremen ME the son of Sockabasin the Doctor at Bremen ME on Tues on 1st inst one of 4 persons drowned while sailing from Long Island in Bremen ME towards Friendship ME [17 Apr 1851]

SOMERS John 18 of Greenock Scotland, fatal shipwreak of the schr *Argus* on Plum Island Capt CROCKETT of Frankfort ME was the captain [2 Jan 1851]

Samuel machinist of the Tremont Theatre in Boston MA on Thurs last lost his life by a dose of corrosive sublimate, which was given to him by his wife, in mistake for some cough drops [1 June 1843]

SOMES David 76 at Edgecomb ME [16 Mar 1848]

Henrietta 14 at Hallowell ME [8 June 1848]

SOOJAH Shah death confirmed he fell by the hand of Zemauh KHAN brother of Dost MAHAMMED [30 Jul 1842]

SOPER Elisha 90 at Orland ME [1 May 1851]

SOPER (Cont.) Mr wounded by the discharge of a cannon, one hand blown off above his wrist and the other near his elbow at Saratoga Springs [25 Jul 1834]

Reuben S 25 at Pittston ME [16 Oct 1851]

Climena 39 w/o Elbridge SOULE & d/o John & Abigail TAYLOR of Winslow ME at Vassalboro ME on 31 Jan [18 Mar 1852]

Joseph steward of ship *Harriet Rockwell* drowned in New Orleans on 1st inst [28 Dec 1848]

Mary L w/o Prof John B L SOULE & only d/o Ethan & Mary STEVENS of Hallowell ME at Terre-Haute IN on 19 June [13 Jul 1848]

Mr suicide on 23d ult at Jefferson ME [*Lincoln Miscellany*] [9 Jan 1851]

two children drowned in the eddy above the Penobscot Bridge gate, the girl was 13y & the boy 11 c/o Jacob SOULE (from the *Bangor Whig*) [4 June 1846]

SOULE - see BAILEY

SOUTHARD Senator of New Jersey at Fredericksburg VA [9 Jul 1842]

William 85 at Thomaston ME [8 Jan 1852]

SOUTHER Simeon a wealthy citizen of Hanover Co VA convicted of beating one of his slaves to death, given 5 yrs in the penitentiary [26 June 1851]

SOUTHWICK George only s/o Jacob SOUTHWICK Esq of Vassalboro ME, a student of Waterville College (Colby College) died [19 June 1845]

Jacob 55 at Vassalboro ME on 7 Feb [13 Feb 1851]

SOUTHWICK - see LANG

SOUTHWORTH Perez s/o Benjamin SOUTHWORTH of cholera in TN graduate of Bowdoin College & formerly Preceptor of Litchfield Academy [2 Aug 1849]

SPAULDING Benjamin 75 at Dover ME [6 Apr 1848]

Cynthia 21 d/o Ashur SPAULDING at Dexter ME [7 Aug 1851]

D H's family a fire broke out in the store & dwelling house at Solon Village (ME) on Mon 4th inst ... Mr S occupied the upper story as a dwelling house & abt 5 a.m. his wife awakened by the smoke. Mother & child threw the beding out the window & both jumped. Her husband was away at the time. (from *Skowhegan Sentinel*) [16 Feb 1839]

Eleazer Mrs 85 at Dover ME [6 Nov 1851]

Ephraim 40 of Norridgewock ME at Dover ME on 22 Jan [6 Feb 1851]

John of North Belgrade ME killed himself [12 June 1845]

Josiah abt 92 AmRev at Norridgewock ME [4 Mar 1852]

Mary 76 w/o Capt Jas SPAULDING at Rockland ME [11 Sept 1851]

Mr the late homicide at Canaan ME [14 Oct 1843]

Otis 57 at Norridgewock ME [21 Dec 1848]

T J fireman of St Charles MO on board the steamboat *George Collier* on the 6th inst on her passage from New Orleans to St Louis MO [25 May 1839]

William M 28 s/o Calvin SPAULDING Esq of Hallowell ME at Sacramento CA on 23 Dec [20 Feb 1851]

William W 23 of Maine at CA on 28 Dec [13 Feb 1851]

SPEAR Jepson O 11 s/o Capt Wellman SPEAR at East Thomaston ME [3 Aug 1848]

Mrs the elderly lady drowned on the Oraloo not named DUNBAR, but SPEAR. So says Charles VANNAH, Selectman of Nobleboro ME, in a letter to Rev Mr BEECHER He says "From the information I have obtained I think the deceased lady is a Mrs SPEAR of Boston MA. If so, she has a son living in Boston by the name of Dr J S SPEAR" [*Eastern Argus*] [24 Jul 1845]

Thomas J likely blinded for life [*N O Picayune* 29th ult] [16 Apr 1846]

Thomas "a reward of $50 will be given to any person or persons who will find Thomas SPEAR s/o William SPEAR, who was lost in the township of Caledon on the night of the 30th Sept 1841. The boy was seen on the 4th of June 1843, by two sons of Daniel

SPEAR (Cont.) McLAUGHLIN, on the town line between Caledon & Albion. He was sitting on a stone looking at his feet which was sure; he was quite naked, excepting the waistband of a pair of trousers of a dark color & about four inches of the thigh in rags corresponding with the same he wore when lost. He was seen again on the 14 June last having on the part of clothing last described by Mrs HOWARD ... Mrs H says that when he turned to run away from her, he had a mane of hair growing down his back." [2 Sept 1843]

    widow of Warren ME dwelling house destroyed by fire [8 Jan 1836]

SPEARIN Albert killed in a saw mill at Milford on Fri last, left a wife & two children [*Bangor Mercury*] [15 Feb 1849]

SPEED Thomas 20 at Belfast ME [22 June 1848]

SPENCE Abram drowned when between Fort Independence & Thompson's Island, one of 27 boys of the Farm School [7 May 1842]

SPENCER Eliza K formerly of North Yarmouth ME 18y 7m at Levant ME on 29 Sept [27 Oct 1840]

    John S Hon U. S. senator from Maryland at his residence in Worcester Co MD on 22 Oct [7 Nov 1840]

    Reed Col 52 at Sebasticock ME [13 Jul 1848]

SPENDLOW - see CRAWFORD

SPOFFORD a child c/o Mr J B SPOFFORD nose completely bitten off by a dog last week at Machester NH [16 Nov 1848]

    Mr of Norridgewock ME drowned on Tues 4 June at the foot of the Grand Falls on the west branch of the main river (the *Bangor Whig*) [22 June 1839]

SPRADBURY Charles an Englishman in the employ of John H SAWYER Esq of South Norridgewock died of an apoplectic fit, caused by drinking cold water [*Skowhegan Press*] [5 Aug 1847]

SPRAGUE Charles A 21 junior publisher of the *Bath Mirror* formerly of Appleton ME at Bath ME [13 Nov 1851]

    Charles F 21 of Boston MA s/o Hon Peleg SPRAGUE at Cuba on 30 May, where he had gone for his health [4 Jul 1840]

    Durenda 17 at Freedom ME on 18 Jul [24 Jul 1851]

    Ezra a blacksmith of Portland ME while sharpening his scythe at Westbrook ME was seized with paralysis. He was a man of intemperate habits [*Portland Advertiser*] [10 Aug 1848]

    John 24, a printer at Gardiner ME on 14th Sept [25 Sept 1851]

    Sarah 54 w/o Marvel SPRAGUE at Gardiner ME [6 Feb 1851]

    William 83 AmRev pensioner at Phipsburg ME [19 Oct 1848]

SPRING Abigail 64 wid/o Samuel SPRING at Winslow ME [22 June 1848]

SPRINGER Alethiea 84 wid/o John SPRINGER at Augusta ME on 24 Nov [7 Dec 1848]

    Fanny Boyd widow 66 at Augusta ME on 25th ult [1 May 1851]

    Laura Ellen 7 d/o Dr Warren W & Susan M SPRIGER at Belgrade ME on 23 Apr [29 May 1851]

    Oliver a native of Sidney ME formerly member of Waterville College ME at Brunswick Missouri of consumption [18 Jan 1840]

    Samuel B Esq of Calais ME at Galveston TX [4 Jan 1840]

SPROUL Caroline 27 w/o William SPROUL Jr at Waldoboro ME [27 Oct 1840]

SPROULE Capt & Rufus CHAPMAN saved; RUSSELL, CHAPMAN, HARVEY, WHEELER, & FORD perished on the schr *Thomas*, SPROULE Capt of Belfast ME. Had they remained on board, a few minutes longer, they would all have been saved, as the life boat was on her way to succor them [25 Mar 1843]

SPROULL - see MURPHY

SPROWL Henry leaving a wife & two children of Bremen ME at Bremen ME on Tues on 1st inst 4 persons drowned while sailing from Long Island in Bremen ME towards Friendship ME [17 Apr 1851]

SPRUILL - see DAVENPORT

SPURZHEIM Dr died in Boston MA a yr ago [8 Aug 1834]

SQUIER Ephraim 94 at Ashford CT on 19th Aug, supposed patriot of the Bunker Hill [16 Oct 1841]

St CLAIR Mr AmRev his last resting place is at Greensburg Westmoreland Co PA. A neat marble pyramid being erected over his remains by his Masonic brethren [16 Sept 1847]

STACKPOLE Harriet 18 at Thomaston ME [30 Nov 1848]

    Maj house fire of his home about one mile west of South West Bend village in Durham ME [*Eastern Baptist*] [26 Feb 1836]

    Peter M Esq of Vassalboro ME wounded fatally by falling of the frame of a sawmill on Mon, legs broken, living yesterday [*Kennebec Journal*] Mr S died on Sun night [16 Nov 1848]

    the firm ADAMS & STACKPOLE in TX were from Portland ME [7 Aug 1851]

    W his tannery on the Kennady brook in Augusta ME burnt [16 Nov 1839]

STACY Sylvester 32 of New Bedford at San Pablo CA of cholera morbus on 22 Dec at Dr Horr's Ranch [13 Feb 1851]

STACY - see FOWLER

STADIN Dr of Saratoga NY death by bite of rattlesnake [3 Oct 1844]

STAFFORD - see WORTH

STAGE - see WISE

STAHL Christian 79 at Waldoboro ME [11 Dec 1851]

STAITES - see McFARLAN

STANDISH Malachi of Rrovidence RI lost when the steam packet *New England* sank on her passage to Gardiner ME. She was opposite Boon Island and came in contact with the schr *Curlew*, Capt CROCKET of Thomaston ME, load with lime. [12 June 1838]

    Miles heirs reside in (ME). Robert CUSHMAN of Belmont ME, one of the nearest heirs, his g-grandmother being Miles STANDISH's grand-dau. A bro living in Belmont & 3 uncles, very aged one in Hartford, 1 in Warren, & 1 in Monson all in ME. Deac Eliashib ADAMS of Bangor ME, holds the same relationship with these uncles, his father's grandfather, Eliashib ADAMS, married the dau/o Miles S [*Bangor Gazette*] [23 Apr 1846]

    Sally Mrs of Lebanon ME(?) thrown from a chaise instantly killed [30 Oct 1851]

STANFORD Isabella 43 (d 21 Oct 1851 d/o Jeremiah STANFORD, see Elder's *History of Lewiston ME*) at Lewiston ME [6 Nov 1851]

STANHOPE Curtis Dr at Steuben ME [27 Jul 1848]

    Lady Hester a long resident of Syria d at Djoun, Syria, on 23d of June [31 Aug 1839]

STANLEY Amanda M 23 only d/o James STANLEY Esq at Farmington ME [23 June 1852]

    Drusilla F 39 w/o Deac Anson STANLEY at Winthrop ME [24 Apr 1851]

    Eliza C 39 w/o Daniel STANLEY at Farmington ME [27 Mar 1851]

    Susannah Mrs 75 at Belfast ME [11 Dec 1851]

STANLEY - see JEWETT

STANWOOD Mr late Pres of Augusta Washington Temperence Society [30 Jan 1845]

STAPLER - see ROSS

STAPLES Betsey 25 w/o Leander STAPLES very suddenly at Limington ME [15 Aug 1840]

    Daniel first mate of ship *Hartley* of Kennebunk ME at New Orleans LA [9 Nov 1848]

STAPLES (Cont.) Harriet H 24 w/o James STAPLES at Belfast ME [15 Apr 1852]

 John Capt had just completed arrangements for a separation with his wife & took his own life at Springfield OH on 17th inst [19 June 1841]

 Mr died of Fall River [6 Feb 1851]

 Roxana 25 at Turner ME [31 Jul 1851]

 W C Dr of Industry ME at San Francisco CA on 27 Jan [18 Mar 1852]

STAPLES - see BOSS, ROSS

STARBIRD J abt 30y a workman in the city mills killed yesterday, left a wife & two children, of Palmyra or St Albans ME [*Bangor Gazette* in Nov] [18 Nov 1843]

 John one evening last week a dispute in a store near the head of Central wharf with John E GOULD of Portland ME. They left together and shortly, STARBIRD was taken up in the street shockingly bruised upon the head and senseless. He died about 4 a.m. the next morning. Gould was arrested & examined. [1 Jan 1839]

 Ruth 97 wid/o William STARBIRD at Brunswick ME [18 Mar 1852]

STARBOARD - see PEARCE

STARK John Esq 82 the 3rd s/o the late Major Gen John STARK at Manchester NH on 24 Nov [12 Dec 1844]

STARKBY Elizabeth 27 wid/o Otis STARKEY of Unity ME at Waterville ME [1 Jan 1852]

STARKEY Dorcas Mrs 45 d/o the late James BLACK at Stetson ME on 11 Jul [24 Jul 1851]

 Horatio A 35 late of Bath ME at Vassalboro ME [6 Jan 1848]

STARRETT Jerusha 72 w/o John STARRETT Jr at Warren ME [18 Dec 1851]

STATEN Amos 46 (born 27 Jul 1805, d 18 Mar 1852 s/o Samuel STATEN, see *History of Lewiston ME* by J G Elder 1989) at Lewiston ME [18 Mar 1852]

STEARNS Jane 3y d/o Mr STEARNS who resides within 30 rods of the railroad at Lynn MA accidentally drank a few swallows of potash water ... One year & 7 months and she has not taken any solid nourishment since ..... (from the *Boston Traveller*) [13 Apr 1839]

 Mr for a number of years a faithful & prudent engineman on the Boston MA & Worcester Railroad, fell a few days since while jumping upon his engine, at Framingham, it passed over his leg. The limb was so severely bruised that it was nessary to amputate it. [22 Oct 1842]

 Silas for many yrs pastor of the Baptist Church at Bath ME [8 Aug 1840]

STEAVENS - see MORSE

STEDMAN Walter abt 24 employed by mercantile house of Freeman, Fisher & Co & his parents reside in Needham [*Mer Journal*] at Ipswich [2 Oct 1835]

STEDMAN - see ADAMS, LANE

STEELE Thomas the friend & co-worker with the late Daniel O'CONNELL died on the 15th ult at Peele's Coffee, Fleet St after a lingering illness [6 Jul 1848]

STEPHENS Edward of Winthrop ME saved from drowning when the steam packet *New England* sank. It left Boston for Bath & Gardiner ME and had an accident with the schr *Curlew* on 31 May [12 June 1838]

 Mr a grocer of New York & Mr CRANE, a young man s/o Dr CRANE of Goshen were killed on the spot in an accident on the Erie Railroad [6 Aug 1846]

 Nathan & J P WILLIAMS escaped from jail at Sampson Co NC on the 11th ult, when they were confined for slave stealing. The latter was under sentence of death. [5 Jul 1849]

STEPHENSON Ambrose of Belfast ME injured at the S C NICKERSON ship yard at the Upper Bridge & died on Tues [*Belfast Signal*] [17 May 1849]

 Sarah an inmate of the alms house at Cambridgeport MA on the morning of Sun the 19th was stabbed with a bread knife by William H BRITTON 57 also an inmate. The

STEPHENSON (Cont.) deceased was 20y, a native of Ireland, handsome, intelligent and much respected. She was admitted in consequence of laboring under a painful disease. [23 Sept 1841]

Susan Jane 34 w/o B F STEPHENSON at Belfast ME [24 Apr 1851]

STETSON Amasa Esq of Boston MA directed the expenditure of about three hundred dollars in transplanting ornamental trees in the town of Stetson ME (from the *Eastern Argus*) [5 June 1841] [N.B. Page 491, *History of Penobscot Co ME*, Williams, Chase & Co., 1882; under section of Stetson, ME, says, "The name it bears was derived from an original proprietor, Mr. Amasa Stetson of Dorchester, MA."]

Elisha 84 AmRev pensioner at Durham ME [24 Feb 1848]

Franklin 23 a mate of Eastport ME lost overboard from schr *William* on passage from Boston MA to Eastport ME [20 Jan 1848]

John 64 at Bremen ME [10 Feb 1848]

Simeon Esq of Hampden ME on Tues last by his sledge running over him [Mec & Farmer] [6 Jan 1837]

STEUBEN Mr the Chevalier Bayard of our Revolution, sans peur et sans reproche, after vainly endeavoring to obtain the fulfillment by Congress of their engagements to him, returned to Utica NY, the legislature of which state voted him a township (six miles square) of land in that neighborhood. Here in a humble log house he died & was buried adjacent in 1797. [16 Sept 1847]

STEVENS Amanda 15 d/o the late Nathan STEVENS at Readfield ME [20 May 1852]

Benjamin abt 38 from Maine on 26 Oct at New Orleans [*Belfast Signal*] [13 Dec 1849]

Charles of Castine ME in a paroxysm of insanity cut the throat of his youngest child & then attempted to cut his own, but was prevented from effecting his purpose fully! The child is dead, but it is thought he may recover. [4 Oct 1849]

E D a druggist having a severe toothache arose in the night ... attemping to destroy the nerve of the tooth by applying Prussic Acid ...swallowed a portion ... at Boston MA [29 Feb 1840]

Ebenezer 70 at Montville ME [9 Oct 1851]

Edward B 48 of ME at Sacramento CA [2 Jan 1851]

Elijah 83 AmRev pensioner at Livermore ME [6 Jul 1848]

Elizabeth 22 of starvation [*New York Commerical*] [23 Nov 1848]

Elizabeth 78 at Vassalboro ME [25 Sept 1851]

Franklin & George W of Pittston ME saved from drowning when the steam packet *New England* sank. It left Boston for Bath & Gardiner ME and had an accident with the schr *Curlew* on 31 May [12 June 1838]

Howard of Winthrop ME on 2 Sept 1844, states "Whereas my wife, Catherine (HUNTON), has without my consent & aganinst my will left my bed & board ..." [5 Sept 1844]

Jacob of Lyme OH all at once on Wed afternoon, a well on his premises commenced overflowing & still continues. It is estimated that the discharge is at least sixty hogsheads per minute. The water is cold & very clear [*Norwalk (OH) Expositor*, 3d Jul] [1 Aug 1844]

James Jr 32 at Pittston ME on 8th Oct [19 Oct 1848]

Jeremiah thrown from a jam of logs, a few weeks since, into the Enchanted Stream, above the Forks (ME) and drowned (copied from the *Mann's Physican* of Industry ME) [29 June 1848]

John Esq 70 at Unity ME [19 Feb 1852]

Julia Rosselle 6 only d/o Melvin & Fanny S at Foxcroft (now Dover-Foxcroft) ME of the canker rash [15 Feb 1840]

L G suicide [*Boston Atlas*] [13 May 1836]

STEVENS (Cont.) Laura of Boston MA saved from drowning when the steam packet *New England* sank. It left Boston for Bath & Gardiner ME and had an accident with the schr Curlew on 31 May [12 June 1838]

Mrs of Auburn ME w/o Moses STEVENS abt 30 yrs ago became insane & for more than 20y she has been confined in a filthy cage, ten or twelve feet square, the threshold of which, for the last half of that period, she has not crossed. [*Lewiston Falls Adv*] [16 May 1844]

Nathan Esq 37 formerly of (Winthrop) at Winslow ME on Mon last [29 Sept 1840]

Oliver capsized with Jonathan TARR in the harbor of Rockport MA drowned [10 Apr 1851]

Ruth 80 w/o Eben STEVENS at Fryeburg ME [7 Sep 1848]

Sarah E 24 d/o the late Abel STEVENS at Eastport ME [3 Aug 1848]

Seth Esq of Hartford Cortland Co m Sylvia HEATH d/o Benjamin HEATH Esq of Locke Cayuga Co NY by Levi HENRY Esq on 22d of Nov. This marriage took place after a 19 year courtship! Mr S 61y & the fair bride 51. The young bridegroom has visited his bride once a month during the above mentioned time, 232 visits, a distance of 20 miles, 9,820 miles, 464 days, an ample opportunity to become acquainted [28 Jan 1843]

Stephen H of Otisfield ME his sons James 7 & Alonzo 9 hurt in cave-in, the younger died [*Norway Advertiser*] [1 Apr 1847]

Timothoy L 67 at Moscow ME [13 Jul 1848]

Wilbur Fisk 10y 9m at Winthrop ME (New Hampshire papers please copy) [22 Jan 1852]

STEVENS - see GALLAGHER, LEMONT, SOULE, THOMPSON

STEVENSON Mr recently, the celebrated English engineer [14 Sept 1848]

Thomas of the 2d Aug brings us the melancholy intelligence that a boat on the morning of 2d inst having on board 25 persons struck upon "Hunt's Rock" ... 19 persons including children drowned ... all of whom resided in Portland (ME) or at York Point. [*Portland Adv*] [*The St Johns City Gazette*] [14 Aug 1838]

STEVENSON - see DURHAM

STEVENSTON Jane Mrs abt 46 the keeper of an American ship-master's boarding house in the Minories at London England on Dec last [26 June 1851]

STEWARD Benjamin abt 16y of Bloomfield ME of lock-jaw on Tues the 4th inst [*Clarion*] [13 June 1844]

STEWARD C F of Nashua NH saved from drowning when the steam packet *New England* sank. It left Boston for Bath & Gardiner ME and had an accident with the schr *Curlew* on 31 May [12 June 1838]

Daniel Esq 82 at Skowhegan ME [3 Oct 1840]

Jonathan 79 at Bloomfield ME [10 Aug 1848]

Nancy C 40 w/o Mansfield STEWARD at Gardiner ME [12 June 1851]

Olive Mrs 75 at Bloomfield ME [23 Mar 1848]

Olive P Jr 16 d/o Hon Daniel STEWARD Jr at Anson ME on 15th ult [18 Jan 1840]

STEWARD - see CRAWFORD

STEWART Adams Dr of Roxbury MA proprietor of patent medicines died [28 Oct 1842]

Fear C 30 widow of D W STEWART at New Vineyard ME [23 Nov 1848]

Timothy U 37 of Bangor ME at Augusta ME on 2 Mar at the insane hospital [27 Mar 1851]

STEWART - see LONG

STICKNEY David MOODY 20 s/o William STICKNEY at Hallowell ME [24 Jul 1851]

Dorothy L 75 at Hallowell ME [26 Sept 1840]

Joseph E in CA a suicide [21 Feb 1850]

STICKNEY (Cont.) Moses of Jaffrey NH walked one day this summer two & 1/2 miles to the centre of town to buy a scythe & home again. He has helped to mow his grass this season & will be one hundred yrs old on the 23d Nov next [28 Aug 1851]

STICKNEY - see SEKINS

STIEVEL George a rope maker of Southwark, a ball entered his neck & passed through one of his lungs & the heart during the Irishmen Riot [16 May 1844]

STIMPSON Rachel 23 w/o Charles STIMPSON at Thomaston ME [11 Dec 1851]

STIMSON Joseph Major 72 at Limerick ME [15 June 1848] & [22 June 1848]

STINCHFIELD - see TARBOX, WHITTIER

STINSON A B MD 30 at Monmouth ME [24 Aug 1848]

Cyrus abt 20 of Farmington ME lost off the fender dam [*Bangor Whig*] [29 May 1835]

Harriet A 3y 10m d/o William F STINSON at Wiscasset ME on 4 Oct [23 Oct 1851]

S G of Bath ME saved from drowning when the steam packet *New England* sank. It left Boston for Bath & Gardiner ME and had an accident with the schr *Curlew* on 31 May [12 June 1838]

William 85 at Deer Isle ME [2 Nov 1848]

STITSEL Mr in Richmond PA, drinking a mug of cider in which there was unperceived, a bee - the bee stung him upon the tongue, and he died in less than an hour [11 Dec 1835]

STOCKBRIDGE - see SEWALL

STODDARD Henrietta 27 w/o Nelson STODDARD & d/o Isaac & Hannah CLARK at Salem ME on 23d Dec [13 Apr 1848]

Russell Esq 84 at Greene ME [21 Aug 1851]

STODDER - see VERY

STONE Amanda M 19 at Gardiner ME [29 Jan 1852]

Baltus 103y 16d a rifleman of the AmRev at Philadelphia PA with WASHINGTON in every campaign Bunker Hill, Trenton, Germantown, Red Bank & others & yet was not wounded [5 Nov 1846]

Charles Col, the 1st settler of Rochester NY died on Wed, built the first house in that city in 1810 [13 Nov 1851]

Col 52 editor of the *NY Commerical Advertiser*, on Thurs morning the 15th inst at the residence of his father-in-law, Rev WAYLAND at Saratoga Springs [22 Aug 1844]

Dr of New Orleans brought a slave with him to Buffalo where he left him & went to Boston MA. The slave fled across to Canada & when the Doctor went over to see him, had a warrent made out & arrested his old master on a case of debt for services. The Doctor thinks this is turning the tables "with a vengeance." [19 Oct 1848]

girl 15y of Dixfield ME went into a saw-mill near her father's house & in sport set the "negro wheel" in motion. While passing her fingers over the cogs she caught by the machinery, her breast was screwed agaist the other wheel and she was crushed to death [3 June 1847]

Hannah F L 22 d/o late Daniel STONE at Brunswick ME [29 Feb 1840]

John Col 76 at Gardiner ME [30 Mar 1848]

Nathaniel Rev 77 at Naples ME [9 Mar 1848]

STORER Henry 38 at Weld ME [20 Feb 1851]

STOREY Mary Eliza 35 w/o William K STOREY at Hallowell ME [6 Apr 1848]

STORRS two girls drowned of Burlington VT d/o Mr Spaulding STORRS, three other ch & Mr STORRS rescued from a watery grave by the manly efforts of a brother of those who perished [1 June 1848]

STORY Joseph Judge 65 of U. S. Supreme Court grad of Harvard 1798 [18 Sept 1845]

Miss of Covington KY married to Mr R SHORT. So the story made short by doubling. "How to Shorten a Story by splicing." [17 Aug 1848]

STOVER Alcot Esq 75 at Bowdoin ME [26 Oct 1848]

STOWELL - see PEARCE

STOWERS Zereda 55 w/o Samuel STOWERS Esq at Madrid ME [24 Jul 1851]

STRAIN Mr swam out to save 2 young ladies of the Charlotte Seminary, drowned with them, had a wife & eight children at Davenport NY [19 Jul 1849]

STRATTON - see MESERVEY

STRAW - see DROWNING

STRICKLAND Mr on the White Mtns, funeral at Trinity Church [*Boston Courier*] [8 Nov 1849]

STRICKLAND - see WHITMAN

STRONG Marshall M house at Madison burned, serving in the legislature from that county & Mrs STRONG with her son & dau perished in the flames! [*The Racine Advocate*, extra of 27 Jan] [19 Feb 1846]

    Moses Judge of Rutland VT on Sat last a husband & father [15 Oct 1842]

    Mr an overseer on the Reading's Plt near Vicksburg by a blow from one of his negroes with an axe. [10 Apr 1851]

STROUT Mary R 23y 8m d/o George H & Polly STROUT at Jay ME on 10 Feb [21 Feb 1851]

    Rebecca 82 at Brunswick ME [29 Apr 1852]

STUART Solomon 74 at Saco ME [15 Apr 1852]

STURDEVANT A W 26 of ME at San Francisco CA on 19 Oct [4 Dec 1851]

STURGIS James of Vassalboro ME on Tues morning last his house for many years occupied as tavern burnt & lost his life. James STURGIS Jr hurt by some article of furniture thrown from the house [*Temperance Gazette*] [16 Nov 1839]

STURGISS David Jr 32 at Norridgewock ME [21 Dec 1848]

STURTEVANT Andrew 83 AmRev at Fayette ME on 10 Jul [10 Aug 1848]

    Anna 64 w/o Alvah STURTLEFF (*sic*) at Paris ME [26 June 1851]

    Leonard saved from drowning when the steam packet *New England* sank. It left Boston for Bath & Gardiner ME and had an accident with the schr *Curlew* on 31 May [12 June 1838]

STURTIVANT Mrs abt 60 w/o Consider STURTIVANT at this town (ME) on Sat last [9 May 1840]

STURTLEFF - see STURTIVANT

SUE - see NILES

SUFFLEBEAU John 109 born on the banks of the Hudson River twelve miles from Albany NY on 15 Feb 1735. His 3rd wife still living at age 82. He was a soldier but paper does not state which war or wars. [*Kaskaska (IL) Republican*] [2 May 1844]

SULLIVAN girl 6 d/o Jere SULLIVAN at Winthrop ME [17 Jul 1851]

    John his house on the 6th inst in Hampden ME burned Mr S, his wife & 7 children barely escaped the flame with their lives, in their night clothes (from the *Bangor Whig*) [25 Dec 1841]

    John in (Lowell MA) on a hand car on the Boston & Lowell railroad and when near the stone bridge, Middlesex St the handle of the car caught in his clothes & threw him violenty onto the tracks ...killing him instantly (copied from *Lowell Vox Populi*) at Billerica MA on Sat evening last [10 June 1852]

    Mary drowned off the ferry boat at Gardiner ME [4 Sept 1851]

    Mr AmRev at Exeter NH [16 Sept 1847]

SUMMER - see ROLERSON

SUMNER - see HASEITH

SUNDERLAND William of Warwich RI drowned on fishing trip at Providence RI on 18th [6 Jul 1839]

SUNDERLAND (Cont.) Judge at Albany NY [*NY Journal of Com*] [22 May 1845]

SUTHERLAND - see FOLLET

SUTTON Capt command the steamboat *Medora*, standing over the boiler when it exploded. He was much injured in the head, & was very doubtful yesterday whether he would recover. [23 Apr 1842]

SWAIN Asa of Sanbornton NH left Franklin on Thurs last for home, found the next morning frozen & dead [2 Mar 1848]

    Mr 2d mate of Nantucket MA crew of whale ship *Awashonks* of Falmouth ME at Fejee Island [6 May 1836]

SWAN Hannah S 3 d/o Benjamin & Eliza SWAN at Augusta ME on 23 Dec [1 Jan 1852]

    Mary Augusta 4y 3m only c/o Francis SWAN Jr & Mary E SWAN at New Sharon ME on 18 Mar [3 Apr 1851]

    Patience 19y 6m d/o Frederick & Patience SWAN at New Sharon ME on 11 Apr [17 Apr 1851]

    Richard Mott 2y bro/o of Patience above on 29 Apr [8 May 1851]

    Robert of cholera at Herman ME [*Bangor Daily Whig*] [16 Aug 1849]

SWANTON John B 59 formerly of Bath ME at Dresden ME [12 June 1851]

SWASEY Caroline Olive 48 d/o the late Dr William SWASEY of Limerick ME at Standish ME [17 Jul 1851]

SWEAT - see KING

SWEET Arnold 59 formerly of Winthrop ME at South Reading MA [5 Feb 1852]

    Benjamin a mulatto boy a pauper of the town kidnapped by Noah ROLLINS & sold to Samuel BENNETT, who was going to AL. Noah R tried and found guilty for kidnapping & selling at Exeter (NH?) [23 Apr 1837]

    Ellis Col 78 at Farmington ME [18 May 1848]

    John abt 24y belonging supposed on the Calais & Houlton ME road drowned, was employed at Hathorne's stream mill at Hampden ME [23 Oct 1851]

    Mr of Somerville MA lost his life at the Cambridge crossing of the Fitchburg Railroad on Wed of last week [13 Sept 1849]

SWEET - see SHORT

SWETT Caroline L of Portland ME "Exchange Street on Sat, smashed Mr H G COLE's bottles, w/o Jere S, repeatedly requested retailers not to sell her husband liquor - & has promised the cowhide if they do [*Argus*] (PS) tried in Portland ME for an assault on Cole's Liquor shop, sentenced to pay a fine of $10 & cost of court, amounting to a little over $50, was ably defended by Gen FESSENDON & Neal DOW Esq [19 Apr 1849] [19 Jul 1849]

    Jesse H of Brunswick ME listed in deaths in CA [23 Sept 1851]

    Joshua 89 AmRev at Gorham ME [22 May 1851]

SWETT - see PEARCE

SWIFT Howard B 30 of Bangor ME at Waterville ME [15 Jan 1852]

SWIFT - see BAILEY, PETERSON

SWIRES Mr shot & killed his son, mistook for a deer in Iowa [13 Dec 1849]

SYLVESTER Alonzo during the thunder storm Thurs 30th Aug, at the blacksmith shop in Livermore ME owned by E PRAY. Alonzo S left a wife & two children. Wm S who was dead to all appearances for 20 minutes except faint beating of a pulse in the left wrist for a few minutes. Mr SAUNDERS, lightly (marked by lightning) on the back of his neck (copied from *Christian Mirror*) [9 Oct 1838]

    Alonzo of Livermore ME by lightning on 30th ult, Deac William SAUNDERS who stood near was struck down, but recovered [18 Sept 1838]

    Joseph s/o Howard SYLVESTER, To all whom it may concern. I hereby relinquish to my son, Joseph Warren SYLVESTER, his time to trade & transact business for himself

SYLVESTER (Cont.) as if he were twenty one yrs of age, signed by Howard SYLVESTER & witness William NOYES at Leeds ME 6 Nov 1835 [13 Nov 1835]
    Marlborough 55 of Hallowell ME at the California mines on 20 Feb [8 May 1851]
    Ruggles 38 at North Leeds ME on 24 Dec [5 Feb 1852]

- T -

TABER Barnabus 71 at Vassalborough ME on 1 Feb [2 Mar 1839]
    Henry of Albion ME in moving a joist in an old abandoned saw mill, a narrow escape, almost a miracle life spared [21 Sept 1848]
    Martha Mrs 100y born in Newport 10 Mar 1744, completed her hundredth year on Sun last, resides with her dau, Mrs KNIGHT on the Long Wharf [*Newport Mercury*] [28 Mar 1844]
    Paul 74 at Vassalough ME [7 Mar 1850]
TABOR Hannah 45 at Gardiner ME [25 Mar 1847]
TAFFT Mr a workman on K & P Railroad a fatal accident on Mon last [10 Apr 1851]
TAFT Leonard & Mr BALSTER & a female burned to death at Uxbridge in the Poor House on Tues night [*Worcester Spy*] [12 Feb 1846]
TAINTER Deborah 48 at Bangor ME [29 Jan 1846]
TALBOT Ann K 24 d/o Deac Peter TALBOT at Waterville ME [6 Apr 1848]
    Asa 79 at Avon ME [1 Mar 1849]
    Elizabeth L w/o George F TALBOT Esq & d/o Col John G NEIL of Skowhegan ME at Machias ME on 25th ult [10 Jul 1845]
    Hester A R 20 at Avon ME on the 3d ult [25 May 1848]
    Isaac Esq 74 at Turner ME [25 Jul 1850]
    Simon 27 native of Canada & citizen of NY belonged to the US ship *Preble* & died with the Africa fever at Porto Grande, Island of St Vincent, Cape Verde on 14 Dec [10 Apr 1845]
TALBOT - see PEARCE
TALCOTT Hannah P 27 at Farmington ME [29 Aug 1850]
    Samuel A formerly attorney general of the state of New York on 19 Mar 1836 [13 Jan 1837]
TALLEYRAND - see BRADSTREET [18 May 1848]
TALLMAN Ann M M 22 d/o Benjamin F TALLMAN Esq of Woolwich ME at Bath ME [11 May 1848]
    Lee of Chester ME? at San Francisco CA [8 Jan 1852]
    Mary B 58 at Woolwich ME [21 May 1846]
    Sarah S 49 at Dresden ME (Swan Island) on 28 Oct [21 Nov 1840]
TAPLEY John 82 at Kennebunk ME [5 Jul 1849]
    Lydia E 32 w/o Lawrence E TAPLEY at Kennebunkport ME [24 Dec 1846]
    Mary A 25 d/o Oliver TAPLEY at Hallowell ME [14 Nov 1840]
TAPPAN Enoch S Dr 63 at (Augusta) ME [*Banner*] [5 Aug 1847]
    Enoch S Dr 66 at Augusta ME on 26th inst [29 Jul 1847]
    Martha 83 formerly of Manchester MA at Augusta ME [22 Feb 1849]
    Mary Mrs 106 at Newburyport MA [28 Jan 1833]
    Samuel Green 6w only s/o Rev S S TAPPAN of Frankfort [25 Sept 1838]
TAPPAN - see SNELL
TAPPEN Catherine H 24 d/o Rev Dr TAPPAN at Augusta ME [29 June 1848]
TARBELL Charles 36 at Gardiner ME [4 Apr 1844]
TARBOX Capt lost in the ship *Mobile* of Bath ME [21 Oct 1852]
    Deliverance 77 at Norway ME [14 May 1846]

TARBOX (Cont.) Frederic C 5y child of Moses & Olive TARBOX at Kennebunkport ME on 13th ult [7 Oct 1847]

infant c/o Samuel TARBOX at Augusta ME on 16 Apr [22 Apr 1847]

Lucretia 22 at Biddeford ME [15 Apr 1852]

Lucy K 3y c/o Moses & Oliver TARBOX at Kennebunkport ME on 20th [7 Oct 1847]

Margaret 98 at Kennebunk ME [2 Mar 1848]

Philip 51 at Bowdoinham ME [23 Feb 1839]

Royal 70 at Gardiner ME [14 Sept 1848]

Samuel of Danville ME had a horse strayed or stolen from his pasture on the night of 6th inst a dark bay horse about ten years old one or both hind feet white, a white stripe in his face, scars on the back part of his thigh, white spots on the back and on the back part of his forelegs near the belly. Whoever will give information to the subscriber in Hartland through the *Maine Farmer* or otherwise, where said horse may be found, shall be suitably rewarded and all necessary charges paid. John STINCHFIELD at Hartland ME 11 July 1840 [18 Jul 1840]

Susan C abt 36 w/o Samuel TARBOX at Augusta ME on 17th Apr [22 Apr 1847]

Zachariah 32 at Topsham ME [12 DEc 1850]

TARLTON John A abt 45 of Portsmouth NH at Thomaston ME has left a wife & 4 children; a member of the Odd Fellows Lodge at Portsmouth NH [*Eastern Argus*] [19 Nov 1846]

TARR George abt 25 of Brunswick ME on his passage from China for New York died on 29 Dec 1844 [20 Nov 1845]

Jacob AmRev at Gloucester ME [12 June 1835]

Jonathan drowned, capsized in a boat with Oliver STEVENS in the harbor of Rockport MA [10 Apr 1851]

Joseph 50 at Litchfiled ME on 1 Aug [14 Aug 1851]

Lucinda A 36 w/o David D TARR at Kingfield ME on 3 May [13 May 1852]

skipper & his two sons & a son-in-law of the fishing schr *William* of Rockport while lying to on the ridges southeast of Baker's land on the 27th ult was run down & all on board perished [21 Aug 1845]

TARR - see FORD

TARRENCE Robert a young man had one hand blown off by the bursting of a cannon at Norriston PA [*The New York Farmer & Mechanic*] [17 Jul 1845]

TASKER Ebenezer abt 27 at Biddeford ME [12 Aug 1852]

Elizabeth M 29 w/o Ebenezer TASKER at Biddeford ME [11 Mar 1852]

TATE Catherine 31 w/o Captain Thomas TATE at Thomaston ME [13 Jan 1848]

William 92 formerly of Westbrook ME at London on 18 Aug, brother of the late Admiral TATE of the Russian Navy [9 Nov 1833]

TAYLOR Aaron 35 native of Maine at Charity Hospital in New Orleans of yellow fever on 28 Aug [2 Nov 1848]

Achsah 22 d/o John TAYLOR at Norridgewock ME [8 Mar 1849]

Albert G 31 at Pittsfield ME on 17 Aug [4 Sept 1851]

Albion of ME in CA [21 Aug 1851]

Aurelia G 40 w/o John R TAYLOR & d/o Noah GREELY Esq at Mt Vernon ME [19 Dec 1840]

Benjamin B abt 22 printer at Bangor ME [28 Aug 1845]

Betsey 35 w/o Samuel TAYLOR formerly of Starks ME at Dover NH [21 Dec 1839]

Betsey 79 w/o Rev Elias TAYLOR at Belgrade ME on 3rd inst [9 May 1844]

Caroline A 11y & 7m at Brunswick ME [11 Feb 1847]

Chalotte R 4y 6m youngest d/o J G N & Margaret TAYLOR at Boston MA on 1st inst [18 Sept 1845]

Charles Otis 3 s/o Otis TAYLOR at Vassalboro ME on 10 Apr [29 Apr 1852]

TAYLOR (Cont.) E Jefferson 41 at Vassalboro ME [28 Oct 1847]

    Ebenezer 82 AmRev pensioner & on the 6th Thankful his wife 76 both buried in the same grave at Yarmouth ME on 5th ult [1 Apr 1843]

    Edward B 25 at Calais ME [11 Dec 1845]

    Ephraim Capt 89 AmRev at Newcastle ME [9 Sept 1847]

    Hannah 26 at Norridgewock ME [14 Nov 1844]

    Harrison Eugene 2y 5m s/o Harrison & Esther TAYLOR at Vassalboro ME on 16 Feb [18 Mar 1852]

    James abt 60 a farmer from Salem Franklin Co came into that city on 29th Jan last with produce for the market died [12 Mar 1846]

    James Gen at his residence in Newport KY on the 7th inst a few minutes only after depositing his vote for President. He was born in 1769 in Carolina Co VA & emigrated to KY in 1792. He was an uncle of the President-elect [23 Nov 1848]

    Jane 59 w/o John TAYLOR at Norridgewock ME [18 Oct 1849]

    Jesse Dr abt 50 at Norridgewock ME [4 APr 1844]

    Joel 26 at Augusta ME on 5th May [21 June 1849]

    John 50 at Bath ME [22 Jan 1839]

    John H 29 at Norridgewock ME [14 Jan 1847]

    Joshua killed by a car breaking loose on the Pennsylvania Railroad over the Alleghany Mtn [4 Jul 1834]

    Judith Ann 18 d/o widow Phebe TAYLOR at Augusta ME on 19th inst [1 Jul 1847]

    Maria 48 at Gardiner ME [14 Aug 1851]

    Martha Ann 18 at Brunswick ME [15 Aug 1844]

    Mary 56 w/o Dimond TAYLOR at Wells [3 Feb 1848]

    Mrs burt to death at Syracuse NY on Sat by the explosion of a spirit gas lamp [1 May 1851]

    Olive 26 d/o the late Samuel TAYLOR Esq at China ME on Sat last [6 Mar 1841]

    Oren W 24 s/o Dismond TAYLOR at Norridgewock ME [15 May 1851]

    Orrin Perley 5y 4m s/o Otis & Sarah TAYLOR at Vassalboro ME on 29th [18 Mar 1852]

    Rebecca 27 at Gardiner ME [22 June 1848]

    Roxana B 23 w/o Jas C TAYLOR at Brunswick ME [25 May 1848]

    Samuel Esq 65 at Porter ME [17 Sept 1846]

    Samuel G 59 formerly of Hallowell ME at Belfast ME [13 Jan 1848]

    Sandford a hand of the schr Ontario of Belfast ME by accident at sea [22 June 1839]

    Sarah 35 w/o Otis TAYLOR at Vassalboro ME on 14 Mar [18 Mar 1852]

    Seth of Lyman ME at his son on Wed last abt 72y [the *Chelsea Pioneer*][14 Dec 1848]

    Simeon abt 70 of Roxbury ME at Rumford ME [10 Apr 1841]

    Thomas Capt abt 45 at Brunswick ME [21 Feb 1837]

    William B G; Wm G TAYLOR, 1st Lt commanding; Mr COOPER of Hingham MA, 2nd Lieut do., Mr Robert COOPER, drowned off West Key on the US cutter *Vigilant*. J C JOHNSON pilot belonging to the *Vigilant* & Robert ARMISTEAD of New Orleans, a passenger, were providentially ashore & thus were saved. The only persons known to be saved from the wreck were Michael DRISCOLL & Henry HOYT, seaman, picked up at sea in a canoe belonging to the cutter. [31 Oct 1844]

    William C 21 of Kennebunk ME at Waterford ME [20 Jul 1848]

    Zachary Gen 56 born in 1790 in KY see biographical sketch [*Traveller*] [4 June 1846] & President died [18 Jul 1850]

TAYLOR - see CARLETON, JOHNSTONE, THUMB, SOULE

TEAGUE baby 2y c/o Asa TEAGUE at New Sharon ME on 5 Sept [9 Oct 1845]

    Mary Jane 8y 5m d/o D M TEAGUE at Mt Vernon ME [12 June 1851]

TEAL Capt killed in the Irish & Native American (not American Indians more likely English born in American) Riots in Philadelphia PA [*Dollar Newspaper*] [18 July 1844]

TEBBETS John P 30 at Belgrade ME [11 Apr 1850]

TEBBETS - see TIBBETTS

TEDFORD Ellis 43 at Topsham ME [22 Aug 1850]

TEGO John 18 at Skowhegan ME [7 May 1846]

TEMPLE James found near Dunlap's wharp in Bath ME last week drowned last winter in crossing the Kennebec river from Bowdoinham, papers and money found about his person may be had of the coroner [*Lincoln Telegraph*] [29 Aug 1837]

Robert Esq President of the Bank of Rutland VT found on the 5th in a field adjoining his residence shot through the heart [17 Oct 1834]

TEN BROECK P S Rev formerly Rector of St Paul's Church at Portland ME at North Danvers MA [1 Feb 1849]

TENANT Margaret Jane 23 formerly of Augusta ME at Portland ME [5 Aug 1843]

TENNEY Charlotte w/o Alonzo TENNEY at Hallowell ME [3 June 1836]

Mrs 102y at Jonesboro ME [25 Apr 1837]

Nathan Dr 79 at Bluehill ME [17 Aug 1848] & [3 Aug 1848]

TENNIS family of New River GA killed by Indians [1 Jan 1839]

TENNY Jane widow mother of Judge TENNY of the supreme court of this state at Byfield MA [23 Apr 1842]

TETFORD Allanson 21 at Topsham ME [13 May 1836]

TETHERLY Robert abt 56 at Eastport ME drowned [22 Nov 1849]

TEWKSBURY Josiah & his wife of Danville, both died within the last three years lived together in the married state 71 yrs [*Exeter News Letter*][*Boston Bee*] [19 Dec 1844]

THACHER Peter O Hon judge of the Municipal Court at Boston MA [4 Mar 1843]

THACHER - see HOWE

THATCHER B B 31 a graduate of Bowdoin College formerly of ME at Boston MA [25 Jul 1840]

Harriet Preble 64 w/o Hon Stephen THATCHER at Lubec ME [10 Jan 1850]

Priscilla J 20 at Lubec ME [12 Sept 1844]

Sarah S 84 at Saco ME [4 APr 1844]

THAXTER Arethusa 77 at Eastport ME [11 Feb 1847]

THAYER Angeline 33 w/o ALexander S THAYER at Paris ME [26 Aug 1852]

H Augusta 22 at Turner ME [26 Aug 1847]

Mrs 38 w/o Phillip THAYER at Waterville ME [16 Apr 1846]

Nathaniel DD pastor of the First Congregational Church & Society of Lancaster at Rochester NY on 22 June [11 Jul 1840]

Sarah W 4m d/o Elias & Elvira A THAYER of Bangor ME at Augusta ME on 8 Jan [23 Jan 1851]

Stephen Dr 72 at Waterville ME [3 June 1852]

Zebediah Capt abt 74 at Dresden ME [4 Feb 1847]

THEOBALD F R of Richmond ME saved from drowning when the steam *packet New England* sank. It left Boston for Bath & Gardiner ME and had an accident with the schr *Curlew* on 31 May [12 June 1838]

Phillip R Dr 63 at Wiscasset ME [23 Jul 1846]

THING Charles H 27 at Hallowell ME [14 Nov 1844]

George R 27 s/o Maj Daniel THING at Mt Vernon ME [29 May 1851]

Gilman of Monmouth ME suicide by hanging in his barn on Wed last his age was abt 50y [24 Oct 1837]

Martha Ann 22 w/o Dr Ira THING at Mt Vernon ME [1 Aug 1844]

THISTLE Issachar 55 formerly of Sangerville ME at Dover ME [18 Sept 1851]

THOMAS Abigail 50 w/o Jedediah THOMAS at Hallowell ME [24 Aug 1848]

Barney of (Thomaston ME?) fell from the main yard of the ship *Franklin King*, & was instantly killed. Amasa MILLER also fell at the same time but caught in some part of the rigging and escaped injury. A third person was saved by Capt L B GILLCHRIST (copied from the *Thomaston (ME) Miscellany*) on Fri the 26th inst [8 Jan 1852]

Charles 79 at Belfast ME [16 Mar 1848]

Charles Col 84 a AmRev pensioner at Brunswick ME [26 Feb 1842]

Charlotte Alice 6m d/o James & Philna THOMAS at Waterville ME [18 Sept 1845]

Cornelio killed on Wed of last week near Utica NY, thrown out of the carriage because of a runaway horse. [27 Jul 1839]

Daniel abt 15 s/o Daniel THOMAS at Hartford ME on 12 Jan [29 Jan 1846]

Elisha 75 at Brownfield ME [8 Jan 1846]

Elizabeth 43 w/o William THOMAS Esq d/o late Jeremiah BROWN of Readfield ME, formerly of Salisbury MA at Augusta ME [1 Aug 1834]

Emily 26 d/o John THOMAS at Brownville ME [22 Jul 1847]

Enoch a long time insane, murdered both his parents, in Woodford Co IL on the night of the 17th Apr & wounded dangerously a younger brother [20 May 1843]

G W of Ellsworth ME at Panama [26 Feb 1852]

Gov of MD published a work of 50 pages all abt his matrimonial troubles. If all the matrimonial troubles were published, Congress would have to "annex" 2 or 3 big planets for a "Library" to put them in [20 Mar 1845]

Hushai at Winthrop ME [3 Apr 1835]

John A Capt at Waldoboro ME [23 Sept 1836]

John W of Augusta ME employed to transport a wagon load of supplies for the Northeastern Boundary Commissioners. During the thunder shower on Wed at Fairfield he mistook the height of the shed & was crushed between his load & the timbers of the building, left a wife & a large family of children [*Kennebec Journal*] [18 Jul 1844]

Joseph AmRev at Portland ME [29 May 1835]

Joseph Esq 84 AmRev a capt of the artillery at Plymouth MA [4 Sept 1838]

Lewis 27 of Eden ME 1st officer of ship *Cabot* at New York [12 Sept 1834]

Lizzie Mary 19m d/o Albert & Mary THOMAS at Hallowell ME [11 Sept 1851]

Lucy (Vaughhan?) 85 of Winthrop ME formerly of Middlebury MA at Wilton ME [4 Oct 1849]

Mary (see p. 628 & 997 Stackpole's *History of Winthrop Maine*, 1994) states her name was Hannah CUSHMAN) widow of the late Capt Hushai THOMAS at Winthrop ME on 3 Feb [13 Feb 1838]

Mr a family in St Jonesbury Railroad accident in the upper parts of Thetford VT on 30th ult, (reported in the *Haverhill Republican* & then reprinted in the *Manchester Mirror*) [6 Nov 1851]

Mr of Delaware perished in shipwreck of the schr *William Polk*, Mr HAMILTON Capt, the capt alone escaped [*Philidelphia Exchange Book*] [23 Jul 1846]

Norton 15m s/o Nicholas J THOMAS Esq at Eden ME [12 Feb 1842]

Peter C 85 at Byron ME [7 Nov 1850]

Philip & two of his hired hands died in Cumberland RI after eating diseased potatoes (from the *Sun*) [3 Oct 1844]

Robert C of East Thomaston ME had his right arm injured by a premature discharge of a gun & was amputated above the elbow [*Belfast Journal*] [12 June 1849]

Stephen H 50 at Windham ME [13 May 1847]

Sylvanus Esq 62 of Winthrop ME at Boston MA after a short illness [25 Dec 1841]

Tryphena 17 d/o widow Mary THOMAS at Augusta ME on 6 Apr [15 Apr 1852]

THOMAS (Cont.) William Hon at East Thomaston ME [31 May 1849]

William Jr 42 at North Yarmouth [2 Mar 1848]

Winslow 11 s/o Winslow & Clarissa THOMAS at Camden ME on 14th Aug of lock-jaw occasioned by a blow upon the head given by another boy [21 Oct 1847]

THOMAS - see ADAMS, COLLAMORE, KING, LORAINE, RUSSELL

THOMASON Betsey 59 w/o Capt William THOMPSON at Embden ME [13 Apr 1848]

THOMASTON James & Henry from Portland ME, bro's left (St Louis MO) on Mon last on way to the gold region, on foot via Independance, taking only the common preparations for a hunting execursion - sending goods by sea to San Francisco CA, expect to reach CA 2 months in advance of those who go with teams or pack mules. [*St Louis Republican*, Jan 24] [15 Feb 1849]

THOMES William of Portland ME lost & drowned left a wife & 3 ch the barque *William Fales*, in Wells Bay ME on Wed evening at 9 o'clock, 13 persons on board, eight lost including every officer. source - George M FREEMAN of Cape Needick (Old York, where the barque drove) [26 Feb 1842]

THOMPSON Aaron 73 at Topsham ME [21 Jan 1843]

Abiagil 71 at Wales ME [14 Jan 1847]

Alhana 23 at Litchfield ME [7 Dec 1839]

Betsey 39 w/o Joseph S THOMPSON at Augusta ME on Apr 26 "*Zion's Advocate* please copy" [4 May 1848]

Caroline 28 w/o Henry THOMPSON at Mercer ME on 11th ult [20 Jul 1848]

Charlotte 64 at Topsham ME [16 Aug 1849]

Daniel 19 s/o Richard THOMPSON at Kennebunk ME [1 Apr 1833]

E F 21y 6m s/o Robert & Susan THOMPSON at Windsor ME on 16 Feb of consumption (Boston MA, Lincoln Co ME and Waldo Co ME papers please copy) [6 Mar 1851]

Eliza 21 at Portland ME [16 Oct 1835]

Elizabeth 27 w/o Jonathan THOMPSON at Searsmont ME [20 Mar 1845]

Elizabeth a deaf & dumb (deaf mute) brought a suit against Mr H PORCH of Cole Co MO, breach of marriage contract, had been entered into between her & PORCH by signs. PORCH entirely deserted the girl & her child, & left them entirely helpless. She recovered $3000 damages [25 Nov 1843]

Eugene 22 s/o Charles THOMPSON at Topsham ME [17 Oct 1850]

Fanny 37 d/o Galen THOMPSON at Jay ME [24 June 1847]

George C 17 s/o Robert THOMPSON at Windsor ME (Lincoln & Waldo Co papers please copy) [5 Oct 1848]

George seaman of Liverpool England lost on the brig *Linden*, a sea disaster, GRIFFITH Capt [19 Nov 1842]

Georgiana 5 d/o James & Louisa THOMPSON of Augusta ME at Westbrook ME on 14th at the res of William STEVENS [1 Jan 1842]

Hannah S 45 w/o David THOMPSON at Topsham ME [15 Oct 1846]

Happy 76 at South Vassalboro ME [1 Aug 1837]

Henry Jr of Machiasport ME at CA at the mines on 12 Nov [14 Mar 1850]

J book-keeper in the commercial house of Carlton R MOORE of (Philadelphia) lost his life at Niagara Falls [*Phil North American*] [5 Sept 1844]

James 48 at East Machias ME [10 Aug 1848]

Joel at Philadelphia jury against George F ALBERTI, James F PRICE & J C MITCHELL kidnapping free, Joel T, infant s/o William T, a colored man of Burlington NJ. The mother of the ch taken from Philadelphia 13 Aug, fugitive slave of Mr MITCHELL of Elkton MD. Child, born in NJ free. Mother sold by master retained the child [16 Jan 1851]

Joel late of Wayne ME estate notice, Rachel THOMPSON adm [11 Nov 1852]

THOMPSON (Cont.) John 25 s/o Archibald THOMPSON Esq of Bridgton ME near the source of the St Croix in the woods [30 May 1837]

John of Bath ME at Havre on board frigate *Constitution* [19 June 1835]

Joseph 24 formerly of North Anson ME at FL [2 Oct 1845]

Josiah of York ME to Kittery with a load of wood in turning a corner, the wheel struck a large stone, and threw his little boy, about five yrs old, from the load, the wheel passed over the boy's head killing him. [12 Nov 1842]

Lauriette 1y 7m d/o Benjamin & Ann THOMPSON at Montville ME on 28 Dec [5 Mar 1846]

Lydia 27 w/o William THOMPSON at Belfast ME [18 May 1848]

Mary 28 w/o Nehemiah THOMPSON at Montville ME [10 Dec 1846]

Mary abt 70y of Topsham ME committed suicide on the night of the 11th inst off the toll bridge between Brunswick & Topsham ME [*Brunswick Advertiser*] [20 Apr 1848]

Mr arrested on the Mississippi charged with attemping to sell a free negro, convicted at Louisville [14 Aug 1841]

Mr of Zanesville OH while ordering some boys from his apple orchard, was struck by one of them named GREEN, with a hammer, and instantly killed [30 Nov 1839

Mrs 86 at Farmington ME [4 Oct 1849]

Phebe 23 at Augusta ME on 2 Sept [16 Sept 1852]

Ray 40 at Gardiner ME [15 Mar 1849]

Robert 43 formerly of Union (ME?) at White Haven PA [5 Mar 1846]

Robert of ME at CA [18 Nov 1852]

Samuel M master of Woolwich ME lost overboard from *schr John Bell* on 4th ult in the Bay of Chaleur by a heavy sea which broke over her while riding at anchor [3 Aug 1848]

Samuel of Pownal ME at Staten Island NY [16 Oct 1845]

Sarah 22 at Wiscasset ME [25 Apr 1844]

Sarah Ann recovered of Amos ADAMS Jr a verdict of $600 for a breach of promise of marriage, Hon WHITMAN was the Judge (from the *Portland Adver*) at Portland ME [6 Jul 1839]

Sarah widow, formerly of Kingston NH 84 "New Hampshire papers please copy" at Rome ME on 26 Mar [20 Apr 1848]

Silas W 35 at Norridgewock ME [5 Nov 1846]

Susannah 73 w/o John THOMPSON at Barnard ME on 20th ult [13 Apr 1848]

W B 33 of Boston MA at San Francisco CA on 5 Oct [20 Nov 1851]

William Esq 84 at Eddington ME [6 Feb 1851]

William on the 1st day of Feb last he attained the age of 111y. He left eleven or twelve children, the oldest of whom was living last summer & is believed to be still in existence, at the advanced age of 91y, his youngest surviving son is 25 years of age. He was honest & temperant [10 Aug 1833]

William seaman 26 of Boston MA belonged to the U. S. ship *Preble* & died with the Africa fever at Porto Grande Island of St Vincent Cape de Verds on 22 Dec [10 Apr 1845]

William W Capt of Calais ME on board of the schr *St Croix* on her passage to Nantucket [10 Sept 1846]

THOMPSON - see RANSOM, SCRIBNER, WOODBURY

THOMS a boy abt 9y s/o Benjamin THOMS, while on a Maying excursion in crossing the Kenduskeag Stream just above Lover's Leap between Bruce's & McQuesten's Mill slipped upon the log fell in and was drowned. The current ran swifty and the efforts of his comrades to rescue him were unavailing. (copied from the *Bangor Mercury*) [15 May 1851]

George E V 6m d/o Nathan J THOMS at Augusta ME [1 Aug 1850]

THOMS (Cont.) Tryphena 17 d/o widow Mary THOMS at Augusta ME on 6 Apr [15 Apr 1852]

THOMSON Dr the author of the Thomsonian system of medical practice at Boston MA [21 Oct 1843]

THORN Sarah widow 80 at South Berwick ME [20 Mar 1851]

THORNDIKE Eben Jr Esq 24 at Unity ME [11 Oct 1849]

Timothy Esq 66 at Brooks ME [30 May 1850]

William 40 late president of the senate of MA at Beverly MA on 8th inst of consumption [24 JUl 1835]

THORNTON Mary S H w/o Dr John H F THORNTON & third d/o the late President HARRISON at North Bend OH on 17 Nov [3 Dec 1842]

THORP Anna 66 at Turner ME [27 Mar 1845]

Benjamin 68 at Turner ME [20 Aug 1846]

Elihu 75 at Gardiner ME [18 Apr 1850]

THUMB Tom "The redoubtable Gen T T offers to bring the Mexican War to a close, by officiating as a spy in the enemy's camp. If taken, he says he would pass for a baby, and remain unsuspected, while he ascertained the policy & designs of the Mexican diplomatists. Like Gen TAYLOR, he says he 'never surrenders' except to the ladies." [17 June 1847]

THURLO Sarah 46 w/o David THURLO at South Deer Isle ME [11 Jul 1850]

THURLOW John 90 formerly of Litchfield at Lee on 3 Aug (MA paper please copy) [23 Sept 1852]

THURSTON Alfred 20 s/o Caleb & Olive THURSTON at China ME on 18 Feb [10 Apr 1851]

Benjamin 30 at Augusta ME on 13 Sept [4 Oct 1849]

Betsey 74 at Gardiner ME [8 Aug 1844]

David an orphan boy & nephew of Richard THURSTON of (Bangor) ME fell overboard (*Bangor Whig*) [17 Oct 1837]

Ira T late of Monmouth ME estate notice Pamela F THURSTON exec [5 Feb 1852]

John R 34 formerly of Exeter NH at Glenburn ME [2 Dec 1843]

Mary Brown 11y 8m d/o Rev David THURSTON of dropsy on the brain at Winthrop ME on 18th ult [6 Feb 1835]

Peleg B abt 27 at Monmouth ME [4 Apr 1834]

Prudence G w/o Samuel THURSTON & d/o Ephraim GOODALE Esq of Orrington ME at Brewer ME on 19th inst [1 Jan 1839]

THURSTON - see BRADLEY

THWING James Rev 53 buried where several members of his family interred at China ME [27 Jul 1848]

TIBBETS Charles G 25 a native of Eastport ME at Tuscaloosa AL on 15th ult of bilious fever [17 Oct 1840]

Mary widow 100y 2m 2d at Newfield (ME?) on 17th inst [28 Dec 1833]

Nathaniel 75 at Belgrade ME on 6 Mar [21 Mar 1850]

Nicholas 73 at Palmyra ME [27 Jul 1848]

TIBBETS - see TEBBETS/TEBBETTS/TIBBETTS

TIBBETTS Benjamin 76 formerly of Vassalboro ME at Augusta ME on 4 June [29 June 1848]

Daniel R 1y 6m s/o William G TIBBETTS at Augusta ME on 21st Apr [25 Apr 1850]

Emery L 15m s/o William TIBBETTS at Augusta ME on 8 May [13 May 1852]

Ephraim 89 AmRev at Berwick ME [23 Jan 1851]

Ephraim Esq 50 at Belgrade ME on 22nd ult [4 Sept 1845]

girl d/o James TIBBETTS at Augusta ME [28 Jan 1847]

TIBBETTS (Cont.) Ichabod 91 formerly of Boothbay ME AmRev at Liberty ME [19 June 1841]

James abt 43 of Bath ME on Sun [*Bath Tribune*] [20 Jan 1848]

James S 18 at Bath ME [20 Jan 1848]

John 26 at Newfield ME? [22 Jul 1847]

John of Boothbay ME on Fri evening 30th ult fell from a wagon in Edgecomb near Wiscasset Bridge & dislocated his neck & died in 15 minutes. Mr T was riding with Mr William K COWING of Lisbon ME by whom he had been summoned to attend court as a witness. [*Bath Times*] [13 Jul 1848]

Juliett G S 4m 12d only c/o John A & Sarah J TIBBETTS of New Sharon ME at Augusta ME on 25th inst [30 Mar 1848]

Mr who belonged to Vassalboro ME jumped into the Kennebec River at Bath ME on the 11th inst and was drowned. Rum, says the *Telegraph*, was the cause of it. [23 Nov 1839]

Nathaniel 93 AmRev the 3rd settler in New Sharon ME on 22nd Sept [30 Oct 1845]

Samuel 42 formerly of Monmouth Me at Richmond ME [16 Dec 1852]

Thomas 22 of Woolwich ME at Waterville ME [20 Feb 1845]

Thomas 64 at Bath ME [16 May 1844]

TIBBETTS - see TEBBETS/TEBBBETTS

TIGHE Lucy Jane 55 w/o John TIGHE at Bath ME [16 Jul 1846]

Mary E 23 of Bath ME at Thomaston ME [27 Jan 1848]

TILDEN Charles 83 at Belfast ME [4 Dec 1851]

Martha 94 a widow at Bowdoin ME [18 Apr 1837]

Ruth B 49 at Belfast ME [31 Oct 1850]

Wales 94 AmRev at North Marshfield [7 Nov 1850]

TILLSON Eliza 46 w/o Emery TILLSON at Belgrade ME [11 Oct 1849]

Perez 88 a Deac at Thomaston ME [28 Cot 1852]

William F 50 at Rockland ME [25 Sept 1851]

TILTON Abigail 83y 2m at Norridgewock ME [25 Apr 1844]

Albert F formerly of Waterville ME at Franklkin IA on 26 Sept [31 Oct 1850]

John 48 at Biddeford ME [11 Mar 1852]

Josiah abt 46 at Monmouth ME on Mon last [15 Apr 1843]

Martha J 22 w/o Charles G TILTON at Belgrade ME [28 Jan 1847]

Mary 85 w/o Rev Nathan TILTON at Scarborough ME [21 Aug 1851]

Mrs 50 w/o Deac Tristram TILTON at Livermore ME [23 Oct 1845]

Samuel of Exeter NH his right arm cut off & horribly torn by a circular saw in the steam mill at Hampton on Mon of last week. [20 Nov 1851]

Sherburne 70 at Saco ME [1 May 1851]

William W abt 30 at Belgrade ME [21 Dec 1848]

TILYOU Peter V 91 AmRev at New York City on 4th inst [14 May 1846]

TIMES - see KILPATRICK

TINKER John Capt 83 of Ellsworth ME injured from a fall [23 Oct 1838]

John 91 at Ellsworth ME [22 Feb 1846]

TINKER - see ABBOTT, WASS

TINKHAM Achsah 53 w/o Deac Orin TINKHAM at Norridgewock ME suddenly [19 Aug 1847]

Amaziah F 32 at Newbury MA on 1 Feb [27 May 1852]

Ariel (early settler in Anson ME, coming from Middleboro MA, extended notice) [8 May 1838]

Ezekiel 83 at Strong ME [18 Dec 1845]

Maria A 26 d/o Amasa TINKHAM Esq at Monmouth ME on 16th ult [17 Feb 1848]

TINKHAM (Cont.) Silas Urbane 26 at Sidney ME on 14th inst [25 Apr 1844]
  Susan 53 w/o the late Arial TINKHAM at Anson ME [6 Aug 1846]
TINSLEY Mr of Woolford fatal railroad accident on the 10th ult on the Lexington & Ohio
  Railroad with Mr WILSON of Madison both were killed [*Louisville (KY) Advertiser*]
  [8 Apr 1836]
TINUM Joseph the postmaster of Kennebunk Depot of Kennebunkport ME in a fit of
  derangement cut his throat (from the *Argus*) [15 May 1851]
TIO Joseph 100y leaving 17 children, 108 granchildren, 77 great grand children at the
  neighborhood of Cornwall Upper Canada [29 May 1838]
TIRRELL William (son of the owner) & William FORD killed in a factory fire of Messrs W
  & O TIRELL (from *Boston Cultivator*) [1 Jan 1846]
TITCOMB Alphia 29 w/o Stephen TITCOMB at Farmington ME [4 Jan 1844]
  Beniah his dwelling house with his & his son's furniture of North Yarmouth ME was
  burnt last Sat (30th inst) [6 June 1840]
  Benjamin Rev 88 published the first paper in Maine - the *Portland Gazette* (sic, the name
  of the paper was the *Falmouth Gazette* in 1785, later named *Cumberland Gazette* &
  in 1785 he co-published & edited with Thomas WAITE) at Brunswick ME [12 Oct
  1848] & [2 Nov 1848]
  Elizabeth 21 w/o Joseph TITCOMB Jr & d/o Thomas WENDELL Jr Esq at Farmington
  ME [29 Mar 1849]
  Eunice 60 w/o William TITCOMB at York ME [3 Jan 1850]
  Everett 5 s/o Samuel TITCOMB Esq at Augusta ME on 9 Mar [20 Mar 1851]
  Joseph Esq 80 of an apoplectic fit at Portland ME on 20th inst [26 Aug 1836]
  Josiah H W abt 20 at Norridgewock ME [8 Feb 1849]
  Mary C 65 w/o Samuel Esq at Belgrade ME on 14th inst [27 Feb 1841]
  Mehitable 51y w/o Jos TITCOMB & d/o the late Supply BELCHER of Farmington ME
  [6 Mar 1838]
  Sarah 46 w/o Rodney TITCOMB at Paris ME [25 Jul 1850]
  Stephen 95 at Farmington ME [6 Jan 1848]
  William 75 at Falmouth ME [1 APr 1833]
  WIlliam Esq abt 50 register of deeds for Somerset Co at Norridgewock ME on 17 Mar
  [28 Mar 1850]
TITCOMB - see PERLEY
TITUS Bathasheba 80 w/o William TITUS at Monmouth ME on 4th inst [28 Jan 1833]
  Theodore his wife & son a lad about 14y on a visit to the husband at his mills, near the
  Lehigh in their own conveyance a truck car to Wilkes-Barre, the wife killed, husband
  bruised, lacerated, senseless & the son dangerously, if not mortally wounded [21 Jul
  1843]
  William 63rd yr of age formerly of Seekonk MA (formerly called Rehoboth, Bristol Co.)
  at Monmouth ME on 12 Apr [18 Apr 1834]
TOBEY Barnabas P abt 40 at Whitefield ME [5 Sept 1840]
  Benjamin 80 at Whitefield ME [15 Apr 1852]
  Charles abt 33 of North Fairhaven MA at Honolulu Sandwich Islands (Hawaii) on 2
  June, was formerly of the Sandwich Islands, but for the last three or four yrs resided
  in China & CA [7 Nov 1850]
  Eben S 22 s/o Nathaniel TOBEY of Jefferson ME at Marine Hospital in New Orleans on
  11th Apr [16 Oct 1845]
  Elizabeth 69 w/o Benjamin TOBEY at Whitefield ME [21 Mar 1850]
  Eunice 29 d/o Hymphus & Anna TOBEY at Vassalboro ME on 31 Dec 1849 [31 Jan
  1850]
  G W Mr death by "excessive drunkenness" on board the ship *Mentor* died suddenly from
  Boston MA at San Francisco on 9th Nov [3 Jan 1850]

TOBEY (Cont.) Hannah 56 w/o Nathaniel TOBEY at Jefferson ME [2 Aug 1849]

John 21 s/o Nathaniel TOBEY at Jefferson ME on 11 Apr [19 Apr 1849]

John 26 at Thomaston ME [19 Oct 1848]

Mary A 36 w/o Robert TOBEY at Fairfield ME [21 Aug 1851] & [7 Aug 1851]

Mary Mrs 89 formerly of Jefferson ME at Patricktown ME [15 Jan 1846]

Ploomy 52 w/o John TOBEY formerly of South Hampton NH at Vassalborough ME on the 23rd ult [11 June 1846]

Sarah Jane 40 w/o Harvey TOBEY at Hallowell ME on 28th inst [5 Jul 1849]

Thankful 90 at Whitefield ME [6 Jan 1848]

William 2d 25 at Norridgewock ME [18 May 1848]

TOBY Isaac Deac abt 96 AmRev at Hawley MA [7 Aug 1845]

Martha 80 at Farmington ME [25 Feb 1843]

TODD Charles S abt 24 formerly editor of the *NY Path-Finder* at Winthrop ME on 23 July [25 Jul 1850]

Elizabeth 65 at Waterville ME [26 Aug 1852]

Hannah Frances 10m d/o William L TODD at Hallowell ME on 7th inst [19 Dec 1837]

Lucy Mrs the only surving sister of Mrs MADISON, at Megerville at the residence of Mr Temple WASHINGTON, her son. She had married in early life George S WASHINGTON, nephew & one of the heirs of Gen WASHINGTON. After the death of WASHINGTON she married Thomas TODD of Kentucky one of the judges of the Supreme Court of the USA [12 Feb 1846]

Mary 45 at Augusta ME [23 Jan 1841]

Mercy 71 at Bath ME on 16 ult [15 APr 1843]

William L 25 of the firm of Sweetser & Todd of Hallowell ME at Augusta ME [13 Feb 1838]

TODD - see ABBOTT

TOLMAN Enoch H 50 to 60y of Greensborough VT on the last committed suicide by blowing out his brains, he was estimated to be worth $50,000. No cause is assigned for the act except he ws greatly troubled on account of being assessed as he thought too high by the town listers [*Portland Eastern Argus*] [7 May 1846]

John Nelson 10 s/o Jos TOLMAN at Camden ME [23 Apr 1842]

Josiah 71 at Rockland ME [2 Dec 1852]

TOLMAN - see OSBORN

TOLSEM Gilman M & his son, Morrill W TOLSEM both drowned in the Androscoggin River by the upsetting of a boat (from the *Coos Co (NH) Democrat*) on 14th Apr [9 May 1840]

TOMPKINS - see DIMMOCK

TOOMEY - see SMITH

TOOTHAKER Abigail 88 wid/o Gideon TOOTHAKER at Brunswick ME [24 Jul 1838]

Harriet 41 w/o David TOOTHAKER at Brunswick ME [1 Aug 1844]

J A of Maine at San Francisco CA [5 Feb 1852]

Seth 91 at Harpswell ME [10 Jan 1850]

TORRENS Leonard 29 of Webster (now Sabattus) ME at Stockton CA [18 Nov 1852]

TORRES Mr & all his family except one child. A letter from an officer of the US brig *Porpoise* dated at Teneriffe 4 Sept states "one fifth of the whole population of Palmas, a port in Gomera, one of the Canaries, which consisted of 18,000 in all, has been swept away by the plague. Amony the number is U. S. Consul, Mr TORRES & family" [6 Nov 1851]

TORREY Azubah 66 formerly of Bath ME at Portland ME [29 Apr 1833]

Charles T Rev died in prison at Baltimore MD [*NY Tribune*] [2 Apr 1846][23 Apr 1846]

TORREY (Cont.) girl abt 3y c/o Charles TORREY at Turner ME on 20 Feb of the canker-
rash [5 Mar 1842]
> Lydia 95y 4m at Plymouth ME on 1st inst a widow [14 May 1842]
> Perkins B 22 s/o Jas TORREY of Turner ME at Milo ME [31 Oct 1834]

TORRY Abigail 42 at Bath ME w/o William TORRY Esq [19 Dec 1834]
> Daniel 36 formerly of Williamston MA at Hallowell ME drowned [20 Sept 1849]
> James of Easton "frozen to death while intoxicated," so says the *Old Colony Reporter*, in
> the woods near Old Colony on Mon of last week [14 Feb 1850]

TORSEY child 2m of Mr Timothy TORSEY at Gardiner ME [20 May 1843]
> Samuel is hereby given, that for a valuable consideration, his father William TORSEY of
> Winthrop ME relinquished said son his time until he shall arrive at the age of 21 yrs
> .... notice dated 22 Jul 1840 [15 Aug 1840]

TOSIER John Esq abt 3y 6m of Corinth ME scalded by falling into a pail of boiling water as
to destroy his life in a few hours, a few days since. [28 Dec 1839]

TOTA - see BELSFORD

TOURNEY Dr one of the bodies recovered of the steamer *Atlantic* shipwreck [24 June
1847]

TOURO Judah a gentleman of New Orleans made a donation of two thousand dollars
towards the completion of the Bunker Hill Monument [13 Feb 1841]

TOWARD James Capt 76 formerly of Vienna ME at Freedom ME on 14 Feb [2 Mar 1848]

TOWARD - see DAVIS

TOWER Capt of ME listed in deaths in CA [23 Sept 1851]
> Issac Capt 29 master of the brig *M'Lellan* in Umpqua River, Oregon on 7 Jul [9 Oct
> 1851]
> Sarah 18m & 4d d/o Samuel & Margaret TOWER at Gardiner ME [18 Sept 1845]

TOWL Jemima Mrs 51 at Millford [18 Apr 1844]

TOWLE boy 10y s/o Robert TOWLE fell from a horse upon a flat rock in the road &
fractured his skull - forcing the broken piece in upon the brain so as to leave a deep
hollow over the place broken ... since when he has been more sensible but by no
means free from danger on the 3rd inst (from the *Gardiner Spectator*) [19 Feb 1842]
> James R 47 at Palmyra ME [20 Sept 1849]
> Mary Ann 36 w/o William H TOWLE at Monmouth ME on 16th ult [2 Jan 1851]
> Mary D 5m d/o Joshua TOWLE at Belfast ME [12 Feb 1846]
> Nancy a town pauper of Monmouth ME will not be supported by William H BOYNTON
> as she has run away on 12 Apr 1838 [8 May 1838]
> Phineas 20 at Buxton ME on 6th inst [11 Jul 1840]
> Ruth M 19 w/o Franklin TOWLE at Augusta ME [22 Feb 1849]
> Sally H B 53 w/o Ira TOWLE at Monmouth ME [25 Apr 1850]
> Sarah 86 wid/o Jenness TOWLE a native of Gilmanton NH at Winthrop ME [18 Mar
> 1852]
> widow abt 70 at Monmouth ME on Fri the 7th inst [15 Apr 1843]
> William M 26 at Augusta ME on 12 Jan [17 Jan 1850]

TOWN Jona G 26 at Norway ME [8 June 1848]

TOWNE child 22m the youngest of David TOWNE at Vassalboro ME [12 Dec 1840]
> Eli Esq 78 one of the 1st settlers of Dover ME? [4 Nov 1852]
> Jacob at Kennebunk ME [29 Apr 1836]

TOWNSEND Almira at Ellsworth [18 Nov 1852]
> David 66 formerly of Abbington MA at Belfast ME [9 Jul 1846]
> Dodovah 78 at Sidney ME on 2nd inst [16 Dec 1852]
> Elijah L his shop in Danville (near Goff's Cr, Auburn ME) consumed by fire together
> with its contents Thurs night the 12th inst [20 Mar 1835]

TOWNSEND (Cont.) Eunice 10m only c/o Asa S & Nancy C TOWNSEND at Sidney ME on 18 Sept [2 Oct 1851]

Francina 29 w/o Solomon TOWNSEND Jr of Turner ME at Greene ME on 11th May [17 May 1849]

Hannah L 37 at Paris ME [13 May 1852]

Hannah Livermore 37 at Paris ME [13 May 1852]

Jane 33 at Turner ME [19 Jul 1849]

John 81 at Auburn ME [14 June 1849]

Lucy Ann 29 d/o Luther TOWNSEND at Farmington ME [28 May 1846]

Luther 63 at Farmington ME [11 May 1848]

Manley B abt 45 s/o D TOWNSEND of Sidney ME & formerly president of the senate of Maine at Alexandria on 7th inst [20 Dec 1849]

Martha 21 at Buxton ME on 9th [1 Apr 1847]

Mrs abt 33 at Turner ME on 22 Sept [16 Oct 1841]

Mrs of Roxbury MA the steam packet *New England* sank. It left Boston for Bath & Gardiner ME and had an accident with the schr *Curlew* on 31 May [12 June 1838]

Nathaniel 53 at Buxton ME on the 11th [1 Apr 1847]

Piam 80 at Carratunk ME [8 Mar 1849]

Reuel B 18m s/o Reuel TOWNSEND at Augusta ME [24 Aug 1848]

Ruth 47 at Buxton ME on 7th inst [1 Apr 1847]

Sarah 69 at Belfast ME [6 June 1850]

Tryphena 70 w/o Dr Amos TOWNSEND at Norridgewock ME [23 Oct 1851]

William 10y s/o Nathaniel & Ruth TOWNSEND at Buxton ME on 23 ult [1 Apr 1847]

TOZER Amos 19 of Waterville ME drowned [7 Oct 1843]

TOZIER Adeline A 3y & 2m d/o Benjamin F & Sibyl L TOZIER at Augusta ME on 27th ult [2 May 1850]

Franklin 41 at Waterville ME [23 May 1850]

Mary M 21 of Brighton ME at Waterville ME [7 Dec 1848]

Phebe 59 w/o Simeon TOZIER at Waterville ME [13 Sept 1849]

TRACY David 43 at Farmington ME [26 June 1845]

Elizabeth J 26 of Farmington ME at Lewiston ME [30 Nov 1848]

James drowned when between Fort Independence & Thompson's Island with a party of 27 of the boys of the Farm School on Thompson's Island accompanied by a teacher & boat-keeper [7 May 1842]

Judge a native of CT died at Macon GA on 21st ult [8 Mar 1849]

Levi W 7y s/o Solomon TRACY at Rome ME [3 Dec 1846]

Lydia w/o Elder Jonathan TRACY at Auburn ME [16 May 1844]

Mary Elizabeth 25 only d/o Wheeler TRACY at Peru ME on 15 Apr [25 Apr 1850]

TRACY - see MORGAN

TRAFTON Eliza 28 w/o Gen Mark TRAFTON at Bangor ME [16 Dec 1843]

Rufus 36 at Kingsbery [7 Oct 1847]

TRANTHAM Betsey Mrs died 10 Jan 1834 at Maury Co TN at the advanced age of 154y, born in Germany and emigrated to the British Colonies in America, at the time of the 1st settlement made in North Carolina in the years 1710. [4 Apr 1834] & 154 the oldest person we have any record of, who died in this country in 1834 in TN [19 Feb 1846]

TRASH/TRASK see LRASH

TRASK Ann 38 at Bath ME [11 Mar 1836]

Caroline L 28 w/o K B TRASK at Gardiner ME [5 Aug 1852]

Eunice D 26 at New Castle ME? [11 Nov 1852]

Joseph of Hallowell ME mate of the schr *Somerset* fell overboard on Sun last near the John Marshall wharf [*Hallowell Cultivator*] [2 Oct 1845]

TRASK (Cont.) Mary E 23y 7m w/o Lyman TRASK at Belgrade ME on 4 Aug [18 Sept 1851]

Naomi w/o Ebenezer TRASK Jr at Belgrade ME [24 Dec 1846]

Thomas J abt 45 at Hallowell ME [4 Apr 1850]

TRACY boy Esq abt 17y of Corinth ME by a thrashing machine amputate both his legs above the knees s/o Philbrook B TRACY Esq (from the Bangor Jeffersonian in ME) [11 Dec 1851]

TREAT Bethiah 29 w/o Washington TREAT at Canton ME [26 Sept 1850]

Harriet 45 at Frankfort ME [30 Apr 1842]

Robert, master of the schr *Pensacola*, Capt BLACK, was missing, found on Sun by grappling in the bed of the stream [*Bangor Whig*][10 June 1847]

Rosanna 53 w/o John TREAT at Enfield ME on the 17th inst of erysipelas [2 Jul 1842]

Rufus 22 at Franfort ME [29 Nov 1849]

TREAT - PATTEN

TREFEATHEREN Hanover of Cornville ME his house blown down a few days since. Mrs T escaped to the trees, & a daughter barely escaped with life by throwing herself from an upper window [3 Feb 1848]

TREFETHEN Mr 72y of Kennebunkport ME at Kennebunk ME accidental [*Boston Bee*] [21 Nov 1844]

TRENCH Mercy 93 at Norridgewock ME [26 Apr 1849]

TREVETT Charles T 4y s/o Teodore S TREVETT at Bath ME [27 Feb 1845]

TREVITT Ruth Ann 25 at Bath ME [18 June 1846]

TRICKEY Elizabeth 65 w/o William TRICKEY of Saco ME at Biddeford ME [29 Mar 1849]

TRIMBLE Mr reported died of sickness near Augusta GA & one negro in the country and the number of new cases are diminishing [16 Nov 1839]

Mrs wid/o John TRIMBLE was appointed as clerk of the Carter circuit in the place of her deceased husband by Judge KINHEAD [*Frankfort (KY) Commonwealth*] [18 June 1846]

TRINIMAN Mrs w/o Capt Robert T & his two daus, she sis/o Miss Maria HALE & Mrs MANITON a boat on the morning of 2d inst having on board 25 persons struck upon "Hunt's Rock" 19 persons including children drowned [*Portland Adv*] [*The St Johns City Gazette* of the 2d Aug] [14 Aug 1838]

TRIPP Elonia 40 w/o Benjamin TRIPP at Searsport ME [11 Nov 1852]

George W 22 at Searsmont ME [23 Jul 1846]

John Rev 86y senior pastor of the Baptist Church at Hebron ME [30 Sept 1847]

John while cutting wood his axe glanced & made wound on the outside of his leg abt two inches long. which caused his death in about three quarters of an hour, supposed by the loss of blood [14 Feb 1837]

Shubael Rev pastor of the Baptist Church at Kennebunk ME [16 May 1837]

TRISTAM Mrs & her child both burnt to death in a house fire on Hobb's Wharf, Broad St, formerly Sea Street [*Boston Bulletin*] [4 Dec 1835]

TRITON Richard of crew shipwreck & four lives lost on the schr *Cevo*, Capt Pelatiah BARTER [25 May 1839]

TRIVETT S Esq his large barn consumed at Frankfort ME on Mon last [1 Oct 1842]

TROTT Esther S 47 at Woolwich ME [7 Jan 1847]

Hannah 80 at Woolwich ME [7 Jan 1847]

James P 41 at Bath ME [7 Sep 1848]

Mary L 25 at Bath ME [29 Jul 1843]

Mehitable Mrs 64 at Woolwich ME on 18th ult [7 Oct 1847]

Sarah 77 at Old Town ME [28 Feb 1850]

TROUANT Elizabeth 20 d/o Samuel TROUANT at Windsor ME [19 Aug 1852]

TROUTMAN Corporal & three others names unknown killed in the Irish & Native American (not American Indians more likely English born in American) Riots in Philadelphia PA [*Dollar Newspaper*] [18 July 1844]

TRUE Aaron 79 at Litchfield ME [2 May 1837]

Asaph 27 at the late fire while passing through the flames to make his escape burnt to cause his death after about twenty hrs of suffering & pain [12 Aug 1847]

Charles S 25 at Sangerville ME [10 Aug 1848]

Ezekiel 87 at Montville ME [28 Aug 1842]

Ezra 83 at Deerfield [6 Nov 1835]

Hannah Elizabeth 22 d/o Major Abner TRUE at Houlton ME on 2 Oct [24 Oct 1850]

Irene 30 deaf & dumb (mute) d/o the late Aaron TRUE at Litchfield ME on 5th ult [16 Nov 1839]

Jeremiah P 34 late assistant engineer on the Western Rail Road an employment in which he was engaged from the commencement of that public work to its close at North Turner ME on 7th ult [11 Mar 1843]

John K 32 formerly of Montville ME at Mt Vernon OH [2 Sept 1847]

Martha 70 w/o Aaron TRUE at Litchfield ME on 19 Apr [2 May 1837]

Martha Avilla 5 only children of Dr James S TRUE at New Sharon ME [25 Feb 1847]

Martha S 31 w/o Otis TRUE Esq at Norway ME [14 Oct 1852]

Mary B 33 w/o John TRUE Esq at Bangor ME [20 Feb 1845]

Mary J 26 w/o Justin TRUE at Litchfield ME [7 Dec 1839]

Nancy 31 w/o Col A M TRUE at Lincoln ME [19 Nov 1842]

Ruth Ann 37 w/o Dr N T TRUE at Bethel ME [5 Apr 1849]

Sarah C 17 d/o Capt Jonathan TRUE at New Gloucester ME of consumption [11 Jan 1840]

Sherburne a carpenter fell into a cistern of hot water in a distillery in Rochester and was scalded to death [11 June 1840]

William of Covington Wyoming Co NY went out on Sun the 25th ult to drive a stake to support the fence, his wife held the stake while he stood upon the fence & aimed a blow at the stake, when his foot slipped & the axe fell with full force upon her head killing her instantly [6 Nov 1851]

TRUFAND Joshua 43 at Winthrop ME on Tues last [31 Oct 1840]

TRUFANT Abigail 77 wid/o Joshua TRUFANT formerly of Bath ME (Bath ME papers please copy) at Winthrop ME [12 Feb 1852]

child of Allen L TRUFANT 7m at Winthrop ME on Tues morning last [27 Jan 1837]

David 74 formerly of Bath ME at Danville (Now part of Auburn ME) on 28th ult [15 Jan 1842]

Joshua 43 at Winthrop ME on Tues last [31 Oct 1840]

Levi a native of Bath ME at Cocho, coast of Africa on 29 Sept 1843 [1 Aug 1844]

Marcia Allen 20 youngest c/o Allen TRUFANT at Winthrop ME on the 27th inst [2 Sept 1842]

Sarah 81 w/o the late David TRUFANT formerly of Bath ME at Lewiston ME [2 Jul 1846]

Sarah F 42 w/o Gilbert C TRUFANT at Bath ME [8 Apr 1852]

Susan S 27 at Winthrop ME [12 Aug 1847]

TRULL Sarah 72 at Sweden ME [22 Nov 1849]

TRULL - see McLAUGHLIN

TRUMBULL Earl accidentally killed of Little Falls NY [20 Feb 1851]

John Col 87 yrs resided until recently at New Haven CT our first great painter and an aide to Gen WASHINGTON New York [18 Nov 1843]

TRUNDAY Mary d/o William TRUNDAY of Wiscasset ME badly burnt on Thurs of last week by her clothes taking fire from the stove, she is not expected to recover [1 Jan 1842]

TRUNDY R F of Damariscotta ME 1st officer lost overboard from bark *Santee* on passage from Boston MA to Mobile AL [22 Feb 1849]

TRYON girl 9 of Glastenbury CT d/o Harvey TRYON accidentally shot by her brother 11 [10 Feb 1848]

Simeon abt 66 at Pownal ME [29 Aug 1844]

TUBBS Alonzo 42 at Hebron ME [21 June 1849]

Charles 67 at Norway ME [26 Jul 1849]

Hannah 17 d/o Charles TUBBS being the 3rd dau Mr T has lost within the space of six months of consumption at Norway Village ME on the 31st ult [10 Sept 1842]

Lydia 61 w/o Charles TUBBS at Norway ME [28 Jan 1847]

TUCK Jacob 27 at Phillips ME [20 Mar 1851]

John Esq 63 at Parsonsfield ME [6 May 1847]

Samuel Esq 75 formerly of Rockingham Co NH at Fayette ME on the 8th of July [29 Sept 1840]

TUCKER Benjamin 67 at Thomaston ME [8 Oct 1846]

boy was drowned in the Cobbossee Stream near Woollen Factory on the 8th inst. He was the s/o Col I N TUCKER (copied from the *Fountain*) [18 Mar 1847]

Eunice 63 w/o George TUCKER at Standish ME [6 Nov 1835]

Frederick of Eastport MA on 2d mate lost overboard from brig *Tarar* on 8th inst on the passage from Mobile to Boston MA [27 Jul 1848]

Henry 44 at Raymond NH on 23 June [23 Aug 1849]

John L of Standish ME on 28th Sat last [*Argus*] [9 Aug 1849]

Mr the colored barber of Centre street to remove the beard of BABE, the pirate, who was sentenced to be hung on the 7th next month, but he refused to shave the BABE (see story) [*New York Herald*] [14 Mar 1844]

Mrs w/o Mason T of Bangor ME, with her paramour, left taking (Mr T's) money, clothing &c offers $20 for information concerning her wherabouts, she is a small woman, cross eyed in her left eye & abt 32, to be sent to Mr Albert G HUNT of Bangor ME or the city Marshall of Boston MA. Papers will confer a favor by copying the above [*Bee*] [2 Dec 1847]

Nancy B 27 at Winthrop ME [28 Mar 1850]

Nason Capt 25 at Harpswell harbor drowned [28 Nov 1850]

Samuel 86 of Bremen ME on Sun last, next to LaFAYETTE, Commodore TUCKER was the highest surviving officer of the AmRev at the time of his death [*Christian Intelligencer*] [25 Mar 1833]

TUCKER - see BARBER, ROLERSON

TUCKERMAN Stephen 51 formerly of Boston MA at Norridgewock ME [11 Mar 1833]

TUELL Gilman was crossing a bridge in the North part of Paris ME on Sun last, in a wagon containing his sister & a child, the horse became frightened & threw him, wagon & riders off the end of the bridge ... he had his leg broken & Miss TUELL had her jaw bone broken & dislocated her frount teeth knocked out The child is thought not to recover [15 Oct 1842]

TUFTS Mary 79 wid/o of Francis TUFTS at Farmington ME [24 Apr 1851]

Pamalia Mrs 72 at Belfast ME [15 Apr 1852]

Peter P while walking with an axe on his shoulder stepped on some ice & fell, the axe cut off two fingers & badly injured the third [*Farmington Chronicle*] [22 Mar 1849]

Simeon 74 at Limerick ME [19 Mar 1846]

TUKESBURY Isaac of Belfast ME, 1st officer on board brig *Watchman* on passage from Wilmington to Boston MA [8 Nov 1849]

TUPPER Cordelia H 21 at Bangor ME on 2nd inst [9 Nov 1833]

Lydia M 35 w/o Holmes TUPPER Esq at Hallowell ME [4 Apr 1850]

TURLEY Judge of Memphis TN from a fall onto his broken cane [10 Jul 1851]

TURNBULL Robert J one of the leading orators & writers of Nullification Party at Charleston SC [29 Jul 1833]

TURNBULL - see HASEITH

TURNER Adam 70 at Paris ME [25 May 1839]

Albion E eld c/o Charles H and Lucy A TURNER in Mt Vernon at Wings Mills on Aug 19 [26 Aug 1852]

Alvin P 2y 6m s/o Elijah TURNER at Augusta ME [23 Aug 1849]

Betsey w/o Capt Robinson TURNER at Peru ME [18 Mar 1852]

boy 3y s/o Dwelly TURNER at Bath ME drowned [24 June 1847]

Briggs A 22 late of North Whitefield ME in Umpqua River, Oregon on 7 Jul [9 Oct 1851]

C R 19 w/o W G TURNER on 14th ult [7 Oct 1836]

Charles Jr 20 s/o Charles TURNER of Augusta ME at Sumner on 24 Feb [4 Mar 1852]

Cornelius Capt 96 at Wiscasset ME at the residence of his son [22 May 1838]

Cornelius 75 at Wiscasset ME [4 May 1848]

Eliza abt 35 at Miltown (Calais) ME [17 Apr 1835]

George C 9m s/o Charles & Eliza TURNER at Augusta ME [12 Aug 1852]

Harriet Ellis 28 w/o Benjamin F TURNER of Lowell MA at Mercer ME on 26th ult [13 May 1847]

Henry 6y s/o Dwelley TURNER at Bath ME drowned [14 Mar 1840]

Henry S 20 at Augusta ME [28 Nov 1834]

Joseph of Ellsworth ME at San Francisco CA [8 Jan 1852]

Julia Ann 16 at Whitefield ME [26 Mar 1835]

L Frederick 4y 5m s/o Joshua S TURNER at Augusta ME [18 Mar 1847]

Lot "his rib in Vermont advertises him as a DRUNKARD BRUTE & a VAGABOND. We reckon Lot wishes she was a pillar of salt" [27 Apr 1839]

Lucinda 32y w/o Charles TURNER at Bloomfield ME [11 Nov 1852]

Lucius C 24 at Leeds ME [31 Oct 1840]

Lydia 63 w/o Capt Asa TURNER at Brighton ME [19 Dec 1840]

Melintha B 18 d/o Charles TURNER at Augusta ME on 28 Jan 1852 [5 Feb 1852]

Minerva Arnold 16 d/o Gilman TURNER Esq at Augusta ME [27 Apr 1848]

Oliver (b 1764 Pembrooke MA) AmRev a pensioner at Sumner ME [6 May 1843]

Otis 26 from Maine drowned on the New Year's night at the foot of Jay St Brooklyn NY [30 Jan 1841]

Phillips 38 Deputy Sheriff at Leeds ME [21 Mar 1844]

Ruth 72 w/o Eph TURNER at Livermore ME [2 Jan 1851]

Samuel B 47 of Whitefield ME at San Francisco CA on 14 Sept [18 Nov 1852]

Sarah 76 wid/o Capt Simeon TURNER at Bath ME [11 Mar 1836]

Susan 55 w/o Nehemiah TURNER at Palermo ME [3 Aug 1839]

Thomas abt 35 of Typhus fever at Turner ME on 4 Nov [10 Dec 1842]

William a ship carpenter at work in the ship yard, head of the Railway wharf, (Fore St) in Portland ME was critically injured on Sat [*Portland Argus*] [5 Apr 1849]

TURNER - see JENNESS, LOMBARD

TURRILL Stephen 101y 4m at the of 15 he joined the army under Gen ABERCROMBIE, was at White Plains, Valley Forge, Monmouth, & Saratoga, a member of the Methodist Church during 78y of his life at Charlotte VT [4 Apr 1844]

TUTTLE Appleton R 11m c/o Jacob & Hannah M TUTTLE at Plymouth NH on 22 May [29 May 1851]

Esther 21? or 23? w/o Moses C TUTTLE at Smithfield ME [10 June 1852]

Frances 28 w/o Joseph TUTTLE at Buckfield ME [14 Mar 1850]

Hiram Esq 52 at Canaan ME on 22d Jan [7 Feb 1850]

Leonder 19 c/o Jacob & Hannah M TUTTLE at Plymouth NH on 30 May [29 May 1851]

Paul 43 at Fairfield ME [17 Oct 1850]

Samuel Esq 94 at Miltown St Stephen New Brunswick Canada [29 May 1845]

TWAMBLEY Palmer A 19 at Saco ME [4 Apr 1850]

TWAMBLY Isaac 52 at Dover ME? [20 Jan 1848]

TWIGG Robert after skinning a cow, supposed died from the effects of poison (from the *Baltimore Sun*) [16 Sept 1843]

TWITCHELL child of Daniel TWITCHELL at Augusta ME [8 Apr 1833]

Eli Esq 88 AmRev at Bethel [20 Nov 1845]

Levi 34 at Paris ME 2d inst very suddenly of the influenza [19 Mar 1842]

Simon abt 73 at Bethel ME on 4th inst [23 May 1844]

TWOMBLY Mary 40 at Farmington ME [4 May 1839]

TYLER David 30 s/o Abraham TYLER of Saco ME drowned on the Penobscot River [16 Apr 1846]

Ellen Moor 15 d/o Isaac TYLER Esq at Weld ME [17 Aug 1848]

Frederick 28 at Dixmont ME [22 Jul 1836]

John father of President TYLER, succeeded Benjamin HARRISON, father of the late President HARRISON, in 1781, as speaker of the Virginia house of delegates. John TYLER, the son the former Speaker TYLER, succeeds William H HARRISON s/o Benjamin HARRISON as President of the USA [1 May 1841]

John Franklin FLYE, Putnam SIMONTON, & Mr DUNCAN. On Sun last 6 young men, about the age of 23 took a boat at Camden harbor to go to French's beach, Lincolnville, where a vessel lay to which some of them belonged. 4 drowned & 2 were saved. The 2 saved were George HODGMAN & a brother of the Mr DUNCAN drowned. [*Belfast Journal*] [20 Apr 1848]

Mary abt 18y at Winthrop ME [22 Oct 1842]

Mary E 19 eldest d/o Isaac TYLER Esq at Weld ME [15 Jul 1847]

Mrs the 1st lady at Washington 52d yr d/o Robert CHRISTIAN of the Co of New York, VA. She was born 13 Nov 1790 & married 29 Mar 1813, a Protestant Episcopal [24 Sept 1842]

Urany Bates 19 d/o Aaron TYLER late of Bath ME at Griggsville IL [2 May 1837]

TYLER - see WOODBURY

TYRILL Judge at Schroon Lake died while speaking at a Free Soil meeting [*Albany Argus*] [28 Sept 1848]

- U -

ULMER Capt an enterprising & active young man. The schr Potomac lost, belonged to East Thomaston ME capsized on Sun afternoon on the 2nd inst in Long Island Sound, opposite Smithtown and all on board perished. [1 Jan 1839]

child 2y c/o Asa ULMER, falling into a tub of hot soap & scalded [5 Feb 1836]

Eliza Mrs 52 at Rockland ME [16 Jan 1851]

Harrison 36 at Rockland ME [7 Nov 1850]

Philip 60 at Thomaston ME [25 Sept 1845]

ULMER - see BUTLER

UMINISKI General at Wiesbaden on 16th of June in the late Polish Revolution [17 Jul 1851]

UNDERHILL Nancy J Miss a devoted teacher washed away by a wave at Isles of Shoals NH [*Cor Portsmouth Journal*] [28 Sept 1848]

UNDERWOOD Joseph H Jr 28 at Fayette ME [20 Feb 1845]
Thomas P 32 s/o Hon Joseph H UNDERWOOD at Fayette ME [5 Feb 1852]
Willaim F of Hallowell ME at sea [16 Dec 1852]

UPHAM Charles A 5m s/o Abijah UPHAM at Readfield ME on 13 Nov [23 Dec 1852] child ae 1y smothered, his father keeps a confectionary shop near the foot of Winthrop Street in (Hallowell) ME [*Hallowell Cult*] [2 Nov 1848]
Gardner 35 at Bristol [20 Nov 1845]
Joanna 22 w/o WIlliam UPHAM at Hallowell ME [24 Aug 1848]
Mary E 9y 11m d/o Abijah UPHAM at Readfield ME on 15 Dec [23 Dec 1852]
William 25 of Maine at Sacramento CA [29 Jul 1852]
William A 31 of Portsmouth NH s/o Gen Timothy UPHAM on 25th ult [19 Aug 1843]

UPSHUR A P Secretary of State T W GILMER, Secretary of the Navy; Virgil MAXCY, late Charge de Affairs to Belgium; Commodore B KENNON & Col Gardiner all passed along the Avenue in hearses, victims of the *Princeton* Calamity [*Washington Capitol*] [14 Mar 1844]

UPSON Marcus of Wolcott CT at San Francisco CA [8 Jan 1852]

UPTON Julia 29 w/o Rufus UPTON of Dixfield ME at Greene ME [17 Jan 1850]
Maria H w/o Rufus P UPTON at St Anthony Minnesota Territory on 3 Nov [23 Dec 1852]
Rachel 80 at Frankfort ME [27 Aug 1846]

URRIOLA Col killed in late revolt in Chili [*Valparaiso Reporter*][19 June 1851]

USHER Abijah 53 at Hollis ME [21 Feb 1841]
Benjamin 10 s/o Samuel USHER of Kingfield ME at Kingfield ME drowned on 21 Oct [30 Oct 1851]
Cyrus K 26 second s/o the late Hon Abijah USHER at Hollis on 10th inst [2 Apr 1842]
Thomas 16 s/o Samuel USHER of Kingfield ME at Kingfield ME drowned on 21 Oct [30 Oct 1851]

- V -

VABSTON Samuel 20 of Thomaston ME at Mobile AL on 1st Nov [18 Jan 1840]

VALE Mr & CASS & YOUNG, three trappers in the vicinity of Morcon River, 1st fire of the Indians, YOUNG shot through the head, VALE & CASS returned the fire & three Indians fell. Vale's relatives reside in Milwaukie. One of the two was buried by the Indians with the name of Eagle Brave. [4 Oct 1849]

VALENTINE Dexter 47 formerly of Westbrook ME at Harmony ME [13 Nov 1851]
Elizabeth F 31 w/o Col Samuel L VALENTINE at Bangor ME [27 May 1833]
Jane one of the last of the Mohegans, charged with drunkenness [18 Mar 1833]
William Major 72 at Saccarappa ME [1 May 1845]

Van BUREN Jane 58 sis/o U. S. president at Kinderhook NY on 10th ult [10 Jul 1838]

VAN BUREN - see GEORGE

Van EVERA Mrs of Canajoharie NY the Lord had spoken to her & commanded her never to eat or drink more, after lingering for fifteen days she died. [24 Aug 1839]

Van HOEZER John 114 of Sullivan Co TN during the last election in that state walked half a mile to vote. He has voted at every presidential election in the United States & means to live as long as he can see anybody alive [16 Sept 1847]

VAN HOOSEN John his house at Farmington MI burnt on 17th ult with his 5 ch perishing in the flames. The father barely escaped being very seriously burnt. Their mother was absent. [20 Mar 1838]

Van HOUTUN - see WICKLIFFE

Van NESS Major of Fort Preble died suddenly [*Portland ME Argus*, 15th] [22 Feb 1849]
 Mrs w/o our Minister at Madrid Spain of chlera on 18 Jul [12 Sept 1834]

Van RESSALAER - see SCHUYLER

Van VORST John born 19 Jan 1740-41, died at Glenville, Schenectady Co on 22d May [*Schenectady Cabnit*] [13 June 1844]

Van WERT - see BALCH

VANCE Elizabeth 40 strangled to death on Tues evening by a piece of meat [*Boston Traveller*] [24 Feb 1848]

Van GORP Peerken the largest man of Europe taken sick at Amsterdam carried to Turnbout, died on the 5th inst 32y 8 ft high. (see also Belgian paper) [*Antwerpt Journal* of the 7th of Sept] [15 Oct 1842]

VANNAH Catharine Mrs 82 at Waldoboro ME [13 May 1843]

VANNAH - see SPEAR

VANSITTART Admiral preceded his family to his new location at Upper Canada at Saratoga Springs [25 Jul 1834]

VANSTON Samuel 20 of Thomaston ME at Mobile AL on 1 Nov [18 Jan 1840]

VANSTONE Melinda 18 at East Thomaston ME [5 Feb 1846]

VARELLA - see DOYLE

VARNEY Mary 53 w/o Enoch VARNEY at Brunswick ME [25 Jan 1849]
 Eliphalet 72 at Bloomfield ME on the 20th inst very suddenly [1 Feb 1840]
 Elizabeth only d/o Wentworth VARNEY after a very short illness with the hooping cough & lung fever at Clinton ME [5 Oct 1839]
 George only s/o Wentworth VARNEY after a very short illness with the hooping cough & lung fever [5 Oct 1839]
 Hatherly 40 at Levant ME [21 Aug 1851]
 Nicholas 70 at Brunswick ME [28 Oct 1843]
 Remington H at Vassalboro ME on 26th Aug [5 Sept 1850]
 Warren P 23 of Bloomfield ME at Orono ME [29 June 1848]

VARNUM Cyrus 42 at Augusta ME [9 Mar 1848]
 Mehitable Mrs d/o Damuel HARVEY at Winthrop ME [20 Mar 1835]
 Mr who recently from New York, now in Bowdoinham ME with the smallpox [*Brunswick Regulator*] [20 May 1836]

VARRICK Ann on the body of hers the inquest on Tues, age abt 70y. Verdict of the jury - death by the visitation of God at Albany NY [23 Nov 1839]

VARSE Mrs similar to the act perpetrated upon Mrs BURDICK, at Greene NY. VARSE married abt a year or two & her husband was suspected in the case of Mrs BURDICK. She had been out near the creek to rest near the mill pond, when two men came up behind her, blindfolded her, tied her hands & then threw her into the pond - The woman was got out alive; who the perpetrators are is a mystery. [*Boston Journal*] [30 Oct 1845]

VASSAL - see WEBSTER

VAUGHAN Benjamin 85 greatly respected through life by all who know him, a member of the British Parliament & a friend of Dr FRANKLIN at Hallowell ME [18 Dec 1835]
 Charles Esq with his brother the late Dr V, of the family among the first settlers of Hallowell ME. In 1792, he & his brother imported some of the best cattle that could be found in England. Later turned his attention to the breeding of sheep at Hallowell ME [1 June 1839] & ae 87 on Wed last [18 May 1839]

VAUGHAN (Cont.) Ellen Stephania 13m d/o Daniel D & Martha R VAUGHAN at Foxcroft ME [20 Mar 1845]

Emily Abbot 2m d/o Charles VAUGHAN Jr at Hallowell ME on Thurs morning the 19 inst [1 May 1838]

Emma Gardiner 8y 6m only d/o William M VAUGHAN at Hallowell ME [14 Mar 1844]

Frances Western 68 w/o Charles VAUGHAN Esq at Hallowell ME [2 Sept 1836]

Joseph 75 at Union ME [16 Oct 1851]

Mary 28 w/o William C VAUGHAN at Elliotsville on the 29th ult [2 Jan 1841]

Sarah B 68 w/o Eben Vaughan at Norridgewock ME [7 Oct 1852]

William 98 at London England bro/o late Benjamin VAUGHAN of Hallowell ME [13 June 1850]

William T Esq abt 65 at Portland ME [22 May 1845]

VAUGHAN - see ABBOTT, THOMAS

VAUX Robert philanthropist of the Society of Friends at Philadelphia PA on 7 Jan 1836 [13 Jan 1837]

VEAZEY Elizabeth 51 w/o Joshua VEAZEY at Calais ME [27 Jul 1848]

VEAZIE Darius 4 at Vienna ME [21 Mar 1844]

George 28 a native of Maine at New Orleans [19 Apr 1849]

J H 42 at Limington ME [17 Feb 1848]

Jason 21 at Camden ME by lightning [15 Aug 1834]

Jerusha abt 22 at Madison ME [17 Jul 1851]

Lydia 35 at Corinna ME very suddenly [10 Aug 1839]

Susan W 60 w/o Gen Samuel VEAZIE at Bangor ME [15 Jul 1852]

VENDERMAKER Rachel 20 married only three weeks cut her throat with a razor on 29th ult [*Saratoga Sentinel*] [10 Feb 1848]

VERNEY Joseph Capt 39 of Pittston ME he was mate of ship *William* at Calcutta on 3 Oct [11 Dec 1851]

VERNEY Susan M 21 6m w/o Levi B VERNEY at Augusta ME on 18 Jan [24 Jan 1850]

VERRILL Aurelia P 26 w/o Davis VERRILL & only c/o Richard D DOWNING at Minot ME [14 Mar 1837]

Elizabeth 31 w/o Davis E VERRILL at Lewiston ME [30 May 1850]

Kimball F Capt 28 at Minot ME [1 June 1848]

William Capt 24 of Camden ME at New Orleans [7 Nov 1837]

VERY Eliza A d/o Mr E C STODDER formerly of Salem at Readfield ME [30 Sept 1843]

VICKERS John Capt, keeper of a public house in McCLELLAN's alley was blown into the air & fell on the wharf. Another death on the *Medora*, Capt SUTTON [23 Apr 1842]

Lyman 2y 9m s/o Joseph & Susan VICKERS at Norridgewock ME on the 18th inst [2 Oct 1845]

VICKERY Matthias Deac 71 at Danville (now Auburn) ME [24 Aug 1848]

VILES Judah 41 w/o Wentworth VILES at Starks ME [8 Jan 1846]

VINAL Joseph 49 at Waldoboro ME [3 Jul 1835]

VINCENT John 86 married Mary BODMAN 82 at Dilton Chapelry England on Mon the 11th inst [11 Sept 1841]

Mrs of Edgartown MA w/o Peter M VINCENT accidentally burnt on Sat 15th inst not likely to recover [27 Mar 1845]

Nicholas 75 chief of the Huron tribe of Indians settled at Lorette, was one of four chiefs who visited England in 1825 & received from George IV, a large silver gift medal [*The Quebec Mercury* of the 5th] [21 Nov 1844]

VINCIENT - WILLIAM

VINEY Warren 39 born in Wiscasset ME at the Marine Hospital in Chelsea MA [14 Jan 1847]

VINING Charles Albert 6 s/o Jeremiah & Susan N VINING at Palermo ME on 2 June of scarlet fever & canker rash [7 June 1849]

David 51 of Strong ME at Readfield ME [19 Aug 1852]

VINSON James of Londonderry Nova Scotia Canada drowned in Lower Steam Mill at Bath ME [26 June 1851]

VINTON Orinda H 34 w/o Rev John A VINTON of Chatham formerly of New Sharon ME at East Bridgewater [28 Aug 1838]

VIRGIN Joseph B abt 22 s/o Eben VIRGIN at Rumford ME of consumption [30 Nov 1839]

VIVIAN Charles Henry 5y 6m s/o William H & Caroline L VIVIAN at Augusta ME on 14 Apr [1 May 1851]

VIVIN child of William VIVIN at Augusta ME on 23rd May [30 May 1850]

Ellah P 2 d/o William at Augusta ME on 18 May [23 May 1850]

VOSE Capt of the brig *Circassian* of Thomaston ME at New Orleans on 23d ult [20 June 1840]

Caroline G wid/o Robert C VOSE Esq of (Augusta) ME. Thurs afternoon while riding with her eldest dau in a one-horse four-wheeled carriage towards Gardiner ME, the carriage turned over. The daughter escaped without much injury but the mother struck upon her head and died after 48 hours. She was 38y (from the *Kennebec Journal* of Augusta ME) [12 Oct 1839]

Caroline S 38 widow of the late Robert C VOSE of Augusta ME at Augusta ME [12 Oct 1839]

David 77 at Hampden ME [19 Jul 1849]

David Deac 71 at Hampden ME [2 Aug 1849]

Edward abt 19 of Thomaston ME at the Marine Hospital on Staten Island [8 Feb 1844]

Elijah 78 at Warren ME [9 May 1840]

Josiah Col 61 formerly a resident of Augusta ME at the U. S. Barracks below New Orleans [7 Aug 1845]

Lucy H 21 at Castine ME [14 Nov 1844]

Mary B 44 of Augusta ME wid/o Gen Rufus C VOSE at Boothbay ME on 27 June [1 Jul 1852]

Nancy J 23 w/o Edwin VOSE at Montville ME [21 Sept 1848]

Peter Thatcher Esq 81 formerly a distinguished merchant of (Augusta ME) at Lancaster MA on 5 Mar [20 Mar 1851]

Robert C Esq 53 at Augusta ME [15 Jul 1836]

Rufus Chandler Gen 44 at Augusta ME on Sun last [28 Aug 1842]

Steven drowned when between Fort Indepance & Thompson's Island with a party of 27 of the boys of the Farm School on Thompson's Island accompanied by a teacher & boat-keeper [7 May 1842]

Thomas Hon 85 at Robbinston ME [7 Dec 1848]

- W -

WADE Abigail 63 w/o Levi WADE at Norridgewock ME [21 Oct 1852]

Albert 14 at Norridgewock ME [22 Jul 1847]

Caroline Augusta 18 d/o William WADE at Augusta ME [11 Dec 1845]

Frederic C infant s/o Selden & Harriet E WADE at Norridgewock ME [1 Jul 1847]

James at Augusta ME [21 Nov 1834]

Margaret H 4y 5m d/o John F WADE at Augusta ME [2 Aug 1849]

Mary A 29 w/o John F WADE at Augusta ME on 3 Jul [17 Jul 1851]

Mary E G 29 d/o Aaron D & Mary WADE at Pittston ME [11 Sept 1851]

Nancy 42 w/o Capt Robert WADE at Woolwich ME [26 Aug 1836]

WADE (Cont.) Polly 59 w/o Roland WADE at Thomaston ME [24 Oct 1834]
> Richard Jr escaped unhurt when water gushed out while digging a well near Findlay. Water burnt like alcohol when lit and still boils. [*Findlay Courier*, Hancock Co OH 3 Aug] [29 Aug 1837]
> Turner 21 at Pittston ME [15 Nov 1849]

WADLEIGH Benjamin 33 at Mt Vernon ME on 8 Mar [27 Mar 1851]
> Daniel G of Belgrade ME brakeman on the Stonington road a few days since was knocked down by a bridge & died of his injuries [*Free American*] [19 Aug 1847]
> John 95y AmRev Battle of Bunker Hill & one of last to leave the scene, one of the founders of society of Shakers at New Gloucester ME 23rd ult [11 Nov 1852]
> Sarah widow 89 at Lovell [14 Oct 1847]

WADLEY Eliza 38 w/o Timothy S WADLEY at Mt Vernon ME on 4th inst [20 Dec 1849]
> William 39 of Mt Vernon ME at Augusta ME on 23 Apr [2 May 1850]
> William 63 at Belgrade ME on 17 Mar [29 Mar 1849]

WADLIN Anna 57 w/o Thomas WADLIN at Hollis ME [25 Dec 1845]•
> Miriam 40 w/o John WADLIN Jr at Northport ME [13 Feb 1845]

WADSWORTH Aaron 73 at Skowhegan ME [20 May 1843]
> Abigail 65 w/o John WADSWORTH at East Winthrop ME on 19 June [21 June 1849]
> Edward K 2y s/o Daniel WADSWORTH at Hallowell ME [5 Sept 1840]
> Harriet Cheney 2y d/o Daniel WADSWORTH at Hallowell ME [18 Sept 1838]
> Jane 29 d/o John WADSWORTH at East Winthrop ME on 12th June [17 June 1843]
> John 22 s/o Moses WADSWORTH at Litchfield ME [29 Oct 1846]
> John 62 at East Winthrop ME on 29 Jan [20 Feb 1851]
> Joseph Benton 14y oldest s/o John WADSWORTH at Hiram ME [21 Dec 1839]
> Moses 78 at Litchfild ME 21 Dec [25 Dec 1851]
> Mrs w/o Jesse WADSWORTH Jr at Livermore Falls ME [25 Jan 1840]
> Sarah Merriam 63 wid/o John WADSWORTH of Winthrop ME at Walpole MA [5 Aug 1843]
> Thomas Albert 2y s/o Thomas WADSWORTH at Augusta ME [2 May 1850]

WAGG Samuel 65y at Danville (now part of Auburn) ME [19 Sept 1850]

WAGGONER John 81y the last of Washington's life Guards where he served for 5yrs, he was 16y when enlisted & served to the end of AmRev d at Lower Sandusky on 15th ult [21 Jan 1843]

WAIT Abigail 17 d/o Holland & Lucy WAIT of North Anson ME at Augusta ME on 17 Sept at the residence of John L DUTTON [9 Oct 1851]
> Hannah w/o Capt John W WAIT at Gardiner ME [6 Aug 1846]
> Joseph 70 formerly a member of the society of Shakers at Belfast ME [5 Aug 1852]

WAITE Alexander 38 from a fall into the hold of the new ship at Portland Pier, left a wife & dau, s/o Ebenezer WAITE of Livermore ME [*Argus*] [13 Dec 1849]
> Ebenezer 75 at Livermore ME [19 Feb 1852]
> Sophronia S 9y 7m d/o Charles W WAITE at Falmouth ME on 12th inst [23 Jul 1842]
> Theo of Delaware perished in shipwreck of the schr *William Polk*, Mr HAMILTON Capt, the Capt alone escaped [*Philidelphia Exchange Book*] [23 Jul 1846]

WAITE - see TITCOMB

WAKEFIELD Abigail H 37 w/o D H WAKEFIELD at Gardiner ME suddenly [23 Mar 1848]
> J Nelson 29 at West Gardiner ME [9 Dec 1852]
> James 41 a member of the Society of Shakers at Poland ME [19 Dec 1844]
> Jeremiah 94 at Gardiner ME [17 Apr 1851]
> John of Gardiner ME passenger drowned from schr *Bunker Hill* on passage from Nassau to Key West on 7th ult [15 Jan 1846]

WAKEFIELD (Cont.) Martha 81 w/o Dominicus WAKEFIELD at Gardiner ME [25 Mar 1847]

Sophronia A 31 w/o Granville WAKEFIELD at Gardiner ME [18 Jul 1850]

William H 5y s/o Grandville A WAKEFIELD at Gardiner ME [29 May 1845]

WALCOTT John Stoughton after taking arsenic & morphine for the toothache at Litchfield CT [25 Apr 1844]

Willard late of Augusta ME, est notice, Jane WALCOTT adm [19 Feb 1852]

WALDO Daniel of Worcester was found dead in his bed [17 Jul 1845]

WALDON Timothy W 28 at Bath ME [3 Aug 1841]

WALDRON Susan abt 22y committed suicide at Milltown ME [16 May 1844]

WALES Henry H 2y 6m only child of the late John W WALES at Hallowell ME on Sat evening on 22d ult [8 May 1838]

John W 28 only son of Benjamin WALES of Hallowell ME at Hallowell ME on Sunday evening the 22nd ult at the residence of his father-in-law Ephraim CARTER [8 May 1838]

WALKER Agnes 80 at Madison ME [6 May 1852]

Almira 23 w/o Leonard WALKER at Embden ME on 15 Dec [2 Jan 1851]

baby 16 days only c/o Leonard H WALKER at Embden ME on 26th [2 Jan 1851]

Betsey 77 w/o George WALKER at Exeter ME [26 Dec 1850]

Betsey P 32 at Belmont ME [31 Oct 1850]

Betsey w/o Capt Robert WALKER in stepping from a wagan broke her leg near the ankle joint at Brooksville ME [8 Jul 1847]

Delia 8 d/o Capt Samuel WALKER at Hallowell ME [18 Jul 1844]

Dexter 67 formerly of Livermore ME at Portland ME [29 Oct 1846]

E P 25 at Farmington ME [13 Nov 1851]

Elizabeth 83 w/o Nathaniel WALKER at Limington ME [30 May 1850]

Floyd 24 of Livermore Falls ME on his way home from CA at Boston MA [23 Jan 1851]

Mrs w/o George, an Irishman was crushed to death when the gable end of the adjoining house on Washington St, New York City fell, one of three children had both legs broken [25 Mar 1843]

Gustavus B 21y 6m s/o Samuel & Elizabeth WALKER of Norridgewock ME at Lowell MA on 16 Aug [18 Sept 1851]

Hannah 13 at Anson ME [22 Aug 1834]

Hezekiah went to his barn to feed his cattle, mis-stepped, fell & died of skull injury 60-70 at Peru Oxford Co ME on 26th ult (formerly of Falmouth ME) [17 Feb 1848]

James 23 at Livermore Falls ME [7 Nov 1840]

James 97 AmRev at Haverhill MA [5 Mar 1846]

James drowned between Fort Independance & Thompson's Island one of 27 boys of the Farm School [7 May 1842]

Jane T 63 w/o Nathaniel WALKER Esq at Topsham ME [28 Aug 1851]

John 70 at Madison ME [5 Apr 1849]

John Esq 62 at Lovell ME [14 Mar 1850]

John Fernderson 31 eldest s/o John & Hannah WALKER at Wilton ME [31 Oct 1850]

John of Madison ME at the house of Eleazer EDDY at Cornville ME on Mon of last week [*Skowhegan Clarion*] [5 Apr 1849]

Joseph B 26 formerly of Limerick ME at Boston ME [28 Feb 1850]

Lavina 24 w/o Willard WALKER at Dresden ME [27 Feb 1845]

Mary Ann 17 d/o Micah WALKER at Augusta ME on 17 Dec [25 Dec 1851]

Minerva 23 w/o Eli C WALKER at Embden [2 Dec 1852]

Mr a wid, fr Gloucester, spent the eve at neighbor's, put his four ch to bed, before his return the house burned, all ch died ... father prob drowned himself (*Norfolk Herald*) [18 Apr 1834]

WALKER (Cont.) Mrs w/o Rev Dr WALKER missionary at Western Africa [14 Sept 1848]
Nancy late of Hallowell(?) ME [29 Jul 1852]
Nathaniel Esq 70 at Topsham ME [28 Aug 1851]
Phinehas Hon 75 at Newport ME on 10th ult [15 Jan 1842]
Robert & S WALKER drowned between Fort Independence & Thompson's Island one of 27 boys of the Farm School [7 May 1842]
Tamson 29 d/o William & Hannah WALKER of Anson ME at St Albans ME [22 Apr 1847]
William 79 at Phillips ME [15 Apr 1847]
William 83 at Madison ME [22 May 1851]
WALKER - see BACON, COWART
WALL Cynthia 74 w/o Capt David WALL at Augusta ME [4 Jan 1849]
David Capt 78 in the house where born and where he had always resided at Augusta ME on 15 Jan [22 Jan 1852]
Ellen 11 d/o Capt Aaron WALL at Thomaston ME [14 May 1846]
Hannah 18 at St George ME [16 Apr 1846]
Susan A 8y d/o Ezra J & Elizabeth WALL at Augusta ME [10 Oct 1844]
WALLACE Abram 78 at Clinton ME [31 Oct 1840]
Dorcas 100y & 6m at Phipsburg ME [25 Feb 1847]
McIntire abt 40 at Phipsburg ME [20 May 1836]
Mr on the whale ship at St Miguel on 1 Jan last [1 Apr 1847]
Mrs 82 at Waldoboro ME [17 Sept 1846]
Mrs on Wed night last 50 to 60 Indians attacked, Mr Wallace's gun didn't fire. He swam across Ancilla R his wife & two dau were murdered by savages. [*Tallahassee Floridian* 4 Feb] [21 Feb 1837]
W one of three of 27 boys of Farm School saved from drowning between Thompson's Island & Fort Independence by schr *H B FOSTER* of Machias ME, coming up from Trinidad [7 May 1842]
William 12 at Turner ME [20 Aug 1846]
William 74 at Phipsburg ME [12 Mar 1846]
WALN Robert an eminent merchant at Philadelphia PA on 24 Jan 1836 [13 Jan 1837]
WALTER child 4y near Rochester choked to death by a bean in the throat on Sat [8 Apr 1843]
Jacob 32 at North Waldoboro ME on 5 Jul [12 Jul 1849]
Mrs d/o Rodney LATHROP of cholera on Fri of last week [13 Sept 1849]
WALTON Abigail w/o Mark WALTON Jr & only child of William COBB of Cape Elizabeth ME on 2nd inst [8 Aug 1840]
Benjamin 91y 8m AmRev at Milo ME on 1 Oct [30 Oct 1851]
David A 25 at Fayette ME on 30 May [10 June 1852]
Ephraim abt 66 of Livermore ME drowned in the Androscoggin River on the 9th at Otis' Falls, near the line of Livermore & Jay [27 May 1843]
Hannah Eliza 15 at Fayette ME [2 Mar 1848]
John H Col formerly mayor of Galveston TX of cholera [*Galveston (TX) Civilian* of the 24th ult] [22 Feb 1849]
Margaret 72 w/o Simeon WALTON at Norway ME [31 Oct 1850]
Melintha 28 d/o Rufus WALTON at Fayette ME on 10 June [28 June 1849]
Moses 66 at Chesterville ME [26 Sept 1850]
Sarah 75 w/o Mark WALTON at Portland ME [8 Feb 1844]
Simeon 73 at Norway ME [17 Oct 1850]
WALTZE Samuel Capt 60 of Nobleboro ME at Chinese Camp Toulumne Co CA on Oct 22 of smallpox [9 Dec 1852]
WARD Betsey C 23 at China ME [18 June 1846]

WARD (Cont.) Edwin 3 s/o Samuel WARD at Augusta ME on 15 Apr [25 Apr 1850]

Elizabeth 16 of Monson ME at Biddeford ME [1 Mar 1849]

James 22 s/o Nehemiah WARD at Windsor ME on 30th Nov [11 Dec 1838]

Joseph engineer near Reading also Jas M'CABE, conductor; Frank TYE & Peter MAHAN, fireman. Mr McCabe's watch stopped at 20 minutes after nine. [*Democratic Rep*] [12 Sept 1844] Mary 21 w/o John E WARD at Windsor ME on 7 Apr [10 Apr 1851]

Mary B 32 w/o Capt John WARD formerly of Columbia ME? died at New York [30 May 1837]

Mary Louisa 24 w/o James WARD at Houlton Aroostook Co ME [30 Mar 1848]

Mr living at Spring St Roxbury MA found near his res last Thurs night, while driving an ox team fell asleep and fell off the wagon, the wheels passed over his head. [23 Nov 1839]

Palmer abt 35 at Madison ME [10 Sept 1846]

Randal of China ME on the Isthmus [29 Nov 1849]

Samuel 19 s/o Nehemiah WARD at Windsor ME on 26th ult [11 Dec 1838]

WARD- see MERCHANT

WARDELL - see PERKINS

WARDEN Charles a baker;charged w/ polygamy, 3 wives m in same city. They appeared against him & he was committed. He is abt 28 yrs; wives are 16, 20, 34, the last a widow [1 Apr 1836]

WARDWELL Eliakim 69 at Penobscot ME [14 Sept 1848]

Joseph Esq 89 at Rumford ME [22 Mar 1849]

WARE Elbridge a poor, sick soldier of Pittston ME on board bark *Shannon* last night (from *Boston Bee* on 20th) [29 June 1848]

oldest d/o Hon Ashur WARE Judge of U. S. District Court was seriously injured on Fri by being knocked down & run over by a wagon in Congress St. [*Argus*] [19 Oct 1848]

Henry I 21 at Athens ME [15 Jul 1847]

Henry Jr 49 a distinguished writer & preacher at Framingham MA [21 Oct 1843]

Henry Rev 80 of Cambridge MA on the 28th inst, the father of William & Henry WARE [31 Jul 1845]

J E of Farmington ME saved from drowning when the steam packet *New England* sank. It left Boston for Bath & Gardiner ME and had an accident with the schr *Curlew* on 31 May [12 June 1838]

Lucy 57 w/o Warren Esq at Orrington ME [25 May 1839]

WARE - see WEBSTER

WARES Lucy abt 20 w/o Hiram WARES at Pittston ME [21 Mar 1850]

WARFIELD John of Maryland had a slave who d week before last ae 124. She retained her sight & usual activity until a few days of her death, always in the same family [5 Feb 1846]

WARLAND J H Mr late editor of the *Manchester American* on Mon admitted to the insane hospital at Concord [26 Feb 1846]

Theodore of Cambridge saved from drowning when the steam packet *New England* sank. It left Boston for Bath & Gardiner ME and had an accident with the schr *Curlew* on 31 May [12 June 1838]

WARNER Capt lost his life on 27th Sept while engaged in ascertaining the feasibility of a railroad route to Oregon. [20 Dec 1849]

Congreve married Elizabeth CROCKETT & a bill passed the Senate of MO declaring the union null & void. They were married as a joke. [20 Feb 1845]

Horace W married Miss Martha Ann SCOLES in Knocks Co OH [1 Apr 1847]

WARR Mr, cmdr of forces in Canada, fell in love with the dau of a chief. Mr W, of noble blood m a Crow or Blackfoot, by a missionary [*Brighton Eng. Herald*] [*Montreal Herald*] [1 Oct 1846]

WARREN Alma abt 18 at Ellsworth ME [23 Oct 1838]

Annis 14y 10m d/o Phineas WARREN at Freedom ME [1 Jan 1846]

Ara 20y at Bangor ME of consumption on 10th inst [26 June 1838]

Charles Newell 2y 8m only s/o M P & Julia Ann B WARREN at West Boylston MA on 11 Aug [6 Sept 1849]

Eliza 68 w/o Josiah WARREN at Norridgewock ME [31 Oct 1850]

Eunice 65 at Saco ME [28 Jan 1847]

Gardiner A 36 at Saco ME [2 Mar 1848]

George Capt 69 at Isleboro ME [16 Sept 1852]

Hannah 21 at Waterboro ME [18 June 1846]

Harriet M 8 c/o William & Louisa WARREN at Vassalboro ME on 20 Sept [23 Nov 1848]

Hellen F 2y 4m c/o William & Louisa WARREN at Vassalboro ME 11 Sept [23 Nov 1848]

Henry Elder 69 at Belfast ME [8 Jul 1836]

Ivory 58 at Durham ME [30 Aug 1849]

John at Albion ME [4 Apr 1850]

John left home abt 3 yrs for South not heard of since 1840 in Kentucky, 28yr tall, lt complexion, lg scar on wrist. Report to, Samuel WARREN of Guilford ME, father. Lost two sons since he left & yearns to see him [24 Jul 1841]

Joseph at Canaan ME of smallpox [5 Feb 1846]

Julia W 19 of Abbott ME on Thurs evening on 7th inst [16 Dec 1843]

Lydia Adeline 29 w/o Cyrus WARREN at Monmouth ME [28 Nov 1844]

Margaret 75 at Gardiner ME [1 May 1845]

Mary abt 36 w/o William WARREN at Skowhegan ME [23 Jan 1845]

Mrs 105y of Oswego Co said to be the oldest pensioner living [1 Oct 1842]

Richard 92y 3m AmRev 13 ch, 84 grandch, & 61 great grandch at Vassalboro ME [18 Mar 1847]

Robert 29 at South Berwick ME [3 Apr 1838]

Sarah 83y widow at Norridgewock ME [10 Aug 1833]

Sarah E 4y 6m c/o William & Louisa WARREN at Vassalboro ME on 10th Sept [23 Nov 1848]

William Gardiner 64 of chronic rheumatism at Gardiner ME [8 Jan 1839]

William W 40 of Jackson ME at Palmyra ME very suddenly [18 Dec 1845]

WARREN - see ROLERSON

WARWICK - see PEARCE

WASHBURN Ebenezer 88y 10m 11d AmRev native of Kingston MA s/o Capt Ebenezer WASHBURN at North Hartford Oxford Co ME on 11 Dec 1850 [30 Jan 1851]

Abiel 91y 9m AmRev, w/ Col BARTON to take PRESCOTT from quarters on RI; taken prisoner & carried to England; at E Bridgewater on 7th inst [*Newport (RI) Herald*] [28 Sept 1848]

E B s/o Israel WASHBURN Esq of Livermore, a lawyer by profession & a printer by trade. Formerly worked at printing in the office of the *Kennebec Journal* [22 Mar 1849]

Hannah E 24 w/o H G O WASHBURN at Belfast ME [29 Feb 1840]

Isaac 53 at Oxford ME [13 Jul 1848]

J C Esq 70 at Calais ME [12 Sept 1850]

Mary A 33 w/o O W WASHBURN Esq at China ME on 27 Apr [9 May 1850]

Royal 35 at Amherst MA [21 Jan 1833]

WASHBURN (Cont.) Sarah D 55 w/o Rev J WASHBURN at Thomaston ME [7 May 1846]

WASHINGTON George his family genealogy [20 Mar 1845]

George 68 President of USA on 10 Dec 1799 [5 Aug 1836]

George only two living "Life Guards" of WASHINGTON were in procession on Fourth of July in Newburg ME. Their names are Benjamin FATON & Robert BLAIR. On entering the church they bore an American flag, followed by six other Revolutionary soldiers - their united ages being 551 years. [3 Aug 1839]

George "WASHINGTON's Farewell Address, orig manuscript copy auctioned in Philadelphia on Feb 12 started at $500 & was sold for $2300, to Rev Dr BOARDMAN who purchased it for a gentleman in New York" [14 Feb 1850]

Lawrence "the old Washington House where Lawrence WASHINGTON, an ancestor of Gen WASHINGTON, lived, still standing in Gadson Wiltshire England, Lawrence d in 1672 [9 Nov 1848]

WASHINGTON - see BERRY, BLACKSNAKE, CARY, CHRYSTLER, CHURCHILL, CODMAN, COLE, DAVIS, EATON, GEORGE, GOUGH, HAMILTON, HANCOCK, HETH, JACKSON, LUFKIN, ROGERS, STONE, TODD, TRUMBULL

WASS John Col 42 at Addison ME [23 Mar 1839]

Lander 20y of Columbia ME injured by a falling tree, speechless when found on Monday last (we learned this report from R TINKER Esq) [*Ellsworth Democrat*] [10 Feb 1848]

WASSON Clarissa 25 w/o Capt Samuel WASSON at Brooksville ME [19 June 1845]

WATERBERY - see SCUDDER

WATERHOUSE Mehitable 67 w/o Major J WATERHOUSE at Scarboro ME [20 Apr 1848]

Abba 4y adopted d/o G G WATERHOUSE at Paris ME on 1st inst [19 Mar 1842]

Benjamin 70 at Richmond ME [11 June 1846]

Benjamin F 22y (b 27 Aug 1827) s/o Col Zebulon & Annar (DYER) WATERHOUSE drowned at Danville (now part of Auburn) ME on 3d inst (see *VR New Gloucester ME*, Book 2, p. 7) [16 May 1850]

Dorothy L 23 d/o Daniel WATERHOUSE of Poland ME at Danville (now part of Auburn) ME [27 Dec 1849]

Emeline H w/o Simeon P WATERHOUSE & d/o Thomas CARLETON Esq at her father's res at Vassalboro ME [8 Apr 1847]

Israel Esq agent of the Maine Stage Company at Portland ME on 29th ult [7 Dec 1839]

James 21 at Durham ME [18 Nov 1847]

James 56 at Bowdoinham ME [26 Mar 1846]

Jane W 35 w/o Gardner WATERHOUSE at Windham ME [27 Dec 1849]

John Capt of Cape Elizabeth of brig *Gazelle* of Portland ME at sea May 26th on passage from Havana for Boston MA of bilious fever [10 June 1843]

John Esq 26 s/o Thomas WATERHOUSE at Durham ME [21 Oct 1847]

WATERMAN Betsey 58 w/o Gen William WATERMAN at Buxton ME [19 Mar 1846]

Charles 10 only s/o Capt Thomas WATERMAN at Turner village [4 Jul 1837]

Hannah B 19 w/o Joseph WATERMAN Esq & d/o Amony LEACH of New Gloucester ME at Gray ME [6 Mar 1838]

John Capt 86 AmRev at Gray ME [8 Jul 1847]

Jonah 72 at Lincolnville ME [3 June 1852]

WATERS Enos killed in the Irish & Native American (not American Indians more likely English born in American) Riots in Philadelphia PA [*Dollar Newspaper*] [18 Jul 1844]

James (a black) of Portland ME saved from the barque *William Fales*, [source George M FREEMAN of Cape Neddick] [26 Feb 1842]

WATERS (Cont.) John of Baltimore MD on the brig *Eastern Star* of Portland ME. Leaped from the deck & was drowned in the attempt to reach shore [13 Apr 1848]

Mary Jane an orphan girl 6y died by catching clothes on fire *[Pittsburgh Visiter]* [28 Oct 1836]

Montain J M 33 at Pittston ME [18 Jul 1844]

Thomas of Bangor ME at San Francisco CA [5 Feb 1852]

WATKINS - see HASEITH

WATSON Abigail S 42 w/o Benjamin WATSON at Farmington ME [13 Jan 1848]

Agnes 83 at Farmington ME [17 June 1852]

Alexander 44 at Saco ME [29 Apr 1847]

Asenath 45 at Thomaston ME [30 Nov 1848]

Austress L 44 w/o Sewall WATSON at Augusta ME [21 Jul 1843]

c/o John WATSON at Hallowell ME [22 Aug 1844]

D D lady of Fayette ME saved from drowning when the steam packet *New England* sank. It left Boston for Bath & Gardiner ME and collided with the schr *Curlew* on 31 May [12 June 1838]

Daniel 82 at Norway ME [8 Jan 1846]

Daniel of Kingston MA accidentally on Tues afternoon while shooting ducks with Wardsworth HUNT [23 Nov 1839]

Edmund Rev 62 at Hodgdon ME [3 Oct 1850]

Elizabeth 32 w/o Stephen WATSON at Saco ME [21 Jan 1847]

Flora Catharine 13w infant d/o Catherine & Noah WATSON at Fayette ME on 15 Aug [26 Oct 1848]

James abt 90 at Thomaston ME [14 Mar 1834]

James second steward lost & missing on 7th inst the steamboat *New York*, bound from Galveston to New Orleans wrecked in a hurricane, 17 persons drowned [24 Sept 1846]

Joseph E 14 at Augusta ME, by a fall through a scuttle in the store of William S HASKELL [26 Nov 1846]

Joshua W 70 at Litchfield ME [7 June 1849]

Josiah M 52 at Readfield ME [22 Aug 1844]

Lucy 29 w/o Sewall WATSON Esq at Fayette ME [11 May 1839]

Mahala w/o John WATSON at Hallowell ME [1 Aug 1844]

Mr of Lewis Co NY a panther entered his house on 27th ult & carried off 11m old ch. 12 yr old sister & other children gave chase, it then dropped the baby unhurt & fled [24 Aug 1839]

Mr the driver from (Eastport ME) to Pembroke fell through the scuttle of the 2nd fl of the stable at Mr LORING's getting hay for his horses, before dawn on Sun morn 2nd inst & broke his his arm in two places. *[Eastport Sentinel]* [13 Jul 1848]

Olive 37 w/o Simeon WATSON at Industry ME on 12 Nov [25 Nov 1852]

Samuel 52 at Richmond ME [22 Oct 1846]

WATSON & HOOPER store a fire broke out on Tuesday morning last the dwelling house near injured, owned by Mr SMITH of 11 at Houlton ME [5 Nov 1841]

WATSON - see FARWELL, ROBERTS

WATTS Amy Jane w/o Capt Samuel WATTS Jr of Hallowell ME at Strafford CT [8 Mar 1849]

Hugh 77 at Warren ME [21 Aug 1842]

Lucy 24 at Jonesboro ME of smallpox [8 Jan 1852]

Lucy 51 w/o Capt Joshua WATTS st George ME [13 Nov 1851]

Samuel Capt 95 at Jonesboro ME [18 Apr 1850]

Samuel Jr Capt 25 at Hallowell ME on 20 Jan [31 Jan 1850]

WAUGH Elizabeth 58 w/o Samuel WAUGH at Readfield ME [16 May 1834]

WAUGH (Cont.) George Col 70 at Levant ME [23 Sept 1847]

Hartley Y 36 at Starks ME [12 June 1851]

Jemima 28 w/o Harrison WAUGH at Starks ME on 9 Sept [4 Nov 1847]

John 74 at Starks ME [20 Feb 1851]

Luther abt 15y, the first green corn that appeared in our market (this year) was brought by s/o Stephen WAUGH of East Winthrop ME on Tues the 31st ult [*Chronicle*] [7 Aug 1838]

Lydia Parker 77 w/o John WAUGH at Starks ME [27 Jan 1848]

Permelia 38 at Starks ME [14 Sept 1839]

Stephen Capt 49 at East Winthrop Me on 24th Jan [31 Jan 1850]

W of Starks ME s/o Wm was accidentally shot in the head while "waking up" a Militia officer for early a.m. training,Sat 17th ult. He d Mon the 24th. [*Somerset Journal*] [14 Oct 1836]

WAWCONCHOCAUNIFCAW Indian a Winnebago chief died at an advanced age [11 Mar 1847]

WAYLAND - see STONE

WAYNE Anthony "Axe found near Cincinnati OH had "U. S." stamped on side. Place Gen WAYNE camped in 1794, going to Greenville, where treaty ended Indian wars of NW [16 Sept 1847]

Mr AmRev at Erie PA buried at a latter date the body transported to Chester Co PA. Although nearly a quarter of a century had elapsed [16 Sept 1847]

Sarah Eliza recovered a verdict of $2000 against Robert BULLOCK for breach of promise of marriage at New Scotland NY [28 Oct 1836]

WAYNE - see MOORE

WEAL - see SAWYER

WEATHERN Benjamin 55 at Farmington ME [20 Aug 1846]

Franklin 22 at Farmington ME [13 Sept 1849]

Willaim Harrison 26 at Farmington ME on 7th inst [19 Jul 1849]

WEAVER Jacob 17 & Sarah SHERMAN 13y 7m married at Poughkeepsie a few day ago [23 Apr 1846]

WEBB Abigail P abt 51 formerly of Augusta ME at Frankfort ME on 4th inst [21 Jan 1843]

Alice 27 w/o Jeremiah WEBB at Knox ME [11 Dec 1851]

Arthur 7m only child of Samuel at Winthrop ME [10 Oct 1850]

Charles W 12 s/o Hanson H WEBB at St Albans ME [16 Jul 1846]

Emily E 38 w/o Convers L WEBB at St Albans ME [25 Sept 1845]

George 23 at Bangor ME [28 Oct 1836]

Hannah 80 at Bath ME [19 Dec 1844]

Hannah G 18 at Skowhegan ME [11 May 1848]

Hiram 20 s/o Joseph B WEBB Esq at Bloomfield ME [12 Nov 1846]

John 92 AmRev at Westbrook ME [30 Jul 1846]

Joshua Jr 17 at Bangor ME [28 Oct 1836]

Matilda C 19y d/o Deacon Robert C WEBB at Waldoboro ME [19 June 1845]

Samuel at Winthrop ME [14 Aug 1840]

Samuel Esq 48 at Winthrop ME suddenly on Fri evening last [25 Apr 1840]

Sarah E 19 at Waldoboro ME [21 Mar 1844]

Sarah Mrs 30 at Pensacola FL d/o Jacob NELSON of Winthrop ME [1 Nov 1849]

WEBB - see KIMBALL

WEBBER Abigail 45 w/o Oliver A WEBBER & d/o the late Isaac HAWES at Vassalboro ME on 14th inst [22 Jan 1846]

boy thrown accidentally from a cart, wheel passed over his neck, s/o Rev Mr WEBBER, Methodist preacher in Portland ME at Portland ME on 24 inst [8 Aug 1840]

WEBBER (Cont.) Charles Edward 3y 4m s/o S R WEBBER at Hallowell ME [5 Sept 1840]

Dorothy w/o Joseph WEBBER at Penobscot ME on 10 Jan [12 Feb 1846]

Ellen P 17 at Gardiner ME [18 Dec 1841]

George Capt 56 after an illness of five days at Vassalboro ME on the 10th inst of a lung fever [21 Dec 1833]

Horatio 7 c/o Charles J WEBBER at Vassalboro ME on 28th [10 June 1847]

Jane 68 at Hallowell ME [13 Sept 1849]

Martha Jane 26 w/o Dr J B WEBBER at Gardiner ME [19 Feb 1846]

Martha Louisa 2y 6m c/o Charles J WEBBER at Vassalboro ME on 16 May [10 June 1847]

Sarah E 22 at Hallowell ME [1 Nov 1849] & [18 Oct 1849]

Sarah T 38 widow of Thomas M WEBBER at Bremen ME [10 Jul 1851]

Stephen 84 AmRev at Acton [22 Apr 1836]

Willard W 3y 1m s/o Jeremiah D & Lois B WEBBER at Chester ME on 31 Aug [30 Sept 1852]

WEBBER - see HAWES

WEBSTER Daniel 86 formerly of Edgecomb ME at Unity ME [24 Aug 1833]

David Col of Fryeburg ME on Mon [*Portland Adv*] [3 June 1847]

George W 16y 4m s/o Francis WEBSTER Esq at Gray ME on 24th ult [3 June 1843]

Hannah 63 at Weld ME [20 Feb 1851]

Ira 17 of Penobscot ME on board schr *Fortune* of Castine ME from Havana [24 Aug 1833]

John 68 formerly of New Gloucester ME at Lewiston ME [10 June 1847]

John W Prof b in Boston MA in 1790, s/o Redford WEBSTER, who resided in the North part of the city. R WEBSTER died in 1834, leaving abt $40,000 [*Boston Herald*] [13 Dec 1849]

Joseph T 40 at Bath ME [14 Feb 1850]

Joshua 26 at Belfast ME [2 Jan 1845]

Josiah Rev 66 at Hampton NH on 27th ult, preached at Newburyport abt 12 days previous at the ordination of his son a seaman's preacher for the port of Constadt Russia [18 Apr 1837

Julia d/o Daniel WEBSTER married to Mr APPLETON of Boston MA [16 Nov 1839]

Major in Mexico [*Boston Journal*] [2 Mar 1848]

Nathaniel 76 at Portland ME [23 Dec 1852]

Noah 85 born 16 Oct 1758, in 1807 commenced compiling his Dictionary, the first edition completed in 1828, at New Haven on Sunday last [10 June 1843]

Richard F Esq 36 at Bangor ME [3 Apr 1845]

Susan 91 at Gray ME [1 Apr 1833]

WEBSTER - see LeROY, FAIRBANK

WEED John m Miss Eliza LANY in Chilicothe [*sic*] OH?. Ephraim Esq pronounces this a Miss E-Lany-ous approximation to the WEED. The question is, did Eliza chews her husband, of her own free will & accord? If so, there will be some biting & scratching between them [*Star*] [23 Jul 1846]

WEED John m Miss Eliza LANY at Bangor ME [*sic*].The *Richmond Star* pronounces this a Miss E-Lany-ous approximation to the WEED. The question is, did Eliza chews her husband, of her own free will & accord? If not so, there will be some biting & scratching between them at Bangor ME [9 Dec 1843]

Mrs w/o Mr WEED of Benton NH assisting her husband in loading hay on a cart, accidentlly killed by a pitchfork [3 Sept 1846]

WEEKS Benjamin 89 at Durham ME [12 Dec 1850]

Beriah 65 at Vassalboro ME [1 Jan 1852]

Elizabeth C 26 w/o Abner B WEEKS at Bath ME [14 May 1846]

WEEKS (Cont.) Hannah 20 at Jefferson ME [19 Aug 1847]

Mrs of Sandwich w/o Amaziah WEEKS Jr shot on Tues by her son a young lad who was playing with a loaded gun [*Boston Bee*] [21 Jan 1847]

Sarah 38 at Lewiston ME [18 Nov 1847]

Truman 44 at Bucksport ME [15 Jul 1847]

Zipporah 64 w/o Uriel WEEKS at Farmington ME [13 Nov 1845]

WEEKS - see ELDERT, JACKSON

WELCH Ann at Waterville ME [30 Sept 1847]

Arthur drowned at Caghnawaga Pond near Monmouth Centre ME was a member of the present Medical Class of Bowdoin College [12 June 1838]

Daniel 65 at Lewiston ME [20 Feb 1851]

Dorcas abt 78 w/o Mark WELCH at Bowdoinham ME [30 Dec 1847]

George W N 18y 6m at New Orleans of yellow fever [30 Sept 1847]

Hannah L 48 w/o James WELCH formerly of Winthrop ME at Danville (now part of Auburn) ME on 6th inst [23 Dec 1852]

John 61 at Monmouth ME [22 Jan 1846]

John 76 at Ossipee NH on 15 Oct [30 Oct 1845]

John N 29 at Bangor ME on 17th inst [5 Feb 1842]

Lydia W 14 at Monmouth ME on 22 Sept [10 Oct 1840]

Mr of Madawaska ME a lumberer had cattle belonging to another, Dep Sheriff WINSLOW, & D BULLOCH executed a search warrant BULLOCH was killed [*Bath Tribune*] [11 Nov 1847]

Mrs G gave birth to three fine healthy boys, averaging six pounds each at Springvale ME on May 1. The lads and their mother are doing well [*Saco Union*] [25 May 1848]

Olive J 18 of Harmony at Hallowell ME [7 Jan 1847]

Oliver Deacon abt 68 author of Welch's Arithmetic at Waterville ME [23 Jan 1845]

Sally 42 w/o George WELCH at Deed River ME [13 June 1850]

Sally Miss 75 at Portsmouth NH on 30 Apr [29 May 1851]

WELCH - see NOLMAN

WELCOME Susanna 36 consort of John B WELCOME at Kingfield ME [4 Jul 1844]

WELD Joseph 18 s/o Zebina WELD of Cornville ME at Skowhegan ME [10 Jul 1851] & employ of Joseph RUSSELL killed by a bull on 24 June (from *Mann's Miscellany*) [3 Jul 1851]

Sarah W 4y d/o Dr George WELD of Somersworth NH at Lebanon on 8 Nov [5 Dec 1834]

WELLINGTON Nathan Capt 54 at East Livermore ME [25 Apr 1850]

Uriah 10 only s/o Capt Nathan WELLINGTON at Livermore ME on 14th inst [27 May 1843]

WELLMAN Benjamin 92 AmRev at Waldoboro ME on 2d inst [13 May 1843]

John Alonzo 19 s/o John P & Martha WELLMAN at Belgrade ME on 28 FEb [1 May 1851]

Justin T 3 s/o John P & Martha C WELLMAN at Belgrade ME on 6 Sept [14 Sept 1848]

Thomas P 36 formerly of Farmington ME at Mainsville OH [10 Jan 1850]

WELLS Charles 22 of Norwich one of the brakeman on the Norwich railroad [31 Jul 1845]

Emily 13 d/o Frederick WELLS at Pittston ME [4 Jul 1844]

George A abt 16y bound to me by the Overseer of the Poor of Belgrade, left without my consent; I hereby forbid any person from harboring or trusting him. Amos ROLLINS [11 Mar 1847]

Harriet H Mrs 27 d/o John MOOERS at Vienna ME [14 Jan 1847]

Hiram 11 s/o Moses WELLS drowned while skating near the bridge at Augusta ME [2 Jan 1838]

WELLS (Cont.) Horace a dentist of New York suicide in prison, left a wife & family in Hartford [*Traveller*] [3 Feb 1848]

Jane 75 widow of Benjamin WELLS at Gardiner ME [17 Aug 1848]

John L Deacon 57 at Sedgwick Bay ME [30 Nov 1848]

John M 47 a native of Waterville ME at Milwaukie WI on 18th ult [16 Dec 1852]

Louis Henry 1y s/o Moses WELLS at Augusta ME [11 Mar 1847]

Lovina 79 w/o Solomon WELLS at Augusta ME on 8 May [16 May 1850]

Lucretia 73 w/o Nathan WELLS at Kennebunk ME [13 Nov 1851]

Maria L 14m d/o Moses WELLS at Augusta ME on 23rd inst [4 Sept 1845]

Martha 20 d/o James N WELLS at Township No 2 Somerset Co (Discontinued Post Office) [15 Aug 1844]

Moses Capt 75 of the oldest shipping masters in the state at Wells ME [14 Oct 1852]

Moses Esq 44y formerly of Wells ME at Wellington ME [1 July 1852]

Mr arrested on the Mississippi charged with attempting to sell a free negro, convicted at Louisville [14 Aug 1841]

Nancy Stuart 30 w/o Moses WELLS at Augusta ME [2 May 1834]

Pamela Mrs of Mount Vernon ME sister to Mrs B (Charlotte BACHELDOR) at Readfield ME [14 Mar 1834]

Samuel Adams 53 late president of the Atlas Insurance Co at Dorchester [29 Aug 1840]

WELLS - see BARNEY, RANKEY

WELMAN John A 19y 6m at Belgrade ME on 28 Feb [13 Mar 1851]

WELSH E Mrs & two children, deck passengers of New Orleans d in a serious accident on board the steamboat *George Collier* on the 6th inst on her passage to St Louis MO [25 May 1839]

Edward 55 at Monmouth ME of the smallpox [2 Jan 1838]

girl almost 2y d/o Maurice WELSH who lives in Half Moon square, rear of Board St was burnt to death [*Boston Post*] [22 Aug 1844]

WELSH - see POWERS

WENDELL - see TITCOMB

WENDENBURG Charles William 21 recently from Germany at Augusta ME on 31 Dec [8 Jan 1852]

WENTWORTH Benjamin 76 at Berwick ME [14 Feb 1837]

Betsey 46y 9m at Strong ME [24 Jul 1845]

Brown 48 at Strong ME [22 Jul 1852]

Catharine 84 w/o Foster WENTWORTH at Webster (now Sabattus) ME [19 Sept 1850]

Charles R 19 at Strong ME [12 Dec 1850]

Charlesmary Sir, Bart, native of Portsmouth NH, & only surviving child of late Sir John WENTWORTH, the last provincial Governor of NH at Kingsand Davenport England [20 June 1844]

Daniel of Harmony on the 1st inst by the wheels of a gun carriage passing over his body while on his way to the general muster at Parkman ME [23 Oct 1838]

David 30 at Gardiner ME [8 May 1851]

Elizabeth 71 w/o David WENTWORTH at Strong ME on 19th ult of apoplexy [8 Jul 1843]

Jane 91 at Buxton ME widow [29 Jul 1843]

John of Chicago IL one of four ed in Congress at present viz Luther SEVERANCE of Augusta ME; Edmund BURKE of Haverhill NH; & Volney E HOWARD of MS [18 Jan 1844]

Lemuel 89 AmRev at Hope ME [8 Feb 1844]

Lydia 77 at Buxton ME [9 Apr 1842]

Mary 45 w/o Leonard WENTWORTH at Hope ME [14 Nov 1850]

Narressa 48y 7m w/o Jacob WENTWORTH at Belgrade ME on 23 Apr [10 May 1849]

WENTWORTH (Cont.) Nehemiah 19 at Ellsworth ME by drowning [24 June 1852]

    S Ellen 20 d/o George WENTWORTH at Farmington ME [6 Feb 1851]

    Susan 30 at Kennebunk ME [29 Aug 1834]

    Susan 45 w/o George WENTWORTH & d/o Hon John REED of Strong ME at Farmington ME on 22 Sept [4 Oct 1849]

    Thurston W 37 formerly of Hope ME at Maumee City OH on 2 Mar of consumption [1 Apr 1852]

    Timothy 55 at Albion ME [25 Feb 1843]

    Timothy 55 at Lebanon [29 Jan 1836]

WENTWORTH - see BARTLETT

WEST Abigail G 38 w/o Reuel WEST formerly of (Augusta) ME at Concord NH of typhoid fever [16 Sept 1852]

    Ammi 50 at (Augusta ME) on 16 Oct [19 Oct 1848]

    Daniel Tracy 21y 3m a member of the sr class of Bowdoin College died at Rochester NY on 15th inst [25 June 1842]

    Edward Capt 91 AmRev formerly of Salem ME at Andover MA on 22d [3 Jul 1851]

    Hannah L w/o Leonard WEST & d/o William & Mary DALTON of Augusta ME at Chelsea ME on 28 Dec [15 Jan 1852]

    infant 5m s/o Leonard & Hannah L (DALTON) WEST at Chelsea ME on 14 Dec [15 Jan 1852]

    Peter Esq 56 at Industry ME on 4th inst [2 Nov 1839]

    Sally 33 w/o William WEST at Winthrop ME [14 Aug 1851]

    Timothy seaman 29 of CT belonged to the U. S. ship *Preble* & died with the Africa fever at Porto Grande Island of St Vincent Cape de Verds on 10 Dec [10 Apr 1845]

    William Capt 33 at Hallowell ME [13 Feb 1835]

    William H 20 at Hallowell ME [4 Apr 1844]

WESTERN - see McFADDEN

WESTON Abel Capt at Bloomfiled ME [21 Sept 1848]

    Anna 82 wid/o John WESTON at Bloomfield ME [8 Jan 1846]

    Benjamin 86 at Madison ME [15 May 1851]

    Benjamin Esq of Madison ME lost two fingers working on the bridge at Norridgewock ME [*Skowhegan Clarion*] [11 Apr 1850]

    Bethiah 7w d/o the late Daniel WESTON Jr at Augusta ME [1 Oct 1846]

    Caroline Eliza 20d Rev J P WESTON at Gardiner ME [19 Sept 1844]

    Caroline F 16 d/o Benjamin WESTON Esq at Madison ME [8 Aug 1850]

    Catherine P 2y d/o Nathan WESTON Jr Esq at Orono ME [17 Sept 1842]

    Daniel Jr 35 of this town at Galveston TX on 21st ult [20 Aug 1846]

    Daniel Sutheric 24 youngest s/o late Rev Daniel WESTON at Gray ME [30 Sept 1843]

    Duane 3y c/o Daniel C WESTON at Augusta ME [24 Jan 1850]

    Edward North 3y 8m s/o Daniel C WESTON Esq at Augusta ME [6 May 1847]

    Edwin 35 at Levant ME [11 May 1848]

    Eli 86 at Bloomfield ME [5 Nov 1846]

    Emily 10y d/o J W WESTON at Bloomfield ME [26 June 1845]

    George 19 at Bloomfield ME [10 Oct 1840]

    George Phillip 9m s/o Daniel WESTON Jr at Augusta ME [23 May 1844]

    Gustavus 17y s/o John B WESTON at Bloomfield ME [31 Oct 1844]

    Harriet W 10 d/o Eusebius WESTON Esq at Bloomfield ME on 29th ult, clothes took fire [15 Oct 1842]

    Henry Livington 1y s/o Daniel C WESTON Esq at Augusta ME on 29 Jan [7 Feb 1850]

    infant d/o W K WESTON at Augusta ME [23 May 1844]

    Jacob 57 at Brunswick ME [20 May 1843]

    Jason 43 at Bangor ME [16 May 1844]

WESTON (Cont.) Love 53 w/o Stephen WESTON at Richmond ME [27 Jul 1848]

Lydia 67 w/o Capt Joseph WESTON at Bloomfield ME [28 Oct 1852]

Mercy 69 w/o Amos WESTON at Frankfort ME [2 Aug 1849]

Phineas in Providence a few days since by Solomon HICKS in a quarrel about a bet [31 Aug 1839]

Ruth R w/o G M WESTON Esq at Augusta ME [23 Oct 1841]

Sally P 45 w/o John W WESTON at Bloomfield ME [30 Jan 1845]

Samuel 20 s/o Stephen WESTON Jr at Madison ME of consumption [13 May 1843]

Samuel Esq 57 at Hallowell ME [9 Jan 1845]

Samuel W 30 at Skowhegan ME [11 Sept 1851]

Stephen 77 at Skowhegan ME [10 June 1847]

William 63 at Bloomfield ME [20 Dec 1849]

William 77 at Norridgewock ME one of 1st white settlers of Somerset Co [16 Jan 1841]

William Capt 83 at Brunswick ME [19 June 1838]

William K of Augusta ME saved from drowning when the steam packet *New England* sank. It left Boston for Bath & Gardiner ME and had an accident with the schr *Curlew* on 31 May [12 June 1838]

WESTON - see BLANCHARD

WETHERBEE John E 37 formerly of Belfast ME at Carrol OH [4 Sept 1845]

WETHERINGTON William S 20 of Newbury MA on board ship *Lenore* at Matanzas on 29 May [3 Jul 1841]

WETHERN Elias late of Vienna ME est notice Charles H RUNDLETT adm [10 June 1852]

Mary 28 w/o Hiram WETHERN at New Portland ME [1 Aug 1840]

WEYMOUTH Harriet N 33 at New Portland ME [19 June 1851]

James 93 AmRev pensioner formerly of Rye NH at Belmont ME [18 Mar 1852]

John 60 taking opium through mistake, supposing it to be powered rhubarb at Vassalboro ME on Sunday the 5th inst [13 May 1833]

Martha at Bloomfield ME [2 May 1850]

Mary F 72 at Georgetown ME on 2d Aug [19 Aug 1847]

Moses Deacon 63 at Alna ME [6 May 1833]

WHARF Wm of Litchfield ME, lightning struck the chimney, struck him on the temple; leaving at right ankle. Life was despaired of, but he's now recovering [*Gardiner Ledger*] [20 May 1843]

WHARFF Irene 38 w/o Capt Joseph WHARFF at Gardiner ME [1 Nov 1849]

WHEATEN James D 81 at Thomaston ME [8 Oct 1846]

Jane Mrs abt 116 at Montville ME [30 Jan 1845]

WHEELER Calvin F 35 at Waterford ME [1 Apr 1847]

Daniel perished on the schr *Thomas*, SPROULE Capt of Belfast ME [25 Mar 1843]

Ester 59 w/o David WHEELER Esq at Waterville ME [14 Aug 1845]

Hannah 18 d/o William L WHEELER at Norridgewock ME [11 June 1846]

J W killed in Buffalo Railroad accident [17 Apr 1851]

James S a native of So Berwick ME 18y drowned at Boston MA [27 Jul 1848]

James T of Waukegan MA drowned bathing Tues 8th inst. NICKERSON, made 3 attempts to save him then said unless released both must be drowned [31 Jul 1851]

John Capt 52 at Belfast ME [23 Sept 1852]

Mahala w/o W H WHEELER Esq at Dixfield ME [19 Mar 1846]

Mary 52 w/o William L WHEELER at Norridgewock ME [2 Apr 1846]

Mary 76 w/o Daniel WHEELER at Dixmont ME [26 Apr 1849]

Morris 115 of Readfield ME died in 1817 (an Irishman) [19 Feb 1846]

Mr alias CURTIS, a juggler, while in the exercise of his vocation, running a sword down his throat preforated some vital part, which caused his instant death [*Buffalo Whig*] [22 May 1835]

WHEELER (Cont.) Peggy 72 at Augusta ME [27 May 1843]
    Phillip M 33 at Rumford ME [1 Oct 1846]
    Sally Miss 40y fell while engaged in her work & died at Fairfield ME [*The Skowhegan
        Clarion*] [3 Jul 1845]
    Samuel Elder 80 at Phillips ME [1 Feb 1849]
    Samuel Esq 71 at Eastport ME [2 Dec 1852]
    Simeon Deacon 69 at Whitefield ME [18 Mar 1852] & [25 Mar 1852]
    Temple Esq 57 at Bangor ME [24 Feb 1848]
WHEELER - see HISCOCK
WHEELRIGHT Abigail 79 at Wiscasset ME [7 Mar 1844]
    Robert 84 at Wiscassett ME [7 Mar 1844]
WHIDDEN James Capt 83 of Greenland NH AmRev fought at Saratoga of the capture of
        BURGOYNE at Deerfield NH on 10 Jul [8 Aug 1844]
    Mrs widow formerly of Hallowell ME 91 at Freedom ME on 6 Mar [16 Mar 1848]
    Nathaniel C Esq abt 47 at Topsham ME on 30 Jul [21 Aug 1851]
WHIPPLE Eleazer 24 of Solon ME lost overboard from the ship *Grecian* on passage from
        New York to San Francisco CA on 9 Jul [23 Sept 1852]
    woman d/o Mr John WHIPPLE of Solon ME by lightning on Sun last, set on fire and
        consumed [*Skowhegan Sentinel*] [19 June 1838]
WHIPPLE - see HAMLIN
Whirling Thunder - see WAWCONCHOCAUNIFCAW
WHITCHER Dearborn of Londonderry by the cars on the Manchester & Lawrence Railroad
    at a crossing in Derry [14 Feb 1850]
WHITCOMB Abraham 85y 5d at the battle of Bunker Hill & also at the surrender of
        BURGOYNE in 1781, died at Stow MA on 23rd ult after a short illness [9 Dec 1843]
    Mrs of Dixmont ME w/o Eli WHITCOMB & mother of 6 ch committed suicide, was a
        member of the Freewill Baptist church [*Bangor Mercury*] [30 Dec 1847]
    Oliver 66 at Dresden ME [21 Feb 1851]
    Susan widow 60 at Fairfield ME [22 Jan 1839]
WHITE a boy s/o Rev Calvin WHITE wounded by accidental discharge of a gun died on
        Tues last [*Gardiner ME Transcript*] [1 May 1851]
    Abigail 78 at Dead River ME [15 Mar 1849]
    Abigail P 26 w/o Samuel WHITE at (Winthrop ME) on Mon last after a short illness [3
        Oct 1840]
    Amelia wid/o Joel WHITE at East Winthrop ME on 7 Mar [13 Mar 1841]
    Amity 27 at Winthrop ME on the 14th of Apr last [9 May 1844]
    Amos Chase c/o William & Lucy WHITE at Canton ME [2 Jul 1846]
    Benjamin Esq 44 at Monmouth ME on Thurs May 15th, Sheriff of Kennebec Co [23 May
        1834]
    Benjamin formerly of Roxbury MA AmRev pensioner at Hallowell ME on 17th ult [24
        Jan 1834]
    Catharine 22 w/o Robert WHITE at Houlton Aroostook Co ME [4 Feb 1847]
    Catharine 2y d/o Jefferson WHITE at Calais ME [14 Mar 1837]
    Clarissa 20 d/o Elder Nathaniel B WHITE at Skowhegan ME [7 Oct 1847]
    Clarissa 37 at Hallowell ME on 14 Apr [25 Apr 1850]
    Clarissa 44 at Readfield ME [24 Jan 1850]
    Cordelia 42 w/o Barzilla WHITE & d/o the late Dr TUPPER at Richmond ME on 4th
        inst [1 May 1835]
    Ebenezer 66 at Brunswick ME [23 Sept 1847]
    Ebenezer Capt 54 at Gardiner ME [17 Dec 1842]
    Edwin Augustus c/o William & Lucy WHITE at Canton ME [2 Jul 1846]
    Eliphalet abt 65 at Winthrop ME on Wed morning last very suddenly [14 Aug 1841]

WHITE (Cont.) Emily Josephine 3y & 2m d/o Gen WHITE at Augusta ME [17 Dec 1846]

Esther 90 at Skowhegan ME [4 Apr 1850]

Frances C 28 w/o Charles K WHITE at Solon ME [18 Dec 1851]

Frances O 18 at Greenfield ME [30 Dec 1847]

George William c/o William & Lucy at Canton ME [2 Jul 1846]

Greenlief 53 at Augusta ME, Adjutant General of the state of Maine [22 Jul 1852]

Hannah Mrs 85 w/o Jacob WHITE at Freeport ME [15 Jan 1846]

Henry convicted of burning the treasury building in Mar 1834 on Fri last sentenced by Washington CC to serve ten yrs [21 Feb 1837]

Hugh L Sen from TN & candidate for the presidency at Knoxville TN on 10th inst [2 May 1840]

James alias WILBER, reputed s/o Mr WILBER of Bethel ME story appeared here. No one can doubt he's white, yet from habit he is happier among Indians [*Zion's Advocate*] [21 Oct 1847]

James alias James WILBUR (see article) [4 Nov 1847]

James S of Maine at San Francisco CA [18 Mar 1852]

Jane Mrs widow 81 at Montville ME [25 Feb 1847]

Jedediah 86 AmRev formerly of Livermore ME at Dead River ME [13 Aug 1846]

Joel 75 formerly of Dcham MA at Winthrop ME [20 Apr 1839]

John 21 of Wiscasset ME at New Orleans on board ship *Hudson* [11 Dec 1851]

John Henry 19y of Windsor ME was struck by lightning while sitting in the door of the house [13 Aug 1846]

John Judge of the 19th judicial district, killed himself at Richmond KY (from the *Lexington KY Observer*) [9 Oct 1845]

John R MD formerly of Montville 54 at Bradley Jackson Co IL on Mar 24th [18 May 1848]

Joseph 52 accident at work left wife & two children at Lowell MA [4 Jan 1849]

Joseph Capt 84 AmRev at Lyman [8 Feb 1844]

Leonard 82 the last survivor of Harvard's class 1787, the direct descendant of the Rev George PHILLIPS [*Salem Gazette*] [22 Nov 1849]

Lucinda C 22 d/o Capt Samuel WHITE at Dresden ME [17 Apr 1851]

Lucius of Maine lost overboard from ship *Halcyon* of Bath on her passage from Mobile to Liverpool [18 Jul 1844]

Lydia 4y 5m d/o Ebenezer WHITE at Brunswick ME [13 Jan 1837]

Lydia Mrs 56 at Weld ME [20 Feb 1851]

Mary Ann Mrs 38 w/o Thomas WHITE at Winthrop ME on 15th inst after a short distressing illness leaving a numerous family to mourn her [23 Jul 1846]

Mary Bangs 45 w/o Nathan WHITE Esq at Bucksport ME [4 May 1848]

Mary Jane 20 w/o John WHITE at Jay ME on the 12th ult [27 May 1843]

Mary Mrs 81 wid/o Maj Benjamin WHITE at Monmouth ME [23 Sept 1843]

Mr with the circus died at Lower Sundusky OH? [5 Sept 1834]

Mrs w/o John WHITE at St Albans ME [3 Apr 1851]

Nathan C 23y 6m s/o Edward WHITE of Brunswick ME at Bangor ME [1 Jan 1846]

Nathan W 23 s/o Henry B & Clarinda F WHITE formerly of Augusta ME at Boscawen NH on 1 Jan [31 Jan 1850]

Oliver 37 of Thomaston ME at New York [28 Sept 1839]

Oliver H G 20 at Hallowell ME [10 Aug 1848]

Peter 75 at Windham ME [26 Apr 1849]

R G drowned between Fort Independence & Thompson's Island, with a party of 27 boys of the Farm School on Thompson's Island accompanied by a teacher & boat-keeper [7 May 1842]

Racheal 77 w/o Samuel WHITE at Readfield ME [7 Dec 1848]

WHITE (Cont.) Robert 30 at Litchfield ME [19 Oct 1839]

    Robert 70 one of the oldest settlers at Belfast ME on 29th ult [15 Aug 1840]

    Rose Jane 23 at Lagrange ME [4 June 1846]

    Sally Mrs 71 w/o Aaron WHITE at Vassalboro ME on 29th ult [2 Apr 1846]

    Samuel 82 at Readfield ME on 11 Dec, while cutting wood at the door [19 Dec 1850]

    Sarah M G 79 at Hallowell ME on 15th ult [20 Jul 1848]

    Sarah Mrs 74 at Bath ME [20 Mar 1845]

    Solomon 84 at Bloomfield ME [16 May 1837]

    William H K 31 formerly of Hallowell ME at New Orleans of cholera [6 Sept 1849]

    William Rev 88 Bishop of the Protestant Episcopal Diocese of PA at Philadelphia PA on
        17 Jul [29 Jul 1836] & [13 Jan 1837]

WHITE - see BURRELL, LARRABEE, GULLIVER

WHITEHEAD John 71 at Paris ME [9 Jan 1851]

    Mary 72 w/o John WHITEHEAD at Paris ME [25 Jan 1849]

    Mr a St Louis lawyer after a suit by a colored man for his freedom in Kaskaskia IL,
        seized by a mob knocked down, kicked & trampled watched by judge, citizens rescued
        him. [23 Sept 1841]

    young man drowned at Philadelphia PA [5 Aug 1843]

WHITEHEAD - see CHANDLER

WHITEHOUSE Andrew abt 79 at Topsham ME [18 Mar 1847]

    Daniel 80 formerly of Berwick ME at Vassalboro ME [19 June 1835]

    Elizabeth Mrs 20 w/o Elbridge G WHITEHOUSE at Augusta ME on 15th inst [28 Aug
        1845]

    Mr at Mercer ME on 2d inst [*Skowhegan Clarion*] [14 Aug 1845]

    William A 3 s/o Edmund Jr & Betsey WHITEHOUSE at Vassalboro ME on 4th inst [14
        Sept 1848]

WHITING Amanda Houghton abt 3y youngest d/o Capt Jonathan WHITING at Winthrop
    ME on 30th ult [4 June 1842]

    Betsey 78 at Augusta ME [18 Jul 1837]

    Emily w/o F P WHITING at Fanning Co TX [4 Mar 1847]

    Frederick P 32 formerly of Union ME at Fanning Co TX [4 Mar 1847]

    John 79 at Union ME [7 Feb 1850]

    Nathaniel 55 formerly of East Winthrop ME at Brockport NY [23 Sept 1847]

    O I form/o of Charleston MA of Leonard STURTEVANT & Co, Mr STURTEVANT
        native of Winthrop ME & lost two partners in four yrs at New Orleans on 12th Nov
        [4 Jan 1849]

WHITMAN Recellar A 50th yr d/o Oren WHITMAN at North Turner ME on 6 Mar [13
    Mar 1841]

    Abel 82 formerly of Bridgewater MA at Frankfort ME [18 May 1848]

    Bernard Rev 38 at Waltham MA [28 Nov 1834]

    David Snow 69 formerly of Livermore ME at Lewiston ME [18 Nov 1843]

    Deborah C 45 w/o Oren WHITMAN at North TURNER [2 Nov 1840]

    Ezra of Winthrop ME formerly of Bridgewater MA last week 81y "had a great taste for
        machinery" (see p. 670 Stackpole's *History of Winthrop ME*) [23 Sept 1851]

    Ford Esq 65 at Bangor ME [30 Dec 1847]

    Harrison Capt abt 33 at Woodstock ME [30 Jan 1845]

    Jason Rev of Lexington MA (Unitarian min) at Portland ME on Tues last, was to attend
        funeral of Sen FAIRFIELD, his wife's bro (had $2000 Life Insurance) [*Portland
        Argus*] [3 Feb 1848]

    John Dea b 25 Mar 1735 at Bridgewater, a temperate man, has not tasted ardent spirits
        for 50y [30 Oct 1841] d in108th yr at E Bridgewater Mon last "undoubtedly oldest
        person in (ME)" [9 Apr 1842] & [30 Apr 1842]

WHITMAN (Cont.) Joseph 88 AmRev at Buckfield ME [29 Jan 1842]
    Luretia 60y w/o Joshua WHITMAN at Turner ME on 7 Feb the mother of Mrs
        SAWTELL & d/o the late Rev John STRICKLAND [26 Feb 1836]
    Oren B abt 2y only s/o Oren WHITMAN at North Turner ME on 3 Dec [13 Mar 1841]
    Rhoda S 43 d/o Ezra WHITMAN at Winthrop ME on Thursday on 14th inst [23 May
        1840]
    Theodore 64 at Sedgwick ME [9 May 1834]
    Zenas 82 at Auburn ME [15 Feb 1849]
WHITMARSH Martha S 23 at Norway ME [21 Nov 1844]
WHITMORE Benjamin 72 at Bowdoinham on 26th ult [16 Sept 1847]
    Daniel 87 at Unity ME [12 Mar 1846]
    Frances D 44 w/o Hon J C WHITMORE at Phipsburg ME [1 Feb 1849]
    Joseph W 33 at Portland ME on 16th inst [27 May 1843]
    Lorenzo of Brunswick ME seaman lost overboard from ship *Elizabeth* on passage from
        Liverpool to Boston MA on 17th ult [23 Aug 1849]
    William 82 at Gardiner ME [13 June 1850]
WHITNEY Aaron 74y 6m at Milltown (Calais) ME [18 Mar 1847]
    Abraham 52 at Lisbon ME [11 Apr 1850]
    Ann D Mrs 48 wid/o Joseph WHITNEY at Lisbon ME [10 Oct 1844]
    Ann Sarah abt 21 w/o Joseph D WHITNEY at Little River Village (Lisbon, Lincoln Co)
        ME [22 Apr 1852]
    Charles 8y s/o Joseph S WHITNEY of Augusta ME fell from a pile of lumber, near
        Williams' sawmill into the Kennebec & drowned. His body was recovered Sat
        afternoon last. [13 Jul 1848]
    Charles Edwin 20 formerly of ME at Briot WI of consumption [23 Oct 1851]
    Charlotte 48 formerly of Portland ME at Searsport ME [1 Aug 1850]
    child infant of Otis WHITNEY at Augusta ME [23 Aug 1849]
    Comfort 47 w/o William WHITNEY at Bath ME [29 Aug 1844]
    Daniel 89 at Oxford ME [19 Feb 1852]
    Edwin 4y 33d s/o A H & Betsey WHITNEY at Augusta ME [27 June 1837]
    Eli memoir of his life, b 3 Dec 1765 at Westborough, MA, his maternal ancestors, name
        of FAY, were also English (*American Journal of Science & Arts*) [30 Nov 1833 to 21
        Dec 1833]
    Elizabeth Mrs 42 w/o Abner WHITNEY at Saco ME [9 Oct 1845]
    Ellen Frances 6 d/o George C WHITNEY ar Winthrop ME [11 Mar 1847]
    George K 3 s/o Otis & Sarah C WHITNEY at Augusta ME on 13 Aug [28 Aug 1851]
    Gustavus F of Whitneyville ME killed by a falling limb from a tree [*Argus*] [12 Feb
        1846]
    Harriet 35 w/o Marshall WHITNEY at Oxford ME [15 Aug 1844]
    Harriet 5 d/o Elias S WHITNEY at Augusta ME on 14th instant [17 Sept 1846]
    Henry 7y 5m s/o Capt William WHITNEY at Bath ME [29 Aug 1844]
    Henry 81y 8m at Chesterville ME on 18 Apr [3 May 1849]
    J P formerly of Belfast ME at New Orleans MA on 30 Jan [9 Mar 1848]
    Jacob 86 AmRev at Phillips ME [18 June 1846]
    James Capt 40 formerly of Gorham ME at Waterford ME [12 Nov 1842]
    James Mae 21 s/o James WHITNEY of Canton ME at Augusta ME on 21st inst of
        smallpox [28 June 1849]
    Joel Esq of Plymouth ME his tannery destroyed by fire on Sat night last, the tannery took
        fire by lightning [*Somerset Journal*] [20 Jul 1839]
    John 19 native of Maine at St Vincent de Paul of yellow fever on 24 June [2 Nov 1848]
    John H 39 at Whitneyville ME of consumption [30 Mar 1848]
    John Perkins a native of Castine ME at New Orleans of yellow fever [7 Sept 1839]

WHITNEY (Cont.) Joseph by lightning at Tuscarawas Co OH on 24th ult [22 June 1839]

Martha 75 w/o Stephen WHITNEY at Bridgton ME formerly of Standish ME [18 Nov 1836]

Mary 15 d/o Ebenezer WHITNEY at Calais ME [20 June 1850]

Mary S K 35y 4m 11d w/o John WHITNEY & d/o the widow Isabel KIMBALL at Lisbon ME on 14th ult [6 May 1843]

Mr of Cambridgeport MA found on the flats of Charles River, near West Boston bridge [*Boston Bee*] [5 Dec 1844]

Nathan 77 at Augusta ME on 24 Nov [7 Dec 1848]

Sarah 100y 8m 20d at Casco ME at the res of her son-in-law, the mother of 12 ch, 4 living, 40 living gch, 123 ggch & 1 gggch [1 Jul 1843]

Silas 69 formerly of Brownfield ME at Moose River ME [25 Jan 1849]

Susan 18 of Maine at Boston MA on 7th inst [16 Oct 1838]

Susannah Mrs 80 wid/o Elias WHITNEY at Portland ME [21 May 1846]

William Atwell 8m only s/o Joseph B & Mary WHITNEY at Thorndike ME [9 Jul 1846]

William Warren 12 of Waterford ME at Burnham ME [21 Oct 1847]

WHITNEY - see BRAGDON, CHAPMAN, CORSON, POWERS, WOODBURY

WHITTAKER Charles L 25 at Ellsworth ME [9 Sept 1847]

WHITTEMORE Abigail abt 22 of Temple ME at Winthrop ME on Thurs the 3d inst [11 Nov 1836]

Enoch 33 at Lisbon ME (died on 26 Apr 1851 ae 32y 11m, see issue of 21 May 1851 *Morning Star*) [8 May 1851]

John D abt 15 eldest s/o Ebenezer WHITTEMORE at East Livermore ME [23 Oct 1845]

N K 74 at Temple ME [5 Aug 1847]

Nancy W 76 wid/o Ebenezer WHITTEMORE of Dexter ME at Topsham ME [6 May 1852]

Samuel 24 at Paris ME [24 Dec 1846]

WHITTEMORE - see WOODBURY

WHITTEN Charles P found floating in the Penobscot River near Bucksport ME Ferry on Thursday last (from *Bangor ME Democrat*) [24 Apr 1851]

Elizabeth M 30 w/o Thomas WHITTEN at Augusta ME [13 Apr 1848]

Joseph 60 at Hollis ME [12 Nov 1846]

Mary 18 at Topsham ME [18 Nov 1852]

WHITTIER Almeda abt 37 d/o Jonathan WHITTIER at Readfield ME on 24 Feb [4 Mar 1852]

Andrew 125y less one month Rev W MARSHALL, states that a year ago last harvest WHITTIER shocked eight sheaves of wheat near Cambridge OH on 25th July [13 Feb 1841]

Augusta Ann 25 w/o Perley M WHITTIER at Dover ME [20 Nov 1851]

David Capt 61 at Belfast ME [1 Nov 1849]

Elisha 66 at Saco ME [19 Mar 1846]

Enoch the dwelling house of his & his son's of South Solon ME consumed by fire [6 Sept 1849]

F H reported of Boston MA 28 of cholera Sacramento CA on 2 Nov [2 Jan 1851]

Hannah Mrs 26 w/o William P WHITTIER at Hollis ME [12 Mar 1846]

Isaac N 38 at Vienna ME on the 29th ult [11 Nov 1847]

Josiah Jr late of Sidney ME est notice Lauriston GUILD adm [11 Mar 1852]

Lydia M 24 w/o Joseph WHITTIER at Augusta ME on 5th Mar [7 Mar 1850]

Lydia T 18 d/o True & Maria WHITTIER at Vassalboro ME on 22 Mar [1 Apr 1852]

Martha 63 w/o S C WHITTIER at Hallowell ME [14 Nov 1850]

Mary 67 w/o Beniah WHITTIER at Readfield ME [28 June 1849]

Mary Smith 53 w/o Capt David WHITTIER at Belfast ME [27 Jul 1848]

WHITTIER (Cont.) Miranda J 4y d/o Isaac F & Mary J WHITTIER at Strong ME [10 Oct 1844]

Mr a mason by occupation, fell from the 4th story of the new machine shop of Wm T MERRIFIELD at Worcester MA, (18 June), left a wife & family in Readfield ME [26 June 1851]

Octavia 22 at Cornville ME on 17 Dec was a member of Myrtle Union, D of T of (Augusta) ME [22 Feb 1849]

Richard 75 at Waterford ME [11 Apr 1850]

Samuel of Portland ME [*Portland Advertiser*] [20 Apr 1848]

Sarah 54 w/o Josiah WHITTIER at Readfield ME [24 Jan 1850]

Sarah B Mrs 29 w/o Franklin WHITTIER formerly of Northfield NH at Bangor ME [19 Dec 1844]

William Esq of Farmington ME house & buildings destroyed by fire abt Sun night, occupied by Eld BAILY & H B STINCHFIELD, best buildings in town, ins for $900 Monmouth Mutual Fire Insurance Office [5 Aug 1843]

WHITTIER - see MELVIN

WHITTREDGE Daniel Capt 27 at Stetson ME [17 Apr 1835]

WHITTUM Ebenezer 69 at Lewiston ME [1 Feb 1849]

WICKLIFFE Robert Jr married Miss Josephine Van HOUTUN of Rotterdam - pronounced a lady of rank & fortune on 7 Apr at Turin [14 May 1846]

WICKS - see SANFORD WICKWIRE Ezekiel Capt 83 formerly of Lebanon CT at Monmouth ME on 29 Nov [13 Dec 1849]

WICKWIRE Sarah 72 wid/o Elisha WICKWARE at Windsor ME on 16 Jan [30 Jan 1851]

WIER Polly Mrs 75 wid/o Robert WIER at Windham ME [19 Feb 1846]

WIGGIN Betsey 79 widow of Nathaniel WIGGIN of Freedom ME at Dover ME [11 Jul 1850]

Daniel H 66 at Lewiston ME [19 Aug 1852]

Martha Ellen 10m only d/o Jacob L & Olive Ann WIGGIN at Albion ME on 20 June [1 Jul 1852]

WIGGINS a boy s/o John WIGGINS at St Albans ME [3 Apr 1851]

Francis S Esq formerly editor of the *Farmer's Cabinet* & late editor of the *American Farmer's Companion* at Philadelphia PA [15 Feb 1840]

Nathaniel 74 at China ME [7 Nov 1850]

WIGGINS - see PEARCE

WIGHT Betsey 57 w/o Jona WIGHT at Monmouth ME on 11 Aug [7 Sep 1848]

Charles Henry 11y 8m s/o Asa & Louisa WIGHT at Vienna ME [15 May 1851]

Charles J 2y s/o Isaac WIGHT at Augusta ME [23 Sept 1852]

T W Leonard 6y s/o Seth WIGHT Esq at Bethel ME [4 Dec 1841]

WILBER - see WHITE

WILBERFORCE William Esq died at London [7 Sept 1833]

WILBUR Adam 76 at East Livermore ME after an illness of 16y [26 Aug 1852]

Asa Elder 87 at Augusta ME on 8th inst [19 Aug 1847]

Eliza A 2y 10m c/o Nahum & Abby WILBUR at Sidney ME of croup [16 Jul 1846]

Eliza L 22 d/o David WILBUR Esq at Augusta ME on 15 Mar [18 Mar 1852] & [25 Mar 1852]

Henry H 4y 8m c/o Nahum & Abby WILBUR at Sidney ME of croup [16 Jul 1846]

Isaiah E 33 of Phillips ME at Bath ME [22 Nov 1849]

James of Bethel ME "Mr WILBUR's daus at Saco factories saw among a body of Indians encamped there, a white young man, recognized a resemblance to their family & soon claimed him as a br, 23y. The Indians encamped at Cape Elizabeth ME opposite this city with the youth & his wife, for he married an Indian girl last Spring. Child was

WILBUR (Cont.) lost in 1827, when family res near Sandy River Pond Franklin Co ME, since then his family had moved to Bethel ME. 20 yrs ago boy was 2y 10m, one day went to meet the other ch but never returned. Perhaps ROBBINS (an old offender) stole the ch, tried for petty thefts, afterwards imprisoned for murder of HINDS & son in 1828, but made his escape." [*Eastern Argus* of Portland ME] [16 Sept 1847]

Mary 36 w/o Ichabod S WILBUR at East Livermore ME [9 May 1850]

Rachel 54 w/o David WILBUR at Augusta ME on 12 Mar [25 Mar 1852] & [18 Mar 1852]

Waitstill 66 w/o Adam WILBUR at East Livermore ME [16 Apr 1846]

WILCOX Elizabeth 30 w/o Charles C WILCOX Esq & d/o Arthems LEONARD Esq of Hallowell ME at Tremont IL [30 Oct 1838]

WILCOX - see JUNKINS

WILDER Arethusa 69 widow of Deacon Thomas WILDER at Dixmont ME [29 Jan 1842]

Betsey 50 w/o John W WILDER at Belfast ME [28 Sept 1848]

Darius 19 at Wiscasset ME [16 Sept 1836]

Ebenezer C 79 at Dennysville ME [30 Oct 1851]

Henry of Greeneville NY died [*Albany Democrat* of the 11th ult] [23 Apr 1846]

John 52 at Pembroke [28 Jan 1847]

Mr killed a bear weight 227 pounds on Fri at Glenburn near Bangor ME after the bear recieved two shots the bruin attacked Mr Wilder & injured one of his hands badly [1 June 1848]

William Henry 22 at Pembroke [28 Jan 1847]

WILDES Benj of Kennebunk ME, form of Kennebunkport drowned Sat a.m. off Kennebunkport. boat belonged to Joshua HERRICK Esq. Left wife & two ch.[*Saco Democrat*] [18 May 1839]

Charles Q 20y 8m at Waldoboro [3 June 1847]

child of Phipsburg ME choked to death by a bean on the 14th instant [24 Aug 1848]

WILEY C W apothecary's shop, BEDLOW's Bookstore & POND's shoe store in building at Main & Milltown St Calais ME, burned yesterday a.m. [*Eastport Sentinel* 10th inst] [19 June 1845]

William 74 at Fryeburg ME [4 Oct 1849]

WILEY - see WOODBURY

WILLAH - see WISEMAN

WILLIAMS boy abt 5 stung in the hollow of his foot by a bee near Vincent Town NJ on 18th inst & d in great agony Tues 22 s/o Mr D P WILLIAMS [*Philadelphia Ledger*] [31 Jul 1851]

WILLARD Aaron 87 long known as manufacturer of clocks at Boston MA on the 20th inst [30 May 1844]

Josiah Jr 27 at Wilton ME [15 Jul 1833]

Prudence Mrs 64 w/o Major Josiah WILLARD of Wilton ME at Bloomfield ME [10 June 1847]

Stephen Capt of Sanford ME his house struck by lightning at Sanford York Co ME on 11th inst, he & his wife were injured [*Saco Union*] [28 Aug 1845]

Stephen Jr 28 at Sanford ME [15 Oct 1846]

WILLET John T 45 at Waldoboro ME [17 June 1852] & [23 June 1852]

WILLETT John Capt 73 at Bridgton ME [3 Dec 1846]

Susan Mrs 25 w/o Capt Thomas B WILLETT at Brunswick ME [5 Nov 1846]

WILLEY Davis on the east side of the river near the dam, while engaged in blasting rocks at Augusta ME [30 Sept 1836]

Lyman 8 only s/o Rev Austin WILLEY editor of the *Liberty Standard* at Hallowell ME [1 Feb 1844]

WILLEY (Cont.) Mary 60 w/o William WILLEY at Athens ME [22 May 1851]

    Moses 43 formerly of Brookfield ME drowned at Farmington ME on 20 May [25 June 1846]

    Mr late editor of the *Free Soil Republican* of Hallowell ME removed to Battle Creek, Michigan & become the editor of the *Liberty Press*, a paper published at that place [19 Jul 1849]

WILLIAM negro severely stabbed by John VINCIENT, another colored person at Mt Joy in Portland ME [27 Jul 1839]

    William of Keene NH in a well about 25 feet deep [4 Oct 1849]

WILLIAMS Abby 54 at Augusta ME on Sunday last [28 Sept 1848]

    Abigail 48 w/o Samuel WILLIAMS at Turner ME [31 Aug 1848]

    Abigail 63 w/o Daniel WILLIAMS Esq at Forks of Kennebec (River) ME [20 Jan 1848]

    Abraham G 24 of the firm of WILLIAMS & MAHON at Portland ME [14 Nov 1840]

    Abram 106y of Kentucky AmRev died recently [8 June 1848]

    Amos 82 one of the 1st settlers of Isleboro ME [4 Apr 1840]

    Anna 93 at North Anson ME [21 Nov 1850]

    Arthur Lowell only child of Joseph H WILLIAMS Esq at Augusta ME [24 Dec 1846]

    B Capt of Washington NC lost his life in the storm [14 Sept 1839]

    Benjamin 60 at Anson ME [7 Dec 1839]

    Charles Esq 54 at Augusta ME [25 Nov 1836]

    Church 75 at Augusta ME on Fri last [17 June 1847]

    Daniel Esq 66 of apoplexy at Solon ME on 8th inst [21 Oct 1847]

    David D s/o Nelson & Elizabeth WILLIAMS at the Forks ME on 28th ult [13 Feb 1845]

    Edward Col 40 at Augusta ME [18 Jul 1837]

    Eleanor Mrs 73 at West Bath ME [26 Feb 1846]

    Elizabeth 64 w/o Col Johnson WILLIAMS at Waterville ME [15 Apr 1852]

    Emily Ann 8m d/o Jos WILLIAMS at Wayne ME on 9 Sept [9 Oct 1845]

    Eunice 71 w/o Paul WILLIAMS at Augusta ME [18 Jul 1840]

    George 37 of Waterville ME at Chesterville ME [1 Mar 1849]

    Hannah 40 w/o Gen John WILLIAMS at Bangor ME [14 Aug 1835]

    Horace s/o Daniel WILLIAMS of Augusta ME left some time ago for the gold mountains in CA [*Banner*] [15 Feb 1849]

    James Rev 68 formerly of Readfield ME & member of the local Masonic Lodge of Readfield (Lafayette Lodge) at Frederickton New Brunswick Canada on 29th ult [16 Jan 1851]

    Joanna 68 widow at Waterville ME [7 Nov 1850]

    Joanna Mrs widow 80y 8m at Embden ME, left 15ch, 106gch, 88ggch [13 Feb 1845]

    Joel H of Skowhegan ME an invalid & cripple, thrown from a wagon in Madison ME on Thurs of last week & had his leg broken between the knee & hip [8 June 1848]

    John 40 a native of Liverpool England at Eastport ME [17 June 1847]

    John 84 AmRev at Wiscasset ME [13 Feb 1845]

    John a colored man while eating his dinner at Center St Boston MA became choked with a piece of meat & died before relief could be administered [25 Dec 1851]

    John fell overboard by the paddles and drowned off the steamboat *Rhode Island* [23 May 1840]

    Joshua of Strong ME at New York City, going to CA but working temporarily at his trade fell from a building & died. Insured for $500 w/ Union Mutual Life of Farmington [22 Aug 1850]

    lad threw a stone at another lad GARDINER wounded him so he died in a few days [15 Nov 1849]

    Lemuel Col 62 at Athens ME [2 Jul 1846]

    Lois 89 wid/o Robert WILLIAMS of Augusta ME at Gardiner ME [25 Dec 1841]

WILLIAMS (Cont.) Lydia 77 wid/o of Thos WILLIAMS at Chesterville ME [24 Apr 1851]

    Margaret widow 85y "colored" at Norridgewock ME, retired to bed on Friday evening last as well as usual & in the morning was found dead [14 Feb 1837]

    Maria 18 d/o George WILLIAMS at York ME [13 Nov 1845]

    Martha Caroline 4 c/o James M WILLIAMS at Augusta ME on 25 Feb [9 Mar 1848]

    Mary G 20 w/o Llewellyn WILLIAMS & d/o Hon C GREENE of Athens ME at Augusta ME 8 Aug [14 Aug 1851]

    Mary S 30 d/o the late Charles WILLIAMS Esq at Augusta ME [13 Dec 1849]

    Mr a missionary to New Zealand eaten by the savages, shared the fate of LYMAN & MUNSON [2 May 1840]

    Mr a native of Springfield MA in a wagon yard at Richmond on 20th ult from intemperance & exposure. [21 Dec 1839]

    Mr drinking on a bet five half pints of clear spirts, principally whiskey in the space of 30 mins & shortly after died. At the Catskill [15 June 1839]

    Mr eloped with d/o R G MORRIS of Amherst MA attacked by young lady's bro & others in Nelson Co. Mr MORRIS & Mr HILL killed & Mr WILLIAMS bro mortally wounded [17 Jul 1851]

    Mr near "Lick Skillet" in Winston Co whipped a negro girl to death. Inquest held but he escaped sheriffs posse [*Ala'a (Miss) Gazette*] [anti slavery comments *Boston Courier*] [31 Dec 1842]

    Otis 19 at Augusta ME on 3 May [9 May 1850]

    Patience (white) 45 w/o Dr Miles WILLIAMS "colored" at Norridgewock ME (see Randolph Stakeman's *Maine Black Population*, Bowdoin College of Brunswick) [30 Jul 1846]

    Sally 67 wid/o Ebenezer B WILLIAMS at Augusta ME on 23d Jan [31 Jan 1850]

    Samuel J printer 70 at Cambridge MA [10 Feb 1848]

    Sarah 21 formerly of Alfred ME at Boston MA [22 Jan 1836]

    Sarah Mrs 53 wid/o Charles WILLIAMS Esq at Augusta ME on 28th ult [4 Apr 1844]

    Seth 40y formerly of Augusta ME at New Orleans on 20th ult [24 May 1849]

    Seth Esq at Augusta ME [23 Jan 1838]

    Tamor claimed as the slave of W P J PURNELL of MD continued. Judge KANE deemed it insufficient & ordered the discharge of the prisoner. [*Philadelphia North American* 10th] [20 Feb 1851]

    Thomas Rev 60 formerly of Brewer ME at Poland ME [10 Dec 1846]

    Timothy Esq 53 at Embden ME [15 Nov 1849]

    William 22 seaman from Maine at New York Hospital [8 May 1835]

    Zilpha Mrs 84 widow at Augusta ME on Sat last [25 Sept 1845]

WILLIAMS - see CUTLER, FOX, HOVEY, JONES, STEPHENS, CRAWFORD

WILLIAMSON Albert M 22y 10m at Mercer ME on 16 Feb [6 Mar 1851]

    Catherine Maria 7y 2m d/o Robert & Mary WILLIAMSON at Gardiner ME [15 Feb 1840]

    Dexter 19 at Augusta ME on 4th inst [11 Oct 1849]

    Ebenezer abt 72 at Starks ME on 25 Oct [4 Nov 1847]

    Hartly 36 s/o Ebenezer & Jemina WILLIAMSON at Starks ME on 3 Oct [4 Nov 1847]

    James V 20 s/o Ebenezer & Jemima WILLIAMSON at Starks ME on 24th Sept [4 Nov 1847]

    John 27 s/o Ebenezer & Jemima WILLIAMSON at Starks ME on 12 Oct [4 Nov 1847]

    Jonathan D Commodore of U. S. Navy died [9 May 1844]

    Levi 22 s/o Ebenezer & Jemima WILLIAMSON at Starks ME on 28 Oct [4 Nov 1847]

    Robert E 19 at Gardiner ME [15 Mar 1849]

    Stephen C Lieut 21y 11m s/o Col Warren WILLIAMS of Gardiner ME of the typhus fever in South Redinton [18 Dec 1841]

WILLIAMSON (Cont.) Warren Col 59 at Gardiner ME [16 Sept 1852]
William D Hom 67 at Bangor ME [11 June 1846]
WILLIAMSON - see CRAWFORD
WILLIS Joseph J 33 at Buckfield ME [13 Feb 1851]
P 69 at Thomaston ME [8 Mar 1849]
WILLISTON Jona 65 at Troy ME [29 Jul 1847]
Miss 25 d/o Mr J WILLISTON, res at the corner of Centre & Hanover Streets, raising bucket of water from a cistern, slipped, fell in head first & drowned [*Boston Transcript*] [24 Jan 1834]
WILLS Betsey F 35 formerly of Northfield NH w/o Elvin A WILLS at Number 2, Lexington ME (NH papers please copy) [10 Jul 1851]
WILSON Anna 93 wid/o Capt James WILSON at Topsham ME [27 Mar 1841]
Arletta 82 formerly of Harpswell ME at Hallowell ME [6 May 1852]
Betsey Mrs 57 w/o Caleb WILSON at Augusta ME [22 Feb 1844]
Caleb 20 at Anson ME [29 Apr 1833]
Caleb 67 at Augusta ME on 16th Jul [29 Jul 1852]
Charles of Boston MA in CA [21 Aug 1851]
Charles seaman crew lost & missing on 7th inst the steamboat *New York*, bound from Galveston to New Orleans was wrecked in a hurricane, 17 persons drowned [24 Sept 1846]
Cyrus F 25 s/o Joshua & Martha WILSON of Bingham ME at Hopkinton MA [17 Jul 1851]
Dr died of cholera at Hampden ME [*Bangor Daily Whig*] [16 Aug 1849]
Eleanor Mrs wid/o Jonathan WILSON at Belfast ME [26 Feb 1846]
Eunice 100 wid/o Eph WILSON at Winslow ME [7 Nov 1850]
Eunice Mrs 65 at Bath ME [10 Aug 1848]
George a party of 7 young men & women went from Campobello I to Casco Bay on a pleasure excursion & drowned with Thankful WILSON, Hannah PARKER & CAMPLIN [24 Jul 1835]
James Deacon 90y 9m 3d at Brunswick ME [4 Sept 1838]
Jane 99 at Bath ME [29 Mar 1849]
Jeannette Mrs 24 w/o Edmund WILSON Jr at Belfast ME [7 Nov 1844]
John 48 at Topsham ME on 2d Aug [22 Aug 1850]
John 71 at Belfast ME [20 Jul 1848]
John Col trial of late Speaker of the House of Rep for murder of Maj J J ___ a member from Randolph Co Dec last. at Little Rock AR [*The Little Rock Gazette* of the 23d inst] [26 June 1838]
John D 56 at Brewer ME [21 Jan 1847]
John form of Nova Scotia Canada found a few days since at the foot of Moosehead Lake (Greenville) ME. He obtained grog at Tom GRANT's shanty & d. [*Skowhegan Press*] [13 Apr 1848]
Joseph W 18 at Augusta ME on 31 Oct [13 Nov 1851]
Lorenzo D abt 22 of East Machias ME the *New York* packet bearing up river at Machias Port on Tues when nearly up to the bridge, was knocked overboard boom & drowned [7 Aug 1851]
Maria (nee JOHNSON) 77 w/o C T (Colin T) WILSON at Portland ME "colored" (see Randolph Stakeman's *Maine Black Population*, Bowdoin College of Brunswick) [13 Feb 1845]
Mary C 34 w/o Alfred WILSON at Newcastle ME [10 Jan 1850]
Mary Mrs 79 at Columbia ME [23 Apr 1846]
Mr discovered on Gull ledge near the wreck of the lighthouse on Minot's ledge by the keeper of the lightship, buried at Cohasset [*Traveller*] [2 Oct 1851]

WILSON (Cont.) Mr of Brunswick ME (one of the carpenter ship builders at the Falls) fell & died of a skull injury at North Yarmouth ME on Sat [3 Oct 1844]

Mr of Madison fatal railroad accident on the 10th ult on the Lexington & Ohio Railroad with Mr TINSLEY of Woolford killed [*Louisville (KY) Advertiser*] [8 Apr 1836]

Mrs w/o Rev Henry R WILSON at the Missionary Station among the Choctaws on 18 Jul [23 Oct 1835]

Mrs & two ch passengers lost or missing on 7th inst the steamboat *New York*, bound from Galveston to New Orleans was wrecked in a hurricane, 17 persons drowned [24 Sept 1846]

Obed Rev 62 of the Methodist Episcopal Church at Skowhegan ME [5 Dec 1840]

Rebecca 69 w/o Isaac WILSON at Livermore ME [25 Oct 1849]

Samuel of Sedgwick ME lost at sea of the schr *Kenduskeag* [26 Apr 1849]

Thankful party of 7 young men & women, going from Campobello I to Casco Bay on a pleasure excursion & drowned with George W, Hannah PARKER & person CAMPLIN [24 Jul 1835]

Theodore 63 at York ME [3 Oct 1850]

Thomas H abt 22 d in Gaol at Alfred ME Wed by suicide, professed to be English, had wallet on which is written "George MONECK or MONCK" containing pieces of paper, on one which is written "Miss Claretta FIELD - Frankfort, blacks P.O. ME" containing a small lock of hair. On another "Mrs FIELD - Frankfort" - said he had friends in New York [29 Jul 1843]

WILSON - see CRAWFORD

WILTBECK - see LUNAR

WILTON John of the steamer *Atlantic* shipwreck [24 June 1847]

WINCHEBACH James of Warren ME a passenger on the schr *May Flower*, HUPPER Capt, James was one of three Maine men who drowned at Norfolk VA [11 Nov 1847]

WINCHELL - see BOLTON

WINCHENBACH Isaac Capt 50 at Waldoboro ME [15 Oct 1846]

WINCHENBACK Elizabeth 77 at Waldoboro ME [15 Aug 1844]

WINCHESTER J B his son fell into the creek while fishing, the lad's mother & grandmother tried to save him but also drowned ... all of the family left is a small inf & a girl abt 3 [17 Jul 1841]

WINES Ruth Mrs at Bloomfield ME [27 Mar 1838]

WING Alexander 38 at Monmouth ME on 31st May [25 June 1846]

Alma M 18 d/o J E WING at Vassalboro ME [31 Aug 1848]

Betsey 77 formerly of Wayne ME at Portland ME [25 Jul 1850]

Catherine Mrs 59 at Lubec ME [7 Aug 1851]

Clara Adelma 1y 10m d/o Ormand T & Octavia A WING at Leeds ME on 29 Feb [18 Mar 1852] & [25 Mar 1852]

Daniel late of Winthrop ME [22 Jan 1836]

Eli of Mt Vernon ME lost his arm on Mon last by having it caught in a shingle machine [18 Jul 1837]

Ella Marr 7 d/o Ormand T & Octavia A WING at Leeds ME on 27 Feb [18 Mar 1852] & [25 Mar 1852]

Frances W 13 d/o Calvin WING of Norkolk VA at Brunswick ME [18 Jul 1844]

Francis Johnson S 5y only s/o William & Louisa WING at Wayne ME [22 Jan 1846]

Ichabod late of Winthrop ME, Cynthia WYMAN, widow [29 June 1839]

Isaac D 36 at Winthrop ME on Tuesday 19th inst after a long & protracted sickness [23 May 1840]

Joan S Mrs 27 w/o William G WING at Belgrade ME [5 Mar 1846]

Mary 38 w/o Levi WING at Wilton ME on 28 Aug [3 Sept 1846]

WING (Cont.) Otis A 24 s/o Joseph WING of Bangor ME drowned in Boston Harbor on 14th inst [3 Aug 1839]

Otis a painter of Bangor ME drowned, the other 5 picked up by an outward bound fishing schooner. A sail boat containing six men was upset in Boston harbor on Sunday last [27 Jul 1839]

Prudence abt 30 at Greene ME on 11th inst [25 Dec 1838]

Sally Mrs 71y d in dwelling house of David WING in Westport near the Hicks' Bridge discovered to be on fire on Tuesday morning [*New Bedford Mercury*] [11 Jan 1849]

Sarah S B 31 w/o C A WING at Winthrop ME on 23 Oct [7 Dec 1848]

Susan 16 at Livermore ME [5 Dec 1837]

Sylvina abt 33 d/o Obed WING of East Livermore ME at St Louis MO on 5th Jul of cholera [6 Sept 1849]

W M 28 formerly of Waterville ME at Matamoras Mexico at the hospital, Nov 1846 [12 Aug 1847]

William 78 at Vassalboro ME [27 May 1847]

WING - see BEAN, BISHOP, PADDOCK,GIFFORD

WINGATE Algernon S 40 at Windsor ME of consumption [22 Jul 1847]

Francis Esq 58 formerly of Portsmouth NH at Brunswick ME [4 Feb 1843]

Francis 59 at Hallowell ME [25 May 1848]

George 75 a s/o the late Judge WINGATE at Stratham NH [23 Sept 1852]

Jonathan 92 AmRev at North Parsonsfield ME [5 Dec 1850]

Joseph at Portland ME on 7th inst [11 Nov 1843]

Joseph Esq 66 at Hallowell ME on 27th ult [2 Oct 1845]

Joshua 97 at Hallowell ME on 11th inst [24 Oct 1844]

Judith Mrs 86 wid/o Joseph WINGATE at Hallowell ME [14 Nov 1844]

Nathan M 27 at Hallowell ME [2 May 1844]

Paine 62 at Hallowell ME on 12th inst [18 Jan 1849]

Sally 68 at Hallowell ME on 20 Nov [27 Nov 1845]

WINGATE - see CRAVEN, MERRILL

WINN M Dr of Farmington ME at Wilton ME [9 Mar 1848]

WINSHIP Amanda abt 4m c/o Albert WINSHIP at Turner ME [3 Sept 1842]

boy by a leopard belonging to the menagerie in the city of Cincinnati OH during the winter s/o Mrs WINTHROP [the *Republican*] [15 Jan 1839]

WINSLOW Aaron 61 formerly of Falmouth ME at Monmouth ME [13 Aug 1842]

Albion K P 25 at Gardiner ME [10 Sept 1846]

Benj 21 formerly of Winthrop ME at Providence RI [27 Apr 1848]

Benjamin 63 at Westbrook ME on Sat of the Society of Friends [29 Apr 1843]

child 9m of Henry WINSLOW at Augusta ME [1 Jul 1836]

Comfort Mrs 26 w/o Nathan WINSLOW of Portland ME at the Island of Madiera [1 Apr 1843]

Eliza 31 w/o Alfred W Esq at West Waterville ME [3 Jan 1850]

Francis was killed on the Worcester Railroad at Westboro [*Leonard's Express*] [16 Apr 1846]

George Edwin 14m s/o William & Esther WINSLOW at Winslow ME [10 Jul 1851]

Harriot L w/o Rev Miron WINSLOW, missionary of the American Board at Ceylon India on the 17th Jan [29 Jul 1833]

Hezekiah 31 at Winthrop ME [11 Mar 1852]

Horace 24 at Brunswick ME [1 Jan 1846]

James of the sloop *Ware* at sea [*Boston Bee*] [8 Mar 1849]

John Hartwell 8m s/o Hezekiah & Nancy C WINSLOW at Winthrop ME on 7 Nov [11 Mar 1852]

Jonathan 84 at Pittston ME [4 Dec 1845]

WINSLOW (Cont.) Judith B 23 at Gardiner ME [30 Jul 1846]

   Kenelm 91 at Windsor ME [20 May 1847]

   Leonard 26 of Strong ME at Andover MA [16 Oct 1845]

   Mary 75 w/o Jona WINSLOW at Albion ME [25 Oct 1849]

   Mary 89 wid/o Nathan WINSLOW of Westbrook ME at Vassalboro ME on 21st ult [15 Mar 1849]

   Mr funeral of an Odd Fellow of Maine Lodge [*Eastern Argus*] [2 Jan 1845]

   Mrs w/o Stephen WINSLOW at Augusta ME [6 Nov 1835]

   Olive d/o Sanford WINSLOW at Hallowell ME [12 Mar 1842]

   Patience A 30 w/o Cyrus WINSLOW at Thomaston ME [2 Dec 1847]

   Sarah T 22 at Gardiner ME [17 Sept 1846]

   William S 18 of Nobleboro ME at Waldoboro ME [24 Oct 1840]

WINSLOW - see WELCH

WINTER Julia H Mrs left her house a few moments on an errand leaving her dau four yrs alone. She returned & found the girl badly burnt who d in two hrs at NY Mon [25 Dec 1841]

WINTHROP Benjamin Esq of N Y, a lineal descendant of Gov John WINTHROP of MA & gr grandson of the Winthrop who was Gov of CT. Mr WINTHROP the last surviving br of the late Adm Robert WINTHROP of the Br Navy & of Lt Gov Thomas Lindall WINTHROP of MA [25 Jan 1844]

   Eliza 33 w/o Hon Robert C WINTHROP & d/o the late Francis BLANCHARD Esq & the adopted d/o Samuel P GARDNER Esq at Boston MA on 14th inst [25 June 1842]

WINTHROP - see DUDLEY

WIRT William 62 formerly Attorney General at Washington City on Tuesday 18 Feb [28 Feb 1834]

WISE Mr in matrimonial difficulty. He attended militia training & at a "kissing party" m "in fun" Martha STAGE. Later he thought she had no claims on him, but she thought otherwise! [8 Jul 1843]

   Robert A of Augusta ME seaman at sea on passage from St Jago [*sic*] to New York on board bark *Saranac* [14 Oct 1847]

WISEMAN Thomas 88y of Fulford, late coachmaker of York ME m Mrs WILLAH 56y of York ME on 16th inst by Rev C CHEETHAM at Centennary Chapel in York ME. [Marriages in the *Wesleyan* of 28th July] [16 Sept 1847]

WISNER Rev Dr formerly of the Old South Church & for several yrs senior secretary of the American Boards of Commissioners for Foreign Missions at Boston MA [20 Feb 1835]

WITCHERELL - see WINSLOW

WITHAM Hannah 63 at Bath ME [23 Dec 1852]

   Jacob R 50 at Carratunk ME [5 Apr 1850]

   Jesse of Starks ME, an aged man, one of his legs so badly broken by a jump from a wagon had to be amputated [25 May 1848]

   Lucy 74 at Washington ME? [5 Sept 1850]

   Lydia Mrs 96 a widow formerly of Alna ME at Embden ME on 8th inst [21 Dec 1839]

   Mary Mrs widow 65 formerly of Kennebunk ME at East Boston MA [30 Dec 1847]

   Mary P 19 at Bath ME [9 Sept 1836]

   Mathew 41 at Bath ME [27 Jul 1848]

   Nathaniel K 17y 9m at Thomaston ME [12 Mar 1846]

   Parsons 25 formerly of New Gloucester ME at Gardiner ME [2 Oct 1851]

   Thomas J 32 at Danville (now part of Auburn) ME [10 Jan 1850]

WITHAM - see COWAN

WITHEE Asa 50 of Hartland ME death from a fall [*Skowhegan Clarion*] [19 Oct 1848]

WITHEE (Cont.) Emily A 21 at Winslow ME on 14th instant [28 Sept 1848] & [5 Oct 1848]

Heber 26 at Solon ME [25 Oct 1849]

Lydia 24y 6m w/o Owen D WITHEE at Madison ME [29 Aug 1850]

Mr fell from the roof of a saw mill abt 50 of Hartland ME [*Skowhegan Clarion*] [19 Oct 1848]

N R 23 at Gardiner ME [11 Mar 1847]

Sarah 79 widow of William WITHEE at Madison ME [18 Oct 1849]

Zoe 78 AmRev at Industry ME [9 Jan 1841]

WITHERBEE John 58 at Castine ME [8 Jul 1847]

Newil Dr 55 at Machias ME [8 Feb 1844]

WITHERELL Elcy 16 at Monmouth ME [25 Oct 1849]

Mary M Mrs 89y 8m w/o John WITHERELL, the mother of 12ch, 66gch, 82 ggch, lived with her husband who survives her, 70y at Monmouth ME on 18 Nov [9 Dec 1847]

Obadiah MAj 98y a native of Pepperell MA, AmRev, the five battles: Bunker Hill, Stony Point, Abraham's Plains, Valley Forge & commanded his company during campaign [25 Jan 1844]

Sarah 18 at Chesterville ME [18 Mar 1852] & d/o John L & Sarah J WITHERELL of Canaan ME at Chesterville ME on 4 Mar [8 Apr 1852]

Sarah G 36 w/o Josiah S WITHERELL of Norridgewock ME at the insane hospital at Augusta ME [21 Jan 1847]

WITHERLEE John 58 at Castine ME [1 Jul 1847]

WITHERN Elias late of Vienna ME est notice, Charles H RUNDLETT, adm [10 June 1852]

Mary 28 w/o Hiram WITHERN at New Portland ME [1 Aug 1840]

WITHIN Samuel 92 AmRev at Wilton ME [29 Mar 1849]

WITHINGTON Mary P 28 at Hallowell ME [24 June 1847]

Wales 54 at Chesterville ME [18 Oct 1849]

WITT Betsey 51 at Norway ME [13 Feb 1851]

Daniel P of Norway ME killed in a railroad accident [20 May 1852]

Sewall 60 at Washington ME [20 Nov 1845]

WOART William Esq abt 45 at Augusta ME on 11 Mar of congestion of the lung [20 Mar 1851]

WOLCOTT Capt of (Augusta ME) in CA sick on 5 Nov & died 16 days later [20 Mar 1851]

WOLF - see REPHENBARK

WOLTS Andrew Capt 37 at Waldoboro ME [2 Mar 1848]

WOMBELL William nephew of the proprietor of WOMBELL's menagerie scalped by a lion, thought he will not recover [31 Aug 1848]

WOMBWELL George at Northallerton Yorkshire on 16 Nov of bronchitis [2 Jan 1851]

WOODBURY - see MILES

WOOD Asa 28 of Vienna ME dead in his well on the 13th inst [*Augusta Age*] [31 Dec 1842]

Betsey 25 at Winthrop ME on 24 Dec [28 Jan 1833]

Charles 17 at Belfast ME [24 Jan 1834]

child 2y of Horace WOOD at Biddeford ME [13 Nov 1845]

Dr & his lady of Orono ME sailed from Boston MA in the ship *Fame* for the Sandwich Islands (from the *Bangor Courier*) [30 Oct 1838]

E G Capt & Capt John PERKINS, Donald CARNELL, Mrs LARKIN & 2 ch, Mrs FITZGERALD, Mr HEWINS, Mr MARKHAM, Charles McKENNEY w & ch, crew consisted of Capt BEDELL, 6 colored seaman, steward, & boy (white) perished of

WOOD (Cont.) brig *Saratoga*, BEDELL Capt; the above named were lost off Orange Key
  on 3rd inst. The only known survivors were Mr Mott SIMINTON 2nd mate & Samuel
  SMITH a passenger who arrived at Boston in bark *Zaidia* from Mansanilla [*Boston
  Post*] [31 Oct 1844]
  Edward Capt 64 at Bath ME on 17th inst [28 Jan 1843]
  Elijah Esq 45 at Palmira ME [23 Jan 1851]
  Elijah on 80th yr a native of Middleborough MA of the early settlers of the town of
  Winthrop ME at Winthrop ME on Thurs evening last [3 Aug 1848]
  Eliza B 24 of Wiscasset ME at Augusta ME on 4 Oct [12 Oct 1848]
  Ellen Lucretia 9 d/o Thomas C WOOD Esq at Winthrop ME [11 Mar 1847]
  Enoch Deacon 67 formerly of Middleboro MA at Winthrop ME on Sat last [19 Feb 1836]
  Enoch Esq 79 at Hallowell ME on Wednesday last [28 Nov 1837]
  Francis J a native of Maine at Pamonkey, descended to the bottom of the Potomac River,
  clothed in a submarine apparatus, to remove a large stone, supposed d by apoplexy.
  [13 Apr 1848]
  George W 18y oldest s/o Sumner WOOD at Auburn ME on 23 Sept of typhus fever [28
  Nov 1844]
  George W Doctor s/o Elijah WOOD Esq of Winthrop ME at Bartholomew Chicot Co
  Arkansas Territory on 15 June [12 Aug 1836]
  Hannah 60 w/o Ralph WOOD at Sidney ME on 27 Sept [10 Oct 1850]
  Hannah Mrs 41 w/o William WOOD at Biddeford ME [17 June 1847]
  Harmon 47 at Augusta ME [21 Oct 1847]
  Harriet Mrs 31 w/o Cyrus WOOD at Kingfield ME [14 Oct 1847]
  Harrison T 6m s/o Amasa WOOD at Winthrop ME on Sat last [13 Nov 1841]
  James Rev the oldest Methodist minister in the world age 89 at Kingswood circuit in
  England [10 Oct 1840]
  Jason Esq 74 at Freedom ME on 15th inst [21 Sept 1848]
  Joseph 72 at Winslow ME [5 Aug 1847]
  Julia Amanda 22 d/o Elisha & Eliza WOOD at Freedom ME on 22 June [11 Jul 1850]
  Martin S Col formerly of Bangor ME at Chicago IL [5 Feb 1846]
  Mary 79 wid/o Andrew WOOD Esq at Winthrop ME [3 Feb 1848]
  Mary N Mrs 43 at Auburn ME [9 Nov 1848]
  Miss recently recovered $10,000 damages for a breach of promise from her faithless
  swain named HERD. "High price for wood, we think." [11 Dec 1835]
  Phebe Mrs 82 consort of Samuel WOOD Esq a native of Middleboro MA at Winthrop
  ME [19 Oct 1839]
  Phineas Esq 68 at Rumford ME [8 May 1845]
  Samuel Esq 89y AmRev native of Middleborough MA & removed to Winthrop ME in
  1784 at Winthrop ME (see obit) [14 Sept 1848]
  Sarah 24 w/o Ariel WOOD Jr at Wiscasset ME [20 May 1833]
  Sarah 78 wid/o Elijah WOOD Esq at Winthrop ME [16 May 1850]
  Sarah Jane 18 w/o Barzillar D WOOD at Sidney ME on Jul 10th [17 Jul 1851]
  Sarah w/o Thomas C WOOD at Winthrop ME [24 May 1849]
  Silas 81y AmRev at Norridgewock ME [2 Jan 1835]
  Susan 27 w/o Josiah WOOD at Belfast ME [31 May 1849]
  Sybil 92 wid/o Capt Silas WOOD of Norridgewock ME at Chesterville ME [29 Jan 1852]
  & 93 at Chesterville ME [22 Jan 1852]
  Sybil Capt of Norridgewock ME at Chesterville ME [29 Jan 1852]
  William 45 printer at New York on 17th ult [10 Jul 1838]
  William 70 formerly of Gorham ME at Baldwin ME [25 Dec 1835]
WOOD - see LORD
WOODARD Noah 24 "a native of Augusta ME" on board the brig *York* [25 Apr 1857]

WOODBINE Col the officer who commanded in FL in 1815, with his family (wife & two sons) were killed at Maraparata on their plantation on 26 Jul supposed by blacks [14 Sept 1833]

WOODBRIDGE Martha M 14 at Hallowell ME [8 Aug 1846]

Sarah 88 wid/o Capt Christopher WOODBRIDGE of Newcastle ME at Hallowell ME [23 Dec 1852]

Thomas 90 formerly of New Castle at Hallowell ME on 31 May [13 June 1837]

WOODBURY Azer abt 42y of Enfield ME drowned in the Penobscot River [15 Apr 1843]

Benjamin 87 AmRev at Buckfield ME [22 Mar 1849]

Charles 18 of Townsend MA & Charles TYLER 22 of Worcester MA both drowned at Worcester MA on Thurs [16 Apr 1846]

child of True WOODBURY at Winthrop ME [14 Sept 1839] & infant child c/o Mr TRUE WOODBURY at (Winthrop ME) on Mon last after a short illness [3 Oct 1840]

Elizabeth Mrs 32 w/o C H B WOODBURY at Dover ME [1 Jul 1852]

Hannah E of Beverly MA jumped from a railroad car near Salem MA, at full speed, escaped w/o injury. Alarmed, her safety was due to passenger catching her dress as she jumped [*Post*] [6 Mar 1851]

Hannah Mrs 28 w/o Charles WOODBURY at Paris ME [26 June 1845]

Hugh 60 at Litchfield ME [3 Oct 1840]

Joseph a bachellor abt 75 with asthma of Beverly MA dropped dead in his yard Monday last sawing up some wood [7 May 1842]

Levi Hon 61 at Portsmouth NH was buried at Francestown (NH?) his native place where lie the remains of his father & grandfather (from the *Traveller*) [11 Sept 1851]

Luke Hon, the Dem cand for Gov of NH at Antrim by hanging (27 Aug) he was abt 50y, graduate of Dartmouth College, left wife but no children, also three brothers reside in Antrim & a mother [4 Sept 1851]

Moses 50 at West Gardiner ME [25 Dec 1845]

Mr engineer, Mr KING & Mr HUNTOON both of Acton, Mr WILEY & Mr THOMPSON of Baldwinville were the five persons killed in an accident of the Vermont and Massachusetts Railroad. Mr WHITNEY of Charleston & Mr A M RAYNOLDS are thought to be very dangerously injured. Joshua LINCOLN of Charlestown had both legs broken, Alfred A WHITTEMORE of Baldwinville was severely injured. The paper was indebted to Charles FIELD Esq of Athol for the particulars [4 Nov 1847]

Susanna 81 at Auburn ME [27 Dec 1849]

WOODBURY - see WEBSTER

WOODCOCK Abram B who will be 19 on the 18th day of Aug next the minor s/o William WOODCOCK of Winthrop ME has been given his right to act etc., witness - Samuel P BENSON [11 Feb 1833]

Hannah S 22 at Sidney ME on 25 Dec [11 Jan 1849]

John M abt 7 s/o Matthew WOODCOCK at Winthrop ME [8 Jul 1833]

Matthew 40 at Winthrop ME on Friday last [17 June 1836]

Patrick 70 of the early settlers of Thomaston ME [19 Aug 1852]

Sarah 11y d/o widow Susan WOODCOCK at Winthrop ME suddenly on Sat last [6 Nov 1841]

Stilman 30 at Albion ME [25 Feb 1843]

Susan widow of Mathew WOODCOCK at Winthrop ME [24 Oct 1830]

Theodore 53 at Searsmont ME [2 Nov 1848]

WOODFORD - see IRVIN, MILES

WOODMAN Benjamin 73 at Upper Stillwater ME [22 Jan 1852]

Charles J married Mrs M L DAVIS by Rev Mr NEALE (were Washingtonians) [28 Oct 1842]

WOODMAN (Cont.) Daniel Esq 70 of Norridewock ME at Westbrook ME on 5 Mar [21 Mar 1850]

David 66 at Leeds ME on 26 Jul [7 Aug 1838]

Frances of Norridgewock ME went to Lowell to work in the cotton mills. She started for home in Nov came as far as Boston MA & there obtained employment, where she remained until her death, by smallpox, a few days since [29 Jan 1846]

Isaac a native of Maine fell from a chimney at the Gray's Iron Foundry at South Boston MA he may recover (*Atlas*) [16 Sept 1847]

J C Esq the large barn built by J C W Esq on the HERRICK farm in Lewiston ME burnt with all the contents by an incendiary on Fri. The loss of Mr WOODMAN is estimated at $650 [17 Dec 1846]

J C Esq of Portland ME, a dwelling house, situated at Minot Corner with the barn & out-buildings owned by him burned, occupied by Oliver MARBLE [*Advertiser*] [4 Nov 1852]

Jabez Capt 50 at Saco ME [4 Apr 1837]

Jabez Rev 67 at New Gloucester ME on 15th inst after a severe illness of three months [10 June 1845]

James Capt 60 at Buxton ME [3 Sept 1846]

Sarah J 27 w/o Albert WOODMAN at Minot ME [16 Nov 1848]

Washington 33 at Norridgewock ME [9 Jul 1846]

WOODS Hannah 24 formerly of Hallowell ME at Detroit MI [22 Feb 1844]

John 16y married a blind old woman, more than 50y at Yaxley in Suffolk [8 Jul 1833]

John 60 at Hallowell ME on 2rd inst [21 Sept 1839]

Lurana 45 w/o Col Nathaniel WOODS at Farmington ME [23 Sept 1852]

Mary 96 wid/o John WOODS at Farmington ME [31 Oct 1844]

Samuel 2 s/o Nathaniel WOODS at Rumford ME [25 Mar 1847]

Sarah Ann 15 oldest d/o Samuel WOODS at Augusta ME [25 Mar 1847]

Sarah Mrs 65 of Hallowell ME at Augusta ME on 11th inst [23 Jul 1846]

Titus R of Waldo ME at Matamoras, belonged to the corps of Sappers & Miners [18 Feb 1847]

WOODS - see HASKELL

WOODSIDE Anthony 25 at Bloomfield ME [25 Nov 1847]

W Lithgow 20 s/o George WOODSIDE at Brunswick ME [23 Dec 1852]

WOODSUM Abiathar Capt 60 at Clinton ME [4 Feb 1847]

Elizabeth A 18 d/o A WOODSUM at Fairfield ME on 10 Jan [16 Jan 1851]

Eunice 56 wid/o Capt Jabez WOODSUM at Saco ME [30 Nov 1848]

Helen S 14y 9m d/o Abner & Eliza A WOODSUM at Augusta ME [11 Dec 1845]

Sally Mrs 75 w/o Abner WOODSUM at Clinton ME [8 Aug 1844]

WOODWARD Daniel Capt 67 at Gardiner ME [15 Apr 1843]

Daniel Sr of (Augusta?) ME went down the (Kennebec) on a fishing excursion last week to visit Woolwich. He had a hat as well as a cap, with him. It is possible that he landed & is safe & that his boat broke from its fastenings. Mr Seth HATHORN of Woolwich on Fri last saw a sailboat coming down the river opposite his farm the boat was picked up by Gilbert EAMES, near Thwing's Point ... [13 Apr 1848]

Deborah S w/o Capt Jordan WOODWARD at Brunswick ME [21 Oct 1836]

Elbridge G of Brunswick at St Jago Cape de Verdes on 31 Sept [14 March 1834]

Gideon R 3y 1m s/o Joseph and Roxanna WOODWARD at Augusta on 1 Oct [11 Oct 1849]

girl d/o Judge WOODWARD of Wilksborough drowned on Sat 19 Jan at Honesdale PA by falling through the ice on which she was sliding, the bodies of two other girls were also recovered [31 Jan 1850]

John 24 at Minot ME [8 June 1848]

WOODWARD (Cont.) Joseph 24 at Buxton [17 May 1849]

    Joseph 78 formerly of Norton MA at Sidney ME on 1 April [5 April 1849]

    Lemuel of Plainfield killed on Sat last while engaged in salting some cattle (from *Norwich Courier*) (from *New Haven Palladium* on 28th) [4 June 1851]

    Melinda 28 eldest d/o Levi & Mary WOODWARD at Dresden ME on 24 May [4 June 1851]

    Mr of Augusta ME a body found supposed to be his, drowned this spring & found on Sat last abt 5 miles above this city [*Bath Tribune*] [25 May 1848]

    Mrs 70 at Brunswick ME [7 Sep 1848]

    Mrs 82 wid/o Elder WOODWARD at Brunswick ME [25 Jan 1849]

    Rufus J 45 formerly of Parkman ME at Great Falls NH [16 July 1842]

    Sarah Jane 19 w/o Barzilla D WOODWARD & only d/o Edwin & Abigail REYNOLDS at Sidney ME on 10 Jul [7 Aug 1851]

    William 23 of Brunswick at sea on passage from Wilmington to Martinique [7 Jan 1847]

WORCESTER George of ME at San Fransisco CA [14 Oct 1852]

    Samuel Rev 51 at Bridgewater MA minister of the New Church [9 Jan 1845]

WORCESTER - see LOMBARD

WORKS Samuel W 25 at New Sharon ME [12 Nov 1846]

WORMELL Francis W 22 of Belfast ME at Burnham ME first officer of schr *Coral* was knocked overboard by the fore boom and drowned [10 Dec 1846]

WORTH Gen his funeral plus Col DUNCAN's & Major GATES at New York City the total of $2,223 for the three military men [3 Jan 1850]

    Mary 68 at China ME w/o John WORTH on 17 Jun [14 Oct 1847]

    Nancy 39 at Vassalboro ME w/o Alex WORTH 30 Oct [11 Nov 1852]

    William J Gen born in Hudson, Columbia Co New York, his ancestors from Devonshire England & settled in MA in 1642, married a d/o the late John STAFFORD of Albany at San Antonio TX on 7th inst died of cholera [*New York Sun*] [31 May 1849]

WORTHEN Mary 22 at China ME d/o John WORTHEN of Belfast ME [24 Aug 1839]

WORTHING Bethiah 42 at Palermo ME w/o C S WORTHING 9 Jul [30 Aug 1849]

    Jacob 71 at Palermo ME [13 Jan 1837]

    John B 6y 5m s/o Clifford S and Bethiah WORTHING at Palermo ME 19 Mar [22 Apr 1847]

WORTHING Mary Abigail 9y 6m at Palermo ME d/o C S WORTHING of bilious fever 4th inst [27 Aug 1846]

WORTHING - see McCURDY

WRAY Louisa B 35 at Abbeville District SC 12th ult w/o H D WRAY d/o late Nathaniel BROWN of Augusta ME [11 Oct 1849]

    Mary a young lady of Philadelphia cut her throat on the 11th inst cause was insanity [10 Jul 1841]

WRIGHT Alice w/o Jonah WRIGHT at Jefferson ME [14 Aug 1841]

    Asher 90 at Coventry CT he was the companion in arms of the lamented Capt Nathan HALE in the army of the Revolution [11 Jul 1844]

    Benjamin F late of Greene ME, est notice Mary E WRIGHT adm [15 Jan 1852]

    Betsey Mrs 22 w/o John WRIGHT of Mt Vernon ME at Belgrade [24 Sept 1846]

    Betsy 57 at Monmouth ME [24 Aug 1848]

    Charity 59 w/o Zebulon WRIGHT at Lewiston ME [8 May 1851]

    Cordelia H w/o Dr Kendell WRIGHT at Weld ME on 21 Nov & youngest d/o Jeremiah HALL Esq of Rumford ME [29 Nov 1849]

    E Eugene 8m only s/o Dr K & Cordelia H WRIGHT at Weld on 9 Mar [11 Apr 1850]

    Eli 23 of the instructors of North Yarmouth Academy at Bethel ME [18 Sept 1841]

    Franklin 35 at Woolwich ME [5 Sept 1850]

WRIGHT (Cont.) Gustavus M G formerly of Queen Anne's Co on Wed evening last in Kent
    Co from the bite or sting of a spider [*The Centreville (MD) Times*] [17 Oct 1844]
    Harriet d/o Horace W l/o Vassalboro ME to pass a team caught by the foot & leg was so
        mutilated by the log passing over it, died two days later at Durham ME [14 Jan 1847]
    John a native of Nova Scotia Canada at Bath ME on the 15th inst from the effects of
        drinking too freely of cold water [24 Aug 1848]
    John AmRev at Woolwick ME [11 Feb 1847]
    Jona Capt 78 at Jackson ME [4 June 1851]
    Joseph 74 at Lewiston ME [9 Jan 1851]
    Lemuel & Levi PALMER perished in the flames at Watertown NY on the 3d ult [6 Apr
        1848]
    Lucy a maid entering St Stephen's Church last Sun. Abel BINGAM, a widower, stepped
        up to Lucy and said "will you marry me to-day?" She blushing said "Yes Abel!" They
        were published & married at noon by Rev Thomas J SALTER *The Middletown CT
        Sentinel* reported [3 Sept 1842]
    Lucy Mrs 80 wid/o John WRIGHT at Woolwich ME [1 Apr 1847]
    Margaret 42 w/o Dr J S WRIGHT at Newcastle ME [21 Mar 1850]
    Maria Mrs w/o Dr O A WRIGHT at Waterville ME [15 Jan 1846]
    O S Rev Methodist Missionary, Rev LAIRD & wife & Rev John CLOUD Presbyterian
        Missionary, had fallen victims to the fevers of that climate in Liberia on 12 May [4
        Jul 1834]
    Oliver Jr 46 at Jay ME [4 Dec 1845]
    Patrick of Addison ME lost overboard from ship *Monmouth* of Bath ME on passage from
        Boston MA to New Orleans [15 Jan 1842]
    Phineas 69 at Lewiston ME [1 Jul 1852]
    Samuel G Hon on 30th ult at Allentown Monmouth Co NJ a member of Congress [14
        Aug 1845]
    Silas elected to Congress in 1826, born 24 May 1795 at Amherst MA his father & family
        removed to Vermont died 52y (see obit) [16 Sept 1847]
    Silas Hon a letter from Prescott Canada East to Horace MOODY Esq at Canton on
        Friday [*Albany Argus*] [2 Sept 1847]
    William 17 of Belfast ME sencond officer of bark *Rio* at Maratti Cuba on 26 Sept of
        yellow fever [12 Nov 1846]
WRIGHT - see ALL, BINGAM, COWART, MOUNTS
WYATT - see MENKIN
WYER Benjamin Franklin 9y 5m [12 Feb 1852] & Charles Frederick 5y 8m c/o Shubael &
    Sally WYER at Vassalboro ME on 4 Jan (*New Bedford Mercury* please copy) [12 Feb
    1852]
    Owen Capt 62 of the lockjaw occasioned by running a splinter in the hand at Nantucket
    MA [22 Apr 1836]
WYMAN Asa Maj 72 at Skowhegan ME on 31 Jul [15 Aug 1850]
    Betsey 59 w/o Maj Abraham WYMAN at Bloomfield ME [5 Dec 1850]
    Charles A 16 at Monmouth ME [20 Sept 1849]
    Cynthia 66 wid/o Asa WYMAN of Skowhegan ME at New York City [11 Sept 1851]
    Daniel struck by lightning & was his house, he was severely injured at Bloomsfield ME
    [23 Jul 1842]
    Dennis of Milford ME at CA [18 Nov 1852]
    Francis 67 at Vassalboro ME [21 May 1846]
    George 20 at St Albans ME [19 Sept 1850]
    Hellen Louisa 2y 6m d/o E G & Loumira WYMAN at Farmington ME [30 Mar 1839]
    Isaiah 80 at Phipsburg ME [1 Apr 1847]
    James 84 at Belgrade ME on 25th ult [11 Mar 1847]

WYMAN (Cont.) Lydia Ann 22 of Bloonfield ME at Waterville ME [11 Oct 1849]

Margaret Mrs 76 w/o Isiah WYMAN Esq at Phipsburg ME [1 Apr 1847]

Mary Caroline 3y 8m d/o J P WYMAN at Augusta ME on 13 Mar [18 Mar 1847]

Mary E 1y 8m d/o Curtis & Nancy WYMAN at Belgrade ME on 25th inst [30 Sept 1847]

Rachel 18 of Fairfield ME at Lowell MA very suddenly [5 Aug 1843]

Rachel 60 w/o Capt Daniel WYMAN at Dover ME [3 Jul 1851]

Reuben 80 at Fairfield ME on the 16th ult [6 June 1840]

Reuben of Calais ME on Mon last suddenly in a fit, left a wife & little ones at Topsfield ME [7 May 1842]

Robert Rev 31y formerly of Cumberland ME at Madras Ceylon on 10 Jan [22 May 1845]

Roderick 7 w/o Bancroft WYMAN at Belfast ME [1 Jan 1839]

Sally 56 at Jay ME [23 Nov 1848] & [9 Nov 1848]

Samuel D 32 s/o James WYMAN at Belgrade ME on 20th ult [17 Aug 1839]

Samuel Jr 24 at Deer River ME [26 Dec 1840]

Sarah 10 d/o George WYMAN of Milford crushed to death on Fri last by falling under two logs which were being drawn to mill [10 Jan 1850]

Sophia 15y 4m at Bloomfield ME [3 Jul 1838]

William 60 at Waterville ME [18 Dec 1841]

William 96 of Phipsburg ME on Fri of last week labored in the hay field .... (not an obit, see story) [*Bath Times*]

WYMAN - see HEYWOOD, WING

- Y -

YALLALEE Hannah H abt 22 of C H YALLALEE & d/o Hanson HIGHT of Norridgewock ME at Williamsburg NY on 23d ult [11 Jan 1849]

YEAGER Mary Mrs 30 w/o Rev W H C YEAGER late of Tallahassee FL & eldest d/o Amherst EATON Esq of Boston MA at Boston MA of consumption [16 Apr 1846]

YEATON Theodore 26 at Augusta ME on 7 Mar [22 Mar 1849]

George N 13m at Augusta ME [11 June 1846]

Hannah Mrs 82 at Minot ME [18 Feb 1847]

Jonathan 82 AmRev at Belgrade ME [9 Nov 1839]

Joseph 29 at Readfield ME on 19th ult of consumption [3 June 1852]

Naomi 47 at New Sharon ME [17 Oct 1850]

William G 28 at Belgrade ME [11 Apr 1850] & [4 Apr 1850]

yellow - see BROWN, slave

YERBY Henry of Old Town Arkansas brutally murdered on the 9th ult, while gunning on his plantation, by two of his negroes. The guilt of the negroes being satisfactorily established, they were taken out, tied to a tree, & burned to death! [13 Dec 1849]

YOHN lad 7y s/o William YOHN severely bitten by a dog belonging to Daniel ENGEL & supposed to have been rabid, the wound latter healed & in good health until Tues last & on Fri died of hydrophobia [*Phil Ledger*] at Reading Berks Co on 37th (*sic*) of Aug last [23 Oct 1845]

YOOSTLING Young killed & s/o Thomas DeMOSS, a lad abt 14 not expected to survive; John BROWN (boy) dangerously hurt, Mr RHOADS injured [*New York American Republican*] on 4th inst the Cumberland Valley Railroad Bridge over the Susquehannah was destroyed by fire [12 Dec 1844]

YORK Benjamin R AmRev at Rumford ME on 20th ult 91y served under Benedict ARNOLD [2 Sept 1852]

Daniel 80 at Farmington ME [12 Aug 1852]

Jeremiah 70 at Frankfort ME [21 Aug 1851]

YORK (Cont.) Joseph Capt 61 formerly of Falmouth ME at Pownal ME [27 Nov 1835]

Rufus s/o Samuel YORK & Mr COLE all on board the vessel loaded with kiln wood in Burrit Cove, South Deer Isle was destroyed by fire last week. The older MR YORK was drowned & the son, Samuel YORK died of burns. Mr COLE was burned badly but may recover [*Age*] [27 Mar 1845]

Sarah Jane 25 eldest d/o Joseph & Mary YORK at Falmouth ME on 30th ult after an illness of five years [15 Apr 1843]

Sarah S 27y 10m w/o Asa F YORK of Bangor ME at Hope ME on 8th ult [3 June 1836]

Solomon Capt 71y 7m AmRev at Sedgwick ME [13 Mar 1835]

YORKE Hannah abt 72 at Weld ME [1 Mar 1849]

YOUNG Albert 30 at Pittston ME [30 Jan 1851]

Albert B 28 by Indians in CA early in Sept [8 Jan 1852]

B Franklin of Newburyport MA the crew of the *Traveller* supposed lost [16 Oct 1851]

Betsey 48 w/o Joshua YOUNG at Mercer ME [30 Nov 1848]

Daniel 64 at Norway ME [23 Apr 1846]

Daniel 67 at Meddybemps ME [7 Aug 1851]

Daniel Jr a Deputy Sheriff of Oxford Co knocked down & robbed, passing over Tukey's Bridge, stopped by a person supposed to be an Irishman & toll demanded, which the bridge was free, refused to pay, proceed toward the city (Portland), recieved a blow on the right side of his head. Mr Y only saw one person, the other person was holding his horse (*Portland Adver*) [31 Jul 1838]

David 82 at Hollis ME [3 Feb 1848]

Dorcas 38 w/o John YOUNG at Portland ME [28 Aug 1845]

Eliza 59 w/o Joseph YOUNG Esq at Augusta ME on 17 Dec [28 Dec 1848]

Elizabeth L 13 d/o James & Dinah YOUNG at Augusta ME on 27 Mar [15 May 1851]

Ellisty E 8m c/o John & Malinda YOUNG at Mercer ME on 5th [23 Sept 1847]

Emily B 28 w/o Stephen YOUNG at Starks ME [18 Mar 1852] & [25 Mar 1852]

Emma Aurora 25 d/o Rev John YOUNG at Augusta ME [27 May 1847]

Florence M 2y 5m c/o John & Malinda YOUNG at Mercer ME on the 1st [23 Sept 1847]

George 75 at Cushing ME [22 Apr 1845]

Harry 42 at Mercer ME [2 Aug 1849]

Ira abt 55y of Bingham ME at starks ME [12 June 1845]

James 59 of Starks ME while driving a team in Norridgewock ME fell from the seat & the wheels of the loaded wagon passed over his body, breaking his back, & otherwise injuring his person. He is not expected to survive [*People's Press*] [7 May 1846] [28 May 1846]

James 89 AmRev pensioner at Fayette ME [28 Sept 1848]

James abt 22 of Turner ME, a painter, threw himself overboard in a state of intoxication [*Bangor Courier*, Jul 3] [15 Jul 1833]

Jonathan 62 at Bath ME [26 Sept 1837]

Joseph 33 at Augusta ME [23 Aug 1849]

Joseph 80 at Thomaston ME [20 Nov 1835]

Joseph Esq 59 at this town (Augusta ME) on 15 Oct [19 Oct 1848]

Joshua 77 at Paris ME [15 Apr 1852]

Joshua 83 of the first settlers on Sandy River at Mercer ME [2 Sept 1847]

Levi 74 of Durham NH while cutting wood killed [*Dover Gazette*] [20 Dec 1849]

Lucinda H 10y 5m d/o James W & Diana YOUNG at Augusta ME on 20 Jul [26 Jul 1849]

Lucy D w/o John L YOUNG at Bath ME [7 Nov 1834]

Margaret 90 wid/o of William YOUNG at Starks ME [11 Jan 1849]

Martin 7y (an Irish lad) fell from a boat near the wharves on Fri & drowned [10 June 1847]

YOUNG (Cont.) Mary 60 w/o John YOUNG at Bath ME very suddenly [10 Feb 1848]

Mary 94 relict of Benjamin YOUNG at Mercer ME [2 Aug 1849]

Moses early this morning the store of his at Frost's Corner in Norway was discovered to be on fire, the goods were destroyed & the store partially damaged [*Norway Advertizer*] [5 Apr 1849]

Mr a deck hand on board the steamer *John Marshall* fell overboard from that boat at Bath ME on Wed evening of last week & was drowned [27 Nov 1845]

Mr (a colored man) men attacked his house on Washington St in Portland ME, which so exasperated him that he discharged a gun loaded with shot at them - the shot taking effect on two of the assailants, wounding one of them badly. The miserable amusement of assailing this poor man received a tragical termination - & should be a lesson not to be forgotten ...[*Portland Argus*] [19 Oct 1848]

Mr of Canaan ME thrown from his horse while on his way home from the general muster at Skowhegan on the 5th inst died the next day [23 Oct 1838]

Mrs a widow & two of her dau recently drowned at Hampden while bathing [25 Jul 1840]

Nancy Mrs 22 w/o Warren YOUNG Esq at Oldtown ME [25 Feb 1847]

Nancy Mrs 32 at Thomaston ME [25 Mar 1833]

Nancy Mrs 70 w/o Jonathan YOUNG at York ME [28 Mar 1844]

Polly 74 at Thomaston ME [12 Jul 1849]

Rachel Mrs 42 at Paris ME [27 Nov 1841]

Reuben & widow GROVES her dwelling house situated about one mile westward from Wiscasset Village was totally destroyed by fire & melancholy to relate, the lady owner & her brother - Mr Reuben YOUNG were both consumed in the flames! They were aged people - upwards of 75y ...[*Bath Times*] [18 Nov 1847]

Simon 45 at Cushing ME [28 May 1846]

Solomon M 2y & 6m s/o Jared YOUNG at Paris ME [12 Feb 1846]

Thomas of Calais ME seaman lost overboard from schr *Warrior* on the passage from Port au Platt to New York on 29th ult [30 Apr 1846]

Warren R Capt late of Old Town ME 32 of cholera Sacramento CA [2 Jan 1851

YOUNG - see Slavery, VALE

YOUNGBLOOD H M Esq editor of the *Southern Watch Tower* married Rebecca M ARMSTRONG by Rev J G JONES near Fayette MS on 29th ult. Who will say now that the rights of the South are not safe, when its "Watch Tower" is fostered by the strong arms of its young bloods! [9 Dec 1843]

YOUNGMAN - see POWERS

- Z -

ZIKER Mr his house eight miles from Baltimore MD burned on the night of 7th, his daughter & wife perished in the flames. [25 Dec 1851]

SELECTED INDEX TO "YOUNG FOLKS" COLUMN

10 December 1870 to 30 December 1886
17 November 1887 to 5 January 1888 and
1 November 1900 to 24 October 1901

The "Young Folks" column was at first overlooked by us as a source of genealogical information. Until about 1884 the "Young Folks" column was a collection of short stories written for children. At about that time, young readers (ages 5 to 18) wrote letters to the editor. Later children wrote essays on historical subjects or notable men or women: Abraham Lincoln, Henry W Longfellow, George Washington etc, most children stated their name, age and address. Now & then a student included the name of their teacher, a little family history, occasionally, as third-generation *Maine Farmer* readers, they named their grandparents.

One example: [19 Feb 1885]
> Dear Mr Editor: I am a girl twelve years old. My home is in St Stephen, New Brunswick Canada, I have three sisters & three brothers. My father is employed in the lumbering business. We are spending the winter with him here on Wissattaquork stream (Wassataquoik stream), Piscataquis Co, State of Maine, it being one of the tributaries of Penobscot river (east branch of the Penobscot River). There are five families living here. We have a school, and I practice on the organ which we brought with us. There are three hundred men and one hundred fifty horses employed cutting and hauling logs. The name of the firm is Tracy & Love. Please send patterns for narrow lace.
> Piscataquis Maud TRACY

ABBOTT Freddie W 10 China ME [2 Dec 1886]
ADAMS Nancy 12 Mattawankeag ME "I boarded with my Uncle James HAMILTON" [2 Dec 1886]
AIKEN Walter Hammond [13 Dec 1900]
ALBEE A S Alna ME [15 Jul 1886]
ALLEN B L ae 11 of Brooklin [22 Oct 1885]
   Eddie L 11 No Dixmont ME "have 3 brothers & two sisters" [26 Aug 1886]
   Ethel M 11 of Burnham ME [1 Apr 1886]
   Eugene teacher of Jonesboro ME [8 Jul 1886]
   Eunice P ae 9 [14 Feb 1901]
   Orrin ae 9 of North Jay ME [4 June 1885]
   Rosa 9 Chesterville ME "home is in Middleboro MA, but I am stopping at my grandpa's this winter with my mamma. My little sister, Gracie, died this winter, ae 5y & now & have no sister or brother" [24 Mar 1887]
   Susie 12 Columbia ME [23 Dec 1886]
ALLISON Mary Dew 9 Newport Nova Scotia "I had a little brother but he died last winter" 27 May 1886
AMES Eva M of Skowhegan ME [25 Dec 1884]
   Evan M [22 Apr 1886]
   F L Skowhegan ME [10 June 1886]
   Luther F 10 of Prospect ME [10 Dec 1885]

ANDERSON Sadie 16 "I saw a letter that Flossie GRACE wrote, well I have 9 bros & 1 sis, 7 older than myself & 4 are married. One brother lives in IL & one in Minnesota" [9 Sept 1886]

Sadie W ae 9 of Warren ME [4 Dec 1884] ae 9 of Warren ME [12 Mar 1885]

ANDREWS Arbella E ae 10 of Caribou ME [5 Nov 1885]

Enna E of Richmond Island Casco Bay ME [21 May 1885]

Etha/Atha J ae 12 of Waterboro ME [18 Dec 1884] of Waterboro ME [19 Mar 1885] ae 14 (b 9 Apr) of Waterboro ME [10 Sept 1885] & Waterboro ME [27 Jul 1886]

ANNES Carrie M 10 of Lincolnville [29 Apr 1886]

ARCHER Edith L ae 9 of Township #8 near Ellsworth Hancock Co ME [19 Mar 1885]

ATKINS Alice E of Garland ME [28 May 1885]

H P of Exeter Mills [11 Feb 1886]

Nellie a teacher of Exeter ME [17 Sept 1885]

AUSTIN Arthur C 9 Parkman ME "have one great grandf, two great grandm, two grandf, two grandm, two step sisters, one step-brother & a pair of twin brothers. I live at my Grandf MERRILL's" [7 Apr 1887]

AVERY Thomas M 13 Benedicta ME [21 Oct 1886]

AYER Mamie A 11 East Pittston ME "my two granfathers (*sic*)died last winter" [3 June 1886]

BABB Abbie E 10 of Oldtown ME [4 Mar 1886] & of W Oldtown ME [6 May 1886]

BABCROFT Ada [4 Apr 1901]

BACHELDER Winnie of Gardiner ME [21 Jan 1886]

BACON S B [22 Apr 1886]

BAGLEY Addie ae 11 of Whiting Washington Co ME [11 Dec 1884] of Whitney ME [9 Jul 1885]

BAILEY Frank M of Deering ME [5 Mar 1885]

Lois A of Cambridge [18 Feb 1886] & of Parkman ME [17 Sept 1885]

Velma E 12 of Deering ME [10 Dec 1885]

BAKER Cora M ae 10 of East Bradford ME [2 Apr 1885]

Georgia A 13 of Wiscasset ME [11 Mar 1886]

Nellie teacher Bingham ME [22 Jul 1886]

BANFORD John H ae 8 [14 Mar 1901]

BANNON Harry of Jefferson ME [11 Dec 1884]

BARKER Abbie M of E Troy ME [8 Apr 1886]

BARRETT Augusta ae 10 of Andover ME [12 Mar 1885] & M Augusta ae 10 last Aug of Andover ME [20 Nov 1884]

Sibyl A 13 of Weld [6 May 1886] & [12 Aug 1886] & ae 11 of Weld ME [23 Apr 1885] & ae 13 of Weld [6 May 1886]

BARRON Effie ae 13 of Ellsworth ME [30 Jul 1885]

BARTLETT Alfred of Elliot ME [16 Jul 1885]

Leslie F 11 of Lee [29 Apr 1886]

Sarah P ae 10 of Eliot ME [27 Aug 1885]

BAYLEY Frank M of Deering ME [15 Oct 1885] & of Riverside [10 Dec 1885]

Mary A of Riverside [26 Nov 1885]

BEAL Angie Mae [23 May 1901] & ae 11 [3 Jan 1901]

BEAN Jennie C Monticello ME [24 Mar 1887]

Lizzie of Presque Isle ME [31 Dec 1885]

BEAR Lizzie May 7 Alfred ME "I have a sister & brother Gertie Emma & Elbridge, both younger than I am" [6 Aug 1886]

BELL Annie B of Blaine ME [6 June 1901]

BEMIS Mayron J ae 6 [14 Mar 1901]

BENNET Della (twin) [13 May 1886]

    Stella (twin) [13 May 1886]

BENNETT Bessie of Augusta ME [7 Mar & 7 Feb 1901]

    Blanche ae 11 of Wells ME [12 Mar 1885]

BENNIS Nellie M 10 of Levant ME [11 Feb 1886]

BENTON Marion A ae 10 granddau of E W FORD of North Berwick ME [13 Dec 1900]

BERRY Gertrude R ae 11 [6 Dec 1900]

    James I [22 Aug 1901]

    Lottie A [2 May 1901]

    Nina R E of Kearny Neb [17 Dec 1885] & ae 8 of Pilot Custer Co Neb [8 Oct 1885]

BICKNELL Lester H 8 East Madison ME [15 Jul 1886]

BILLINGS E V of Eastbrook [7 Jan 1886] & Ella V 11, 12 & 13 Eastbrook "have 3 brothers
    & one sister, my oldest brother has a small crew in the Woods Mr PHILLIPS, Harvey
    BRAGDON, Gleason SCAMMONS & Meltiah BRAGDON" [22 Jan 1885] & [4 Nov
    1886] & [17 Feb 1887]

    Lucy May 10 Eastbrook "have 3 brothers & one sister Fred, Willie, Henry & Ella" [7 Jan
    1886] [4 Nov 1886][17 Feb 1887]

BISHOP Clara L 9 of Brownville ME [19 Nov 1885]

    Isa M 13 of Brownville ME [19 Nov 1885]

BLACKWELL Clyde H ae 9 of Madison ME [28 Mar 1901]

    J Harvie Jr 8 Corinth ME "I have 2 big sisters & one little brother" [8 Jul 1886]

    William H 10 of Corinth ME [14 Jan 1886]

BLAISDELL Minnie of East Cornville ME [8 Oct 1885] & [17 Dec 1885]

BLAKE May Athinson ME [17 June 1886]

BLANEY Annie 12 Little Ridgton "have 2 bros Jerred ae 11 & George ae 9" [27 Jan 1887]

BOND Millie 7 Exeter [9 Dec 1886] & Millie M 8 Exeter "4 bros & 2 sis" [7 Apr 1887]

BOOBER Maud E ae 12 of Sherman Aroostook Co ME [2 Apr 1885]

BOOKER Lizzie [13 May 1886] & of Norridgewock [4 Feb 1886]

BOOTHBAY Lillian R 7 of East Parsonsfield ME [11 Mar 1886] & "no bro or sis, my
    mother is dead, & my father is in FL. I like to have grammy read the children's
    column in the *Farmer*" [19 Aug 1886]

BOSTON Lucy ae 13 of Canaan ME [25 June 1885]

BOWIE C H of Winnegance [23 Apr 1885]

BOYINGTON C Marshall Cooper's Mills ME [27 May 1886]

    Eddie Cooper's Mills ME [27 May 1886]

    Edith M 12 Cooper's Mills ME [27 May 1886]

    George Cooper's Mills ME [27 May 1886]

    John E Cooper's Mills ME [27 May 1886]

BOYNTON Annie May 5 South Jefferson ME [3 June 1886]

    Gladie G 13 Medway ME "I live on a farm with my grandparents" [27 Jan 1887] & 12 of
    Medway ME [18 Mar 1886]

BRACKETT Ida A ae 12 [17 Jan 1901]

    Shelden [28 Mar 1901]

BRADBURY Carrie B 9 of Limerick ME [21 Jan 1886]

    Ethel M New Limerick ME [22 Jul 1886]

    Eva May ae 10 [30 May 1901]

    May L ae 12 of Limerick ME [7 May 1885] & ae 13 of Limerick ME [15 Apr 1886]

BRADFORD Lettie M 9 St Albans ME "live with my grandparents, papa dead 6y, my
    mamma works in the insane hospital in RI. I have a sister, Nellie. We have a cousin,
    Charlie CHRISTIE, he lives with us" [7 Apr 1887]

BRAGG Ernest A of Plymouth ME [6 Dec 1900]

BRAGG (Cont.) Mabel E ae 7 of Dixmont ME [16 Apr 1885]
BRIDGES Ansel H 12 of Sprague's Mills [1 Apr 1886]
BRIGGS Ernest [16 May 1901]
 Jr Alexander H 9 of Blue Hill Falls [11 Feb 1886]
 Stella A of Carrying Place ME [22 Nov 1900]
BRISON Harry little boy to do chores Maple Grove [6 Aug 1886]
BRITT John M ae 11 [28 Feb 1901]
BROOKS Amina Ann 10 North Newport [3 Feb 1887]
BROWN Addie L ae 14 of Round Pond ME [2 Jul 1885]
 Hattie A 8 West Camden ME [11 Mar 1886]
 Ida O of North Searsmont ME [26 Feb 1885]
 Lizzie of No Searsmont [26 Feb 1885]
 Minnie of No Searsmont [26 Feb 1885]
 Sarah 11 Caribou ME "My sister is going to be married next Christmas" [4 Nov 1886]
 Willie G 11 of North Searsmont ME [7 Jan 1886]
 Willie G ae 10 of North Searsmont ME [26 Feb 1885] & ae 11 of North Searsmont ME
  [7 Jan 1886]
BRUCE Carrie E 14y South Hollis ME "I have two brothers & one sister: Harry, Willie &
 Sadie" [15 Jul 1886]
BUCK Annie E 7 Lincoln ME "I have 4 sisters & 3 brothers" [26 Aug 1886]
 Edwina T ae 11 of Saco ME [25 June 1885]
 Everett A 8 Lincoln ME "have 4 sisters & 2 brothers, Jane is the youngest" [29 Jul 1886]
 Lizzie E 11 Lincoln ME [22 Jul 1886]
BUGBEE Sadie W of North Perry [18 Dec 1884][14 May 1885][7 Jan 1886][22 Apr 1886]
 & ae 14 (b 7 Oct) of North Perry [8 Oct 1885]
BUKER Celia B 10 St Albans ME "have 3 sisters Minnie, May & Ida" [10 Feb 1887]
BULGNOR Edgar W of Perry ME [10 Dec 1885]
BULL LeBaron ae 8 last Oct of Woodstook ME [8 Jan 1885]
 William A of Woodstock ME [26 Feb 1885]
BULMER Edgar W of Perry ME [5 Feb 1885]
 Lizzie E 13 Perry ME "2 sis & 2 bros, oldest sister is Susan May who lives with
  Grandmother MORRISON, youngest sister is Alice Victoria, & oldest brother is
  Everett" [3 Feb 1887]
BUNNER Edgar W of PErry ME [23 Jul 1885]
BURGESS Lola D 8 Oakland ME "my sister is Sadie ae 5y & a brother, Hart ae 20m" [16
 June 1887]
BURNS Vador teacher Madison ME [10 June 1886]
BUSHER Mark E Jr of Freedom ME [16 Apr 1885]
BUSSELL John H [4 Apr 1901]
BUTLER Alice M 10 Bingham ME [22 Jul 1886]
 Beth H [28 Mar 1901]
 Mina O ae 11 of Springfield ME [1 & 15 Jan 1885]
BUTTERFIELD Archie L D of South Presque Isle Aroostook Co ME [4 June 1885]
BUZZELL Roscoe of Cornville ME [6 Aug 1885]
CAIN Laura E 8y Codyville Washington Co ME "my sis is going to school at Pittsfield ME,
 my papa died two years ago, he was a soldier of the 15th Maine. We live on a farm
 east of Topsfield ME. I have two grandmas & 2 grandpas living. My grandpa is 94y
 & grandmy [*sic*] is 84, they used to live with us but now live in Portland ME. My
 sister's name is Jennie & brother is Gilbert B" [24 Mar 1887]
CALDWELL Mabel ae 13 of Cambridge (Kings Co) "75 miles from Halifax" (Nova Scotia)
 [9 Jul 1885]

CAMPBELL Augustus E 12 North Leeds ME [22 Jul 1886]
  Mennie M of Winterport ME [25 June 1885]
CANDER Lillian D ae 11 of Stratton [27 Aug 1885]
CARLETON Ethel Henry 10 Etna Centre ME "my father is dead, I live with my
  grandparents" [14 Jul 1887]
  Percy O 10 of Winterport ME [7 Jan 1886]
  Willie E [22 Apr 1886]
CARVER Myrtie ae 11 [18 Apr, 9 23 May 1901]
CARY Susie A ae 9 of East Pittston ME [24 Sept 1885]
CHADBORNE Alton L 13 of Harmony ME [31 Dec 1885]
CHADBOURN Grace [30 May 1901]
CHADBOURNE Carrie M teacher Denmark ME [3 Mar 1887]
  Mira ae 11 of Princeton ME [19 feb 1885]
CHAMPMAN Frankie G of Limerick ME [6 Aug 1885]
CHANDLER G J ae 9 of New Sharon ME [11 Dec 1884]
  Leslie T ae 9 [31 Jan 1901]
CHAPMAN Frankie G ae 9 of Limerick ME formerly of Windham ME [23 Apr 1885]
  Walter L Damariscotta ME [3 June 1886]
CHASE Etta ae 15 [25 Apr 1901]
  Freddy A ae 12 of Etna [23 Jul 1885]
  Jennie Bell 6 Canaan ME "I am stopping at my grandpa's in Belgrade ME" "My little
    brother is one year old last Mar" [30 June 1887]
  Maud G ae 10 of Swanville ME [16 Apr 1885]
CHICK Isla Maude of Mountain ME [9 May, 6 June 1901]
CHIPMAN Wardie A 7 of Skowhegan ME [6 Aug 1886] & 8 of Skowhegan ME "have one
    grandma & one grandpa & one g-grandpa but my grandma died the 15 of last month.
    I have never seen my great gf or g-gm" [27 Jan 1887]
CHRISTIE Chester C ae 8 of Oak Hill St James New Brunswick Canada [23 Apr 1885]
CHRISTY Hannah of East Washburn ME [13 Aug 1885]
CLARK Alice J ae 11 of Fort Fairfield ME [22 Jan 1885]
  Amy G 9 of Unity ME [7 Jan 1886]
  Annie M 11 Fort Fairfield, Aroostook Co ME "7 bros living & 3 dead, & no sis" [21 Oct
    1886]
  Edith A of St George ME [22 Oct 1891]
  Grace H ae almost 16 of Bangor ME [14 Mar 1901]
  Horace ae 9 of Mattawamkeag ME [26 Mar 1885]
  Lizzie Mrs teacher North Perry ME [3 June 1886]
  Lottie T 9 of Somerset Mills [4 Mar 1886]
  Mildred ae 14 of Bangor ME [27 Dec 1900]
  Perly A [22 Apr 1886]
CLARKE Annie M 11 Fort Fairfield ME [8 Jul 1886]
CLAY Grace ae 5 of So Thomaston [19 Mar 1885]
  Sadie E of So Thomaston ME [19 Mar 1885]
CLEMONS Grace P of Lee ME [13 Aug 1885]
COBB Florence Evelyn ae 5 of Chelsea ME [5 Mar 1855]
  Junia E of White Rock [10 Dec 1891]
  Mabel ae 9 of Chelsea ME [4 Dec 1884]
COBURN Daisy M ae 7 of Carthage ME [21 May 1885]
COLE Amanda 13 Etna Centre ME "2 sis & 3 bros" [14 Jul 1887]
  Annie L 11 of Wells ME [10 Dec 1885]
  Elsie M of Kennebunk ME [15 Oct 1885]

COLE (Cont.) Ida May 11 Etna Centre ME [14 Jul 1887]

    Lizzie A ae 11 of Wells ME [15 Jan 1885] & ae 12 of Wells ME [10 Dec 1885]

    Mamie 7 Saco ME "have 2 grandmas ae 75 & one g-gm ae 90" [13 Jan 1887]

    Morris Herbert 7 Etna Centre ME [14 Jul 1887]

COLLINS Etta [27 June 1901]

COMENS Lulu ae 9 of Phipsburg ME [18 Dec 1884]

CONANT Daisy M [22 Aug 1901]

    Gladys A ae 9 [31 Jan 1901]

CONVERSE Walter H 11 Beatrice NE "my grandfather in Fairfield NE, is a native of
    Maine & move to Nebraska 16 yrs ago. I was born in MA" [6 Aug 1886]

COOK Abbie Lou 10 of Unity ME [11 Mar 1886]

    Maggie B 13 of Rockland ME [29 Apr 1886]

    Mary Addie ae 13 of N Vassalboro ME [6 Aug 1885]

COOKSON Eva L ae 13 of Oakfield ME [19 Mar 1885]

    Nellie M 12 Burnham ME "have brother, Charlie E ae 7" [22 Jul 1886]

COOPER Josie ae 13 of Pittston ME [22 Oct 1885] & Josie L of Pittston [6 May 1886]

COPELAND Edith L 9 Holden ME "my home is in Lynn MA, I spend summers with my
    grandpa in Holden ME" [9 Sept 1886]

COPP Lilly G [25 Feb 1886] & Lily G ae 9 of Skowhegan ME [16 Apr 1885]

CORSON Rose A 13 West Athens ME "I have four sisters & three brothers, one of my
    sisters is married & lives in Skowhegan & I am stopping with her now" [9 Sept 1886]

    Walter H 10 Athens ME [6 Aug 1886]

COTTLE Jennie teacher Augusta ME [23 Dec 1886]

CRABTREE Mabel E ae 10 [21 Mar 1901]

CROOKER Annie B [14 Feb 1901][25 Apr 1901]

CROSBY Lizzie A ae 11 of Temple Mills ME [18 June 1885]

CROWELL R Henry of Canaan ME [18 Dec 1884][14 May 1885]

CULVER Eddie M 11 of Medford MA [1 Apr 1886]

CUMMINGS A L ae 15 of Livermore Centre ME [19 Feb 1885]

CUNLIFF Margie ae 10 of Smithfield ME [18 Dec 1884]

CUNNINGHAM Cyrus A 12 of Washington [8 Apr 1886]

CURRIER E D [11 Apr 1901]

CURTIS Eliza H 13 of Sprague's Mills [7 Jan 1886]

    Elizabeth E ae 6 [18 Apr 1901]

    Harnie May 6 of Winthrop ME [18 Feb 1886]

CUSHING Myra May ae 10 of Blue Hill ME [30 Jul 1885]

CUSHMAN Celia M ae 15 of Lincoln Academy [13 Dec 1900]

DAGGET Annabel M 7 of Morrill ME [18 Mar 1886]

DAGGETT Elsie M ae 11 of New Portland ME [30 Jul 1885]

DAISY Lottie E 10 of Medway [29 Apr 1886] & ae 9 of Medway [4 Mar 1886]

DALEY Hattie ae 11 [25 Apr 1901]

    Mamie T ae 14 [3 Jan 1901][7 Feb 1901]

DANFORTH Harold E of Madison ME [2 May 1901]

    R Pearl of Blackwell ME [11 Apr 1901][31 Jan 1901]

DANVENPORT Elbridge 8 Phillips ME 27 May 1886

    Sadie M 11 Phillips ME 27 May 1886

DARING Gussie L ae 11 of Rangeley ME [26 Mar 1885]

DAVIDSON Laura T 10 of Falmouth Nova Scotia [28 Jan 1886]

DAVIS Edith A of Warren ME [24 Dec 1885]

    Ernest A Liberty ME [17 June 1886]

    Iva P of New Haven [16 Jul 1885]

DAY Florence A [21 Mar 1901]

DeCOSTA Hazel ae 11 [28 Mar 1901]

DEERING J P ae 11 of Saco ME [6 Aug 1885]

DELAND L Maud ae 7 of Skowhegan ME [21 May 1885]

DELANO Susie W ae 8 of Skowegan ME [28 May 1885]

DENNET Charlie D 9 of Etna ME weighs 95 lbs [25 Feb 1886]

DENNETT Abie G of Deering ME [9 Apr 1885]

Frank J teacher South Hollis ME [15 Jul 1886]

DENNIS Albert 12 Madison ME [15 Jul 1886]

DERHAM Gracie B 10 of Fairfield ME [12 Nov 1885]

DEVEREN Percy R [22 Apr 1886]

DILLINGHAM Austin A ae 6 of Newburgh CT [16 Apr 1885]

Sumner I 8 Sebago Lake, Naples ME [3 June 1886]

DOANE Levi 10 Aurora ME [3 June 1886]

DODGE Archie H of Newcastle ME [18 Mar 1886]

Myra B of New Castle ME [6 Aug 1885]

DOMON Anson C 12 of South Charlotte [8 Apr 1886]

DONOVAN Sadie M 11 of Norway Lake [12 Nov 1885]

DOW C M almost 9 Hartland ME [8 Jul 1886]

Mittie A ae 6 [5 Feb 1885] & Mittie A ae 7 of Plymouth [25 Feb 1886]

Nena N ae 10, sister of C M, of Hartland ME [8 Jul 1886]

Nina N 10 Hartland ME "I have one brother, 3 years old, C M DOW is my sister." [8 Jul 1886]

DOWNEY John B [27 Dec 1900]

DOWNS John teacher Smithfield ME [21 Oct 1886]

Myrtie E 13 Winterport ME [17 June 1886]

DREW Mattie May 10 Etna Centre ME "have 4 brothers" [14 Jul 1887]

Ruth F/Ruth ae 9 [13 Dec 1900][14 Feb 1901]

DUDLEY Jeanette A ae 7 [21 Feb 1901]

Maggie D 10 of Augusta ME [18 Feb 1886]

Nettie of Castle Hill ME [15 Jan 1885]

DULEY Susie May 9 Parker's Head ME "have one sister ae 7 & no brothers" [17 Feb 1887]

DUNBAR F Marion of Vinalhaven [15 Apr 1886] & F Marion of Winterport ME [25 June 1885]

DUNCAN Mary M E 11 of Augusta ME [25 Mar 1886]

DUNNING Herbert A ae 11 of Levant ME [21 May 1885]

DURGAIN Mildred Ethel 6 of North Sedgwick ME [19 Nov 1885]

DURGIN Lillie E 11 Forks ME "a sister, Gracie & brother, Ira" [23 Dec 1886]

DURRELL Bertha M ae 15 of Kingfield ME [6 Aug 1885]

DUTTON Stella and Myrtie [13 May 1886]

DYER Lillias teacher in Etna [14 Jul 1887]

EAMES Lulie B [13 May 1886]

EASTMAN Lottie M ae 12 of Clinton ME [10 Dec 1891]

EDGECOMB Alice R 9 of Richmond [6 May 1886]

EDMUNDS Evie "gone to Burnham ME, to stay this winter, her grandfather gone to Los Angeles CA" [25 Nov 1886]

ELLIOT E W [22 Apr 1886]

ELLIOTT Johnnie of Lincoln Co [11 June 1885]

Mamie ae 7 of East Bradford [2 Apr 1885]

ELLIS Helen [9 May 1901]

Maude [9 May 1901]

EMERSON Bertha A of Indian River Washington Co [20 Nov 1884]
   Elmira ae 10 of So Norridgewock ME [18 Apr 1901]
   Eunice ae 16 of So Norridgewock ME [18 Apr 1901][13 June 1901]
EMERY Bertha M 11 of Salisbury [7 Jan 1886]
   Faith R 10 of Owls Head [31 Dec 1885]
EVANS Esther F [15 Aug 1901]
FABIAN Jennie ae 9 of Ornesville Piscataquis Co ME [8 Jan 1885]
FALOON Sadie North Woodville ME "two bros, George & the other not named. I had 3,
   but one died. My sister are Ellen & Esther" [1 Sept 1887]
FARNHAM Augusta R ae 11 of East Boothbay ME [2 Jul 1885]
   Mae B of No Belgrade ME [28 Jan 1886]
FARRAR Clarence B [22 Apr 1886]
   Clarence R 9 Wellington ME "I have two little brothers ae 6y & 2y" [8 Jul 1886]
FARWELL Fred 11 of Bethel ME [1 Apr 1886]
FAUGHT Alice M of North Belgrade ME [5 Mar 1855]
FAULKNER Ella ae 12 of Orient [5 Nov 1885] & 13 of Orient ME my mother died a year
   ago last Mar, I have a little brother [27 Jul 1886]
   Gracie A 12 Grand Pre, Nova Scotia, Canada "my brother takes the *Maine Farmer*" [22
   Jul 1886]
FAUNICE Leon T ae 11 of Abbot ME [9 Jul 1885]
FELIX Lulu of North Perry ME [12 Nov 1885]
FELKER Hattie ae 11 of Searsport ME [4 Dec 1884] ae 12 of Searsport ME [2 Jul 1885]
FELLOWS Frank Cony 11 Sidney ME "I live in Malden MA, visiting my uncle in Sidney
   ME, my grandmother lives on a farm 1.5 miles out of the city. My grandfather died
   last May" [6 Aug 1886]
FENDERSON Frank D 7 East Parsonsfield ME [3 June 1886]
FERNALD Addie M ae 14 of Lincolnville ME [19 Nov 1891]
   Bertha C 11 East Dixmont ME "I have 5 sisters Mira, Alice, Julia, Lena & Nellie" [12
   Aug 1886]
   Minnie E Lincolnville ME [24 Feb 1887]
   Vesta Winterport ME 13 May 1886
FIELD Wyman of Presque Isle ME [13 Aug 1885]
FIFIELD Irvin D ae 11 of Augusta ME [8 Jan 1885]
FILES Freda [*sic*] teacher Caribou ME [10 June 1886]
FISH May D 12 of Weston ME [5 Nov 1885]
FISHER Wealthy L 14 of Belfast ME [31 Dec 1885]
FISK Ammie L [22 Apr 1886]
FISKE Ruth Stevens [22 Aug 1901]
FITCH Sadie 13 of Topsfield ME [6 May 1886]
FLAGG Nina Maud 7 Unity ME "have no brother or sisters, my papa has gone down to
   Waldo to work" [16 Dec 1886]
FLINT Annie N of Nobleboro ME [26 Nov 1891]
FOGG Abbie L ae 14 of Limerick ME [2 Jul 1885]
   Evelyn ae 11 of Cornville ME [31 Jan 1901]
   Gennia A of W Chester NY [25 Feb 1886]
   Laura A of Limerick ME [10 Dec 1885] & Lura A ae 8 of Limerick ME [19 Feb
   1885][15 Apr 1886][6 Aug 1886]
FOLSOM G J 8 Exeter Mills [24 Mar 1887]
FOOTMAN Gertrude 11 Exeter ME "born in Boston MA, moved to Exeter to live with
   grandparents at age 1y. Have one brother, Russell ae 9y & no sisters" [2 Sept 1886]
FORBES Edith C/L of Brooks ME [22 Apr 1886] & ae 10 of Brooks ME [28 Jan 1886]

FORD Alice M 8 of Red Beach [11 Feb 1886]

FOSS Ethel Maud of Brooks ME [8 Jul 1886]
    Ina Minerva 10 Brooks ME "I have one sister Ethel Maud" [8 Jul 1886]

FOSTER M B 14 Amherst ME? "got a father, 7 sisters & two brothers. Mamie & I are twins & are the youngest of the family. My mother died when I was ten days old..." [24 June 1886]
    Mary M 11 of Columbia ME [28 Jan 1886]

FOWLER Harrie Edgar of Medway Penobscot Co ME [14 May 1885]
    Huldah M ae 8 of Skowhegan ME [27 Aug 1885]
    Lina A 10 Medway ME [27 Jan 1887]

FREDERICK Nellie C New Sharon ME [6 Aug 1886]

FREEMAN F W teacher Saco ME 27 May 1886
    Florence H 10 of Vassalboro ME [18 Mar 1886]

FRENCH Fannie V 8 Hammonton NJ "one brother & one sister, both younger than I" [19 Aug 1886]
    Maud A 9 of Palmyra ME [25 Mar 1886]

FROST Blanche E 8 North Mariaville [29 Jul 1886]

FURBER Merle M ae 10 [16 May 1901]

GAGE Lura ae 8 of Plymouth ME [3 Sept 1885] & Lura M 9 Plymouth ME [8 Jul 1886]

GALUSHA Emma L ae 11 [6 June 1901]

GARLAND Miss M L 10 [16 Dec 1886]

GAY Verdie C ae 9 of Augusta ME [21 May 1885]

GEE Daisy Belle almost 9 Hartland ME "have 2 brother & three sisters. Two of my sisters are married" [13 Jan 1887]

GERALD Winnie 7 Albion ME [12 Aug 1886]

GERRISH Maggie M ae 11 of Oakfield Aroostook Co ME [5 Feb 1885]

GETCHELL E L 11 Somerset Mills [8 Jul 1886] & Ervie L of Somerset Mills (former name of Shawmut Post Office in Fairfield ME) [26 Feb 1885]
    Maggie C 12 Somerset Mills ME [20 May 1886]

GILE Walter C/E of Readfield ME [15 Oct 1885][29 Apr 1886]

GILES Bertha L 6 Aurora ME [19 Aug 1886]
    Ethel M 8 Aurora ME [17 June 1886] & "my great grandmother lives with us, she will be 87y old next August" [22 Jul 1886]

GILLPATRICK Caleb 10 "my father is dead, I live with the Mr LORD's family" [10 Mar 1887]

GILMAN Flossie May 8 of Dexter ME [4 Feb 1886]
    Horace E 10 [4 Mar 1886]
    Lottie J ae 8 of North Sidney ME [4 June 1885]

GILPATRIC Frank A ae 10 of Biddeford ME [15 Jan 1885]

GINN Fannie/Fannie S of Bucksport ME [16 Jul 1885] ae 11 [12 Feb 1885]

GIVEN Fannie S Bucksport ME [21 Oct 1886]
    Harry L 10 of South Windsor ME [14 Jan 1886]

GLASS Mertie E ae 8 of East Bucksport ME [11 June 1885]

GLAZIER Phillip L 10 of Hallowell ME [1 Apr 1886]

GLIDDEN Ida [27 Dec 1900]
    Marcia [21 Feb 1901]

GLITTEN Jessie C ae 12 [15 Oct 1885]

GOODRICH Cyrus Mrs teacher East Madison ME [15 Jul 1886]

GOODRIDGE Linnie of Canaan [3 Dec 1885]

GOODWIN Alma F ae 11 of Canaan ME [30 Apr 1885]
    Ethel I ae 9 of Glenburn ME [13 June 1901]

GOODWIN (Cont.) Eva M ae 10 of Canaan ME [19 Mar 1885]

GORDON Alice Bell 12 Sweden ME "have two sisters & one brother Lillian May, Lottie Eva & Walter Ervin" [10 Mar 1887]

Ellen F 13 of Thorndike ME [1 Apr 1886]

Ernest L ae 11 of Readfield Depot ME [7 May 1885][17 Dec 1885] ae 12 [6 May 1886]

G Ernest 9 of Jefferson ME [14 Jan 1886]

Gracie May ae 8 of Moscow ME [16 Jul 1885]

Lottie Eva 10 Sweden ME "have two sisters & one brother Lillian May, Alice Bell & Walter Ervin, my oldest sister works in a store at Cambridge MA" [10 Mar 1887]

GOSS Austin A of South Deer Isle ME [11 June 1885]

GOULD Maud 12 Prospect ME [17 June 1886]

Olive 9y & 81 lb Princeton ME "my brother, four years older than myself, accidentally shot me last Nov, causing the loss of my left eye" [9 June 1887]

GOVE Clarence C 13 East Palermo ME [24 June 1886]

GOWELL Jodie 6 in Dec Orlando FL "I spent the summer in Litchfield ME at my granfather's (*sic*), William WYMAN" [25 Nov 1886]

GRACE Flossie 16 Portland ME "I have 8 brothers & two sisters all under 25 yrs of age, my brother, Bertie is 10y & weighs 150 lbs..." (see ANDERSON) [26 Aug 1886]

GRAFFAM Florence M [18 Apr 1901]

Gracie Edith 5 Bangor ME "have a brother,Harry Bion ae 9m, a sister, Ida May & a grandpa, Joseph GRANT of East Bangor ME. I have a little brother, Frank Lewis, he is dead" [28 July 1887]

Ida May 9 East Bangor ME "I am visiting my grandparents" [28 July 1887]

GRAHAM Hazel Birdell ae 10 weight 91 pounds [7 Mar 1901]

GRANT Annie L [2 May 1901]

John W [2 May 1901]

Wilber H [4 Apr 1901]

GRAY A L 9 South Hiram ME [29 Jul 1886]

Eugenie A 12 Sweden ME "have a little baby brother ae 9m & three others Harold Leslie, Charlie Prentiss, Johnnie Heald" [21 Jul 1887]

Florence of Readfield Depot [20 June 1901]

GREEN Harry E ae 9 next Fri of Pittston ME [23 Apr 1885] & of No Pittston ME [30 Jul 1885] & Harry Edgar [3 Dec 1885]

Harry L of So Windsor [29 Apr 1886]

Lillie A 5 of North Pittston ME [3 Dec 1885]

Phila N 9 Stratton "have one little sister, Edna, ae 2y & 2 bro 5y old twins, Perham & Percy" [7 Oct 1886]

GRIFFEN Linnie M ae 11 of Lyman ME [10 Sept 1885]

GRINDAL Sarah teacher of Orland ME [8 Jul 1886]

GROSS Austin A ae 11 (b 9 June) of South Deer Isle [9 Jul 1885]

GUPTILL Katie H ae 12 of Cherryfield ME [24 Dec 1892]

Orville J of Waterville ME [4 Mar 1886] & ae 10 of Waterville ME [31 Dec 1885] & "I have a brother Roscoe" [1 Jul 1886]

HACKETT Amos C 10 of Freeman ME [25 Mar 1886]

Sadie 11 Damascus ME [3 Mar 1887]

HADLEY Ana M ae 12 of Peterboro NH [17 Jan 1901]

Lora E 10 of Bar Harbor ME [7 Jan 1886]

HADLOCK Bessie Warren ae 9 of Kennebunk ME [31 Jan 1901]

HAINES Julia A 13 Fort Fairfield ME [6 Aug 1886]

Martha J 11 Fort Fairfield ME "have 4 brothers & two sisters, my youngest sister is 16m" [6 Aug 1886]

HALE Nora S 9 of Cumberland ME [26 Nov 1885]

HALEY Millard ae 7 (born 9 Feb) of Princeton ME [11 Mar 1886]
Olive 10 of Princeton ME [11 Mar 1886]

HALL Inez C of East Jefferson ME [4 Feb 1886] & ae 9 of East Jefferson ME [15 Oct 1885]
Mary B of Lawrencetown [14 Jan 1886]
Samuel C [10 Dec 1885]

HALLETT Nettie 13 Eureka [15 Jul 1886]

HAM Carrie M ae 10 of Parkman ME [23 Apr 1885][13 May 1886]
Sadie N ae 11 of Kineo Shore of Moosehead Lake ME [16 Jul 1885] & [27 Jul 1886]

HAMILTON Bennie ae 9 [9 Jul 1885]

HAMMOND Freddie E ae 5y on 19 Jan last Hermon ME "have a brother, Roland Bodwell" [28 July 1887]
Herbert L ae 7 of Hammond's Grove Manchester ME [18 June 1885]
Mamie E 6 Paris Hill ME "I have an aunt who will be 7 yrs old in June, we go to school together" [6 Aug 1886]

HANSCON Almon ae 11 of Mt Chase [9 Jul 1885]

HARDING Merton 6 Etna Centre ME [14 Jul 1887]
Minnie ae 13 of Bethel ME [22 Jan 1885] of Bethel ME [2 Apr 1885]
Winfield 9 Etna Centre ME "have 3 brothers" [14 Jul 1887]

HARDY Abbie R ae 13 of Temple ME [5 Feb 1885]
Cora L 9 of Temple ME [18 Mar 1886][5 Feb 1885]
Eugenie 16 of Madrid ME [7 Jan 1886]

HARMON Jennie M 13 of Porter ME [16 Apr 1885]

HARPER Gracie E ae 9 of East Waterboro ME [5 Feb 1885]
Mary S ae 14 of Aurora ME [12 Mar 1885][16 Jul 1885]

HARRIMAN Florence L ae 9+ of East Bucksport ME [15 Jan 1885]
Gracie 10 of Orland ME [31 Dec 1885]
Hattie L ae 10 of Orland ME [16 Apr 1885]

HARRIS Mertie M 12 Skowhegan ME [17 June 1886]
Millie ae 12 of Lee ME [18 Dec 1884]

HART Malcolm C 10 Willimantic [13 Jan 1887] & [17 Feb 1887]
Maud E 8 of Cushing ME [18 Feb 1886]

HARVEY Cora A 8 of So Berwick [4 Feb 1886]

HASKELL Ella C ae 10 of Liberty ME [30 Apr 1885] ae 11 [4 Mar 1886]
Frank H ae 13 of Windham ME [2 Apr 1885]

HASTINGS Emma A of So Hope ME [28 May 1885]
Ralph L 8 of So Hope [6 May 1886]

HATCH Margie M 12 of Lovell Centre [14 Jan 1886]
Miriam of Castine ME [15 Oct 1885]
Miss teacher of Castine ME Columbia Falls ME [27 Jul 1886]

HATHORN Iva May [6 June 1901]

HAWES Frank D Colony, Kansas "left Maine when 5, lived in Kansas 5y" [17 Feb 1887]
Phebe E [13 June 1901]

HAWKES Alice S 7y Appleton ME "I live in Swampscott MA, but am stopping at Appleton ME now. My Uncle Judson takes the *Maine Farmer*." [23 June 1887]

HAYDEN Charlotte E ae 5 [28 Feb 1901]
Laban 8 Madison Centre ME 20 May 1886
Ron 10 Madison Centre ME [1 Apr 1886]
Roy ae 9 of Madison ME [23 Jul 1885]

HAYES Arthur 7 Pittston ME [2 Dec 1886]

HAYNES Clara M of Chelsea ME [20 Nov 1884] [8 Jan 1885]

HAYNES (Cont.) Dora A 7 of Alhambra Montana [1 Apr 1886]
    George S 9 of Alhambra Montana Territory [25 Mar 1886]
    Walter S ae 8 of Rockport MA [15 Jan 1885]
HAYWARD Melvina ae 12 of Otsego MN [1 Oct 1885]
HEALY Bessie Concord ME [10 June 1886]
    Cynthia Felker 9 Concord ME [10 June 1886]
    Joel Concord ME [10 June 1886] & Joel Gray 11 of Concord [11 Mar 1886]
HEATH Arthur P ae 10 of Woodland ME [7 May 1885]
    Leon J 7 of Princeton ME [19 Nov 1885]
HELMERSHAUSEN Edna 9 Jefferson ME [29 Jul 1886]
HEWETT Lloyd F [16 May 1901]
HIGGINS Eva C 7 of Thorndike ME [21 Jan 1886]
    Ida B 13 of Columbia Falls [11 Feb 1886]
    Ross C teacher Thorndike ME [15 Jul 1886]
HIGHT Ethel F 6 [1 Apr 1886]
HILL Carlick ae 6 Stockton CA [5 Nov 1885]
    Ernest ae 9 of East Bradford ME [11 Dec 1884]
    Orrin J ae 8 [28 Feb 1901]
    Walter 9 of Lyman ME [10 Dec 1885]
HILLS Nellie M ae 10 of Belmont ME [3 Sept 1891]
HILTON Mamie J 8 Madison ME "I have two brothers, the oldest David ae 5 this June &
    the other is six months old, he hasn't any name, but can sit alone & is very
    cunning..." [17 June 1886] & Mamie of No Boothbay ME [7 Jan 1886]
HINCKLEY J Frank ae 11 [4 Apr 1901]
HINKLEY Irving L ae 10 of Litchfield ME [1 Oct 1885]
    Maggie S ae 8 of Phillips ME [25 Dec 1884]
HISLER Inez Viola ae 9 of Week's Mills ME [31 Jan 1901][11 Apr 1901]
HOBBS Ethel teacher Somerset Mills ME [20 May 1886][8 Jul 1886]
HOBERT Anna L West Farmington ME "You made a mistake in my name, You had it
    "Annie L ROBERTS" [21 Oct 1886] & 8 West Farmington ME "I have one sister,
    Ida & three brothers Hiram, Mark, Forrest" [16 Sept 1886]
HODGKINS Beula [16 May 1901]
    Ethel ae 4 of No Lamoine [24 Sept 1885]
HOLDEN Carrie D 11 Moose River ME [12 Aug 1886]
HOLMAN Andrew [22 Aug 1901][30 May 1901]
HOLMES Frank Caribou ME [3 June 1886]
    Harry Caribou ME [3 June 1886]
    Idella 11 Caribou ME [3 June 1886]
    Maud Caribou ME [3 June 1886]
    S Harry S 13 Caribou ME [10 June 1886]
HOLTON Jay 9 "2 sisters Minnie & Mabel" [28 July 1887]
HOOKER Grace of Gardiner ME [23 Jul 1885]
HOPKINS Nelson E of Indian Point ME [11 Dec 1884][8 Jan 1885]
HOUSE E M of Corinna ME [13 Aug 1885] & Elwood M of Corinna ME [5 Feb 1885]
HOUSTON Mary Miss teacher West Bath ME [15 Jul 1886]
    Rose Mabel 7y North Etna ME "have a brother, Elmer, ae 5" [3 Mar 1887]
HOWARD Allie E 7 of Dexter ME [14 Jan 1886]
    Celestia M teacher East Palermo ME [24 June 1886]
    Edna E ae 10 [14 Feb 1901]
    Ernest G ae 13 of Winthrop ME [19 Nov 1891]
    Gracie L of Etna Montana [9 Jul 1885]

HOWARD (Cont.) Myrtle 12 of Medway [21 Jan 1886]

HOWARD - see REED

HOXIE Carrie L Skowhegan ME [3 June 1886]

HOYT Bertha V of Mountain (Raymond?) ME [18 Jul 1901]

    Mary G ae 12 of North Rumford ME [2 Sept 1891]

HUGHES Lyda K of Frankfort ME [28 Jan 1886]

HUMPHREY Annie A 12 Silver Ridge, Aroostook Co ME "have 4 brothers Herman, Freeland, Alfred & Joseph" [9 June 1887]

    Estelle [4 Apr 1901]

    Vinnie 11 of Sprague's Mills [25 Mar 1886]

HUNTER Bessie [11 Apr 1901]

    Lenwood A ae 9 [28 Feb 1901]

HUNTINGTON Alice R of Bridgewater ME [22 Jan & 30 Apr 1885]

    Josie Estella 8y on last day of Jan next Richmond ME "in my brother George E HUNTINGTON's letter you got my little sister's name Caroline, it should have been Carrie Lina, they are two separate names. I have two brothers & three sisters George Elmer, Roy Lester, & Carrie Lina, Lettie, Ada & the little darling we call Pet, no other name as yet." [23 Dec 1886]

HUNTINGTON Roy L 10 Richmond ME "I have a baby sister 4mos old" "My brother George studies all my studies, my sister, Josie Estelle is in the 3rd reader" [23 Dec 1886][17 Feb 1887]

HUNTON Hartwell 14 New Vineyard ME "late of Augusta ME, my father having been employed in the Maine Central Rail Road repair shop." [27 Jan 1887]

HUSE Millie L ae 11 of Lagrange ME [7 May 1885]

HUSSEY Alma ae 12 of Canaan ME [26 Mar 1885]

    Leon R [6 Dec 1900]

HUSSEY Rosa Lee ae 11 of Albion ME [25 June 1885] & [21 Jan 1886] & [1 Jul 1886] & of North Palermo ME [2 Dec 1886]

HUTCHINGS Mary teacher Orland ME [22 Jul 1886]

HUTCHINS Harry Lee ae 12 Lovell Village [8 Oct 1885]

IRELAND Bertie M ae 12 of Chester ME [4 June 1885]

    Jennie M ae 9 of Atkinson ME [23 Jul 1885]

JACKSON Lilla E teacher at Concord [2 Apr 1885]

    Nellie M ae 5 of Castle Hill Aroostook Co ME [11 Dec 1884]

    Nettie C 12 Liberty ME [8 Jul 1886]

    Silas C ae 12 of Augusta ME [19 Feb 1885]

JACOBS Lizzie A [4 Apr 1901]

JAMESON Alice V of No Warren ME [14 Jan 1886]

    Angie B 8 of No Warren ME [29 Apr 1886]

JELLISON Gracie A ae 8 of Kennebunk ME [24 Dec 1892]

    Otha H ae 13 of Mariaville [6 & 27 Aug 1885]

JENKINGS Loten D ae 7 of Wayne ME [23 Apr 1885]

JEWETT Minnie C teacher Sidney ME [22 Jul 1886]

    Ora May ae 6 of Skowhegan ME [4 Dec 1884] ae 7 [12 Mar 1885]

JOHNSON Blanch ae 7 of Winslow ME [25 June 1885]

    Edith A 7 Readfield ME "my mother died when I was 4 years old & my oldest sister keeps house for papa, I have 2 brothers & three sisters, one of my sisters is married" [9 Sept 1886]

    I V 10 of W Harrington [29 Apr 1886]

    Laura A 10 of So Bridgeton ME [4 Mar 1886]

    Millie A ae 12 of Winslow ME [18 June 1885] ae 13 [10 Dec 1885]

JOHNSON (Cont.) Minnie L of East Bucksport ME [26 Mar 1885]
JOHONNETT Mabel F 10 of Palmyra ME [13 Aug, 12 Nov, 17 Dec 1885][18 Feb, 18 Mar
    1886] & Mabel of Palmyra ME "my brother, Leslie is at work on the hay press" [2
    Dec 1886]
JONES Albert W ae 12 [7 Mar 1901]
    Cora E 8 of Princeton ME [4 Mar 1886]
    Doris C [14 Feb 1901]
    Edward A ae 9 [14 Mar 1901]
    Mabel L [2 May 1901]
    Nelly A [16 May 1901]
    Vira A ae 9 of West Gardiner ME [30 Jul 1885]
JORDAN Alice D of Bowery Beach [18 Mar 1886]
    Avis ae 9+ of Caribou ME [21 May 1885]
    C W Mrs very old & cannot write well Saco ME [20 May 1886]
    Clarence L 9 [24 June 1886]
    Ethel H ae 14 [14 Mar 1901]
    Florrie E ae 12 of Bowery Beach [5 Nov 1891]
    Hattie B 13 East New Portland ME [24 June 1886]
    Hattie L ae 13 of Bangor ME [21 May 1885]
JOSE Flossie G 9 (born on 4 July) of Dexter ME [18 Feb 1886]
JUDKINS Bertie ae 13 of Cornville ME [23 Jul 1885]
    Sadie B 6 Lakeside "I live with grandpa CUMMINGS, my 'big' grandma is 85y & is
        mamma's grandmother. There is four generations living in this house, I have one
        sister, Edna" [9 Sept 1886]
    Daisy M ae 12 of Ripley ME [30 Apr 1885]
    Edna L 8 Belgrade ME "I live with grandpa CUMMINGS ... my papa works in the
        scythe shop at Oakland ME, my sister is Sadie ae 6y" [15 Jul 1886]
KALLOCK Augusta H [13 June 1901][18 Apr 1901]
KEEF Bellie M ae 9 of East Benton ME [24 Sept 1885][30 Jul 1885]
KEENE Lillian P 11 Avon ME [16 Dec 1886]
KEENLAND Marion [2 May 1901]
KEEP(?) Mary Isabelle 10 Freedom ME "I live with my aunt & uncle, my aunt was married
    recently, we are living at grandpa's" [3 June 1886]
KELLEY William E ae 9 of North Newburgh ME [7 May 1885]
KENISTON Stella L [21 Mar 1901][30 May 1901]
KENNEY Henry 12 of Bluehill Falls ME [8 Apr 1886]
KENNISTON Herbert L 6y Warren ME "one brother & two sisters" [3 Feb 1887]
    Mabel L ae 9 of Amherst [8 Apr 1886][7 Jan 1886]
KEZER Ruth ae 14 of Santa Barbara CA [12 Feb 1885]
KILPATRICK Nettie D 9 of Florenceville NB [15 Apr 1886]
KIMBALL Clarence L 5 Sweden ME "have 2 brothers & one sister" [28 July 1887]
    Hattie E 13 Sweden ME "have three brothers & one of them is married" [28 July 1887]
    M D of Parkman ME [15 Jan 1885] & Morris D ae 11 of Parkman ME [27 Aug 1885]
    Rose A 11 Parkman ME "I have 3 brothers & one sister, her name is Daisy G ae 5, my
        oldest brother is 15y, my next is 14, my youngest alive is 12. I had a little brother die
        about 8 years ago, he was 7 months old when he died, I had a little brother last
        summer but he died" [2 Dec 1886]
    Ruthie G 9 of Herman ME [18 Mar 1886]
    Seth 12 Parkman ME "I have 2 brothers & two sisters. My oldest brother is 16y & the
        next is 14 & my oldest sister is 11 & my youngest is 5. Oldest brother is Reuel W &
        next is Morris D, my oldest sister is Rose" [23 Dec 1886]

KINCAID Alice Maude ae 6 of North Bangor ME [2 Jul 1885]
    Georgia S ae 10 of Bangor/ No Bangor ME [2 Jul 1885] ae 11 [28 Jan 1886]
KINCAIDE Ida M 14 Wiscasset ME [24 June 1886]
KING Lacordie M 9 of Lamrine [18 Mar 1886]
KNAPP Lottie P ae 8 of Kingfield ME [9 Jul 1885]
KNIGHT Jennie M [27 June 1901]
KNOWLES Allen M 6 of Corinna [15 Apr 1886]
    George F 12 of Corinna [29 Apr 1886]
    Harold G of Wilton ME [24 Oct 1901
    Lula M of Corinna Centre ME [7 Jan 1886]
    M A Hallowell ME "I am spending my vacation at my grandfather's in Manchester, he
        will be 93y next Sept" [10 June 1886]
LADD Hattie M ae 10 of Garland ME [28 May 1885]
LAMSON Florence E 8 of Joice [15 Apr 1886]
    Ida M 12 of Joice [28 Jan 1886]
    Sarah A 9 of Liberty [12 Nov 1885]
LANCASTER Fannie of Corinna ME [14 Jan 1886]
LANDER Bertha E ae 13 of Eustis ME [13 Aug 1885]
    Charles A of Thorndike ME [16 Jul 1885] ae 12 [2 Apr 1885] & [27 May 1886]
LANE Abbie A ae 12 of Ripley ME [10 Sept 1885][5 Nov 1885] & Arbie A ae 11 Ripley
    ME [16 Jul 1885]
    Lillie M 10 [10 Feb 1887]
    Sadie ae 9 of Ripley ME [3 Sept 1885]
LANG Carrie Zell ae 12 of St Albans ME [13 Aug 1885]
LARRABEE Charlie 13 Parkman ME "I live with my grandfather, brothers Arthur &
    Willie & one sister, Hattie. One of my brothers is working in Dexter ME. My father
    lives in the Aroostook." [7 Apr 1887]
LAWRENCE Addie M ae 12 of Somerset Mills (former name of Shawmut Post Office in
    Fairfield) ME [15 Jan 1885]
LEATHERS Mae E 12 Winn ME 27 May 1886
LEAVITT Edna ae 15 [7 Mar 1901]
    Ernest C ae 10 of Palmyra ME [2 Jul 1885]
    Susie Sultana ae 7 [21 Feb 1901][23 May 1901]
    Viola Myrtle [2 May 1901] (twin) [21 Feb 1901]
    Violet May [2 May 1901] (twin) [21 Feb 1901]
LEIGHTON Arvilla E 14 of Steuben ME [1 Apr 1886] & "I have two brothers & one sister,
    but they are all dead." [15 Jul 1886]
    Bertie F 9 of Stillwater CA, moved from ME a year ago my Grandmother came with us,
    but died last month [22 Jul 1886]
    Blanche of Cherryfield ME [8 Apr 1886]
    Fred A ae 12 of Sidney ME [11 Mar 1886]
    George B 10 Augusta ME [23 Dec 1886]
    Grace [11 Jul 1901]
    Lizzie ae 9 of Ft Fairfield ME [2 Jul 1885]
    Mildred Lowe ae 9 of North Yarmouth ME [7 Mar 1901][6 June 1901]
    Minnie E 14 Steuben ME "I have had five brothers, & two are dead. I have one sister." [8
    Jul 1886]
LEVENSELLER Georgia H in High School of Holden ME [15 Jan 1885] & Georgia H of E
    Eddington ME [18 Feb 1886]
LEWIS Ernest W ae 10 of Sidney ME [30 Apr 1885]
    Susie A ae 13 of North Falmouth ME [5 Nov 1885][29 Apr 1886]

LIBBEY Cordelia ae 12 of Albion ME [28 May 1885]
LIBBY Annie M Minot ME [17 June 1886]
    Harold [21 Mar 1901]
    Hertha L ae 7 [4 Apr 1901]
    Jessie Wynona 7 White Rock [24 June 1886]
    Lottie M ae 12 of Augusta ME [30 Apr 1885]
LIMD Sarah H ae 11 of Augusta ME [3 Sept 1885]
LINNELL Charley, brother of Florence E, in CO with her father [8 Jul 1886]
    Florence E 9 West Levant ME " I have four brothers, my papa & my oldest brother,
        Charley, are in Colorado. My other brothers are Virgil, Waldo & Johnnie" [8 Jul
        1886]
    Johnnie of West Levent ME [8 Jul 1886]
    Virgil of West Levant ME [8 Jul 1886]
    Waldo of West Levent ME [8 Jul 1886]
LINSCOTT George E teacher Jefferson ME [27 Jul 1886]
    Hattie M 10 South Windsor ME [3 Mar 1887] & "three brothers & one sister: Charles,
        Herbert, Ray & Belle" [22 Jul 1886]
    Hattie May ae 10 of Brunswick ME [12 Mar 1885]
LINT Alice Mabel 8 Richmond ME [23 Dec 1886]
LITTLEFIELD Andrew C of Prospect [29 Apr 1886]
    Beckie H L 6 of Prospect ME [25 Feb 1886]
    Etta 12 North Berwick ME "have 3 sister & 2 brothers & two half brothers" [2 Dec 1886]
    Herbert W of Wells ME [26 Feb 1885][15 Jan 1885]
    Jennie H of Wells Beach ME [18 Mar 1886]
    Minnie E 9 [3 Dec 1885] & Minnie E ae 8 of Athens ME [20 Nov 1884]
LITTLEHALE Harrison Morton [9 May 1901]
    Iona [16 May 1901]
    Walter E [16 May 1901]
LOGAN Katie 10y next Aug Weston ME my oldest sister is married & my 2nd sister is a
    dressmaker in Boston MA, I have three brothers [29 Jul 1886]
LONGLEY Charles S ae 10 of Plymouth ME [4 June 1885]
    Florence A ae 13 of Lake Shore [7 Mar 1901][21 Mar 1901]
    Frank D ae 8 [4 June 1885]
LOOK Amie 6 of Jonesboro ME [8 Apr 1886]
LOVEJOY Minnie E almost 12y Augusta ME, near Coombs Mills "I have 3 sisters, Mabel,
    Alice & Hattie" [25 Nov 1886]
MacNULTY Gertie of Washington DC [8 Oct 1885]
MACOMBER Zella C 8 of Fall River [17 Dec 1885]
MADDOX Edgar H 10 North Ellsworth ME [24 Feb 1887]
    Mabel C ae 11 of Orland ME [24 Sept 1885]
MAGRATH Roy 5 Saco ME "have 2 sisters, one older, Gertrude & one younger, Lillian"
    [10 Feb 1887]
MAILEY Herbert M 10 Columbia ME [1 Jul 1886]
MANSFIELD Angie M ae 10 of Orono ME [7 May 1885]
    Burnie D 6 Orono ME [24 June 1886]
    Ned R 8 Orono ME [10 June 1886]
MARBEL Fannie S a teacher at Ripley ME [12 Mar 1885]
MARCIA Ada A ae 13 Benton Falls [8 Oct 1885]
MARDEN H C teacher Swanville ME [10 June 1886]
    Maria E ae 11 of West Winterport ME [26 Mar 1885]
    Stella ae 13 of Parsonsfield ME [30 Jul 1885]

MARSHALL Merton A of North Bradford ME [27 Aug 1885]

MARSTON Grace ae 13 of Andover ME [2 Jul 1885] & Gracie ae 12 of Andover ME [5 Feb 1885]

MARTIN Lillie E ae 14 of Albion ME [26 Mar 1885][28 May 1885]

Maud S 8 Mattawamkeag ME "have five sisters & three brothers" [28 Oct 1886]

N A teacher Maple Grove [15 Jul 1886]

MASON Bennie 10 of Woodville [4 Feb 1886]

MATHEWS Addie L ae 9 of North Boothbay ME [22 Oct 1885]

MAXIM Camilla [9 May 1901]

MAXWELL M C of Cornville ME [3 Sept 1885]

Mabel C [4 Dec 1884] ae 10y 6m of East Cornville ME [3 Sept 1885][12 Nov 1885]

MAY Ida 12 of So Etna [21 Jan 1886]

Lillie ae 11 of Dedham [1 Oct 1885]

Sadie of Otis ME [10 Sept 1885]

McALLISTER Cliston ae 11 [7 Mar 1901]

N Blanche ae 12 [14 Mar 1901]

McALPIN Almira ae 12 of Maple town ME [28 May 1885]

McAVOY Thomas J Benedicta ME "my brother is Finnie" [25 Nov 1886]

McCARTER George A ae 9 of Cushing ME [19 Feb 1885]

McCASLIN Adella ae 13 of Medway ME [8 Jan 1885]

McCLURE Eliza Olie 12 20 mi from Katahdin (Mtn) [12 Nov 1885]

McCOLLOM William fieldhand Maple Grove [6 Aug 1886]

McGEE Mont M ae 11 of Somerville NB Canada [16 Jul 1885]

Unic B 7 of Somerville New Brunswick Canada [11 Mar 1886]

McGUIRE Beryl ae 9 [13 June 1901]

McKECHNIE Perley R [13 June 1901]

Prudie ae 13 [28 Feb 1901]

McKEEN R D teacher Prospect ME [17 June 1886]

Rillia Beryl ae 7 [21 Feb 1901]

McLINTOCK Charlie ae 11 of East Winslow ME [25 June 1885]

MERRILL Amy M 12 of Lee ME [11 Mar 1886]

Gertie B of Chelsea [28 Jan 1886]

Hattie J of East Eddington ME [18 Dec 1884]

Ira A 9 Parkman ME "have 2 grandmothers & 2 grandfathers, one g-gf ae 85y, two g-gm, one ae 87 & the other ae 90 & a brother, C Harry ae 4 & a sister, Florence May" [17 Feb 1887]

MERROW Angie N ae 12 [21 Feb 1901]

Flora B ae 9 of Fairfield Centre ME [2 Apr 1885] ae 10 [4 Mar 1886]

MESSER Daise R 9 Passadumkeag ME 3 June 1886

Harry 18 Passadumkeag ME 3 June 1886

Herbert E 18 North Union "I go to the sea shore every summer with my cousin, Bert L STEVENS from New Haven CT" [1 Jul 1886]

MICKELL Jinks 10 West Bath ME "My step-father takes the *Farmer*" [15 Jul 1886]

MILL Carrie ae 11 of Saco ME [16 Jul 1885]

MILLER Alice 9 Miller's Creek "I have a sister Ada Blanche ae 4y, I live in Nova Scotia, I have a brother in Boston MA, he works in a moulding factory, he was in Maine last summer. I have two little brothers Grant & Austin." [17 June 1886]

Frank B teacher Columbia ME [21 Oct 1886]

MILLS A P of NB [21 Jan 1886]

Hattie G 12 Mercer ME "I have 2 sisters & one brother: May, Minnie & Leslie" [30 Dec 1886]

MILLS (Cont.) Lonnie P of Tracy Mills New Brunswick Canada [27 Aug 1885]

MILTON Frank M Augusta ME [25 Nov 1886]

MINOT Elizabeth R ae 11 of North Sidney ME [11 Apr 1901]

    Marica P 7 Belgrade ME "have one sister, Rosa Dell ae 6" [2 Dec 1886]

MONROE Maude Mt Vernon ME [26 Aug 1886]

MOODY Alice May 8 of Whitefield ME [25 Mar 1886]

    Bertie A 12 North Palermo ME [3 Feb 1887]

    Clara ae 11 of Newcastle ME [11 June 1885] & Clara G ae 12 No Newcastle [4 Feb 1886]

    Sallie ae 12 of York ME [16 Apr 1885]

MOOERS Charles W 8 Pittston ME "my father is Fred C MOOERS, I have a sister, Edith ae 5y" [26 Aug 1886]

    Edith Evelyn ae 5 of Pittston ME [28 May 1885]

MOORE Edward M 7 Moore's Mills, New Brunswick, Canada "I have one sister, Gertie & two brothers, Walker & John" [25 Nov 1886]

    Mildred ae 9 of Moore Mills ME [12 Feb 1885]

    Tinnie 8 of Ellsworth Falls ME [11 Mar 1886]

MOPP Molly J [11 Feb 1886]

MORAN Bennie F 11 North Woodville "have a little nephew ae 8mos, Leslie FALOON" [17 Feb 1887] & Bennie F ae 9 of No Woodville ME [4 June 1885]

    Clara B of North Woodville [22 Jan 1885]

MOREY Bina of Morrell ME [4 Mar 1886]

    D W Morrill ME [15 Jul 1886]

MORGAN Glen Vernon ae 10 of Garland ME [18 June 1885]

MORGRIDGE Gussie B ae 8 (born 26 Feb) of Island Falls ME [6 Aug 1885]

MORRILL Gertie B of Chelsea ME [29 Apr 1886]

MORRISON Annie E ae 14 of Hartland ME [4 June 1885]

    Edna 11 of Hartland ME [19 Nov 1885]

    Jennie 10 Golden Ridge ME "have sisters Minnie, Alice, & Lena" [30 June 1887]

    Lilla 8 (born on 6 May) of Hartland ME [6 May 1886]

MORSE Inez V teacher Searsport ME [17 June 1886]

    Lottie [7 Feb 1901]

MORTON L K teacher North Union ME [1 Jul 1886]

MOSHER Nellie ae 9 of Ashland ME [19 Mar 1885]

MOULTON Cora J 9 of Pomeroy Ridge NB Canada [26 Nov 1885]

    George W ae 12 of Concord [1 Apr 1886] ae 12 of Concord ME [2 Apr 1885] ae 12 of Concord [1 Oct 1885]

MOWER Marion ae 9 [14 Mar 1901]

MURPHY James T 9 West Deer Isle ME "My sister Lucy is going to tell about our baby brother" [9 Dec 1886]

    Lucy H 11y on 22 Sept last West Deer Isle ME "live on a farm at Burnt Cove, we have lived in Ohio 5 yrs & have lived here 3 yrs, I have two sisters Minnie & Lizzie, a brother James & a half brother, he is a baby 14m Erwin. I have a step-sister, Cora May ae 9y, she lives with her grandma" [25 Nov 1886]

NANSON Lucy M ae 7 of North Sidney ME [9 Jul 1885]

NARNUM R L ae 19 at Pittsfield ME of Pittsfield ME [12 Mar 1885]

NASH Georgie A 9 Columbia ME "have 2 bro & no sisters" [21 Oct 1886] & [23 Dec 1886]

NASON Jamie Nason ae 9 of Brownville ME [12 Mar 1885]

NELSON Flora E ae 11 of Canaan ME [18 June 1885]

    Katie G 13 East Winn ME "I have 3 sisters & one brother, but I had 4 sisters & two brothers, 1 sister & brother & mother died, I live with my aunt & uncle" [9 Dec 1886]

NICHOLS Everett E ae 11 of Highland [8 Jan 1885]
   Rena ae 10 [25 Apr 1901]
   Robert [15 Aug 1901]
NICKERSON Fred H teacher Winterport ME [17 June 1886]
NILE Nettie N of Rangeley ME [25 Mar 1886]
NORTON Clarence A ae 10 [14 Mar 1901][25 Apr 1901]
   Ella F Mt Vernon ME [15 Jul 1886]
   Leroy W ae 12 [21 Feb 1901]
NOTTAGE Eunice [13 June 1901]
NOYES Daniel 15 Jefferson ME 20 May 1886
   Frank W ae 10 of Talmadge [30 Jul 1885]
   Mary Ada 8 of Jefferson ME [25 Feb 1886]
NYE Annie E ae 10 of Canaan ME [17 Sept 1885]
   Linnie E ae 9 of Canaan ME [19 Mar 1885]
   Rena E ae 9 of St Albans ME [23 Apr 1885]
ORCUTT Mattie R 12 Wood Island Light Station (My address is Biddeford Pool, ME) "My
   youngest brother, Georgie is 7y" & "my sister, younger than I am is larger, taller &
   weighs 11 pounds more. We study at home & my oldest sister hears our lessons" &
   "my sister Minnie E ae 10, only weigh 90s pounds" [24 Feb 1887][13 Jan 1887][9
   June 1887]
OSBORNE Mabel M 7 of Manchester [3 Dec 1885]
OSGOOD Charlie S ae 11 of Houlton ME [19 Mar 1885]
OTIS H Mott ae 10 of Otis Ridge ME [25 June 1885]
   L Mabel ae 11 weight 102 pounds of Fairfield Centre ME [2 JUl 1885]
PACKARD A B of Rockville [10 Dec 1885]
   Bertie E 9 of So Litchfield ME [25 Mar 1886]
   Bertram E 9 So Litchfield ME [10 Dec 1885]
PAGE Lilla M 8 of Hallowell ME [31 Dec 1885]
PAINE Charlie E 8 of Salisbury Cove [4 Feb 1886]
   Minnie M ae 11 of Troy ME [27 Aug 1885]
PALCHY Lerrona 13 Fort Fairfield ME [25 Mar 1886]
PAPT Helen teacher Steuben ME [8 Jul 1886]
PARSONS Ina M ae 12 of New Portland ME [6 Aug 1885]
PARTRIDGE Bart 10 of No Whitefield ME [4 Feb 1886]
PATRIDGE Lottie L ae 7 of Augusta ME [9 Jul 1885]
PATTEN Agnes 8 of Sullivan ME [18 Mar 1886]
PAUL Florence A 10 of Kittery ME [7 Jan 1886]
   Gertrude Bradbury 7 of Kittery ME [25 Mar 1886]
PEABODY Mabel E ae 10 [7 Feb 1901]
   Myron C [21 Mar 1901]
PEASE Harry F of Schuylerville NY [26 Feb 1885]
   Hattie 11 North New Portland ME "I have a brother, Alton. I have been sick with
   diptheria this winter." [24 Feb 1887]
PENNELL Cora M ae 16 of Palmyra ME [8 Oct 1885]
PENNEY Mabel ae 12 of Princeton ME [9 Jul 1885]
   Nettie of Hampden [4 Feb 1886]
PEPPER Lydia E ae 12 of Point Reyes Marin Co CA [12 Mar 1885]
PERCY Lee ae 7 of Canaan ME [2 Jul 1885]
PERHAM Gracie B 10 of Fairfield ME [17 Dec 1885] & Gracie Beulah 11 Fairfield ME
   "have 2 brother & one sister James, George & Martha" [13 Jan 1887]
PERKINS Albro H of Riverside [27 June 1901]

PERKINS (Cont.) Bessie E of Nobleboro ME [24 Dec 1892]
    Caddie ae 12 of Acton ME [3 Sept 1885]
    Edith [23 May 1901]
    Ethel A ae 8 of Orono ME [12 Mar 1885]
    Isabel ae 8 of Fairfield ME [22 Jan 1885]
    Lizzie M ae 9 of South Smithfield ME [30 Apr 1885]
PERLEY John of Unity ME teacher at Thorndike ME [2 Apr 1885]
PETTENGILL Hattie S ae 13 [1 Jan 1885]
PETTERSON Bernie Columbia Falls ME "have 4 brothers & one sister, she is 5y old. Three
    of my brothers are married. The eldest lives in Biddeford ME, the next lives ib
    Jonesport ME & the youngest is in Portland Oregon [29 Jul 1886]
PHILBRICK Alison ae 13 of Woodland ME [7 May 1885]
    Ella Mt Vernon ME [15 Jul 1886]
PHILBROOK Ada of South Thomaston ME [11 Mar 1886] & [27 May 1886]
    Olivia [16 May 1901]
PHILLIPS Ida M ae 11y of Fairfield ME [27 Dec 1900]
PHINNEY Georgia S ae 11 of Palmyra ME [5 Feb 1885]
PICKARD Elva 7 (born on 16 Feb) of W Hampden ME [18 Feb 1886]
PIERCE Carrie C [20 June 1901]
    Helen Margaret Pierce [6 June 1901]
PIKE Frances 12 of Wayne ME [1 Apr 1886]
    Hattie V [28 Mar 1901]
    Mabel A of Harrison ME [29 Aug 1901][13 Dec 1900]
    Rhoda Y 11 Princeton ME [24 June 1886]
PINKHAM Clara Myrtie 6y on the 11 Jul last West Gardiner ME [9 Dec 1886]
PIPER Dellie M 7 Simpson's Corner "have 2 brothers & 2 sisters, Frank & Charlie, Vivin
    [sic] & Hattie" [19 Aug 1886]
PIPPER Eda A of Eastbrook [3 Sept 1891]
PLUMMER Bert teacher of the Somerset Mills (former name of Shawmut Post Office in
    Fairfield ME)[26 Feb 1885]
    James S ae 7 [21 Feb 1901]
    Linwood C born in 1876 June 11 Fort Fairfield ME "I have 3 brothers & one sister, my
    elder brother is an operator & is at work in the telegraph office in Keawic, New
    Brunswick, Canada." [15 Jul 1886]
POLK Frank S 8 of Ledge [25 Feb 1886]
POND Amy E ae 11 of Mattawamkeag ME [25 Dec 1884]
POOR Anna G ae 14 of Biddeford ME [21 May 1885]
    Annah of Saco ME [1 Oct 1885]
    Gennie A of Saco ME [25 June 1885]
    Lura Oketo Kansas "It is about 30y since my father came to Kansas" [16 June 1887]
PORTER Rebie E 12 W Oldtown ME [6 May 1886] & Rebie E of Upper Stillwater (Orono)
    ME [26 Mar 1885] of Upper Stillwater [1 Oct 1885] & ae 12 W Oldtown ME [6 May
    1886]
POTTLE Mamie M 11 North Perry ME "I have a brother in San Diego CA" [3 June 1886]
POWE Alice M ae 5 of Mattawamkeag [27 Aug 1885] & 6 "my papa is very sick with
    typhoid fever, but is better now, my brother is 17y, William B POWE Jr & a sister
    Amy, which will be going to school in Bangor ME" [4 Nov 1886]
    Amy E Mattaweamkeag ME [3 June 1886] & of East Branch [1 & 8 Apr 1886] & in the
    Maine Woods "I don't think I shall go into the woods this winter, papa has bought a
    house in Bangor ME, we are going to move there in the spring" [16 Sept 1886] & of
    East Branch [8 Apr 1886]

PRATT Sadie H 9 Fairfield ME [12 Aug 1886] & 8 of Fairfield ME [2 Apr 1885]
PREBLE Elwin ae 11 of Carmel ME [24 Sept 1885]
    Wilbur ae 13 of Carmel ME [24 Sept 1885]
PRESCOTT Lillian G 13 of Liberty ME [8 Apr 1886]
PULLEN Cora Dexter ME [10 June 1886]
    Harry Dexter ME [10 June 1886]
    Nellie Dexter ME [10 June 1886]
    Tina 11 Dexter ME [10 June 1886]
PUTNAM Ralph B [21 Mar 1901]
QUIMBY Harvey R ae 12 of Starks ME [3 Sept 1885]
    Winslow F ae 9 [12 MAr 1885]
QUINBY Ada C of East Bucksport ME [12 Feb 1885]
RAMSAY Nettie M of Center Montville ME
RAMSEY Annie L ae 10 of Monticello ME [16 Jul 1885]
RAMSON Ida M of West Paris ME [23 Jul 1885]
RAND Nellie B ae 12 of Ripley ME [12 Mar 1885]
    Nina S 11 Thorndike ME "My father & mother are Patrons of Husbandry, members of Grange # 57, I have a brother, Fred Blaine ae 3y & sister, Eda [*sic*] ae 5y" [3 MAr 1887]
RAYMOND Stanley H [11 Apr 1901]
REDIKER Phylena [30 May 1901]
REDLON Harrison Gray of Buxton ME [4 June 1885]
    Harry G ae 12 of Buxton Centre ME [12 Mar 1885]
    Mabel F ae 9 of Buxton Centre ME [5 Mar 1885][3 Dec 1885]
    Rosa Bell Albion ME "my grandparents live with us & are both sick. Father is a poor man, but has a large family of seven." [17 Feb 1887]
REDMAN Roddie E 10 Bucksport ME "I hope my cousin from Wood Island will write again soon" see - ORCUTT [16 June 1887]
REED Addie E ae 12 of Medway ME [2 Apr 1885]
    George B ae 10 of Mexico ME [22 Jan 1885]
    Josiah A J almost ae 10 Mexico ME "I have three brothers & one sister George, John, Gerald & Grace" [24 Feb 1887]
    Nellie M ae 11 of Medway ME [11 Mar 1886]
    Nettie M 12 Medway ME "I have two gradmothers Ann REED ae 86 & Maria HOWARD ae 79 ... I have a cousin Myrtle HOWARD..." & "my brothers are not at home this winter. Alvah is at Millinockett lake at work in the woods & Fred is at Rapagnous." [24 June 1886][3 Feb 1887]
REYNOLDS Addie R of Fort Fairfield ME [1 Oct 1891]
RHODES Bessie 11 Saco ME "have 5 bro & 3 sisters" [7 Oct 1886]
    Grace 14 Saco ME "have 5 bro & 3 sisters" [7 Oct 1886]
RICE Ethel [16 May 1901]
RICH Annie of Thorndike ME [18 Mar 1886]
    Becca Bowdoinham ME [22 Jul 1886]
    Davie E ae 6 [21 Feb 1901]
    Fred P [11 Jul 1901]
RICHARDSON Abbie A of North Presque Isle ME [27 Aug 1885]
    Helen E [14 Feb 1901]
    Maggie B 7 of Wayne ME [4 Feb 1886]
    Walker M [28 Mar 1901]
RICHARSON Eva E Kingman ME "have 4 brothers Melvin, Alpheus, Avery, & Herbert & a sister Lizzie" [9 Dec 1886]

RICHMOND Walter E [17 Jan 1901]
RIDEOUT Fred M [6 June 1901]
RIDER Annie M Holden ME "I have two brothers & no sisters, my brother, WIllie, is 6y,
     my grandmother is 62y [25 Nov 1886]
     Willie B 7y old next month Holden ME "have a sister & brother" [10 Mar 1887]
RIDLEY Edward H ae 9 [7 Mar 1901]
     Inez E 14 [9 June 1887] & 12 of Springvale ME [5 Feb 1885][16 Apr 1885]
     Mabel P ae 8 of Springvale ME [22 Jan 1885]
     Nellie ae 13 of Springvale ME [5 Feb 1885]
RIDLON Rosa Bell 11 Albion ME "have 2 sisters & 1 brother, Orsaville [sic], Clara &
     James, my oldest sister is married" [21 Oct 1886]
RILEY Jennie L 6 Monroe ME "I have a brother, Almon & two sisters Lillie & Emma" [8
     Jul 1886]
RITCHIE Myra E 10 Aurora ME [27 Jan 1887] & Myra E ae 9 of Aurora ME [11 Mar
     1886]
ROBBINS Fred W Ellsworth Falls ME [27 Jul 1886]
     Grace 8 of Brooklin [19 Nov 1885]
     H Genie 10 Winthrop ME [3 June 1886]
     Pearl A [30 May 1901]
ROBERTS Eva ae 12 [31 Jan 1901]
     Orville ae 10 of Augusta ME [2 Apr 1885]
ROBERTSON Lizzie ae 9 of Monroe ME [14 Jan 1886]
ROBINSON Annie L 10 of Ripley ME [12 Nov 1885]
     Coney N ae 15 of Concord ME [30 Jul 1885]
     Gersham C ae 9 of Albion ME [28 May 1885] ae 10 [3 Dec 1885]
     Herman D ae 7 of Somerville New Brunswick Canada [27 Aug 1885]
     Mrs D G an aunt Hastings, Mich [16 Dec 1886]
     Myra L 12 Palmyra ME [31 Dec 1885]
     Otis A ae 8 of Cushing ME [18 June 1885]
     Walter 7 of Palmyra ME [31 Dec 1885]
ROCKWELL Laura 11 of Cornwallis NS [11 Feb 1886]
ROGERS Mildred ae 11 [16 May 1901]
ROLLINS Fred W 10 of Ellsworth Falls [22 Apr 1886] & [16 Dec 1886] & 29 July 1886
     Harry E ae 11 [21 Feb 1901][14 Mar 1901][11 Apr 1901]
ROSS Walter and Winnie 8 (twins) 2 1/2mi from Presque Isle [29 Apr 1886]
ROWE Amy E of Mattawamkeag ME [15 Jan 1885]
RUSH Bertha of Mattawamkeag ME [12 Feb 1885][7 May 1885]
RUSSELL Clarence 14 Fairfield ME "I live in Boston MA, but I am now living with Moses
     GREEN in Fairfield ME" [30 Dec 1886]
     Eva teacher Madison ME [15 Jul 1886]
     Katie E 11 Fort Fairfield ME [14 Jan 1886]
     Mary J ae 11 of Ft Fairfield ME [8 Jan 1885]
     Meda A 13 of Fort Fairfield ME [28 Jan 1886]
RYDER Susie Brownville ME "have three sisters & three brothers" [7 Apr 1887]
SADLER Josie 9 Cooper ME [9 Sept 1886]
SAINTCLAIR Etta ae 8 of So Hope [12 Feb 1885]
     George ae 10 of So Hope ME [12 Feb 1885]
SALSBURY Everett F ae 8 of Canaan ME [18 June 1885]
SAMPSON Belle G ae 10 of Phillips ME [2 Apr 1885]
SANBORN Oscar H ae 10 [25 Apr 1901]
     Susie L ae 4 of East Machias ME [13 Aug 1885]

SANFORD James A ae 10 of West Bath ME [19 Feb 1885]

SARGENT Mamie ae 8 of Monroe ME [18 June 1885]

SCAMMON Wesley [11 Jul 1901]

SCOTT Dora 9 Medway ME "have brother & sister Melvin ae 8 & Maud ae 7" [24 Mar 1887]

SEAVEY Harry ae 11 [14 Mar 1901]

SEDGELY Daisy M 12 of Maranokook [1 Apr 1886]

SEVERANCE Edith M 6 Bangor ME "spending time at grandpappa's Ephraim NOYES in Jefferson ME, my grandmother who is 81 ..." [19 Aug 1886]

SHARDON Cora Bell 11 of Buxton ME [29 Apr 1886]

SHATTUCK Maggie M 11 Newcastle ME "have 2 brothers & 2 sisters" [10 Feb 1887]

SHAW Angie A 8 of North Newburgh "I have 4 brothers & 2 sisters" [19 Aug 1886]
    Elinah B 12 of Victoria Corner New Brunswick Canada [1 Apr 1886]
    Mildred [4 Apr 1901]

SHEPHERD Freemetta 10 of Belfast ME [31 Dec 1885]

SHERMAN Grace S 12 Appleton ME "have 2 sister Edith M & Helen Judson. Edith is married & lives in Fremont Nebraska" [23 June 1887]

SHOREY Ida C East Lowell [26 Aug 1886]
    Lulu M 8 of Lowell MA "I have five brothers & four sisters Arthur, Oscar, Elmer, Ernest, Thaddeus, Lilla, Josie, Ida & one in Heaven named Mattie. Lilla & Josie live in Bangor ME & Oscar in Foxcroft ME" [29 Jul 1886]
    Lulu M "every one of my brothers & sisters are gone. Ida has gone to Bangor ME to see Lilla & Josie. Lilla has got a little boy, Gussie RAMSDELL, ae 1y in Feb" [3 Mar 1887]

SILSBY Mr Aurora ME [3 June 1886]

SIMONDS Carrie E 9 of Etna ME "my papa's name is Benjamin W SIMONDS" [1 Sept 1887]
    Ida E 11 of Etna ME "have two sisters Carrie Emma & Sarah Etta. I had a little sister, Lula May ae 10m died 20 May" [1 Sept 1887]

SKILLIN Clifford A ae 7 of Hartford ME [28 Feb 1901]

SKILLINGS Lena E of Yarmouth ME [14 Jan 1886]
    Lyna E 7 of Yarmouth ME [1 Jul 1886]

SMALL Bessie of Mountain ME [22 Aug 1901]
    Ella H ae 7 of Cherryfield ME [2 Apr 1885]
    George F ae 12 of Biddeford ME [5 Mar 1855]
    Lena 7 of Pittsfield ME "have one brother" [28 Oct 1886]
    Lina E 7 of Pittsfield ME "My papa has been dead 6 yrs. I have one brother ae 13y [10 Feb 1887]

SMART Mary A ae 14 of Oakfield Aroostook Co ME [5 Feb 1885]
    Myrtle F [18 Apr 1901]

SMILEY Mabel L 9 Sidney ME I have no little sister, my sister is married & two brothers [22 Jul 1886]

SMITH Albert S ae 9 of Winham ME [4 June 1885]
    Anna I [15 Aug 1901]
    B Effie of Presque Isle ME [13 Aug 1885]
    Brida May 10 of Hartland ME "I have two sisters" [16 Dec 1886]
    Callie M 8 of Brownville ME [15 Jul 1886]
    Carrie 13 [16 Dec 1886]
    Cory R [10 Oct 1901]
    Edgar H ae 14 [21 Feb 1901]
    Edwin 8 of Cornwallis Nova Scotia "have 2 bro, Hugh & Fred" [7 Oct 1886]

SMITH (Cont.) Effie B of Presque Isle ME [7 May 1885]
    Effie Blanchie Sprague's Mills "my father sold farm in Presque Isle ME" [26 Aug 1886]
    Eugene I ae 10 of Ossipee Mills [20 Nov 1884]
    Flora Flagstaff ME 27 May 1886
    Frank E 10 of Brownville [29 Apr 1886]
    Fred O 12 of N Kennebunkport ME [31 Dec 1885]
    George [21 Feb 1901]
    George E [25 Apr 1901]
    Gracie E [22 Aug 1901]
    Hugh 11 of Cornwallis Nova Scotia "have 2 bro " [7 Oct 1886]
    Ida M of West Farmington ME, relatives in Portland ME [16 Apr 1885][19 Feb 1885][18 Dec 1884]
    Isaac A 11 of Sherman ME [6 May 1886]
    Kathie E 9 Flagstaff ME 27 May 1886
    Lillie B of Ellsworth ME [18 Mar 1886]
    Lillie of Winterport ME [18 Mar 1886]
    Lizze A Steuben ME "my cousin, George SMITH, is going to teach school, I have two sisters, Clara & Gertie" [7 Oct 1886]
    Lizzie A of Steuben ME [25 Mar 1886] & ae 10 of Steuben ME [8 Oct 1885]
    Mabel O 11 of Lincolnville ME [1 Apr 1886]
    Mildred F [13 June 1901]
    Millard [24 Oct 1901]
    Minnie A 9 of Pittsfield ME [17 Dec 1885]
    Nellie A ae 12 of Brownville ME [21 May 1885][16 Jul 1885][29 Apr 1886]
    Sadie A 10 of Sherman Mills ME [7 Jan 1886] & [6 May 1886]
    Samuel M [13 May 1886]
    Simeon [10 Oct 1901]
    Susie Flagstaff ME 27 May 1886
    Victor R ae 13 of North Hancock ME [19 Mar 1885][2 Jul 1885]
SNOW Jessie R of Bucksport [11 Feb 1886]
SNOWMAN Freddie Albea [*sic*] ae 6m, brother of Rosie & Lydia [*sic*], of Orland ME [8 Jul 1886]
    Linda 10 Orland ME "I have a sister, Rosie ae 8y & a brother, Freddie Albea ae 6m" [8 Jul 1886]
    Rosie ae 8 of Orland ME [8 Jul 1886]
    Rosie L 9 Orland ME "I have a little brother, Albea [*sic*], ae 11m & a sister, Linda, ae 11" [22 Jul 1886]
SOULE Carrie N of Phillips ME [27 Aug 1885]
    G B M of No Palermo ME [18 Mar 1886]
SPARROW E W 12 Hampden Cor ME [10 June 1886]
    Florence of Orland ME [5 Feb 1885]
SPINNEY Mamie D ae 8 of Phipsburg ME [18 Dec 1884]
SPOFFORD Ida C of Milton Plt [7 Jan 1886]
SPRAGUE Clara A teacher of South Princeton ME [8 Jul 1886]
    George L 13 Washington ME [17 June 1886]
    Marcia ae 10 of South Princeton ME [8 Jul 1886]
SPRING Ella of So Hiram ME [22 Oct 1885][24 Dec 1885]
    Walter M [2 May 1901]
SPRINGER Martie U [13 May 1886]
STANDLEY Norris E ae 8 of South Hiram ME [12 MAr 1885]
STANLEY Addie A ae 10 of Kingfield ME [23 Apr 1885]

STANLEY (Cont.) Alice [17 Oct 1901]

Bertha E [2 May 1901]

Carlton ae 13 of Kingfield ME [23 Apr 1885]

Hattie of Starks ME [11 Feb 1886]

Myrtie A ae 6 of So Hiram ME [19 Mar 1885]

Newton ae 16 of Kingfield ME [23 Apr 1885]

STANWOOD Mabel E of Freeport ME [8 Jan 1885]

STAPLES Vinnie M of North Penobscot ME [18 Dec 1884]

Willie W ae 8 of Campello MA [5 Nov 1891]

STEVENS Annie E 8 Augusta ME "I live with my grandma & grandpa, this summer I went up country to see my aunt & called on my great great grandma, 92y old. She told me she was married 10 Mar 1816 in Albion ME by Rev James CROSBY & raised 10 children. There were nine great grandchildren of us, I have one brother" [28 Oct 1886]

Daisy 7 of Augusta ME [31 Dec 1885]

Inez G 13y 2m of Philadelphia PA [28 Jan 1886]

Iva Lillian [9 May 1901]

Ralph ae 9 [9 May 1901]

STEWARD Stella M ae 11 of Skowhegan ME [5 Nov 1885]

STILSON Ada M 8 (born on 18 Feb) of Sidney ME [18 Feb 1886]

Fred E 11 of Sidney ME [18 Feb 1886]

STINCHFIELD Rufus ae 13 of Princeton ME [24 Dec 1885]

STINSON Mabel E of New Sharon ME [14 May 1885]

STODDARD Eva Winnieford ae 7 last Jul of Hallowell ME [20 Nov 1884]

Harry A Vassalboro ME [2 Dec 1886]

Harry ae 11 next Dec of Hallowell ME [20 Nov 1884]

Winnie E Vassalboro ME "living in Windsor ME this summer, my brother Fred is 12" [23 Sept 1886]

STOVER Gladys M 10 of Auburn ME [14 Jan 1886]

STROUT Amy [11 Apr 1901][13 June 1901]

Eva M ae 13 [30 May 1901]

Lida ae 8 [5 Nov 1885]

Rollo G ae 10 of East Bradford ME [8 Jan 1885]

STUART Bertha M ae 13 of South Hollis ME [11 June 1885]

SULLIVAN Asa H ae 13 Charlotte Co Canada [30 Apr 1885]

SWEET Dana of Avon ME [8 Jul 1886]

SWEETSER Clarence L ae 11 of Hermon Centre ME [5 Feb 1885]

SWIFT Hattie [13 May 1886] & Hattie B 9 West Sidney ME [25 Nov 1886] & ae 7 of West Sidney ME [11 Dec 1884]

SYLVESTER Iva [25 Jul 1901]

Ivah ae 12 [13 June 1901]

TABOR Vivian H 6 of Unity [22 Apr 1886]

TARBOX Agnes E [21 Mar 1901]

Clara W 9 of Fryeburg ME [4 Mar 1886]

TARR Leroy E 12 of Wayne ME [24 Dec 1885]

TAYLOR Annie teacher Athens ME [22 Jul 1886]

Ethie 11 Leedville CO "I have a brother ae 14 & two cousins in Augusta ME, but no sisters. I have a grandmother ae 73, who lives in Norridgewock ME, I have not seen her in 4 yrs" [6 Aug 1886]

Gleason E [13 May 1886]

TAYLOR (Cont.) Lelia S 8 Hope ME "My sister taught our school. I have one sister & 2 brothers. My youngest brother is away to one of our aunts, our uncle has gone to VA cutting ship timber" [24 Feb 1887]

TENNEY Bertha ae 9 of Hampden Corner ME [2 Jul 1885]

TENNIE Nellie of Hampden Corner ME [5 Nov 1885]

TEWKSBURY Evelyn M 12 South Atkinson ME "my aunt Mary HUTCHINS takes the *Maine Farmer*" [24 June 1886]

    Lottie A 11 South Atkinson ME [8 Jul 1886]

THAYER Maud ae 7 of Presque Isle ME [9 Jul 1885]

THOMAS Leon A ae 8 of Phillips ME [6 Aug 1885]

THOMPSON Maurice of Montville ME [8 Apr 1886]

    Nina S 12 of Mattawamkeag ME [31 Dec 1885]

THORNTON Mary of Princeton ME [2 Apr 1885]

THURBER Abbie E 11 of Salisbury's Cove ME [25 Mar 1886]

THURSTON Annie L ae 11 of South Deer Isle [11 June 1885]

    Lucy H 11 West Deer Isle ME "I joined the Band of Hope when I lived in Ohio" [24 Mar 1887]

TIBBETTS Celia [23 May 1901]

    Hattie teacher Waterville ME [1 Jul 1886]

    Mamie Agnes 6 Corinna ME "have 2 brothers, Everett E ae 4 & Harold Willis ae 9mos" [17 Feb 1887]

    O A 10 Searsmont ME [3 June 1886]

TODD Myrtie M 12 Caribou ME [3 June 1886]

TOLMAN Helen G ae 7 [8 Jan 1885]

TOMPLAINS Hannie E ae 12 at Maysville [5 Nov 1885]

TOOTHAKER Lizzie B of Harpswell ME [14 May 1885]

TOWLE Emma E of West Fryeburg [10 Dec 1891]

    Mittie 10 of Searsport ME [17 Dec 1885]

TOWNS Albion Victor 12 of Winthrop ME [18 Feb 1886]

TOZIER Abbie M ae 11 of Albion ME [26 Mar 1885]

    Fannie E ae 9 of Albion ME [26 Mar 1885]

    Susie E ae 9 of Canaan ME [2 Apr 1885]

TRACY Alfred L 11 of Sherman ME [28 Jan 1886]

    Macolm ae 11 [31 Dec 1885]

    Maud ae 12 of St Stephens NB Canada [19 Feb 1885]

    Maud E of Sherman ME [28 Jan & 15 Apr 1886]

TRAFTON Norris M 9 St Albans ME "have one sister ae 4y. Mother is dead most 4y, we live with Uncle Charles & Aunt Phronie, they have one girl ae 5y" [17 Feb 1887]

TRASK Blanche ae 13 [9 Apr 1885]

    Llewellyn B 18 Presque Isle ME "have two brothers Henry & John. Henry is in Colorado; John is only 8y. My father is a lame man." [30 June 1887]

    Susie C 11 Presque Isle ME "my father is a lame man" [24 Mar 1887]

TREAT Harry L ae 10 at Bucksport Centre ME [22 Jan 1885]

TREWORGY Bertha E 11 [14 Jan 1886] & almost 12 of South Surry ME in the part some call Newbury Neck [28 Oct 1886]

TRIPP Annie C 13 will be 14 next June of Pine Point "one brother ae 5 & one sister ae 11" [9 Dec 1886]

TRUE Anne Mae 13 Monmouth ME [22 Jul 1886]

    Annie May ae 11 of Monmouth ME [30 Apr 1885]

    E E teacher Lee ME 20 May 1886

TRUEWORTHY Raymond A of Waldoboro ME [9 May 1901]

TUCKER Alice M ae 9 of West Parsonsfield ME [26 Feb 1885][8, 16 Apr & 13 Aug 1885]
Grace 8 Hollis Center ME "I live in Boston MA, spending my vacation at granfather's (*sic*), James KNIGHTS. I have one brother, Fred" [6 Aug 1886]
Lura J 8 Parsonsfield ME [8 Apr 1886]

TURNER F E Belfast ME [17 June 1886]
Jusie D ae 9 of Palermo ME [19 Mar 1885]

TUSCAN Gracie E ae 8 of Bingham ME [21 May 1885]

TYLER Hattie of Farmington ME [28 Jan 1886]

UNDERHILL Carrie B 11 Charlestown MA "I am visiting with my Aunt Ann in Windsor ME, my Uncle Amos takes the *Maine Farmer*" [12 Aug 1886]

UNDERWOOD Alberta teacher from Fayette ME, moved from ME 6y ago Hammonton NJ [17 Aug 1886]

UPTON Gertrude L ae 10 of Points Reyes Marin Co CA [22 Jan 1885]

VARNEY E G 13 of Vienna ME [8 Apr 1886]

VAUGHAN Albert T of So Union ME [11 Mar 1886]
Blanchie 11 Bean's Corner "my papa is dead, he died when I was 3, he was a soldier. My mamma went to Boston MA two years ago & is working in a large store & did not return until last summer. I live with Mr Horace W RANGER for the past 2 yrs. I have a brother, Arthur, ae 16, my other brother, Fred, is working in a silk factory in Canton MA, I have not seen him for three years." [17 Feb 1887]

VOSE Mason J 10 New Portland ME "I live with my father, mother, grandmother, two sisters & two brothers. My grandfather, Jesse VOSE is eighty years old today. He has taken the *Maine Farmer* 53 yrs (since 1833). He walked two miles to see us today" [22 Jul 1886]

VOTER Edith W 9 of W Farmington ME [21 Jan 1886]
Nellie G 10y West Farmington ME [10 Mar 1887]

WAKEFIELD Annie E 13 of West Harrington ME [8 Apr 1886]
Horatio D ae 12 of Steuben ME [5 Nov 1885]

WALKER David P [18 Apr 1901]
Ella M of Canton ME [6 Dec 1900]
Lillian M [4 Jul 1901]
Lottie ae 12 of Embden ME [4 June 1885]
Richard A [28 Mar 1901]

WARD Clara E 12 of Searsport ME [18 Mar 1886]
Clara E 8 Troy ME [17 June 1886]
Earle A [18 Jul 1901][22 Aug 1901]
Ira T 11 Thorndike ME [15 Jul 1886]
May ae 10 of Stockton CA [24 Sept 1885]

WARREN Maud M 9 Denmark ME "have 8 sisters & one brother, we live near Pleasant Mtn" [3 Mar 1887]

WASSON Lucy 12 of West Brooksville [8 Apr 1886]

WATERHOUSE Fred W of Mechanic Falls ME [4 Feb 1886]
Homer T 12 of Lyman ME [26 Nov 1885]

WATSON Lubertha H 6 No Belgrade ME [15 Apr 1886]

WEATHERBY Hannah L 11 of Little Bridgeton NB [4 Feb 1886]

WEBBER Calvin E 9 Mt Vernon ME [28 July 1887]
Charlie ae 9 of Etna Center ME [14 Jul 1887]
Elmer H 6 Mt Vernon ME "I am a twin to Annie Rose WEBBER, we have a baby sister, Myra" [21 Jul 1887]
Emma A ae 11 of Mt Vernon ME [7 May 1885]
Fred M of Mt Vernon ME [26 Mar 1885]

WEBER Louis [11 Jul 1901]
WEBSTER Annie 10 of Carratunk ME [26 Nov 1885]
    Daisy C ae 10 of Bangor ME [11 Dec 1884]
    Josie ae 10 of Cambridge (Kings Co Nova Scotia)? [9 Jul 1885]
WEED Mamie E 6 Knox ME "My cousin Annah is here from Sherman Mills ME" [25 Nov
    1886]
WEEKS Lilla ae 14 of Westbrook ME [9 Jul 1885]
    Percy 8 Sand Point Idaho "I used to live in CA. I have 3 cousins in CA" [1 Sept 1887]
WELCH Abbie Ellen ae 11 of Dead River ME [22 Oct 1891]
WELTS Aramenta E 11 of Caribou ME [1 Apr 1886]
WENTWORTH D G teacher Searsmont ME [3 June 1886]
    Flora B ae 7 of Freedom [9 Apr 1885]
    Nellie M ae 10 of Weld ME [9 Apr 1885]
WESCOTT Alice Maria ae 6 [24 Sept 1885]
    Ward W ae 9 of Hancock Co [23 Apr 1885]
WEST Etta of Egypt [4 Mar 1886]
WETHERBY Hannah 12 Little Ridgton [27 Jan 1887]
WEYMOUTH Maud F 15 East New Portland ME [24 June 1886]
WHITE Ellis A of Winthrop ME [10 & 31 Dec 1885]
WHITMORE Harry E ae 10 [25 Apr 1901]
    Raymond V of Fort Fairfield [25 Apr 1901]
WHITNEY Bertha A 8 of Lee ME [20 May 1886][31 Dec 1885]
    Charlene a teacher at Sprague's Mills Aroostook Co ME [12 Mar 1885]
    Lilla F ae 10 of Bangor ME [9 Jul 1885]
    Llewellyn H of Jonesboro ME [24 Dec 1885][18 Mar 1886]
    Luie M of Presque Isle ME [5 Nov 1885]
    Margie I teacher at Windham ME [2 Apr 1885]
    Nettie 12 of Bangor ME [9 Jul 1885]
WHITTIER A M 15 of Vienna ME [21 Jul 1887] & 13 of Vienna ME [20 Aug 1885]
    Ella F 12 of Eastbrook [26 Nov 1885]
    Mabel A ae 9 of Carnville [*sic*] ME [8 Jan 1885]
WIGHT Mary A ae 13 of Northport ME [16 Apr 1885]
WILBUR Ethel V ae 14 of No Lamoine ME [28 Jan 1886][29 Apr 1886]
WILEY Lucy W 12 of Martinsville [22 Apr 1886]
WILLEY Hattie Miss teacher East Madison ME [15 Jul 1886]
    Jennie ae 8 of Cherryfield ME [11 June 1885]
    Lottie C ae 13 of Cherryfield ME [6 Aug 1885]
    Nannie ae 6 of Cherryfield ME [11 June 1885]
WILLIAMS Belle E ae 9 of Winthrop ME [7 May 1885] & [18 Feb 1886]
    Bertha ae 5, sister of Leroy E, of Bowdoinham ME [8 Jul 1886]
    Cora V ae 10 of Embden ME [5 Mar 1855]
    Leroy E 8 Bowdoinham ME "a little sister, Bertha ae 5 & a brother (Nattie) most four" [4
        June 1885] & ae (8y this month) [8 Jul 1886]
    Nattie ae 3 (almost 4) brother of Leroy E, of Bowdoinham ME [8 Jul 1886]
WILLS May J ae 10 of Vienna ME [19 Feb 1885][12 Nov 1885]
WILSON Annie [20 June 1901]
    Neddie C [11 Apr 1901]
WINSLOW Eddie H 11 of W Bristol [4 Feb 1886] & 12 (will be 13y in Mar of 1887) West
    Bristol ME "I used to live in Augusta ME, but my father & mother are both dead
    now, I live on a farm with Mr CURTIS. my brother, Arthur R, age 10y & lives with
    my grandpa & grandma in Pittston ME near the bridge." [7 Oct 1886] [3 Mar 1887]

WOLTZ Bertie Waldoboro ME [29 Jul 1886]

WOOD Florence C ae 9 [13 June 1901]

    Irving A ae 12 of Winslow ME [5 Feb 1885]

    M Helen [22 Apr 1886]

    Mary H of Mercer ME [22 Oct 1885]

WOODARD Charles S ae 10 of Augusta ME [7 May 1885]

WOODBURY Hannie W 8 Round Pond ME [25 Mar 1886]

    Marion Jessie Hastings, MI "live with my Aunt & Uncle now, for my mamma ia dead, I have 3 brothers & they are with papa in Toronto [16 Dec 1886]

WOODCOOK Eva teacher at Cushing ME [12 Feb 1885]

WOODMAN Frank 9 Searsport ME "I live on a farm with my grandfather & grandmother; my mother died 4 years ago, my father has not been at home but once since" [17 June 1886]

WOODWARD Amanda E Jonesboro ME [8 Jul 1886]

WOOSTER Helen A of South Hancock ME [19 Nov 1885]

WRIGHT Addie M of Caribou ME [25 Dec 1884]

WYLLIE Ralph C 11 of Warren ME [29 Apr 1886]

WYMAN Freeman L a teacher at West Paris [5 Mar 1855]

    Mabel ae 10 of Dead River ME [13 Aug 1885]

YORK Beulah F ae 12 [27 Dec 1900]

    Eliza J ae 11 of Porter ME [4 Dec 1884] ae 12 of Porter ME [12 Feb 1885]

    Jennie E Porter ME "I have one sister ae 10y & no brothers" [15 Jul 1886]

    Josie 10 South Medway ME "have five brothers Osborne, Arthur, Jimmie, Johnnie & Freddie" [1 Sept 1887]

    Mary E ae 9 of Kezar Falls ME [4 Dec 1884] & of Porter ME [12 Feb 1885]

    Myra M ae 11 of Medway ME [8 Jan 1885]

    Stella M [21 Mar 1901]

    Walter J 11 West Forks ME "my twin brother, Wallace E, were 11y old on 8 Apr last, we have 3 sisters Blanche, who has gone to Newton NH, the others are Edith Belle & Nera Lee YORK" [16 June 1887]

YOUNG Angie W ae 12 next August of Trenton ME [24 June 1886]

    Arthur B ae 8 of Prospect ME [19 Feb 1885]

    Ernest L of W Troy ME [18 Feb 1886]

    Florence [21 Mar 1901]

    Gracie A 13 South Surry ME "have one sister, Nannie ae 11y" [4 Nov 1886]

    Harry ae 10 of Ashland ME [21 May 1885]

    Hattie M 12 (born on 15 Feb) of No Warren ME [25 Feb 1886]

    Irving M 8 of Columbia Falls [29 Apr 1886]

    Lizzie M 9 of Bar Harbor ME [4 Feb 1886]

    Mabel I 10 of Columbia Falls ME [17 Dec 1885]

    N M 11 South Surry ME "have 2 brothers & & two sisters" [4 Nov 1886]

    Wilbur W 10 of No Warren ME [25 Feb 1886]

INDEX TO NEWS ARTICLES:

1833 - 1911
and
1912 - 1924

We have indexed the articles titled "Communications" and "Editorial Correspondence" related to Maine and New England. The articles contain brief histories of Maine towns in the form of travelogues. Also indexed are historical or genealogical articles buried in the newspaper. No effort was made to index all the letters under an article headed "Editorial Correspondence" from Maine servicemen of the Civil War (1861-1865). County Farmer Club news is not indexed, as one can expect to find something published at least once a month. Some of the other column titles are: "Excursions in Maine and Thoughts by the Way" by Cyril Pearl; "More about the State of Maine," from the *Hill's Monthly Visitor* (*Maine Farmer* new series 2-26 (1843); "Down East," 1834 to 1835, copied from the *Hancock Advertiser*; and "Stray Leaves from our Log-Book" (1845).

Mr. Daniel Stickney of Augusta, Maine, was secured as a traveling canvassing agent and correspondent of the *Farmer* to visit Penobscot, Piscataquis, and Aroostook counties. The items of news facts, general interest, and historical memoranda started in 1872. "Old Times" column started in 1879, and published vital records and journals of the Revolutionary period. Also in 1887, "Choice of Miscellany" and "Curious Things" columns were started. They printed articles of historical and genealogical interest.

ABBOT Maine [28 Jul 1859]
ADAMS F S (photo) [21 Dec 1899] [19 Dec 1901] of Bowdoin ME (photo) [10 Dec 1903] of
    Bowdoinham ME (photo) [13 Dec 1906]
    Frank S of Bowdoinham ME, photo, Candidates for Commissioner of Agr [26 Sept 1912]
        & photo & story on his farm [19 Dec 1912]
    Ogden, drawing [2 Mar 1893]
ADDISON Maine, Jottings from Our Correspondent [19 Nov 1885]
ADDITION E E of Leeds ME, photo, Candidates for Commissioner of Agr [26 Sept 1912]
        & photo w/story of Farm at Leeds [24 Oct 1912] & (photo) [29 Dec 1910]
    F L at Greene ME (photo of farm) 12 Aug 1909]
AFRICA (Batongo Co) Brown People of [16 Sept 1847]
ALABAMA BASINS [5 Sept 1861]
ALBANY Maine, Grants of Land in [13 Dec 1879]
ALBION Maine, [Vol 8-61 (1840)] a brief history [10 Nov 1881]
ALDEN Benjamin, farmhouse in Greene ME built 1791, see Ziba Alden GILBERT farm [5
    Aug 1909]
    Rutillus of Winthrop ME (photo of home) [18 Jan 1900] [22 Mar 1900] (photo) [4 Dec
    1902] (photo) [3 Dec 1903]
ALEY Robert J Dr (photo) [8 Sept 1910]
ALFRED Court House ME, Ancient Court Records [30 Aug 1873]
ALLAGASH, Aroostook Co ME [28 Jan 1871]
ALLEMAN Dudley, was editor of the *Maine Farmer* [1 Sept 1923]
ALLEN Abby W ae 88 [24 Nov 1887]
    Farm of Pittsfield MA, a visit [2 Jan 1896]
ALVA Aroostook Co ME [1 Jul 1871]

AMERICA one hundred years ago [17 Oct 1895]
AMERICAN FLAG, history of [17 June 1909]
AMERICAN PORTRAIT PAINTER - Gilbert STUART [25 Oct 1879]
AMES James H of Unity & his potato field (photo) [11 Nov 1897]
AMHERST Maine - historical memo [3 May 1873]
ANDOVER Maine [23 & 30 June 1864] Ed Corr [11 Jul 1867]
ANDROSCOGGIN Co Maine - The Crops in [21 Nov 1868]
    Intervals - Mt Zircon &c [1 Aug 1861]
    River Valley - Editorial Correspondence travelogue [10 Jan 1867]
APPLE TREE, photo of the largest one of U. S., in CT [2 Jul 1891]
APPLES, Jumping on, Ben DAVIS [26 Jan 1899] [30 Oct 1902]
ARNOLD Benedict, his family genealogy [5 Sept 1874] & Benedict & Aaron BURR [19 Feb
    1885] & March Through Norridgewock 4 Oct 1775 to Mon 9 Oct [26 Jul 1873]
AROOSTOOK, #1 a trip to [7 Aug 1880] & #2 a trip to Caribou & Perham [14 Aug 1880]
    & #3, a trip to Ft Fairfield & Presque Isle [21 Aug 1880]
    About # 1 [11 Mar 1871]
    An excursion in # 4 [22 Nov 1873]
    Another Voice from by Stephen S BRAGDON of Easton [1 Apr 1871]
    Article [24 Nov 1859]
    August Wanderings #5 [20 Sept 1883]
    Cutting Wood in by O B GRIFFIN of Caribou [5 Feb 1920]
    Emigrants - Information to [29 Aug 1861]
    Farming [28 Jul 1859]
    French settlers, Suffering along the St John River [31 May 1855] & French settlers,
        Aroostook Co ME [16 Nov 1878]
    Future of [21 Nov 1868]
    Good news from [2 Sept 1852]
    Lands [26 June 1856]
    Letter by J F BLAKE of Winterport [28 Jan 1871]
    Letter from Fort Fairfield by GWH [16 May 1867]
    Letter from Island Falls [19 Apr 1866]
    Letter from James W AMBROSE of Sherman Mills [28 Mar 1868] & [13 Nov 1869] &
        More About by J W AMBROSE of Sherman [8 Apr 1871] & My Experince in, by
        James W AMBROSE of Sherman Mills [2 May 1867]
    Letter from [9 Oct 1875]
    Life in Northern by Cyrus SPRAGUE of Gardiner ME [25 Sept 1884]
    Notes from [16 Oct 1875]
    Notes of a Round Trip [16 Nov 1878]
    Notes #2 from Caribou [20 Nov 1880]
    Scenes in the Wilderness - No 3, Aroostook Mtn & Godfrey's Falls [10 Apr 1845]
    Sept Wanderings #1 [11 Oct 1883]
    Settling Lands [5 June 1856]
    Starch Factories [11 Oct 1883]
    Sugar Beets in [15 June 1899]
    Thoughts on Emigration #3 [3 Apr 1856]
    Towns & Villages by Mr FARLEY [1 & 29 Jul 1871]
    Trip Through #1 to 3 [21 Jan 1864] [4 Feb 1864] [11 Feb 1864]
    Trip to, by Elisha PURINGTON of East Embden [14 Nov 1868]
    Written by Mr FARLEY [29 Apr 1871]
AROOSTOOK MTN, Scenes in the Wilderness - No 3 [10 Apr 1845]
AROOSTOOK PROSPECTS, Masardis ME [27 Jul 1916]

AROOSTOOK VALLEY - in the Winter (5 Apr 1855)

ASHLAND Maine, visit to #1 [4 Sept 1884] visit #2 [16 Oct 1884] [21 Jan 1864]

ASHLEY Charles S (photo) [22 Feb 1906]

ATHENS Maine [1 Sept 1859]

ATHERTON W P, orchardist of Hallowell ME (photo) [7 Sept 1899]

ATWOOD Blanche, drawing [22 Mar 1894]

AUBURN Jct (Danville Jct) Maine - ed corr [23 Mar 1868]

AUBURN Maine - DILLINGHAM Genealogy [25 Jan 1873]

AUGUSTA Maine [24 Nov 1859] [15 Apr 1876] [27 May 1876] [4 Nov 1876] [Vol 8-69
    (1840)] [new series 2-26 (1843)]
    100th [20 May 1897] [3 June 1897] [10 June 1897]
    As it was & is [29 Dec 1892]
    Augusta House, new at State St & Western Ave (photo) [10 Dec 1908]
    Boy in a whaler #1-3 [16 30 Mar 1893] [8 Feb 1894]
    Centennial [10 Sept 1896] [10 Dec 1896]
    Civil War Soldiers' Monument [30 Oct 1880]
    Climate & Products of 1788 [25 Jan 1873]
    Death of James W NORTH [8 June 1882]
    Death rate 1852-1855 [2 Jan 1890]
    Fort Burying Ground at Cushnoe [3 Oct 1861]
    Forty Years ago, Its changes [12 May 1853]
    Historical Sketches of (#3-5), by Hon James W NORTH [1 Mar 1866] [8 Mar 1866] [15
        Mar 1866]
    Hotel North at 264 Water St (photo) [10 Dec 1908]
    Lithgrow Library of Augusta ME [18 Jul 1895] [2 Jan 1896] Library & reading room at
        Augusta ME photo [6 Feb 1896]
    Masonic Temple, drawing & story [21 June 1894]
    Mortuary Records names 112 causes of Death & Ages [12 Apr 1883]
    Old & New 1-5 by E B GETCHELL [20 Jul, 3 17 Aug, 21 Sept, 19 Oct 1893]
    Old People of Augusta - see: ALLEN, BOSTON, BRADBURY, BRITT, CHISAM,
        CLAPP, CLARK, CUSHING, EASON, EATON, EVELETH, FARRINGTON,
        GILLEY, GRANT, GREEN, HAMLIN, HEWINS, KINSMAN, LITTLE, PHILLIPS,
        POWERS, ROBBINSON, ROBINSON, TOWNE, WOLCOTT, YOUNG [24 Nov
        1887] [22 Feb 1894] [10 Jan 1901]
    Old Time Settlers, Notes of [15 Apr 1876] [27 May 1876]
    Post Office of other days by Charles M MORSE [16 Sept 1897]
    Savings Bank, unclaimed deposits [29 Nov 1906] [12 Dec 1907] [3 Dec 1908] [18 Nov
        1909] [1 Dec 1910]
    Traders 39 years ago [28 Mar 1889]
    Trust Co (photo) [31 May 1906]
    Universalist Church History [7 Mar 1868]
    "Winthrop Hall," an old landmark [21 June 1873]
    Winthrop House (photo) at 90 State St corner of Winthrop [10 Dec 1908]

AUSTRALIAN BALLOT [28 Jul 1898] [4 Aug 1898] [6 Oct 1898] [20 Oct 1898] [24 Nov
    1898]

AUSTRALIAN NEWSPAPER States "Wives Wanted" [1 Feb 1849]

AUTO, A twist at the Problem [21 June 1906] another view of the [26 Apr 1906] Can see
        Nothing but Disaster in the [7 June 1906] Wanted - an Automobilist Educator [18 Jul
        1907]

AUTOMOBILE, on the Farm [20 Jan 1910] A Voice from the other side [31 May 1906]

AVON Maine, Glimpses from the Road-side [1 Mar 1849] [17 Sept 1857]

BACHELDER N J (photo) [14 Nov 1901] [25 Aug 1904]
BAGLEY, Jonathan ae 94y of Troy ME [24 Apr 1875]
BAILEYVILLE, now called Winthrop Center, a travelogue [2 June 1887]
BAKER A (photo) [25 Aug 1904]
BALL Albert of Mapleton ME, photo & story on farm [17 Apr 1913]
BALLOT LAW, How it works [2 Mar 1899]
BANCROFT George, a great Historian is gone [22 Jan 1891]
BANCROFT MILLS Maine [21 Jan 1864]
BANGOR Maine, in 1818 - hist memo [8 Feb 1873] & [28 Apr 1859] [28 Jul 1859] &
    Natural History Society [Vol 8-365 (1840)] & [Vol 8-37 (1840)]
BARNABY Alvin P of Hartsville College Indiana (photo) [29 Apr 1897]
BARTELME Mary M, 1st woman public guardian of Cook Co IL (drawing) [10 June 1897]
BASIN FALLS [Vol 9-133 (1841)]
BATCHELDER'S Grant [5 Sept 1861]
BATH Maine, Ancient Georgetown & its Second Parish [21 Aug 1880] [28 Aug 1880] & to
    Augusta, travel log [21 Apr 1859] & [4 Jul 1861]
BATTLE OF MONTEREY 1846 [22 Oct 1846]
BEACHER, Henry Ward, story on the widow [2 Apr 1896]
BEALE J W Mrs of Worcester MA (Drawing) [28 Jan 1897]
BEARCE Boyden (photo) [19 Dec 1901] [20 Dec 1906]
BELFAST Maine, Journal old diaries Apr & May 1832-1870 (weather) [13 Mar 1875]
BELGRADE Maine [17 July 1845] Jottings by the Way [10 Mar 1892]
BELL Alexander Capt of Portland ME, drawing [13 Oct 1892]
    Anna M ae 15 d/o W G BELL of Madison ME, (photo with a steer) [3 Oct 1907]
BEN DAVIS APPLE DOOM [30 Oct 1902] & [26 Jan 1899]
BENEDICTA, Aroostook Co [18 Dec 1884] [11 Nov 1850]
BENSON Franklin of West Hollis ME, drawing [20 Apr 1893]
BENTON A Mr [8 Mar 1894]
BERAW Eva of Bradford MA, drawing [27 Apr 1893]
BERRY Elizabeth D of Hampton NH, drawing [3 Nov 1892]
    Genealogy - see Kittery ME
    Ira printer of the *E Argus* ae 90 [24 Sept 1891]
    Levi of Pownal ME, drawing [16 Mar 1893]
    S R Mrs of Lebanon NH, drawing [30 Mar 1893]
BETHEL HILL Maine [8 Aug 1861] Bethel House [1 Aug 1861]
BETHEL Maine [8 Aug 1861] [11 Jul 1867] [22 Aug 1861] [6 Oct 1877] Centennial [4
    June 1896]
BIBLE, Ages of Men Before the Flood (Noah) [22 June 1882]
BINGHAM VILLAGE Maine, Jottings by the Way [29 Oct 1891]
BISHOP Nathaniel of Winthrop ME, Another Old Pioneer Gone [20 Apr 1854]
BLACK George D of Kansas, new State Master (drawing & article) [25 Jul 1907]
    H C of Henron ME (photo) [17 Nov 1910]
    J H Dr of Readfield ME, drawing [2 Mar 1893]
BLACKMAN Clifford [3 Nov 1892] [23 Mar 1893]
BLACKSTONE VALLEY, Aroostook Co, ME the first settlers in the [26 Sept 1874]
BLACKSTRAP MONUMENT of Falmouth ME drawn by Ola O FIELD ae 12 of
    Woodfords Station [19 Mar 1908]
BLACKWELL Pauline Mrs & child, drawing [16 Nov 1893]
    William Mr & Mrs, diamond wedding (of Fairfield ME) [9 Apr 1896]
BLAIR Lyman at Greenville ME (photo of house) [7 Jul 1904]
BLAKE Dudley of Hallowell ME, drawing [4 May 1893] [14 Sept 1893]

BLANCHARD Albert Mrs & Helena Miss, drawing [18 Jan 1894]

BLANCHARD Maine [1 Sept 1859]

BLETHIN, Jeanette b 1783 at Salem MA ae 92 of Thorndike ME [24 Apr 1875];

BLUEHILL Maine - Hancock Co the scenery about [8 Jul 1871] Our State [10 Aug 1872]
the Granite Quarries [8 Jul 1871]

BOGART E S Mrs, drawing [1 Dec 1892]

BOND'S BROOK [24 June 1858]

BOOTHBAY ASSOCIATION, Old Maine Town Remembered at Elsmere estate
Dorchester MA [21 June 1894]

BOOTHBY Merritt A of Clinton ME, drawing [5 Jan 1893] [11 May 1893]

BOSTON Edward ae 83 [24 Nov 1887]

BOSTON Mass, Dr Benjamin Shurtleff letter to Dr Cony of Augusta ME [25 Jan 1873]
1630-1824 Great Fires [11 Jan 1873]

BOUNTY LAND FOR MARRIAGE, The Congress of Texas have passed a law granting
2,982 acres of good land to every woman, who will marry, during the present year, a
citizen of that Republic, & who was such at the time of the declaration of their
Independence [23 Nov 1839]

BOVINE TUBERCULOSIS in Maine, Review for 20yrs [31 Dec 1908]

BOW town Somerset Co ME [17 Aug 1878]

BOWDOIN COLLEGE, The Necrology 1887-88 [14 June 1888] & College Centennial [5
Jul 1894]

BOWDOINHAM Maine, early history [29 Nov 1883] [Vol 8-85 (1840)] [14 Mar 1867]

BOWEN George A (photo) [14 Nov 1901]

BOWNESS E F, farmer in Turner ME [26 Sept 1912]

BOYDSTOWN so called in 1820 but, changed to Milton, then Almond see Orneville [13
May 1871]

BRADBURY James W died ae 99y [10 Jan 1901] & James W of Hallowell & Gardiner ME
ae 97, his recollections [1 June 1899]

BRADFORD Maine [22 Dec 1859] [29 Dec 1859]

BRADLEY C E (photo haying at Barker's Ridge farm) at Island Falls ME summer of 1909
[26 May 1910]

BRAIN Annie ae 3 the youngest cyclist, drawing [23 Jul 1896]

BREWER Maine [Vol 8-37 (1840)] Brick Co - Our State [18 May 1872]

BREWER N Howard of Hockanum CT (photo) [18 Nov 1909]

BRIDGES James b 17 Jul 1804 [24 Nov 1887]

BRIDGEWATER Aroostook Co ME [1 Jul 1871]

BRIGGS B F & F H their farm, Maple Grove Farm in Auburn ME [8 June 1893] & B F of
Auburn ME (obit & photo) [18 May 1899]

Nannie M, drawing of a granddaughter of Iowa at Semicentenniel [5 Nov 1896]

BRIGHTON Maine [1 Sept 1859]

BRITT Jacob ae 80 said to be the grandson of one of Burgoyne's Hessians who deserted &
then came to the Kennebec [24 Nov 1887]

BROAD BAY RIVER, "ZITZ," German for SIDES, an old Document [28 June 1873]

BROOKLIN Hancock Co ME - Our State [10 Aug 1872]

BROOKS Maine, Sketches of Early Settlers of [25 Sept, 9 16 Oct, 6 Nov 1880, 6 Jan, 3 17
24 Feb 1881]

BROWN F L, Riverside Stock farm between Sebasticook River & Maine Central Railroad
[21 Aug 1913]

George V of Caribou ME (photo) [29 Dec 1910]

Mary Ellen, (Negro notary) 1st commissioned in KY (drawing) [17 June 1897]

BROWN PEOPLE of Africa [16 Sept 1847]

BROWNVILLE Maine [2 June 1859] [28 Jul 1859]

BRUCE Robert of Chicago IL, drawing [8 Dec 1892]

BRUNSWICK Maine [Vol 8-173 (1840)]

BRYAN William J (photo) [13 Aug 1908]

BRYANT C of Keene's Mills with his team (photo) [7 Apr 1910]

Carroll A of Livermore ME, story on Farm [3 Apr 1913]

BRYANT'S POND Maine [22 Sept 1877]

BUCK Elijah Mr & Mrs of Saco ME, drawing [15 Mar 1894]

Florence Rev of Cleveland Unitarian (Drawing) [31 Dec 1896]

BUCKFIELD Maine, a letter from D S a Veteran [31 Aug 1893] [Vol 9-133 (1841)] [15 Sept 1877] [24 June 1880] & a corr ed [25 Apr 1867] & Prop Records [23 & 30 Aug 1879] [6 Sept 1879]

Marriages by Isaac PARSONS Esq 1794 [18 Sept 1880]

BUCKLEY J P of Stroudwater ME, photo concrete block silo [7 Apr 1910]

BUCKSPORT Maine village [30 June 1859] ed corr [15 Feb 1868] Our State [20 Jul 1872]

BUKER farm at Bowdoinham ME, photo of haying with article [15 Aug 1907]

John F of Bowdoin Centre ME (photo of Farm) [3 Sept 1903]

BUNKER HILL MONUMENT [10 Jul 1835]

BURLINGTON Maine by J P Clark of Springfield ME [12 Sept 1874]

BURNT JACKET Maine [1 Sept 1859]

BUSH - see WOMAN, Suffrage

BUTTERFIELD, Jacob W b 12 Mar 1783 ae 92 of Chesterville ME [24 Apr 1875];

BUXTON Maine, historic paper by Eugene C CARIL [22 Oct 1908] & "Editorial Notes" [4 June 1891]

BUZZELL Charles E Gen of Lakeport NH photo [6 Feb 1896]

CALAIS Maine, Facts About the Enterprising Young Fair [28 Aug 1913]

(view from St Stevens NB) [16 Jul 1899]

CALDWELL E E of Leeds ME, Grandview Farm [16 Sept 1915]

CALIFORNIA, Dairy by Geo R SNEATH near Menlo Park CA [16 Apr 1896]

Death Valley [8 Jan 1891]

Early Discoveries of Gold, in 1721 [1 Feb 1849]

Early History of [1 Feb 1849]

Expedition, over 50 names men from Belfast, Bangor, Hampden, Boston Lee, Lincolnville, Waterville, Camden, Brooks, Orono, Waldo, Unity, Oldtown, China & Orrington leaving Waldo Co [8 Feb 1849]

Passengers list of Mainer's going to [1 Feb, 20 Sept, 15 22 Nov 1849]

CALL Frank L Mr & Mrs of West Troy (60th wedding yr) [18 Feb 1897]

CALL - see ODLIN

CAMPBELL John J of Lewiston ME, drawing [13 Apr 1893] [19 Oct 1893]

Percy A Prof [19 Mar 1908] [8 Dec 1910]

CANAAN Maine [18 May 1865] [6 Jul 1865]

CANADIAN, Cornwallis Valley [3 Aug 1878]

Immigration [23 Oct 1913]

Montreal Canada - ed corr [20 Aug 1868] [27 Aug 1868] [3 Sept 1868]

People who sleep in coffins, The Strange Discovery in Montreal [2 June 1892]

CANTON Maine [Vol 9-251 & 9-349 (1841)] [24 June 1880] [31 Jul 1880]

Canton Point ME, Indian Village by Myrtic CARVER ae 11 [23 May 1901] & [27 Aug 1857] [1 Aug 1861]

CAPE ELIZABETH, A shipwreck in 1703 [30 June 1877]

An Island History of Richmond Island, ME 1583-1906 [11 Jan 1906]

Early History of, [18 Jan, 22 Feb, 15 Mar 1873]

CAPE ELIZABETH (Cont.) Marriages by Clement JORDAN Esq 1786 [2 Oct, 25 Sept
    1880]
    Marriages by David STROUT Esq 1788 [2 Oct 1880]
    Marriages by Rev Ephraim CLARK 1786-87, 1787-88, 1789-95 [18 25 Sept, 2 Oct 1880]
    Marriages by Samuel CALEF Esq 1786-1794 [2 Oct 1880]
CAPE SMALL POINT Maine [22 Jul 1886]
CAPT KIDD'S TREASURE [5 Jul 1873]
CAPT THUNDERBOLT, a forgotten celebrity of half a century ago by Hon William
    GOULD [11 Aug 1887]
CARIBOU, Aroostook Co ME [16 Nov 1878] [16 Oct 1875] [29 Jul 1871] [20 Nov 1880]
    August Wandering # 2 [30 Aug 1883]
    Excursion to Aroostook Co [8 Aug 1895]
    Grange Hall (photo) [10 May 1906]
    Upper Aroostook Co ME [7 Nov 1889]
CARMEL Maine [28 Jul 1859]
CARR J T Rev of Pittsfield ME, drawing [14 Sept 1893]
CARRATUCK Maine, Jottings by the Way [29 Oct 1891]
CARRYING PLACE Somerset Co ME [17 Aug 1878]
CARTHAGE Maine [31 Jul 1880]
CASCADE GRANGE HALL of Oakland ME (photo) [5 Nov 1903]
CASTINE Maine, new History of Castine, Penobscot & Brooksville ME by George A
    Wheeler of Castine [20 Mar 1875]
    One Hundred Years at [16 Jul 1896]
CASTLE HILL, Visit to Ashland # 2 [16 Oct 1884]
CENTURY AGO (1780) Extreme Cold [1 May 1880]
CHARLESTON [19 May 1859]
CHASE Solon, sketch [13 Jan 1910]
CHASE & SANBORN's Coffee ad [21 May 1903]
CHATHAM NH, the Valley at [3 Nov 1904]
CHENEY F S of Augusta ME (photo of farm building) [30 Jan 1908]
CHEROKEE GOLD [24 Apr 1845]
CHERRYFIELD Maine, Down East from Ellsworth to the Jumping Off place [26 Dec
    1834] & Jottings from Our Correspondant [19 Nov 1885]
CHESTERVILLE Maine, Glimpses from the Road-side [15 Mar 1849] [30 Oct 1880]
CHICAGO IL - ed corr [19 26 Sept, 10 Oct 1868]
CHICK Abbie T Mrs of New Portland ME, drawing [12 Jan, 18 May 1893]
CHILCOTT J C obit of the editor of the Ellsworth American [20 Apr 1893]
CHINA Maine [Vol 8-61 (1840)] Incidents in the Settlement [17 Oct 1867] History of [7
    Nov 1874]
CHINESE EXCLUSION [25 May 1893]
CHISAM William Mrs ae 81 [24 Nov 1887]
CHOATE genealogy - Early settlers in Poland ME [1 Mar 1873]
CIVIL WAR 19th ME Veteran Assoc, by William A WOOD, Experience of a Veteran #1-6
    [2 16 Mar, 6 Apr, 11 May, 24 Aug, 2 Nov 1893]
    3rd Maine Reunion [29 Sept 1887]
    3rd ME Reg Muster Roll [20 June 1861]
    3rd ME Reg - deaths [1 Aug 1861]
    3rd ME Reg - letter from [1 Aug 1861] [4, 11, 18 Jul 1861] [12 Sept 1861]
    7th Maine Battery [9 Jul 1885]
    20th Maine at Gettysburg [28 Dec 1865]
    20th Maine Reunion at Waterville ME [1 Sept 1887]

CIVIL WAR (Cont.) 21st ME Reunion [1 Aug 1901]
   7th ME Reg - Letter from # 2 & #4 [12 Sept 1861] [5, 26 Sept 1861]
   Battle of Big Bethel, the first Dead Rebel [17 Aug 1882]
   Battle of Fredericksburg [20 Nov 1890]
   Battle of Missionary Ridge [31 Jul 1869]
   Campaign in Virginia, Complete List of Casualities in Maine Reg [2 June 1864]
   Dakotah, letter from a man in Co B, 13th Iowa Vol (Mr CLARK formerly of New
      England) [20 Mar 1862]
   Departure of the 7th ME Reg [29 Aug 1861]
   Departure of the 8th ME Reg [12 Sept 1861]
   Departure of the 9th ME Reg [26 Sept 1861]
   GAR in Maine [8 Feb 1894]
   Grand Army Reunion [14 Aug 1884]
   Killed & Wounded Maine Soldier & many issues followed [12 June 1862]
   Letters from Maine Reg's Weekly 1861-1864
   Life in Libby Prison, Co B 4th ME [15 Sept 1892]
   Maine Prisoners of War in New Orleans [5 Dec 1861]
   Peace meeting in Saybrook in 1861 [11 Dec 1890]
   Red River Battles - The Maine Troops in [12 May 1864]
   Return of Invalid Maine Soldiers [15 May 1862]
   Second Maine Cavalry Reunion [12 Oct 1893]
   Serving the Country #1 - 23, Sketches of the Service of a Veteran ME Reg from ME to
      FL by John W LANG Co B 9th ME Vet Vol Inf [13 20 27 Apr, 4 11 18 25 May, 1 8
      15 22 29 Jun, 6 20 27 Jul, 3 10 31 Aug, 7 21 28 Sep, 5 19 Oct 1893]
   The Battles of the Wilderness [19 May 1864]
   The Boys who saved the Nation [18 Feb 1886]
   The Old Third Maine [14 Sept 1893]
   The Soldier Boys in Council [23 Aug 1883]
   The Turning Point, Gettysburg [13 Jul 1893]
   The Youngest Soldier [2 Aug 1888]
   Twelfth Maine Reunion [25 Aug 1892]
   Vet Reunions, 6th ME, 15th ME at Eastport ME & Kennebunk ME, 7th ME & 1st ME
      Heavy Artillery [31 Aug 1893]
   View of a section of Fort Sedgwick, alias Fort Hell, front of Petersburg VA [13 Jan 1881]
CLAIR Octave, drawing [22 Dec 1892]
CLAPP Joseph H ae 81 [24 Nov 1887]
CLARK George H of North Anson (photo) [20 Jan 1898]
   George M of Higganum CT (photo of home & drawing of G M CLARK [27 Sept 1900]
   Linwood E (photo) [2 Dec 1909]
   Mrs ae 93y formerly Mrs CROSS [24 Nov 1887]
CLARRY Reunion [27 Aug 1896]
CLEAVELAND E L at Houlton ME, Seed Potato Farm [25 Sept 1913]
CLEVELAND Motor Tractor (photo) [19 Apr 1917]
CLIFFORD E T of Winthrop ME (photo) [29 Dec 1910]
COAL in Maine, Discovery of (in Palmyra) [22 Jan 1836]
COBB William T (photo) [21 Jul 1904] [28 June 1906]
COHEN S Miss, drawing [4 Jan 1894]
COBURN family, Miscellany [24 June 1886]
COCHRANE J H Major obit, drew the heading for the *Maine Farmer* [8 Aug 1895]
COLBY F W of Augusta ME (photo of poultry house) [6 Feb 1908]

COLEMAN Charles M of Vassalboro ME (drawing & story by Mrs Mary F FOSSETT) family genealogical data [6 May 1897]

COLUMBUS & what has followed by H K BAKER [17 Nov 1892]

CONANT family of Oxford Co, photo bros: Clarles B, Albert A, Harry L, Wilson H, George I, Walter G, & Everett E [11 Jan 1912]

CONDENSED MILK BUSINESS [22 June 1893]

CONTINENTAL MONEY 1775-1781 [29 Jul 1847]

CONY Judge - a letter from [13 Dec 1879]
    Female Academy #1, Revolutionary Story & history of the School [16 Aug 1879] #2 History [23 Aug 1879]
    House (photo) at 214 Water St [10 Dec 1908]

COOK A S [8 Dec 1910]
    Alfred S of Canton ME (photo) [20 Jan 1910]
    Elijah Prof of Vassalboro ME (photo) [23 Dec 1897] [22 Dec 1898] [21 Dec 1899] (obit w/ photo) [4 Jan 1900]
    George W of St Johnsburg VT, drawing [8 Dec 1892] [16 Feb 1893]

COPELAND R L (photo) [28 Oct 1909]

COPPER MINE in Troy ME [24 Aug 1833]

CORINNA Maine [28 Jul 1859] [31 Jul 1875]

CORINTH Maine [12 19 May 1859] [31 Jul 1875]

CORNELIUS Nancy 1st Indian woman to graduate as a trained nurse of the Oneida Tribe of Wisconsin [5 Nov 1896]

CORNVILLE Maine [1 Sept 1859]

COTTON MILLS, early by Wm B WINSOR of Naples ME [7 Mar 1874]

COULTER Harry E of Mansfield OH, drawing [27 Oct 1892]

CRAIG Elmer Mrs of LeRoy IL, drawing [2 Mar 1893]

CROUCH Charles S (photo) [3 Mar 1898]

CROWLEY William, photo & story on farm at South Lewiston ME [5 Sept 1912]

CRYSTAL PLT, Aroostook Co ME [9 Oct 1875] & (#4R5) [5 Jul 1860]

CUBA, History [16 May 1901] the country [21 Feb 1901]

CULBERTON Frank Watters at Monmouth ME (photo) [1 June 1899]

CUMBERLAND Maine Vol 8-221 (1840)

CUSHING John S ae 80 born in Brunswick ME [24 Nov 1887]

CUSHMAN Samuel of West Mansfield MA, photo of poultry farm [5 Apr 1900]

CUSHNOC, Historical [17 Nov 1892] more about [10 Nov 1892]
    Creamery Co [30 Jul 1896]
    Heights, New School House (drawing) [23 Apr 1891]
    House, Old - A Glance at its History [27 Oct 1892]

DAGGETT, William b 9 Apr 1785 at Tisbury MA, res Bremen ME [24 Apr 1875]

DALTON, Aroostook Co ME [9 Oct 1875] Dalton/Ashland - see Number 11

DAMARISCOTTA Creamery [9 Apr 1896]

DANCING Viewed Historically [8 Mar 1873]

DANIELSON DeForest Mrs (photo with her horse) [24 Mar 1904]

DANVILLE Jct, Grange Hall Dedication [27 Jan 1898]
    Letter from [17 Jan 1867]

DANVILLE Maine, families: VICKERY [27 Dec 1879] families: HOLLIS, MOODY, ARNOLD, ACKLEY, PENLEY, MOODY [6 Dec 1879] families: MOODY, JORDAN [13 Dec 1879] & [Vol 9-85 (1841)] see Auburn

DAVENPORT George H Capt, GAR veteran, drawing & story [11 Oct 1894]

DAVIS Abbie M Mrs, drawing [27 Jul 1893]

DAVIS (Cont.) Cyrus W Hon of Waterville ME (photo) [21 Jul 1904] (photo of farm) [25 Aug 1904] (photo) [28 June 1906]

Fred at Newport ME (farm photo) [9 Jul 1903]

Henry G (photo) [27 Oct 1904]

Lizzie May Miss, drawing [13 Jul 1893]

DAVISSON Estelle Mae, a lawyer in Nebraska (drawing) [24 Dec 1896]

DEAD RIVER, Somerset Co ME [17 Aug 1878]

Valley [1 Feb 1855]

& Flag Staff #1 [12 Sept 1861] & #2 [3 Oct 1861]

DEARBORN George E of North Vassalboro ME, drawing [15 Dec 1892]

DEARBORN Maine [17 July 1845]

DEATHS of 1882 [4 Jan 1883] of 1883 [3 Jan 1884]

DeCASTINE D Baron - Men, Something about our Public, in the olden time by J W LANG [12 Jan 1893]

DEDHAM Maine [Vol 8-37 (1840)]

DEER ISLAND Maine [1 Sept 1859] Our State [10 Aug 1872]

DENISON FIBRE CO [31 Jul 1880]

DENNIS Manson W staff of the *Maine Farmer* (photo) [25 May 1905]

DENNYSVILLE Maine Vol 3-35 (1835)

DEXTER Maine, [31 Oct 1850] ed corr [12 Dec 1867] Notes of a Missionary Tour #1 [26 Feb 1870] [28 Jul 1859] [31 Jul 1875] & School punishment of Mr BEMENT at ae 15, he is now over 80y [25 May 1893]

DIARY of 70 years ago, the writer lived in East Bradford, now Groveland [10 Feb 1887]

DINSMORE Reunion [27 Aug 1896]

DIVORCE - see Law

DIXFIELD Maine [Vol 9-259 (1841)] [1 Aug 1861] [23 & 30 June 1864] & [31 Jul 1880]

DIXMONT Maine, Journal of a tour "Up East" by J WHITMAN of North Turner [19 Feb 1842]

DOANE Mattie of Hampden Centre ME drawing [27 Apr 1893] [7 Sept 1893]

DOHERTY Edward O of Dover NH, drawing [4 Jan 1894]

DOUGLASS F W (photo of farm) [8 Apr 1909]

DOVER Maine, Historical Sketch Business Resources by S E COBURN at the Pomona at South Dover Grange [16 May 1895] & [31 Oct 1850] ed corr [14 21 Nov 1867] [19 May, 28 Jul 1859]

DOW E C of Belfast ME story of apple farm with photo [15 May 1913]

DOWNEAST, letter respecting Eastport & Pembroke ME [6 May 1833]

Copied from the *Hancock Advertiser* [1834 to 1835]

From Ellsworth to the Jumping Off place [19 Dec 1834]

Description [Vol 3-35 (1835)] [Vol 2-379, 387, 505 (1834)]

Maine, Map of [20 Jul 1899]

DOWNING, Jack Maj, Letter to Mr HOLMES [8 Aug 1834]

DOWNS Z L, drawing [17 Aug 1893] [23 Mar 1893]

DRESDEN, Alna & Wiscasset & Swan Island - see Old Pownalboro [7 Feb 1850] & [Vol 8-85 (1840)]

DREW William A Rev, obit [6 Dec 1879]

DUBY J J Mrs, woman undertaker, drawing [10 Sept 1896]

DUNNS of Poland ME [5 Apr 1873]

DUNNVILLE (North Wayne ME) [29 Jul 1847]

DURHAM Maine [Vol 8-317 (1840)] [Vol 9-85 (1841)]

DUXBURY (MA), History of [6 Dec 1849]

DYER L W (photo) of Cumberland ME [19 Dec 1901] [4 Dec 1902] [3 Dec 1903] L W Mrs (photo) [26 Dec 1901]

EAGAN Walter ae 14 of South Thomaston ME letter to the editor [31 Mar 1892]

EARL of CLARENDON, Historical Fact [28 Aug 1835]

EASON Mr (colored) died a few years ago ae abt 115y [24 Nov 1887]

EAST CORINTH Maine [28 Jul 1859]

EAST DIXMONT Maine (many taverns) [17 Jan 1861]

EAST LIVERMORE Maine, Glimpses from the Road-side [15 Feb 1849]

EAST MACHIAS Maine [Vol 3-35 (1835)]

EASTPORT Maine, Letter from [31 Oct 1874] Financial Matters [5 Jul 1855] in Ashes [21 Oct 1886]

EATON Russell b 19 Feb 1800 at Worcester MA ae 88 [24 Nov 1887]
    Samuel H 49 of Oxford ME, a Mason, Knight of Pyhthia & Granger, obit with photo [12 Dec 1918]

EDGARTOWN Mass, Martha's Vineyard, An Ancient Town [7 Aug 1884]

EDISON, when was young [6 Jul 1893]

EDITORIAL Jotting & Sketches #1 - 9 [4 11 18 25 Jul, 1 8 15 22 Aug, 5 Sept 1861]

ELECTRIC, Farm of A O & E E Ramsdell near Lewiston & Mechanic Falls electric line (photos) [26 Nov 1908]
    Light - under Miscellaneous [25 Apr 1867]
    Railroads in ME [14 Oct 1897]

ELLIS R W of Embden ME (photo) [23 Dec 1897]

ELLSWORTH Maine to the Jumping over place [Vol 3-43 (1835)]

ELMWOOD FARM, Lewiston Jct ME (photo) [16 Jan 1896] [5 Mar 1903]

EMBDEN Maine [12 June 1845]

EMBREE C E obit w/photo [11 Mar 1920]

EMERSON Isaiah Mrs of Manchester NH, drawing [18 May, 23 Nov 1893]
    Thomas C of Perham ME, drawing [23 Feb, 29 June 1893]

ENFIELD Penobscot Co ME by J P Clark of Springfield ME [12 Sept 1874] by B F WILBUR visited [24 Dec 1842] [7 Nov 1850] Letter from Peobscot Co description [17 Jan 1867]

ETHER, first man to take (1846) Ebenezer Hopkins FROST [3 Dec 1896]

ETNA Maine [22 Mar 1860]

EVELETH E G of Auburn ME photo of Maine State Fair Officer [15 Aug 1895]
    Joseph J b 14 Nov 1805 at Augusta ME [24 Nov 1887]

EXETER Maine [12 Jan 1860] [25 Aug 1859]

FAIRBANKS Charles Warren (photo) [27 Oct 1904]

FAIRFIELD Maine, An Excursion #1 [6 Jul 1878] [30 Nov 1854] [18 May, 6 Jul 1865]
    Historical sketch 100 yrs [11 Oct 1888]
    Library dedication of [1 Aug 1901]
    Victor Grange Hall at Fairfield Centre (photo) [15 Oct 1903]

FALMOUTH Maine [Vol 8-253 (1840)] - see Portland

FARMS ABANDONED, "Vacated Farms on Door Roads," a letter from *Portland Press Herald* from Frank SMITH of Damiriscotta Mills [27 Jul 1922]

FARMING, "Looking Backward" by B Walter McKEEN [27 Nov 1919]
    100 yrs ago in Maine by E C CARLL [26 June 1913]
    Now & then (farming) by C B SMITH [5 Apr 1900]

FARMINGTON Maine, Brigade Orders, 1st Brigade 8th dist in 1818 [25 Oct 1879]
    resolutions 1809 [6 Dec 1879] [18 Jul 1861]

FARNHAM Annie Hayward staff of the *Maine Farmer* (photo) [25 May 1905]

FARNSWORTH A S (photo) [19 Dec 1901]

FARRINGTON Mrs, mother of Marshal FARRINGTON, ae 80 [24 Nov 1887]
FARWELL Porter of Bethel ME, photo of home [12 Apr 1900]
FAYETTE Maine, Glimpses from the Roadside [11 Jan 1849]
FELLOWS George Emory Dr (photo) [19 Mar 1908] [8 Sept 1910]
FEMALE ABOLITION SOCIETY [29 Oct 1885]
FERNALD Bert M of Poland ME (photo) [26 May 1904] [23 Jul 1908] [7 Jul 1910]
FERON Edward T drawing [14 Sept 1893]
FIELD Mary French drawing [13 Aug 1896]
FISH Fernald J, a sailor's obit with photo [3 Oct 1918]
FISHER, Elijah - Journal & introduction [27 Dec 1879] & his Journal 5 May 1775 to Feb
      1785 [3 Jan 1880 to 3 Apr 1880]
    William J & Mrs, drawing [1 Nov 1894]
FIVE ISLANDS Maine (7 Nov 1850)
FLAGS, Colonial & Revolutionary [6 May 1876]
FLAX, Premium on [10 May 1849]
    Culture in Maine [22 Feb 1849] [27 Apr 1848]
    Seed or Linseed, tariff of 1846 [21 Oct 1847]
FORESTVILLE PLT Aroostook Co ME, In a Log house - ed corr [12 Dec 1868]
FORT FAIRFIELD Aroostook Co ME, August Wanderings # 2 [30 Aug 1883] [16 Nov
      1878] a letter [7 Mar 1861] [1 Jul 1871] ed corr [28 Nov, 5 Dec 1868] [29 Jul 1871]
      [5 June 1856] [5 Dec 1850] Excursion to Aroostook Co [8 Aug 1895]
FORT HALIFAX [14 Mar 1867] Old Block House of Winslow ME (photo) [22 Dec 1898]
FORT KNOX Maine built 1844 [30 June 1859]
FORT WILLIAM HENRY [22 Jul 1915]
FOSS W L of Augusta ME, drawing [26 Jan, 1 June 1893]
FOSTER Daniel E (photo) [18 Aug 1910]
    Mary Jane Mrs of New York NY, drawing [9 Mar 1893]
    W A of Newry Oxfrod Co ME, orchards [1 Jan 1914]
FOXCROFT Piscataquis Co ME [1 Jul 1871] [31 Oct 1850] ed corr [28 Nov 1867] & the
      Spool Works of L H DWELLEY & Co [8 Jul 1886]
FRANKFORT Maine [Vol 8-53 & 8-381 (1840)] (from the *Eastern Republican*) [Vol 3-99
      (1835)] [30 June 1859]
FRANKLIN Benjamin [20 Dec 1879]
FRANKLIN CO Maine to Rangeley Lakes by W B LAPHAM [21 Jul & 4 Aug 1892] old
      Petition Lower Plt on Sandy River [9 Feb 1882] #1 & 2 Jotting from New Vineyard
      [30 Oct & 20 Nov 1880] Among the Hills [17 Sept 1857] Farming Lands [10 Apr
      1862] Gold Mines of [18 May 1854]
FRANKLIN PLT Maine [2 June 1864]
FRASER Nellie, drawing [22 Feb 1894]
FREEDOM Waldo Co ME [24 Apr 1875]
FREEMAN Maine, Glimpses from the Road-side [8 Mar 1849]
FREEPORT Maine - ed corr [4 Apr 1867] & [Vol 8-173 (1840)]
FREIGHT CARS to the West, Agricultural Development for Central ME (photo) [27 Jan
      1910]
FRENCH George H staff of the *Maine Farmer* (photo) [25 May 1905]
FRESHET, Damage on the Androscoggin River [9 Apr 1846]
    Machias 1779 & 1846 [9 Apr 1846]
    Maine Rivers [13 May 1843]
    Saco River [9 Apr 1846]
FROST E C, story & photo of Kennecook Farm at Readfield ME [10 Nov 1921]

FRYEBURG, Echoes from (more History) by HKB [15 Sept 1892] & ed corr [11 Jul 1867] [25 Apr, 9 May 1868]

FRYEBURG ACADEMY [9 Aug 1879] Centennial of [25 Aug 1892] Old [5 MAy 1892]

FUGGLE Charles N (photo) [4 Aug 1904]

GALLUP Christopher, new mgr editor of *Maine Farmer* [2 Sept 1909]

GAMMON Warren of Freeman ME, biography, the originator of the Polled Hereford [19 May 1921]

GARDINER Maine [new series 2-26 (1843) [4 Jul 1861] [Vol 8-77 (1840)]

GARDINER Obadiah of Rockland ME (photo) New State Grange Master [30 Dec 1897] & (photo) [21 Dec 1899] [20 Dec 1900] [14 Nov 1901] [21 Dec 1905] [20 Dec 1906] [23 Jul 1908]

GARDINER Robert H Hon - see BRADBURY "Personal Recollections" [1 June 1899]

GARDNER Willie of Canaan ME & steers (photo) [8 Jan 1903]

GARLAND Maine - ed corr [5 Dec 1867] [7 Nov 1867] Notes of a Missionary Tour # 1 [26 Feb 1870] [31 Jul 1875]

GARRISON MOB of Boston MA [29 Oct 1885]

GATES R H of West Parus (photo) [20 Jan 1910]

GEOLOGY, The Kames of Maine [9 Oct 1880]

GERMAN EMIGRANTS, Progress of Society of the (from the *Philadelphia Daily Advertiser* 18 Mar 1811) [5 Sept 1874]

GIFFORD E E (photo) [27 Oct 1910]

GILBERT Clarence s/o Z A GILBERT, (photo of Lumbering at Greene ME) [18 Jul 1907] Z A died at Greene ae 79 (see obit) [15 Aug 1912] & Ziba Alden (photo) [25 May 1905] [17 May 1894] [13 Nov 1902] a visit to his farm [5 Jan 1905] [14 Nov 1907] [5 Aug 1909] retires after 27 yrs with the *Maine Farmer* [29 Sept 1910] & Ziba elected into the Hall of Fame at UMO [12 Mar 1914]

GILE E E, Hillside Stock Farm at Fayette ME [31 Jul 1913]

GILEAD Maine [22 Aug 1861]

GILLEY John a native of Ireland ae 124 [24 Nov 1887] & d 9 July 1813 ae 124 [22 Feb 1894]

GILMAN A W of Foxcroft ME (photo) [21 & 28 Mar 1901] [4 Dec 1902] [3 Dec 1903] (residence photo) [4 Oct 1906] (photo) [8 Nov 1906] (photo) [12 Dec 1907]

GILPATRICK Jennie Mrs of West Hollis ME, drawing [1 June 1893]

GLANCE BACKWARD (one year) [12 Jan 1888]

GLASS COFFINS (from the *Chicago Chronicle*) [28 May 1896]

GLENBURN Maine [28 Jul 1859]

GODDARD Mary Aunt of South Durham ME, photo, the oldest person in Maine (Courtesy of *Brunswick Record*) [23 Mar 1916]

GODFREY'S FALLS Scenes in the Wilderness - No 3 [10 Apr 1845]

GOLD, Fever in Canaan ME [15 22 Feb 1849]

    Madrid ME [29 Sept 1853]

    Mine in Maine [1 Feb 1849]

    Mines of Franklin Co ME [18 May 1854]

GOLDEN RIDGE Aroostook Co ME [5 Oct 1859] [11 Nov 1850] [26 June, 2 Oct 1856] [7 June 1860]

GOLDING John H, drawing [5 Oct 1893]

GOODELL Ex-Gov D H of Antrim OH, photo of Maple Grove Stock Farm [29 Nov 1894]

GORHAM Maine [Vol 8-405 (1840)] Our State # 6 [8 Feb 1873]

GOSS A L & E F Co of Lewiston ME (photo of both at Fair) [9 Sept 1897]

GOVERNORS OF NH [12 JUl 1873]

GRAFFAM A D (photo) [24 Mar 1910]

GRAHAM J C at Presque Isle ME (farm photo) [2 Jul 1903]
GRAND ARMY at Bangor ME [15 Feb 1894] [21 Feb 1895]
GRANGE, Brief History of the Origin of the Patrons of Husbandry [26 Dec 1912]
 Early Days of the by W H COPELAND of Brewer ME [7 Apr 1910]
 List of Active in Maine [2 June 1887] List of Dormant in Maine [24 Mar 1887]
 Maine State Patrons of Husbandry [15 Dec 1887]
 Named with 200 or more members [20 Dec 1906]
 Patrons of Husbandry, a brief History [16 Dec 1886]
 Supplement to the *Maine Farmer* w/photos [8 Dec 1921]
GRANITE - Large slabs [17 Jan 1867]
GRANT C C ae 82 [24 Nov 1887]
GRAY Maine, settlement of, by S P M of Cape Elizabeth ME [24 Oct 1874]
 Marriages by Nathan MORRILL 1789-1790 [18 Sept 1880]
GREAT FALLS NH, the Dam [9 Apr 1846]
GREEN Mrs, mother of Moses SAFFORD, ae 85 [24 Nov 1887]
GREENBACK PARTY MOVEMENT, "A Bit of History" [2 Nov 1916]
GREENLAW S C at Presque Isle ME (farm photo) [2 Jul 1903]
GREENVILLE Maine [1 Sept 1859]
GREENWICH CT, History of the Old CT Church [23 Jan 1896]
GREGORY James J H of Marblehead MA (photo)
GRIFFIN O B of Caribou ME, Bee Keepers Association [9 Sept 1915] & photo, Candidates
 for Commissioner of Agr [26 Sept 1912]
GUILFORD Maine [28 Jul 1859]
GUIOUS J F of Presque Isle, farm [16 Oct 1913]
GYPIES [28 Feb 1850]
HADLEY Mary C Mrs of Otter Creek ME, drawing [6 Apr 1893]
HALE Nathan, a centennial story [18 Nov 1876]
 Sarah Josepha photo [18 Nov 1920]
HALL A W of Bunker Hill ME [23 Mar 1893]
 C A Miss photo [26 Dec 1912]
 John Goff b 1791 at Newcastle ME ae 89 [30 Dec 1880]
HALLOWELL HOUSE (photo) [10 Dec 1908]
HALLOWELL Maine, [4 Nov 1876] [Vol 8-77 (1840)] [new series 2-26 (1843)]
 Celebration [2 Jul 1896]
 Granite works [14 June 1888]
 Reunion & Dedication [13 Jul 1899]
 Old letter dated 21 Nov 1791 by Samuel HOWARD Jr [15 Mar 1873]
 Random Thoughts & Recollections #3-#26 of Hallowell ME [4 11 18 25 Nov 1876] [2 16
  23 30 Dec 1876] [13 20 27 Jan, 3 10 17 24 Feb, 3 10 17 31 Mar, 7 14 21 28 Apr, 5
  May 1877]
HAMDEN Maine, Journal of a tour "Up East" by J WHITMAN of North Turner [19 Feb
 1842]
HAMILTON John b at Vassalboro ME ae 83 [30 Dec 1880]
HAMLIN Chester P of East Wilton ME (photo with his ram) [19 Jan 1905]
 Hannibal obit [9 Jul 1891]
 Lewis B b 30 June 1800 at Barnstable MA ae 88y [24 Nov 1887]
HAMLIN's of Augusta ME [5 Jan 1893]
HANCOCK CO Maine - Letter from [8 Jul 1871]
HANCOCK POINT, Maine (photo) of Strawberry Valley Fruit Farm, E W WOOSTER,
 manager [24 Feb 1898]
HANOVER NH (15 Sept 1853)

HANSON George Mrs of Sebago ME, drawing [8 June 1893] & [2 Feb 1893]
HAPGOOD'S ADJUSTABLE SNOW ROLLER, drawing, for making roads in winter [12 May 1898]
HARLOW Marion, staff of the *Maine Farmer* (photo) [25 May 1905]
HARMON Frank staff of the *Maine Farmer* (photo) [25 May 1905]
HARPSWELL Maine, Fishing Smack/Lobster/Cod Fisheries, Birds, geology Vol 8-173 (1840)
    Marriages by Benjamin DUNNING Esq 1790 [3 Mar 1881]
    Marriages by Isaac SNOW Esq 1791-1792 [3 Mar 1881]
    Marriages by Rev Samuel EATON 1788-1791 & 1792 [3 Mar 1881] & 1792-1793 [3 Mar 1881]
HARRIMAN'S Point Maine - Our State [10 Aug 1872]
HARRIS F W of West Farmington ME (photo of home with his dahlias) [19 May 1910]
HARRISON, when was a boy [24 Nov 1892]
HARTFORD Maine [Vol 9-235 (1841)] [24 June 1880]
HATHAWAY Arthur T [1 Dec 1910]
HAUER Charles N, drawing [8 June 1893]
HAVEN Etta E, drawing [2 Feb 1893]
HAWAII, a Bloodless Revolution [2 Feb 1893]
    Annexation [24 June 1897]
    Affair [23 Nov 1893]
    A Glimpse of a trip by Mrs Horace NORTH [8 June 1893]
HAWAIIAN QUESTION [23 Nov 1893] [9 Feb 1893]
HAYFORD Columbus of Maysville Centre (photo of house) Aroostook Potato farm [30 Dec 1897] (farm home photo) [20 Aug 1903]
HAYNESVILLE Maine [28 Jul 1859]
HEALY George F of Waterville ME, drawing [1 Dec 1892]
HEBRON Maine, Among the Oxford Hills [16 Feb 1893] ed corr [10 Oct 1867] [17 Oct 1867]
HEED Harvey Mr of Laceyville OH, drawing [1 Dec 1892]
HEMMERICH Joseph, drawing [29 June 1893]
HEMP, a correct chemical analyse [16 Sept 1847]
    Gigantic "Lomocorchasus" [10 May 1849]
HENDERSON Ira Mrs, drawing [20 Apr 1893]
    Kate (Alpine) Mrs (drawing & story) [8 Jul 1897]
    Mary Mrs, drawing [25 Jan 1894]
HERMAN Maine [28 Jul 1859]
HERRICK A A Mrs, drawing [5 Apr 1894]
HEWINS Daniel b 11 Aug 1800 at Sharon MA [24 Nov 1887]
HICHBORN C S (photo) [2 Apr 1908]
HICKS Herman of Rochester NY, drawing [26 Jan 1893]
HIGHMOOR FARM, Maine State Experimental Farm Building (photo) [29 July 1909]
HIGHWAYS OF STEEL, a Steel Track Road [27 Sept 1906]
HILL John F of Augusta ME (photo) [28 June 1900]
HIRAM Maine - Early History by Llewellyn A WADSWORTH [25 Jan 1873]
HISTORICAL FACT - Charles I to James II [28 Aug 1835]
HISTORY, "Our Anglo-Saxon Heritage" by Ralph M BACON of Bryant Pond [19 Dec 1918]
    1896, the Events of & the Grim Reaper Busy [31 Dec 1896]
    Bethel ME by Willian B Lapham, a book review [7 Apr 1892]
    Breeds of Cattle of Kennebec Co Maine [14 Mar 1834]

HISTORY (Cont.) Dairy Cow in Maine by Frank S ADAMS [4 June 1914]
    Grass [14 Oct 1847]
    Maine 1 World We Live in, 2 From Flame to Soil, 3 1st People in ME, 4 Noble Red Man,
       5 Norsemen, 6 Champlain, 7 Norumbega, 7 Columbus, 8 Discoveries, 9 Anglo-
       Saxons, 10 Religious Liberty, 11 ME Paid, 12 Fernando Gorges, 13 MA Colony, 14
       Early Indian Wars, 15 Indians' Defeat, 16 Last of the French, 17 *Lexington* of the
       Seas, 18 Attack on Canada, 19 Maine a State, 20 A Century of Statehood [11 Jan
       1923 to 2 June 1923]
    Music in New England 1741-1770 by Mr HOOD [17 June 1847]
    Potato by Mrs Helen SAMPSON SMITH of Excelsior Pomona Grange at Temple ME on
       25 Jan [22 Feb 1917]
    Should begin at Home, How to write a town History [9 Mar 1893]
HODGES A E of North Fairfield ME, farm [16 Oct 1913]
    Lancaster of Brownfield ME a 102y living mulatto [22 Feb 1873]
HOLDEN Maine, early history [17 May 1873]
HOLMES Ezekiel Dr, Reminiscences of by Samuel L BOARDMAN [2 Jan 1913]
    memory of [23 Jan 1896] & biography of [14 Mar 1912] & [21 Mar 1912] & memorial
       with oil painting of HOLMES in 1832 [2 May 1912] (photo) [2 June 1904] & Men,
       Something about our Public, in the olden times by J W LANG [12 Jan 1893] &
       drawing 1833 [2 Jan 1913]
HOLMES Hall, the New Agricultural Building at Orono (photo) [26 May 1904] & 1st
    elected in to the Agricultural Hall of Fame [29 Feb 1912]
HOLWAY Melvin S staff of the *Maine Farmer* (photo) [25 May 1905]
    Oscar of Fairfield ME (photo) [24 Jul 1901]
HOMAN Joseph A former owner of the *Maine Farmer*, obit [6 May 1909]
HONOLULU, the position at [20 Apr 1893]
HORSELESS Carriage [4 June 1896]
HORSES, "Maine has Written Chapter in History of Horse Racing" [21 Dec 1922]
    Equine Etchings, some Maine Roadsters of years agone [4 Jan 1923]
    "Reminiscences" by G H HATCH [26 Jan 1922]
    Winthrop Messenger & his Descendants in Maine (a Genealogy of a horse) [8 June
       1872]
HOULTON Aroostook Co [2 Oct 1856] - ed corr [7 Nov 1868] [1 July, 11 Nov 1871]
    Excursion to [8 Aug 1895]
HULETT Warren of Pawlet VT, drawing [9 Nov 1893]
HUNT William H Mrs of Readfield ME, drawing [16 Feb 1893]
HUNTON W G of Readfield ME (photo) [9 Dec 1909] [8 Dec 1910]
HURD E E at Madison ME, story & photo on farm [17 May 1917]
    William D Prof (photo) [13 Aug 1903] [19 Mar 1908]
HUTCHINS H Wesley of Auburn ME, photo of Maine State Fair Officer [15 Aug 1895]
HUTCHINSON Joseph, settled on Lot #25 Readfield ME in 1790 "Century Dairy Farm
    Notes" [8 Aug 1912]
HYNES Wellington of Elizabethtown NY (photo) [2 Feb 1899]
ICE HOUSE, small [25 Jan 1906]
INDIAN, A Brave (from the Pittsbury Gazette) [22 Feb 1855]
    Burial of Cochise, an Indian Chief [8 Aug 1874]
    Customs of Mourning [7 Jul 1853]
    Election at Perry ME [25 Oct 1888]
    Family tree of Phillip [2 Sept 1876
    Fort & Graves in Marblehead MA, 45 Indian graves found, paper by James J H Gregory
       [13 Mar 1875]

INDIAN (Cont.) Hanging, under Cherokee law [27 Nov 1845]
 In Auburn "Discovery of Human Bones" [28 June 1855]
 Justice - Pequawket Country, central NH near Fryeburg village [13 Oct 1864]
 Lo! The Poor [10 Apr 1869]
 Mollocket - ed corr [11 Jul 1867]
 Names, souvenirs of the Red Man, title of Place & their significance [2 Jul 1891]
 Names on the Kennebec River [20 Nov, 2 23 Dec 1880] [6 Jan, 3 24 Mar 1881]
 Of Maine by Dr Nathaniel True of Bethel ME [3 Mar 1864]
 Old Point ME (24 July 1845)
 Oldtown ME [21 Jul 1859] [17 Oct 1868]
 Passamaquody tribe, Sleigh Ride to Louis' Island [6 Feb 1835]
 Penobscot, Passamaquoddy & Micmacs of New Brunswick Canada by Charles G
  LELAND [6 Nov 1884]
 Raid in Bethel ME in 1781 [28 Mar 1874]
 St Francis Indians [6 Oct 1877]
 Troubles of the Early Plymouth Colony [2 Dec 1886]
 Village (see Canton Point ME) [27 Aug 1857]
 Wars, in Canada none [12 Mar 1896]
INSANE HOSPITAL New Barn erected 1895, photo [16 Apr 1896]
 Photo of new piggery [24 Dec 1896]
 Purchase of the Hoyt Farm so called in Augusta ME [24 Jul 1835]
IRELAND W M photo [26 Dec 1912]
IRISH LEAGUE, annual Convention in Boston MA [21 Aug 1884]
ISLAND FALLS Maine [13 Oct 1859] [5 Jul 1860] & Stand up for Your Town [22 Dec
 1898]
ISLAND POND VT - ed corr [13 Aug 1868
ISLE OF SHOALS, History of [28 June 1873]
ISRAEL CRUSHED BY EQYPT, a great Historic Tablet found by PETRIC [3 Sept 1896]
JACKSON, the death of "Stonewall" in 1863 [8 Jul 1886]
JACKSON Maine Vol 8-53 (1840)
JAY Maine, Glimpses from the Road-side [22 Feb 1849] (Philips Canada) [2 Aug 1879] [11
 Jul 1861]
JEFFERSON Maine, a trip to [8 June 1882] [2 June 1887]
JERRARD S G Col of Levant ME (Kenduskeag PO) photo of Maine State Fair Officer [15
 Aug 1895]
JERUSALEM Maine [1 Feb 1855]
JOHNSON W E (photo) [17 Mar 1904]
JONES Aaron of South Bend Indiana (photo) [23 Aug 1900] [14 Nov 1901] [25 Aug 1904]
JONESBORO Maine, Down East from Ellsworth to the Jumping Off place [9 Jan 1835]
JORDAN David M, drawing [10 Nov 1892] of Edmest NY, drawing [30 Mar 1893]
 Peter Capt ae 91y of Brunswick ME [24 Apr 1875]
JOTTING BY THE WAY # 1-7 trip to Washington DC [27 Jan 1859 to 7 Apr 1859]
JOURNAL OF A TOUR "UP EAST" by Dr HOLMES (19 Feb 1842) & by J WHITMAN
 of North Turner [19 Feb 1842]
JOURNALISM 2000 years ago [27 Nov 1875]
KASKASKIA, IL (a sketch) [1 Aug 1844]
KATAHDIN, a brief account of, by Dr YOUNG [20 Apr 1848]
 Horseback Maine, notes by the way [8 Mar 1879]
 Iron Works ME by Moses CHANDLER [28 May 1870] & [1 Jul 1871]
KEENE Walter S, story & photo of his farm of Palmyra ME [30 Aug 1900] & [25 Jul 1901]
 & (photo of Home) [24 Sept 1903]

KELLEY O H photo [26 Dec 1912]

KENDUSKEAG Maine [31 Jul 1875]

KENNEBEC, Arsenal at Augusta ME (painting by Joseph PEARSON) [16 Mar 1905
    Patent ME [1 Nov - 29 Nov 1879]
    Purchace ME [9 Aug 1879] & hist memo [8 Feb 1873]
    Valley, Old People at Riverside: HALL, HAMILTON, & WING [30 Dec 1880]:
        Kennebecer, Recollections of, Old Taverns, the Grocery & the lazy Pole by E B
        GETCHELL [26 Aug 1897]

KENNEBEC RIVER [12 June 1845] Early Times - List of Brunswick men 1757 [1 Sept
    1881]
    On the upper [30 June 1887]
    Opening & Closing 1785-46 [15 Apr 1847] & opening & closing of the River 1785 to
        1877 [12 Jan 1878] & 1785-1886 Opening & closing of [5 May 1887]
    Old Times on the Kennebec River by E B GETCHELL [21 Feb 1895]

KENNEBECER, Recollections of, Seven Mile Brook etc by E B GETCHELL [27 May
    1897]

KENT'S HILL, a Methodist School [16 June 1887] & Maine Wesleyan Seminary at
    Readfield ME (photo) [5 Jul 1900] & ed corr [16 Apr 1867]

KEYSER H L of Greene ME, Candidate of Commissioner of Agr [2 Jan 1913]

KIMBALL John A, drawing [17 Aug 1893]

KING Hattie of Ithaca NY (photo) [23 Sept 1897]
    S M Mr (Kingleside Farm of South Paris ME with photo) [2 Dec 1897]
    William H of Haverhill MA, drawing [11 May 1893]
    Wm Gen - Men, Something about our Public, in the olden time by J W LANG [12 Jan
        1893]

KINGFIELD Maine [17 Sept 1857]

KINGSBERY Maine [1 Sept 1859]

KINSMAN John b 11 Oct 1800 at Limerick ME ae 87 [24 Nov 1887]

KITTERY Maine, Births in 1700's [23 Oct 1880] [25 Nov 1880] [3 Mar 1881]
    BERRY Genealogy of Kittery/Falmouth/Lisbon ME [1 Feb 1873]

KNOWLTON D H (photo) [14 Nov 1907]
    Lizzie A Mrs of Liberty ME, drawing [4 May 1893]

KNOX, Gen - letter by [13 Dec 1879]

KOSSUTH Louis b 27 Apr 1802, the Hungarian Patriot [29 Mar 1894]

LADD William L drawing [13 Apr 1893]

LANCASTER NH - ed corr [6 June 1867] & [20 June 1867]

LANG John W, authored article see Men, Something about our Public [12 Jan 1893]

LANGFORD Henry Rev, drawing [23 Nov 1893]

LAPHAM William Berry Dr, long obit of an Historian, Genealogist & Free Mason [1 Mar
    1894]

LAW - Divorces in Maine [23 Jan 1869]

LEARMONTH Cora, drawing [7 Sept 1893]

LEARNED George E, Orford NH Dep Sheriff (photo) [26 Jan 1899]

LEAVITT R D (photo) [19 Dec 1901]

LEE Maine - ed corr [17 Oct 1868]

LEEDS Maine, The STINCHFIELD family by Myrtie CARVER [9 May 1901]

LELAND W E staff of the *Maine Farmer* (photo) [25 May 1905]

LENFEST Edgar R of Manchester ME (photo) [19 Dec 1907]

LETTER, D Maine (5 Dec 1850) H Aroostook Co ME (9 Dec 1847)

LEWISTON Maine Centennial [11 Jul 1895]

LEWISTON (Cont.) Falls Mining & Trading Co 11 men from Androscoggin Valley & one from Old Town [1 Feb 1849]

Fire at Barker's Mill Village [16 Sept 1852]

Journal, article on it [12 Dec 1907] & *Journal & Evening Journal* [7 Feb 1899]

Maine State Fair grounds, photo of Cattle Sheds [15 Sept 1904]

Original land Grant 28 Jan 1768 [14 Dec 1782]

The Great Land Sale [31 May 1855]

Water power, Rail Roads in Maine [28 Aug 1845] & Water Power [21 Aug 1845]

LEXINGTON KY, how it was named [29 May 1875]

LIBBEY R H of Newport ME & his fruit trees (photo) [19 Jul 1900] [14 Jul 1904] [5 Feb 1903] [9 Jul 1903] [19 Dec 1901]

LIBBY A J of Embden ME photo of Maine State Fair Officer [15 Aug 1895]

Alonzo of Westbrook ME, photo of Maine State Fair Officer [15 Aug 1895]

E H (photo) [22 Dec 1898] [21 Dec 1899] [19 Dec 1901] [20 Dec 1906] [22 Dec 1910]

F J of Richmond ME (photo & story) [17 Mar 1898]

Fred B, North Deering ME, Riverview Farm [23 Jul 1914]

LIBERTY, Waldo Co Maine [24 Apr 1875] Libraries, Free Public [27 Aug 1896]

LIGHTHOUSES [28 Feb 1850]

LILY BAY Maine [1 Sept 1859]

LINCOLN, Abraham by Olive E DANNA [16 Feb 1899] & Lincoln's Gettysburg Address [21 Feb 1895]

Enoch - Men, Something about our Public, in the olden time by J W LANG [12 Jan 1893]

Mr at Bull Run [23 Jul 1891]

LINCOLN Maine - [7 Nov 1850] by J P CLARK of Springfield ME [12 Sept 1874]

LINNEUS Maine [21 Jan 1864] & More about Aroostook Co [11 Nov 1871]

LITCHFIELD Maine, an ancient (SPRINGER) Homestead by P P CURTIS [26 Oct 1905]

Centennial [29 Aug 1895]

LITTLE Thomas ae 83 [24 Nov 1887]

LIVERMORE FALLS Maine [11 Jul 1861] [25 Jul 1861]

LIVERMORE Maine, Notes by Hon Israel WASHBURN [22 Aug 1874] [Vol 9-235 (1841)] [20 Aug 1857] [11 Jul 1861]

LOCKE'S MILLS Maine [29 Sept 1877]

LOCOMOTIVE, 1st West of the Mississippi [23 Dec 1852]

LOCOMOTION, Early modes of 25 BC to 1845 AD [9 Aug 1873]

LOCUSTS, General Intelligence [21 Jul 1843]

LOHR William, drawing [1 June 1893]

LONGLEY Farm at Plymouth ME [25 Aug 1921]

LORD Samuel D of Biddeford ME for Governor (drawing) [19 Jul 1900]

LORING L W, photo & story on the Orchard at Pownal ME [6 Mar 1913]

LOUI'S ISLAND, Sleigh Ride to [6 Feb 1835]

LOVEJOY Walter S of Macon GA, drawing [9 Feb 1893]

LOVEWELL Genealogy [28 Aug 1880]

LOWELL Frank & Son's Growers of seed potatoes [9 Jan 1913]

J L of Auburn ME, photo, Candidates for Commissioner of Agr [26 Sept 1912]

LUBBOCK Violet C drawing [30 Jul 1896]

LUMBER CAMP, a Visit to by Mary F FOSSETT [6 Apr 1893]

LYNDON (CARIBOU) Maine [11 Feb 1864]

LYTLE Mary Frances Mrs, drawing [15 Dec 1892]

MACHIAS Maine, Down East from Ellsworth to the Jumping Off place [9 Jan 1835] photo [16 Jul 1899]

MacKENZIE Constance photo [3 Dec 1896]

MACOMBER Arthur of Dryden ME, story of Farm [7 Jul 1923]

MADAWASKA Maine, August Wanderings #3 [6 Sept 1883]

MADISON Maine (17 July 1845)

MADRID Maine - Gold in [29 Sept 1853] [18 May 1854]

MAINE, 75 Years ago by Daniel STICKNEY of Presque Isle ME

    Agriculture by B W McKEEN, Society in Hallowell in 1787 [23 Jul 1914] [30 Jul] Dr E HOLMES [6 Aug] Work of ME Board of Agr [27 Aug] Sketch of Conditions [3 Sept] Advanced Work of Board of Agr, Aroostook Conditions [22 Sept] Advancement in Farm practices [12 Nov] Home markets for Farm ProductS, Proposed Bills for UMO [29 Jul] College of Agr [6 Jan] Education for the Farmer [10 Feb] Locating of College of Agr [10 Aug 1916?]

    At Gettysburg [3 Feb 1887] [12 May 1887]

    Cheese Factories in 1875 [4 Mar 1876]

    Early Times in Somerset Co, by William ALLEN [18 May 1865] [6 Jul 1865] [1 Aug 1867]

    Emigration to [2 Jan 1868]

    Man close to the Pole [26 Oct 1893]

    Men in Oakland, Alameda Co CA [18 May 1878]

    More about the State of Maine - from the Hill's Monthy Visitor (*Maine Farmer* new series 2-26 (1843))

    Our State #1-7 [11 May 1872] [18 May 1872] [20 Jul 1872] [10 Aug 1872] [18 Jan 1873] [8 Feb 1873] [22 Feb 1873]

    Patent Medicine Law in [*Boston Medical Journal*] [11 Mar 1847]

    Reform School at Cape Elizabeth - ed corr [28 Mar 1868]

    Relocation of state House 1827 to _____ [13 Sept to 25 Oct 1879]

    Son's & daughters of, residing in Dover annual Banquet [29 Apr 1897]

    The Grange in (history) [17 May 1883]

    The Growth of Industries [17 Nov 1892]

    The Upper St John River [7 Aug 1880]

    Town Histories a list of [16 Aug 1879]

    Travels in the Dirigo State #1 to 3 [2 June 1864] [23 June 1864] [30 June 1864]

    Volunteers, list of officers Company A to K [22 Apr 1847]

    Wild Lands in [18 June 1896]

MAINE FARMER, 1833-1912 by Dr G M TWICHELL [2 Jan 1913]

    Agents listed by town [17 June 1833] History of the Paper [23 Nov 1882] & [29 Aug 1912] Editors & staff (photo) [25 May 1905]

    In other days [10 Nov 1892]

    Its Agricultural editors 1833-1913 [2 Jan 1913]

    New Press (drawing) [26 Feb 1903]

MAINE INDUSTRIAL SCHOOL & Workshop for the Blind, a proposed plan (drawing) [2 Feb 1905]

    For Girls at Hallowell ME [23 Apr 1896]

MAINE INSANE ASYLUM at Augusta ME, photo of Milking room, Percy GREIG, mgr [30 July 1903]

    Hospital Report for [17 Jan 1867]

    Photo of the Edwin C Burleigh Pavilion [8 Mar 1906]

Maine Patriot & State Gazette of 1827, reviewed by Joseph W PATERSON [21 May 1891]

MAINE STATE, #8 [1 Mar 1873]

    Board of Ag, photo of members of 1895 [14 Feb 1895]

    Capitol new photo [5 Jan 1911]

    Fair Then & Now 1860 & 1895 [25 Apr 1895] & (photo) [5 Sept 1901]

MAINE STATE (Cont.) Grange Headquarters (photo) [28 Dec 1899]
    House to reconstructed (drawing) [2 Oct 1909]
    Society for the Prevention of Cruelty to Animals [7 Jul 1887]
MAINE STATE COLLEGE, [18 May 1893]
    Buildings at Orono: Coburn Hall, The Farm House, Dairy Building, Forcing House [31 Jan 1895]
    Class of 1883, name age weight height politics & religion [5 Jul 1883]
    Drawing of the forcing house [2 June 1892]
    New Agricultural Building to be built U of Maine at Orono [23 Jan 1908] [21 Jan 1909]
    Pensions, 112 lists of persons with residence [7 Apr 87 to 30 Sept 1897]
    Photographs of Barns & The Poultry Plant [17 Jan 1901]
MAINE's First Homeseekers Edition [7 May 1914]
MANLEY J H of Augusta ME, Haying in 1906 (photo) [30 May 1907]
    Joseph H of Augusta ME drawing [17 Sept 1896] & [3 Apr 1902] & [14 Jan 1904] & (drawing & obit) [9 Feb 1905]
    Susan Cony w/o Joseph M (see obit) [20 Feb 1896]
    Samuel C (photo) Treas & Mgr of *The Maine Farmer* [25 May 1905]
MAP, Plan of the North Eastern Part of Maine, Settling Lands 1858 [extra 1858]
    Trunk Line Roads, Tentative System for Maine by John Clark SCATES of Westbrook ME [22 Feb 1912]
    Washington County Railroad & connections 1899 [20 Jul 1899]
MAPLE GROVE, Aroostook Co ME [12 Jul 1855] Masardis (21 Nov 1850)
MAPLE GROVE FARM the home of B F BRIGGS of Auburn ME [14 May 1896]
MAPLETON Maine, photo of the Bee Farm of E TARR [4 Aug 1898]
    Visit #2 to Asland [16 Oct 1884]
MARRIAGES - Curious Things, reprinted, a dozen in number 1788-1853 [6 June 1889]
MARRIED WOMAN'S REIGN [22 June 1893]
MARS HILL Aroostook Co ME [1 Jul 1871]
MARSHALL W C Hon of Belfast ME, photo of Maine State Fair Officer [15 Aug 1895]
MARSHFIELD MA, Purchase of [17 May 1873] old meeting House [8 Mar 1873]
MARTIN Carrie E, drawing [13 Oct 1892] & [6 Apr 1893]
    Willard S photo [3 Dec 1896]
MARYSVILLE New Brunswick Canada [22 Mar 1888]
MASARDIS Maine [26 Jul 1860]
MASON & DIXON's LINE [11 Mar 1847] & [9 Aug 1873]
MASONRY, Origin of [13 Mar 1880]
MASSACHUSETTS, Ancient Laws, the Blue Laws [23 Oct 1880] [13 Nov 1880] [25 Nov 1880]
MATTAWAMKEAG POINT Maine (7 Nov 1850)
MAYFIELD Maine Slate Quarries [26 Sept 1874]
MAYFLOWER, The log of the [3 June 1897]
MAYO Alice staff of the *Maine Farmer* (photo) [25 May 1905]
McDOWELL F M photo [26 Dec 1912]
McDONALD Coro M drawing [6 Aug 1896]
    Marguerite drawing [16 Jul 1896]
    Morris (photo) [23 Jan 1908]
McGEE Mattie Mrs photo ME [23 Jul 1896]
McINTIRE, Henry b 1782 at York ME of New Sharon ME [24 Apr 1875]
    I E of Waterford ME [8 Dec 1910]
    L E of Greenfields, Oxford Co ME, on farm [25 Jul 1912] & of East Waterford his farm [10 Jul 1919]

McKEEN B Walker of Fryeburg ME (photo) [29 Dec 1910]

McKERVEY Gertrude of Saint John New Brunswick Canada, drawing [20 Apr 1893]

McLELLAN papers Revolutionary letters of Brunswick ME [19 Apr 1873]

McVEY Jessie Miss, drawing [30 Nov 1893]

MEDWAY Maine Tanneries [15 Nov 1879]

MEEHAM James & Mary, drawing [29 Sept 1892]
    Mary of West Concord NH (drawing) [14 Jan 1897]

MELLEN Prentiss, Chief Justice of Portland ME - Men, Something about our Public, in the
    olden time by J W LANG [12 Jan 1893]

MERCER Maine [31 Oct 1834] [17 July 1845] [30 Nov 1854]

MERRILL Leon S Dr (photo) [9 Dec 1909] & [12 Dec 1907]

MESSER Elizabeth Mrs of Baltimore MD, drawing [5 Jan 1893] [16 Mar 1893]

METHODISM IN MAINE by Rev Allen, a review [10 Nov 1887]

MEXICAN WAR, A Costly Job [26 Aug 1847]
    A Historic Cannon was in the [18 June 1896]

MIDDLEBURY VT, haying at, drawing [15 Feb 1894]

MILLER Ann of Puhring PA, drawing [19 Apr 1894]
    Minnie Mrs, drawing [28 Sept 1893]

MILO Maine [31 Oct 1850] [28 Jul 1859] [9 June 1859]

MILTON Plt Maine [2 June 1864]

MINISTERS, How the Parson was Paid [23 Dec 1880]

MINNESOTA - notes from Howard M Atkins [25 Sept 1869]

MINOT Maine [Vol 9-117 (1841)]

MITCHELL Maria Prof [3 Sept 1896]
    R G of Patten ME, drawing [6 APr 1893]

MOLUMKUS Maine [21 Jan 1864] [7 Nov 1850]

MONMOUTH Maine, Glimpses from the Road-side [8 Feb 1849]
    Grange Hall (photo) [16 May 1907]
    "Mechanic's Grove" [12 June 1845]
    see Highmoor Farm

MONROE MILLS Maine [Vol 8-53 (1840)]

MONSON Maine, Journal of a tour "Up East" by J WHITMAN of North Turner [19 Feb
    1842]
    Slate Quarries [10 Aug 1878]

MONTANA, Letter from a Maine native [19 Jul 1883]

MONTICELLO Aroostook Co ME [1 Jul 1871]

MONTVILLE, Waldo Co ME [24 Apr 1875]

MOOSE RIVER Somerset Co ME [17 Aug 1878]

MOOSEHEAD LAKE Maine
    Gen Dearborn's Tour in Maine [6 Sept 1849]
    Kineo House [1 Sept 1859]
    Letter from [19 Nov 1870] & [15 Jul 1871]
    Sanatorium at Greenville Jct ME (photo) [17 Jan 1907]

MORAN Benie (drawing) [17 Dec 1896]

MORGAN, William Capt the Free Masons by Thurlow WEED [10 Jan 1884]

MORGAN HORSE, Origin of the [26 Aug 1883]

MORMAN BIBLE, the maker of the [30 Aug 1873]

MORSE A E (photo) [25 Aug 1904]
    Moses drawing [30 Mar 1893]

MORTON Agnes S of Charlestown MA [23 Mar 1893]

MOUNT BIGELOW Maine [1 Feb 1855]

MOUNT DESERT ISLAND Maine [26 May 1887]

MOUNT VERNON Maine, Establishment of free grammer school in 1802 [3 Apr 1880] & Free Grammer School an ancient Document dated 3 Apr 1802 [3 Feb 1887]

MOUNT VERNON VA Visit to [5 Dec 1844]

MOUNT ZIRCON HOUSE Oxford Co - An Echo from the Hills [18 Jul 1861] & a visit to [7 Feb 1861] & [23 & 30 June 1864]

MOUNTAIN MEADOWS MASSACRE of 1858 [12 Dec 1874]

MOUNTAINS & MOUNTAIN SCENERY in Maine #1-#4 (19 Sept 1850-10 Oct 1850)

MOWER Charles W of E Vassalboro ME, drawing [5 Jan 1893]

MUSTER ROLLS 1757 & 1762 Maine [21 Aug 1880]

NAPLES Maine, a Charming Inland Town in Maine [8 June 1899] & Our State # 7 & 8 [22 Feb 1873] [1 Mar 1873]

NATIONAL EMBLEM, How it was adopted 112 yrs ago on 14 June 1777 [20 June 1889]

NEGRO, Minstrelsy [5 Apr 1873]

Religion of the Southern [26 Jul 1883]

Voice not adapted to the singing of White Man's Music (racial statement) [9 May 1895]

NEGROES "Spotted Negroes" [4 Nov 1847]

NESS J A & R (photo of Maple Grove Farm of Auburn ME) [18 June 1908]

NEW BRUNSWICK CANADA, Photo of Turnip Field, article by Hon W S TOMPKINS, Middle Southampton [5 May 1898]

Notes from #1 & 2 [26 Sept 1861] [10 Oct 1861]

NEW ENGLAND, Then & Now (17yrs ago) [28 May 1896]

Telephone & Telegraph Co, cost 2 cents a day [25 Aug 1910]

NEW GLOUCESTER Maine, Drawing of the residence of the late Nicholas Rideout [10 Dec 1885]

Ed corr [5 Sept 1867] [19 Dec 1867] [26 Dec 1867]

Marriages by Isaac PARSONS Esq 1786-1795 [11 Sept 1880]

Marriages by Rev Samuel FOXCROFT 1787-1790 [11 Sept 1880] & 1790-1794 [18 Sept 1880]

Marriages by William WIDGERY Esq 1785-1794 [18 Sept 1880]

NEW HAMPHIRE AGRICULTURAL COLLEGE, Photo & story of Barn [7 June 1894]

Photo of Buttermakers [29 Mar 1900]

NEW SHARON Maine, copy of Original Deed [19 Jul 1879]

NEW SWEDEN Aroostook Co & its Founder [24 Dec 1865]

30th Anniversary [28 June 1900] & August Wanderings #3 [6 Sept 1883]

NEW VINEYARD Franklin Co ME [20 Nov 1880] & 1802-1808) Extracts from Records [2 Aug 1879]

NEWBURGH Maine, Journal of a tour "Up East" by J WHITMAN of North Turner [19 Feb 1842]

NEWFOUNDLAND - Its Inhabitants &c [14 Oct 1847]

NEWRY Maine [15 Aug 1861]

NEWPORT Maine [28 Jul 1859] & (photo of High St & Sebasticook Lake) [9 Jul 1903] & Condensed Milk Factory (photo) [8 Jan 1903]

NEWSPAPER STATISTICS: number of papers by Country [27 Jan 1837]

NICATOU, Penobscot Co ME [7 June 1860]

NILES Family of Rangeley Lakes by Rudie McKECHNIE ae 13y [28 Feb 1901]

NONOGENARIANS see: BAGLEY, BLETHIN, BUTTERFIELD, DAGGETT, JORDAN, McINTIRE, SCOTT, TUCK, WELCH & WOODMAN [24 Apr 1875]

NORLANDS, South Livermore ME, the Washburn family [13 Aug 1885]

NORRIDGEWOCK, Bridge 1777 to 1850 (article from *People's Press*) [11 Apr 1850] &
    Destruction of [1 Mar 1873] & ed corr [22 Feb 1868] & letter from [17 Jan 1867] &
    [18 May 1865] [6 Jul 1865] & [17 & 24 July 1845]
NORTH ANSON Maine - ed corr [7 Mar 1868]
NORTH BRIDGTON Maine - ed corr [31 Oct 1867]
NORTH DIXMONT Maine - Good Taverns [25 Aug 1859]
NORTH JAY Maine [11 Jul 1861]
NORTH VASSALBORO Maine - Ed Corresp, letter from [31 Jan 1867]
NORTH WATERFORD Maine [5 Sept 1861]
NORTH WAYNE Maine [29 Jul 1847]
    Dunnville ME, Glimpses from the Road-side [1 Feb 1849]
NORTH YARMOUTH Maine [Vol 8-173 (1840)]
    Marriages by David MITCHELL Esq 1787-1788 [9 Oct 1880] & 1788-1789 [6 Nov
        1880] & 1789-1793 [13 Nov 1880] & 1793-1794 [23 Dec 1880]
    Marriages by Isaac PARSONS Esq 1787 [9 Oct 1880]
    Marriages by John LEWIS Esq 1789 [13 Nov 1880] & 1795 [30 Dec 1880]
    Marriages by Rev Rufus ANDERSON 1794-1795 [30 Dec 1880]
    Marriages by Rev Tristram GILMAN 1777 (*sic*, should be 1787) & 1788 [9 Oct 1880] &
        1787 [2 Oct 1880] & 1788 [16 Oct 1880] & 1789 [23 Oct 1880] & 1790 [6 Nov 1880]
        & 1790-1791 [13 Nov 1880] & 1791-1792 [2 Dec 1880] & 1792-1794 & 1795 [23
        Dec 1880] & 1794-1795 [30 Dec 1880]
    Marriages by Samuel MERRILL Esq 1789 [6 Nov 1880] & 1791-1792 [2 Dec 1880] &
        1792 [23 Dec 1880]
    Marriages by Samuel MORRILL Esq 1787-1789 [16 Oct 1880]
    Marriages by William SYLVESTER Esq 1787 [9 Oct 1880]
NORTHERN MAINE - Good Change for Settlers [2 Oct 1856]
NORTON N F of Penobscot ME, photo of Bellflowers in the Orchard [14 June 1900]
    Norway ME - ed corr [24 Oct 1867]
NORWAY Maine [8 Sept 1877]
NOTES BY THE WAY [12 Sept 1874]
NOTES FROM THE COUNTY [8 Sept 1877] [15 Sept 1877] [22 Sept 1877] [29 Sept
    1877] [6 Oct 1877]
NOTES OF THE EASTERN TRIP VI [3 Aug 1878]
NOURSE S W Esq of Hudson MA, drawing [26 Jan 1893]
NOVA SCOTIA - Notes from 1605-1713 [10 Sept 1870]
NOYES Charles J, drawing [8 Mar 1894]
    David of Manchester NJ, a Free Mason (drawing) [22 Sept 1892]
    Reuel J staff of the *Maine Farmer* (photo) [25 May 1905]
    Wallace W, drawing [8 Feb 1894]
NUMBER 11 (Ashland) Maine [21 Nov 1850] & [5 June 1856]
NUTTING James, obit, printer of Lewiston Journal 10th ME in 1862 [23 Feb 1893]
OAKLAND Maine history [5 June 1884]
ODD FELLOWSHIP, History of [7 Mar 1874]
ODLIN W W of Cambridge ME "Taken the (*Maine) Farmer* 50y, 76y old on 4 Jan, my step-
    grandfather was Samuel CALL" [31 Mar 1921]
OLD POWNALBORO Maine, a history [7 Feb 1850]
OLD STAGE TIMES in Piscataquis & Penobscot Co's ME [31 Jul 1884]
OLD TIMES COLUMN - a Historical Reminiscence [19 July 1879]
OLD WINTHROP HALL by Walter D STINSON read before the Kennebec Natural
    History & Antiquarian Society [7 Apr 1892]
OLDTOWN Maine [21 Jul 1859]

OLNEY Andrew H Esq, drawing [10 Nov 1892]
ORDER OF THE REDMAN [26 Apr 1894]
ORIGIN OF OUR FLAG [28 July 1898]
ORLAND Maine - ed corr [1 Feb 1868] & Our State [20 Jul 1872]
ORNEVILLE - A sketch of by A W CLARK [13 May 1871]
ORONO Maine Herrick Stock Farm (photo) [27 Apr 1899]
    Stock Judging Pavilion at U of Maine [18 Mar 1909]
    View of Laboratory Building at Maine State College (UMO) [29 Dec 1877]
ORRINGTON Maine [Vol 8-45 (1840)] [23 June 1859]
OTISFIELD Maine Marriages by George PIERCE Esq 1787-1789 [18 Sept 1880]
OXFORD CO Maine [Vol 9-235 (1841)]
O'FALLON Mary F, drawing [24 Nov 1892] & [2 Feb 1893]
PACKARD E R, drawing [16 Mar 1893]
    George E of Dover ME, photo of farm & story [22 Aug 1918]
PAISLEY Amanda Mrs, drawing [27 Oct 1892]
PALERMO Maine & its Farmers [17 Feb 1898]
PALMYRA Somerset Co ME, Notes by the Way, Walter S KEENE's Farm [16 June 1898]
    Discovery of Coal in ME [22 Jan 1836]
PANTHERS in Maine [3 Jan 1889]
PAN-AMERICAN EXPOSITION (photo) [24 Jan 1901]
PARCELS POST LAW, Took effect Jan 1st, Photo of Delivery Auto [2 Jan 1913]
PARIS HILL Maine, notes of [1 Sept 1877]
PARIS Maine, A History of by William LAPHAM, a review [5 Feb 1885]
    Scraps from Early History [18 Oct 1873]
    Court House - ed corr [16 Sept 1867]
    Marriage Records 1795 to 1801 [29 Nov 1879] & [27 Dec 1879]
PARKER Alton B (photo) [27 Oct 1904]
    G F (photo) [6 Jan 1910]
    R Francis (photo) [13 Feb 1908]
PARKMAN Maine [28 Jul 1859] & Letter from [29 Jul 1871]
PARRIS Albion K - Men, Something about our Public, in the olden time by J W LANG [12 Jan 1893]
PARSONS Seth E of Albany NY, drawing [12 Jan 1893]
PARSONSFIELD Maine - Early settlers [5 Apr 1873] & letter from L S STAPLES [7 Fev 1867]
PATRIC Jeanie G Mrs, drawing [23 Mar 1893]
PATTEN E C of Topsham ME (photo) [18 Feb 1904]
    Edwin C of Topsham ME (photo) [29 Dec 1910]
PATTEN Maine [11 Nov 1850] [2 Oct 1856] [5 Jul 1860] [21 Jan 1864] & [13 Oct 1859]
PATTEN Roland T (photo) [13 Feb 1908]
PATTERSON Joseph W obit [16 Mar 1893]
PEABODY RIVER NH & Gorham NH - ed corr [23 May 1867]
PEAKE Edith Mrs Rev of San Francisco CA drawing [10 Dec 1896]
PEJEPSCOT PROPRIETORS [15 Sept 1892]
PEMAQUID, to restore old (History) [14 May 1896]
PEMBROKE Mass - Copies of Old Records [18 Jan 1873] & extract from records [8 Feb 1873]
PENNEY Charles F Rev (obit) of New Gloucester ME [11 May 1899]
PENOBSCOT CO Maine, [21 Jul 1859] & Notes from [31 Jul 1875] & Joel HUTCHINGS family reunion [20 Oct 1881]
PENOBSCOT VALLEY Maine [Vol 8-37 (1840)]

PENSIONERS, a notice to [13 Jul 1893]

PEPPERELL Col Wm - Men, Something about our Public, in the olden time by J W LANG [12 Jan 1893]

PERU Maine [23 June 1864] & [31 Jul 1880]

PHILBRICK Lovina Mrs, drawing [9 Mar 1893]

PHILLIPS Franklin Co ME [10 Sept 1857] & [17 Sept 1857] & Academy Boys from ME [27 Dec 1879] & Inscriptions copied from Headstones [20 Dec 1879]

PHILLIPS Gardiner b 1806 [24 Nov 1887]

PHINNEY C S of Standish ME (photo) [4 Feb 1904]

PILOTRO Adele, Cuba's woman Col, drawing & story [9 Jul 1896]

PINKHAM Mrs of Lynn MA (drawing of residence) [16 Jul 1899]

PISCATAQUA Ancient [7 Sept 1893]

PISCATAQUIS Co Maine, Fifty years ago & now by J L BENNETT [11 Jan 1906]
   Letter from [1 Jul 1871]
   New Mines in, lead, silver & copper [27 June 1867]
   Settling Lands in [2 Aug 1860]

PITTSFIELD POULTRY FARM (photo) [2 Jan 1908]

PITTSTON Maine [Vol 8-77 (1840)] & [new series 2-26 (1843)]

PLAISTED Frederick W (photo) [7 Jul 1910] [15 Sept 1910]

PLEASANT POND Maine, Jottings by the Way [29 Oct 1891]

PLEASANT RIDGE township Somerset Co ME [17 Aug 1878]

PLYMOUTH COLONY longevity (some *Mayflower* people) [5 Apr 1873]

POLAND Maine, 1st settlers [5 Apr 1873] & Early settlers in [1 Mar 1873]

POLAND SPRINGS on the Map, Pan-American Exposition, shows New England & New York Rail lines [13 June 1901]

POLLS, Then & Now (1793 & 1803) number of Polls in Maine by selected towns [8 May 1880]

POMPILLY Isaiah of Auburn (photo) [20 Jan 1898]

PONT A BUOT (Buots Bridge) New Brunswick Canada, the battle June 1755 [1 Feb 1873]

POPE Charles S of Manchester ME, Cream Manufactory [25 JUne 1914]

POPHAM BEACH Maine, A Much Discussed Subject [16 Dec 1880]

POPULATION of the USA in 1848 [22 Mar 1849]

PORTER L W Mr of West Berlin VT, drawing [11 Jan 1894]

PORTLAND Maine, [4 Jul 1861] Abstract of Seasons, weather &c from the Journal of Rev Thomas SMITH 1722-1788 (1 Oct 1842 to 12 Nov 1842) Portland - drawn picture of New Mechanics Hall [16 June 1859]
   Ed corr [21 Mar 1868]
   Great Fire in 1866 [16 Aug 1873]
   History, the 4th of July [12 Jul 1883]
   Obit of Nathaniel DEERING [7 Apr 1881]
   Observatory [24 Oct 1874]
   Our State #5 [18 Jan 1873]
   The Growth [4 Oct 1855]

PORTSMOUTH NH, Extracts from Church Records in 1671 [25 Oct 1879]

POWDERHORNS, Historic 1755 to 1760, last used in 1848 [15 Oct 1896]

POWER CO, Central Maine Completes New Station at Skowhegan [20 Jan 1921]

POWERS Llewellyn Gov (drawing) [7 Jan 1897]
   Sarah died past yr ae 106y [24 Nov 1887]

POWNAL Maine [Vol 8-317 (1840)] [Vol 9-85 (1841)]

PRESCOTT John R Hon of Maine, drawing [2 Nov 1893] & of Rome ME, drawing [27 Apr 1893]

PRESENT & THE PAST by H R SMILEY of Sidney ME [3 Dec 1896]

PRESQUE ISLE, Aroostook Co ME, Letter to Dr HOLMES from J B HALL [9 Dec 1847]
    & [5 June 1856] & [26 Jul 1860] & [11 Feb 1864] & [29 Jul 1871] & [11 Mar 1871]
    August Wandering # 3 [6 Sept 1883]
    Excursion to Aroostook Co [8 Aug 1895]
    Ed corr [14 Nov 1868] [21 Nov 1868] & [21 28 Nov, 5 Dec 1850]

PROHIBITION, Half Century of [6 June 1901]

PROVINCETOWN Mass Records of Death [25 Nov 1880]

PUFFER W R Rev of Richford VT, drawing [4 May 1893]

PULSIFER genealogy - Early settlers in Poland ME [1 Mar 1873]

PUZZLE Mtn (Newry) Maine [15 Aug 1861]

QUAKER, Some Boys of 1776 [22 Dec 1877]

RAILROADS in Maine [28 Aug 1845]

RAIL SERVICE, Aroostook Co ME [16 Nov 1878]

RANGELEY, James Esq by Seward DILL of Phillips ME [31 Oct 1874]

RANGELEY Maine, letter from [8 Dec 1877]

RAWSON (#1R5) Maine [7 June 1860]

RAY John of Waterville ME, drawing [26 Jan 1893]

RAYMOND EXCURSION # 4, Niagara village & history [19 Nov 1885]

READFIELD Maine "Century Dairy Farm Notes" [8 Aug 1912]

RED CENT, the old [3 Apr 1880]

REDIKER Melinda A Mrs of Washburn ME, drawing [9 Mar 1893]

REDMAN R W (photo) [17 Nov 1910] & [8 Dec 1910]

REED Charles of Belfast ME born 1809, a biographical letter [17 Nov 1898] [3 Nov 1898]
    T Brooks, staff of the *Maine Farmer* (photo) [25 May 1905]

REUNION, of the 4th ME Bat [24 June 1897]
    of Civil War Regimental 32rd ME, 17th ME, 2nd Cavalry, 7th ME, 1st ME artillery [27
        Aug 1896]

REVOLUTIONARY, Diary of Paul LUNT of Newburyport MA, Summer of 1775 at
        Bunker Hill [13 Mar 1875]
    Officers [16 Sept 1847]
    Relics by Rev Dr CHICKERING [*Transcript*] [18 Jan 1873]
    Soldiers at Bunker Hill [1 July 1843]
    War, a story 1781 [2 June 1887] & Feb 1779 [22 Feb 1879] & the 1st victim [8 Jan 1876]
        & 1780, Order book [20 Dec 1879]

REYNOLDS J C Mr & Mrs married 50yrs at Sidney ME [23 Apr 1896]

RICHARDS Granville E, drawing [6 Apr 1893]

RICHMOND ISLAND - see Cape Elizabeth

RICHMOND ME - ed corr [28 Mar 1867] & [Vol 8-85 (1840)]

RICKER W J (photo) [4 Nov 1909]

RIDEOUT Nicholas, drawing of his residence at New Gloucester ME [10 Dec 1885]

ROAD PROJECT [2 Aug 1906]

ROBBINS Family Reunion [14 Sept 1893]

ROBBINSON Hannah (KENNEY) (RICHARD) b 30 Apr 1796 at Hallowell ME [24 Nov
    1887]

ROBERTS John A of Norway ME (photo) [17 Dec 1903] & obit w/photo b 10 Sept 1852 [4
    Mar 1920]

ROBINSON Hannah of Augusta ME ae 102 (drawing & story) [6 May 1897] & ae 101 [7
    May 1896]
    Harriet drawing [9 Nov 1893]
    Mrs, the mother of Mrs Joseph PIPER, is in her 90th yr [24 Nov 1887]

RODD Lucien of Whitehall NY, drawing [4 May 1893] & drawing [26 Oct 1893]

ROGERS E A of Brunswick candidate for Commissioner of Agr [7 Nov 1912] & (photo) [4 Dec 1902]

Lillian of New York drawing [26 Nov 1896]

ROKOMEKO TRIBE OF INDIANS (see Canton Point) [27 Aug 1857]

ROOSEVELT Theodore (photo) [27 Oct 1904] & obit [9 Jan 1919]

RUMFORD FALLS Maine, Developments at [22 Dec 1892]

RUMFORD Maine [Vol 9-259 (1841)] & first settlers [25 Oct 1879]

RUSSELL family early settlers of Bingham ME by Francis RUSSELL of Mexico ME [12 Apr 1873]

RUSSIA, Exiles from [1 Mar 1894]

RYDER C W Mrs of Holden ME drawing [13 Apr 1893]

SACO, Editorial Correspondence [27 Dec 1866] & [4 Jul 1861]

Slate Quarry, Notes from York Co [10 June 1876]

Valley Settlement by G T RIDLON Sr, a book review [19 Sept 1895]

SAGADOHOC, Two Hundred seventy-three Anniversary of [4 Sept 1880] [11 Sept 1880] [16 Dec 1880]

SALEM Maine [17 Sept 1857] & Gold Mines [18 May 1854] & Glimpses from the Roadside [8 Mar 1849]

SALEM OH - Letter from Moses TABER, formerly of Maine [29 May 1869]

SANBORN James S (photo & obit) [14 May 1903]

J S, Elmwood Farm Lewiston Jct with horses [15 Aug 1901] [29 Aug 1901]

Prof J W, formerly of New Hampshire College talked at Turner ME Grange [28 Feb 1895]

SANBORN's horses [26 Mar 1896]

SANDWICH ISLANDS, the New Acquisition - Hawaiian [23 Feb 1893]

SANDY RIVER Maine, History by Myrtie CARVER Ae 11 [23 May 1901]

SANDY RIVER VALLEY Maine [30 Nov 1854] [25 Jul 1861] & (see Canton Point) ME [27 Aug 1857]

SANFORD Justin O of Stamford VT (drawing) [11 Feb 1897]

L L [17 Nov 1910]

SARSFIELD Plt Aroostook Co ME - Letter from [22 Nov 1866]

SAUNDERS William photo [26 Dec 1912]

SAVAGE A R Judge of Auburn ME (drawing) [13 May 1897]

SAWTELLE J R, Letter from a Kennebec man from Ogden Utah [14 Sept 1892]

SCARBORO Maine, Death Records by Capt Zebulon LIBBY, 5 Dec 1803 to May 1819 [26 Jul 1879] & 1820-1823 [9 Aug 1879] & Feb 1823-1825 [6 Sept 1879]

SCHOONER, Origin of the word [5 Sept 1874]

SCOTT, John Capt b 27 Apr 1785 at Wiscasset ME ae 93 [5 June 1875]

SEVEN MILE RIVER Maine (1 Feb 1855)

SEWALL Gen Henry Diary the intro 1776 to 1783 [29 June 1872]

SEWALL's Diary Mar 1776 to May 1776 [6 Jul 1872] May 1776 to Oct 1776 [13 July 1872] Oct 1776 to Mar 1777 [20 July 1872] Mar 1777 to Jul 1777 [27 Jul 1872] July 1777 to Sept 1777 [3 Aug 1872] Sept 1777 to Jan 1778 [10 Aug 1872] Jan 1778 to Jul 1778 [17 Aug 1872]

SEWALL's Diary Jul 1778 to Dec 1778 [24 Aug 1872] Dec 1778 to Jul 1779 [31 Aug 1872] Jul 1779 to Jan 1780 [7 Sept 1872] Jan 1780 to May 1780 [14 Sept 1872] Jul 1781 to Dec 1781 [26 Oct 1872] Dec 1781 to Aug 1782 [2 Nov 1872] May 1780 to Nov 1780 [21 Sept 1872]

SEWALL's Diary Nov 1780 to Apr 1781 [5 Oct 1872] Apr 1781 to Jul 1781 [19 Oct 1872] Aug 1782 to Mar 1783 [9 Nov 1872] Aug 1783 to Dec 1783 [30 Nov 1872] Mar 1783 to Aug 1783 [23 Nov 1872]

SHAKERS, About the Enfield NH [20 Feb 1875]

SHEEP, Account of the 19th century sheep raisers in Vermont by A L HARLOW [29 Dec 1923]

SHERIDAN Maine, Visit to Ashland #2 [16 Oct 1884]

SHERMAN Aroostook Co ME, sketch of [9 Oct 1875] & (see Golden Ridge Plt) & [11 Feb 1864]

SHIP BUILDING, The 1st in Maine [26 Sept 1874]

SHIRLEY Maine [1 Sept 1859]

SHORTHORN BULL in Maine & Dr E HOLMES by E C CARLL [28 Nov 1912]

SHUMWAY Mr S, drawing [14 Sept 1893]

SIDNEY Maine & her people Glimpses in Sidney & Belgrade ME [1 Dec 1887] & [17 July 1845]

SILLOWAYE William A H Col of Bellows Falls VT, drawing [16 Mar 1893] & [15 Mar 1894]

SIMPSON, Thomas as 91y native of Brunswick ME [24 Apr 1875]
   Reunion at Brunswick ME, descendants of William & Agnes Lewis SIMPSON settled abt 1735 [9 Aug 1900]

SKILLIN H E Mrs of North Yarmouth ME,drawing [19 Jan 1893]

SKOWHEGAN, Grange (photo) [13 Feb 1908] & ed corr [14 Mar 1868]

SLATE in Foxcraft ME [10 June 1836]

SLAVE, the Story of a by E B GETCHELL [7 Sept 1893]
   Traffic, Chinese women, San Francisco CA [15 Dec 1898]

SLAVERY, Negroes in the SC city just before the War [14 June 1894] & Days [13 Dec 1894]

SLAVES in New England [12 Apr 1894]

SLAYTON John A Esq, drawing [15 Feb 1894]

SMALL J B, inventor & manufacturer now of Boston MA (photo) [21 Feb 1901] Smallpox [9 Feb 1899]

SMITH William R of Gardiner ME, drawing [9 Feb 1893] & Esq obit, formerly of *Lincoln Intelligencer* & the *Age* [18 Jan 1894]

SMITHFIELD Maine [17 July 1845] & (formerly East Pond) [30 Nov 1854]

SOLLER Mrs & Mrs M M's children of Atoona PA, drawing [22 Dec 1892]

SOLON Maine [12 June 1845] & Grange Hall (photo) [13 Jan 1910]

SOMERSET Co Maine Agricultural Society (picture of all men) [1 Feb 1906]
   Excursion #1 & 3 [6 Jul 1878] [17 Aug 1878]
   Notes of [4 Aug 1877]
   Notes #3 [1 Feb 1855]
   Notes [30 Nov 1854]

SONS OF VETERANS [22 June 1893]

SOULE James of Palermo ME, drawing [19 Jan 1893] & [25 May 1893]

SOUTH POLAND Maine, a Day at Elmwood Farm [24 May 1895]

SOUTH VASSALBORO Maine, photo of cows of S F COBB [11 Aug 1898]

SPARHAWK family of Kittery ME & the burning of Falmouth ME [14 Dec 1872]

SPEAR Robert A Mrs of West Warren ME, drawing [30 Mar 1893]

SPENCER BAY [1 Sept 1859]

SPINNEY John Rev of Industry ME, drawing [5 Apr 1894]

SPRAGUE Lita Frost Rev of Boston MA, ass't pastor to husband, drawing [9 Jul 1896]

SPRINGFIELD Maine - ed corr [31 Oct 1868]

ST ALBANS, Early History of (a paper read by W H SNELL) [9 Jan 1896]
ST ALBANS VT Creamery building, drawing [1Oct 1891]
ST CROIX RIVER, Sleigh Ride to Loui's Island [6 Feb 1835]
ST JOHN, the valley of [22 Nov 1873] & [11 Feb 1892]
STAGE COACH, The Old Days, Traveling in Maine 50 years ago [11 Nov 1886]
STANTON Secretary, drawing [15 Mar 1894]
STAPLES Simeon, drawing [31 Aug 1893] & [6 Jul 1893]
STARKS Maine [30 Nov 1854]
STATE FAIR, photo of 1897 [2 Sept 1897]
STEAM, Carriages #1 [18 Mar 1833]
   Condensed History of (abt 280 BC to 1810 AD) [2 Aug 1866]
   Mill at Canton ME [24 June 1880]
STEAMER *HERCULES* on the Kennebec River, drawing [20 Apr 1893]
STEARNS Austin at Paris Hill (farm house photo) [6 Aug 1903]
STETSON C S of Alto ME (photo) [23 Dec 1909] & of Greene ME (photo) [17 Dec 1903]
   & (photo) [26 Dec 1907] & [17 Dec 1908] & [22 Dec 1910]
STETSON Maine, Notes by the Way [16 Oct 1880]
STEVENS Charles H Esq of South Effingham NH (drawing) [21 Jan 1897]
STEWART A A (photo) [11 Feb 1909]
STEWART Estella of Springfield MA, drawing [20 Apr 1893]
STONE QUARRIES in Maine [27 Aug 1885]
STONEHAM Maine [5 Sept 1861]
STORY F of Augusta ME, drawing [24 Nov 1892]
STRANGE NAMES OF TOWNS [31 May 1894]
STRICKLAND L P Hon, drawing [1 Feb 1894]
STRONG Maine [17 Sept 1857]
STROUT of Poland ME [5 Apr 1873]
STURGIS Brothers of Auburn ME (photo of the farm) [2 Apr 1891]
SUGAR ISLAND Maine [1 Sept 1859]
SULLIVAN Hancock Co ME [7 JUl 1859]
SUMNER Oxford Co ME [3 Sept 1857]
SUTHERLAND Anna Mrs, drawing [22 June 1893]
SWEDEN Aroostook Co ME [28 Jan 1871]
SWEET, Job Dr photo [30 Jan 1896]
SWEETSIR S F (photo) [19 Dec 1901]
SWIFT I O his Orchard [8 Jan 1914]
TAFT William P (photo) [13 Aug 1908]
TALMAGE T DeWit Rev (drawing) [10 Mar 1898]
TANNERY - the Winn ME [8 Mar 1866]
TELEGRAPH, Who invented the ? by L M Mooers [17 Aug 1872]
TELEGRAPHY, Wireless [9 Nov 1899]
TELLER H A, drawing [15 Dec 1892]
TEMPERANCE 40yrs ago [26 Apr 1873]
TEMPLE Christina Mrs of Bangor ME, drawing [21 Dec 1893]
TEMPLE Maine, Glimpses from the Road-side [1 Mar 1849] & sheep farmer [24 Apr 1913]
   & Grange (photo) [30 Mar 1905]
TENNEY Albert G 37 yrs editor of the *Brunswick Telegraph* [5 Jul 1894]
TEWSBURY MA's Almshouse, drawing of the barn [16 Mar 1893]
TEXAS, Past & Present [14 Jul 1881]
THAMES, drawing of an excursion on [5 Sept 1874]

THANKSGIVING, the 1st [28 Nov 1912] & Day Among the Lumberjacks [28 Nov 1912]
    & Origin of [1 Mar 1873]

THOMAS, Ichabod of Sidney ME letter to Duxboro MA dated 22 May 1794 [14 Dec 1872]
    Genealogy - historical memoranda [14 Dec 1872]

THOMAS Gen, oldest Gen of the Civil War ae 92 (photo) [18 Apr 1901]

THOMASTON Maine - ed corr [9 Jan 1868]

THOMASTON STATE PRISON - ed corr [2 Jan 1868]

THOMPSON S C (photo) [4 June 1903]
    W J of South China ME, photo of oat field [12 Sept 1907] & (photo) [19 Dec 1901] &
    [20 Dec 1906]

THORNDIKE Maine [Vol 8-61 (1840)]

THORPE B Frank W editor (photo) [25 May 1905] goes to Cornell (photo) [2 Sept 1909]

TIDENS genealogy, The TIDENS of Scituate MA Marriages 1661-1864 & Births 1649-
    1846 [10 Feb 1881]

TIMBLE John Rev Jr photo [26 Dec 1912]

TOBACCO GROWING IN MAINE [5 Apr 1849] [26 Nov 1908]

TOGUS Maine - National Military Asylum near Augusta, drawing & story [8 Jul 1871]

TOGUS SPRINGS [2 Dec 1858]

TOPSHAM Sagadahoc Co ME - ed Corr [7 Mar 1867] & Something about the old town of
    [3 Mar 1887]

TORNADO in ME [23 June 1892]

TORONTO Canada West - ed corr [10 Sept 1868]

TOWN C C Mrs, drawing [12 Oct 1893]

TOWN POUND, the old by Will P WINSLOW [15 Feb 1917]

TOWNE Charles ae 83 [24 Nov 1887]

TOWNSHIP LETTER A #2 Maine (19 Sept 1850)

TRACY Reunion [27 Aug 1896]

TRAFTON D O (farm horse & person photo) of Newport ME [9 Jul 1903]

TRASK Jonathan of Exeter NE died ae 99y 1m 6d "State News" [22 Feb 1900]

TROLLEY CAR Winthrop - Gardiner electric [27 Sept 1906]

TROY, Maine, copper mine [24 Aug 1833]

TRUE Nathaniel T Dr (obit) [19 May 1887]

TRUE's Pin Worm Elixir of Auburn ME, advertisement [1 June 1893]

TUBERCULOSIS, Human [29 Apr 1909] & Panic [11 Feb 1909] & Vaccination for the
    Prevention of [17 Feb 1910]

TUCK, Jeremiah b 22 June 1780 at Kensington NH, res Fayette ME [5 June 1875]

TUCKER Herbert M, on farm at Livermore ME [4 Apr 1912]

TUPPER Mary A of Wilton ME, drawing [12 Apr 1894]

TURNER George W, drawing [29 Dec 1892] & [9 Mar 1893]

TURNER Maine [Vol 9-117 (1841)] & [24 June 1880]
    New Grange Hall (photo) [17 Nov 1898] & [26 May 1898]
    The Flag Outrage [3 Oct 1861]
    The Timely Shot (Lewiston Journal) [5 Apr 1849]
    Turner Creamery, Turner Center ME (photo) [7 Dec 1899] & [25 Sept 1919]

TWICHELL George W Dr of Augusta ME, photo of Maine State Fair Officer [15 Aug
    1895] & (photo) Pres of the *Maine Farmer* Publishing Co [25 May 1905] goes to the
    Portland Express [6 Oct 1910] & Secret of his success at Inglenook, Monmouth ME
    w/photo [27 Nov 1919]

UNCLE TOM'S CABIN, How written [16 June 1898]

UNITY, Waldo Co ME [24 Apr 1875] & [Vol 8-61 (1840)] & Journal of a tour "Up East" by
    J WHITMAN of North Turner [19 Feb 1842]

UPPER STILLWATER Maine - Our State [18 May 1872]
USA EXTINCTION OF THE NATIONAL DEBT 1791-1835 [26 Dec 1834]
VAN BUREN Aroostook Co ME [16 Nov 1878] & August Wanderings #3 [6 Sept 1883]
VARNEY Alfre M staff of the *Maine Farmer* (photo) [25 May 1905]
VASSALBORO Maine, [Vol 8-69 (1840)] Emigrant & genealogy of Philip FAUGHT [5
    June 1880]
    North Vassalboro Manufacturing Co [14 Apr 1859]
    Oak Grove Seminary (Photo & story) [23 Aug 1900] & (photo) [17 Nov 1898]
    Then & now by J H SMILEY [26 Oct 1899]
VERMONT by H K BAKER [5 Jan 1893]
VIENNA Maine, Glimpses from the Road-side [29 Mar 1849]
VIEW/DRAWING OF
    Aroostook Falls ME [2 Jan 1848]
    Aroostook Mountain from Upper Sebois Lake (6 Feb 1845)
    Bryant's Pond ME from Dudley Hill [29 June 1882]
    Carritunk Falls ME [12 June 1845] & Solon & Embden ME [2 Sept 1876]
    Castle at West Corner of Fort William Henry [22 Jul 1915]
    Chase's Mountains from the summit of Sugar Loaf [6 Aug 1846)
    Colby University & story [24 May 1879]
    Farm Buildings of Calvin CHAMBERLAIN of Foxcroft ME [15 Jul 1858]
    Godfrey's Falls [10 Apr 1845]
    Group of Centennial Prize Jersey's at Echo Farm Litchfield CT [30 Nov 1878]
    Holmes & Robbins, Machine Shop & Iron Foundry, Gardiner ME [3 June 1833]
    Ice Fields of the Kennebec River with a story [16 Feb 1882]
    Kendall & Whitney's Agricultual Warehouse & Seed Store at Portland ME [15 Mar
        1888]
    Kennebec Ice-houses [5 Mar 1885]
    Mapleton Aroostook Co ME, a Farm Scene [30 Dec 1897]
    Mary, an Indian Doctress of the Penobscot Tribe [1 Jul 1833]
    New Agricultural building at State College [18 Aug 1887]
    New Hampshire College of Agriculture & Mechanic Arts [8 Aug 1889]
    North Vassalboro ME, the farm buildings of Ira E GETCHELL [22 June 1878]
    Prof E W STEWART [14 Apr 1887]
    Rumford Falls ME & story [9 Aug 1879]
    Sugar Loaf from Mt Katahdin [29 Jan 1846] Visit to Aroostook Co # 1-# 6 [31 Oct 1850
        to 5 Dec 1850]
    Sugar-loaf Mtn from Seboois River, Scenes in the Wilderness # 4 [13 Nov 1845]
    The Androscoggin Falls at Jay ME Bridge [11 Jul 1874
    Thomas HIGGINS Esq of Liverpool England & story
    Tisonic Falls & covered bridge at Waterville ME [30 Aug 1879]
    Walter B Pierce, national Lecturer Farmer's League [12 June 1890]
    Works of Richardson Manufacturing Co Worcester MA [17 May 1888]
WADSWORTH Eli C, photo of the residence a *Maine Farmer* Summer Home [20 Jan
    1898]
WALDO Co, Grange [30 Nov 1882] [14 Dec 1882] & Notes from [24 Apr 1875]
WALDO Gen Samuel - Men, Something about our Public, in the olden time by J W LANG
    [12 Jan 1893]
WALES Maine, Jottings by the Way by CSA [3 Oct 1895]
WAR MAP of Harbin & vicinity [3 Mar 1904]
WAR of 1812 [19 Jul 1879] & "Hay foot! Straw foot!" [26 Jul 1879]
WARREN M S Mrs, on jury in Colorado photo [18 June 1896]

WARREN Maine - ed corr [16 Jan 1868] [23 Jan 1868]

WASHBURNE family [19 Apr 1873]

WASHINGTON George by F Story TAYLOR [2 Mar 1899]

WASHINGTON, Mrs Booker T (story) [15 Oct 1896]

WASHINGTON Co & its Possibilities, the Sunrise Rout [20 Jul 1899]

WATER POWER in Maine, Lewiston [21 Aug 1845]

WATERBORO Maine, "Early Maine Settlers" by John Chich MURRAY [24 June 1920]
Deering Ridge ME, Jotting by the way [4 Dec 1884]

WATERFORD Maine, Centennial at [11 Sept 1875]
Marriages by George PIERCE Esq 1787 [18 Sept 1880]

WATERVILLE Maine [new series 2-26 (1843)] & ed Corr [21 Feb 1867] & [26 Dec 1868]

WATTS' Hymns [17 June 1847]

WAUGH family records, Somerset Co [4 Aug 1877]

WAYNE Maine, Glimpses from the Road-side [1 Feb 1849] & (Beech Hill) [11 Jul 1861] &
[25 Jul 1861] & 100th Celebration [25 Aug 1898]

WAYSIDE NOTES OF TRAVEL #2-18, 20, 22-30, & 33 [21 28 Apr, 12 19 May, 2 9 23
30 June, 7 21 28 Jul, 4 11 25 Aug, 1 Sept, 5 13 Oct, 24 Nov, 22 29 Dec 1859] [12
Jan, 22 Mar 1860] [7 June 1860] [5 Jul 1860] [26 Jul 1860] [17 Jan 1861]

WEATHER, and the Crops [14 Sept 1893]
How to Foretell [27 Dec 1860]
Journal 1810-1849 by Joshua WHITMAN of North Turner Bridge (7 Mar 1850)
Journal Progress of Vegetation &c for 35y (1800-1835) by Joshua WHITMAN of North
Turner ME [10 June 1836]
Observations of the, 1 Sept 1816 to 30 June 1817 by Lewis B HAMLEN [19 Mar 1891]
Probabilities [13 Jul 1893]

WEBSTER Daniel, his ancestry [14 Sept 1893]

WEBSTER Maine, Jottings by the Way by CSA [3 Oct 1895]

WELCH, Nancy ae 92y at York d/o David & Mary GERALD [24 Apr 1875]

WELLINGTON Maine [25 Aug 1859]

WENTWORTH C V Mrs, drawing [21 Sept 1893]
Mrs C D (drawing of a portrait painter) [1 Oct 1903]

WEST BATH Maine Grange Hall (photo) [30 Jan 1902]

WEST BIGHTON Mass, rye field of J H HORTON, photograph & article [1 Mar 1894]

WEST LEBANON Maine Academy [24 Oct 1874]

WEST PARIS Maine Grange Hall (photo) [17 Mar 1910]

WEST POLAND Maine - Visit to the Shakers [9 Aug 1860]

WEST SUMNER Maine [30 June 1864]

WEST WATERVILLE Maine, Ed Corr, letter from [24 Jan 1867] & view of the Cascade
[2 Dec 1876]

WEST William Dr of Belfast ME, photo, Candidates for Commissioner of Agr [26 Sept
1912]

WESTBROOK Maine - ed corr [4 Apr 1868] & [4 Jul 1861] & [Vol 8-405 (1840)]
Seminary organized 1831, a drawing [18 Feb 1871]

WESTON Homestead & Farm at Skowhegan, story & genealogical data [1 Mar 1917]

WHIPPLE Mary drawing [3 Sept 1896]

WHITE MTNS, Glen House a letter from S J [19 Sept 1867] Glen House burned flat [17
Aug 1893] & Glen House, a corr ed [4 Apr 1867]

WHITE PEOPLE of 21y plus, counted by state can not read [18 Dec 1845]

WHITNEY POND of Canton ME [Vol 9-349 (1841)]

WHITTIER Wilmont R (photo) [13 Feb 1908]

WIGGIN Edward, master of Maine State Grange [20 Dec 1894]

WILLARD Nathaniel of Strong ME, farm [29 Jan 1914]

WILLIAMS A A Mrs, drawing [15 Dec 1892] & of Lynn MA, drawing [23 Feb 1893]

WILLIAMSBURG Maine, Rambles through the Country [24 Jul 1875]

WILLIAMSTOWN VT - A trip to Mt Mansfield VT [27 Aug 1868]

WILSON B Mrs, drawing [12 Oct 1893]

   Barney, drawing [16 Feb 1893]

   George S (photo) [3 Feb 1898]

   J A of Brunswick ME, farm [30 Oct 1913]

   James Prof of Iowa (photo) [25 Mar 1897]

   Oliver Mrs, drawing [1 Dec 1892]

WILTON Maine, Congregational Church Vital Records [25 Oct 1879]

   Glimpses from the Road-side [22 Feb 1849]

   Letter from Maj J H WILLARD [29 May 1869]

   Notes #1-6 on History by John H WILLARD [21 Feb, 7 21 Mar, 4 Apr, 2 May, 6 June 1867]

WINDHAM Maine, [7 Apr 1853]

   Farming in with photos [29 Nov 1917]

   Letter from [5 Nov 1870]

   Marriages by Benjamin DUNNING Esq 1787 [24 Feb 1881]

   Marriages by Edmund PHINEY Esq [6 Jan 1881]

   Marriages by Joseph HOOPER Esq 1790 [6 Jan 1881]

   Marriages by Paul LITTLE Esq 1791-1792 [6 Jan 1881] & 1792-1794 [17 Feb 1881]

   Marriages by Rev Peter SMITH 1786-1787 [30 Dec 1880] & 1787-1789 [6 Jan 1881]

   Marriages by Samuel EATON 1787-1788 [24 Feb 1881] & 1786-1787 [17 Feb 1881]

   Marriages by William SYLVESTER Esq 1786-1789 [24 Feb 1881]

   Windemere farm (photo 1898 & 1908) [26 Mar 1908]

WING Asa W b at Vassalboro ME ae 70 [30 Dec 1880]

WINN Maine [21 Jul 1859]

WINTERPORT Maine "Charming" [11 Oct 1888]

WINTHROP Maine, A letter from S P MAYBERRY of Cape Elizabeth [20 Dec 1866]

   Condensed Milk Factory [18 May 1893]

   Editorial Correspondence [27 Dec 1866] & [24 June 1880] & [new series 2-26 (1843)]

   Journal of a tour "Up East" by J WHITMAN of North Turner [19 Feb 1842]

   Oldest Methodist in Maine (11 Jul 1850)

   Winthrop ME to Farmington ME [11 Jul 1861]

WITCHCRAFT, Modern [17 Nov 1892]

WOLCOTT Jane (HUNTRESS) b 12 Jul 1796 at Berwick ME [24 Nov 1887]

WOMAN By Rev Wm T BRIGGS [25 May 1893]

   In Business [27 Apr 1893]

   Lawyers in Canada [10 Sept 1896]

   Officals, a Kansas town that is ruled by [11 June 1896]

   On the Farm, essay read at York Co Pomona Grange at Kennebunk ME by Mrs A E McKENNEY [26 Mar 1891]

   Woman Suffrage, Mrs Abigail BUSH, drawing [13 Aug 1896]

   Only on the Jury 90y ago, it asked clemency for a colored sister at Lexington KY [2 Aug 1894]

   Reform Wrought by Chicago [7 Sept 1893]

   Successful Farmers [30 Aug 1888]

   Suffrage by Mrs C A CUNNINGHAM at Cascade Grange, Oakland ME [6 Apr 1893] & in Maine [13 Feb 1869] & [14 Nov 1895]

   Suffrage equal, Kansas Women [24 Dec 1896]

WOMAN (Cont.) The Federation of [17 Oct 1895]
    Voting in Topeka KS [14 Apr 1887]
    What they can do [25 Oct 1888]
    What the Southern had to endure in the 60's [18 Jul 1889]
WOOD Joanna E (drawing) [21 Jan 1897]
WOODCOOK H N, drawing [2 Mar 1893]
WOODMAN, Lydia ae 91y of South Norridgewock ME [24 Apr 1875]
WORKERS of Maine [26 Jan 1888]
WRIGHT Jean of Louisville (drawing) [17 Dec 1896]
WYLIE Lollie Belle drawing [17 Sept 1896]
YANKEE DOODLE, where was it written [1 JUl 1909]
YMCA, Shore of Lake Cobbosseecontee [Reconstruction Supplement to *Maine Farmer* 3
    Apr 1919]
YORK George H (photo) [27 Oct 1910]
YOUNG John M, photo of farm building at Calais ME [24 Jan 1907]
    Thomas ae 93y in 1880 census native of Wiscasset ME [24 Nov 1887]

SELECTED NEWS ARTICLES 1833-1911

AGED PERSONS, in the United States 476 white males aged 100 years and upwards - 315 white females. Also 286 colored males (free) & 361 colored females (free). Also, 753 male slaves - and 580 females, all aged one hundred years & upwards. The blacks, it would therefore seem, are longer lived than the whites. [23 Oct 1841]

COLORED FREE MASONRY, The three Grand Lodges of colored Free Masons of the States of MD, NY & PA made a turn-out ... [NY Express] [13 Jul 1848]

COLORED SETTLEMENT, in New York Some time since, Gerrit SMITH gave away a large tract of land in Oneida Co NY to colored settlers. The settlement is called "Florence" and is said to be very flourishing, among the recent improvements is the setting up of a printing press. [14 Feb 1850]

COLORED 5 men drowned in Merrymeeting Bay on Thurs of last week, while on their way from Bowdoinham village to this place. Four of the persons colored, & we believe all belonged here. Names not known to us [Bath Telegraph] [7 Oct 1843]

CALIFORNIA PILGRIMS, families to join husbands and fathers who have for some time been in the golden land .... many new adventurers to the new State on the Pacific and a few who have been there before. The barque J W Paige, fitted out by Messrs James DUNNING and ATWOOD & NICKERSON sailed for California from Frankfort on Saturday last. She had seventy-two passengers in all. (copied from Bangor Whig) [15 Apr 1852]

DEAF MUTES, The Deaf & Dumb Asylum at Hartford contains 162 pupils; 88 males & 74 females - Of these, 21 are supported by their friends, 25 by Maine, 16 by NH, 17 by VT, 46 by MA, 29 by CT, 3 by SC, & 5 by GA [5 Feb 1846]

EASTPORT ME, Almost the whole business part of (Eastport) destroyed by fire on Sat last, started in Water Street # 9 owned by Col B B LEAVITT and occupied as a dwelling house & grocery by an Irish family & the store of Messrs G & J HOBBS on the east side and the office of D T GRANGER on the west side inclusive A number of dwelling houses back of the Street, were also burnt (from the Eastport Sentinel) [13 Jul 1839]

EASTPORT ME The people of St John New Brunswick Canada have subscribed one thousand dollars and forwarded it for the relief of sufferers of the late disastrous fire at Eastport ME [27 Jul 1839]

ELLSWORTH ME, fire broke out on Tues night in the store owned by T ROBINSON Esq & occupied by J S LORD. The store was consumed together with the new store of W C BLACK & Co. The town books & papers and also the books & papers of the law office of T ROBINSON Esq were consumed. [14 Feb 1850]

FEMALES, The Congress of Texas passed a law granting 2,982 acres of good land to every woman, who will marry, during the present year, a citizen of that republic, & who was such at the time of the declaration of their independence. [23 Nov 1839]

FREE NEGROES, in Alabama by a law of the last session of the Alabama Legislature all the free persons of color who remain in the state after the 1st of Aug next are liable to be enslaved [21 Sept 1839]

FREE NEGROES, The Legislature of VA has passed the bill appropriating $30,000 per annum for the removal of free negroes from the state. The same bill levies a tax of $1 upon all males free negroes over 21 & under 55 yrs of age [28 Mar 1850]

FREE SUFFRAGE, "at the recent election in WI free suffrage voted. Establishes the right of every male citizen, of whatever color, over 21 years to vote at all elections in that state" [24 Jan 1850]

GENEALOGY, English nobleman undertook to ridicule passion of Welch, tracing their ancestry down to profoundest depths of antiquity. To a gentleman boating could carry his family lineage back to Noah, he stated by way of offset, that when in Wales he shewn the pedigree of a family that filled above five large skins of parchment, about the middle of it note in the margin, About this time, the world was created. [25 Mar 1847]

HEMP: can be made as white as snow, to make finest white paper, this kind of hemp will be soon sought after by the paper makers. Linen rags have always been very scarce in the West & the importation of them has nearly ceased in the East since the tariff. Supply the place of linen rags, worth 6 to 9 cents a pound. It will afford a new supply of raw material to paper manufactories at the East as well as in the West [21 Jan 1843]

HEMP: The most carefully formed estimates of the hemp crop of the Missouri river 13,000 tons. Product of the whole West beside, 17,000 tons & an amount equal to 30,000 tons - from this deduct the quanity used in the west in manufacturer, 12,000 tons and for export 18,000 to 20,000 tons or more than equal to the requirements of all northern seaports & leaving a considerable quantity for export [*Cincinnati Gazette*][2 Dec 1847]

INDIANS OF CANADA, By returns made to the British Parliment, it appears that the whole number of Indians in Canada is 13,241 [29 Mar 1849]

IRISHMEN, Rogers, Ketchum & Groomer of Patterson trying a new locomotive, boiler burst, hurling the fragments blowing off the roof and one side of the a brick building. When the accident occurred, the shop filled with workmen still buried in the ruins. Three or four taken out dead & ten or fifteen badly wounded. The persons killed were Irish [*The Daily Advertiser* of May 7] [15 May 1851]

JEWISH SETTLEMENT, The *Jewish Chronicle* says that several Jewish families have emigrated to the United States from Bohemia, with the view of founding a Jewish settlement in the State of Wisconsin. [6 Dec 1849]

JOKE: Consistent spelling A western writer thinks if the proper way to spell tho is "Though" ate "eight" and bo "beau" then the proper way to spell "Potatoes" is Pougheighteaux [8 May 1851]

JOKE: Dean SWIFT remarks doubtless with much truth, that in the establishing of colonies, the French commence with a fort, the Spaniards with a church & the English with a grog shop [11 May 1843]

JOKE: pretty Riddle "I will consent to all you desire," said a young female to her lover, "on condition that you give me what you have not, what you can never have, and yet can give away." What did she ask him for? A husband. [1 Aug 1840]

JOKE: Sent to execute a writ against a Quaker, an officer saw the Q's wife. She requested him to be seated & her husband would speedily see him. The officer waited, but the Q didn't make his appearance & when the fair Q came into the room, he reminded her of her promise. "Nay, friend, I promised that he would see thee, He has seen thee. He did not like thy looks; therefore he avoided thy path, & left the house by another road." [31 Aug 1848]

JOKE: The schoolmaster asked poor Tom, the idiot, how long a man could live without brains, Tom, laying ho'd of the domine's button, & gazing for a few moments in his face, replied; "How long have you lived, dominie?" [10 Dec 1842]

JOKE: "A Jeu D'Esprit - A poor devil by the name of Judah was up before the Recorder for being found drunk, and a facetious Frenchman said,'twas only a Judah spree!" [11 May 1843]

MAINE, information Islands of Maine, Hon Elijah L HAMLIN states before the Bangor Lyceum on the subject of "The Islands & the Islanders of Maine" there are nearly 1000 islands & inlets belonging to the State & they have a population of about twenty thousand. The islanders are in general an intelligent people & are remarkable for their hospitality & generosity. [*Bangor Whig*][*Thomaston Gazette*] [15 Feb 1849]

MAINE, information The sea coast of Maine extends in a direct line over 221 miles but following its indentations, the distance is increased to more than 600 miles. There are scattered along the coast with in a space of 130 miles east of Cape Elizabeth ME about 1000 islands & inlets - the largest of the first named being Mount Desert, which contains over 60,000 acres. *[Portland Advertiser]* [8 Mar 1849]

MARRIAGES - see TEXAS & females [23 Nov 1839]

MASONIC "A Mason or an Odd Fellow is bound to render assistance to his brother in need in any part of the world - why is it not so among Christians? But let a Christian go from this state to New Orleans, and be taken sick & needy, & make himself known to the churches, as a Christian, & who would come to his aid on that account. *[Gospel Banner]*" [1 Jan 1846]

METEOR "of a monstrous meteor, 3 times as big as the great ball rolled into the Baltimore Convention? It is rumored that such a phenomenon occurred this morning about 3 o'clock, the light from the meteor illuminated the city equal to the sun at noonday (from *Boston Transcript* of Wed) The meteor seen by many in this city, who happened to be awake at that hour in the morning. (from *Portland Advertiser*) [23 May 1840]

NEGRO settlement in Cass Co MI, a large settlement of "colored" people mostly from the Southern States. They have a fine location, well-tilled farms, neat & comfortable cottages & buildings & live an industrious & happy life [27 Dec 1849]

NEGRO "the City Court of Baltimore on Friday, petition of a negro man for his freedom, brought into the state from Delaware. The laws of Delaware declare that a slave purchased for the intention of exportation shall be free. The court sustained that law, and declared the man to be free." [25 Jul 1840]

NEGROES, a free colored man was ordered by a court in KY to be sold as a slave. His crime was simply coming into that state, it being against the law for a free colored man to do so [28 Sept 1848]

NEGROES, The Legislature of DE, a law to prevent free negroes from coming into that state hereafter to reside under a penalty of $50. The law is not to affect seafaring men, servants or persons entering the state temporarily for the purpose of trade. Any Captain of a vessel taking a free negro to attend a camp or other meeting is subject under this law to a fine of $200 [10 Apr 1851]

NEGROES - *The Galveston Civilian*, 18th said McCULLOCH's company of mounted Rangers overtook on the 10th ult a gang of runaway negroes, near the river Neuces, on their way to Mexico. The negroes were challenged by the Rangers to surrender, but refused and in return opened a fire upon the Rangers, killing two & wounding a third very badly. A general engagement then ensued in which all the negroes were killed. [8 May 1851]

NEW BRUNSWICK & ANNEXATION "The St Johns New Brunswick Canada Morning News is out for annexation to the USA. It says there are strong & growing sentiments among the people in favor of the measure, complains of the evils under which they suffer by mal-administration & declares that next summer there will go up from the people an universal cry for separation" [31 Jan 1850]

NEWS List of Revolutionary battles, exception of a few in the southern states *[New Bedford Mer]* Concord, 19 Apr '75; Bunker Hill, 15 June '75; Old Hampton VA, Nov '75; Great Bridge, near Norfolk, VA 18 Dec '75; Long Island 27 Aug '76; Fort Washington 17 Nov '76; Fort Lee 19 Nov '76; Trenton, when 1000 Hessians captured 26 Dec '76; Princeton 2 Jan '77; Bennington, 16 Aug '77; Brandywine, 11 Sept '77 Germantown, 4 Oct '77; Burgoyne's army taken near Saratoga, 17 Oct '77; Red Banks, 22 Oct '77; Monmouth, 28 June '78; Stony Point, 16 Jul '79; Camden 10 Aug '80; Cowpens, 17 Jan '81; Gilford NC 15 Mar '81; Groton CT Massacre 6 Sept '81; Entaw Springs 9 Sept '81; King's Mountain 7 Oct '81; Cornwallis & his army taken 19 Oct 1781[5 Aug 1836]

NEWS: A letter from New Orleans of the 9th in speaking of mortality at that place says By two cholera & two fevers, New Orleans has lost twelve thousand persons - one fourth of its population [7 Dec 1833]

NEWS: Adulterated Drugs. There are several manufacturers of adulterated drugs in England. They are shipped to this & other countries & sold. This is most infamous. It is bad enough to be under the necessity of using genuine drugs. [15 June 1848]

NEWS: Cash for Negroes - built a private jail for the keeping of slaves, in Pratt street. The male & female appartments completely separate - the rooms large light & air & all above ground, 25 cents per head a day N.B. Cash will at times be given for likely slaves of both sexes, would do well to see me before they sell, as I am always purchasing for New Orleans market..... Hope H SLATER [24 Jul 1838]

NEWS: English are extending their military operation down the Madawaska River, constructing barracks on the North & South side of the St John's River at the confluence of the Madawaska in violation of the argeement made by Sir John HARVEY & Gen Winfield SCOTT [*The Bangor Democrat*] [18 Jan 1840]

NEWS: Female Wages - It was stated at a meeting of the seamstresses of Boston MA, that some of the girls received only one cent an hour for hard work, & this was paid in copper coin purchased at the toll houses at a discount [4 Nov 1843]

NEWS: Hemp & Flax cleaner - a machine invented by BILLINGS & HARRISON which rots & breaks & scutches & turns out 400 pounds of clean flax or hemp per day, equal to any foreign article. This must produce a revolution in this business & instead of being importers of flax & hemp we must become manufacturers of them & extensive exporters for the other portions of the World. (written by Dr E HOLMES, editor) [11 Jan 1849]

NEWS: How to Ruin a Son, Let him have his own way, allow him free use of money, suffer him to rove where pleases on the Sabbath day, give him access to wicked companions, call him to no account for his evenings, funish him with no stated employment. Pursue any one of these ways & you will experience a most marvellous, if you have not to mourn over a debased & ruined child. (from the *Philadelphia Presbyterian*) [29 Jul 1843]

NEWS: Hyman versus Bacchus - passed the Legislature of OH authorizing the Supreme Court to grant divorces to applicants if can prove either party a habitual drunkard for two years. (*Baltimore Gazette*) [16 May 1834]

NEWS: In Sweden they deprive a man of a right to vote who gets drunk a third time. We don't [20 Nov 1841]

NEWS: Institutions for the Deaf & Dumb - There now are eleven institutions in the USA devoted exclusively to the education of the deaf & dumb (deaf mutes) [23 Sept 1851]

NEWS: Need of the Montreal Road. Not less than three large English ships have been wrecked & totally destroyed, this summer in going up the St Lawrence River. In the last one hundred nineteen persons perished. When that road is done, persons need not run risk of that most dangerous of all places, the Gulf of St Lawrence, as they can come in to Portland ME and take the cars for Canada in double quick time. [15 Jul 1847]

NEWS: Shoeing the Army. A shoe manufacturer, who had a contract to supply shoes for the army at $1.05 per pair, had a large lot of them condemned as unsuitable by the Government Agent in Philadelphia. Yankee packed them up & started off South, and sold them to another Government Agent for $1.50 per pair. That's the way they pick that old goose of an Uncle Sam [27 May 1847]

NEWS: slavery A Man convicted married 3 woman all 3 living & not divorced arrested in Baltimore. Proved the man s/o colored woman, a slave at Annapolis, a slave himself, not subject to the law. No punishment can legally overtake him. That a slave may commit, with impunity, a crime for which the social laws punish a free man most severely! [*The Mirror*] [6 Mar 1845]

NEWS: Spurious Opium, a large quantity of spurious opium was sold at auction in Boston MA last week. It was the dregs, or what is left after the morphine had been extracted. Look out for such stuff, ye who are wanting the real "Simon Pure" article. [25 May 1848]

NEWS: The Female Kings a sect in OH, "the last shall be first" woman the lord of creation and man her servant. They sit in judgment upon the saints; endowed with eternal life; proof to injury, have left their families and are wandering about without purse, taking no thought of the morrow, led, as they think, by the Spirit to follow the Lamb whithersoever he goeth [*NY Mirror*] [9 Apr 1846]

NEWS: The number of petitions in the Bankruptcy filed in the clerk's office of Maine District on which notices have been published is 1453, total people were over 1500. [9 Jul 1842]

NEWS: Treasury Dept nearly all corresp from the establishment to 31st ult destroyed. All officers of USA, past or present by Mr McLANE to copy letters to & from. Corresp saved: written to the Pres & Cashiers of banks 1 Oct 1819 to 20 Feb 1833; relating to AmRev claims under 1828, claims of AmRev act of 1832 & to apps insolvent debtors passed in Mar & Jul 1832. [*Boston Patriot*] [6 May 1833]

NEWS: Widows of Pensioners ... "who chanced to marry an AmRev soldier before 1 Dec 1794, aged, wounded, destitute and crippled, who achieved our liberties may have been nursed, fed, supported & cherished by one of these worthy dames, to whom he plighted his troth long years before..." [29 Jan 1846]

NEWS: "a man having fallen into a well in Chelsea MA, rescued by his friends, by a rope fastened about his neck! He died the next day the effects of the rescue" [28 Dec 1848]

NEWS: "New leather from old shoes of the Abingdon Yankees, invented a mode of grinding them over mixing them up with some adhesive liquor & plating them out again into fine new fresh leather. It is said to be very strong & suitable for many purposes. If this be the case, why not run the leather, while liquid, into shoes & boots, into harnesses & other things into which leather is made & thus save the shoe thread? [28 Aug 1851]

NEWS: "Served 'em Right" By the ancient laws of Hungary, a man convicted of bigamy was condemned to live with both wives in the same house; the crime was in consequence, extremely rare. [29 Jul 1843]

NO DEATHS, reported wreck of the British brig *Margaret & Jane*, near Moose river ME in Nov last [30 Mar 1848]

NORTHWESTERN TERRITORY, in 1788, NW Territory comprising OH, IN, IL, & MI (part of MN), but 5000 white male inhabitants. Now the population reckoned by millions. (N.B. 1790 census for the NW Territory was not done, excused from making a count, hands full fighting the Indians. [17 Apr 1851]

PRINTERS, The editor of the *Great Falls (NH) Gazette* recently advertised for a practical printer for a partner. By the last Olive Branch we notice that Miss Lucy, a practical printer in that establishment, tenders her services to the editor of the *Gazette* - Take her, man. Don't back out of so fair a proposal, and bid the ready partner, "O take your time, Miss Lucy." [16 Sept 1847]

REVOLUTIONARY SOLDIER, *The Providence Journal* gives the names, places of residence & ages of twenty-four of the venerab'e soldiers of the Revolution who dined with the city authorities of Providence on the 4th (July). The ages run from 74 to 94. [18 Jul 1840]

RUSSIANS, 200 flying from religious persecution in their own country are about settling in the territory of Wisconsin [*Peoria Register*][23 Nov 1839]

SCAMPS, A Pennsylvania paper says that a young scamp in Reading dressed himself in woman's clothes & went with another scamp to a priest & were married. They paid the priest with a counterfeit note. They should commence housekeeping in the state prison. [31 Aug 1848]

SCRAPS OF HISTORY, reign of Henry VIII, didn't grow any vegetable or eatable root: carrots, parsnips, cabbage, &c. Turkeys, fowls, &c intro abt 1524. The currant shrub brought from the Island of Zante, AD 1553. Pocket watches from Germany, AD 1577. Abt 1580, coaches intro; Saw mill erected near London in 1633, but demolished, that it might not deprive the laboring poor of employ. [25 Jul 1834]

SCRAPS OF HISTORY, Tea intro 1666, and soon became a fashionable drink it sold then for 60s per lb. It was boiled in a large iron pot until it was tender and then sauced with butter, and served up in a large deep dish. [25 Jul 1834]

Ship *Aid-de Camp* from Londonderry bound to St John's Canada w/ 305 on board, wrecked on Briar's Island on 19th ult --16 emigrants drowned of whom 3 men & the remainder women and ch. The survivors arrived at Halifax on 24th in a wretchedly destitute situation, having lost their all in wreck some of them being half naked. Measures immediately taken for their relief, and many of them obtained employment at Halifax. [27 Jul 1839]

SLAVES Georgia & Maine. The legislature of Maine having "declined taking any measures to give satisfaction to the state of GA for the violation of its constitutional rights, by the refusal of Governor DUNLAP & Gov KENT to deliver up to its authorities upon their demand, the fugitives from its justice, PHILBROOK & KELLERAN" Gov GILMER says the latter state will be justified in declaring by law, that all citizens of Maine who may come within its jurisdiction on board of any vessel as owners officers or mariners, shall be considered as doing so with the intent to commit the crime of seducing negro slaves from their owners, and be dealt with accordingly by the officers of justice. Robert DUNLAP, a Democrat of Brunswick Gov of Maine 1834-38 Edward KENT, a Whig of Bangor Gov of Maine 1838-39 [23 Nov 1839]

SNAKE: Mrs WIGHT of Hallowell ME in a vomiting spasm throwed from her stomach a live snake measuring seven inches in length, swallowed some months since in drinking water from a spring. The snake lived two or three days in a bottle of water & is now preserved in spirits [*Hallowell Gazette*] [2 Nov 1848]

SOLDIERS' widows "Congress has passed an act giving five years half pay to the widows & orphans of each non-commissioned officer & soldier who served during the Mexican War & was honorably discharged or continued in service till the time of his death & whose death was in consequence of wounds received or disease contracted within the line of duty" [15 Feb 1849]

STORY, A woman arrested & committed to prison in Troy, for appearing in male attire. They must have singular laws in Troy; in other places the women are allowed to wear the breeches and nobody objects [23 Sept 1841]

STORY, Edward BONTON walking along Cross St, Mary RILEY invited him to walk up stairs through a trap door, introduced him to 5 men, who seized him, and tearing his pantaloons, robbed him of his pocket-book, containing $102 in city bills, & then left him. He made his case known to the officers who arrested RILEY & 3 of the men all of whom were identified by Mr B were all committed in full for trial (*Boston Times*) [23 Sept 1841]

TEXAN, legislators of the Republic passed a law granting a bonus of two thirds of a league of good land to every woman who will marry during the present year, any citizen of this republic, who was such at the time of our declaration of independence. [2 Oct 1838] & see also females [23 Nov 1839]

TOWN HISTORIANS, the *Christian Mirror* recommends that every town employ a person, to collect historical items and also to keep a record of such transactions as take place from time to time. By small expence much valuable histical matter would be saved, & being recorded while everything is fresh, it could not be otherwise than authentic. [4 Nov 1847]

WEATHER: A flock of 100 sheep were dug out of a snow drift on Fisher's Island, where they had been buried to the depth of 16 feet [5 Feb 1846]

WEBSTER Daniel "Once Webster was standing in company with several southern gentlemen, in front of the capital at Washington, as a drove of mules was going by. 'Webster,' says one of the southern gentlemen, 'there goes some of your constituents' 'Yes,' instantly replied Mr W., 'they are going to teach school at the South.'" (copied from *Boston Path-Finder*) [29 June 1848]

WEBSTER Henry, heirs of England, granted by Plymouth Co, belong to Gen John DAVIS of Washington, (formerly Spec DAVIS of Augusta ME) "citizen heir of Florentinus VASSAL." tract 5 by 1 miles in Pittston, another 15 by & 1 miles, commencing on Kennebec in Fairfield embracing the "Low Farm" & running through Smithfield & Mercer to Sandy River; a tract of 2 miles in Bowdoin & Webster, large tracts in Windsor & Alna. [11 Nov 1847]

WEBSTER Henry, The suit brought against Peter COOPER of Pittston ME. At least 25,000 acres of improved farming lands embraced in this claim ...500 farms with their families upon them ...The case laid before the Dist Court in Portland lately but the Judges WOODBURY & WARE not being agreed, carried up to the Supreme Court of the USA. [11 Nov 1847]

WHITMAN Ezra Jr in Baltimore MD, formerly of Winthrop ME runs Agricultural Warehouse. "No Down-Easter thinks of going through Baltimore without calling at his shop ...." (not an obit) "a Yankee in Baltimore MD" [7 May 1846] & [2 Sept 1847]

WINSLOW Josiah one of the early governors of MA Colony. It is said that at his funeral, Rev Mr WITHERELL of Scituate prayed that "the Governor's son might be made half equal to his father." The Rev Dr Gad HITCHCOCK observed afterwards "that the prayer was so very reasonable, it might be hoped that God would grant it - but He did not." [*NY Observer*] [26 Oct 1848]

LIST OF NEWSPAPERS USED BY THE *MAINE FARMER*

Advocate of Freedom 1841
(Augusta) Age 1839-1845
Ala's (Miss) Gazette 1842
Albany Argus 1842 & 1848
Albany Daily Advertiser 1844
Albany Democrat 1846
Albany Evening Journal 1845
Alexandria Gazette 1850
Alton IL Observer 1837
American Daily Advertiser 1844
American Farmers' Companion 1840
American Journal of Science & Arts 1833
American Whig Review 1847
Amherst (NH) Cabinet 1851
Arkansas Intelligencer 1844
Baltimore American 1848
Baltimore Gazette 1834
Baltimore Patriot 1841
Baltimore Sun 1840
Bangor Courier 1833 - 1848
Bangor Daily Whig 1849
Bangor Democrat 1840 & 1849 & 1851
Bangor Gazette 1846
Bangor Mechanic & Farmer 1836
Bangor Mercury 1847 - 1851
Bangor Whig 1837 - 1848
Bath Inquirer 1836
Bath Telegraph 1839, 1843, 1846
Bath Times 1847 - 1851
Bath Tribune 1847 - 1849
Bay State Democrat
Belfast Advertiser 1834
Belfast Advocate 1835
Belfast Republican Journal 1843 - 1848
Belfast Signal 1848 - 1851
Bellows Falls Gazette 1841
Biddeford ME Herald 1848
Biddeford ME Advertizer 1851
Boston Advertiser 1843 - 1849
Boston Atlas 1836 - 1849
Boston Bee 1844 & 1849
Boston Bulletin 1835
Boston Courier 1833, 1842 - 1851
Boston Cultivator 1846
Boston Daily Advertiser 1849
Boston Herald 1849
Boston Journal 1845 & 1848

Boston Mail 1849
Boston Path Finder 1848
Boston Patriot 1837
Boston Post 1837, 1844 & 1845
Boston Times 1841
Boston Transcript 1845, 1849
Boston Traveller 1839 - 1848
Brighton England Herald 1846
Bristol (RI) Phenix 1844
Brockport Sentinel 1843
Brooklyn Daily Advertiser 1849
Brunswick Advertiser 1848
Brunswick Journal 1846
Brunswick Regulator 1836
Buffalo Commercial Advertizer 1844
Buffalo Whig 1835
Burington Free Press 1847, 1848
Burlington (Iowa) Hawkeye
Caddo Gazette 1842
Calais Advertiser 1846 - 1850
Calais Democrat 1840
Calais Journal 1847 & 1851
Centrevill MD Times 1844
Charleston Courier 1844
Charleston Mercury 1846
Charleston News 1848
Charlestown MA Aurora
Chelsea Pioneer 1848
Chicago Democrat 1847
Christian Freeman 1840
Christian Intelligencer 1833
Christian Mirror (Congregational paper
    of Portland, ME) 1838-1847
Chronicle 1846
Cincinnati Advertiser 1847
Cincinnati Chronicle 1841
Cincinnati Gazette 1845 & 1849
Clarion 1844 - 1847
The Cleveland Plaindealer 1849
Comcord NH Stateman 1848
Commerical Gazette 1848
Concord Freeman 1842
County Herald 1839
Danvers Courier 1845
Democratic Rep 1844
Dollar Newspaper 1844
Dover Observer 1848, 1849

Dover (NH) Gazette 1844
Eastern Argus 1844, 1845, 1847, 1848
Eastern Baptist 1838
Eastern Republican 1837
Eastport Democrat 1834, 1835
Eastport Sentinel 1834 - 1851
Elizabeth City NC Advocate 1842
Ellsworth Advertiser 1834
Ellsworth Democrat 1848
Exeter News Letter 1844, 1848
Farmer's Cabinet 1840
Farmington Chronicle 1849
Farmington Register 1843
Fountain & Journal (formerly "Cold
    Water Fountain & Gardiner News-
    Letter") 1847 & 1852
Frankfort Argus 1839
Frankfort (KY) Commonwealth 1846
Franklin Journal 1848
Free American 1847
Free Press & Advocate 1835
Free Soil Republican 1849
Frontier Journal 1845
Galveston TX Civilian 1849
Gardiner Advertiser 1850
Gardiner Blade 1843, 1845, 1846
Gardiner Fountain (see Fountain &
    Journal) 1847 & 1848
Gardiner Ledger 1842 1843
Gardiner Spectator 1842
Gardiner Transcript 1851
Gazette des Triburaus of Paris Frane 1834
Georgia Enquire 1840
Germanton PA Telgraph 1848
Gospel Banner (Universalist at Augusta
    ME) 1838 & 1845 - 1852
Greenfield MA Gazette 1844
Greenfield Courier 1843
Hallowell ME Advertiser 1833
Hallowell ME Advocate 1833
Hallowell ME Cultivator 1845
Hallowell ME Gazette 1847 - 1851
Hallowell ME Standard 1844
Hampden Post 1843
Hampden Whig 1834
Hancock Co Democrat 1847
Hargerstown Torchlight 1844
Hartford Times 1851
Hartford Columbia 1844
Hartford Courant 1848
Haverhill republican 1851 Hill's New
    Hampshire Patriot 1843

Holden's Dollar Magazine 1849
Independent Messenger 1835
Iowa Reporter 1845
Ithaca Chronicle 1846
Journal du Bas Rhin (in Germany)
Kaskaska IL Republican 1844
Keene NH Sentinel 1838, 1846
Kennebeck ME Journal 1839
Kennebunk ME Gazette 1835
Keokuk Iowa papers 1949
Lebanon NH Whig 1851
Lewiston Falls ME Adv 1844
Lewiston ME Journal 1847 - 1851
Lewiston Sun Journal 1995
Lexington KY Observer 1845
Lexington (MO) Telegraph 1846
Liberty Gazette 1846
Liberty Press 1849
Lime Rock Gazette 1847
Limerick ME Freewill Baptist Repository
    1847
Lincoln Miscellany 1851
Lincoln Observer 1847
Lincoln Patriot 1836, 1839
Lincoln Telegraph 1837 & 1845
Little Rock Gazette Arkansas 1838
London Times 1835
Louisville KY Advert 1836
Louisville Journal 1838
Lowell Courier 1848
Lowell Herald 1844
Lowell Journal 1849
Lowell Mercury 1834
Lowell Vox Populi 1852
Lynn Forum 1848
Lynn Record 1834
MacKennzie's British, Irish & Canadian
    Gazette 1838
Magnetic Telegraph 1846
Maine Inquirer (Bath ME) 1833 1844
Maine Journal (formerly Fountain &
    Journal)
Maine Temperance Gazette 1840
Manchester American 1846 1852
Manchester Mirror 1851
Mann's Miscellany 1851
Mann's Physician 1848
Maysville Monitor 1837
Mechanic & Farmer 1837
Mercantile Journal 1839
Mercury Journal 1843
Meredith Bridge Democrat 1851

Middletown CT Sentinel 1842
Missionary Herald 1850
Missouri Courier 1843
Missouri Reporter 1845
Mobile Tribune 1846
Montreal Gazette 1833
Montreal Herald 1846
Morgantown VA Journal 1843
Morning Star (Freewill Baptist of Dover
    NH) 1847 & 1851
Nashua Oasis 1848
National Intelligencer 1833, 1845, 1846
New Bedford Mercury 1848
New England Farmer 1851
New Hampshire Patriot 1844
New Haven Herald 1840
Natchez Free Trader 1849
New Haven Palladium 1841, 1851
New Orleans Delta 1851
New Orleans Picayune 1846 & 1848
New Orleans Republican 1840's
New York American Republican 1844
New York Commericial 1837, 1844, 1851
New York Courier & Enquirer 1835,
    1837
New York Daily Advertiser 1834 & 1846
New York Express 1845
New York Farmer & Mechanic 1845
New York Herald 1844
New York Journal of Commerce 1845,
    1846
New York Mirror 1851
New York Observer 1848
New York Standard 1833
New York Star 1834
New York Sun 1841 & 1849
New York Tribune 1846
Newark (NJ) Advertiser 1844, 1848
Newburyport Herald 1842, 1844, 1848
Newport Mercury 1844
Newport RI Herald 1848
Niagara Reported 1843
Norfolk Beacon 1846
Norfolk Democrat 1845
Norfolk Herald 1834
Norridgewock Journal 1834-1835
Norridgewock Workingman 1844
Norristown PA Herald 1844
North State Whig 1846
Northampton Courier 1835 - 1846
Norway Advertiser 1846 - 1849
Norwich Courier 1851

OH Statesman 1844
Old Colony Reporter 1850
Olive Branch 1847 & 1852
Oxford Democrat 1840, 1848, 1851
Paris ME Democrat 1848
Penn Yan Democrat 1846
People's Press 1846, 1847, 1849
Philadelphia Bulletin 1851
Philadelphia Chronicle
Philadelphia Commerical Herald 1834
Philadelphia Exchange Book 1846
Philadelphia Ledger 1843, 1845
Philadelphia North American 1844
Philadelphia Presbyterian 1843
Philadelphia Sat Courier
Pictou Mechanic & Farmer 1841
Pictou Nova Scotia Chronicle 1851
Piscataquis Observer 1848 - 1851
Piscataquis Farmer 1844
Pitsburgh Visiter 1836
Plymouth Rock MA 1846
Point Coupee Tribune 1846
Portland ME Advertiser 1833 & 1845
Portland American 1844
Portland ME Eastern Argus 1844
Portland ME Bulletin 1843
Portland ME Courier 1833
Portland ME Jeffersonian 1835
Portland ME Transcript 1846 1848
Portland ME Umpire 1848
Portsmouth NH Journal 1848 - 1849
Portsmouth Messenger 1849
Pottsville PA Emporium 1844
Providence Courier 1838
Providence Journal 1836, 1843
Providence Sentinel 1846
Providence Transcript 1849
Quebec Mercury 1844
Racine Advocate 1846
Recorder 1842
Repository 1851
Richmond KY News Letter 1849
Richmond Star 1841
Rochester (NY) Democrat 1844
Rockingham (VA) Register 1846
Saco ME Democrat 1839 - 1848
Saco ME Herald 1842
Saco ME Repository 1844
Saco ME Union 1848, 1851
Sag Harbor Corrector 1840
Salem Advertiser 1841
Salem Freeman newspaper 1851

Salem Gazette 1849
Salem Register 1844
Sandwich Observer 1850
Saratoga Sentinel 1848
Sat Courier 1839
Schenectady Cabinet 1844
Scioto OH Gazette 1838 & 1843
Skowhegan Clarion 1845 - 1850
Skowhegan Press 1847 - 1849
Skowhegan Sentinel 1837 - 1839
Somerset Journal 1836 - 1839
Southern Watch Tower 1843
Springfield Gazette 1844
Springfield MA Republican 1847, 1851
Spy 1845
St. Andrews NB Standard 1849
St Croix Courier 1834
St John New Brunswick Morning News 1850
St John's City Gazette 1838
St Louis Republican 1838 & 1849
Summit OH Beacon 1847
Sundusky OH Clarion 1834
Taunton Currier of England 1834
Temperance Advocate 1834
Temperance Gazette 1839 - 1841
Temperance Herald 1842
Temperance Recorder 1840
Thomaston Gazette 1846 - 1848

Thomaston ME Recorder 1834 (1837?) - 1846
Transcript 1835
U.S. Gazette 1846
Vermont Watchmen and Journal 1839
Vicksburg 1848
Vicksburg MO Paper 1834
Vicksburg Whig 1840
Voice of Freedom 1844
Waldo Signal 1843
Washington Capitol 1844
Washington Globe 1834
Washington Herald 1842
Washington Union 1846
Washingtonian 1841
Watchman 1844
Watervillonian 1842
Waterville Mail 1848 & 1851
Wesleyan (Maine Wesleyan Journal) 1847
Woodstook VA Tenth Legion 1849
Woodwill MI Republican 1846
Woonsocket Patriot 1847
Worcester Spy 1849
Worcester Telegraph 1847
Worcester Transcript 1845
Yankee Blade 1848
Zaneville Journal 1846
Zion's Advocate 1847 - 1848

SHIPS, 1833-1852

Names of barks, brigs, schooners and ships named in the *Maine Farmer* 1833-1852. To save space in most cases we give only the year of the issue for your reference.

Steamboat Law "After the first of Oct next by an act passed at the late session of Congress all owners of Steamboats are required to take out a license under penalty of $500. The boat must be inspected every twelve months and the boilers and machinery every 6 months ...." [2 Oct 1838]. This law was passed likely in reaction to the many steamboat accidents which we notice were reported in the newspapers.

Acadia steamer 1840
Accumulator schr 1846
Adams brig 1847
Ajax brig 1836
Ajax ship 1834
Alabama Dread & Caution of Mystic lost schr. The survivor Joseph NOBLE [16 Oct 1838]
Albion ship 1837
Alexander schr 1841
Alleghany, U.S. 1849
Allston brig 1840
Ann brig 1844
Architect schr 1849
Argus schr 1851
Arturus schr 1848
Arvum ship 1844
Asia steamer 1851
Atlantic steamer 1847
Atlas schr from Portland ME for Cuba was lost [16 Oct 1838]
Awashonks whaleship 1836
Bangor schr of Hingham vessel ashore and crew saved [16 Oct 1851]
Bangor steamer 1837
Bay State steamer 1847
Belfast brig 1850
Bellino schr 1833
Ben Sherrod steamer 1837
Berlin schr 1849
Blonde bark 1852
Bloomfield schr of Boston MA vessel ashore and crew saved [16 Oct 1851]
Bolivar ship 1840
Buckeye State steamer 1851
Buckeye steamer burst her boilers five miles above Randolph 6 persons killed 1839
Cactus bark 1847
Caledonia schr of Portland ME vessel ashore and crew saved [16 Oct 1851]

Capital ship 1849
Carmeltita bark 1847
Caroline schr of Key West FL lying at anchor off Caezar's Creek during the gale struck & sunk Master & crew all lost. [16 Oct 1838]
Catherine Nicholas brig 1847
Cevo schr 1839
Challenge schr 1846
Charles L Vose schr 1848
Choctaw steamer 1834
Clara C Bell bark 1851
Cleveland brig 1851
Columbia brig 1847
Columbia ship 1849
Columbia steamer 1851
Columbia U.S. Frigate 1846
Commerce schr of Harwich vessel ashore and crew saved [16 Oct 1851]
Condor ship 1848
Constitution schr of Gloucester vessel ashore and crew saved [16 Oct 1851]
Constitution steamer 1851
Copeland F & Co. schr 1851
Cortez ship 1848
Courier de Vera Cruz schr Jules JULIAN Capt only 7 out of 16 souls saved. The survivors rescued from the devouring ocean were soon visited by a large party of armed Indians who spared their lives because they were Frenchmen saying they only killed Americans. [16 Oct 1838]
Curlew schr 1838
Danube brig 1840
Dart schr 1849
Delta schr 1833
Detroit bark 1844
Diligence bark 1850
Don Nicholas schr 1847

Dudley bark 1847

Durock schr of Amesbury vessel ashore and crew saved [16 Oct 1851]

Eagle brig 1841

Eastern Star brig 1844

Edward schr 1840

Ellen Perkins schr 1846

Elvira schr 1850

Empire bark 1849

Export schr C M MORRILL master of Kennebunk ME struck on Ledberry Reef no lives loss but the cargo was a total loss [16 Oct 1838]

Falcon steamer 1851

Falmouth US Frigate 1849

Fame schr 1849

Favorite schr 1844

Felecina sloop 1851

Flint schr of Gloucester (MA) had lost 14 hands [16 Oct 1851]

Forest schr of Gloucester MA RICH Capt lost on Cape Cod with all on board eight in number Upwards of forty children have been left fatherless in this single instance. [30 Oct 1841]

Forest schr of Newburyport MA lost all hands [16 Oct 1851]

Formosa whaleship 1849

Fortune schr of Castine 1833

France ship 1852

Francis Robinson schr 1839

Franklin Dexter schr of Harwich lost ten hands [16 Oct 1851]

Franklin King ship 1852

Gazelle brig of Portland ME 1843

General Waven ship

George Collier steamer 1839

Glen bark 1851

Golden Gate steamer 1852

Golden Grove schr vessel ashore and crew saved [16 Oct 1851]

Golden Rule schr vessel ashore and crew saved [16 Oct 1851]

Granite brig 1839

Granville schr 1837

Harriet Newell schr of Harwich had lost two hands [16 Oct 1851]

Harriet Rockwell ship 1848

Harriet ship 1852

Hartley ship of Kennebunk ME 1848

Henry Clay ship 1842

Henry Freeling schr 1848 & 1851

Henry Knox schr of Cohasset vessel ashore and crew saved [16 Oct 1851]

Hollander brig 1835

Hope bark 1847

Hope schr 1846

Houston brig 1847

Hylas schr 1842

Illuminator schr 1844

Independence schr 1843

India ship 1842

Island brig 1846

Jacob Perkins ship 1835

James & Alma schr of Newburyport MA vessel ashore and crew saved [16 Oct 1851]

James Crooper schr 1837

Jane bark 1846

John Bell schr 1833

Kedron brig 1848

Kennebec steamer 1851

Kossuth ship 1850

Lady Of The Lake steamer 1834

Lenity schr 1844

Leonidas ship 1844

Levant brig 1847

Lexington schr many lives were lost [1 Feb 1840]

Lexington schr the *Providence Journal* relates: "...loss of the *Lexington* a milk man called on one of his customers. The mother of 9 children - & with tears in her eyes told him her husband was lost to them no means to pay him & better not leave any more as he must lose what she already owned. He replied for as long as he had the means she should not want for milk. And truly has he kept his word." [15 Feb 1840]

Linden brig 1842

Lucretia schr 1851

Lucy Blake schr 1837

Lucy H Chase brig 1852

Lucy schr 1847

Lyon schr of Castine ME master mate & six hands lost [16 Oct 1851]

Maine schr 1841

Margaret Ann schr 1847

Margaret brig 1843

Martha schr 1851

Mary Ann schr a slaver has arrived at New York from Sierra Leone. She was taken by the British brig of War *Benetta* on the

Mary Ann (Cont.)
coast of Africa being then under
American colors delivered over to Lieut
PAINE of the US schr *Grampus* and by
him sent to U States. The Captain died
on the passage. [23 May 1840]
Mary Averill brig 1835
Mary bark 1845
Mary Carver schr - see FARWELL
Mary Eleanor schr 1849
Mary Moulton schr of Castine ME lost all
hands [16 Oct 1851]
Mary Scotchburn schr vessel ashore and
crew saved [16 Oct 1851]
Massachusetts ship 1840
Mayflower schr 1847
Medore steamer 1842
Michigan steamer 1849
Minnesota schr 1849
Minstool schr - see Outerbridge
Minstool schr 1841
Missouri U.S. steamer 1852
Mobile ship 1852
Mt Hope schr of Hingham MA vessel ashore
and crew saved [16 Oct 1851]
Naiad Queen schr of Cohasset vessel ashore
and crew saved [16 Oct 1851]
Nancy Maria schr 1839
Narragansett steamer 1839
Neptune whaleship 1846
New England packet 1838
New York steamer 1846
Norman ship 1850
North Star schr 1841
Northerner steamer for Chagres 1849
Ocean Monarch ship 1848
Olive Branch schr 1840
Oliver schr 1852
Oliver Thompson brig 1851
Ontario schr 1839
Oraloo wreck of 1845
Orbit schr 1851
Oregon steamer 1849
Orlinda schr 1848
Orpheus ship 1847
Osage schr 1842
Oscar Coles schr of Boston MA vessel
ashore and crew saved [16 Oct 1851]
Ottoman schr 1848
Ovando bark 1850
Panama ship 1835
Paul Jones ship 1847

Perdonnet ship 1844
Peru schr 1847
Pilot schr 1849
Potomac schr 1839
Powhattan schr vessel ashore and crew
saved [16 Oct 1851]
Preble US Ship 1845
Prize schr Mr RUIZ the owner of the slaves
on board the schooner taken to New
London resided in Boston MA several
months last year & his connections in
Principe are highly repectable. [14 Sept
1839]
Proxy brig 1842
Regulus schr 1842
Richard Bon Homme ship of (Revolutionary
War) 1844
Rival & Nettle schr of Truro MA vessel
ashore and crew saved [16 Oct 1851]
Rochester ship 1847
Rolla schr 1835
Rothchild bark 1842
Rousseau ship 1840
Royal Tar ship 1836
Ruth S Hodgdon schr 1850
Sarah brig of Bangor ME 1850
Sarah schr 1834 & 1851
Saratoga brig 1844
Saxonville ship 1849
Scott Dyer bark 1851
Sea Belle schr 1846
Sea Gull steamer 1851
Seaflower schr 1841
Senate schr 1851
Serapis ship (Revolutionary War) 1844
Sidney schr 1838
Somerset schr 1845
South American steamer 1851
Splendid brig 1842
Splendid schr 1836
Splendid ship 1846
St Louis ship 1842
State Of Maine steamer 1849
Superior schr 1848
Swallow steamer 1845
Telegraph schr of Boston MA had lost 18
hands [16 Oct 1851]
Thomas schr 1843
Tilton brig 1839
Traveller brig 1851
Traveller schr the vessel was not lost and all
hands supposed lost [16 Oct 1851]

Triumphant schr of Cape Elizabeth ME
  vessel ashore and crew saved [16 Oct
  1851]
United States ship 1840
Vahalle bark 1844
Virginia brig 1843
Wanderer brig 1852
Ware sloop 1849
Washington brig 1835
Watchman schr 1848
Wave schr LEWIS Capt of Hallowell ME
  from St Marks via Key West for New
  York with cotton tobacco & cigars was
  found ashore at Metemphia Beach
  Accomack Co VA on 22d ult. The mate
  died about ten days before; & the Capt

Wave (Cont.)
  being dangerously ill his crew exhausted
  his sails blown away & no one to
  navigate the vessel had run her ashore.
  Capt LEWIS was taken to the house of
  Mr Thomas CROPPER commissioner of
  wrecks and died on 25th. [16 Oct 1838]
William Crawford brig 1852
William Fales bark 1840 & 1842
William M Meir schr 1851
William Polk schr 1846
William Purington brig 1846
William schr 1848
William Tell bark 1840
Wilmington steamer 1839
Zandia bark 1844